Multicore and GPU Programming

Multicore and GPU Programming
An Integrated Approach
Second Edition

Gerassimos Barlas

MORGAN KAUFMANN PUBLISHERS

ELSEVIER AN IMPRINT OF ELSEVIER

Morgan Kaufmann is an imprint of Elsevier
50 Hampshire Street, 5th Floor, Cambridge, MA 02139, United States

Library of Congress Cataloging-in-Publication Data
A catalog record for this book is available from the Library of Congress

British Library Cataloguing-in-Publication Data
A catalogue record for this book is available from the British Library

ISBN: 978-0-12-814120-5

For information on all Morgan Kaufmann publications
visit our website at https://www.elsevier.com/books-and-journals

Publisher: Stephen Merken
Editorial Project Manager: Angie Breckon
Production Project Manager: Karthikeyan Murthy/Manikandan Chandrasekaran
Designer: Miles Hitchen

Typeset by VTeX

Printed in the United States of America

Last digit is the print number: 9 8 7 6 5 4 3 2

Working together
to grow libraries in
developing countries

www.elsevier.com • www.bookaid.org

Dedicated to my late parents, Dimitris and Maria,
for making it possible,
and my loving wife Katerina and my two sons
Alexandros and Dimitris, for making it worthwhile.

Contents

PART 1 Introduction

PART 2 Programming with threads and processes

PART 3 Higher-level parallel programming

List of tables

Preface

Parallel computing has been given a fresh breath of life since the emergence of multi-core architectures in the first decade of the new century. The new platforms demand a new approach to software development; one that blends the tools and established practices of the network of workstations (NoW) era with emerging software platforms such as CUDA.

This book tries to address this need by covering the dominant contemporary tools and techniques, both in isolation and, most importantly, in combination with each other. We strive to provide examples where multiple platforms and programming paradigms (e.g., message passing and threads) are effectively combined. "Hybrid" computation, as it is usually called, is a new trend in high-performance computing, one that could possibly allow software to scale to the "millions of threads" required for exascale performance.

All chapters are accompanied by extensive examples and practice problems. Whenever possible multiple design alternatives are pursued and compared. All the little details that can make the difference between productive software development and a futile exercise are presented in an orderly fashion.

The book covers the latest advances in tools that have been inherited from the 1990s (e.g., the OpenMP and MPI standards), but also more cutting-edge platforms, such as the C++11 thread support, the Qt library with its sophisticated thread management, and the Thrust template library with its capability to deploy the same software over diverse multicore architectures, including both CPUs and GPUs.

We could never accomplish the feat of covering all the tools available for multi-core development today. Even some of the industry standard ones, like POSIX threads, are omitted.

Our goal is to sample the dominant paradigms (ranging from OpenMP's semiautomatic parallelization of sequential code to the explicit communication "plumbing" that underpins MPI), while at the same time explaining the rationale and how-to behind efficient multicore program development.

What is in this book

The book is separated into the following logical units:

- **Introduction, designing multicore software**: Chapter 1 introduces multicore hardware and examines influential instances of this architectural paradigm. Chapter 1 also introduces speedup and efficiency, which are essential metrics used in the evaluation of multicore and parallel software. Amdahl's law and Gustafson–Barsis's rebuttal cap up the chapter, providing estimates of what can be expected from the exciting new developments in multicore and many-core hardware.

Chapter 2 is all about the methodology and the design patterns that can be employed in the development of parallel and multicore software. Both work decomposition patterns and program structure patterns are examined.

- **Programming with threads and processes**: Dealing explicitly with the individual paths of execution in the form of threads or processes is the most elementary form of parallel programming. In this part we examine how this paradigm is used to program CPUs (with C++11 threads), GPUs (with CUDA and OpenCL), and even clusters of networked machines (using MPI).

  C++11 threads have been a long-awaited addition to the C++ standard, establishing a firm foundation for cross-platform, high-performance, parallel software development for CPUs. Chapter 3 covers C++11 facilities, along with commonly used synchronization mechanisms such as semaphores and monitors. Also, frequently encountered design patterns, such as producers–consumers and readers–writers, are explained thoroughly and applied in a range of examples.

  Chapter 4 is dedicated to shared-memory parallel data structures and how we can ensure correctness when multiple actions are attempted on a program's data.

  In Chapter 5 we cover MPI, which is the de facto standard for distributed memory parallel programming. MPI provides the foundation for utilizing multiple disjoint multicore machines as a single virtual platform, designed to scale from a single shared-memory multicore machine to a million-node supercomputer. The features that are covered include both point-to-point and collective communication, as well as one-sided communication. A section is dedicated to the Boost.MPI library, as it does simplify the proceedings of using MPI, although it is not yet feature-complete.

  GPU software development is covered in great detail, including kernel design, memory management, grid-block/index space configurations, and optimization techniques. Both CUDA (Chapter 6) and OpenCL (Chapter 7) are examined both in isolation and in combination with other platforms such as C++11 threads and MPI.

- **High-level parallel programming**: Parallel software suffers from high development and maintenance costs. Some of this burden can be alleviated by utilizing tools that handle the more esoteric details of "how" and "where" to execute costly computations.

  The OpenMP standard in its latest incarnation (v5.0) manages to address these problems by requiring only "hints" from the programmer, while also allowing both CPUs and GPUs to be targeted. There are still complications that need to be addressed, such as loop-carried dependencies, which are also examined in Chapter 8.

  OpenMP's design philosophy is to take advantage of multi- and many-core hardware, while requiring minimum alterations to the source code of a sequential program. The Qt library covered in Chapter 9 offers another solution to the design problem by supporting high-level abstractions in the form of map, filter, and reduce operations that can be applied to collections of data, without the need to instantiate or manage any threads.

Chapter 10 covers the Thrust template library which follows suit, requiring a software redesign, so that computations can be expressed as transformations, reductions, or in general the application of function objects on data. The STL-like approach to program design affords Thrust the ability to target both CPUs and GPU platforms.

- **Advanced topics**: Chapter 11 is dedicated to an often underestimated aspect of multicore development: load balancing. In general, load balancing has to be seriously considered once heterogeneous computing resources come into play. For example, a CPU and a GPU constitute such a set of resources, so we should not think only of clusters of dissimilar machines as fitting this requirement. Chapter 11 briefly discusses the Linda coordination language, which can be considered a high-level abstraction of dynamic load balancing.
  The main focus is on static load balancing and the mathematical models that can be used to drive load partitioning and data communication sequences. A well-established methodology known as divisible load theory (DLT) is explained and applied in a number of scenarios. A simple C++ library that implements parts of the DLT research results that have been published over the past two decades is also presented.

Using this book as a textbook

The material covered in this book is appropriate for senior undergraduate or postgraduate coursework. The required student background includes programming in C++, basic operating system concepts, and at least elementary knowledge of computer architecture.

Depending on the desired focus, an instructor may choose to follow one of the suggested paths listed below. The first two chapters lay the foundations for the other chapters, so they are included in all sequences:

- **Emphasis on parallel programming** (undergraduate):
  - Chapter 1: Flynn's taxonomy, contemporary multicore machines, performance metrics. Sections 1.1–1.5.
  - Chapter 2: Design, PCAM methodology, decomposition patterns, program structure patterns. Sections 2.1–2.5.
  - Chapter 3: Threads, semaphores, monitors. Sections 3.1–3.10.
  - Chapter 5: MPI, point-to-point communications, collective operations, object/structure communications, debugging and profiling. Sections 5.1–5.12, 5.16–5.18, and 5.20.
  - Chapter 6: CUDA programming model, memory hierarchy, GPU-specific optimizations. Sections 6.1–6.6, 6.7.1, 6.7.3, and 6.7.4.2.
  - Chapter 10: Thrust basics. Sections 10.1–10.5.

- **Emphasis on multicore programming** (undergraduate):
  - Chapter 1: Flynn's taxonomy, contemporary multicore machines, performance metrics. Sections 1.1–1.5.
  - Chapter 2: Design, PCAM methodology, decomposition patterns, program structure patterns. Sections 2.1–2.5.
  - Chapter 3: Threads, semaphores, monitors. Sections 3.1–3.10.
  - Chapter 8: OpenMP basics, work-sharing constructs, correctness and performance issues. Sections 8.1–8.9 and 8.12.
  - Chapter 6: CUDA programming model, memory hierarchy, GPU-specific optimizations. Sections 6.1–6.10.
  - Chapter 10: Thrust basics. Sections 10.1–10.5
- **Advanced multicore programming**:
  - Chapter 1: Flynn's taxonomy, contemporary multicore machines, performance metrics. Sections 1.1–1.5.
  - Chapter 2: Design, PCAM methodology, decomposition patterns, program structure patterns. Sections 2.1–2.5.
  - Chapter 3: Threads, semaphores, monitors, advanced thread management. Sections 3.1–3.13.
  - Chapter 4: Parallel data structures, lock-based and lock-free design approaches. Sections 4.1–4.3.
  - Chapter 5: MPI, point-to-point communications, collective operations, object/structure communications, debugging and profiling. Sections 5.1–5.12, 5.16–5.18, 5.21–5.22, and 5.25.
  - Chapter 6: CUDA programming model, memory hierarchy, GPU-specific optimizations. Sections 6.1–6.15.
  - Chapter 8: OpenMP basics, work-sharing constructs, correctness and performance issues. Sections 8.1–8.14.
  - Chapter 11: Load balancing, "divisible load theory"-based partitioning. Sections 11.1–11.5.

Also, if FPGAs or other non-NVidia accelerators are targeted, Chapter 7 on OpenCL can replace Chapter 6 on CUDA.

Software and hardware requirements

The book examples have been developed and tested on Ubuntu Linux. All the software used throughout the book is available in free or open source form. These include:

- GNU C/C++ Compiler Suite 9.x (for CUDA compatibility) and 10.x (for OpenMP 5.0 compatibility)
- OpenMPI 4.x
- NVidia's CUDA SDK 11.x (includes Thrust)
- Qt 5.x library

- Tau
- Scalasca

A reasonably recent Linux installation with the above or newer versions of the listed software should have no problem running the sample code provided. Although we do not provide makefiles or instructions for compiling and executing them using Visual Studio on a Windows platform, users without access to a Linux installation[1] should be able to port the examples with minimum changes. Given that we use standard C/C++ libraries, the changes – if any – should affect only header files, i.e., which ones to include.

In terms of hardware, the only real restriction is the need to have a compute capability 3.5 or newer NVidia GPU for Chapter 6. Earlier-generation chips are no longer supported by the CUDA SDK. Users without an NVidia GPU can still take advantage of their GPU hardware with OpenCL (Chapter 7).

Sample code

The programs presented in this book are made available in a compressed archive form from the publisher's website.

The programs are organized in dedicated folders, identified by the chapter name, as shown in Fig. 0.1.

Each listing in the book is headed by the location of the corresponding file, *relative* to the chapter's directory.

Single-file programs contain the command that compiles and links them in their first-line comments. Multi-file projects reside in their own directories, which also contain a makefile or a project (.pro) file. Sample input data are also provided wherever needed.

Several examples in the book are accompanied by command-lines that explain how they can be compiled and/or executed. For example:

```
$ g++ hello.cpp -lpthread -o hello
$ ./hello
Main thread waiting...
Hello from thread 139981974968064
```

Please note that the dollar sign "$" in all the commands shown represents the command prompt and should not be entered as part of the command.

---

[1] Linux can be easily installed without even modifying the configuration of a machine via virtualization technology. The freely available Virtualbox software from Oracle can handle running Linux on a host Windows system with minimal resource consumption.

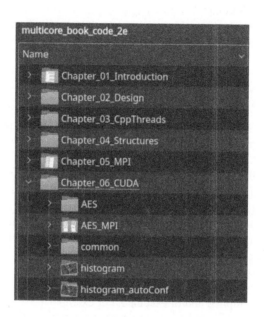

FIGURE 0.1

Screenshot showing how sample code is organized in chapter-specific folders.

Introduction

Introduction

In this chapter you will:

- Understand the current trends in computing machine design and how these influence software development.
- Learn how to categorize computing machines based on Flynn's taxonomy.
- Learn the essential tools used to evaluate multicore/parallel performance, namely speedup and efficiency.
- Learn the proper experimental procedure for measuring and reporting performance.
- Learn Amdahl's and Gustafson–Barsis' laws and apply them in order to predict the performance of parallel programs.

1.1 The era of multicore machines

Digital computers have been the cornerstone of much of the technological and scientific advancements that we have experienced since the 1980s. The speed with which they can process information has been increasing exponentially, as originally observed by Moore in the 1970s and expressed by the now famous – but mistakenly called so – "law," allowing us to tackle ever more complex problems.

It is surprising that Moore's law is describing the industry trends even today, but for a small clarification that is easily overlooked by popular science: it is the transistor count that grows exponentially and not the operational speed! A depiction of Moore's "law" is shown in Fig. 1.1.[1]

It was an easy mistake to make, as the increase in transistor count was accompanied by leaps in operating frequency (also known as the "clock") that circuit miniaturization accommodated. However, increased clock frequencies resulted in elevated heat generation. Chip designers responded by lowering the operating voltages of the electronic circuits (currently running with as low as 1.29 V!) but this was not enough to counter the problem. This inevitably stalled the increase in clock frequencies, which have remained in the 2–5 GHz range since the mid 2000s.

So, the only route left to meet the demand for more computational power was to squeeze more computational logic, more computing cores inside a chip. Since the

---

[1] The data plotted originate from https://en.wikipedia.org/wiki/Transistor_count.

Multicore and GPU Programming. https://doi.org/10.1016/B978-0-12-814120-5.00009-3
Copyright © 2023 Elsevier Inc. All rights reserved.

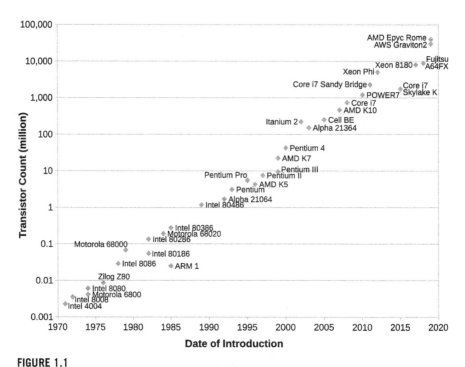

FIGURE 1.1

A logarithmic plot of CPU transistor count versus year of introduction.

first dual-core, single-die chip introduced by IBM in 2001 (Power 4), a large variety of multicore chips have been released, including both *homogeneous* chips with a large number of cores, like the 64-core Tilera TILE64,[2] and *heterogeneous* chips, like the Cell BE, which is powering among other things the Sony Playstation 3 (PS3).

These chips were a natural evolution of the multi-socket platforms, i.e., machines that could host several CPUs each on a separate chip, of the mid to late 1990s. What was unexpected though was the emergence of GPGPU computing, the paradigm of doing general-purpose computing using a graphical processing unit (GPU). While a single GPU core compared with a contemporary CPU core is underpowered, GPUs boast massively parallel architectures with hundreds or thousands of cores, "fed" by high-bandwidth, high-speed RAM. The outcome is orders of magnitude higher computational speeds!

GPGPU offers an additional distinct advantage in a world where energy resources are dwindling: it provides superior GFlop/Watt performance, i.e., you can get more computation done per energy unit spent. This is especially critical in the server and

---

[2] http://www.tilera.com/products/processors/TILE64.

cloud infrastructure domain, where the energy consumed by a CPU over its operational lifetime can be much higher than its actual price.

GPGPU technology is considered a *disruptive* one, and this is true in many levels: it enables the pursuit of solutions to problems that are out of reach with contemporary single- or even multicore CPU technology, but it also demands new software design and development tools and techniques. It is projected that in the near future, millions of threads will be required to master the computing power of the next-generation high-performance computing hardware that will become available!

All this performance that multicore chips avail to us does not come for free: it requires an explicit redesign of algorithms, which traditionally have been operating based on a single deterministic sequence of steps.

1.2 A taxonomy of parallel machines

The quest for squeezing more performance out of contemporary computing technology by utilizing multiple resources is not a new one. It has begun as early as in the 1960s, so finding a way of describing the architectural characteristics of parallel machines became essential. Michael Flynn introduced a taxonomy of computer architectures in 1966, where machines are classified based on how many data items they can process concurrently and how many different instructions they can execute at the same time. The answer to both of these criteria can be either single or multiple, which means that their combination can produce four possible outcomes:

- **S**ingle **i**nstruction, **s**ingle **d**ata (SISD): a simple sequential machine that executes one instruction at a time, operating on a single data item. Surprisingly, the vast majority of contemporary CPUs do not belong to this category. Even microcontrollers nowadays are offered in multicore configurations. Each of their cores can be considered a SISD machine.
- **S**ingle **i**nstruction, **m**ultiple **d**ata (SIMD): a machine where each instruction is applied on a collection of items. Vector processors were the very first machines that followed this paradigm. GPUs also follow this design at the level of the streaming multiprocessor (SM)[3] (SM) for NVidia or the SIMD unit for AMD.
- **M**ultiple **i**nstruction, **s**ingle **d**ata (MISD): this configuration seems like an oddity. How can multiple instruction be applied to the same data item? Under normal circumstances it does not make sense. However, when fault tolerance is required in a system (military or aerospace applications fit this description), data can be processed by multiple machines and decisions can be made on a majority principle.
- **M**ultiple **i**nstruction, **m**ultiple **d**ata (MIMD): the most versatile machine category. Multicore machines, including GPUs, follow this paradigm. GPUs are made from a collection of SMs/SIMD units, whereby each can execute its own program. So while each SM is an SIMD machine, collectively they behave as an MIMD one.

---

[3] For more info see Section 6.3.

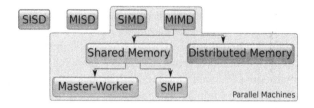

FIGURE 1.2

Flynn's – extended – taxonomy of computing systems.

This taxonomy has been refined over the years, with the addition of subcategories especially under the MIMD slot, as presented in Fig. 1.2.

MIMD can be separated into two broad subcategories:

- Shared-memory MIMD: machine architecture having a universally accessible shared memory space. The shared memory simplifies all transactions that need to take place between the CPUs with a minimum amount of overhead, but it also constitutes a bottleneck that limits the scalability of the system. One solution to this problem is to partition memory between the CPUs, so that each CPU "owns" a part of the memory. Thus a CPU gets faster access to its local memory but it can still access albeit more slowly non-local memory belonging to other CPUs. The partitioning does not affect the addressing scheme, which is universal. This design is known as non-uniform memory access (NUMA), and it permits shared memory machines to scale up to a few tens of CPUs.
- Distributed-memory or shared-nothing MIMD: a machine that is made up of processors that communicate by exchanging messages. The communication cost is high, but since there is no single medium to be contested, such machines can scale without any practical limit apart from space and energy bounds.

Shared-memory machines can be further subdivided into master–worker and symmetric multiprocessing platforms. In the latter, all the participating CPUs are identical and capable of executing any program in the system, including system and application software. In a master–worker setup some of the processors are dedicated for the execution of specialized software, i.e., we can treat them as co-processors. GPU equipped systems can be considered as belonging to this category, although the majority of high-performance GPU platforms have distinct memory spaces for the CPU and GPU. As such, they are not shared-memory platforms, despite recent driver software advances that hide much of the complexity involved in moving data between the two memories.

The same arrangement exists in machines equipped with the Intel Xeon Phi co-processor. The initial release of the Intel Xeon Phi co-processor contains 61 Pentium cores operating as a shared-memory MIMD platform. It is installed on a PCIe card, and although it resides on the same enclosure/chassis as the host CPU, the most appropriate classification of the combined CPU/co-processor system is the distributed memory MIMD one.

1.3 A glimpse of influential computing machines

Contemporary machines blur the lines between the categories laid out by Flynn. The drive for more performance has led to machines that are both MIMD and SIMD, depending on the level at which they are examined.

There are currently two trends in utilizing the increased transistor count afforded by miniaturization and advancements in semiconductor materials:

1. Increase the on-chip core count, combined with augmented specialized SIMD instruction sets (e.g., SSE and its subsequent versions, MMX, AESNI, AVX, etc.) and larger caches. This is best exemplified by Intel's Xeon Phi co-processor and by AMD's Ryzen and Epyc lines.
2. Combine heterogeneous cores in the same package, typically CPU and GPU ones, each optimized for a different type of task. This is best exemplified by AMD's line of Accelerated Processing Unit (APU) chips, which are commonly found in game consoles such as Sony's PS4 and PS5 and Microsoft's XBox One. Intel is also offering OpenCL-based computing on its line of CPUs with integrated graphics.

But why is the pairing of CPU and GPU cores on the same die an important feature? Before we answer this question, let us discuss what exactly GPUs bring to the game!

GPUs, also known as graphics accelerator cards, have been developed as a means of processing massive amounts of graphics data very quickly, before they are placed in the card's display buffer. Their design envelope dictated a layout that departed from the one traditionally used by conventional CPUs. CPUs employ large on-chip (and sometimes multiple) memory caches, few complex (e.g., pipelined) arithmetic and logical processing units (ALUs), and complex instruction decoding and prediction hardware to avoid stalling (going idle) while waiting for data to arrive from the main memory.

Instead, GPU designers chose a different path: small on-chip caches, with a big collection of simple ALUs capable of parallel operation, since data reuse is typically low for graphics processing and programs are relatively simple. In order to feed the multiple cores on a GPU, designers also dedicated very wide, fast memory buses for fetching data from the GPU's main memory.

The contrast between the two worlds is evident in Fig. 1.3. Although the block diagrams are not scaled properly relative to each other, it is clear that while memory cache dominates the die in the CPU case, compute logic dominates in the case of the GPU.

GPUs have been proven to offer unprecedented computing power. However, their use in a system in the form of a dedicated graphics card communicating with the main CPU over a slow bus such as PCIe compromises their effectiveness. The reason is that data have to be transferred to (and from) the main computer memory to the GPU's memory before the GPU can process them. This effectively creates a data size threshold, below which GPUs are not an effective tool. The case study of Sec-

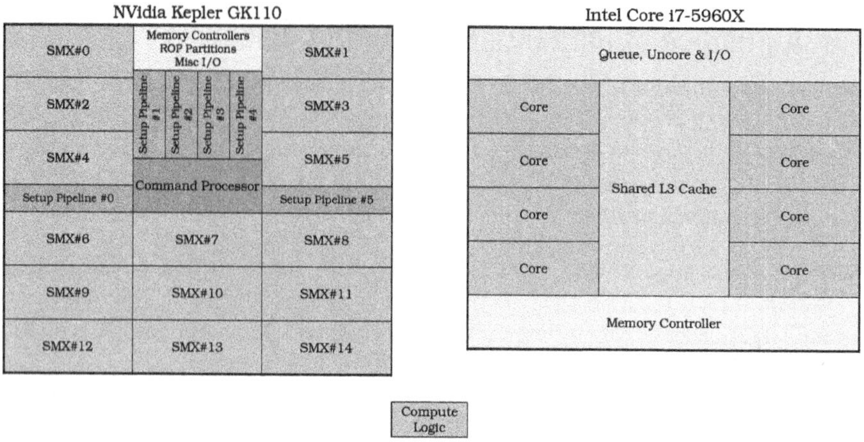

NVidia Kepler GK110

	Memory Controllers ROP Partitions Misc I/O	
SMX#0		SMX#1
SMX#2	Setup Pipeline #1 / Setup Pipeline #2 / Setup Pipeline #3 / Setup Pipeline #4	SMX#3
SMX#4	Command Processor	SMX#5
Setup Pipeline #0		Setup Pipeline #5
SMX#6	SMX#7	SMX#8
SMX#9	SMX#10	SMX#11
SMX#12	SMX#13	SMX#14

Intel Core i7-5960X

	Queue, Uncore & I/O	
Core		Core
Core	Shared L3 Cache	Core
Core		Core
Core		Core
	Memory Controller	

Compute Logic

FIGURE 1.3

Block diagrams of the NVidia Titan GPU and the Intel i7-5960X octa-core CPU, derived from silicon die photographs. The diagrams are not scaled relative to each other. They are only supposed to show the relative real estate devoted to compute logic. Each SMX SIMD block contains 192 cores and 64 KiB of cache/shared memory. Each i7 core contains its own private 32 KiB data and 32 KiB instruction L1 caches and a 256 KiB L2 cache. The shared L3 cache in i7-5960X is 20 MiB.

tion 11.5.2 highlights this problem (see Fig. 11.16 for execution times versus data size on sample CPU and GPU cores).

Now it becomes obvious why having CPU and GPU cores share and access the same memory space is an important feature. In principle, this arrangement promises better integration of computing resources and potentially greater performance, but only time will tell.

In the following sections we review some of the most influential designs in multicore computing, some contemporary and some of historical importance. These provide insights into the direction in which processor designs are moving.

1.3.1 The Cell BE processor

The Cell BE (Broadband Engine) processor, famous for powering Sony's PS3 gaming console, was introduced in 2007, the outcome of a joint venture among Sony, Toshiba, and IBM. Cell features a design well ahead of its time: a master–worker, *heterogeneous*, MIMD machine on a chip. The chip variant that equips the PS3 console contains the following:

- The master is a 64-bit PowerPC core (called the Power Processing Element [PPE]) capable of running two threads. It is responsible for running the operating system and managing the workers.
- The workers are eight 128-bit vector processors (called the Synergistic Processing Elements [SPEs]). Each SPE has its own dedicated on-chip local – not cache –

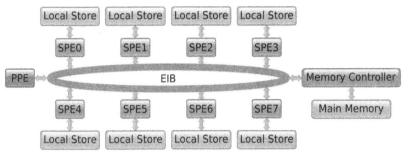

FIGURE 1.4

Block diagram of the Cell BE processor.

memory (256 KiB) called the "local store," used to hold the data and code it is running.

The SPE cores are not binary compatible with PPE: they have their own instruction set designed for SIMD operation. The PPE is responsible for initializing them and starting jobs on them. SPEs communicate via a high-speed ring interconnect called the Element Interconnect Bus (EIB), shown in Fig. 1.4. SPEs do not have direct access to the main memory, but they can perform DMA transfers between the main memory and their local store.

The hardware was designed for maximum computing efficiency, but at the expense of programming ease. The Cell is notorious for being one of the most difficult platforms to program on.

At the time of its introduction, the Cell was one of the most powerful processors available on the market, with a peak performance in double-precision arithmetic of 102.4 GFlops for the combined total of the eight SPEs. It very quickly became a component for building "budget-supercomputers" in the form of PS3 clusters. Applications that run on these machines included astrophysics simulations, satellite imaging, and biomedical applications. It should be noted that the IBM Roadrunner supercomputer, which was the world's fastest during 2008–2009, contained 12,240 PowerXCell 8i and 6562 AMD Opteron processors. PowerXCell 8i is an enhanced version of the original Cell with improved double-precision floating point performance.

The Cell processor is no longer being developed, probably a victim of its programming complexity and the advances in GPU computing.

1.3.2 NVidia's Ampere

Ampere is the eighth GPU architecture NVidia has designed specifically for compute applications. The new architecture is as surprising to the uninitiated as the previous ones! The departure from the "traditional" SMP chips becomes obvious only when one tries to program an incarnation of such a design. In this section we will just

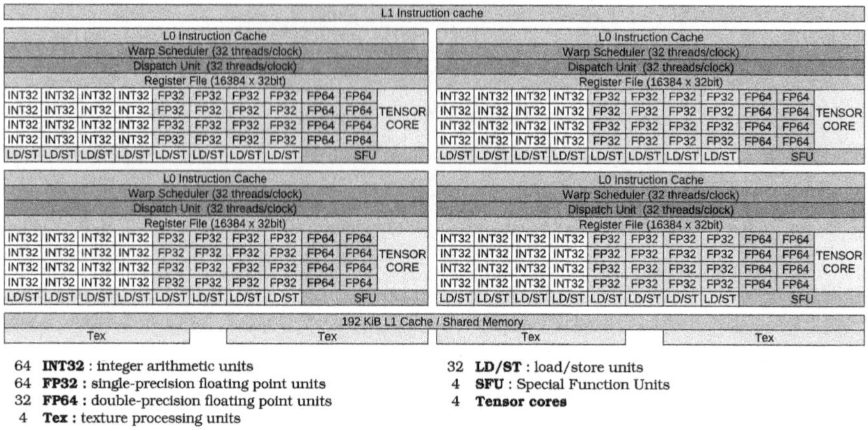

L1 Instruction cache

| L0 Instruction Cache |
| Warp Scheduler (32 threads/clock) |
| Dispatch Unit (32 threads/clock) |
| Register File (16384 x 32bit) |

INT32	INT32	INT32	INT32	FP32	FP32	FP32	FP32	FP64	FP64	
INT32	INT32	INT32	INT32	FP32	FP32	FP32	FP32	FP64	FP64	TENSOR
INT32	INT32	INT32	INT32	FP32	FP32	FP32	FP32	FP64	FP64	CORE
INT32	INT32	INT32	INT32	FP32	FP32	FP32	FP32	FP64	FP64	
LD/ST	LD/ST	LD/ST	LD/ST	LD/ST	LD/ST	LD/ST	LD/ST		SFU	

| L0 Instruction Cache |
| Warp Scheduler (32 threads/clock) |
| Dispatch Unit (32 threads/clock) |
| Register File (16384 x 32bit) |

INT32	INT32	INT32	INT32	FP32	FP32	FP32	FP32	FP64	FP64	
INT32	INT32	INT32	INT32	FP32	FP32	FP32	FP32	FP64	FP64	TENSOR
INT32	INT32	INT32	INT32	FP32	FP32	FP32	FP32	FP64	FP64	CORE
INT32	INT32	INT32	INT32	FP32	FP32	FP32	FP32	FP64	FP64	
LD/ST	LD/ST	LD/ST	LD/ST	LD/ST	LD/ST	LD/ST	LD/ST		SFU	

| L0 Instruction Cache |
| Warp Scheduler (32 threads/clock) |
| Dispatch Unit (32 threads/clock) |
| Register File (16384 x 32bit) |

INT32	INT32	INT32	INT32	FP32	FP32	FP32	FP32	FP64	FP64	
INT32	INT32	INT32	INT32	FP32	FP32	FP32	FP32	FP64	FP64	TENSOR
INT32	INT32	INT32	INT32	FP32	FP32	FP32	FP32	FP64	FP64	CORE
INT32	INT32	INT32	INT32	FP32	FP32	FP32	FP32	FP64	FP64	
LD/ST	LD/ST	LD/ST	LD/ST	LD/ST	LD/ST	LD/ST	LD/ST		SFU	

| L0 Instruction Cache |
| Warp Scheduler (32 threads/clock) |
| Dispatch Unit (32 threads/clock) |
| Register File (16384 x 32bit) |

INT32	INT32	INT32	INT32	FP32	FP32	FP32	FP32	FP64	FP64	
INT32	INT32	INT32	INT32	FP32	FP32	FP32	FP32	FP64	FP64	TENSOR
INT32	INT32	INT32	INT32	FP32	FP32	FP32	FP32	FP64	FP64	CORE
INT32	INT32	INT32	INT32	FP32	FP32	FP32	FP32	FP64	FP64	
LD/ST	LD/ST	LD/ST	LD/ST	LD/ST	LD/ST	LD/ST	LD/ST		SFU	

192 KiB L1 Cache / Shared Memory

Tex　　Tex　　Tex

64 **INT32** : integer arithmetic units
64 **FP32** : single-precision floating point units
32 **FP64** : double-precision floating point units
4 **Tex** : texture processing units

32 **LD/ST** : load/store units
4 **SFU** : Special Function Units
4 **Tensor cores**

FIGURE 1.5

Block diagram of Ampere's Streaming Multiprocessor building block. An A100 GPU has 108 SMs enabled.

look at architectural features that make this and other GPUs a formidable computing machine.

The cores in an Ampere GPU are arranged in groups called **Streaming Multiprocessors** (**SMs**). Each Ampere SM contains 64 cores that execute in an SIMD fashion, i.e., they run the same sequence of instructions but on different data. Each SM can run its own program though. The total number of SM blocks is the – primary – differentiating factor between different chips of the same family. Currently, the most powerful chip in the Ampere family is the A100 GPU that comes with a total of 108 SMs enabled out of a maximum possible of 128, in order to improve production yields. This means that each A100 GPU comes with a total of $108 \cdot 64 = 6912$ cores! These are rated at a peak performance of 9.7 TFlops for double-precision arithmetic, boosted to 19.5 TFlops when tensor cores are employed [43]. A tensor core is a specialized unit designed to perform multiply-and-accumulate operations fast, as required by artificial intelligence (AI) applications. Tensor cores were introduced for the first time in NVidia's Volta architecture. Fig. 1.5 shows the block diagram of an Ampere SM.

The details of how such a "beast" can be programmed are covered in Chapter 6. As a short introduction to the topic, a GPU is used as a co-processor, assigned work items from the main CPU. The CPU is referred to, in this context, as the *host*. It would be awkward to have code spawning a separate thread for each of those 6912 cores. Instead, the GPU programming environment allows the launch of special functions called **kernels**, that run with distinct, intrinsic/built-in variables. In fact, the number of threads that can be generated with a single statement/kernel launch comes to tens of thousands or even millions. Each thread will take its turn running on a GPU core.

The sequence can be summarized to the host (a) sending data to the GPU, (b) launching a kernel, and (c) waiting to collect the results.

Table 1.1 The top nine most powerful supercomputers as of June 2021, sorted in descending order of their maximum delivered TFlop/KW ratio.

Rank	Site	System	Cores	Rmax (TFlops)	Power (kW)	Tflop/KW
5	Perlmutter, DOE/SC/LBNL/NERSC, United States	AMD EPYC 7763 64C 2.45GHz, NVIDIA A100 SXM4 40 GB, Slingshot-10	706304	64590	2528	25.550
8	JUWELS, Atos Forschungszentrum Juelich (FZJ), Germany	AMD EPYC 7402 24C 2.8GHz, NVIDIA A100, Mellanox HDR InfiniBand	449280	44120	1764	25.011
6	Selene, NVIDIA Corp. United States	AMD EPYC 7742 64C 2.25GHz, NVIDIA A100, Mellanox HDR InfiniBand	555520	63460	2646	23.983
9	HPC5, Dell EMC Eni S.p.A., Italy	Xeon Gold 6252 24C 2.1GHz, NVIDIA Tesla V100, Mellanox HDR Infiniband	669760	35450	2252	15.742
1	Fugaku, RIKEN Center for Computational Science, Japan	Fujitsu A64FX 48C 2.2GHz, Tofu interconnect D	7630848	442010	29899	14.783
2	Summit, Oak Ridge National Laboratory, United States	IBM POWER9 22C 3.07GHz, NVIDIA Volta GV100, Dual-rail Mellanox EDR Infiniband,	2414592	148600	10096	14.719
3	Sierra, DOE/NNSA/LLNL United States	IBM POWER9 22C 3.1GHz, NVIDIA Volta GV100, Dual-rail Mellanox EDR Infiniband	1572480	94640	7438	12.724
4	Sunway TaihuLight, NRCPC National Supercomputing Center in Wuxi, China	Sunway SW26010 260C 1.45GHz	10649600	93014.6	15371	6.051
7	Tianhe-2A, NUDT National Super Computer Center in Guangzhou, China	Intel Xeon E5-2692v2 12C 2.2GHz, TH Express-2, Matrix-2000	4981760	61444.5	18482	3.325

To assist in the speedy execution of threads, the on-chip memory configuration is designed for keeping data "close" to the cores. This on-chip memory subsystem includes a large register file that can dedicate 255 32-bit registers per thread and a 40 MiB L2 cache to reduce latency. The thing that definitely sets Ampere apart from a traditional CPU is the combined L1 cache/shared memory. This is specific to each SM and its partitioning can be programmatically controlled by the host. Shared memory is not transparent to the applications in the way cache memory is. It is addressable memory and it can be considered a form of user-managed cache.

The 192 KiB L1 cache/shared memory is a huge leap from not so distant GPU designs that had a mere 16 KiB shared memory per SM. What we have witnessed over the years in GPU design is the incorporation of bigger and more complex cache hierarchies, more powerful cores (Kepler, a 2012 architecture, had 192 cores per SM), and the inclusion of specialized hardware/instruction sets (tensor cores). GPUs are becoming more CPU-like and the reverse is also true!

A feature which is characteristic of GPUs in general is the ability to perform more for less: more computation for less energy. This is of paramount importance in the field of high-performance computing (HPC), where the energy costs dwarf the cost of the hardware itself, making GPUs a prime candidate for number crunching. This is evident in Table 1.1, where the top performing machine in terms of measured TFlop/KW is Perlmutter, an Ampere A100 equipped machine, followed by two systems equipped with the same chip.

In the case of the A100, efficiency is boosted further by attaching the device memory with the GPU on the same substrate. The GPU is coupled with six modules of second-generation high bandwidth memory (HBM2), reducing the energy required to transfer data to and from the GPU. Fig. 1.6 shows a photograph of the actual chip packaging.

FIGURE 1.6

Photo of NVidia's A100 GPU.

1.3.3 Multicore to many-core: TILERA's TILE-Gx8072 and Intel's Xeon Phi

GPUs have been hosting hundreds or thousands of – admittedly simple – computing cores for more than a decade. But they can do so while being effective under special circumstances typical of graphics workloads. Achieving the same feat for a general-purpose CPU, capable of running operating system tasks and application software, is a different ball game. The two designs that have managed to accomplish this feat are putting in silicon, well-known network configurations that have been used to build parallel machines in the past decades. It is a miniaturization success story.

The first manifestation of the many-core paradigm came in the form of TILERA's TILE64 co-processor, released in August 2007. TILE64 offered 64 cores arranged in a 2D grid. Later designs offered by TILERA came in different configurations, including 9, 16, 36, and 72 cores. The block diagram of the 72-core variant, i.e., TILE-Gx8072,[4] is shown in Fig. 1.7. The 2D grid of communication channels called the iMesh Interconnect comes with five independent mesh networks that offer an aggregate bandwidth exceeding 110 Tbps. The communication is done via non-blocking, cut-through switching with one clock cycle per hop. Each core has 32 KiB data and 32 KiB instruction L1 caches and a 256 KiB L2 cache. An 18 MiB L3 coherent cache is shared between the cores. Access to the main RAM is done via four DDR3 controllers.

The TILE-Gx8072 CPU is targeting networking (e.g., filtering, throttling), multimedia (e.g., transcoding), and cloud applications. Networking receives a lot of attention as attested to by the 32 1-Gbps ports, the eight 10-Gbps XAUI ports, and the two dedicated compression and encryption acceleration engines (MiCA).

As with a GPU, TILERA's chip can be used as a co-processor to offload heavy computational tasks from the main CPU/host. Four multi-lane PCIe interfaces are available to accelerate the transfer of data from/to the host. It can also be used as

---

[4] http://www.tilera.com/sites/default/files/productbriefs/TILE-Gx8072_PB041-03_WEB.pdf, last accessed in July 2014.

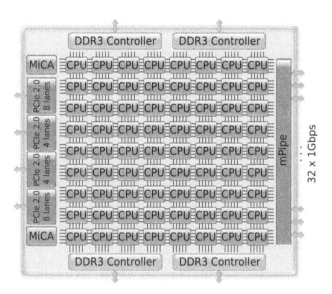

FIGURE 1.7

Simplified block diagram of TILERA's TILE-Gx8072 chip.

a stand-alone platform because it runs a Linux kernel. TILERA offers its Multi-core Development Environment (MDE) as a software development platform for its chips. MDE is built upon OSS tools, such as the GNU C/C++ compiler, the Eclipse IDE, Boost, Thread Building Blocks (TBB), and other libraries. Hence, it leverages existing tools for multicore development, keeping compatibility with a wealth of languages, compilers, and libraries. Chapters 3 and 8 cover tools and techniques that are suitable for developing software for TILERA's chips.

Intel's entry in the many-core arena came at a much later date (2012), but it was not less spectacular. It is a telling fact that at the time of its introduction, the Intel Xeon Phi was a building block of 2 of the 10 supercomputers topping the Top500 list.[5]

Xeon Phi comes equipped with 61 x86 cores that are heavily customized Pentium cores. The customizations include the ability to handle four threads at the same time in order to hide pipeline stalls or memory access delays and a special 512-bit wide Vector Processing Unit (VPU) that operates in SIMD mode to process 16 single-precision or 8 double-precision floating point numbers per clock cycle. The VPU also has an Extended Math Unit (EMU) to handle transcendental functions such as reciprocal, square root, and exponential functions on vectors. Each core comes equipped with 32 KiB data and 32 KiB instruction L1 caches and 512 KiB L2 coherent cache.

---

[5] June 2014 Top500 list: https://top500.org/lists/top500/2014/06/.

The cores are connected with another well-known communication architecture, which has been used also in the Cell BE chip: the ring (see Fig. 1.8).

The ring is bidirectional and it is actually made of six individual rings, three in each direction. Each direction has one 64-byte wide (!) data ring and two narrower rings: an address (AD) ring and an acknowledgment (AK) ring. The AD ring is used to send read/write commands and memory addresses. The AK ring is used for L2 cache coherence.

The coherency is managed by distributed tag directories (TDs), which contain information about every L2 cache line on the chip.

When a core gets an L2 cache miss, it sends an address request on the AD ring to the tag directories. If the requested data block is found in another core's L2 cache, a forwarding request is sent to that core's L2 cache over the AD ring and the requested block is subsequently forwarded over the data ring. If the requested data is not on the chip, the memory address is sent from the tag directory to the memory controllers.

The redundancy, that is, having two from each type of ring, ensures scalability, since testing has shown that using only one of the AK and AD type rings causes performance to level off at around 30 to 35 cores.

The GDDR5 memory controllers are interleaved across the cores and accessed through these rings. Memory addresses are equally distributed between the controllers to avoid making any one of them a bottleneck.

The hardware is impressive. But how is it to program 61 cores? The Xeon Phi co-processor is available as a PCIe card that runs Linux. A special device driver makes the PCIe bus appear as a network interface, which means that the co-processor appears to the host machine as another machine to which it is connected over the network. A user can use SSH to log in the Xeon Phi machine!

Applications can either be run on the host machine and parts of them offloaded to the Xeon Phi card, or they can run entirely on the co-processor, in which case they are referred to as running in "native mode." Xeon Phi leverages all the existing shared- and distributed-memory tools' infrastructure. One can use threads, OpenMP, Intel TBB, MPI, etc., to build applications for it. This also constitutes a major advantage of the many core architectures compared with GPUs, since the latter require the mastering of new tools and techniques.

As a last word, it is worth noting one characteristic that is common to all architectures that host many cores: relatively low clock frequencies. This feature is shared by GPUs (0.8–1.5 GHz), TILE-Gx8072 (1.2 GHz), and Intel Xeon Phi (1.2–1.3 GHz). It is the price one has to pay for cramming billions of transistors on the same die, as the signal propagation delays increase.

Intel stopped developing Xeon Phi in 2017. However, many of the architectural features developed for it have trickled down to mainstream desktop and server CPU designs.

1.3.4 AMD's Epyc Rome: scaling up with smaller chips

Cramming more and more compute logic inside a CPU or GPU chip package is a driving principle in the industry. This results in huge chips in terms of surface area,

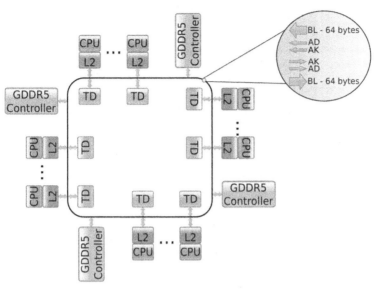

FIGURE 1.8

Block diagram of the Intel Xeon Phi co-processor.

despite the evolution of 7-nm and soon to be 5-nm node processes. For example, the Intel 8086 CPU, a popular choice for 1980s microcomputers, was manufactured using a 3-μm = 3000-nm process and had a surface area of 16 mm². In contrast, Intel's Ice Lake CPU with integrated graphics, manufactured using a 10-nm process, has a surface area of ∼ 122 mm². In turn, bigger chips tend to get more manufacturing defects, producing lower yields (percent of good versus defective chips produced) and driving prices up.

AMD's solution to this problem came in 2017 in the form of the multi-chip module (MCM) for the production of the first-generation Epyc Naples CPU. Instead of having a monolithic CPU with all the logic on a single silicone chip, an MCM CPU is comprised of several smaller chips (chiplets) connected together to provide the full functionality intended. Chiplets, by virtue of being small in size, can be produced with far superior yields, and as a side benefit, they can be connected in a different configuration to produce CPUs of different capabilities and price points.

The second-generation Epyc CPU revealed at the end of 2019 was a revelation: the 7742 model has 64 cores and 256 MiB of L3 cache in a single package, running at a base clock speed of 2.25 GHz with a 3.4 GHz boost. Fig. 1.9 shows a block diagram of this CPU. Each chiplet is officially called a core complex die (CCD) and it contains two core complex (CCX) parts. Each CCX contains four Zen2 cores, their dedicated L2 cache, and their shared L3 cache [42].

In effect this design uses a system-on-chip (SoC) to implement the complex and expensive circuitry of multi-socket server platforms of the past. Although this is technically a single CPU package, the existence of disjoint L3 caches means that data

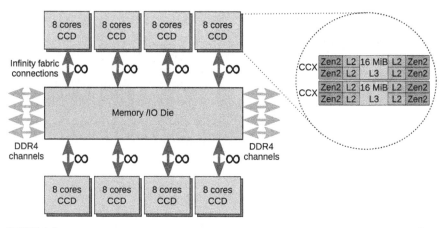

FIGURE 1.9

Block diagram of AMD's Epyc Rome 7742 CPU.

cache locality can be a significant decision factor for thread placement. For this reason the chip can be configured in software as a NUMA platform in four different ways, from treating the whole CPU as a single NUMA domain (i.e., as if all nodes have equal cost access to all available memory), to breaking it into one NUMA domain per CCX [42], for a total of 16 groups of four cores.

1.3.5 Fujitsu A64FX: compute and memory integration

Fujitsu's A64FX is an ARM-based processor that powers the most powerful machine in the world at the time of this writing: Japan's Fugaku. A64FX delivers this performance by (a) implementing the ARMv8.2-A instruction set with 512-bit Scalable Vector Extensions (SIMD instructions similar to Intel's AVX) and more importantly (b) tightly integrating the CPU with 32 GiB of HBM2 memory, able to deliver a bandwidth of 1 TiB/sec to the cores (256 GiB per HBM2 module). This approach is similar to how memory is attached to NVidia's A100 accelerator (see Fig. 1.10), and it is not the only similarity between this CPU and contemporary GPUs.

A block diagram of A64FX can be seen in Fig. 1.11. A64FX is made up of four core memory groups (CMGs), offering a total of 52 cores [52]. Each CMG contains 12 compute cores and one helper core that is responsible for executing OS duties, performing I/O, etc. As each CMG is attached directly to an HBM2 module, an L3 cache is unnecessary, saving both silicon real estate and the energy required to run it. The four CMG modules are connected internally by a network in a similar fashion to the Cell BE and Xeon Phi before it.

Having the memory and the CPU share the same substrate means that the memory capacity and speed is no longer a design capability or concern, but it offers a huge advantage in speed, energy efficiency, cooling, and packaging, all key factors in HPC installations.

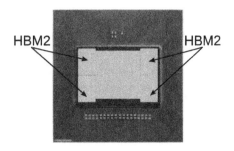

FIGURE 1.10

Photo of Fujitsu's A64FX. Source [45].

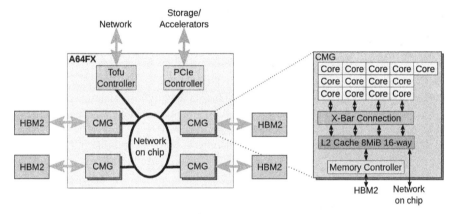

FIGURE 1.11

Block diagram of Fujitsu's A64FX.

1.4 Performance metrics

The motivation driving the multicore hardware and software efforts is the extraction of more performance: shorter execution time, bigger problems and datasets, etc. It is clear that an objective criterion or criteria are needed to be able to assess how effective or beneficial such efforts are.

At the very least, a parallel program should be able to beat in terms of execution time its sequential counterpart (but this is not something you can take to the bank every time). The improvement in execution time is typically expressed as the **speedup**, which is formally defined as the following ratio:

$$\text{speedup} = \frac{t_{seq}}{t_{par}}, \tag{1.1}$$

where t_{seq} is the execution time of the sequential program and t_{par} is the execution time of the parallel program for solving the same instance of a problem.

Both t_{seq} and t_{par} are wall-clock times, and as such they are not objective. They can be influenced by:

- the skill of the programmer who wrote the implementations,
- the choice of compiler (e.g., GNU C++ versus Intel C++),
- the compiler switches (e.g., turning optimization on/off),
- the operating system,
- the type of filesystem holding the input data (e.g., EXT4, NTFS, etc.),
- the time of day (different workloads, network traffic, etc.).

In order to have some level of confidence on reported speedup figures, one should abide by the following rules:

1. All programs (sequential and parallel) should be tested on identical software and hardware platforms and under similar conditions.
2. The sequential program should be the fastest known solution to the problem at hand.

The second one is the least obvious of the two, but it is a crucial requirement: parallel algorithms are completely different beasts than their sequential counterparts. In fact, a sequential algorithm may not have a parallel derivative. It is even possible that a parallel derivative is infeasible to create.

The reason behind the second requirement is a fundamental one: the elevated – and expensive in terms of development cost – effort required to implement a parallel program is justified only if it yields tangible benefits.

The speedup offered by a parallel algorithm for a given number of processors can still vary based on the input data (an example illustrates this point later in this section). For this reason, it is customary to report average figures for the speedup after testing the two programs on a wide collection of inputs of the same size, or even the average, maximum, and minimum observed.

Speedup tells only part of the story: it can tell us if it is feasible to accelerate the solution of a problem, e.g., if speedup > 1. It cannot tell us if this can be done efficiently, i.e., with a modest amount of resources. The second metric employed for this purpose is efficiency. **Efficiency** is formally defined as the following ratio:

$$\text{efficiency} = \frac{\text{speedup}}{N} = \frac{t_{seq}}{N \cdot t_{par}}, \tag{1.2}$$

where N is the number of CPUs/cores employed for the execution of the parallel program. One can interpret the efficiency as the average percent of time that a node is utilized during the parallel execution. If efficiency is equal to 100%, this means that the speedup is N, and the workload is equally divided between the N processors, which are utilized 100% of the time (they are never idle during execution). When speedup $= N$, the corresponding parallel program exhibits what is called **linear speedup**.

This, unfortunately, is an ideal scenario. When multiple processors work towards the accomplishment of a goal, they spend time coordinating with each other, either

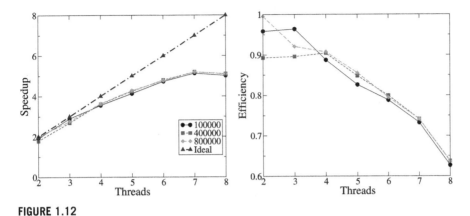

FIGURE 1.12

(a) Speedup and (b) efficiency curves for the execution of a parallel integral calculation by a variable number of threads on a multicore CPU. Each curve corresponds to a different number of divisions of the x-range (as shown in the legend). The ideal speedup line in (a) provides a measure of the performance deterioration, which is a common problem with increased coordination costs.

by exchanging messages or by handling shared resources. The activity related to coordination robs CPU time that ultimately reduces speedup below N.

Fig. 1.12 shows speedup and efficiency curves for a sample program that calculates the definite integral of a function by applying the trapezoidal rule algorithm. The computational load is controlled by the number of trapezoids used for the calculation. The results plotted in Fig. 1.12 were obtained on an i7 950 quad-core CPU and averaged over 10 runs.

There is a discrepancy here for the cautious reader: if we only have a quad-core CPU, how can we test and report speedup for eight threads?

The i7 950 quad-core CPU supports a technique called **hyperthreading**,[6] which allows a CPU core to run two software threads by duplicating parts of the CPU hardware. A CPU that has this feature enabled appears as having twice the number of physical cores it actually has. Unfortunately, the performance is increased on average by only 30%, which is very different from the twofold increase suggested. In that regard, the results reported in Fig. 1.12 are skewed, since on the given platform we do not have eight distinct physical CPUs on which to run eight threads.

However, the deterioration observed in efficiency with an increased number of threads is not bogus: it is typical behavior for parallel applications, although the degree of deterioration is application-specific. It all comes down to what we can generally call the coordination cost, and this can only increase when more parties/CPUs talk to each other.

---

[6] Hyperthreading is a marketing term coined by Intel, for what is otherwise known as hardware threads.

In that regard, Fig. 1.12 serves two purposes: (a) it illustrates what typical speedup and efficiency curves look like and (b) it raises awareness about proper experimentation techniques. Measuring performance should involve real hardware resources and not the virtual provided by hyperthreading.

The ideal speedup curve in Fig. 1.12(a) acts as a measure of how successful our parallel program is. As we mentioned, this is the upper bound of performance. But not always!

There are situations where speedup $> N$ and efficiency > 1, in what is known as a **superlinear speedup** scenario. According to the interpretation we gave to efficiency, this seems like an impossible case. However, we should keep in mind that sequential and parallel programs process their input data in different ways, following different execution paths. So, if the aim of a program is the acquisition of an item in a search space, a parallel program may reach this point far sooner than the number of computing resources utilized would suggest, just by following a different route to reach it.

This is of course not a typical case that can materialize under application- and input data-specific circumstances. As an example, let us consider the problem of acquiring the encryption key of a ciphertext. In the DES encryption standard, a secret number in the range $[0, 2^{56} - 1]$ is used as the key to convert a message (plaintext) to a scrambled unreadable mess (ciphertext). A brute force attack on a ciphertext would involve trying out all the keys until the decoded message could be identified as a readable text. If we assume that each attempt to decipher the message costs time T on a single CPU, if the key was the number 2^{55}, then a sequential program would take $t_{seq} = (2^{55} + 1)T$ time to solve the problem.

If we were to employ two CPUs to solve the same problem and we partitioned the search space of 2^{56} keys equally among the two CPUs, i.e., range $[0, 2^{55} - 1]$ to the first one and range $[2^{55}, 2^{56} - 1]$ to the second one, then the key would be found by the second CPU after only one attempt! We would then have $speedup_{2p} = \frac{(2^{55}+1)T}{T} = 2^{55} + 1$ and $efficiency_{2p} = \frac{2^{55}+1}{2} \approx 2^{54}$!

It would seem quite natural to expect that throwing more computing resources to a problem, i.e., increasing N, would reduce the execution time. This is a fallacy! And our simple example can prove it: what happens if three CPUs are utilized? The first CPU would be assigned the range $[0, \lfloor \frac{2^{56}}{3} \rfloor - 1]$, the second one the range $[\lfloor \frac{2^{56}}{3} \rfloor, \lfloor 2 \frac{2^{56}}{3} \rfloor - 1]$, and the third the range $[\lfloor 2 \frac{2^{56}}{3} \rfloor, 2^{56} - 1]$. So the second processor will find the solution after $2^{55} - \lfloor \frac{2^{56}}{3} \rfloor$ tries, resulting in a speedup of $speedup_{3p} = \frac{(2^{55}+1)T}{(2^{55}-\lfloor\frac{2^{56}}{3}\rfloor)T} = 3\frac{2^{55}+1}{3 \cdot 2^{55}-2^{56}} = 3\frac{2^{55}+1}{2^{55}+2 \cdot 2^{55}-2^{56}} = 3\frac{2^{55}+1}{2^{55}} \approx 3$, which is substantially inferior to $speedup_{2p}$.

Speedup covers the efficacy of a parallel solution: is it beneficial or not? **Efficiency** is a measure of resource utilization: how much of the potential afforded by the computing resources we commit is actually used? A low efficiency indicates a poor design, or at least one that should be further improved.

Finally, we would like to know how a parallel algorithm behaves with increased computational resources and/or problem sizes: *does it scale*?

In general, **scalability** is the ability of a (software or hardware) system to handle a growing amount of work efficiently. In the context of a parallel algorithm and/or platform, scalability translates to being able to (a) solve bigger problems and/or (b) incorporate more computing resources.

There are two metrics used to quantify scalability: strong scaling efficiency (related to (b)) and weak scaling efficiency (related to (a)).

Strong scaling efficiency is defined by the same equation as the generic efficiency defined in equation (1.2):

$$\text{strong scaling efficiency } (N) = \frac{t_{seq}}{N \cdot t_{par}}. \tag{1.3}$$

It is a function of the number N of processors employed to solve the same problem as a single processor.

Weak scaling efficiency is again a function of the number N of processors employed, defined by

$$\text{weak scaling efficiency } (N) = \frac{t_{seq}}{t'_{par}}, \tag{1.4}$$

where t'_{par} is the time to solve a problem that is N times bigger than the one the single machine is solving in time t_{seq}.

There are a number of issues with calculating scaling efficiency when GPU computing resources are involved: what is the value of N that should be used? GPUs typically have hundreds or thousands of cores but it would be awkward or just bad science to report as t_{seq} the time of executing on a single GPU core. If we choose to report as t_{seq} the time of execution of a single CPU core, are we justified to use the total number of GPU cores as N when calculating efficiency? Also, a GPU is a hosted device, i.e., it needs a CPU to perform I/O on its behalf. Does that CPU count?

It is clear that efficiency can be calculated in many different ways under such circumstances. To avoid the controversy, we report only speedup figures in the case studies covered that involve heterogeneous platforms.

1.5 Predicting and measuring parallel program performance

Building a parallel application is substantially more challenging than its sequential equivalent. A programmer has to tackle coordination problems, such as proper access to shared resources, load balancing issues, i.e., dividing the workload among the available computing resources so as to minimize execution time, termination problems, i.e., halting the program in a coordinated fashion, and others.

Embarking on such an endeavor should be attempted only when the application can actually benefit from it by providing an accelerated problem solution. Development costs dictate that one cannot just implement multiple alternative designs and test them in order to select the best one, or worse, evaluate the feasibility of the project. This might be possible for the simplest of problems, but even then it would be preferable if we could determine a priori the best development route to follow.

The development of a parallel solution to a problem starts with the development of its sequential variant! This seems like an oxymoron, but just try to answer these questions: how can we know how much faster a parallel solution to a problem is if we do not have a sequential solution to compare against? We need a baseline and this can only be obtained from a sequential solution. Also, how can we check if the solution produced by the parallel program is correct? Not that the output of a sequential program is guaranteed to be correct, but it is much easier to get it to be correct.

The development of the sequential algorithm and associated program can also provide essential insights into the design that should be pursued for parallelization. The issue is a practical one, as we need to answer the following questions related to the feasibility and cost effectiveness of the parallel program:

- *Which are the most time-consuming parts of the program?* These should be the prime candidates for parallel execution.
- Once these parts are identified and assuming that they can be parallelized, *how much performance gain can be expected?*

A clarification is needed here: the sequential program that is required is not just any sequential program that solves the same problem. It has to be the sequential implementation of the same algorithm that is being parallelized.[7] For example, if we need to sort data in parallel, an algorithm that is suited for a parallel implementation is bucket sort. A sequential implementation of bucket sort can help up predict the parallel performance and also pinpoint the most time-consuming parts of the algorithm. A sequential implementation of quicksort can provide baseline performance information but it cannot contribute to any of the two questions posed above.

Once the sequential version is implemented, we can use a **profiler** to answer these questions. A profiler is a tool that collects information about how frequently parts of a program are called, how long their duration is, and how much memory is used. Profilers use a number of different techniques to perform their task. The most commonly used techniques are:

- **Instrumentation**: modifies the code of the program that is being profiled, so that information can be collected, e.g., incrementing a special counter before every instruction to be executed. This results in very accurate information, but at the same time increases the execution time substantially. This technique requires re-compilation of the target program.
- **Sampling**: the execution of the target program is interrupted periodically, in order to query which function is being executed. Obviously, this is not as accurate as

---

[7] We still need the best sequential solution for proper speedup calculations.

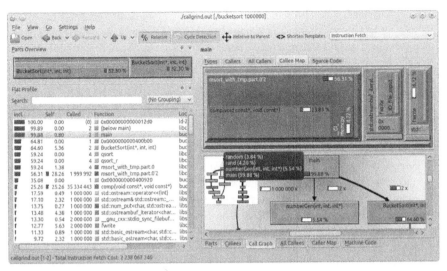

FIGURE 1.13

A sample screenshot of `kcachegrind`, showing the results of the profiling of a sequential bucket sort implementation that switches to quicksort for smaller buckets.

instrumentation, but the program does not require recompilation and the execution time is only slightly disturbed.

The `valgrind` analysis tool collection contains an instrumentation-based profiler. The instrumentation is performed right before the profiling takes place, which means there is no need for user intervention. This is an example of how it can be called:

```
$ valgrind --tool=callgrind ./bucketsort 1000000
```

where `./bucketsort 1000000` are the program to be profiled and its arguments.

The outcome is a file called "`callgrind.out`," which holds the results of the analysis. This can be visualized by a front-end program like `kcachegrind`. A sample screenshot is shown in Fig. 1.13.

Experience and intimate knowledge of the problem domain are assets that can allow someone to pinpoint the "hotspots" that need to be parallelized without profiling a sequential program.

However, the profiler can help us answer the second question posed above, about the potential performance we can extract from a parallel solution. Traditionally, this is done by approximate mathematical models that allow us to capture the essence of the computation that is to be carried out. The parameters of these models can be estimated via profiling the sequential application. In the following section, we describe Amdahl's law, which is based on such a simple model.

Regardless of the mathematical model performance predictions, real-life testing of the implemented parallel design must be conducted for two reasons: correctness and performance. The correctness of the parallel implementation must be verified. Parallel programs can behave in a non-deterministic manner, as events occurring in an unspecified order relative to each other may influence the outcome of the computation. Non-determinism – unless planned for – is an undesirable characteristic that must be rooted out if it exists. Also, testing can reveal weaknesses with the original design or performance problems that need to be addressed.

The following list contains guidelines for conducting a proper experimental procedure:

- The duration of the whole execution should be measured, unless specifically stated otherwise. For example, if only a part of a program is to be parallelized, speedup and efficiency could be calculated only for that particular part of the execution timeline. However, overall times could serve to put into perspective the impact of the parallel solution and whether it is cost-effective or not. For example, a program that needs 100 seconds for solving a problem would still require 90+ seconds if a 10% part of it was executed with a speedup of $100\times$.
- Results should be reported in the form of averages over multiple runs, possibly including standard deviations. The number of runs is application-specific, as for example repeating an experiment that lasts for 3 days 100 times and for many different scenarios would be totally unrealistic. However, to counter this, averaging over three runs can only produce unreliable statistical figures. So, a careful balance must be struck.
- Outliers, i.e., too big or too small results, should be excluded from the calculation of the averages as they typically are expressions of an anomaly (e.g., running out of main memory or changes in the workload of the machines). However, care should be given so that unfavorable results are not brushed away instead of being explained.
- Scalability is paramount, so results should be reported for a variety of input sizes (ideally covering the size and/or quality of real-life data) and a variety of parallel platform sizes.
- Test inputs should vary from very small to very big, but they should always include problem sizes that would be typical of a production environment, if these can be identified.
- When multicore machines are employed, the number of threads and/or processes should not exceed the number of available *hardware* cores, if efficiency is to be calculated. Hyperthreading is a special case, as this technology makes a CPU appear to the operating system as having twice (or more) the number of cores it actually has. However, these *logical* cores do not match the capabilities of full-blown cores. So, although the operating system may report the availability of, e.g., eight cores, the corresponding hardware resources are just not there, in effect compromising any scalability analysis. Ideally, hyperthreading should be disabled for measuring scalability or the number of threads should be limited to the number of hardware cores.
  There are cases where having more threads than cores is beneficial: if some of them block for whatever reason, the remaining can still utilize the CPUs. However,

when efficiency is calculated, N in equation (1.2) should be the number of cores and not the number of threads/processes.

Out of the desire to predict parallel performance without going through the expensive step of implementing and testing a parallel program came the two laws described in the sections that follow. Especially, Amdahl's law remains still influential, although it has been shown to be flawed.

1.5.1 Amdahl's law

In 1967 Gene Amdahl formulated a simple thought experiment for deriving the performance benefits one could expect from a parallel program. Amdahl assumed that:

- We have a sequential application that requires T time to execute on a single CPU.
- The application consists of a $0 \leq \alpha \leq 1$ part that can be parallelized. The remaining $1 - \alpha$ has to be done sequentially.
- Parallel execution incurs no communication overhead, and the parallelizable part can be divided evenly among any chosen number of CPUs. This assumption suits particularly well multicore architectures where cores have access to the same shared memory.

Given the above assumptions, the speedup obtained by N nodes should be upper-bounded by

$$\text{speedup} = \frac{t_{seq}}{t_{par}} = \frac{T}{(1-\alpha)T + \frac{\alpha \cdot T}{N}} = \frac{1}{1 - \alpha + \frac{\alpha}{N}} \tag{1.5}$$

as we are ignoring any partitioning/communication/coordination costs. Eq. (1.5) can give us the maximum possible speedup as well if we obtain the limit for $N \to \infty$:

$$\lim_{N \to \infty}(\text{speedup}) = \frac{1}{1 - \alpha}. \tag{1.6}$$

Eq. (1.6) is a rare gem. In a simple, easy to remember form, it solves a difficult question: how much faster can a problem be solved by a parallel program? And it does so in a completely abstract manner, without consideration of the computing platform idiosyncrasies. It relies only on the characteristics of the problem, i.e., α.

Fig. 1.14 visualizes the predictions of Amdahl's law for different values of α. It is immediately striking that the predicted speedup is severely restricted. Even for modest values of α, the maximum speedup is low. For example, if $\alpha = 0.9$, speedup < 10 regardless of the number of processors thrown at the problem.

The miserable predictions are also reflected in the efficiency curves of Fig. 1.15, where efficiency drops rapidly even for $\alpha = 95\%$.

Amdahl's law has an interesting consequence, which might have been the motivation behind its creation. Amdahl's law was formulated during an era that saw the introduction of the mini-computer. Mini-computers were much cheaper than the then-dominant mainframes, but were also less powerful. A natural question popped

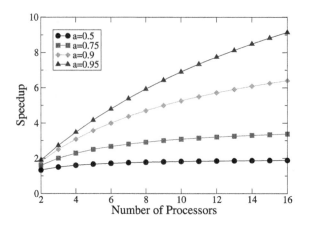

FIGURE 1.14

Speedup curves for different values of α, i.e., the part of an application that can be parallelized, as predicted by Amdahl's law.

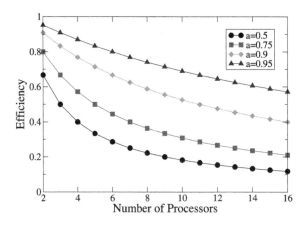

FIGURE 1.15

Efficiency curves for different values of α, as predicted by Amdahl's law.

up: which is the best investment for speeding up the solution of a problem? A few powerful but expensive machines, or many more less powerful but inexpensive ones?

The metaphor used to describe this dilemma predicated the outcome without much doubt: "an army of ants versus a herd of elephants"! The mathematical proof based on the same assumptions as above is as follows: assuming that we have a program that can execute in time T_A on a single powerful CPU and in time T_B on a less powerful, inexpensive CPU. We can declare, based on the execution time, that CPU A is $r = \frac{T_B}{T_A}$ times faster than B. If we can afford to buy N_B CPUs of the inexpensive type, the best speedup we can get relative to the execution on a single CPU of type A is

$$\text{speedup} = \frac{T_A}{(1-\alpha)T_B + \frac{\alpha T_B}{N_B}} = \frac{1}{(1-\alpha)r + \frac{\alpha \cdot r}{N_B}}. \tag{1.7}$$

For infinite N_B, we can get the absolute upper bound on the speedup

$$\lim_{N_B \to \infty}(\text{speedup}) = \frac{1}{(1-\alpha)r}, \tag{1.8}$$

which means that the speedup will never be above 1, no matter how many "ants" you use, if

$$\frac{1}{(1-\alpha)r} \leq 1 \Rightarrow r \geq \frac{1}{1-\alpha}. \tag{1.9}$$

So if $\alpha = 90\%$ and $r = 10$ we are better off using a single expensive CPU than going the parallel route with inexpensive components.

The problem is that this conclusion does not reconcile with the reality of high-performance computing. The list of the top 500 most powerful supercomputers in existence worldwide, as compiled in June 2021,[8] is populated exclusively by machines that have tens of thousands to millions of CPU cores (7,630,848 for the machine holding the top spot, Fugaku). If the army of ants won, there must be a flaw in our approach. This is revealed in the following section.

1.5.2 Gustafson–Barsis' rebuttal

Amdahl's law is fundamentally flawed as it has been repeatedly shown to fail to explain empirical data: parallel programs routinely exceed the predicted speedup limits.

Finally, two decades after Amdahl's law was published, Gustafson and Barsis managed to examine the problem from the proper point of view.

A parallel platform does more than just speed up the execution of a sequential program. It can accommodate bigger problem instances. So instead of examining what a parallel program could do relative to a sequential one, one should examine how a sequential machine would perform if it were required to solve the same problem that a parallel one can solve.

Assume the following:

- We have a parallel application that requires T time to execute on N CPUs.
- The application spends $0 \leq \alpha \leq 1$ of the total time running on all machines. The remaining $1 - \alpha$ has to be done sequentially.

Solving the same problem on a sequential machine would require a total time:

$$t_{seq} = (1-\alpha)T + N \cdot \alpha \cdot T \tag{1.10}$$

as the parallel parts have to be done sequentially.

---

[8] Available at http://www.top500.org/lists/2021/06/.

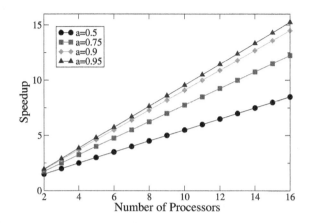

FIGURE 1.16

Speedup curves for different values of α as predicted by Gustafson–Barsis' law.

The speedup would then be

$$\text{speedup} = \frac{t_{seq}}{t_{par}} = \frac{(1-\alpha)T + N \cdot \alpha \cdot T}{T} = (1-\alpha) + N \cdot \alpha \qquad (1.11)$$

and the corresponding efficiency would be

$$\text{efficiency} = \frac{\text{speedup}}{N} = \frac{1-\alpha}{N} + \alpha. \qquad (1.12)$$

The efficiency has a lower bound of α as N goes to infinity.

The resulting speedup curves as shown in Fig. 1.16 are worlds apart from the ones in Fig. 1.14. Given the total disregard for the communication costs, the results are obviously overambitious, but the potential truly exists.

In the efficiency curves of Fig. 1.17 the picture remains a rosy one. Even for $\alpha = 50\%$, efficiency does not drop below 50% for up to 16 CPUs. This is just too good to be true. Even for the so-called embarrassingly parallel problems, communication overheads become a defining factor when N increases, diminishing speedup gains and plummeting efficiency. In general, obtaining efficiency above 90% in practice is considered a worthwhile achievement.

Exercises

1. Study one of the top 10 most powerful supercomputers in the world.

- What kind of operating system does it run?
- How many CPUs/GPUs is it made of?

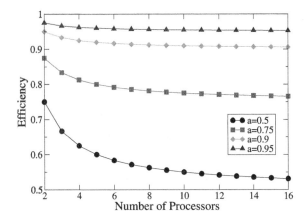

FIGURE 1.17

Efficiency curves for different values of α as predicted by Gustafson–Barsis' law.

- What is its total memory capacity?
- What kind of software tools can be used to program it?

2. How many cores are inside the top GPU offerings from NVidia and AMD? What is the GFlop rating of these chips?

3. The performance of the most powerful supercomputers in the world is usually reported as two numbers, $Rpeak$ and $Rmax$, both in TFlops (tera floating point operations per second). Why is this done? What are the factors reducing performance from $Rpeak$ to $Rmax$? Would it be possible to ever achieve $Rpeak$?

4. A sequential application with a 20% part that must be executed sequentially is required to be accelerated threefold. How many CPUs are required for this task? If the required speedup factor was 5, what would be the number of CPUs required?

5. A parallel application running on five identical machines has a 10% sequential part. What is the speedup relative to a sequential execution on one of the machines? If we would like to double that speedup, how many CPUs would be required?

6. An application with a 5% non-parallelizable part is to be modified for parallel execution. Currently on the market there are two parallel machines available: machine X with four CPUs, each CPU capable of executing the application in 1 hour on its own, and machine Y with 16 CPUs, with each CPU capable of executing the application in 2 hours on its own. Which is the machine you should buy if the minimum execution time is required?

7. Create a simple sorting application that uses the mergesort algorithm to sort a large collection (e.g., 10^7) of 32-bit integers. The input data and output results should be stored in files, and the I/O operations should be considered a sequential part of the application. Mergesort is an algorithm that is considered appropriate for parallel execution, although it cannot be equally divided between an arbitrary number of processors, as Amdahl's and Gustafson–Barsis' laws require.

Assuming that this equal division is possible, estimate α, i.e., the part of the program that can be parallelized, by using a profiler like `gprof` or `valgrind` to measure the duration of mergesort's execution relative to the overall execution time. Use this number to estimate the predicted speedup for your program.

Does α depend on the size of the input? If it does, how should you modify your predictions and their graphical illustration?

8. A parallel application running on 10 CPUs spends 15% of its total time in sequential execution. What kind of CPU (how much faster) would we need to run this application completely sequentially, while keeping the same total time?

9. A company is running an application with a 10% non-parallelizable part on a sequential machine. Needing to speed up the execution of this application, a parallel machine with 10 CPUs is planned to replace the existing hardware. According to Amdahl, how much faster should the new machine's CPUs be than the older one to guarantee a speedup?

10. The weather service is planning to upgrade their parallel machine used for weather prediction. The existing 10-core machine is running an application that runs sequentially for 5% of the time and takes 5 hours to complete. The CPU that will be the basis of the new machine is three times faster than the old one. How many CPUs will be required for the new machine so that it runs the same application in 1 hour or less?

11. The archive containing the book's code samples has a program named `terminProdConsMess.cpp`. The program uses a user-specified number of threads arranged in a producer–consumer pattern to calculate the definite integral of a function using the trapezoid rule. The program accepts two parameters: (a) the number of threads (1 for sequential execution) and (b) the number of trapezoids to use. It reports the total execution time in milliseconds. Test this program with a varying number of threads and calculate the speedup and efficiency achieved.

Multicore and parallel program design

2

In this chapter you will:

- Learn the PCAM methodology for designing parallel programs.
- Use task graphs and data dependency graphs to identify parts of a computation that can be executed in parallel.
- Learn popular decomposition patterns for breaking down the solution of a problem into parts that can be executed concurrently.
- Learn major program structure patterns for writing parallel software, such as master–worker and fork/join.
- Understand the performance characteristics of decomposition patterns, such as pipelining.
- Learn how to combine a decomposition pattern with an appropriate program structure pattern.

2.1 Introduction

The transition to multicore programming is never an easy one, even for seasoned professional programmers. Multicore and parallel programming in general break the legacy of the sequential program that executes its statements in a strict order. When many things happen at the same time, as is the case for parallel programs, the possible ordering of statements is far from unique. Unless the program is carefully designed, problems like erroneous updates to data, out-of-sync communications that block programs, can creep in.

In this chapter we delve into the development of multicore software by addressing the most fundamental aspect of the problem: *the design*.

Our objectives are twofold:

- correctness and
- performance.

Turning a sequential program into a parallel one is not necessarily the way to go. Parallel execution may require a completely new algorithm. In fact, GPUs impose so many restrictions on the program structure so that we can squeeze out their potential, that a complete redesign is typically necessary.

Multicore and GPU Programming. https://doi.org/10.1016/B978-0-12-814120-5.00010-X

2.2 **The PCAM methodology**

PCAM stands for **p**artitioning, **c**ommunication, **a**gglomeration, and **m**apping, and it is a four-step process for the design of parallel programs that was popularized by Ian Foster in his 1995 book [26].[1] Foster's book remains the definitive resource for understanding and properly applying PCAM. The core ideas of PCAM are still relevant today, even for multicore platforms.

The steps are as follows:

1. **Partitioning**: The first step involves the breakup of the computation in as many individual pieces as possible. This step brings out the parallelism – if it exists – in the algorithm. The granularity of the pieces is application-specific. The breakup can be function-oriented, i.e., separate the different steps that take place (called **functional decomposition**), or data-oriented, i.e., split the data that are to be processed (called **domain or data decomposition**). A rule of thumb is that the number of pieces should be one to two orders of magnitude bigger than the number of compute nodes available. This allows more flexibility in the steps that follow.

2. **Communication**: Ideally, the tasks that result from the breakup of the previous step are totally independent. However, it is usually the case that the tasks have interdependencies: for one to start, another one has to complete, etc. This dependence may include the passing of data: *communication*. In this step, the **volume of data** that need to be communicated between the tasks is determined. The combination of the first two steps results in the creation of the **task dependency graph**, with nodes representing tasks and edges representing communication volume.

3. **Agglomeration**: Communication is hampering parallel computation. We can reduce it or eliminate it by grouping tasks together.[2] Each group will be ultimately assigned to a single computational node, which means communication within the group is eliminated. The number of groups produced at this stage should be as a rule-of-thumb one order of magnitude bigger than the number of compute nodes available.

4. **Mapping**: For the application to execute, the task groups produced by the third step must be assigned/mapped to the available nodes. The objectives that need to be achieved at this stage are to: (a) load balance the nodes, i.e., they should all have more or less the same amount of work to do as measured by execution time, and (b) reduce communication overhead even further by mapping groups with expensive data exchange between them to the same nodes: communication over shared memory is virtually free.

How each of the steps can be performed is application-dependent. Furthermore, it is known that the mapping step is an NP-complete problem, which means that in

---

[1] Available online at http://www.mcs.anl.gov/~itf/dbpp/text/book.html.

[2] Communication can be also eliminated by duplicating tasks, i.e., performing the same task more than once but on different machines. This is an option we do not consider in this chapter.

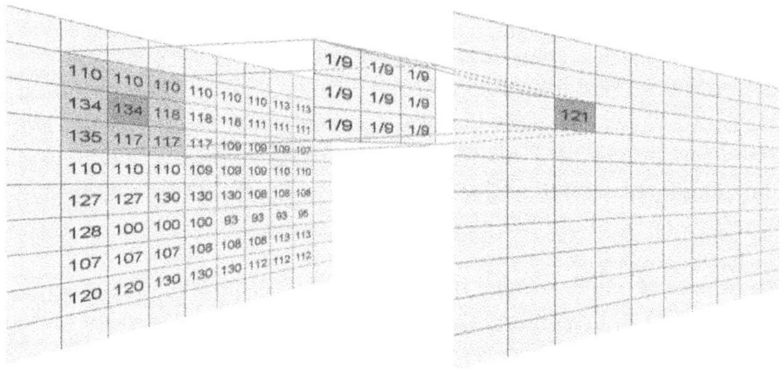

FIGURE 2.1

An illustration of how a 3×3 kernel is applied to the pixel values of an image to produce a desired effect. The shown 3×3 matrix produces a blurring effect. The new pixel values for the image on the right are produced by accumulating the products of the kernel weights and the pixel values of the area surrounding the pixel's location.

its general form it cannot be optimally solved for non-trivial graphs. A number of heuristics can be employed instead.

Additionally, performance can be improved by duplicating computations, thus eliminating the need to communicate their results [10].

As an example of how PCAM can be applied, let us consider the problem of parallelizing a low-level image processing algorithm such as image convolution, which can be used for noise filtering, edge detection, or other applications, based on the kernel used. The kernel is a square matrix with weights that are used in the calculation of the new pixel data. An illustration for a blur effect kernel is shown in Fig. 2.1.

Convolution between a kernel K of – odd – size n and an image f is defined by the formula

$$g(x, y) = \sum_{i = n2}^{n2} \sum_{j=-n2}^{n2} k(n2 + i, n2 + j) f(x - i, y - j), \qquad (2.1)$$

where $n2 = \lfloor \frac{n}{2} \rfloor$. If for example a 3×3 kernel is used,

$$K = \begin{vmatrix} k_{0,0} & k_{0,1} & k_{0,2} \\ k_{1,0} & k_{1,1} & k_{1,2} \\ k_{2,0} & k_{2,1} & k_{2,2} \end{vmatrix}, \qquad (2.2)$$

then for each pixel at row i and column j, the new pixel value $v'_{i,j}$ resulting from the convolution is determined by the values of the pixel and its eight neighbors according to the formula

$$v'_{i,j} = v_{i-1,j-1} \cdot k_{2,2} + v_{i-1,j} \cdot k_{2,1} + v_{i-1,j+1} \cdot k_{2,0} +$$
$$v_{i,j-1} \cdot k_{1,2} + v_{i,j} \cdot k_{1,1} + v_{i,j+1} \cdot k_{1,0} +$$
$$v_{i+1,j-1} \cdot k_{0,2} + v_{i+1,j} \cdot k_{0,1} + v_{i+1,j+1} \cdot k_{0,0}, \quad (2.3)$$

where v are original pixel values.

The pseudocode for a program applying a convolution-based filter is shown in Listing 2.1. To avoid handling boundary pixels (i.e., pixels on the four edges of the image) as special cases, the array holding the image data is enlarged by two rows and two columns. How these extra pixels are initialized is determined by how convolution is set to be calculated for the boundaries. For example, they can be initialized either to zero or to the value of the image pixel closest to them.

Listing 2.1: Pseudocode for image filtering using convolution. The image is assumed to be of size IMGX × IMGY and the kernel of size $n \times n$.

```
1   int img[IMGY+2][IMGX+2];
2   int filt[IMGY][IMGX];
3   int n2 = n/2;
4   for(int x=1;x <= IMGX; x++) {
5     for(int y=1; y <= IMGY ; y++)  {
6       int newV=0;
7       for(int i= -n2; i<= n2; i++)
8         for(int j= -n2; j<= n2; j++)
9           newV += img[ y - j][ x - i ] * k[n2 + j][n2 + i];
10      filt[y-1][x-1] = newV;
11      }
12    }
```

Unrolling the first two for loops in Listing 2.1 and treating their body as a single task provides us with a task graph of size IMGX × IMGY. This is an example of domain decomposition as each task is responsible for calculating the value of a single pixel. However, only the original value of the pixel is not sufficient for the calculation. The values of the neighboring pixels are also required, producing the graph that is shown in Fig. 2.2.

The total communication operations required for the computations in Fig. 2.2 to proceed are equal to

$$
\begin{aligned}
totalComm = {} & 8 \cdot IMGX \cdot IMGY - 3 \cdot 2 \cdot (IMGX - 2) \\
& - 3 \cdot 2 \cdot (IMGY - 2) - 4 \cdot 5 \\
= {} & 8 \cdot IMGX \cdot IMGY - 6 \cdot (IMGX + IMGY) + 4.
\end{aligned} \tag{2.4}
$$

The first term accounts for the eight communications per pixel required, as in the example shown in Fig. 2.2 the red task (dark gray in print version) receives data from the eight blue tasks (light gray in print version). The last three terms are corrections for the top and bottom pixel rows [each doing three fewer communications, for a total of $3 \cdot 2 \cdot (IMGX - 2)$[, the left and right pixel columns [$3 \cdot 2 \cdot (IMGY - 2)$], and the four corner pixels ($4 \cdot 5$).

Fig. 2.2 is the outcome of applying the first two steps of the PCAM methodology. The number of communication operations is obviously quite large. Grouping together tasks, as per the third phase of PCAM, aims to reduce this overhead by making required data local to a task. There are many ways that tasks can be grouped:

- 1D: group together tasks along the x- or y-axis;
- 2D: group together neighboring tasks to form rectangular groups of fixed size.

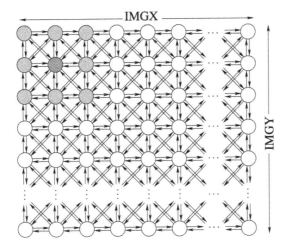

FIGURE 2.2

Task graph resulting from performing domain decomposition of the image convolution algorithm.

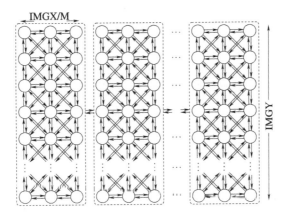

FIGURE 2.3

Task graph resulting from performing agglomeration on the graph of Fig. 2.2 by grouping together columns of tasks into M groups.

The sides of each group should evenly divide – if possible – the corresponding image dimension. Otherwise, the resulting groups will be unequal in terms of workload. This can in turn cause nodes to become idle while others keep computing when the mapping phase is done.

If the agglomeration is done across the x-axis, assuming that the number of groups M divides evenly the number of image columns, we get the task graph of Fig. 2.3. Here, the communication operations are reduced to just $2(M-1)$, but each operation now carries $IMGY$ pixel values. The number of groups for our simple example can match the number of available compute nodes, making the mapping stage trivial. It is also a possibility that the agglomeration is not uniform, i.e., the groups are not identical in size, if the execution platform is not homogeneous. The possibilities are endless and are obviously driven by the problem, the data representation, and the execution platform.

2.3 Decomposition patterns

The most challenging and at the same time critical part of the design process is arguably the decomposition phase, i.e., determining the parts of the computation that can proceed concurrently. While the task graph approach is the most generic, it does not let developers gain from previous experience. This is where patterns come in. Mattson et al. [47] list a number of decomposition patterns (identified in their book as "algorithm structure design space patterns") that can cover the basic ways a workload can be decomposed for eventual distribution to the nodes of a parallel/multicore platform. Fig. 2.4 shows the decision tree that leads to one of the six possible patterns.

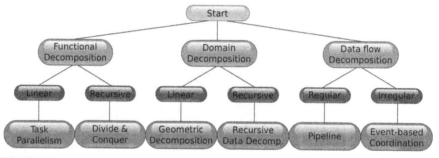

FIGURE 2.4

Decision tree for the decomposition of an algorithm. The bottom layer lists the possible decomposition patterns.

The two categories of decomposition identified in the previous section, i.e., functional and domain decomposition, are joined by an additional one: data flow decomposition. This category of patterns is applicable when the application is supposed to process a **stream of data** that pass through a number of processing stages. In that sense, it can be regarded as an extension of functional decomposition. The data may follow a predetermined sequence of steps leading to the use of the pipeline pattern, or they may follow irregular patterns as in the case of discrete event simulations, leading to the use of the event-flow decomposition.

The next decision step has to do with the a priori knowledge (or absence of knowledge) of the tasks that need to be executed towards the solution of a problem. A priori knowledge implies the ability to statically partition the jobs at the data or functional level (linear decomposition). In the opposite situation, run-time partitioning has to be utilized.

The following sections describe each of the six patterns in detail. It should be noted that there is no strict separation between the different decomposition patterns. A problem can in general be decomposed in several different ways. The variety of patterns allows us to think about the parallelization problem from different perspectives.

2.3.1 **Task parallelism**

Many sequential codes are structured in modules that interoperate towards the solution of a problem. As an example, let us consider the main loop of a game:

```
while(true) {
    readUserInput();
    drawScreen();
    playSounds();
    strategize();
    }
```

An easy approach to parallelism would be to assign each of the individual modules to a different compute node:

```
Task1 {
  while(true) {
      readUserInput();
      barrier();
      }
Task2 {
  while(true) {
      drawScreen();
      barrier();
      }
Task3 {
  while(true) {
      playSounds();
      barrier();
      }
Task4 {
  while(true) {
      strategize();
      barrier();
      }
```

The `barrier` synchronization primitive is supposed to ensure that all tasks co-ordinate together by forcing them to wait until all complete a loop before the next iteration begins.

As long as complex dependencies do not exist between the tasks, concurrent execution is possible. This is, however, a scheme that does not scale well with the number of compute nodes, as the maximum number of nodes cannot exceed the usually limited number of tasks.

2.3.2 **Divide-and-conquer decomposition**

A large collection of sequential algorithms are elegantly expressed recursively, i.e., the solution is expressed as the combination to the solutions of smaller disjoint sub-problems.

The sequence of steps for a typical divide-and-conquer algorithm is shown below:

```
// Input: A
DnC(A) {
  if(A is a base case)
    return solution(A);
  else {
    split A into N subproblems B[N];
    for(int i=0;i<N;i++)
      sol[i] = DnC( B[i] );      // solve each subproblem
    return mergeSolution(sol);
  }
}
```

A simple example is the top-down mergesort algorithm, partially shown in pseudocode below:

```
// Input: array A and endpoints st, end
mergeSort(A, st, end) {
  if(end > st) {
    middle = (st+end) / 2;
    mergeSort(A, st, middle);
    mergeSort(A, middle+1, end);
    mergeLists(A, st, middle, end);
  }
}
```

The `mergeLists` call is the one that is actually doing the sorting, but the above listing reveals how the algorithm breaks up the input into ever decreasing size pieces that it subsequently joins together once they are sorted.

It should be stressed that the dependency graph, which allows us to explore the concurrency potential, does not coincide with the function call graph, so care should be exercised when such a graph is generated. Fig. 2.5 shows the sequence of calls made by a sequential program for sorting an array of eight items. The parallelism is revealed when the dependency graph between those function calls is drawn as shown in Fig. 2.6.

In general, the divide-and-conquer pattern is governed by the dynamic generation of tasks at run-time. The generation is performed until either we reach down to a

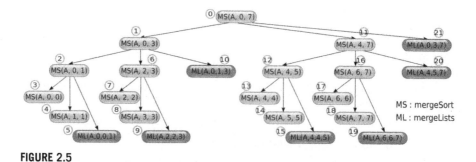

FIGURE 2.5

Call graph for a sequential execution of the top-down mergesort algorithm for an input of eight items. The circled numbers next to each node represent the call order.

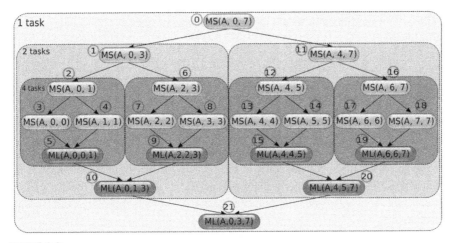

FIGURE 2.6

Dependency graph for the function calls made by the top-down mergesort algorithm for an input of eight items. The dashed gray boxes represent possible task assignments. In our example, the maximum level of concurrency is four tasks, as the mergeSort calls for an array of size 1, return immediately, and do not represent any actual workload.

specific problem size or the number of tasks that can run concurrently reaches the number of available compute nodes. This approach can be summarized in the form of pseudocode as shown below:

Listing 2.2: Pseudocode for parallelizing a generic divide-and-conquer algorithm.

```
1   // Input: A
2   DnC(A) {
3     if(isBaseCase( A ))
4       return solution(A);
5     else {
6       if( bigEnoughForSplit( A ) ) { // if problem is big enough
7         split A into N subproblems B[N];
8         for(int i=0;i<N;i++)
9           task[i] = newTask( DnC( B[i] ) );   // non-blocking
10
11        for(int i=0;i<N;i++)
12          sol[i] = getTaskResult( task[i] );  // blocking results wait
13
14        return mergeSolution( sol );
15      }
16      else {                        // else solve sequentially
17        return solution( A );
18      }
19    }
20  }
```

In the loop of lines 8–9, non-blocking calls are made to generate N tasks that will solve the subproblems created in line 7. The execution will only block when it is time to collect the results of the child task executions (lines 11–12). It is also possible that the parent task solves one of the subproblems, generating $N - 1$ new tasks, instead of idling. This modification would require the change of lines 8–12 in Listing 2.2 to the following:

```
for(int i=0;i<N-1;i++)
    task[i] = newTask( DnC( B[i] ) );    // non-blocking

DnD( B[N-1] );  // solve one of the subproblems

for(int i=0;i<N-1;i++)
    sol[i] = getTaskResult( task[i] );  // blocking results wait
```

The actual scheduling or mapping of the tasks to the available compute nodes is another problem, which is largely platform-specific as it depends on the associated costs of migrating tasks and communicating data. Therefore, it will be examined in later chapters.

2.3.3 Geometric decomposition

Many algorithms involve the repetition of a sequence of steps on a collection of data. If the data are organized in linear structures such as arrays, 2D matrices, etc., then the data can be split along one or more dimensions and assigned to different tasks. Hence the name "geometric" decomposition.

If there are no dependencies between the data, we have an **embarrassingly parallel** problem, since all the resulting tasks can be executed in parallel, maximizing the potential speedup.

For example, let us consider the problem of simulating heat diffusion on a 2D surface. The equation that governs the temperature change of an isotropic and homogeneous medium is

$$\frac{\partial u}{\partial t} = \alpha \nabla^2 u = \alpha \left(\frac{\partial^2 u}{\partial x^2} + \frac{\partial^2 u}{\partial y^2} \right), \tag{2.5}$$

where $u = u(x, y, t)$ is the temperature as a function of space and time and α is a constant related to the material's thermal conductivity.

A simulation can be performed by dividing the surface into a discrete mesh of cells, each of size $h \cdot h$. Each cell's temperature can be updated over a number of time steps by using the following approximation to the Laplacian operator of Eq. (2.5):

$$u'[i, j] = u[i, j] + \delta t \cdot \frac{u[i-1, j] + u[i+1, j] + u[i, j-1] + u[i, j+1] - 4u[i, j]}{h^2},$$
$$\tag{2.6}$$

where $u'[i, j]$ is the new temperature and $u[i, j]$ the old one at grid location $[i, j]$; δt is the time step.

Eq. (2.6) means that in order to calculate the temperature at every time step, four neighboring values must be collected as shown in Fig. 2.7.

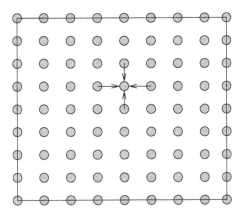

FIGURE 2.7

Data dependencies for the calculation of a cell's new temperature value in the simulation of heat transfer.

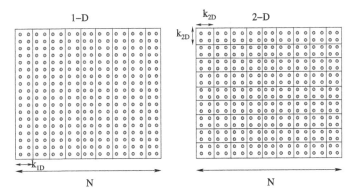

FIGURE 2.8

Geometric decomposition of the data in the simulation of heat transfer.

The geometric decomposition of this problem's data can proceed in one or two dimensions as shown in Fig. 2.8. But which one is preferable?

This is a question that can be answered only by taking into consideration the target execution platform. Fortunately, this can be accomplished without having to build and test multiple versions of the parallel program.

Let us assume that the execution platform is homogeneous, with single-port, full-duplex communication links, and that the following parameters describe the problem:

- N: the number of cells per dimension,
- k_{1D}: the number of cells per division along the x-axis,
- k_{2D}: the number of cells per side of a 2D partition,
- P: the number of compute nodes,

- t_{comp}: the processing cost per single update for a single cell,
- t_{comm}: the communication cost per data item sent between two compute nodes,
- t_{start}: the communication startup latency.

Then, if 1D decomposition is used, we end up with $P = \lceil \frac{N}{k_{1D}} \rceil$ groups that are supposed to be mapped to individual nodes. For the sake of simplicity we will assume that k_{1D} divides N evenly. For each time step, each node will have to spend for execution and communication:

$$comp_{1D} = k_{1D} \cdot N \cdot t_{comp} = \frac{N^2}{P} \cdot t_{comp}, \tag{2.7}$$

$$comm_{1D} = 2 \cdot (t_{start} + t_{comm} N). \tag{2.8}$$

The communication time is calculated based on the need to send and receive a total of four batches of N values. The full-duplex links allow for simultaneous send and receive operations to take place, hence the constant 2 in Eq. (2.8). Boundary nodes are an exception that can be ignored, since the other nodes dominate the overall execution time. The exception becomes the rule if we only have two nodes! Then, the coefficient in Eq. (2.8) is reduced from 2 to 1.

If 2D decomposition were used, each node would be responsible for a k_{2D}^2-sized group of cells. The cells should be evenly divided between the compute nodes, hence k_{2D} should be chosen so that $k_{2D}^2 = \frac{N^2}{P}$. Each node would have to spend for execution and communication per time step:

$$comp_{2D} = k_{2D}^2 t_{comp} = \frac{N^2}{P} t_{comp}, \tag{2.9}$$

$$comm_{2D} = 4 (t_{start} + t_{comm} \cdot k_{2D}) = 4 \left(t_{start} + t_{comm} \cdot \frac{N}{\sqrt{P}} \right). \tag{2.10}$$

As in the 1D case, boundary nodes are an exception that can be ignored, unless we have only four nodes ($N = 4$). In that case, each node performs two concurrent receive and send operations (for a total of four), reducing the coefficient in Eq. (2.10) to 2.

So, if we have more than four nodes to utilize, 1D decomposition would be superior to the 2D case because of the communication overhead if

$$comm_{1D} + comp_{1D} < comm_{2D} + comp_{2D} \Rightarrow$$

$$2 \cdot (t_{start} + t_{comm} N) + \frac{N^2}{P} \cdot t_{comp} < 4 \left(t_{start} + t_{comm} \cdot \frac{N}{\sqrt{P}} \right) + \frac{N^2}{P} t_{comp} \Rightarrow$$

$$t_{comm} N < t_{start} + 2 t_{comm} \frac{N}{\sqrt{P}} \Rightarrow$$

$$t_{start} > t_{comm} N \left(1 - \frac{2}{\sqrt{P}} \right). \tag{2.11}$$

So, as long as the communication startup delay exceeds the threshold of Eq. (2.11), 1D decomposition is preferable, given the communication setup described above.

It should be noted that Eq. (2.6) can be also modeled as a convolution of an image with pixels representing the temperature of the cells and a 3×3 kernel:

$$K = \begin{vmatrix} 0 & 1 & 0 \\ 1 & -4 & 1 \\ 0 & 1 & 0 \end{vmatrix}. \tag{2.12}$$

The discussion of Section 2.2 would apply in this case, giving us the same results.

2.3.4 Recursive data decomposition

Recursive data structures such as trees, lists, or graphs cannot be partitioned in the straightforward manner of the previous section. In recursive data decomposition the data structure is decomposed into individual elements. Each element (or groups of elements) is then assigned to a separate compute node.

The process may involve a modification of the original algorithm so that concurrent operations can take place. The way of operation mimics *dynamic programming*, where bigger problems are solved based on the stored solutions of smaller problems.

As an example, let us consider the problem of calculating the partial sums of an array: given an input array A with N elements, calculate the partial sums $S_i = \sum_{j=0}^{i} A_j$. This is also known as the prefix-sum problem, which serves as a preprocessing component of many algorithms. The precise term is inclusive prefix-sum. The exclusive prefix-sum variant leaves out of the sum the item itself: $S_i^{(excl)} = \sum_{j=0}^{i-1} A_j$, with $S_0 = 0$. A demonstration of these two calculations is shown in Table 2.1.

Table 2.1 Example of exclusive and inclusive prefix-sum calculations.

Input

1	2	3	4	5	6	7

Exclusive prefix-sum

0	1	3	6	10	15	21

Inclusive prefix-sum

1	3	6	10	15	21	28

The linear-complexity sequential algorithm for the inclusive prefix-sum is the following:

Listing 2.3: Sequential pseudocode for the calculation of partial sums of an array.

```
S[0] = A[0];
for(int i=1; i< N; i++)
    S[i] = S[i-1] + A[i];
```

A variation to this algorithm (proposed by Hillis and Steele [31]) would be to calculate partial sums of ever increasing groups of numbers: first of groups of size two, then of groups of size four, then of groups of size eight, etc.:

Listing 2.4: Alternative sequential pseudocode for the calculation of partial sums of an array of integers.

```
1   // Input array A of size N
2   // Uses two arrays for calculating the sum, each of size N
3   int S[2][N];
4
5   S[1][0] = A[0];
6   S[0][0] = A[0];
7
8   int *Snew, *Sold, *aux;
9   Snew = S[0];
10  Sold = A;
11  aux = S[1];
12
13  int step=1;
14  int oldStep=0;
15  while(step < N) {
16    int pos=oldStep;
17
18    // copy the elements not to be updated
19    while(pos < step) {
20      Snew[ pos ] = Sold[ pos ];
21      pos++;
22    }
23
24    // accumulate pairs of elements distance "step" apart
25    while(pos < N) {
26      Snew[pos] = Sold[pos - step] + Sold[pos];
27      pos ++;
28    }
29
30    Sold = Snew;
31    Snew = aux;
32    aux = Sold;
33    oldStep = step;
34    step *= 2;
35  }
36
37  // result is in array Sold
38  }
```

A tracing of the code in Listing 2.4 for an array of size $N = 9$ is illustrated in Fig. 2.9. The use of two arrays for holding the values of the result array as it is being computed is mandated by the fact that each iteration of the while loop of line 14 must be done without touching the old S values.

The swapping code of lines 30–32 ensures that the newly calculated values of S will be used for the next calculations. For the very first iteration of the loop (for step=1), the input array A is used instead of Sold, eliminating the need to initially copy A into Sold.

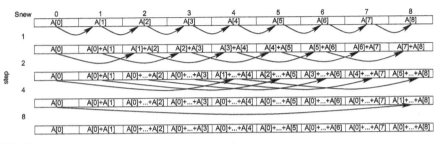

FIGURE 2.9

An illustration of the steps involved in the execution of the code in Listing 2.4 for an array of size $N = 9$. The step variable marks the sets of additions conducted. Each edge represents the accumulation of cell values, the arrow pointing at the destination cell.

Listing 2.4 does not improve on the time complexity of Listing 2.3. On the contrary actually: its time complexity is $O(N \lg N)$ steps,[3] which is a substantial increase over $N - 1$. However, it lends itself to parallel execution! Each of the maximum N steps of each iteration of the while loop of line 15 can be done in parallel. Before the next iteration starts, all nodes should synchronize (via a barrier) so that the updated values of the S array can be used in the next iteration.

If $N - 1$ processors were available, they could run the algorithm of Listing 2.4 in $O(\lg N)$, yielding a potential speedup of

$$\text{speedup} = \frac{N - 1}{\lceil \lg N \rceil}. \tag{2.13}$$

Of course, having that many processors is an unrealistic proposition for any real-life problem, which in turn means that each of the P available nodes should be assigned a group of the updates done in each iteration. The parallel pseudocode is shown below:

Listing 2.5: Pseudocode of a parallel program for partial sums calculation of an array of integers by P nodes. It is assumed that the individual nodes are identified by a unique ID that starts from 0.

```
1   // Input array A of size N
2   // Uses two arrays for calculating the sum, each of size N
3   int S[2][N];
4
5   S[1][0] = A[0];
6   S[0][0] = A[0];
7
8   int *Snew, *Sold, *aux;
9   Snew = S[0];
10  Sold = A;
```

---

[3] Number of steps is $\sum_{i=0}^{\lfloor \lg N \rfloor} (N - 2^i) \approx \sum_{i=0}^{\lg N} (N - 2^i) = N(\lg N + 1) - \sum_{i=0}^{\lg N} 2^i = N(\lg N + 1) - (2^{\lg N + 1} - 1) = N(\lg N + 1) - 2N + 1 = N \lg N - N + 1.$

```
11    aux = S[1];
12
13    int step=1;
14    int oldStep=0;
15
16    while(step < N) {
17
18      parallel do
19        {
20          int pos=oldStep + ID;
21
22          // copy the elements not to be updated
23          while(pos < step) {
24            Snew[ pos ] = Sold[ pos ];
25            pos += P;
26          }
27
28          // accumulate pairs of elements distance "step" apart
29          while(pos < N) {
30            Snew[pos] = Sold[pos - step] + Sold[pos];
31            pos += P;
32          }
33        }
34
35      barrier();
36
37      Sold = Snew;
38      Snew = aux;
39      aux = Sold;
40      oldStep = step;
41      step *= 2;
42    }
43
44    // result is in array Sold
45  }
```

In the parallel loop of lines 18–33 in Listing 2.5, each compute node identified by ID updates the partial sum of elements S[ID+oldStep], S[ID+P+oldStep], S[ID+2*P+oldStep], etc. As long as N is a power of 2 and evenly divided by P, each node is assigned the same workload.

The barrier call of line 35 ensures that all nodes will proceed to the next iteration only when everyone has finished with the parallel do loop.

However, a question that naturally arises given the increased complexity of the parallel algorithm is whether the parallel code can deliver a speedup larger than 1.

The while loop of lines 16–42 in Listing 2.5 is executed $\lceil lgN \rceil$ times. In each iteration, the total number of elements of the Snew array that are updated is equal to $N - oldStep$, with $step - oldStep$ being just copies. If we assume that the cost t_c of line 30 in the above listing dominates the execution time and that N is a power of 2, we can estimate the total execution time as being equal to

$$t_{par} = t_c \left(\lceil \frac{N-1}{P} \rceil + \lceil \frac{N-2}{P} \rceil + \cdots + \lceil \frac{N-2^{lgN-1}}{P} \rceil \right) =$$

$$= t_c \sum_{i=0}^{lgN-1} \lceil \frac{N-2^i}{P} \rceil \approx t_c \sum_{i=0}^{lgN-1} \frac{N-2^i}{P} =$$

$$= t_c \left(\frac{N}{P} \sum_{i=0}^{lgN-1} 1 - \frac{1}{P} \sum_{i=0}^{lgN-1} 2^i \right) = t_c \left(\frac{N}{P} lgN - \frac{1}{P} \left(2^{lgN} - 1 \right) \right) =$$

$$= t_c \left(\frac{N}{P} lgN - \frac{N}{P} + \frac{1}{P} \right) = t_c \left(\frac{N}{P} (lgN - 1) + \frac{1}{P} \right). \quad (2.14)$$

So, a speedup greater than one would require

$$speedup = \frac{t_{seq}}{t_{par}} = \frac{t_c(N-1)}{t_c \left(\frac{N}{P}(lgN-1) + \frac{1}{P} \right)} > 1 \Rightarrow$$

$$(N-1) > \frac{N}{P}(lgN-1) + \frac{1}{P} \Rightarrow \text{(multiplying both sides by } \frac{P}{N-1})$$

$$P > \frac{N}{N-1}(lgN-1) + \frac{1}{N-1}. \quad (2.15)$$

For large problem sizes the above threshold can be approximated by $lgN - 1$, e.g., for 2^{20} items, the number of nodes should exceed 19.

As the prefix-sum calculation is a very frequently encountered component of many algorithms, it is worthwhile to consider an alternative (but a bit more complex) solution to parallelizing this computation. Blelloch [20] proposed a solution comprised of two phases: a **reduction** phase and a **down-sweep** phase. The algorithm works on arrays that have a size which is a power of 2, but the upside is that it is more work-efficient than the Hillis–Steele algorithm.

The Blelloch algorithm works by treating the array as the leaf level of an implicit perfect binary tree. During the reduction phase, we sum up the children of each internal node and store the result in their parent. By doing this level-by-level, we can get to the root where the total sum of all the data will be. With some clever manipulation of the indices, we can get away with storing the internal node results in the original data array.

During the down-sweep phase, we replace the root with zero and we traverse the "tree" in reverse, starting from the root and descending to the leaves. At each level, we switch the values of left and right children of an internal node and deposit their sum in the right child. Again with proper manipulation of the indices all the calculations are in place.

Both phases are depicted in Fig. 2.10 and the pseudocode of the algorithm is provided in Listing 2.6. The algorithm calculates the exclusive prefix-sum, but keeping a copy of the "tree root" is sufficient for extending the calculation to the inclusive version.

Listing 2.6: Pseudocode of Blelloch's parallel algorithm for prefix-sum calculation.

```
1   // Input array A of size N which is a power of 2
2   // The exclusive prefix sum is stored in-place in array A
3
4   // reduction phase
5   int step = 2;
```

```
6     int smallStep = 1;
7     while (smallStep < N)
8     {
9         // assume that the for is partitioned between the nodes
10        parallel for (int i = 0; i < N; i += step)
11            d[i + step - 1] += d[i + smallStep - 1];
12
13        smallStep = step;
14        step *= 2;
15    }
16
17    // down-sweep phase
18    d[N - 1] = 0;
19    step = smallStep;
20    smallStep /= 2;
21    while (smallStep > 0)
22    {
23        parallel for (int i = 0; i < N; i += step)
24        {
25            int temp = d[i + smallStep - 1];
26            d[i + smallStep - 1] = d[i + step - 1];
27            d[i + step - 1] += temp;
28        }
29
30        step = smallStep;
31        smallStep /= 2;
32    }
```

The algorithm is made of two sequences of parallel steps: the parallel for loops in lines 10 and 23 which process one level at a time in parallel. There is no need to

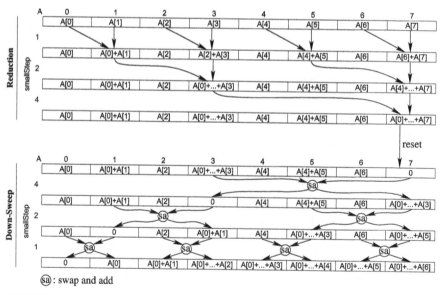

ⓢⓐ : swap and add

FIGURE 2.10

Going through the steps of Blelloch's algorithm for computing the prefix-sum of an eight-element array.

have explicit barriers before lines 13 and 30, as these lines are part of the sequential execution.

In terms of complexity, we have two phases consisting of $M = \lceil lg(N) \rceil$ steps. The ceiling in this expression serves the case where N is not a power of 2 and padding with zeros is required to get the appropriate array size. If we have 2^{M-1} processors, we can complete the additions and swaps required in logarithmic time. If we assume that t_c is also the cost of the swap operation in lines 25–26, we can estimate the total execution time as

$$t_{par}^{(Blel)} = t_c \cdot M + t_c \cdot 2 \cdot M = 3 \cdot t_c \cdot M, \qquad (2.16)$$

which translates into a speedup of

$$\text{speedup}^{(Blel)} = \frac{t_{seq}}{t_{par}^{(Blel)}} = \frac{t_c(N-1)}{3 \cdot t_c \cdot M} = \frac{N-1}{3 \cdot lg(N)}. \qquad (2.17)$$

The speedup is clearly less than for the Hillis–Steele algorithm, but we need roughly half the number of processors. Using $\frac{N}{2}$ processors is still an unrealistic scenario even for modest input data, so we could partition the two parallel for loops of Listing 2.6 between P processors. The estimated execution time would then be

$$t_{par}^{(Blel)} = 3 \cdot t_c \left(\lceil \frac{N/2}{P} \rceil + \lceil \frac{N/4}{P} \rceil + \cdots + \lceil \frac{1}{P} \rceil \right) =$$

$$= 3 \cdot t_c \sum_{i=0}^{lgN-1} \lceil \frac{2^i}{P} \rceil \approx \frac{3 \cdot t_c}{P} \sum_{i=0}^{lgN-1} 2^i =$$

$$= \frac{3 \cdot t_c}{P} (2^{lg(N)} - 1) \approx \frac{3 \cdot t_c}{P} N, \quad (2.18)$$

where the summation terms correspond to the work performed for each level of the "tree," evenly split between the P processors.

The result from Eq. (2.18) is a rough lower bound that also shows that the overall work performed by the algorithm is closer to the sequential one (only enlarged by a factor of 3) than the Hillis–Steele algorithm (which is enlarged by $lg(N)$). So the Blelloch algorithm should be faster for large inputs.

2.3.5 Pipeline decomposition

A pipeline is the software/hardware equivalent of an assembly line. An item can pass through a pipeline made up of several *stages*, each stage applying a particular operation on it.

The pipeline is a popular pattern, encountered in many domains:

- **CPU architectures**: machine instructions in modern CPUs are executed in stages that form a pipeline. This allows the concurrent execution of many instructions, each running in a different stage of the pipeline.

- **Signal processing**: many signal processing algorithms are formulated as pipelines. For example, a fast Fourier transform (FFT)-based filter may be designed around three stages executed in sequence: FFT transform, FFT coefficient manipulation, and inverse FFT transform.
- **Graphics rendering**: contemporary GPUs have graphics or rendering pipelines that receive as input 3D vertices and produce as output 2D raster images. The pipeline stages include lighting and shading, clipping, projection transformation, texturing, etc.
- **Shell programming**: *nix provides the capability to feed the console *output* of one command at the console *input* of another, thus forming a command pipeline. This seemingly unsophisticated technique can make the simple *nix command-line tools perform highly complex tasks. For example, the following three-stage pipeline lists the commands executed by user guest, with superuser privileges. This could be used by a system administrator to detect hacking attempts:

```
$ sudo grep sudo /var/log/auth.log | grep guest | gawk −F ":" '{print $4}'
```

The first stage in the pipeline filters lines containing the word sudo in the /var/log/auth.log log file. The next stage limits the output of the first stage to the lines containing the word guest. Finally the third stage parses the lines output from the second stage to produce the commands used by user guest.

Pipeline stages perform a variation of the following pseudocode, where sending and receiving operations are usually *synchronous* and concurrent in order to reduce any CPU idle times:

```
initialize();
while( moreData ) {
   readDataFromPreviousStage();
   process();
   sendDataToNextStage();
}
```

But what exactly is the benefit of arranging for a computation to take place as a sequence of communicating discrete stages? It turns out there is no benefit unless the stages can run concurrently, operating on different data items at a time. But even then, care must be taken to ensure that the stages' durations are very close or identical: the slowest (longest duration) stage dictates the speed of the pipeline.

A simple example followed by its analysis can shed light on pipeline behavior. Let us assume that we have five stages, arranged in a linear pipeline. Each stage gets its next input as soon as it has sent its output to the next stage. For simplicity we will assume that the *communication costs are negligible*. Then the processing of four data items might resemble the Gantt chart of Fig. 2.11.

It is immediately obvious from Fig. 2.11, that the longest-lasting stage (stage 3) dictates the rate at which the pipeline can process data.

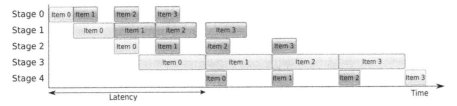

FIGURE 2.11

A Gantt chart of a five-stage pipeline with unequal stage durations, processing a collection of four data items. The highlighted sequence of stage executions dictates the total execution time.

In general, if we have N data items to be processed by an M-stage pipeline, with each stage S_i taking t_i time to process its input and S_l being the slowest stage, then the total execution time (see the highlighted group of stage executions in Fig. 2.11) is

$$t_{total} = \sum_{j=0}^{l-1} t_j + N \cdot t_l + \sum_{j=l+1}^{M-1} t_j. \qquad (2.19)$$

The processing rate of the pipeline (i.e., data items processed per time unit) is

$$rate = \frac{N}{\sum_{j=0}^{l-1} t_j + N \cdot t_l + \sum_{j=l+1}^{M-1} t_j}. \qquad (2.20)$$

The latency of the pipeline is defined as the time required until all stages are having some input to process:

$$latency = \sum_{j=0}^{M-2} t_j. \qquad (2.21)$$

If all the pipeline stages are identical in duration, each lasting time t, then the above equations can be simplified:

$$t_{total} = \sum_{j=0}^{M-2} t + N \cdot t = (N + M - 1)t, \qquad (2.22)$$

$$rate = \frac{N}{(N + M - 1)t}, \qquad (2.23)$$

$$latency = (M - 1)t. \qquad (2.24)$$

If N is much larger relative to M, then the pipeline can achieve an almost perfect speedup[4] score of

$$\text{speedup} = \frac{N \cdot M \cdot t}{(N + M - 1)t} \approx M. \tag{2.25}$$

An example of a linear pipeline is the pipeline sort[5]: for sorting N data items, create N stages that read an item from the previous stage, compare it with their current holding (if any), and send the biggest of the two items to the next stage. Each i-numbered stage (for $i \in [0, N - 1]$) runs for a total of $N - i - 1$ iterations. The pseudocode describing the behavior of each stage is shown below:

Listing 2.7: Pseudocode of a single stage of a pipeline sort algorithm.

```
void stage(int sID)                    // sID is the stage ID
  T item = readFromStage(sID-1);       // for sID equal to 0 this reads from the ↩
       input
  for(int j=0; j< N - sID -1 ; j++ ) {
    T newItem = readFromStage(sID-1);
    if(newItem < item)                 // decide which should be send forth
      swap(item, newItem);
    sendToStage(sID+1, newItem);
  }
  result[sID] = item;                  // deposit result in destination array
}
```

If we were able to execute all the stages in parallel, then the total execution time would be equal to $2N - 1$ times the duration of the loop's body in Listing 2.7. Because the loop body has a constant duration, the time complexity of pipeline sort would be linear $O(N)$. However, having N stages is impractical. An alternative would be to have fewer stages that process batches of data items instead of comparing just two of them.

This formulation leads to the following adaptation of Listing 2.7, where we have K stages, each receiving batches of $\frac{N}{K}$ data – assuming N is divided evenly by K – from its previous stage:

Listing 2.8: Pseudocode of a single stage of a pipeline sort algorithm that processes batches of data items.

```
void stage(int sID)                     // sID is the stage ID
  T part1[] = readFromStage(sID-1);  // reads an array of data
  if(sID == 0) MergeSort(part1);     // a typical sequential sort
  for(int j=0; j< K - sID -1 ; j++ ) {
    T part2[] = readFromStage(sID-1);
    if(sID == 0) MergeSort(part2);
    MergeLists(part1, part2);        // merge part2 into part1
    sendToStage(sID+1, secondHalf(part1));
  }
  store(result , part1, sID);         // deposit partial result
}
```

---

[4] Assuming that communication costs are negligible makes this possible.
[5] There are many algorithms that can be designated as "pipeline sort." This is just one of the available variants.

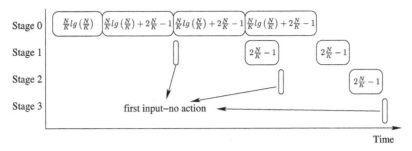

FIGURE 2.12

Gantt chart of a four-stage sorting pipeline, as described in Listing 2.8. The worst-case numbers of key comparisons per stage are shown.

The time complexity of the mergesort algorithm in lines 3 and 6 is $O(\frac{N}{K} lg \frac{N}{K})$. The merging of the two subarrays at line 7 has a worst-case complexity of $O(2\frac{N}{K} - 1) = O(\frac{N}{K})$. A parallel execution of all the K stages would result in a timing similar to the one shown in Fig. 2.12, as the duration of the first stage would dominate the proceedings. The total execution would be proportional to the number of key comparisons performed in the parts that dominate the total time:

$$K\frac{N}{K}lg\left(\frac{N}{K}\right) + (K-1)\left(2\frac{N}{K} - 1\right) + (K-2)\left(2\frac{N}{K} - 1\right) =$$

$$Nlg\left(\frac{N}{K}\right) + (2K-3)\left(2\frac{N}{K} - 1\right) \approx N \cdot lg\left(\frac{N}{K}\right). \quad (2.26)$$

This is admittedly a poor result as the speedup would be upper-bounded by

$$speedup_{max} = \frac{Nlg(N)}{Nlg\left(\frac{N}{K}\right)} = log_{\frac{N}{K}}(N). \quad (2.27)$$

However, this is an example that is counter to a pipeline's best practices: processing long streams of data (much longer than the pipeline's length) and keeping the stages equal in duration.

2.3.6 Event-based coordination decomposition

The previously examined decomposition patterns share an implicit common trait: communication flow is fixed and can be taken into consideration in the design and performance evaluation of a parallel algorithm. In a number of applications though, this is not true.

It is possible that we can identify a number of tasks or groups of tasks that interact dynamically by making decisions during run-time. In such cases, communication patterns are not fixed, and neither can the execution profile (frequency, duration, and idle times) of tasks be known a priori.

A typical example of such a scenario is a discrete-event simulation of a system. Discrete-event simulations are based on the modeling of system components or agents by objects or software modules that interact by generating "events." An event is a *time-stamped message* that can represent a status change in the state of a module, a trigger to change the state, a request to perform an action, a response to a previously generated request, or the like.

2.4 Program structure patterns

Patterns can assist not only in the selection of an appropriate workload decomposition approach, but also in the program development. This is the purpose of the program structure patterns. In the following sections we examine and analyze a few of the most prominent ones.

We can distinguish the parallel program structure patterns into two major categories:

- **Globally parallel, locally sequential** (GPLS): this means that the application is able to perform multiple tasks concurrently, with each task running sequentially. Patterns that fall in this category include:
    - single program, multiple data (SPMD),
    - multiple program, multiple data (MPMD),
    - master–worker,
    - map-reduce.
- **Globally sequential, locally parallel** (GSLP): this means that the application executes as a sequential program, with individual parts of it running in parallel when requested. Patterns that fall in this category include:
    - fork/join,
    - loop parallelism.

The distinction between the two categories is made more clear by the depiction of Fig. 2.13. The GPLS patterns tend to offer greater scalability and are particularly suited for shared-nothing architectures. On the other hand, GSLP tends to be employed for converting sequential programs into parallel ones by parallelizing the parts of the program that mostly affect performance.

2.4.1 Single program, multiple data

In the SPMD pattern all the nodes of the execution platform run the same program, but they apply the same operations on different data and/or they follow different execution paths within the program.

Keeping all the application logic in a single program promotes easier and bug-free development, which makes it a popular choice among programmers. The typical program structure involves the following steps:

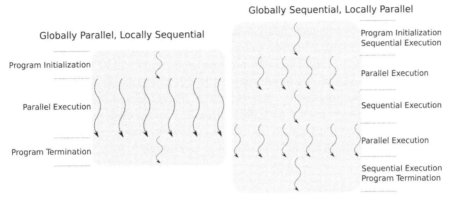

FIGURE 2.13

An illustration of how GPLS and GSLP paradigms work.

- **Program initialization**: this step usually involves deploying the program to the parallel platform and initializing the run-time system responsible for allowing the multiple threads or processes to communicate and synchronize.
- **Obtaining a unique identifier**: identifiers are typically numbered starting from 0, enumerating the threads or processes used. In certain cases, the identifier can be a vector and not just a scalar (e.g., CUDA). Identifier lifetime follows the thread or process lifetime they correspond to. Identifiers can be also persistent, i.e., exist for the duration of the program, or they can be generated dynamically whenever they are needed.
- **Running the program** by following the execution path corresponding to the unique ID. This could involve workload or data distribution, diversification of roles, etc.
- **Shutting down the program**: shutting down the threads or processes, possibly combining the partial results generated into the final answer.

The SPMD approach is convenient but it has a weakness: all the application's code and static (i.e., global) data are replicated in all the nodes. This can be an advantage, but it can also be a drawback, when said items are not required.

2.4.2 Multiple program, multiple data

The SPMD approach is flexible enough to cover most scenarios. It comes up short only when:

- The execution platform is heterogeneous, mandating the need to deploy different executables based on the nodes' architecture.
- The memory requirements of the application are so severe that memory space economy dictates a reduction of the program logic uploaded to each node to the bare essentials.

The MPMD pattern covers these cases by allowing different executables, possibly generated from different tool chains, to be assembled into one application. Each compute node is free to run its own program logic and process its own dataset. However, the sequence of steps identified in the previous section may still be followed.

Most major parallel platforms support the MPMD pattern. A special case is CUDA, where the program is compiled into a single file, but it actually contains two different binaries: one for the CPU host and one for the GPU co-processor.

In most cases, a configuration file mapping the different executables to the appropriate compute nodes is all that is needed. Such an example is shown in Section 5.5.2.

2.4.3 Master–worker

The master–worker paradigm (also referred to as "master–slave") separates the roles of the computational nodes into two distinct ones. The responsibilities of the master node(s) can involve:

- handing out pieces of work to workers,
- collecting the results of the computations from the workers,
- performing I/O duties on behalf of the workers, i.e., sending them the data that they are supposed to process or accessing a file,
- interacting with the user.

In each simplest form, an implementation of the master–worker pattern involves a single master node and multiple worker nodes. However, this arrangement does not scale with the number of nodes, as the master can become the bottleneck. In that case we can have hierarchical schemes that incorporate a number of master modes, each commanding a part of the available machines and being accountable to a higher-authority master. Such an arrangement is shown in Fig. 2.14(b).

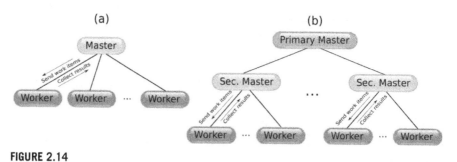

FIGURE 2.14

(a) A simple master–worker architecture. (b) A hierarchical master–worker setup, with two types of master nodes, primary and secondary.

The master–worker setup is very simple in its inception and can be naturally applied to a number of problems if the overall computation can be broken up into disjoint independent pieces that do not require internode communication. An added benefit is that this setup can provide implicit load balancing, i.e., it feeds workloads to the idle nodes, ensuring that overall, there is little or no imbalance as far as work assignments are concerned.

The workloads can be described in a variety of ways, from the most *specific*, e.g., providing parameters for the execution of a known function, to the most *generic*, e.g., providing instances of classes with any kind of computation portfolio.

2.4.4 Map-reduce

Map-reduce is a popular derivative of the master–worker pattern. It was made popular by Google's implementation for running its search engine. The context for the application of the map-reduce pattern is having to process a large collection of independent data (embarrassingly parallel) by applying ("mapping") a function on them. The collective results of all the partial computations have to be "reduced" by the application of a second function.

The map-reduce pattern as evangelized by Google's tutorial [65] works in its generic form, as shown in Fig. 2.15. A user program spawns a master process that oversees that whole procedure. A number of workers are also spawned; they are responsible for (a) processing the input data and producing intermediate results and (b) combining the results to produce the final answer.

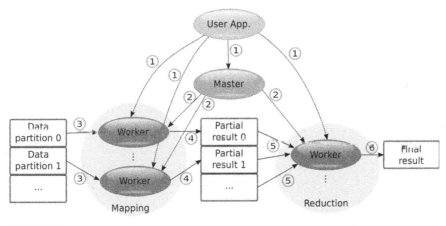

FIGURE 2.15

Generic form of the map-reduce pattern. The steps involve: (1) spawning of the master and worker threads, (2) task assignments by the master, (3) data input by the workers performing the mapping, (4) saving of the partial results, (5) reading of the partial results from the "reducing" workers, and (6) saving the final result.

In practice, the workers applying the map and the reduce stages do not have to be different. Also, the data storage between the two types of workers can be persistent (e.g., a file) or transient (e.g., a memory buffer).

The main difference between the map-reduce pattern and a typical master–worker setup is that the formulation allows for the use of automated tools that take care of the deployment and load balancing of the application. The **Apache Hadoop**[6] project is an example of a framework employing a map-reduce engine. The Hadoop map-reduce engine provides two types of processes: *JobTracker*, which is equivalent to the master in Fig. 2.15, and *TaskTracker*, which is equivalent to the worker type in Fig. 2.15. These processes are spawned as system services (daemons). The JobTracker is responsible for assigning work to TaskTracker nodes, keeping track of their progress and state (e.g., if they die, the work is scheduled elsewhere). Each TaskTracker maintains a simple first-in, first-out (FIFO) queue of assigned tasks and executes them as separate processes (i.e., in separate Java Virtual Machines).

2.4.5 Fork/join

The fork/join pattern is employed when the parallel algorithm calls for the dynamic creation (forking) of tasks at run-time. These child tasks (processes or threads) typically have to terminate (join) before the parent process/thread can resume execution.

The generated tasks can run either by spawning new threads or processes or by using an existing pool of threads to handle them. The latter is an approach that minimizes the overhead associated with the creation of threads and can potentially manage the processing resources of a machine optimally (by matching the number of threads to the number of available cores).

An example of the fork/join pattern in action is shown below in the form of a parallel quicksort implementation[7]:

Listing 2.9: Pseudocode outline of a parallel version of the quicksort algorithm. The fork/join pattern is used to spawn new sorting tasks for different pieces of the input data.

```
1   template <typename T>
2   void QuickSort<T>(T [] inp, int N) {
3     if(N <= THRES)  // for small input sort sequentially
4         sequentialQuickSort(inp, N);
5     else {
6         int pos = PartitionData(inp, N);         // split data into two parts
7         Task t = new Task( QuickSort(inp, pos)); // create new task to sort one ↩
              of the parts
8         t.run();
9         QuickSort(inp + pos+ 1, N-pos -1);        // keep sorting the second part
10        waitUntilDone(t);                          // the sort is complete only if ↩
              the child task is finished
11    }
12  }
```

The `PartitionData` call of line 6 separates the input data into two regions, one containing elements smaller than or equal to a chosen element called the "pivot" and

---

[6] http://hadoop.apache.org/.

[7] The details of how partitioning works in the context of quicksort can be found in most algorithm design textbooks.

one containing elements bigger or equal to the pivot. The `pos` index points to the position where the pivot element is placed, effectively separating the two regions, which span the ranges $[0, pos)$ and $[pos + 1, N)$. The two regions are subsequently sorted in parallel, one by spawning a new task (lines 7–8) and the other by the original thread/process (line 9). As long as the size of the array to be sorted exceeds the `THRES`, a new task will be generated for the task.

Reiterating a point made earlier, the generation of a new task does not necessarily mean that a new thread or process is created to handle it. This would be a recipe for disaster if a very large array were to be sorted, because that would very likely overwhelm the operating system. To illustrate how big an issue this can be, let us consider how many tasks are generated during the execution of the parallel quicksort of Listing 2.9.

If we represent as $T(N)$ the total number of tasks generated for an input of size N (excluding the first, "parent" one) and we assume that the `PartitionData` function manages to separate the input data into two equal-size parts (a best-case scenario), then we have

$$T(N) = \begin{cases} 0 & \text{if } N \leq THRES, \\ 1 + 2T(\frac{N-1}{2}) \approx 1 + 2T(\frac{N}{2}) & \text{if } N > THRES. \end{cases} \tag{2.28}$$

Backward substitution can solve the above recurrence relation. If we assume that N and $THRES$ are powers of 2, then the expansion

$$T(N) = 1 + 2T(\frac{N}{2}) = 1 + 2 + 2^2 T(\frac{N}{2^2}) =$$
$$= \sum_{i=0}^{k-1} 2^i + 2^k T(\frac{N}{2^k}) = 2^k - 1 + 2^k T(\frac{N}{2^k}) \tag{2.29}$$

will stop when $\frac{N}{2^k} = THRES \Rightarrow k = lg(\frac{N}{THRES})$. Substituting this value of k in Eq. (2.29) yields

$$T(N) = 2^k - 1 + 2^k \cdot T(THRES) = 2^{lg(\frac{N}{THRES})} - 1 = \frac{N}{THRES} - 1 \tag{2.30}$$

as $T(THRES) = 0$. If for example we have $N = 2^{20}$ and $THRES = 2^{10}$, we will need $2^{10} - 1 = 1023$ tasks. A better approach would be to use a pool of threads to execute the tasks generated. This approach is explored thoroughly in Section 3.12.

There is also another point of view for the result we got for $T(N)$: in practice, the optimum or near-optimum number of threads is determined by the number of available cores. Thus we could use this number, e.g., T, and the size of the problem as determined by N to calculate a threshold that yields the best possible utilization of the available hardware, i.e., $THRES = \frac{N}{T}$, allowing us in turn to optimize the execution according to the problem instance.

2.4.6 Loop parallelism

The migration of software to multicore architectures is a monumental task. The loop parallelism pattern addresses this problem by allowing the developer to port existing sequential code by parallelizing the loops that dominate the execution time.

This pattern is particularly important for the OpenMP platform, where the loops are semiautomatically parallelized with the assistance of the programmer. The programmer has to provide hints in the form of directives to assist with this task.

Loop parallelism is a pattern with limited usability in the sense that it does not promote the design of a ground-up new parallel solution to a problem, but instead it focuses on the evolution of a sequential solution into a parallel one. This is also a reason that the performance benefits are usually small, but at least the development effort involved is equally minimal.

2.5 Matching decomposition patterns with program structure patterns

A question that naturally arises is: given a decomposition pattern, which is the best way to structure the program? The answer is highly dependent on the application. Additionally, a number of platforms impose a particular program structure pattern on developers. For example, MPI uses the SPMD/MPMD pattern, whereas OpenMP promotes the loop parallelism pattern.

Still, given a specific decomposition pattern, certain program structure patterns are better suited for implementation purposes. Table 2.2 summarizes these pairings.

Table 2.2 Decomposition patterns and the most suitable program structure patterns for implementing them.

	Decomposition Patterns					
Program Structure Patterns	Task Parallelism	Divide and Conquer	Geometric Data	Recursive Data	Pipeline	Event-based Coordination
Single-Program Multiple Data	√	√	√	√	√	√
Multiple-Program Multiple Data	√	√	√	√	√	√
Master-Worker	√	√	√	√		
Map-Reduce		√	√	√		
Fork/Join	√	√	√	√	√	√
Loop Parallelism		√	√			

Exercises

1. Perform a 2D agglomeration step for the image convolution problem of Section 2.2. What is the resulting number of communication operations?
2. Perform the comparison between the 1D and 2D decompositions of the heat diffusion example in Section 2.3.3 by assuming that (a) half-duplex communication links are available and (b) n-port communications are possible, i.e., all communications can take place at the same time over all the links.
3. How would communication costs affect the pipeline performance? Derive variations of Eqs. (2.19) to (2.21) that take into account a constant communication overhead between the pipeline stages.
4. The total number of tasks calculated in Section 2.4.5 for the parallel quicksort of Listing 2.9, is based on the best-case assumption that the input is split in equal halves by every call to the `PartitionData` function. What would be the result if the worst case (i.e., one part gets $N - 1$ elements and the other part 0) were considered?
5. Use a simple problem instance (e.g., a small array of integers) to trace the execution of the parallel quicksort of Listing 2.9. Create a Gantt graph for the tasks generated assuming an infinite number of compute nodes is available for executing them. Can you calculate an upper bound for the speedup that can be achieved?
6. What is the decomposition pattern employed by the parallel quicksort of Listing 2.9?
7. Mergesort comes in two varieties: top-down and bottom-up. Suggest a decomposition pattern for the bottom-up flavor of the algorithm. What would be an appropriate program structure for implementing the algorithm in parallel?
8. Propose a program structure pattern that would be appropriate for the prefix-sum operation. The prefix-sum or scan operation takes a binary associative operator $\oplus$ and an ordered set of N elements $[x_0, x_1, \cdots, x_{N-1}]$ and returns the ordered set $[x_0, x_0 \oplus x_1, \cdots, x_0 \oplus x_1 \oplus \cdots \oplus x_{N-1}]$.
9. A pipeline is composed of four stages, each taking 1 ms, 2 ms, 4 ms, and 1 ms, respectively. If 1000 data items are to be processed by the pipeline, calculate the overall execution time by assuming that the communication time is zero. Draw a diagram showing the processing of the first three data items.

Programming with threads and processes

Threads and concurrency in standard C++

3

In this chapter you will:

- Learn what threads are and how you can create them.
- Learn how to initialize threads in order to perform a desired task.
- Learn how to terminate a multi-threaded program using different techniques.
- Understand problems associated with having threads access shared resources, like race conditions and deadlocks.
- Learn what semaphores and monitors are and how you can use them in your programs.
- Become familiar with classical synchronization problems and their solutions.
- Learn how to create and use a pool of threads.
- Learn effective debugging techniques for multi-threaded programs.

3.1 Introduction

The concurrent execution of multiple programs has been commonplace since the 1960s, when MIT introduced the Compatible Time Sharing System (CTSS) operating system (OS). Operating systems achieve this feat by interrupting the currently executing program and giving the control of the CPU to another one. The switch which effectively "shares" the CPU time (hence the name *time-sharing*) can be triggered by:

- regular hardware interrupts generated by a clock/timer,
- irregular hardware interrupts, e.g., coming from a device requesting attention,
- a call to the OS itself, e.g., a request to perform I/O.

Each running program constitutes a process, i.e., an OS entity that encapsulates the code, data, resources, and execution state required by the OS for managing the program.

Thus, each process takes control of the CPU for a "time slice," before surrendering it to the OS, which hands over the CPU to another process, etc. The timing for a single CPU machine would be similar to Fig. 3.1(a).

Time-sharing allows the efficient use of computational resources but it cannot speed things up for each individual process. On the contrary, time sharing can slow

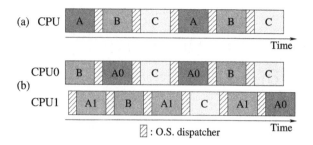

FIGURE 3.1

An example of the concurrent execution of multiple processes by (a) a single CPU and (b) multiple CPUs. (b) A program running as two processes, A0 and A1.

down the execution of a process by directly reducing the CPU time given to it and by indirectly diluting the available CPU time with the frequent execution of the OS/task switcher (also known as the "dispatcher").

In order for a program to get a bigger share of computational time (bar scheduling directives that affect a program's priority), it has to be broken up into multiple processes. The same is true if the execution platform has more than one core. Such an example is shown in Fig. 3.1(b). The mechanism that was originally used for creating or "spawning" multiple processes was the fork call. An example is shown below:

Listing 3.1: Skeleton for "forking" a process.

```cpp
// File : fork.cpp
#include <cstdlib>
#include <iostream>
#include <unistd.h>

using namespace std;

int main (int argc, char **argv)
{
  pid_t childID;

  childID = fork ();
  if (childID == 0)
    {
      cout << "This is the child process\n";
    }
  else
    {
      cout << "This is the parent process\n";
    }
  return 0;
}
```

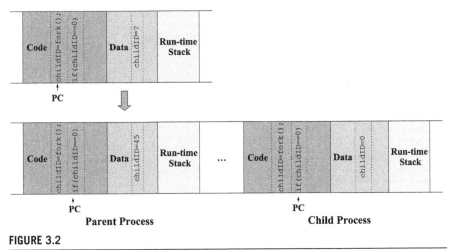

FIGURE 3.2

Memory layout that results from "forking" a process. "PC" stands for program counter.

"Forking" a process results in the creation of a verbatim copy of the process's memory, including all code and data, as they were at the moment of the call (see Fig. 3.2). The only thing different between the original (*parent*) and copy (*child*) is that the child process, which continues execution from the line following the call to fork, does not receive the return value from it (the pid_t type is just an alias for int). Hence, the childID for the child process in line 13 of Listing 3.1 is 0. This allows the creation of logic similar to the one starting at that line, to differentiate the actions of the two processes (it would not make sense to have them do the same thing).

Some obvious questions pop up by observing how the fork mechanism works:

- Why should one copy the code? Is this part of the memory mutable?
- The child process has private copies of all the parent's data. How can the two exchange information?

The answer to the first question is that there are instances of programs that modify their code at run-time. This feature is most prominent among viruses but it cannot be excluded as a valid program behavior. For the latter question, system designers have provided mechanisms that solve this problem (such as pipes or shared-memory regions), but none is that easy or convenient as just assessing a common set of variables.

The overhead associated with reserving and copying a process's image makes the fork call an expensive approach to achieving concurrency. Fortunately, an alternative exists in the form of threads, as explained in the following section.

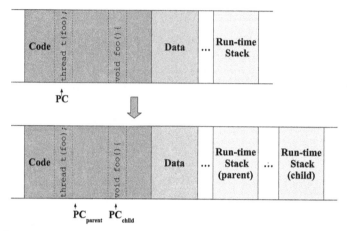

FIGURE 3.3

Memory layout that results from spawning a new thread from the main thread of a process.

3.2 Threads

3.2.1 What is a thread?

A thread can be considered to be a light-weight process. A more precise definition is that it is an execution path, a sequence of instructions, that is managed separately by the operating system scheduler as a unit. There can be multiple threads per process.

Threads alleviate the overhead associated with the fork mechanism by copying only the bare essentials needed: the run-time stack. The run-time stack cannot be shared between two threads as it contains the activation frames (or activation records) for the functions/methods being called. A shared stack would mean – among other things – that upon returning from a function, control could return to a point different than the one who called it.

When the *main* (or initial) thread of a process spawns a new thread, the resulting arrangement would be similar to the one shown in Fig. 3.3. The "parent" and "child" relationships apply here also.

The additional overhead associated with reserving and copying a process's image makes the fork call an expensive approach to achieving concurrency. Having separate processes can be beneficial, like, e.g., in providing enhanced memory protection or more flexible scheduling, but for the most part the drawbacks outweigh the benefits.

3.2.2 What are threads good for?

Threads are usually associated with GUI programming. One cannot maintain a re-sponsive user interface while performing a task initiated by the user, without having a UI-dedicated thread. However, the gamut of their uses is much richer. Threads can be used for:

- **Improving performance**: By breaking up an application's load into multiple threads, one can get to utilize multiple cores in a system, boosting performance substantially.
- **Background tasks**: Interactive applications can use threads to perform background tasks, i.e., tasks that do not require user interaction, while at the same time continuing to respond to user requests.
- **Asynchronous processing**: Sending a request to a server over a network involves substantial latency. By spawning a thread to handle the transaction with the server asynchronously (i.e., without waiting for the response), an application can continue doing useful work, improving performance and resource (e.g., CPU time) utilization.
- **Improving program structure**: A typical attribute of games is the need to perform concurrently a large collection of periodic tasks. Such tasks include screen redraw, sound playback, user input detection, and strategy making. These tasks do not have to run with the same frequency as the rest (e.g., strategy), and putting them inside the same loop and ensuring that they can run at the screen refresh rate is an extreme requirement that can only be satisfied with increased program complexity. Assigning the various tasks to different threads allows for much better structured code that is also more maintainable.

3.3 Thread creation and initialization

Threads have been a neglected part of the C++ ecosystem for a long time, in the sense that thread creation and management was not part of the standard C++ library. A rich collection of third-party libraries filled this void, with notable members being:

- pThreads: a C-based library that is considered the common denominator for threading support. The C++11 thread library is built on top of it.
- winThreads: a Windows-only C++-based library.
- Qt threads: a part of the Qt (pronounced "cute") cross-platform C++-based libraries and tools. It is characterized by ease-of-use and a rich API.

Since the C++11 standard was introduced, threads have become a part of the standard C++ library, alongside a collection of tools and libraries that have expanded with the introduction of each new standard since.

In the previous edition of this book, threads were covered using the Qt cross-platform library (currently being offered by The Qt Company https://www.qt.io), which still offers a better vehicle out of the box for someone to master concurrency than the "native" C++ threads. However, simple steps can make using the native C++ threads as easy as using Qt.

The code necessary for creating a thread in C++11 is minimal, as can be seen in Listing 3.2.

Listing 3.2: Skeleton for creating a C++11 thread.

```cpp
// File : hello.cpp
#include <iostream>
#include <thread>

using namespace std;
void f()
{
  cout <<"Hello from thread " << this_thread::get_id() << "\n";
  this_thread::sleep_for(1s);
}

int main(int argc, char **argv)
{
  thread t(f);
  cout << "Main thread waiting...\n";
  t.join();
  return 0;
}
```

In order to have GCC compile and run the above program, one has to type:

```
$ g++ hello.cpp -lpthread -o hello
$ ./hello
Main thread waiting...
Hello from thread 139981974968064
```

which indicates the use of the pThreads library as the underpinning implementation.

Listing 3.2 illustrates a few key components of how the thread class can be used:

- Line 14 is the one creating the thread object and starting the corresponding thread's execution. There is no separate statement for accomplishing the latter action. The only thing required is the address of the function to be executed by the thread.
- The main thread has to wait for the child thread to complete execution, as the termination of the main thread causes the immediate termination of all generated threads.[1] The join() method call on line 16 is, as expected, a blocking one.
- C++11 defines a this_thread namespace that can be used to inquire or act upon the executing thread. On line 8 this is used to get the identifier of the executing thread. On line 9 the sleep_for function puts the thread to sleep for one second.[2]

Once join() is called on a thread, the corresponding object is destroyed, so no further actions can be performed on the thread.

In the simple example shown above, the thread was given no data to operate upon, which is atypical of most scenarios. In most data-parallel applications (see Sec-

---

[1] This applies to all threads, even "detached" ones (see Section 3.3).

[2] The "s" suffix is an operator defined in the chrono header file (operator""s()), along with a set of others, allowing us to specify time units with literal constants.

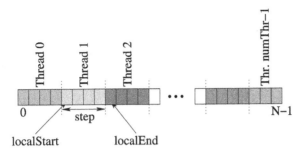

FIGURE 3.4

A geometric decomposition of an N-element array into $numThr$ groups, each containing $step = \lceil \frac{N}{numThr} \rceil$ elements. The last group is the exception to this rule, with a size of $step = N - (numThr - 1) \cdot \lceil \frac{N}{numThr} \rceil$. $localStart$ and $localEnd$ correspond to the iterators used in Listing 3.3.

tion 2.3.3) we desire to have a collection of threads, each running the same function but operating on different data.

Two possible alternatives for accomplishing this would be:

- **Using global variables**: A bad idea in terms of design, compounded by the fact that the **get_id**() function shown in Listing 3.2 returns an object – not a number – which is suitable for comparison purposes only (i.e., check if two threads are the same) and cannot be used to partition data (see the sample output in the previous section).
- **Passing parameters to the function to be executed by the thread**: The thread constructor can accept an arbitrary number of parameters, that are passed to the function specified upon invocation.

If, for example, we would like to calculate the average of some data array, summing up the elements using multiple threads can be accomplished with a geometric decomposition as shown in Fig. 3.4.

Implementing this decomposition pattern by using the second approach detailed above, produces:

Listing 3.3: Calculating the average of N data using multiple threads.

```
1   // File : aver.cpp
2   #include <thread>
3   #include <numeric>
4   #include <vector>
5
6   using namespace std;
7
8   void partialSum(vector<double>::iterator start, vector<double>::↩
        iterator end, double *res)
9   {
10      *res =0;
```

```
11        for(auto i=start; i<end; i++)
12            *res += *i;
13    }
14    //————————————————————————————————————
15    int main(int argc, char **argv)
16    {
17      int numThr=atoi(argv[1]);
18      int N = atoi(argv[2]);
19      int step=(int)ceil(N*1.0/numThr);
20      double res[numThr];
21
22      vector<double> data(N);
23      iota(data.begin(), data.end(), 1);
24      thread *thr[numThr];
25      vector<double>::iterator localStart = data.begin();
26      vector<double>::iterator localEnd;
27      for(int i=0;i<numThr;i++)
28      {
29          localEnd=localStart+step;
30          if(i==numThr-1) localEnd=data.end();
31          thr[i] = new thread(partialSum, localStart, localEnd, res+i);
32          localStart += step;
33      }
34
35      double total=0;
36      for(int i=0;i<numThr;i++)
37      {
38          thr[i]->join();
39          delete thr[i];
40          total += res[i];
41      }
42      cout << "Average is : " << total/N << endl;
43      return 0;
44    }
```

The above program accepts two command-line parameters, namely the number of threads (line 17) and the size of the data array (line 18), allowing us to test performance and correctness for a variety of scenarios.

The key points of Listing 3.3 are:

- In order to be able to launch multiple threads using a loop, an array of pointers to thread objects is created on line 24. Each member of that array is initialized on line 31, which also spawns the corresponding thread.
- Each thread deposits the partial result it calculates in a separate element of the res array (defined on line 20). Once each thread terminates, following the join() statement on line 40, the partial result is accumulated in a local variable of the main thread.
- Each thread is assigned an equal portion of the data array (calculated as the step variable on line 19), using the iterators localStart and localEnd. The latter

points to one element past the assigned part, following the `begin()` and `end()` iterator semantics of the STL library.

- The `vector` data repository is initialized by the `iota` function (defined in the numeric header) on line 23 to contain the sequence 1, 2, 3, ..., N. This allows an easy verification of the calculation outcome, as the expected result should be $\frac{N+1}{2}$.

It is important to note that all parameters to the thread constructor are passed by value. If one would like to pass the `vector` object and integer indices to the function to be called, instead of the two iterators, calling by reference would require the following changes to the signature of the `partialSum` and the `thread` constructor call:

```
1  #include <functional>
2  ...
3  void partialSum(const vector<double> &data, int start, int end, ↵
       double &res)
4  ...
5    thr[i] = new thread(partialSum, cref(data), localStart, localEnd, ↵
       ref(res[i]));
6  ...
```

The functions `ref()` and `cref()`, which are declared in the `functional` header, return a reference and a constant reference to their parameter, respectively.

A more elegant way of approaching the problem of thread creation is the use of a function object or **functor**, i.e., a class or structure that provides an implementation of the "()" operator. By encapsulating all the related data that a thread will need inside a separate object, we can perform initialization and post thread-termination result collection with ease. In most of the examples of this chapter, we are using a functor approach. A functor-based derivative of Listing 3.3 is:

Listing 3.4: Calculating the average of N data using functors. Only the differences from Listing 3.3 are shown.

```
1  // File : aver2.cpp
2  #include <memory>
3  ...
4  struct PartialSumFunctor
5  {
6    vector < double >::iterator start;
7    vector < double >::iterator end;
8    double res = 0;
9
10   void operator() ();
11 };
12
13 void PartialSumFunctor:: operator() ()
14 {
15   for (auto i = start; i < end; i++)
16     res += *i;
17 }
18 //─────────────────────────────────
19 int main (int argc, char **argv)
```

```
20   {
21       ...
22       unique_ptr < thread > thr[numThr - 1];
23       PartialSumFunctor f[numThr];
24       for (int i = 0; i < numThr - 1; i++)
25         {
26           localEnd = localStart + step;
27           f[i].start = localStart;
28           f[i].end = localEnd;
29           thr[i] = make_unique < thread > (ref (f[i]));
30           localStart += step;
31         }
32       f[numThr - 1].start = localStart;
33       f[numThr - 1].end = data.end ();
34       f[numThr - 1] ();  // using the main thread to process part of the ⤶
             workload
35       double total = f[numThr - 1].res;
36
37       for (int i = 0; i < numThr - 1; i++)
38         {
39           thr[i]->join ();
40           total += f[i].res;
41         }
42       ...
```

While the overall code length is slightly increased, it is arguably a less cluttered and far less error-prone approach. The key changes to the code are:

- The introduction of the `PartialSumFunctor` structure on lines 4–17 to hold the parameters necessary for the execution of each thread, which will run the `operator()` function. As the corresponding instances are managed separately from the threads (array of functors is declared on line 23), we can keep the local results internally (data member on line 8) and collect them after the threads finish (line 40).
- Each functor is explicitly *passed by reference* to the thread constructor (line 29). Otherwise, they would be passed by value, and while the computation would still take place with all the right parameters, it would not use the functors that the main thread has created, making the results inaccessible.
- The `unique_ptr` class template and `make_unique` function (defined in the `memory` header) allow the elimination of the explicit memory de-allocation seen in Listing 3.3, following the Resource Acquisition Is Initialization (RAII) principle.
- A final optimization present in Listing 3.4 is the use of the main thread to compute the last part of the load by reducing the limit in the `for` loops of lines 24 and 37 and calling the `partialSum` function directly on line 34.

Instances of the `thread` class have the peculiarity of being unable to be copied. If, for example, one has a function that serves to set up threads, these threads can be returned to the caller only in the form of pointers, or by *moving* the objects.

It is also possible to "fire-and-forget" a thread, by "detaching" it from its parent. This allows the thread to continue execution even if the thread object that was used to start it is destroyed.

For example, in the following function, the threads keep running, even though the thr object is a local variable that is destroyed at the end of the for-loop block:

```
template <typename T>
void setup(vector<T> &input)
{
    for(auto i : input)
    {
        thread thr(process,i); // call function "process" for parameter ↩
            i
        thr.detach();
    }
}
```

This makes the call to join() unnecessary, and it allows a thread to survive beyond the lifetime of a function that sets it up. The above example hides in its simplicity the issue of data access: how can the created threads access safely the parent thread's data, and how can the parent thread collect the results of the execution?

For one, the default behavior of the thread constructor is to receive parameters by value. This is a feature that allows a thread to decouple from the context where it was created, but it can be very inefficient. These questions are thoroughly answered in the sections that follow.

Another way to avoid the explicit "joins" is to follow the RAII principle and wrap a thread with an object that will implicitly call join() upon its destruction. A possible implementation that relies upon a custom destructor is shown below:

```
1   class ThreadGuard
2   {
3   private:
4       thread &thr;
5   public:
6       explicit ThreadGuard(thread &t) : thr(t) {}
7       ~ThreadGuard()
8       {
9           if(thr.joinable())
10              thr.join();
11      }
12
13      ThreadGuard & operator=()(const ThreadGuard &o) = delete;
14      ThreadGuard(const ThreadGuard &o) = delete;
15  };
```

The constructor of the class ThreadGuard can only be called explicitly by passing a reference to a thread that it stores internally (line 6). When a ThreadGuard instance is destroyed, it checks if the thread can still be joined (in case other operations were performed on it), before waiting for the thread to terminate (lines 9 and 10).

The copy assignment operator and the copy constructor are marked as deleted (lines 13 and 14) to avoid having the compiler automatically generate default versions of them. Otherwise, copies of `ThreadGuard` instances could live outside their intended scope and that could be problematic (e.g., if the corresponding thread objects have been already destroyed).

The following example illustrates this principle, although in a not optimum manner, as the topic of sharing data in an error-free way is left for the next section.

Implementing RAII for the previous section's program, utilizing the `ThreadGuard` class, can be done as follows:

Listing 3.5: Calculating the average of *N* data using functors and RAII for thread management. Only the differences from Listing 3.4 are shown.

```
1   // File : aver3.cpp
2   . . .
3   void process_aux(vector<double> &data, int numThr, vector<↵
        PartialSumFunctor> &f)
4   {
5       int N=data.size();
6       int step = (int) ceil (N * 1.0 / numThr);
7
8       unique_ptr < thread > thr[numThr];
9       unique_ptr < ThreadGuard > tg[numThr];
10
11      vector < double >::iterator localStart = data.begin ();
12      vector < double >::iterator localEnd;
13      for (int i = 0; i < numThr; i++)
14        {
15          localEnd = localStart + step;
16          if (i==numThr-1)
17              localEnd = data.end();
18          f[i].start = localStart;
19          f[i].end = localEnd;
20          thr[i] = make_unique<thread>(ref(f[i]));
21          tg[i] = make_unique<ThreadGuard>(ref(*thr[i]));
22          localStart += step;
23        }
24  }
25  //————————————————————————————————————
26  double process(vector<double> &data)
27  {
28      int numThr = thread::hardware_concurrency();
29      vector<PartialSumFunctor> f;
30      f.resize(numThr);
31      process_aux(data, numThr, f);
32
33      double total=0;
34      for (int i = 0; i < numThr; i++)
35        total+= f[i].res;
36
37      return total/data.size();
38  }
```

```
39   //----------------------------------------------------
40   int main (int argc, char **argv)
41   {
42     int N = atoi (argv[1]);
43
44     vector < double >data (N);
45     iota (data.begin (), data.end (), 1);
46     double aver = process(data);
47
48     cout << "Average is : " << aver << endl;
49     return 0;
50   }
```

In Listing 3.5 we use a pair of functions, process and process_aux, to perform the desired computations. The key points are:

- The process function (lines 26–38) gets the number of available hardware threads on line 28, by calling the thread::hardware_concurrency() static method. Subsequently, it creates a vector of functors that can be used by threads, while retaining their results after the threads complete their execution.
- The vector of PartialSumFunctor structures is passed by reference to the process_aux function (lines 3–24), where the structures are initialized (lines 15–19) and they are used to create threads (line 20) and ThreadGuard instances (line 21).
- Once the loop of lines 13–23 finishes and process_aux is about to return, the destructors of the ThreadGuard objects are called, which forces the main thread to wait for all the child threads to finish.
- When the line 31 call to process_aux returns, lines 33–35 collect the partial results from the functors and return the computed average.

3.4 Sharing data between threads

Sharing of global data, as it is shown in Fig. 3.3, simplifies a thread's access to common data repositories. However, there is a *precondition*: access must be read-only. Otherwise, special mechanisms must be employed to ensure that when a thread is writing to a shared variable, it does so in isolation, i.e., no other thread should be allowed to do this at the same time. When a modification is being made, reading operations should be also blocked, as an inconsistent state could be retrieved otherwise. It is often the case that making write operations "atomic" (i.e., indivisible, uninterruptible) is not sufficient. It may be required that an object or data structure become locked (i.e., completely inaccessible) for the duration of a state-modifying operation.

As an example, consider two threads that operate on a bank account object. One is trying to withdraw funds and pay for a utility bill and the other is trying to deposit the monthly salary. Assuming that the account is represented by a simple data structure

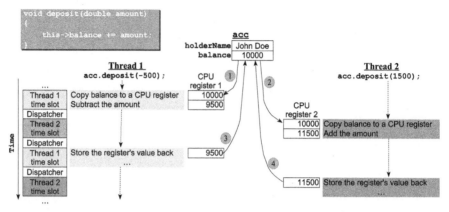

FIGURE 3.5

One of the possible outcomes, resulting from having two threads modify a bank account object, without any means of coordination. The read and write operations to the `balance` field are numbered in the sequence they occur. The value stored back by operation #4 eliminates the change done by #3, placing the object in a wrong state (should be 11,000 and not 11,500).

consisting of a string (for the holder's name) and a double (for the balance), then one of the possible outcomes of having the two threads run at the same time is shown in Fig. 3.5. It is important to stress that this is one possible outcome, with the account updated correctly being another. The problem is that there is no way to predict the outcome of maintaining an account in this fashion.

Fig. 3.5 illustrates a *race condition that is caused by a data race*. The race qualifier in both names hints to the contention between threads for access to shared data. A **data race** occurs when two or more threads access the same memory location and at least one of those accesses is a write. This constitutes a problem as uncoordinated modifications can lead to data corruption.

A **race condition** on the other hand is *an abnormal program behavior caused by dependence of the result on the relative timing of events in the program*. A race condition can exist even if there is no data race and the opposite is also true, i.e., a data race can exist without producing a race condition.

Data races can be eliminated by forcing data operations to be atomic, but this is not sufficient for eliminating race conditions, especially if operations involve complex data structures whose consistency goes beyond atomic access to their individual data members. To illustrate these points further, let us assume that the `deposit` method shown in Fig. 3.5 became:

Listing 3.6: Pseudocode of a method that has a race condition but not a data race.

```
void deposit(double amount)
{
  double temp;
  atomic{ temp = this->balance; }
```

```
    temp += amount;
    atomic{ this ->balance = temp; }
}
```

where `atomic` is supposed to represent the execution of the enclosed block in an atomic fashion. This method does not have a data race because access to the `balance` is atomic and `temp` is a local variable. However, we can still get a sequence as the one in Fig. 3.5, hence a race condition still exists.

Assuming we used a Boolean flag to keep track of the changed accounts for audit purposes, we could have:

Listing 3.7: Pseudocode of a method that has no race condition but has a data race.

```
void deposit(double amount)
{
    this -> modified = true;
    atomic{ this ->balance += amount; }
}
```

The above code has no race condition any more. Still multiple threads could simultaneously write to the `modified` flag, but this data race should present no problem to the program correctness.

Finally, if all the changes occurred in an atomic fashion as:

Listing 3.8: Pseudocode of a method that has neither a race condition nor a data race.

```
void deposit(double amount)
{
    atomic{
        this -> modified = true;
        this ->balance += amount; }
}
```

we would eliminate all the races, but the issue would be that `deposit` would cease to be something multiple threads could execute concurrently! And this explains why we do not go about converting all shared data access to atomic.

Data races are easy to detect and to this end, a compiler can provide assistance. On the other hand, race conditions are more difficult to discover and deal with, as they depend on relative event timings that cannot be triggered on a deterministic or consistent basis.

The example we have explored so far is a simple instance of the readers–writers problem that is thoroughly treated in Section 3.7.4. We can easily illustrate the ill effects of uncoordinated shared data access by modifying the code of Listing 3.3 to use a single repository for threads to place their partial results in the average calculation, as shown below:

Listing 3.9: Example of a race condition caused by a data race, when calculating the average of data. Only the differences from Listing 3.3 are shown.

```
1   // File : aver0.cpp
2   ...
3   int main(int argc, char **argv)
4   {
5       ...
6       double res=0;
7       ...
8       for(int i=0;i<numThr;i++)
9       {
10          ...
11          thr[i] = new thread(partialSum, localStart, localEnd, &res);
12      }
13      ...
14      cout << "Average is : " << res/N << endl;
15      ...
```

Then we would get results similar to the following:

```
$ ./aver0  4  1000
Average is :  462.998
$ ./aver0  4  1000
Average is :  469.364
$ ./aver0  4  1000
Average is :  500.5
```

which are all erroneous except the last one. So getting the correct result is a possibility. Unfortunately, in most cases one would never be able to easily verify a program's output the same way we have done for our "doctored" sample input.

The solution to this problem is the elimination of the "racing" by having each thread modify the shared resource (variable res in our example) under conditions of exclusivity, i.e., each thread should perform the modifications in isolation, while all other threads are prevented to access that resource at the same time. Each section of code responsible for the modifications is called a **critical section** and the notion of exclusivity prompts the use of some kind of barrier or lock.

In the following sections we will cover the most commonly used locking mechanisms in shared-memory programming. It is also possible to eliminate race conditions without blocking or locking a data item/structure, but this is not a trivial exercise as we will see later.

3.5 Design concerns

The problem illustrated in the previous section can be boiled down to the following: *How can you make a multi-threaded program behave in the same manner as a sequential one?*

This is where different **consistency models** come into play. A consistency model is a set of rules that enforce a system to behave in a specific way. A number of

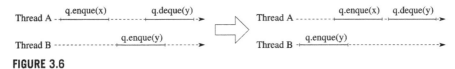

FIGURE 3.6

An example of reordering the timelines of two threads operating on a FIFO queue, without changing the program order, that makes the sequence of events (shown on the left) equivalent to using a sequential queue.

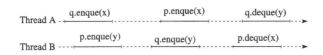

FIGURE 3.7

An example showing that the composition of two sequentially consistent objects (p and q FIFO queues) is not sequentially consistent.

consistency models have been proposed, each offering a different trade-off between efficiency and strictness. One of the many models that have been proposed is the **sequential consistency** model.

In the sequential consistency model, all the events that operate on shared-memory objects should appear to happen in a one-at-a-time order. Also, these events should appear to take effect in program order, as far as each thread is concerned. The events that take place in different threads can be shifted so that the overall history (sequence of events/method invocations) of an object satisfies its sequential specification (i.e., how it behaves when run by a single thread). An example of this reordering is shown in Fig. 3.6.

The sequential consistency model is problematic in the sense that it is not compositional: combining two software modules that observe sequential consistency does not guarantee the production of a composite that is sequentially consistent. An example of how sequential consistency fails is shown in Fig. 3.7, where the sequence shown in Fig. 3.6 is duplicated for a second queue q. While each individual queue is sequentially consistent, there is no way that the two timelines shown in Fig. 3.7 can satisfy sequential consistency.

A more strict consistency model is that of **linearizability** [30]: events should appear to happen in one-at-a-time order and should appear to take place **instantaneously**. The last requirement is modeled by the introduction of so-called **linearization points**. A linearization point is a time instance within the duration of a method call, where the effect of the call is considered to take effect. The introduction of the linearization points has two implications:

1. The methods can be *totally ordered* according to their linearization points. A linearization point can be arbitrarily chosen within the time frame between a method call invocation and its return. The resulting ordering must be equivalent to a sequential execution for the concurrent execution to be considered linearizable.

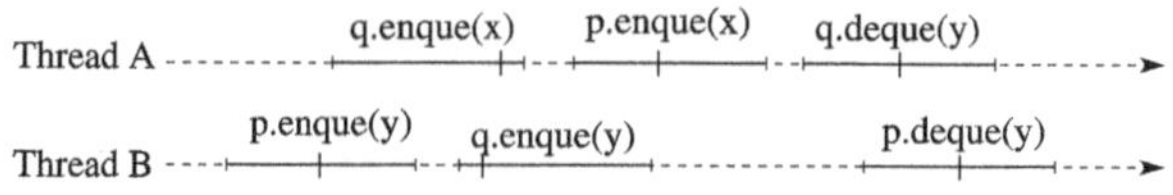

q.enque(x)   p.enque(x)   q.deque(y)

Thread A

p.enque(y)   q.enque(y)   p.deque(y)

Thread B

FIGURE 3.8

An example of a linearizable execution by two threads operating on two FIFO queues.

2. Although locking is not mandated (and actually it should be avoided for performance reasons), locking down an object while a method is performed is the equivalent of having its effect take place instantaneously as far as everyone else is concerned. The simplest thing is to use locking mechanisms, and for this reason these are explored in the following sections.

Every linearizable execution is sequentially consistent, but the reverse is not true. An example of a linearizable execution is shown in Fig. 3.8.

In the following sections we will explore two locking mechanisms that, although equivalent in functionality, promote dramatically different paradigms for synchronizing threads. Also in Section 3.8 we describe the memory consistency model that C++11 has introduced.

3.6 Semaphores

A semaphore is a software abstraction proposed by the late Dutch computer scientist Edsger Dijkstra that supports two **atomic** operations:

- P[3] or lock,
- V or unlock.

Various semaphore implementations use different naming conventions for replacing the cryptic P and V (e.g., `lock-unlock` and `acquire-release` are popular choices), but the semantics remain the same according to the type of semaphore implemented: **binary** or **counting**.

A **binary semaphore** has a state indicating whether it is locked or unlocked. Here is what happens when a thread calls P or V:

- P: If the semaphore is unlocked, it becomes locked and the call returns, allowing the thread to continue. If the semaphore is locked, then the thread is blocked and placed in a queue Q of waiting threads.
- V: If the semaphore's queue is empty, the semaphore becomes unlocked. Otherwise, a thread T is dequeued from Q and allowed to continue execution. Effec-

---

[3] P and V names come from the Dutch language phrases "Probeer te verlagen" (try to decrease) and "verhogen" (to increment).

tively, this is the time instance thread T's P call returns. Can you guess when the state of the semaphore will switch back to the unlocked state?

If the queue employed by a semaphore is a FIFO queue, then the semaphore is called **strong**. Otherwise, it is called **weak**. In this case, there is no priority maintained between blocked threads, which could potentially lead to an indefinite block of a thread (a phenomenon called **starvation**, also discussed later in this section).

A **counting semaphore** (also known as a general semaphore) has a counter C as a state, indicating how many resources of some type are available (e.g., messages, file handles, buffers, etc.). Here is what happens when a thread calls P or V on a counting semaphore:

- P: C is decremented.[4] If its new value is negative, the thread is blocked and placed in the waiting-threads queue Q.
- V: C is incremented. If the new value is zero or negative, a thread T is dequeued from Q and allowed to continue execution.

A **mutex** (coming from **MUT**ual **EX**clusion) is a restricted variant of the binary semaphore which permits the lock–unlock sequence to be called by a single thread each time. Once a thread succeeds in a lock call, it "owns" the mutex and it is the only one that can call the unlock method. A binary semaphore on the other hand has no such restriction, i.e., one thread can call lock and another can call unlock.

C++11 added a `mutex` class in the standard library, providing the methods `lock` and `unlock`, as well as `try_lock`, which is a non-blocking version of the lock operation. `try_lock` returns a Boolean indicating whether the lock was acquired or not.

A counting semaphore implementation has been added to the C++20 standard in the form of the `counting_semaphore` class template. A binary semaphore is just a specialization of this class template:

```
using binary_semaphore = std::counting_semaphore<1>;
```

where "1" is the semaphore's maximum allowed value.

However, at the moment of this writing, `counting_semaphore` is not supported by all compilers. Fortunately, creating such a class is not difficult and we actually describe such an implementation in Section 3.9.3.

The example in Fig. 3.9 shows the changes in the state of a counting semaphore, being shared by three threads.

Armed with the `mutex` class, we can solve the race condition that plagues the program of Listing 3.9 by using a mutex to ensure atomicity to the changes applied to the `res` variable. The mutex must be shared by all the participating threads, which means that it has to be:

---

[4] It is possible to have only non-negative values for a counting semaphore. The implementation gets a bit more complex and that is why it is not considered further.

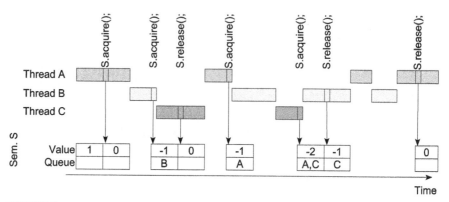

FIGURE 3.9

An example that shows the changes in the state of a general semaphore in response to acquire/release calls by three threads.

- defined as a global variable (should be avoided), or
- passed by reference to the function called by each thread, or
- passed by reference to the constructor of the functor to be called by each thread.

Going with the first option produces the smallest amount of change to Listing 3.9:

```
1  mutex l;  // global lock
2  void partialSum(vector<double>::iterator start, vector<double>::↩
       iterator end, double *res)
3  {
4      for(auto i=start; i<end; i++)
5      {
6          l.lock();
7          *res += *i;
8          l.unlock();
9      }
10 }
```

Because mutices serve as locks they are by default initialized as open/unlocked. For general semaphores the initial counter value is 0 unless explicitly specified otherwise. The introduction of the lock–unlock pair surrounding line 7 above creates a critical section. A **critical section** is a part of the program where access to the different threads is mutually exclusive, i.e., only one thread at any time can be inside it. Critical sections allow us to safely access shared resources, without the risk of putting them in an inconsistent state when writing or getting wrong data when reading. In principle, critical sections have to remain small in length or time duration, because they defeat the purpose of introducing concurrency by forcing threads to execute them sequentially.

The above code would produce correct results, but would be performing significantly slower than a sequential program! The reason is that the introduction of the critical section forces threads to execute the corresponding code in a sequential manner. If we factor in the overhead of acquiring and releasing the lock, we end up with a slowdown instead of a speedup.

In order to avoid a performance hit, critical sections should be minimized both in frequency (how many times they get executed) and in time duration. A proper alternative is given below, where we also eliminate the global mutex variable, by passing it by reference to the thread constructor (line 23):

Listing 3.10: A solution to the race condition problem of Listing 3.9 that utilizes a mutex (for brevity only the changes from the original code are shown).

```
1   // File : aver1.cpp
2   #include <functional>
3
4   void partialSum(vector<double>::iterator start, vector<double>::↩
        iterator end, double &res,  mutex &l)
5   {
6       double partialRes = 0;
7       for(auto i=start; i<end; i++)
8           partialRes += *i;
9
10      l.lock();
11      res += partialRes;
12      l.unlock();
13  }
14  //————————————————————————————————
15  int main(int argc, char **argv)
16  {
17      . . .
18  mutex l;
19  for(int i=0;i<numThr;i++)
20      {
21          localEnd=localStart+step;
22          if(i==numThr-1) localEnd=data.end();
23          thr[i] = new thread(partialSum, localStart, localEnd, ref(res)↩
                , ref(l));
24          localStart += step;
25      }
26      . . .
```

In the `partialSum` function given above, we perform all calculation using disjoint parts of the input vector and a local variable, which by being automatic is allocated on the run-time stack of each thread. Hence we have as many `partialRes` variables as there are threads. The critical section is limited to line 11, which updates the shared `res` repository only once during a thread's execution.

Sharing can be problematic if a **lazy initialization** of the shared resource is desired. Lazy initialization is a tactic where the creation of an object, the calculation of a value, or any expensive computation is delayed until the first time it is needed.

Of course, a lazy-initialized shared object raises the question of which thread will initialize it. An easy way to address this issue is to guard the construction via a mutex, prior to any operation:

```
mutex l;  // global lock
shared_ptr< resource > ptr;

// function called by all threads
void foo( param t )
{
    l.lock();
    if( !ptr )  // first to get the lock sets ptr
        ptr.reset( new resource() ); // executed once
    l.unlock();
    // use the object now
    ptr->do_something( t );
}
```

The first thread to acquire the "l" lock uses the `reset` method to initialize the shared pointer with whatever is passed as a parameter. This solution works but it involves a costly lock–unlock sequence for all the involved threads. C++11 has introduced an alternative mechanism for such a scenario in the form of the `call_once` function (also defined in the `mutex` header):

```
template< class Callable, class... Args >
void call_once( once_flag& flag,   // flag to record if the call ↩
    happened

               Callable&& f,       // function, functor, etc. to ↩
                  call
               Args&&... args );  // parameters for f
```

For each call that must be made only once, a `once_flag` object needs to be used for proper thread coordination. The resulting modifications on our previous small example would be:

```
once_flag f;  // global lock
shared_ptr< resource > ptr;

// function called by all threads
void foo( param t )
{
    call_once( f, [](){
        ptr.reset( new resource() ); // executed once
        });

    // use the object now
    ptr->do_something( t );
}
```

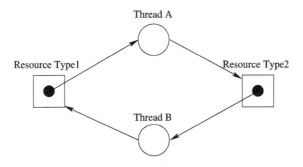

FIGURE 3.10

A resource allocation graph that shows a deadlock between two threads. Rectangles represent resource types and the dots inside them represent available resources of that type. Edges going from threads to rectangles represent pending requests, while edges going from resources to threads indicate resource ownership.

Recursive locks

C++11 allows what could be regarded as a programming error: the same thread can be allowed to lock a mutex multiple times. Such a mutex is called **recursive** and for the lock to become open, the thread has to unlock it the same number of times. The `mutex` class is not a recursive implementation. If such a behavior is desired, like for example inside a recursive function that locks the same semaphore every time it calls itself, one has to employ the `recursive_mutex` class (also defined in the `mutex` header file). This provides the same methods as the normal `mutex` class.

3.7 Applying semaphores in classical problems

So far, our use of a mutex has been rather straightforward. However, the use of semaphores is a challenge not to be underestimated. Semaphores are a *fine-grain* mechanism for controlling concurrency, and as such they offer the potential of extracting great performance but at the expense of development effort. Not only are race conditions difficult to detect, but also the mutual exclusion required to eliminate them can produce side effects in the form of deadlocks or starvation.

A **deadlock** is a phenomenon involving multiple threads (two or more), where threads wait to get access to resources indefinitely, while holding and not releasing other resources. An example is shown in Fig. 3.10 in the form of a resource allocation graph.

Starvation on the other hand can affect individual threads. Starvation happens when the execution of a thread or a process is suspended/disallowed for an indefinite amount of time, although it is capable of continuing execution. Starvation is typically associated with enforcing of priorities or the lack of fairness in scheduling or access to resources.

Here are some examples of things that can go wrong:

- Acquiring (locking up) a resource and forgetting to release it.
- Locking a mutex in one thread and unlocking it in another. Most implementations describe such a sequence as producing undefined results (it may or it may not work).
- Releasing a resource that was never acquired.
- Using a resource without locking it up. Even read-only access can require a lockup.

Unfortunately, there is no magic recipe for learning how to properly use semaphores. We will start by distinguishing what are the roles a semaphore can play and identifying what are the software patterns involved for each of the roles. We will then proceed to apply these to a number of classical problems that have wide applicability in software design.

In our discussion we will refer to an implementation of a general semaphore that is described in Section 3.9.3. One can also use the excellent implementation provided by Qt's `QSemaphore` class, or the C++20's `counting_semaphore` if it is supported.

If your compiler does implement the `counting_semaphore` class template, one can replace the following lines (as used in the examples that follow):

```
#include "semaphore.h"
. . .
semaphore s(10);
```

with these:

```
#include <semaphore>
. . .
std::counting_semaphore s(10);
```

The only limitation when employing C++20 `counting_semaphore` instances is that the `acquire` and `release` methods have no parameters, hence the value of a semaphore can only be adjusted by -1 or $+1$ at a time.

A semaphore can be utilized in three distinct ways:

1. As a **lock**. Suitable semaphore type: **binary** or **mutex**.
2. As a **resource counter**. Suitable semaphore type: **general**.
3. As a **signaling mechanism**. In principle, both binary and counting semaphores can be used depending on the application (but not a mutex). However, as a general guideline, binary semaphores should be avoided in this case, as they cannot accumulate multiple signals/increments.

As will be demonstrated, a semaphore can serve multiple of the above roles at one time.

For each of the above uses, there is a pattern on how they can be deployed. These patterns are shown for the case of two threads in Table 3.1.

Table 3.1 Software patterns employed for using a semaphore in each of its three distinct roles.

	Use	Sem. Initialization	Thread1	Thread2	Thread Relationship

S1	Lock	mutex l;	l.lock();
			...
			l.unlock();
				l.lock();
				...
				l.unlock();
					Threads compete for acquiring the lock to a shared resource.

S2	Resource Counter Scenario 1	semaphore s;	s.release();	s.acquire();	One thread produces resources (Thread 1) and another consumes them (Thread 2). Initially there are no available ones.

S3	Resource Counter Scenario 2	semaphore s(N);	s.acquire();
			...
			s.release();
				s.acquire();
				...
				s.release();
					Thread compete for acquiring resources from a pool of N available ones.

S4	Signaling Mechanism	semaphore s;	s.release();	s.acquire();	One thread (Thread 2) waits for a signal from the other (Thread 1).

Table 3.1 will serve as a guideline, as we explore how semaphores can be properly used via the study of a number of classical problems in the sections that follow. These serve two purposes:

- They represent scenarios that are widely encountered in practice.
- They introduce special conditions that can be observed or anticipated in real-life.

3.7.1 Producers–consumers

The producers–consumers problem concerns the synchronization of two types of threads via a shared buffer. The buffer is used for holding resources made by the producer threads, until they are requested by the consumer threads. In its most generic form the problem involves n producers and m consumers.

The pseudocode of how the two types of threads operate – based on a functor setup – is shown in Listing 3.11.

Listing 3.11: Pseudocode for producer–consumer functors, without any synchronization logic. The buffer is a circular one, which means that producers and consumers operate on different positions in the buffer's space.

```
1  const int BUFFSIZE=100;
2  class Resource {...};
3
4  Resource buffer[BUFFSIZE];
5  int in=0, out=0, resCount=0;
6
7  class Producer
8  public:
9    void operator() () {
10     while(1) {
11        Resource item = produce();
```

```
12          while(resCount == BUFFSIZE) ;    // wait for an empty slot in ↵
               the buffer
13          buffer[in] = item;               // store the item
14          in = (in+1) % BUFFSIZE;          // update the in index
15          resCount++;                      // increment the resource ↵
               counter
16        }
17     }
18  };
19
20  class Consumer
21  public :
22    void operator() ()   {
23       while(1) {
24          while(resCount == 0) ;         // wait for an available item
25          Resource item = buffer[out];// take the item out
26          out = (out+1) % BUFFSIZE;    // update the out index
27          resCount--;                  // decrement the resource ↵
               counter
28          consume(item);
29        }
30     }
31  };
```

We begin by laying out the requirements that the two types of threads must satisfy given the bounded nature of the buffer and the need to safely access shared variables:

- When a producer stores an item in the buffer, it must lock down the "in" parameter. Related pattern in Table 3.1: S1.
- When a consumer removes an item from the buffer, it must lock down the "out" parameter. Related pattern in Table 3.1: S1.
- If the buffer is empty, consumers must wait for resources to be generated by the producers. Related pattern in Table 3.1: S2.
- If the buffer is full, producers must wait for resources to be removed by the consumers. Related pattern in Table 3.1: S2.

The above can be summarized to needing *two binary semaphores or mutices* for locking down in and out and *two counting semaphores* for alerting the threads when it is appropriate to operate on the buffer. The suggested solution, which is illustrated in Listing 3.12, overcomes one particularly inefficient aspect of Listing 3.11: the *busy-waiting* loops of lines 12 and 24 in Listing 3.11 are converted to acquire calls on lines 16 and 31 of Listing 3.12, respectively. As a semaphore can block a thread until a resource is made available, the while loops can be discarded, saving CPU time.

Listing 3.12: Pseudocode for properly synchronizing *n* producers and *m* consumer threads using semaphores.

```
1  const int BUFFSIZE=100;
2  class Resource {...};
3
```

```
4   Resource buffer[BUFFSIZE];
5   int in=0, out=0;
6
7   semaphore slotsAvail(BUFFSIZE);    // counts how many buffer slots ↩
        are free
8   semaphore resAvail(0);             // counts how many buffer slots ↩
        are taken
9   mutex l1, l2;                      // by default initialized open
10
11  class Producer {
12  public:
13    void operator() () {
14      while(1) {
15        Resource item = produce();
16        slotsAvail.acquire() ;   // wait for an empty slot in the ↩
            buffer
17        l1.lock();
18        buffer[in] = item;       // store the item
19        in = (in+1) % BUFFSIZE;  // update the in index safely
20        l1.unlock();
21        resAvail.release();      // signal resource availability
22      }
23    }
24  };
25
26  class Consumer {
27  public:
28    void operator() () {
29      while(1) {
30        resAvail.acquire() ;     // wait for an available item
31        l2.lock();
32        Resource item = buffer[out];// take the item out
33        out = (out+1) % BUFFSIZE;// update the out index
34        l2.unlock();
35        slotsAvail.release();    // signal for a new empty slot
36        consume(item);
37      }
38    }
39  };
```

Comparing Listings 3.11 and 3.12 side-by-side, raises some questions:

- **Q.**: What about the `resCount` counter? It is a shared variable, yet it is not protected by a mutex. Instead it is completely removed!
  A.: It is removed because the busy-waiting loops where it served are no longer needed. If the counter were to be kept in the code, it would require a mutex.
- **Q.**: Is it possible to replace the `resAvail` and `slotsAvail` counting semaphores with a single one? It should be that `resAvail` + `slotsAvail` = BUFFSIZE.
  A.: In a sequential program it would be always true that `resAvail` + `slotsAvail` = BUFFSIZE. However, while a thread or two (one of each type) are interacting with the buffer, it may actually be the case that

$$\mathtt{resAvail + slotsAvail = BUFFSIZE-1}$$

or even

$$\mathtt{resAvail + slotsAvail = BUFFSIZE-2.}$$

The additional reason that prevents the elimination of these semaphores is that they serve a signaling purpose, waking up threads waiting for a slot or a resource.[5]

- **Q.**: Can we replace the two mutices with one? The only thing they seem to do is lock the buffer.

  A.: This is possible but inefficient, as it will force a producer to wait on a consumer to update the `out` index and vice versa. It is, however, possible to eliminate one or both of the mutices if there is only one instance of a thread type. So, if there is only one producer, `l1` (and the related logic) can be eliminated, and if there is only one consumer, `l2` can be eliminated. Table 3.2 summarizes this discussion.

- **Q.**: Could we release the locks to `in` and `out` before an item is stored or taken out of the buffer? We could accomplish this by using temporary variables to hold the buffer locations to use for deposit/extraction as in:

```
class Producer {
public:
  void operator() () {
    while(1) {
      Resource item = produce();
      slotsAvail.acquire() ;    // wait for an empty slot in the ↩
          buffer
      l1.lock();
      int tmpIn = in;
      in = (in+1) % BUFFSIZE;  // update the in index safely
      l1.unlock();
      buffer[tmpIn] = item;    // store the item
      resAvail.release();      // signal resource availability
    }
  }
};

class Consumer {
public:
  void operator() () {
    while(1) {
      resAvail.acquire() ;     // wait for an available item
      l2.lock();
      int tmpOut=out;
      out = (out+1) % BUFFSIZE;// update the out index
      l2.unlock();
      Resource item = buffer[tmpOut];// take the item out
```

---

[5] The `slotAvail` semaphore and the associated statements can be eliminated only if the buffer is always big enough to hold the resources deposited. This is the equivalent of having an infinite buffer. See Exercise 11 for an example.

```
        slotsAvail.release();      // signal for a new empty slot
        consume(item);
    }
  }
};
```

A.: This approach does provide better performance by shrinking the critical section duration. However, there are two scenarios – remote but they exist – where it does not work. One of the two scenarios is shown in Fig. 3.11. When Prod1 is interrupted after line 5, before actually placing an item, Prod2 can come in, place an item, and trigger a consumer to extract from the position that was reserved but not yet initialized by Prod1.

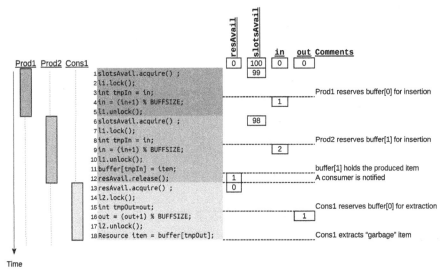

Time

FIGURE 3.11

Sequence diagram for a scenario that shows that insertion and/or extraction of buffer items outside of a critical section is erroneous. The right side of the figure shows the values of the most significant shared variables, after each of the shown statements is executed.

One might argue about Listing 3.11 that further gains in code simplicity can be made by making the buffer a proper class, with methods protected by mutices. This would relegate the synchronization problem to the buffer itself, making the threads completely unaware of any concurrency issues. This is a fair comment that will be explored further in Section 3.9.

3.7.2 Dealing with termination

A significant problem in shared-memory and distributed applications is program termination. It is often the case that a complex condition needs to be evaluated, which

Table 3.2 A summary of the required number and type of semaphores needed to solve the producers–consumers problem.

		Producers	
		1	N
Consumers	1	2 counting semaphores for signaling	2 counting semaphores and 1 binary semaphore for the producers
	M	2 counting semaphores and 1 binary semaphore for the consumers	2 counting semaphores and 2 binary semaphores

renders the continuation of execution unnecessary. This condition is usually evaluated locally (e.g., finding a matching hash value in a password cracking program or a GUI thread reacting to a press of the Exit button) and it is propagated to the other threads. In this section we present two methods that can be used to facilitate proper multi-threaded program termination.

There are two key elements in both of the suggested solutions:

- The termination signal – in whatever form – should reach all threads.
- The threads should be able to detect it within a reasonable amount of time.

The two solutions are presented in the context of the producers–consumers problem, but they can be adjusted to fit other situations. The only real restriction is that each thread should periodically check if the termination condition has been met or not.

3.7.2.1 Termination using a shared data item

Using a shared data item for termination seems like a trivial approach, but there are a few caveats! Contemporary CPU designs use multi-level caches for speeding up access to main memory. The consistency models employed in these caches may not be strict, i.e., cached copies of a shared variable may not be invalidated and updated immediately after one of the copies is modified. Most *cache coherence* implementations follow the **weak consistency**, which means that synchronization variables (e.g., semaphores) have a globally consistent state, but read–write operations in ordinary data may appear in any order to the threads of a program.

So, to be able to properly support termination based on a flag, we must either use an atomic data type (covered in Section 3.8) or force the compiler to avoid caching copies of the flag by using the `volatile` keyword.[6]

In the context of the producers–consumers problem, there are two design alternatives, based on whether the threads need to perform a fixed or variable number of iterations. We distinguish two cases:

---

[6] The `volatile` keyword deserves a word of caution: while it works as expected with primitive data types (e.g., bool or int), with structure or class instances it does not prevent race conditions. If multiple threads access a shared structure or class, then they must do so inside a critical section.

(a) *The number of iterations is known a priori.* In this case, a counting semaphore can be used for each type of thread, replacing their infinite while(1) loops with a while(sem.try_acquire()) statement. The try_acquire method is a non-blocking version of the acquire one that returns true if decrementing the semaphore was successful, or false otherwise. The resulting code is shown in Listing 3.13, which contains working code incorporating class templates for the producer and consumer threads.

Listing 3.13: Generic solution to the *n*-producer and *m*-consumer problem, with a fixed number of iterations. For the sake of brevity, the more significant parts are shown.

```cpp
// File : terminProdCons.cpp
. . .
#include "semaphore.h"

const int BUFFSIZE = 100;

template <typename T>
class Producer {
private:
    int ID;
    static semaphore * slotsAvail;
    static semaphore * resAvail;
    static mutex l1;
    static semaphore * numProducts;
    static T* buffer;
    static int in;
public:
    static T(*produce)();
    static void initClass(int numP, semaphore *s, semaphore *a, T* b
        , T(*prod)());
    Producer<T>(int i) : ID(i) {};
    void operator()();
};
//-------------------------------------------------
template <typename T> void Producer<T>::initClass(int numP, semaphore
    *s, semaphore *a, T* b, T(*prod)()) {
    numProducts = new semaphore(numP);
    slotsAvail = s;
    resAvail = a;
    buffer = b;
    produce = prod;
}
//-------------------------------------------------
template <typename T>
void Producer<T>::operator()() {
    while (numProducts->try_acquire()) {
        T item = (*produce)();
        slotsAvail->acquire(); // wait for an empty slot in the
            buffer
        l1.lock();
```

```
38        buffer[in] = item; // store the item
39        in = (in + 1) % BUFFSIZE; // update the in index safely
40        l1.unlock();
41        resAvail->release(); // signal resource availability
42      }
43  }
44  //─────────────────────────────────────────────
45  template <typename T>
46  class Consumer  {
47  private:
48      int ID;
49      static semaphore * slotsAvail;
50      static semaphore * resAvail;
51      static mutex l2;
52      static T* buffer;
53      static int out;
54      static semaphore *numProducts;
55  public:
56      static void (*consume)(T i);
57      static void initClass(int numP, semaphore *s, semaphore *a, T* b↩
            , void (*cons)(T));
58      Consumer<T>(int i) : ID(i) {};
59      void operator()();
60  };
61  //─────────────────────────────────────────────
62  template <typename T> void Consumer<T>::initClass(int numP, semaphore↩
        *s, semaphore *a, T* b, void (*cons)(T)) {
63      numProducts = new semaphore(numP);
64      slotsAvail = s;
65      resAvail = a;
66      buffer = b;
67      consume = cons;
68  }
69  //─────────────────────────────────────────────
70  template <typename T> void Consumer<T>::operator()() {
71      while (numProducts->try_acquire()) {
72          resAvail->acquire(); // wait for an available item
73          l2.lock();
74          T item = buffer[out];  // take the item out
75          out = (out + 1) % BUFFSIZE; // update the out index
76          l2.unlock();
77          slotsAvail->release(); // signal for a new empty slot
78          (*consume)(item);
79      }
80  }
81  //─────────────────────────────────────────────
82  template <> int (*Producer<int>::produce)() = NULL;
83  template <> void (*Consumer<int>::consume)(int) = NULL;
84  . . .
85
86  int produce() {
87      // to be implemented
```

```
88          return 1;
89   }
90   //─────────────────────────────────────
91   void consume(int i) {
92          // to be implemented
93   }
94   //─────────────────────────────────────
95   int main(int argc, char *argv[]) {
96          if (argc == 1) {
97                cerr << "Usage " << argv[0] << " #producers #consumers #↩
                         iterations\n";
98                exit(1);
99          }
100         int N = atoi(argv[1]);
101         int M = atoi(argv[2]);
102         int numP = atoi(argv[3]);
103         int *buffer = new int[BUFFSIZE];
104
105         unique_ptr<thread > thr[M+N];
106
107         semaphore avail(0);
108         semaphore buffSlots(BUFFSIZE);
109
110         Producer<int >::initClass(numP, &buffSlots, &avail, buffer, &↩
                      produce);
111         Consumer<int >::initClass(numP, &buffSlots, &avail, buffer, &↩
                      consume);
112
113         shared_ptr<Producer<int >> p[N];
114         shared_ptr<Consumer<int >> c[M];
115
116         for (int i = 0; i < N; i++) {
117                p[i] = make_shared<Producer<int >>(i);
118                thr[i] = make_unique<thread >(ref(*p[i]));
119         }
120         for (int i = 0; i < M; i++) {
121                c[i] = make_shared<Consumer<int >>(i);
122                thr[i+N] = make_unique<thread >(ref(*c[i]));
123         }
124
125         for (int i = 0; i < N+M; i++)
126                thr[i]->join();
127   . . .
128   }
```

The program in Listing 3.13 is run by providing the numbers of producers and consumers and the number of iterations as in the example below:

```
$ ./terminProdCons
Usage ./terminProdCons #producers #consumers #iterations

$ ./terminProdCons 3 4 1000
```

Its key points are the following:

- Both the `Producer` and `Consumer` classes are defined as generic types (templates), capable of handling any class of resource.
- Class invariants such as the semaphores, buffer reference, and the in/out indices are declared as static members of each class (lines 11–16 and 49–54) and are initialized by the `initClass` static methods. The latter are called before any thread can be spawned (lines 110–111) and once the `main` function allocates all the necessary data.
- The resource-specific parts, i.e., the creation and consumption of the handled items, is done by two functions, pointers to which are passed as parameters to the `initClass` methods. The actual functions used in the code are just stubs.
- The `avail` and `buffSlots` semaphores are shared between both classes, and that is why they have to be declared outside of them. In contrast, the `l1` and `l2` mutices are class-specific, declared on lines 13 and 51, respectively.
- Static template function pointer syntax in C++ forces the specialization of lines 82–83. For use with another *concrete* data type `T`, the `int` specifier in these lines must be replaced by `T`.
- Thread objects are managed by using an array of unique pointers (line 105). Since the producer and consumer functors are also managed by pointers, we pass their reference to the thread constructors, using `std::ref` (lines 118 and 122).

(b) *The number of iterations is determined at run-time.*

In this case we can have an arrangement similar to:

```
. . .
static volatile bool *exitFlag; // declared as a pointer to allow  ↩
    sharing between classes
. . .
void Producer<T>::run() {
    while (*exitFlag == false) {
. . .
```

But another issue comes up: threads cannot terminate unless they are able to check the status of the shared `exitFlag`. How can we wake up threads which *may be* blocked in a semaphore's queue when termination is detected? Unblocking threads requires that the corresponding semaphores are incremented, permitting threads to resume execution.

An obvious choice for this task is to assign it to the first thread that detects the end of the execution. In the implementation partly shown for brevity, in Listing 3.14 the termination is triggered by the `consume` function and detected by one of the `Consumer` threads which proceeds to set the termination flag to true (line 66).

Listing 3.14: Generic solution to the *n*-producers and *m*-consumers problem, when the number of iterations is unknown. For the sake of brevity, only the parts different from Listing 3.13 are shown.

```cpp
// File : terminProdCons2.cpp
. . .
template <typename T>
class Producer {
private:
    . . .
    static volatile bool *exitFlag;
public:
    static T(*produce)();
    static void initClass(semaphore *s, semaphore *a, T *b, T(*prod)↩
        (), bool *e);
    Producer<T>(int i) : ID(i) {}
    void operator()();
};
//————————————————————————————————
. . .
template <typename T>
void Producer<T>::operator()() {
    while (*exitFlag == false) {
        T item = (*produce)();
        slotsAvail->acquire(); // wait for an empty slot in the ↩
            buffer

        if (*exitFlag) return; // stop immediately on termination

        ll.lock();
        buffer[in] = item; // store the item
        in = (in + 1) % BUFFSIZE; // update the in index safely
        ll.unlock();
        resAvail->release(); // signal resource availability
    }
}
//————————————————————————————————

template <typename T>
class Consumer {
private:
    static volatile bool *exitFlag;
    . . .
public:
    static bool (*consume)(T i);
    static void initClass(semaphore *s, semaphore *a, T* b, bool (*↩
        cons)(T), int N, int M, bool *e);
    Consumer<T>(int i) : ID(i) {}
    void operator()();
};
//————————————————————————————————
. . .
```

```
47   template <typename T> void Consumer<T>:: operator () () {
48       while (*exitFlag == false) {
49           resAvail->acquire(); // wait for an available item
50
51           if (*exitFlag) return; // stop immediately on termination
52
53           l2.lock();
54           T item = buffer[out]; // take the item out
55           out = (out + 1) % BUFFSIZE; // update the out index
56           l2.unlock();
57           slotsAvail->release(); // signal for a new empty slot
58
59           if ((*consume)(item)) break; // time to stop?
60       }
61
62       // only the thread initially detecting termination reaches here
63       *exitFlag = true;
64       resAvail->release(numConsumers - 1);
65       slotsAvail->release(numProducers);
66   }
67   //————————————————————————————————
68   . . .
69   int produce() {
70       // to be implemented
71       int aux = rand();
72       return aux;
73   }
74   //————————————————————————————————
75   bool consume(int i) {
76       // to be implemented
77       cout << "@"; // just to show something is happening
78       if (i % 10 == 0) return true;
79       else return false;
80   }
81   //————————————————————————————————
82   int main(int argc, char *argv[]) {
83       . . .
84       bool exitFlag = false;
85
86       Producer<int>:: initClass(&buffSlots, &avail, buffer, &produce, &↩
                exitFlag);
87       Consumer<int>:: initClass(&buffSlots, &avail, buffer, &consume, N↩
                , M, &exitFlag);
88       . . .
89   }
```

Other key differences between Listings 3.13 and 3.14 are:

- The thread that detects the end of execution (line 59) makes sure that all the other threads of both types are able to terminate by incrementing appropriately both resAvail and slotsAvail (lines 64–65).

- Because the termination is carried out by a `Consumer` thread, the class is initialized to contain the number of both `Consumer` and `Producer` threads (line 87).
- The declared-as-`volatile` *exitFlag Boolean is shared between both types of threads, allowing them to terminate with a simple `while(*exitFlag == false)` loop control statement (lines 18 and 48).
- The threads that are woken up check the termination condition immediately before proceeding to interact with the buffer (lines 22 and 51). This prevents any undesirable side effects or overhead.
- The `produce` function (lines 69–72) returns random integers. Once a multiple of 10 is picked up from a consumer, the `consume` function returns `true` to indicate it is time to stop (line 78).

3.7.2.2 Termination using messages

A very elegant approach that can be also extended to distributed-memory applications is the delivery of termination messages. In our consumers–producers setup, we can treat the items that are exchanged via the shared buffer as implicit messages. A special (i.e., invalid in the application context) item (e.g., a negative number in an application that expects only positive ones or a null pointer when the consumers expect pointers to objects) can be used to indicate the end of the program. As an example, let us assume that the producer threads generate and deposit in the buffer, instances of the class:

```
class Triangle3D{
  public:
      float point1[3];
      float point2[3];
      float point3[3];
};
```

Then a Triangle3D instance with two equal points could be considered by the consumer threads as a termination signal.

The only restriction we have is that termination has to be handled by the producers, as the flow of resources is unidirectional. If the consumer threads were to be used for this purpose, then a technique from the ones described in the previous sections should be applied.

To illustrate this concept, in the example shown in Listing 3.15, a multi-threaded integration of a function is performed. The producer thread deposits in the shared buffer the specifications that should be followed by the consumer threads in calculating the result for a particular part of the range, i.e., the range boundaries and the number of divisions. The program loosely follows the map-reduce pattern described in Section 2.4.4.

The integration is performed using the trapezoidal rule: the integration region $[a, b]$ is split into n equal-width slices of length h as shown in Fig. 3.12. The area for

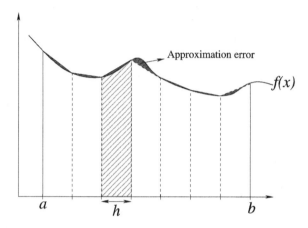

FIGURE 3.12

An illustration of the trapezoidal rule application to the calculation of a function's integral. The red (gray in print version) area represents the approximation error, which can be substantially reduced by shrinking the size of h.

each slice between points x_i and x_{i+1} is approximated by $h \cdot \frac{f(x_i)+f(x_{i+1})}{2}$. The whole area between $[a, b]$ is then

$$\sum_{i=0}^{n-1} h \cdot \frac{f(x_i) + f(x_{i+1})}{2} = h \left(\frac{f(a) + f(b)}{2} + \sum_{i=1}^{n-1} f(x_i) \right), \qquad (3.1)$$

where $x_0 = a$, $x_n = b$, $x_i = a + i \cdot h$, and $h = \frac{b-a}{n}$.

Listing 3.15: Multi-threaded integration of a function, with message termination of worker/consumer threads.

```cpp
// File : terminProdConsMess.cpp
. . .
const int BUFFSIZE = 10;
const double LOWERLIMIT = 0;
const double UPPERLIMIT = 10;
//------------------------------------------------
typedef struct Slice {
    double start;
    double end;
    int divisions;
} Slice;
//------------------------------------------------
double func(double x) {
    return fabs(sin(x));
}
//------------------------------------------------
// acts as a consumer
class IntegrCalc {
```

```
19  private:
20      int ID;
21      static semaphore *slotsAvail;
22      static semaphore *resAvail;
23      static mutex 12;
24      static mutex resLock;
25      static Slice *buffer;
26      static int out;
27      static double *result;
28      static semaphore numProducts;
29  public:
30      static void initClass(semaphore *s, semaphore *a, Slice *b, ←
            double *r);
31
32      IntegrCalc(int i) : ID(i) {};
33      void operator()();
34  };
35  //————————————————————————————————————————
36  . . .
37  void IntegrCalc::initClass(semaphore *s, semaphore *a, Slice *b, ←
            double *res) {
38      slotsAvail = s;
39      resAvail = a;
40      buffer = b;
41      result = res;
42      *result = 0;
43  }
44  //————————————————————————————————————————
45  void IntegrCalc::operator()() {
46      while (1) {
47          resAvail->acquire(); // wait for an available item
48          12.lock();
49          int tmpOut = out;
50          out = (out + 1) % BUFFSIZE; // update the out index
51          12.unlock();
52
53          // take the item out
54          double st = buffer[tmpOut].start;
55          double en = buffer[tmpOut].end;
56          int div = buffer[tmpOut].divisions;
57
58          slotsAvail->release(); // signal for a new empty slot
59
60          if (div == 0) break; // exit
61
62          //calculate area
63          double localRes = 0;
64          double step = (en - st) / div;
65          double x;
66          x = st;
67          localRes = func(st) + func(en);
68          localRes /= 2;
```

```
69          for(int i=1; i< div; i++)   {
70              x += step;
71              localRes += func(x);
72          }
73          localRes *= step;
74
75          // add it to result
76          resLock.lock();
77          *result += localRes;
78          resLock.unlock();
79      }
80  }
81  //———————————————————————————————————————
82  int main(int argc, char *argv[]) {
83      . . .
84      int N = atoi(argv[1]);
85      int J = atoi(argv[2]);
86      Slice *buffer = new Slice[BUFFSIZE];
87      semaphore avail, buffSlots(BUFFSIZE);
88      int in = 0;
89      double result;
90
91      IntegrCalc::initClass(&buffSlots, &avail, buffer, &result);
92
93      unique_ptr<thread> thr[N];
94      shared_ptr<IntegrCalc> func[N];
95      for (int i = 0; i < N; i++) {
96          func[i] = make_shared<IntegrCalc>(i);
97          thr[i] = make_unique<thread>(ref(*func[i]));
98      }
99
100     // main thread is responsible for handing out 'jobs'
101     // It acts as the producer in this setup
102     double divLen = (UPPERLIMIT — LOWERLIMIT) / J;
103     double st, end = LOWERLIMIT;
104     for (int i = 0; i < J; i++) {
105         st = end;
106         end += divLen;
107         if (i == J — 1) end = UPPERLIMIT;
108
109         buffSlots.acquire();
110         buffer[in].start = st;
111         buffer[in].end = end;
112         buffer[in].divisions = 1000;
113         in = (in + 1) % BUFFSIZE;
114         avail.release();
115     }
116
117     // put termination sentinels in buffer
118     for (int i = 0; i < N; i++) {
119         buffSlots.acquire();
120         buffer[in].divisions = 0;
```

```
121        in = (in + 1) % BUFFSIZE;
122        avail.release();
123      }
124   . . .
125  }
```

The key points of the above program are the following:

- The `IntegrCalc` class defined at lines 18–34 acts as a consumer, receiving `Slice` structures (defined between lines 7–11) from the program's main thread as assignments for calculation.
- The main thread assumes the responsibility of the producer, preparing `Slice` structures and flagging their availability (lines 109–114).
- The class invariants are initialized by the `initClass` method. References to the semaphores shared between the main and consumer threads are also passed as parameters (line 91).
- The `operator()` method sports an infinite loop (line 46) that is terminated when a `Slice` structure with `div` equal to zero is received (line 60).
- The termination of the program is the responsibility of the main thread. After all slices have been deposited in the shared buffer, the main thread deposits as many "sentinel" structures as the number of spawned threads (lines 118–123). Please observe that the termination loop is structured in the exact same fashion as the one producing slice assignments above it, i.e., waiting for available space and indicating the presence of new `Slide` instances. It could not be otherwise, given the nature of the shared buffer.
- The `IntegrCalc`-running threads extract the calculation parameters from the `Slice` structure they acquire and proceed to calculate the area using the trapezoidal method. The partial result calculated is accumulated in the `*result`. The latter, being shared between all the `IntegrCalc` threads, sits inside a critical section (lines 76–78).

3.7.3 The barbershop problem – Introducing fairness

The barbershop problem is a thread/process synchronization problem that has been described in various forms in the literature. In its simplest incarnation, the problem is the following.

We have a hypothetical barbershop with one barber. The shop has one barber chair and a waiting room with a fixed number of chairs in it. A customer entering the barbershop would sit in a chair in the waiting room and proceed to sit in the barber's chair when called by the barber. When the barber completes a customer's haircut, he lets the customer go and gets the next customer from the waiting room.

Based on the specifics of how the customers and barber behave and the number of corresponding threads, there can be many possible solutions. We will explore one particular problem setting that brings out the issue of **fairness**. Fairness is usually used in the context of a scheduler, e.g., a scheduler is fair if all ready-to-run processes of the same priority get the same allocation of CPU time. In this context, fairness means that signals meant for a particular thread should be delivered to it.

To illustrate the problem, we assume that we have two barbers in the shop, each using one of two available barber chairs. The pseudocode of the solution is shown below:

Listing 3.16: Pseudocode for solving the barbershop problem, assuming two barber threads.

```
1   semaphore waitChair(NUMCHAIRS);
2   semaphore barberChair(2);
3   semaphore barberReady;
4   semaphore barberDone;
5   semaphore customerReady;
6
7   class Customer {
8    public:
9      void operator()() {
10       waitChair.aquire();      // wait for a chair
11       barberReady.acquire();   // wait for a barber to be ready
12       waitChair.release();     // get up from the chair
13       barberChair.acquire();   // wait for an available barber chair
14       customerReady.release(); // signal that customer is ready
15       barberDone.aquire();     // wait for barber to finish haircut
16       barberChair.release();   // get up from barber's chair
17     }
18  };
19
20  class Barber {
21   public:
22     void operator()() {
23       while(1){                // live to cut hair!
24       barberReady.release();   // signal availability
25       customerReady.acquire(); // wait for customer to be seated
26       barberDone.release();    // signal that hair is done
27     }
28    }
29  };
```

The solution in Listing 3.16 works but has a fatal flaw. The timing diagram in Fig. 3.13 illustrates a scenario where a barber cutting a customer's hair signals that he is done and the customer in the other chair gets up! This sequence can be produced by having a difference in the speed between the two barber threads. Once Cust1 increases customerReady and releases Barb1 from the corresponding queue, the two threads become implicitly associated. Barb1 is too slow to finish the job, so when Barb2 increases barberDone, Cust1 leaves his chair. This is clearly an unfair solution.

The only way this problem can be addressed is to establish an association between a customer and the barber serving him. There are two alternatives that can create this connection:

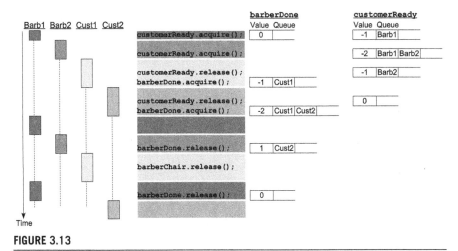

FIGURE 3.13

Sequence diagram of a possible interaction between two barber and two customer threads. The right side of the figure shows the value and queues of two of the semaphores employed, after each of the shown statements is executed.

1. A customer has to acquire the ID of the barber thread that will serve him.
2. A barber has to acquire the ID of the customer he is to serve.

Both solutions require that some of the semaphores in the original solution are replaced by arrays of semaphores, with as many elements as the number of threads that need to be identified. Obviously, the more economical solution is to use the first approach, where we have arrays of two elements, one for each barber.

For a customer to be able to acquire the ID of a barber, we will have to establish a buffer where the IDs of the available barbers are deposited. In that respect, this part of the solution has to follow the producers–consumers pattern. There is a twist to the circumstances surrounding how this pattern is applied: if the buffer holding the IDs is as big as the number of IDs, the barbers (producers) do not have to wait until there is an available slot in the buffer. From the barber's perspective, the buffer is infinite, so the associated counting semaphore can be eliminated! The essential parts of the solution are shown in Listing 3.17.

Listing 3.17: A fair solution to the barbershop problem. Each customer collects the ID of the barber that will serve him and through it uses a set of semaphores specific to that barber.

```cpp
// File : fairBarber.cpp
. . .
#include <boost/make_shared.hpp>
//—————————————————————————————
void concurPrint(int cID, int bID) {
    static mutex l;
    l.lock();
```

```
 8      cout << "Customer " << cID << " is being serviced by barber " <<↵
            bID << endl;
 9      l.unlock();
10  }
11  //————————————————————————————————————
12
13  class Barber {
14  private:
15      int ID;
16      static semaphore *barberReady;
17  //      static boost::shared_ptr<semaphore[]> customerReady;
18      static boost::shared_ptr<semaphore[]> customerReady;
19      static boost::shared_ptr<semaphore[]> barberDone;
20
21      static mutex l1;
22      static semaphore customersLeft;
23      static boost::shared_ptr<int[]> buffer;
24      static int in;
25      static int numBarbers;
26  public:
27      static void initClass(int numB, int numC, semaphore *r, boost::↵
            shared_ptr<semaphore[]> &c, boost::shared_ptr<semaphore[]> &↵
            d, boost::shared_ptr<int[]> &b);
28
29      Barber(int i) : ID(i) {}
30      void operator()();
31  };
32  //————————————————————————————————————
33  . . .
34  void Barber::initClass(int numB, int numC, semaphore *r, boost::↵
        shared_ptr<semaphore[]> &c, boost::shared_ptr<semaphore[]> &d, ↵
        boost::shared_ptr<int[]> &b) {
35      customersLeft.release(numC);
36      barberReady = r;
37      customerReady = c;
38      barberDone = d;
39      buffer = b;
40      numBarbers = numB;
41  }
42  //————————————————————————————————————
43
44  void Barber::operator()() {
45      while (customersLeft.try_acquire()) {
46          l1.lock();
47          buffer[in] = ID;
48          in = (in + 1) % numBarbers;
49          l1.unlock();
50          barberReady->release(); // signal availability
51          customerReady[ID].acquire(); // wait for customer to be ↵
                seated
52          barberDone[ID].release(); // signal that hair is done
53      }
```

```
54    }
55    //————————————————————————————————————
56
57    class Customer {
58    private:
59        int ID;
60        static semaphore *barberReady;
61        static boost::shared_ptr<semaphore[]> customerReady;
62        static boost::shared_ptr<semaphore[]> barberDone;
63        static semaphore waitChair;
64        static semaphore barberChair;
65        static mutex l2;
66        static boost::shared_ptr<int[]> buffer;
67        static int out;
68        static int numBarbers;
69        static semaphore numProducts;
70    public:
71        static void initClass(int numB, semaphore *r, boost::shared_ptr<↵
              semaphore[]> &c, boost::shared_ptr<semaphore[]> &d, boost::↵
              shared_ptr<int[]> &b);
72
73        Customer(int i) : ID(i) {}
74        void operator()();
75    };
76    //————————————————————————————————————
77    semaphore Customer::waitChair(NUMCHAIRS);
78    . . .
79    void Customer::initClass(int numB, semaphore *r, boost::shared_ptr<↵
              semaphore[]> &c, boost::shared_ptr<semaphore[]> &d, boost::↵
              shared_ptr<int[]> &b) {
80        barberReady = r;
81        customerReady=c;
82        barberDone = d;
83        buffer = b;
84        numBarbers = numB;
85        barberChair.release(numB);
86    }
87    //————————————————————————————————————
88
89    void Customer::operator()() {
90        waitChair.acquire(); // wait for a chair
91        barberReady->acquire(); // wait for a barber to be ready
92        l2.lock();
93        int bID = buffer[out];
94        out = (out + 1) % numBarbers;
95        l2.unlock();
96        waitChair.release(); // get up from the chair
97        barberChair.acquire(); // wait for an available barber chair
98        customerReady[bID].release(); // signal that customer is ready
99        concurPrint(ID, bID);
100       barberDone[bID].acquire(); // wait for barber to finish haircut
101       barberChair.release(); // get up from barber's chair
```

```
102  }
103  //————————————————————————————————————
104
105  int main(int argc, char *argv[]) {
106      if (argc == 1) {
107          cerr << "Usage " << argv[0] << " #barbers #customers\n";
108          exit(1);
109      }
110      int N = atoi(argv[1]);
111      int M = atoi(argv[2]);
112      boost::shared_ptr<int[]> buffer(new int[N]);
113
114      semaphore barberReady;
115      boost::shared_ptr<semaphore[]> customerReady (new semaphore[N]);
116      boost::shared_ptr<semaphore[]> barberDone (new semaphore[N]);
117
118      Barber::initClass(N, M, &barberReady, customerReady, barberDone,↵
                  buffer);
119      Customer::initClass(N, &barberReady, customerReady, barberDone, ↵
                  buffer);
120
121      unique_ptr<thread> thr[N+M];
122
123      shared_ptr<Barber> b[N];
124      shared_ptr<Customer> c[M];
125      for (int i = 0; i < N; i++) {
126          b[i] = make_shared<Barber>(i);
127          thr[i] = make_unique<thread>(ref(*b[i]));
128      }
129      for (int i = 0; i < M; i++) {
130          c[i] = make_shared<Customer>(i);
131          thr[i+N] = make_unique<thread>(ref(*c[i]));
132      }
133
134      for (int i = 0; i < N+M; i++)
135          thr[i]->join();
136
137      return 0;
138  }
```

The key points of Listing 3.17 solution are:

- The dynamic arrays required for the code are managed with `unique_ptr` and `shared_ptr` objects, keeping with the RAII principle. For handling shared pointers to arrays, we utilize Boost[7] library's `boost::shared_ptr` class template (lines 112, 115, and 116), as C++ standard support for this feature has been relegated to C++20 (unavailable at the time of this writing).

---

[7] Boost (available at https://www.boost.org) is a high-quality free library that offers a wide variety of application-specific functions. It is the staging ground for many to-be additions to the C++ standard library.

- Each barber is associated with an element in two semaphores arrays, `customer-Ready` and `barberDone`, defined on lines 115 and 116, respectively.
- The `waitChair` and `barberChair` semaphores serve the purpose of keeping with the scenario's simulation (customer sits in a chair before a barber chair becomes available, etc.) and are meant to be only used by customers. `barberChair` is initialized accordingly on line 85.
- As with previous solutions in this chapter, the data shared between the two types of threads are allocated in `main()` and passed as parameters to methods initializing the two classes' data members (lines 110–119).
- A buffer is set up to hold the available barber IDs. The customer threads extract the IDs in a setup reminiscent of producers–consumers. The only thing missing is the equivalent of the `slotsAvail` semaphore as the buffer is as big as the number of barbers; hence, there is always going to be a slot available. The "producers"/barbers part is on lines 46–50, and the "consumers"/customers part is on lines 91–95.
- The `Customer` threads do not perform any looping, so the termination responsibility lies with the `Barber` threads. To facilitate this functionality, the `customersLeft` semaphore is initialized to the number of customers on line 35 and decremented/tested on line 45 of the `Barber::operator()` method.
- Last but not least, lines 5–10 define the `concurPrint` function that is used to generate non-mangled console output by restricting the use of the `cout` object only inside a critical section.

3.7.4 **Readers–writers**

The readers–writers problem manifests itself whenever a shared resource is accessed by threads trying to modify it alongside threads trying to read it. In its simplest form, the problem is governed by the following two conditions:

- Each writer must have exclusive access to the resource while it is modifying it. All other threads, including readers, are blocked.
- If a reader is accessing the resource, other readers may do so as well. Obviously, adhering to the previous condition, writer threads cannot access the resource while a reader is doing so.

These two rules allow us to preserve the resource in a consistent state, avoiding race conditions and erroneous changes. What they do not specify though, is **the order** in which the threads are allowed to access the resource.

Should there be a priority given to one or the other kind of thread? Priorities entail the danger of *starvation*, but under certain circumstances priorities can be an application requirement. The key to solving this problem is the management of the queue of threads that try to access the resource.

The three distinct possibilities in how the threads' ordering problem can be solved are analyzed in the sections that follow.

3.7.4.1 A solution favoring the readers

Favoring the readers means that when a reader tries to access the resource and the resource is currently being read by other readers, the reader is allowed to proceed regardless of any writer threads waiting.

Listing 3.18 shows the core of the solution in pseudocode:

Listing 3.18: A solution to the readers–writers problem favoring the readers.

```
 1  mutex writerLock;
 2  mutex countLock;
 3  int numReaders =0;
 4
 5  void Reader::operator()()
 6  {
 7    countLock.lock();
 8    numReaders++;
 9    if(numReaders == 1)
10      writerLock.lock();
11    countLock.unlock();
12
13    // reader critical section
14
15    countLock.lock();
16    numReaders --;
17    if(numReaders == 0)
18      writerLock.unlock();
19    countLock.unlock();
20  }
21
22  void Writer::operator()()
23  {
24    writerLock.lock();
25    // writer critical section
26    writerLock.unlock();
27  }
```

The design of the above solution is fairly simple:

- The writer threads share a mutex (writerLock) that controls entry to their critical section.
- The readers also share a mutex (countLock) that controls access to a shared counter (numReaders). Before the counter is modified on lines 8 and 16, the mutex must be locked.
- The first reader to acquire the countLock tries to also acquire the writerLock mutex. If there is a writer inside its critical section, the reader thread will wait (any other incoming reader threads will also block on trying to acquire the countLock). Otherwise, the reader thread will continue, effectively blocking any writer threads from entry.
- After the last reader thread exits its critical section, the writers' mutex is released (line 18).

The solution favors the readers because once a reader enters its critical section, any other incoming readers can join in, bypassing waiting writers.

3.7.4.2 Giving priority to the writers

Favoring the writers means that any writer in the queue of threads waiting to access their critical section will bypass any waiting readers. The solution is very similar to the previous one despite the more complex appearance! Listing 3.19 shows the core of the solution in pseudocode:

Listing 3.19: A solution to the readers–writers problem, favoring the writers.

```
1    mutex writerLock;
2    mutex readerLock;
3    mutex countLock;
4    mutex writerCountLock;
5    int numReaders=0;
6    int numWriters=0;
7
8    void Reader::operator()()
9    {
10     readerLock.lock();
11     countLock.lock();
12     numReaders++;
13     if(numReaders == 1)
14       writerLock.lock();
15     countLock.unlock();
16     readerLock.unlock();
17
18     // reader critical section
19
20     countLock.lock();
21     numReaders--;
22     if(numReaders == 0)
23       writerLock.unlock();
24     countLock.unlock();
25   }
26
27   void Writer::operator()()
28   {
29     writerCountLock.lock();
30     numWriters++;
31     if(numWriters==1)
32       readersLock.lock();
33     writerCountLock.unlock();
34
35     writerLock.lock();
36     // writer critical section
37     writerLock.unlock();
38
39     writerCountLock.lock();
40     numWriters--;
41     if(numWriters==0)
```

```
42          readersLock.unlock();
43        writerCountLock.unlock();
44    }
```

At first glance, the readers part is identical to the one shown in Listing 3.18, with the sole addition of a seemingly inconsequential lock–unlock pair on a `readersLock` mutex. It is actually this mutex that allows the writers to exercise control over readers entry. Going into more detail:

- The `readerLock` has no other purpose but to inhibit reader threads from entering their critical section. That is why readers release it almost immediately (line 16). Writers exercise this control when they first start running (line 32).
- Only the first writer needs to block the readers, hence the line 31 condition. The last of the writers to leave unblocks the readers (lines 41 and 42).
- The need to enumerate the waiting writers via the `numWriters` variable also necessitates the use of a mutex (`writerCountLock`) to prevent race conditions.
- The readers that start execution before the arrival of the first writer operate in the same fashion as in the previous solution.
- It may seem that having both `readerLock` and `countLock` (and the way they are used in the Reader class) is redundant. Would it be possible for a writer to just acquire `countLock` instead? Could that solve the priority problem without the need for one more lock?
  Well, the answer is no: if `countLock` is acquired by a writer, any reader inside its critical section will be unable to proceed past line 20. The result would be a deadlock as pictured in Fig. 3.10!

3.7.4.3 A fair solution

A fair solution dictates the application of a strict FIFO policy on the queue of waiting threads. This means that threads are allowed in their critical section in the order they request entry, while always abiding by the two conditions set in Section 3.7.4.

The trick that we can use to solve the problem fairly is to use one more semaphore that all the threads will have to acquire once they start running. Both types of threads should release this semaphore once they are allowed to enter their critical section. As long as we use a strong semaphore, the order is FIFO and there is no danger of starvation.

The pseudocode of the fair solution is shown in Listing 3.20:

Listing 3.20: A fair solution to the readers–writers problem.

```
1    mutex writerLock;
2    mutex fairLock;
3    mutex countLock;
4    int numReaders=0;
5    int numWriters=0;
6
7    void Reader::run()
8    {
```

```
9    fairLock.lock();
10   countLock.lock();
11   numReaders++;
12   if(numReaders == 1)
13     writerLock.lock();
14   countLock.unlock();
15   fairLock.unlock();
16
17   // reader critical section
18
19   countLock.lock();
20   numReaders--;
21   if(numReaders == 0)
22     writerLock.unlock();
23   countLock.unlock();
24  }
25
26  void Writer::run()
27  {
28    fairLock.lock();
29    writerLock.lock();
30    fairLock.unlock();
31
32    // writer critical section
33
34    writerLock.unlock();
35  }
```

Some key observations about the solution:

- The code for the readers is almost identical to the one used to give priority to the writers. However, the introduction of the `fairLock` mutex forces all types of threads in the same queue.
- When a reader acquires `fairLock`, it proceeds to increment the `numReaders` counter and possibly acquire the `writerLock` mutex. It releases `fairLock` immediately before entering its critical section, allowing other readers to also proceed.
- If a writer follows a reader in the `fairLock` queue, it will block at line 29 and prevent any other thread from acquiring `fairLock`.

3.7.4.4 C++17 provisions

C++17 provides a `shared_mutex` class that can be used for a readers–writers scenario. The class provides, along with the known `lock`, `unlock`, and `try_lock` methods, which are used for locking the mutex exclusively, the following list of methods:

- `lock_shared`: locks the mutex for shared ownership. If the mutex is locked exclusively, it blocks.
- `try_lock_shared`: tries to lock the mutex for shared ownership. Returns true if the acquisition was successful.
- `unlock_shared`: unlocks the mutex.

Thus, our code could be simplified to:

Listing 3.21: A solution to the readers–writers problem using C++17.

```
1   #include <shared_mutex>
2   shared_mutex rwlock;
3
4   void Reader::operator()()
5   {
6     rwlock.lock_shared();
7
8     // reader critical section
9
10    rwlock.unlock_shared();
11  }
12
13  void Writer::operator()()
14  {
15    rwlock.lock();
16
17    // writer critical section
18
19    rwlock.unlock();
20  }
```

The code can be made even more robust by using a wrapper object around the shared_mutex, as shown below:

Listing 3.22: Readers–writers solution using C++17 and RAII.

```
1   #include <shared_mutex>
2   #include <mutex>  // For std::unique_lock
3
4   shared_mutex rwlock;
5
6   void Reader::operator()()
7   {
8     shared_lock readGuard(rwlock); // shared lock for readers
9
10    // reader critical section
11  }
12
13  void Writer::operator()()
14  {
15    unique_lock writeGuard(rwlock); // exclusive lock for writers
16
17    // writer critical section
18  }
```

Listing 3.22 avoids abnormal effects to other threads if one of them produces an exception or returns abnormally. The shared_lock and unique_lock objects call the appropriate lock methods upon construction and the corresponding unlock methods upon their destruction, alleviating the need to explicitly unlock the mutex. These classes allow us to automate the release of locks when a complex critical section (such as a function that has multiple return points or generates exceptions) is involved.

3.8 **Atomic data types**

C++11 and subsequent versions of the standard have incorporated an `atomic` class template and a number of specializations (i.e., concrete implementations for specific data types) as shown in Table 3.3. The atomic data types offer data-race free access to threads without needing to resort to explicit locking. For example, the `atomic` class template can be used to implement lock-free concurrent data structures (see Chapter 4).

Locking can be done behind the scenes based on what the target CPU architecture supports. But on certain machines it can be completely avoided and in any case it alleviates this burden from the programmer, resulting in more efficient code development and execution.

As `atomic` is a template, one might be inclined to go for a definition such as:

```
class FooClass { . . .};
atomic<FooClass> obj;      // does not compile
atomic<FooClass *> ptrObj;  // works fine
```

in the hope that access to `obj` would be atomic. However, this approach works only for the specializations of the template shown in Table 3.3.

The `atomic` class template provides the following atomic methods:

- `store`/`load`: saves/retrieves the value of the atomic object.
- `fetch_add`/`fetch_sub`: adds/subtracts the argument from the stored value. The method returns the previous value.
- `fetch_and`/`fetch_or`/`fetch_xor`: performs bitwise AND/OR/XOR between the argument and the value of the atomic object. The previous value is returned.
- `exchange`: replaces the value of the atomic object and returns the previous value.
- `compare_exchange_weak`/`compare_exchange_strong`: compares the value of the atomic object with the argument and performs an `exchange` operation if they are equal or a `load` operation otherwise. The "weak" variant may fail spuriously, i.e., even when the memory contents match the expected value, due to architecture implementation issues. Using the "weak" variant in a loop may yield better performance in some platforms. The "strong" variant will try to perform the operation again in the case of a spurious failure. The reason for the failure has to do with the implementation of the exchange operation (see sidebar on "LL/SC and compare-and-swap").
- `is_lock_free`: returns true if the atomic object is lock-free, i.e., a lock is not used to implement the aforementioned methods.

Table 3.3 A sample of the C++11 `atomic` class template specializations and their associated aliases. Unsigned type variants (e.g., `uint`) and pointers to any type T (`atomic<T*>`) are covered as well.

Alias	Specialization
std::atomic_bool	std::atomic<bool>
std::atomic_char	std::atomic<char>
std::atomic_short	std::atomic<short>
std::atomic_int	std::atomic<int>
std::atomic_long	std::atomic<long>
std::atomic_llong	std::atomic<long long>
std::atomic_char16_t	std::atomic<char16_t>
std::atomic_char32_t	std::atomic<char32_t>
std::atomic_int8_t	std::atomic<std::int8_t>
std::atomic_int16_t	std::atomic<std::int16_t>
std::atomic_int32_t	std::atomic<std::int32_t>
std::atomic_int64_t	std::atomic<std::int64_t>
std::atomic_int_least8_t	std::atomic<std::int_least8_t>
std::atomic_int_least16_t	std::atomic<std::int_least16_t>
std::atomic_int_least32_t	std::atomic<std::int_least32_t>
std::atomic_int_least64_t	std::atomic<std::int_least64_t>
std::atomic_int_fast8_t	std::atomic<std::int_fast8_t>
std::atomic_int_fast16_t	std::atomic<std::int_fast16_t>
std::atomic_int_fast32_t	std::atomic<std::int_fast32_t>
std::atomic_int_fast64_t	std::atomic<std::int_fast64_t>
std::atomic_intptr_t	std::atomic<std::intptr_t>
std::atomic_size_t	std::atomic<std::size_t>
std::atomic_ptrdiff_t	std::atomic<std::ptrdiff_t>
std::atomic_intmax_t	std::atomic<std::intmax_t>

LL/SC and compare-and-swap

Atomic memory operations in the presence of multi-level cache hierarchies and multi-threaded execution depend on performing checks before modifications are committed. There are two approaches:

- **Compare-and-swap**, also known as compare-and-exchange: this refers to a single command where the contents of a memory location are compared against a value. If there is a match, a new supplied value is stored. In any case, the previous value is returned. x86-64 chips follow this approach using the CMPXCHG command, which supports 8, 16, 32, and 64 bit operands.
- **Load-link and store-conditional** (LL/SC): most RISC architectures (such as PowerPC and ARM) follow this approach, where a sequence of two commands is performed. The load-link command returns the contents of the memory location specified. The store-conditional command *attempts* to store a new value to the same location. The SC command will fail if any other modification to that location has been performed since the LL command or if there has been a context switch interrupting the LL/SC sequence.

A list of atomic augmented assignment and increment/decrement operators is also provided: ++, −−, +=, −=, &=, |=, ^=, but they are not universal, as for example the &= operator makes no sense for an atomic pointer.

The atomic types can be used to build locks, to replace locks, or to complement them. For example, we achieve mutual exclusion for our threads by using an atomic Boolean as shown below:

Listing 3.23: Achieving mutual exclusion by using an atomic Boolean.

```
atomic<bool> lock; // should be accessible from all concerned ↩
    threads

// entry section
while(true)
{
    bool tmp = false;
    if(lock.compare_exchange_weak(tmp, true))
        break;
    this_thread::yield();
}

// critical section
. . .

// exit section
lock.store(false);
```

The loop between lines 4 and 10 ensures that we are able to compare successfully the value of the `lock` variable with `false` (the default initial state of an `atomic<bool>`) and exchange it with `true` (line 7), before continuing to the critical section. The use of the `compare_exchange_weak` variant is meant to offer better performance in some hardware platforms. If the check fails, we can surrender the CPU (line 9) instead of wasting CPU cycles busy-waiting.

The `tmp` variable needs to be initialized every time before executing line 7, as the `compare_exchange_*` methods swap the value of the atomic variable with the first parameter passed to them, hence `tmp` would be set to `true` if the comparison fails.

Finally, the exit section is as simple as restoring the default value of the atomic Boolean (line 16).

Of course, line 9 is optional and it can be accompanied by extra logic that, for example, repeats the loop a number of times before yielding:

```
// entry section
int iter=0;
while(true)
{
    bool tmp = false;
    if(lock.compare_exchange_weak(tmp, true))
        break;
    if(++iter > MAX_ITER)
        {
```

```
        iter=0;
        this_thread::yield();
      }
  }
  . . .
```

We can take these ideas further by creating a simple readers–writers "lock" that is not based on blocking, i.e., changing the execution state, of threads:

Listing 3.24: A readers–writers lock utilizing atomic types.

```
1   // File : atomic_rw_lock.cpp
2   #include <atomic>
3   . . .
4   const int UNLOCKED = 0;
5   const int WRITERIN = -1;
6   //--------------------------------------------------
7   class RWLock
8   {
9   private:
10    atomic < int >lockState;
11
12  public:
13    void lockRead ();
14    void lockWrite ();
15    void unlock ();
16      RWLock ()
17      {
18        lockState.store (UNLOCKED);
19      }
20    RWLock (RWLock &) = delete;
21  };
22
23  //--------------------------------------------------
24  void RWLock::lockRead ()
25  {
26    while (true)
27      {
28        int currState = lockState.load ();
29        if (currState >= 0)
30          if (lockState.compare_exchange_weak (currState, currState + ↵
              1))
31            return;
32        this_thread::yield ();
33      }
34  }
35
36  //--------------------------------------------------
37  void RWLock::lockWrite ()
38  {
39    while (true)
40      {
41        int currState = lockState.load ();
```

```
42        if (currState == UNLOCKED)
43          if (lockState.compare_exchange_weak (currState, WRITERIN))
44            return;
45        this_thread::yield ();
46      }
47  }
48
49  //————————————————————————————————————————
50  void RWLock::unlock ()
51  {
52    while (true)
53      {
54        int currState = lockState.load ();
55        if (currState == WRITERIN)
56          {
57            if (lockState.compare_exchange_weak (currState, UNLOCKED))
58              return;
59          }
60        else
61          {
62            if (lockState.compare_exchange_weak (currState, currState ↩
                   - 1))
63              return;
64          }
65      }
66  }
```

The key points of Listing 3.24 are:

- An atomic integer (lockState defined on line 10) is used to keep track of the lock's state. The value of lockState can be one of the following:
  - *Zero*: represented by the UNLOCKED symbolic constant, declared at line 4.
  - *Negative 1*: represented by the WRITERIN symbolic constant, which corresponds to a writer holding the lock
  - *Positive*: corresponds to the number of readers holding the lock.
- The same while - compare_exchange_weak loop structure as shown in Listing 3.23 is used wherever we need to change the state of the lock. The only difference is that we are now having multiple states instead of just two, which also means that some extra checking is necessary before a compare-and-exchange is attempted. For example, in the lockRead() method, we need to check that the lock is not owned by a writer (line 29) before trying to increment lockState. Similarly, in lockWrite() we need to make sure that the lock is UNLOCKED before trying to acquire it.
- Just a single unlock() method is required, as the value of lockState is enough to determine what change needs to be performed (line 57 for writers and line 62 for readers).

Using our new `RWLock` is as simple as:

```cpp
// File : atomic_rw_lock.cpp
. . .
void Reader::operator () ()   // reader thread
{
  l->lockRead ();
  // reader critical section
  printf ("Reader %i runs critical section\n", ID);
  l->unlock ();
}
. . .
void Writer::operator () ()   // writer thread
{
  l->lockWrite ();
  // writer critical section
  printf ("Writer %i runs critical section\n", ID);

  l->unlock ();
}
```

Compiling and running the above program requires linking against the `atomic` library in GCC and Clang:

```
$ g++ atomic_rw_lock.cpp —pthread —latomic —o atomic_rw_lock
$ ./atomic_rw_lock 5 20
. . .
```

Our `atomic<int>`-based solution can work well enough in circumstances of low contention, i.e., the threads will not waste much time waiting in the while loops. Otherwise a lock-based solution would be more efficient.

3.8.1 Memory ordering

The atomic methods listed above include in their signature one or more optional parameters that have to do with **memory ordering**. Memory ordering is concerned with interthread coordination, i.e., how memory operations performed in one thread are perceived by other threads, or, in other words, how modifications to shared variables are communicated to the threads that access them. These settings have no effect on the operations conducted within one thread, in the sense that one thread is always up-to-date with the changes it has performed.

To understand why this is an issue that a programmer has to be concerned with, we have to understand the root of the problem: the existence of multi-level disjoint caches and register files in use by modern microprocessors. At any point in time, multiple copies of a variable/memory location may exist across those caches and/or registers (on different cores). The proper thing to do is to somehow make sure that all the copies stay consistent, i.e., are identical throughout the lifetime of a program and its threads. However, cache coherency protocols (see also Section 8.12.2) can be expensive, forcing CPU cores to wait while changes are propagated across all cores.

The alternative is to have inconsistent copies, but construct the program logic so that such differences can be tolerated without influencing the correctness of the program. This is where "memory ordering" comes into play. We can specify alternative ways of handling change propagation to other threads, based on the operation performed on an atomic variable. This way a programmer can fine-tune what kind of mechanism is sufficient while incurring the minimum amount of overhead.

The C++11 standard established the following memory orderings:

- `memory_order_relaxed`: there are no synchronization or ordering constraints imposed on other threads' reads or writes.
- `memory_order_acquire`: used in a load operation, to make sure that all writes in other threads to the concerned atomic variable are visible in the current thread.
- `memory_order_consume`: this is identical in functionality to `memory_order_acquire`, but it may be more efficient in certain hardware platforms. The gain in performance is achieved by having data dependencies that ensure change propagation from other threads, instead of requiring a memory fence operation to ensure all changes become available.
- `memory_order_release`: used in a store operation to ensure that the changes from the current thread become visible in other threads that acquire/read the same atomic variable.
- `memory_order_acq_rel`: used in read–modify–write operation (e.g., `compare_exchange_*`), where both an acquire operation is performed for the read part and a release operation is performed for the write part. Hence changes from other threads become visible before the read, and the change from the current thread becomes visible to other threads after the write.
- `memory_order_seq_cst`: short for "sequentially consistent," i.e., a load operation performs an acquire and a write operation performs a release. This is the most strict ordering, and it is the default one in order to ensure program correctness.

These settings can be used to establish three different modes of operation:

1. **Relaxed**: using the `memory_order_relaxed` setting, the changes are not forcefully propagated to the other cores, allowing each thread to see different values and value sequences of a variable. This is akin to maintaining a linear list of values for each variable/memory location. Each thread can "see"/read from the list when trying to read the variable, either the last value it wrote (existing in its cache) or any of the values that were subsequently written to that variable by other threads (signifying that a change in the value reached its CPU cache).
2. **Acquire–release**: by using `memory_order_acquire` and `memory_order_release`, changes are propagated between pairs of threads. The thread that does the writing needs to use `memory_order_release`, and the thread that does the reading needs to use `memory_order_acquire`. `memory_order_acq_rel` and `memory_order_consume` belong to this mode as well, utilized by methods other than `store` and `load`.
3. **Sequentially consistent**: using `memory_order_seq_cst` all threads see the same values of a variable by forcing change propagation. This is the default operation,

but it can be costly on architectures that do not have proper hardware support for memory consistency.

To better appreciate what all the above mean, the following example illustrates the kind of behavior relaxed ordering can produce:

Listing 3.25: An illustration of relaxed memory ordering operation.

```cpp
1  // File : relaxed.cpp
2  #include <cassert>
3  . . . .
4  atomic<bool> x, y;
5
6  void thr1()
7  {
8    x.store(true, memory_order_relaxed);
9    y.store(true, memory_order_relaxed);
10 }
11 //------------------------------------------------
12 void thr2()
13 {
14   bool temp=false;
15   while(!temp)
16       temp=y.load(memory_order_relaxed);
17   assert(x.load(memory_order_relaxed)==true);
18 }
19 //------------------------------------------------
20 int main (int argc, char **argv)
21 {
22     thread t1(thr1);
23     thread t2(thr2);
24     t1.join();
25     t2.join();
26     return 0;
27 }
```

The thread executing `thr2()` above performs a busy-waiting loop until the change to atomic Boolean y from `thr1()` is detected. It then proceeds to verify that the x atomic Boolean is also `true` (line 17). It is possible for the above code to trigger the `assert` function, abnormally terminating the program, despite having the x variable set prior to y in `thr1()`. The reason is of course the use of the relaxed memory ordering in all atomic variable operations. To compile and test the above code, one needs to type (more on why optimization is required to follow):

```
$ g++ relaxec.cpp -o relaxed -pthread -latomic -O2
$ ./relaxed
```

Unfortunately, getting the assertion to fail requires an architecture that does not offer strong memory consistency, which is not the case for the x86-64 architecture.

To prevent triggering the assertion while avoiding the overhead of sequential consistency, we could have:

Listing 3.26: An illustration of relaxed memory ordering operation.

```
// File : acquire−release.cpp
void thr1()
{
  x.store(true, memory_order_release);
  y.store(true, memory_order_release);
}

void thr2()
{
  bool temp=false;
  while(!temp)
      temp=y.load(memory_order_acquire);
  assert(x.load(memory_order_acquire) ==true);
}
```

where store operations "release" and load operations "acquire."

We can also use the acquire–release mode to produce a spinlock that does not block the calling thread, similar to the RWLock of Listing 3.24:

Listing 3.27: A lock based on atomic operations.

```
1  // File : atomic_lock.cpp
2  . . .
3  class ALock
4  {
5  private:
6    atomic < bool >lockState;
7
8  public:
9    void lock();
10   void unlock ();
11   ALock ()
12   {
13     lockState.store (false);
14   }
15   ALock (ALock &) = delete;
16   ALock &operator=()(const ALock &o) = delete;
17 };
18
19 //——————————————————————
20 void ALock::lock()
21 {
22   while (true)
23     {
24       bool temp=false;
25       if (lockState.compare_exchange_weak (temp, true, ↩
              memory_order_acq_rel ))
26           return;
27       this_thread::yield ();
28     }
29 }
```

```
30
31   //──────────────────────────────────────────────────
32   void ALock::unlock ()
33   {
34       lockState.store(false, memory_order_release);
35   }
```

The novelty in this code is the use of the `memory_order_acq_rel` ordering on line 25, which is a combination of "acquire" for reading the `lockState` atomic Boolean and "release" for storing the new value if the comparison succeeds. The rest of the logic and code structure is a simplification of the `RWLock`. Thus, the while loop of lines 22–28 in the `lock()` method will try to switch the state of the lock until it succeeds and returns. Otherwise, it yields the CPU before another attempt.

In turn, the `unlock()` method just switches the state of the lock, making sure the change is observed by other threads by utilizing the "release" mode.

It is worth noting that the code generated for each ordering depends on the optimization setting of the compiler, something that can trigger inconsistent code behavior seemingly based only on the compiler flags. For example, when compiling without optimization, GCC follows each atomic operation with a memory fence, which makes all the orderings indistinguishable. A memory fence is a *serializing* operation that commits all memory operations that precede it so that they become globally available. Only when optimization is enabled (e.g., with `-02`) does the compiler reserve the memory fence only for the `memory_order_seq_cst` setting.

In conclusion, relaxed or acquire–release orderings can lead to code that behaves differently based on the executing hardware platform. As such, unless dictated otherwise by the lack of performance, sticking with the default memory ordering is recommended. Interested readers can also take a look at the book "C++ Concurrency in Action" by Anthony Williams [63] for a more in-depth look into memory ordering.

3.9 Monitors

Semaphores offer a great deal of flexibility and *if* properly used, one can extract the maximum amount of parallelism from a multi-threaded application. However, this is a big "if"! Semaphores are notoriously difficult to use properly, as they offer very fine-grained concurrency control, with program logic that can be spread across multiple threads. In the era of OO programming, semaphores seem out of place.

Using atomics on the other hand is not an exercise for the faint of heart as there are many more things that can go wrong, and the code can get quite complex and full of pitfalls, as illustrated in the cases examined in Chapter 4.

Fortunately, an alternative solution exists in the form of a monitor. A **monitor** is an object or module that is designed to be accessed safely from multiple threads. To accomplish this feat only one thread at a time may be executing any of the public methods of a monitor. In order to be able to block a thread, or signal a thread to continue (both essential functionalities for establishing critical sections), monitors provide a mechanism called a **condition variable**.

A condition variable, which is typically accessed only inside a monitor, has a queue and supports two operations:

- A **wait** operation: if a thread executes the wait operation of a condition variable, it is blocked and placed in the condition variable's queue.
- A **signal** operation: if a thread executes the signal operation of a condition variable, a thread from the condition variable's queue is released (i.e., it becomes ready). If the queue is empty, the signal is ignored.

The wait and signal operations resemble the semaphore ones. However, there are distinct differences: a wait operation on a condition variable results in the *unconditional* blocking of the thread, whereas for a semaphore the block depends on its value. Also, a condition variable signal may be ignored, while in the case of a semaphore a release always increments it.

A condition variable is always associated with a condition, i.e., a set of rules that dictate when a thread will block or continue execution. This is actually one of the biggest advantages of monitors over semaphores, as any complex condition can be easily handled without an interwoven sequence of semaphore acquisitions, as the ones we saw in the readers–writers problem.

As a simple example, let us consider a monitor class for performing transactions to a bank account. The *pseudocode* of the `withdraw` and `deposit` methods would be similar to this:

```
class AccountMonitor
{
   private:
      Condition insufficientFunds;
      Mutex m;
      double balance;
   public:
      void withdraw(double s) {
        m.lock();
        if(balance < s)
          {
            m.unlock();
            insufficientFunds.wait();
            m.lock();
          }

        balance -= s;

        m.unlock();
      }

      void deposit(double s) {
        m.lock();
        balance += s;
```

```
25          insufficientFunds.signal();
26        m.unlock();
27      }
28  };
```

In order to ensure that only one thread will be running inside an `AccountMonitor` instance, a mutex is locked on entry on both methods. This mutex is released upon exit (line 19) or when a thread is about to be blocked – upon finding insufficient funds to withdraw – and placed in the condition variable's queue (line 12). A blocked thread wakes up when funds are deposited in the account (line 25).

What if the deposited funds are still insufficient when a thread wakes up? What if there are multiple pending withdraw operations and it is possible that at least one could be completed, but not necessarily the one released by the `signal` statement?

Obviously, the program logic shown above does not cover these circumstances. The answers will come as a direct consequence of the following paragraph.

The exact moment when a woken-up thread will run depends on the monitor's implementation. Two possibilities exist:

1. The thread runs immediately. Because a monitor cannot have two active threads running its methods, this automatically leads to the suspension of the thread which issued the signal. This thread will run as soon as the woken-up one exits the monitor. This approach follows the **Hoare** monitor specification, named after the scientist who originally suggested the monitor concept in the early 1970s.

2. The woken-up thread waits until the signal-issuing thread exits the monitor. Because of the delay until the thread is handed control of the monitor, the condition on which it was waiting originally may have been modified again. This necessitates a re-check, replacing the `if` statement controlling the wait with a `while` statement. This approach follows the **Lampson–Redell** monitor specification, and it offers some distinct advantages over the Hoare one. These include the ability to have timed-out waits and the ability to wake all the threads which are waiting on a condition variable. Both of these are enabled by having the condition a thread is waiting for reevaluated whenever it starts running again.

To indicate the difference in behavior, the signal method is called "**notify**," and the signal to all waiting threads of a condition variable is called "**notify all**."

The majority of monitor implementations, including the ones available in C++11, Qt, and Java, follow the Lampson–Redell specification, as the extra functionality is coupled by an intrinsically simpler implementation. Equipped with such a monitor, we can complete the bank account monitor example so that we also cover the two questions posed above. We will rewrite the code after exploring the monitor facilities provided.

C++11 provides a `condition_variable` implementation, which supports the following set of methods:

- wait: forces a thread to block. To eliminate the need for the programmer to separately unlock–lock the mutex controlling entry to the monitor, a reference to this mutex is passed to the method for performing these operations automatically.
- wait_for: forces a thread to block for a specified amount of time or until it receives a signal.
- wait_until: similar to wait_for, but the time-out is triggered when a specific time point is reached.
- notify_one: notifies one of the blocked threads.
- notify_all: notifies all blocked threads. They will all run, one-by-one, inside the monitor.

C++11 offers an overloaded version of the wait() method that allows the checking of the condition that blocks a thread within the wait() call itself. For example, one could write:

```
while(someCondToWait)
    waitCond.wait(lock);
```

or equivalently, using a lambda expression (notice the reversal of the condition logic):

```
waitCond.wait(lock, [](){return !someCondToWait;});
```

There is just one last clarification that we need to do before we can write a proper example using the condition_variable class. The "lock" that needs to be passed to the wait methods in order to release the monitor while a thread is blocked needs to be a unique_lock instance (first discussed in Section 3.7.4.4), so as to ensure the release of the lock upon termination of a monitor method. Otherwise, the monitor would become inaccessible.

For methods that do not block the calling thread (i.e., wait is not called), a lock_guard instance is sufficient. The constructor of a lock_guard instance locks the mutex passed as a parameter. The mutex is subsequently unlocked when the lock_guard is destroyed, same as the unique_lock class we saw earlier in Section 3.7.4.3. The difference being the two is that the latter allows locking and unlocking the mutex during the lifetime of the unique_lock instance.

Thus a typical monitor class structure would be similar to:

```
class Monitor
{
  private:
    mutex l;        // monitor lock
    condition_variable cv, . . .; // one or more condition variables
  public:
    void foo1();
    void foo2();
    . . .
};
void foo1()
{
  unique_lock< mutex > ul( l );
```

```
. . .
cv.wait( ul, [](){ return someCondition; } );
. . .
}
void foo2()
{
  lock_guard< mutex > guard( l );
  . . .
  cv.notify_one());
  . . .
}
```

We are now ready to rewrite the bank account monitor class:

Listing 3.28: A monitor-based bank account class.

```
1   // File : accountmonitor.cpp
2   #include <condition_variable>
3   . . .
4
5   class AccountMonitor
6   {
7     private:
8       condition_variable insufficientFunds;
9       mutex m;
10      double balance=0;
11    public:
12      void withdraw(double s) {
13        unique_lock<mutex> ml(m);
14        while(balance < s)
15            insufficientFunds.wait(ml);
16        balance -= s;
17      }
18
19      void deposit(double s) {
20        lock_guard<mutex> ml(m);
21        balance += s;
22        insufficientFunds.notify_all();
23      }
24  };
```

The key points of our `AccountMonitor` class are:

- All methods (except the constructor as each object is constructed once by a single thread) start by locking the mutex. This is done by utilizing a `lock_guard` instance in the `deposit()` method (line 20), where there is no possibility for a thread to block inside the method, while for the `withdraw()` a `unique_lock` is employed. Both `unique_lock` and `lock_guard` will unlock the mutex upon exiting their respective methods.
- `withdraw()` can block a thread when the requested amount exceeds the available balance (lines 14–15). In such a scenario, the mutex locked by the `unique_lock`

instance needs to be released, hence the pass by reference of the `ml` object to the `wait` method (line 15).

Lines 14–15 in the previous Listing can be also replaced by:

Listing 3.29: A monitor-based bank account class.

```
1   // File : accountmonitor1.cpp
2   . . .
3   insufficientFunds.wait(ml, [&](){
4         return balance < s;   }
5       );
6   . . .
```

One can easily distinguish three parts in a monitor's method, with two of them being optional:

1. **Entry** (optional): checking if the conditions are right for a thread to proceed.
2. **Mid section** : manipulating the state of the monitor to the desired effect, plus performing any operations that require mutual exclusion.
3. **Exit** (optional): signaling to other threads that it is their turn to enter or continue execution in the monitor.

Can you identify these parts in the methods of Listing 3.28?

The mutual exclusion offered by a monitor simplifies the design of multi-threaded applications to a large extent, as it encapsulates the corresponding program logic in a central location, making it easier to understand and modify.

Monitors and semaphores have been proven to be equivalent in the sense that any program using semaphores can be transformed into one using monitors and vice versa. Alas, the complexity of the solutions is a different aspect of the problem.

A monitor-based solution can follow two possible paradigms based on where the critical sections are maintained. One option is to keep the critical sections inside the monitor. The second option is to use the monitor for gaining and releasing entry to the critical sections. Each of these design approaches has its set of advantages and disadvantages. We set out to explore them in the following sections.

3.9.1 Design approach #1: critical section inside the monitor

Putting a critical section inside a monitor makes perfect sense as threads are forced to execute one at a time. However, this is a strategy that works only if the critical section is relatively short. Otherwise, efficiency is sacrificed and in extreme cases it may very well turn a multi-threaded program into a sequential one. The bank account example presented above follows this design approach, justifiably so, as the duration of both `deposit` and `withdraw` methods is negligible.

Another scenario where this design would be also suitable is the use of a monitor for serializing output to a console or a file:

```
1   class ConsoleMonitor
2   {
3     private:
4       mutex m;
5     public:
6       void printOut(string s) {
7         lock_guard< mutex > g(m);
8         cout << s;
9       }
10  };
```

A twist to the above example brings up the Achilles heel of this approach: what if the output was destined to a collection of different files? Would the solution below still work if only one instance of the class was employed?

```
1   class FileOutputMonitor
2   {
3     private:
4       mutex m;
5     public:
6       void writeOut(string s, ofstream &out) {
7         lock_guard< mutex > g(m);
8         out << s;
9       }
10  };
```

The answer depends on the frequency of the writeOut calls and the number of output streams being used. In principle though, this is a suboptimal solution. A better solution would be to have a different monitor object for each output stream or design a monitor in the fashion described in the next session.

3.9.2 Design approach #2: monitor controls entry to critical section

In this approach, a monitor is used as a mutex, i.e., it is designed with a pair of methods, one for allowing entry to the critical section (getting a permit) and one for signaling exit from the critical section (releasing the permit). While this may seem like an overcomplicated approach that mimics the lock–unlock sequence of a simple mutex, the reality is that a monitor is able to exercise much finer control over critical section entry than a simple mutex can.

As an example, let us consider the "cigarette smokers problem." The problem consists of three smoker threads and one agent thread. Each smoker continuously makes a cigarette and smokes it. But to make a cigarette, a smoker needs three ingredients: tobacco, paper, and a match. Each of the three smokers has an infinite supply of only one of the ingredients: one has only paper, another has only tobacco, and the third has only matches. The agent thread has an infinite supply of everything and places two randomly selected ingredients on the table. Then, it signals the availability of the two ingredients and blocks. The smoker who misses the two ingredients on the table takes them, makes a cigarette, and smokes it for a random amount of time. Upon finishing his cigarette, he signals the agent who then repeats the cycle.

It should be stressed that the problem definition used here is far more challenging than the typical setup described in the literature. In the literature, the agent signals the appropriate smoker to start making a cigarette. Here it is the smokers who must decide who should continue.

The solution is shown in Listing 3.30:

Listing 3.30: A monitor-based solution to the cigarette smokers problem.

```cpp
// File : smokers.cpp
. . .
#define TOBACCO_PAPER 0
#define TOBACCO_MATCHES 1
#define PAPER_MATCHES 2
#define MAXSLEEP 1000

const char *msg[]={"having matches", "having paper", "having tobacco↩
    "};
// *****************************************************
class Monitor
{
  private:
      mutex l;
      condition_variable w, finish;
      int newingred;
      int exitf;
  public:
      Monitor();
      // return 0 if OK. Otherwise it means termination
      int canSmoke(int);
      void newIngredient(int );
      void finishedSmoking();
      void finishSim();
};
//————————————————————————
Monitor::Monitor(): newingred(-1), exitf(0) {}
//————————————————————————
void Monitor::newIngredient(int newi)
{
  unique_lock< mutex > ul(l);
  newingred = newi;
  w.notify_all();
  finish.wait(ul); // wait for smoker to finish
}
//————————————————————————
int Monitor::canSmoke(int missing)
{
  unique_lock< mutex > ul(l);
  while(newingred != missing && ! exitf)
    w.wait(ul);
  return exitf;
```

```
42    }
43    //————————————————————————————————————————
44    void Monitor::finishedSmoking()
45    {
46      lock_guard< mutex > lg(l);
47      newingred = -1;
48      finish.notify_one();
49    }
50    //————————————————————————————————————————
51    void Monitor::finishSim()
52    {
53      lock_guard< mutex > lg(l);
54      exitf=1;
55      w.notify_all();
56    }
57    // *************************************************
58    class Smoker
59    {
60      private:
61        int missing_ingred;
62        Monitor *m;
63        int total;
64      public:
65        Smoker(int, Monitor *);
66        void operator()();
67    };
68    //————————————————————————————————————————
69    Smoker::Smoker(int missing, Monitor *mon) : missing_ingred(missing),↵
           m(mon), total(0){}
70    //————————————————————————————————————————
71    void Smoker::operator()()
72    {
73      while((m->canSmoke(missing_ingred)) ==0)
74      {
75        total++;
76        cout << "Smoker " << msg[missing_ingred] << " is smoking\n";
77        this_thread::sleep_for(chrono::duration<int, milli>(rand() % ↵
             MAXSLEEP));
78        m->finishedSmoking();
79      }
80    // cout << "Smoker " << msg[missing_ingred] << " smoked a total of "↵
           << total << "\n";
81    }
82    // *************************************************
83    class Agent
84    {
85      private:
86        int runs;
87        Monitor *m;
88      public:
89        Agent(int, Monitor *);
90        void operator()();
```

```
91    };
92    //————————————————————————————————————
93    Agent::Agent(int r, Monitor *mon) : runs(r), m(mon){}
94    //————————————————————————————————————
95    void Agent::operator()()
96    {
97      for(int i=0;i<runs; i++)
98      {
99        int ingreds = rand() % 3;
100       m->newIngredient(ingreds);
101     }
102    m->finishSim();
103    }
104    // ****************************************************
105    int main(int argc, char **argv)
106    {
107      Monitor m;
108      Smoker *s[3];
109      unique_ptr<thread> tp[4];
110
111      for(int i=0;i<3;i++)
112      {
113        s[i] = new Smoker(i, &m);
114        tp[i] = make_unique< thread >(ref(*s[i]));
115      }
116      Agent a(atoi(argv[1]), &m);
117      tp[3] = make_unique< thread >(ref(a));
118
119      for(int i=0;i<4;i++)
120        tp[i]->join();
121
122      return EXIT_SUCCESS;
123    }
```

The solution is made up of three classes: a Smoker class, whose instances are identified by the type of resources they require (resources are enumerated on lines 3–5), an Agent class, which runs for a predetermined number of iterations (defined in the constructor), and a Monitor class, which is used for letting the other two communicate. The key points of the solution are:

- The Monitor provides two sets of public methods:
  - A canSmoke and finishedSmoking pair employed by the Smoker threads. They correspond to a "get" and "release permit" type of methods.
  - The newIngredient and finishSim methods used by the Agent thread.
- The Agent calls the Monitor's newIngredient method by passing the type of resources that become available. The Monitor proceeds to wake up any waiting threads (line 32) and then forces the Agent thread to block until a Smoker is done (line 33).
- The Agent thread is given responsibility for program termination. After the specified number of runs is completed, the finishSim method of the monitor is called.

This in turn switches on a Boolean flag (exitf, line 54) inside the monitor and wakes up all threads waiting on the condition variable w.

- Each Smoker thread runs a loop that terminates when the value returned by the Monitor's canSmoke method is non-zero. The latter method returns the value of the exitf flag.

This is what a sample run of this program looks like:

```
$ ./smokers 3
Smoker having paper is smoking
Smoker having matches is smoking
Smoker having tobacco is smoking
```

3.9.3 General semaphores revisited

In this section we present a more powerful alternative to the C++20 counting_semaphore class template.

There are three components that are required: an integer for holding the value of the semaphore, a mutex for controlling access to the monitor, and a condition variable for blocking threads when attempting to decrement the value of a non-positive semaphore. The implementation of the basic acquire and release functionality, along with all the extra methods typically expected from modern implementations (such as releasing or acquiring multiple resources or non-blocking acquisitions), can be done as shown below:

Listing 3.31: A general semaphore implementation using two mutex objects and an integer.

```cpp
// File : semaphore.h and semaphore.cpp
#include <mutex>
#include <condition_variable>

class semaphore
{
private:
    int value = 0;
    std::mutex l;
    std::condition_variable block;

public:
    semaphore (int i = 0);
    semaphore (const semaphore &) = delete;
    semaphore (const semaphore &&) = delete;
    semaphore & operator= (const semaphore &) = delete;
    semaphore & operator= (const semaphore &&) = delete;
    void acquire ();
    void acquire (unsigned int i);
    void release (unsigned int i = 1);
    int available ();
    bool try_acquire (unsigned int i = 1);
```

```
23  };
24  //————————————————————————————
25  semaphore::semaphore (int i)
26  {
27    value = i;
28  }
29  //————————————————————————————
30  void semaphore::acquire ()
31  {
32    std::unique_lock < std::mutex > ul (l);
33    value--;
34
35    if (value < 0)
36      {
37        block.wait (ul);
38      }
39  }
40  //————————————————————————————
41  void semaphore::acquire (unsigned int i)
42  {
43    std::unique_lock < std::mutex > ul (l);
44    block.wait( ul, [&](){ return value >= i;} );
45    value -= i;
46  }
47  //————————————————————————————
48  void semaphore::release (unsigned int i)
49  {
50    std::lock_guard < std::mutex > guard (l);
51    while (i--)
52      {
53        value++;
54        block.notify_one ();
55      }
56  }
57  //————————————————————————————
58  int semaphore::available ()
59  {
60    std::lock_guard < std::mutex > guard (l);
61    return value;
62  }
63  //————————————————————————————
64  bool semaphore::try_acquire (unsigned int i)
65  {
66    std::lock_guard < std::mutex > guard (l);
67    bool res = false;
68    if (value >= (int) i)
69      {
70        value -= i;
71        res = true;
72      }
73    return res;
74  }
```

In Listing 3.31 the "l" mutex defined on line 9 is used to provide atomicity to the methods of the class. The "block" condition variable is utilized for blocking a thread when the value is zero or negative (line 37). When the value of the semaphore becomes negative, its absolute value corresponds to the number of blocked threads. This property is utilized on lines 51–55 of the release() method, to wake up the "sleeping" threads.

The try_acquire() method works with any non-negative integer parameter, while acquire() comes in two flavors based on whether one or more "resources" need to be reserved. The second version (lines 41–46) acquires all resources at once, instead of trying to acquire them one at a time as in the following code:

```
void semaphore::acquire (unsigned int i)
{
  while (i--)
    this->acquire ();
}
```

The reason for not going this route is that it opens the possibility of *deadlock*. For example, if we have a semaphore res initialized to two and two threads trying to perform res.acquire(2);, we could end up with each one holding one and neither being able to proceed.

The version given in Listing 3.31 is not without problems either, as it does allow for *starvation*. For example, if we have one thread trying to execute res.acquire(2); in competition with other threads, the possibility of getting all the resources free at one time diminishes as the number of competing threads and/or the frequency of acquire() calls increases.

3.10 Applying monitors in classical problems

3.10.1 Producers–consumers revisited

The manipulation of the buffer in the producers–consumers context is a typically lightweight affair. However, for the sake of completeness we will explore monitor-based solutions sporting both of the aforementioned designs.

3.10.1.1 Producers–consumers: buffer manipulation within the monitor

In this case, the monitor just needs to publish *put* and *get* methods for the producers and consumers to use. The expressive power of the monitor construct, especially in comparison to the simplicity of semaphores, becomes apparent from the solution described below:

Listing 3.32: A monitor-based solution to the producers–consumers problem, where the buffer is encapsulated within the monitor.

```
// File : monitor1ProdCons.cpp
. . .
```

```
3   template <typename T>
4   class Monitor {
5   private :
6       mutex l;
7       condition_variable full, empty;
8       int in, out;
9       int N;
10      int count;
11      T *buffer;
12  public :
13      void put(T);
14      T get();
15      Monitor(int n = BUFFSIZE);
16      ~Monitor();
17  };
18  //————————————————————————————————
19  . . .
20  template <typename T>
21  void Monitor<T>::put(T i) {
22      unique_lock <mutex> ul(l);
23      while (count == N)
24          full.wait(ul);
25      buffer[in] = i;
26      in = (in + 1) % N;
27      count++;
28      empty.notify_one();
29  }
30  //————————————————————————————————
31  template <typename T>
32  T Monitor<T>::get() {
33      unique_lock <mutex> ul(l);
34      while (count == 0)
35          empty.wait(ul);
36      T temp = buffer[out];
37      out = (out + 1) % N;
38      count--;
39      full.notify_one();
40      return temp;
41  }
42  //*************************************************************
43  template <typename T>
44  class Producer {
45  private :
46      static semaphore numProducts;
47      int ID;
48      static Monitor<T> *mon;
49  public :
50      static T(*produce)();
51      static void initClass(int numP, Monitor<T> *m, T(*prod)());
52
53      Producer<T>(int i) : ID(i) {}
54      void operator()();
```

```
55    };
56    //————————————————————————————————
57    . . .
58    template <typename T> void Producer<T>::initClass(int numP, Monitor<T↩
      > *m, T(*prod)()) {
59        mon = m;
60        numProducts.release(numP);
61        produce = prod;
62    }
63    //————————————————————————————————
64    template <typename T>
65    void Producer<T>::operator()() {
66        while (numProducts.try_acquire()) {
67            T item = (*produce)();
68            mon->put(item);
69        }
70    }
71    //————————————————————————————————
72
73    template <typename T>
74    class Consumer {
75    private:
76        int ID;
77        static Monitor<T> *mon;
78        static semaphore numProducts;
79    public:
80        static void (*consume)(T i);
81        static void initClass(int numP, Monitor<T> *m, void (*cons)(T));
82
83        Consumer<T>(int i) : ID(i) {}
84        void operator()();
85    };
86    //————————————————————————————————
87    . . .
88    template <typename T> void Consumer<T>::initClass(int numP, Monitor<T↩
      > *m, void (*cons)(T)) {
89        numProducts.release(numP);
90        mon = m;
91        consume = cons;
92    }
93    //————————————————————————————————
94    template <typename T> void Consumer<T>::operator()() {
95        while (numProducts.try_acquire()) {
96            T item = mon->get(); // take the item out
97            (*consume)(item);
98        }
99    }
100   //————————————————————————————————
101   . . .
102   int main(int argc, char *argv[]) {
103       . . .
104       int N = atoi(argv[1]);
```

```
105    int M = atoi(argv[2]);
106    int numP = atoi(argv[3]);
107    Monitor<int> m;
108
109    Producer<int>::initClass(numP, &m, &produce);
110    Consumer<int>::initClass(numP, &m, &consume);
111    . . .
```

The producers and consumers code is reduced to the bare minimum (lines 64–70 and 94–99), while all the intricate details of buffer manipulation are encapsulated inside the put (lines 20–29) and get (lines 31–41) Monitor methods. Listing 3.32 shares many features with Listing 3.13, in the way producers and consumers terminate (i.e., by giving them the total number of resources to operate upon) and the use of class templates to facilitate a generic solution.

In contrast to Listing 3.13 though, the producers and consumers are not aware of the inner workings of the shared buffer, nor are they signaling each other via semaphores. All the communication is implicitly done through the Monitor class.

The Monitor class uses two condition variables, full and empty, to block producers when the queue is full (lines 23 and 24) and consumers when the queue is empty (lines 34–35) respectively. Please notice that the Monitor class uses a large collection of variables that were previously shared between threads in Listing 3.13, without the need to protect them against race conditions. Now the only thing shared by the two types of threads is a Monitor instance, to which they become aware via the initClass methods of their respective classes. These are called prior to creating any Producer or Consumer instances on lines 109–110.

Each producer/consumer thread attempts to decrement a semaphore before calling the monitor (lines 66 and 95), providing an easy termination logic. There are two semaphores defined, one for each of the Producer and Consumer classes. In general, semaphores and monitors do not mix as they constitute different design approaches, but for this particular example they are a convenience.

As a matter of principle, semaphores are never used inside a monitor. Doing so would make no sense, as they could be easily replaced by integer variables, and their signal/wait facilities could interfere with normal monitor operations (e.g., blocking a thread inside a monitor without releasing the monitor's mutex).

In Listing 3.13 we could replace the semaphores with atomic integers. This is left as an exercise.

3.10.1.2 Producers–consumers: buffer insertion/extraction exterior to the monitor

If the addition or removal of resources from the shared buffer takes a considerable amount of time (e.g., requires copying objects instead of references), using the second design approach can improve performance. Getting and releasing a permit from the monitor means that the run methods will be a bit longer than the minuscule ones of the previous design.

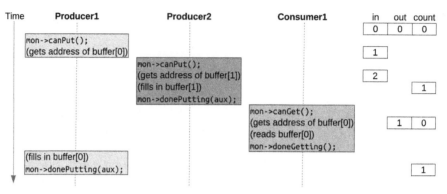

FIGURE 3.14

A sequence diagram of a possible interaction between two producer threads and one consumer thread that deposit/extract items outside the monitor when a single circular queue is used. The values of the `in`, `out`, and `count` variables are shown after each call to the monitor.

The idea is that producers and consumers will use a pair of functions to first acquire exclusive access to a buffer's location and then release the location back to the monitor to utilize.

There is one major difference though: the acquisition and release of buffer elements potentially out-of-order means that we can no longer treat the buffer as a circular queue. For example, it would be possible to have a producer release an element prior to another producer that acquired one at an earlier time, thus allowing a consumer to get an item that is not there. This scenario is depicted in Fig. 3.14.

For this reason, two separate queues have to be maintained, one for the free buffer elements (`emptySpotsQ`) and one for the occupied ones (`itemQ`).

Listing 3.33: A monitor-based solution to the producers–consumers problem, where the buffer elements are directly manipulated by the producer and consumer threads, under the supervision of the monitor. For the sake of brevity, only the differences with Listing 3.32 are shown.

```cpp
// File : monitor2ProdCons.cpp
. . .
template <typename T>
class Monitor {
private:
    mutex l;
    condition_variable full, empty;
    queue<T *> emptySpotsQ;
    queue<T *> itemQ;
    T *buffer;
public:
    T* canPut();
    T* canGet();
    void donePutting(T *x);
```

```
15        void doneGetting(T *x);
16        Monitor(int n = BUFFSIZE);
17        ~Monitor();
18   };
19   //─────────────────────────────────────────
20
21   template <typename T>
22   Monitor<T>::Monitor(int n) {
23        buffer = new T[n];
24        for(int i=0;i<n;i++)
25            emptySpotsQ.push(&buffer[i]);
26   }
27   //─────────────────────────────────────────
28
29   template <typename T>
30   Monitor<T>::~Monitor() {
31        delete []buffer;
32   }
33   //─────────────────────────────────────────
34
35   template <typename T>
36   T* Monitor<T>::canPut() {
37        unique_lock< mutex > ul(l);
38        while (emptySpotsQ.size() == 0)
39            full.wait(ul);
40        T *aux = emptySpotsQ.front();
41        emptySpotsQ.pop();
42        return aux;
43   }
44   //─────────────────────────────────────────
45
46   template <typename T>
47   T* Monitor<T>::canGet() {
48        unique_lock< mutex > ul(l);
49        while (itemQ.size() == 0)
50            empty.wait(ul);
51        T* temp = itemQ.front();
52        itemQ.pop();
53        return temp;
54   }
55   //─────────────────────────────────────────
56
57   template <typename T>
58   void Monitor<T>::donePutting(T *x) {
59        lock_guard< mutex > lg(l);
60        itemQ.push(x);
61        empty.notify_one();
62   }
63   //─────────────────────────────────────────
64
65   template <typename T>
66   void Monitor<T>::doneGetting(T *x) {
```

```
67      lock_guard< mutex > lg(1);
68      emptySpotsQ.push(x);
69      full.notify_one();
70  }
71  //————————————————————————————
72  . . .
73  template <typename T>
74  void Producer<T>::operator()() {
75      while (numProducts.try_acquire()) {
76          T item = (*produce)();
77          T* aux = mon->canPut();
78          *aux = item;
79          mon->donePutting(aux);
80      }
81  }
82  //————————————————————————————
83  . . .
84  template <typename T>
85  void Consumer<T>::operator()() {
86      while (numProducts.try_acquire()) {
87          T* aux = mon->canGet();
88          T item = *aux; // take the item out
89          mon->doneGetting(aux);
90          (*consume)(item);
91      }
92  }
```

The key points of the solution in Listing 3.33 are:

- The Monitor class provides two pairs of methods:
  - canPut and donePutting for Producer threads and
  - canGet and doneGetting for Consumer threads.

  The bodies of these methods essentially contain the two halves (unevenly divided) of the put and get methods, respectively, of Listing 3.32.
- The canPut and canGet methods return pointers to buffer locations that can be used for storage or retrieval of resources. The in, out, and count variables are no longer necessary as they would introduce a race condition. Instead the typical FIFO queue operations push, front, and pop are used to hold and extract the buffer elements from queues emptySpotsQ and itemQ.
- All the addresses of the initially empty buffer elements are placed in the emptySpotsQ queue via the Monitor constructor (lines 24 and 25). The buffer is still allocated and freed as an array for convenience.
- The Producer and Consumer threads can take their time to store or extract a resource after the canPut and canGet methods return. The Monitor is able to serve other threads at that time.
- The donePutting/doneGetting methods require the address of the buffer element that was placed/removed from the buffer, as illustrated on lines 79 and 89 of the operator() methods. Once the corresponding queues are updated, a waiting Consumer/Producer is alerted via the empty/full condition variables.

3.10.2 **Readers–writers**

Monitor-based solutions also shine in the context of the readers–writers problem. Assigning priority to one or the other type of thread is much simpler using a monitor than using semaphores. The nature of the problem mandates the use of the second design approach, i.e., each thread will have to acquire a permit to access the resource and then release this permit when all is done.

The threads do not have to be concerned with priorities or about the existence of other threads running in their critical sections. This functionality is embedded in the monitor's methods.

In all three solutions described in the following sections, the `Reader` and `Writer` threads execute a fixed number of operations as shown below:

```
void Reader::operator()() {
    for(int i=0;i<NUMOPER;i++)
    {
        mon->canRead();
        // critical section
        coord->finishedReading();
    }
}
void Writer::operator()() {
    for(int i=0;i<NUMOPER;i++)
    {
        mon->canWrite();
        // critical section
        coord->finishedWriting();
    }
}
```

In the next sections we analyze the details of the monitor's implementations.

3.10.2.1 *A solution favoring the readers*

In order to assign priority to the reader threads, one has to just keep track of the waiting reader threads `readersWaiting` and prevent a writer from entering its critical section if `readersWaiting > 0`.

Listing 3.34: A monitor implementation favoring the `Reader` threads.

```
1   // File : readersFav.cpp
2   . . .
3   class Monitor
4   {
5   private:
6     mutex l;
7     condition_variable wq;        // for blocking writers
8     condition_variable rq;        // for blocking readers
9     int readersIn;                // how many readers in their ↵
          critical section
10    bool writerIn;                // set if a write is in its critical ↵
          section
```

```
11    int readersWaiting;
12  public:
13    Monitor ():readersIn (0), writerIn (0), readersWaiting (0) {}
14    void canRead ();
15    void finishedReading ();
16    void canWrite ();
17    void finishedWriting ();
18  };
19
20  //************************************
21  void Monitor::canRead ()
22  {
23    unique_lock < mutex > ul (l);
24    while (writerIn == true)
25      {
26        readersWaiting++;
27        rq.wait (ul);
28        readersWaiting--;
29      }
30    readersIn++;
31  }
32
33  //************************************
34  void Monitor::canWrite ()
35  {
36    unique_lock < mutex > ul (l);
37    while (writerIn == true || readersWaiting > 0 || readersIn > 0)
38      wq.wait (ul);
39
40    writerIn = true;
41  }
42
43  //************************************
44  void Monitor::finishedReading ()
45  {
46    lock_guard < mutex > lg (l);
47    readersIn--;
48    if (readersIn == 0)
49      wq.notify_one ();
50  }
51
52  //************************************
53  void Monitor::finishedWriting ()
54  {
55    lock_guard < mutex > lg (l);
56    writerIn = false;
57    if (readersWaiting > 0)
58      rq.notify_all ();
59    else
60      wq.notify_one ();
61  }
```

The important points of the solution shown in Listing 3.34 are:

- The monitor incorporates two condition variables: wq for queuing up waiting writers and rq for waiting readers.
- A running count of the readers inside their critical sections is maintained. It is incremented at line 28 and decremented at line 47 once a reader leaves. If the count reaches 0, a signal is sent to any waiting writers (line 49).
- A writer thread blocks if readers are inside their critical section or they are waiting to enter it (line 37).
- The last part which completes the shift in priority to readers is the management of the condition variable queues in the finishedWriting method: a writer is woken up only if there are no readers waiting (lines 57–60).

3.10.2.2 Giving priority to the writers

In order to assign priority to the writer threads, one has to just keep track of the waiting writer threads writersWaiting and prevent a reader from entering its critical section if writersWaiting > 0.

The two monitor classes in Listings 3.34 and 3.35 are nearly identical. Their differences are concentrated at the lines that control entry to the critical section and queue management upon exit from the critical section. In Listing 3.35, line 24 forces readers to block if there are writers waiting to enter their critical section. Handing priority over to writers is completed by lines 58–61, where a writer leaving its critical section picks a waiting writer if there is one over the readers. However, if there are no waiting writers, all readers are woken up (line 61).

Listing 3.35: A monitor implementation favoring the Writer threads.

```
1   // File : writersFav.cpp
2   . . .
3   class Monitor
4   {
5   private:
6     mutex l;
7     condition_variable wq;        // for blocking writers
8     condition_variable rq;        // for blocking readers
9     int readersIn;                // how many readers in their ←
          critical section
10    bool writerIn;                // set if a write is in its critical←
          section
11    int writersWaiting;           // how many writers are waiting to ←
          enter
12  public:
13      Monitor ():readersIn (0), writerIn (0), writersWaiting (0) {}
14    void canRead ();
15    void finishedReading ();
16    void canWrite ();
17    void finishedWriting ();
18  };
19  . . .
```

```
20   // ************************************
21   void Monitor::canRead ()
22   {
23     unique_lock < mutex > ul (1);
24     while (writerIn == true || writersWaiting > 0)
25       rq.wait (ul);
26
27     readersIn++;
28   }
29
30   // ************************************
31   void Monitor::canWrite ()
32   {
33     unique_lock < mutex > ul (1);
34     while (writerIn == true || readersIn > 0)
35       {
36         writersWaiting++;
37         wq.wait (ul);
38         writersWaiting--;
39       }
40
41     writerIn = true;
42   }
43
44   // ************************************
45   void Monitor::finishedReading ()
46   {
47     lock_guard < mutex > lg (1);
48     readersIn--;
49     if (readersIn == 0)
50       wq.notify_one ();
51   }
52
53   // ************************************
54   void Monitor::finishedWriting ()
55   {
56     lock_guard < mutex > lg (1);
57     writerIn = false;
58     if (writersWaiting > 0)
59       wq.notify_one ();
60     else
61       rq.notify_all ();
62   }
```

3.10.2.3 A fair solution

Creating a fair solution to the readers–writers problem is a challenge. Although it has never been a consideration in our previous examples, the order in which threads are released from the queue of a condition variable is crucial for achieving a FIFO order in serving critical section entry requests.

Reading the C++11 online documentation on the `notify_one` method reveals: "If more than one [thread is blocked], it is unspecified which of the threads is selected." This means that a single condition variable cannot provide the FIFO wakeup schedule required for fairness. *But if one cannot, could a bunch of them do?*

The solution shown in Listing 3.36 exhibits this feature exactly: threads that are forced to block do so on different condition variables, allowing us precise control on which will be woken up and in what order. A fixed array of condition variables is allocated and managed as a circular queue (with `in` and `out` indices and a `counter` for how many are used). It is accompanied by a Boolean array (`writeflag`) that helps us distinguish what type of thread is blocked in each condition variable. If all the condition variables are used, threads are forced to queue up in a generic condition variable (`quefull`). This is actually the only departure from a completely fair solution (because threads leaving this queue do not do so in a FIFO manner), but it is a small compromise.

Listing 3.36: A fair monitor implementation for the readers–writers problem.

```
1   // File : readWriteFair.cpp
2   const int QUESIZE = 100;
3   // ****************************************
4
5   class Monitor
6   {
7   private :
8     mutex l;
9     condition_variable c[QUESIZE]; // a different condition for each ↩
          waiting thread
10    bool writeflag[QUESIZE];        // what kind of threads wait?
11    condition_variable quefull;     // used when queue of waiting ↩
          threads becomes full
12    int in, out, counter;
13    int readersIn;                  // how many readers in their ↩
          critical section
14    int writersIn;                  // how many writers in their ↩
          critical section (0 or 1)
15   public :
16
17    Monitor ():in (0), out (0), counter (0), readersIn (0), writersIn ↩
          (0) {}
18    void canRead ();
19    void finishedReading ();
20    void canWrite ();
21    void finishedWriting ();
22   };
23
24   // ****************************************
25   void Monitor::canRead ()
26   {
27     unique_lock < mutex > ul (l);
28     while (counter == QUESIZE)
29       quefull.wait (ul);
```

```
30
31    if (counter > 0 || writersIn)
32      {
33        int temp = in;
34        writeflag[in] = false;
35        in = (in + 1) % QUESIZE;
36        counter++;
37        c[temp].wait (ul);
38      }
39    readersIn++;
40  }
41
42  //**************************************
43  void Monitor::canWrite ()
44  {
45    unique_lock < mutex > ul (l);
46    while (counter == QUESIZE)
47      quefull.wait (ul);
48
49    if (counter > 0 || writersIn > 0 || readersIn > 0)
50      {
51        int temp = in;
52        writeflag[in] = true;
53        in = (in + 1) % QUESIZE;
54        counter++;
55        c[temp].wait (ul);
56      }
57    writersIn++;
58  }
59
60  //**************************************
61  void Monitor::finishedReading ()
62  {
63    lock_guard < mutex > lg (l);
64    readersIn--;
65    if (readersIn == 0 && counter > 0)
66      {
67        c[out].notify_one ();        // it must be a writer that is being←
                                            woken up
68        out = (out + 1) % QUESIZE;
69        counter--;
70        quefull.notify_one ();
71      }
72  }
73
74  //**************************************
75  void Monitor::finishedWriting ()
76  {
77    lock_guard < mutex > lg (l);
78    writersIn--;
79    if (counter > 0)
80      {
```

```
81        if (!writeflag[out])
82          {
83            while (counter > 0 && !writeflag[out])        // start  ⤸
                 next readers
84              {
85                c[out].notify_one ();
86                out = (out + 1) % QUESIZE;
87                counter--;
88              }
89          }
90        else                          // next writer
91          {
92            c[out].notify_one ();
93            out = (out + 1) % QUESIZE;
94            counter--;
95          }
96        quefull.notify_all ();
97      }
98  }
```

Other major points in the monitor of Listing 3.36 are the following:

- All threads requesting entry into their critical section first inspect the status of the queue of condition variables and the type of threads currently in their critical section.
- Reader threads are allowed to proceed in canRead only if there is no writer inside and the queue of condition variables is empty[8] (counter == 0). If the latter is false (line 31), this means that at least one writer is ahead of this thread in the service order.
- A writer thread is allowed to proceed in canWrite if the queue of condition variables is empty and there are no readers or a writer inside (line 49).
- If the conditions on lines 31 and 49 are true, a thread is blocked using an element of the c array and the corresponding element in writeflag is set/reset to indicate a writer/reader is blocked.
- When finishWriting is called and the queue of condition variables is not empty (counter >0), the type of thread at the head of the queue (pointed by out) is examined (line 81). If the first element is a reader, all the readers up to the end of the queue or the encounter of the first writer are signaled (lines 83–88). Otherwise a writer is woken up (lines 92–94).

The ability to manage the threads requesting entry into their critical section with such a fine-grained approach opens up a number of possibilities that go beyond the simple readers–writers scenario. For example, arbitrary objective functions can be used to evaluate which thread will proceed next (e.g., based on priority, monetary considerations, etc.). A fitting example would be the case of a multi-threaded DBMS

---

[8] The term "empty queue" is used loosely here. Literally, the queue is "empty" if none of the condition variables has a non-empty queue of threads.

system, serving incoming client requests. These could be ranked based on client rank, request urgency, or any other set of criteria.

3.11 Asynchronous threads

The name of this section seems like an oddity: are threads not supposed to be asynchronous anyway? What the title is actually referring to is the capability of the C++11 standard library to launch threads in a "background mode" by calling the `async` template function. These threads are also known as background threads, although this is also kind of a misnomer.

The effect of an `async` call is that a function is "requested" to run asynchronously, the key word here being "requested." What actually happens i.e., whether a thread is launched to do the bidding of the caller or the function is just executed by the same thread, depends on the implementation of the library. Fortunately, there is an overloaded version of the `async` function that allows the programmer to specify exactly what will happen.

So one might ask, "how is this different from using the thread class constructor directly?" The major difference is that the result of the executed function can be explicitly returned to the caller, something we have been doing implicitly so far with the use of functors or reference parameters.

The following is a simple example of the `async` template function:

Listing 3.37: A multi-threaded average-finding program, using "background" threads.

```
1   // File : aver_async0.cpp
2   #include <future>
3   . . .
4   double partialSum(vector<double>::iterator start, vector<double>:: ←
        iterator end)
5   {
6       double partialRes = 0;
7       for(auto i=start; i<end; i++)
8           partialRes += *i;
9
10      return partialRes;
11  }
12  //────────────────────────────────────────
13  int main(int argc, char **argv)
14  {
15      . . .
16      future<double> f[numThr];
17      vector<double>::iterator localStart = data.begin();
18      vector<double>::iterator localEnd;
19      for(int i=0;i<numThr;i++)
20      {
21          localEnd=localStart+step;
22          if(i==numThr-1) localEnd=data.end();
```

```
23        f[i] = async(partialSum, localStart, localEnd);
24        localStart += step;
25    }
26
27    for(int i=0;i<numThr;i++)
28        res += f[i].get();
29    cout << "Average is : " << res/N << endl;
30    return 0;
31 }
```

The above performs the same function as the code in Listing 3.10, but we do not have to use a mutex or wait for the threads to terminate explicitly. Instead, for each `async` call we make – in the place where we previously launched threads (line 23) – we just keep a "tab" to the request made via a `future` object. The `future` class template instances (defined on line 16) are used to query the status of a "background" thread and to get whatever is returned from the called function. The `future` template parameter specifies what kind of result is expected.

As observed on line 23, the call to `async` is identical in terms of parameters to the thread constructor call. As such, objects are passed by value. If we wish to pass by reference, the `ref()` and `cref()` functions are required as usual. If a method needs to be executed, then the first parameter is the address of the method, the second the object on which it will be called, and the remaining parameters are passed to the method. The different syntax for calling a method can be seen on line 25 below:

Listing 3.38: A variation of Listing 3.37 where we request the execution of a method as a background thread. Only the differences from Listing 3.37 are shown.

```
1  // File : aver_async1.cpp
2  . . .
3  using namespace std;
4  class Aver
5  {
6  private:
7    vector < double >::iterator start, end;
8  public:
9    // pass iterators as constructor parameters
10   Aver (vector < double >::iterator s, vector < double >::iterator e↩
          ):start (s), end (e) {}
11   double partialSum ()
12     . . .
13 };
14
15 //————————————————————————————————
16 int main (int argc, char **argv)
17 {
18   . . .
19   for (int i = 0; i < numThr; i++)
20     {
21       localEnd = localStart + step;
22       if (i == numThr − 1)
23         localEnd = data.end ();
```

```
24        Aver temp (localStart, localEnd);
25        f[i] = async (&Aver::partialSum, temp); // temp is copied
26        localStart += step;
27      }
28    . . .
29  }
```

One thing that both the above listings fail to do is to specify the execution policy for the `async` calls, i.e., how the request call will be executed. There are two options:

- `launch::async`: forces the spawning of a new thread to execute the function.
- `launch::deferred`: no new thread is created. When the caller thread tries to get the result of the function via the `future` object, the function is executed. This is also known as *lazy evaluation*.

The default behavior when no execution policy is specified is implementation-specific. But if a multi-threaded execution is needed, the first option should be explicitly passed as the first parameter of the `async` call, e.g., for Listing 3.38 we should have:

```
f[i] = async (launch::async, &Aver::partialSum, temp); // temp is ↩
   copied
```

The methods supported by the `future` class include:

- `get`: blocks until the function executes and returns the result of the call,
- `wait`: blocks the calling thread until the result becomes available,
- `wait_for`: blocks the calling thread for a specific amount of time or until the result becomes available,
- `wait_until`: blocks the calling thread until the specified time point is reached or until the result becomes available.

The timed `wait_*` methods return one of the following values:

- `future_status::deferred`: function not called yet
- `future_status::ready`: result is ready. So this can be followed by a get() call.
- `future_status::timeout`: result is unavailable.

So if for example we would like to wait for 1 second, attempting to get a socket descriptor to a remote site, we could have:

```
future< int > f;
f = async (launch::async, getConn, ip, port); // launch a thread to ↩
   try and get a connection
if( f.wait_for( chrono::duration<int>( 1 ) ) == future_status::ready↩
   ) // duration defaults to seconds
  {
    int sockfd = f.get(); // retrieve the socket file descriptor
    . . .
  }
```

The `future` class template is also used in conjunction with the `packaged_task` class template. The `packaged_task` is the C++11 mechanism for encapsulating any callable target (e.g., function, function object, lambda expression, etc.) in an object that can be stored and passed around. In comparison with the `async` call, the `packaged_task` is just a container, i.e., creating an instance does not create a new thread or run the callable target.

In order to execute a `packaged_task`, it must be explicitly called, or passed as a parameter to a `thread` constructor, as shown below:

Listing 3.39: An example of using `packaged_task`.

```
1   // File : packaged_task_example.cpp
2   #include <future>
3   . . .
4   double maxf (double a, double b)
5   {
6     return (a > b) ? a : b;
7   }
8
9   //─────────────────────────────
10  void explicitRun ()
11  {
12    packaged_task < double (double, double) > pt (maxf);
13    future < double >res = pt.get_future ();
14    pt (1, 2);
15    cout << res.get () << endl;
16  }
17
18  //─────────────────────────────
19  void threadRun ()
20  {
21    packaged_task < double (double, double) > pt (maxf);
22    future < double >res = pt.get_future ();
23    thread t (move (pt), 1, 2);
24    t.join ();
25    cout << res.get () << endl;
26  }
```

The `packaged_task` constructor calls of lines 12 and 21 must have the signature of the target passed as a template parameter. Given the signature of the `maxf` function used in our example, the `future` instance used to retrieve the result of the call will return a `double` (lines 13 and 22).

In the `explicitRun` function of line 10, we call the `packaged_task` instance as if it was a function, passing it the parameters that will be passed on to the target function. In the `threadRun` function we start a thread for running the target, retrieving the `future` prior to the thread constructor, as the `packaged_task` instance is moved to the thread. The `join` call on line 24 is essential in order to avoid having the thread throw an exception. An alternative would be to detach the thread. In any case though, the result will be available to print on line 25 only after the execution is complete, which means that we could swap lines 24 and 25 without an ill effect.

As a final comment, if we would like to have the parameters to the target saved in the `packaged_task`, we could use either a function object or the `bind` function template to masquerade the target. This way, we could rewrite `explicitRun` above as:

```
#include <functional>
void explicitRun ()
{
  packaged_task < double () > pt (bind(maxf,1,2)); // <==
  future < double >res = pt.get_future ();
  pt ();                                           // <==
  cout << res.get () << endl;
}
```

3.12 Dynamic vs. static thread management

In all the examples we have seen so far, whenever some work needed to be done separately from the main thread, a child thread was launched either explicitly (using the `thread` class) or implicitly (using the `async` call). While this *dynamic* approach is adequate for most scenarios, it can be a performance-sapping one if thread creation – and destruction – is done frequently. This can be the case for an Internet server that can receive thousands of requests per second. But why could this be counter to performance? The reason is that thread creation might be cheaper than process creation (see Section 3.2), but it is not free: memory regions need to be allocated and initialized, kernel structures need to be updated, etc.

The dynamic creation of threads can be also problematic if done without consideration of what the target machine is capable of. For example, an algorithm that calls for the creation of 10,000 threads in order to better balance the load of the available CPUs[9] will likely fail to deliver because the accumulated overhead from creating and destroying threads will slow the proceedings down. Of course we might not get to find this out, because it is very probable that the operating system would not allow the creation of so many threads (there are usually limits on the concurrent threads/processes a kernel can handle).

And this brings us to the alternative: having a static/fixed set of threads that run job/task requests from a queue. This set of threads that are started only once and just feed from a queue is also known as a *pool of threads*. The *static* approach has several things going for it:

✓   There is no overhead for starting each task, other that the one initially incurred for starting the pool.

---

[9] Some threads may take more time than others to finish. So having a large number of them tends to balance times out among the cores.

✓ The number of threads in the pool can be customized to better suit the workload at hand. For example, I/O-bound tasks may require more threads to fully utilize the CPU, whereas CPU-bound ones might manage with one kernel thread per hardware thread/logical CPU core.

✓ Thousands of tasks can be generated to allow for better load balancing, without being restricted by the operating system.

✓ System resource consumption (e.g., main memory and kernel structures) is minimized. This also produces time benefits, e.g., better utilization of CPU caches, less time needed for garbage collection, etc.

And some that are against it:

✗ Tasks must be packaged in a suitable way that would allow them to be inserted and removed from a container, ideally a queue. We also need a way to collect the results they produce.

✗ There is no – easy – way to enforce task precedence, i.e., having some tasks completed before others. Also having tasks that generate other tasks that they have to wait for to complete before they are done is not straightforward. This could be feasible with fibers (see Section 3.13) or by using multiple pools.

✗ Having cooperative tasks can be a problem. For example, if we had N producer and M consumer tasks, the pool would have to be at least $N + M$ threads big.

So it comes as no surprise that there is no free lunch here and that dynamic and static thread creation are each best suited for separate application domains.

Using the tools described in Section 3.11, we can package and communicate a task, signal its termination, and collect the result of its execution, so the first item in the negatives list is not a real issue. Hence, we can proceed to describe the implementation of a pool of threads.

Our implementation is based on two class templates: one (CustomThread) for setting up the threads that will constitute our pool and one (CustomThreadPool) for setting up a shared queue for depositing and extracting tasks, in a producer–consumer fashion.

The CustomThread class template shown below serves as the *consumer* in our solution, running a loop where it retrieves a unique pointer to a packaged_task instance from the CustomThreadPool class, dereferences it to get the task, runs it, and repeats the loop (lines 20–24):

Listing 3.40: A class template for the creation of a pool of threads.

```
1   // File :   customThreadPool.h
2   . . .
3   template < typename T > class CustomThreadPool;
4   // *******************************************************
5   template < typename T > class CustomThread
6   {
7   public:
8     static CustomThreadPool < T > *tpool;
9     void operator () ();
```

```
10   };
11
12   //————————————————————————————
13   template < typename T >
14   CustomThreadPool < T > *CustomThread < T >::tpool;
15   //————————————————————————————
16   template < typename T >
17   void CustomThread < T >::operator () ()
18   {
19     unique_ptr < packaged_task < T () >> tptr;
20     while (tpool->get (tptr))
21       {
22         packaged_task < T () > task = move (*tptr);
23         task ();
24       }
25   }
```

The template parameter is the type of result expected from the `packaged_task` instances. The callable object used in the `packaged_task` should receive no parameters (line 19).

Access to the `CustomThreadPool` instance is provided by a static pointer (line 14). This pointer is initialized (line 62) when the `CustomThread` instances are created by the constructor of the `customThreadPool` class (lines 63–64):

Listing 3.41: A class template for managing tasks following a producer–consumer pattern.

```
26   // File :  customThreadPool.h
27   . . .
28   const int __BUFFERSIZE = 100;
29   const int __NUMTHREADS = 16;
30
31   //***************************************************************
32   template < typename T >
33   class CustomThreadPool
34   {
35   private:
36     condition_variable empty;      // for blocking pool threads if ↩
            buffer is empty
37     condition_variable full;       // for blocking calling thread if ↩
            buffer is empty
38     mutex l;
39     atomic < bool > done;          // flag for termination
40     unique_ptr < packaged_task < T () >> *buffer; // pointer to array ↩
            of pointers to objects
41     int in = 0, out = 0, count = 0, N, maxThreads;
42
43     unique_ptr < thread > *t;      // threads RAII
44   public:
45     CustomThreadPool (int nt = __NUMTHREADS, int n = __BUFFERSIZE);
46     ~CustomThreadPool ();
47
```

```
48    bool get (unique_ptr < packaged_task < T () >> &);      // to be ↵
        called by the pool threads
49
50    future < T > schedule (unique_ptr < packaged_task < T () > >);   //↵
        to be called for work request
51  };
52
53  // ************************************************************
54  template < typename T >
55  CustomThreadPool < T >::CustomThreadPool (int numThr, int n)
56  {
57    N = n;
58    done.store (false);
59    buffer = new unique_ptr < packaged_task < T () >>[n]; // buffer ↵
        init.
60    maxThreads = numThr;
61    t = new unique_ptr < thread >[maxThreads];      // thread pointers ↵
        array alloc.
62    CustomThread < T >::tpool = this;
63    for (int i = 0; i < maxThreads; i++) // starting pool threads
64      t[i] = make_unique < thread > (CustomThread < T > ());
65  }
66
67  //————————————————————————————————————
68  template < typename T >
69  CustomThreadPool < T >::~CustomThreadPool ()
70  {
71    done.store (true);               // raise termination flag
72    empty.notify_all ();             // wake up all pool threads that ↵
        wait
73
74    for (int i = 0; i < maxThreads; i++)
75      this ->t[i]->join ();
76
77    delete []t;
78    delete []buffer;
79  }
80
81  //————————————————————————————————————
82  template < typename T >
83  future < T > CustomThreadPool < T >::schedule (unique_ptr < ↵
        packaged_task < T () > >ct)
84  {
85    unique_lock < mutex > ul (l);
86    while (count == N)
87      full.wait (ul);
88    buffer[in] = move (ct);
89    future < T > temp = buffer[in]->get_future ();
90    in = (in + 1) % N;
91    count++;
92
93    empty.notify_one ();
```

```
94
95    return move (temp);
96  }
97
98  //─────────────────────────────────────
99  template < typename T >
100 bool CustomThreadPool < T >::get (unique_ptr < packaged_task < T () ↩
        >> &taskptr)
101 {
102   unique_lock < mutex > ul (1);
103   while (count == 0 && (done != true))
104     empty.wait (ul);
105
106   taskptr = move (buffer[out]);
107   out = (out + 1) % N;
108   count--;
109
110   full.notify_one ();
111   if (done.load () == true && count < 0)          // thread should ↩
          call get again until there are no more pending tasks
112     return false;
113   else
114     return true;
115 }
```

The `CustomThreadPool` instance maintains a circular queue of unique pointers to `packaged_task` objects, implementing a producer–consumer monitor. The queue is modified by methods:

- `schedule`: deposits a `packaged_task` pointer in the queue.
- `get`: dequeues a task pointer from the queue and moves it to the parameter passed on by the caller.

Other key points of Listing 3.41 are:

- The `schedule` method is supposed to be called by the producers and the `get` method by the consumers. The `schedule` method returns a `future` instance for the submitted `packaged_task`, so that the producer/caller can get the result when it becomes available. Also the `get` method returns a Boolean to indicate the successful retrieval of a `packaged_task` or not. This allows threads to terminate when no more tasks are available (line 20 in Listing 3.40).
- The part on lines 85–93 and the part on lines 102–110 are typical examples of producer/consumer logic as explained in Section 3.10.1.1. The `empty`/`full` condition_variables are used to signal consumers/producers, respectively.
- The termination of the thread pool is initiated by calling the `CustomThreadPool` destructor (lines 68–79). The threads become aware of the termination when they check the `done` atomic Boolean inside the `get` method. Setting the `done` flag (line 71) will make the `get` method return false when no more tasks are available in the buffer (lines 111–112). After setting the `done` flag, the `CustomThreadPool`

destructor waits for all the threads to join (lines 74 and 75), thus making sure that all the submitted work is complete.

- All objects managed by a `CustomThreadPool` instance, i.e., `packaged_task` and `thread` instances, are maintained via `unique_ptr` objects, which simplifies memory management. The corresponding arrays are allocated on lines 59 and 61.
- The threads are allocated and start executing `CustomThread` function objects (lines 63 and 64), once the `CustomThread::tpool` pointer is set (line 62).

The size of the `packaged_task` buffer and the number of pool threads are easily customizable by parameters to the constructor of the `CustomThreadPool` class. A typical definition for having as many threads as the number of hardware threads/logical cores in the system would be:

```
CustomThreadPool<void> tp(thread::hardware_concurrency());
```

As an example on the use of the `CustomThreadPool` class template, the following program generates a number of independent tasks for calculating the Mandelbrot fractal set. Seemingly, this is not the most appropriate example, because the load can be partitioned and assigned to a fixed number of threads a priori, which is not a recipe for a problem requiring dynamic thread spawning. However, if we did stick with a fixed number of threads, we could end up with a substantial load imbalance.

The Mandelbrot set[10] is a set of points $c = x + i \cdot y$ on the complex plane that produce a bounded sequence of numbers $z_0, z_1, z_2, \ldots$ when the recursive formula

$$z_{n+1} = z_n^2 + c \tag{3.2}$$

with $z_0 = c$ is applied, i.e., $z_n = \sqrt{x_n^2 + y_n^2} < \infty \ \forall n$.

The famous Mandelbrot fractal image is produced by calculating for each point c on the complex plane the number of iterations n at which the sequence diverges: $|z_n| > 2$, because if the magnitude goes above 2 the sequence is known to diverge. The number n is used to pseudocolor the point. Obviously, for the Mandelbrot set of points the number of iterations has to be bounded as they never diverge.

If we did break up the complex plane into a fixed number of regions (for example we could perform 1D geometric partitioning along the x-axis) and assigned each region to a thread, it is very likely that every thread will require a very different amount of time to complete. The reason is that each thread will most likely be assigned a different part of the Mandelbrot set, accumulating a different total number of iterations that have to be performed.

But if we could break up the plane in a very large – compared with the number of logical cores – number of regions and use our pool of threads, we could even out the imbalance that heavy computational regions can cause.

The following program implements this exact approach for the complex plane area specified in the command-line in the form of the upper left and bottom right corner coordinates. For each disjoint region produced by the breakup, a `MandelCompute`

---

[10] http://en.wikipedia.org/wiki/Mandelbrot_set.

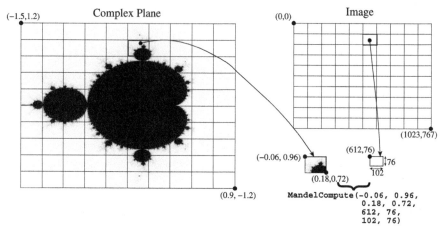

FIGURE 3.15

An illustration of the parameters required to generate an instance of the `MandelCompute` class in Listing 3.42. The parameters include a description of both the "source" area in the complex plane and the "destination" part of the image to be computed. The actual code also includes a reference to a `QImage` object.

function object is created. Fig. 3.15 shows how a functor is initialized. The required constructor parameters include (a) the upper left and lower right corners of the part of the complex plane to examine and (b) the top left corner coordinates, the height and the width in pixels of the part of the image to be generated.

Listing 3.42: A Mandelbrot fractal set calculator that generates a task for each part of the image to be computed.

```cpp
// File(s) : mandelbrot_threadPool/main.cpp
#include <QImage>
#include <QRgb>
#include "customThreadPool.h"
. . .

// *****************************************************************
class MandelCompute {
private:
    static const int MAXITER;
    int diverge(double cx, double cy);

    double upperX, upperY, lowerX, lowerY;
    int imageX, imageY, pixelsX, pixelsY;
    shared_ptr<QImage> img;

public:
    MandelCompute(double, double, double, double, shared_ptr<QImage
        >, int, int, int, int);
    void operator()();
```

```
20  };
21  const int MandelCompute::MAXITER = 255;
22
23  //————————————————————————————————————————
24  int MandelCompute::diverge(double cx, double cy) {
25      int iter = 0;
26      double vx = cx, vy = cy, tx, ty;
27      while (iter < MAXITER && (vx * vx + vy * vy) < 4) {
28          tx = vx * vx − vy * vy + cx;
29          ty = 2 * vx * vy + cy;
30          vx = tx;
31          vy = ty;
32          iter++;
33      }
34      return iter;
35  }
36
37  //————————————————————————————————————————
38  MandelCompute::MandelCompute(double uX, double uY, double lX, double ↵
          lY, shared_ptr<QImage> im, int iX, int iY, int pX, int pY) {
39      upperX = uX;
40      upperY = uY;
41      lowerX = lX;
42      lowerY = lY;
43      img = im;
44      imageX = iX;
45      imageY = iY;
46      pixelsX = pX;
47      pixelsY = pY;
48  }
49
50  //————————————————————————————————————————
51  void MandelCompute::operator()() {
52      double stepx = (lowerX − upperX) / pixelsX;
53      double stepy = (upperY − lowerY) / pixelsY;
54
55      for (int i = 0; i < pixelsX; i++)
56          for (int j = 0; j < pixelsY; j++) {
57              double tempx, tempy;
58              tempx = upperX + i * stepx;
59              tempy = upperY − j * stepy;
60              int color = diverge(tempx, tempy);
61              img->setPixel(imageX + i, imageY + j, qRgb(256 − color, ↵
                  256 − color, 256 − color));
62          }
63  }
64
65  // ************************************************************
66  int main(int argc, char *argv[]) {
67      double upperCornerX, upperCornerY;
68      double lowerCornerX, lowerCornerY;
69
```

```
70      upperCornerX = atof(argv[1]);
71      upperCornerY = atof(argv[2]);
72      lowerCornerX = atof(argv[3]);
73      lowerCornerY = atof(argv[4]);
74      double partXSpan, partYSpan;
75
76      int Xparts = 10, Yparts = 10;
77      int imgX = 4096, imgY = 2160;
78      int pxlX, pxlY;
79
80      if(argc>5) // optional specification of partitioning
81      {
82        Xparts=atoi(argv[5]);
83        Yparts=atoi(argv[6]);
84      }
85
86      partXSpan = (lowerCornerX - upperCornerX) / Xparts;
87      partYSpan = (upperCornerY - lowerCornerY) / Yparts;
88      pxlX = imgX / Xparts;
89      pxlY = imgY / Yparts;
90      shared_ptr<QImage> img = make_shared<QImage>(imgX, imgY, QImage
          ::Format_RGB32);
91      CustomThreadPool<void> tp(thread::hardware_concurrency());
92      future<void> f[Xparts][Yparts];
93
94      // iterate over each region
95      for (int i = 0; i < Xparts; i++)
96          for (int j = 0; j < Yparts; j++) {
97              double x1, y1, x2, y2;
98              int ix, iy, pX, pY; //image coords. and pixel spans
99
100             x1 = upperCornerX + i * partXSpan;
101             y1 = upperCornerY - j * partYSpan;
102             x2 = upperCornerX + (i + 1) * partXSpan;
103             y2 = upperCornerY - (j + 1) * partYSpan;
104
105             ix = i*pxlX;
106             iy = j*pxlY;
107             pX = (i == Xparts - 1) ? imgX - ix : pxlX;
108             pY = (j == Yparts - 1) ? imgY - iy : pxlY;
109
110             unique_ptr<MandelCompute>  t = make_unique<MandelCompute
                  >(x1, y1, x2, y2, img, ix, iy, pX, pY);
111             unique_ptr<packaged_task<void()> > pt = make_unique<
                  packaged_task<void()> >(*t);
112             f[i][j] = tp.schedule( move(pt));
113         }
114
115     // now wait for all threads to stop
116     for (int i = 0; i < Xparts; i++)
117         for (int j = 0; j < Yparts; j++) {
118             f[i][j].get();
```

```
119        }
120
121      img->save("mandel.png", "PNG", 0);
122      return 0;
123  }
```

The main points of the program in Listing 3.42 are:

- The part of the complex plane to be examined (as specified by command-line parameters that are extracted at lines 70–73) is split into $Xparts * Yparts$ disjoint pieces. For each piece, a separate function object is generated (line 110), encapsulated in a `packaged_task` instance (line 111), and deposited in the `CustomThreadPool` queue (line 112).
- The tasks contain instances of the `MandelCompute` class. The calculations take place inside the `compute` and `diverge` methods.
- The main thread, after creating the `CustomThreadPool` singleton `tp` (line 91), deposits the generated tasks in `tp`'s queue and keeps the returned future instances in a 2D array (line 112), which mirrors the plane partitioning. These `future` instances are subsequently used to check that the tasks are completed (lines 115–118), before the generated image is saved to a file.
- A `QImage` instance (courtesy of the Qt library) is used for handling the generated image data and finally storing the complete image in a file (line 121). All the methods in class `QImage` are **re-entrant**, which means it is safe to call them from multiple threads. Because each of the threads is instructed to operate on a different part of the `QImage` object, there are no race conditions or data races to worry about.

3.13 **Threads and fibers**

Threads offer compelling advantages in performance and space economy over processes, while also accommodating a better program structure when multiple activities are pursued. During the early years of adopting threads for multi-programming, threads were implemented with the assistance of third-party libraries, due to the absence of native operating system support. The threading libraries provided calls for thread creation, communication, and thread switching. Switching between threads was done on a cooperative basis, i.e., the running thread called the threading library in order to surrender the CPU and allow the selection and execution of another thread, all within the context of a single process. This is the reason why this approach to thread support is also known as cooperative multi-threading. Another term used is *user-level* or *userland* threads, because all thread-related operations are conducted in user mode without the knowledge or cooperation of the operating system kernel.

In contrast, all contemporary operating systems support threads at the system level (e.g., schedulers are aware of threads), and these implementations are known as *kernel-level* threads.

User-level threads have a number of distinct advantages:

✓ The time and space overhead for all thread-related operations, including spawning, communication, and switching, is a fraction of what is incurred for kernel-level threads. This feature earned user-level threads the names "lightweight threads," "green threads," or "microthreads."

✓ Hundreds or thousands of threads can be easily created and managed.

✓ Custom thread schedulers can be employed or even written by the programmer.

✓ As a third-party library is used, it is easier to port the software to different operating systems.

But not everything is rosy:

✗ If a thread makes an operating system call that blocks the process, all the threads block. This means that non-blocking I/O calls should be preferred if fibers are involved.

✗ Only a single core can be utilized by all the threads, as only one can be active at any time instance.

The inability to use multiple cores seems like a tombstone for the future of user-level threads. But what if we could combine kernel-level and user-level threads? This is the idea behind the concept of the *fiber*: while we can still use our kernel-level threads to create execution entities that can saturate the available cores of a system, each of these threads can create multiple user-level threads (fibers), for fine-tuning with minimum cost what each core will perform. In this section we will use the term *thread* to refer to the kernel generated and supported execution units and we will use the term *fiber* for the userland threads that the Boost fiber library creates and manages.

Fibers are provided by the `boost::fiber` library. This is a cross-platform library that utilizes native fiber support if available at the host operating system, like, e.g., Windows fibers, which benefits performance. Its API is very similar to the one provided by the `std::thread` standard class. So, creating a fiber is as simple as passing a callable object to the `fiber` constructor. The parameters are passed by value, so if passing by reference is desired, the `ref()` and `cref()` functions can be utilized. Some examples:

```cpp
#include <boost/fiber/all.hpp>

class CallableFoo {
    . . .
    void operator()();
};

void fooFunc(int i);

boost::fibers::fiber fiberSetup(CallableFoo &x)
{
    boost::fibers::fiber  f( ref( x ) );
    return f;  // a move operation is performed. Fibers cannot be ↩
        copied
```

```
}
boost::fibers::fiber fiberSetup2() {
    CallableFoo x;
    // setting up x
    . . .
    boost::fibers::fiber f( x );   // x is copied and maintained by ←
        the fiber.
                                   // ref() cannot be used for x here ←
                                     , because
                                   // x will be destroyed upon ←
                                     exiting the function
    return f;
}
. . .
boost::fibers::fiber f = fiberSetup2();
. . .
boost::fibers::fiber f2( fooFunc, 1);
```

Waiting for a fiber to finish requires a join operation:

```
boost::fibers::fiber f2( fooFunc, 1);
. . .
f2.join(); // blocking call
```

Alternatively, fibers can be detached:

```
boost::fibers::fiber( fooFunc, 1).detach(); // detaching an unnamed ←
    fiber
```

A word of caution though: a detached fiber cannot run unless another fiber surrenders the CPU. Also, detached threads that are not finished will block the parent thread from exiting. So the following code snippet will result in a blocked program after the message is printed, as none of the fiber gets a chance to run.

```
int main()
{
    boost::fibers::fiber f[10];
    for(int i=0;i<10;i++)
    {
        f[i] = boost::fibers::fiber(foo);
        f[i].detach();
    }
    cout << "Finishing...\n";
    return 0;
}
```

The following modification would allow the program to terminate, but only if the fibers never give up the CPU until they are finished, i.e., they do not yield or go to sleep:

```
int main()
{
    boost::fibers::fiber f[10];
    for(int i=0;i<10;i++)
    {
        f[i] = boost::fibers::fiber(foo);
        f[i].detach();
    }
    boost::this_fiber::yield();  // parent thread calls the fiber ↩
        library that in turn runs all the fibers
    cout << "Finishing...\n";
    return 0;
}
```

In effect, in the above code we are just running the fibers one after the other. Hopefully, it becomes clear that detached fibers should be used with great care.

Fibers can communicate by using `boost::fibers::mutex` and `boost::fibers::condition_variable` class instances. These classes provide the same methods as the `std::mutex` and `std::condition_variable` classes, but they are meant to be used between fibers, as blocking a single fiber will not result in blocking all the others. In contrast, if a fiber blocks on an `std::mutex`, all the fibers of that thread will be blocked. In other words, for *intrathread* fiber synchronization one should use `boost::fibers::mutex` and `boost::fibers::condition_variable`, while for *interthread* synchronization `std::mutex` and `std::condition_variable` are the proper choice.

Fibers can be also put to sleep with the `boost::this_fiber::sleep_for` and `boost::this_fiber::sleep_until` methods, which will result in the execution of another fiber (the thread will not sleep). Switching to another fiber can be also done by calling `boost::this_fiber::yield()`. However, as you might have guessed, calling `std::this_thread::yield()` would cause all fibers of the current thread to give up the CPU.

Each fiber can be identified by a unique ID, which can be retrieved by calling the `boost::this_thread::get_id()` method:

Listing 3.43: "Hello World" example using fibers.

```
1  // File : fiber_hello.cpp
2  #include <boost/fiber/all.hpp>
3  . . .
4  void msg()
5  {
6      boost::this_fiber::sleep_for(chrono::duration<int, milli>(rand()↩
           %100));
7      cout <<"Hello from fiber " << boost::this_fiber::get_id() << endl↩
           ;
8  }
9
10 int main()
11 {
```

```
12    boost::fibers::fiber f[10];
13    for(int i=0;i<10;i++)
14        f[i] = boost::fibers::fiber(msg);
15
16    for(int i=0;i<10;i++)
17        f[i].join();
18 }
```

The above program can be compiled and run with the commands:

```
$ g++ -std=c++17 fiber_hello.cpp -o fiber_hello -lboost_fiber -↩
    lboost_context
$ ./fiber_hello
Hello from fiber 0x5655577bd700
Hello from fiber 0x56555781d700
Hello from fiber 0x5655577dd700
. . .
```

Fibers are handled by a fiber manager provided by the library. The manager employs a scheduling algorithm for selecting the next fiber to run when the currently executing one gives up the CPU or blocks. The default scheduling algorithm is the round-robin. Additionally, one can select from these built-in ones:

- work_stealing: If the local ready queue of fibers is empty, fibers from other queues are "stolen."
- numa::work_stealing: If the local ready queue of fibers is empty, fibers from other queues that belong to threads running on the same NUMA node (see Section 1.2) are "stolen."
- shared_work: Fibers are shared between all threads. This is a poor choice for NUMA architectures or for maximizing CPU cache utilization.

One can change the scheduling algorithm by invoking the use_scheduling_algorithm function, prior to any fiber construction. For example, the following call will allow the exchange of the fibers between as many threads as the logical cores:

```
boost::fibers::use_scheduling_algorithm< boost::fibers::algo:: ↩
    work_stealing >( thread::hardware_concurrency());
```

Of course, as many threads have to be created in the first place and each thread will have to make the same use_scheduling_algorithm call in order for fibers to be able to migrate between threads.

We can thus combine threads and fibers to create a pool of threads that alleviates some of the issues listed above. For example, if a fiber were to block by calling the fiber library (e.g., using lock() on a boost::fibers::mutex), the library would switch to another fiber, preventing the thread from blocking. This means that a hierarchy of fibers can be handled by multiple cores with no problem.

The following example of a thread-fiber combo pool illustrates the steps that have to be performed:

Listing 3.44: A pool of threads that combines kernel- and user-level threads.

```cpp
// File : fiber_pool.cpp
#include <boost/fiber/all.hpp>
#include "semaphore.cpp"

thread workerSetup (boost::fibers::barrier & b, semaphore &done, int
    n)
{
  return move (thread ([&]()
                {
                    boost::fibers::use_scheduling_algorithm < boost::
                        fibers::algo::shared_work > ();
                    b.wait ();
                    while(done.try_acquire()==false)
                        boost::this_fiber::yield();
                }
            ));
}

// ********************************************
void foo ()
{
  for(int i=0;i<10;i++)
  {
    boost::this_fiber::sleep_for (chrono::duration < int, milli > (
        rand () % 100));
    cout << "Hello #" << i << " from fiber " << boost::this_fiber::
        get_id () << " running on thread " << this_thread::get_id ()
        << endl;
    boost::this_fiber::yield();
  }
}

// ********************************************
int main ()
{
  int numThr = thread::hardware_concurrency ();
  boost::fibers::barrier b {static_cast < size_t > (numThr)};
  semaphore done (0);
  unique_ptr < thread > t[numThr - 1];

  boost::fibers::use_scheduling_algorithm < boost::fibers::algo::
      shared_work > ();

  for (int i = 0; i < numThr - 1; i++)
    t[i] = make_unique < thread > (workerSetup (b, done, numThr));

  // block until all threads set the fiber scheduler
  b.wait ();

  // create the fibers
  boost::fibers::fiber f[100];
```

```
46      for (int i = 0; i < 100; i++)
47        {
48          f[i] = boost::fibers::fiber (foo);
49  //        f[i].detach ();
50        }
51
52      // waiting for all work to complete
53      for(int i=0;i<100;i++)
54          f[i].join();
55
56      // let threads know that they can stop.
57      done.release (numThr-1);
58
59      for (int i = 0; i < numThr - 1; i++)
60        t[i]->join ();
61      return 0;
62  }
```

The main thread performs the following sequence:

(a) After finding the number of logical cores (line 31) a matching number of threads (including the main thread) is set up by calling the workSetup() function to create each individual thread (loop on lines 38–39).

(b) All the threads (including the main thread) create a fiber scheduler for sharing the fiber load (lines 36 and 9) by making the same use_scheduling_algorithm call. This has to be completed by all threads before any fibers are created. To ensure that this is done, a barrier is set up (line 32) to force all the threads to synchronize by waiting on lines 42 and 10.

(c) Once execution gets past the barrier on line 42, a number of fibers is set up to execute the foo() function. We can either detach them after creation (line 49) or wait for them to finish (lines 53–54).

(d) The done semaphore is increased to indicate to the worker threads that no more work is pending (line 57). Semaphores are better than condition variables for signaling in this case, because the "signal" is not lost if the thread is not blocked, waiting for it.

(e) If the fibers are detached, waiting for the threads to finish (lines 59–60) also ensures that the fibers are done. Otherwise we have to wait for the fibers to complete with the loop of lines 53–54 before incrementing the semaphore.

The worker threads after creating the fiber scheduler (line 9) perform a loop where they wait for a signal to come from the main thread (condition of line 11). As long as the work is not complete, they call the boost::fiber::yield() method, which switches to another active fiber.

A sample output from the above program reveals that the fibers execute on all the generated threads, including the main thread. Also a fiber can switch between threads from one iteration of the lines 20–25 loop to the next, as per the work-sharing fiber scheduler used:

```
$ ./fiber_pool
Hello 0 from fiber 0x565557ba5200 running on thread 139620449462016
Hello 0 from fiber 0x565557ca5300 running on thread 139620684326656
Hello 0 from fiber 0x5655578d4d00 running on thread 139620570351360 ←
   <===
Hello 0 from fiber 0x5655579f4e00 running on thread 139620709504768
Hello 1 from fiber 0x5655578d4d00 running on thread 139620578744064 ←
   <===
. . .
```

It should be noted that the `this_fiber::yield()` call of line 24 is superficial, as calling the `this_fiber::sleep_for()` method on line 22 is enough for switching to another fiber. This would not be true if `this_thread::yield()` and `this_thread::sleep_for()` were used instead.

3.14 Debugging multi-threaded applications

Debugging of multi-threaded applications goes way beyond merely having a debugger capable of managing multiple threads. Most contemporary debuggers support the execution and individual debugging of threads, with thread-specific breakpoints, watch windows, etc. In this section, we are not concerned primarily with how a debugger can be utilized. As an example, Fig. 3.16 shows the DDD, GNU DeBugger (GDB) front-end, executing the fair readers–writers solution of Listing 3.36. The only requirement for being able to use DDD and GDB (for the CLI aficionados) in Unix/Linux is to compile your program with debugging information support, i.e., use the -g switch of the compiler.

Bugs in multi-threaded programs typically manifest sporadically, only under special circumstances that have to do with the precise timing of events. A debugger disrupts timings by pausing or slowing down the execution of threads, making bug reproduction and discovery a challenge. Ultimately, finding the bugs becomes a matter of experience and intuition, but also appropriately instrumented program code can be of great help.

In the following list, we enumerate a number of steps a developer can take to ensure a bug-free multi-threaded application:

- The first step in eliminating bugs in multi-threaded applications is of course to not introduce them in the first place! A sound software design that precedes the writing of the code is critical in this regard.
- The classical problems studied in this chapter are not just of educational value. The majority of the concurrency problems one can encounter in real-life are either instances of these problems or can be reduced to them with a few simple steps. Utilizing the solutions presented in this chapter can eliminate problems that stem from trying to reinvent the wheel.

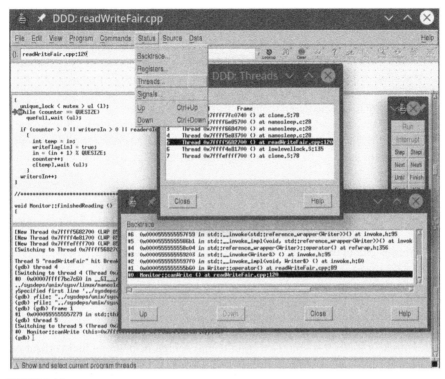

FIGURE 3.16

A screenshot of the DDD debugger, which is a GDB front-end, running an instance of the fair solution to the readers–writers problem of Listing 3.36. The program is currently running seven threads as shown in the dialog window: the main thread (currently spawning more threads), three readers, and three writers. A breakpoint has stopped a writer thread at line 120 in the code. The backtrace of the selected thread is also shown.

- The application should be modified to produce some type of log or trace history that can be examined off-line. This would permit the collection of information about the run-time behavior of the application.
- Having too many threads in an application can complicate the interpretation of the logs produced. It is generally a good design to have the application parameterized as far as the number of threads is concerned. By limiting the threads to 1, bugs not specific to timings can be discovered. Also, by limiting them to 2 or 3, one can reduce the overhead of extracting information from the logs substantially.

Peppering your code with `printf` or `cout` statements to keep track of the execution path and state of the program is not sufficient. Having multiple threads produce console (or file) output at the same time typically results in mangled messages that cannot be deciphered. The solution is to treat the console (or the file stream) as a shared resource and place the output statements inside a critical section.

Some authors advocate keeping the debugging/tracing information in a memory buffer (called a *trace buffer*) to be saved upon termination of the program. This is a questionable approach for misbehaving programs. It requires that (a) the program terminates normally (i.e., does not crash or hang), (b) the buffer is big enough to accommodate whatever is generated, and (c) the buffer is not corrupted by memory errors.

A better solution is to dump the trace messages to the console as soon as they are generated. This can work for a file also, but for the additional overhead of opening and closing the file for every message that is to be saved. Otherwise, one risks losing the last changes made to the file if the program crashes, along with possibly important information.

In order to differentiate normal program output from trace messages, one can utilize the standard error stream. But what if the debugging output needs to be processed further, e.g., filtered according to the thread that generated it, etc.? The solution is simple: *stream redirection*. This is a capability common to both the *nix and Windows worlds. So, in order to redirect the standard error output to file `trace.log`, one would have to use the following syntax:

```
$ myprog 2> trace.log
```

It is also a good idea to stamp any debugging messages with the time that they were generated. For this purpose, the normal time functions (like `clock`) that come with 1-msec or lower resolution are insufficient. A high-resolution timer is required, and a number of them are available through different APIs (please see Appendix C.2 for more details). For the remainder of the section we will assume that there is a function called `hrclock` (high-resolution clock) that returns a time stamp in seconds, of type `double`.

Listing 3.45 shows a sample that implements the guidelines laid down in the discussion above, using the C++11 `chrono` package for timing support:

Listing 3.45: A sample of how a multi-threaded application can be set up for debugging. The code contains a data race between threads attempting uncoordinated modifications to a shared counter.

```
1   // File : debugSample.cpp
2   . . .
3   #include <chrono>
4
5   #define DEBUG
6
7   //*****************************************************
8   chrono::high_resolution_clock::time_point time0;
9   mutex l;
10  double hrclock ()
11  {
12    chrono::high_resolution_clock::time_point t;
13    t = chrono::high_resolution_clock::now();
14    return chrono::duration<double>(t-time0).count(); //defaults to ↩
          seconds
```

```
15    }
16
17    // ************************************************
18    void debugMsg (string msg, double timestamp)
19    {
20      l.lock ();
21      cerr << timestamp << " " << msg << endl;
22      l.unlock ();
23    }
24
25    // ************************************************
26    int counter = 0;
27
28    class MyThread
29    {
30    private:
31      int ID;
32      int runs;
33    public:
34      MyThread (int i, int r):ID (i), runs (r) {}
35      void operator()()
36      {
37        cout << "Thread " << ID << " is running\n";
38        for (int j = 0; j < runs; j++)
39          {
40    #ifdef DEBUG
41            ostringstream ss;
42            ss << "Thread #" << ID << " counter=" << counter;
43            debugMsg (ss.str (), hrclock ());
44    #endif
45            this_thread::sleep_for(chrono::duration < int, milli > (rand↩
                () % 4 + 1));
46            counter++;
47          }
48      }
49    };
50
51    int main (int argc, char *argv[])
52    {
53    #ifdef DEBUG
54      time0 = chrono::high_resolution_clock::now();
55    #endif
56      . . .
57    }
```

The key points of the sample program are:

- The additional code segments are inside C++ preprocessor conditional blocks (lines 40–44 and 53–55). One just has to comment out line 5 to get a production-ready version of the program.
- A global-scope mutex is used to ensure that the body of the debugMsg function is a critical section.

- Time is measured from the moment the program starts execution. The time stamp of that instance is stored in the time0 variable, which is subsequently subtracted from every time stamp calculated (line 14).

A sample run of this program and a close inspection of the debugging output reveals the data race at work:

```
$ ./debugSample 10 100 2> log
Thread Thread Thread Thread Thread Thread Thread 6419 is running
Thread 8 is running
Thread 3 is running
 is running
7 is running
5 is running
Thread 2 is running
0 is running
 is running
 is running
994
$ sort log
. . .
0.0033443 Thread 5 counter=216
0.00335193 Thread 7 counter=218
0.00335193 Thread 8 counter=217          <———
0.00335503 Thread 3 counter=219
. . .
```

Finally, a word of caution for properly debugging a program: you should *disable compiler optimizations*. An optimizing compiler can change the execution order of statements or even discard variables that you declare in your program, in its effort to streamline execution. As a result, debugging an optimized executable can produce surprising results, like jumps between statements, which can strain the programmer. In rare cases, it can be the compiler optimizations that cause a bug to appear. Although this is an extraordinary event, there are a number of compiler optimizations that are characterized as "unsafe." Developers who desire to push a compiler to its limits should ensure that the resulting executable behaves in the same way as an unoptimized one.

For example, the -ftree-loop-if-convert-stores GCC compiler switch converts conditional memory writes into unconditional memory writes. Here is a sample taken from the manual page of the compiler:

```
for (i = 0; i < N; i++)
   if (cond)
      A[i] = expr;
```

would be transformed to

```
for (i = 0; i < N; i++)
   A[i] = cond ? expr : A[i];
```

Both the original and the transformed code provide opportunity for a race condition if the A array is a shared resource. In the transformed version though, the problem is exaggerated.

Exercises

1. Enumerate and create the other timing diagrams that show the alternatives of Fig. 3.5 when it comes to the final balance of the bank account.
2. Research the term "fork bomb" and write a program that performs as such.
3. Modify the producer–consumer example shown in Listing 3.14 so that the threads terminate after the number 100 is generated.
4. Suggest a modification to the program of Listing 3.15 so that the `IntegrCalc` threads can use any function that returns a double and takes a double as a parameter.
5. In a remote region of Siberia there are single tracks joining railroad stations. Obviously only one train can use a piece of track between two stations. The other trains can wait at the stations before they do their crossings. The following graph indicates the track and station layout:

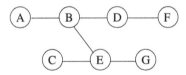

Write a multi-threaded program that simulates the journey of three trains with the following schedules:

   - $A \to B \to E \to C$
   - $D \to B \to E \to G$
   - $C \to E \to B \to D \to F$

As each train arrives at a station display a related message. You can assume that a station can hold any number of trains waiting.
6. Modify the program of the previous exercise so that each station can hold only two trains. Can this lead to deadlocks?
   If you have not done so already, make sure that your program uses only one thread class.
7. A desktop publishing (like PageMaker) application has two threads running: one for running the GUI and one for doing background work. Simulate this application in Qt. Your implementation should have the thread corresponding to the GUI send requests to the other thread to run tasks on its behalf. The tasks should be (obviously just printing a message is enough for the simulation):

- printing,
- mail merging, and
- PDF generation.

After performing each requested task, the second thread should wait for a new request to be sent to it. Make sure that the first thread does not have to wait for the second thread to finish before making new requests.

8. A popular bakery has a baker that cooks a loaf of bread at a time and deposits it on a counter. Incoming customers pick up a loaf from the counter and exit the bakery. The counter can hold 20 loaves. If it is full the baker stops baking bread. If it is empty, a customer waits. Use semaphores to solve the coordination problem between the baker and the customers.

9. Because of customer demand, the bakery owner is considering the following enhancements to his shop:
   a. Increase the capacity of the counter to 1000.
   b. Hire three more bakers.

   Modify the solution of the previous exercise to accommodate these changes. Which is the easiest to implement?

10. A bank account class is defined as follows:

```
class BankAccount {
  protected:
      double balance;
      string holderName;
  public:
      double getBalance();
      void deposit(double);
      void withdraw(double, int); // the highest the second ↩
          argument, the higher the priority of the request
};
```

Write the implementation of the three methods given above so that withdraw operations are prioritized: if there are not enough funds in the account for all, the withdrawals must be done in order of priority regardless if there are some that can be performed with the available funds. You can assume that the priority level in the `withdraw` method is by default equal to 0 and that it is upper-bounded by a fixed constant MAXPRIORITY.

11. The IT department of a big corporation is equipped with five high-speed printers that are used by a multitude of threads. The threads are part of the same accounting process. Each of the threads is supposed to perform the following (pseudocode) sequence in order to print out any material:

```
...
printerID = get_available_printer();
// print to printerID printer
releasePrinter(printerID);
...
```

Write an appropriate implementation for the two functions listed above using semaphores. You can assume that the available printer IDs are stored in a shared buffer.

12. Create three threads, each printing out the letters "A," "B," and "C." The printing must adhere to these rules:

    - The total number of "B"s and "C"s that have been output at any point in the output string cannot exceed the total number of "A"s that have been output at that point.
    - After a "C" has been output, another "C" cannot be output until one or more "B"s have been output.

    Use semaphores to solve the problem.

13. Modify the previous exercise so that the printing is governed by this set of rules:

    - One "C" must be output after two "A"s and three "B"s are output.
    - While there is no restriction on the order of printing "A" and "B," the corresponding threads must wait for a "C" to be printed when the previous condition is met.

    Use a monitor to solve the problem.

14. Address the termination problem in the previous exercise. How can the three threads terminate after, e.g., a fixed number of "A"s has been output? Or when a fixed total number of character has been output?

15. Create four threads, each printing out the letters "A," "B," "C," and "D." The printing must adhere to these rules:

    - The total number of "A"s and "B"s that have been output at any point in the output string cannot exceed the total number of "C"s and "D"s that have been output at that point.
    - The total number of "A"s that have been output at any point in the output string cannot exceed twice the number of "B"s that have been output at that point.
    - After a "C" has been output, another "C" cannot be output until one or more "D"s have been output.

    Solve the problem using (a) semaphores and (b) a monitor.

16. Use semaphores to solve the typical cigarette smokers problem, where the agent signals directly the smoker missing the two ingredients placed on the table.

17. Solve the cigarette smokers problem as described in Section 3.9.2 using semaphores.

18. Model the movie-going process at a multiplex cinema using a monitor. Assume the following conditions:

    - There are three different movies played at the same time in three halls. The capacity of each hall is four, five, and seven, respectively.
    - One hundred customers are waiting to see a randomly chosen movie.

- A cashier issues the tickets.
- If a hall is full a movie begins to play.
- A customer cannot enter a hall while a movie is playing or while the previous viewers are exiting the hall.
- A movie will play for the last customers even if the corresponding hall is not full.

19. Write a multi-threaded password cracker based on the producer–consumer paradigm. The producer should generate plaintext passwords according to a set of rules and the consumers should be hashing each password and checking whether it matches a target signature. All the threads should terminate upon the discovery of a matching password. You can use the MD5 cryptographic hash function for this exercise.

20. Write a multi-threaded program for finding the prime numbers in a user-supplied range of numbers. Compare the following design approaches:

  a. Split the range in equal pieces and assign each one to a thread.

  b. Have a shared `QAtomicInt` variable that holds the next number to be checked. Threads should read and increment this number before testing it.

  c. Have a shared "monitor" object that returns upon request a range of numbers to be tested. This can be considered a generalization of the previous design.

Which of the designs is more efficient? Explain your findings.

21. Which type of thread is favored by the solution to the readers–writers problem in Listing 3.22? If either of the readers or writers are favored, modify the code to produce a fair solution.

22. Modify Listing 3.13 so that termination of the producer and consumer threads is accomplished via atomic integers.

23. Justify the statement at the end of Section 3.13 about the use of the `yield` and `sleep_for` methods in Listing 3.44.

24. Devise a benchmark for testing how much faster spawning a fiber is compared to spawning a thread.

Parallel data structures

4

In this chapter you will:

- Learn how to create thread-safe data structures, such as stacks, queues, and lists.
- Utilize different synchronization techniques, such as fine-grained, optimistic, and lazy synchronization, to build concurrent structures.
- Understand synchronization issues arising from concurrency, such as the ABA problem.
- Design and build lock-free data structures.
- Understand the differences and design trade-offs concerning lock-using and lock-free concurrent structures.

4.1 Introduction

Chapter 3 is largely devoted to how threads can coordinate by using semaphores, monitors, and atomics. So why is a separate chapter on parallel data structures required? Well, the answer is, it is not, if you are willing to compromise on performance. The mechanisms covered so far are quite sufficient for creating a thread-safe data structure: all we have to do is turn all access to the data structure into critical sections.

An entity (data structure or function) is called thread-safe if there are no race conditions present when multiple threads access it. Another more formal definition for a data structure is that the *invariants* of the structure, i.e., properties that have to be preserved, are maintained during access by multiple threads.

For example, a stack's invariants are:

- An item that has been pushed N times can only be popped N times.
- If a thread pushes item A followed by item B onto the stack, and no other thread pushes these values, B must be popped before A.

For example, the simplest way to create a thread-safe stack is to turn the stack class into a monitor:

Listing 4.1: A concurrent stack modeled after a monitor.

```
// File : stack_coarse.hpp
class empty_stack : std::exception
{
```

Multicore and GPU Programming. https://doi.org/10.1016/B978-0-12-814120-5.00013-5

```
4    public:
5      virtual const char* what() const noexcept {return "Stack is empty"↩
         ;};
6    };
7    //*************************************************
8    template <typename T>
9    class stack{
10   private:
11       std::vector<T> store;
12       std::mutex l;
13   public:
14       bool empty();
15       int size();
16       void push(T &);
17       T pop();
18   };
19
20   template<typename T> bool stack<T>::empty()
21   {
22       std::lock_guard<std::mutex> lg(l);
23       return store.empty();
24   }
25
26   template<typename T> int stack<T>::size()
27   {
28       std::lock_guard<std::mutex> lg(l);
29       return store.size();
30   }
31
32   template<typename T> void stack<T>::push(T & i)
33   {
34       std::lock_guard<std::mutex> lg(l);
35       store.push_back(i);
36   }
37
38   template<typename T> T stack<T>::pop()
39   {
40       std::lock_guard<std::mutex> lg(l);
41       if(store.size()==0)
42           throw empty_stack();
43       T temp = std::move(store.at[store.size()-1]);
44       store.pop_back();
45       return std::move(temp);
46
47   }
```

In the tradition of the C++ Standard Library's stack class template, which is designated as a *container adaptor*, our class relies on a vector for actually storing the data. As each method locks down the stack via the mutex (defined on line 12) before any change or inspection of the structure is attempted, there is no possibility of a race condition.

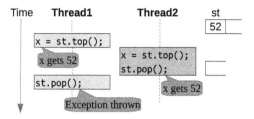

FIGURE 4.1

An example of a race condition produced when `top()` and `pop()` stack calls are interrupted.

There is however a noticeable absence in the methods shown above: `top()` is missing. Instead `pop()` serves as a combination of top and pop, by removing and returning the top of the stack, throwing an exception in case the stack is empty (lines 41–42). The omission is necessitated by the fact that having separate top and pop methods would introduce a race condition as illustrated in Fig. 4.1.

Apart from this small inconvenience of missing the `top` method, getting a thread-safe stack seems fairly straightforward. We could even modify/enhance the semantics of pop, to have a thread wait for an item to be pushed on the stack as shown below:

Listing 4.2: A concurrent stack that allows signaling between "pusher" and "popper" threads.

```
// File : stack_coarse_v2.hpp
template<typename T>
class stack{
private:
    std::condition_variable c;
    . . .
};

template<typename T> void stack<T>::push(T & i)
{
    std::lock_guard<std::mutex> lg(l);
    store.push_back(i);
    c.notify_one();
}

template<typename T> T stack<T>::pop()
{
    std::unique_lock<std::mutex> ul(l);;
    while(store.size()==0)
        c.wait(ul);
    T temp = std::move(store.at[store.size()-1]);
    store.pop_back();
    return std::move(temp);

}
```

However, our stack is a special case: the methods are small in duration, and enforcing mutual exclusion would not sacrifice performance in most scenarios. But imagine having a linked list that holds millions of nodes, being searched by multiple threads.

Thus, while it is quite easy to encapsulate a regular, non-concurrent container such as `list`, `dequeue`, etc., and regulate access to its methods using a mutex, this coarse approach of locking the entire structure for the exclusive use of one thread would lose its appeal pretty fast.

In the following sections we explore four alternative designs that are suited for different usage scenarios:

- **Fine-grained** synchronization: Structures can be made of several components that do not need to be locked at once. In this design we selectively lock down the concern parts, possibly allowing more threads to access the structure.
- **Optimistic** synchronization: Locking is reserved for the final phase of an operation. For example, searching through a list would be done without locking. Only when the item is found, a lock is acquired and a check performed to ensure that while searching was done the item was not modified (e.g., deleted).
- **Lazy** synchronization: Certain operations can be divided in phases. For example, deleting a node can be performed logically by flagging it as being removed. The physical removal that requires locking can occur less frequently.
- **Non-blocking** synchronization: Using atomic operation to avoid race conditions without locking.

The methods that are presented for non-blocking synchronization can be either *lock-free* or *wait-free*. A lock-free method guarantees that at least some of the threads calling it can complete within a finite number of steps. So while it is possible that some threads could starve, overall the system is progressing. A wait-free method on the other hand guarantees that all the threads calling it can complete within a finite number of steps. Satisfying the wait-free condition is obviously harder than the lock-free one.

The simple data structures discussed in the following sections are implemented based on two designs alternatives: using pointers or using arrays. The latter allows for faster memory management but creates "bounded" structures, i.e., structures that have an upper size limit imposed by the underlying array. Using pointers on the other hand allows for "unbounded" structures, but it can be problematic in terms of memory management, especially when it comes time to deallocate or reuse nodes. In both cases we employ sentinel nodes, i.e., placeholders for the beginning and end (if required) of our structures, that allow special cases, such as empty structures, to be handled gracefully.

Fig. 4.2 shows an example of what these two design alternatives look like for a sorted list of integers. Assuming that the 32 bit numbers to be stored in the list are in the range $[0, 10^6]$, we can use -1 and $2^{31} - 1$ as sentinel values. The array-based representation still uses a "next" field in each node to avoid having to move data around during addition/removal operations, but the "pointers" are now array indices.

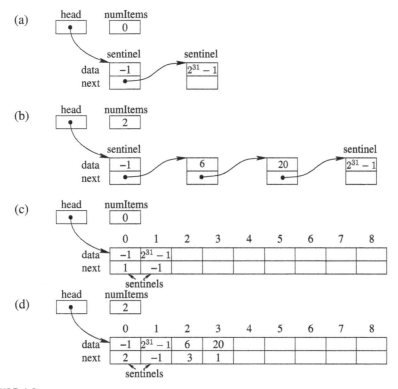

FIGURE 4.2

A sorted list of non-negative integers implemented as (a),(b) a linked list using pointers and as (c),(d) an array of nodes. In (a) and (c) we have an empty list, while in (b) and (d) we have two numbers contained.

The component missing from the array-based representation is the one concerning the management of free nodes. This and other fine details will be examined in the following sections.

4.2 Lock-based structures

4.2.1 Queues

The C++ standard library `queue` class template is a container adaptor in the same fashion as the stack is. However, if we are to allow multiple threads concurrent access to a queue, we cannot settle for a black box, but instead we must provide our own implementation. In order to avoid the problem highlighted in Fig. 4.1 for a stack, we are not considering the implementation of distinct `front` and `back` methods, which only query the corresponding items.

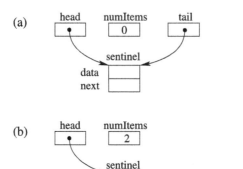

FIGURE 4.3

(a) An empty queue. (b) A queue<int> after inserting items 20 and 6.

Our implementation is based on a linked list. As operations take place only on the two endpoints of the list, we need to have two separate locks, one for the head and one for the tail. This separation can double the number of threads concurrently accessing the queue. The only complication exists when the queue is empty, where both the head and the tail of the queue would need to be modified.

To avoid this special case, we introduce a sentinel node in the queue constructor, i.e., an empty node that is just there to keep the head and tail pointers untangled. An illustration of the queue's node layout is shown in Fig. 4.3.

The code is shown below:

Listing 4.3: A concurrent queue using fine-grained locking.

```
1   // File : queue_fine.hpp
2   template <typename T>
3   class queue{
4   private:
5
6       template <typename W>
7           struct Node{
8               W data;
9               std::unique_ptr<Node<W>> next;
10          };
11
12      std::unique_ptr<Node<T>> head;
13      Node<T> *tail;
14      std::mutex hl, tl;
15      std::atomic<int> numItems =0;
16  public:
17      bool empty();
18      int size();
19      void push_back(T &);
20      T pop_front();
```

```
21        queue();
22 };
23
24 //----------------------------------------------------------------
25 template<typename T> queue<T>::queue()
26 {
27     std::unique_ptr<Node<T>> sentinelNode = std::make_unique<Node<T↩
           >>();
28     head = std::move(sentinelNode);
29     tail = head.get();
30 }
31
32 //----------------------------------------------------------------
33 template<typename T> bool queue<T>::empty()
34 {
35     return numItems.load()==0;
36 }
37
38 //----------------------------------------------------------------
39 template<typename T> int queue<T>::size()
40 {
41     return numItems.load();
42 }
43
44 //----------------------------------------------------------------
45 template<typename T> void queue<T>::push_back(T & i)
46 {
47     std::unique_ptr<Node<T>> newNode = std::make_unique<Node<T>>();
48     newNode->data = i;
49
50     std::lock_guard<std::mutex> lg(tl);
51     tail->next = std::move(newNode);
52     tail = tail->next.get();
53     numItems++;
54 }
```

Our queue incorporates an atomic count of the items present (numItems), effectively eliminating the need to access any of the pointers to check the size of the container. Additionally, the use of the atomic integer eliminates the need to obtain any of the locks for the empty() and size() methods.

Some extra points about the code in Listing 4.3 are explained below:

- As can be observed in Fig. 4.3, the head pointer always points to the sentinel node, making the task of popping the front requiring an extra pointer dereference operation (i.e., head->next = head->next->next, instead of head=head->next). This is a small price to pay though, for making the code easier to maintain and for effectively doubling the concurrency capability of the structure.
- In order to automate the node memory management, smart pointers are used (lines 9 and 12). To avoid the extra overhead of a counter that a shared_ptr needs,

we use `unique_ptr`, but this means that we cannot use a smart pointer type for `tail`, as this would violate the `unique_ptr` specifications.

- In the `push_back` method, there is no need to obtain the lock for the tail (`tl`) before we allocate the node needed to store the new item. Hence the corresponding `lock_guard` definition is left for line 50.

What is missing from Listing 4.3 is the implementation of the `pop_front` method. A naive implementation is shown below. Although it seems to be working, it can lead to problems when two threads simultaneously access both ends of a queue containing a single item. Popping the last item before enqueueing the next one will cause a null pointer exception, as the tail keeps pointing to a now-deleted node.

Listing 4.4: A naive implementation of `pop_front` for a concurrent queue using fine-grained locking.

```
55  template<typename T> T queue<T>::pop_front()
56  {
57      std::lock_guard<std::mutex> lg(hl);
58
59      if(numItems==0)
60          throw empty_queue();
61
62      T temp = std::move(head->next->data);
63      head->next = std::move(head->next->next);
64      numItems--;
65      return std::move(temp);
66  }
```

A working `pop_front` method is shown below, with the added feature that a thread is made to wait for an item to become available in the queue. This is accomplished with the loop of lines 71–72, where the `numItems` atomic integer has to be decremented as long as it is not zero, before execution can continue.

Listing 4.5: A proper implementation of `pop_front` for a concurrent queue using fine-grained locking.

```
67  template<typename T> T queue<T>::pop_front()
68  {
69      std::lock_guard<std::mutex> lg(hl);
70
71      int tmp=numItems;
72      while(tmp ==0 || !numItems.compare_exchange_strong(tmp, tmp-1))↩
            ;
73
74      T temp = std::move(head->next->data);
75      if(head->next->next==nullptr)
76      {
77          std::lock_guard<std::mutex> lg2(tl);
78          if(numItems==0)
79              tail = head.get();
80      }
```

```
81      head->next = std::move(head->next->next);
82      return std::move(temp);
83  }
```

To avoid the shortcomings of the previous `pop_front`, if we detect that we are about to dequeue the last item from the queue (check on line 75), we lock down the `tail` (line 77) and check if the queue is about to become empty (line 78). If it is, `tail` must point to the sentinel node (line 79). This check will fail if a new item has been enqueued. Subsequently, it is time to advance the pointer of the sentinel to the next node (line 81).

Move semantics are used to transport items out of the queue (line 82). This should minimize the cost of the respective operation.

4.2.2 **Lists**

The list structure covered in this section is supposed to represent a set of elements in the way STL's `set` class template does: a container of unique elements, following a particular order. A linked list representation is used as in the previous section, but we have no use for a tail pointer.

In order to support fast comparison between the stored elements, the node structure used here is augmented with an extra field that is supposed to be the hash value of the stored item:

Listing 4.6: Core node structure used in the concurrent lists.

```
1  template <typename W>
2  struct Node{
3      W data;
4      size_t key;
5      std::unique_ptr<Node<W>> next;
6  };
```

The ordering of the nodes within the list is performed based on the `key` field, which is of type `size t`, as the `std::hash` function object template returns a `size_t` result.

In an effort to simplify the code by eliminating the treatment of special cases (i.e., boundary insertions or empty list), the list is having two sentinel nodes: one with the smallest possible value (0) as a key and one with the largest possible value (`std::numeric_limits<size_t>::max()`). This means that none of the items in the list can have a key matching any of these two values. Fortunately, constructing a hash function meeting this criterion is trivial.

4.2.2.1 *List using coarse-grain locks*

The first implementation we consider is the one using a single lock to serialize threads' access, as previously used in Listing 4.1 for a stack. The concurrency part of the structure is pretty straightforward, so we use this section for explaining the core logic for inserting and removing items. The same logic is shared with the remaining synchronization approaches.

The declaration of the class is shown below:

Listing 4.7: A parallel list using coarse-grained synchronization.

```
1    // File : list_coarse.hpp
2
3    template <typename T>
4    class list_coarse{
5    private:
6
7    template <typename W>
8        struct Node{
9            W data;
10           size_t key;
11           std::unique_ptr<Node<W>> next;
12       };
13
14       std::unique_ptr<Node<T>> head;
15       std::mutex lck;
16       int numItems=0;
17   public:
18       bool empty();
19       int size();
20       bool insert(T &);
21       bool erase(T &);
22
23       list_coarse();
24       list_coarse(list_coarse &) = delete;   // delete the default ←↩
             copy constructor and copy assignment
25       list_coarse & operator=(const list_coarse &) = delete;
26   };
27
28   //————————————————————————————————————
29   template <typename T> list_coarse<T>::list_coarse()
30   {
31       std::unique_ptr<Node<T>> smallestSentinel = std::make_unique<Node←↩
             <T>>();
32       smallestSentinel->key=0;
33       std::unique_ptr<Node<T>> biggestSentinel = std::make_unique<Node<←↩
             T>>();
34       biggestSentinel->key = std::numeric_limits<size_t>::max();
35       smallestSentinel->next = std::move(biggestSentinel);
36       head = std::move(smallestSentinel);
37   }
38
39   //————————————————————————————————————
40   template <typename T> bool list_coarse<T>::empty()
41   {
42       std::lock_guard<std::mutex> lg(lck);
43       return numItems==0;
44   }
45
46   //————————————————————————————————————
```

```
47   template <typename T> int list_coarse<T>::size()
48   {
49       std::lock_guard<std::mutex> lg(lck);
50       return numItems;
51   }
```

The layout resulting from the constructor is shown in Fig. 4.4(a). The `next` field for the second sentinel is not initialized as it is never dereferenced.

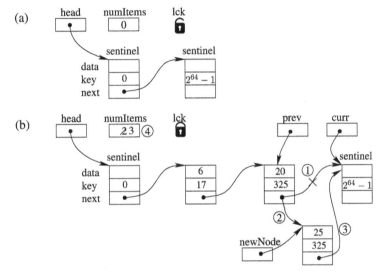

FIGURE 4.4

(a) An empty list assuming a 64-bit architecture. (b) Inserting item 25 in a list of length two. The circled numbers represent the sequence of events after the proper insertion location, as flagged by the prev and curr pointers, is found.

Both insertion and removal logic incorporate a search through the list to locate the node that either equals or exceeds – in terms of its hash value – the item we are trying to add or remove. This is necessary to keep the list ordered. Two pointers "walk over" the list in unison, namely "prev" and "curr," allowing us to interject a new node between two existing ones, or just pop one out. The loop condition using the hash value (`curr->key < ikey`) is found on line 64 below:

Listing 4.8: Insertion in a coarse-grained parallel list.

```
52   template <typename T> bool list_coarse<T>::insert(T & i)
53   {
54       std::lock_guard<std::mutex> lg(lck);
55       std::hash<T> h;
56
57       size_t ikey = h(i);
58       if(ikey==0) ikey++;   // make sure there is no interference with ↩
                the sentinels
```

```
59      else if( ikey== std::numeric_limits<size_t >::max()) ikey--;
60
61      Node<T> *curr, *prev;
62      prev = head.get();
63      curr = head->next.get();
64      while( curr->key < ikey || ( curr->key == ikey && curr->data < i↩
            ))
65      {
66          prev = curr;
67          curr = curr->next.get();
68      }
69      if(curr -> data == i) return false;   // item already exists in ↩
            the list
70
71      std::unique_ptr<Node<T>> newNode = std::make_unique<Node<T>>();
72      newNode->key = ikey;
73      newNode->data= i;
74      newNode->next = std::move(prev->next);
75      prev->next = std::move(newNode);
76      numItems++;
77      return true;
78  }
```

Before traversing the list, lines 55–59 calculate the hash value of the item to be inserted (ikey), making sure we never get a value that coincides with one of the sentinel keys (lines 58–59).

The list traversal starts from the first non-sentinel node (curr pointer initialization on line 63). Checking the hash values alone does not suffice though, as they are not unique. In the case where two different items have the same hash value we need the additional check curr->key == ikey && curr->data < i to keep the loop going. Fig. 4.4(b) illustrates how the loop behaves during insertion to the list if the keys match for unequal items. The loop will continue as long as the keys match and the stored item is smaller than the item to be inserted.

Once the loop exits and there is no duplicate item in the list (line 69), a new node is constructed, populated, and inserted as per the sequence shown in Fig. 4.4(b).

Deleting an item from the list closely resembles the insertion procedure as they both search through the list:

Listing 4.9: Deleting an item from a coarse-grained parallel list.

```
79  template<typename T> bool list_coarse<T>::erase(T &i)
80  {
81      std::lock_guard<std::mutex> lg(lck);
82      std::hash<T> h;
83
84      size_t ikey = h(i);
85      if(ikey==0) ikey++;   // make sure there is no interference with ↩
            the sentinels
86      else if( ikey== std::numeric_limits<size_t >::max()) ikey--;
87
88      Node<T> *curr, *prev;
```

```
89     prev = head.get();
90     curr = head->next.get();
91     while( curr->key < ikey || ( curr->key == ikey && curr->data < i↩
          ))
92     {
93         prev = curr;
94         curr = curr->next.get();
95     }
96     if( curr -> data != i || curr->key == std::numeric_limits<size_t↩
          >::max()) return false;
97
98     prev->next = std::move( curr->next);
99     numItems--;
100    return true;
101 }
```

Code diverges after line 96, where if `curr` does not point to the node containing the desired item, we return `false` for failure. The second part of the condition on line 96 caters for the extraordinary scenario where the uninitialized `data` field of the second sentinel contains a value matching – by accident – the item to be deleted. If that were to happen, in the absence of this check the sentinel node would be deleted, an obviously not sane thing to do!

The coarse-synchronized list will perform adequately if there are not many threads trying to access it and the list stays small in size. As long as the mutex used is a strong one, no starvation will be experienced by the threads as well.

4.2.2.2 List using fine-grain locks

During any single list modification only two nodes are modified: the one preceding in order the one to be inserted/deleted and the one moved in or out of the list. As such, locking the entire list is a complete overkill, as we could just lock down only the preceding node. In addition, we would need to lock down the following node so it is not removed before our operation is complete. This is the principle behind the operation of the fine-grained list. Locking individual nodes requires that the node structure is augmented with a `mutex` field:

Listing 4.10: Node structure for fine-grain locking.

```
1  // File : list_fine.hpp
2  . . .
3  template <typename T>
4  class list_fine{
5  private:
6
7  template <typename W>
8      struct Node{
9          W data;
10         size_t key;
11         std::unique_ptr<Node<W>> next;
12         std::mutex lck;
13     };
```

```
14
15      std::atomic<int> numItems=0;
16  . . .
```

The only modification we need to make to the previous section's code is the locking–unlocking of the *prev and *curr nodes as the list is being traversed, in a "hand-over-hand" way, as shown below:

Listing 4.11: Insert and erase methods for fine-grained list container.

```
17  // File : list_fine.hpp
18  . . .
19  template<typename T> bool list_fine<T>::insert(T & i)
20  {
21      std::hash<T> h;
22      size_t ikey = h(i);
23      if(ikey==0) ikey++;  // make sure there is no interference with ←
            the sentinels
24      else if(ikey== std::numeric_limits<size_t>::max()) ikey--;
25
26      Node<T> *curr, *prev;
27      head->lck.lock();
28      prev = head.get();
29
30      prev->next->lck.lock();
31      curr = head->next.get();
32      while( curr->key < ikey || ( curr->key == ikey && curr->data < i←
            ))
33      {
34          prev->lck.unlock();
35          prev = curr;
36          curr = curr->next.get();
37          curr->lck.lock();
38      }
39      bool res=true;
40      if(curr -> data != i) // item does not exist in the list
41      {
42          std::unique_ptr<Node<T>> newNode = std::make_unique<Node<T>>()←
                ;
43          newNode->key = ikey;
44          newNode->data= i;
45          newNode->next = std::move(prev->next);
46          prev->next = std::move(newNode);
47          numItems++;
48      }
49      else
50          res=false;
51
52      curr->lck.unlock();
53      prev->lck.unlock(); // unlocked last
54      return res;
55  }
56
```

```
57   //————————————————————————————————————————
58   template <typename T> bool list_fine<T>::erase(T &i)
59   {
60       std::hash<T> h;
61       size_t ikey = h(i);
62       if(ikey==0) ikey++;   // make sure there is no interference with ↵
                 the sentinels
63       else if(ikey== std::numeric_limits<size_t>::max()) ikey--;
64
65       Node<T> *curr, *prev;
66       head->lck.lock();
67       prev = head.get();
68
69       prev->next->lck.lock();
70       curr = head->next.get();
71       while( curr->key < ikey || ( curr->key == ikey && curr->data < i↵
                 ))
72       {
73           prev->lck.unlock();
74           prev = curr;
75           curr = curr->next.get();
76           curr->lck.lock();
77       }
78       bool res=true;
79       if(curr -> data == i && curr->key != std::numeric_limits<size_t↵
                 >::max())
80       {
81           prev->next = std::move( curr->next);
82           numItems--;
83       }
84       else
85           res=false;
86
87       curr->lck.unlock();
88       prev->lck.unlock(); // unlocked last
89       return res;
90   }
```

This creates a "pipeline" effect (shown in Fig. 4.5(a)) where threads traverse the list in the order they enter it, forming an implicit traffic queue inside it. So for example, Thread A in Fig. 4.5(a) controls indirectly the progress of Thread B, as Thread B cannot lock its *curr node and advance until Thread A unlocks node "32."

Lines 21–38 of the insert() method are identical to lines 60–77 of erase(), as they represent the list traversal portion of the code. One key aspect of the sequence is that the lock acquisition sequence has to be identical between all threads regardless of the operation they are trying to accomplish. Otherwise, a deadlock is a possibility, as shown in Fig. 4.5(b), where we assume that the lock operations of lines 66 and 69 in erase() have been switched. So, after we unlock the *prev node (line 34), we advance prev and curr (lines 35 and 36) and lock down *curr (line 37).

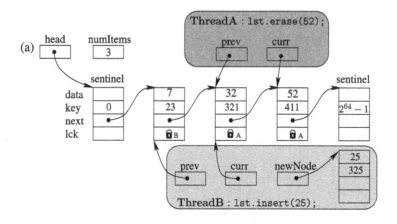

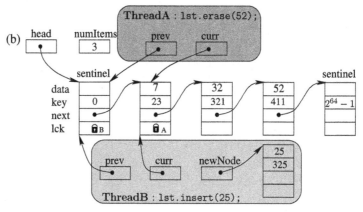

FIGURE 4.5

(a) Fine-grained list being accessed by two threads. Thread A is further ahead down the list and has locked nodes "32" and "52." Thread B cannot proceed until Thread A unlocks node "32." (b) If erase() and insert() acquired the initial nodes in a different order, a deadlock could occur.

Both nodes are unlocked upon termination of the methods, regardless of the successful or not outcome (lines 52–53 and 87–88).

One last modification to the list_fine class compared to list_coarse is that numItems is now an atomic integer (declared on line 15), to ensure data-race-free operation in the absence of a list lock.

4.2.2.3 List using optimistic synchronization

There are two major drawbacks in the fine-grained synchronization list: (a) it still requires a large number of lock–unlock operations, with each causing the kernel to intervene, and (b) threads can form a traffic queue inside the list, with threads unable to pass by one another, even if they eventually act on totally different parts of the list.

The optimistic synchronization approach calls for locking the nodes only when the insertion/deletion point is reached. This constitutes a dramatic reduction in lock-related overhead, and threads do not have to form a traffic queue. What we are optimistic about is that other threads will not modify the list at the locations we are going to act upon. So is this the equivalent of a flying car for our list problems? It could very well be, but there is a caveat: when *prev and *curr are finally locked pending further action, they may not be part of the list anymore! Optimism can fail us sometimes.

To address this new problem, we must reaffirm that *prev and *curr are parts of the list by traversing the list once more. Most of the code is carried over unchanged from the previous section – sans the lock operations:

Listing 4.12: A list container using optimistic synchronization and its insertY method. Only the changes from Listing 4.11 are shown.

```cpp
// File : list_opt.hpp
template < class T > class list_opt
{
private:
  template < class W > class Node
  {

    . . .

    std::shared_ptr < Node < W >> next;
  };

  std::shared_ptr < Node < T >> head;
  bool validate (std::shared_ptr < Node < T >> prev, std::shared_ptr
      < Node < T >> curr);
  . . .
};

//------------------------------------------------
template < class T > bool list_opt < T >::insert (T & i)
{
  std::hash < T > h;
  size_t ikey = h (i);
  if (ikey == 0)  ikey++; // make sure there is no interference with
      the sentinels
  else if (ikey == std::numeric_limits < size_t >::max ()) ikey--;

  bool res;
  while (true)
    {
      std::shared_ptr < Node < T >> prev = atomic_load (&head);
      std::shared_ptr < Node < T >> curr = atomic_load (&(head->next
          ));
      while (curr->key < ikey || (curr->key == ikey && curr->data < 
          i))
        {
          prev = atomic_load (&curr);
          curr = atomic_load (&(curr->next));
```

```
33              }
34          std::lock_guard < std::mutex > lg1 (prev->lck);
35          std::lock_guard < std::mutex > lg2 (curr->lck);
36          if (validate (prev, curr))          // if false repeat from ↵
                  scratch
37          {
38              if (curr->key == ikey && curr->data == i)
39                res = false;
40              else
41                {
42                  std::shared_ptr < Node < T >> newNode = std::↵
                        make_shared < Node < T >> ();
43                  newNode->key = ikey;
44                  newNode->data = i;
45                  newNode->next = atomic_load (&(prev->next));
46                  atomic_store (&(prev->next), newNode);
47                  numItems++;
48                  res = true;
49                }
50              return res;
51          }
52      }
53  }
54
55  //—————————————————————————————————————————
56  template < class T > bool list_opt < T >::validate (std::shared_ptr ↵
        < Node < T >> prev, std::shared_ptr < Node < T >> curr)
57  {
58    std::shared_ptr < Node < T >> np = atomic_load (&head);
59    while (np != nullptr && np != prev && np->data != std::↵
          numeric_limits < size_t >::max ())
60      np = atomic_load (&(np->next));
61    return np == prev && np->next == curr;
62  }
```

As per our discussion so far, once we locate the node candidate for insertion, we lock down the *prev and *curr nodes (lines 34 and 35) and check whether these two are still part of the list by calling the validate method. If the validation comes back affirmative, we conduct the remaining checks (is the item already there?) and potential changes (adding the node). If the validation fails, then we have to repeat the whole process from the beginning (while(true) loop of lines 25–52). Because the lock_guard instances have the block scope of the outer while loop's body, they are destroyed and they release the locks upon the end of the iteration.

The validate method traverses the list until it locates the prev node. When it does, it checks if the following node is pointed to by curr (line 61). Given that these two nodes are already locked and they cannot be modified or removed from the list by another thread, this affirms the validity of the two pointers.

A major difference from the previous implementations is the use of "shared" smart pointers (see lines 8 and 11). The reason for this change is that it is possible for a thread to reach a deleted node and try to access its next field. If unique_ptr were used, dereferencing the `next` pointer would cause a protection fault, as `next` would have been set equal to `nullptr` upon physical deletion of the node. Apart from the small overhead of an additional counter per pointer, this approach still offers automatic memory deallocation, which was the goal of using smart pointers in the first place.

There is just one penalty for using smart pointers: `shared_ptr` is not thread-safe; hence, we must resort to using atomic operations for copying/moving the pointer values between the `shared_ptr` instances (probably involving mutices). This can be seen in many lines of Listing 4.12 (e.g., lines 27, 28, 31, etc.), both in the `insert()` and `validate` methods. The C++20 standard has deprecated the use of the `atomic_load` and `atomic_store` function templates, in favor of the `atomic< shared_ptr >` class template. Unfortunately, at the moment of writing there are no compilers that implement this part of the new standard.

The `erase` method follows the pattern of the previous sections, in that it shares a large portion of the code with the `insert` method: lines 19–36 are identical to lines 67–84 below.

Listing 4.13: The `erase` method of a list container using optimistic synchronization.

```
63   // File : list_opt.hpp
64
65   template < class T > bool list_opt < T >::erase (T & i)
66   {
67     std::hash < T > h;
68     size_t ikey = h (i);
69     if (ikey == 0)  ikey++; // make sure there is no interference with↩
            the sentinels
70     else if (ikey == std::numeric_limits < size_t >::max ()) ikey--;
71
72     bool res;
73     while (true)
74       {
75         std::shared_ptr < Node < T >> prev = atomic_load (&head);
76         std::shared_ptr < Node < T >> curr = atomic_load (&(head->next↩
              ));
77         while (curr->key < ikey || (curr->key == ikey && curr->data < ↩
              i))
78           {
79             prev = atomic_load (&curr);
80             curr = atomic_load (&(curr->next));
81           }
82         std::lock_guard < std::mutex > lg1 (prev->lck);
83         std::lock_guard < std::mutex > lg2 (curr->lck);
84         if (validate (prev, curr))          // if false repeat from ↩
            scratch
85           {
86             bool res = true;
87             if (curr->data == i && curr->key != std::numeric_limits < ↩
                size_t >::max ())
88               {
```

```
89          atomic_store (&(prev->next), curr->next);
90          numItems--;
91        }
92      else
93        res = false;
94
95      return res;
96    }
97  }
98 }
```

Once the two locked nodes are "validated," we can then proceed to remove the desired item. If validation fails, we have to repeat the whole process from the very beginning, just as in the case of `insert`.

But why is it imperative to do the validation in the first place? The example shown in Fig. 4.6 shows a scenario where failure to validate would pretty much render the list corrupted.

More things can go wrong if validation is not performed. These are left as an exercise.

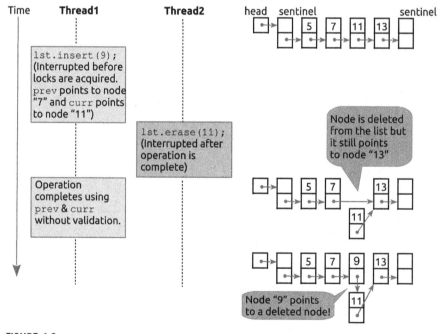

FIGURE 4.6

A possible scenario that shows what would happen if a thread used the locations found during an "optimistic" traversal without validating them first. The state of the list is shown after each modification. After the second thread removes node "11," Thread1 should no longer use what `curr` points to.

It should be noted that the `while(true)` logic in both the `insert` and `erase` methods raises the possibility of starvation. A thread discovering changes during the validation process may – although unlikely – repeat this cycle forever.

This can be an issue in high-contention scenarios, where a large number of threads attempt modifications in a relatively small part of a list. If this is known beforehand, the fine-grain lock approach of the previous section would be a preferable design choice. An alternative could also be to impose a back-off time period, where a thread has to wait before attempting the list traversal again. This is similar to the back-off (exponential or otherwise) techniques employed by communication protocols such as the Internet Protocol. This can be easily incorporated by pairing the `if` statement of line 84 with an `else` block.

4.2.2.4 *List using lazy synchronization*

The optimistic synchronization list solves the problems associated with the fine-grained one, but introduces a new one: the list has to be traversed again just to verify that nothing has changed since the nodes were locked. And the process could be repeated multiple times if it happens that other threads modified the nodes we need to lock.

We could reduce the number of traversals which could be costly if the list is long, if we knew at the moment of locking that the nodes have been modified or dropped from the list. The former we can check just by seeing if `*curr` is still pointed to by `*prev`. The latter we could check if we had a flag that indicated that the node(s) has been removed.

This is the principle behind the operation of the lazy synchronized list: by introducing a Boolean flag to the node structure, we can track its state even after it has been dropped from the list:

Listing 4.14: The `Node` structure for a list container using lazy synchronization.

```
1   // File : list_lazy.hpp
2   template < class W > class Node
3   {
4   public:
5     W data;
6     size_t key;
7     std::shared_ptr < Node < W >> next;
8     bool marked;  // true if node is removed
9     std::mutex lck;
10    Node (): marked{false}, next{nullptr} {};
11  };
```

And as a consequence, we can simplify the `validate` procedure to the following:

Listing 4.15: The `validate` method of a lazy-synchronized list.

```
12  // File : list_lazy.hpp
13  template < class T > bool list_lazy < T >::validate (std::shared_ptr↩
        < Node < T >> prev, std::shared_ptr < Node < T >> curr)
14  {
```

```
15    return !prev–>marked && !curr–>marked && prev–>next == curr;
16  }
```

The `insert` method remains the same as the one shown in Listing 4.12, but the `erase` needs to be slightly augmented to handle the `marked` flag:

Listing 4.16: The `erase` method of a lazy-synchronized list.

```
17  // File : list_lazy.hpp
18  template < class T > bool list_lazy < T >::erase (T & i)
19  {
20    std::hash < T > h;
21    size_t ikey = h (i);
22    if (ikey == 0)  ikey++; // make sure there is no interference with↩
          the sentinels
23    else if (ikey == std::numeric_limits < size_t >::max ()) ikey––;
24
25    bool res;
26    while (true)
27      {
28        std::shared_ptr < Node < T >> prev = atomic_load (&head);
29        std::shared_ptr < Node < T >> curr = atomic_load (&(head–>next↩
            ));
30        while (curr–>key < ikey || (curr–>key == ikey && curr–>data < ↩
            i))
31          {
32            prev = atomic_load (&curr);
33            curr = atomic_load (&(curr–>next));
34          }
35        std::lock_guard < std::mutex > lg1 (prev–>lck);
36        std::lock_guard < std::mutex > lg2 (curr–>lck);
37
38        if (validate (prev, curr))         // if false repeat from ↩
            scratch
39          {
40            bool res = true;
41            if (curr–>data == i && curr–>key != std::numeric_limits < ↩
                size_t >::max ())
42              {
43                curr–>marked = true;       // logical removal
44                atomic_store (&(prev–>next), curr–>next); // physical ↩
                    removal
45                numItems––;
46              }
47            else
48              res = false;
49
50            return res;
51          }
52      }
53  }
```

As can be observed on line 43, before we physically remove a node from the list, we mark it as deleted for other threads to detect. The order of the physical and logical removals is inconsequential as the node is locked during this operation. Another thread will not inspect the `marked` flag of a node it does not "own."

Not everything is rosy though: we still have to repeat the traversal of the list in both the `insert` and `erase` methods if the validation fails. This means that the lazy list is susceptible to causing starvation as in the case of the optimistic list.

4.3 Lock-free structures

After discussing lock-free access to data in the previous chapter, it comes as no surprise that structures can be built to provide concurrent access without using locks.

Lock-free data structures can improve concurrency and scalability by eliminating blocking. Also deadlocks can be disposed of, as we no longer work by locking down resources, but in a way that ensures changes are done in isolation, keeping our data in a consistent state.

The problem of how lock-free structures can be implemented is far from trivial, as a data container is not a single item that we can modify atomically in the same way as an atomic integer. The biggest issue is change detection: how changes perpetrated by other threads can be *reliably* detected and accounted for.

Change detection may entail loops that can be expensive, more so than even locking/unlocking. That is why the question whether locks should be used or not is difficult to answer. It depends on the application domain, the number of threads, and the relative frequency of the operations performed. At the end of this chapter we attempt an evaluation of all the different techniques, but it is definitely not an answer to all the questions one might pose.

The task at hand seems an impossible one: how can a thread assert that a structure is in a particular state when after it accesses it, another thread can modify it at will, making the acquired information invalid? There are a number of steps one can take towards this goal:

- Whenever a thread is reading the state of the structure or the part that is desired to change, this has to be done in one atomic step, even if this involves the acquisition of several pieces of information.
- Any change has to be applied in a way that "appears" to be atomic to the other threads, i.e., as if happening at a single instance in time, the so-called linearization point (see also Section 3.5). For example, inserting a new node in a linked list may take a number of steps like creating the node, populating its fields, etc. However, making the node appear in the list, i.e., become visible to the other threads, has to be an atomic operation.
- A memory reclamation scheme should be used to avoid having threads access deleted memory.

- Sequential consistency memory ordering should be used, at least at the prototyping stage.
- Testing has to be rigorous. Something that "seems" to work for a dozen threads can fail catastrophically for a few hundred threads. Let us elaborate:
  - Putting the structure "under stress" in order to verify that it works means using as many threads as possible.
  - For bounded structures, i.e., structures that have a maximum a priori specified size, making them smaller will magnify the possibility of failure if one exists.
  - Insertion and deletion can be tested separately in initial testing. Mixing them at a later stage can reveal unseen problems.

The algorithms presented in the following sections are adaptations from the seminal book by Herlihy and Shavit [30].

The stack is the simplest of the containers we are examining, so we will begin our discussion with it.

4.3.1 Lock-free stacks

4.3.1.1 A lock-free stack with explicit memory management

A stack is special amongst our considered containers, in the sense that we have only one point of contention between our threads: the top of the stack. The result is that we can ensure a thread-safe operation just by making all changes to the top atomic.

To achieve this feat we can implement our stack as a linked list and employ an atomic pointer to point to the head of the list, as shown below:

Listing 4.17: A lock-free stack.

```cpp
// File : stack_lock_free.hpp
template <typename T>
class stack_lock_free
{
private:
template <typename W>
    struct Node{
        W data;
        Node<W> * next;
    };

    std::atomic<Node<T> *> head;

public:
    T pop();
    void push(const T&);
    stack_lock_free(){ head.store(nullptr);}
    stack_lock_free(const stack_lock_free &) = delete;
    stack_lock_free & operator=(const stack_lock_free &) = delete;
};

//
```

```
23   template <typename T>
24   void stack_lock_free<T>::push(const T&i)
25   {
26       Node<T> *newNode = new Node<T>;
27       newNode->data = i;
28       newNode->next = head.load();
29       while(! head.compare_exchange_weak( newNode->next, newNode) );
30   }
31
32   //--------------------------------------------------
33   template <typename T>
34   T stack_lock_free<T>::pop()
35   {
36       Node<T> *candidate = head.load();
37       while(candidate != nullptr && !head.compare_exchange_weak(↩
             candidate, candidate->next));
38       if(candidate == nullptr) throw empty_stack();
39       T tmp = candidate->data;
40       delete candidate;
41       return std::move(tmp);
42   }
```

In order to push an item onto the stack, a new node is created, populated, and made to initially point to where head points to (lines 26–28). To complete the push operation, we need to make the head point to the new node. To ensure that head was not modified by another thread after executing line 28, a compare_exchange_weak operation is performed on the head atomic pointer, updating the next pointer of the new node, until a match is accomplished and the head is made to point to newNode.

A similar approach is followed for the pop operation: the head pointer is copied, then atomically compared with the value retrieved, and if successful, set to point to the next node (line 37). As long as the list is not empty that is.

Then, after having successfully extracted the node from the stack, we can return its contents to the caller.

The use of the while loops on lines 29 and 37 is not mandated just by the semantics of the "weak" compare-and-exchange variant, but also by the need to repeat the operation until the head can be successfully modified. This makes our implementation lock-free but not wait-free, as there is no upper bound on the iterations required to enact the change in the stack. This is a common feature of all the implementations in this section, including the one in Section 4.3.1.2.

A major difference from our previous lock-based linked lists is that memory is explicitly managed via regular pointers. The continuous creation (line 26) and deletion (line 40) of nodes in push and pop, respectively, creates a significant overhead that could be mitigated by having a custom memory management for Node instances.

The idea is to keep a list of the Node instances when they get popped from the stack and reuse them in subsequent push operations. This way we can postpone the deallocation of the nodes until the stack is destroyed.

All we need in terms of implementation is to add an extra atomic pointer in our stack class to handle the list of free nodes and methods for inserting and removing nodes to it. Inserting and deleting from the list of free nodes work in a very similar fashion to the push and pop stack methods seen above:

Listing 4.18: A lock-free stack with built-in custom node memory management.

```
1   // File : stack_lock_free_v2.hpp
2   template < typename T > class stack_lock_free
3   {
4   private:
5     template < typename W > struct Node
6     {
7       W data;
8       Node < W > *next;
9     };
10
11    std::atomic < Node < T > *>head;
12    std::atomic < Node < T > *>freeNodes;
13
14  //————————————————
15    Node < T > *getFree ()
16    {
17      Node < T > *tmp = freeNodes;
18      while (tmp != nullptr && !freeNodes.compare_exchange_weak (tmp, ↩
              tmp->next));
19      if (tmp == nullptr)
20        tmp = new Node < T > ();
21      return tmp;
22    }
23  //————————————————
24    void releaseNode (Node < T > *n)
25    {
26      n->next = freeNodes;
27      while (!freeNodes.compare_exchange_weak (n->next, n));
28    }
29  //————————————————
30
31  public:
32    . . .
33    stack_lock_free ()
34    {
35      head.store (nullptr);
36      freeNodes.store (nullptr);
37    }
38    ~stack_lock_free ();
39    stack_lock_free (const stack_lock_free &) = delete;
40    stack_lock_free & operator= (const stack_lock_free &) = delete;
41  };
42
43  //————————————————————————————
44  template < typename T > stack_lock_free < T >::~stack_lock_free ()
45  {
46    Node < T > *tmp, *aux;
47    tmp = freeNodes;
```

```
48    while (tmp != nullptr)
49      {
50        aux = tmp->next;
51        delete tmp;
52        tmp = aux;
53      }
54    tmp = head;
55    while (tmp != nullptr)
56      {
57        aux = tmp->next;
58        delete tmp;
59        tmp = aux;
60      }
61  }
62
```

The `releaseNode` method of lines 24–28 adds to the list of free nodes by performing an atomic compare-and-exchange operation on the `freeNodes` pointer.

In turn, the `getFree` method of lines 15–22 tries to get one of the unused nodes from the free list by doing a compare-and-exchange operation to make the `freeNodes` pointer advance to the next node. If no free nodes exist, the `new` operator is invoked (line 20) to create a `Node` instance we can return to the caller.

An explicit destructor is needed to avoid memory leaks. The one on lines 44–61 traverses both lists pointed by `head` and `freeNodes`, respectively, and frees each individual node.

Another issue with the solution of Listing 4.17 is the program-terminating exception that is thrown if the stack is empty (Listing 4.17, line 38). The exception is an improper way to flag this condition. If we would like to stick with the lock-free theme and avoid the use of a condition variable for signaling "poppers" from "pushers," we can have a working pop method by modifying its signature to `bool pop(T &)`, allowing us to return false in the case of a failure.

With this modification and the use of `getFree()` and `releaseNode()`, we can write the new push and pop methods:

Listing 4.19: Push and pop methods for a lock-free stack with built-in custom node memory management.

```
63  // File : stack_lock_free_v2.hpp
64  template < typename T > class stack_lock_free
65  {
66      . . .
67  public:
68    bool pop (T &);
69      . . .
70  };
71
72  //-----------------------------------------------
73  template < typename T > void stack_lock_free < T >::push (const T & ↩
        t )
74  {
```

```
75    Node < T > *newNode = getFree ();
76    newNode->data = i;
77    newNode->next = head.load ();
78    while (!head.compare_exchange_weak (newNode->next, newNode));
79  }
80
81  //————————————————————————————————
82  template < typename T > bool stack_lock_free < T >::pop (T &i)
83  {
84    Node < T > *candidate = head.load ();
85    while (candidate != nullptr && !head.compare_exchange_weak (↵
          candidate, candidate->next));
86    if (candidate == nullptr)
87      return false;
88    i = std::move(candidate->data);
89    releaseNode (candidate);
90    return true;
91  }
```

The changes are located on line 89, where we now call `releaseNode` instead of `delete`, and on line 75, where we call `getFree` instead of `new`.

4.3.1.2 A lock-free stack using smart pointers

We can automate the node-related memory management for our list via smart pointers. The only condition is that the standard library implementation provides lock-free atomic operations on smart pointers. We can verify that this is the case by using a code snippet similar to:

```
1  shared_ptr<int> aux;
2  cout << "Is lock free " << atomic_is_lock_free( &aux ) << endl;
```

If the output of the above call is "1," then the following implementation is lock-free. Otherwise, every atomic operation on our shared pointers involves the acquisition of a lock:

Listing 4.20: A linked-list stack implementation using smart pointers. Only the differences from Listings 4.18 and 4.19 are shown.

```
1   // File : stack_lock_free_smart.hpp
2   template < typename T > class stack_lock_free_smart
3   {
4   private:
5     template < typename W > struct Node
6     {
7       W data;
8       std::shared_ptr<Node < W >> next;
9     };
10
11    std::shared_ptr<Node<T>> head;
12    . . .
13  };
```

```
14    //─────────────────────────────────────────
15    template < typename T > void stack_lock_free_smart < T >::push (↩
          const T & i)
16    {
17      std::shared_ptr<Node < T >> newNode = std::make_shared<Node<T>>();
18      newNode->data = i;
19      newNode->next = std::atomic_load(&head);
20      while (!std::atomic_compare_exchange_weak (&head, &(newNode->next)↩
          , newNode));
21    }
22
23    //─────────────────────────────────────────
24    template < typename T > bool stack_lock_free_smart < T >::pop (T &i)
25    {
26      std::shared_ptr<Node < T >> candidate = std::atomic_load(&head);
27      while (candidate != nullptr && !std::atomic_compare_exchange_weak ↩
          (&head, &candidate, candidate->next));
28      if (candidate == nullptr)
29        return false;
30      i = std::move(candidate->data);
31      return true;
32    }
```

The `atomic_compare_exchange_weak` function calls of lines 20 and 27 behave similarly to their atomic method counterparts.

The signature of the function is:

```
template< class T >
bool atomic_compare_exchange_weak( std::atomic<T>* obj,
            typename std::atomic<T>::value_type* expected,
            typename std::atomic<T>::value_type desired ) noexcept;
```

If the value of `*obj` matches the value of `*expected`, `desired` is stored in `*obj` and `true` is returned. Otherwise, `*obj` is stored in `*expected` and `false` is returned. Starting with C++20, the comparison is based on the binary representation of the objects. The value copies are performed in binary as well, so shallow object copies are performed.

Although this is clearly a shorter implementation, it might not be the best-performing one. Avoiding allocation/deallocation of nodes by "recycling" them, as in Listings 4.18 and 4.19, is the best way to go.

4.3.2 A bounded lock-free queue: first attempt

Queues present double the challenge of a stack (literally!), as we now have two endpoints to worry about. And to this we also have to add the hassle of properly maintaining the nodes used to build the structure, as we cannot afford to deallocate them before all the threads that could access them are done.

In this section we present a variation of the memory management scheme discussed in Section 4.3.1.1, in the form of a *bounded* queue. The term "bounded" refers to limiting the queue to a maximum size, beyond which it cannot grow. While a bounded queue may be undesirable for some applications, this design sports a fast memory management that could boost performance significantly.

The layout of our queue is similar to the one depicted in Fig. 4.3, i.e., a head and a tail pointer initialized to point to a sentinel node. However, the "bounded" attribute allows us to incorporate two significant changes to the design:

(1) All nodes are preallocated by the constructor as a single array. To maintain the nodes, the structure keeps two internal queues: one for holding the actual data (delimited by pointers head and tail) and one for holding the free/unused nodes (delimited by pointers freeHead and freeTail).

(2) As the nodes can be identified by their index in the node array, all pointers are integers. The ones that need to be atomically modified, such as head and tail, are defined as atomic<int>.

Each of the two queues starts with a sentinel node that is never actually used to store data. The sentinels are merely keeping the queues from running out of nodes and thus simplifying the code. As such, head always points to node 0 and freeHead always points to node 1 in the array of nodes:

Listing 4.21: Class definition for a bounded lock-free queue class template.

```cpp
// File : queue_lock_free_bound.hpp
//————————————————————————————————
template < typename T > class queue_lock_free_bounded
{
private:

  template < typename W > struct alignas (2) Node
  {
    W data;
    std::atomic < int >next;
    std::atomic < int >delNext;
  };

  std::atomic < int >head;
  std::atomic < int >tail;
  std::atomic < int >freeHead;
  std::atomic < int >freeTail;
  std::atomic < int >numItems = 0;
  std::atomic < int >numFreeItems;

  int getFree ();
  void makeFree (int);
  Node < T > *store;
  int storeSize;        // size of array store
public:
  bool empty ();
  int size ();
  void enqueue (T &);
  T dequeue ();
```

```
30
31     queue_lock_free_bounded (int ss = 100);
32     ~queue_lock_free_bounded ();
33     queue_lock_free_bounded (queue_lock_free_bounded &) = delete; // ↩
           delete the default copy constructor and copy assignment
34     queue_lock_free_bounded & operator= (const queue_lock_free_bounded↩
           &) = delete;
35   };
36
37   //─────────────────────────────────────────────
38   template < typename T > queue_lock_free_bounded < T >::↩
           queue_lock_free_bounded (int ss)
39   {
40     store = new Node < T >[ss];
41     storeSize = ss;
42     freeHead = 1;                      // unused nodes
43     freeTail = storeSize − 1;
44     for (int i = 1; i < ss − 1; i++)
45       store[i].delNext = i + 1;
46     store[ss − 1].delNext = −1;
47
48     numFreeItems.store (storeSize − 2);
49     store[0].next = −1;
50     head = 0;
51     tail = 0;
52   }
53
54   //─────────────────────────────────────────────
55   template < typename T > queue_lock_free_bounded < T >::~↩
           queue_lock_free_bounded ()
56   {
57     delete [] store;
58   }
59
60   //─────────────────────────────────────────────
61   template < typename T > bool queue_lock_free_bounded < T >::empty ()
62   {
63     return numItems == 0;
64   }
65
66   //─────────────────────────────────────────────
67   template < typename T > int queue_lock_free_bounded < T >::size ()
68   {
69     return numItems;
70   }
```

The two internal queues are initialized in the constructor (lines 38–52), using −1 as a termination constant for the linked lists. The node structure is equipped with two "pointers" for each of the two lists (next and delNext), allowing the traversal of the two lists independently.

The exact memory layout corresponding to the code shown above is illustrated in Fig. 4.7.

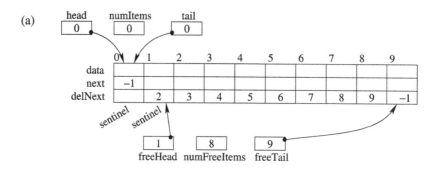

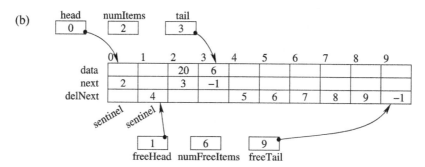

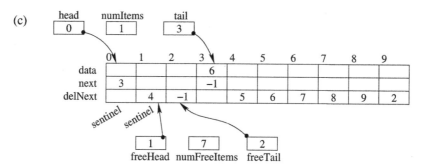

FIGURE 4.7

(a) An empty `queue_lock_free_bounded<int>`, with a maximum capacity of 8. Node "0" is used as a sentinel for the data queue and node "1" is used as a sentinel for the free node queue. (b) The queue after inserting items 20 and 6. The free node queue sentinel now points to node "4". Node "2" is at the head of the data queue. (c) The state of the queue after dequeuing 20. Node "2", which was dequeued, is now at the tail of the free node queue.

The two internal queues are managed in the same exact fashion, so we analyze the inner workings of just one of them. The `enqueue` and `dequeue` methods for the data queue map to the `makeFree` and `getFree` methods, respectively, for the free nodes queue. The latter are called by the former to get or release a node.

The enqueue logic for both internal queues is shown below:

Listing 4.22: Enqueue logic for a bounded lock-free queue class template.

```cpp
// File : queue_lock_free_bound.hpp
//------------------------------------------
// Enqueue for the free nodes list
template < typename T > void queue_lock_free_bounded < T >::makeFree↩
    (int currIdx)
{
  store[currIdx].delNext = −1;
  while (true)
    {
      int tmpIdx = freeTail.load ();
      int nextIdx = store[freeTail].delNext;
      if (tmpIdx == freeTail.load ())
        {
          if (nextIdx == −1)
            {
              if (store[tmpIdx].delNext.compare_exchange_strong (↩
                  nextIdx, currIdx))
                {
                  freeTail.compare_exchange_strong (tmpIdx, currIdx)↩
                    ;   // if it fails next iteration will advance↩
                     it
                  numFreeItems++;
                  return;
                }
            }
          else
            freeTail.compare_exchange_strong (tmpIdx, nextIdx);
        }
    }
}

//------------------------------------------
template < typename T > void queue_lock_free_bounded < T >::enqueue ↩
    (T & i)
{
  int newIdx;
  newIdx = getFree ();
  store[newIdx].data = i;  // init fields of new node
  store[newIdx].next = −1;

  while (true)
    {
      int lastIdx = tail.load ();
      int nextIdx = store[tail].next;   // should be =−1
      if (lastIdx == tail.load ())
        {
          if (nextIdx == −1)
            {
              if (store[tail].next.compare_exchange_strong (nextIdx,↩
                  newIdx))
                {
```

```
116              tail.compare_exchange_strong (lastIdx, newIdx);
117              numItems++;
118              return;
119            }
120          }
121        else
122          tail.compare_exchange_strong (lastIdx, nextIdx);
123        }
124      }
125  }
```

The key points of the `enqueue` method are as follows:

- We begin by acquiring a free node from the corresponding list on line 102.
- The queue modification process is enclosed in a `while(true)` loop, so that if any change that is incoherent with the thread's knowledge about the status of the queue is detected, we start all over again.
- Checks for changes perpetrated by other threads are conducted at:
  - Line 110: Is the index of the last node read still stored at the `tail`?
  - Line 112: Is the index stored in the `next` field of the last node still −1? Otherwise another node has been added to the queue.
  - Line 114: Were we successful at atomically changing the `next` field of the last node to point to our newly enqueued node?
- If the last check succeeds, we have enqueued a new node. We can then atomically update the `tail` (line 116), but this is not a step where failure should result in restarting the process, as the new node is already in the queue. Thus, restarting at this point would insert multiple copies of the same data in the queue. If the `tail` update fails, we get one more chance to update it when another thread runs the check of line 112. If a discrepancy is discovered, the body of the else on line 122 ensures that the `tail` will point to the proper node.
- The reason all the methods in this section utilize the `compare_exchange_strong` call for atomic changes is that the weak variant can produce spurious failures. These would be detrimental for performance, as in almost all cases they would lead to a restart of the whole process.

The `dequeue` and `getFree` methods also mirror each other:

Listing 4.23: Dequeue logic for a bounded lock-free queue class template.

```
126  // File : queue_lock_free_bound.hpp
127  //────────────────────────────────────────
128  template < typename T > int queue_lock_free_bounded < T >::getFree ↵
          ()
129  {
130    int newIdx;
131    int succIdx;
132    while (true)
133      {
134        newIdx = store[freeHead].delNext;
```

```
135       if (numFreeItems == 0 || newIdx == -1)
136         {
137            std::this_thread::yield ();
138            continue;
139         }
140       if (store[freeHead].delNext == newIdx)
141         {
142            succIdx = store[newIdx].delNext;
143            if (succIdx == -1)
144              if (!freeTail.compare_exchange_strong (newIdx, freeHead)↩
                       )    // free list became empty
145                continue;
146            if (store[freeHead].delNext.compare_exchange_strong (↩
                     newIdx, succIdx))
147                break;
148         }
149     }
150   numFreeItems--;
151   return newIdx;
152 }
153
154 //————————————————————————————————
155 template < typename T > T queue_lock_free_bounded < T >::dequeue ()
156 {
157   int poppedIdx;
158   int nextIdx;
159   while (true)
160     {
161       poppedIdx = store[head].next;
162       if (numItems == 0 || poppedIdx == -1)
163         {
164            std::this_thread::yield ();
165            continue;
166         }
167       if (store[head].next == poppedIdx)
168         {
169            nextIdx = store[poppedIdx].next;
170            if (nextIdx == -1)
171              if (!tail.compare_exchange_strong (poppedIdx, head))    ↩
                     // tail should point to where head points to when ↩
                     queue becomes empty
172                continue;
173            if (store[head].next.compare_exchange_strong (poppedIdx, ↩
                     nextIdx))
174                break;
175         }
176     }
177   T tmp = std::move (store[poppedIdx].data);
178   makeFree (poppedIdx);
179   numItems--;
180   return std::move (tmp);
181 }
```

The key points of the dequeue method are as follows:

- As with the enqueue method, the modification process is enclosed in a while(true) loop, to allow for the process to restart in the event of discovering a discrepancy.
- The "sanity" checks are conducted at:
  - Line 167: Is the sentinel still pointing to the node to be dequeued (indexed by poppedIdx)?
  - Line 170: If there is nothing following the node to be dequeued (nextIdx == -1), then the list will become empty. Thus tail has to be made to point at the sentinel. If the tail update fails on line 171 we start all over.
  - Line 173: If we can make the sentinel point to the next node, the node has been dequeued and we can break the infinite loop to deliver the data to the caller. Otherwise, the process is repeated.
- Once we remove the node from the list, we can move its data contents to a temporary variable (line 177), before handing the node over to the free node list (line 178).
- A thorny issue in the design of the dequeue method is what should happen if there are no data in the queue. The condition of line 162 uses both the numItems atomic counter and the poppedIdx to verify if this is happening. Out of all the possible actions, our design choice is to make the thread wait for an item to become available. Similarly, in the getFree method, a thread is made to wait for a free node to become available when the queue has reached its maximum capacity.

So what is the key design strategy behind the methods described above? It boils down to two things: (a) Perform a series of tests to ensure that the state of the queue was not modified by another thread. If any such modification is detected the process starts again. (b) Modify the state of the queue in a critical single step known as the *linearization point*. Once we successfully perform this step, all other threads will be able to detect and react to the change performed. The linearization point for enqueue is line 114 (changing the tail node's next pointer), while for dequeue it is line 173 (changing the sentinel's next pointer). Once line 114 succeeds, even if line 116 (tail update) fails, the next thread to attempt an enqueue operation will detect the discrepancy and "assist" by changing the tail (line 122).

Having gone through all these checks, the previous methods seem bulletproof. Alas, they are actually broken, as they are susceptible to the ABA problem.

4.3.3 The ABA problem

ABA refers to a list node removal/insertion scenario that leads to the corruption of the list, on the condition that *nodes are reused*, as in our bounded lock-free queue.

Such a sequence of steps is shown in Fig. 4.8 for a generic list. Although it is really difficult for such a scenario to materialize, it is certainly not impossible and the consequences are dire.

One way to eliminate the ABA problem is to not recycle the nodes. However, another problem is raised then: when is it allowed to delete a node? How do you

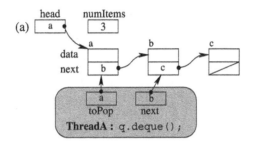

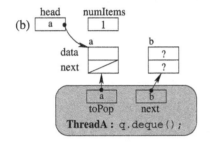

FIGURE 4.8

(a) Thread A has called the `dequeue` method and has been interrupted after acquiring references to the first and second node in the list. (b) While Thread A was not running, other threads emptied the list from all the nodes, and one inserted the "recycled" node at address "a," which is now again at the head of the list. Executing a compare-and-exchange operation to modify the `head` would be successful. But then it would point to "b," which is no longer part of the list!

know there is no other thread trying to access it at that moment or shortly after? Access to deleted memory is according to the C++ standard producing "undefined behavior," or in other words it can get us into trouble, the least of which is a program crash because then we would know that something is wrong. Techniques for dealing with this problem are discussed later.

Several techniques exist for solving the ABA problem. One is to tag the nodes with an integer stamp, i.e., a counter that is incremented every time the node is inserted into the list. A recycled node would have a different stamp from the one originally acquired by a thread that was interrupted and facing an ABA scenario. The problem in implementing this solution is that the node addresses/references and their stamps have to be accessed in an atomic fashion. In C++ this would require either the use of a lock or bit manipulation of the address bits.

This last sentence requires a bit more elaboration: in contemporary 64-bit architectures, a bunch of higher-order bits remain unused, either by design or by technology limitations. At the moment of this writing, the largest HPC "fat" node one can buy can have up to 4 TiB of memory, which requires 42 address bits. Also, the AMD64 architecture uses 48 of the 64 address bits, "sign extending" the 47th bit (bit count starts from zero) to the remaining higher-order 16 address bits. This means that we could store a 16-bit integer in a pointer, as long as we extract and reset the counter bits prior to dereferencing it.

Another solution is to hold off committing deleted nodes to the free nodes list, until there are no threads trying to remove nodes from the data list. This is the easiest solution by far, as we can detect that this condition is true by maintaining an atomic integer that is incremented whenever a thread calls dequeue/remove and decremented as it exits the method. This solution is explained further in the following section.

4.3.4 A fixed bounded lock-free queue

The ABA problem affects the bounded lock-free queue of Listings 4.21–4.23, as the released nodes can be recycled and reenter the data queue before an interrupted thread resumes execution.

Initially we take a look at the "popper" threads, i.e., the ones trying to dequeue an item by attempting to advance the head of the data queue to the next node.

The changes that we need to introduce are shown below:

Listing 4.24: A modified bound lock-free queue that solves the ABA problem for the "popper" nodes. Only the changes from Listings 4.21–4.23 are shown.

```
1   // File : queue_lock_free_bound_aba.hpp
2   //————————————————————————————————————
3   template < typename T > class queue_lock_free_bounded
4   {
5   private :
6     std :: atomic < int >numContestedFreeNodes=0;
7     std :: atomic < int >numPoppers =0;
8       . . .
9   };
10
11  //————————————————————————————————————
12  template < typename T > void queue_lock_free_bounded < T >::makeFree↩
         (int currIdx)
13  {
14    store[currIdx].delNext = −1;
15    while (true)
16      {
17        int tmpIdx = freeTail.load ();
18        int nextIdx = store[freeTail].delNext;
19        if (tmpIdx == freeTail.load ())
20          {
21            if (nextIdx == −1)
22              {
23                if (store[tmpIdx].delNext.compare_exchange_strong (↩
                     nextIdx, currIdx))
24                  {
25                    freeTail.compare_exchange_strong (tmpIdx, currIdx)↩
                       ;   // if it fails next iteration will advance↩
                         it
```

```cpp
26                    numContestedFreeNodes++; // for the newly freed ↩
                          node
27
28                    if(numPoppers==0)
29                    {
30                        int tmp = numContestedFreeNodes;
31                        // make sure numContestedFreeNodes is modified↩
                              atomically
32                        while(!numContestedFreeNodes.↩
                              compare_exchange_weak(tmp, 0));
33                        numFreeNodes += tmp;
34                    }
35                    return;
36                }
37            }
38            else
39                freeTail.compare_exchange_strong (tmpIdx, nextIdx);
40        }
41    }
42 }
43
44 //————————————————————————————————————
45 template < typename T > T queue_lock_free_bounded < T >::dequeue ()
46 {
47    int poppedIdx, nextIdx;
48    numPoppers++;
49    while (true)
50      {
51        poppedIdx = store[head].next;
52        if (numItems == 0 || poppedIdx == −1)
53          {
54            numPoppers−−;
55            std::this_thread::yield ();
56            numPoppers++;
57            continue;
58          }
59        if (store[head].next == poppedIdx)
60          {
61            nextIdx = store[poppedIdx].next;
62            if (nextIdx == −1)
63              if (!tail.compare_exchange_strong (poppedIdx, head)) // ↩
                      tail should point to where head points to when queue↩
                      becomes empty
64                continue;
65            if (store[head].next.compare_exchange_strong (poppedIdx, ↩
                  nextIdx))
66              break;
67          }
68      }
69    T tmp = std::move (store[poppedIdx].data);
70    numPoppers−−;
71    makeFree (poppedIdx);
```

```
72    numItems--;
73    return std::move (tmp);
74  }
```

There are two additions to our class: one atomic integer counting the number of "popper" threads (line 7) and one atomic integer counting the number of "contested" free nodes (line 6). The latter are released nodes that have been *added to the free nodes* list, but they are not ready yet for "consumption," i.e., they cannot reenter the data queue. Only `numFreeNodes` nodes of those present in the free node list are allowed to reenter the data queue.

The contested free nodes are allowed to switch to really free ones, if there are no "popper" threads active. Whenever a node is released by calling `makeFree`, it is firstly added to the free list, before checking if the `numPoppers` counter is zero. If this is true, we should be able to do:

```
numFreeNodes += numContestedFreeNodes +1;
numContestedFreeNodes.store(0);
```

However, if multiple threads are executing this code, we would end up with a race condition despite having no data races, courtesy of the atomic variables. The reason is of course that these two statements are not indivisible, so we could have two threads execute the first one, before either reaches the second.

The solution is to reset `numContestedFreeNodes` using the `compare_exchange_weak` operation on line 32, which allows keeping the old value in `tmp` for adding to `numFreeNodes`.

The `numPoppers` counter, which is critical for running `makeFree` properly, is modified in the `dequeue` method. It is incremented on entry (line 48) and decremented on exit (line 70) after the required data list manipulation is complete. It is also modified on lines 54 and 56, before interrupting and after resuming the execution of the thread, as when this happens we effectively restart the `dequeue` method from the beginning, leaving no room for ABA to materialize.

Alas, we are not done. Our bound lock-free queue features two internal queues. The modifications shown in Listing 4.24 solve the ABA problem for the "poppers" of the data queue. What about the "poppers" of the free nodes list, i.e., the threads which call `enqueue`? These data-queue "pusher" threads could certainly fall victim to the ABA problem on the free nodes list. We can solve this problem mirroring the changes we did for the data queue:

Listing 4.25: A modified bound lock-free queue that solves the ABA problem for the "pusher" nodes. Only the additions to Listing 4.24 are shown.

```
75  // File : queue_lock_free_bound_aba.hpp
76  //----------------------------------------------
77  template < typename T > class queue_lock_free_bounded
78  {
79  private:
80    std::atomic < int >numContestedItems=0;
81    std::atomic < int >numPushers=0;
```

```
82      . . .
83    };
84
85    //————————————————————————————————————
86    template < typename T > int queue_lock_free_bounded < T >::getFree ↩
          ()
87    {
88      int newIdx;
89      int succIdx;
90      numPushers++;
91      while (true)
92        {
93          newIdx = store[freeHead].delNext;
94          if (numFreeNodes == 0 || newIdx == −1)
95            {
96              numPushers−−;
97              std::this_thread::yield ();
98              numPushers++;
99              continue;
100           }
101         if (store[freeHead].delNext == newIdx)
102           {
103             succIdx = store[newIdx].delNext;
104             if (succIdx == −1)
105               if (!freeTail.compare_exchange_strong (newIdx, freeHead)↩
                    )   // free list became empty
106                 continue;
107             if (store[freeHead].delNext.compare_exchange_strong (↩
                  newIdx, succIdx))
108               break;
109           }
110       }
111     numPushers−−;
112     numFreeNodes−−;
113     return newIdx;
114   }
115
116   //————————————————————————————————————
117   template < typename T > void queue_lock_free_bounded < T >::enqueue ↩
          (T & i)
118   {
119     int newIdx;
120     newIdx = getFree ();
121     store[newIdx].data = i;
122     store[newIdx].next = −1;
123
124     while (true)
125       {
126         int lastIdx = tail.load ();
127         int nextIdx = store[tail].next;   // should be =−1
128         if (lastIdx == tail.load ())
129           {
```

```
130          if (nextIdx == -1)
131            {
132              if (store[tail].next.compare_exchange_strong (nextIdx,↩
                    newIdx))
133                {
134                  tail.compare_exchange_strong (lastIdx, newIdx);
135                  numContestedItems++; // add one for the newly ↩
                      enqueued node
136
137                  if (numPushers==0)
138                    {
139                      int tmp = numContestedItems;
140                      // make sure numContestedItems is modified ↩
                          atomically
141                      while (!numContestedItems.compare_exchange_weak↩
                          (tmp, 0));
142                      numItems += tmp;
143                    }
144
145                  return;
146                }
147            }
148          else
149            tail.compare_exchange_strong (lastIdx, nextIdx);
150        }
151    }
152 }
```

The changes in `enqueue` reflect those in `makeFree`, and the changes in `getFree` mirror the ones made in `dequeue`. So, we have two additional atomic counters, one measuring the "pusher" threads (`numPushers` defined on line 81) and one for the new data nodes that have been added to the queue but are not safe to be released yet (`numContestedItems` defined on line 80).

The `numPushers` counter is incremented as soon as a thread enters the `getFree` method (line 90), which pops a node from the free node list, and decremented on exit (line 111). Also, if there are no free nodes that can be popped and a thread is forced to restart after surrendering the CPU, `numPushers` is decremented before the interrupt (line 96) and incremented when execution resumes (line 98).

Once the "pusher" threads complete the changes to the data queue, they check the value of `numPushers`. If it is zero, it is safe to make the `numContestedItems` newly added items available for dequeuing. To avoid a race condition, this is accomplished by atomically changing `numContestedItems` to zero while keeping its value in a temporary variable (lines 139–142).

4.3.5 An unbounded lock-free queue

Reusing nodes in list-based structures is arguably the way to go, despite the slight complication that dealing with the ABA issue brings. However, a bounded queue is not the proper solution for all problem domains, especially when the size of the queue can vary wildly from one problem instance to the next and there is no reliable way of calculating it a priori.

An unbounded queue can be built on the same memory recycling principles as our bounded queue. There are a few things that need to be modified in the `queue_lock_free_bounded` class template to this end:

(a) Change all index-based node access to pointer-based.
(b) Allocate a new node when there is no free one we can recycle.

The result of the first change affects mostly the constructor and destructor of the class as shown below:

Listing 4.26: An unbounded lock-free queue that solves the ABA problem.

```
// File : queue_lock_free_unbound_aba.hpp
//---------------------------------------------------------------
template < typename T > class queue_lock_free_unbound
{
private:
  template < typename W > struct Node
  {
    W data;
    std::atomic < Node<T> * >next;
    std::atomic < Node<T> * >delNext;
  };

  std::atomic < Node<T> * >head;
  std::atomic < Node<T> * >tail;
  std::atomic < Node<T> * >freeHead;
  std::atomic < Node<T> * >freeTail;

  std::atomic < int >numItems = 0;
  std::atomic < int >numFreeNodes = 0;
  std::atomic < int >numContestedFreeNodes =0;
  std::atomic < int >numContestedItems =0;
  std::atomic < int >numPoppers =0;
  std::atomic < int >numPushers =0;

  Node<T> * getFree ();
  void makeFree (Node<T> *);
public:
  bool empty ();
  int size ();
  void enqueue (T &);
  T dequeue ();

  queue_lock_free_unbound ();
  ~queue_lock_free_unbound ();
  queue_lock_free_unbound (queue_lock_free_unbound &) = delete; // ↩
      delete the default copy constructor and copy assignment
  queue_lock_free_unbound & operator= (const queue_lock_free_unbound↩
      &) = delete;
```

```
37   };
38
39   //————————————————————————————————————
40   template < typename T > queue_lock_free_unbound < T >::↵
           queue_lock_free_unbound ()
41   {
42     Node<T> *tmp = new Node<T>(); // sentinel for data queue
43     tmp->next = nullptr;
44     head = tail = tmp;
45
46     tmp = new Node<T>(); // sentinel for free nodes queue
47     tmp->next = nullptr;
48     freeHead = freeTail = tmp;
49   }
50
51   //————————————————————————————————————
52   template < typename T > queue_lock_free_unbound < T >::~↵
           queue_lock_free_unbound ()
53   {
54     Node<T> *tmp = head.load();
55     Node<T> *next;
56     while(tmp != nullptr)
57     {
58       next = tmp->next;
59       delete tmp;
60       tmp = next;
61     }
62
63     tmp = freeHead.load();
64     while(tmp != nullptr)
65     {
66       next = tmp->next;
67       delete tmp;
68       tmp = next;
69     }
70   }
```

The constructor inserts two sentinel nodes, one for the data queue and one for the free node queue. The destructor, on the other hand, has to traverse both linked lists and erase the nodes present, one-by-one. Obviously these two methods can only be called by a single thread.

For the remaining methods, because of the close resemblance of the unbounded queue code to the bounded one, we only show and discuss a representative subset:

Listing 4.27: Methods enqueue and getFree for an unbounded lock-free queue that solves the ABA problem.

```
71   // File : queue_lock_free_unbound_aba.hpp
72   //————————————————————————————————————
73   template < typename T > queue_lock_free_unbound<T>::Node<T>*  ↵
           queue_lock_free_unbound < T >::getFree ()
74   {
```

```
75    Node<T>* newPtr;
76    Node<T>* succPtr;
77    numPushers++;
78    while (true)
79      {
80        newPtr = freeHead.load()->delNext;
81        if (numFreeNodes == 0 || newPtr == nullptr)
82          {
83                if(numPoppers==0 && numContestedFreeNodes>0) // is there
                     one we can retrieve from previous released nodes?
84                  {
85                    int tmp = numContestedFreeNodes;
86                    // make sure numContestedItems is modified
                         atomically
87                    while(!numContestedFreeNodes.compare_exchange_weak(
                         tmp, 0));
88                    numFreeNodes+= tmp;
89                    continue;
90                  }
91                else
92                  {
93                    // return a newly allocated node
94                    numPushers--;
95                    return new Node<T>();
96                  }
97          }
98        if (freeHead.load()->delNext == newPtr)
99          {
100           succPtr = newPtr->delNext;
101           if (succPtr == nullptr)
102             if (!freeTail.compare_exchange_strong (newPtr, freeHead)
                   )   // free list became empty
103               continue;
104           if (freeHead.load()->delNext.compare_exchange_strong (
                 newPtr, succPtr))
105             break;
106         }
107     }
108   numPushers--;
109   numFreeNodes--;
110   numContestedFreeNodes.load());
111   return newPtr;
112 }
113
114 //--------------------------------------------------------------
115 template < typename T > void queue_lock_free_unbound < T >::enqueue
      (T & i)
116 {
117   Node<T>* newPtr;
118   newPtr = getFree ();
119   newPtr->data = i;
120   newPtr->next = nullptr;
```

```
121
122   while (true)
123     {
124       Node<T>* lastPtr = tail.load ();
125       Node<T>* nextPtr = tail.load()->next;     // should be = nullptr
126       if (lastPtr == tail.load ())
127         {
128           if (nextPtr == nullptr)
129             {
130               if (tail.load()->next.compare_exchange_strong (nextPtr ↩
                    , newPtr))
131                 {
132                   tail.compare_exchange_strong (lastPtr, newPtr);
133                   numContestedItems++; // for the newly enqueued ↩
                        node
134
135                   if (numPushers ==0)
136                     {
137                       int tmp = numContestedItems;
138                       // modify numContestedItems atomically
139                       while (!numContestedItems.compare_exchange_weak ↩
                            (tmp, 0));
140                       numItems+= tmp;
141                     }
142                   return;
143                 }
144             }
145           else
146             tail.compare_exchange_strong (lastPtr, nextPtr);
147         }
148     }
149 }
```

The enqueue method is nearly identical to the one shown in Listing 4.25, the only differences coming from switching the integer indices and array elements to node pointers.

The only major change is in the getFree method. Previously, when no free node was available for use by a "pusher" thread, that thread was forced to surrender the CPU and try again later. For our unbounded queue, we have two alternative actions: if there are no "popper" threads and there are some contested free nodes waiting (condition of line 83), we shift those contested free nodes to the free ones and repeat the process from the beginning. Otherwise, a new node is allocated and returned to the caller (line 95).

The bounded and unbounded code bases are so similar that one may wonder if it is even worth considering the restricted bounded queue as a concurrent data structure component. Their performance should be pretty similar after all. However, the contiguous memory space occupied by the bounded queue is more CPU cache-friendly and it could prove to be somewhat faster. The exact difference depends of course on the application and problem instance.

4.4 **Closing remarks**

It is easy for someone to think that lock-free structures are the solution to the performance issues that can plague shared-memory parallel applications. However, this is not always the case as blocking is replaced by something that can be detrimental to performance as well.

Also, designing and implementing lock-free structures is not a job for the faint-hearted. There are many things that can go wrong. For example, even changing the order in condition checking in an `if` or `while` statement can completely change the semantics of the code.

In principle, low contention scenarios, i.e., when threads have few chances of competing in accessing the shared resources, lock-free designs should be better. The opposite is typically true in high-contention scenarios. Of course, if low contention is the case, how much of an overhead would locking introduce?

Ultimately, the application, problem scenario, and platform settings are the ones that determine which is the best solution.

As an illustration of what kind of difference one can expect, we timed the execution of one million total operations divided evenly amongst threads, on a "fine-grained" queue (see Section 4.2.1) and a lock-free unbounded queue (see Section 4.3.5). Each thread either performed all the enqueueing operations first, followed by dequeueing (scenario 1), or alternated/flip-flopped between enqueue/dequeue operations (scenario 2). The results of the following code, timed on an AMD Ryzen 9 3900X and compiled using GNU C++ 9.2.1 with the -O2 switch, are shown in Fig. 4.9.

Listing 4.28: The code used to test a high-contention scenario (scenario 1) of threads sharing a queue.

```
1   // File : queue_performance_test.cpp
2   #include "queue_fine.hpp"
3   . . .
4     auto t1 = high_resolution_clock::now ();
5     unsigned int seed = 0;
6     queue < int >q_fine;
7     for (int iter = 0; iter < Niter; iter++)
8       {
9         for (int i = 0; i < numThr; i++)
10          t[i] = make_unique < thread > ([&]()
11                                         {
12                                           for (int j = 0; j < numOper; ↩
                                               j++)
13                                           {
14                                           int x;
15                                           if (j <= numOper / 2)
16                                           {
17                                             x = rand_r (&seed) % 100;
18                                             q_fine.push_back (x);
19                                           else
20                                             x = q_fine.pop_front ();
```

```
21                                              }
22                                         }
23          );
24          for (int i = 0; i < numThr; i++)
25             t[i]->join ();
26       }
27    auto t2 = high_resolution_clock::now ();
28    cout << "Fine : " << duration_cast < milliseconds > (t2 - t1).↩
         count ();
29    // repeat for lock-free unbounded queue...
```

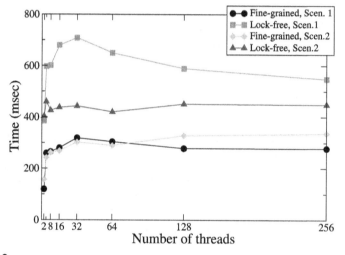

FIGURE 4.9

Time required to perform a total of one million operations on a fine-grained and a lock-free unbounded queues versus the number of threads, averaged over 100 runs. In scenario 1 all the enqueueing operations are done first, followed by dequeueing (scenario 1). In scenario 2 threads alternate between enqueue/dequeue operations.

It should be stressed that both scenarios, even when only two threads are used, are high-contention ones. So Fig. 4.9 is not there to dismiss lock-free structures as inefficient, but to indicate that a right choice on which structure to use can be critical. The code in Listing 4.28 is not what one can expect from a normal application. Scenario 2 is a lower-contention case than scenario 1, and the lock-free queue clearly benefits from this, as seen in Fig. 4.9.

Exercises

1. Modify the queue structure of Listing 4.3, so that a thread trying to dequeue from an empty container will wait for a signal, instead of throwing an exception.

2. In Fig. 4.6 a possible scenario of list corruption is described if validation is not performed. Suggest other possible ways the list could be corrupted.

3. Someone suggests that in the lazy synchronization list, we could replace the `marked` flag by setting the `next` field to `nullptr`. Could this modification be a viable alternative?

4. Modify the stack implementation of Listing 4.18 to support the `empty` and `size` methods.

5. In Listing 4.18 we have a stack that manages node memory allocation, one node at a time. Modify the code so that a bunch of `Node` instances are created initially as an *array* and kept in the `freeNodes` list. What are the advantages and disadvantages of this solution?

6. What would happen in the lazy synchronization list of Section 4.2.2.4 if an item was inserted to the list after it was erased by another thread?

7. Design and implement a binary search tree structure that uses fine-grained locks.

8. Implement an `includes` method for the list structure. It should return true or false based on the item being in the list.

Distributed memory programming

5

In this chapter you will:

- Learn what the Message-Passing Interface (MPI) is and how you can use it to create applications that run on distributed-memory platforms.
- Understand how an MPI program can be deployed for execution.
- Learn how to perform point-to-point communications using MPI.
- Learn how to perform collective communications using MPI.
- Utilize non-blocking and/or buffered communication primitives to increase the performance of your application.
- Learn to use Remote Memory Access (RMA) functions to implement one-sided communications.
- Learn how to use C and C++ MPI bindings via the Boost.MPI library.
- Combine threads and MPI processes to maximize the performance of distributed platforms with multicore nodes.

5.1 Introduction

What makes distributed memory programming relevant to multicore platforms is scalability: stand alone, shared-memory, multicore systems just do not have the potential to scale beyond the performance envelope of their memory bus. Attaining even higher performance is thus relegated to collections of systems that communicate over a network.

The Message-Passing Interface (MPI) covered in this chapter can be considered as the "glue" that makes such distributed memory systems operate as cohesive platforms. MPI facilitates both point-to-point communication and efficient collective communication operations that improve performance and reduce program clutter. Starting with version 3.0, MPI provides a Remote Memory Access (RMA) mechanism that enables one-sided communications to take place in a fashion which resembles shared resource access using semaphores.

In this chapter we explore the capabilities of MPI as made available by both C and C++ bindings. The latter, in the form of the Boost.MPI library, constitute a more user-friendly implementation of the MPI standard.

Multicore and GPU Programming. https://doi.org/10.1016/B978-0-12-814120-5.00014-7

231

The chapter includes a wide range of case studies that show both how to employ MPI to build parallel applications and how to combine MPI with threads for more efficient use of multicore architectures.

The emergence of the workstation platform and networking capabilities in the 1980s prompted the creation of libraries that could be used to deploy and manage programs over intranets. The core concept was to run multiple processes that could communicate by exchanging messages. The libraries alleviated the troubles of node discovery, message routing, and process identification that plain-vanilla socket-based approaches had to contend with. One of the first popular examples was the Parallel Virtual Machine (PVM) library, which was developed during the summer of 1989 at Oak Ridge National Laboratory and was released to the public in early 1991.

However, those early attempts more often than not duplicated each other and led to the construction of software that was pretty much non-portable. This prompted a common initiative by academia and industry partners that resulted in the creation of the first MPI standard (MPI-1) in 1994.

5.2 MPI

The Message-Passing Interface (MPI) is considered the de facto standard for distributed-memory, or shared-nothing programming. MPI is not a programming language but a set of functions (i.e., an API) that can be used from a variety of languages. It should also be stressed that MPI is not a specific library but a standardized specification for one. The latest MPI version is 4.0, published in June 2021. The standard defines the syntax and semantics of a core of library routines.

A number of vendors, both government institutions and private corporations, have developed MPI implementations that adhere to a lesser or greater degree to one or more MPI specifications. The reason for partial compliance is the size and complexity of the complete standard, which also entails some infrequently used features (such as, e.g., dynamic process management). Over the years a number of different MPI implementations have come and gone. Currently, the two prominent OSS implementations that stand out are:

- OpenMPI: MPI-3.1 fully compliant OSS implementation. It is developed and maintained by a number of academia and industry partners.
- MPICH: implements the MPI-3.1 standard. It is a continuation of the MPICH2 project that provided MPI-2 support. A number of industry (e.g., IBM, Intel, Microsoft) and academic partners work with MPICH on derivative implementations. MPICH is currently offering a beta implementation of MPI 4.0.

At the moment of this writing (November 2021) there are only beta implementations of the MPI 4.0 standard. Throughout the following sections we will be referring to the 4.0 additions where relevant, although in the absence of a proper implementation release, running examples are impossible.

Many Linux distributions (Ubuntu being one of them) offer installation packages for OpenMPI and MPICH. Installation in Ubuntu Linux can be as simple as:

Listing 5.1: Installing OpenMPI in Ubuntu.

```
$ sudo apt install openmpi*
```

Differences between the libraries lay not only in the degree of compliance to the standard, but also in the level of optimization, the architectures supported (custom or otherwise, like, e.g., support of Infiniband), and the toolsets used for program development, deployment, management, and instrumentation.

MPI uses a language-independent specification to describe the semantics of the supported calls. These are made available to programmers via specific language bindings or APIs. MPI-1 implementations typically offered bindings for C and Fortran. Later C++ bindings also became available, but they were completely removed from the standard later. In the sections that follow we offer examples that use the C bindings as provided by the MPI library and the C++ bindings as implemented by the Boost.MPI wrapper library wherever possible. The Boost set of libraries is considered the breeding ground for libraries that could later become part of the C++ Standard Library. The Boost.MPI library offers a welcome level of abstraction in comparison to the C bindings.[1]

While it is possible to learn to use MPI only via the Boost.MPI classes, study of the C bindings reveals certain aspects of the MPI operations that are critical for a thorough understanding of the standard. It is therefore recommended that the reader does not skip over the C-only sections of the text. Additionally, Boost.MPI currently covers only a subset of the full MPI standard.

MPI remains relevant even today in the era of multiple cores, due to its flexible design. The primary concern of a software engineer is to decompose the target application into parts that can be executed as separate processes. The MPI runtime environment will take care of the actual mapping (guided or otherwise) of processes to physical nodes/CPUs. The underlying machine can be easily switched between a multicore PC and an intranet of homogeneous or even heterogeneous machines.

It is indicative of the importance of MPI that NVidia's CUDA toolkit supports (since version 4.1) MPI communication primitives involving GPU memory. This opens up a whole new world of possibilities for GPU programming, as we explore in Chapter 6.

---

[1] Boost.MPI offers a different set of C++ bindings than the ones originally introduced in the MPI standard. The latter are considered deprecated as of MPI-2.2 and they have been completely removed from MPI-3.0. The rationale is that they barely offer anything different from their C counterparts.

5.3 Core concepts

The abstraction MPI presents is one of processes that can exchange messages with each other, just by specifying the other end of the communication operation. The processes could be just as easily deployed over a single machine or a network of *heterogeneous* machines without needing to modify or recompile the code. A configuration file and/or command-line parameters allow the control of the deployment at launch-time. The MPI library and runtime environment are responsible for:

- **Process identification**: A unique non-negative number per process, also known as a *rank* in MPI nomenclature, is used for this purpose. This identification number is defined within the context of a group of processes, known as a communicator. By default, all processes in an MPI program belong to the global communicator identified by the symbolic constant `MPI_COMM_WORLD`. In the following sections we also use the term node to refer to an MPI process.
- **Message routing**: MPI takes care of efficiently delivering the messages to their destinations by using either sockets (for intermachine communications) or shared buffers (for intramachine communications).
- **Message buffering**: Once a message has been dispatched by its sender, it is typically buffered by MPI on its way to its destination. Multiple messages can await collection in a receiver's MPI buffer space. MPI provides mechanisms for delegating buffering duties to the application. This can be useful for managing very big messages.
- **Data marshaling**: MPI accommodates the construction of parallel machines from heterogeneous architectures (e.g., big-endian and small-endian) by converting data representations to suit the message's destination. This is the reason why MPI calls require the explicit declaration of the data types being communicated.

In the following sections we use the C-language bindings exclusively to present and explain the different functions offered by MPI. Fortran bindings are almost identical with the C ones (the naming is different in the sense that all function names are upper-case). C++ bindings have been completely removed from the standard since MPI 3.0. C++ users can either use the C bindings or resort to the excellent Boost.MPI library which is presented in Section 5.22.

5.4 Your first MPI program

The typical structure of a C MPI program is shown below:

Listing 5.2: Skeleton of a C MPI program.

```
#include <mpi.h>
...
int main(int argc, char **argv)
{
  . . .
```

```
// No MPI calls prior to this point
MPI_Init(&argc, &argv);

// MPI statements

MPI_Finalize();
// No MPI calls beyond this point
. . .
}
```

The `MPI_Init` function initializes the MPI execution environment by, for example, allocating the memory space necessary for message buffering. Command-line parameters are also parsed in order to extract any directives to MPI, hence the parameter list of `MPI_Init`. `MPI_Finalize` terminates the MPI execution environment and frees up any resources taken up by MPI.

The naming convention used by MPI for C is that functions start with the `MPI_` prefix and only the first letter of the remaining function name is capital. If the name is made of multiple components, they are separated by an underscore, e.g., `MPI_Comm_size`. Constants follow the same rule, with the exception that all characters are upper-case.

Along the lines of the traditional "Hello World" programs, the "`mpihello.c`" program in Listing 5.3 prints a greeting from every MPI process spawned.

Listing 5.3: MPI's "Hello World" in C.

```
1   #include <mpi.h>
2   #include <stdio.h>
3   int main (int argc, char **argv)
4   {
5     int rank, num, i;
6     MPI_Init (&argc, &argv);
7     MPI_Comm_rank (MPI_COMM_WORLD, &rank);
8     MPI_Comm_size (MPI_COMM_WORLD, &num);
9     printf ("Hello from process %i of %i\n", rank, num);
10    MPI_Finalize ();
11    return 0;
12  }
```

Line 7 in Listing 5.3 is where each MPI process requests to find out its ID/rank in the global communicator `MPI_COMM_WORLD`. The communicator's size, i.e., the total number of processes, is determined on line 8. Processes are numbered from 0 to $N - 1$, where N is the communicator size. To compile the above program, the `mpicc` command can be used to automate the process[2]:

---

[2] Please note that in all the examples of this chapter, the files (source code, binary, or otherwise) are assumed to be in the current directory and the current directory is in the ${PATH} environmental variable. If this is not the case, a relative or an absolute pathname has to be used.

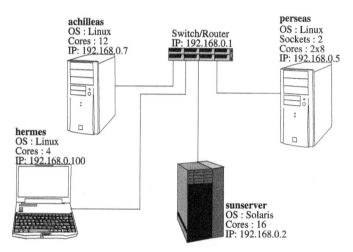

FIGURE 5.1

Intranet example used for explaining MPI execution configurations.

```
$ mpicc mpihello.c —o mpihello
```

where the -o flag determines the filename of the executable generated.

The same can be accomplished by calling the GNU C compiler (gcc) directly:

```
$ gcc hello.c —o hello2 —I /usr/include/mpi —lmpi
```

The benefit of using mpicc is that we avoid the hassle of having to specify where the header files are located (with the -I switch) and which libraries to link with (the -lmpi switch).

The execution environment is determined during program launch via the mpirun command.[3] In order to explore both intra- (i.e., single) and internode (i.e., over multiple machines) deployment, we will assume that we have at our disposal the heterogeneous network shown in Fig. 5.1. Assuming that the user is running the program from a console window in the **hermes** laptop, spawning a group of four processes is as simple as entering:

```
$ mpirun —np 4 mpihello
```

This will in turn produce an output which may or may not resemble the ones shown in Table 5.1, as there is no guarantee on the relative timing of the different processes. The third column in Table 5.1 clearly reveals the problems that uncoordinated console output can cause in this case. The solution to this problem would be to designate only one of the processes to output to the console (for more see Section 5.18).

---

[3] mpiexec and orterun are synonyms of mpirun in OpenMPI.

Table 5.1 A sample of the possible outputs that can be generated from a run of the program in Listing 5.3, using four processes.

Output #1	Output #2	Output #3
Hello from process 1 of 4	Hello from process 3 of 4	Hello from process 2 of 4
Hello from process 2 of 4	Hello from process 2 of 4	Hello from process 1 of 4
Hello from process 0 of 4	Hello from process 0 of 4	Hello from process 0 of 4
Hello from process 3 of 4	Hello from process 1 of 4	Hello from process 3 of 4

This simple execution command that uses only the `-np` switch is sufficient for debugging programs on a stand-alone machine. Under normal circumstances, we would not expect much of a speedup from such an execution, unless the machine used was a multicore one!

In the latest incarnation of OpenMPI, the `-np` parameter cannot exceed the number of cores in the system (cores not hardware threads). If one is trying to test with more processes, the `--oversubscribe` switch must be also given.

An important issue that has to be addressed is how the different nodes in your intranet access the code and data needed. The simplest approach is to have all the machines mount a shared NFS or CIFS volume that contains the required files. If your Linux home directory is handled by an NFS server and the accounts are handled by NIS or LDAP, there is nothing more to be done. If a shared volume is not used, then the files will have to be transferred with FTP or SSH protocols to all the nodes.

Running a program on a remote host requires a particular security setup that is outlined step-by-step in Appendix B.1. Failure to do so will result in a sequence of credential (login) requests for each of the processes that are to be executed.

In order to deploy the program over multiple machines, a "hostfile" has to be specified. The hostfile is a text file containing a list (one per line) of the IPs (or DNS names) of the machines that will host the executing processes. For the network of Fig. 5.1, the hostfile would contain (please notice the absence of `sunserver`'s IP):

```
192.168.0.5
192.168.0.7
192.168.0.100
```

or a permutation of the above. If these lines are saved in file "`hosts`," distributing four processes over the three available nodes would require:

```
$ mpirun —hostfile hosts —np 4 mpihello
```

The processes would be distributed in a round-robin fashion starting from the first entry in the hostfile and the process with rank 0. Thus, the `perseas` machine would end up with two processes, ranked 0 and 3.[4] The optional "**slots**" modifier for each

---

[4] A "**rankfile**" can be used to fine-tune the mapping of processes to the available nodes/cores. The interested reader should consult the `mpirun`'s manual page for more information.

Table 5.2 Examples of process distributions for different `mpirun` switches for the example platform of Fig. 5.1.

Launch command (`mpirun`) switches	Process rank distribution		
	192.168.0.5	**192.168.0.7**	**192.168.0.100**
`-np 8`	0 1 2 3 4 5 6 7		
`-np 8 --map-by node`	0 3 6	1 4 7	2 5
`-np 8 --map-by socket`	0 1 4 5	2 6	3 7

node in the hostfile can allow us to set the maximum number of processes per node. If the number of processes exceeds the total number of slots, an error is generated by `mpirun`.

```
192.168.0.5   slots=8
192.168.0.7   slots=4
192.168.0.100 slots=2
```

Normally, the above would get all four processes running on `perseas`. We would need to specify more than eight processes before they would spill over to the other machines. However, for this particular example it would cause the generation of an error, i.e., the program would not start, as the machine from which the program is launched – in our case the `hermes` laptop – must participate in the execution.

Some rudimentary form of load balancing can be achieved by using the `--map-by X` switch, where X can be one of `node`,[5] `socket`, `core`, `hwthread`, etc. (see the `mpirun` manual page). Sample results for the above hostfile are shown in Table 5.2. The `-display-devel-map` switch can be used to display information about the process mapping before execution.

The construction and maintenance of the hostfile is a simple matter when static IPs are used. Dynamic IPs present a challenge that is actually trivial if a sequence of simple steps is employed. These steps, which can also be automated with the use of a script, are described in detail in Appendix B.2.

5.5 Program architecture

5.5.1 SPMD

MPI software can be constructed according to the Single-Program, Multiple-Data (SPMD) paradigm or the Multiple-Program, Multiple-Data (MPMD) one discussed in the next section. The former one facilitates easy source code management and dictates that the nodes query their rank and adjust their behavior accordingly. Consequently, the `main` function is made up of `switch` or `if-else` statements that navigate

---

[5] The term "node" here refers to a network node. However, in this chapter we use the terms "node" and "process" interchangeably.

```
① #include<mpi.h>
   #include<string.h>
   #include<stdio.h>
   #define MESSTAG 0
   #define MAXLEN 100

   int main (int argc, char **argv) {
②    MPI_Init (&argc, &argv);
③    int rank, num, i;
      MPI_Comm_rank (MPI_COMM_WORLD, &rank);
      MPI_Comm_size (MPI_COMM_WORLD, &num);
④    if (rank == 0) {
          char mess[] = "Hello World";
          int len = strlen(mess)+1;
          for (i = 1; i < num; i++)
⑤            MPI_Send (mess, len, MPI_CHAR, i, MESSTAG, MPI_COMM_WORLD);
      } else {
          char mess[MAXLEN];
          MPI_Status status;
⑥        MPI_Recv (mess, MAXLEN, MPI_CHAR, 0, MESSTAG, MPI_COMM_WORLD, &status);
          printf ("%i received %s\n", rank, mess);
      }
⑦    MPI_Finalize ();
      return 0;
   }
```

Key:

①	MPI-related header files
②	MPI initialization. Any command-line parameters destined for the MPI runtime are passed on.
③	Rank query.
④	Code branching based on process identity/rank
⑤	Basic send operation.
⑥	Basic MPI receiving operation. The *MPI_Status* structure holds information about the message.
⑦	MPI termination and cleanup.

FIGURE 5.2

An SPMD "Hello World" MPI program using the C bindings.

the nodes to their workloads. The node with rank 0 (typically representing the node that controls the terminal managing the standard I/O streams) is usually reserved to play the role of the work coordinator or "master." SPMD is the typical approach used by MPI programs.

An example along the guidelines set above is shown in Fig. 5.2. Code sections ③ and ④ in Fig. 5.2 serve to differentiate node behavior. The syntax and semantics of the communication calls in ⑤ and ⑥ are explained in Section 5.6.

5.5.2 MPMD

MPMD programs are appropriate when either heterogeneous machines make up the execution platform (hence the need for different executable binaries) or the code and static data are just too large to be forcefully propagated to all nodes/processes. MPMD programs require more housekeeping than SPMD ones, but because they do not need to incorporate code and data that will not be used, the memory footprint of each process can be minimized. Another way to look at this is that available memory is maximized.

One can specify different executables to use for groups of processes in two ways, which are pretty similar:

1. Using command-line parameters: In this approach, the `mpirun` should be accompanied by two or more `-np #` exec specifications separated by a colon (":"), each specifying how many copies of the `exec` binary to run. Example:

```
$ mpirun —np 2 pr1 : —np 5 pr2
```

will run two processes with the `pr1` and five processes with the `pr2` executable, all part of the same global communicator.

2. Using an *appfile* (**app**lication **file**): An *appfile* is a text file containing all the parameters required by `mpirun`. If an appfile is specified, all other command-line parameters are ignored. Hence, an appfile needs to contain also the IPs or DNS names of the hosts as a "`-hostfile`" parameter will be ignored.

Assuming that we would like to use the `sunserver` of Fig. 5.1 in our execution platform, we should prepare two executables: one for `sunserver` and one for the other nodes. This can be done by using a cross-compiler on one machine or by running the native compiler on each platform. If the binaries produced are named "`myapp.linux`" and "`myapp.solaris`," the following appfile would suffice for running eight copies of "`myapp.solaris`" on sunserver and two copies of "`myapp.linux`" on each of the other three nodes.

Listing 5.4: A sample appfile for executing an MPI program on a heterogeneous platform.

```
—host 192.168.0.2 —np 8 myapp.solaris
—host 192.168.0.5 —np 2 myapp.linux
—host 192.168.0.7 —np 2 myapp.linux
—host 192.168.0.100 —np 2 myapp.linux
```

As can be observed in the above example, the contents of the appfile are just normal parameters that could have been given directly to `mpirun` (although it would be a very long line!). If the name of the appfile is "appconf," then the execution could be initiated by:

```
$ mpirun —app appconf
```

An MPMD example is given in Listing 5.5 in the following section. A more extensive example that combines computations on CPU and GPU nodes is given in Section 6.15.2.3.

The only difference between OpenMPI and MPICH as far as MPMD functionality is concerned is that the latter uses a different switch for designating the so-called "configuration file," as shown below:

```
$ mpirun —configfile appconf    # In MPICH
```

The contents of the appfile/configuration file share the same semantics and syntax in both libraries.

5.6 Point-to-point communication

Fig. 5.2 and the ⑤ and ⑥ statements in particular are examples of the functionality for which MPI is most famous, i.e., the easy exchange of information between processes/nodes. MPI provides a diverse variety of send and receive primitives that allow programmers to select the ones which are most suitable in every imaginable scenario. The simplest are the ones used in Fig. 5.2. The syntax of MPI_Send is

```
int MPI_Send(void       *buf,   // Address of the send buffer (IN)
             int        count,  // Number of items in message (IN)
             MPI_Datatype dtype, // MPI-based symbolic constant
                                //    representing the type of data
                                //    being communicated (IN)
             int        dest,   // Destination process rank (IN)
             int        tag,    // Label identifying the type
                                //    of message (IN)
             MPI_Comm   comm    // Identifies the communicator
                                //    context of 'dest' (IN)
)
```

MPI_Send (as most of MPI calls) returns an error value. If this value is 0 (or the symbolic constant MPI_SUCCESS) no error has occurred.

The first half of the parameters serve to describe the message and the second half to describe the destination process. MPI_Send follows the footsteps of other standard C library functions that operate on arrays of arbitrary data, like, e.g., qsort, which implements the quicksort algorithm. The syntax of qsort is

```
void qsort(void    *base,     // Address of data buffer to sort
        size_t    nmemb,     // Number of items in buffer
        size_t    size,      // Size of each item in buffer
        int(*comp)(const void *, // Pointer to a function that can
                    const void *) //    compare the items pairwise
        )
```

The similarities are many but so are the differences. Why is MPI_Send requiring the specification of the datatype, whereas qsort is happy with the size of each item? The answer can be given through another question: if a little-endian machine, like, e.g., an i7 processor, were sending data to a big-endian machine, like, e.g., a PowerPC processor, how would the latter be able to read the data? One would need to go over the buffer and change the byte ordering. But what if a 32-bit machine was sending data to a 64 bit one? Clearly, this is a burden that should not be left to the application programmer.[6]

MPI can do the job automatically if we explicitly specify the data types in a machine-agnostic (i.e., MPI-based) fashion. Such translations do not take place for homogeneous platforms, but forcing the source code to be written in such a manner means that it will never need to be modified, regardless of the target execution platform. Table 5.3 lists some of the MPI datatypes. A noteworthy addition in MPI-3 is the inclusion of C++-specific data types, identified by the CXX part of the symbolic name, despite having the C++ bindings removed.

Table 5.3 A partial list of MPI datatypes.

MPI datatypes	C datatypes
MPI_CHAR	signed char
MPI_UNSIGNED_CHAR	unsigned char
MPI_INT	signed int
MPI_LONG	signed long int
MPI_FLOAT	float
MPI_DOUBLE	double
MPI_LONG_DOUBLE	long double
MPI_CXX_BOOL	bool
MPI_CXX_FLOAT_COMPLEX	std::complex<float>

The second half of MPI_Send parameters relate to the routing of the message as the destination process is identified through the pair of (communicator, rank) values. The tag parameter (which should be a non-negative number[7]) is used so that two processes can identify and filter the different messages that are exchanged between them. The filtering takes place on the receiving side that should obviously execute an MPI_Recv call. The syntax is:

```
int MPI_Recv(void      *buf,       // Receive buffer address (OUT)
             int        count,      // Buffer capacity in items (IN)
             MPI_Datatype datatype, // Same as in MPI_Send (IN)
             int        source,     // Rank of sending process (IN)
             int        tag,        // Label identifying the type
                                    //   of message expected (IN)
             MPI_Comm   comm,       // Identifies the communicator
                                    //   context of 'source' (IN)
```

---

[6] Data representation and type size are some of the nastiest sources of bugs in computer software. The Y2K bug is such an example.

[7] MPI-1 specifies that it should be between 0 and MPI_TAG_UB.

```
                         MPI_Status    *status  //  Pointer  to  structure  holding
                                                //     message  parameters  (OUT)
                  )
```

The syntax of `MPI_Recv` mirrors the one by `MPI_Send` with the exclusion of the `MPI_Status` structure pointer. Its purpose will be explained shortly. The buffer used by the receiving process must be big enough so as to accommodate the data sent. Obviously, the datatype should match the actual type of items being communicated. The `source` parameter can be either a non-negative integer, in which case it identifies the `(comm, source)` process, or set to the symbolic constant `MPI_ANY_SOURCE` (a quick search in the `mpi.h` header file reveals this to be equal to -1). In the latter case any process from the specified communicator can be the source of the message. The communicator identifier must match the one used by the sender process.

The `tag` can be set to a non-negative number to select a particular type of message, or it can be set to `MPI_ANY_TAG` (again representing -1) to just get any incoming message from the `source`, regardless of its `tag`.

The above means that there is a bit of flexibility to how a process receives messages. So after a successful message acquisition, how can the process know where the message came from? What is its exact length? And what is the `tag` that the sender attached?

Fortunately, all this information is stored in the `MPI_Status` structure that the receiver provides. Its declaration is:

```
typedef struct ompi_status_public_t MPI_Status;
struct ompi_status_public_t {
  int MPI_SOURCE;    // The rank of the source
  int MPI_TAG;       // The tag set by the source
  int MPI_ERROR;     // If not 0, it indicates an error
  int _count;        // Size of message in bytes
  int _cancelled;
};
```

The last two data members of the `MPI_Status` structure are not meant to be directly accessible. Instead, the `MPI_Get_count` function can be used to return the length of the message in data items:

```
int MPI_Get_count(MPI_Status *status,  // Address of a structure
                                       //    set by MPI_Recv (IN)
                  MPI_Datatype dtype,  // MPI datatype expected (IN)
                  int *count           // Number of items read (OUT)
                  )
```

If a developer chooses to ignore this information, the `MPI_Status` reference can be replaced with the `MPI_STATUS_IGNORE` symbolic constant.

Having become acquainted with the intricacies of the basic communication primitives in MPI, we can put them to work in the following MPMD program, where the rank-0 process receives and prints out messages from the other running processes.

Listing 5.5: An MPMD example made up of two files, master.c and worker.c, that makes use of MPI_Send, MPI_Recv, and MPI_Status.

```
1   //——————— master.c ———————
2   #include <mpi.h>
3   #include <stdio.h>
4   #include <string.h>
5
6   #define MAXLEN 100
7   char buff[MAXLEN];
8
9   int main (int argc, char **argv)
10  {
11    MPI_Status st;
12    int procNum;
13
14    MPI_Init (&argc, &argv);
15    MPI_Comm_size (MPI_COMM_WORLD, &procNum);
16    while (--procNum)
17      {
18        MPI_Recv (buff, MAXLEN, MPI_CHAR, MPI_ANY_SOURCE, MPI_ANY_TAG,
19                  MPI_COMM_WORLD, &st);
20        int aux;
21        MPI_Get_count (&st, MPI_CHAR, &aux);
22        buff[aux] = 0;
23        printf ("%s\n", buff);
24      }
25    MPI_Finalize ();
26  }
27
28
29  //——————— worker.c ———————
30  #include <mpi.h>
31  #include <stdio.h>
32  #include <string.h>
33  #include <stdlib.h>
34  #define MAXLEN 100
35  char *greetings[] = { "Hello", "Hi", "Awaiting your command" };
36  char buff[MAXLEN];
37
38  int main (int argc, char **argv)
39  {
40    int grID, rank;
41    srand (time (0));
42    MPI_Init (&argc, &argv);
43    grID = rand () % 3;
44    MPI_Comm_rank (MPI_COMM_WORLD, &rank);
45    sprintf (buff, "Node %i says %s", rank, greetings[grID]);
46    MPI_Send (buff, strlen (buff), MPI_CHAR, 0, 0, MPI_COMM_WORLD);
47    MPI_Finalize ();
48  }
```

The worker processes initialize the pseudorandom number generator on line 41 before randomly selecting one of the three greeting messages on line 43. The node rank (retrieved on line 44) and the selected message are printed to a character array on line 45, before being sent to process 0 on line 46.

The master process, on the other hand, waits for as many incoming messages as the communicator size minus 1, via the line 16 loop. The messages are read in the random order in which they arrive and are subsequently printed out (line 23) after a zero termination character is appended at the end of the received string (line 22). The actual size of the message is needed for this purpose and that is why it is retrieved on line 21.

The Listing 5.5 program can compile and execute with the following sequence of commands:

```
$ mpicc master.c —o master
$ mpicc worker.c —o worker
$ mpirun —np 1 master : —np 3 worker
```

Because the execution will be done on the same machine (a -hostfile parameter is absent above), one can expect to get the same greeting – most of the time – from all workers as the pseudorandom number generator is initialized with the same value (current time in seconds on line 41), e.g.:

```
Node 2 says Hi
Node 3 says Hi
Node 1 says Hi
```

When two processes exchange messages back and forth, the ordering of – blocking – send and receive operations is critical.

5.7 Alternative point-to-point communication modes

As reported in the previous section, MPI_Send returns MPI_SUCCESS if no error has occurred. Is this an indication that the message was delivered successfully to its destination? In MPI nomenclature, MPI_Send is called a *blocking send* operation, implying that the sender blocks until the message is delivered. However, this is misleading as the function may return before the message is delivered!

MPI_Send uses the so-called **standard communication mode**. What really happens is that MPI decides based on the size of the message, whether to block the call until the destination process collects it or to return before a matching receive is issued. The latter is chosen if the message is small enough, making MPI_Send **locally blocking**, i.e., the function returns as soon as the message is copied to a local MPI buffer, boosting CPU utilization. The copy is necessary so as to release the buffer used by the source process for subsequent operations, as with this form of send, there is no way for the sender process to know when the message is delivered.

There are three additional communication modes:

- **Buffered**: In buffered mode the sending operation is always locally blocking, i.e., it will return as soon as the message is copied to a buffer. The second difference with the standard communication mode is that the buffer is user-provided.
- **Synchronous**: In synchronous mode, the sending operation will return only after the destination process has initiated and started the retrieval of the message (the receiving may not be complete though). This is a proper **globally blocking** operation.
- **Ready**: The send operation will succeed only if a matching receive operation has been initiated already. Otherwise the function returns with an error code. The purpose of this mode is to reduce the overhead of handshaking operations.

In order to distinguish the different communication modes, a single letter is prefixed before Send: **B** for buffered, **S** for synchronous, and **R** for ready. All the additional functions share the same signature with the standard MPI_Send.

```
int [ MPI_Bsend | MPI_Ssend | MPI_Rsend ] (void *buf, int count, ↩
     MPI_Datatype datatype, int dest, int tag, MPI_Comm comm);
```

Buffered and synchronous modes constitute the two opposite ends of what a send operation could do. The first one mandates the use of a buffer (a user-supplied one so that it is always sufficiently large) while the latter forgoes the need of a buffer by forcing the sender to wait for the message to reach the destination.

The buffered mode requires a bit of setup work in order to be deployed. The details are supplied below.

5.7.1 Buffered communications

The buffered communication mode requires that the user allocates a dedicated buffer for MPI to hold the messages that are sent via *buffered* send calls. Each process can specify only one buffer, and thus it is important that this buffer is big enough to accommodate all the communication needs of the buffered communication calls. If the specified buffer overflows, MPI will signal an error. Non-buffered send calls are handled natively by MPI, i.e., by using MPI's own buffers, if it is deemed to be necessary. A typical sequence is:

```
MPI_Buffer_attach(...);
...
MPI_Bsend(...);
...
MPI_Buffer_detach(...);
```

MPI_Bsend has the same signature as MPI_Send and there is no modification required to the receiving end of the communication, i.e., MPI_Recv is used as normal.

The MPI_Buffer_attach function informs MPI of the location and size of the user-provided buffer space. This memory can be reclaimed and either used for another purpose or freed by calling the MPI_Buffer_detach function. Caution should be taken when passing parameters to the latter. While in MPI_Buffer_attach the pointer is an input parameter, in `MPI_Buffer_detach` the double pointer is an output parameter, i.e., the address of a pointer variable is expected.

An example along the lines of the "Hello World" program explained previously is given in Listing 5.6.

Listing 5.6: A variation to the "Hello World" program that uses buffered communications on node 0.

```c
#include <mpi.h>
#include <stdio.h>
#include <stdlib.h>
#include <string.h>

#define COMMBUFFSIZE 1024    /* This would be too small under most ←
    circumstances */
#define MAXMSGSIZE 10
#define MSGTAG 0

int main (int argc, char **argv)
{
  int rank, num, i;
  MPI_Init (&argc, &argv);
  MPI_Comm_rank (MPI_COMM_WORLD, &rank);
  MPI_Comm_size (MPI_COMM_WORLD, &num);

  if (rank == 0)
    {
      // allocate buffer space and designate it for MPI use
      unsigned char *buff = (unsigned char *) malloc (sizeof (←
          unsigned char) * COMMBUFFSIZE);
      MPI_Buffer_attach (buff, COMMBUFFSIZE);
      char *msg = "Test msg";
      for (i = 1; i < num; i++)
          MPI_Bsend (msg, strlen (msg) + 1, MPI_CHAR, i, MSGTAG, ←
              MPI_COMM_WORLD);

      // detach and release buffer space
      unsigned char *bptr;
      int bsize;
      MPI_Buffer_detach (&bptr, &bsize);
      free (bptr);
    }
  else
    {
      MPI_Status status;
      char msg[MAXMSGSIZE];
      MPI_Recv (msg, MAXMSGSIZE, MPI_CHAR, 0, MSGTAG, MPI_COMM_WORLD←
          , &status);          // no change at receiving end
      printf ("%s\n", msg);
    }

  MPI_Finalize ();
```

```
    return 0;
}
```

5.8 Non-blocking communications

In general, buffered sends as described in the previous section are considered a bad practice because of the explicit need to perform a memory copy. A copy is not mandated by the normal send primitive. Performance can be enhanced if no copy ever takes place (as in the synchronous communication mode) or when we are allowed to continue execution without worrying about the progress of the communication. The latter is the domain of the "immediate," non-blocking functions, which strive to improve concurrency by overlapping communication and computation. The transition is as simple as using the `MPI_Isend` function in the place of `MPI_Send`.

On the receiving side, concurrency can be improved if the `MPI_Recv` function is replaced by the `MPI_Irecv` one, which does not block. However, this is no free lunch! Both immediate functions initiate the communication but upon their return to the caller, the status of the message is unknown. This is a problem for both parties, as the sender would not know when it is possible to reuse/modify the area holding the data being sent, and the receiver would not know when it can use the buffer designated for holding the message.

To overcome this problem, polling has to be used, i.e., both parties have to query the MPI environment on the status of the initiated action. For this purpose, a special handle is returned to the two processes upon completion of the corresponding functions in the form of an `MPI_Request` structure. The signatures of the two aforementioned functions are:

```
typedef int MPI_Request;
```

```
int MPI_Isend(void        *buf,      // Address of data buffer (IN)
              int         count,     // Number of data items (IN)
              MPI_Datatype datatype, // MPI-encoded datatype of
                                     //   "buf" (IN)
              int         dest,      // Destination proc. rank (IN)
              int         tag,       // Message label (IN)
              MPI_Comm    comm,      // Identifies the communicator
                                     //   context of 'dest' (IN)
              MPI_Request *req       // Placeholder for handle needed
                                     //   for checking status (OUT)
             )
```

```
int MPI_Irecv(void        *buf,      // Receive buff. address (OUT)
              int         count,     // Buffer capacity in items (IN)
              MPI_Datatype datatype, // MPI-encoded datatype of
                                     //   "buf" (IN)
              int         source,    // Rank of sending process (IN)
```

```
int          tag,      // Message label (IN)
MPI_Comm     comm,     // Identifies the communicator
                       //    context of 'source' (IN)
MPI_Request  *req      // Placeholder for handle needed
                       //    for checking status (OUT)
)
```

Polling can be performed via the `MPI_Wait` and `MPI_Test` functions, which are blocking and non-blocking, respectively. Both can set an `MPI_Status` structure which for the receiver holds crucial message information:

```
int MPI_Wait(MPI_Request *req, // Address of the handle identifying
                               //    the operation queried (IN/OUT)
                               //    The call invalidates *req by
                               //    setting it to MPI_REQUEST_NULL.
             MPI_Status *st    // Address of the structure that will
                               //    hold the comm. information (OUT)
)
```

```
int MPI_Test(MPI_Request *req, // Address of the handle identifying
                               //    the operation queried (IN)
             int     *flag,    // Set to true if operation is
                               //    complete (OUT).
             MPI_Status *st    // Address of the structure that will
                               //    hold the comm. information (OUT)
)
```

A side effect of `MPI_Wait` (and `MPI_Test` upon a successful return) is that the `MPI_Request` handle is destroyed and the corresponding pointer is set to the symbolic constant `MPI_REQUEST_NULL`.

The proper use of the immediate communication primitives is illustrated through the following example. It is assumed that a range of numbers is to be partitioned and assigned to the participating nodes by the master node. In the code that follows, we assume that the partitioning is homogeneous, i.e., everyone gets an equal share of the work (including the master), but in practice this can be easily changed. An illustration of the communication involved for a total of three nodes is shown in Fig. 5.3.

Listing 5.7: An immediate communications example, where a range of numbers is evenly split among the nodes. The master sends the range that each node is responsible for.

```
1  // File : isend_example.c
2  #include <mpi.h>
3  #include <stdio.h>
4  #include <stdlib.h>
5  #include <string.h>
6
7  #define RANGEMIN 0
8  #define RANGEMAX 1000
9  #define MSGTAG 0
```

```
10
11    int main (int argc, char **argv)
12    {
13      int rank, num, i;
14      int range[2];
15      MPI_Init (&argc, &argv);
16      MPI_Comm_rank (MPI_COMM_WORLD, &rank);
17      MPI_Comm_size (MPI_COMM_WORLD, &num);
18      MPI_Status status;
19
20      if (rank == 0)
21        {
22            MPI_Request rq[num-1];
23            int rng[2*num];
24            int width = (RANGEMAX - RANGEMIN) / num;
25            rng[0] = RANGEMIN;                  // left limit
26            rng[1] = rng[0] + width - 1;   // right limit
27            for(i=1;i<num;i++)
28                {
29                    rng[i*2] = rng[i*2-1] + 1;        // message preparation
30                    rng[i*2+1] = (i==num-1) ? RANGEMAX : rng[i*2] + width-1;
31                }
32
33            for(i=1;i<num;i++)              // initiate all send operations
34                MPI_Isend(rng+i*2, 2, MPI_INT, i, MSGTAG,MPI_COMM_WORLD,
35                          &(rq[i-1]));
36
37            for(i=1;i<num;i++)             // block until all are complete
38                MPI_Wait(&(rq[i-1]), &status);
39
40          range[0] = rng[0];                 // master's limits
41          range[1] = rng[1];
42        }
43      else
44        {
45            MPI_Request rq;
46            MPI_Irecv (range, 2, MPI_INT, 0, MSGTAG, MPI_COMM_WORLD,&rq);
47            MPI_Wait(&rq, &status);
48        }
49
50      printf ("Node %i's range : ( %i, %i )\n", rank, range[0], range↩
         [1]);
51
52      MPI_Finalize ();
53      return 0;
54    }
```

Key points of the above program are:

- Multiple send operations can be initiated at the same time (lines 33–35). However, each can be tracked only by maintaining a separate handle for it, hence the need to have an array of type `MPI_Request` (line 22).

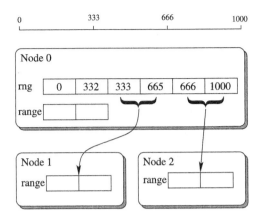

FIGURE 5.3

An illustration of the distribution taking place in Listing 5.7 for three nodes.

- If multiple operations are initiated, their associated data buffers are free for modification only after `MPI_Wait` returns. In order to allow multiple concurrent communications to take place, each message is designated its own buffer (line 23).
- If an `MPI_Irecv` is immediately followed by a call to `MPI_Wait` (lines 46 and 47), the two calls can be replaced by a normal `MPI_Recv` call.

The above program is in no way optimum. MPI provides very powerful *collective* (i.e., involving more than two nodes) communication operations that could reduce the loops of lines 33–38 to a single line (see Section 5.11), not to mention that for static partitionings like the one shown, no communication is really necessary, as each node can calculate its own range, replacing lines 20–48 with:

```
int width = (RANGEMAX - RANGEMIN) / num;
range[0] = RANGEMIN + rank * width;
range[1] = (rank == num-1) ? RANGEMAX : range[0] + width - 1;
```

The same could apply if the range limits were given as command-line parameters (e.g., via the `argv` array), as these become available to all MPI processes.

Immediate communications can also employ one of the three alternative modes explained in Section 5.7. So we have immediate buffered, synchronous, and ready modes. To distinguish them, a single letter is sandwiched between "I" and "s" in Isend: **b** for buffered, **s** for synchronous, and **r** for ready. All the additional functions share the same signature with the standard `MPI_Isend`.

```
int [ MPI_Ibsend | MPI_Issend | MPI_Irsend ] (void *buf, int count, ↩
    MPI_Datatype datatype, int dest, int tag, MPI_Comm comm, ↩
    MPI_Request &req);
```

Their semantics are identical to the alternative calls discussed in Section 5.7.

It should be noted that blocking sends can be matched will non-blocking receives and vice versa, e.g., a message sent by an MPI_Send call can be received by an MPI_Irecv call. The crucial parts that need to match are the endpoints as identified by the (communicator, rank, message tag) tuple.

5.9 Point-to-point communications: summary

Under normal circumstances this wide gamut of different communication modes is redundant. But in the case where MPI_Send is not good enough for your purposes, the decision comes down to one of the following choices:

A sending process ...	Function
... must block until the message is delivered	MPI_Ssend
... should wait only until the message is buffered	MPI_Bsend
... should return immediately without ever blocking	MPI_Isend
... should maximize concurrency by avoiding blocking and provide efficiency by eliminating buffer copies	MPI_Issend

5.10 Error reporting & handling

MPI provides rudimentary error reporting facilities, especially in comparison with the exception hierarchy that platforms such as Java provide. MPI is designed to offer reliable communications so developers do not have to check if errors happened during data transmissions. However, if MPI functions are called with the wrong parameters they can still malfunction.

All MPI calls (except MPI_Wtime and MPI_Wtick, which are explained in Section C.6 of Appendix C) return an integer value which represents an error condition. If the returned value is equal to MPI_SUCCESS (0), then no error was detected, at least locally. An example of what this means is that we can have an MPI_Send call returning successfully, after copying the message to a local MPI buffer, but the message may never be delivered to a destination for a number of reasons. Such reasons include the use of a mismatched tag, wrong destination rank, etc.

By default, MPI calls that detect an error fail catastrophically, i.e., they abort the application.

MPI-2 provides the capability to change this behavior by calling the MPI_Comm_set_errhandler function[8]:

---

[8] MPI-1 provides an alternative in the form of the MPI_Errhandler_set function. This function is considered deprecated in MPI-2 and it should not be used. Most deprecated functions in MPI-2 have been completely removed from later standards.

```
int MPI_Comm_set_errhandler(MPI_Comm comm, // Communicator (IN)
               MPI_Errhandler errhandler) // structure identifying
                                          // the error handler (IN)
```

One can either switch to one of the predefined handlers or define his/her own error handler. The predefined handlers which can be passed as parameters to `MPI_Comm_set_errhandler` are:

- `MPI_ERRORS_ARE_FATAL`: the default, terminate-upon-error handler.
- `MPI_ERRORS_RETURN`: MPI calls return with an error code but the program is not aborted. MPI will try, but it is not guaranteed to be able, to recover from the error condition.

A custom error handler can be registered with MPI to handle errors in a different manner. The error handling function must be defined as a variadic function (i.e., allowing a variable number of parameters) with the following signature:

```
void my_handler(MPI_Comm *comm, int *errcode, ...);
```

The parameters beyond the second one can be accessed with the `stdarg` standard C library. However, MPI does not specify what is supposed to come after the second parameter, so any attempt to access them results in code that is non-portable across different MPI implementations.

The custom handler must be registered with MPI with the following function:

```
int MPI_Comm_create_errhandler(
        MPI_Comm_errhandler_fn *function,  // Pointer to a handler
                                           // function (IN)
        MPI_Errhandler         *errhandler)// Pointer to a
                                           // MPI_Errhandler
                                           // structure, to be used
                                           // for registration (OUT)
```

Example:

Listing 5.8: A variation of the "Hello World" example, with a custom error handler. The `MPI_Send` call on line 21 will cause the `customErrHandler` function to execute in response to using an invalid/uninitialized communicator.

```
1  // File : errorHandling.c
2  . . .
3  void customErrHandler(MPI_Comm *comm, int *errcode, ...) {
4    printf("Error %i\n", *errcode);
5  }
6
7  int main (int argc, char **argv) {
8    MPI_Init (&argc, &argv);
9    MPI_Errhandler eh;
10
11   MPI_Comm_create_errhandler(customErrHandler, &eh);
```

```
12   MPI_Comm_set_errhandler(MPI_COMM_WORLD, eh);
13   MPI_Comm c;
14
15   int rank, num, i;
16   MPI_Comm_rank (MPI_COMM_WORLD, &rank);
17   MPI_Comm_size (MPI_COMM_WORLD, &num);
18   if (rank == 0) {
19       char mess[] = "Hello World";
20       for (i = 1; i < num; i++)
21           MPI_Send (mess, strlen (mess) + 1, MPI_CHAR, i, MESSTAG, c);
22   }
23   else {
24       char mess[MAXLEN];
25       MPI_Status status;
26       MPI_Recv (mess, MAXLEN, MPI_DOUBLE, 0, MESSTAG, MPI_COMM_WORLD ↩
                , &status);
27       printf ("%i received %s\n", rank, mess);
28   }
29   . . .
```

MPI-2 and later versions provide three different types of error handlers: for communicators, for windows (used in remote memory access), and for files (for parallel I/O). In this section we discussed explicitly only communicator-specific error handling. However, the functions discussed above have direct equivalents in the other two cases. The only thing that changes is that the Comm part of the function name is replaced by Win and File, respectively: MPI_Win_set_errhandler, MPI_File_create_errhandler, etc.

5.11 Collective communications

The term "collective communications" refers to operations that involve more than two nodes. Communication time is idle time for compute nodes, so it is of critical importance to minimize it. The non-blocking variants of our point-to-point primitives allow for overlap between computation and communication. Collective primitives go one step further, by also allowing *communications that involve multiple parties to take place concurrently.*

Here is an example that illustrates the necessity of having such operations: the 0-ranked process in MPI has exclusive access to the standard input stream. So, if the user enters a parameter required by all the nodes of an application, the only way it can be made accessible to the other MPI nodes is if process 0 sends/**broadcasts** it to them:

```
. . .
MPI_Comm_rank (MPI_COMM_WORLD, &rank);
MPI_Comm_size (MPI_COMM_WORLD, &num);
MPI_Status status;

if (rank == 0)
```

```
    {
        int param;
        cin >> param;
        for(i=1;i<num;i++)
            MPI_Send(&param, 1, MPI_INT, i, MSGTAG, MPI_COMM_WORLD);
    }
    else
    {
        int param;
        MPI_Recv (&param, 1, MPI_INT, 0, MSGTAG, MPI_COMM_WORLD, &↩
            status);
        . . .
    }
```

The communication cost of the above code snippet is proportional to the number of processes involved, as it requires $\Theta(N)$ individual communication operations conducted in sequence. This is obviously an expensive approach. Using `MPI_Isend` would not solve our problem, as what matters is the completion of the communication, and not just the availability of node 0.

If, however, we make the nodes that have already received the data act as repeaters, we could reduce the overall communication duration, as shown in Listing 5.9.

Listing 5.9: An efficient broadcasting approach that takes $\Theta(\lceil lgN \rceil)$ steps to complete.

```
1   // File : broadcast.c
2   . . .
3   // Returns the position of the most significant set bit of its ↩
        argument
4   int MSB(int i)
5   {
6       int pos = 0;
7       while (i != 0) {
8           i >>= 1;
9           pos++;
10      }
11      return pos-1;
12  }
13
14  // ******************************************
15
16  int main(int argc, char **argv) {
17      MPI_Init(&argc, &argv);
18
19      int rank, num, i;
20      MPI_Comm_rank(MPI_COMM_WORLD, &rank);
21      MPI_Comm_size(MPI_COMM_WORLD, &num);
22      MPI_Status status;
23
24      if (rank == 0) {
25          int destID = 1;
```

```
26      double data;
27      scanf("%lf", &data);
28      while (destID < num) {      // a subset of nodes gets a ↩
            message
29          MPI_Send(&data, 1, MPI_DOUBLE, destID, MESSTAG, ↩
                MPI_COMM_WORLD);
30          destID <<= 1;
31      }
32    } else {
33      int msbPos = MSB(rank);
34      int srcID = rank ^ (1 << msbPos);     // the message is not ↩
            coming from 0 for all
35      printf("#%i has source %i\n", rank, srcID);
36
37      // receive the message
38      double data;
39      MPI_Recv(&data, 1, MPI_DOUBLE, srcID, MESSTAG, ↩
                MPI_COMM_WORLD, &status);
40      printf("Node #%i received %lf\n", rank, data);
41
42      // calculate the ID of the node that will receive a copy of ↩
            the message
43      int destID = rank | (1 << (msbPos + 1));
44      while (destID < num) {
45          MPI_Send(&data, 1, MPI_DOUBLE, destID, MESSTAG, ↩
                MPI_COMM_WORLD);
46          msbPos++;
47          destID = rank | (1 << (msbPos + 1));
48      }
49    }
50  . . .
```

The program of Listing 5.9 works by treating the nodes of the MPI program as being arranged in a hypercube. Every node sends a message to one of its neighbors using a dimension that has not been used yet to carry a message. To accomplish this feat, the destination's rank is calculated by switching one of the zero bits of the source's rank that are above its most significant set bit. The same is true for the 0-ranked node. The source ID for a node that is expecting a message (line 39) is calculated by resetting the most significant bit of its own rank.

For example, if a node's rank is 7 (111 in binary), it will receive its message from node 3 (011 in binary) and it will proceed to send this message to nodes 15 (1111 in binary), 23 (10111 in binary), 39 (100111 in binary), etc. These calculations can be clearly observed in Fig. 5.4, which traces an execution of the above code.

The second broadcast variation performs better, needing only a cost proportional to $\Theta(\lceil lg N \rceil)$ to complete, as long as there is a direct communication link between all nodes. The proof is easy, as at the end of every iteration of the above algorithm, the number of nodes that have received the message doubles.

After k iterations we would be able to reach the following number of nodes:

$$1 + 2 + 4 + \cdots + 2^{k-1} = 2^k - 1. \tag{5.1}$$

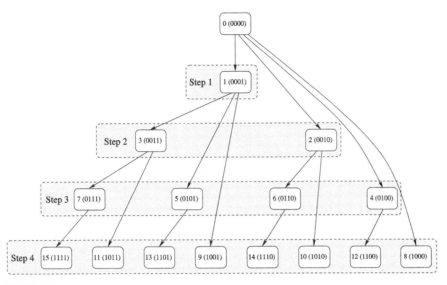

FIGURE 5.4

An illustration of how a message is broadcast according to the program in Listing 5.9 to 15 nodes in four steps. The nodes are decorated by their ranks, with their binary representation in parentheses.

Starting with node 0, reaching the remaining $N-1$ nodes would require

$$N-1 = 2^k - 1 \Rightarrow k = lg(N) \tag{5.2}$$

steps to complete. Obviously, because k needs to be an integer, we have to round up to $k = \lceil lg(N) \rceil$.

This is, however, a complex solution! Additionally, there is a problem with architectures where the communication links do not form a complete graph, or hypercube as required by Listing 5.9, but a subset of it, like, e.g., a 2D or a 3D mesh, a cylinder, or even have an irregular communication network, like a Network of Workstations (NoW). The above program would still work, but it would not be optimized any more, and our analysis would be flawed as far as the total cost is concerned.

Fortunately, MPI collectives solve this problem also: MPI implementations can provide *optimized* collective operations, specifically tuned to perform as efficiently as possible, given the execution platform's communication infrastructure.

MPI provides its own optimized implementation of a broadcast operation, via the `MPI_Bcast` function:

```
int MPI_Bcast( void       *buffer,  // Address of the buffer that
                                    //     either holds or receives
                                    //     the data (IN/OUT)
               int         count,   // Size of buffer (IN)
               MPI_Datatype dtype,  // MPI type of the elements
```

```
                                        //     in the buffer (IN)
           int          root,    // Rank of source process (IN)
           MPI_Comm     comm     // Communicator (IN)
        )
```

Equipped with `MPI_Bcast`, we can provide the same functionality as Listing 5.9, with the code shown in Listing 5.10.

Listing 5.10: Broadcasting using the `MPI_Bcast` function.

```
1   // File : broadcast2.c
2   . . .
3   if (rank == 0) {
4       double data;
5       scanf("%lf", &data);
6       MPI_Bcast( &data, 1, MPI_DOUBLE, 0, MPI_COMM_WORLD);
7   } else {
8       double data;
9       MPI_Bcast( &data, 1, MPI_DOUBLE, 0, MPI_COMM_WORLD);
10      printf("Node #%i received %lf\n", rank, data);
11  }
12  . . .
```

Lines 6 and 9 in Listing 5.10 are identical, as this is a requirement for the use of `MPI_Bcast`. Having common or compatible parameters is actually a requirement for using any of the collective MPI operations.

MPI collective operations have distinct traits in comparison to regular point-to-point operations. These are:

- Operations are not distinguished by a tag. They apply *universally* to all the nodes of a *communicator*. If multiple operations are used, they will be executed in the order they are called.
- The calls must be identical for all participating processes, regardless if they are sources or sinks.

  The parameters used must be identical, or at least "compatible." Compatibility has a different meaning for input and output message-related parameters, depending on whether they are used in the source or the destination nodes. The typical rules, unless stated otherwise in the MPI documentation, are:

  - Input parameters, source nodes: The type and number of items (if arrays are used) must be identical.
  - Input parameters, destination nodes: These are ignored. If pointers are expected, a null reference can be used instead.
  - Output parameters, source nodes: These are ignored. If pointers are expected, a null reference can be used instead.
  - Output parameters, destination nodes: The type and number of items (if arrays are used) must be identical.

A deviation from the above may cause a call to fail (best case) or produce erroneous results (worst case).

MPI_Bcast can be also used to provide *multicasting* functionality, i.e., sending a message to a subset of the available processes. This can be achieved by creating a custom communicator. This option is explored further in Section 5.16.

MPI provides a large variety of collective operations that we explore in the following sections. They can be divided into:

- **one-to-all**: MPI_Bcast, MPI_Scatter, MPI_Scatterv,
- **all-to-one**: MPI_Gather, MPI_Gatherv, MPI_Reduce,
- **all-to-all**: MPI_Allotall, MPI_Alltoallv, MPI_Allreduce, MPI_Allgather, MPI_Barrier.

MPI-3 adds immediate versions of the above functions to the standard. The naming convention follows the one used for MPI_Isend, etc., so the function names are produced by replacing MPI_ with MPI_I and making the rest of the name lower-case. The parameters and their order are identical, with the exception of the addition of an extra argument of type MPI_Request* at the end. The request parameter allows the caller process to check if the call is complete or not via the functions MPI_Test and MPI_Wait (see Section 5.8).

In the following sections we will explore the above operations, going beyond the mere syntax of the commands. The study of the inner workings of the collective operations constitutes a valuable educational tool as it exposes a number of important techniques about managing processes and orchestrating communications between them.

5.11.1 Scattering

Scattering refers to the distribution of a dataset to the processes of a communicator. The MPI function is:

```
int MPI_Scatter(void        *sendbuf,   // Address of the data to be
                                        //    sent (IN)
                int         sendcnt,    // Number of sendbuf items to
                                        //    send per process(IN)
                MPI_Datatype sendtype,  // MPI type of sendbuf
                                        //    elements (IN)
                void        *recvbuf,   // Address of receiving
                                        //    buffer (OUT)
                int         recvcnt,    // Size of recvbuf (IN)
                MPI_Datatype recvtype,  // MPI type of recvbuf
                                        //    elements (IN)
                int         root,       // Source process rank (IN)
                MPI_Comm    comm)       // Communicator (IN)
```

Two buffers are designated: a send buffer that contains the data to be evenly distributed among the processes, including the root, and a receive buffer where the data will be deposited. The sendcnt parameter specifies how many elements will be sent to each process. As a consequence, sendcnt is a lower bound for the size of recvbuf

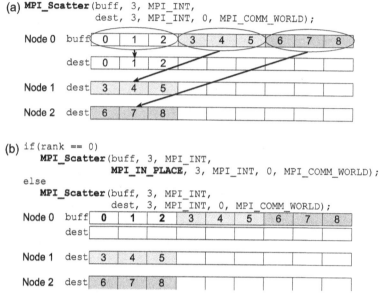

(a) **MPI_Scatter**(buff, 3, MPI_INT,
                  dest, 3, MPI_INT, 0, MPI_COMM_WORLD);

(b) if(rank == 0)
      MPI_Scatter(buff, 3, MPI_INT,
                    MPI_IN_PLACE, 3, MPI_INT, 0, MPI_COMM_WORLD);
    else
      MPI_Scatter(buff, 3, MPI_INT,
                    dest, 3, MPI_INT, 0, MPI_COMM_WORLD);

FIGURE 5.5

An illustration of how scattering an array works when (a) the root has a destination buffer and (b) the scatter is in place for the root.

and `sendbuf` should contain at least $N \cdot recvcnt$ elements, where N is the size of the communicator.

Two datatypes need to be specified, one for the sending and one for the receiving buffer. Typically, these should be identical. There are however a number of cases where they can be different, but only if they are derived types based on the same primitive type. Such a scenario is examined in Section 5.15.

The scatter operation has a memory copy overhead for the root process. This can be avoided by specifying in the place of `recvbuf` the symbolic constant `MPI_IN_PLACE` for the call made by the root. This option does not move the part assigned to the root process. An illustration of `MPI_Scatter` in action is shown in Fig. 5.5.

As an example for the use of `MPI_Scatter`, let us consider the problem of matrix–vector multiplication, i.e., multiplying an $M \times M$ matrix A by an M-element vector B. A parallel solution can be easily designed by applying the geometric data decomposition pattern (see Section 2.3.3). We can split matrix A row-wise into blocks and assign each of the blocks to one MPI node. This decomposition pattern is also favored by the fact that C/C++ use a row-major memory allocation for 2D arrays.

The calculations taking place in matrix–vector multiplication are illustrated in Fig. 5.6.

If M is not evenly divided by the number of MPI processes, a memory protection fault is likely to be produced when `MPI_Scatter` tries to access the data destined

$$
\begin{pmatrix}
A_{0,0} & A_{0,1} & \cdots & A_{0,M-1} \\
A_{1,0} & A_{1,1} & \cdots & A_{1,M-1} \\
\vdots & \vdots & & \vdots \\
A_{M-1,0} & A_{M-1,1} & \cdots & A_{M-1,M-1}
\end{pmatrix}
\cdot
\begin{pmatrix}
B_0 \\
B_1 \\
\vdots \\
B_{M-1}
\end{pmatrix}
=
$$

$$
\begin{pmatrix}
A_{0,0} \cdot B_0 + A_{0,1} \cdot B_1 + \cdots + A_{0,M-1} \cdot B_{M-1} \\
A_{1,0} \cdot B_0 + A_{1,1} \cdot B_1 + \cdots + A_{1,M-1} \cdot B_{M-1} \\
\vdots \\
A_{M-1,0} \cdot B_0 + A_{M-1,1} \cdot B_1 + \cdots + A_{M-1,M-1} \cdot B_{M-1}
\end{pmatrix}
$$

FIGURE 5.6

An illustration of how a matrix–vector multiplication is performed.

for the last process. In that case, we can still use `MPI_Scatter` to perform the data distribution if we make sure that the input buffer holding A is padded with enough extra rows to avoid this error. `MPI_Bcast` can be used for sending vector B, as shown in Listing 5.11.

Listing 5.11: Matrix–vector multiplication that uses `MPI_Scatter` and `MPI_Bcast` for data distribution.

```cpp
// File : matrix_vector.cpp
. . .
const int M = 100;

// ********************************************
// Performs C=A*B with A a matrix "rows X columns", and B a vector ↩
    with "columns" elements
void MV (double *A, double *B, double *C, int columns, int rows)
{
  for (int i = 0; i < rows; i++)
    {
      double temp = 0;
      for (int j = 0; j < columns; j++)
        temp += A[i * columns + j] * B[j];

      C[i] = temp;
    }
}

// ********************************************
int main (int argc, char **argv)
{
  MPI_Init (&argc, &argv);

  int rank, N;
```

```
25    MPI_Comm_rank (MPI_COMM_WORLD, &rank);
26    MPI_Comm_size (MPI_COMM_WORLD, &N);
27    MPI_Status status;
28
29
30    int rowsPerProcess;              // size of block per MPI process
31    int rowsAlloc = M;
32    if (M % N != 0)
33      rowsAlloc = (M / N + 1) * N;
34    rowsPerProcess = rowsAlloc / N;
35
36    if (rank == 0)
37      {
38        double *A = new double[M * rowsAlloc];
39        double *B = new double[M];
40        double *C = new double[M];         // result vector
41
42        for (int i = 0; i < M * M; i++)  A[i] = i; // initialize A & B
43        for (int i = 0; i < M; i++)       B[i] = 1;
44
45        MPI_Scatter (A, M * rowsPerProcess, MPI_DOUBLE, MPI_IN_PLACE, ←
              0, MPI_DOUBLE, 0, MPI_COMM_WORLD);
46        MPI_Bcast (B, M, MPI_DOUBLE, 0, MPI_COMM_WORLD);
47        MV (A, B, C, M, rowsPerProcess);  // root does its share of ←
              the computation
48
49        // collect results now
50        for (int i = 1; i < N - 1; i++)
51          MPI_Recv (C + rowsPerProcess * i, rowsPerProcess, MPI_DOUBLE ←
              , i, RESTAG, MPI_COMM_WORLD, &status);
52
53        // last process treated differently
54        MPI_Recv (C + rowsPerProcess * (N - 1), M - (N - 1) * ←
              rowsPerProcess, MPI_DOUBLE, N - 1, RESTAG, MPI_COMM_WORLD, ←
              &status);
55
56        for (int i = 0; i < M; i++)
57          cout << C[i] << " ";
58        cout << endl;
59      }
60    else
61      {
62        double *locA = new double[M * rowsPerProcess];
63        double *B = new double[M];
64        double *partC = new double[rowsPerProcess]; // partial result ←
              vector
65
66        MPI_Scatter (NULL, M * rowsPerProcess, MPI_DOUBLE, locA, M * ←
              rowsPerProcess, MPI_DOUBLE, 0, MPI_COMM_WORLD);
67        MPI_Bcast (B, M, MPI_DOUBLE, 0, MPI_COMM_WORLD);
68
69        if (rank == N - 1)
```

```
70        rowsPerProcess = M - (N - 1) * rowsPerProcess;  // strip ↩
             padded rows for the last process

71
72        MV (locA, B, partC, M, rowsPerProcess);
73        MPI_Send (partC, rowsPerProcess, MPI_DOUBLE, 0, RESTAG, ↩
             MPI_COMM_WORLD);

74    }
75    . . .
```

These are the fine points of Listing 5.11:

- The program calculates the product of a 100×100 matrix with a 100-element vector. The sizes are controlled by line 3, which defines the symbolic constant M. In a real-life situation, one would expect that the problem data would be read from a file, instead of having them initialized to dummy values on lines 42–43. However, there is a substantial benefit to using properly manipulated dummy data at the testing phase of an application: you can easily verify the correctness of your parallel algorithm implementation. Given the values used on lines 42–43, the above program should output a sequence of numbers that represent the sum of the rows of the A matrix. The ith element of the resulting vector, with $i \in [0, M)$, should be equal to

$$i \cdot M + (i \cdot M + 1) + \ldots + ((i+1) \cdot M - 1) = \frac{(M-1)M}{2} + i \cdot M^2.$$

  For $M = 100$ we should get "4950 14950 24950 34950 44950 54950 64950 74950 ..."
- The MV function on lines 7–17 calculates a matrix–vector product, given the addresses and sizes of the matrix and vector involved. Each process calls it once the input data are collected from the root process (line 72).
- The 0-rank process (root) uses in-place scatter to distribute matrix A to all the processes (line 45). The vector is sent via MPI_Bcast (lines 46 and 67).
- The – partial – results are collected via point-to-point communications (lines 50–54 and 73).
- The scenario of having M not evenly divided by the number of processes N is addressed by padding the A matrix with extra rows (lines 32–33). Thus, every process gets the same number of matrix rows (rowsPerProcess). During product calculation and result collection, the last process adjusts the rows according to the true size of A and the actual rows that can be used (lines 69–70).
- In order to pass references to multi-dimensional arrays to functions, C/C++ requires that all but one of the dimension sizes (the higher one) are fixed and declared in the function header. To overcome this limitation and pass arbitrary-sized matrices to the MV function, the A matrix is defined as a 1D array (lines 38 and 62). In order to access the x-column and y-row element (numbering starting from 0) of A, one has to use the index $y \cdot numColumns + x$, since the elements are stored row after row consecutively in memory, and the beginning of row y starts at index $y \cdot numColumns$.

One thing that can be considered as a potential pitfall of `MPI_Scatter` is the need to send the same volume of data to all the members of a communicator. But what if the execution platform is not homogeneous? Faster CPUs should be assigned a larger portion of the workload if execution time is to be minimized. This need is addressed by `MPI_Scatterv`, where the "v" suffix stands for vector. `MPI_Scatterv` syntax requires two additional arrays as input, so that the precise amount of data each process will get can be specified. The exact syntax is:

```
int MPI_Scatterv(void      *sendbuf,  // Address of the buffer to
                                      // be sent (IN)
                 int        *sendcnts,// Array with as many elements
                                      // as the communicator size.
                                      // Contains the number of items
                                      // to send to each process (IN)
                                      // Significant only at the root
                 int        *displs,  // Same array size as sendcnts
                                      // Contains the offsets in
                                      // sendbuf where each of the
                                      // parts resides (IN)
                                      // Significant only at the root
                 MPI_Datatype sendtype, // MPI type of sendbuf
                                      // elements (IN)
                 void       *recvbuf, // Address of receiving
                                      // buffer (OUT)
                 int        recvcnt,  // Size of recvbuf (IN)
                 MPI_Datatype recvtype, // MPI type of recvbuf
                                      // elements (IN)
                 int        root,     // Rank of source process (IN)
                 MPI_Comm   comm)     // Communicator (IN)
```

Equipped with `MPI_Scatterv`, we can avoid having to pad the matrix A. Instead, the code in Listing 5.12 would have to be used.

Listing 5.12: A variation of Listing 5.11 that uses `MPI_Scatterv`. Only the major differences with the original code are shown.

```
1   // File : matrix_vector2.cpp
2   . . .
3     int rowsPerProcess;              // size of block per MPI process
4     rowsPerProcess = M/N;
5
6     if (rank == 0) {
7         double *A = new double[M * M];
8         double *B = new double[M];
9         double *C = new double[M];        // result vector
10        . . .
11        int displs[N];
12        int sendcnts[N];
13        for(int i=0;i<N;i++)  {
14            sendcnts[i] = rowsPerProcess*M;
15            displs[i] = i*rowsPerProcess*M;
16            if(i==N-1)
```

```
17          sendcnts[i] = (M - (N-1)*rowsPerProcess)*M;
18        }
19
20      MPI_Scatterv (A, sendcnts,displs, MPI_DOUBLE, MPI_IN_PLACE, 0,↵
                MPI_DOUBLE, 0, MPI_COMM_WORLD);
21      MPI_Bcast (B, M, MPI_DOUBLE, 0, MPI_COMM_WORLD);
22      MV (A, B, C, M, rowsPerProcess);
23        . . .
24      }
25   else
26      {
27      if (rank == N - 1)
28        rowsPerProcess = M - (N - 1) * rowsPerProcess;
29        . . .
30      MPI_Scatterv (NULL, NULL, NULL, MPI_DOUBLE, locA, M * ↵
                rowsPerProcess, MPI_DOUBLE, 0, MPI_COMM_WORLD);
31        . . .
32      }
33   . . .
```

The major addition to Listing 5.11 is the calculation of the send counts and displacement arrays on lines 13–18. These parameters are not required in any other process but the root, so on line 30 all the corresponding arguments used by the receiving processes are NULL.

Finally, Listing 5.11 has one flaw: result collection is effectively a collective all-to-one operation. The details of how this can be accomplished with a single statement are discussed in the following section.

5.11.2 **Gathering**

Gathering is the exact anti-symmetric operation of scattering: it collects data from all the processes of a communicator into the destination process's repository. Similarly to scattering, MPI provides two functions accommodating uniform and variable data collection: MPI_Gather and MPI_Gatherv. Their syntax is:

```
int MPI_Gather(void        *sendbuf,   // Address of the buffer to be
                                       // sent. Separate in each
                                       // source process. (IN)
               int          sendcnt,   // The number of items to be
                                       // sent from each process.(IN)
               MPI_Datatype sendtype,  // MPI type of sendbuf
                                       // elements (IN)
               void        *recvbuf,   // Address of receiving
                                       // buffer (OUT)
                                       // Significant only at the root.
               int          recvcnt,   // Reserved space in recvbuf
                                       // per sending process (IN).
                                       // Significant only at the root.
               MPI_Datatype recvtype,  // MPI type of recvbuf
                                       // elements (IN)
               int          root,      // Rank of destination (IN)
```

```
                   MPI_Comm      comm)      // Communicator (IN)
```

```
int MPI_Gatherv(void        *sendbuf, // Address of the buffer to be
                                      // sent. Separate in each
                                      // source process. (IN)
                int         sendcnt,  // The number of items to be
                                      // sent from each process.(IN)
                MPI_Datatype sendtype, // MPI type of sendbuf
                                      // elements (IN)
                void        *recvbuf, // Address of receiving
                                      // buffer (OUT)
                                      // Significant only at the root.
                int         *recvcnts,// How many items to get from
                                      // each source. (IN)
                                      // Significant only at the root.
                int         *displs,  // Location offsets in recvbuf
                                      // for each of the sources (IN)
                                      // Significant only at the root.
                MPI_Datatype recvtype, // MPI type of recvbuf
                                      // elements (IN)
                int         root,     // Rank of destination (IN)
                MPI_Comm    comm)     // Communicator (IN)
```

Adopting Listing 5.12 to use gathering instead of point-to-point communications is straightforward. Given the need to treat the last process in the communicator differently, even during the result collection phase, MPI_Gatherv is deemed more suitable for the circumstances.

In Listing 5.13, we are reusing the sending counts (sendcnts) and displacements arrays (displs) for specifying how MPI_Gatherv will collect data from the processes.

Listing 5.13: Modifications to Listing 5.12 so that MPI_Gatherv can be used to collect the matrix–vector product.

```
1  // File : matrix_vector3.cpp
2  . . .
3    int rowsPerProcess;              // size of block per MPI process
4    rowsPerProcess = M/N;
5
6    if (rank == 0) {
7        . . .
8        MV (A, B, C, M, rowsPerProcess);
9
10       for(int i=0;i<N;i++)
11       {
12           sendcnts[i] = rowsPerProcess;
13           displs[i] = i*rowsPerProcess;
14           if(i==N−1)
15               sendcnts[i] = M − (N−1)*rowsPerProcess;
16       }
17
18       MPI_Gatherv(C, rowsPerProcess, MPI_DOUBLE, C, sendcnts, displs ↩
               , MPI_DOUBLE, 0, MPI_COMM_WORLD);
```

```
19        // print out C
20        . . .
21     }
22  else
23     {
24        . . .
25        MPI_Scatterv (NULL, NULL, NULL, MPI_DOUBLE, locA, M * ↵
                 rowsPerProcess, MPI_DOUBLE, 0, MPI_COMM_WORLD);
26        MPI_Bcast (B, M, MPI_DOUBLE, 0, MPI_COMM_WORLD);
27        MV (locA, B, partC, M, rowsPerProcess);
28
29        MPI_Gatherv(partC, rowsPerProcess, MPI_DOUBLE, NULL, NULL, ↵
                 NULL, MPI_DOUBLE, 0, MPI_COMM_WORLD);
30     }
31  . . .
```

5.11.3 **Reduction**

An operation that is frequently taking place in the processing of large collections of data is *reduction*: selecting, extracting, or deriving one or a subset of data items. Some of the simplest examples include summation and finding the minimum or maximum of a set of items.

As an example of reduction, let us consider an MPI version of the multi-threaded function integration program presented in Section 3.7.2. Instead of dynamically assigning parts of the input range and focusing on how to terminate the program, we can do a static uniform partitioning and assign $\frac{1}{N}$ of the input range to each process, where N is the number of processes. Effectively we switch our focus from problem data distribution, to result collection.

The shared static variable *result of the IntegrCalc class of Listing 3.15 is no longer available in our distributed-memory platform. In order to be able to accumulate the final result, the root could use point-to-point communication to collect the individual partial results and add them up in a $\Theta(N)$ time complexity operation. However, this process can be sped up considerably by having pairs of processes sum up their results in successive steps as shown in Fig. 5.7. As illustrated, N does not have to be a power of 2 to be able to use this *tournament tree* pattern to solve the problem in $\Theta(\lceil lgN \rceil)$.

The mechanics of how the tree in Fig. 5.7 is constructed are revealed if the binary representation of the process ranks are taken into consideration. The communications taking place in Fig. 5.7 are depicted using a different visualization technique in Fig. 5.8.

The reduction operation is taking place over $\lceil lgN \rceil$ steps, one step for each of the bits required to represent the process ranks. During step i, the ith bit of a process is examined. If it is 1, it sends its partial sum to the process with the same ID as itself, but with the ith bit reset. Subsequently, it takes no action. These steps can be more concisely expressed as the code in Listing 5.14.

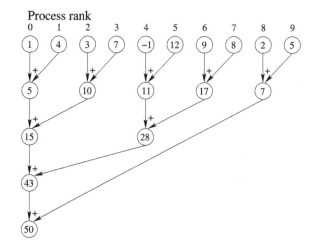

FIGURE 5.7

Calculating a summation using a tournament tree pattern.

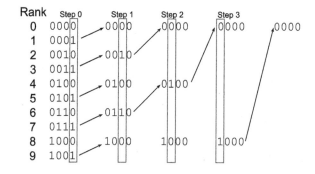

FIGURE 5.8

Graph illustrating the pairings of processes that take place in the tournament tree of Fig. 5.7. Edges represent data communications and the frames highlight the bits considered during each step of the reduction.

Listing 5.14: Summing up the partial results in MPI processes by performing reduction.

```
1   // File : manual_reduction.cpp
2   . . .
3     int rank, N;
4     MPI_Comm_rank (MPI_COMM_WORLD, &rank);
5     MPI_Comm_size (MPI_COMM_WORLD, &N);
6     MPI_Status status;
7
8     int partialSum = rank; // just a sample value
9     int bitMask = 1;
```

```
10    bool doneFlag = false; // set when a process sends its partial sum
11    while (bitMask < N && !doneFlag) {
12        int otherPartyID;    // process rank of communication endpoint
13        if ((rank & bitMask) == 0) { // destination process
14            otherPartyID = rank | bitMask;
15            if (otherPartyID >= N) { // invalid otherPartyID indicates
16                bitMask <<= 1;        // that process is not involved
17                continue;            // in current step
18            }
19            int temp;
20            MPI_Recv (&temp, 1, MPI_INT, otherPartyID, MPI_ANY_TAG, ↩
                MPI_COMM_WORLD, &status);
21            partialSum += temp;
22        }
23        else {                          // source process
24            otherPartyID = rank ^ bitMask;
25            doneFlag = true;
26            MPI_Send (&partialSum, 1, MPI_INT, otherPartyID, 0, ↩
                MPI_COMM_WORLD);
27        }
28        bitMask <<= 1;
29    }
30
31    if (rank == 0)
32        cout << partialSum << endl;
33    . . .
```

MPI provides a built-in reduction function that allows us to perform the magic of Listing 5.14 in a single statement. The syntax of MPI_Reduce, which reduces the values in all the provided buffers to a single value stored at the specified root, is the following:

```
int MPI_Reduce(void        *sendbuf, // Address of the buffer to be
                                     // sent. Separate in each
                                     // source process. (IN)
               void        *recvbuf, // Address of receiving
                                     // buffer (OUT)
                                     // Significant at the root.
               int          count,   // Number of elements to send
               MPI_Datatype datatype, // MPI type of sendbuf and
                                     // recvbuf elements (IN)
               MPI_Op       op,      // Symbolic constant identify-
                                     // ing the type of reduction
                                     // to be performed (IN)
               int          root,    // Rank of destination (IN)
               MPI_Comm     comm)    // Communicator (IN)
```

The fifth parameter specifies the operator to be applied during the reduction. The list of predefined reduction operators is given in Table 5.4.

Equipped with MPI_Reduce, we can complete the distributed-memory function integration example, as shown in Listing 5.15.

Table 5.4 List of predefined reduction operators in MPI.

Symbolic name	Description
MPI_SUM	Summation
MPI_MIN	Minimum
MPI_MAX	Maximum
MPI_PROD	Product
MPI_LAND	Logican AND
MPI_BAND	Bitwise AND
MPI_LOR	Logican OR
MPI_BOR	Bitwise OR
MPI_LXOR	Logican exclusive OR
MPI_BXOR	Bitwise exclusive OR
MPI_MAXLOC	Maximum and its location
MPI_MINLOC	Minimum and its location

Listing 5.15: Function integration example that uses MPI_Reduce to accumulate the partial results of the MPI processes.

```cpp
// File : integration_reduction.cpp
. . .
double testf (double x) {
  return x * x + 2 * sin (x);
}

//----------------------------------------------
//calculate and return area
double integrate (double st, double en, int div, double (*f) (double↩
    )) {
  double localRes = 0;
  double step = (en - st) / div;
  double x;
  x = st;
  localRes = f (st) + f (en);
  localRes /= 2;
  for (int i = 1; i < div; i++) {
      x += step;
      localRes += f (x);
    }
  localRes *= step;

  return localRes;
}

//----------------------------------------------
int main (int argc, char *argv[]) {

  MPI_Init (&argc, &argv);
```

```
29
30   int rank, N;
31   MPI_Comm_rank (MPI_COMM_WORLD, &rank);
32   MPI_Comm_size (MPI_COMM_WORLD, &N);
33   MPI_Status status;
34
35   if (argc == 1) {
36       if (rank == 0)
37           cerr << "Usage " << argv[0] << " start end divisions\n";
38       exit (1);
39   }
40   double start, end;
41   int divisions;
42   start = atof (argv[1]);
43   end = atof (argv[2]);
44   divisions = atoi (argv[3]);
45
46   double locSt, locEnd, rangePerProc;
47   int locDiv;
48   locDiv = ceil (1.0 * divisions / N);
49   rangePerProc = (end - start) / N;    // range part per process
50   locSt = start + rangePerProc * rank; // local range start
51   locEnd = (rank == N - 1) ? end
52                : start + rangePerProc * (rank + 1); //local range ↩
                      end
53   double partialResult = integrate (locSt, locEnd, locDiv, testf);
54   double finalRes;
55   MPI_Reduce (&partialResult, &finalRes, 1, MPI_DOUBLE, MPI_SUM, 0, ↩
         MPI_COMM_WORLD);
56
57   if (rank == 0)
58     cout << finalRes << endl;
59   . . .
```

Listing 5.15 has a peculiarity in that the computations can start and complete in all the processes without the root needing to send any kind of initializing messages. As all processes have access to the command-line parameters, lines 42–44 can extract all the information required for the computation to commence. Processes then proceed to calculate the subrange of the desired [*start, end*] that they will operate upon by splitting the range evenly between them (lines 48–52). The partial integrals are subsequently calculated by calling the integrate function, with the process-local range and a pointer to the function that is to be integrated. MPI_Reduce on line 55 accumulates the final result by using the MPI_SUM reduction operator. The only special duties assigned to the root process are simple error-handling (lines 36–37) and final result reporting (lines 57–58).

5.11.4 All-to-all gathering

In Section 5.11.2, we used matrix–vector multiplication as an example of the need to gather results efficiently. A number of applications require that the result of the

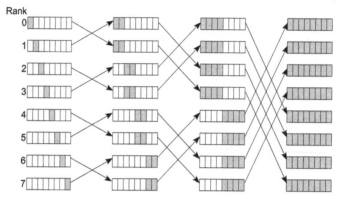

Rank

FIGURE 5.9

Implementation of an all-to-all gathering operation, using a "butterfly" communication scheme. The shaded boxes represent parts of the data present at a node.

gathering operation is propagated back to the MPI processes for subsequent steps. For example, we could be applying a sequence of transformations to a vector $\vec{x}$:

$$\vec{y} = A_{k-1} \cdot A_{k-2} \ldots A_0 \cdot \vec{x} = A_{k-1}(A_{k-2}(\ldots(A_0 \cdot \vec{x}))). \tag{5.3}$$

In order to calculate $\vec{y}$, each new vector that is produced by one multiplication must be made available to all the processes. One solution would be to have one gathering step, followed by a broadcasting step, as in the following code (with N representing the number of processes and M the size of the vector):

```
double *y = new double[M];
double *newY = new double[M];
. . .
MPI_Gather(y, M/N, MPI_DOUBLE, newY, M/N,  MPI_DOUBLE, 0, ↵
    MPI_COMM_WORLD);
MPI_Bcast(newY, M, MPI_DOUBLE, 0, MPI_COMM_WORLD);
```

This sequence of statements would amount to a total of $2\lceil lgN \rceil$ steps, each step involving a number of concurrent message exchanges. An alternative communication scheme can be employed to effectively cut this cost in half (as far as the number of steps is concerned), as long as duplex communications are supported, i.e., it is possible for two processes to send and receive messages between them concurrently. The only restriction to the **butterfly** communication pattern, as it is known due to its appearance (see Fig. 5.9), is that the number of processes must be a power of 2.

The pattern illustrated in Fig. 5.9 is performed over $\lceil lgN \rceil$ steps. During each ith step, the processes which have their ranks different in the ith bit only exchange the *data they have collected so far*. Eventually, all the processes end up having a complete copy of the data to be gathered. The operation is reminiscent of the way the tournament tree is built in the reduction implementation of Listing 5.14, with the difference that in our all-to-all gathering the data communicated double in volume with every step.

The following code snippet implements the butterfly communication pattern using point-to-point communications to gather K-sized arrays from all the processes:

Listing 5.16: MPI implementation of the butterfly pattern using point-to-point communication for achieving an all-to-all gathering operation.

```cpp
// File : allgather.cpp
const int K = 10;
const int ALLGATHERTAG = 0;
. . .
  unique_ptr<double[]> localPart = make_unique<double[]>(K);
  unique_ptr<double[]> allParts = make_unique<double[]>(K*N);

  // test data init.
  for (int i = 0; i < K; i++)
    localPart[i] = rank;
  int bitMask = 1;
  int acquiredCount = K;
  int acquiredStart = rank * K;

  // copy local data to array that will hold the complete data
  memcpy (&allParts[rank * K], &localPart[0], sizeof (double) * K);
  while (bitMask < N)
    {
      int otherPartyID = rank ^ bitMask;
      if ((rank & bitMask) == 0)
        {
          MPI_Send (&allParts[acquiredStart], acquiredCount, ←
              MPI_DOUBLE, otherPartyID, ALLGATHERTAG, MPI_COMM_WORLD←
              );
          MPI_Recv (&allParts[acquiredStart + acquiredCount], ←
              acquiredCount, MPI_DOUBLE, otherPartyID, ALLGATHERTAG,←
              MPI_COMM_WORLD, &status);
          acquiredCount *= 2;
        }
      else
        {
          MPI_Recv (&allParts[acquiredStart - acquiredCount], ←
              acquiredCount, MPI_DOUBLE, otherPartyID, ALLGATHERTAG,←
              MPI_COMM_WORLD, &status);
          MPI_Send (&allParts[acquiredStart], acquiredCount, ←
              MPI_DOUBLE, otherPartyID, ALLGATHERTAG, MPI_COMM_WORLD←
              );
          acquiredStart -= acquiredCount;
          acquiredCount *= 2;
        }
      bitMask <<= 1;
    }
```

```
36   // printout/verification step
37   if (rank == 0)
38     {
39       for (int i = 0; i < K * N; i++)
40         cout << allParts[i] << " ";
41       cout << endl;
42     }
43   . . .
```

For the first time in this chapter, we have in the above listing C++11-specific source code, with the use of smart pointers. The only change that needs to be done for compiling the above program is to enable the compiler's C++11 extensions. For GCC, this means a command similar to:

```
$ mpic++ −std=c++17 allgather.cpp −o allgather
```

The key variables in Listing 5.16 are:

- localPart: array that is contributed in the gathering by all processes. Each localPart contains K elements for a total of $K \cdot N$ items that have to be gathered. localPart is initialized to the rank of the process, in order to produce an output on lines 35–37, which is easily checked for correctness.
- allParts: placeholder for the gathered data. Initially each process places in the appropriate offset in allParts its own data parts, which are originally in array localPart (line 16). At the end of the procedure, all processes will hold a verbatim copy of allParts.
- acquiredCount: counts how many of the desired data are already resident in a process. Initialized to K.
- acquiredStart: index in the allParts array, where a process's resident data are.
- bitMask: serves as a loop control variable and as a bit mask for determining the rank of the process to pair with during each communication step, given one's own rank (line 19).

The allParts array fills up in the fashion observed in the boxes of Fig. 5.9 (memory addresses growing from right to left). During each iteration of the loop on lines 17–31, a process determines the rank of the other process that it should exchange data with (line 19), performs the exchange (lines 22–23 and 28–29), updates the offset of the resident data (if need be, line 30), and increases the number of items currently resident (lines 24 and 31).

One noteworthy feature of Listing 5.16 is that the two parties exchanging messages follow a different send/receive sequence: one is sending and then receiving, while the other is following the opposite order. This arrangement would guarantee that our processes would not face a deadlock, even if the sending call would block. Of course, as explained in Section 5.7, MPI_Send is locally blocking, but even if we were to use MPI_Ssend, our program would still function properly.

A sample run of the program in Listing 5.16 is shown below:

```
$ mpirun -np 8 ./allgather
0 0 0 0 0 0 0 0 0 0 1 1 1 1 1 1 1 1 1 1 2 2 2 2 2 2 2 2 2 2 3 3 3 3 ↩
    3 3 3 3 3 3 4 4 4 4 4 4 4 4 4 4 5 5 5 5 5 5 5 5 5 5 6 6 6 6 6 6 ↩
    6 6 6 6 7 7 7 7 7 7 7 7 7 7
```

MPI provides two all-to-all gathering functions, for uniform and variable data collection, respectively: MPI_Allgather and MPI_Allgatherv. Their syntax is:

```
int MPI_Allgather(void      *sendbuf,   // Address of the buffer to
                                        // be sent. (IN)
                  int       sendcount,  // Number of elements to
                                        // send per process. Should
                                        // be identical in all. (IN)
                  MPI_Datatype sendtype,// MPI type of sendbuf
                                        // elements. (IN)
                  void      *recvbuf,   // Address of receiving
                                        // buffer (OUT)
                  int       recvcount,  // Space available in
                                        // recvbuf per process. (IN)
                  MPI_Datatype recvtype,// MPI type of recvbuf. (IN)
                  MPI_Comm  comm)       // Communicator (IN)
```

and

```
int MPI_Allgatherv(void     *sendbuf,   // Address of the buffer
                                        // to be sent. (IN)
                   int      sendcount,  // Count of items to
                                        // send (IN)
                   MPI_Datatype sendtype,// MPI type of sendbuf
                                        // elements. (IN)
                   void     *recvbuf,   // Address of receiving
                                        // buffer (OUT)
                   int      *recvcnts,  // Array of counters that
                                        // indicate the available
                                        // space in recvbuf, per
                                        // sending process. Array
                                        // is as big as the commu-
                                        // nicator size. (IN)
                   int      *displs,    // Array of indices that
                                        // mark the beginning in
                                        // recvbuf of the dest.
                                        // blocks. (IN)
                   MPI_Datatype recvtype,// MPI type of recvdbuf
                                        // elements. (IN)
                   MPI_Comm comm)       // Communicator (IN)
```

Naturally, in both functions the recvcnt (or the contents of array recvcnts) should be at least equal to sendcnt (sendcnts). The MPI_Allgather function would reduce much of the code in Listing 5.16 to a single line, alleviating also the restriction on the number of processes, as shown in Listing 5.17.

Listing 5.17: An alternative implementation of the example of Listing 5.16, using the `MPI_Allgather` function.

```cpp
// File : allgatherMPI.cpp
const int K = 10;
. . .
  unique_ptr<double[]> localPart = make_unique<double[]>(K);
  unique_ptr<double[]> allParts = make_unique<double[]>(K * N);

  // test data init.
  for (int i = 0; i < K; i++)
    localPart[i] = rank;

  MPI_Allgather(localPart.get(), K, MPI_DOUBLE, allParts.get(), K, ↵
      MPI_DOUBLE, MPI_COMM_WORLD);

  // printout/verification step
  if (rank == 0)
    {
      for (int i = 0; i < K * N; i++)
        cout << allParts[i] << " ";
      cout << endl;
    }
. . .
```

5.11.5 All-to-all scattering

Occasionally, the need arises to collect and distribute data to and from all the processes. This would be the equivalent of using N distinct `MPI_Scatter` operations, one from each of our processes. Fig. 5.10 shows what the outcome of an all-to-all scattering is when it involves four processes.

MPI provides two functions catering for the uniform and variable block distribution, respectively:

```
int MPI_Alltoall(void      *sendbuf, // Address of the buffer to
                                     // be sent (IN)
                 int       sendcount,// Number of elements to send
                                     // per process Should be
                                     // identical in all (IN)
                 MPI_Datatype sendtype, // MPI type of sendbuf
                                     // elements (IN)
                 void      *recvbuf, // Address of receiving
                                     // buffer (OUT)
                 int       recvcount,// Available elements in
                                     // recvbuf per process (IN)
                 MPI_Datatype recvtype, // MPI type of recvbuf (IN)
                 MPI_Comm  comm)     // Communicator (IN)
```

and

```
int MPI_Alltoallv(void      *sendbuf,  // Address of the buffer to
                                       // be sent (IN)
                  int       *sendcnts, // Array holding the number
                                       // of items to send to each
                                       // process (IN)
                  int       *sdispls,  // Array of indices, marking
                                       // the beginning in sendbuf,
                                       // of the data blocks (IN)
                  MPI_Datatype sendtype, // MPI type of sendbuf
                                       // elements (IN)
                  void      *recvbuf,  // Address of receiving
                                       // buffer (OUT)
                  int       *recvcnts, // Array of counters.
                                       // Indicates the available
                                       // space in recvbuf, per
                                       // sending process (IN)
                  int       *rdispls,  // Array of indices, marking
                                       // the beginning in recvbuf,
                                       // of the dest. blocks (IN)
                  MPI_Datatype recvtype, // MPI type of recvdbuf
                                       // elements (IN)
                  MPI_Comm   comm)     // Communicator (IN)
```

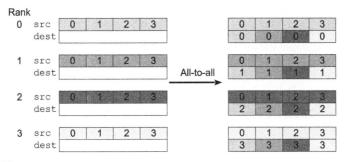

FIGURE 5.10

Outcome (on the right side) of an all-to-all scattering operation, involving four processes. Data blocks are numbered to indicate their order in their source array and colored to indicate their origin.

As an example for the use of MPI_Alltoallv, we will consider parallelizing the **bucket sort** algorithm. Bucket sort works by scanning the input data and placing the items to be sorted in separate bins/buckets, based on the range they fall into. A fixed number of bins is used, implying that the data input range must be known a priori. Each individual bucket can be subsequently sorted by recursively calling bucket sort or another non-recursive algorithm if the contents of the bucket fall below a predetermined threshold.

If we assume that we have M items to be sorted, B buckets are used, and the items are uniformly distributed over their input range, then the time complexity of bucket sort is governed by the recurrence relation

$$C(M) = \begin{cases} M + B \cdot C(\frac{M}{B}) & \text{if } N > 1 \\ 0 & \text{if } N = 1 \end{cases} \tag{5.4}$$

as each bucket is expected to get the same amount of items $\frac{M}{B}$ and each bucket is to be subsequently recursively sorted. It can be easily shown that $C(M) = M \cdot \log_B(M)$, making the complexity asymptotically approach a linear one as the number of buckets increases.

What makes bucket sort particularly interesting among sorting algorithms is that it can be easily parallelized[9] by applying the geometric data decomposition pattern (see Section 2.3.3). The required steps which amount to assigning one bucket per process are[10]:

1. Split the input data into N groups and distribute (**scatter**) them to the processes.
2. Each process scans and separates the $\frac{M}{N}$ data into N buckets.
3. Processes exchange the data that are supposed to be handled by other processes (**all-to-all scatter**).
4. Each process sorts its part of the data, using any sorting algorithm.
5. Sorted data are collected using a **gather** operation.

A sample implementation of this algorithm is shown in Listing 5.18.

The inner workings of Listing 5.18 can be more easily comprehended via the simple tracing example shown in Fig. 5.11, where nine integers in the range $[1, 9]$ are sorted.

Listing 5.18: A parallel implementation of bucket sort in MPI, using collective communications. Once the buckets are split, they are sorted using quicksort.

```
1   // File : bucketsort.cpp
2   . . .
3   int rank, N;
4   MPI_Comm_rank (MPI_COMM_WORLD, &rank);
5   MPI_Comm_size (MPI_COMM_WORLD, &N);
6   MPI_Status status;
7
8   if (argc == 1)
9      {
10       if (rank == 0)
11          cerr << "Usage " << argv[0] << " number_of_items\n";
```

---

[9] The communication overhead involved in parallelizing a sorting algorithm makes the latter a dubious endeavor, especially if the algorithm is a linear-complexity one. However, there are cases where it is a worthwhile consideration, such as when the input data do not fit in a single machine or when practicing collective communications in MPI!

[10] This is not the only way parallelization can be accomplished. An alternative is considered in the Exercises section at the end of the chapter.

```
12        exit (1);
13      }
14
15    int M = atoi (argv[1]);
16    int maxItemsPerBucket = ceil (1.0 * M / N); // used in case M is ↩
          not evenly divided by N
17
18    int deliveredItems;
19    int bucketRange = ceil (1.0 * (MAX − MIN) / N);
20    unique_ptr<int[]> data = make_unique<int[]>(N * maxItemsPerBucket)↩
          ; // array allocation exceeds M to allow easy scattering
21
22    unique_ptr<int[]> buckets = make_unique<int[]>(N * ↩
          maxItemsPerBucket);
23    unique_ptr<int[]> bucketOffset = make_unique<int[]>(N); // where ↩
          do buckets begin?
24    unique_ptr<int[]> inBucket = make_unique<int[]>(N);      // how ↩
          many items in each one?
25
26    unique_ptr<int[]> toRecv = make_unique<int[]>(N);    // counts how ↩
          many items will be received from each process
27
28    unique_ptr<int[]> recvOff = make_unique<int[]>(N);   // offsets for↩
          sent data
29
30    if (rank == 0)
31      initData (MIN, MAX, data, M);
32
33    // initialize bucket counters and offsets
34    for (int i = 0; i < N; i++)
35      {
36        inBucket[i] = 0;
37        bucketOffset[i] = i * maxItemsPerBucket;
38      }
39
40    // step 1
41    MPI_Scatter (data.get(), maxItemsPerBucket, MPI_INT, data.get(), ↩
          maxItemsPerBucket, MPI_INT, 0, MPI_COMM_WORLD);
42    deliveredItems = (rank == N − 1) ? (M − (N − 1) * ↩
          maxItemsPerBucket) : maxItemsPerBucket;
43
44    // step 2
45    // split into buckets
46    for (int i = 0; i < deliveredItems; i++)
47      {
48        int idx = (data[i] − MIN) / bucketRange;
49        int off = bucketOffset[idx] + inBucket[idx];
50        buckets[off] = data[i];
51        inBucket[idx]++;
52      }
53
54    // step 3
```

```
55    // start by gathering the counts of data the other processes will ←
          send
56    MPI_Alltoall (inBucket.get(), 1, MPI_INT, toRecv.get(), 1, MPI_INT ←
          , MPI_COMM_WORLD);
57    recvOff[0] = 0;
58    for (int i = 1; i < N; i++)
59      recvOff[i] = recvOff[i − 1] + toRecv[i − 1];
60
61    MPI_Alltoallv (buckets.get(), inBucket.get(), bucketOffset.get(), ←
              MPI_INT, data.get(), toRecv.get(), recvOff.get(), MPI_INT, ←
              MPI_COMM_WORLD);
62
63    // step 4
64    // apply quicksort to the local bucket
65    int localBucketSize = recvOff[N − 1] + toRecv[N − 1];
66    sort(data.get(), data.get()+localBucketSize);
67
68    // step 5
69    MPI_Gather (&localBucketSize, 1, MPI_INT, toRecv.get(), 1, MPI_INT ←
          , 0, MPI_COMM_WORLD);
70    if (rank == 0)
71      {
72        recvOff[0] = 0;
73        for (int i = 1; i < N; i++)
74          recvOff[i] = recvOff[i − 1] + toRecv[i − 1];
75      }
76
77    MPI_Gatherv (data.get(), localBucketSize, MPI_INT, data.get(), ←
              toRecv.get(), recvOff.get(), MPI_INT, 0, MPI_COMM_WORLD);
78
79    // print results
80    if (rank == 0)
81      {
82        for (int i = 0; i < M; i++)
83          cout << data[i] << " ";
84        cout << endl;
85      }
86    . . .
```

The five steps identified above for our parallel bucket sort are clearly marked in the code. The following discussion fills in the implementation details:

- Bucket sort is not an in-place algorithm. A separate buffer is required for holding the data while they are being distributed to buckets. Each bucket should have enough space allocated for it to be able to hold the complete input data. Because the M data are uniformly scattered to our N processes (line 41), each process must allocate $N \cdot \frac{M}{N} = M$ bucket space. Buckets are allocated as a single array (buckets). The beginning of each individual bucket within the single array and the number of items it contains are the job of arrays bucketOffset and inBucket,

PC	Variable	Process 0	Process 1	Process 2
34 (Step)	data	2 7 3 8 7 6 9 1 4		
42 (Step 1)	data	2 7 3 8 7 6 9 1 4	8 7 6	9 1 4
55 (Step 2)	buckets	2 3 _ _ _ _ 7 _ _	_ _ _ 6 _ _ 8 7 _	1 _ _ _ 4 _ 9 _ _
	inBucket	2 0 1	0 1 2	1 1 1
57	toRecv	2 0 1	0 1 1	1 2 1
61 (Step 3)	recvOff	0 2 2	0 0 1	0 1 3
65	data	2 3 1	6 4	7 8 7 9
69 (Step 4)	data	1 2 3	4 6	7 7 8 9
70	toRecv	3 2 4		
77 (Step 5)	recvOff	0 3 5		
80	data	1 2 3 4 6 7 7 8 9		

FIGURE 5.11

A trace of the parallel bucket sort of Listing 5.18 upon sorting nine integers using three processes. PC stands for Program Counter and it represents the *next line* of code in Listing 5.18 to be executed. Time runs from top to bottom. The corresponding steps and the variables that are affected by them in each process are shown.

respectively. The former may seem redundant, as a bucket's offset is a matter of a simple calculation (line 37), but it is actually required for calling MPI_Alltoallv (line 61).

- Processes exchange the data that belong to other buckets with their respective "owner" processes. In this case, an all-to-all scatter would be the ideal candidate for minimizing the communication overhead. Because there is typically a non-uniform distribution of the data in the buckets, using MPI_Alltoall would require the transmission of dummy data and it would result in a non-contiguous storage of data in each process.

  To overcome this problem, the processes initially exchange the number of data that they intend to send to the other ones (line 56). With this information, each process calculates the offsets where the incoming data will be stored (lines 57–59) and proceeds to use MPI_Alltoallv for the exchange (line 61). This results in contiguous data storage in the data array that can then be sorted (line 66).

- A similar problem with the data exchange of step 3 exists for the gathering of the data to the root process. The root initially collects the amount of data each process will submit using MPI_Gather (line 69). Appropriate receive offsets can then be calculated (lines 70–75), prior to using MPI_Gatherv (line 77) to complete the parallel sorting operation.

5.11.6 All-to-all reduction

The all-to-all reduction operation has no difference from the reduction discussed in Section 5.11.3, other than the fact that all participating processes get a copy of the reduction result and not just the root. The syntax of the MPI_Allreduce function reflects this feature by the removal of the "root" parameter:

```
int MPI_Allreduce(void      *sendbuf, // Address of the buffer to
                                      // be sent. Separate in each
                                      // source process. (IN)
                  void      *recvbuf, // Address of receiving
                                      // buffer (OUT)
                                      // Significant in all proc.
                  int        count,   // Number of elements to send
                  MPI_Datatype datatype, // MPI type of sendbuf and
                                      // recvbuf elements (IN)
                  MPI_Op     op,      // Symbolic const. identify-
                                      // ing the type of reduction
                                      // to be performed (IN)
                  MPI_Comm   comm )   // Communicator (IN)
```

Similar to the all-to-all gathering operation, an all-to-all reduction can be accomplished by using the butterfly communication pattern. The only difference with the scheme discussed in Section 5.11.3 is that between steps/stages of the algorithm, reduction is performed on the so far received data. In that respect, butterfly-based, all-to-all reduction requires a much smaller amount of data to be communicated overall.

An example of the use of the all-to-all reduction operation would be a parallel genetic algorithm. Genetic algorithms are heuristic optimization techniques that describe possible solutions to an optimization problem as a population of "individuals," each solution modeled as an individual. This population "evolves" over several iterations (called generations) by applying changes to the individuals inspired by biology: crossover and mutation. The best individuals of a population are selected to survive into the next iteration/generation of the algorithm.

A parallel genetic algorithm could be designed around the partitioning of the population (data decomposition), whereas each node/process evolves a subset of the individuals. The best individuals can be selected and used for the next generation by employing an all-to-all reduction.

5.11.7 Global synchronization

Some algorithms, like Jacobi's method for solving a system of linear equations, require that data are collected and updated prior to continuing with the next iteration. This data collection and synchronization step can be done via the MPI_Alltoall function or some other form of collective operation. If no data need to be exchanged though, synchronization can be accomplished by the MPI_Barrier function.

MPI_Barrier receives as a parameter a communicator:

```
int MPI_Barrier( MPI_Comm comm )
```

All processes of that communicator must call the function, and the function returns only when it has been called by all of them.

5.12 Persistent communications

A regular pattern that is encountered in many applications, including master–worker designs, is having repeated communications involving messages of different content but of the same size. MPI 4.0 optimizes the exchange of such messages by introducing the mechanism of persistent communications. The core idea is that MPI will reserve in such cases the necessary resources for the communications to take place, while the processes will just initiate the transfers and wait for their completion.

The deployment of persistent communications involves four distinct steps:

I. **Creation**: During this step a process informs MPI about the setup that will govern the persistent exchanges. This involves the send/receive buffer and its length, datatype, destination/source process, and message tag. Alternative modes are also supported in the form of buffered, synchronous, and ready send operations. A limitation of persistent communication is that these parameters have to remain fixed, e.g., changing the message length is not allowed.

The setup involves calling an appropriate "*init" function. Samples of these functions that also cover collective operations are shown below:

- `MPI_Send_init`
- `MPI_Bsend_init`
- `MPI_Ssend_init`
- `MPI_Rsend_init`
- `MPI_Recv_init`
- `MPI_Bcast_init`
- `MPI_Gather_init`
- `MPI_Gatherv_init`
- `MPI_Scatter_init`
- `MPI_Scatterv_init`
- `MPI_Allgather_init`
- `MPI_Allgatherv_init`
- `MPI_Reduce_init`

These mirror the signatures of their corresponding normal send/receive counterparts, with the exception of having an additional pointer to an `MPI_Request` instance as a final parameter. This serves as a handle to be used for identifying the operation in all the subsequent steps. For example:

```
int MPI_Send_init(void      *buf, // Address of data buffer (IN)
                  int       count,// Number of data items (IN)
                  MPI_Datatype dtype,// buf elements datatype (IN)
                  int       dest, // Destination proc. rank (IN)
```

```
          int           tag,  // Message type label (IN)
          MPI_Comm      comm, // Communicator ID (IN)
          MPI_Request   *req) // Comm. request handle(IN/OUT)
```

In the case of collective operations, there is also an `MPI_Info` parameter. `MPI_Info` is an opaque object holding an unordered collection of pairs of (key, value) strings. It is used for allowing users to provide optimization-related hints to the MPI runtime. MPI provides a large collection of functions for creating, populating, and querying `MPI_Info` containers. For example:

```
int MPI_Bcast_init(void      *buf,  // Address of the buffer that
                                     // either holds or receives
                                     // the data (IN/OUT)
                   int        count, // Buffer size (IN)
                   MPI_Datatype dtype,// Buffer elements type (IN)
                   int        root,  // Source process rank (IN)
                   MPI_Comm   comm   // Communicator (IN)
                   MPI_Info   info,  // Info object handle (IN)
                                     // Can use MPI_INFO_NULL
                   MPI_Request *req) // Comm. request handle(IN/OUT)
```

If no info needs to be provided, a user may use the `MPI_INFO_NULL` constant for the `info` parameter.

II. **Sending/receiving**: Once the desired communication is described to MPI with the previous step, it can be initiated by calling the `MPI_Start` function. The `MPI_Startall` alternative can be used for launching a collection of operations:

```
int MPI_Start(MPI_Request  *req)   // Handle for communication
                                   // request (IN/OUT)

int MPI_Startall(int count,        // Size of "req" array (IN)
                 MPI_Request req[]) // Array of request
                                   // handles (IN/OUT)
```

Once these functions return, one cannot expect that the communications are complete, only that the corresponding request or requests have become *active*. For the same reason, the contents of the buffer cannot be modified (if sent) or accessed (if received) before the next step.

III. **Waiting**: To inquire about the status of an initiated persistent communication, the `MPI_Wait` and/or `MPI_Test` functions can be used (see Section 5.8).

IV. **Ending**: The resources associated with a persistent operation can be released by calling the `MPI_Request_free` function:

```
int MPI_Request_free(MPI_Request  *req) // Handle for comm. ↩
    request (IN/OUT)
```

This function should be invoked only after an operation is complete, or as per the MPI jargon, the request has become *inactive*.

An example of the sequence of calls required is also shown in Fig. 5.12.

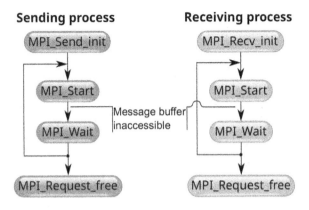

Sending process   **Receiving process**

FIGURE 5.12

Example of persistent communications sequence in MPI 4.0. Regular communication functions can be also used for either end.

This sequence is also applied in the following "Hello World" variation program, where process 0 sends a sequence of strings to process 1:

Listing 5.19: "Hello World" using persistent communications.

```cpp
// File : hello_persistent.cpp
. . .
#define MESSTAG 0

int main (int argc, char **argv)
{
  MPI_Init (&argc, &argv);
  MPI_Request req;

  int rank, num, i;
  num = atoi(argv[1]);

  MPI_Comm_rank (MPI_COMM_WORLD, &rank);
  char mess[] = "Hello no 9999"; // enough space for up to 10000
  const int MAXLEN = sizeof(mess);
  if (rank == 0)
    {
      MPI_Send_init(mess, MAXLEN, MPI_CHAR, 1, MESSTAG, ←
          MPI_COMM_WORLD, &req);
      for (i = 0; i < num; i++)
      {
        sprintf(mess,"Hello no %i",i);
        MPI_Start(&req);
        MPI_Wait(&req, MPI_STATUS_IGNORE);
      }
      MPI_Request_free(&req);
    }
  else
```

```
28      {
29          MPI_Status status;
30          MPI_Recv_init(mess, MAXLEN, MPI_CHAR, 0, MESSTAG, ↩
                MPI_COMM_WORLD, &req);
31          for (i = 0; i < num; i++)
32          {
33              MPI_Start(&req);
34              MPI_Wait(&req, MPI_STATUS_IGNORE);
35              printf ("%i received %s\n", rank, mess);
36          }
37          MPI_Request_free(&req);
38      }
39      MPI_Finalize ();
40      return 0;
41  }
```

The program reads the number of messages to be sent at line 11, and both processes run loops with this limit (lines 19 and 31). The key point in Listing 5.19 is lines 14 and 15, which allocate the character array to hold the message and calculate its maximum length under the assumption that the maximum number of messages is 10,000. Given that persistent communications fix the message parameters a priori (lines 18 and 30), we must make sure that the declared message length will cover all the possibilities.

5.13 Big-count communications in MPI 4.0

The MPI 4.0 standard introduces a large collection of variants to all the point-to-point and collective communication functions, in order to support the exchange of data where the count parameter needs to exceed the maximum of a signed 32-bit integer ($2^{31} - 1$). The so-called "big count" variants share the same signatures, names, and semantics with the regular functions, with two differences:

(a) All the new functions have a _c suffix in their name for differentiation.

(b) The count parameter is of type MPI_Count instead of int.

MPI_Count is an MPI library-defined type, which means it can be an alias for anything bigger than a regular 32-bit integer.

For example, the big-count variant of MPI_Send is:

```
1  int MPI_Send_c(void        *buf,      // Address of data buffer (IN)
2                 MPI_Count    count,    // Number of data items (IN)
3                 MPI_Datatype datatype, // buf elements datatype (IN)
4                 int          dest,     // Destination proc. rank (IN)
5                 int          tag,      // Message label (IN)
6                 MPI_Comm     comm)     // Communicator identifier (IN)
```

The same apply for the receiving calls, e.g., for MPI_Irecv we have:

```
1  int MPI_Irecv_c(void        *buf,    // Address of data buffer (OUT)
2                  MPI_Count    count,  // Number of data items (IN)
```

```
3              MPI_Datatype datatype,// buf elements datatype (IN)
4              int          source,  // Rank of source proc. (IN)
5              int          tag,     // Message label (IN)
6              MPI_Comm     comm,    // Communicator identifier (IN)
7              MPI_Request  *req)    // Handle for checking
8                                    // status (IN/OUT)
```

And the same convention extends to persistent operations, collective operations, and their combinations. For example:

```
1   int MPI_Send_init_c(void    *buf,      // Address of data buffer (IN)
2              MPI_Count    count,     // Number of data items (IN)
3              MPI_Datatype datatype,// buf elements datatype (IN)
4              int          dest,     // Destination proc. rank (IN)
5              int          tag,      // Message label (IN)
6              MPI_Comm     comm,     // Communicator identifier (IN)
7              MPI_Request  *req)     // Placeholder for comm. request
8                                     // handle (IN/OUT)
9   //
10  int MPI_Bcast_c(void        *buf,      // Buffer to be sent or
11                                     // received (IN/OUT)
12             MPI_Count    count,     // Size of buffer (IN)
13             MPI_Datatype dtype,     // Buffer elements type (IN)
14             int          root,      // Rank of source process (IN)
15             MPI_Comm     comm)      // Communicator (IN)
16  //
17  int MPI_Bcast_init_c(void   *buffer,   // Broadcast buffer(IN/OUT)
18             MPI_Count    count,     // Buffer size (IN)
19             MPI_Datatype dtype,     // Buffer elements type (IN)
20             int          root,      // Source process rank (IN)
21             MPI_Comm     comm       // Communicator (IN)
22             MPI_Info     info,      // Info object handle (IN)
23             MPI_Request  *req)      // Placeholder for comm. request
24                                     // handle (IN/OUT)
```

Obviously, the above concerns only functions that have "count" parameters. So `MPI_Start`, etc., have no "big-count" counterparts.

These functions are direct replacements for the regular ones, so all the guidelines regarding their use as mentioned earlier apply here as well.

5.14 Partitioned communications

Partitioned communications are a fine-grained communication mechanism introduced in MPI 4.0, where a message can be transmitted/received in small partitions. Breaking up a message in smaller parts allows (a) the receiving process to be notified about the delivery of each individual partition (and possibly proceed to immediately use the corresponding data using multiple threads) and (b) the sending process to involve multiple threads, each responsible for setting up a subset of the partitions. The threads can be spawned using C++11 threads or OpenMP.

Of course in order for multiple threads to populate or read a partitioned message, we must have an MPI implementation that supports being called by multiple threads. As discussed in Section 5.19, we must have MPI_Init_thread return MPI_THREAD_SERIALIZED or ideally MPI_THREAD_MULTIPLE. However, having this support available is not a prerequisite.

The partitioned communications API is based on MPI_Request objects and operates in a similar way to persistent communications: there is a creation phase, multiple send initiations and/or delivery checks, a completion phase, and a cleanup phase.

The sender creation phase is performed by calling the MPI_Psend_init function:

```
int MPI_Psend_init(void      *buf,     // Address of data buffer (IN)
                   int        partnum, // Number of partitions. Must be
                                       // a non-negative number (IN)
                   MPI_Count  count,   // Data items per partition (IN)
                   MPI_Datatype datatype,// "buf" elements datatype (IN)
                   int        dest,    // Destination proc. rank (IN)
                   int        tag,     // Message type label (IN)
                   MPI_Comm   comm,    // Communicator identifier (IN)
                   MPI_Info   info,    // Info handle (IN)
                   MPI_Request *req)   // Placeholder for comm. request
                                       // handle (IN/OUT)
```

The returned MPI_Request handle is used for identification processes in subsequent steps. The initialization has to be done by just one thread if multiple ones are going to be involved in setting the message contents.

Once a partition is ready to be sent, the corresponding thread can call MPI_Pready or one of the related functions:

```
int MPI_Pready(int partitionNum,     // Ready partition number (IN)
               MPI_Request *req)      // Comm. request handle (IN/OUT)
//─────────────────────────────────────────────────────────
// Equivalent to calling MPI_Pready in a loop
int MPI_Pready_range(int partLow,    // Smallest ready partition
                                     // number (IN)
                     int partHigh,   // Largest ready partition
                                     // number (IN)
                     MPI_Request *req) // Comm. request handle (IN/OUT)
//─────────────────────────────────────────────────────────
int MPI_Pready_list(int num,         // Size of partsNo array (IN)
                    int partsNo[],    // Array of partition numbers
                                     // that are ready(IN)
                    MPI_Request *req) // Comm. request handle (IN/OUT)
```

The actual sending is done by calling MPI_Start or MPI_Startall, as with persistent communications. The call to MPI_Start can be done as soon as MPI_Psend_init returns, or even after a bunch of partitions are declared ready.

As with persistent communications, the *complete* message transfer can be queried via MPI_Wait and/or MPI_Test.

On the receiving process, a partitioned communication is set up by calling `MPI_Precv_init`:

```
1   int MPI_Precv_init(void    *buf,       // Address of data buffer (IN)
2                      int      partnum,   // Number of partitions. Must be
3                                          // (non-negative)(IN)
4                      MPI_Count count,    // Data items per partition (IN)
5                      MPI_Datatype datatype,// "buf" elements datatype (IN)
6                      int      source,    // Rank of source proc. (IN)
7                      int      tag,       // Message type label (IN)
8                      MPI_Comm comm,      // Communicator identifier (IN)
9                      MPI_Info info,      // Info handle (IN)
10                     MPI_Request *req)   // Comm. request handle (IN/OUT)
```

The message can start to be received once `MPI_Start` is called. Testing if a partition has been delivered is the purpose of the non-blocking `MPI_Parrived` function:

```
1   int MPI_Parrived(MPI_Request *req,  // Comm. request handle (IN/OUT)
2                    int          partnum, // Partition to be tested (IN)
3                    int          *flag) // Set to true/false to indicate
4                                        // delivery status (IN/OUT)
```

Again a communication is completed when `MPI_Wait` is invoked or `MPI_Test` returns true.

The cleanup for both the sender and receiver processes is a matter of calling `MPI_Request_free` (see Section 5.12).

An example of the sequence of function calls involved is shown in Fig. 5.13.

5.15 Communicating objects

MPI communication functions cater for the communication of arrays of primitive data types via their second parameter. However, it is frequently desirable to be able to communicate structures or objects. One can of course break up the structures that need to be communicated into individual elements or arrays of elements and then proceed to perform a series of send operations. This is a viable but costly and counterproductive approach. From a software engineering perspective, breaking data encapsulation, among other things, complicates the code and thus it does not constitute a recommended solution.

From a cost perspective, it is well known that multiple communication operations result in a higher overall communication cost than it would have been if one operation was used to carry the same amount of data. The culprit lies in what is sometimes referred to as the **startup latency** or just **latency**. This more or less fixed cost incorporates the activation of multiple OS layers, the network interface, etc. So, while the actual over-the-wire times may be identical, the accumulation of the extra latencies penalizes this approach.

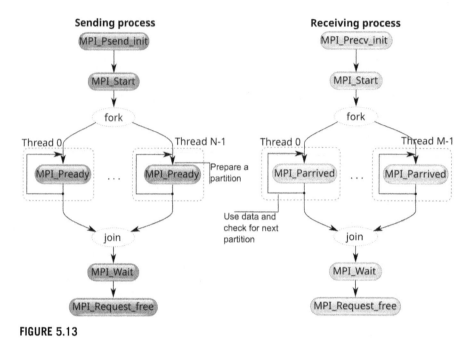

FIGURE 5.13

Example of partitioned communication sequences for the sender and receiver processes. The numbers of threads on the two sides do not have to match.

A quick hack could be something like this:

```
const int N = ...;

typedef struct Point
  {
    int x;
    int y;
    int color;
  };

Point image[N];
. . .
MPI_Send(image, N*sizeof(Point), MPI_BYTE, dest, tag, MPI_COMM_WORLD↩
    );
```

But this solution would not work all the time. It is a viable option only if the execution platform is homogeneous, i.e., all the machines use the same data representation. This requirement extends to the compiler optimizations used to compile the executables, in case an MPMD approach is employed. The reason is the alignment of structures in memory which may change based on the optimization level, as extra padding may be used.

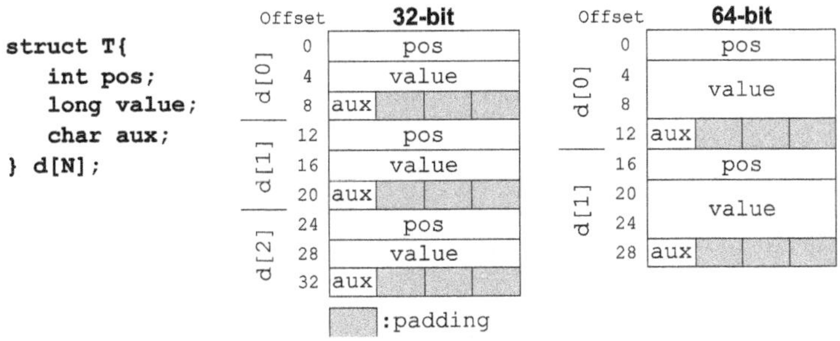

FIGURE 5.14

Two possible memory layouts for the array of structures shown on the left: one for a 32-bit architecture (where type `long int` is 4 bytes long) and one for a 64-bit architecture (where type `long int` is 8 bytes long). By default, the GNU C compiler uses padding to ensure that all access to memory is aligned at 4-byte boundaries, for x86 binaries.

MPI provides two mechanisms that can be used to communicate structures between heterogeneous machines:

- creating MPI derived datatypes,
- packing/unpacking data.

Both are preferable to the hack presented above, in that they ensure the validity of the program even if it was to run on a different platform. Anticipating change is always a prudent thing to do.

5.15.1 Derived datatypes

Fig. 5.14 displays the memory layouts of the same data structure when used in a 32-bit and a 64-bit program. There are differences in the size of the individual data members of the structure and naturally their relative location in regard to the beginning of the structure (different offsets). Consequently, if MPI were to be able to transfer and translate an instance of a structure from one machine to another, it would need all the information listed below:

- The number and types of all the data members/fields.
- The relative offset of the fields from the beginning of the structure (where to deposit data).
- The total memory occupied by a structure, including any padding necessary to align it to specific boundaries. This is needed so that arrays of structures can be communicated.

MPI provides a variety of functions for creating "derived" or general datatypes. A general datatype is an opaque object that is capable of describing all the above information. Once a derived datatype is defined, a reference to this object can be used in any communication function that requires a datatype specification parameter.

Derived datatypes must be declared individually/locally in all the processes that will employ them.

Two of the most commonly used functions for creating derived datatypes are `MPI_Type_vector` and `MPI_Type_create_struct`. The first one comes handy for extracting blocks of data from single- or multi-dimensional arrays of a single datatype, in the form of a vector. The second one is the most generic of the available functions, allowing the use of blocks made of different datatypes. Their syntax is the following:

```
int MPI_Type_vector(int            count,     // Number of blocks
                                             // making up vector (IN)
                    int            blklength,// Size of each block in
                                             // number of items (IN)
                    int            stride,    // Number of items
                                             // between the start of
                                             // successive blocks (IN)
                    MPI_Datatype old_type,   // MPI datatype of each
                                             // item (IN)
                    MPI_Datatype *newt_p)    // Placeholder for the
                                             // derived datatype (OUT)
```

```
int MPI_Type_create_struct(int        count,     // Number of blocks
                                                 // making up structure.
                                                 // It is also the size
                                                 // of the three array
                                                 // parameters that
                                                 // follow next. (IN)
                          int         blklen[],// Number of elements
                                                 // per block (IN)
                          MPI_Aint    displ[], // Offset of each
                                                 // block in bytes (IN)
                          MPI_Datatype types[], // Type of elements
                                                 // in each block (IN)
                          MPI_Datatype *newt)    // Address for storing
                                                 // the derived type (OUT)
```

Each specification of a derived datatype must be followed by a call to the `MPI_Type_commit` function for having MPI store the specification internally. Once a datatype is committed, it can be used repeatedly in communication functions. `MPI_Type_commit` takes just a single parameter which is a reference to the `MPI_Datatype` object:

```
int MPI_Type_commit(MPI_Datatype *datatype) // Reference to derived
                                            // datatype. (IN)
```

As an example for the use of `MPI_Type_vector`, we will consider the problem of dense matrix to matrix multiplication, i.e., multiplying a $K \times M$ matrix A by an $M \times L$ matrix B. A parallel solution can be easily designed by applying the geometric data decomposition pattern (see Section 2.3.3). Among the variety of ways we can partition the data, in this example we will use a 2D decomposition of the result matrix

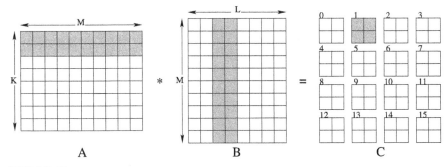

FIGURE 5.15

Illustration of a 2D partitioning of the result matrix C, in a matrix A by matrix B multiplication. The highlighted cells indicate dependencies that must be resolved by communicating the corresponding rows of A and columns of B to the process calculating that part of C. Process ranks are shown next to C's blocks, in the order they are assigned in the program of Listing 5.20.

C as shown in Fig. 5.15, which necessitates that a subset of A's rows and a subset of B's rows are communicated to the available processes.

The communication of A's rows is a simple matter, given the row-major memory allocation used for 2D arrays by C/C++. However, B's columns reside in noncontiguous memory locations. This can be dealt with either by transposing matrix B so that columns become rows or by creating a derived datatype that can extract the columns from their existing memory location. The latter is the preferable approach, especially if very large matrices are involved.

The code shown in Listing 5.20 uses the exact same method as Listing 5.12 for propagating the rows of matrix A to the available processes. The only difference in the communication of A is that the move from 1D to 2D partitioning of the data necessitates the use of a nested loop for calculating the displacements and send counts (lines 37–46). Careful manipulation of these arrays allows us to send the same rows of A multiple times, as required. Each set of rowsPerProcess rows of A is sent procX times.

Listing 5.20: Part of an MPI program for multiplying a $K \times M$ matrix A with an $M \times L$ matrix B. The program uses derived data types to simplify the communication of blocks of data between the processes. The K and L matrix dimensions must be multiples of procY and procX, respectively.

```
1   // File : matrixMult.cpp
2   . . .
3     MPI_Datatype columnGroup;    // Datatype for communicating B's ↩
          columns
4     MPI_Datatype matrBlock;      // Datatype for communicating C's ↩
          blocks
5
6     int procX, procY;
```

```
7    procX = atoi (argv[1]);        // expects an X*Y grid of processes
8    procY = atoi (argv[2]);        // for calculating the product
9    if (procX * procY != N)        // It will abort if there are not ↩
         enough processes to form the grid
10     MPI_Abort (MPI_COMM_WORLD, 0);
11
12   int rowsPerProcess;            // size of block related to A
13   int columnsPerProcess;         // size of block related to B
14   rowsPerProcess = K / procY;    // each process will calculate
15   columnsPerProcess = L / procX; // rowsPerProcess*columnsPerProcess ↩
         elements of C
16
17   // K and L must be multiples of procY and procX, respectively
18   assert(rowsPerProcess * procY == K && columnsPerProcess * procX ==↩
         L && N == procX * procY);
19
20   if (rank == 0)
21     {
22       MPI_Type_vector (M, columnsPerProcess, L, MPI_DOUBLE, &↩
             columnGroup);
23       MPI_Type_commit (&columnGroup);
24       MPI_Type_vector (rowsPerProcess, columnsPerProcess, L, ↩
             MPI_DOUBLE, &matrBlock);
25       MPI_Type_commit (&matrBlock);
26       unique_ptr<double[]> A = make_unique<double[]>(K * M);
27       unique_ptr<double[]> B = make_unique<double[]>(M * L);
28       unique_ptr<double[]> C = make_unique<double[]>(K * L);
29
30       // A and B are initialized to values that can be used to check
31       // the correctness of the result.
32       for (int i = 0; i < K * M; i++)  A[i] = i;
33       for (int i = 0; i < M * L; i++)  B[i] = 0;
34       for (int i = 0; i < M; i++)      B[i * L + i] = 1;  // B is ↩
             the identity matrix
35
36       // distribute A first
37       int displs[N];
38       int sendcnts[N];
39       int cntr = 0;
40       for (int i = 0; i < procY; i++)
41         for (int j = 0; j < procX; j++)
42           {
43             sendcnts[cntr] = rowsPerProcess * M;
44             displs[cntr] = i * rowsPerProcess * M;
45             cntr++;
46           }
47
48       MPI_Scatterv (A.get(), sendcnts, displs, MPI_DOUBLE, ↩
             MPI_IN_PLACE, 0, MPI_DOUBLE, 0, MPI_COMM_WORLD);
49
50       // now distribute B
51       cntr = 1;
```

```
52        for (int i = 0; i < procY; i++)
53          for (int j = 0; j < procX; j++)
54            if (i + j != 0)
55              {
56                MPI_Send (B.get() + j * columnsPerProcess, 1, ↵
                     columnGroup, cntr, 0, MPI_COMM_WORLD);
57                cntr++;
58              }
59
60        // partial result calculation
61        MMpartial (A, B, C, rowsPerProcess, M, columnsPerProcess, L);
62
63        // now collect all the subblocks of C
64        cntr = 1;
65        for (int i = 0; i < procY; i++)
66          for (int j = 0; j < procX; j++)
67            if (i + j != 0)
68              {
69                MPI_Recv (C.get() + i * L * rowsPerProcess + j * ↵
                     columnsPerProcess, 1, matrBlock, cntr, 0, ↵
                     MPI_COMM_WORLD, &status);
70                cntr++;
71              }
72
73        printMatrix (C, K, L);
74      }
75    else
76      {
77        MPI_Type_vector (M, columnsPerProcess, columnsPerProcess, ↵
             MPI_DOUBLE, &columnGroup);
78        MPI_Type_commit (&columnGroup);
79        MPI_Type_vector (rowsPerProcess, columnsPerProcess, ↵
             columnsPerProcess, MPI_DOUBLE, &matrBlock);
80        MPI_Type_commit (&matrBlock);
81
82        unique_ptr<double[]> locA = make_unique<double[]>(↵
             rowsPerProcess * M);
83        unique_ptr<double[]> locB = make_unique<double[]>(M * ↵
             columnsPerProcess);
84        unique_ptr<double[]> partC = make_unique<double[]>(↵
             rowsPerProcess * columnsPerProcess);   // partial result ↵
             matrix
85
86        MPI_Scatterv (NULL, NULL, NULL, MPI_DOUBLE, locA.get(), ↵
             rowsPerProcess * M, MPI_DOUBLE, 0, MPI_COMM_WORLD);
87
88        MPI_Recv (locB.get(), 1, columnGroup, 0, 0, MPI_COMM_WORLD, &↵
             status);
89
90        MMpartial (locA, locB, partC, rowsPerProcess, M, ↵
             columnsPerProcess, columnsPerProcess);
91
```

```
92        MPI_Send (partC.get(), 1, matrBlock, 0, 0, MPI_COMM_WORLD);
93    }
94  . . .
```

The key points of Listing 5.20 are listed below:

- The program requires that `procX * procY` processes are available for distributing the workload. Parameters `procX` and `procY` are supplied by the user in the command-line.
- Each process receives `rowsPerProcess` rows of matrix `A` and `columnsPerProcess` columns of matrix `B` in order to calculate a `rowsPerProcess x columnsPerProcess` block of the result matrix `C`.
- Two derived datatypes are defined on lines 22–25 and 77–80. These must be declared in all the processes that use them. While each *must account for the same amount of data, the actual layout of a derived datatype can be different in each process*. In the root process, the layout has to account for the extra rows and columns of data present in `B` and `C` (lines 22–25), while in the worker processes there are no such extra items (lines 77–80). So, while in the root process the "stride" parameter for the `columnGroup`-derived datatype is `L`, in the worker processes it is equal to `columnsPerProcess`. This difference is also obvious if one compares the array memory layouts established on lines 26–28 with the local ones established on lines 82–84.
- The `columnGroup`-derived datatype is used to extract columns of data from matrix `B`. The derived "vector" is made up of M individual blocks (as many as the rows of `B`), and each block consists of `columnsPerProcess` items of type `MPI_DOUBLE`. The blocks are L distance apart in process 0, i.e., as many items as the total number of columns. This distance is exactly `columnsPerProcess` in the other processes. Fig. 5.16 illustrates this difference.
  Once `columnGroup` is defined, the root process can send blocks of columns to the other processes by manipulating the starting offset in the `B` matrix (line 56). The processes that receive the data are waiting for just one element of type `columnGroup` (line 88).
- The `matrBlock` derived datatype is used for collecting the computed partial results. The derived "vector" is made up of `rowsPerProcess` blocks, each `columnsPerProcess` items of type `MPI_DOUBLE` wide. The distance between the blocks in the root process is L, the length of `C`'s row.

As an example of the use of the `MPI_Type_create_struct` function, we will consider the problem of communicating the following data structure:

```
struct Pixel {
  int x;
  int y;
  unsigned char RGB[3];
};
```

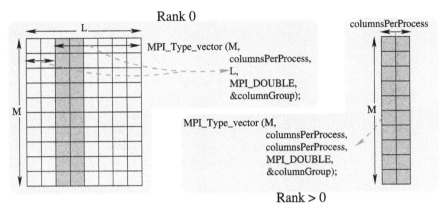

FIGURE 5.16

Illustration of how the derived datatype `columnGroup` is defined for the 0-ranked process and all other processes in the program of Listing 5.20, based on the memory layout of matrices `B` (left) and `locB` (right).

`MPI_Type_create_struct` requires a much more explicit setup for the creation of a derived datatype than `MPI_Type_vector`. Each of the data members of a structure must be documented: their individual datatypes, their size, and their offset from the beginning of the structure must be declared. The length of the associated code means that it is a good idea to encapsulate the details in a separate function, as shown below:

Listing 5.21: A function for defining a derived datatype for the communication of a `Pixel` structure.

```cpp
// File : derivedExample.cpp
void deriveType (MPI_Datatype * t)
{
  struct Pixel sample;

  int blklen[3];
  MPI_Aint displ[3], off, base;
  MPI_Datatype types[3];

  blklen[0] = 1;
  blklen[1] = 1;
  blklen[2] = 3;

  types[0] = MPI_INT;
  types[1] = MPI_INT;
  types[2] = MPI_UNSIGNED_CHAR;

  displ[0] = 0;
  MPI_Get_address (&(sample.x), &base);
  MPI_Get_address (&(sample.y), &off);
  displ[1] = off-base;
  MPI_Get_address (&(sample.RGB[0]), &off);
```

```
23    displ[2] = off - base;
24
25    MPI_Type_create_struct (3, blklen, displ, types, t);
26    MPI_Type_commit (t);
27  }
```

MPI_Aint is an alias for a signed int or a signed long integer, depending on whether the system architecture is 32 or 64 bit. Variables of this type are typically used with the MPI_Get_address function to extract the address of a memory location. The results are usually the same as the outcome of the address-of (&) C operator, although this does not need to be true for systems with word-addressable memory (versus byte-addressable). The syntax of MPI_Get_address is:

```
int MPI_Get_address(void      *location, // Address of a memory
                                         // location (IN)
                    MPI_Aint *address)  // Storage for the
                                         // address (OUT)
```

Lines 10–12 in Listing 5.21 document the length of each of the three components of the Pixel structure, i.e., the sizes of the corresponding arrays. Lines 14–16 document their type, and lines 18–23 calculate their offset from the beginning of the structure. For the offset calculations a sample instance of the structure is allocated (line 4) and its base address is calculated at line 19.

5.15.2 Packing/unpacking

In the case of an unstructured message, e.g., a collection of data that are not part of the same structure or array or a message that is communicated only once or very infrequently, one can skip the process of creating a derived datatype. A byte array can be prepared with all the data that need to be transmitted, kind of similar to a serialization buffer, and sent to its destination. The destination process will need to follow the same order of insertion to extract the data one-by-one from the byte array.

MPI provides two functions for inserting/packing and extracting/unpacking data from a byte array:

```
int MPI_Pack(void       *inbuf,    // Address of data to store in
                                   // byte array (IN)
             int        incount,   // Count of data in *inbuf (IN)
             MPI_Datatype datatype, // Datatype of *inbuf (IN)
             void       *outbuf,   // Address of byte array (IN)
             int        outcount,  // Size of outbuf in bytes (IN)
             int        *position, // Position of first available
                                   // free space in *outbuf.
                                   // Function both reads and
                                   // updates it (IN/OUT)
             MPI_Comm   comm)      // Communicator (IN)
```

```
int MPI_Unpack(void     *inbuf,    // Address of byte array to
                                   // read from (IN)
```

```
     int          insize,    // Size of *inbuf in bytes (IN)
     int          *position,// Position in *inbuf to read
                            // from. Function updates
                            // *position after extracting
                            // to *outbuf (IN/OUT)
     void         *outbuf,   // Address of array to store
                            // extracted data (IN)
     int          outcount,  // Num. of items to extract(IN)
     MPI_Datatype datatype,  // Datatype of *outbuf (IN)
     MPI_Comm     comm)      // Communicator (IN)
```

Apart from this being a rather code-intensive approach to communicating arbitrary data, the only real challenge in using this pair of functions is to correctly estimate the space necessary to hold the byte buffer. An underestimate, i.e., a too small buffer, would produce a crashing program in the best case and a misbehaving one in the worst case.

If we were to communicate the `Pixel` structure used as an example in the previous section, the code sequence in Listing 5.22 would be required for packing/unpacking.

Listing 5.22: Using `MPI_Pack`/`MPI_Unpack` to communicate an instance of a `Pixel` structure.

```cpp
// File : packUnpack.cpp
. . .
  unsigned char *buffer = new unsigned char[100];
  if (rank == 0)
    {
      struct Pixel test; // followed by initialization code
      . . .
      // pack everything up
      int position=0;
      MPI_Pack(&(test.x), 1, MPI_INT, buffer, 100, &position, ←
          MPI_COMM_WORLD);
      MPI_Pack(&(test.y), 1, MPI_INT, buffer, 100, &position, ←
          MPI_COMM_WORLD);
      MPI_Pack(test.RGB, 3, MPI_UNSIGNED_CHAR, buffer, 100, &←
          position, MPI_COMM_WORLD);
      MPI_Send (buffer, position, MPI_UNSIGNED_CHAR, 1, 0, ←
          MPI_COMM_WORLD);
    }
  else
    {
      struct Pixel test;
      int position=0;
      MPI_Recv (buffer, 100, MPI_UNSIGNED_CHAR, 0, 0, MPI_COMM_WORLD←
          , &status);

      // now start unpacking
      MPI_Unpack(buffer, 100, &position, &(test.x), 1, MPI_INT, ←
          MPI_COMM_WORLD);
      MPI_Unpack(buffer, 100, &position, &(test.y), 1, MPI_INT, ←
          MPI_COMM_WORLD);
```

```
24        MPI_Unpack(buffer, 100, &position, test.RGB, 3, ↵
              MPI_UNSIGNED_CHAR, MPI_COMM_WORLD);
25        . . .
26      }
27    . . .
```

As can be observed in Listing 5.22, the sequences of packing and unpacking mirror each other completely. When the packing process is done, the value of the position variable reflects the total length of the assembled message. Hence, we can use it in the place of the count parameter in MPI_Send (line 13).

On the receiving process, once the buffer is collected (line 19), a sequence of unpacking calls extract the data in the same order they were inserted. The position variable is updated by each call to point to the next data item to be retrieved.

In summary, when one faces the task of communicating collections of data in MPI, one should use:

- *count* **parameter**: if data are an array of primitive types.
- **Derived datatypes**: if data are heterogeneous and/or in non-contiguous but regularly spaced memory locations (e.g., subset of the columns of a matrix, as in MPI_Type_vector), and are communicated often.
- **Packing/unpacking**: if data are heterogeneous and/or in non-contiguous memory locations (e.g., referenced by pointers), and are not communicated often.

5.16 Node management: communicators and groups

The communicator is the fundamental object that is used for message exchange in MPI. Upon initializing MPI with the MPI_Init call, the global communicator MPI_COMM_WORLD is created, which encompasses all running processes. A communicator is a container for information concerning communication routing (virtual topologies), process identification, message caching, and differentiation based on tagging (called contexts in MPI terminology), as well as other information that might be used by the system.

MPI_COMM_WORLD is a predefined **intracommunicator**, i.e., it serves communications taking place between processes belonging to its own group of processes. MPI defines also another kind of communicator: an intercommunicator. An **intercommunicator** is used for sending messages between processes that belong to two separate logical groups. This functionality can come in handy if in a big application processes are split in separate – typically disjoint – groups, each responsible for a different part of the application. It is definitely easier to have processes in the same group communicate using ranks starting from 0 up to the size of the group minus 1. For this a new intracommunicator must be created.

Intercommunicators are then used to bridge processes belonging to two different intracommunicators/groups. In this section we focus only on the creation of intracommunicators and groups, as especially the latter are required for one-sided communications (see Section 5.17).

5.16.1 Creating groups

A group is an ordered set of process identifiers. Each process in a group is associated with an integer rank. Ranks are contiguous starting from zero, in the same fashion as communicator ranks. Ranks are not unique, but they are relative to a group or communicator. *One can think about ranks as if they were array indices, used to access inside a group the process ID and host IP that uniquely identify a process.*

MPI uses the MPI_Group opaque object to represent this information. MPI defines two symbolic group constants: MPI_GROUP_EMPTY, which is used to represent an empty group, and MPI_GROUP_NULL, which is used to represent an invalid group. The latter is returned upon freeing up a group object with the MPI_Group_free function.

A group can be created in a variety of ways:

- From a **communicator**: We can extract all the process info of a communicator into a group for further manipulation:

```
int MPI_Comm_group(MPI_Comm  comm,    // Communic. to access (IN)
                   MPI_Group *group)  // Reference to store comm's
                                      // group (OUT)
```

- From an **existing group**: We can start from an existing group and extract by inclusion or exclusion a new set. The corresponding functions are:

```
int MPI_Group_incl(MPI_Group group,    // Existing group (IN)
                   int       n,        // Size of *ranks (IN)
                   int       *ranks,   // Address of array with
                                       // ranks to include in
                                       // new group (IN)
                   MPI_Group *newgroup)// New group refer. (OUT)
```

The new ranks of the processes in newgroup produced by MPI_Group_incl are in the order of inclusion, i.e., the order in which they are listed in the ranks array. For example, the process in ranks[0] gets rank 0 in newgroup.

```
int MPI_Group_excl(MPI_Group group,    // Existing group (IN)
                   int       n,        // Size of *ranks (IN)
                   int       *ranks,   // Address or array with
                                       // ranks to remove from
                                       // new group (IN)
                   MPI_Group *newgroup)// New group refer. (OUT)
```

The new ranks of the processes in newgroup produced by MPI_Group_excl are in the order in which they appear in the original group. So, for a group of five processes, if n=2 and ranks[0]=0, ranks[1]=2, then the processes with original ranks 1, 3, 4 are included in newgroup with ranks 0, 1, and 2, respectively.

- From the **union of two groups**:

```
int MPI_Group_union(MPI_Group group1,
                    MPI_Group group2,
                    MPI_Group *newgr) // Address for storing new
                                      // group (OUT)
```

- From the **intersection of two groups**. The syntax of the `MPI_Group_intersection` function is the same as that of the `MPI_Group_union` one.
- From the **difference of two groups**. The syntax of the `MPI_Group_difference` function is the same as that of the `MPI_Group_union` one.

As an example for the use of these functions, the program in Listing 5.23 separates the odd and even ranked processes into two groups. The program illustrates the use of two more accessor functions: `MPI_Group_size`, which returns the size of a group, and `MPI_Group_rank`, which returns the group rank of the calling process or `MPI_UNDEFINED` if the process does not belong to the group. Their syntax is identical to the communicator-related ones:

```
int MPI_Group_size(MPI_Group group, // Group structure (IN)
                   int       *size) // Address to store size (OUT)
```

```
int MPI_Group_rank(MPI_Group group, // Group structure (IN)
                   int       *rank) // Address to store rank
                                    // or MPI_UNDEFINED (OUT)
```

Listing 5.23: A program that splits the processes into two groups, one for the even-ranked and one for the odd-ranked.

```
1   // File : groupExample.cpp
2   . . .
3     int num, i, rank;
4     MPI_Group all, odd, even;
5
6     MPI_Init (&argc, &argv);
7     // copy all the processes in group "all"
8     MPI_Comm_group (MPI_COMM_WORLD, &all);
9     MPI_Comm_size (MPI_COMM_WORLD, &num);
10    MPI_Comm_rank (MPI_COMM_WORLD, &rank);
11
12    int grN = 0; // group N (number)
13    int ranks[num / 2];
14
15    for (i = 0; i < num; i += 2)
16      ranks[grN++] = i;
17
18    // extract from "all" only the odd ones
19    MPI_Group_excl (all, grN, ranks, &odd);
20    // sutract odd group from all to get the even ones
21    MPI_Group_difference (all, odd, &even);
22
23    // print group sizes
```

```
24    if (rank == 0)
25      {
26        MPI_Group_size (odd, &i);
27        printf ("Odd group has %i processes\n", i);
28        MPI_Group_size (even, &i);
29        printf ("Even group has %i processes\n", i);
30      }
31
32    // check group membership
33    MPI_Group_rank (odd, &i);
34    if (i == MPI_UNDEFINED)
35      printf ("Process %i belongs to even group\n", rank);
36    else
37      printf ("Process %i belongs to odd group\n", rank);
38
39    // free up memory
40    MPI_Group_free (&all);
41    MPI_Group_free (&odd);
42    MPI_Group_free (&even);
43    . . .
```

5.16.2 Creating intracommunicators

An intracommunicator can be constructed from an existing intracommunicator, either through duplication or through selection of a subset of processes. The three functions that support these approaches are:

```
// Duplicates a communicator
int MPI_Comm_dup(MPI_Comm comm,        // Original communicator (IN)
                 MPI_Comm *newcomm),   // Placeholder for copy (OUT)
```

```
// Creates a communicator according to the group membership
int MPI_Comm_create(MPI_Comm  comm,    // Original communicator (IN)
                    MPI_Group group,   // Set of processes to include
                                       // in new communicator (IN)
                    MPI_Comm *newcomm) // Address of new commun.(OUT)
```

And finally, `MPI_Comm_split`, which creates an array of communicators according to how many different values the `color` parameter gets. Each process, though, gets to participate in just one of them.

```
int MPI_Comm_split(MPI_Comm comm,     // Original communicator (IN)
                   int       color,   // Property of processes that
                                      // places in the same group
                                      // those that match (IN)
                   int       key,     // Rank of process in new
                                      // communicator (IN)
                   MPI_Comm *newcomm) // Pointer to comm. storage.
                                      // One new communicator per
                                      // color is created (OUT)
```

A simple example that extends the code in Listing 5.23 is shown below:

Listing 5.24: A program that splits the processes into two groups, creates two communicators based on the groups and performs broadcasting within each of the two groups.

```cpp
// File : commExample.cpp
. . .
  int num, i, rank, localRank;
  MPI_Group all, odd, even;
  MPI_Comm oddComm, evenComm;
  char mess[11];

  MPI_Init (&argc, &argv);
  // copy all the processes in group "all"
  MPI_Comm_group (MPI_COMM_WORLD, &all);
  MPI_Comm_size (MPI_COMM_WORLD, &num);
  MPI_Comm_rank (MPI_COMM_WORLD, &rank);

  int grN = 0;   // size of group
  int ranks[num / 2];

  for (i = 0; i < num; i += 2)
    ranks[grN++] = i;

  // extract from "all" only the odd ones
  MPI_Group_excl (all, grN, ranks, &odd);
  // sutract odd group from all to get the even ones
  MPI_Group_difference (all, odd, &even);

  MPI_Comm_create (MPI_COMM_WORLD, odd, &oddComm);
  MPI_Comm_create (MPI_COMM_WORLD, even, &evenComm);

  // check group membership
  MPI_Group_rank (odd, &localRank);
  if (localRank != MPI_UNDEFINED)
    {
      if (localRank == 0)        // local group root, sets up message
        strcpy (mess, "ODD GROUP");
      MPI_Bcast (mess, 11, MPI_CHAR, 0, oddComm);
      MPI_Comm_free (&oddComm);  // free communicator in processes ↩
          where it is valid
    }
  else
    {
      MPI_Comm_rank (evenComm, &localRank);
      if (localRank == 0)        // local group root, sets up message
        strcpy (mess, "EVEN GROUP");
      MPI_Bcast (mess, 11, MPI_CHAR, 0, evenComm);
      MPI_Comm_free (&evenComm);
    }
```

```
46    printf ("Process %i with local rank %i received %s\n", rank, ↵
          localRank, mess);
47
48    // free up memory
49    MPI_Group_free (&all);
50    MPI_Group_free (&odd);
51    MPI_Group_free (&even);
52    . . .
```

The groups that are created on lines 21 and 23 are used to create two intracommunicators on lines 25 and 26. These communicators are valid only in the processes that are their members, and that is why their deallocation is inside the if-else structure of lines 30–44. The deallocation takes place via the MPI_Comm_free function (lines 35 and 43), but the actual cleaning up of the memory takes place only after all pending communications are completed. In contrast, the deallocation of the groups takes place in all the nodes (lines 49–51).

The approach used in Listing 5.24 is the most generic in the sense that very complex criteria can be used to separate the processes into groups and communicators. In the case of simple rules, a shorter path to follow is to use MPI_Comm_split. With this function we can transform Listing 5.24 into the following:

Listing 5.25: A program that splits MPI_COMM_WORLD into two intracommunicators based on whether their rank is even or odd. Broadcasting is performed within each of the two communicators.

```
1    // File : commExampleSplit.cpp
2    . . .
3    int num, i, rank, localRank;
4    MPI_Comm newComm;
5    char mess[11];
6
7    MPI_Init (&argc, &argv);
8    MPI_Comm_size (MPI_COMM_WORLD, &num);
9    MPI_Comm_rank (MPI_COMM_WORLD, &rank);
10
11   MPI_Comm_split(MPI_COMM_WORLD, rank%2, rank/2, &newComm);
12
13   if (rank == 0)        // root of even group
14       strcpy (mess, "EVEN GROUP");
15   else if(rank == 1)    // root of odd group
16       strcpy (mess, "ODD GROUP");
17
18
19   MPI_Bcast (mess, 11, MPI_CHAR, 0, newComm);
20   MPI_Comm_rank (newComm, &localRank);
21   MPI_Comm_free (&newComm);   // free communicator in processes where ↵
          it is valid
22
23   printf ("Process %i with local rank %i received %s\n", rank, ↵
          localRank, mess);
24   . . .
```

The `color` and `key` parameters to `MPI_Comm_split` in Listing 5.25 are as shown in Table 5.5.

Table 5.5 The `color` and `key` parameters to `MPI_Comm_split` as they are calculated in Listing 5.25.

rank	0	1	2	3	4	5	6	7	8	9
color	0	1	0	1	0	1	0	1	0	1
key	0	0	1	1	2	2	3	3	4	4

5.17 One-sided communication

Two-sided communications, i.e., ones that need explicitly designated source and destination processes, pose two challenges for developers:

- **Correctness**: each send must be coupled with a receive operation with compatible parameters. Small deviations can be difficult to detect.
- **Performance**: it is difficult to overlap communication and computation, although the alternative forms of `MPI_Send` and `MPI_Recv` examined in Section 5.7 contribute to a solution.

Since MPI-2 (and with substantial extensions in MPI-3) an alternative communication paradigm is available that facilitates accessing a process's memory remotely. MPI's Remote Memory Access (RMA) mechanism allows the use of one-sided communication, whereas there can be only one process specifying all the transaction parameters that will affect a remote memory location.

RMA is an attractive alternative to two-sided communications, especially when the communication patterns vary during runtime and a two-sided communication could require polling or global operations before it could take place.

The procedure for conducting RMA operations is the following:

1. Create a **window**. "Window" is the term used to refer to a structure/object exposing a specified memory area for remote access.
2. Perform a sequence of communication operations. Communications are finished only when synchronization calls are made and completed.
3. Destroy the window.

The `MPI_Win_create` function is used for creating a window using preallocated memory:

```
int MPI_Win_create(void      *base,     // Address of the memory to be
                                          // remotely accessed (IN)
                    MPI_Aint size,       // Memory size in bytes (IN)
                    int      disp_unit,  // Displacement between
                                          // successive elements of the
```

```
                                    // type of data  stored  in  the
                                    // memory  region  (IN)
            MPI_Info info,          // Object  handle  used  for
                                    // optimization  hints  (IN)
            MPI_Comm comm,          // Communicator  (IN)
            MPI_Win  *win)          // Window  object  address
                                    // to  be  initialized  (OUT)
```

MPI_Win_create is a collective call, so it must be called by all processes in a communicator. Each process may specify different parameters for its own local buffer that is exposed via the window object. One-sided communication calls require the specification of both the window reference and the target's rank. As long as remote memory accesses fit inside the prescribed buffer, there should be no problem.

The disp_unit parameter should be set to the size of the data type of the buffer. Its purpose is to simplify access to individual array elements.

The MPI_Info parameter is an opaque object (object of an unspecified type) that serves as a placeholder for (key, value) pairs that can assist MPI in optimizing the related operations. MPI provides a set of functions for setting or querying the pairs in an MPI_Info object (MPI_Info_create, MPI_Info_get, etc.). For our purposes, we can simply use the MPI_INFO_NULL symbolic constant instead.

A window object is destroyed by the call:

```
int MPI_Win_free(MPI_Win  *win) // Window obj. address  (IN/OUT)
```

Upon a successful execution, win is set to MPI_WIN_NULL.

RMA distinguishes between two types of functions: **communication** and **synchronization**. RMA suffers from the same consistency problems that are examined in Section 3.5. MPI provides a set of synchronization functions that allow the developers to implement strict or loose consistency models, as best suited for the application at hand.

5.17.1 **RMA communication functions**

RMA provides three communication functions:

- MPI_Put: copies data from the caller memory to the target memory.
- MPI_Get: copies data from the target memory to the caller memory.
- MPI_Accumulate: adds local data to the target memory.

All the above functions are non-blocking: the call initiates the transfer but there is no way to know when it will be complete, other than calling the synchronization functions discussed in the next section. This behavior opens up an opportunity for optimizations, as MPI can choose to send aggregate access requests (i.e., a bunch of them together), instead of individual ones. It also opens the backdoor for programming errors due to memory corruption: a process should not access a buffer it has exported via a window, until it is known that RMA calls have been completed.

The syntax of these functions and an explanation of their parameters is given below:

```
int MPI_Get(void        *origin_addr,// Address of buffer to store
                                     // retrieved data (OUT)
            int         origin_count,// Buffer size in number of
                                     // items (IN)
            MPI_Datatype origin_dtype,// *origin_addr datatype(IN)
            int         target_rank, // Rank of process to read
                                     // from (IN)
            MPI_Aint    target_disp, // Displacement/array index
                                     // to start getting data
                                     // from. Displacement is in
                                     // datatype units. (IN)
            int         target_count,// Number of items to
                                     // retrieve (IN)
            MPI_Datatype target_dtype,// Source buffer datatype
                                     // Actual address is inferred
                                     // from the window(IN)
            MPI_Win     win)         // Window object (IN)
```

```
int MPI_Put(void        *origin_addr,// Address of data to be
                                     // sent (IN)
            int         origin_count,// Buffer size in number of
                                     // items (IN)
            MPI_Datatype origin_dtype,// *origin_addr datatype.(IN)
            int         target_rank, // Rank of process to send
                                     // data (IN)
            MPI_Aint    target_disp, // Displacement/array index
                                     // to start putting data
                                     // in (IN)
            int         target_count,// Storage size in number
                                     // of items (IN)
            MPI_Datatype target_dtype,// Target buffer datatype
                                     // Actual address is inferred
                                     // from the window(IN)
            MPI_Win     win)         // Window object handle (IN)
```

```
int MPI_Accumulate(void  *origin_addr,// Buffer address of data
                                     // to be sent (IN)
            int         origin_count,// Buffer size in number
                                     // of items (IN)
            MPI_Datatype orig_type,  // *origin_addr type (IN)
            int         target_rank, // Rank of process to send
                                     // data to (IN)
            MPI_Aint    target_disp, // Starting array index in
                                     // destin. process (IN)
                                     // Actual target address
                                     // is inferred from the
                                     // window
            int         target_count,// Storage size in number
                                     // of items (IN)
            MPI_Datatype target_type, // Target buffer datatype
            MPI_Op      op,          // Reduction operation
```

```
                                       //  Symbolic  constant ,  same
                                       //  as  in  MPI_Reduce  (IN)
             MPI_Win        win)       //  Window  object  handle  (IN)
```

`MPI_Accumulate` behaves in a similar manner to `MPI_Reduce`, taking local and remote data and storing their reduction in the remote process buffer. `MPI_Accumulate` allows the simple implementation of shared counters, among other things.

An example of the use of these functions will be presented following the discussion of the synchronization functions.

MPI-3 has added request-based versions of the above functions that return a reference to an `MPI_Request` structure that can be used to check when the operation is complete. These versions are only valid for use in passive target operations (see Section 5.17.2).

5.17.2 RMA synchronization functions

MPI provides two different approaches to implementing RMA, each coming with its own set(s) of functions for synchronization:

- **Active target**: the process having its memory accessed is actively participating in the data exchange. The time span during which a process is allowed to perform RMA communications is called **exposure epoch**, and it is controlled by the *target* process, i.e., the owner of the memory exported through the window. Two sets of functions can be used in this case. Their difference lies in how the exposure epoch is set up.
- **Passive target**: only the process performing the get, put, or accumulate operation(s) is controlling the proceedings. Similarly to the active target case, all RMA communications have to take place within a time span identified as **access epoch**. This time period is controlled by the *origin* process, i.e., the one conducting the operations.

The epochs (exposure for the target and access for the origin) essentially mark periods of time where changes are allowed in the shared memory of the target process, and any attempt to use the data by the target process may result in incoherent results. The end of an epoch marks the application of all the pending/requested changes and the implied permission to start using the data at the target process.

When exactly communications take place during an epoch is not specified by the MPI standard, leaving room for optimizations by the MPI implementations. The only certain thing is that when an epoch is closed, the corresponding calls (e.g., `MPI_Win_complete`, `MPI_Win_fence`, etc.) will return when any modifications made to the window data are committed, both at the target processes and at any local copies that may be privately kept by MPI at the origin processes.

The three sets of synchronization functions are:

1. `MPI_Win_fence`: this function is used for **active target** RMA. The access epoch in the origin process and the exposure epoch in the target process are started and

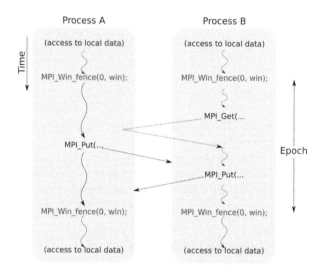

FIGURE 5.17

An example of the interaction between two processes when `MPI_Win_fence` is used to establish and terminate an epoch. The slanted dashed lines represent communications. The vertical dotted lines represent idle times.

completed by a call to `MPI_Win_fence`. `MPI_Win_fence` is similar to `MPI_Barrier` in the sense that all the processes in a communicator used to create a window must call it. The syntax is the following:

```
int MPI_Win_fence(int        assert,  // Assertion flags, used for
                                      // optimization (IN)
                  MPI_Win win)        // Window object handle (IN)
```

The `assert` parameter, which is also found in other synchronization functions, is a bitwise OR of symbolic constants that represent conditions (assertions) that could be taken into consideration in streamlining the communications taking place during synchronization. A value of 0 can be safely used in the place of the `assert` flag, which indicates that no condition is guaranteed.

The MPI standard declares that the `MPI_Win_fence` call both ends the preceding epoch and starts a new epoch, so a sequence of `MPI_Win_fence`, `MPI_Put`, `MPI_Win_fence`, `MPI_Get`, `MPI_Win_fence` is possible. In general, `MPI_Win_fence` calls should enclose RMA communication calls.

During an access epoch, a process *P* may access any of the remote memory blocks exported via the window, and any other process may access *P*'s own local memory block. This kind of synchronization is best suited for applications that exhibit interleaved periods of computation and global data exchange. An example of the interaction taking place in this case is shown in Fig. 5.17.

Because `MPI_Win_fence` is a collective operation, it suffers from high synchronization costs.

2. `MPI_Win_start`, `MPI_Win_complete`, `MPI_Win_post`, `MPI_Win_wait`: this set of functions was introduced to allow *pairwise* synchronization between origin and target processes. This reduces the communication overhead involved, thus making it a far more scalable approach. An additional benefit is that fine-grained control over the ordering of local and remote accesses to a target's memory is allowed by forcing the declaration at the beginning of an exposure (access) epoch by the processes that will serve as targets (origins).

This **active target** approach requires that the origin calls `MPI_Win_start` and `MPI_Win_complete`, while the target calls `MPI_Win_post` and `MPI_Win_wait` to start and end the access and exposure epochs, respectively.

The `MPI_Win_start` call can be blocking until the target processes issue a corresponding `MPI_Win_post` call. Also, the termination of the exposure epoch in a target process via `MPI_Win_wait` will block until all origin processes issue a matching `MPI_Win_complete` call.

Their syntax is as follows:

```
// to begin an exposure epoch
int MPI_Win_post(MPI_Group group, // Group of origin proc. (IN)
                 int       assert,// Flags that can be used for
                                  // optimization. Zero can be
                                  // used for default. (IN)
                 MPI_Win   win)   // Window object (IN)
```

```
// to terminate an exposure epoch
int MPI_Win_wait(MPI_Win win) // Window object. (IN)
```

```
// to begin an access epoch
int MPI_Win_start(MPI_Group group, // Group of target proc. (IN)
                  int       assert,// Flags that can be used for
                                   // optimization. Zero can be
                                   // used for default. (IN)
                  MPI_Win   win)   // Window object (IN)
```

```
// to terminate an access epoch
int MPI_Win_complete(MPI_Win win) // Window object (IN)
```

An example of the interaction taking place in this case is shown in Fig. 5.18.

3. `MPI_Win_lock`, `MPI_Win_unlock`: these functions behave in a similar manner to the signal and wait methods of a semaphore. The origin process may use them to get exclusive access to the target's shared memory (at least as far as MPI-controlled access is concerned), without the explicit cooperation of the target (**passive target**). Unless access to the shared buffer is done through appropriate RMA calls, there is no guarantee that these calls will operate as specified.

Their syntax is as follows:

```
int MPI_Win_lock(int       lock_type, // Lock type (IN). One of:
                                       // MPI_LOCK_EXCLUSIVE
```

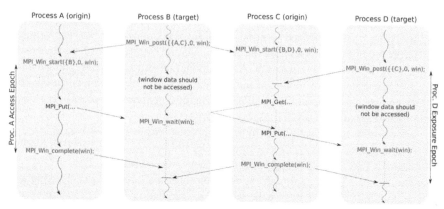

FIGURE 5.18

An example of the interaction between four processes when `MPI_Win_post` and `MPI_Win_start` are used to begin epochs. The slanted dashed lines represent communications. The { } notation is used to represent groups of processes without deviating too much from the C-language syntax. `MPI_Win_start` calls can block until the corresponding targets issue `MPI_Win_post` statements, as shown. However, this is not the default behavior. The exact action depends on the `assert` flags specified and the particular MPI implementation. The vertical dotted lines represent idle times.

```
                                    // MPI_LOCK_SHARED
        int     rank,               // Rank of target. (IN)
        int     assert,             // Assertion flag. (IN)
        MPI_Win win)                // Window object (IN)
```

```
int MPI_Win_unlock(int      rank,// Rank of target. (IN)
                   MPI_Win win) // Window object. (IN)
```

The `MPI_LOCK_SHARED` lock type can be used to implement "reader" functionality, i.e., allow multiple processes to get data from the target while preventing any modifications from taking place.

On the other hand, the `MPI_LOCK_EXCLUSIVE` lock type can be used to implement "writer" functionality, preventing access to the window data from any other process while they are being modified.

As with previous synchronization functions, an `assert` flag of 0 can be used as default.

Fig. 5.19 shows a possible interaction scenario between three processes that utilize `MPI_Win_lock` to acquire exclusive access to a window's memory.

In order to demonstrate the use of the RMA functions, we show how the bucket sort implementation of Listing 5.18 can be converted to use RMA. For educational purposes, we use all the three different methods of RMA synchronization.

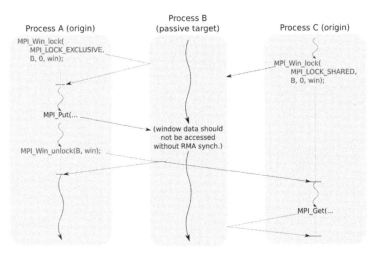

FIGURE 5.19

An example of the interaction between three processes when `MPI_Win_lock` and `MPI_Win_unlock` are used to establish passive target synchronization. Process A is trying to get an exclusive lock in order to modify the target's memory, while process C is trying to get a shared lock in order to read the target's memory. The slanted dashed lines represent communications, while the vertical dotted lines represent idle times.

The initial steps shown below entail the allocation of memory for the data array (line 23), the buckets (line 24), the bucket offsets (line 25), the bucket content counters (line 26), the receive counters (line 28), and the offsets for data retrieval (line 29).

Lines 42–44 create and populate two process groups: one containing all the processes (`all`) and one containing all the processes but the calling one (`allOtherGroup`). These two groups are used for commencing the exposure epochs.

Also three windows are created: one for accessing the buckets (`bucketWin`, line 46), one for the bucket counters (`cntWin`, line 47), and one for the unsorted, initial data arrays (`dataWin`, line 48).

Listing 5.26: A parallel bucket sort implementation that uses RMA for data exchange between the processes.

```
1   // File : bucketsortRMA.cpp
2   . . .
3   int main (int argc, char **argv)
4   {
5      MPI_Init (&argc, &argv);
6
7      int rank, N;
8      MPI_Comm_rank (MPI_COMM_WORLD, &rank);
9      MPI_Comm_size (MPI_COMM_WORLD, &N);
10     MPI_Status status;
11
12     if (argc == 1)
```

```
13   {
14     if (rank == 0)
15       cerr << "Usage " << argv[0] << " number_of_items\n";
16     exit (1);
17   }
18
19   int M = atoi (argv[1]);
20   int maxItemsPerBucket = ceil (1.0 * M / N);
21   int deliveredItems;
22   int bucketRange = ceil (1.0 * (MAX - MIN) / N);
23   unique_ptr<int[]> data = make_unique<int[]>(M);
24   unique_ptr<int[]> buckets = make_unique<int[]>(N * ←
         maxItemsPerBucket);
25   unique_ptr<int[]> bucketOffset = make_unique<int[]>(N);        // ←
         where do buckets begin?
26   unique_ptr<int[]> inBucket = make_unique<int[]>(N);   // how many ←
         items in each one?
27
28   unique_ptr<int[]> toRecv = make_unique<int[]>(N);        // how many ←
         items to receive from each process
29   unique_ptr<int[]> recvOff = make_unique<int[]>(N);       // offsets ←
         for sent data
30
31   if (rank == 0)
32     initData (MIN, MAX, data, M);
33
34   // initialize bucket counters and offsets
35   for (int i = 0; i < N; i++)
36     {
37       inBucket[i] = 0;
38       bucketOffset[i] = i * maxItemsPerBucket;
39     }
40
41   // three windows created, one for the bucket counts, one for the ←
         buckets themselves and one for the data
42   MPI_Group all, allOtherGroup;
43   MPI_Comm_group (MPI_COMM_WORLD, &all);
44   MPI_Group_excl (all, 1, &rank, &allOtherGroup);
45   MPI_Win cntWin, bucketWin, dataWin;
46   MPI_Win_create (buckets.get(), N * maxItemsPerBucket * sizeof (int←
         ), sizeof (int), MPI_INFO_NULL, MPI_COMM_WORLD, &bucketWin);
47   MPI_Win_create (inBucket.get(), N * sizeof (int), sizeof (int), ←
         MPI_INFO_NULL, MPI_COMM_WORLD, &cntWin);
48   MPI_Win_create (data.get(), M * sizeof (int), sizeof (int), ←
         MPI_INFO_NULL, MPI_COMM_WORLD, &dataWin);
```

The first step following the data allocation and initialization is to scatter the data that initially reside in process 0 to all the other processes. This is a step that uses the `MPI_Put` function to remotely access the remote `data` arrays (line 57). The remote access is enclosed in `MPI_fence` calls (executed by all processes on lines 51 and 60) that start and end the exposure/access epochs. As these are collective calls, all the processes will have to wait for the root process to finish the data distribution before continuing.

```
49   // step 1
50   // replacing MPI_Scatter (data, maxItemsPerBucket, MPI_INT, data, ↩
         maxItemsPerBucket, MPI_INT, 0, MPI_COMM_WORLD);
51   MPI_Win_fence (0, dataWin);
52   if (rank == 0)
53     {
54       for (int i = 1; i < N; i++)
55         {
56           deliveredItems = (i == N - 1) ? (M - (N - 1) * ↩
                 maxItemsPerBucket) : maxItemsPerBucket;
57           MPI_Put (&(data[bucketOffset[i]]), deliveredItems, MPI_INT ↩
                 , i, 0, N * maxItemsPerBucket, MPI_INT, dataWin);
58         }
59     }
60   MPI_Win_fence (0, dataWin);
61   deliveredItems = (rank == N - 1) ? (M - (N - 1) * ↩
         maxItemsPerBucket) : maxItemsPerBucket;
```

One might question the necessity of the first `MPI_Win_fence` call on line 51. After all, it is followed by an `if` block that is executed by the 0-ranked process only and a second `MPI_Win_fence` call that surely prevents all processes from continuing before the data are distributed. However, we cannot make the `MPI_Put` call of line 57 before we start an epoch. While `MPI_Win_fence` behaves as `MPI_Barrier`, it has different semantics.

In the next step, which does not involve any communication, the processes go over their local data items and sort them into N buckets, as many as the number of processes.

```
62   // step 2
63   // split into buckets
64   for (int i = 0; i < deliveredItems; i++)
65     {
66       int idx = (data[i] - MIN) / bucketRange;
67       int off = bucketOffset[idx] + inBucket[idx];
68       buckets[off] = data[i];
69       inBucket[idx]++;
70     }
```

At the next step, the buckets have to be redistributed so they end up to their appropriate process. Mirroring the bucket sort implementation in Listing 5.18 that used collective operations, we start by having each process get from all the other processes the sizes of the buckets that it needs to retrieve. Each process starts an exposure epoch (line 75) so that its bucket counters can be accessed by all other processes, and then it starts an access epoch (line 76) in order to access the remote bucket counters. Changing the order of these two statements will not necessarily cause a deadlock, as it is up to the MPI implementation to have a blocking or non-blocking `MPI_Win_start`. However, the order we use below is prudent and makes more sense.

The `allOtherGroup` MPI_Group variable is used to control which processes are granted access rights in the exposure epoch or are to be accessed in the access epoch. These epochs end (line 80 for access and line 81 for exposure) after all counters are retrieved by the loop of lines 77–79.

The loop of lines 83–85 is then used to calculate where each of the to-be-retrieved buckets should be stored in local memory.

```
71   // step 3
72   // start by gathering the counts of data the other processes will ↩
        send
73   // replacing MPI_Alltoall (inBucket, 1, MPI_INT, toRecv, 1, ↩
        MPI_INT, MPI_COMM_WORLD);
74   toRecv[rank] = inBucket[rank];
75   MPI_Win_post (allOtherGroup, 0, cntWin);
76   MPI_Win_start (allOtherGroup, 0, cntWin);
77   for (int i = 0; i < N; i++)
78     if (i != rank)
79       MPI_Get (&(toRecv[i]), 1, MPI_INT, i, rank , 1, MPI_INT, ↩
          cntWin);
80   MPI_Win_complete (cntWin);
81   MPI_Win_wait (cntWin);
82
83   recvOff[0] = 0;
84   for (int i = 1; i < N; i++)
85     recvOff[i] = recvOff[i - 1] + toRecv[i - 1];
```

The remote buckets are then retrieved by starting a new exposure epoch for all the processes (line 87). The use of the `all` MPI_Group allows for simpler code in the loop of lines 89–90, as there is no need for a special check that distinguishes between local and remote bucket arrays. `MPI_Get` can be used even for copying the local bucket to the appropriate offset of the `data` array.

The last step before sorting the individual buckets in their respective processes is to lock the `dataWin` window (line 94), so that the root process will have to wait for the sorting to complete before starting to copy the buckets to its memory.

```
86   // replacing MPI_Alltoallv (buckets, inBucket, bucketOffset, ↩
        MPI_INT, data, toRecv, recvOff, MPI_INT, MPI_COMM_WORLD);
87   MPI_Win_post (all, 0, bucketWin);
88   MPI_Win_start (all, 0, bucketWin);
89   for (int i = 0; i < N; i++)
90     MPI_Get (&(data[recvOff[i]]), toRecv[i], MPI_INT, i, ↩
          bucketOffset[rank], toRecv[i], MPI_INT, bucketWin);
91   MPI_Win_complete (bucketWin);
92   MPI_Win_wait (bucketWin);
93
94   MPI_Win_lock (MPI_LOCK_EXCLUSIVE, rank, 0, dataWin); // limit ↩
        access to data array until it is sorted
```

The sorting can be done with STL's `sort` algorithm (line 98) before unlocking the `dataWin` window (line 100).

```
95    // step 4
96    // apply quicksort to the local bucket
97    int localBucketSize = recvOff[N - 1] + toRecv[N - 1];
98    sort(data.get(), data.get()+localBucketSize);
99
100   MPI_Win_unlock (rank, dataWin);          // data array is available ↩
         again
```

Finally, the root process gathers the sizes of the individual buckets (line 102) and calculates the offsets where each one will have to be copied (lines 103–108). Line 102 holds the only collective function remnant of the original Listing 5.18. The reason is just simplicity. Replacing collective communication functions with RMA operations tends to enlarge the code as a direct comparison to Listing 5.18 can reveal.

Once the bucket sizes are known to the root process, it can start to lock each individual bucket (line 115) before copying the remote, sorted subarray to its proper place in its local memory (line 116). The passive target RMA is terminated by line 117.

```
101   // step 5
102   MPI_Gather (&localBucketSize, 1, MPI_INT, toRecv.get(), 1, MPI_INT ↩
         , 0, MPI_COMM_WORLD);
103   if (rank == 0)
104     {
105       recvOff[0] = 0;
106       for (int i = 1; i < N; i++)
107         recvOff[i] = recvOff[i - 1] + toRecv[i - 1];
108     }
109
110   // replacing MPI_Gatherv (data, localBucketSize, MPI_INT, data, ↩
         toRecv, recvOff, MPI_INT, 0, MPI_COMM_WORLD);
111   if (rank == 0)
112     {
113       for (int i - 1; i < N; i++)
114         {
115           MPI_Win_lock (MPI_LOCK_EXCLUSIVE, i, 0, dataWin);        // ↩
               gain access to remote data array
116           MPI_Get (&(data[recvOff[i]]), toRecv[i], MPI_INT, i, 0, ↩
               toRecv[i], MPI_INT, dataWin);
117           MPI_Win_unlock (i, dataWin); // release lock to remote ↩
               data array
118         }
119     }
120
121   // print results
122   if (rank == 0)
123     {
124       for (int i = 0; i < M; i++)
125         cout << data[i] << " ";
126       cout << endl;
127     }
```

The window and group memory cleanup (lines 128–132) is the last operation preceding `MPI_Finalize`. If one neglects to do so, MPI can produce runtime errors informing of this fact.

```
128    MPI_Group_free (&all);
129    MPI_Group_free (&allOtherGroup);
130    MPI_Win_free (&cntWin);
131    MPI_Win_free (&bucketWin);
132    MPI_Win_free (&dataWin);
133    MPI_Finalize ();
134    return 0;
```

The comparison of the RMA-based bucket sort implementation with Listing 5.18 is not a flattering one, as far as the complexity and the length of the code are concerned. This is a natural consequence of replacing collective operations with individual memory accesses. RMA-based implementations are not much different in that respect from point-to-point communication-based ones, i.e., they lack expressiveness. The choice of tool is ultimately the prerogative of the programmer, given performance and other application-specific restrictions.

5.18 I/O considerations

In MPI the root process has the special privilege of exclusive use of the standard input, i.e., it is the only one that can read user input from the keyboard. However, all processes have access to the standard output and the command-line parameters used to launch the application. So, if the command-line contains a set of parameters critical for the execution of the program, these can be accessed and parsed directly instead of having the root process parse them and broadcast them.

The real issue lays elsewhere: how can we maximize the I/O speed from secondary storage to MPI processes? Keeping the processes busy means that they must have easy and fast access to the problem's data. The least common denominator is to have universal access to a common filesystem, such as an NFS volume. This would guarantee that all processes can access the problem's data without requiring special action from the root process, e.g., reading and scattering of file data. Additionally, a parallel filesystem like IBM's Elastic Storage [53], the Parallel Virtual File System (PVFS) [4], the Lustre [2], or BeeGFS [1] can be used to maximize the I/O data rates that can be achieved.

A parallel filesystem can improve I/O performance at the system level. However, there is one more facet of the problem that needs to be addressed: **parallel access to data at the application or process level**. Fig. 5.20 illustrates the issue at hand by showing three different I/O configurations. Clearly, Fig. 5.20(b) provides the greatest performance potential, but it might also make it necessary to postprocess the program's output (e.g., joining the files into one). Fig. 5.20(c) would then seem to be the best compromise, although special support needs to be provided to avoid having processes step on each other's toes!

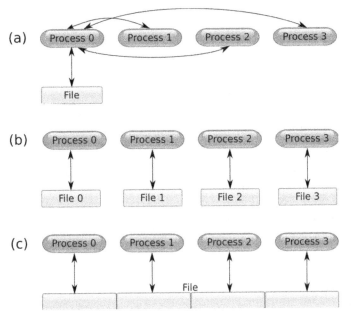

FIGURE 5.20

MPI applications with different I/O configurations: (a) root process controls access to the data file, (b) each process has access to a separate file, (c) all processes have access to the same file concurrently. Configurations (b) and (c) qualify as parallel I/O.

MPI provides a set of parallel I/O functions aiming at solving this problem. These functions should be used instead of the typical POSIX file library to open, close, read, and write to a file or files from multiple processes. MPI uses a special nomenclature to describe its I/O functions:

- **etype**: is the elementary datatype, i.e., the fundamental data unit that a file is made of. All I/O is performed in etype units. Also, when MPI accesses a file, the size of the declared etype is used for calculating offsets and file pointers. Any primitive or derived datatype can be used as the etype of a file.
- **filetype**: a filetype is a single etype or a collection of etypes in the form of a derived datatype. A filetype forms the basis for partitioning a file among processes.
- **view**: a view defines what is currently accessible in a file from a process. A view is defined on the basis of three things: (a) a displacement or offset from the beginning of a file, (b) an etype, and (c) a filetype. The pattern defined by the filetype is repeated, starting at the declared offset, to define the view. Fig. 5.21(a) shows the relationship between the etype, the filetype, and the view.

A group of processes that access a file can have the same etype, but different filetypes and views, so that each one gets a distinct part of the file as shown in Fig. 5.21(b).

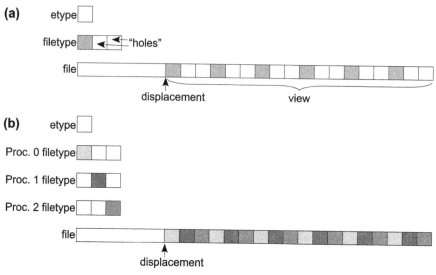

FIGURE 5.21

(a) Relationship between etype, filetype, and view for MPI I/O functions. (b) Each MPI process can have a different filetype associated with a file, in order to be able to partition the file into disjoint sets.

The files to be accessed by MPI I/O must be binary ones, with fixed lengths per etype. Text files, generally, do not satisfy this requirement.

The most commonly used MPI I/O functions are as follows:

```
int MPI_File_open(MPI_Comm comm,      // Communicator (IN)
                  char     *filename, // Path to file (IN)
                  int      amode,     // Mode of operation (IN)
                  MPI_Info info,      // Info object handle (IN)
                  MPI_File *fh)       // File handle (OUT)
```

MPI_File_open is a *collective* function, so it has to be called by all the processes in the declared intracommunicator. The amode parameter is a bitwise OR of different constants (some are mutually exclusive) that direct MPI on how the file will be opened. A list of these constants is shown in Table 5.6.

All files opened by MPI must be closed before MPI_Finalize is called, using:

```
int MPI_File_close(MPI_File *mpi_fh) // File handle (IN)
```

For reading and writing collections of etype data, one can use:

```
int MPI_File_read(MPI_File      mpi_fh,   // File handle (IN)
                  void          *buf,     // Data buffer address (OUT)
                  int           count,    // Number of elements in
                                          // *buf (IN)
                  MPI_Datatype  datatype, // Etype (IN)
                  MPI_Status    *status)  // Status object (OUT)
```

Table 5.6 A list of file opening modes that can be used in `MPI_File_open`.

Mode	Description
MPI_MODE_RDONLY	read only
MPI_MODE_RDWR	read & write
MPI_MODE_WRONLY	write only
MPI_MODE_CREATE	create the file if it does not exist
MPI_MODE_EXCL	error will be flagged if file exists when trying to create it
MPI_MODE_DELETE_ON_CLOSE	delete file upon closing it
MPI_MODE_UNIQUE_OPEN	file will be exclusively accessed
MPI_MODE_APPEND	file pointer set at end of file
MPI_MODE_SEQUENTIAL	file will be accessed sequentially

```
int MPI_File_write(MPI_File    mpi_fh,   // File handle (IN)
                   void        *buf,     // Data buffer address (IN)
                   int         count,    // Number of elements in
                                         // *buf (IN)
                   MPI_Datatype datatype,// Etype (IN)
                   MPI_Status  *status)  // Status object (OUT)
```

Finally, a view can be specified for a file via the following function:

```
int MPI_File_set_view(MPI_File    mpi_fh,   // File handle (IN)
                      MPI_Offset  disp,     // File offset in etype
                                            // units (IN)
                      MPI_Datatype etype,   // Etype handle (IN)
                      MPI_Datatype filetype,// Filetype handle (IN)
                      char        *datarep, // Data represent-
                                            // ation (IN)
                      MPI_Info    info)     // Info object handle
                                            // for optimization
                                            // hints (IN)
```

As mentioned previously, the `etype` parameter is an MPI datatype symbolic constant or an MPI-derived datatype as described in Section 5.15.1.

The `*datarep` string can have one of the following values:

- "native": Data are stored as if they were dumped from memory. This is appropriate only for homogeneous environments. As there is no data conversion performed, a platform change from big- to little-endian or a change in the length of the representation (32 to 64 bit) would render the data unreadable.
- "external32": Data on the file are stored in a canonical representation that allows them to be converted appropriately for I/O in a heterogeneous environment. The compromise for ensuring the cross-platform readability of the data is that I/O performance deteriorates. Also, a loss of precision is possible.

As a simple example of the use of MPI I/O, let us consider the distribution of data to processes for sorting. In our bucket sort example of Listing 5.26, the sample data are generated at the root process. One would normally expect that the data reside in a file. Breaking up the file into roughly equal parts can be accomplished with the code in Listing 5.27. For this simple example, the structure of the code mimics closely what would be required if POSIX calls were used.

Listing 5.27: An example of a roughly equal block distribution of int-type data via MPI I/O.

```
1   // File : fileIO.cpp
2   . . .
3     MPI_Init (&argc, &argv);
4
5     int rank, N;
6     MPI_Comm_rank (MPI_COMM_WORLD, &rank);
7     MPI_Comm_size (MPI_COMM_WORLD, &N);
8     MPI_Status status;
9
10    if (argc == 1)
11      {
12        if (rank == 0)
13          cerr << "Usage " << argv[0] << " filetoload\n";
14        exit (1);
15      }
16
17    MPI_File f;
18    MPI_File_open (MPI_COMM_WORLD, argv[1], MPI_MODE_RDONLY, ←
          MPI_INFO_NULL, &f);
19
20    int blockSize;
21
22    MPI_Offset filesize;
23    MPI_File_get_size (f, &filesize); // get file size in bytes
24    filesize /= sizeof(int);          // convert to number of items
25    blockSize = filesize / N;         // calculate size of block to ←
          read per process
26    int pos = rank * blockSize;       // initial file position per ←
          process
27    if(rank == N-1)
28        blockSize = filesize - pos;   // get all remaining in last ←
            process
29
30    unique_ptr<int[]> data = make_unique<int[]>(blockSize);
31    MPI_File_seek(f, pos*sizeof(int), MPI_SEEK_SET);
32    MPI_File_read (f, data.get(), blockSize, MPI_INT, &status);
33    MPI_File_close (&f);
34
35    sleep (rank);
36    cout << rank << " read " << blockSize << " numbers." << endl;
37    for (int i = 0; i < 30; i++)
38      cout << data[i] << " ";
39    cout << " .... Last one is : " << data[blockSize - 1];
40    cout << endl;
41
```

```
42    MPI_Finalize ();
43    return 0;
44 }
```

Line 18 opens the file provided as a command-line parameter in read-only mode. The size of the file in bytes is queried on line 23 with the result stored in variable `filesize`. The `MPI_Offset` type is just a typedef for type `long long`. The actual number of integers in the file is calculated on line 24, so that the size of the blocks that will be assigned to each process and the initial position to read from can be calculated (lines 25 and 26, respectively). The last ($N - 1$-ranked) process is treated separately (lines 27–28) in order to be able to get all the data in the file, regardless if the file size is evenly divided by the size of the communicator or not.

The data are read on line 32, after the *local* file pointer is moved to the appropriate offset in the file with the `MPI_File_seek` function (line 31). `MPI_File_seek` and the respective constants used for placing the file pointer (`MPI_SEEK_SET`, `MPI_SEEK_CUR`, and `MPI_SEEK_END`) mirror the corresponding C99 function `fseek` and its constants (`SEEK_SET`, `SEEK_CUR`, and `SEEK_END`), resulting in a fairly familiar setup.

Finally, line 35 delays each process for a sufficient amount of time to allow for a tidy output to the console of some debugging information (lines 36–40). Running the program of Listing 5.27 on a file containing a sequence of 10,000 integers from 0 to 9999 would produce the following output:

```
$ mpirun -np 3 ./fileIO  data
0 read 3333 numbers.
0 1 2 3 4 5 6 7 8 9 10 11 12 13 14 15 16 17 18 19 20 21 22 23 24 25 ←
    26 27 28 29 .... Last one is: 3332
1 read 3333 numbers.
3333 3334 3335 3336 3337 3338 3339 3340 3341 3342 3343 3344 3345 ←
    3346 3347 3348 3349 3350 3351 3352 3353 3354 3355 3356 3357 3358←
    3359 3360 3361 3362 .... Last one is: 6665
2 read 3334 numbers.
6666 6667 6668 6669 6670 6671 6672 6673 6674 6675 6676 6677 6678 ←
    6679 6680 6681 6682 6683 6684 6685 6686 6687 6688 6689 6690 6691←
    6692 6693 6694 6695 .... Last one is: 9999
```

A **cyclic block distribution** of the file's contents to the available processes can be accomplished by declaring a filetype and view for a file, as shown in Listing 5.28. A cyclic block distribution means that fixed-sized blocks of the data are assigned to the processes in a round-robin fashion.

Listing 5.28: An example of a cyclic block distribution of data via MPI I/O.

```
1 // File : viewExample.cpp
2 . . .
3 const int BLOCKSIZE = 10;
4
5 // *****************************************
6 int main (int argc, char **argv)
7 {
8    MPI_Init (&argc, &argv);
```

```
9
10   int rank, N;
11   MPI_Comm_rank (MPI_COMM_WORLD, &rank);
12   MPI_Comm_size (MPI_COMM_WORLD, &N);
13   MPI_Status status;
14
15   if (argc == 1)
16     {
17       if (rank == 0)
18         cerr << "Usage " << argv[0] << " filetoload\n";
19       exit (1);
20     }
21
22   MPI_File f;
23   MPI_File_open (MPI_COMM_WORLD, argv[1], MPI_MODE_RDONLY, ↵
         MPI_INFO_NULL, &f);
24
25   MPI_Datatype filetype;
26   int sizes = N * BLOCKSIZE, subsizes = BLOCKSIZE, starts = 0;
27   MPI_Type_create_subarray (1, &sizes, &subsizes, &starts, ↵
         MPI_ORDER_C, MPI_INT, &filetype);
28   MPI_Type_commit (&filetype);
29   MPI_File_set_view (f, rank * BLOCKSIZE * sizeof (int), MPI_INT, ↵
         filetype, "native", MPI_INFO_NULL); // MPI_INT is the etype
```

Lines 25–29 above constitute the first major difference with Listing 5.27. A derived datatype is created for establishing a filetype for the opened file. The `MPI_Type_create_sub-array` function is useful for extracting a portion of a multi-dimensional array. Its syntax is:

```
int MPI_Type_create_subarray(
        int          ndims,      // Number of array dimensions (IN)
        int          sizes[],    // Size of each dimension (IN)
        int          subsizes[], // Number of elements to extract
                                 // from each dimension (IN)
        int          starts[],   // Starting offsets in each
                                 // dimension (IN)
        int          order,      // Array storage order (IN)
        MPI_Datatype oldtype,    // Array element datatype (IN)
        MPI_Datatype *newtype)   // Address for storing the
                                 // derived datatype (OUT)
```

The array storage order can be set to one of `MPI_ORDER_C` or `MPI_ORDER_FORTRAN`. This is significant only for 2D or higher dimensional arrays.

By creating a subarray type of `BLOCKSIZE` elements from a 1D array N times as big as that (line 27) and by setting the byte offset to start reading from the file to `rank*BLOCKSIZE*sizeof(int)` (line 29), each process is made to read a different block of data. Fig. 5.22 illustrates the resulting effect.

Although the amount of data each process will read can be computed a priori, in the remaining of the code we use a type `vector<int>` object for having a dynamically grown data repository, as the data are read one block at a time.

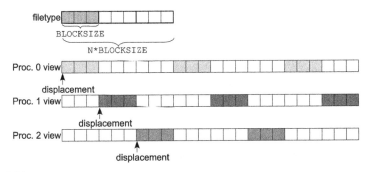

FIGURE 5.22

An illustration of the filetype and views associated with three processes, as used in Listing 5.28 to achieve a cyclic block distribution of a file's data.

```
30    vector < int >data;
31    int temp[BLOCKSIZE];
32
33    MPI_Offset filesize;
34    MPI_File_get_size (f, &filesize); // get size in bytes
35    filesize /= sizeof (int);          // convert size in number of ↩
          items
36    int pos = rank * BLOCKSIZE;        // initial file position per ↩
          process
37    while (pos < filesize)
38      {
39        MPI_File_read (f, temp, 1, filetype, &status);
40        int cnt;
41        MPI_Get_count (&status, filetype, &cnt);
42
43        pos += BLOCKSIZE * N;
44        for (int i = 0; i < cnt * BLOCKSIZE; i++)
45          data.push_back (temp[i]);
46      }
47
48    MPI_File_close (&f);
49
50    sleep (rank);
51    cout << rank << " read " << data.size () << " numbers." << endl;
52    for (int i = 0; i < 30; i++)
53      cout << data[i] << " ";
54    cout << " .... Last one is : " << data[data.size () - 1];
55    cout << endl;
56
57    MPI_Finalize ();
```

The pos variable, which is defined on line 36 and updated on line 43, keeps track of the file pointer so that the loop of lines 37–46 can terminate when all the data have been read. The data are read temporarily in the temp array, before being appended at the end of the `data` vector. The `status` variable allows us to know the exact number of items read (line 41), which should be normally equal to one.

Running the program of Listing 5.28 on a file containing a sequence of 10,000 integers from 0 to 9999 would produce the following output:

```
$ mpirun —np 3 ./viewExample  data
0 read 3340 numbers.
0  1  2  3  4  5  6  7  8  9  30  31  32  33  34  35  36  37  38  39  60  61  62  63  64  65 ↩
     66  67  68  69  .... Last one is: 9999
1 read 3330 numbers.
10  11  12  13  14  15  16  17  18  19  40  41  42  43  44  45  46  47  48  49  70  71  72↩
     73  74  75  76  77  78  79  .... Last one is: 9979
2 read 3330 numbers.
20  21  22  23  24  25  26  27  28  29  50  51  52  53  54  55  56  57  58  59  80  81  82↩
     83  84  85  86  87  88  89  .... Last one is: 9989
```

5.19 Combining MPI processes with threads

MPI is primarily concerned with communication although it does provide the means for dynamic process creation. However, it is arguably preferable to spawn multiple threads on multicore systems than to spawn individual MPI processes with all the additional memory and management overhead. The only downside one might consider when using threads in MPI programs is that only one of the threads may have access to MPI for communications. This has nothing to do with function thread safety, but rather with the fact that MPI identifies/ranks processes, and thus it cannot address individual threads.

In this section we discuss the setup required for deploying multiple threads from each MPI process. The spawning mechanism is nothing special. A variety of libraries can be used, including the pthreads, Qt threads, or C++11 threads. The challenge is to properly compile and link the executable, a process which is somewhat complicated by the fact that `mpicc/mpiCC/mpic++/mpicxx` are actually compiler front-ends that hide much of the compilation inner workings from the developers.

Ultimately, `mpicc/mpiCC/mpic++/mpicxx` just call the C/C++ compiler with the appropriate switches for locating the header files during compilation and locating and linking in the MPI library. A simple way to integrate MPI and threads is to create a makefile or modify the project (.pro) file so that all compiler and linker invocations are handled via the `mpicc/mpiCC/mpic++/mpicxx` programs. In this way, a developer does not have to worry about MPI-specific include and library files locations and/or switches.[11]

A simple program that demonstrates the use of C++11 threads and MPI processes is given in Listing 5.29, where each process spawns as many threads as the

---

[11] This setup has been tested with OpenMPI 4.0.2, QMake 5.9.5, and GCC 9.2.1, on Ubuntu Linux 18.10. However, it should work with other configurations as well.

number of available cores. A process can query the number of available cores via the POSIX function `sysconf`, which returns a number of runtime system configuration information, based on the parameter passed to it. In our case the parameter is `_SC_NPROCESSORS_ONLN`.

Listing 5.29: An example of an MPI program spawning C++11 threads.

```cpp
 1  // File : mpiAndThreads.cpp
 2  . . .
 3    MPI_Init (&argc, &argv);
 4
 5    int rank, N;
 6    MPI_Comm_rank (MPI_COMM_WORLD, &rank);
 7    MPI_Comm_size (MPI_COMM_WORLD, &N);
 8
 9    int numThreads = sysconf (_SC_NPROCESSORS_ONLN);
10    unique_ptr<thread> thr[numThreads];
11    for (int i = 0; i < numThreads; i++)
12      {
13        thr[i] = make_unique<thread>([=](){
14            cout << "Thread " << i << " is running on process " << ↵
                 rank << "\n";
15                              }
16                            );
17      }
18
19    for (int i = 0; i < numThreads; i++)
20      thr[i]->join();
21
22    MPI_Finalize ();
```

This program can be compiled and subsequently executed using `mpirun` by providing a project file similar to the one shown below:

```
#File : mpiAndThreads.pro
SOURCES += mpiAndThreads.cpp
QMAKE_CXXFLAGS += -std=c++17
LIBS += -pthread
TARGET = mpiAndThreads
QMAKE_CXX = mpic++
QMAKE_CC = mpicc
QMAKE_LINK = mpic++
```

The three last lines are the key to successfully making `qmake` use the MPI compiler front-end for compilation and linking. These lines effectively force `qmake` to generate a `Makefile` that uses `mpic++` for compiling C++ programs (by setting `QMAKE_CXX`), `mpicc` for compiling C programs (by setting `QMAKE_CC`), and `mpic++` for linking object and library files into the target executable (by setting `QMAKE_LINK`).

Compiling and running the program is then as simple as (see Appendix A for more details on the use of `qmake`):

```
$ qmake mpiAndThreads.pro
$ make
$ mpirun —np 2 ./mpiAndThreads
```

If only the main thread of an MPI process will perform MPI calls, then the above discussion is the end of the story. However, MPI can be configured to allow multiple threads from an MPI process to perform MPI calls. Enabling threading support takes place during the compilation phase of an MPI library. OpenMPI has enabled threading support since version 3 by default, so if you are using a recent release there is nothing more to do.

The MPI standard defines four levels of threading support:

- `MPI_THREAD_SINGLE`: Only one thread per process is allowed.
- `MPI_THREAD_FUNNELED`: Multiple threads are allowed, but only one is supposed to make MPI calls (all MPI calls are "funneled" to the main thread).
- `MPI_THREAD_SERIALIZED`: Multiple threads making MPI calls are allowed, but only one of them can do so at any given time.
- `MPI_THREAD_MULTIPLE`: Multiple threads are allowed, all of them making concurrent MPI calls.

The thread-level support that an MPI implementation provides can be queried by the `MPI_Query_thread` function or by the `MPI_Init_thread` function that should be used instead of the typical `MPI_Init` to initialize MPI in a multi-threaded setup. The syntax of `MPI_Init_thread` is the following:

```
int MPI_Init_thread(int  *argc,    // Pointer to the number of
                                   // program arguments (IN)
               char ***argv,   // Pointer to the argument
                                   // pointer vector (IN)
                int  required,  // Required thread—level support.
                                   // One of the above listed cons—
                                   // tants should be specified.(IN)
                int  *provided)// Level of provided threading
                                   // support (OUT).
```

`MPI_Init_thread` should be called once by the main thread of an MPI process as a replacement to `MPI_Init`. The threads spawned by an MPI process still share a single identifier (the process rank) through which they can communicate with the other nodes.

An extensive example on the use of MPI and threads is provided in Section 5.25.2.

5.20 Timing and performance measurements

In terms of timing, MPI provides two functions: `MPI_Wtime` (wall time) and `MPI_Wticks`. The first reads the system clock while the second returns the clock's resolution in seconds per tick. Their syntax is the following:

```
double MPI_Wtime( void );
double MPI_Wtick( void );
```

MPI_Wtime returns the time since an unspecified time in the past. Therefore, a single returned value has no meaning, but by subtracting two readings of the function, we can measure a time span.

```
double timeStart, timeEnd;
timeStart = MPI_Wtime();
. . . // do something
timeEnd = MPI_Wtime();
cout << "Total time spent : " << timeEnd - timeStart << endl;
```

In retrospect, there is no practical reason to prefer these functions to any others provided natively by C/C++ or external libraries, as long as CPU-specific mechanisms are not employed (such as the RDTSC x86 command). Ultimately, it all comes down to the system clock and its resolution that these libraries are reading.

5.21 **Debugging, profiling, and tracing MPI programs**

Debugging MPI programs presents the same challenges as the debugging of multi-threaded applications. Using console output is still a developer's primary weapon for detecting bugs and fixing them. A useful trick that can be used to distinguish the output of the different processes on the console is to have them generated at staggered intervals by making them sleep for an amount of time proportional to their rank:

```
MPI_Comm_rank (MPI_COMM_WORLD, &rank);
do_some_work();
sleep(rank);      // puts the process to sleep for "rank" seconds
outputDebugInfo();
```

A convenient approach that can be used to check each and every error code returned by MPI functions is to define the following preprocessor macro:

```
#define MEC(call) {int res; \
                   res = call; \
                   if(res != MPI_SUCCESS) { \
                       fprintf(stderr, "Call "#call" return error ↩
                           code %i\n", res); \
                       MPI_Abort(MPI_COMM_WORLD, res);}   }
```

and use the MEC (**MPI Error Check**) macro to encapsulate all MPI function calls. The #call expression in the fprintf statement expands to a string containing the macro argument without trying to execute the command. For example:

```
MEC(MPI_Send(&data, k, dest, tag, MPI_COMM_WORLD));
```

MPI errors are by default fatal. The `MEC` macro can only be useful if the default behavior is changed to `MPI_ERRORS_RETURN` as explained in Section 5.10.

There are a number of profiling and tracing tools available for high-performance computing (HPC), which also encompass MPI. Profiling refers to getting how much time is consumed by different parts of the program, while tracing refers to getting when events take place during the execution. Profiling can help us determine where most time is spent, while tracing allows us to pinpoint where load imbalances occur or communication delays take place.

Profiling and tracing offer complimentary views on the performance of a software system, and although very similar techniques are used to perform them, their requirements are quite different. Tracing in general is a much more expensive technique in terms of time and system resource consumption.

The following is a list of some of the most prominent open source profiling and tracing tools today:

- Scalasca is a joint project of several German academic institutions, hosted by the Technical University of Darmstadt (https://www.scalasca.org/). Scalasca uses the Score-P system for instrumenting code. Score-P also allows manual code instrumentation, i.e., the programmer can flag the region or regions of interest, making the analysis reports more intuitive. Scalasca offers a GUI front-end for examining the analysis reports. Scalasca's main feature is that it automatically detects inefficiencies in communication patterns. Scalasca through Score-P also offers analyses of MPI, CUDA, OpenMP, OpenCL, and OpenACC programs.
- Tuning and Analysis Utilities (TAU), by the University of Oregon (http://tau.uoregon.edu/), is a highly portable profiling and tracing toolkit that runs on most HPC platforms. It is a mature set of tools (development started in 1997) that can analyze programs in C/C++, Fortran, Python, and Java. TAU uses the Program Database Toolkit (PDT) to instrument (i.e., annotate with timing code) programs that employ MPI, CUDA, OpenMP, and OpenCL, providing a comprehensive solution to code analysis. TAU can also perform instrumentation without recompiling the code by library preloading. This way though, only the calls to the selected libraries can be traced.

Both TAU and Scalasca are offered under a BSD-style license. In the following sections we provide a brief introduction to both toolkits, as they compliment each other nicely. TAU on the one hand can provide detailed execution tracing, while Scalasca focuses on communication pattern analysis, partially automating the detection of problem areas. Both are quite sophisticated tools that can be customized/configured to perform in different ways.

5.21.1 Brief introduction to Scalasca

Scalasca has a lengthy but straightforward installation process, as the software consists of several modules that have to be installed separately in sequence. In this section we are not considering the installation specifics.

Scalasca operates in three phases:

1. "Skin" phase: preparing the code for measurements. This is done by using the `scorep` command or `scalasca -instrument`.
2. "Scan" phase: running the application under the control of Scalasca and collecting the measurements, using the `scan` or `scalasca -analyze` commands.
3. "Square" phase: interactively exploring the measurements analysis report, using the `square` or `scalasca -examine` commands.

In the "skin" phase, the code is compiled under the control of Score-P, so that measurement code is inserted at places of interest (e.g., surrounding MPI calls). This means that a compilation command such as:

```
$ mpic++ -O2 foo.cpp -o foo
```

would need to change to any of the following:

```
$ scalasca -instrument mpic++ -O2 foo.cpp -o foo
# OR
$ scorep mpic++ -O2 foo.cpp -o foo
# OR
$ scorep-mpicxx -O2 foo.cpp -o foo
```

The change in the executable's size reflects the added instrumentation code.

In case a QMake project is used to build the program, the only change required is to the symbolic names identifying the compiler and linker:

```
QMAKE_CXX = scorep mpic++
QMAKE_CC = scorep mpicc
QMAKE_LINK = scorep mpic++
```

During phase 2, execution also needs to be performed under the control of Scalasca. For sequential or OpenMP programs this means:

```
$ scalasca -analyze ./foo foo_parms
# OR
$ scan ./foo foo_parms
```

For MPI programs, the `mpirun` launcher needs to be involved as well:

```
$ scan mpirun -np 4 ./foo foo_parms
```

The execution results in the creation of a so-called *experiments* archive folder (inside the working directory) for holding the measurement files. The folder name reflects to a degree the experiment setting (e.g., includes the name of the executable and the number of MPI nodes), and it cannot be overwritten by another experiment. Keeping the experiment results in separate repositories allows comparisons between runs.

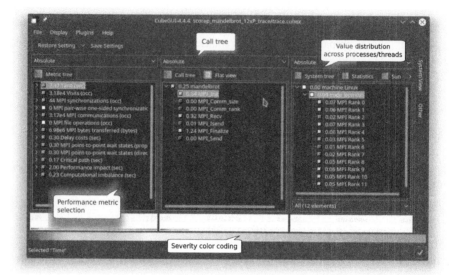

FIGURE 5.23

A screenshot of the CubeGUI results brower. The trace displayed corresponds to a run of the Mandelbrot fractal generating program explained in Section 5.25.1.

By default, Scalasca performs only profiling. If tracing is required, the -t switch must be used during the program launch, e.g.:

```
$ scan —t mpirun —np 4 ./foo foo_parms
```

Finally, the collected results can be analyzed and inspected by calling:

```
$ scalasca —examine scorep_foo_4xP_trace
#OR
$ square scorep_foo_4xP_trace
```

The only parameter required is the name of the experiments archive folder. This launches a GUI similar to the one shown in Fig. 5.23.

The results are displayed in three panes that are coupled/connected. Each pane shows a tree view of the results, with internal tree nodes showing the overall/cumulative value of their content (e.g., execution time) and the leaf nodes showing their exclusive values. The left pane shows a list of performance metrics, color-coded according to their severity. These include execution time, MPI calls, critical path analysis, etc. Once one of these metrics is selected, the middle pane displays a call tree, with each call again color-coded with its contribution to the corresponding metric. Upon selecting one of these calls, the program displays on the right pane how the call performed on each of the processes used in the run. The right pane can display alternative views of the data, such as statistical plots.

Score-P also provides the means for a programmer to define regions of code that need to be instrumented by using the following pairs of preprocessor macros:

- `SCOREP_USER_FUNC_BEGIN()` and `SCOREP_USER_FUNC_END()` for functions.
- `SCOREP_USER_REGION_BEGIN()` and `SCOREP_USER_REGION_END()` for arbitrary blocks of code.

These must be provided in matching pairs, but they can also be nested. In the first case, measurements are associated with the function name. In the second case, an identifier must be defined before the beginning of the region, so that it can be associated with the corresponding measurements, using the `SCOREP_USER_REGION_DE-FINE()` macro. This identifier becomes a region's "handle."

The `SCOREP_USER_REGION_BEGIN()` macro takes three parameters:

```
SCOREP_USER_REGION_BEGIN(handle, // as  defined  by
                                 // SCOREP_USER_REGION_DEFINE
                         name,   // a  unique  string  naming  the  region
                         type)   // symbolic  constant  declaring  the
                                 // region's type, or a bitwise OR
                                 // combination of them.  Options:
                                 // SCOREP_USER_REGION_TYPE_COMMON,
                                 // SCOREP_USER_REGION_TYPE_FUNCTION,
                                 // SCOREP_USER_REGION_TYPE_LOOP,
                                 // SCOREP_USER_REGION_TYPE_DYNAMIC,
                                 // SCOREP_USER_REGION_TYPE_PHASE
```

The `SCOREP_USER_REGION_END()` needs only the region's handle passed as a parameter to properly match the opening macro.

For example, to examine the matrix multiplication performance in Listing 5.20, we would have to do the following modifications:

Listing 5.30: Modifications to the matrix multiplication example of Listing 5.20 in order for Scalasca to instrument the `MMpartial` function loops.

```
1   // File : matrixMult_scalasca.cpp
2   #include <SCOREP_User.h>
3   . . .
4   void MMpartial (unique_ptr<double[]> &A, unique_ptr<double[]> &B, ←
        unique_ptr<double[]> &C, int rowsA, int colsA, int colsB, int ←
        trueBcols)
5   {
6     SCOREP_USER_REGION_DEFINE(test_r);  // test_r does not need to be ←
          defined
7
8     SCOREP_USER_REGION_BEGIN(test_r, "mm", ←
          SCOREP_USER_REGION_TYPE_LOOP); // labeled with "mm"
9     for (int i = 0; i < rowsA; i++)
10      for (int j = 0; j < colsB; j++)
11        {
12          double temp = 0;
13          for (int n = 0; n < colsA; n++)
14            temp += A[i * colsA + n] * B[n * trueBcols + j];
15
16          C[i * trueBcols + j] = temp;
```

```
17        }
18    SCOREP_USER_REGION_END(test_r);
19  }
20  . . .
```

In the above example, given that a whole function is enclosed in the macros, we could also use the SCOREP_USER_FUNC_BEGIN() and SCOREP_USER_FUNC_END() pair.

In order to enable the user-supplied instrumentation, scorep has to be called with a parameter of --user during the compilation phase. The next two phases are as before:

```
$ scorep —user mpic++ —std=c++17 matrixMult_scalasca.cpp —o ↩
    matrixMult_scalasca
$ scan —t mpirun —np 4 matrixMult_scalasca 2 2
$ square scorep_matrixMult_scalasca_4_trace
```

The "mm" label will be used in the square browser for examining the results.

5.21.2 Brief introduction to TAU

TAU operates in a very similar fashion to Scalasca (at least in one of its modes of operation), in that the code needs to be recompiled. This involves replacing the compiler command with a TAU front-end shell script, as the following example:

```
$ tau_cxx.sh —std=c++17 foo.cpp —o foo
```

A major difference from Scalasca is that the operation of TAU is controlled via environment variables. In order for the above command to succeed, we need to set up the TAU_MAKEFILE environment variable so that it points to the makefile that TAU will use for compilation:

```
# In BASH :
$ export TAU_MAKEFILE=${TAU_HOME}/x86_64lib/Makefile.tau—mpi
#
# In CSH:
$ setenv TAU_MAKEFILE=${TAU_HOME}/x86_64lib/Makefile.tau—mpi
```

The exact naming of the makefile depends on the configuration settings of TAU.

TAU can utilize PDT for parsing the code or use the compiler to automatically create instrumentation calls in the generated executable by setting:

```
$ export TAU_OPTIONS="—optCompInst"
```

Tracing needs to be explicitly enabled via:

```
$ export TAU_TRACE=1
```

Once the code is compiled, it can execute as normal, without the invocation of another command. Upon termination, TAU generates a number of files inside the working directory. These have to be consolidated (because there are multiple files per

MPI process) and possibly converted, before the measurements can be inspected by one of the visualization packages that TAU can utilize, like `jumpshot` or `vampir`.

As an example, compiling and tracing the reduction program of Listing 5.14 with:

```
$ tau_cxx.sh  manual_reduction.cpp -o manual_reduction
$ mpirun -np 8 ./manual_reduction
$ tau_treemerge.pl                        # measurement ↩
    consolidation.
                                          # Produces tau.trc & tau.↩
                                            edf
$ tau2slog2 tau.trc tau.edf -o app.slog2  # convertion to slog2 ↩
    format
$ jumpshot app.slog2
```

produces the output of Fig. 5.24, which allows us to inspect the timing of events and the interaction – depicted as arrows – between the processes. Each function is represented as a rectangle. Rectangles can be nested, representing call dependencies.

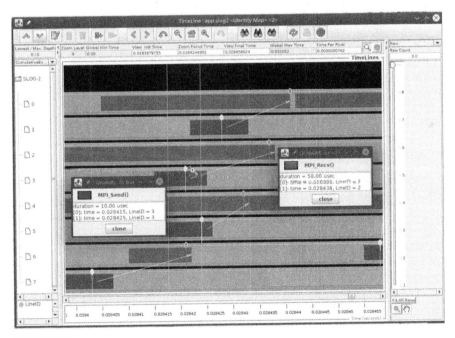

FIGURE 5.24

A screenshot of `jumpshot` displaying the (zoomed-in) trace of a reduction operation on eight processes. The arrows represent communication. Right-clicking on any "box" brings up the details of the corresponding function call.

5.22 The Boost.MPI library

The Boost.MPI wrapper library constitutes a major departure towards simplicity and elegance from the C/Fortran idiosyncrasies of MPI. The only problem is that at the moment of this writing, Boost.MPI does not support/provide abstractions for the full spectrum of communication primitives made available by MPI. Additionally, at present (as of Boost V1.71) only the MPI 1.1 standard is supported. This means that the C bindings are still the best vehicle to extract the maximum of performance from your parallel platform, but it is also arguably true that Boost.MPI is the best way of extracting the maximum performance from your programming effort!

Boost.MPI is a small part of the Boost library that is primarily made of class templates, but also some binary library files. Apart from abstracting and encapsulating MPI functionality, it offers a rich variety of classes for serialization, regular expression evaluation, image processing, etc. Compared with MPI, the available documentation covering Boost.MPI is relatively scant. Fortunately, the source code of the library itself is handsomely commented.

The typical structure of a Boost.MPI program is shown below:

Listing 5.31: Skeleton of a Boost.MPI program.

```
#include <boost/mpi.hpp>
. . .
int main (int argc, char **argv)
{
  // No MPI calls prior to this point
  boost::mpi::environment env (argc, argv);
  boost::mpi::communicator world;

  // MPI statements
  . . .
  return 0;
}
```

The MPI library is initialized with the construction of the `boost::mpi::environment` object. In contrast to the C bindings case, the MPI environment is terminated implicitly, with the destruction of the `boost::mpi::environment` object. Also, there is no symbolic constant representing the global communicator, but the default constructor of the `boost::mpi::communicator` class returns an object that can be in turn queried for rank information.

The Boost.MPI program that would correspond to the one shown in Listing 5.3 is:

Listing 5.32: "Hello World" in Boost.MPI.

```
1  // File : mpihello.cpp
2  #include <boost/mpi.hpp>
3  #include <iostream>
4
5  using namespace std;
```

```
6
7   int main (int argc, char **argv)
8   {
9     boost::mpi::environment env (argc, argv);
10    boost::mpi::communicator world;
11    cout << "Hello from process " << world.rank() << " of " << world.↵
          size() << endl;
12    return 0;
13  }
```

The `mpi.hpp` header file includes all the Boost.MPI header files. Individual header files can also be used if the compilation time is critical.

The program in Listing 5.32 can be compiled with OpenMPI:

```
$ mpic++ mpihello.cpp -o mpihello -lboost_mpi
```

The two differences from the C case are the need to specify the shared object files (.so) containing the Boost library[12] and the use of the C++ compiler (invoked by the `mpic++` command).

Obviously, the appropriate compilation command depends on the MPI implementation used and the configuration of the Boost library. For example, if `libboost_mpi` was not compiled as a shared library and MPICH was used, we would need (assuming Boost was installed under `/usr/local/`):

```
$ mpic++ mpihello.cpp -o mpihello /usr/local/lib/libboost_mpi.a
```

The procedure for execution is identical to the ones detailed in Sections 5.4 and 5.5.2.

In Fig. 5.25, we compare side-by-side the program of Fig. 5.2 with its Boost/MPI equivalent. What is immediately obvious is that the use of Boost.MPI reduces clutter substantially.

The capabilities offered by Boost.MPI include:

- point-to-point communication abstractions,
- collective operations,
- communicator management,
- serializing structures for communication.

A table detailing the mapping from MPI C bindings to Boost.MPI is given in Appendix D.

5.22.1 Blocking and non-blocking communications

Boost.MPI makes good use of the OO capabilities of C++ to simplify MPI communication calls. For example, in the place of the single `MPI_Send` function, Boost.MPI

---

[12] `-lboost_mpi` refers to the `libboost_mpi.so` file, located in one of the system-declared library directories.

MPI C Bindings	Boost.MPI
① `#include<mpi.h>`	`#include<boost/mpi.hpp>`
`#include<string.h>`	`#include<iostream>`
`#include<stdio.h>`	`#include<string>`
`#define MESSTAG 0`	`using namespace std;`
`#define MAXLEN 100`	`using namespace boost;`
	`#define MESSTAG 0`
`int main (int argc, char **argv) {`	`int main (int argc, char **argv) {`
② `  MPI_Init (&argc, &argv);`	`  mpi::environment env (argc, argv);`
③ `  int rank, num, i;`	`  mpi::communicator world;`
`  MPI_Comm_rank (MPI_COMM_WORLD, &rank);`	`  int rank = world.rank ();`
`  MPI_Comm_size (MPI_COMM_WORLD, &num);`	
④ `  if (rank == 0) {`	`  if (rank == 0) {`
`    char mess[] = "Hello World";`	`    string mess ("Hello World");`
`    int len = strlen(mess)+1;`	
`    for (i = 1; i < num; i++)`	`    for (int i = 1; i < world.size (); i++)`
⑤ `      MPI_Send (mess, len, MPI_CHAR,`	`      world.send (i, MESSTAG, mess);`
`          I,MESSTAG, MPI_COMM_WORLD);`	
`  } else {`	`  } else {`
`    char mess[MAXLEN];`	`    string mess;`
`    MPI_Status status;`	
⑥ `    MPI_Recv (mess, MAXLEN, MPI_CHAR, 0,`	`    world.recv (0, MESSTAG, mess);`
`        MESSTAG, MPI_COMM_WORLD, &status);`	
`    printf ("%i received %s\n", rank,`	`    cout << rank << " received " << mess`
`        mess);`	`                              << endl;`
`  }`	`  }`
⑦ `  MPI_Finalize ();`	`  return 0;`
`  return 0;`	`}`
`}`	
⑧ `mpicc hello.c -o hello`	`mpic++ hello.cpp -lboost_mpi \`
	`       -lboost_serialization -o hello`

Key:

①	MPI-related header files
②	MPI initialization. Any command-line parameters destined for the MPI runtime are passed on.
③	Rank query. The default constructor in Boost.MPI returns the *MPI_COMM_WORLD* equivalent.
④	Code branching based on process identity/rank
⑤	Basic send operation. In Boost, the data type is implicitly passed, via polymorphism.
⑥	Basic MPI receiving operation. The *MPI_Status* structure holds critical information about the message.
⑦	MPI termination. In Boost, the destruction of the *boost::mpi::environment* object does the same.
⑧	Compilation command

FIGURE 5.25

Comparison of a "Hello World" MPI program using the C bindings and the Boost.MPI wrapper classes. The side-by-side comparison clearly highlights the differences between the two platforms.

offers a set of overloaded template methods of the `mpi::communicator` class, allowing the programmer to skip the declaration of the type of data being communicated.

Point-to-point communications are handled as methods of an `mpi::communicator` class instance. The `send`, `recv`, `isend`, and `irecv` methods provide a consistent interface, as far as the order and semantics of their first parameters are concerned. The first one is always the rank of the destination/source process and the second the message tag. The remaining parameters describe the data to be sent or the buffer to receive the message.

A sample of the available `send` methods is shown below:

```
void send(int dest, int tag) const;   // Sends an empty message

template <typename T>                  // Sends a single data item
  void send(int dest, int tag, const T& value) const;

template <typename T>                  // Sends an array of n elements
  void send(int dest, int tag, const T* values, int n) const;
```

The matching `recv` methods follow similar guidelines. The only difference is that they return a `status` object:

```
status recv(int source, int tag) const; // Receives an empty message

template <typename T>                    // Receives a single item
  status recv(int source, int tag, T& value) const;

template <typename T>
  status recv(int source, int tag,       // Receive an array of
                                          // values
              T* values, int n) const;   // The size of buffer
                                          // *values is n
```

A receiving node can get any incoming message by using the constants `mpi::any_source` and `mpi::any_tag` in place of the `MPI_ANY_SOURCE` and `MPI_ANY_TAG` ones used in C.

The `status` class offers a number of methods:

```
int source(); // Returns the message source
int tag();    // Returns the message tag
int error();  // Returns the error code, or 0
template <typename T> // Returns the number of items T transfered
  optional<int>       // if they can be determined, hence the
    count() const;    // optional<int> return object
```

Immediate versions of the `send` and `recv` methods are provided, with almost identical signatures: the only difference is that they return a `request` object that can be queried about the progress of the communication. The `request` class provides `wait` and `test` methods, which are equivalent to `MPI_Wait` and `MPI_Test`. Method `wait` returns a `status` object upon completion. Method `test` returns an `optional<status>` object, which means that the status is returned only if the operation is complete. For example:

```
string message;
. . .
mpi::request r = world.irecv(0, MESSTAG, message);
mpi::status s = r.wait();                        // block until ↩
    communication is done
cout << s.count<int>() << " items received\n";   // Type of items ↩
    must be supplied
```

Boost.MPI also provides a set of `wait*` and `test*` template functions, for performing blocking and non-blocking reporting of communication progress, respectively, of collections of `request` objects. These methods can operate on ranges of `request` arrays or vectors, as specified by two delimiting references/iterators. They allow checking of all or any of the supplied request objects for completion. Their syntax is shown below:

```
// Waits until all communication are complete
template<typename ForwardIterator>
    void wait_all(ForwardIterator first, ForwardIterator last)

// Waits until any communication is complete. Returns a pair ↩
    containing the status object corresponding to the completed ↩
    operation and an iterator pointing to the completed request.
template<typename ForwardIterator>
    std::pair<status, ForwardIterator>
      wait_any(ForwardIterator first, ForwardIterator last)

// Tests if any of the supplied requests are complete. Returns an ↩
    optional pair type identical to the one described for wait_any()
template<typename ForwardIterator>
    optional< std::pair<status, ForwardIterator> >
        test_any(ForwardIterator first, ForwardIterator last)
```

Listing 5.33 contains a variation of the "Hello World" program explained above, with the master using non-blocking communication and the `test_any` function to check the completion of the operations. The `optional` class template that is used as a type for the return value of `test_any` allows the return of an object that evaluates to a `std::pair<status, ForwardIterator>` object or a NULL reference if nothing is returned.

In the example of Listing 5.33, if any of the communications described by the `r` vector is completed (check of line 30), then the position of that request object in the `r` vector (calculated on line 32) is used to get which node was the target of the operation and print an assorted message (line 33). The vectors are trimmed on lines 34 and 35 so that the completed operation's request object is not returned again.

The receiver processes use `irecv` and the simple `wait` method of the `mpi::request` class to block until the operation is complete (lines 42 and 43). The `status` object returned by the `wait` method is used on line 44 to print out the number of data items of type `string` received.

Listing 5.33: A Boost.MPI-based "Hello World" program that uses non-blocking communications.

```cpp
// File : boostnonblock.cpp
#include <boost/mpi.hpp>
#include <boost/optional.hpp>
. . .
using namespace boost;
#define MESSTAG 0
int main (int argc, char **argv)
{
  mpi::environment env (argc, argv);
  mpi::communicator world;

  int rank = world.rank ();
  int N = world.size ();

  if (rank == 0)
    {
      string mess ("Hello World");
      vector < mpi::request > r; // a vector for the request objects
      vector < int >dest;        // a vector for the destination IDs
      for (int i = 1; i < N; i++)    // initiate the sending and ←
            store the request objects
        {
            r.push_back (world.isend (i, MESSTAG, mess));
            dest.push_back (i);
        }

        // loop until all communications are done
        while (r.size() >0)
          {
            optional < pair < mpi::status, vector < mpi::request >::←
                iterator > > res = mpi::test_any < vector < mpi::←
                request >::iterator > (r.begin (), r.end ());
            if (res)  // if return value is initialized
              {
                int idx = (res->second) - r.begin ();
                cout << "Message delivered to " << dest[idx] << endl;
                r.erase (res->second);   // remove completed ←
                    operations from the vector
                dest.erase (dest.begin () + idx);
              }
          }
    }
  else   // receiver code
    {
      string mess;
      mpi::request r = world.irecv (0, MESSTAG, mess);
      mpi::status s = r.wait ();          // block until communication←
            is done
      cout << rank << " received " << mess << " - " << s.count < ←
            string >() << " item(s) received\n";
```

```
45        }
46
47      return 0;
48  }
```

5.22.2 Data serialization

Boost.MPI brings something new to MPI communications when we consider the exchange of non-primitive datatypes. While MPI's approach is lengthy and cumbersome, Boost.MPI uses C++ features to hide most of the details involved from the user.

As with the plain-vanilla MPI, Boost effectively offers two methods for communicating objects and/or data structures: one based on *serialization*, which is equivalent to using MPI_Pack/MPI_Unpack, and one based on the separation of structure (*skeleton*) and content, which is equivalent to the definition of derived MPI datatypes.

Serialization is appropriate for data that are communicated infrequently, or their structure is dynamic in nature. To turn a class into a serializable one, one has to define a serialize method that sends an object's data members one-by-one to a stream (Archive in Boost's jargon). For example:

```cpp
class MyData
{
  private:
    int num;
    string s;
  public:
    template<class Archive>
      void serialize(Archive & ar, const unsigned int version);
};

template<class Archive>
  void MyData::serialize(Archive & ar, const unsigned int version)
{
    ar & num;
    ar & s;
}
```

The reverse process of deserialization calls the same method, as the & operator behaves differently based on the type of Archive object used: similar to operator >> for input streams and operator << for output streams.

The (de)serialization of an object is called automatically by Boost.MPI's point-to-point and collective operations. So, in order for an instance of the above class to be communicated between two processes, one would just need to write:

```cpp
. . .
MyData item;
int r = world.rank();
if(r==0)
  {
```

```
      // initialization code for item
      ...
      world.send(1, 0, item);  // send to process 1, with tag 0
    }
else
      world.recv(0, 0, item);  // receive from process 0
```

The separation of structure and content is suitable for data structures that keep a fixed memory layout (e.g., a fixed size array) throughout the program's execution. It is essentially the same restriction that permits the creation of MPI's derived datatypes. However, Boost.MPI greatly simplifies this approach, requiring just the use of two functions:

- `mpi::skeleton()`: for capturing and communicating the structure, memory layout, or skeleton of an object.
- `mpi::get_content()`: for communicating the actual data that populate the skeleton.

The user must still supply a `serialize` function along the lines described previously. Serializing an instance of a class allows Boost.MPI to extract all the necessary information about the location and size of its data members, which is mirroring the procedure followed for the definition of a derived datatype (see Section 5.15.1).

The example in Listing 5.34 serves as a guideline for the use of these two functions, and it is in no way complete or optimized. It shows the outline of a master–worker configuration, where the master distributes work items to the worker processes in a round-robin fashion. Section 5.25 offers a more complete coverage of this scenario.

Listing 5.34: A Boost.MPI-based outline of a master–worker setup that uses skeleton communications to speed up data exchange.

```
1  // File : boostSkeleton.cpp
2  . . .
3  struct WorkItem
4  {
5  public:
6    int param1;
7    double param2;
8    string param3;
9
10   template < class Arch > void serialize (Arch & r, int version)
11   {
12     r & param1;
13     r & param2;
14     r & param3;
15   }
16 };
17
18 //=============================================================
19 int main (int argc, char **argv)
```

```
20  {
21    mpi::environment env (argc, argv);
22    mpi::communicator world;
23
24    WorkItem item;
25    item.param3 = "work";
26    int rank = world.rank ();
27    int N = world.size ();
28    int numWork = atoi (argv[1]);
29
30    if (rank == 0)
31      {
32        for (int i = 1; i < N; i++)
33          world.send (i, TAGSKELETON, mpi::skeleton (item));
34
35        int destID = 1;
36        for (int i = 0; i < numWork; i++)
37          {
38            item.param1 = i;
39            world.send (destID, TAGWORKITEM, mpi::get_content (item));
40            destID = (destID == N - 1) ? 1 : destID + 1;
41          }
42
43        // signal end of execution
44        item.param3 = "done";
45        for (int i = 1; i < N; i++)
46          world.send (i, 1, mpi::get_content (item));
47      }
48    else
49      {
50        world.recv (0, TAGSKELETON, mpi::skeleton (item));
51        world.recv (0, TAGWORKITEM, mpi::get_content (item));  // read↩
                first work item
52        while (item.param3 != "done")
53          {
54            // process work item
55            cout << "Worker " << rank << " got " << item.param1 << ↩
                endl;
56
57            // read next one
58            world.recv (0, TAGWORKITEM, mpi::get_content (item));
59          }
60      }
61
62    return 0;
63  }
```

Lines 3–17 in Listing 5.34 define a structure with a variety of fields to represent a work item. The `serialize` template function (lines 10–15) saves/reads these fields in sequence to/from a supplied data stream. The layout of an instance of the class `WorkItem` is communicated from the master process (lines 32 and 33) to all the worker processes (line 50).

Once the layout is known, it is repeatedly used to accelerate the communication of the work items the master process generates (line 38) and sends (line 39). The number of work items is determined by the command-line parameter supplied by the user (line 28). The termination of the worker processes is triggered by having the master process send work items with `param3` set to "done" (lines 44–46).

A sample output of the above program would look like this:

```
$ mpirun —np 3 ./boostSkeleton 4
Worker 2 got 1
Worker 1 got 0
Worker 1 got 2
Worker 2 got 3
```

5.22.3 Collective operations

Broadcasting, reduction, scattering, and gathering are all implemented in Boost.MPI in the form of template functions. Overloading allows the handling of different scenarios, e.g., gathering of scalars and arrays, with the same function names.

Table 5.7 lists a sample of them, just to get the reader familiar with the syntax. The naming gives away their correspondence to MPI functions. The semantics of each function are discussed thoroughly in Section 5.11, which introduces the collective operations. In any case, the Boost.MPI collective functions are just wrappers of the corresponding MPI ones.

All the functions shown in Table 5.7 have overloaded versions where `in_values` parameter's type is switched from a pointer to an array (T*) to a `vector<>` reference. The use of `vector<>` for out-parameters (i.e., for the receiving end) is preferred, as a vector will be automatically resized if its capacity is insufficient.

The `Op` parameter for the `reduce` functions can be any binary function. A collection of commonly used ones is defined within the `boost/mpi/operations.hpp` header file. These include:

- `maximum`,
- `minimum`,
- `bitwise_and`, `bitwise_or`, `bitwise_xor`, and
- `logical_and`, `logical_or`, `logical_xor`.

A user-supplied function can also be used in a reduction operation. Functions used with `reduce` must be associative, i.e., $f(x, f(y, z)) = f(f(x, y), z)$; otherwise the results will be inconsistent, e.g., they will depend on the ordering of the partial reductions.

An example on how a custom reduction operation can be implemented is provided in Listing 5.35. The starting point of the procedure is the subclassing of the `std::binary_function` class template. The `std::binary_function` class serves as a base class for *function objects*, i.e., for objects that provide an `operator()` method.

Table 5.7 A selection of collective operations supported by Boost.MPI.

Broadcast	```template<typename T> void broadcast(const communicator& comm, T& value, int root); template<typename T> void broadcast(const communicator& comm, T* values, int n, int root);```
Gather	```template<typename T> void gather(const communicator& comm, const T& in_value, std::vector<T>& out_values, int root); template<typename T> void gather(const communicator& comm, const T* in_values, int n, std::vector<T>& out_values, int root);```
Scatter	```template<typename T> void scatter(const communicator& comm, const std::vector<T>& in_values, T& out_value, int root); template<typename T> void scatter(const communicator& comm, const std::vector<T>& in_values, T* out_values, int n, int root);```
All-Gather	```template<typename T> void all_gather(const communicator& comm, const T& in_value, std::vector<T>& out_values); template<typename T> void all_gather(const communicator& comm, const T* in_values, int n, std::vector<T>& out_values);```
All-to-all	```template<typename T> void all_to_all(const communicator& comm, const std::vector<T>& in_values, std::vector<T>& out_values); template<typename T> void all_to_all(const communicator& comm, const std::vector<T>& in_values, int n, std::vector<T>& out_values);```
Reduce	```template<typename T, typename Op> void reduce(const communicator& comm, const T& in_value, T& out_value, Op op, int root); template<typename T, typename Op> void reduce(const communicator& comm, const T* in_values, int n, T* out_values, Op op, int root);```
All-Reduce	```template<typename T, typename Op> void all_reduce(const communicator& comm, const T& in_value, T& out_value, Op op); template<typename T, typename Op> void all_reduce(const communicator& comm, const T* in_values, int n, T* out_values, Op op);```

Parameters index:

comm : communicator to apply the operation on
in_value : a single T item to be sent
in_values : an array or vector of items to be sent
n : number of items to be collected from each process
op : binary function to be applied during the reduction operation
out_value : buffer for a single T item
out_values : array or vector buffer for collected items of type T
root : source/destination process of broadcast/gather operation

The specialization of the class template `std::binary_function` requires the specification of three types: the types of the first and second arguments and the type of the `operator()` method's result.

For example:

```
struct LabelEnumClass : public binary_function<string, int, string> ↩
    {
    string operator() (string a, int b) {return (a==b);}
}
. . .
LabelEnumClass o;    // creating a function object
string base;
int ID;
. . .
string label = o(base, ID); // calling operator()
```

In the case of a reduction operator, all the types passed to the `binary_function` template should be identical. In Listing 5.35, the `CenterOfMass::operator()` method is used to calculate the center of mass of two objects, each described by a vector (x, y, z) and a mass. If each process in the application computes the center of mass of a subset of objects, then the reduction operation can yield the center of mass of the whole set. The mass M and center of mass $\vec{R}$ of a set of objects described by the tuples $(m_i, \vec{r}_i)$, where m_i and $\vec{r}_i$ are the mass and location of object i, are calculated as follows:

$$M = \sum_{\forall i} m_i \qquad (5.5)$$

and

$$\vec{R} = \frac{\sum_{\forall i} m_i \vec{r}_i}{M}. \qquad (5.6)$$

It can be easily shown that these functions and the operator based on them are both commutative and associative.

As the `CenterOfMass::operator()` will use exclusively `CenterOfMass` instances, the `binary_function` class is specialized using the `CenterOfMass` type (line 3). The above equations are implemented by the code of lines 27–40, while the `serialize` method of lines 18–25 allows Boost.MPI to communicate `CenterOfMass` instances.

The `main` function serves only to initialize one `CenterOfMass` instance per process with dummy data (line 56) and perform the reduction (line 59). The fourth parameter of the `reduce` function is an unnamed or anonymous `CenterOfMass` instance. A process will use this instance to execute the `operator()` method and perform a phase of the reduction.

Listing 5.35: A reduction example in Boost.MPI, using a user-supplied reduction operation. The reduction operation produces the center of gravity of two masses.

```cpp
// File : boostReduction.cpp
. . .
class CenterOfMass:public std::binary_function < CenterOfMass, ↩
    CenterOfMass, CenterOfMass >
{
public:
  double x, y, z, mass;

  CenterOfMass (double a, double b, double c, double m):x (a), y (b)↩
    , z (c), mass (m) {}

  CenterOfMass () {}

  template < class Archive > void serialize (Archive & ar, const ↩
    unsigned int version);

  const CenterOfMass & operator () (const CenterOfMass & o1, const ↩
    CenterOfMass & o2) const;
};


//------------------------------------------------------------
template < class Archive > void CenterOfMass::serialize (Archive & ↩
    ar, const unsigned int version)
{
  ar & x;
  ar & y;
  ar & z;
  ar & mass;
}


//------------------------------------------------------------
const CenterOfMass & CenterOfMass:: operator () (const CenterOfMass &↩
    o1, const CenterOfMass & o2)
    const
    {
      CenterOfMass *res = new CenterOfMass ();
      res->x = o1.x * o1.mass + o2.x * o2.mass;
      res->y = o1.y * o1.mass + o2.y * o2.mass;
      res->z = o1.z * o1.mass + o2.z * o2.mass;
      double M = o1.mass + o2.mass;
      res->x /= M;
      res->y /= M;
      res->z /= M;
      res->mass = M;
      return *res;
    }


//============================================================
ostream & operator << (ostream & out, const CenterOfMass & obj)
{
```

```
45   out << obj.mass << " at (" << obj.x << ", " << obj.y << ", " << ↵
         obj.z << ") " << endl;;
46   }
47
48   //=============================================================
49   int main (int argc, char **argv)
50   {
51     mpi::environment env (argc, argv);
52     mpi::communicator world;
53
54     int rank = world.rank ();
55
56     CenterOfMass m1(1.0 * rank, 1.0 * rank, 1.0 * rank, 1.0 * rank + ↵
           1);
57     CenterOfMass m2;
58
59     reduce (world, m1, m2, CenterOfMass (), 0);
60     if (world.rank () == 0)
61       cout << m2 << endl;
62     return 0;
63   }
```

5.23 A case study: diffusion-limited aggregation

Diffusion-limited aggregation (DLA) is a crystal formation process, whereby particles performing Brownian motion (i.e., random motion in all directions) are "glued" together to form aggregates. The formations that result from this process are also known as Brownian trees.

DLA can be simulated in two dimensions by having a 2D grid of cells populated by moving particles and crystal parts. In the simulation code described below, we assume that each cell can be occupied by one or more free moving particles for simplicity. A particle becomes part of the crystal (and stops moving) when it moves into a cell that is in proximity of the already formed crystal. A visualization of the formed crystal over multiple iterations is shown in Fig. 5.26.

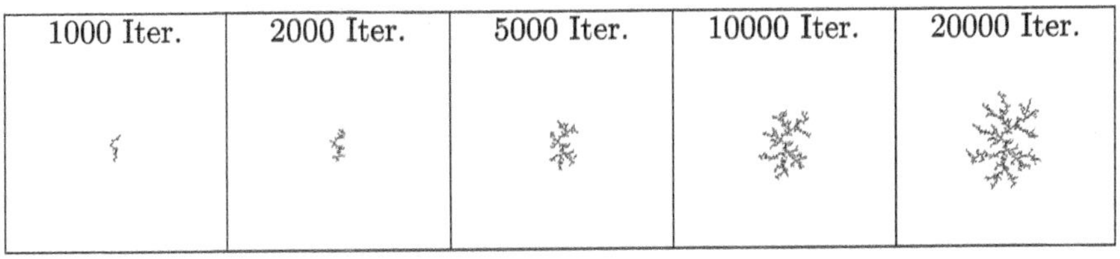

1000 Iter.	2000 Iter.	5000 Iter.	10000 Iter.	20000 Iter.

FIGURE 5.26

The output of a DLA simulation for a grid of 200 × 200 cells with an initial population of 1000 particles, for different numbers of iterations.

The simulation's basic parameters are the size of the 2D grid, the initial number of particles, the number of iterations, and the initial crystal "seed," i.e., the fixed part to which particles will start attaching as the simulation progresses. In the code provided below, the seed is a cell fixed in the center of the 2D grid, while the remaining parameters can be provided as command-line parameters. The following structure definition is used for holding the positions of moving particles:

```
typedef struct PartStr
{
  int x;
  int y;
} PartStr;
```

If the particles are maintained in an array of type PartStr, then a single simulation step can be done with the following function:

```
1  // File : dla_core.c
2  /* Parameters:
3  *       pic: (in) pointer to a 2D array of type int
4  *       rows: (in) number of rows in array pic
5  *       cols: (in) number of columns in array pic
6  *       p: (in/out) array holding particles
7  *       particles: (in/out) pointer to particle counter
8  *       changes: (out) pointer to array holding pending changes
9  *                     to pic array
10 *       numChanges: (out) pointer to the counter of pending changes
11 */
12 void dla_evolve_plist (int *pic, int rows, int cols, PartStr *p, int↩
       *particles, PartStr *changes, int *numChanges)
13 {
14   int i;
15   *numChanges =0;
16
17   for (i = 0; i < *particles; i++)
18     {
19       int new_x = p[i].x + three_way ();
20       if (new_x == 0)   // bounce off boundaries
21         new_x = 1;
22       else if (new_x == cols - 1)
23         new_x = cols - 2;
24
25       int new_y = p[i].y + three_way ();
26       if (new_y == 0)   // bounce off boundaries
27         new_y = 1;
28       else if (new_y == rows - 1)
29         new_y = rows - 2;
30
31       if (pic[new_y * cols + new_x] == 0)    // steps into empty ↩
           space
32         {
33           int turnCrystal = check_proxim (pic, cols, new_x, new_y);
34           if(turnCrystal <0)
```

```
35              {
36                  // record crystal change
37                  changes[*numChanges].x = new_x;
38                  changes[*numChanges].y = new_y;
39                  (*numChanges) ++;
40                  // erase particle from list
41                  p[i] = p[(*particles) - 1];
42                  i--;   // re-examine position i
43                  (*particles)--;
44              }
45          else   // change particle position
46              {
47                  p[i].x=new_x;
48                  p[i].y=new_y;
49              }
50          }
51      }
52  }
```

The function goes over all the available particles, updating their position (lines 18–28) and then checking their proximity to an aggregate formation as represented by the (rows x cols) 2D array pic. The position update is based on the three_way() function which returns −1, 0, and 1 with equal probability:

```
inline int three_way ()
{
  return (random() % 3)-1;
}
```

The check_proxim() function returns −1 if the new position of a particle lies next to the crystal. By surrounding the grid by empty single boundary rows and rows (keeping them empty is the task of lines 19–22 and 25–28 in the above code), check_proxim() can be simplified to:

```
// Checks the 3x3 cell neighborhood in 2D array pic,
// around coordinate (x,y)
int check_proxim (int *pic, int cols, int x, int y)
{
  int *row0, *row1, *row2;
  row0 = pic+(y - 1) * cols + x - 1;
  row1 = row0 + cols;
  row2 = row1 + cols;
  if (*row0 < 0 || *(row0+1) < 0 || *(row0+2) < 0 ||
      *row1 < 0 || *(row1+1) < 0 || *(row1+2) < 0 ||
      *row2 < 0 || *(row2+1) < 0 || *(row2+2) < 0    )
    return (-1);
  else
    return (1);
}
```

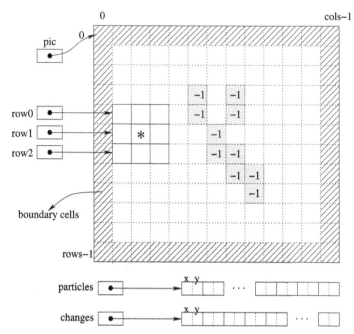

FIGURE 5.27

A visualization of the structures and variables used in functions dla_evolve_plist() and check_proxim(). An asterisk (*) represents a particle that is screened for proximity to the formed crystal (represented by the gray cells). Its proximity range is represented by the nine solid rectangles.

where *row0, *row1, and *row2 represent the leftmost cells of the three rows making up the neighborhood of a particle. Fig. 5.27 serves to visualize the aforementioned details.

The output of the dla_evolve_plist() function is stored in a preallocated array of type PartStr, which is passed via pointer changes (lines 36–42). The actual array part used is stored in the *numChanges counter, while as a side effect the array holding the particles and their number (*particles) are also updated.

A *sequential* program (provided as dla_sequential.c) can perform the simulation by running the following loop:

```
while (−−iter)
{
  dla_evolve_plist (pic, rows, cols, p, &particles,
                    changes, &numChanges);
  apply_changes (pic, rows, cols, changes, numChanges);
}
```

where the apply_changes() function updates the state of the aggregate formation with the latest cells to become part of it:

```
void apply_changes(int *pic, int rows, int cols,
                   PartStr *changes, int numChanges)
{
  int i;
  for(i=0;i<numChanges;i++)
     pic[changes[i].y * cols + changes[i].x] = -1;
}
```

Parallelizing the sequential program comes down to figuring out how to partition the problem's data. These can be partitioned space-wise or particle-wise. In the former approach, each MPI process is responsible for a disjoint part of the 2D grid and whatever lies within it. The decomposition can be made in a regular and homogeneous way (i.e., all processes take an equal share of the rows[13] of the grid) if the participating nodes are homogeneous, but it is complicated by the need to exert special care on the particles "living" on boundary rows, e.g., right on the edge of the grid's division lines.

The alternative of splitting the particles produces a smaller challenge. In the case of a homogeneous platform, the particles can be evenly split among the available processes:

```
53  // File : dla_mpi.c
54  . . .
55     int rank, num;
56     MPI_Init (&argc, &argv);
57     MPI_Comm_rank (MPI_COMM_WORLD, &rank);
58     MPI_Comm_size (MPI_COMM_WORLD, &num);
59     ...
60     int particlesPerNode = particles / num;
61     if (rank == num - 1)        // assign remaining particles in
62                                 // case they cannot be split evenly
63        particlesPerNode = particles - particlesPerNode * (num - 1);
```

Still, the processes have to maintain a copy of the state of the aggregate formation, implicitly mandating a barrier at the end of each iteration. During this synchronization phase, each process must communicate to all the others any changes it did to the aggregate. Using point-to-point communications in an N-process communicator would require each process to execute $2(N - 1)$ individual send and receive operations for a grand total of $2N^2 - N$ operations per iteration!

A faster solution is to use collective communications. Because the changes need to propagate to all processes, a natural choice is the MPI_Allgather function, which can be completed in $\lceil \log_2(N) \rceil$ steps. The only complication is that the number of changes is not the same in all processes, which prompts the use of the MPI_Allgatherv alternative. MPI_Allgatherv allows each process to contribute a different size part to the collection being assembled and communicated.

---

[13] At first glance a column-wise partitioning seems equally plausible. Is it really? Does the way C/C++ allocates 2D arrays have any influence in this regard?

The last piece of the puzzle for making the communication of an array of `PartStr` structures possible is the declaration of an MPI data type. This is accomplished with:

```
64   PartStr *p = (PartStr *) malloc (sizeof (PartStr) *
65                                    particlesPerNode);
66   int lengths[2] = { 1, 1 };
67   MPI_Datatype types[2] = { MPI_INT, MPI_INT };
68   MPI_Aint add1, add2;
69   MPI_Aint displ[2];
70   MPI_Datatype Point;
71
72   MPI_Get_address (p, &add1);
73   MPI_Get_address (&(p[0].y), &add2);
74   displ[0] = 0;
75   displ[1] = add2 - add1;
76
77   MPI_Type_create_struct (2, lengths, displ, types, &Point);
78   MPI_Type_commit (&Point);
```

The – universally – declared `Point` datatype can then be used inside our main loop:

```
79   while (--iter)
80   {
81      dla_evolve_plist (pic, rows, cols, p, &particlesPerNode,
82                        changes, &numChanges);
83
84      //exchange information with other nodes
85      MPI_Allgather (&numChanges, 1, MPI_INT, changesPerNode, 1,
86                     MPI_INT, MPI_COMM_WORLD);
87
88      //calculate offsets
89      numTotalChanges = 0;
90      for (i = 0; i < num; i++)
91      {
92         buffDispl[i] = numTotalChanges;
93         numTotalChanges += changesPerNode[i];
94      }
95
96      if(numTotalChanges >0)
97      {
98         MPI_Allgatherv (changes, numChanges, Point,
99                         totalChanges, changesPerNode, buffDispl,
100                        Point, MPI_COMM_WORLD);
101        apply_changes (pic, rows, cols, totalChanges, numTotalChanges↩
                         );
102     }
103  }
```

Because the size of the data each process will contribute needs to be known ahead of time, a separate collective operation is required (line 85 above), where the number of changes per process is collected. Subsequently, the location where each set of changes will be deposited in array `totalChanges` can be calculated using the loop of lines 89–94 and stored in the integer array `buffDispl`. A beneficial side effect of this additional communication step is that no changes need to be collected if the `numTotalChanges` counter is found to be zero (line 96).

5.24 A case study: brute-force encryption cracking

Encryption – and how to crack it – has always been a fascinating subject among computer science scholars. Our study of the subject is admittedly rather superficial, and it is only performed as an example of how one can synchronize and load-balance MPI processes.

The Data Encryption Standard (DES) is a widely used encryption method that entails the use of a 56-bit secret key for encrypting and decrypting data. While the length of the key allows for $2^{56} = 7.2 \cdot 10^{16}$ possible keys, DES is not considered safe enough for contemporary applications. In 1998, the Electronic Frontier Foundation (EFF) showed a custom-built machine called "Deep Crack," capable of going through all the DES keys in a matter of days. The idea was to show that the DES key length was not secure enough. Since then considerably cheaper and faster tools have been developed for the task. It is no wonder that the Advanced Encryption Standard (AES) has been gradually replacing DES since its ratification as a standard in 2001.

In this section we will see how a brute-force cracking of a DES-encrypted message can be performed using MPI.

DES is implemented in Unix/Linux by the `ecb_crypt()` function. The encryption/decryption process of a message requires the calculation of the key's parity, as in the function shown below:

```
1   // File : decrypt.cpp
2   #include <rpc/des_crypt.h>
3   ...
4   void decrypt(long key, char *ciph, int len)
5   {
6      // prepare key for the parity calculation. Least significant bit ↵
             in all bytes should be empty
7      long k = 0;
8      for(int i=0;i<8;i++)
9      {
10        key <<= 1;
11        k += (key & (0xFE << i*8));
12     }
13
14     des_setparity((char *)&k);
15
16     // Decrypt ciphertext
17     ecb_crypt((char *)&k,(char *) ciph, len, DES_DECRYPT);
18  }
```

The parameters of the `decrypt()` function are more or less self-explanatory. The `ciph` pointer points to the byte buffer containing the ciphertext of total length `len`. The

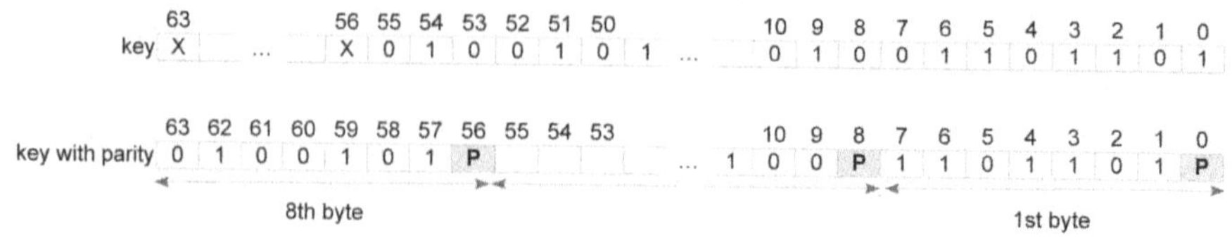

	63			56	55	54	53	52	51	50			10	9	8	7	6	5	4	3	2	1	0
key	X	...		X	0	1	0	0	1	0	1	...	0	1	0	0	1	1	0	1	1	0	1

	63	62	61	60	59	58	57	56	55	54	53			10	9	8	7	6	5	4	3	2	1	0
key with parity	0	1	0	0	1	0	1	P				...		1	0	0	P	1	1	0	1	1	0	1	P

8th byte   1st byte

FIGURE 5.28

An example showing how the key must be preprocessed prior to DES encryption/decryption. "X" represents unused bits and "P" represents the parity bits calculated by the `des_setparity()` function.

length of the buffer should be a multiple of 8 bytes, although no check is performed to that effect.

Lines 7–12 prepare the key by shifting its contents to the left, so that the low-order bit in every byte is left empty. These bits are filled up with the parity when the `des_setparity()` function is called on line 14. Fig. 5.28 shows the outcome of these lines.

The decryption is performed on line 17. Encryption can be performed just by replacing the `DES_DECRYPT` constant with `DES_ENCRYPT`. The produced output overwrites the original input.

In order to decide whether the plaintext produced by trying out a key is the correct one, we will assume that part of the message is known, i.e., we will filter out keys that do not produce a plaintext that contains a given substring. In effect we can utilize the `decrypt()` function shown above to build a function that will return true when a key is a candidate for producing the correct plaintext:

```
19   char search[]=" the ";
20   //──────────────────────────────────────────────
21   // Returns true if the plaintext produced containes the "search" ↩
          string
22   bool tryKey(long key, char *ciph, int len)
23   {
24     char temp[len+1];
25     memcpy(temp, ciph, len);
26     temp[len]=0;
27     decrypt(key, temp, len);
28     return strstr((char *)temp, search)!=NULL;
29   }
30   ...
```

On line 25 the ciphertext is copied to a temporary buffer so that it can be decrypted (line 27). The produced string is null-terminated (line 26) so that it can be checked against the known substring (stored in the global array `search`) using the `strstr()` C-library string function. This function returns a pointer to the first occurrence of the substring or NULL if none is found.

In the worst-case scenario, one would have to try all the 2^{56} possible keys before finding the correct one. The problem is how can we partition the key search space in a way that minimizes the overall execution time. There are two general possibilities, although many variations of each can be implemented:

- **Static** partitioning: The division of the workload is done a priori. We can have both equal and unequal partitioning based on the capabilities of the nodes that make up the execution platform.
- **Dynamic** partitioning: The division and assignment of the workload is done at runtime, permitting load-balancing to be performed, albeit at the cost of a more complicated solution.

Dynamic partitioning is examined in far greater detail in Section 5.25. In this section we will deal only with static partitioning.

The only lingering question that needs to be answered is what should happen once a candidate solution has been found. One could either continue until all the keys are exhausted or terminate the program. The early termination is a more challenging problem to tackle, and for this reason it is the approach chosen in the solutions discussed below.

An easy solution to the partitioning problem would be to have each MPI process calculate which part of the key search-space it will be responsible for:

Listing 5.36: A static key search-space partitioning solution for DES cracking.

```
31   // File : decrypt.cpp
32   ...
33   unsigned char cipher[] = {251, 37, 207, . . . , 170, 0};
34
35   char search[] = " live ";
36   //------------------------------------------------
37   int main(int argc, char **argv)
38   {
39     int N, id;
40     long upper=(1L << 56); // upper bound for keys
41     long mylower, myupper;
42     MPI_Status st;
43     MPI_Request req;
44     int flag;
45     int ciphLen = strlen(cipher);
46
47     MPI_Init(&argc, &argv);
48
49     MPI_Comm_rank(MPI_COMM_WORLD, &id);
50     MPI_Comm_size(MPI_COMM_WORLD, &N);
51     int range_per_node = upper / N;
52
53     mylower = range_per_node * id;
54     myupper = range_per_node * (id + 1) - 1;
55     if(id == N-1)
56       myupper = upper;
```

```
57
58      long found = 0;
59      MPI_Irecv(&found, 1, MPI_LONG, MPI_ANY_SOURCE, MPI_ANY_TAG, ↩
            MPI_COMM_WORLD, &req);
60      for(int i=mylower; i<myupper && found==0;i++)
61      {
62        if(tryKey(i, (char *)cipher, ciphLen))
63        {
64          found=i;
65          for(int node=0; node<N; node++)
66            MPI_Send(&found, 1, MPI_LONG, node, 0, MPI_COMM_WORLD);
67          break;
68        }
69      }
70
71      if(id==0)
72      {
73        MPI_Wait(&req, &st);
74        decrypt(found, (char *)cipher,ciphLen);
75        printf("%li %s\n", found, cipher);
76      }
77
78      MPI_Finalize();
79  }
```

The range of keys that each MPI process should test is calculated on lines 52–55. The if statement of lines 54–55 eliminates the possibility of missing keys at the end of the $[0, 2^{56})$ range due to round-off errors.

Each process sets up an immediate receive operation on line 58 that targets the found flag. The found flag can be set either by discovering a key on line 61 or by receiving the "news" of the discovery by the process that accomplished this feat, via the loop of lines 64 and 65. The solution is printed out by process 0 on lines 70–75. The MPI_Wait() call on line 72 ensures that the communication of the found key is complete, before any attempt to use the corresponding variable is made.

The main problem with the solution of Listing 5.24 is that the speedup that can be achieved depends on the actual key used for the encryption. The following list of scenarios depicts the chaotic, seemingly unpredictable behavior that is to be expected:

- **Scenario 1**: For $key = 2^{20}$, a two-node MPI program will have an expected speedup of 1. The same would be true for any key in the range $[0, 2^{55} - 1]$. If the program executed on N *homogeneous* nodes, this would hold for any key in the range $[0, \frac{2^{56}}{N})$.
- **Scenario 2**: For $key = 2^{55}$, a two-node MPI program will have an expected speedup $= \frac{2^{55}+1}{1} = 2^{55} + 1$! The second MPI process terminates after just one attempt, while the sequential program would have to perform a total of $2^{55} + 1$

attempts before reaching the same solution. Generalizing for N nodes (assuming N divides 2^{56} evenly), for $key = \frac{N-1}{N}2^{56}$ the expected speedup would be $\frac{\frac{N-1}{N}2^{56}+1}{1} = \frac{N-1}{N}2^{56} + 1$. This is clearly a **super-linear speedup**.

- **Scenario 3**: A two-node MPI program will have an expected speedup of 2, only for $key = 2^{56} - 1$. The same key is the only one that would yield a 100% efficiency for N homogeneous nodes (assuming N divides 2^{56} evenly).

An easy fix to this problem that also allows for a shorter and simpler program to be implemented is to have each MPI process "stagger" through the range of keys as shown in Listing 5.37.

Listing 5.37: An alternative static key search-space partitioning solution for DES cracking.

```
80  // File : decrypt2.cpp
81  ...
82  //────────────────────────────────────────────
83  int main (int argc, char **argv)
84  {
85    int N, id;
86    long upper=(1L << 56);
87    long found = 0;
88    MPI_Status st;
89    MPI_Request req;
90    int flag;
91    int ciphLen = strlen((char *)cipher);
92
93    MPI_Init (&argc, &argv);
94    MPI_Comm_rank (MPI_COMM_WORLD, &id);
95    MPI_Comm_size (MPI_COMM_WORLD, &N);
96    MPI_Irecv ((void *)&found, 1, MPI_LONG, MPI_ANY_SOURCE, ↵
               MPI_ANY_TAG, MPI_COMM_WORLD, &req);
97    int iterCount=0;
98    for (long i = id; i < upper; i += N)
99      {
100       if (tryKey (i, (char *) cipher, ciphLen))
101         {
102           found = i;
103           for (int node = 0; node < N; node++)
104             MPI_Send ((void *)&found, 1, MPI_LONG, node, 0, ↵
                       MPI_COMM_WORLD);
105           break;
106         }
107       if(++iterCount % 1000 == 0) // check the status of the pending↵
                receive
108         {
109           MPI_Test(&req, &flag, &st);
110           if(flag) break;
111         }
112     }
113
```

```
114   if (id == 0)
115     {
116       MPI_Wait (&req, &st); // in case process 0 finishes before the↩
                key is found
117       decrypt (found, (char *) cipher, ciphLen);
118       printf ("%li %s\n", found, cipher);
119     }
120   MPI_Finalize ();
121 }
```

The major differences with Listing 5.24 are two: the for-loop of line 97 and the regular check for the completion of the immediate receive operation on lines 106–110. The loop structure is very simple in its inception: every process starts from a key equal to its rank and goes through the key range with a step equal to the total number of processes. This ensures that the whole range is covered in a wave-like fashion that makes the runtime behavior better match our performance expectations.

The regular test of lines 106–110 ensures that the communication completion will be acknowledged, even if a stale value of found is kept in the CPU's cache memory. The frequency of the test is a completely ad hoc choice, driven by the desire to not burden the overall execution with too frequent tests, while at the same time permitting a timely termination of the program. Please note that line 97 no longer contains a check on the value of found, as the mere completion of the communication is adequate for the loop's termination.

Testing of the program of Listing 5.37 with a message encrypted with the key 107481429 produced the results in Table 5.8. It is clear that the intended purpose of predictability as far as performance improvement is concerned is accomplished.

Table 5.8 Average encryption cracking time for the program of Listing 5.37 on a Ryzen 9 3900x, 12 core CPU. The message was encrypted with the key 107481429. Reported numbers are averaged over 10 runs.

Processes	Exec. time (sec)	Speedup	Efficiency
1	101.30	-	-
2	51.24	1.98	0.989
4	25.58	3.96	0.990
8	12.82	7.90	0.987
12	8.77	11.54	0.962

The typical problem with our static partitioning solutions is that they fail to properly exploit heterogeneous execution platforms. Dynamic partitioning is the obvious answer to this problem, although as shown in Chapter 11, a more elaborate static partitioning technique would also fit the bill.

5.25 A case study: MPI implementation of the master–worker pattern

The master–worker pattern (see also Section 2.4.3) is a popular choice for laying out the structure of an MPI program. In general, there are two choices for the partitioning of the workload:

- **Static partitioning**: The master node calculates a priori the workload that will be assigned to each of the worker processes and possibly to itself. In order for the distribution to be balanced, relatively accurate cost models of the computation and communication involved must be employed to predict the total execution time of all the nodes. This also entails detailed knowledge about the performance characteristics of the execution platform. A balanced distribution is not necessarily one that assigns the same workload in terms of execution time to all the nodes, as communication overheads can be substantial. The ultimate purpose is to minimize the overall execution time of the program and as such a balanced distribution is typically skewed, varying the workload according to the characteristics of the execution platform and the communication overheads.

  A static partitioning has the potential to minimize the communication costs, as master–worker communication is limited to the beginning and end of the computation.

- **Dynamic partitioning**: The master node distributes workload in discrete pieces to the workers in a round-robin, a first-come, first-served, or some other application-specific order, until the work is complete. This approach is simpler than the static partitioning approach as there is no need for the derivation of cost models and an a priori partitioning of the load. This is a heuristic that can provide implicit workload balancing, with however some performance penalty due to increased communication traffic between the master and worker nodes.

While the Achilles heel for static partitioning is the need to derive accurate cost models, for dynamic partitioning it is the choice of the **work item size**, i.e., how much workload will be assigned as a unit to a process. A too small work item can produce extraordinary amounts of communication traffic, while a too big work item can leave nodes idle or underutilized. Getting it right is the major challenge in the deployment of dynamic partitioning.

The workloads can be described in a variety of ways, from the most *specific*, e.g., providing parameters for the execution of a known function, to the most *generic*, e.g., providing instances of classes with any kind of computation portfolio. In the following sections we explore sample implementations of the master–worker pattern that use dynamic partitioning.

5.25.1 A simple master–worker setup

In this section we show how a simple dynamic partitioning, master–worker setup that utilizes round-robin distribution can be implemented in MPI. The target application

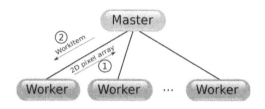

FIGURE 5.29

An overview of the software architecture and communication protocol used in Listing 5.38. Circled numbers indicate message order. The seemingly reverse order is essential for a proper handshake between the master and the workers.

is the calculation of the Mandelbrot fractal set, which is a problem that is examined in Section 3.12.

The work item for workload distribution is a rectangular portion of the desired fractal image. The sides of the work item are provided by the user in the command-line that launches the program, allowing us to test the performance of the program as a parameter of the work item size.

The master and worker processes operate using a simple protocol:

1. The worker sends to the master the result of a computation. In the beginning, a special null result is used to commence the transaction by using an appropriate message tag.
2. The master responds by sending a work item to the worker. If there are no more available, a special null work item is sent by using an appropriate message tag.

An overview of the system architecture and the communication traffic involved is shown in Fig. 5.29.

A large portion of the code is carried over from Listing 3.42, with the necessary adaptations. Many of them stem from the fact that in a distributed memory setup there cannot be a shared QImage object, nor can object references be exchanged between the nodes. In order to preserve the cross-platform compatibility offered by MPI, the essential information that defines a work item are encapsulated in a structure (struct WorkItem) and communicated using a derived datatype. If the execution platform was homogeneous, object serialization could be employed for communicating work items. However, it is quite doubtful that any performance gains could be had from such an approach, which essentially equates to using MPI_Pack/MPI_Unpack. Additionally, the code itself would not also gain anything in terms of length or complexity.

The code is shown over several parts in Listing 5.38. The program uses MPI and a couple of Qt classes for image manipulation. For this reason, the compilation process is accomplished with the techniques discussed in Section 5.19. The first part of the program is devoted to the definition of a set of symbolic constants to be used as communication tags (lines 10–13). Lines 17–21 define the structure that encapsulates the data that define a work item. A work item is defined by:

- the boundaries of the complex plane where calculation is to take place as defined by the upper left (upperX, upperY) and lower right (lowerX, lowerY) corners,
- the size of the image part to be calculated (pixelsX x pixelsY),
- the location of the image part in the "bigger" picture (imageX, imageY).

Lines 25–87, which are mostly unchanged from Listing 3.42, contain a class for calculating the pixel values that correspond to a work item. The only changes relate to the need to initialize the class from a work item structure, hence the change from a constructor to a method-based initialization. The init method, starting at line 58, also performs some basic memory management by allocating the memory required for holding the image-part data (lines 65–68).

Listing 5.38: A master–worker implementation of a Mandelbrot fractal set calculator.

```cpp
1   //  File :  mandlebrot/mandlebrot.cpp
2   . . .
3   #include "mpi.h"
4   #include <QImage>
5   #include <QRgb>
6   using namespace std;
7
8   // ***************************************************************
9   // Communication tags
10  #define NULLRESULTTAG 0
11  #define RESULTTAG       1
12  #define WORKITEMTAG     2
13  #define ENDTAG          3
14
15  // ***************************************************************
16  struct WorkItem
17  {
18    double upperX, upperY, lowerX, lowerY;
19    int pixelsX, pixelsY, imageX, imageY;
20  };
21
22  // ***************************************************************
23  // Class for computing a fractal set part
24  class MandelCompute
25  {
26  private:
27    double upperX, upperY, lowerX, lowerY;
28    int pixelsX, pixelsY;
29
30    static int MAXITER;
31    int diverge (double cx, double cy);
32
33  public:
34    unique_ptr<int[]> img=nullptr;
35
36    void init (WorkItem * wi);
37    void compute ();
38  };
```

```
39   int MandelCompute::MAXITER = 255;
40
41   //————————————————————————————————
42   int MandelCompute::diverge (double cx, double cy)
43   {
44     int iter = 0;
45     double vx = cx, vy = cy, tx, ty;
46     while (iter < MAXITER && (vx * vx + vy * vy) < 4)
47       {
48         tx = vx * vx - vy * vy + cx;
49         ty = 2 * vx * vy + cy;
50         vx = tx;
51         vy = ty;
52         iter++;
53       }
54     return iter;
55   }
56
57   //————————————————————————————————
58   void MandelCompute::init (WorkItem * wi)
59   {
60     upperX = wi->upperX;
61     upperY = wi->upperY;
62     lowerX = wi->lowerX;
63     lowerY = wi->lowerY;
64
65     if (img == nullptr || pixelsX != wi->pixelsX || pixelsY != wi->↵
         pixelsY)
66       {
67         img = make_unique<int[]>((wi->pixelsX) * (wi->pixelsY));
68       }
69     pixelsX = wi->pixelsX;
70     pixelsY = wi->pixelsY;
71   }
72
73   //————————————————————————————————
74   void MandelCompute::compute ()
75   {
76     double stepx = (lowerX - upperX) / pixelsX;
77     double stepy = (upperY - lowerY) / pixelsY;
78
79     for (int i = 0; i < pixelsX; i++)
80       for (int j = 0; j < pixelsY; j++)
81         {
82           double tempx, tempy;
83           tempx = upperX + i * stepx;
84           tempy = upperY - j * stepy;
85           img[j * pixelsX + i] = diverge (tempx, tempy);
86         }
87   }
```

In order to be able to communicate a WorkItem structure, a derived datatype is created and committed on lines 88–109. It should be noted that only part of the structure needs to be communicated, as a worker is not concerned with putting the image together. As imageX and imageY do not need to be communicated, the size of the int block on line 97 is limited to 2 instead of 4.

This "stitching" of the individual images resulting from the processing of the work items is reserved for the master node. This task is done by the savePixels function on lines 113–121.

```
88   void registerWorkItem (MPI_Datatype * workItemType)
89   {
90     struct WorkItem sample;
91
92     int blklen[2];
93     MPI_Aint displ[2], off, base;
94     MPI_Datatype types[2];
95
96     blklen[0] = 4; // treating the 4 individual doubles as an array of↩
                 4
97     blklen[1] = 2; // the part's location in the final image is not ↩
                 communicated
98
99     types[0] = MPI_DOUBLE;
100    types[1] = MPI_INT;
101
102    displ[0] = 0;
103    MPI_Get_address (&(sample.upperX), &base);
104    MPI_Get_address (&(sample.pixelsX), &off);
105    displ[1] = off — base;
106
107    MPI_Type_create_struct (2, blklen, displ, types, workItemType);
108    MPI_Type_commit (workItemType);
109  }
110
111  // ****************************************************************
112  // Uses the divergence iterations to pseudocolor the fractal set
113  void savePixels (QImage * img, int *imgPart, int imageX, int imageY,↩
          int height, int width)
114  {
115    for (int i = 0; i < width; i++)
116      for (int j = 0; j < height; j++)
117        {
118          int color = imgPart[j * width + i];
119          img->setPixel (imageX + i, imageY + j, qRgb (256 — color, ↩
                256 — color, 256 — color));
120        }
121  }
122
123  // ****************************************************************
124  int main (int argc, char *argv[])
125  {
126    int N, rank;
```

```
127    double start_time, end_time;
128    MPI_Status status;
129    MPI_Request request;
130
131    start_time = MPI_Wtime ();
132
133    MPI_Init (&argc, &argv);
134    MPI_Comm_size (MPI_COMM_WORLD, &N);
135    MPI_Comm_rank (MPI_COMM_WORLD, &rank);
136
137    MPI_Datatype workItemType;
138    registerWorkItem (&workItemType);
```

The master node is responsible for retrieving the user-supplied parameters from the command-line and customizing the resulting image size so that it is made up of an integer number of work items (lines 154–164). The structures representing work items are allocated and initialized before any communications take place on lines 171–186. The benefit of doing this is twofold:

- MPI_Issend can be used to communicate work items without worrying about the overhead of buffer copies or the overwriting of message memory before it is sent out.
- An association can be established and maintained between assigned work items and worker processes. This allows the master node to place incoming results in the appropriate place of the target image, without requiring that placement information (i.e., imageX and imageY) is communicated back-and-forth between the master and the worker.

```
139    if (rank == 0)    // master code
140      {
141        if (argc < 6)
142          {
143            cerr << argv[0] << " upperCornerX upperCornerY ↩
                    lowerCornerX lowerCornerY workItemPixelsPerSide\n";
144            MPI_Abort (MPI_COMM_WORLD, 1);
145          }
146
147        double upperCornerX, upperCornerY;
148        double lowerCornerX, lowerCornerY;
149        double partXSpan, partYSpan;
150        int workItemPixelsPerSide;
151        int Xparts, Yparts;
152        int imgX = 4096, imgY = 2160;
153
154        upperCornerX = atof (argv[1]);
155        upperCornerY = atof (argv[2]);
156        lowerCornerX = atof (argv[3]);
157        lowerCornerY = atof (argv[4]);
158        workItemPixelsPerSide = atoi (argv[5]);
159
```

```
160        // make sure that the image size is evenly divided in work ↩
               items
161        Xparts = (int) ceil (imgX * 1.0 / workItemPixelsPerSide);
162        Yparts = (int) ceil (imgY * 1.0 / workItemPixelsPerSide);
163        imgX = Xparts * workItemPixelsPerSide;
164        imgY = Yparts * workItemPixelsPerSide;
165
166        partXSpan = (lowerCornerX − upperCornerX) / Xparts;
167        partYSpan = (upperCornerY − lowerCornerY) / Yparts;
168        QImage *img = new QImage (imgX, imgY, QImage::Format_RGB32);
169
170        // prepare the work items in individual structures
171        unique_ptr<WorkItem[]> w = make_unique<WorkItem[]>(Xparts * ↩
               Yparts);
172        for (int i = 0; i < Xparts; i++)
173          for (int j = 0; j < Yparts; j++)
174            {
175              int idx = j * Xparts + i;
176
177              w[idx].upperX = upperCornerX + i * partXSpan;
178              w[idx].upperY = upperCornerY − j * partYSpan;
179              w[idx].lowerX = upperCornerX + (i + 1) * partXSpan;
180              w[idx].lowerY = upperCornerY − (j + 1) * partYSpan;
181
182              w[idx].imageX = i * workItemPixelsPerSide;
183              w[idx].imageY = j * workItemPixelsPerSide;
184              w[idx].pixelsX = workItemPixelsPerSide;
185              w[idx].pixelsY = workItemPixelsPerSide;
186            }
```

The assignedPart array has one element per process, and it is used for holding the index of the work item that has been assigned to a process. Once the master receives a result message from a worker, it saves the pixel values in the QImage object used for this purpose (lines 199–202) and sends the next available work item to that worker. The worker's ID is retrieved from the MPI_Status structure set by the MPI_Recv function (line 193).

The placement of the returned image portion (*imgPart) is controlled by the imageX and imageY fields of the work item assigned to that worker (work item index on line 195).

Once all the work items have been distributed, the master waits for the last results and sends back to each worker a message with a tag that flags the termination of the program (lines 206–220).

```
187        // now distribute the work item to the worker nodes
188        unique_ptr<int[]> assignedPart = make_unique<int[]>(N);    // ↩
               keep track of what its worker is assigned
189        unique_ptr<int[]> imgPart = make_unique<int[]>( ↩
               workItemPixelsPerSide * workItemPixelsPerSide);
190        for (int i = 0; i < Xparts * Yparts; i++)
191          {
```

```
192        MPI_Recv (imgPart.get (), workItemPixelsPerSide * ↩
               workItemPixelsPerSide, MPI_INT, MPI_ANY_SOURCE, ↩
               MPI_ANY_TAG, MPI_COMM_WORLD, &status);
193        int workerID = status.MPI_SOURCE;
194        int tag = status.MPI_TAG;
195        int widx = assignedPart[workerID];
196        assignedPart[workerID] = i;
197        MPI_Issend (&(w[i]), 1, workItemType, workerID, ↩
               WORKITEMTAG, MPI_COMM_WORLD, &request);
198
199        if (tag == RESULTTAG)
200          {
201            savePixels (img, imgPart.get (), w[widx].imageX, w[widx↩
                 ].imageY, workItemPixelsPerSide, ↩
                 workItemPixelsPerSide);
202          }
203      }
204
205    // now send termination messages
206    for (int i = 1; i < N; i++)
207      {
208        MPI_Recv (imgPart.get (), workItemPixelsPerSide * ↩
               workItemPixelsPerSide, MPI_INT, MPI_ANY_SOURCE, ↩
               MPI_ANY_TAG, MPI_COMM_WORLD, &status);
209
210        int workerID = status.MPI_SOURCE;
211        int tag = status.MPI_TAG;
212
213        if (tag == RESULTTAG)
214          {
215            int widx = assignedPart[workerID];
216            savePixels (img, imgPart.get (), w[widx].imageX, w[widx↩
                 ].imageY, workItemPixelsPerSide, ↩
                 workItemPixelsPerSide);
217          }
218        assignedPart[workerID] = -1;
219        MPI_Isend (NULL, 0, workItemType, workerID, ENDTAG, ↩
               MPI_COMM_WORLD, &request);
220      }
221
222    img->save ("mandel.png", "PNG", 0); // save the resulting ↩
             image
223
224    delete img;
225    end_time = MPI_Wtime ();
226    cout << "Total time : " << end_time - start_time << endl;
227  }
```

The worker nodes first establish communication with the master on line 231. This can be considered as an implicit availability message: "We are here waiting for your commands!" This is preferable to having the master just assign work items in order of rank, for the simple reason that during program initialization not all MPI processes start at the same time instance, as they are affected by network traffic and system loads. By having the "faster starting" workers receive work earlier, performance can be boosted.

```
228   else       // worker code
229     {
230       MandelCompute c;
231       MPI_Send (NULL, 0, MPI_INT, 0, NULLRESULTTAG, MPI_COMM_WORLD); ↩
                    // establish communication with master
232       while (1)
233         {
234           WorkItem w;
235           MPI_Recv (&w, 1, workItemType, 0, MPI_ANY_TAG, ↩
                    MPI_COMM_WORLD, &status); // get a new work item
236           int tag = status.MPI_TAG;
237           if (tag == ENDTAG)
238             break;
239           c.init (&w);
240           c.compute ();
241           MPI_Send (c.img.get (), w.pixelsX * w.pixelsY, MPI_INT, 0, ↩
                    RESULTTAG, MPI_COMM_WORLD); // return the results
242         }
243     }
244
245   MPI_Finalize ();
246   return 0;
247 }
```

5.25.2 **A multi-threaded master–worker setup**

In this section we improve on the master–worker code of Listing 5.38 in two major ways:

- Each worker spawns a number of threads with the aim to more effectively utilize multicore execution platforms.
- A separate thread (the main one) in each worker is responsible for the communication with the master node, making sure that communication and computation overlap as much as possible.

In order for the code presented in this section to work properly, your MPI implementation must be compiled with threading support enabled (see Section 5.19).

The overall architecture of the code that follows is shown in Fig. 5.30. Two individual FIFO queues are used inside each worker *process*:

- *inque[14]: for holding work items arriving from the master node.

---

[14] inque and outque are actually pointers to QueueMonitor<> objects. The "*" notation is used to maintain consistency.

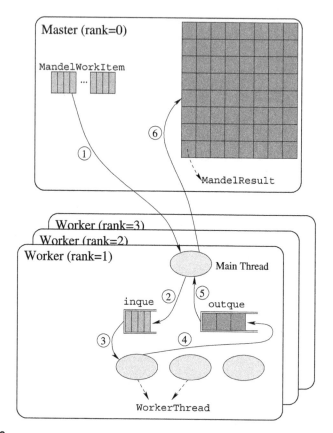

FIGURE 5.30

An overview of the software architecture used in Listing 5.40. Circled numbers indicate event order.

- *outque: for holding results that are produced from the threads and are waiting to be forwarded to the master.

The sequence of events that leads to the transformation of a work item into a partial result, as shown in Fig. 5.30, is the following:

- ①: The master node distributes work items (represented by instances of class MandelWorkItem) to the worker processes.
- ②: The main thread in each worker process deposits the received work items in queue *inque.
- ③: When a worker thread is done with a work item, it collects the next available one from *inque.
- ④: When a work item is complete, the result (represented by an instance of class MandelResult) is deposited in queue *outque.

- ⑤: The main thread reads any available results from outque and sends them to the master process.
- ⑥: The master process consolidates the partial results as they arrive.

Due to the size of the code, we proceed to discuss the individual building blocks separately. The two queues are central to the proper coordination of the threads in a worker process, so we begin by discussing this component. Both queues are instances of the class template QueueMonitor shown in Listing 5.39. As they are shared by the worker threads, QueueMonitor is a monitor-based class (see Section 3.9 for a discussion on monitors), with methods protected by a mutex. QueueMonitor offers a FIFO interface with a twist: both enqueue and dequeue operations are two-step affairs.

This design was prompted by the need to eliminate memory allocation overhead. Work item and result structures are preallocated and managed by the queues, which maintain two lists: one for the structures currently being populated (queue, defined on line 8) and one for the structures being free (freeList, defined on line 7). A pre-allocated array of structures is passed as a parameter to the constructor of the class (lines 22–26) and its elements are used to populate the freeList.

Listing 5.39: A monitor-based class template that implements a FIFO interface, with two-stage enqueue and dequeue operations. A header file is used for this class, as C++ templates do not generate code unless they are instantiated.

```
1   // File : mandlebrot_mt/sharedQue.h
2   . . .
3   template <typename T>
4   class QueueMonitor
5   {
6   private :
7       list<T> freeList;
8       list<T> queue;
9
10      mutex l;
11      condition_variable full, empty;
12
13  public :
14      QueueMonitor(int , T prealloc);
15      T reserve(); // reserve an item for management. reserve and ↩
            enque are supposed to be used in tandem
16      void enque(T);
17      T deque();        // deque and release are supposed to be used in ↩
            tandem
18      void release(T); // returns an item to the free list
19      int availItems();
20  };
21  //————————————————————————————————
22  template <typename T> QueueMonitor<T>::QueueMonitor(int s, T prealloc↩
        )
23  {
24      for(int i=0;i<s;i++)
```

```
25        freeList.push_back(prealloc+i);
26    }
```

When a thread wishes to deposit an item in a `QueueMonitor` instance, it should (a) reserve one of the items managed by the object by calling the `reserve` method, (b) populate the item with the needed data, and (c) deposit the item by calling the `enque` method.

```
27    //----------------------------------------------------------------
28    // reserves an item so that its fields can be populated before it is ⤶
              enqueued
29    template<typename T> T QueueMonitor<T>::reserve()
30    {
31        unique_lock< mutex > ul(1);
32        while(freeList.empty())
33            full.wait(ul);
34        T tmp = freeList.front();
35        freeList.pop_front();
36        return tmp;
37    }
38    //----------------------------------------------------------------
39    // this is non-blocking because the item has been reserved before
40    template<typename T> void QueueMonitor<T>::enque(T item)
41    {
42        lock_guard<mutex> lg(1);
43        queue.push_back(item);
44        empty.notify_one();
45    }
```

When a thread wishes to withdraw an item from a `QueueMonitor` instance, it should (a) reserve one of the available items managed by the object by calling the `deque` method, (b) extract the information required from the item, and (c) release the acquired item back to the object by calling the `release` method.

```
46    //----------------------------------------------------------------
47    template<typename T> T QueueMonitor<T>::deque()
48    {
49        unique_lock< mutex > ul(1);
50        while(queue.empty())
51            empty.wait(ul);
52        T tmp = queue.front();
53        queue.pop_front();
54        return tmp;
55    }
56    //----------------------------------------------------------------
57    template<typename T> void QueueMonitor<T>::release(T item)
58    {
59        lock_guard<mutex> lg(1);
60        freeList.push_back(item);
61        full.notify_one();
62    }
63    //----------------------------------------------------------------
```

```
64  template <typename T> int QueueMonitor<T>::availItems ()
65  {
66      lock_guard<mutex> lg(l);
67      return queue.size ();
68  }
```

The main file of the program holds the classes that describe the work items and result sets. The `MandelWorkItem` class encapsulates the data describing a work item. It also provides MPI registration for the successful communication of class instances between the master and worker processes. The static `init` method needs to be called for a derived datatype to be created and registered.

Listing 5.40: A multi-threaded master–worker implementation of a Mandelbrot fractal set calculator.

```
69   // File : mandlebrot_mt / mandlebrot_mt .cpp
70   . . .
71   //*******************************************************
72   class MandelWorkItem
73   {
74   public:
75       double upperX, upperY, lowerX, lowerY;
76       int imageX, imageY, pixelsX, pixelsY;
77       static MPI_Datatype type;
78
79       static void initType ();
80   };
81   MPI_Datatype MandelWorkItem::type;
82
83   //*******************************************************
84   void MandelWorkItem::initType ()
85   {
86       MandelWorkItem sample;
87
88       int blklen[2];
89       MPI_Aint displ[2], off, base;
90       MPI_Datatype types[2];
91
92       blklen[0] = 4;
93       blklen[1] = 4;
94
95       types[0] = MPI_DOUBLE;
96       types[1] = MPI_INT;
97
98       displ[0] = 0;
99       MPI_Get_address (&(sample.upperX), &base);
100      MPI_Get_address (&(sample.imageX), &off);
101      displ[1] = off - base;
102
103      MPI_Type_create_struct (2, blklen, displ, types, &type);
104      MPI_Type_commit (&type);
105  }
```

The MandelResult class is responsible for representing the partial results that are generated from the worker threads. Similarly to the MandelWorkItem class, a static init method is provided for registering an MPI-derived datatype (lines 138–153) and for declaring the size in pixels of the subpicture each work item will generate (data member numItems).

A slight complication exists with the fact that MPI will not traverse pointers in communicating a data structure, i.e., it performs what is known as a *shallow copy*. In order to be able to communicate back to the master process the pixel values (stored in a dynamically created array) of a subpicture and the coordinates where it belongs, the following approach is used:

- The *imgPart array, which is used for holding the pixel values, is extended upon allocation by 2 elements (lines 126 and 133). The extra space is used to hold the imageX and imageY subpicture coordinates (lines 127–128 and 134–135). The init method of lines 131–136, which is separate from the constructor, allows the initialization of an object past its construction (e.g., after an array of MandelResult objects is created).
- The derived datatype is basically a 1D array of integers, which is defined by the static initType method (lines 138–153). Method initType is called once by all nodes during setup (line 315).

Given this design, the use of the derived datatype is superfluous: it is just an array. The idea is this code could be used as the foundation for another master–worker application, where a different type of result would need to be communicated. Along these lines, the MandelResult class is also equipped with a getResultSize method which currently returns one by default. This could be used in a future extension of the code, if variable-size work items were to be used, resulting in variable-size result sets.

The alternative to the above would be to use MPI_Pack/MPI_Unpack with all the additional overhead that is entailed.

```
106   // ******************************************************************
107   class MandelResult
108   {
109   public:   // public access is not recommended but it is used here to ↩
                  shorten the code
110       unique_ptr<int[]> imgPart=nullptr;
111       // the needed imageX and imageY parameters, i.e., the location ↩
                  of computed image in bigger picture, are placed at the end ↩
                  of the pixel buffer
112       static int numItems;        // not part of the communicated data
113       static MPI_Datatype type;
114
115       MandelResult(){};
116       MandelResult(int , int );
117       void init(int , int );
118       int getResultSize() {return 1;}
119       static void initType(int blkSize);
```

```
120   };
121   MPI_Datatype MandelResult::type;
122   int MandelResult::numItems;
123   //————————————————————————————————————————————————————————
124   MandelResult::MandelResult(int iX, int iY)
125   {
126       imgPart = make_unique<int[]>(numItems+2); // +2 to hold imageX ↵
                  and imageY
127       imgPart[numItems] = iX;
128       imgPart[numItems+1] = iY;
129   }
130   //————————————————————————————————————————————————————————
131   void MandelResult::init(int iX, int iY)
132   {
133       imgPart = make_unique<int[]>(numItems+2); // +2 to hold imageX ↵
                  and imageY
134       imgPart[numItems] = iX;
135       imgPart[numItems+1] = iY;
136   }
137   //————————————————————————————————————————————————————————
138   void MandelResult::initType(int s)
139   {
140       numItems = s;
141       int blklen;
142       MPI_Aint displ;
143       MPI_Datatype types;
144
145       blklen = numItems + 2;
146
147       types = MPI_INT;
148
149       displ = 0;
150
151       MPI_Type_create_struct (1, &blklen, &displ, &types, &type);
152       MPI_Type_commit (&type);
153   }
```

The `MandelCompute` class is fairly unchanged from the version used in List-ing 5.38. The main difference is that it is now operating on a `MandelWorkItem` object and a `MandelResult` object, which are supplied before the computation takes place.

```
154   // *****************************************************************
155   // Class for computing a fractal set part
156   class MandelCompute
157   {
158   private:
159       double upperX, upperY, lowerX, lowerY;
160       int pixelsX, pixelsY, imageX, imageY;
161       MandelResult *res;
162
163       static int MAXITER;
164       int diverge (double cx, double cy);
165
```

```
166   public:
167       void compute();
168       void init(MandelWorkItem *, MandelResult *);
169       MandelResult* getResult();
170   };
171   int MandelCompute::MAXITER = 255;
172
173   //--------------------------------------------------
174   int MandelCompute::diverge (double cx, double cy)
175   {
176       int iter = 0;
177       double vx = cx, vy = cy, tx, ty;
178       while (iter < MAXITER && (vx * vx + vy * vy) < 4)
179       {
180           tx = vx * vx - vy * vy + cx;
181           ty = 2 * vx * vy + cy;
182           vx = tx;
183           vy = ty;
184           iter++;
185       }
186       return iter;
187   }
188
189   //--------------------------------------------------
190   void MandelCompute::init (MandelWorkItem* wi, MandelResult *r)
191   {
192       upperX = wi->upperX;    //local copies are used to speed up ↵
                  computation
193       upperY = wi->upperY;
194       lowerX = wi->lowerX;
195       lowerY = wi->lowerY;
196       imageX = wi->imageX;
197       imageY = wi->imageY;
198
199       res = r;
200
201       pixelsX = wi->pixelsX;
202       pixelsY = wi->pixelsY;
203   }
204
205   //--------------------------------------------------
206   void MandelCompute::compute ()
207   {
208       double stepx = (lowerX - upperX) / pixelsX;
209       double stepy = (upperY - lowerY) / pixelsY;
210
211       int *img = res->imgPart.get();  // shortcut
212       for (int i = 0; i < pixelsX; i++)
213           for (int j = 0; j < pixelsY; j++)
214           {
215               double tempx, tempy;
216               tempx = upperX + i * stepx;
```

```
217              tempy = upperY - j * stepy;
218              img[j * pixelsX + i] = diverge (tempx, tempy);
219          }
220      img[pixelsX * pixelsY] = imageX;
221      img[pixelsX * pixelsY + 1] = imageY;
222  }
223
224  //-----------------------------------------------------------
225  MandelResult*  MandelCompute::getResult()
226  {
227      return this->res;
228  }
```

Following the best practices for thread setup, established in Section 3.3, the threads running on the worker nodes use a WorkerThread *function object*. Each WorkerThread instance is supplied references to the *inque and *outque objects (declared on lines 428 and 429, respectively), which are used in the worker process to traffic messages to and from the master process.

A thread runs for as long as a non-null MandelWorkItem reference is withdrawn from the inque (check at line 261). Upon termination, a thread deposits a NULL reference in the outque to signal the end of its stream of results.

```
229  // ***************************************************************
230  // Function object for use by the threads
231  class WorkerThread
232  {
233  private:
234      int ID;
235      int runs;
236      shared_ptr<QueueMonitor<MandelWorkItem *> > in;
237      shared_ptr< QueueMonitor<MandelResult *> > out;
238  //       QueueMonitor<MandelWorkItem *> *in;
239  //       QueueMonitor<MandelResult *> *out;
240
241  public:
242      WorkerThread(int i, shared_ptr<QueueMonitor<MandelWorkItem *> > ↵
                 &, shared_ptr< QueueMonitor<MandelResult *> > &);
243      void operator()();
244  };
245  //-----------------------------------------------------------
246  WorkerThread::WorkerThread(int id, shared_ptr<QueueMonitor<↵
             MandelWorkItem *> > &i, shared_ptr< QueueMonitor<MandelResult *>↵
             > &o)
247  {
248      ID = id;
249      in = i;
250      out = o;
251      runs=0;
252  }
253
254  //-----------------------------------------------------------
255  void WorkerThread::operator()()
```

```
256  {
257      unique_ptr<MandelCompute> c = make_unique<MandelCompute>();
258      while(1)
259      {
260          MandelWorkItem * work = in->deque();
261          if(work==NULL) break;
262
263          MandelResult *res = out->reserve();
264          c->init (work, res);
265          in->release(work);
266
267          c->compute ();
268
269          out->enque(res);
270      }
271      out->enque(NULL);
272  }
273  // ***********************************************************
274  // Uses the divergence iterations to pseudocolor the fractal set
275  void savePixels (QImage * img, int *imgPart, int imageX, int imageY, ↩
         int height, int width)
276  {
277      for (int i = 0; i < width; i++)
278          for (int j = 0; j < height; j++)
279          {
280              int color = imgPart[j * width + i];
281              img->setPixel (imageX + i, imageY + j, qRgb (256 − color↩
                 , 256 − color, 256 − color));
282          }
283  }
```

The most notable differences of the initial statements in the main function are that `MPI_Init_thread` is used to initialize the MPI runtime and that thread support is checked (rather forcefully) by an assertion on lines 297 and 298, respectively. In this version of the code, we use a single thread per process to conduct communications, thus requiring the `MPI_THREAD_FUNNELED` support. Using multiple threads for communication is left as an exercise.

The number of available cores is discovered via the call of line 293, and this is subsequently used to generate as many worker threads and to size the FIFO structures *inque and *outque accordingly.

The class method calls of lines 314–315 ensure that derived datatypes are available for MPI communications.

```
284  // ***********************************************************
285  int main (int argc, char *argv[])
286  {
287      int N, rank, numCores;
288      double start_time, end_time;
289      MPI_Status status;
290      MPI_Request request;
291
```

```
292
293     numCores = sysconf (_SC_NPROCESSORS_ONLN);
294
295     // init MPI and check thread support
296     int provided;
297     MPI_Init_thread (&argc, &argv, MPI_THREAD_FUNNELED, &provided);
298     assert(provided >= MPI_THREAD_FUNNELED);
299     start_time = MPI_Wtime ();
300
301     MPI_Comm_size (MPI_COMM_WORLD, &N);
302     MPI_Comm_rank (MPI_COMM_WORLD, &rank);
303
304     // check that all parameters are supplied
305     if (rank == 0 && (argc < 6))
306     {
307         cerr << argv[0] << " upperCornerX upperCornerY lowerCornerX ↵
                lowerCornerY workItemPixelsPerSide\n";
308         MPI_Abort (MPI_COMM_WORLD, 1);
309     }
310
311     int workItemPixelsPerSide = atoi (argv[5]);
312
313     // create samples of the work item and result classes and ↵
                register their types with MPI
314     MandelWorkItem::initType();
315     MandelResult::initType(workItemPixelsPerSide * ↵
                workItemPixelsPerSide);
```

The master process (as in Listing 5.38) prepares the work items in the array *w declared on line 340, before starting to distribute them to the worker processes. Each worker process initially receives twice as many work items as the number of its host machine's available cores (lines 380–385). The rationale is to have load available so as to keep the threads busy, while communications take place. Each result that is received by the master prompts the sending of more work items, so as to keep the *inque of the corresponding worker full.

To be able to accomplish this, each worker process starts its execution by sending to the master its host's available core count (line 420). These numbers are collected (line 363) and kept in the nodeCores array (line 368). Every result message that is delivered to the master triggers the sending of more work items, so that *inque remains full (lines 380–385). Also, a RESULTTAG-labeled message causes a call to the savePixels function that "lights up" the resulting image pixels based on the worker results (line 377).

Once all the work items have been distributed (condition i != Xparts * Yparts fails on lines 361 and 380), the master starts listening for the last results from each worker process (the expected number is reflected in the workItemsAssignedToNode array elements), using the loop of lines 394–411. Once these are received, an ENDTAG-labeled message is sent (line 410) that will propagate to all the worker threads in the form of a NULL MandelWorkItem reference (lines 451–456).

The busyNodes variable counts down the worker processes remaining with assigned work (line 394). Once this reaches 0, the master process terminates the program by saving the resulting image (line 413) and shutting down the MPI runtime.

```
316    if (rank == 0)      // master code
317    {
318        double upperCornerX, upperCornerY;
319        double lowerCornerX, lowerCornerY;
320        double partXSpan, partYSpan;
321        int Xparts, Yparts;
322        int imgX = 4096, imgY = 2160;
323
324        upperCornerX = atof (argv[1]);
325        upperCornerY = atof (argv[2]);
326        lowerCornerX = atof (argv[3]);
327        lowerCornerY = atof (argv[4]);
328
329        // make sure that the image size is evenly divided in work ↵
               items
330        Xparts = (int) ceil (imgX * 1.0 / workItemPixelsPerSide);
331        Yparts = (int) ceil (imgY * 1.0 / workItemPixelsPerSide);
332        imgX = Xparts * workItemPixelsPerSide;
333        imgY = Yparts * workItemPixelsPerSide;
334
335        partXSpan = (lowerCornerX - upperCornerX) / Xparts;
336        partYSpan = (upperCornerY - lowerCornerY) / Yparts;
337        unique_ptr<QImage> img = make_unique<QImage> (imgX, imgY, ↵
               QImage::Format_RGB32);
338
339        // prepare the work items in individual structures
340        unique_ptr<MandelWorkItem[]> w = make_unique<MandelWorkItem↵
               []>(Xparts * Yparts);
341        for (int i = 0; i < Xparts; i++)
342            for (int j = 0; j < Yparts; j++)
343            {
344                int idx = j * Xparts + i;
345
346                w[idx].upperX = upperCornerX + i * partXSpan;
347                w[idx].upperY = upperCornerY - j * partYSpan;
348                w[idx].lowerX = upperCornerX + (i + 1) * partXSpan;
349                w[idx].lowerY = upperCornerY - (j + 1) * partYSpan;
350
351                w[idx].imageX = i * workItemPixelsPerSide;
352                w[idx].imageY = j * workItemPixelsPerSide;
353                w[idx].pixelsX = workItemPixelsPerSide;
354                w[idx].pixelsY = workItemPixelsPerSide;
355            }
356
357        // now distribute the work item to the worker nodes
358        unique_ptr<int[]> nodeCores = make_unique<int[]>(N);
359        unique_ptr<int[]> workItemsAssignedToNode = make_unique<int↵
               []>(N);
```

```
360    unique_ptr<MandelResult> res = make_unique<MandelResult>(0, ↩
           0);
361    for (int i = 0; i < Xparts * Yparts; i++)
362    {
363        MPI_Recv (res->imgPart.get(), res->getResultSize(), ↩
               MandelResult::type, MPI_ANY_SOURCE, MPI_ANY_TAG, ↩
               MPI_COMM_WORLD, &status);
364        int workerID = status.MPI_SOURCE;
365        int tag = status.MPI_TAG;
366        if(tag == CORESAVAILTAG)
367        {
368            nodeCores[workerID] = res->imgPart[0];
369            workItemsAssignedToNode[workerID]=0;
370        }
371        else if (tag == RESULTTAG)
372        {
373            workItemsAssignedToNode[workerID]--;
374            int idx = res->numItems;
375            int imageX = res->imgPart[idx];  // extract location↩
                   of image part
376            int imageY = res->imgPart[idx+1];
377            savePixels (img.get(), res->imgPart.get(), imageX, ↩
                   imageY, workItemPixelsPerSide, ↩
                   workItemPixelsPerSide);
378        }
379
380        while(workItemsAssignedToNode[workerID] != 2*nodeCores[↩
               workerID] && i != Xparts*Yparts)
381        {
382            MPI_Isend (&(w[i]), 1, MandelWorkItem::type, ↩
                   workerID, WORKITEMTAG, MPI_COMM_WORLD, &request)↩
                   ;
383            i++;
301            workItemsAssignedToNode[workerID]++;
385        }
386        i--;
387    }
388
389    // now send termination messages
390    int busyNodes=0;
391    for(int i=1;i<N;i++)
392        if(workItemsAssignedToNode[i]!=0) busyNodes++;
393
394    while(busyNodes != 0)
395    {
396        MPI_Recv (res->imgPart.get(),1,MandelResult::type, ↩
               MPI_ANY_SOURCE, MPI_ANY_TAG, MPI_COMM_WORLD, &status↩
               );
397
398        int workerID = status.MPI_SOURCE;
399        int tag = status.MPI_TAG;
400
```

```
401                 if (tag == RESULTTAG)
402                 {
403                     int idx = res->numItems;
404                     int imageX = res->imgPart[idx];
405                     int imageY = res->imgPart[idx+1];
406                     savePixels (img.get(), res->imgPart.get(), imageX, ↩
                            imageY, workItemPixelsPerSide, ↩
                            workItemPixelsPerSide);
407                     workItemsAssignedToNode[workerID]--;
408                     if(workItemsAssignedToNode[workerID]==0) busyNodes ↩
                            --;
409                 }
410                 MPI_Isend (NULL, 0, MandelWorkItem::type, workerID, ↩
                        ENDTAG, MPI_COMM_WORLD, &request);
411             }
412
413             img->save ("mandel.png", "PNG", 0); // save the resulting ↩
                    image
414
415             end_time = MPI_Wtime ();
416             cout << "Total time : " << end_time - start_time << endl;
417         }
```

Each worker process starts by allocating the work items and result structures memory (lines 422–423) and setting up the FIFO queues (lines 428 and 429) that serve the threads. The threads are spawned with the loop of lines 433–437.

Once the threads are started, the main thread serves as the communication funnel between the worker threads and the master process, via the loop of lines 443–488. The body of the loop is split into a sequence of two steps:

- Lines 446–462 receive work items from the master process and deposit them in *inque. If an ENDTAG-labeled message is received, as many as numCores NULL references are deposited to act as flags to the worker threads, and the endOfWork flag is set to avoid performing this step again.
- Lines 465–484 send back results to the master node if there are available items in *outque (condition on line 466). An MPI_Issent call is used to avoid the overhead of copying the message data to an MPI buffer.

The loop terminates only when all the results have been sent to the master process, indicated by having the numWorkerThreads counter become zero. The counter is decremented every time a thread deposits a NULL reference in the *outque, which indicates its termination (lines 469–472).

```
418     else        // worker code
419     {
420         MPI_Send (&numCores, 1, MPI_INT, 0, CORESAVAILTAG, ↩
                MPI_COMM_WORLD);        // publish available cores to master
421
422         unique_ptr<MandelWorkItem[]> w = make_unique<MandelWorkItem↩
                []>(2*numCores); // preallocated work items
```

```
423    unique_ptr<MandelResult[]> r = make_unique<MandelResult↵
           []>(2*numCores);      // preallocated result items
424    for(int i=0;i<2*numCores;i++)
425        r[i].init(0,0);
426
427    // populate the two queues with the preallocated objects
428    shared_ptr< QueueMonitor<MandelWorkItem *> > inque = ↵
           make_shared< QueueMonitor<MandelWorkItem *> >(2*numCores↵
           , w.get());
429    shared_ptr<QueueMonitor<MandelResult *>> outque = ↵
           make_shared<QueueMonitor<MandelResult *>>(2*numCores,r.↵
           get());
430
431    unique_ptr < thread > thr[numCores];
432    unique_ptr<WorkerThread> workFunc[numCores];
433    for(int i=0;i<numCores;i++)
434    {
435        workFunc[i] = make_unique<WorkerThread>(i, inque, outque↵
               );
436        thr[i] = make_unique<thread>(ref(*workFunc[i]));
437    }
438
439    // one loop for sending and recv messages
440    bool endOfWork=false;
441    int numWorkerThreads = numCores;
442    int assigned=0;
443    while (1)
444    {
445        // receiving part
446        if(!endOfWork  && assigned != numCores )
447        {
448            MandelWorkItem *w = inque->reserve();
449            MPI_Recv (w, 1, MandelWorkItem::type, 0, MPI_ANY_TAG↵
                   , MPI_COMM_WORLD, &status); // get a new work ↵
                   item
450            int tag = status.MPI_TAG;
451            if (tag == ENDTAG)
452            {
453                for(int i=0;i<numCores;i++)
454                    inque->enque(NULL);
455                endOfWork=true;
456            }
457            else
458            {
459                inque->enque(w);
460                assigned++;
461            }
462        }
463
464        // sending part
465        MandelResult *res;
466        if(outque->availItems() >0)
```

```
467                  {
468                      res = outque->deque();
469                      if(res == NULL)
470                      {
471                          numWorkerThreads--;
472                      }
473                      else
474                      {
475                          MPI_Request r;
476                          MPI_Status s;
477
478                          MPI_Issend (res->imgPart.get(), res->↩
                                 getResultSize(), MandelResult::type, 0, ↩
                                 RESULTTAG, MPI_COMM_WORLD, &r); // return ↩
                                 the results
479                          MPI_Wait(&r, &s);
480
481                          outque->release(res);
482                          assigned--;
483                      }
484                  }
485
486                  if(!numWorkerThreads) // terminate the loop
487                      break;
488              }
489
490          for(int i=0;i<numCores;i++)
491              thr[i]->join();
492      }
493      MPI_Finalize ();
494      return 0;
495  }
```

The code shown above can be easily modified to serve other scenarios. The core changes would mostly affect classes `MandelWorkItem`, `MandelResult`, and `MandelCompute` and the lines that modify or initialize their instances.

Exercises

1. Write an MPMD version of the "Hello World" program of Fig. 5.2, in effect eliminating the `if/else` structure around which the program is built. You may use the C or C++ bindings.

2. Write an SPMD version of the two programs shown in Listing 5.5.

3. Modify the program shown in Listing 5.5 so that the master node prints out a list of the processes IDs for which the message has not been read yet. Your output should be similar to:

```
1  $ mpirun -np 1 master : -np 3 worker
2  Node 2 says Hi. Awaiting nodes : 1 3
```

```
3   Node 3 says Hi. Awaiting nodes : 1
4   Node 1 says Hi. Awaiting nodes :
```

4. Create a model of the characteristics of the communication link joining two processes running on two different machines, i.e., calculate the startup latency and communication rate, by implementing and testing a **ping-pong** benchmark program. A ping-pong program measures the time elapsed between sending a message, having it bounce at its destination and receiving it back at its origin. By varying the message size, you can use statistical methods (least-squares) to estimate the startup latency and rate as the intercept and slope, respectively, of the line fitted to the experimental data.

5. How would we need to modify the broadcasting program of Listing 5.9 if the source of the message was an arbitrary process and not the one with rank 0?

6. Assuming that the execution platform of your program consists of four machines with identical architecture but different CPU clocks: one with 4 GHz, one with 3 GHz, and two with 2 GHz. How should you split matrix A used in the example of Section 5.11.1 in order to solve the matrix–vector product problem in the smallest possible time?

7. Write a program that performs gathering as efficiently as possible using point-to-point communications, i.e., the equivalent of MPI_Gather. What is the *time complexity* of your algorithm?

8. Write a program that performs scattering as efficiently as possible using point-to-point communications, i.e., the equivalent of MPI_Scatter. What is the *volume* of data collectively communicated if each process is to receive K number of items? Express this number as a function of K and the number of processes N.

9. The amount of data exchanged during every step of the butterfly pattern in Fig. 5.9 doubles in relation to the previous step. If initially every process had data of size K bytes to exchange, what is the total time required for the operation to complete if we assume that each message exchange takes time $t_s + l \cdot V$, where t_s is the link's startup latency, V is the volume of data to be sent, and l is the inverse of the communication speed?

10. An alternative parallel bucket sort algorithm would have the root process of an N-process run, scan the input data, and split them into N buckets before scattering the buckets to the corresponding processes. Implement this alternative design and compare its performance with the version presented in Section 5.11.5.

11. Write a function that could be used for providing multicasting capabilities to a program, i.e., to be able to send a message to a subset of the processes of a communicator. Use an appropriate collective operation for the task.

12. Write the equivalent of the ping-pong program using RMA functions and measure the communication speed achieved versus the size of the message used. Compare your results with the data rates accomplished with point-to-point communications.

13. Modify the program of Listing 5.7 so that the partitioning of the range depends on the relative speed of the participating nodes. One easy approach is to make the ranges proportional to the CPU operating frequency, or the calculated bogomips.

Both numbers are available in the /proc/cpuinfo pseudofile on a Linux machine. The master can collect the numbers and reply back to the worker nodes with the calculated ranges. If we represent as m_i the i node's bogomips, the percent of the range α_i that should be assigned to node i can be calculated as $\alpha_i = \frac{m_i}{\sum_{\forall k} m_k}$.

14. The butterfly communication scheme that is outlined in Section 5.11.4 is only one of the possible strategies for an all-to-all or all-reduce data exchange. A different approach would be mandated if the underlying communication infrastructure did not provide the required links, making the procedure inefficient. An example of such an architecture is the ring, where each node is directly connected to just two others.
    (a) Write an MPI program that would implement an efficient all-to-all exchange of data on a ring of machines.
    (b) How many steps would be required in comparison to a butterfly scheme if the number of nodes/processes were $N = 2^k$?
    (c) If we assume that the time taken to send V bytes over a communication link is given by $l \cdot V$, where l is the (inverse of the) link speed in sec/byte, how does your algorithm compare against the butterfly scheme in terms of overall communication time?

15. The case study on Diffusion-Limited Aggregation in Section 5.23 decomposes the problem's data on a particle-wise basis. Explore the alternative of partitioning the 2D grid and assigning it to the processes involved. What are the benefits and drawbacks of this approach? Is the communication pattern involved different in this case? Does this approach produce similar results to the sequential program and alternative parallel programs?

16. Implement a 3D-space Diffusion-Limited Aggregation simulation by extending the solutions provided in Section 5.23.

17. It is not unusual in NoWs setups to have machines with different capabilities. Create an MPI program that would have each process read from a file a number of integers that is proportional to its CPU speed as indicated by the operating frequency (its "clock"). Use appropriate *filetypes* and *views* to perform the data distribution in a cyclic-block manner.

18. The details of the trapezoidal rule for computing a function integral are discussed in Section 3.7.2. Implement an MPI-based version of the trapezoidal rule using: (a) dynamic partitioning and (b) static partitioning. For part (a) you can base your solution on master–worker implementation of Section 5.25.1.

19. Use the master–worker code provided in Section 5.25 as a basis for the creation of a hierarchical master–worker configuration, where nodes are organized in a three-level (or higher) tree instead of the two-level tree of the simple setup. The secondary master nodes of the middle tree layer(s) should be responsible for managing the load distribution in their subtrees, while the primary master at the root of the tree should be responsible for the overall workload distribution.

20. Modify the multi-threaded master–worker code of Section 5.25.2 so that there are two separate threads in each worker process for communication: one for

receiving work items and one for sending back results. What are the benefits and drawbacks of this arrangement?

21. Conway's Game of Life is played on a rectangular grid of cells that may or may not contain an organism. The state of the cells is updated at each time step by applying the following set of rules:

- Every organism with 2–3 neighbors survives.
- Every organism with 4 or more neighbors dies from overpopulation.
- Every organism with 0–1 neighbors dies from isolation.
- Every empty cell adjacent to 3 organisms gives birth to a new one.

Create an MPI program that evolves a board of arbitrary size (dimensions could be specified at the command-line) over several iterations. The board could be randomly generated or read from a file.

Try applying the geometric decomposition pattern to partition the work among your processes. One example could be to evenly split the board row-wise. It is clear that each process can update its part of the board only by knowing the state of the bottom board row resident in the previous process and the state of the top board row resident in the next process (the boundary processes being an exception).

22. Radix sort is a linear complexity non-comparison based sorting algorithm that is suitable for concurrent execution. Radix sort sorts data by separating them into groups based on their digits (for integers) or characters (for strings). The data must be of fixed range, i.e., the number of bits or characters used must be known a priori.

Radix sort comes in two forms: Least-Significant Digit radix sort (LSD) or Most-Significant Digit radix sort (MSD). The latter is suitable for parallel execution, as data which are partitioned in groups can be operated independently in subsequent phases of the algorithm. The MSD algorithm, which is very close to bucket sort,[15] can be implemented recursively as shown in the following pseudocode for binary data. An extension for data with non-binary digits (strings) is straightforward. The use of the auxiliary array B allows the sorting to be *stable*.

```
1   // Input: array A, with N elements, each D bits long.
2   // Output: A holds sorted data
3   radix_sort(A, N)
4       allocate memory B equal in size to A
5       tmp <- radix_aux(A, N, B, D-1)
6       if tmp <> A    // if sorted data end up in B array
7           copy B to A
8
9   // Auxiliary recursive function
10  // Use of temporary array B for a stable sort
```

---

[15] The major difference between radix sort and bucket sort lies in how the keys are examined: piecewise in radix sort and as a whole in bucket sort. In the latter, an arbitrary number of buckets can be prescribed.

```
11   // Returns location of sorted data
12   radix_aux( A, N, B, k)
13      if k = -1 Or N<2      // base case for termination
14         return A
15      else
16         let r be the number of items in A, with k-th bit set to 0
17         resetIdx <- 0
18         setIdx <- r
19         for i <- 0 to N-1      // separate data in two bins
20            if k-th bit of A[i] is set
21               store A[i] in B[ setIdx ]
22               setIdx <- setIdx + 1
23            else
24               store A[i] in B[ resetIdx ]
25               resetIdx <- resetIdx + 1
26
27         tmp1 <- radix_aux(B, r, A, k-1)          // sort bin with a 0↩
                  k-th bit, using the (k-1)-th bit
28         tmp2 <- radix_aux(B+r, N-r, A+r, k-1) // sort bin with a 1↩
                  k-th bit, using the (k-1)-th bit
29         if tmp1 + r <> tmp2      // pointer comparison
30            if r > N - r      // make the smallest copy
31               copy N-r elements from tmp2 to tmp1+r
32               return tmp1
33            else
34               copy r elements from tmp1 to tmp2-r
35               return tmp2-r
36         else
37            return tmp1
```

Use divide & conquer decomposition as your decomposition pattern (see Section 2.3.2) to design and implement an MPI radix sort.

GPU programming: CUDA

6

In this chapter you will:

- Understand the memory hierarchy of GPUs and how the different memories can be utilized.

- Learn how computations are mapped to threads in CUDA using grids and blocks.

- Learn how to use streams and zero-copy memory to maximize the utilization of a GPU.

- Synchronize threads across blocks, grids, and devices using cooperative groups.

- Reduce the cost of intrawarp communications using warp primitives and cooperative groups.

- Accelerate the launch of complex workflows using CUDA graphs.

- Combine CUDA and MPI to handle big workloads over a cluster of GPU-equipped machines.

- Learn to use a step-by-step approach in the development of CUDA programs via two case studies.

6.1 Introduction

GPUs devote a big portion of their silicon real estate to compute logic, whereas conventional CPUs devote large portions of it to on-chip cache memory. This results in having hundreds or thousands (!) of cores in contemporary GPUs, as already shown in Section 1.3.2.

But if the GPU hardware is so powerful, why are we not seeing all the software being ported and run on them? In order to put all this computational power to use, one has to create at least one separate thread for each core. Even more are needed so that computation can be overlapped with memory transfers. This obviously mandates a shift in the programming paradigm used. Going from a handful of threads to thousands requires a different way of partitioning and processing loads. Also, not all computations can benefit from multiple threads. There are many tasks which are inherently sequential and GPU cores are a poor match for these type of tasks. This means that CPUs and GPUs have to coexist for building a system that can excel in all possible scenarios.

Multicore and GPU Programming. https://doi.org/10.1016/B978-0-12-814120-5.00015-9

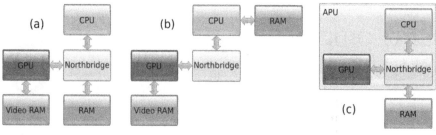

FIGURE 6.1

Existing architectures for CPU-GPU systems: (a) and (b) represent discrete GPU solutions, with a CPU-integrated memory controller in (b). Diagram (c) corresponds to integrated CPU-GPU solutions, as AMD's Accelerated Processing Unit (APU) chips.

GPU program deployment has a characteristic which can be considered a major obstacle: GPU and host memories are typically disjoint, requiring explicit (or implicit, depending on the development platform) data transfer between the two. Only some low-cost, entry-level systems violate this rule by having a portion of the main memory allocated for display and GPU purposes, at the expense of performance, as CPU and GPU compete for memory access.

The existing architectures are shown in Fig. 6.1. Fig. 6.1(a) represents a typical arrangement for discrete GPU solutions. AMD's Athlon 64 and later Intel's Nehalem architectures reduced the latency associated with main memory access by integrating the memory controller in the CPU die (as seen in Fig. 6.1(b)). AMD's Accelerated Processing Unit (APU) chips integrate CPU and GPU in a single chip (as seen in Fig. 6.1(c)). This is a breakthrough with great potential, especially with the introduction of the heterogeneous Unified Memory Access (hUMA) technology that unifies the memory spaces of CPU and GPU and even maintains cache coherence between them.

However, at present, the wafer real estate compromises that these chips have to endure (sharing the same chip limits the amount of functionality that can be incorporated for both CPU and GPU alike), along with their coupling with slow memory subsystems, delegates them to low-cost market segments. The situation may change in the near future with the use of chiplet technology, which "glues" together many smaller components into a package. Chiplet-based products were made commercially available for the first time in 2017 with AMD's Epyc CPUs. The first chiplet-based CPU-GPU combo came in the form of Intel's i7-8809G CPU that combined a quad-core CPU with a Radeon RX Vega M GPU.

Having disjoint memories means that data must be explicitly transferred between the two, whenever data need to be processed by the GPU or results collected by the CPU. Considering that memory access is a serious bottleneck in GPU utilization (despite phenomenal speeds like a maximum theoretical memory bandwidth of 616 GiB/s for NVidia's RTX 2080 Ti and 1024 GiB/s for AMD's Radeon VII), communicating data over relatively slow peripheral buses like the PCIe[1] is a major problem.

In NVidia's A100, the first product based on the Ampere architecture, second-generation High Bandwidth Memory (HBM2) is utilized to push the memory bandwidth to 1.56 TiB/sec [32]. An impressive number, until one considers that this is used to feed 6912 cores, which does not produce a very impressive ratio of bandwidth per core. In subsequent sections we will examine how this communication overhead can be reduced or "hidden" by overlapping it with computation.

A second characteristic of GPU computation is that GPU devices may not adhere to the same floating point representation and accuracy standards as typical CPUs. This can lead to the accumulation of errors and the production of inaccurate results. Although this is a problem that has been addressed by the latest chip offerings by NVidia and AMD, it is always recommended – as a precaution during development – to verify the results produced by a GPU program against the results produced by an equivalent CPU program. For example, CUDA code samples available with NVidia's SDK typically follow this approach.

GPU programming has been advancing with leaps and bounds since the first early attempts. Current tools cover a wide range of capabilities as far as problem decomposition and expressing parallelism are concerned. On one side of the spectrum we have tools that require explicit problem decomposition such as CUDA and OpenCL, and on the other extreme we have tools like OpenACC that let the compiler take care of all the data migration and thread spawning necessary to complete a task on a GPU.

Some of the most prominent GPU development platforms are:

- **CUDA**: **C**ompute **U**nified **D**evice **A**rchitecture[2] was introduced by NVidia in late 2006 as one of the first credible systems for GPU programming that broke free of the "code-it-as-graphics" approach used until then. CUDA provides two sets of APIs (a low- and a higher-level one) and it is available freely for Windows and Linux operating systems. Although it can be considered to be too verbose, for example, requiring explicit memory transfers between the host and the GPU, it is the basis for the implementation of higher-level third-party APIs and libraries as explained below. CUDA, in its 11th incarnation since the summer of 2020, is specific to NVidia hardware only.
- **OpenCL**: **Open C**omputing **L**anguage[3] is an open standard for writing programs that can execute across a variety of heterogeneous platforms that include GPUs, CPU, DSPs, or other processors. OpenCL has a very wide industry support that includes AMD, Apple, Intel, and NVidia. It is covered in detail in Chapter 7.

---

[1] PCIe 3.0 has a theoretical speed of 8 GT/s (giga-transfers per second) per lane, which over a typical 16-lane interface, as the ones available in the majority of motherboards, translates to a maximum data rate of 16 GB/s. PCIe 4.0 doubles that to 16 GT/s per lane.

[2] https://developer.nvidia.com/category/zone/cuda-zone.

[3] http://www.khronos.org/opencl/.

- **OpenMP**: The Open Multi-Processing standard was originally developed for shared-memory parallel CPU programming. Since the OpenMP 4.0 specification published in 2013, it can also target GPUs. OpenMP is covered in Chapter 8.
- **OpenACC**: An open specification[4] for an API that allows the use of compiler directives (e.g., `#pragma acc`, in a similar fashion to OpenMP) to automatically map computations to GPUs or multicore chips, according to a programmer's hints.
- **Thrust**: A C++ template library[5] that accelerates GPU software development by utilizing a set of container classes and a set of algorithms to automatically map computations to GPU threads. Thrust used to rely solely on a CUDA back-end, but since version 1.6 it can target multiple device back-ends, including CPUs. Thrust has been incorporated in the CUDA SDK distribution since CUDA 4.1. It is covered in detail in Chapter 10.
- **ArrayFire**: A comprehensive GPU function library[6] that covers mathematics, signal and image processing, statistics, and other scientific domains. ArrayFire functions operate on arrays of data, in a similar fashion to Thrust. ArrayFire relies on a CUDA back-end also. A "gfor" construct is provided that allows the parallel execution of a loop's iterations on the GPU.

In the following sections we explore CUDA. The Thrust platform which contributes in a big way towards the elimination of much of the logistical overhead (i.e., memory allocation and transfers) involved in GPU programming is covered in Chapter 10. Appendix E addresses issues related to CUDA installation.

6.2 CUDA's programming model: threads, blocks, and grids

The CUDA programming model follows the Globally Sequential Locally Parallel pattern (see Section 2.4). As GPUs are essentially co-processors that can be used to accelerate parts of a program, a CUDA program executes as shown in Fig. 6.2.

In order to properly utilize a GPU, the program must be decomposed into a large number of threads that can run concurrently. GPU schedulers can execute these with minimum switching overhead and under a variety of configurations based on the available device capabilities. However, there are two challenges that need to be overcome:

(i) How do we spawn the hundreds or thousands of threads required?
CUDA's answer to this is to spawn all the threads as a group, running the same function with a set of parameters that apply to all.
(ii) How do we initialize the individual threads so that each one does a different part of the work?

---

[4] http://www.openacc-standard.org.

[5] http://code.google.com/p/thrust/.

[6] https://arrayfire.com/.

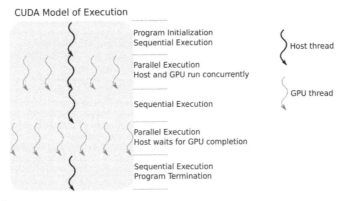

FIGURE 6.2

The GSLP CUDA execution model. The host machine may continue execution (default behavior) or may block, waiting for the completion of the GPU threads.

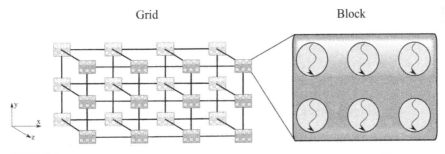

FIGURE 6.3

An example of the grid/block hierarchy used to describe a set of threads that will be spawned by CUDA. The figure illustrates a $4 \times 3 \times 2$ grid, made by 3×2 blocks. The grid connections are there only for illustrative purposes.

CUDA solves this problem by organizing the threads in a 6D structure (lower dimensions are also possible)! Each thread is aware of its position in the overall structure, via a set of intrinsic variables/structures. With this information a thread can map its position to the subset of data that it is assigned to.

Threads are organized in a hierarchy of two levels as shown in Fig. 6.3. At the lower level threads are organized in **blocks** that can be of one, two, or three dimensions. Blocks are then organized in **grids** of one, two, or three dimensions. The sizes of the blocks and grids are limited by the capabilities of the target device. The rationale behind this organization, which lies partly in hardware issues and partly in software engineering issues, is revealed in Sections 6.3 and 6.6.

NVidia uses the **compute capability** (CC) specification to encode what each family/generation of GPU chips is capable of. The part that is related to grid and block sizes is shown in Table 6.1. Devices of compute capability 1.x & 2.x are no longer

Table 6.1 Compute capabilities and associated limits on block and grid sizes.

Item	Compute capability			
	5.x	**6.x**	**7.x**	**8.0**
GPU family	Maxwell	Pascal	Turing	Ampere
Sample GPU	980	1080	2080	A100
Max. grid dimensions	3			
Grid maximum x-dimension	$2^{31} - 1$			
Grid maximum y/z-dimension	$2^{16} - 1$			
Max. block dimensions	3			
Block max. x/y-dimension	1024			
Block max. z-dimension	64			
Max. threads per block	1024			

supported by NVidia's SDK, since v9.0. Although the numbers look consistent across the whole range shown, this is not the case for a big number of other features. For example, compute capability 7.x and above devices are equipped with ray-tracing (RT) cores. The compute capability of a GPU can be discovered by running the device-Query utility that comes with the CUDA SDK samples. Devices with the same major revision number are of the same core architecture. For example, all devices based on the Volta/Turing architecture have a major revision number of 7. The minor revision numbers correspond to incremental improvements.

The programmer has to provide a function that will be run by all the threads in a grid. This function in CUDA terminology is called a **kernel**. During the invocation of a kernel, one can specify the thread hierarchy with a special *execution configuration* syntax ($<<<$ $>>>$). For example, running a kernel called foo() by a set of threads as the one depicted in Fig. 6.3 would require the following lines:

```
dim3 block(3,2);
dim3 grid(4,3,2);
foo<<<grid, block>>>();
```

The CUDA-supplied dim3 type represents an integer vector of three elements. If fewer than three components are specified, the rest are initialized by default to 1. In the special case where a 1D structure is desired, integers can be used as well, e.g., running a grid made up of five blocks, each consisting of 256 threads is possible with:

```
foo<<<5, 256>>>();
```

Many different grid–block combinations are also possible. Some examples are shown below:

```
dim3 b(3,3,3);
dim3 g(20,100);
foo<<<g, b>>>();    // Run a 20x100 grid made of 3x3x3 blocks
foo<<<10, b>>>(); // Run a 10-block grid, each block made by 3↵
    x3x3 threads
```

```
foo<<<g, 256>>>(); // Run a 20x100 grid, each block made of 256 ↵
    threads
foo<<<g, 2048>>>();// An invalid example: maximum block size is ↵
    1024 threads even for compute capability 7.x
foo <<<5, g>>>();    // Another invalid example, that specifies a ↵
    block size of 20x100=2000 threads
```

The following is the CUDA equivalent of a "Hello World" program:

Listing 6.1: A "Hello World" CUDA program.

```
1  // File : hello.cu
2  #include <stdio.h>
3  #include <cuda.h>
4
5  __global__ void hello()
6  {
7      printf("Hello world\n");
8  }
9
10 int main()
11 {
12    hello<<<1,10>>>();
13    cudaDeviceSynchronize();
14    return 0;
15 }
```

The program can be compiled and executed as follows (CUDA programs should be stored in files with a .cu extension):

```
$ nvcc hello.cu -o hello
$ ./hello
```

and it will produce 10 lines of output. The **NVidia CUDA Compiler** (nvcc) is a compiler front-end or compiler driver. It accepts a number of parameters that are passed to the C/C++ compiler and other tools (like the GPU assembler) verbatim.

The key points of Listing 6.1 are the following:

- The kernel hello() is just like any other C function. The only difference is the decoration with the __global__ directive, which specifies that the hello function is supposed to be called from the host and run on the device. This means that nvcc will create two functions: one that will run on the GPU, as expected, and one *stub* function that will run on the CPU and will set up and invoke the GPU one. In devices of compute capability 3.5 and above, a __global__ function can be also called from the device, i.e., from other kernels running on the GPU.
- Kernels which are called from the host (i.e., __global__) are not supposed to return any value. They must be declared void. Any results that a kernel computes are stored in the device memory and must be explicitly transferred back to host memory as discussed in Section 6.6.

- GPU execution is *asynchronous* (as implicitly indicated in Fig. 6.2), i.e., the statement of line 12 specifies the execution configuration, but the time instance the threads will terminate (or even spawn) is undetermined. If the host requires that the GPU computation is done before proceeding (e.g., results are needed), an explicit *barrier* statement is needed (cudaDeviceSynchronize on line 13). If line 13 in commented out, there will be no output from the program. Can you guess why?

CUDA supports two more function specifiers: __device__ and __host__. A __device__ function can only be called from within a kernel, i.e., not from a host. A __host__ function can only run on the host. The __host__ is typically omitted, unless used in combination with __device__ to indicate that the function can run on both the host and the device. This means that two binary executables must be generated: one for execution on the CPU and one for execution on the GPU. The CUDA toolkit conveniently packages all the generated binary codes inside the same executable file.

Each of the CUDA threads is aware of its position in the grid/block hierarchy via the following intrinsic/built-in structures, all having three dimension components x, y, and z:

- blockDim: Contains the size of each block, e.g., (B_x, B_y, B_z).
- gridDim: Contains the size of the grid, in blocks, e.g., (G_x, G_y, G_z).
- threadIdx: The (x, y, z) position of the thread within a block, with $x \in [0, B_x - 1]$, $y \in [0, B_y - 1]$, and $z \in [0, B_z - 1]$.
- blockIdx: The (b_x, b_y, b_z) position of a thread's block within the grid, with $b_x \in [0, G_x - 1]$, $b_y \in [0, G_y - 1]$, and $b_z \in [0, G_z - 1]$.

The purpose of making a thread aware of its position in the hierarchy is to allow it to identify its workload.

threadIdx is not unique among threads as there could be two or more threads in different blocks with the same index. Deriving a unique scalar ID for each of the threads would require the use of all the above information. Each thread can be considered as an element of a 6D array with the following definition[7]:

```
Thread t[gridDim.z][gridDim.y][gridDim.x][blockDim.z][blockDim.y][↩
    blockDim.x];
```

Getting the offset of a particular thread from the beginning of the array would produce a unique scalar ID:

---

[7] The index arrangements seems strange, with z-components coming before the x-components. However, this is a definition compatible with the thread hierarchy depicted in NVidia's CUDA C Programming Guide. Additionally, the mapping of the x-, y-, and z-components of a thread's ID to a part of the data/workload is completely application-specific, i.e., alternative/different ID calculations are also possible.

Listing 6.2: Calculation of a unique ID for a thread in a grid of blocks.

```
int myID = ( blockIdx.z * gridDim.x * gridDim.y +
             blockIdx.y * gridDim.x +
             blockIdx.x ) * blockDim.x * blockDim.y * blockDim.z +
             threadIdx.z *  blockDim.x * blockDim.y +
             threadIdx.y * blockDim.x +
             threadIdx.x;
```

There are two distinct components in the above expression: the first three lines correspond to the number of threads contained in the blocks preceding the current one; the last three lines correspond to the local ID of the thread within its block.

An alternative way for the calculation of a thread's global ID is to assume that each thread is an element of a 3D array with dimensions:

```
Thread t [ gridDim.z * blockDim.z ]
         [ gridDim.y * blockDim.y ]
         [ gridDim.x * blockDim.x ];
```

A thread's global coordinates would be:

```
// start of block + local component
int x = blockIdx.x * blockDim.x + threadIdx.x;
int y = blockIdx.y * blockDim.y + threadIdx.y;
int z = blockIdx.z * blockDim.z + threadIdx.z;
```

The following ID calculation based on the above formulation produces the same results as Listing 6.2:

```
int altMyID = threadIdx.x + blockIdx.x * blockDim.x +
              (blockIdx.y * blockDim.y + threadIdx.y) * gridDim.x * ↩
                 blockDim.x+
              (blockIdx.z * blockDim.z + threadIdx.z) * gridDim.x * ↩
                 blockDim.x * gridDim.y * blockDim.y;
```

The first three lines in Listing 6.2 relate to the interblock offset (i.e., getting to the beginning of the block a thread belongs to) and the last three to the intrablock offset (i.e., the distance from the beginning of the block).

Fortunately, in most cases the layout of the threads uses a small subset of dimensions, allowing the simplification of this formula (treating the missing grid/block dimensions as equal to 1 and the corresponding coordinates as 0), or there is a direct association between the thread and data-to-be-processed layouts (e.g., processing points in a 3D lattice by an equal-size grid of threads), making the calculation of a scalar ID unnecessary. A more convenient way of getting a thread's scalar ID is discussed in Section 6.10.1, using the thread_rank method of a thread_block object.

Based on the above, we can modify the program of Listing 6.1 so that each thread prints out its ID:

Listing 6.3: A variation to the "Hello World" program of Listing 6.1. Only the changes are shown.

```
1   // File : hello2.cu
2   . . .
3   __global__ void hello()
4   {
5     int myID = ( blockIdx.z * gridDim.x * gridDim.y +
6                  blockIdx.y * gridDim.x +
7                  blockIdx.x ) * blockDim.x +
8                  threadIdx.x;
9
10    printf ("Hello world from %i\n", myID);
11  }
12  . . .
```

In the vast majority of scenarios, the host is responsible for I/O operations, including console output, as generating messages from each of the kernel threads could be overwhelming. Kernel console output can be an option for debugging purposes, if it is combined with conditional statements to properly filter what is shown to the user. Section 6.6 presents the process of moving data in and out of the GPU memory in detail, as well as the memory hierarchy of CUDA devices. A clear understanding of the latter is essential for optimizing GPU performance.

6.3 CUDA's execution model: streaming multiprocessors and warps

GPU cores are essentially vector-processing units, capable of applying the same instruction on a large collection of operands. So, when a kernel is run on a GPU core, the same instruction sequence is *synchronously* executed by a large collection of processing units called Streaming Processors (SPs). A group of SPs that execute under the control of a single control unit is called a Streaming Multiprocessor (SM). A GPU can contain multiple SMs, each running its own kernel. Since each thread runs on its own SP, we will refer to SPs as cores (NVidia documentation calls them CUDA cores), although a more purist approach would be to treat SMs as cores. NVidia calls this execution model Single Instruction Multiple Threads (SIMT).

SIMT is analogous to SIMD. The only major difference is that in SIMT the size of the "vector" that the processing elements operate upon is determined by the software, i.e., the block size.

The computational power of a GPU (and consequently its target market) is largely determined at least within the members of a family, by the number of SMs available. As an example, Table 6.2 lists a number of legacy and more recent GPU offerings.

Threads are *scheduled* to run on an SM as a block. The threads in a block do not *run* concurrently though. Instead they are executed in groups called **warps**. The size of a warp is hardware-specific. The current CUDA GPUs use a warp size of 32 but this could change in future GPU generations (the intrinsic integer variable warpSize

Table 6.2 A sample list of GPUs and their SM capabilities in terms of INT32 cores. In Ampere INT32 and FP32 cores can execute in parallel, which justifies NVidia in reporting 10496 cores in the RTX 3090 official documentation. In reality we have 5248 INT32 and 5248 FP32 cores.

Archit.	GPU	Cores	Cores/SM	SM	CC
Ampere	RTX 3090	5248	64	82	8.6
Ampere	A100	6912	64	108	8.0
Turing	RTX 2080 Ti	4352	64	68	7.5
Turing	RTX 2070 Super	2560	64	40	7.5
Pascal	GTX 1080 Ti	3584	128	28	6.1
Pascal	GTX 1070	1920	128	15	6.1
Maxwell	GTX 980	2048	128	16	5.2
Kepler	GTX Titan	2688	192	14	3.5
Kepler	GTX 780	2304	192	12	3.5

can be used to query this number). The benefit of interleaving the execution of warps is to hide the latency associated with memory access, which can be significantly high.

Threads in a block are split into warps according to their intrablock thread-ID as calculated by the formula in Listing 6.2, if we set to zero the grid-related terms:

```
int myID = threadIdx.z * blockDim.x * blockDim.y +
           threadIdx.y * blockDim.x +
           threadIdx.x;
```

An SM can switch seamlessly between warps as each thread gets its own set of registers. Each thread actually gets its own private execution context that is maintained on-chip. This contradicts the arrangement used by multi-threading on CPUs, where a very expensive context switch (involving the saving of CPU registers) accompanies thread switching.

Each SM can have multiple warp schedulers, e.g., in Ampere there are four. This means that up to four independent instruction sequences from four warps can be issued simultaneously. Additionally, each warp scheduler can issue up to two instructions as long as they are independent, i.e., the outcome of one does not depend on the outcome of the other. This is known as **instruction-level parallelism** (ILP). As an example, let us consider the following code:

```
a = a * b;
d = b + e;
```

These two statements can be executed concurrently, while the following example does not present such an opportunity due to the dependency between the two statements:

```
a = a * b;
d = a + e;   // needs the value of a
```

Table 6.3 Select compute capabilities and associated limits on kernel and thread scheduling.

Item	Compute capability						
	3.5	**5.0**	**6.0**	**6.1**	**7.0**	**7.5**	**8.0**
Concurrent kernels/device	32		128	32		128	
Max. resident blocks/SM	16		32			16	32
Max. resident warps/SM	64					32	64
Max. resident threads/SM	2048					1024	2048
32-bit registers/SM	64k						
Max. registers/thread	255						

Once an SM completes the execution of all the threads in a block, it switches to a different block in the grid. Each scheduler is permanently assigned to a group of 32 cores, simplifying scheduling and improving efficiency. In reality, each SM may have a large number of *resident blocks* and *resident warps*, i.e., executing concurrently.

The number of resident kernels, blocks, and warps depends on the memory requirements of a kernel and the limits imposed by the compute capability of a device. These limits are shown in Table 6.3 for a subset of the available GPUs.

As an example of how these numbers are significant, let us assume that we have a kernel that requires 48 registers per thread, and it is to be launched on an RTX 2070 Super card, as a grid of $4 \times 5 \times 3$ blocks, each 100 threads long. The registers demanded by each block are $100 \times 48 = 4800$, which is below the 64k/SM available on this compute capability 7.5 card. The grid is made of $4 \times 5 \times 3 = 60$ blocks that need to be distributed to the 40 SMs of the card. Although NVidia does not publish how the blocks are distributed to the SMs, we can safely assume that it should be a form of round-robin assignment. This means that there will be 20 SMs that will receive two blocks and 20 SMs that will receive one block. Obviously, this would be a source of inefficiency as during the time the 20 SMs process the second of the two blocks they were assigned, the remaining 20 SMs are idle.

Additionally, each of the 100-thread blocks would be split into $\lceil \frac{100}{warpSize} \rceil = 4$ warps, as warpSize = 32 for the Turing architecture. The first three warps would have 32 threads and the last would have four threads! If we assume that the warps execute in pairs on the 64 core/SM machine, when the last warp of each block executes (alongside the third warp), $\frac{64-(32+4)}{64} = 43.75\%$ of each SM would be idle.

These issues indicate that kernel design and deployment is critical for extracting the maximum performance from a GPU. These issues are addressed in Section 6.7.

The mechanics of the thread scheduling can be safely ignored by a programmer as there is no control that can be exercised on when or in what sequence the threads in a kernel invocation will run. Care should be given only to the case where multiple threads modify the same memory location. Operation atomicity should be maintained, but this is a concern shared by multicore CPU software as well.

There is however a significant reason why one needs to understand how threads and warps are executed, and that reason is *performance*. Threads in a warp may ex-

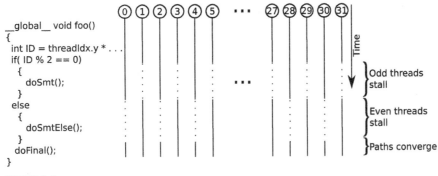

FIGURE 6.4

An illustration of the execution of the kernel in Listing 6.4 by a warp of threads. The dotted lines indicate a stall.

ecute as one, but they operate on different data. So what happens if the result of a conditional operation leads them to different paths? The answer is that all the divergent paths are evaluated (if threads branch into them) in sequence until the paths merge again. The threads that do not follow the path currently being executed are stalled. So, given the kernel in Listing 6.4, the execution of a warp would be as shown in Fig. 6.4.

Listing 6.4: An example of a kernel that would slash the utilization of an SM in half, by keeping half of the threads in a warp stalled.

```
__global__ void foo()
{
    int ID = threadIdx.y * blockDim.x + threadIdx.x;
    if( ID % 2 == 0)
    {
        doSmt();
    }
    else
    {
        doSmtElse();
    }
    doFinal();
}
```

A solution to this problem is discussed in Section 6.7.2.

6.4 CUDA compilation process

In this section we examine the process behind the compilation of a CUDA program into a form that can be deployed on a GPU. The nvcc compiler driver tool certainly makes the process transparent to the programmer, but there are many cases where intimate knowledge of this process can be beneficial and/or critical.

We begin by examining the different file formats that are handled or generated during the compilation process. A peculiarity of `nvcc` is that it will fail to process a file that does not have one of the recognized file prefixes:

- `.cu`: Source files for device and host functions. Since CUDA 5.0 multiple .cu files can be part of a project. Previously, all device code had to be placed in a single file.
- `.cc`, `.cpp`, `.cxx`: C++ source code.
- `.c`: C source code.
- `.h`, `.cuh`: Header files.
- `.o` (Linux), .obj (Windows): Object files. These are the products of the compilation process and they serve as the input of the linking phase.
- `.a` (Linux) .lib (Windows): Static library files. During the linking phase, static libraries become part of the final binary executable file.
- `.so`: Shared object or dynamic library files. These are not embedded in the executable files.
- `.cubin`: CUDA binary file targeting a specific GPU. It should be stressed that NVidia does not preserve binary compatibility across GPU families, as this would seriously hinder its ability to innovate and produce radical new designs.
- `.ptx`: A portable, device assembly format. PTX stands for Parallel Thread Execution. PTX code has to be compiled with a just-in-time compiler (JIT) before execution. PTX files are text files.
- `.fatbin`: CUDA "fat" binary file. It is used to encapsulate multiple PTX and cubin files.

As can be deduced from the above list, a CUDA executable can exist in two forms: a binary one that can only target specific devices (i.e., a specific GPU architecture like Turing or Ampere) and an intermediate assembly one that can target any device by JIT compilation. In the latter case, the PTX Assembler (`ptxas`) performs the compilation during execution time, adding a startup overhead, at least during the first invocation of a kernel.

A CUDA program can still target different devices by embedding multiple cubins into a "fat binary." The appropriate cubin is selected at runtime. If none is found, a PTX file matching the target architecture would be needed. Although PTX files are just intermediate code, they can still target specific features of an architecture (like, e.g., atomic operation support).

Fig. 6.5 shows an abstracted overview of the compilation process (as of CUDA SDK 11). More details are available in NVidia's `nvcc` Reference Guide, located at `${CUDA}/doc/pdf/CUDA_Compiler_Driver_NVCC.pdf`.[8] Since CUDA 11.2, NVidia

---

[8] As a matter of convention, we refer to the location where the CUDA SDK is installed as `${CUDA}`. This is platform-specific and it can be modified during SDK installation. If in doubt, finding the location of the `nvcc` tool will reveal this location, as `nvcc` is typically installed under `${CUDA}/bin`.

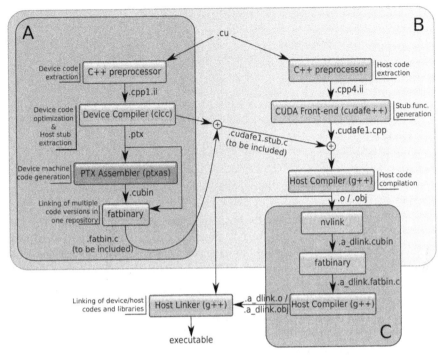

FIGURE 6.5

A high-level view of CUDA's compilation process. The "A" box needs to be executed for each targeted device architecture. The "B" box (which covers "A" as well, but not "C") needs to be executed for each .cu file. The optional "C" part is used when the project contains multiple .cu files, mandating the use of a dedicated linking phase for the device code. Otherwise the generated object file can be directly linked with the system libraries for the generation of the executable, bypassing box "C." The "+" signs indicate that files are combined by using #include preprocessor directives.

is no longer providing downloadable copies of the SDK documentation. These are instead available online at https://docs.nvidia.com/cuda.

The compilation process is subject to change by NVidia between SDK releases. An interested reader can observe the sequence of commands in detail, by calling the nvcc compiler driver with the -dryrun switch, forcing just the display but not the execution of the programs/tools involved as well as the environment parameters used, as shown in the following example:

```
$ nvcc —dryrun hello.cu
#$ _NVVM_BRANCH_=nvvm
#$ _SPACE_=
#$ _CUDART_=cudart
#$ _HERE_=/opt/cuda/bin
#$ _THERE_=/opt/cuda/bin
#$ _TARGET_SIZE_=
```

```
#$ _TARGET_DIR_=
#$ _TARGET_DIR_=targets/x86_64−linux
#$ TOP=/opt/cuda/bin/..
#$ NVVMIR_LIBRARY_DIR=/opt/cuda/bin/../nvvm/libdevice
#$ LD_LIBRARY_PATH=/opt/cuda/bin/../lib
#$ PATH=/opt/cuda/bin/../nvvm/bin:/opt/cuda/bin
#$ INCLUDES="−I/opt/cuda/bin/../targets/x86_64−linux/include"
#$ LIBRARIES=  "−L/opt/cuda/bin/../targets/x86_64−linux/lib/stubs" ↩
   "−L/opt/cuda/bin/../targets/x86_64−linux/lib"
#$ CUDAFE_FLAGS=
#$ PTXAS_FLAGS=
#$ gcc −D__CUDA_ARCH__=520 . . .
```

Fig. 6.5 conveys the essence of the process, which is the separate compilation of the host and device parts, prior to joining them in one executable. The two distinct paths followed (for the device and the host) are connected in multiple places in order to facilitate the generation of the stub host functions. These functions are called upon the invocation of a kernel by the host, to set up and launch the respective device code.

CUDA can embed both cubin and PTX versions of the device code in the produced executable. This is the default behavior, but device code can also reside in a separate file that is loaded during runtime by using the CUDA Driver API.

The tricky part is that nvcc defaults to generating code that adheres to the compute capability 5.2 specification (since SDK 11.0). This default leaves all architectures prior to compute capability 5.2 unsupported, while being suboptimal for more recent GPU designs.

Thankfully, nvcc accepts a number of parameters that control the code generation, allowing us to negate these problems. The most significant of these are:

- -arch: controls the "virtual" architecture that will be used for the generation of the PTX code, i.e., it controls the output of the nvopencc command. The possible values for this parameter are shown in the first column of Table 6.4.
- -code: specifies the actual device that will be targeted by the cubin binary, i.e., it controls the output of the ptxas command. The possible values for this parameter are shown in the second column of Table 6.4.
- -gencode: can combine the two previous settings in one by specifying both arch and code requirements.

As can be seen from Table 6.4, there is a one-to-one correspondence between -arch and -code parameters. While the first one enables the use of specific hardware capabilities during PTX generation, the second one allows the compilation process to adapt to (optimize for) the peculiarities of a specific device and take this into account during the cubin generation.

The -arch parameter can take a single value, but the -code parameter can have a list of values, in which case a cubin is generated for each of the specified machines and embedded in the fat binary. The list of values for the -code parameter can include a single virtual architecture, in which case the corresponding PTX code is also added to the fat binary. Obviously, the architecture targeted by -code should never

Table 6.4 Possible values for the `-arch` and `-code` parameters of the `nvcc` command. As of SDK 11.0, compute capabilities lower than 3.5 are no longer supported.

Virtual architecture (`-arch`)	Streaming multipr. code (`-code`)	Feature enabled
compute_35	sm_35	Dynamic parallelism
compute_50	sm_50	Maxwell support
compute_52	sm_52	
compute_53	sm_53	
compute_60	sm_60	Pascal support
compute_61	sm_61	
compute_62	sm_62	
compute_70	sm_70	Volta support
compute_72	sm_72	
compute_75	sm_75	Turing support
compute_80	sm_80	Ampere support

be below the compute capability of the virtual architecture specified. Otherwise, the compilation will fail.

For example:

- PTX generation code for compute capability 5.0. The fat binary incorporates two cubins, one for sm_70 and one for sm_50 (but no PTX):

```
$ nvcc hello.cu —arch=compute_50 —code=sm_50,sm_70
```

- Same as the above example, with the addition of the PTX code in the fat binary:

```
$ nvcc hello.cu —arch=compute_50 —code=compute_50,sm_50,sm_70
```

Or (note the use of quotes for the code value):

```
$ nvcc hello.cu —gencode arch=compute_50,code=\"compute_50,sm_50,↩
    sm_70\"
```

- An example that fails to compile (cannot turn PTX code for compute capability 7.0 into a cubin for compute capability 5.0):

```
$ nvcc hello.cu —arch=compute_70 —code=sm_50,sm_70
```

- Default compilation settings:

```
$ nvcc hello.cu
```

Are equivalent to:

```
$nvcc hello.cu —arch=compute_52 —code=compute_52,sm_52
```

Or:

```
$ nvcc hello.cu —gencode arch=compute\_52,code=\"compute_52,sm_52↩
  \"
```

• Targeting a Turing device:

```
$ nvcc hello.cu —arch=sm_75
```

Which is shorthand for:

```
$ nvcc hello.cu —arch=compute_75 —code=compute_75,sm_75
```

• Same as the previous example, without a cubin generation (only PTX):

```
nvcc hello.cu —arch=compute_75 —code=compute_75
```

On Linux platforms, nvcc defaults to using the GNU C/C++ compiler (gcc, or g++). On Windows it defaults to using the command-line version of the Visual Studio C/C++ compiler (cl). The compiler program should be in the executable path. Alternative compilers can be tested with the -compiler-bindir option.

6.5 Putting together a CUDA project

The CUDA SDK provides a wealth of sample projects for someone to study CUDA and its application in a large array of domains.[9] Starting a new CUDA project under Linux can be as easy as calling the CUDA C/C++ Project wizard in the Eclipse IDE. Starting with SDK 11, CUDA support can be installed in Eclipse using the SDK-bundled plugin, instead of the previously provided Nsight IDE (an Eclipse derivative). The process is documented in the ${CUDA}/doc/pdf/Nsight_Eclipse_Plugins_Installtion_Guide.pdf file, or at https://docs.nvidia.com/cuda/nsightee-plugins-install-guide/index.html. Windows users can also use Microsoft Visual Studio for working with CUDA.

With the latest CUDA plugin, Eclipse can import an existing CUDA sample project inside a newly created one, allowing for easy experimentation. The process to do this is shown in Fig. 6.6.

For programmers with a more hands-on approach, there is also the possibility of working with a makefile, an arrangement that makes it easier to integrate together a multitude of tools (e.g., MPI, threads, etc.) without the explicit support of an IDE. In this section we will explore this option, as it also enables a closer understanding of the process of building a CUDA application.

---

[9] The sample projects location is OS- and installation-specific. Consult NVidia's documentation and/or your site's administrator for this information.

FIGURE 6.6

Sequence of Eclipse dialogs for creating a project based on the NVidia-supplied samples.

The SDK provides a template project that can be used as a starting point for working with a makefile. This is available under the 0_Simple/template location in samples. Unfortunately, trying to modify the template manually can be a source of mistakes and frustration.

For this reason we proceed to discuss how one can easily set up a makefile from scratch for working with the CUDA Toolkit.

CUDA supports the split of the device source code into multiple files. This is obviously beneficial for the structure and maintainability of a project, although certain limitations apply:

- No PTX version of the code can be embedded in the fat binary.
- Device code modules that are compiled separately must be compiled with the same parameters (-code) and must produce *relocatable device code* by specifying the nvcc's option -rdc=true. The combination of the -c (compile only) and -rdc=true switches can be shortened to -dc.

The process for *separate compilation* requires the use of the "C"-labeled box in Fig. 6.5 that merges together/links all the device code in a single fat binary. An example of this augmented process is shown in Fig. 6.7.

Fortunately, most of the details are taken care of by nvcc with the use of appropriate parameters, effectively turning the process of going from a bunch of .cu files to an executable into a black-box. Thankfully, NVidia has made sure that many of nvcc's

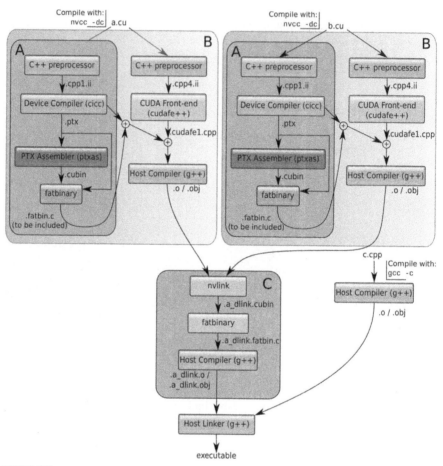

FIGURE 6.7

An example of CUDA's separate compilation process. It is assumed that the project is made up of three source code files: two containing device code (`a.cu` and `b.cu`) and one containing host code only (`c.cpp`). The box labels ("A," etc.) match the ones used in Fig. 6.5.

parameters match the ones that are typically used by the GNU C/C++ compiler. These include `-o` for specifying the output destination file, `-l` for specifying libraries, `-c` for restricting the process to compilation but not linking, `-O` for optimization, `-g` for debugging information inclusion, `-I` for specifying include file directories, and `-L` for specifying library file directories.

As an example, let us consider a project made up of the following source code files, that will run on a Turing device:

- `d.cuh`: Header file for the device functions defined in `a.cu` and `b.cu`.
- `a.cu`: File containing a set of kernels.

- `b.cu`: File containing another set of kernels.
- `hostFE.cu`: File containing the host functions that call the kernels in `a.cu` and `b.cu`.
- `main.cpp`: C++ code that calls the front-end functions in `hostFE.cu`, using a C++11 thread.

The compilation can be done with the following sequence of commands (note that include and library directories are obviously platform- and system-specific and that the "`-device-c`" switch is equivalent to "`-dc`"):

```
# Compile file a.cu
nvcc —device—c —arch=sm_75 —o a.o a.cu

# Compile file b.cu
nvcc —device—c —arch=sm_75 —o b.o b.cu

# Compile front—end file hostFE.cu, that calls the kernels in a.cu ←
    and b.cu
nvcc —device—c —arch=sm_75 —o hostFE.o hostFE.cu

# Compile file main.cpp
g++ —c main.cpp —fPIC

# Link everything together. Notice the extra option for the threads ←
    library. Multiple lines are used to highlight the sets of ←
    different switches and options
nvcc —rdc=true —arch=sm_75    \\
    —L/usr/lib/x86_64—linux—gnu —lpthread    \\
    main.o a.o b.o hostFE.o —o demo_prj
```

The creation of a makefile capable of utilizing CUDA and other tools in the same project is discussed in Appendix E.3.

6.6 Memory hierarchy

As discussed in Section 6.1, GPU memory is typically disjoint from the host's memory. So passing chunks of data to a kernel in the form of a pointer to an array in the host's memory is not possible[10]:

```
int *mydata = new int[N];
. . . // populating the array
foo<<<grid, block>>>(mydata, N);   // NOT POSSIBLE!
```

---

[10] This is not entirely accurate, but special provisions are required to enable direct device access to host memory. Read Section 6.7.4.2 for the details.

Instead, data have to be explicitly copied from the host to the device and back once the required processing has been completed. This entails the allocation of two regions of memory for every array that needs to be processed on the device:

1. One region on the host. This can be allocated with the new operator or the malloc and calloc functions, as usual. Smart pointers can be used as well.
2. One region on the device. This can be allocated and released with the cudaMalloc and cudaFree functions. The proper coupling of cudaMalloc with cudaFree calls cannot be stressed enough. Leaked device memory cannot be automatically recovered, given the absence of a full-blown operating system/garbage collector running on the device. The only remedy is a reboot!

```
// Allocate memory on the device.
cudaError_t cudaMalloc ( void** devPtr,    // Host pointer address,
                                           // where the address of
                                           // the allocated device
                                           // memory will be stored
                         size_t size )     // Size in bytes of the
                                           // requested memory block

// Frees memory on the device.
cudaError_t cudaFree ( void* devPtr );     // Parameter is the host
                                           // pointer address
                                           // returned by cudaMalloc
```

In the listings that follow, in order to keep track of what kind of memory each pointer references, we prefix the pointers to host memory with h_ or h and the pointers to device memory with d_ or d.

The transfer of data between the two memory spaces can be done with the cudaMemcpy function:

```
// Copies data between host and device.
cudaError_t cudaMemcpy ( void* dst,        // Destination block ↩
    address
                         const void* src,   // Source block address
                         size_t count,      // Size in bytes
                         cudaMemcpyKind kind )  // Direction of copy.
```

cudaError_t is an enumerated type. If a CUDA function returns anything other than cudaSuccess, which is a symbolic name for 0, an error has occurred.

The cudaMemcpyKind parameter of cudaMemcpy is also an enumerated type. The kind parameter specifies the direction of the copy, and it can take one of the following values:

- cudaMemcpyHostToHost = 0, host to host;
- cudaMemcpyHostToDevice = 1, host to device;
- cudaMemcpyDeviceToHost = 2, device to host;
- cudaMemcpyDeviceToDevice = 3, device to device (for multi-GPU installations);

- `cudaMemcpyDefault` = 4, used when Unified Virtual Address space capability is available (see Section 6.7).

A simple data transfer example is shown in Listing 6.5, in the form of a vector addition program. The host is responsible for generating two random integer arrays that are passed to the device. Upon completion of the vector addition on the device, the result data are transferred back to the host:

Listing 6.5: Adding two 2000-element vectors using CUDA.

```
1   // File : vectorAdd.cu
2   . . .
3   #include <cuda.h>
4   #include <memory>
5
6   using namespace std;
7
8   static const int BLOCK_SIZE = 256;
9   static const int N = 2000;
10
11  #define CUDA_CHECK_RETURN( value ) {                                 \
12      cudaError_t _m_cudaStat = value;                                 \
13      if (_m_cudaStat != cudaSuccess) {                                \
14          fprintf(stderr, "Error %s at line %d in file %s\n", \
15                  cudaGetErrorString(_m_cudaStat),                     \
16                  __LINE__, __FILE__);                                 \
17          exit(1);                                                     \
18      } }
19
20  __global__ void vadd (int *a, int *b, int *c, int N)
21  {
22    int myID = blockIdx.x * blockDim.x + threadIdx.x;
23    if (myID < N)
24      c[myID] = a[myID] + b[myID];
25  }
26
27  int main (void)
28  {
29    unique_ptr<int[]> ha, hb, hc; // host (h*) and
30    int *da, *db, *dc;            // device (d*) pointers
31    int i;
32
33    // host memory allocation
34    ha = make_unique<int[]>(N);
35    hb = make_unique<int[]>(N);
36    hc = make_unique<int[]>(N);
37
38    // device memory allocation
39    CUDA_CHECK_RETURN (cudaMalloc ((void **) &da, sizeof (int) * N));
40    CUDA_CHECK_RETURN (cudaMalloc ((void **) &db, sizeof (int) * N));
41    CUDA_CHECK_RETURN (cudaMalloc ((void **) &dc, sizeof (int) * N));
42
43    for (i = 0; i < N; i++)
```

```
44        {
45          ha[i] = rand () % 10000;
46          hb[i] = rand () % 10000;
47        }
48
49    // data transfer, host -> device
50    CUDA_CHECK_RETURN (cudaMemcpy (da, ha.get (), sizeof (int) * N, ←
            cudaMemcpyHostToDevice));
51    CUDA_CHECK_RETURN (cudaMemcpy (db, hb.get (), sizeof (int) * N, ←
            cudaMemcpyHostToDevice));
52
53    int grid = ceil (N * 1.0 / BLOCK_SIZE);
54    vadd <<< grid, BLOCK_SIZE >>> (da, db, dc, N);
55
56    CUDA_CHECK_RETURN (cudaDeviceSynchronize ());
57    // Wait for the GPU launched work to complete
58    CUDA_CHECK_RETURN (cudaGetLastError ());
59
60    // data transfer, device -> host
61    CUDA_CHECK_RETURN (cudaMemcpy (hc.get (), dc, sizeof (int) * N, ←
            cudaMemcpyDeviceToHost));
62
63    // correctness check
64    for (i = 0; i < N; i++)
65      {
66        if (hc[i] != ha[i] + hb[i])
67          printf ("Error at index %i : %i VS %i\n", i, hc[i], ha[i] + ←
                hb[i]);
68      }
69
70    CUDA_CHECK_RETURN (cudaFree ((void *) da));
71    CUDA_CHECK_RETURN (cudaFree ((void *) db));
72    CUDA_CHECK_RETURN (cudaFree ((void *) dc));
73    CUDA_CHECK_RETURN (cudaDeviceReset ());
74
75    return 0;
76  }
```

One striking feature of the above program is the use of the CUDA_CHECK_RETURN preprocessor macro, which was generated by the Nsight IDE. Similar macros are employed by the CUDA SDK sample programs aiming to catch and report a CUDA call failure as early as possible. Once a CUDA function returns a non-zero value, the program is terminated after printing out to the console the source code file name and line where the error occurred.

The macro can be made to call a function to the same effect, as done in the following code, which is part of the helper_cuda.h header file employed in the SDK 11.0 sample projects:

```
#define checkCudaErrors(val) check((val), #val, __FILE__, __LINE__)

template <typename T>
```

```
void check(T result, char const *const func, const char *const file,
        int const line) {
  if (result) {
    fprintf(stderr, "CUDA error at %s:%d code=%d(%s) \"%s\" \n", ↵
        file, line,
            static_cast <unsigned int >(result), _cudaGetErrorEnum(↵
                result), func);
    exit(EXIT_FAILURE);
  }
}
```

These macros clearly obscure the program structure and for this reason we do not use them in the remaining sample programs of this chapter. However, it is *very strongly recommended that these macros are used in practice.* An erroneous call can produce a cascade of errors which can go undetected otherwise.

Other key points of the above program are:

- The program manages six pointers, three smart ones pointing to host memory addresses and three pointing to device memory addresses. By convention and in order to easily identify them, host pointers are prefixed by "h" and device pointers by "d."
- Data are copied from the host to the device prior to calling the kernel (lines 50 and 51) and from the device to the host after the kernel completes (line 61). The device memory that holds our data is called **global memory**. The reservation of the required space in global memory is done on lines 39–41.
- Each CUDA thread calculates just a single element of the result vector (line 24). This is not an advisable design in general, but it clearly illustrates that CUDA threads can be extremely lightweight.
- Each thread calculates its global position/ID in the grid (line 22) and uses it to index the parts of the input that it will operate upon.
- Each core proceeds with the calculation only if its ID permits (line 23). This check is required when the workload is not evenly distributed between the thread blocks. In this case we have a grid of eight blocks (lines 53 and 54), but in the last block of 256 threads, we have an "assignment" for only $2000 - 7 \times 256 = 208$ of them. An illustration of the grid/block arrangement and how they relate to the input arrays is shown in Fig. 6.8.
- The cudaGetLastError function on line 58 is used to detect any errors that occurred during the execution of the kernel.
- The cudaDeviceReset call of line 73 destroys and cleans up all resources associated with the current device in the current process. This should be called only before program termination.
- Lines 64–68 check the results generated by the GPU against the ones calculated by the CPU for the same input. This validation step is required during the development phase in order to detect any anomalies introduced by erroneous algorithms/coding, rounding errors, or GPU failure to conform to the IEEE Standard for Floating-Point Arithmetic (IEEE 754). Fortunately, compute capability 2.x and

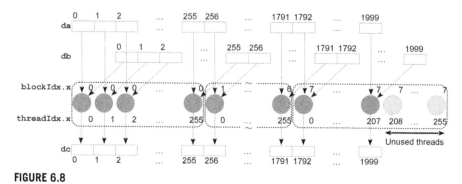

FIGURE 6.8

The computation conducted by the vector addition code in Listing 6.5.

above devices comply to IEEE 754,[11] but this does not guarantee that the GPU-generated results will match the CPU ones, as modern CPUs tend to exceed the requirements of IEEE 754 in terms of accuracy. It is obvious that such checks should not be carried over to the production version of a software system.

GPUs follow a different paradigm from CPUs in the architectural design of their memory subsystem. In order for CPUs to operate at full speed, they need to have quick access to seemingly random data locations in main memory. Contemporary main memory technology (DDR4 and even DDR5 RAM) is relatively slow, thus requiring the incorporation of big on-chip memory caches (multiple levels of caches are a common feature). For example, AMD's Ryzen 9 5950X has a total of 73 MiB of on-chip cache, organized in three levels.

On the other hand, GPUs as part of their job to filter and transform huge amounts of graphical information need to process big collections of contiguous data that are to be read and operated upon once, without requiring that they are kept on chip for subsequent operations. This means that GPUs benefit from big data buses and they can do with small or no on-chip cache memories. This picture has changed slightly since the introduction of CUDA, with on-chip memories getting bigger and incorporating caches in order to more efficiently support generic computation.

The biggest discrepancy between CPU and GPU memory organizations lies in the fact that the GPU memory hierarchy is not transparent to the programmer. GPUs have faster on-chip memory which occupies a separate address space than the off-chip one. CUDA programs can – and should – take advantage of this faster memory by moving frequently used data to it. CPU programs can be designed to exploit cache locality (e.g., by restricting the amount of data they work on at a time, so that they all fit in the cache), but in the GPU world we have to explicitly manage data movement between the two types of memory.

---

[11] A very useful discussion on the sensitive issue of IEEE 754 compliance is available at https://developer.nvidia.com/sites/default/files/akamai/cuda/files/NVIDIA-CUDA-Floating-Point.pdf.

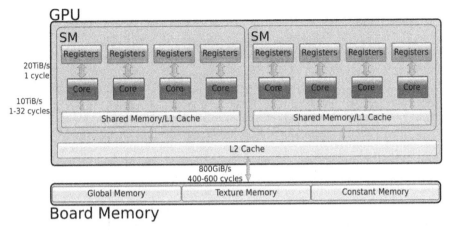

FIGURE 6.9

GPU memory hierarchy. Each bus is labeled with typical bandwidth and latency values. The global memory latency can be as low as 32 cycles if an L1 cache hit happens [40].

Data movement between the host and the device can only involve what is identified as **global memory**. GPUs also employ other types of memory, most of them residing on-chip and in separate address spaces. These, along with their typical performance characteristics, are illustrated in Fig. 6.9 [40]. Each of the memory types has a unique set of characteristics that make it suitable for particular tasks:

- **Local memory/registers**: Used for holding automatic variables.
- **Shared memory**: Fast on-chip RAM that is used for holding frequently used data. The shared on-chip memory can be used for data exchange between the cores of the same SM.
- **Cache memory**: Cache memory is transparent to the programmer. Level 1 cache and shared memory are actually part of the same fast on-chip RAM that each SM has, and it is SM-specific (only the threads running on that SM can use it). This RAM is divided and designated to act as cache or shared memory based on programmer directives. Level 2 cache is shared among the SMs.
- **Global memory**: Main part of the off-chip memory. High capacity, but relatively slow. The only part of the memory that is accessible to the host via the CUDA library functions.
- **Texture and surface memory**: Part of the off-chip memory. Its contents are handled by special hardware that permits the fast implementation of some filtering operations.
- **Constant memory**: Part of the off-chip memory. As its name suggests, it is read-only. However, it is cached on-chip, which means it can provide a performance boost.

Table 6.5 summarizes the different kinds of memories from the point of view of the lifetime and scope of the data residing in them.

Table 6.5 Summary of the memory hierarchy characteristics.

Type	Location	Access	Scope	Lifetime
Register	On-chip	R/W	Thread	Thread
Local	Off-chip	R/W	Thread	Thread
Shared	On-chip	R/W	Block	Block
Global	Off-chip	R/W	Grid	Controlled by host
Constant	Off-chip	R	Grid	Controlled by host
Texture	Off-chip	R	Grid	Controlled by host

In the following sections we discuss how these different memory types can be effectively incorporated in our kernel designs, with the ultimate goal of extracting more GPU performance. The optimization of their use is reserved for later sections, allowing the reader to absorb the information at a more relaxed pace.

6.6.1 Local memory/registers

As discussed in Section 6.3, each multiprocessor gets a set of registers that are split amongst the resident threads. These are used to hold automatic variables declared in a kernel, speeding up operations that would otherwise require access to the global or shared memories.

A device's compute capability determines the maximum number of registers that can be used per thread. If this number is exceeded, local variables are allocated in the runtime stack which resides in off-chip memory and it is thus slow to work with. This off-chip memory is frequently called **local memory**, but it is actually the global memory that is used for this purpose. The "local" specifier just conveys the fact that whatever resides there is only accessible to a particular thread. Local memory locations can be cached by the L1 cache, so performance may not suffer much, but the outcome is application-specific.

The NVidia compiler will automatically decide on which variables will be allocated to registers and which will *spill over* to local memory. The nvcc compiler driver can be instructed to report the outcome of this allocation process with the -Xptxas -v or -ptxas-option=-v switches:

```
$ nvcc —Xptxas —v warpFixMultiway.cu
ptxas info: 14 bytes gmem
ptxas info: Compiling entry function '_Z3foov' for 'sm_30'
ptxas info: Function properties for _Z3foov
    8 bytes stack frame, 0 bytes spill stores, 0 bytes spill loads
ptxas info: Used 14 registers, 320 bytes cmem[0]
```

In the above example, the generated code uses 14 registers and 0 bytes are spilled over to local memory.

The number of registers used per thread influences the maximum number of threads that can be resident at an SM. For example, let us assume that a kernel is using 100 registers and it is invoked as blocks of 256 threads, which means each block requires $100 \cdot 256 = 25{,}600$ registers. If the target GPU for running the kernel is a Turing chip (e.g., RTX 2080), sporting 64k registers per SM, then each SM could have only two resident blocks (requiring $2 \cdot 25,600 = 51,200$ registers) as three would exceed the available register space ($3 \cdot 25,600 = 76,800 > 65,536$). This in turn means that each SM could have $2 \cdot 256 = 512$ resident threads running, which is well below the maximum limit of 1024 threads per SM for this device. This undermines the GPU's capability to hide the latency of memory operations by running other ready warps.

In fact, NVidia calls occupancy the ratio of resident warps over the maximum possible resident warps:

$$occupancy = \frac{resident\_warps}{maximum\_warps}. \tag{6.1}$$

In our example, occupancy is equal to $\frac{2 \cdot \frac{256 \text{ threads}}{32 \text{ threads/warp}}}{32 \text{ warps}} = \frac{16}{32} = 50\%$. In general, an occupancy close to 1 is desirable, although other factors also influence the performance that can be "extracted" from a GPU. In order to raise the occupancy in our example, we could reduce the number of required registers by rewriting the kernel code. Getting a GPU with a bigger register file is not an option at the moment, as the only devices with more registers (128k per SM) were the compute capability 3.7 ones. If the required registers per kernel fell to 64, then we could have four resident blocks (requiring a total of $4 \cdot 64 \cdot 256 = 65,536$ registers), resulting in an occupancy of $\frac{4 \cdot 8}{32} = 50\%$, as each block is made up of eight warps.

NVidia provides an occupancy calculator tool in the form of an Excel spreadsheet[12] that allows the calculation of the occupancy, given the characteristics of the kernel and the target device. This tool provides not only single point calculations (e.g., what is the current occupancy), but it also provides guidance about how to modify the kernel and deployment characteristics by plotting the resulting effects on the occupancy.

6.6.2 Shared memory

Shared memory is a block of fast on-chip RAM that is shared between the cores of an SM. Each SM gets its own block of shared memory, which can be viewed as a user-managed L1 cache. Shared memory and L1 cache are actually part of the same on-chip memory that can be programmatically partitioned in different ways. In compute capability 7.5 devices, each SM is equipped with 96 KiB RAM that can be partitioned as 32 KiB/64 KiB (32 KiB for shared and 64 KiB for L1) or 64 KiB/32 KiB to serve these two roles. In compute capability 8.0 devices, each SM comes with 192 KiB of memory, with the option of dedicating 164 KiB to shared memory, leaving the rest to serve as L1. For the less fortunate ones who cannot get their hands on an A100, RTX 3000 series GPUs (compute capability 8.6) have SMs that can dedicate 100 KiB to shared memory.

---

[12] Available at $\{CUDA\}/tools/CUDA_Occupancy_Calculator.xls.

A programmer can specify the *preferred* device-wide arrangement by calling the cudaDeviceSetCacheConfig function. A *preferred* kernel-specific arrangement can be also set with the cudaFuncSetCacheConfig function. Both of these functions set only a preference. The CUDA runtime will ultimately decide for the appropriate configuration, given the shared memory requirements of a kernel.

Shared memory can be used in the following capacities:

- As a holding place for very frequently used data that would otherwise require global memory access (read/write operations), e.g., a counter.
- As a fast *mirror* of data that reside in global memory, if they are to be accessed multiple times (for reading access), e.g., a lookup table.
- As a fast way for cores within an SM, to share data.

The first two items in the above list would be naturally handled by the cache memory in CPUs. So, why do we not let the GPU cache handle these as well? There are two considerations: firstly GPU cache memory is limited in size and fragmented (each SM has its own L1), and secondly shared memory allows us to programmatically select what will stay on-chip for further use. It is always about eking out the maximum performance.

So, how can one specify that the holding place of some data will be the shared memory of the SM, and not the global memory of the device?

The answer is: via the __shared__ specifier. Shared memory can be statically or dynamically allocated. **Static allocation** can take place if the size of the required arrays is known at compile time. **Dynamic allocation** is needed if shared memory requirements can be only calculated at runtime, i.e., upon kernel invocation. To facilitate this mode of operation, the execution configuration has an alternative syntax, with a third parameter holding the size in bytes of the shared memory to be reserved.

For example, let us consider the problem of calculating the histogram of a collection of integers, i.e., counting the number of elements that belong to each one of a set of disjoint categories or bins/buckets. The histogram is a popular tool in image processing, so we will proceed to develop our example in this context.

If we were to calculate the histogram of a grayscale image consisting of N pixels, each taking up one byte in an array (in), the CPU code for performing this task could be in the form of this function:

Listing 6.6: CPU histogram calculation.

```
1  // File : histogram/histogram.cu
2  . . .
3  void CPU_histogram (unsigned char *in, int N, int *h, int bins)
4  {
5    int i;
6    // initialize histogram counts
7    for (i = 0; i < bins; i++)
8      h[i] = 0;
9
```

```
10    // accummulate counts
11    for (i = 0; i < N; i++)
12      h[in[i]]++;
13  }
```

The `bins`-sized array `h` holds the result of the calculation. Obviously, the one byte per pixel restricts the number of categories: $bins \leq 256$.

A multi-threaded solution to this problem would require the partitioning of the image data into disjoint sets, the calculation of partial histograms by each thread, and finally the consolidation of the partial histograms into the complete one.

The CUDA solution described below follows the same guidelines more or less, but with some key differences that go beyond the explicit data movement between the host and device memories:

- The data partitioning is *implicit*. All the spawned CUDA threads have access to all the image data, but go through them using a different starting point and an appropriate stride that makes it possible to cover all the data, while coalescing memory accesses (more on this topic in Section 6.7). This difference is highlighted in Fig. 6.10.
- To speed up the update of the local counts, a "local" array is set up in shared memory. Because multiple threads may access its locations at any time, atomic addition operations have to be used for modifying its contents.
- Because threads execute in blocks and each block executes warp-by-warp, explicit synchronization of the threads must take place between the discrete phases of the kernel, e.g., between initializing the shared-memory histogram array and starting to calculate the histogram, etc.

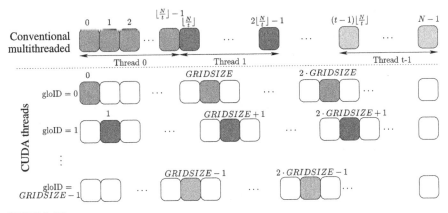

FIGURE 6.10

An illustrated comparison between the input data, access patterns of a multi-threaded CPU solution with *t* threads, for histogram calculation, and a CUDA solution. The symbols used reference the variables of Listing 6.7.

- The global histogram array, i.e., the one that holds the final result, is also updated concurrently by multiple threads. Atomic addition operations have to be employed so that the results stay consistent.

If the number of bins are known a priori, then we can allocate a fixed amount of local memory per block, as shown in the Listing below. The GPU_histogram_static kernel assumes that its execution configuration calls for a 1D grid of 1D blocks:

Listing 6.7: CUDA histogram calculation kernel, using **static** shared memory allocation.

```
14   // File : histogram/histogram.cu
15   . . .
16   static const int BINS = 256;
17
18   __global__ void GPU_histogram_static (int *in, int N, int *h)
19   {
20     int gloID = blockIdx.x * blockDim.x + threadIdx.x;
21     int locID = threadIdx.x;
22     int GRIDSIZE = gridDim.x * blockDim.x;   // total number of threads
23     __shared__ int localH[BINS];             // shared allocation
24     int i;
25
26     // initialize the local, shared-memory bins
27     for (i = locID; i < BINS; i += blockDim.x)
28       localH[i] = 0;
29
30     // wait for all warps to complete the previous step
31     __syncthreads ();
32
33     //start processing the image data
34     for (i = gloID; i < N; i += GRIDSIZE)
35       {
36         int temp = in[i];
37         atomicAdd (localH + (temp & 0xFF), 1);
38         atomicAdd (localH + ((temp >> 8) & 0xFF), 1);
39         atomicAdd (localH + ((temp >> 16) & 0xFF), 1);
40         atomicAdd (localH + ((temp >> 24) & 0xFF), 1);
41       }
42
43     // wait for all warps to complete the local calculations, before ↩
              updating the global counts
44     __syncthreads ();
45
46     // use atomic operations to add the local findings to the global ↩
              memory bins
47     for (i = locID; i < BINS; i += blockDim.x)
48       atomicAdd (h + i, localH[i]);
49   }
```

The array declared as __shared__ on line 23 above is shared between all the threads of a block. Although it is an automatic variable, it is not thread-specific. As such, all the threads in the block contribute to its initialization with the loop of lines 27 and 28. Other key observations about the structure of GPU_histogram_static are:

- Each thread calculates its position in the block it belongs to (locID) and its position in the grid (gloID). The former is used as a starting point in the initialization of the localH array (line 27) and the updating of the h array in global memory (line 47). The gloID variable is used as a starting point in scanning the image data (line 34). The total number of threads (GRIDSIZE) is used as a stride.
- The image data are passed as individual pixels to the CPU_histogram function, but as groups of four in GPU_histogram_static (in is passed as an array of int). The goal is to speed up/optimize the access of data from global memory.[13] Having lines 37–40 as the equivalent of the single statement on line 12 is effectively a partial unrolling of the loop. The bitwise shifts and ANDs of these lines isolate the individual pixel values, which are subsequently used as offsets to the base of the localH array.
- The peculiarities of CUDA's execution model mean that (a) the completion of phases must be followed by explicit synchronization (lines 31 and 44) to ensure the validity of data and (b) shared locations must be *atomically updated* (lines 37–40 and 48) to ensure **linearizability**.

The __syncthreads() function can be called inside a kernel to act as a barrier for all the threads in a *block*. The cudaDeviceSynchronize() used in a previous section is called by the host to wait for a *grid* of threads to complete.

The atomicAdd is an overloaded function that belongs to a set of atomic operations supported mostly by devices of compute capability 2.x and above. The int version shown below has analogous versions for unsigned int, long long int, and float operands:

```
int atomicAdd(int* address,  // Location to modify
              int val);      // Value to add
```

If the number of histogram bins is not known, then the shared memory has to be allocated by the CUDA runtime based on the execution configuration parameters, as shown in Listing 6.8.

Listing 6.8: CUDA histogram calculation kernel, using **dynamic** shared memory allocation.

```
50  // File : histogram/histogram.cu
51  . . .
52  __global__ void GPU_histogram_dynamic (int *in, int N, int *h, int ↩
       bins)
53  {
54    int gloID = blockIdx.x * blockDim.x + threadIdx.x;
```

---

[13] The same could be done in the CPU code of Listing 6.6, but it was left on purpose in the simplest, unoptimized form possible.

```
55    int locID = threadIdx.x;
56    extern __shared__ int localH[];
57    int GRIDSIZE = gridDim.x * blockDim.x;
58    int i;
59
60    // initialize the local bins
61    for (i = locID; i < bins; i += blockDim.x)
62      localH[i] = 0;
63
64    // wait for all warps to complete the previous step
65    __syncthreads ();
66
67    //start processing the image data
68    for (i = gloID; i < N; i += GRIDSIZE)
69      {
70        int temp = in[i];
71        atomicAdd (localH + (temp & 0xFF), 1);
72        atomicAdd (localH + ((temp >> 8) & 0xFF), 1);
73        atomicAdd (localH + ((temp >> 16) & 0xFF), 1);
74        atomicAdd (localH + ((temp >> 24) & 0xFF), 1);
75      }
76
77    // wait for all warps to complete the local calculations, before ↩
             updating the global counts
78    __syncthreads ();
79
80    // use atomic operations to add the local findings to the global ↩
             memory bins
81    for (i = locID; i < bins; i += blockDim.x)
82      atomicAdd (h + i, localH[i]);
83  }
```

The main difference between kernel `GPU_histogram_dynamic` and `GPU_histogram_static` lies on lines 23 and 56 and the use of the `extern` keyword. The reservation of shared memory and the initialization of the `localH` pointer take place by the CUDA runtime, when the kernel is invoked on line 119. The change in the kernel signature was necessitated by the need to also pass the number of bins, which are in turn calculated (line 99) after an image is read (line 88):

Listing 6.9: `main()` function for the memory management and launch of the kernels in Listings 6.7 and 6.8.

```
84  // File : histogram/histogram.cu
85  . . .
86  int main (int argc, char **argv)
87  {
88    PGMImage inImg (argv[1]);
89
90    int *d_in, *h_in;
91    int *d_hist, *h_hist, *cpu_hist;
92    int i, N, bins;
93
```

```
94    h_in = (int *) inImg.pixels;
95    N = ceil ((inImg.x_dim * inImg.y_dim) / 4.0);
96
97    bins = inImg.num_colors + 1;
98    h_hist = (int *) malloc (bins * sizeof (int));
99    cpu_hist = (int *) malloc (bins * sizeof (int));
100
101   // CPU calculation used for testing
102   CPU_histogram (inImg.pixels, inImg.x_dim * inImg.y_dim, cpu_hist, ←
          bins);
103
104   cudaMalloc ((void **) &d_in, sizeof (int) * N);
105   cudaMalloc ((void **) &d_hist, sizeof (int) * bins);
106   cudaMemcpy (d_in, h_in, sizeof (int) * N, cudaMemcpyHostToDevice);
107   cudaMemset (d_hist, 0, bins * sizeof (int));
108
109   GPU_histogram_static <<< 16, 256 >>> (d_in, N, d_hist);
110   cudaDeviceSynchronize ();        // Wait for the GPU launched work to ←
          complete
111
112   cudaMemcpy (h_hist, d_hist, sizeof (int) * bins, ←
          cudaMemcpyDeviceToHost);
113
114   for (i = 0; i < BINS; i++)
115     if (cpu_hist[i] != h_hist[i])
116       printf ("Calculation mismatch (static) at : %i\n", i);
117
118   cudaMemset (d_hist, 0, bins * sizeof (int));
119   GPU_histogram_dynamic <<< 16, 256, bins * sizeof (int) >>> (d_in, ←
          N, d_hist, bins);
120   cudaDeviceSynchronize ();        // Wait for the GPU launched work to ←
          complete
121
122   cudaMemcpy (h_hist, d_hist, sizeof (int) * bins, ←
          cudaMemcpyDeviceToHost);
123
124   for (i = 0; i < BINS; i++)
125     if (cpu_hist[i] != h_hist[i])
126       printf ("Calculation mismatch (dynamic) at : %i\n", i);
127
128   cudaFree ((void *) d_in);
129   cudaFree ((void *) d_hist);
130   free (h_hist);
131   free (cpu_hist);
132   cudaDeviceReset ();
133
134   return 0;
135 }
```

The PGMImage class used in the above code is available in the common directory and it facilitates access to Portable Gray Map (PGM) formatted images. The class constructor allows the reading of a PGM image from a file, and public data members allow access to the image data, such as the dimensions (x_dim, y_dim), the number of gray levels allowed (num_colors), and the actual pixels (*pixels).

The main function is responsible for the allocation of the host and device arrays, the movement of data between the host and device memories, and the initialization of the device histogram array (lines 107 and 118) via the cudaMemset function, which is modeled after the standard C library function memset:

```
cudaError_t cudaMemset (void *devPtr, // pointer to device memory
                        int value,    // value to set each byte
                        size_t count) // number of bytes
```

A question that arises is: *what if a kernel needs to dynamically allocate multiple arrays in shared memory?* The solution to this problem is awkward: the size of all the arrays needs to be passed as a parameter to the execution configuration. Subsequently, this lump of shared memory needs to be divided manually between the arrays that use it, once the kernel starts executing.

As an example, let us consider a kernel that needs to set up three dynamically allocated arrays in shared memory: int a[K], double b[L], and unsigned int c[M]. Then, the code snippet shown in Listing 6.10 would suffice.

Listing 6.10: An example of dynamically setting up multiple shared-memory arrays.

```
1  __global__ void foo(int *arraySizes)
2  {
3      int K,L,M;
4      extern __shared__ int a[];
5      double *b;
6      unsigned int *c;
7
8      K = arraySizes[0];
9      L = arraySizes[1];
10     M = arraySizes[2];
11
12     b = (double *)(&a[K]);
13     c = (unsigned int *)(&b[L]);
14     . . .
15 }
16
17 int main (void)
18 {
19     int K=100, L=20, M=15;
20     int ha[3]={K,L,M};
21     int *da;
22
23     cudaMalloc ((void **) &da, sizeof (int) * 3);
24     cudaMemcpy(da, ha, sizeof (int) * 3, cudaMemcpyHostToDevice);
25     foo<<< 1, 256, K*sizeof(int) + L*sizeof(double) + M*sizeof(↩
           unsigned int) >>>(da);
26     . . .
27 }
```

Bank

	0	1	2	3	4	5	6	7	8	9	10	11	12	13	14	15
	0	4	8	12	16	20	24	28	32	36	40	44	48	52	56	60
	64	68	72	76	80	84	88	92	96	100	104	108	112	116	120	124
	128	132	136	140	144	148	152	156	160	164	168	172	176	180	184	188

(Address, left axis)

FIGURE 6.11

An illustration of how shared memory is divided into banks. For brevity only 16 banks are shown.

The array sizes could be passed as parameters to the kernel (as is done above), or they could be calculated inside the kernel making the passing of the `arraySizes` parameter redundant. In both cases, the total of required shared memory must be reserved upon invoking the kernel (line 25 above). The array sizes can then be used inside the kernel to infer the beginning of each array (lines 12 and 13). As an alternative, the `arraySizes` parameter could hold the starting offset in bytes of each array, allowing appropriate padding to be incorporated for aligned memory accesses. A third alternative would be to pass K, L, and M as individual parameters.

Another reason that would mandate the use of dynamic allocation of shared memory is the need to allocate data in excess of 48 KiB. Maxwell GPUs were the first to have 96 KiB shared memory per SM, but NVidia restricted access to one thread block to just 48 KiB. With two resident thread blocks, one could of course utilize the whole of shared memory, having each block use its own dedicated 48 KiB chunk.

In Volta/Turing and Ampere devices this restriction also exists for *statically* allocated shared memory. If dynamic allocation is used, Turing devices can use up to 64 KiB per block, Volta up to 96 KiB per block, Ampere compute capability 8.0 up to 163 KiB per block (not 164 KiB as 1 KiB is reserved for system use), and Ampere compute capability 8.6 up to 99 KiB, via the following call:

```
// Device code
__global__ void fooKernel(. . .) {
. . .
// Host code
int maxbytes = 98304; // 96 KiB for Volta
cudaFuncSetAttribute(fooKernel, ↵
    cudaFuncAttributeMaxDynamicSharedMemorySize, maxbytes);
fooKernel <<<gridDim, blockDim, maxbytes>>>(. . .);
```

A feature of shared memory that is not utilized by our histogram example is its division into **banks**. The division is driven by the fact that shared memory has to be accessed simultaneously by multiple cores. Compute capability 2.0 devices and above have 32 banks, while all earlier devices had 16 banks. Fig. 6.11 illustrates the bank concept.

A collision is produced when two or more threads try to access different addresses that reside in the same bank. This in turn forces these threads to go in sequence.

However, unlike access to global memory, access to shared memory does not cause the execution of another ready warp, in order to hide the delay, which makes shared-memory bank collisions a problem.

Section 6.7.3 provides more information on the handling of banks and how a modification of our histogram example can eliminate bank conflicts.

6.6.3 Constant memory

Constant memory may sound like a variation of ROM, but in reality it is just a portion of the off-chip device memory that is dedicated for holding constant data. Current specifications restrict constant memory to 64 KiB. Constant memory offers two important characteristics: firstly it is cached and secondly it supports broadcasting a single value to all the threads of a warp. NVidia GPUs provide 8 KiB of cache memory per multiprocessor for the contents of the constant memory (compute capability 6.0 is an exception with just 4 KiB). These characteristics make constant memory a good candidate for placing frequently reused data that are not to be modified, saving in the process the precious little shared memory available.

Constant memory also serves for holding the function parameters that are passed to a kernel. These parameters cannot exceed a total maximum of 4 KiB.

A variable can be allocated in constant memory, via the __constant__ specifier.[14] For example:

```
__constant__ int ITERLIMIT=1000;
```

Since the introduction of the Fermi architecture, all NVidia GPU offerings sport an L2 cache which handles all memory transactions and not just the ones involving constant memory. This makes the use of constant memory specifically a less attractive prospect on newer machines.

The only serious restriction involves the 64 KiB size limit. If the data to be processed exceed this limit, then one solution to making them available via the constant memory is to break them into "tiles" or blocks that satisfy the limit and process them one after the other. The host has the capability to change the contents of constant memory (after all it is only "viewed" as constant from the device), via the cudaMem-cpyToSymbol template function:

```
template<class T > cudaError_t cudaMemcpyToSymbol (
        const T & symbol, // destination of copying operation
        const void *src,  // Source address
        size_t count,     // Number of bytes to copy
        size_t offset = 0,// Offset from start of symbol
        enum cudaMemcpyKind kind = cudaMemcpyHostToDevice);
```

---

[14] **Pitfall**: Variables that are allocated in constant memory should not be passed by reference from the host as parameters to a kernel. The compiler will not complain but the kernel will fail when trying to access the variable.

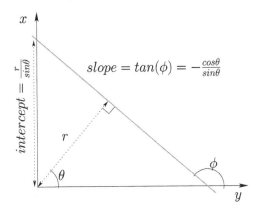

FIGURE 6.12

Describing a line in the 2D plane.

As an example for the use of constant memory, we will explore the implementation of the Hough transform. The Hough transform is an image feature extraction technique that allows the detection of straight lines in an image. More elaborate shapes, both ones with analytical and non-analytical representations, can be also detected with the use of the generalized Hough transform that has been proposed in 1981 by D.H. Ballard [9]. Our example focuses on the simple line-detecting version.

The linear Hough transform operates on black-and-white images that are typically the product of an edge detection filter that helps eliminate from further consideration pixels that are not part of a line. The Hough transform is essentially a pixel voting system, where each possible line in a discrete space is "voted for" by the pixels that can potentially belong to it. The lines that get the most votes are the ones that are detected. The theory behind it is explained below.

The (x, y) Cartesian coordinates of a point belonging to a straight line are bound by the following equation:

$$y = slope \cdot x + intercept.$$

If r is the distance of the line from the origin and θ is the angle formed as illustrated in Fig. 6.12, then (x, y) are connected via:

$$y = -\frac{cos(\theta)}{sin(\theta)}x + \frac{r}{sin(\theta)},$$

which can in turn be written as follows:

$$r = x \cdot cos(\theta) + y \cdot sin(\theta). \tag{6.2}$$

During the application of the Hough transform, each lit pixel (x, y) of the image examined could be a part of a whole family of lines as shown in Fig. 6.13. By iterating

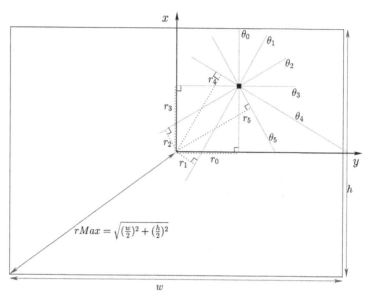

FIGURE 6.13

An example of six (θ_i, r_i) pairs of line parameters that would be associated with the pixel shown. The maximum possible line distance $rMax$ for a $w \times h$ image is also shown, assuming the axes' origin is at the image center.

over the possible angles θ, we can calculate the corresponding $r(\theta)$ via Eq. (6.2). To make the calculation tractable, the possible angles are taken from a limited set (e.g., from 0 to 180 degrees in 1-degree increments). The final piece of the puzzle is the "accumulator, a matrix of counters indexed by θ and $r(\theta)$, which are incremented when a pixel that "fits" the corresponding line is examined.

Obviously, a similar "quantization" process is applied for the calculated distances $r(\theta)$, so that the accumulator matrix can be accessed. The number of bins to be used for r is dictated by the desired accuracy, but in our case it is actually restricted by the size of available shared memory, since maintaining a local accumulator per thread block would benefit the speed of the calculation.

A simple CPU implementation of the linear Hough transform is shown in Listing 6.11. A key observation to understanding the implementation(s) discussed in this section is that the axes' origin is assumed to be on the image center, making the distance of the lines examined ranging between $[-rMax, rMax]$ (see Fig. 6.13).

Listing 6.11: A simple CPU implementation of the linear Hough transform.

```
1  // File : hough/hough.cu
2  . . .
3  const int degreeInc = 2;
4  const int degreeBins = 90;
5  const int rBins = 100;
```

```
6    const float radInc = degreeInc * M_PI / 180;
7    //**********************************************************
8    void CPU_HoughTran (unsigned char *pic, int w, int h, int **acc)
9    {
10     float rMax = sqrt (1.0 * w * w + 1.0 * h * h) / 2;
11     *acc = new int[rBins * 180 / degreeInc];
12     memset (*acc, 0, sizeof (int) * rBins * 180 / degreeInc);
13     int xCent = w / 2;
14     int yCent = h / 2;
15     float rScale = 2 * rMax / rBins;
16
17     for (int i = 0; i < w; i++)
18       for (int j = 0; j < h; j++)
19         {
20           int idx = j * w + i;
21           if (pic[idx] > 0)
22             {
23               int xCoord = i - xCent;
24               int yCoord = yCent - j;   // y-coord has to be reversed
25               float theta = 0;          // actual angle
26               for (int tIdx = 0; tIdx < degreeBins; tIdx++)
27                 {
28                   float r = xCoord * cos (theta) + yCoord * sin (theta↩
                         );
29                   int rIdx = (r + rMax) / rScale;
30                   (*acc)[rIdx * degreeBins + tIdx]++;
31                   theta += radInc;
32                 }
33             }
34         }
35   }
```

As discussed previously, the two nested loops of lines 17 and 18 iterate over all the pixels of the examined image and update the accumulator matrix for any pixel found to be lit (condition of line 21). The (i, j) indices used to access a pixel's state are converted to appropriate (xCoord, yCoord) coordinates by lines 23 and 24, before the loop of lines 26–33 calculates and "quantizes" the (θ, r) values of the possible lines to produce the (tIdx, rIdx) indices for updating the accumulator matrix (line 30). Line 29 quantizes r, while θ escapes the need for conversion by maintaining a separate variable for tIdx.

The expression for converting $r(\theta)$ into rIdx (line 29) incorporates an offset (+ rMax as r could be negative and rIdx has to start from zero), and a scaling operation (divided by the full extent of the range $2\,rMax$ and multiplied by rBins) so that the $[-rMax, rMax]$ range is mapped to $[0, rBins)$

The GPU implementation shown in Listing 6.12 uses two arrays (d_Cos and d_Sin) allocated in constant memory for holding the precomputed values of the sine and cosine functions. As only a small subset of angles are tested (a number of degreeBins that cover the range $\in [0, 180°]$ in increments of degreeInc), there is no need to calculate the cosine and sine terms of line 28 multiple times. The host calculates these values (lines 98–106) and transfers the results in the constant memory arrays (lines 112 and 113) via two `cudaMemcpyToSymbol` calls.

This approach utilizes both characteristics of constant memory, i.e., values are cached and broadcasted.

Listing 6.12: A GPU implementation of the linear Hough transform that uses constant memory.

```
36   // File : hough/hough.cu
37   . . .
38   __constant__ float d_Cos[degreeBins];
39   __constant__ float d_Sin[degreeBins];
40
41   // ******************************************************************
42   // GPU kernel. One thread per image pixel is spawned.
43   // The accummulator memory needs to be allocated by the host in ←
         global memory
44   __global__ void GPU_HoughTran (unsigned char *pic, int w, int h, int←
         *acc, float rMax, float rScale)
45   {
46     int i;
47     int gloID = blockIdx.x * blockDim.x + threadIdx.x;
48
49     int locID = threadIdx.x;
50     int xCent = w / 2;
51     int yCent = h / 2;
52
53     int xCoord = gloID % w − xCent;
54     int yCoord = yCent − gloID / w;
55
56     __shared__ int localAcc[degreeBins * rBins];   // each block is ←
           using a shared memory, local accummulator
57
58     // initialize the local, shared−memory accumulator matrix
59     for (i = locID; i < degreeBins * rBins; i += blockDim.x)
60       localAcc[i] = 0;
61
62     // wait for all warps to complete the previous step
63     __syncthreads ();
64
65     if (gloID < w * h && pic[gloID] > 0) // first condition for the ←
           case of extra threads
66       {
67         for (int tIdx = 0; tIdx < degreeBins; tIdx++)
68           {
69             float r = xCoord * d_Cos[tIdx] + yCoord * d_Sin[tIdx];
70             int rIdx = (r + rMax) / rScale;
71             atomicAdd (localAcc + (rIdx * degreeBins + tIdx), 1);
72           }
73       }
74
75     // wait for all warps to complete the local calculations, before ←
           updating the global counts
```

```
76      __syncthreads ();
77
78      // use atomic operations to add the local findings to the global ↩
           memory accummulator
79      for (i = locID; i < degreeBins * rBins; i += blockDim.x)
80        atomicAdd (acc + i, localAcc[i]);
81    }
82
83    // *********************************************************************
84    int main (int argc, char **argv)
85    {
86      int i;
87
88      PGMImage inImg (argv[1]);
89
90      int *cpuht;
91      int w = inImg.x_dim;
92      int h = inImg.y_dim;
93
94      // CPU calculation
95      CPU_HoughTran (inImg.pixels, w, h, &cpuht);
96
97      // compute values to be stored in device constant memory
98      unique_ptr<float[]> pcCos = make_unique<float[]> (degreeBins);
99      unique_ptr<float[]> pcSin = make_unique<float[]> (degreeBins);
100     float rad = 0;
101     for (i = 0; i < degreeBins; i++)
102       {
103         pcCos[i] = cos (rad);
104         pcSin[i] = sin (rad);
105         rad += radInc;
106       }
107
108     float rMax = sqrt (1.0 * w * w + 1.0 * h * h) / 2;
109     float rScale = 2 * rMax / rBins;
110
111     // copy precomputed values to constant memory
112     cudaMemcpyToSymbol (d_Cos, pcCos.get(), sizeof (float) * ↩
           degreeBins);
113     cudaMemcpyToSymbol (d_Sin, pcSin.get(), sizeof (float) * ↩
           degreeBins);
114
115     // setup and copy data from host to device
116     unsigned char *d_in, *h_in;
117     int *d_hough;
118     unique_ptr<int[]> h_hough;
119
120     h_in = inImg.pixels; // h_in is just an alias here
121
122     h_hough = make_unique<int[]>(degreeBins * rBins);
123
124     cudaMalloc ((void **) &d_in, sizeof (unsigned char) * w * h);
```

```
125    cudaMalloc ((void **) &d_hough, sizeof (int) * degreeBins * rBins)↩
         ;
126    cudaMemcpy (d_in, h_in, sizeof (unsigned char) * w * h, ↩
         cudaMemcpyHostToDevice);
127    cudaMemset (d_hough, 0, sizeof (int) * degreeBins * rBins);
128
129    // execution configuration uses a 1D grid of 1D blocks, each made ↩
         of 256 threads
130    int blockNum = ceil (w * h / 256);
131    GPU_HoughTran <<< blockNum, 256 >>> (d_in, w, h, d_hough, rMax, ↩
         rScale);
132
133    cudaDeviceSynchronize ();        // Wait for the GPU launched work to↩
         complete
134
135    // get results from device
136    cudaMemcpy (h_hough.get(), d_hough, sizeof (int) * degreeBins * ↩
         rBins, cudaMemcpyDeviceToHost);
137
138    // compare CPU and GPU results
139    for (i = 0; i < degreeBins * rBins; i++)
140      {
141        if (cpuht[i] != h_hough[i])
142          printf ("Calculation mismatch at : %i %i %i\n", i, cpuht[i],↩
               h_hough[i]);
143      }
144  . . .
145  }
```

The key points of Listing 6.12 are:

- The GPU_HoughTran kernel essentially encompasses the logic of the body of the two nested for loops of lines 17–34. It is operating on a single pixel which is indexed by the global ID (gloID) of each thread running it. A minimum of $w \times h$ threads are required. Because each block is set to 256 threads (lines 130 and 131), the size of the grid becomes $\lceil \frac{w \cdot h}{256} \rceil$ blocks. In the case that $w \cdot h$ is not a multiple of 256, extra threads without an assigned work item will be spawned, hence the need for the extra condition on line 65.
- Each block of threads uses a shared memory accumulator matrix (declared on line 56) that is initialized by the loop of lines 59–60 in a staggered way as described in detail in Section 6.7.3.
- The local accumulator matrix is added to the global one at the end of each block's execution (lines 79–80).
- The GPU-generated results are compared against the CPU ones with the loop of lines 139–143. This is a recommended approach during the development phases of a CUDA program. Even if program correctness is not an issue (if only that was true!) hardware and software architectural differences between CPU and GPU can lead to discrepancies in the results. Detecting them and understanding their source is a very important step in producing reliable GPU software.

It should be stressed that it is unclear by how much our CUDA program could accelerate the Hough transform calculation: it all depends on the input data. A mostly empty image will result in the majority of threads exiting early. Our example primarily serves the purpose of showing how constant memory can be set up and utilized.

6.6.4 Texture and surface memory

Texture memory is accessed through two sets of special functions:

- **Texture Reference API** and
- **Texture Object API** for compute capability 3.x and above devices.

When a kernel calls one of these functions to read texture memory, it performs a *texture fetch*. A texture fetch is no ordinary memory read though: it can perform filtering and/or translation of values by treating the texture residing in memory as the sampled/discrete representation of a 1D, 2D, or 3D function.

These special access functions are implemented in hardware, making them very fast and efficient to use. However, there are both size and representation limitations on the textures that can be stored in texture memory, making the use of texture memory rather limited in the GPGPU domain. For this reason we will not explore it further in this chapter.

6.7 Optimization techniques

CUDA is not known for its easy learning curve. However, it is not the language itself or the thoroughly documented toolkit functions that make CUDA a challenge. This comes from the need to accommodate specific hardware traits in your programs if you are to extract the performance which a GPU is capable of. In the following paragraphs we discuss these essential techniques that span from kernel structure and execution configuration design to asynchronous execution of device commands.

6.7.1 Block and grid design

The optimization of the grid and block design depends on both the data layout of the problem and the hardware capabilities of the target device. In that regard, it is advisable to design an algorithm that adapts to the available CUDA hardware and dynamically deploys the threads as required to minimize the total execution time.

One of the aspects of the execution minimization problem is that the available computing hardware should be "occupied/busy" as much as possible. Two things must happen:

1. Enough work should be *assigned* to the CUDA cores (deployment/execution configuration phase).

2. The assigned work should allow *execution* with the minimum amount of stalling due to resource contention or slow memory access (execution phase).

Block and grid design influence the first of the above, while the second one is a multi-faceted aspect of CUDA program design that is addressed in the sections that follow. In this section we discuss the sizes of the grid and block without regard to the dimensions used, i.e., as if they are both one dimensional. The reason is that the number of dimensions has no effect on the execution efficiency. The total number of threads per block and the total number of blocks in the grid do.

The first step in designing a host front-end function that adjusts the execution configuration to the capabilities of the target device is the discovery of said capabilities and primarily the number of available SMs. Central to querying the capabilities of a device is the cudaDeviceProp structure, which is populated by a call to the cudaGetDeviceProperties() function[15]:

```
cudaError_t cudaGetDeviceProperties(
          struct cudaDeviceProp *prop,  // Pointer to structure for
                                        //    storing info
          int device);                  // Integer identifying the
                                        //    device to be queried.
                                        //    For systems with one
                                        //    GPU, 0 can be used.
```

Here is a small subset of the fields included in the cudaDeviceProp structure (the field names are self-explanatory):

```
struct cudaDeviceProp{
   char name[256]; // A string identifying the device
   int major;       // Compute capability major number
   int minor;       // Compute capability minor number
   int maxGridSize [3];
   int maxThreadsDim [3];
   int maxThreadsPerBlock;
   int maxThreadsPerMultiProcessor;
   int multiProcessorCount;
   int regsPerBlock; // Number of registers per block
   size_t sharedMemPerBlock;
   size_t totalGlobalMem;
   int warpSize;
   . . .
};
```

For example, a generic approach that could be used for listing the names of the GPUs in a system equipped with multiple devices would be:

---

[15] The $CUDA/samples/1_Utilities/deviceQuery sample project provides a very good starting point for anyone trying to query the capabilities of a device.

```
int deviceCount = 0;
cudaGetDeviceCount(&deviceCount);
if(deviceCount == 0)
   printf("No CUDA compatible GPU exists.\n");
else
{
   cudaDeviceProp pr;
   for(int i=0;i<deviceCount;i++)
      {
          cudaGetDeviceProperties(&pr, i);
          printf("Dev #%i is %s\n", i, pr.name);
      }
}
```

The `multiProcessorCount` field can be used to derive the minimum number of blocks a grid should be made of if it is to use all the SMs in a GPU. Obviously we need at least as many blocks as the number of SMs, and ideally an integer multiple of this number, in order to get multiple *resident* blocks on each SM. The number of resident blocks depends on the block size and on how many resources (e.g., registers and shared memory) each block will need to consume.

If the number of blocks cannot reach the number of SMs, another kernel could possibly run on the remaining SMs by scheduling it on a separate stream (see Section 6.7.5).

One of the myths surrounding kernel deployment optimization is that the best approach is the one maximizing occupancy [defined in Eq. (6.1)]. This probably came to be due to the importance NVidia documentation gave to said subject. However, it has been proven that lower occupancy can lead to better performance [60].

A key point here is that there are cases where lower occupancy and a smaller number of threads per block can provide better performance if the kernel is properly designed to take advantage of the more available resources per thread. Summarizing the general guidelines that one should follow:

- Do more parallel work per thread. Ideally, this should be composed by items that can be executed concurrently by the warp schedulers.
- The grid should be big enough to provide multiple (e.g., three or four) blocks per SM.
- Threads per block should be a multiple of warp size to avoid wasting computing resources on underpopulated warps. An initial choice of between 128 and 256 threads is a good one for experimentation.
- Use big enough blocks to take advantage of multiple warp schedulers. All devices since the introduction of compute capability 3.0 have four warp schedulers per SM, which means we should have at least $4 \cdot warpSize$-sized blocks.
- Use more registers per thread to avoid access to shared memory. This may mean that the number of threads has to be smaller than suggested above if the register file is not big enough (e.g., 64). This contradiction can be resolved through testing.

The number of threads per block can be derived from the `warpSize`, the `maxThreadsPerBlock`, and the register and shared memory demands per thread of the kernel, given the `sharedMemPerBlock` and `regsPerBlock` fields of the `cudaDeviceProp` structure.

The following formula that incorporates the above list of guidelines can be used to calculate an initial estimate for the number of threads per block:

$$threadsPerBlock = min \begin{pmatrix} numWarpSchedulers \cdot warpSize, \\ \frac{regsPerBlock}{registersPerThread}, \\ \frac{sharedMem}{sharedPerThread}, \\ maxThreadsPerSM, \end{pmatrix} \quad (6.3)$$

where the first line corresponds to our above suggestion of $numWarpSchedulers \cdot warpSize$ per block, the second line considers register restrictions, and the third line incorporates the limit imposed by shared memory consumption. The fourth line is there for completeness, as the result should never exceed the target device's hardware limitation on the block size. We are assuming that these are given/supplied:

- `numberOfThreads`: The total number of threads that need to be executed.
- `sharedPerThread`: The total amount of shared memory needed by each thread (in bytes).
- `registersPerThread`: The total number of registers per thread needed. The output of "`nvcc -Xptxas -v`" can be used to get this information.

The rest are retrieved by calling `cudaDeviceProperties()` on the target device.

The `threadsPerBlock` can be turned into a multiple of the `warpSize` via this simple calculation:

$$threadsPerBlock = warpSize \cdot \lceil \frac{threadsPerBlock}{warpSize} \rceil. \quad (6.4)$$

Given the $threadsPerBlock$, we can then calculate the size of the grid:

$$totalBlocks = \lceil \frac{numberOfThreads}{threadsPerBlock} \rceil. \quad (6.5)$$

Listing 6.13 shows a function that implements Eqs. (6.3)–(6.5) in an attempt to automate the process of execution configuration calculation. However, mixed results can be expected. The reason is that the optimum execution configuration is intimately interwoven with the structure of the kernel. Small changes to one can profoundly affect the other, leaving experimentation as the ultimate approach for optimization.

Listing 6.13: A function for calculating the execution configuration of a kernel.

```
1  // File : executionConfHeur.cu
2  //-------------------------------------------------------------
3  // In : numberOfThreads, registersPerThread, sharedPerThread
4  // Out : bestThreadsPerBlock, bestTotalBlocks
5  void calcExecConf (int numberOfThreads, int registersPerThread, int ↩
       sharedPerThread, int &bestThreadsPerBlock, int &bestTotalBlocks)
6  {
7    cudaDeviceProp pr;
8    cudaGetDeviceProperties (&pr, 0);      // replace 0 with ↩
         appropriate ID in case of a multi-GPU system
9    int maxRegs = pr.regsPerBlock;
10   int SM = pr.multiProcessorCount;
11   int warp = pr.warpSize;
12   int sharedMem = pr.sharedMemPerBlock;
13   int maxThreadsPerSM = pr.maxThreadsPerMultiProcessor;
14   int totalBlocks;
15   float imbalance, bestimbalance;
16   int threadsPerBlock;
17   int numWarpSchedulers = 4; // default for all CCs
18
19   bestimbalance = SM;
20
21   // initially calculate the maximum possible threads per block. ↩
         Incorporate limits imposed by:
22   // 1) SM hardware
23   threadsPerBlock = maxThreadsPerSM;
24   // 2) registers
25   threadsPerBlock = min(threadsPerBlock, maxRegs /registersPerThread↩
         );
26   // 3) shared memory size
27   threadsPerBlock = min(threadsPerBlock, sharedMem /sharedPerThread)↩
         ;
28
29   // make sure it is a multiple of warpSize
30   int tmp = threadsPerBlock / warp;
31   threadsPerBlock = (tmp + 1)* warp;
32
33   for (; threadsPerBlock >= numWarpSchedulers * warp && ↩
         bestimbalance != 0; threadsPerBlock -= warp)
34     {
35       totalBlocks = (int) ceil (1.0 * numberOfThreads / ↩
           threadsPerBlock);
36
37       if (totalBlocks % SM == 0)
38         imbalance = 0;
39       else
40         {
41           int blocksPerSM = totalBlocks / SM;   // some SMs get this↩
               number and others get +1 block
42           imbalance = (SM - (totalBlocks % SM)) / (blocksPerSM + ↩
               1.0);
```

```
43        }
44
45        if (bestimbalance >= imbalance)
46        {
47            bestimbalance = imbalance;
48            bestThreadsPerBlock = threadsPerBlock;
49            bestTotalBlocks = totalBlocks;
50        }
51    }
52 }
```

Lines 7–17 collect information about the target device and define the variables used in the subsequent calculations.

Lines 23–27 use the second to fourth line of Eq. (6.3) to get an upper bound on the number of threads per block that can be utilized. Lines 30 and 31 then make sure that the number found is a multiple of the warpSize, before different block sizes (all multiples of the warpSize) are tested.

Function calcExecConf() couples the threadsPerBlock calculation to the number of blocks that will be distributed per SM (blocksPerSM). The rationale is that we should assign the same number of blocks to all SMs to achieve a perfect balance of the workload. For this reason we use the loop of lines 33–52 to test a number of configurations before settling into the one that causes the least amount of "imbalance" in the load distribution, i.e., the one that gives to all SMs the same amount of work if possible. The imbalance is defined by the formula

$$imbalance = \begin{cases} 0 \text{ if } totalBlocks \text{ is a multiple of } SM, \\ \frac{SM-(totalBlocks \% SM)}{blocksPerSM+1} \text{ otherwise,} \end{cases} \quad (6.6)$$

where $blockPerSM = \lfloor \frac{totalBlocks}{SM} \rfloor$ is the number of blocks all SMs get, with $totalBlocks \% SM$ of them getting one more. This means that $SM - (totalBlocks \% SM)$ multiprocessors remain idle for $\frac{1}{blocksPerSM+1}$ percent of the total execution time, assuming that all blocks have the same execution time. So the imbalance, as defined, translates to the accumulation of relative idle time of all SMs. Obviously, other metrics could be derived to quantify the imbalance caused by uneven workload distribution at the block or even individual thread level.

The loop of lines 33–52 ends either when the minimum $numWarpSchedulers \cdot warpSize$ is reached or a configuration with 0 imbalance is found.

Odd inputs to the calcExecConf() function, like, e.g., a number of threads which is not a multiple of the warpSize, can produce suboptimal results. Instead of trying to derive a do-all function, we hope that this function will serve as a starting point to anyone writing his/her own derivative.

Since CUDA 6.5, NVidia has added a number of functions to the runtime API to assist programmers in the selection of the execution configuration. These are:

```
// Returns in *minGridSize and *blocksize suggested grid / block
// sizes, for achieving the best potential occupancy
template < class T > cudaError_t
cudaOccupancyMaxPotentialBlockSize (
        int *minGridSize,   // Smallest grid size for maximum
                            // occupancy (OUT)
        int *blockSize,     // Block size for maximum occup. (OUT)
        T func,             // Kernel for which the calculation is
                            // done  (IN)
        size_t dynamicSMemSize, // Amount of memory (bytes) that is
                            // dynamically allocated in shared
                            // memory (IN)
        int blockSizeLimit); // Maximum block size allowed for
                            // 'func.' Zero means no limit (IN)
//------------------------------------------------------------
// Variation of cudaOccupancyMaxPotentialBlockSize, for kernels that
// have different dynamic memory requirements, based on block size
template < typename UnaryFunction, class T > cudaError_t
cudaOccupancyMaxPotentialBlockSizeVariableSMem (
        int *minGridSize,   // Smallest grid size for maximum
                            // occupancy (OUT)
        int *blockSize,     // Block size for maximum occup. (OUT)
        T func,             // Kernel for which the calculation is
                            // done  (IN)
        UnaryFunction blockSizeToDynamicSMemSize, // Unary function
                            // that gets the block size as input,
                            // and returns the shared memory requi-
                            // rements in bytes as output (IN)
        int blockSizeLimit ); // Maximum block size allowed for
                            // 'func.' Zero means no limit (IN)
```

The difference between these functions is that they apply to different types of kernels: `cudaOccupancyMaxPotentialBlockSize()` should be used when shared memory is statically allocated with a declaration such as:

```
__global__ myKernel(int *data, int N)
{
__shared__ int local[ 256 ];
. . .
```

or the allocation is dynamic but with a *fixed size* per block.

If, on the other hand, the shared memory required depends on the size of the block, as in:

```
__global__ myKernel(int *data, int N)
{
  extern __shared__ int local[];
  . . .
}
. . .
int sharedReq = block * 10;
myKernel<<< grid, block, sharedReq * sizeof(int) >>>( d, N );
```

the `cudaOccupancyMaxPotentialBlockSizeVariableSMem()` function should be used instead.

In both cases, CUDA uses the kernel information, the declared shared memory requirements, and any limit on the block size to return suggested grid and block sizes. The limit on the block size could be derived from the algorithm design, or it could be associated with the maximum number of threads we could run, i.e., the problem size.

For example, modifying the histogram calculating example of Section 6.6.2, using the suggestions of `cudaOccupancyMaxPotentialBlockSize()` results in the following code:

Listing 6.14: CUDA execution configuration calculation for the histogram kernels of Listings 6.7 and 6.8 using static and dynamic fixed-per-block, shared memory allocation, respectively. Only the modifications to the `main()` function of Listing 6.9 are shown.

```
1  // File : histogram_autoConf/histogram.cu
2  . . .
3  static const int BINS = 256;
4
5  // ***********************************************************************
6  __global__ void GPU_histogram_static (int *in, int N, int *h)
7  {
8    __shared__ int localH[BINS];
9    . . .
10 }
11 // ***********************************************************************
12 __global__ void GPU_histogram_dynamic (int *in, int N, int *h, int ↩
      bins)
13 {
14   extern __shared__ int localH[];
15   . . .
16 }
17
18 // ***********************************************************************
19 int main (int argc, char **argv)
20 {
21   . . .
22   int blockSize, gridSize;
23   cudaOccupancyMaxPotentialBlockSize (&gridSize, &blockSize, (void ↩
        *) GPU_histogram_static, BINS * sizeof (int), N);
24   gridSize = ceil(1.0 * N / blockSize);
```

```
25
26   GPU_histogram_static <<< gridSize, blockSize >>> (d_in, N, d_hist)↩
        ;
27   . . .
28
29   cudaOccupancyMaxPotentialBlockSize (&gridSize, &blockSize, (void ↩
        *) GPU_histogram_dynamic, bins * sizeof (int), N);
30   gridSize = ceil(1.0 * N / blockSize);
31
32   GPU_histogram_dynamic <<< gridSize, blockSize, bins * sizeof (int)↩
        >>> (d_in, N, d_hist, bins);
33   . . .
```

A notable difference between the calcExecConf() function presented above and cudaOccupancyMaxPotentialBlockSize() is that the latter does not actually return a proper grid size (nor does the variable shared memory variant). Instead, it returns a grid size that would maximize occupancy, under the assumption that each thread will process multiple data items. Because this is not the case for the given kernel, we have to calculate the proper grid size on lines 24 and 30.

Our next example uses a shared memory allocation that depends on the block size. The kernel calculates the number of odd numbers in the input by having each thread in a block keep a shared-memory counter. These counters are subsequently reduced to a single number per block, before being added to the global memory location holding the final result:

Listing 6.15: A CUDA program for counting the odd numbers in an input array. A shared memory counter with a size equal to the block size constitutes a variable shared memory arrangement.

```
34   // File : odd.cu
35   . . .
36   __global__ void countOdds (int *d, int N, int *odds)
37   {
38     extern __shared__ int count[];
39
40     int myID = blockIdx.x * blockDim.x + threadIdx.x;
41     int localID = threadIdx.x;
42     count[localID] = 0;
43     if (myID < N)
44       count[localID] = (d[myID] % 2);
45     __syncthreads ();
46
47     // reduction phase: sum up the block
48     int step = 1;
49     int otherIdx = localID | step;
50     while ((otherIdx < blockDim.x) && ((localID & step) == 0) )
51       {
52         count[localID] += count[otherIdx];
53         step <<= 1;
54         otherIdx = localID | step;
55         __syncthreads ();
```

```
56        }
57
58      // add to global counter
59      if (localID == 0)
60        atomicAdd (odds, count[0]);
61    }
62
63    //————————————————————————————————————————————
64    int sharedSize (int b)
65    {
66      return b * sizeof (int);
67    }
68
69    //————————————————————————————————————————————
70    int main (int argc, char **argv)
71    {
72      int N = atoi (argv[1]);
73
74      unique_ptr<int[]> ha; // host (h*) and
75      int *da;              // device (d*) pointers
76      int *dres;
77      int hres;
78
79      ha = make_unique<int[]>(N);
80
81      cudaMalloc ((void **) &da, sizeof (int) * N);
82      cudaMalloc ((void **) &dres, sizeof (int) * 1);
83
84      numberGen (N, MAXVALUE, ha.get());
85
86      cudaMemcpy (da, ha.get(), sizeof (int) * N, cudaMemcpyHostToDevice↵
            );
87      cudaMemset (dres, 0, sizeof (int));
88
89      int blockSize, gridSize;
90      cudaOccupancyMaxPotentialBlockSizeVariableSMem (&gridSize, &↵
            blockSize, (void *) countOdds, sharedSize, N);
91
92      gridSize = ceil (1.0 * N / blockSize);
93      printf ("Grid : %i    Block : %i\n", gridSize, blockSize);
94      countOdds <<< gridSize, blockSize, blockSize * sizeof (int) >>> (↵
            da, N, dres);
95
96      cudaMemcpy (&hres, dres, sizeof (int), cudaMemcpyDeviceToHost);
97
98      // correctness check
99      int oc = 0;
100     for (int i = 0; i < N; i++)
101       if (ha[i] % 2)
102         oc++;
103
104     printf ("%i %i\n", hres, oc);
```

```
105
106   cudaFree ((void *) da);
107   cudaFree ((void *) dres);
108   cudaDeviceReset ();
109
110   return 0;
111 }
```

The kernel on lines 36–61 is relatively straightforward. Each thread uses its global ID to check if the corresponding array element is odd and increment its own shared memory counter (line 44). Once all the threads in a block have completed this step (ensured via the __syncthreads() call on line 45), a reduction process begins that consolidates all the partial counters into a single one, stored in count[0]. The first thread in the block can then add this value, using an atomic operation, to the global counter (line 60).

The execution configuration is calculated in 90, via the call to the cudaOccupancyMaxPotentialBlockSizeVariableSMem() function, as our kernel has variable shared memory requirements, i.e., the size of the count array is equal to the block size. In order to feed this information to the CUDA runtime, the sharedSize() function (lines 64–67) is used to return for an input block size the corresponding shared memory requirements in bytes. As in the previous example, once we have the suggested block size, we calculate the grid size on line 92.

The two cudaOccupancyMaxPotentialBlockSize* functions are complemented by the following function, which calculates the number of blocks per SM that will maximize occupancy *if the block size is fixed*:

```
// Returns in  *numBlocks the number of blocks per SM
// for achieving the best potential occupancy
template < class T > cudaError_t
cudaOccupancyMaxActiveBlocksPerMultiprocessor(
    int *numBlocks,   // Number of blocks per SM to maximize
                      // occupancy (OUT)
    const void *func, // Pointer to kernel to be launched (IN)
    int blockSize,    // Block size (IN)
    size_t dynamicSMemSize); // Shared memory in bytes per SM (IN)
```

Normally, one would need to use just one of the three functions for finding the execution configuration. To be able to honor the result returned by the above function, we need to have a kernel that can operate on multiple input data points. If we were to modify our odd counting example in this regard, the result would be:

Listing 6.16: A CUDA program for counting the odd numbers in an input array that uses cudaOccupancyMaxActiveBlocksPerMultiprocessor for finding the execution configuration. Only the changes from Listing 6.15 are shown.

```
112   // File : odd_maxActive.cu
113   . . .
114   __global__ void countOdds (int *d, int N, int *odds)
115   {
```

```
116    extern __shared__ int count[];
117
118    int myID = blockIdx.x * blockDim.x + threadIdx.x;
119    int totalThr = blockDim.x * gridDim.x;
120    int localID = threadIdx.x;
121    count[localID] = 0;
122    for(int i=myID; i < N; i+= totalThr)
123       count[localID] += (d[i] % 2);
124    __syncthreads ();
125
126    // reduction phase: sum up the block
127    . . .
128 //------------------------------------------------
129 int main (int argc, char **argv)
130 {
131    . . .
132    cudaDeviceProp pr;
133    cudaGetDeviceProperties (&pr, 0);       // replace 0 with ↵
          appropriate ID in case of a multi–GPU system
134    int SM = pr.multiProcessorCount;
135
136    int blockSize = 256;
137    int blockPerSM, gridSize;
138    cudaOccupancyMaxActiveBlocksPerMultiprocessor(&blockPerSM, (void ↵
          *) countOdds, blockSize, sharedSize(blockSize));
139
140    gridSize = min( (int)ceil (1.0 * N / blockSize), blockPerSM * SM);
141
142    countOdds <<< gridSize, blockSize, blockSize * sizeof (int) >>> (↵
          da, N, dres);
143    . . .
```

The kernel modifications are on lines 122 and 123, where threads go through the input data using a loop. The block size is fixed on line 136 and the optimum number of blocks per SM is calculated on line 138.

In order to calculate the size of the grid, we need the number of SMs available (retrieved on lines 132–134) and the maximum number of blocks that can be used to tackle the given problem ($\lceil \frac{N}{blockSize} \rceil$). Using these two numbers, we can calculate the grid size on line 140.

In summary, this section provides an initial approach to solving the execution configuration problem via a custom function and via the library functions provided by NVidia for the same purpose. Neither is perfect. The best execution configuration can only be determined by experimentation, as performance depends on many factors and not just occupancy (e.g., register consumption). Thus it is imperative that the application is tested for various configurations and inputs. NVidia's Visual Profiler is an indispensable tool in this quest (see Section 6.13).

6.7.2 **Kernel structure**

The structure of a kernel influences how efficiently an SM is utilized. A branching operation leads to the stalling of the threads that do not follow the particular branch, as illustrated in Fig. 6.4. Listing 6.17 is a slight variation of the code in Listing 6.4, so that the work done by each thread depends explicitly on its ID:

Listing 6.17: An example of a kernel that causes half of the threads in a warp to stall.

```
__global__ void foo()
{
  int ID = threadIdx.y * blockDim.x + threadIdx.x;
  if( ID % 2 == 0)
    {
      doSmt( ID );
    }
  else
    {
      doSmtElse( ID );
    }
  doFinal( ID );
}
```

Starting with the Volta architecture, NVidia introduced a mechanism called Independent Thread Scheduling that modifies the way divergent threads are scheduled by incorporating a separate program counter and a separate call stack for each thread in a warp. This is a huge departure from the single program counter and stack per warp of the previous architectures. However, divergence is still a performance issue that plagues the more recent GPU designs, so the discussion in this section applies equally well. How exactly the new design affects warp scheduling is discussed in Section 6.7.2.1.

A way around the stalling problem would be to modify the condition so that all the threads in a warp follow the same execution path, but they diversify across warps or blocks. An alternative ID can be calculated for each thread (called IDprime in the code samples that follows) that alternates between being universally even or universally odd for each warp. The new ID can be calculated with the formula

$$ID' = (ID - warpSize \cdot \lceil \frac{warpID}{2} \rceil) \cdot 2 + (warpID\%2), \qquad (6.7)$$

where ID is the original thread ID and $warpID$ enumerates the warps using the formula $warpID = \lfloor \frac{ID}{warpSize} \rfloor$. Eq. (6.7) can be broken down and explained as follows:

*   The last term, $(warpID\%2)$, forces all the threads in a warp to alternate between even or odd ID's, matching the even or odd property of the $warpID$.
*   The multiplier of the first term ($\cdot 2$) makes the threads form groups whose ID's are different by 2 (effectively all the odd or all the even ones).
*   The offset in the first term ($-warpSize \cdot \lceil \frac{warpID}{2} \rceil$) of the equation adjusts the beginning of each new even (odd) warp, so that it is warpSize-distant from the previous even (odd) warp.

Eq. (6.7) can be easily calculated as:

```
int warpID = ID / warpSize;
int IDprime = (ID - (warpID + 1) / 2 * warpSize)*2 + (warpID % 2);
```

Or, by sacrificing a bit of portability by assuming a fixed warp size of 32, we can efficiently implement the ceiling and floor functions of Eq. (6.7) with bitwise operators, making the calculation much faster:

```
const int offPow=5;   // reflects a warp size of 32
. . .
int warpID = ID >> offPow;
int IDprime = ((ID - (((warpID + 1) >> 1) << offPow )) << 1) + (↵
    warpID & 1);
```

The following code shows the complete modifications that result in a non-stalling kernel, despite the use of the if-else blocks:

Listing 6.18: An example of a kernel that would not cause intrawarp branching, while doing the same work as the one in Listing 6.17.

```
1   // File : warpFix.cu
2   . . .
3   __global__ void foo ()
4   {
5     int ID = threadIdx.y * blockDim.x + threadIdx.x;
6     int warpID = ID >> offPow;
7     int IDprime = ((ID - (((warpID + 1) >> 1) << offPow )) << 1) + (↵
        warpID & 1);
8
9     if( (warpID & 1) ==0 )   // modulo-2 condition
10    {
11      doSmt(IDprime);
12    }
13    else
14    {
15      doSmtElse(IDprime);
16    }
17    doFinal(IDprime);
18  }
```

This solution works only if the block size is a multiple of 2 times the warp size, e.g., 64, 128, 192, etc. If for example we have a block of size B, with

$$2 \cdot k \cdot warpSize \leq B \leq 2 \cdot (k+1) \cdot warpSize,$$

then the warps made of the threads with ID between $2 \cdot k \cdot warpSize - 1$ and $B - 1$ cannot use the program logic utilizing the IDprime.

What if the kernel involves a multiway decision? An example would be a switch statement with N outcomes. In this case, it is still possible to arrange threads in warps that follow the same path. The only caveat is that blocks must have a size which is a multiple of `N*warpSize`. Then we could use the following ID' calculation:

$$ID' = grpOff +$$
$$(ID - grpOff - (warpID\%N) \cdot warpSize) \cdot N +$$
$$(warpID\%N), \quad (6.8)$$

where

$$grpOff = \lfloor \frac{warpID}{N} \rfloor \cdot warpSize \cdot N.$$

Eq. (6.8) can be broken down and explained as follows:

- $grpOff$ represents the first thread ID of successive groups of $N \cdot warpSize$ threads. Beginning from this position, the second term in Eq. (6.8) adjusts the ID's to the desired effect, i.e., making successive threads acquire ID's different by N.
- The multiplier of the second term ($\cdot N$) makes the threads form groups whose ID's are different by N. The terms which are subtracted from ID (i.e., $-grpOff - (warpID\%N) \cdot warpSize$) adjust ID' so that it begins from the $grpOff$ starting point.
- The last term, $(warpID\%N)$, forces all the threads in a warp to get an ID' that leads them to the same path.

Listing 6.19 implements Eq. (6.8) for a three-way decision control structure.

Listing 6.19: A solution to the stalling problem for a three-way decision structure.

```
1  // File : warpFixMultiway.cu
2  . . .
3  const int N = 3;
4
5  __global__ void foo ()
6  {
7    int ID = threadIdx.x;
8    int warpID = ID / warpSize;
9    int grpOff = (warpID / N) * warpSize * N;
10   int IDprime = grpOff + (ID - grpOff - (warpID % N) * warpSize) * N↩
          + (warpID % N);
11
12   printf ("Thread %i %i\n", ID, IDprime); // just for illustration ↩
          purposes
13
14   switch (warpID % N)
15     {
16     case 0:
17       doSmt (IDprime);
```

```
18          break;
19       case 1:
20          doSmtElse (IDprime);
21          break;
22       default:
23          doSmtElse2 (IDprime);
24       }
25     doFinal (IDprime);
26  }
```

The ID, $ID's$ pairs generated for a 192-thread block and $N = 3$ are shown in Table 6.6.

Unfortunately, the change in ID does not solve the path divergence problem if the decision is based on input data properties, e.g., if the data are even or odd. In that case, a possible solution could be a rearrangement of the input data, so that all the data items leading to one or the other path are grouped together. The feasibility of this solution, and whether it can result in overall performance benefits (because of the extra overhead associated with the rearrangement on the host), is problem-dependent.

Listing 6.20 illustrates the idea behind data rearrangement: the decision that will be made on the device (line 11) is first performed on the host (line 43) and used to shift around the data in order to group them together (loop of lines 41–56). The origPos array is used to keep track of the position change, so that a reordering of the results according to the original placement of the input data can be performed (lines 68–69).

Listing 6.20: An example of a solution to the path divergence problem for a two-way decision based on the input data.

```
1   // File : warpFix_dataRearr.cu
2   . . .
3   __device__ int doSmt (int x) { return x; }
4   __device__ int doSmtElse (int x) { return x; }
5   //---------------------------------------------
6   __global__ void foo (int *d, int N, int *r)
7   {
8     int myID = blockIdx.x * blockDim.x + threadIdx.x;
9     if (myID < N)
10      {
11        if (d[myID] % 2 == 0)
12          r[myID] = doSmt (d[myID]);
13        else
14          r[myID] = doSmtElse (d[myID]);
15      }
16  }
17
18  //---------------------------------------------
19  int main (int argc, char **argv)
20  {
21    int N = atoi (argv[1]);
22
```

```
23    unique_ptr<int[]> ha, hres, hresOrdered; // host (h*) pointers
24    int *da, *dres;                           // device (d*) pointers
25
26    ha = make_unique<int[]>(N);
27    hres = make_unique<int[]>(N);
28    hresOrdered = make_unique<int[]>(N);
29
30    cudaMalloc ((void **) &da, sizeof (int) * N);
31    cudaMalloc ((void **) &dres, sizeof (int) * N);
32
33    numberGen (N, MAXVALUE, ha.get());
34
35    // rearrange data
36    int evenIdx = 0, oddIdx = N - 1;
37    int *origPos = new int[N];
38    for (int i = 0; i < N; i++)
39       origPos[i] = i;
40
41    for (int i = 0; i < N && evenIdx < oddIdx; i++)
42       {
43          if (ha[i] % 2 != 0)
44             {
45                int tmp = ha[i];
46                ha[i] = ha[oddIdx];
47                ha[oddIdx] = tmp;
48                tmp = origPos[i];
49                origPos[i] = origPos[oddIdx];
50                origPos[oddIdx] = tmp;
51                i--;
52                oddIdx --;
53             }
54          else
55             evenIdx++;
56       }
57
58    cudaMemcpy (da, ha.get(), sizeof (int) * N, cudaMemcpyHostToDevice↵
          );
59    cudaMemset (dres, 0, sizeof (int));
60
61    int blockSize = 256, gridSize;
62    gridSize = ceil (1.0 * N / blockSize);
63    foo <<< gridSize, blockSize >>> (da, N, dres);
64
65    cudaMemcpy (hres.get(), dres, N * sizeof (int), ↵
          cudaMemcpyDeviceToHost);
66
67    // restore original placement
68    for (int i = 0; i < N; i++)
69       hresOrdered[origPos[i]] = hres[i];
70    . . .
```

Table 6.6 Pairs of ID and ID' values, for each of six warps running the program of Listing 6.19 for $N = 3$.

Warp											
0		1		2		3		4		5	
ID	ID'	ID	ID'	ID	ID'	ID	ID'	ID	ID'	ID	ID'
0	0	32	1	64	2	96	96	128	97	160	98
1	3	33	4	65	5	97	99	129	100	161	101
2	6	34	7	66	8	98	102	130	103	162	104
3	9	35	10	67	11	99	105	131	106	163	107
4	12	36	13	68	14	100	108	132	109	164	110
5	15	37	16	69	17	101	111	133	112	165	113
6	18	38	19	70	20	102	114	134	115	166	116
7	21	39	22	71	23	103	117	135	118	167	119
8	24	40	25	72	26	104	120	136	121	168	122
9	27	41	28	73	29	105	123	137	124	169	125
10	30	42	31	74	32	106	126	138	127	170	128
11	33	43	34	75	35	107	129	139	130	171	131
12	36	44	37	76	38	108	132	140	133	172	134
13	39	45	40	77	41	109	135	141	136	173	137
14	42	46	43	78	44	110	138	142	139	174	140
15	45	47	46	79	47	111	141	143	142	175	143
16	48	48	49	80	50	112	144	144	145	176	146
17	51	49	52	81	53	113	147	145	148	177	149
18	54	50	55	82	56	114	150	146	151	178	152
19	57	51	58	83	59	115	153	147	154	179	155
20	60	52	61	84	62	116	156	148	157	180	158
21	63	53	64	85	65	117	159	149	160	181	161
22	66	54	67	86	68	118	162	150	163	182	164
23	69	55	70	87	71	119	165	151	166	183	167
24	72	56	73	88	74	120	168	152	169	184	170
25	75	57	76	89	77	121	171	153	172	185	173
26	78	58	79	90	80	122	174	154	175	186	176
27	81	59	82	91	83	123	177	155	178	187	179
28	84	60	85	92	86	124	180	156	181	188	182
29	87	61	88	93	89	125	183	157	184	189	185
30	90	62	91	94	92	126	186	158	187	190	188
31	93	63	94	95	95	127	189	159	190	191	191

6.7.2.1 Kernel structure and Independent Thread Scheduling

NVidia introduced the Independent Thread Scheduling (ITS) technology with the Volta GPU family [25], where for each of the threads of a warp a separate program counter and a separate call stack were made available. Although ITS does not eliminate the performance penalty of thread divergence, it allows divergent threads to continue executing in an interleaved fashion, in turn permitting intrawarp cooperation (e.g., signaling or data exchange) between threads on different execution paths.

Threads do continue to execute as groups, but these groups can be interleaved, allowing threads to progress while executing different paths, without the requirement that one group reaches a convergence point. Consider the following example:

Listing 6.21: An example of a kernel where threads diverge.

```
1   __global__ void foo ()
2   {
3     int myID = blockIdx.x * blockDim.x + threadIdx.x;
4     if (myID % 2 )
5     {
6        A( myID );
7        B( myID );
8     }
9     else
10    {
11       C( myID );
12       D( myID );
13    }
14    E( myID );
15  }
```

The two different ways in which the above kernel will be executed by a warp are shown in Fig. 6.14. The traditional execution means that one group of threads will wait for the other one to reach the point of convergence (the execution of the E() call).

On the other hand, ITS interleaves the execution of the two groups, as seen in Fig. 6.14(b). A schedule optimizer is responsible for grouping together threads that execute the same code in SIMT groups, so that an SM is utilized as efficiently as possible. The only issue is that the two groups may not reconverge, but they may continue execution separately until the end of the kernel. This scheduling policy has to do with the goal that ITS tries to fulfill, i.e., to allow threads in one path of execution to produce results and/or to signal threads in another execution path. As such, it is possible that the E() call on line 14 is such an operation.

One can forcefully reconverge the separate thread groups by using the __syncwarp() call. This is an intrawarp *barrier* function that forces all threads in a warp to execute it before they can proceed. If this call is issued before the E() call (after line 13), the execution will be as shown in Fig. 6.14(c). As such, __syncwarp() is *essential* for restoring the warp to a fully synchronous operation.

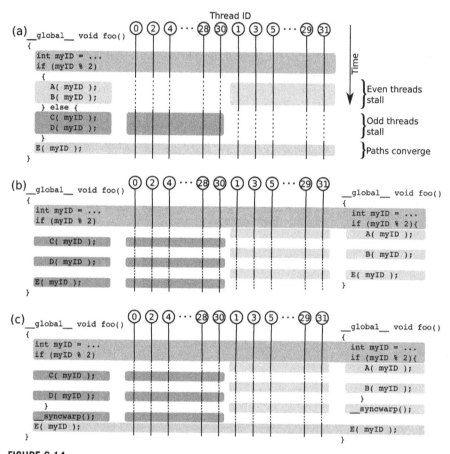

FIGURE 6.14

(a) Execution of the Listing 6.21 kernel by a pre-Volta SM. (b) Execution of the same kernel using Independent Thread Scheduling. (c) Execution using Independent Thread Scheduling, when convergence is forced after the if-else construct, via __syncwarp(). Dotted lines represent idle times.

syncwarp() is also essential for correctness, as the break from the previous warp execution model means that any modifications to memory (shared or otherwise) are not necessarily visible across the warp threads automatically.

At first glance, the example of Fig. 6.14 does not reveal the potential of ITS, because the threads are made to follow one of two paths. This can be far from the case in a kernel, where threads can descend down a hierarchy of conditional statements, leading to a much bigger set of possible paths. ITS will be able to keep the threads that execute the same code in one group.

One scenario where ITS shows its potential is the use of locks in order to synchronize threads. This is of course not a recommended use for a GPU, but it is a plausible scenario. Assuming we have a fine-grained linked list (see Section 4.2.2.2), inserting a new node in the list requires the acquisition of two locks, one for the node before and one for the node following the insertion point:

Listing 6.22: An example of a kernel that uses locks to manage a linked list in a fine-grained manner.

```
__global__ void foo2 (T *data, int N)
{
  int myID = blockIdx.x * blockDim.x + threadIdx.x;
  if(someCondition( data[myID] ))
  {
    Node *prev, *next;
    findLoc(data[myID], &prev, &next); // find location to insert ↵
        data[myID]
                                   // When findLoc returns , ↵
                                      prev and next are locked
    Node *newNode = getFreeNode();
    newNode->info = data[myID];
    prev->next = newNode;
    newNode->next = next;
    prev->l.unlock();
    next->l.unlock();
  }
  __syncwarp();
}
```

If threads were to operate in a lock-step manner as before, a deadlock is a possibility if two threads in the same warp acquire the locks to two neighboring nodes that they access through their `prev` pointers. With ITS, we can have threads wait for other warp threads to finish, without deadlock becoming an issue.

6.7.3 Shared memory access

Concurrent access to shared memory can lead to performance deterioration if threads try to access the same memory bank. The rules are:

- If threads in a warp access data in different banks, access is instantaneous (1-cycle).
- If two or more threads access different elements that reside within the same bank, there is a bank conflict and access is serialized, forcing threads to stall. If each thread of a warp accesses a different part of the same bank, access for the whole warp will require 32 cycles.
- If two or more threads *read* from shared-memory locations that reside within the same 32-bit word (e.g., byte at address 0xF1 and byte at address 0xF2 are part of the same 32-bit data at address 0xF0), data are broadcast to them and there is no conflict.
- If two or more threads *write* to the *same* shared-memory location, there is still no conflict, but only one write will be performed and the eventual value to be

stored is non-deterministic, as this is a data race. If, however, the writes are done to different parts of the same 32-bit word, there is no conflict and no data race. For example, the testShared kernel below will not report an error when the check is conducted on lines 16–21:

```
1   // File : sharedMemoryTest.cu
2   __global__ void testShared ()  // assuming 256-thread 1D block
3   {
4     __shared__ unsigned char count[256];  // one byte per element
5
6    int myID = threadIdx.x;
7    count[myID]=0;  // shared memory initialization
8    __syncthreads();
9
10   for(int i=0;i<100;i++)
11       count[myID]++;  // four threads write to different parts of ↩
                the same 32-bit word
12
13     __syncthreads();
14
15     // check for discrepancies
16     if(myID==0)
17     {
18       for(int i=0;i<256;i++)
19           if(count[i]!=100)
20               printf ("Error at %i\n", myID);
21     }
22   }
23
24   //——————————————————————————————————
25   __global__ void testShared2 ()  // assuming 256-thread 1D block
26   {
27     __shared__ int count[64];  // 32-bits per element
28
29     int myID = threadIdx.x;
30     if(myID<64) count[myID]=0;
31     __syncthreads();
32     for(int i=0;i<100;i++)
33         count[myID / 4]++; // four threads write to the same 32-bit ↩
                word
34
35     __syncthreads();
36     if(myID==0)
37     {
38       for(int i=0;i<64;i++)
39           if(count[i]!=400)
40               printf ("Error2 at %i (%i)\n", i, count[i]);
41     }
42   }
```

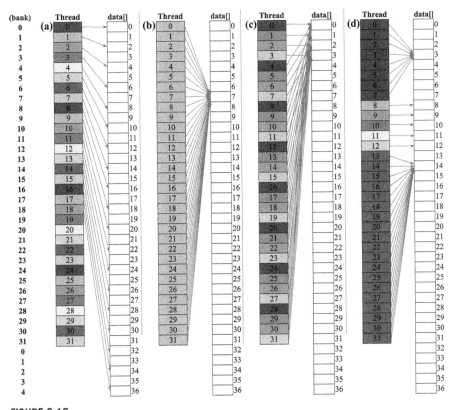

FIGURE 6.15

Four different shared memory access patterns and their effect on bank conflicts for a 32-thread warp. Threads are colored to reflect the bank they access. (a) Each thread accesses the `data[2*ID]` element, resulting in two-way bank conflicts. (b) All threads try to access element `data[7]` (no conflicts). (c) Each thread accesses the `data[ID % 4]` element, resulting in a conflict-free access. (d) Conflict-free access, as threads access different banks, even if two groups access `data[3]` and `data[14]`, respectively. A conflict would exist if, e.g., thread 12 accessed `data[35]`.

In contrast, the `testShared2` kernel (line 25) that has multiple threads write to the same 32-bit word will report errors for all `count` array locations, as instead of the expected value 400, all the elements will have the value 100.

Fig. 6.15 explores four different access patterns and their effects on bank conflicts.

We proceed to examine how a bank conflict-free design can be applied for the case of the histogram calculation example presented in Section 6.6.2.

The kernel design in Listing 6.7 does not consider the organization of shared memory into banks, leaving it open to bank conflicts. The random nature of the input data presents a challenge as we cannot predict which bank will be accessed by each

Table 6.7 An estimation of the shared memory needed per SM to provide conflict-free access during a histogram calculation of an image, assuming each counter is a 32-bit integer.

Maximum gray levels	Compute Capability	Shared Memory Banks	Shared memory capacity	Memory requirements	Conflict-free Solution Feasible
256	3.x, 5.x	32	48KiB	32768	√
512				65536	X
768				98304	X
1024				131072	X
256	7.0	32	96KiB	32768	√
512				65536	√
768				98304	√
1024				131072	X
256	7.5	32	64KiB	32768	√
512				65536	√
768				98304	X
1024				131072	X
256	8.0	32	163KiB	32768	√
512				65536	√
768				98304	√
1024				131072	√
256	8.6	32	99KiB	32768	√
512				65536	√
768				98304	√
1024				131072	X

thread at any time instance. The only way we can prevent conflicts from happening is to *force each thread to use a different bank*, which in turn means that we need a separate histogram count array *for every thread in the active warp*. This would raise the shared memory requirements by a `warpSize` factor! Depending on the number of our input image's maximum gray levels, we get the requirements listed in Table 6.7.

The memory requirement calculations in Table 6.7 are based on the formula

$$sharedMemReq = numBanks \cdot sizeof(int) \cdot grayLevels.$$

A conflict-free solution mandates a staggered array allocation for each thread, in a manner similar to how input data are fetched from the global memory (see Fig. 6.10), guaranteeing that each thread has exclusive use of one bank. This arrangement is shown in Fig. 6.16.

The "trick" to restricting each thread to its own part of the `localH` array is to multiply the offset provided by a pixel's gray level by `warpSize` (or shift to the left by 5 bits for `warpSize=32`).

The resulting kernel is shown in Listing 6.23.

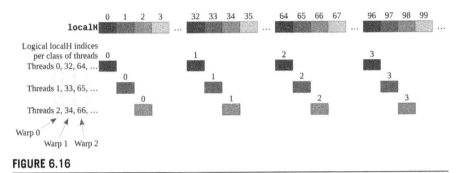

FIGURE 6.16

Assigning a different bank of shared memory to each thread in a warp, by doing a staggered allocation of the local histogram array.

Listing 6.23: A conflict-free shared memory access, histogram calculating kernel, with each thread in a warp using a private part of the `localH` array. The code assumes a fixed warp size of 32.

```
1   // File : histogram_noConflict/histogram_V1.cu
2   . . .
3   const int BINS4ALL = BINS * 32;
4
5   //****************************************************************
6   __global__ void GPU_histogram_V1 (int *in, int N, int *h)
7   {
8     int gloID = blockIdx.x * blockDim.x + threadIdx.x;
9     int locID = threadIdx.x;
10    int GRIDSIZE = gridDim.x * blockDim.x;
11    __shared__ int localH[BINS4ALL];
12    int bankID = locID & 0x1F ; // Optimized version of locID % ↵
          warpSize;
13    int i;
14
15    // initialize the local, shared-memory bins
16    for (i = locID; i < BINS4ALL; i += blockDim.x)
17      localH[i] = 0;
18
19    // wait for all warps to complete the previous step
20    __syncthreads ();
21
22    //start processing the image data
23    for (i = gloID; i < N; i += GRIDSIZE)
24      {
25        int temp = in[i];
26        int v = temp & 0xFF;
27        localH[bankID + (v << 5) ]++;  // Optimized version of localH[↵
            bankID + v * warpSize]++
28        v = (temp >> 8) & 0xFF;
29        localH[bankID + (v << 5) ]++;
30        v = (temp >> 16) & 0xFF;
```

```
31        localH[bankID + (v << 5) ]++;
32        v = (temp >> 24) & 0xFF;
33        localH[bankID + (v << 5) ]++;
34      }
35
36    // wait for all warps to complete the local calculations, before ↩
           updating the global counts
37    __syncthreads ();
38
39    // use atomic operations to add the local findings to the global ↩
           memory bins
40    for (i = locID; i < BINS4ALL; i += blockDim.x)
41      atomicAdd (h + (i >> 5), localH[i]); // Optimized version of ↩
           atomicAdd (h + (i/warpSize), localH[i]);
42  }
```

A side effect of eliminating the bank conflicts is that the `atomicAdd` operations become redundant (see lines 27, 29, 31, and 33 above), providing an additional improvement to the overall execution speed.

A close examination of lines 25–33 in Listing 6.23 reveals that there are dependencies between successive lines, which prevents ILP. A simple solution is to rearrange the computations and introduce a few local variables.

Before we show the resulting kernel, we have to address one more issue: all NVidia GPU architectures since Fermi support the concurrent execution of multiple warps in an SM. This means that for these devices and for thread blocks that exceed the `warpSize`, the kernel in Listing 6.23 is wrong. The failure stems from the race conditions created between threads belonging to different warps, through the sharing of the 32 local histograms. An easy fix is to limit the block size if the device has such capabilities, as seen below:

Listing 6.24: Part of the main function that launches the kernel in Listing 6.23.

```
43  // File : histogram_noConflict/histogram_V1.cu
44  . . .
45  int main (int argc, char **argv)
46  {
47  . . .
48    cudaDeviceProp pr;
49    cudaGetDeviceProperties (&pr, 0);       // replace 0 with ↩
           appropriate ID in case of a multi-GPU system
50    int SM = pr.multiProcessorCount;
51    int blockSize = 32;
52    int gridSize = min( SM, (int)ceil (1.0 * N / blockSize));
53    . . .
54    GPU_histogram_V1 <<< gridSize, blockSize, 0 >>> (d_in, N, d_hist);
55    . . .
```

Lines 48–50 query the device capabilities so as to launch as many blocks as the number of SMs, if possible. We cannot launch more than $\lceil \frac{N}{blockSize} \rceil$ blocks, hence the minimum expression on line 52.

Of course this raises the question of how efficient such an approach is, as a Turing GPU has 64 cores per SM, half of which would stay idle.

There are two solutions to this problem: (a) create as many local histograms as the number of threads in a block or (b) use atomic operations.

The first option puts restrictions on the maximum block size, as 8-bit grayscale images would demand $grayLevels \cdot sizeof(int) = 256 \cdot 4$ bytes $= 1$ KiB of shared memory per thread. We can reduce the footprint per histogram if the maximum number of pixels examined per thread stays below 256. Then, a single byte per counter can be used, reducing the memory per histogram to 256 bytes and bringing the maximum size of a block to $\frac{maximum\,Shared\,Mem}{mem\,Per\,Histogram} = \frac{64\ \text{KiB}}{256\ \text{B}} = 256$ threads for Volta/Turing devices. Unfortunately, this solution eliminates the bank conflict-free arrangement. The implementation of this alternative is shown in Listing 6.25.

Listing 6.25: A variation of the kernel in Listing 6.23, that avoids atomic operations by ensuring that each thread in a block has its own histogram. This kernel also caters for ILP, by breaking interdependencies between successive statements. A total of 64KiB shared memory is used, which means that this kernel can run only on compute capability 7.x devices and above.

```
56   // File : histogram_noConflict/histogram_V2.cu
57   . . .
58   const int BINS = 256;
59   const int BLOCKSIZE = 256;   // reduce to run on pre-Volta machines
60   const int MAXPIXELSPERTHREAD = 255; // to avoid overflowing a byte  ↩
         counter
61   const int BINS4ALL = BINS * BLOCKSIZE;
62
63   //*******************************************************************
64   __global__ void GPU_histogram_V2 (int *in, int N, int *h)
65   {
66     int gloID = blockIdx.x * blockDim.x + threadIdx.x;
67     int locID = threadIdx.x;
68     int GRIDSIZE = gridDim.x * blockDim.x;
69     extern __shared__ unsigned char localH[];
70     int bankID = locID;
71     int i;
72
73     // initialize the local, shared-memory bins
74     for (i = locID; i < BINS4ALL; i += blockDim.x)
75       localH[i] = 0;
76
77     // wait for all warps to complete the previous step
78     __syncthreads ();
79
80     //start processing the image data
81     unsigned char *mySharedBank = localH + bankID;
82     for (i = gloID; i < N; i += GRIDSIZE)
83       {
84         int temp = in[i];
85         int v = temp & 0xFF;
```

```
86          int v2 = (temp >> 8) & 0xFF;
87          int v3 = (temp >> 16) & 0xFF;
88          int v4 = (temp >> 24) & 0xFF;
89          mySharedBank[v * BLOCKSIZE]++;
90          mySharedBank[v2 * BLOCKSIZE]++;
91          mySharedBank[v3 * BLOCKSIZE]++;
92          mySharedBank[v4 * BLOCKSIZE]++;
93        }
94
95     // wait for all warps to complete the local calculations, before ↩
          updating the global counts
96     __syncthreads ();
97
98     // use atomic operations to add the local findings to the global ↩
          memory bins
99     for (i = locID; i < BINS4ALL; i += blockDim.x)
100       atomicAdd (h + (i/BLOCKSIZE), localH[i]);
101   }
102
103   // ************************************************************
104   int main (int argc, char **argv)
105   {
106     . . .
107     int blocks = (int)ceil(N*4.0/(BLOCKSIZE * MAXPIXELSPERTHREAD));
108
109     cudaFuncSetAttribute(GPU_histogram_V2, ↩
            cudaFuncAttributeMaxDynamicSharedMemorySize, BINS4ALL); // ↩
            remove line for pre-Volta machines
110     GPU_histogram_V2 <<< blocks, BLOCKSIZE, BINS4ALL >>> (d_in, N, ↩
            d_hist);
111     . . .
```

The notable differences of Listing 6.25 compared to Listing 6.23 are:

- The introduction of an ILP-friendly block in the for-loop of lines 82–93.
- The dynamic calculation of the grid size based on the need to keep each thread doing no more than MAXPIXELSPERTHREAD pixel calculations (line 107).
- The individual elements of each histogram are BLOCKSIZE bytes apart, instead of warpSize positions.[16]

The second option, i.e., using atomic operations, is implemented in the kernel of Listing 6.26. The two notable changes relative to the original kernel of Listing 6.23, are the use of atomicAdd() on lines 141–144 (obviously) and the introduction of the if construct on line 132, which allows us to avoid using the costly atomic operations if the block size is not above the warpSize. In that case, we revert to the for-loop of

---

[16] It is possible to maintain the conflict-free access to shared memory by using 128 threads per block and storing four histogram counters per int element of the localH array. This scheme is quite complex, requiring lengthy code modifications, without providing much benefit, due to the time-consuming bitwise manipulations required. For this reason, we do not elaborate more on it.

lines 147–159, which is identical to the one used in Listing 6.23. The mySharedBank pointer serves the elimination of the repeated calculation of localH+bankID, as done on lines 27, 29, 31, and 33 of Listing 6.23.

Listing 6.26: A variation of the kernel in Listing 6.23 that uses atomic operations to eliminate the race conditions caused by having multiple concurrently running warps access the shared memory partial histograms.

```
112  // File : histogram_noConflict/histogram_atomic.cu
113  . . .
114  __global__ void GPU_histogram_atomic (int *in, int N, int *h)
115  {
116    int gloID = blockIdx.x * blockDim.x + threadIdx.x;
117    int locID = threadIdx.x;
118    int GRIDSIZE = gridDim.x * blockDim.x;
119    __shared__ int localH[BINS4ALL];
120    int bankID = locID % warpSize;
121    int i;
122
123    // initialize the local, shared-memory bins
124    for (i = locID; i < BINS4ALL; i += blockDim.x)
125      localH[i] = 0;
126
127    // wait for all warps to complete the previous step
128    __syncthreads ();
129
130    //start processing the image data
131    int *mySharedBank = localH + bankID;
132    if (blockDim.x > warpSize) // if the blocksize exceeds the ↩
           warpSize, it is possible multiple warps run at the same time
133      for (i = gloID; i < N; i += GRIDSIZE)
134        {
135
136          int temp = in[i];
137          int v = temp & 0xFF;
138          int v2 = (temp >> 8) & 0xFF;
139          int v3 = (temp >> 16) & 0xFF;
140          int v4 = (temp >> 24) & 0xFF;
141          atomicAdd (mySharedBank + (v << 5), 1);
142          atomicAdd (mySharedBank + (v2 << 5), 1);
143          atomicAdd (mySharedBank + (v3 << 5), 1);
144          atomicAdd (mySharedBank + (v4 << 5), 1);
145        }
146    else
147      for (i = gloID; i < N; i += GRIDSIZE)
148        {
149
150          int temp = in[i];
151          int v = temp & 0xFF;
152          int v2 = (temp >> 8) & 0xFF;
153          int v3 = (temp >> 16) & 0xFF;
154          int v4 = (temp >> 24) & 0xFF;
```

```
155        mySharedBank[v << 5]++;   // Optimized version of localH[↵
               bankID + v * warpSize]++
156        mySharedBank[v2 << 5]++;
157        mySharedBank[v3 << 5]++;
158        mySharedBank[v4 << 5]++;
159      }
160
161    // wait for all warps to complete the local calculations, before ↵
           updating the global counts
162    __syncthreads ();
163
164    // use atomic operations to add the local findings to the global ↵
           memory bins
165    for (i = locID; i < BINS4ALL; i += blockDim.x)
166      atomicAdd (h + (i >> 5), localH[i]); // Optimized version of ↵
           atomicAdd (h + (i/warpSize), localH[i]);
167  }
168
169  // ********************************************************************
170  int main (int argc, char **argv)
171  {
172    . . .
173    cudaDeviceProp pr;
174    cudaGetDeviceProperties (&pr, 0);        // replace 0 with ↵
           appropriate ID in case of a multi-GPU system
175    int SM = pr.multiProcessorCount;
176    int blockSize = 256;
177    int gridSize = min( SM, (int)ceil (1.0 * N / blockSize));
178    . . .
179    GPU_histogram_atomic <<< gridSize, blockSize, 0 >>> (d_in, N, ↵
           d_hist);
180    . . .
181  }
```

Which of the above versions is quicker depends ultimately on the characteristics of the target GPU architecture. For instance, atomic operations on shared memory have become cheaper/faster in recent GPUs. Table 6.8 summarizes the results of testing on an RTX 2060 Super GPU, a compute capability 7.5 device with 34 SMs. The software environment involved CUDA 10.2 and GCC 7.4.

The results are only indicative as we did not attempt to optimize the launch configurations. However, the differences in performance are so distinct that we can safely conclude that the version employing the atomic operations is the best for the given device.

6.7.4 Global memory access

GPU memory subsystems are designed to perform transactions in large batches: 32, 64, or 128 bytes at a time. This allows GPUs to access memory at very high speeds, but with a catch: any memory access operation can involve only a single such block

Table 6.8 Average and standard deviation of kernel execution times over 100 runs, for different histogram-calculating kernels. Input data consisted of a 3264×2448, 8-bit, grayscale image. Reported times exclude the data transfer to/from the GPU.

Kernel (Listing #)	Launch conf. (grid, block)	Execution time (msec)
GPU_histogram_V1 (6.23)	34, 32	0.9003 ± 0.0035
GPU_histogram_V2 (6.25)	123, 256	4.40 ± 0.21
GPU_histogram_atomic (6.26)	34, 256	0.2539 ± 0.0037

of memory, starting at an address which is a multiple of this size. It is as if memory is segmented and one can access only one of these segments at any point in time.

When a warp executes an instruction involving access to global memory, the GPU **coalesces**/groups together the individual thread requests into operations involving these blocks. This creates two challenges:

(a) Warp threads should better access items within the same block of memory. Otherwise, they will be forced to execute in as many groups as the blocks being accessed.
(b) Data should be arranged/aligned in memory so that they do not cross between two consecutive memory blocks if possible. Also, in order to maximize the number of threads that can access items in a collection in a "coalesced" manner, that collection should begin at the starting point of a block.

But what exactly is the size of a block so that a kernel can be designed to meet the first challenge? Current generation GPUs access memory by generating *128-byte requests*. How these requests are fulfilled depends on the memory subsystem that will carry them out: L1 cache, L2 cache, or global memory. The L1 cache is SM-localized, as it is part of the shared memory, while L2 is GPU-wide.

The rules that apply for compute capability 3.x and higher devices, and in the context of a warp's execution, are:

- If the data that the warp threads request exist in the L1 cache, then a single 128-byte wide access operation is performed. The L1 cache is organized into 128-byte segments that map to global memory segments. Otherwise, data go through the L2 cache in 32-byte operations. This reduction in the cache line size aims to improve the utilization of the L2 memory by avoiding over-fetching. Obviously, in the case of a cache hit, the access is performed at the speed of the corresponding cache. Otherwise, access is performed at the speed of global memory.
  L2 is used for caching global memory, while L1 is used for caching local memory or global data that are read-only for the lifetime of a kernel. The exact behavior of

L1 depends on the compute capability of the device.[17] By making the L1 cache read-only, the SM-shared L2 serves the purpose of keeping all SMs up-to-date with data modifications.

The compiler automatically selects which data items will be cached in the L1 cache by issuing different instructions for fetching the data from global memory. A programmer can provide hints to the compiler for L1 use by decorating variables with the const keyword and pointers with the __restrict__ keyword. The __restrict__ qualifier declares that the corresponding pointer is the only way to access the referenced data, i.e., there is no pointer aliasing, or two pointers pointing to overlapping memory regions. For example:

```
1  __global__ void foo( const int * __restrict__ data, int N) {
2  . . .
```

- Data may be accessed in any order within the range of a 32-byte (uncached or cached in L2) or 128-byte (cached in L1) block. This includes requests for the same memory location by multiple threads.
- If the collective size of the data exceeds the block size (e.g., when the size of each item is more than 4 bytes), then the requests are split into separate 32-byte or 128-byte operations, again depending on cache residency.

Fig. 6.17 illustrates the effects of coalesced memory access using a variety of scenarios.

Meeting the second challenge is a matter of properly aligning and/or padding data structures. To this end, the __align__ qualifier can be used, so that the compiler can perform the alignment/padding automatically. The __align__ qualifier expects a parameter corresponding to the size in bytes of the memory reserved for the structure. An example is shown in Listing 6.27.

Listing 6.27: An example of a padded and aligned data structure. It occupies 16 bytes in memory, so that when it is used in an array, all array elements start at an address which is a multiple of 16.

```
struct __align__(16) point{
    int x,y;
    unsigned char color[3];
};
. . .
point *d_p;
cudaMalloc ((void **) &d_p, sizeof (point) * DATASIZE);
```

The above example would reserve a global memory block as shown in Fig. 6.18, with cudaMalloc returning a block suitable for coalesced access.

Things get more "interesting" when a 2D array is required. For memory requests to be coalesced, we must have both a thread-block size and a matrix width, which

---

[17] The best source of information for this topic on each individual compute capability is NVidia's "CUDA C Programming Guide."

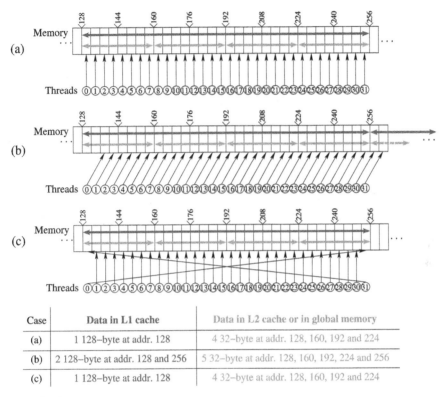

Case	Data in L1 cache	Data in L2 cache or in global memory
(a)	1 128–byte at addr. 128	4 32–byte at addr. 128, 160, 192 and 224
(b)	2 128–byte at addr. 128 and 256	5 32–byte at addr. 128, 160, 192, 224 and 256
(c)	1 128–byte at addr. 128	4 32–byte at addr. 128, 160, 192 and 224

FIGURE 6.17

An example of how different global memory access patterns are serviced according to cache residency for compute capability 3.x and higher devices. It is assumed that each thread is trying to access a 4-byte data item.

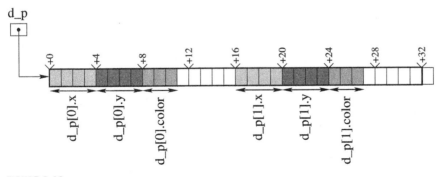

FIGURE 6.18

Memory layout produced from the allocation of the "aligned" data structure of Listing 6.27.

are a multiple of the warp size. To ensure the second requirement, the `cudaMallocPitch()` function can be used:

```
cudaError_t cudaMallocPitch(
            void ** devPtr,    // Address of allocated memory (OUT)
            size_t * pitch,    // Actual size of row in bytes (OUT)
            size_t width,      // Requested table width in bytes (IN)
            size_t height);    // Requested table height in rows (IN)
```

The `pitch` parameter, which is returned upon a successful allocation, can be used for calculating the offset of individual matrix elements. If for example, the following code segment is executed on the host:

```
int *d_matr, pitch;
cudaMallocPitch((void **)&d_matr, &pitch, 200, 100);
```

then the total device memory allocated would be $pitch \cdot 100$ bytes. A kernel trying to access d_p elements should receive as an additional parameter the **pitch** value and calculate the address of a matrix element (i, j) using one of the following two alternatives:

```
// (a) Start by getting how many elements are in one row
// Assuming int is the type of each element:
pitch /= sizeof(int); // works only if there is no remainder
. . .
int *p = d_matr + (j * pitch + i);

// (b) Or without a division that changes the value of pitch by
// casting to a type char:
int *p = (int *)((char *)d_matr + (j*pitch + i*sizeof(int)));
```

However, this is not the end of the story as far as coalesced access to data structures is concerned. There is nothing wrong with defining an **Array of Structures** (**AoS**) and passing it as a parameter to a kernel, until it is time to access its members. Alignment and padding may be fine, but when the following kernel is applied to an array of `point` structures, as the one defined in Listing 6.27:

```
// Eucledian distance calculation
__global__ void distance( point *data, float *dist, int N)
{
    int myID = blockIdx.x * blockDim.x + threadIdx.x; // assuming a 1↵
        D grid of ID blocks
    if (myID >= N) return;
    dist[ myID ] = sqrt( data[myID].x * data[myID].x + data[myID].y *↵
        data[myID].y );
}
```

then upon accessing `data[myID].x`, the threads of a warp will cause the initiation of 16 successive global memory operations (assuming `warpSize` is 32), since only two structures fit within a 32-byte block. The same goes for the y-part of the formula.

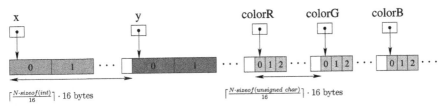

FIGURE 6.19

An illustration of the Structure of Arrays alternative of the Array of Structures shown in Fig. 6.18. Empty cells represent padding based on the assumption that the __align__(16) qualifier were used in the definition of x, y, etc. The memory reserved for each array is also shown.

An alternative – although counterintuitive – solution to this problem is to organize the data as a **Structure of Arrays (SoA)**, i.e., each of the structure components should reside in a separate array. The resulting kernel that truly provides coalesced memory access would be:

```
// Euclidean distance calculation for a Structure of Arrays
__global__ void distance2( const int * __restrict__ x, const int * ↩
    __restrict__ y, float* __restrict__ dist, int N)
{
    int myID = blockIdx.x * blockDim.x + threadIdx.x; // assuming a 1↩
        D grid of 1D blocks
    if (myID >= N) return;
    dist[ myID ] = sqrt( x[myID] * x[myID] + y[myID] * y[myID] );
}
```

which would require just four global memory operations for a warp to access the x-component for the first time. The second access (as mandated by the x[myID] * x[myID] term) would utilize the L1/L2 cache, or by a simple rewrite (using an automatic temporary variable) it could be eliminated/replaced by a register access.

The resulting memory layout, which also has the side effect of utilizing approximately $\frac{16-11}{16} = 31\%$ less device memory because of the much reduced demand for padding, is shown in Fig. 6.19. Padding needs to be inserted only between the individual array memory spaces.

6.7.4.1 Page-locked and zero-copy memory

The term **page-locked** or **pinned** memory refers to host memory that cannot be swapped out as part of the regular virtual memory operations employed by most contemporary operating systems. Pinned memory is used to hold critical code and data that cannot be moved out of the main memory, e.g., like the O.S. kernel. It is also needed for performing Direct Memory Access (DMA) transfers across the PCIe bus. When one uses regular memory for holding the host data upon a request to transfer the data to the device, the NVidia driver allocates paged-locked memory, copies the data to it, and upon completion of the transfer frees up the pinned memory. This buffering overhead can be eliminated by using pinned memory for all data that are to be moved between the host and the device.

Pinned memory can be allocated with:

- malloc() followed by a call to mlock(). Deallocation is done in the reverse order, i.e., calling first munlock() and then free().
- Or by calling the cudaMallocHost() function. Memory allocated in this fashion has to be deallocated with a call to cudaFreeHost(). Otherwise, the program may behave in an unpredictable manner:

```
cudaError_t cudaMallocHost(
            void ** ptr,   // Addr. of pointer to pinned
                           //    memory (IN/OUT)
            size_t size); // Size in bytes of request (IN)

cudaError_t cudaFreeHost (void * ptr);
```

The only potential problem with pinned memory is that if it is used in excess, it could lead to performance degradation due to the inability of the host to use virtual memory effectively.

The performance gain that page-locked memory can yield depends on the hardware platform and, most importantly, on the size of the data involved. In the experiments reported by Cook in [24], there is virtually no gain for transfers below 32 KiB, and the bus becomes saturated (i.e., reaches maximum throughput) when transfers go beyond 2 MiB. For the plateaus Cook got beyond the 2 MiB mark, the performance gain ranged between 10% and a massive 2.5×.

Zero-copy memory is just a term used to convey that no explicit memory transfer between the host and the device needs to be initiated. Another, less fashionable term used for the same concept is **mapped memory**. Mapped memory is page-locked memory that can be mapped to the address space of the device. So we have a memory region with two addresses: one for access from the host and one for access from the device. A transfer across the PCIe bus will be initiated by the CUDA runtime upon the first attempt to access a region of memory that is designated as mapped memory, stalling the active kernel while it is taking place.

This may sound inefficient but there is still justification for using mapped memory:

- It makes the program logic simpler as there is no need to separately allocate device memory and transfer the data from the host. This can be a viable option for early development phases that involve porting CPU code to CUDA. Devoting lengthy parts of the code for memory transfers may be a distraction that can be reserved for the later stages, when the core logic of the program behaves as expected.
- The CUDA runtime can automatically overlap kernel-originated memory transfers with – another – kernel execution. This can boost performance without the need of streams (see Section 6.7.5).

- For low-end systems where the CPU and the GPU share the same physical RAM, no transfer ever takes place, making the use of mapped memory in such cases a no-brainer.

To set up a mapped memory region, one has to call the cudaHostAlloc() function:

```
cudaError_t cudaHostAlloc(
        void ** pHost,          // Addr. of pointer to mapped
                                //   memory (IN/OUT)
        size_t size,            // Size in bytes of request (IN)
        unsigned int flags);    // Options for function (IN)
```

using the symbolic constant cudaHostAllocMapped for the flags parameter.

As mapped memory is also page-locked memory, its release is done with the cudaFreeHost() function.

Mapped memory is referenced by two pointers: one on the host and one on the device. The device pointer, which is the one to be passed to a kernel, can be retrieved from the host pointer with the cudaHostGetDevicePointer function:

```
cudaError_t cudaHostGetDevicePointer(
        void ** pDevice,        // Address where the returned device
                                //   pointer is stored (IN/OUT)
        void * pHost,           // Address of host pointer (IN)
        unsigned int flags)     // Currently should be set to 0
```

So we can have:

```
int *h_data, *d_data;
cudaHostAlloc((void **)&h_data, sizeof(int)* DATASIZE, ←
    cudaHostAllocMapped);
cudaHostGetDevicePointer((void **)&d_data,(void *)h_data, 0);
doSmt<<< gridDim, blkDim >>>(d_data);
```

The above sequence is unnecessary for 64-bit applications running under Windows or Linux. In that case, a **Unified Virtual Addressing** (UVA) space is formed, incorporating both device and host memory. Then, the above sequence could be simplified, as the device pointer would be no different from the host pointer:

```
int *h_data;
cudaHostAlloc((void **)&h_data, sizeof(int)* DATASIZE, ←
    cudaHostAllocMapped);
doSmt<<< gridDim, blkDim >>>(h_data);
```

One can check if UVA is enabled via the canUseHostPointerForRegisteredMem field in the cudaDeviceProp structure returned by the cudaGetDeviceProperties() call. If it is non-zero, then UVA is enabled.

UVA has significant implications for the performance of third-party devices and libraries, as it can eliminate otherwise redundant data buffer copies (see Section 6.14). UVA simplifies the application code by delegating some of the work details to the libraries. For example, under UVA cudaMemcpy() can be used just by specifying the source and destination pointers, without needing to explicitly specify the type of copy operation. So the last line in the following sequence:

```
int *h_in;
int *h_out, *d_out;
. . . .
cudaHostAlloc((void **)&h_in, sizeof(int)* DATAINSIZE, ←
     cudaHostAllocMapped); // Allocate mapped memory
cudaMalloc((void **) &d_out, sizeof (int) * DATAOUTSIZE); ←
                    // Allocate device memory
doSmt<<< gridDim, blkDim >>>(h_in, d_out);
cudaMemcpy(h_out, d_out, sizeof(int) * DATAOUTSIZE, ←
   cudaMemcpyDeviceToHost); // Device-to-host transfer
```

can be replaced with:

```
cudaMemcpy(h_out, d_out, sizeof(int)* DATAOUTSIZE, cudaMemcpyDefault←
   ); // "Implied" device-to-host transfer
```

making the use of the cudaMemcpyDefault flag exclusive, regardless of the "direction" of the copy. Please note that as shown above we still have to "manually" get the output data from the device.

6.7.4.2 Unified memory

The separate memory spaces of host and device necessitate the explicit (or implicit via zero-copy memory) transfer of data between them, so that a GPU can process the designated input and return the outcome of a computation. This results in a sequence of cudaMemcpy() operations, as seen in the examples of the previous sections. Unified memory is a facility introduced in CUDA 6.0 that allows implicit transfers to take place both to and from the device, without the need for lengthy and error-prone cudaMemcpy() sequences.

Unified memory introduces the concept of managed memory, which for compute capability devices before 6.x is essentially memory allocated on both host and device, under the control of the device driver. The device driver ensures that the two memory ranges stay coherent, i.e., contain the same data, when they are being accessed by either CPU or GPU.

The "unified memory" term is justified by the fact that a program needs to maintain just a single-pointer to the data, which is similar to the zero-copy memory described in Section 6.7.4.1. The difference (again for pre-6.x devices) is that for zero-copy memory, the transfer is triggered by access, i.e., during kernel execution, while in the unified memory case the transfer is initiated immediately before the launch and promptly after the termination of a kernel.

Unified memory does not reduce the execution time of a program, as the transfers take place like in a typical CUDA program, albeit implicitly. In that regard, we can consider it an optimization technique, but only as far as the program structure and programming effort are concerned.

Managed memory can be allocated in two ways:

- Dynamically, via a call to the `cudaMallocManaged()` function, which is just a variant of `cudaMalloc()`.
- Statically, by declaring a global variable as being `__managed__`.

In both cases, the resulting pointer/variable can also be accessed from the host, indicating the second host-side allocation. The key though is *when* this access is possible. The managed memory is "handed over" to the GPU for the duration of a kernel's execution. This includes all managed regions/items, regardless if they are passed or not in the parameter list of a kernel. The host-side of the memory is inaccessible while the kernel is being executed, actually generating a protection fault if access is attempted.[18]

The syntax of `cudaMallocManaged()` is as follows:

```
template < class T > cudaError_t cudaMallocManaged (
     T **devPtr,      // Address for storing the memory pointer
                      // (IN/OUT)
     size_t size,     // Size in bytes of the required memory (IN)
     unsigned flags)// Creation flag, defaults to
                      // cudaMemAttachGlobal (IN)
```

The flag must be either `cudaMemAttachGlobal`, which means the allocated memory is accessible by all kernels (and locked when any is running and using it), or `cudaMemAttachHost`, which means that the memory is accessible only to kernels launched by the thread that allocated this block.

To show exactly how unified memory affects the source code, we contrast in Fig. 6.20 two versions of the atomic operations-based histogram calculation program that we covered in Section 6.7.3. While the kernel is unchanged, the host code for preparing the input and collecting the output is significantly simplified. In fact, the host can use native functions (not CUDA library calls) to prepare the input and examine the output.

Comparing the two codes side-by-side, one can immediately spot the "thinning" of the variable definitions on lines 6 and 7, as in unified memory there is no need for separate host and device allocations.

The `cudaMallocManaged()` call of line 19 allocates space for the input on the host and the device, accessible by the single `in` pointer. The histogram array is statically allocated via the `__managed__`-decorated declaration on line 1. The host-side input is initialized by line 21 (the only spot where the unified memory version has to perform extra work), while the device-side output is initialized by line 22. When `cudaMemset()` is applied to a managed memory pointer, it always affects the device-side memory region. The input data are implicitly transferred to the device upon the launch of the kernel on line 24.

---

[18] For devices of compute capability 6.x and above, managed memory that is allocated *statically* can still be accessed by the CPU during kernel execution, via the page-faulting mechanism (read below).

Explicit memory Management

```
1
2  int main (int argc, char **argv)
3  {
4    PGMImage inImg (argv[1]);
5
6    int *d_in, *h_in;
7    int *d_hist, *h_hist, *cpu_hist;
8    int i, N, bins;
9
10   h_in = (int *) inImg.pixels;
11   N = ceil ((inImg.x_dim * inImg.y_dim) / 4.0);
12
13   bins = inImg.num_colors + 1;
14   h_hist = (int *) malloc (bins * sizeof (int));
15   cpu_hist = (int *) malloc (bins * sizeof (int));
16
17   CPU_histogram (inImg.pixels, inImg.x_dim *
                    inImg.y_dim, cpu_hist, bins);
18
19   cudaMalloc ((void **) &d_in, sizeof (int) * N);
20   cudaMalloc ((void **) &d_hist, sizeof (int) * bins);
21   cudaMemcpy (d_in, h_in, sizeof (int) * N,
                 cudaMemcpyHostToDevice);
22   cudaMemset (d_hist, 0, bins * sizeof (int));
23
24   GPU_histogram_atomic <<< 16, 256 >>> (d_in, N, d_hist);
25
26   cudaMemcpy (h_hist, d_hist, sizeof (int) * bins,
                 cudaMemcpyDeviceToHost);
27
28   cudaFree ((void *) d_in);
29   cudaFree ((void *) d_hist);
30   free (h_hist);
31   free (cpu_hist);
```

Unified Memory

```
__device__ __managed__ int hist[BINS];
int main (int argc, char **argv)
{
  PGMImage inImg (argv[1]);

  int *in;
  int *cpu_hist;
  int i, N, bins;

  N = ceil ((inImg.x_dim * inImg.y_dim) / 4.0);

  bins = inImg.num_colors + 1;

  cpu_hist = (int *) malloc (bins * sizeof (int));

  CPU_histogram (inImg.pixels, inImg.x_dim *
                 inImg.y_dim, cpu_hist, bins);

  cudaMallocManaged ((void **) &in, sizeof (int) * N);

  memcpy (in, inImg.pixels, sizeof (int) * N);

  cudaMemset (hist, 0, bins * sizeof (int));

  GPU_histogram_atomic <<< 16, 256 >>> (in, N, hist);

  cudaDeviceSynchronize ();   // Wait for the GPU to finish

  cudaFree ((void *) in);

  free (cpu_hist);
```

FIGURE 6.20

Explicit memory management (bottom/left) and managed memory-based (top/right) main functions for calculating the histogram of an image.

In order to ensure that the kernel has terminated, before the managed memory regions can be accessed, *an explicit synchronization is required* via the `cudaDeviceSynchronize()` call of line 26. Finally, the managed memory is released by `cudaFree()` call on line 28.

The code is undoubtedly shorter, but there are some shortcomings: in the explicit memory management version, the input is copied directly from the internal buffer of the `PGMImage`-type object `inImg` to the device memory (see lines 10 and 21 in the left/bottom pane of Fig. 6.20). In the managed memory version, the input data have to be copied twice, the first time going from the `inImg`'s buffer to the host's portion of the managed memory (line 21 in the right/top pane of Fig. 6.20). This is a problem that could be overcome by a redesign of the `PGMImage` class, so that the image data are read into managed memory, or by mixing unified and explicit memory management. So this is not a deficiency of managed memory, but rather something to be taken into account during the design phase. What is important is that one understands the unified memory mechanism in order to avoid making choices that deteriorate performance.

The only real issue with unified memory is that the programmer loses the fine control that he/she can exercise over what, when, and in which direction data will move. This can be a key design feature in order to unlock the full potential of a GPU's power. For example, in the block cipher encryption case study of Section 6.15.2, the input data are transferred in batches to the GPU and not in one go.

NVidia has tried to remove this deficiency by introducing a *GPU page-faulting* mechanism that is supported by compute capability 6.x devices and above. Currently this mechanism is available only on machines running 64-bit Linux. It works by unifying the CPU-GPU memory into a single virtual address space. If a kernel tries to access a page that is not present in global memory, a page-fault is triggered and the corresponding memory is transferred from the CPU. The same mechanism works in the opposite direction, i.e., for moving data from the GPU to the CPU. The unification is accomplished by using a 49-bit virtual addressing scheme[19] that is big enough to incorporate the memory space of the current generation of AMD64 CPUs (which are limited to 48 bits) and any GPUs present.

This unification of the CPU and GPU(s) address spaces in compute capability 6.x and above devices and the page-faulting mechanism creates some fascinating side effects:

• Managed memory allocated on one GPU is automatically visible on all GPUs (and CPUs) in the system, without requiring explicit transfers. A page-fault will carry out the action needed.
• Device memory is not limited by the physical RAM available on the GPU board, but rather by the total system memory across all devices, CPUs and GPUs combined. This means that we can allocate more device memory than is physically present on the board (called **memory oversubscription**).

---

[19] Enough for addressing 512 TiB.

NVidia has also developed the Address Translation Services (ATS) mechanism that is currently available for Volta devices on IBM Power 9 systems using NVLink. ATS allows a GPU to have full access to the system memory (not just the managed one), amazingly making the following code feasible:

```
int *data = new int[N];
kernel<<<grid, block>>>(data, N);
```

Support for this feature can be checked through the `pageableMemoryAccessUsesHostPageTables` field of the `cudaDeviceProp` structure:

```
cudaDeviceProp pr;
cudaGetDeviceProperties (&pr, 0);
cout << "Access to host memory : " << pr.↩
    pageableMemoryAccessUsesHostPageTables << endl;
```

6.7.5 Asynchronous execution and streams: overlapping GPU memory transfers and more

As a general guideline, memory transfers between the host and the device should only take place when absolutely necessary. Contemporary GPUs are equipped with gigabytes of global memory that can be used to preserve intermediate data between the successive invocations of different kernels. The term **kernel fusion** is used to refer to the approach of replacing multiple kernel invocations by a single one in an attempt to minimize data transfers. However, register file and shared memory restrictions may prevent the creation of a single kernel as a replacement to others (see Section 6.7.1). Factorizing the algorithm in disjoint kernels is still doable and with small performance (if at all) penalties as long as the program data do not traverse the PCIe bus before/after every kernel invocation.

Alternatively, one could "hide" the cost of memory transfers by overlapping them with kernel execution. A **stream** is a sequence of commands (including device memory copies, memory setting, and kernel invocations) that are executed in order. A CUDA program can explicitly control device-level concurrency by managing streams. Each stream will execute sequentially, but the commands from different streams (with commands possibly deposited by different host threads) can be issued concurrently. Thus, the relative execution order of commands residing in different streams is unknown. Execution is of course influenced by the availability – or not – of the resources needed: if one tries to execute concurrently two kernels that, combined, require more than the total available device memory, the allocation directive for one of them will fail.

Streams are represented by the `cudaStream_t` type. There is a default stream (a.k.a. the `NULL` stream) associated with all the requests that have no stream reference attached.

By default, `nvcc` generates code that will use the `NULL` stream regardless of the number of threads running on the host. There is an option to create one stream for each of the host threads by using the "`-default-stream per-thread`" switch or defining the `CUDA_API_PER_THREAD_DEFAULT_STREAM` macro before including the CUDA header(s) in the source file:

```
$ nvcc —default—stream per—thread —lpthread src.cu
```

Or:

```
#define CUDA_API_PER_THREAD_DEFAULT_STREAM
#include <cuda.h>
. . .
```

Explicit use of streams involves the following steps:

1. **Creation**: A stream can be created by a call to the `cudaStreamCreate()` function:

```
cudaError_t cudaStreamCreate(cudaStream_t * pStream); // Pointer ↩
    to a new stream identifier
```

2. **Use**: A third version of the execution configuration syntax exists that can enqueue a kernel invocation in a chosen stream:

```
kernelFunction <<< gridDim, blockDim, sharedMem, stream >>> ( ↩
    list_of_parameters );
```

Additionally, there is a set of asynchronous (i.e., non-blocking) CUDA memory functions (all having the `Async` suffix) that accept an additional stream parameter so that they can be queued in a particular sequence. For example:

```
// Same as cudaMemcpy, with the addition of the cudaStream_t last↩
    parameter. If the last parameter is omitted, the command is ↩
    deposited in the default stream (stream 0)
cudaError_t cudaMemcpyAsync(void *dst,
                            const void *src,
                            size_t count,
                            enum cudaMemcpyKind kind,
                            cudaStream_t stream=0);

// Same as cudaMemSet, with the addition of the cudaStream_t last↩
    parameter
cudaError_t cudaMemsetAsync(void *devPtr,
                            int value,
                            size_t count,
                            cudaStream_t stream=0);
```

In contrast, `cudaMemcpy` (but not `cudaMemset`) is a synchronous/blocking operation for data exceeding 64 KiB.

3. **Destruction**: A stream can be destroyed via a call to the `cudaStreamDestroy()` function:

```
cudaError_t cudaStreamDestroy(cudaStream_t stream); // Stream ↩
    identifier
```

This is a non-blocking function that returns immediately. The resources associated with the stream will be released when all its pending operations are complete. For synchronization purposes one should use the `cudaStreamSynchronize()` call:

```
cudaError_t cudaStreamSynchronize (cudaStream_t stream) ; // ↩
    Stream identifier
```

In the following example, two streams are used to coordinate two sequences involving a host-to-device data transfer, a kernel invocation, and a device-to-host results transfer:

```
1  // File : streamTest.cu
2  . . .
3    cudaStream_t str[2];
4    int *h_data[2], *d_data[2];
5    int i;
6
7    for(i=0;i<2;i++)
8    {
9      cudaStreamCreate(&(str[i]));
10     h_data[i] = (int *)malloc(sizeof(int) * DATASIZE);
11     cudaMalloc((void ** )&(d_data[i]), sizeof(int) * DATASIZE);
12
13     // initialize h_data[i]....
14
15     cudaMemcpyAsync(d_data[i], h_data[i], sizeof(int) * DATASIZE, ↩
           cudaMemcpyHostToDevice, str[i]);
16
17     doSmt <<< 10, 256, 0, str[i] >>> (d_data[i]);
18
19     cudaMemcpyAsync(h_data[i], d_data[i], sizeof(int) * DATASIZE, ↩
           cudaMemcpyDeviceToHost, str[i]);
20   }
21
22   cudaStreamSynchronize(str[0]);
23   cudaStreamSynchronize(str[1]);
24   cudaStreamDestroy(str[0]);
25   cudaStreamDestroy(str[1]);
26
27   for(i=0;i<2;i++)
28   {
29     free(h_data[i]);
30     cudaFree(d_data[i]);
31   }
```

The blocking calls of lines 22 and 23 ensure that by the time we get to free the allocated memory (loop of lines 27–31), all pending commands in our two streams have been completed.

There are two significant problems with the above listing. First, on devices that do support bi-directional transfers from and to the device, the host data **must be on page-locked** memory. This means that the copy of line 19 for `str[0]` and the copy of line 15 for str[1] could run concurrently only if h_data point to pinned memory. On the other hand, the two memory copy operations of line 15 (one for str[0] and one for str[1]) have to go in sequence regardless, because they require the use of the same communication medium.

The second problem is that page-locked host and device memory allocation are on a list of operations that block concurrency from taking place at the time of their execution. The complete list includes:

- Page-locked host memory allocations (cudaMallocHost).
- Device memory allocation (cudaMalloc).
- Device memory setting (cudaMemset).
- Any CUDA command that is added to the default stream.
- Memory copy between two areas of the same device.
- A change in the L1/shared memory configuration.

To address these issues, we should modify the above code as follows:

```
1   // File : streamTest2.cu
2   . . .
3   cudaStream_t str[2];
4   int *h_data[2], *d_data[2];
5   int i;
6
7   // Allocate memory first in both host and device
8   for(i=0;i<2;i++)
9   {
10      cudaMallocHost ((void **) &(h_data[i]), sizeof(int) * DATASIZE)↩
           ; // has to be pinned
11      cudaMalloc((void ** ) &(d_data[i]), sizeof(int) * DATASIZE);
12   }
13
14    // initialize h_data[i]....
15
16   // Now start populating the streams
17   for(i=0;i<2;i++)
18   {
19      cudaStreamCreate(&(str[i]));
20
21      cudaMemcpyAsync(d_data[i], h_data[i], sizeof(int) * DATASIZE, ↩
           cudaMemcpyHostToDevice, str[i]);
22
23      doSmt <<< 10, 256, 0, str[i] >>> (d_data[i]);
24
25      cudaMemcpyAsync(h_data[i], d_data[i], sizeof(int) * DATASIZE, ↩
           cudaMemcpyDeviceToHost, str[i]);
26   }
27
28   // Synchronization and cleanup
29   cudaStreamSynchronize(str[0]);
30   cudaStreamSynchronize(str[1]);
31   cudaStreamDestroy(str[0]);
```

```
32    cudaStreamDestroy(str[1]);
33
34    for(i=0;i<2;i++)
35    {
36      cudaFree(h_data[i]);
37      cudaFree(d_data[i]);
38    }
```

We have seen previously that one can use the `cudaDeviceSynchronize()` call to wait for the default stream queue to become empty. In fact, `cudaDeviceSynchronize()` waits for all streams on a device to become empty. A number of CUDA functions and mechanisms are available to extend this functionality for explicitly or implicitly synchronizing individual streams. These functions, which are examined in the next section, allow us to establish coordination between different streams or simply detect the completion of a command or a set of commands.

A more meaningful example of stream execution and a quantification of the benefits one can get is shown in Section 6.15.2.2.

6.7.5.1 Stream synchronization: events and callbacks

The time instance a command – and everything preceding it in a stream – completes can be captured in the form of an **event**. CUDA uses the `cudaEvent_t` type for managing events. The available actions associated with `cudaEvent_t` instances are:

- Creation:

```
cudaError_t cudaEventCreate (cudaEvent_t *event);
```

- Destruction:

```
cudaError_t cudaEventDestroy (cudaEvent_t event);
```

- Recording the time an event takes place:

```
cudaError_t cudaEventRecord(
        cudaEvent_t event,      // Event identifier (IN)
        cudaStream_t stream=0);// Stream identifier (IN)
```

Essentially, this is a command enqueued in the specified stream.

- Finding the elapsed time between two events:

```
cudaError_t cudaEventElapsedTime(
        float *ms,              // Storage for elapsed time
                                //   in msec units (OUT)
        cudaEvent_t start,// Start event identifier (IN)
        cudaEvent_t end); // End event identifier (IN)
```

`cudaEventRecord` and `cudaEventElapsedTime` can be used for instrumenting a CUDA program.

- Waiting for an event to occur:

```
cudaError_t cudaEventSynchronize (cudaEvent_t event);
```

This is a blocking call that can be used for explicit synchronization.

An example of how events can be used to instrument a CUDA program is provided in Listing 6.28 in the form of a program that measures the PCIe transfer speed as experienced through a series of cudaMemcpy calls.

Listing 6.28: An example of how a CUDA program can be instrumented with the use of events.

```
1   // File : memcpyTest.cu
2   . . .
3   const int MAXDATASIZE = 1024 * 1024;
4
5   int main (int argc, char **argv)
6   {
7     int iter = atoi (argv[1]);
8     int step = atoi (argv[2]);
9     cudaStream_t str;
10    int *h_data, *d_data;
11    int i, dataSize;;
12    cudaEvent_t startT, endT;
13    float duration;
14
15    cudaMallocHost ((void **) &h_data, sizeof (int) * MAXDATASIZE);
16    cudaMalloc ((void **) &d_data, sizeof (int) * MAXDATASIZE);
17    for (i = 0; i < MAXDATASIZE; i++)
18      h_data[i] = i;
19
20    cudaEventCreate (&startT);
21    cudaEventCreate (&endT);
22    cudaStreamCreate (&str);
23    for (dataSize = 0; dataSize <= MAXDATASIZE; dataSize += step)
24      {
25        cudaEventRecord (startT, str);
26        for (i = 0; i < iter; i++)
27          {
28            cudaMemcpyAsync (d_data, h_data, sizeof (int) * dataSize, ←
                cudaMemcpyHostToDevice, str);
29          }
30        cudaEventRecord (endT, str);
31        cudaEventSynchronize (endT);
32        cudaEventElapsedTime (&duration, startT, endT);
33        printf ("%i %f\n", (int) (dataSize * sizeof (int)), duration /←
            iter);
34      }
35
36    cudaStreamDestroy (str);
37    cudaEventDestroy (startT);
38    cudaEventDestroy (endT);
```

```
39
40     cudaFreeHost (h_data);
41     cudaFree (d_data);
42     cudaDeviceReset ();
43     . . .
```

The program of Listing 6.28 performs a series of varying data size, memory copy operations from the host to the device. The program expects two command-line parameters (read at lines 7 and 8) which are the number of iterations used for averaging the results for each data size and the step used to iterate from data size 0 to data size MAXDATASIZE. Lines 25 and 30 are the essential parts of the instrumentation, enclosing all the commands that are enqueued in the stream used. Line 31 waits for the endT event to occur, which effectively translates to the completion of a set of tests for a specific data size.

The above code could be simplified a bit by using "0" in place of the str parameter (on lines 25, 28, and 30), forcing the use of the default stream.

Another mechanism pertaining to synchronization is the **callback**. A callback is a *host* function that is called in response to the detection of an event. In terms of expressiveness, a callback is a much more generic – if expensive – mechanism than events. A function that is to be called as a callback must have the following signature:

```
void callback(cudaStream_t stream, // Stream calling the function (←
    IN)
              cudaError_t status,  // Error condition (IN)
              void *userData);     // Pointer to arbitrary data (IN)
```

A function can be registered to be called when all the preceding commands have been completed in a stream by the cudaStreamAddCallback() function:

```
cudaError_t cudaStreamAddCallback(
              cudaStream_t stream,             // Stream that will ←
                  trigger
                                               //   the function (IN)
              cudaStreamCallback_t callback,// Pointer to callback
                                               //   function (IN)
              void *userData,                  // Data to be supplied to
                                               //   the callback (IN)
              unsigned int flags);             // Should be zero (←
                  reserved
                                               //   for future use)
```

The stream operations following the callback will wait for the callback function to return.

A variation of Listing 6.28 using a callback function is shown below:

Listing 6.29: A variation of Listing 6.28, illustrating the use of callback functions.

```
1    // File : memcpyTestCallback.cu
2    . . .
3    const int MAXDATASIZE = 1024 * 1024;
```

```
4   //------------------------------------------------------------
5   void myCallBack (cudaStream_t stream, cudaError_t status, void *↩
        userData)
6   {
7     float *t = (float *) userData;
8     clock_t x = clock();
9     *t = x*1.0/CLOCKS_PER_SEC;
10  }
11  //------------------------------------------------------------
12  int main (int argc, char **argv)
13  {
14    int iter = atoi (argv[1]);
15    int step = atoi (argv[2]);
16    cudaStream_t str;
17    int *h_data, *d_data;
18    int i, dataSize;;
19
20    cudaStreamCreate(&str);
21    cudaMallocHost ((void **) &h_data, sizeof (int) * MAXDATASIZE);
22    cudaMalloc ((void **) &d_data, sizeof (int) * MAXDATASIZE);
23    for (i = 0; i < MAXDATASIZE; i++)
24      h_data[i] = i;
25
26    float t1, t2;
27    cudaStreamAddCallback (str, myCallBack, (void *) &t1, 0);
28    for (dataSize = 0; dataSize <= MAXDATASIZE; dataSize += step)
29      {
30        for (i = 0; i < iter; i++)
31          {
32            cudaMemcpyAsync (d_data, h_data, sizeof (int) * dataSize, ↩
                cudaMemcpyHostToDevice, str);
33          }
34        cudaStreamAddCallback (str, myCallBack, (void *) &t2, 0);
35        cudaStreamSynchronize(str);
36        printf ("%i %f\n", (int) (dataSize * sizeof (int)), (t2 - t1) ↩
            / iter);
37        t1 = t2;
38      }
39
40    cudaStreamDestroy (str);
41
42    cudaFreeHost (h_data);
43    cudaFree (d_data);
44    cudaDeviceReset ();
45  . . .
```

The `myCallBack()` function of lines 5–10 uses a pointer to `float` to return the time instance it is called. Two different pointers are specified as callback parameters on lines 27 and 34, allowing us to measure and output a time difference on line 36. Admittedly, the use of the `clock()` function on line 8 limits the accuracy of the results, but it should be stressed that callback functions should refrain from using CUDA functions.[20]

6.8 Graphs

A CUDA graph is a new way of submitting work to a GPU that consists of describing the operations that need to take place, including memory transfers and kernel launches, in the form of a graph. The graph nodes correspond to the operations and the edges to their dependencies. The benefit of using a CUDA graph is that once the graph is defined, CUDA enables a number of optimizations that are not possible to be implemented otherwise. A CUDA graph can minimize the setup time required to perform a series of computations on a GPU, while maximizing the concurrency by overlapping non-competing or dependent operations. It is an optimization strategy worth considering especially for operations which are repetitive.

Working with a CUDA graph requires three steps:

1. **Definition**: Describing the nodes and edges connecting them.
2. **Instantiation**: Performing the setup work associated with launching the graph. The result of this step is an *executable graph*.
3. **Execution**: An executable graph can be launched into a stream like any other regular operation.

During the definition phase, one can declare the nodes and their dependencies, either separately (nodes followed by edges) or jointly. The node types supported are:

- kernel,
- host function call,
- memory copy,
- memory initialization (e.g., `cudaMemset`),
- a child graph (graphs can be nested),
- an empty node (placeholder for establishing dependencies).

A graph can be created in two ways:

(a) by using the graph API or
(b) by capturing a stream.

The first method is the most powerful and expressive of the two, but it also requires substantial programmer effort. The second one provides most of the graph benefits with minimum code, but because the graph is implicitly generated, it is typically suboptimal.

---

[20] ◈ **Pitfall**: although a callback function can make CUDA calls, these cannot be directed to the same stream that the callback is placed in, as this would lead to a deadlock.

6.8.1 Creating a graph using the CUDA graph API

A graph object can be constructed via a call to the cudaGraphCreate function:

```
cudaError_t cudaGraphCreate (
    cudaGraph_t *pGraph,    // Graph object to be initialized (IN/OUT)
    flags );                // Creation flags, must be 0
```

Nodes and dependencies can be subsequently added by using a set of functions that correspond to the node type, as listed above. For example, adding a kernel node can be done via:

```
// Creates a kernel node and adds it to a graph.
cudaError_t cudaGraphAddKernelNode(
    cudaGraphNode_t *pGraphNode,    // Address of node object to be
                                    // created (IN/OUT)
    cudaGraph_t graph,              // Graph object to add the node
                                    // to (IN)
    const cudaGraphNode_t *pDepend,// Array of pointers to other node
                                    // objects that correspond to
                                    // operations that preceed this
                                    // node (IN)
    size_t numDependencies,         // Size of pDepend array (IN)
    const cudaKernelNodeParams *params); // Pointer to a structure
                                    // that specifies how the launch
                                    // will take place (IN)
```

The most intricate of the parameters required in the last one: the cudaKernelN-odeParams structure encapsulates all the information required for a kernel launch, including the execution configuration and the parameter list:

```
struct cudaKernelNodeParams
{
    void* func;                     // Pointer to kernel function (IN)
    dim3 gridDim;                   // Grid size (IN)
    dim3 blockDim;                  // Block size (IN)
    unsigned int sharedMemBytes;    // Dynamically allocated shared
                                    // memory in bytes (IN)
    void **kernelParams;            // Pointer to array of pointers.(IN)
                                    // Each points to one kernel
                                    // parameter (IN)
    void **extra;                   // Used in parameter specification.
                                    // Can be set to NULL (IN)
};
```

For a kernel that requires N parameters, the kernelParams points to an array of N pointers. Each of them points to a memory location from where the corresponding kernel parameter can be retrieved. The size and type of the data stored there are retrieved by CUDA from the kernel's image.

Similarly, adding a memory transfer node can be done with:

```
cudaError_t cudaGraphAddMemcpyNode(
   cudaGraphNode_t *pGraphNode,   // Address of node object to be
                                  // created (IN/OUT)
   cudaGraph_t graph,             // Graph object to add the node
                                  // to (IN)
   const cudaGraphNode_t *pDepend,// Array of pointers to other
                                  // node objects that correspond
                                  // to operations that preceed
                                  // this node (IN)
   size_t numDependencies,        // Size of pDepend array (IN)
   const cudaMemcpy3DParms *params);// Pointer to a structure that
                                  // specifies how the transfer will
                                  // take place (IN)
```

The first four parameters' semantics are identical to the ones in `cudaGraphAddKernelNode`. The last one, in the form of a pointer to a `cudaMemcpy3DParms` instance, specifies the transfer details:

```
struct cudaMemcpy3DParms {
   cudaArray_t srcArray;             // Source address
   struct cudaPos srcPos;            // Starting position
   struct cudaPitchedPtr srcPtr;     // Source address alternative
   cudaArray_t dstArray;             // Destination address
   struct cudaPos dstPos;            // Starting position in destination
   struct cudaPitchedPtr dstPtr;     // Destination address alternative
   struct cudaExtent extent;         // Size of memory to transfer
   enum cudaMemcpyKind kind;         // Direction of copy
};
```

The source of the transfer can be specified with either `srcArray` or `srcPtr`. The same rule applies for the destination. Given that `cudaArray`'s purpose is for providing access to texture data, we can just utilize the `*Ptr` parameters only.

`cudaMemcpy3DParms` has a slew of structure fields that makes it tedious to use. To avoid overcomplicating things, CUDA provides a set of `make_*` functions for creating the structure instances needed:

```
// Returns a cudaPitchedPtr structure, initialized according to ↩
    passed parameters
static __inline__ __host__
 struct cudaPitchedPtr make_cudaPitchedPtr(
    void *d,     // Pointer to memory (IN)
    size_t p,    // Pitch of allocated memory in bytes (IN)
    size_t xsz,  // Logical width of allocation in elements (IN)
    size_t ysz); // Logical height of allocation in elements (IN)
// *************************************
// Returns a cudaPos instance for specifying a location offset in 1D↩
    , 2D and 3D arrays
static __inline__ __host__
 struct cudaPos make_cudaPos(
    size_t x,    // Offsets in the x, y and z dimensions (IN)
    size_t y,
```

```
      size_t z);
// ****************************************
// Returns a cudaExtend instance for specifying a 1D, 2D or 3D block
// of data. Parameters are in bytes if the block is not a cudaArray
static __inline__ __host__
 struct cudaExtent make_cudaExtent(
     size_t w,    // Block width (IN)
     size_t h,    // Block height (IN)
     size_t d);   // Block depth (IN)
```

The last of the nodes we will examine is the memset node. A memset node can be created with the – very similar to the above – `cudaGraphAddMemsetNode`:

```
cudaError_t cudaGraphAddMemsetNode(
    cudaGraphNode_t *pGraphNode,  // Address of node object to be
                                  // created (IN/OUT)
    cudaGraph_t graph,            // Graph object to add the node
                                  // to (IN)
    const cudaGraphNode_t *pDepend,// Array of pointers to other
                                  // node objects that correspond
                                  // to operations that preceed
                                  // this node (IN)
    size_t numDependencies,       // Size of pDepend array (IN)
    cudaMemsetParams *params);    // Parameters for how memory
                                  // will be set (IN)
```

The `cudaMemsetParams` structure is composed of the following fields:

```
struct __device_builtin__
 cudaMemsetParams {
    void *dst;                  // Pointer to device memory
    size_t pitch;               // Pitch of destination device pointer.
                                // Unused if height is 1
    unsigned int value;         // Value to be used for initialization
    unsigned int elementSize;// Size of each element in bytes. Must
                                // be 1, 2, or 4
    size_t width;               // Width in bytes
    size_t height;              // Number of rows (1 for 1D array)
};
```

Dependencies can be added at a later stage, i.e., after node construction, by using the `cudaGraphAddDependencies()` function:

```
// Connect graph nodes with dependency edges
cudaError_t cudaGraphAddDependencies(
    (cudaGraph_t graph,           // Target graph
    const cudaGraphNode_t *from,  // Array of "source" nodes
    const cudaGraphNode_t *to,    // Array of "target" node
    size_t numDependencies);      // Size of "from" and "to" arrays
```

Multiple calls to `cudaGraphAddDependencies` can be made.

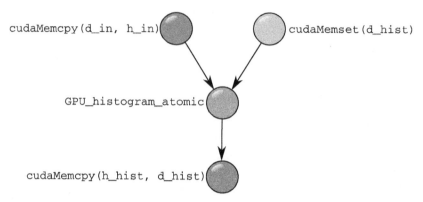

FIGURE 6.21

Graph corresponding to the histogram calculation of Listing 6.26.

Once a graph is created and populated, it needs to be instantiated by calling cudaGraphInstantiate(). As instantiation also entails validation of the graph description, this function is set up to return diagnostic information:

```
// Returns an instantiation of a graph, ready for execution
cudaError_t cudaGraphInstantiate(
    cudaGraphExec_t *pGraphExec,  // Pointer to executable graph to be
                                  // created (IN/OUT)
    cudaGraph_t graph,            // Graph (IN)
    cudaGraphNode_t *pErrorNode,  // Pointer to a graph node object
                                  // that will be made to point to the
                                  // graph node that caused the error
                                  // in case of failure (IN/OUT)
    char *pLogBuffer,             // Buffer for storing diagnostic
                                  // messages(IN)
    size_t bufferSize);           // Size of pLogBuffer (IN)
```

Finally, a graph can be executed by inserting an instance to a stream:

```
// Inserts an executable graph in a stream
cudaError_t cudaGraphLaunch(
    cudaGraphExec_t graphExec,  // Exec. graph (IN)
    cudaStream_t stream);       // Stream in which to launch (IN)
```

After listing the intricacies for implementing the three main types of nodes in a CUDA graph and connecting them, we can proceed to a simple example. The histogram calculation of Listing 6.26 can be represented by the graph shown in Fig. 6.21.

The graph which consists of two memory copy nodes, a single kernel node and a single memset node, can be implemented as follows:

Listing 6.30: CUDA graph-based implementation of the histogram calculation program in Listing 6.26 (only the changes are shown).

```
1   // File : histogram_noConflict/histogram_graph.cu
2   . . .
3   int main (int argc, char **argv)
4   {
5     // memory allocation and execution configuration calculation are ←
          carried out as usual
6     . . .
7     cudaStream_t str;
8     cudaStreamCreate (&str);
9
10    // ********************************************************************
11    // Creation phase
12    cudaGraph_t gr;
13    cudaGraphCreate (&gr, 0);
14
15    //—————————————————
16    // Kernel node:
17    cudaGraphNode_t kern;
18    cudaKernelNodeParams kernParms;
19    void *paramList[3] = { &d_in, &N, &d_hist };
20
21    kernParms.func = (void *) GPU_histogram_atomic;
22    kernParms.gridDim = gridSize;
23    kernParms.blockDim = blockSize;
24    kernParms.sharedMemBytes = 0;
25    kernParms.kernelParams = paramList;
26    kernParms.extra = NULL;
27
28    cudaGraphAddKernelNode (&kern, gr, NULL, 0, &kernParms);
29
30    //—————————————————
31    // Host—to—device transfer node:
32    cudaGraphNode_t h2d;
33    cudaMemcpy3DParms h2dParms;
34
35    h2dParms.srcArray = NULL;
36    h2dParms.srcPtr = make_cudaPitchedPtr ((void *) h_in, sizeof (int)←
          * N, N, 1);
37    h2dParms.srcPos = make_cudaPos (0, 0, 0);
38    h2dParms.dstArray = NULL;
39    h2dParms.dstPtr = make_cudaPitchedPtr ((void *) d_in, sizeof (int)←
          * N, N, 1);
40    h2dParms.dstPos = make_cudaPos (0, 0, 0);
41    h2dParms.extent = make_cudaExtent (sizeof (int) * N, 1, 1);
42    h2dParms.kind = cudaMemcpyHostToDevice;
43
44    cudaGraphAddMemcpyNode (&h2d, gr, NULL, 0, &h2dParms);
45
46    //—————————————————
47    // Device memory set node:
```

```
48    cudaGraphNode_t dset;
49    cudaMemsetParams dsetParms;
50
51    dsetParms.dst = d_hist;
52    dsetParms.value = 0;
53    dsetParms.elementSize = 4;
54    dsetParms.width = bins;
55    dsetParms.height = 1;
56
57    cudaGraphAddMemsetNode (&dset, gr, NULL, 0, &dsetParms);
58
59    //------------------------------
60    // Device-to-host transfer node:
61    cudaGraphNode_t d2h;
62    cudaMemcpy3DParms d2hParms;
63
64    d2hParms.srcArray = NULL;
65    d2hParms.srcPtr = make_cudaPitchedPtr ((void *) d_hist, sizeof (↩
          int) * bins, bins, 1);
66    d2hParms.srcPos = make_cudaPos (0, 0, 0);
67    d2hParms.dstArray = NULL;
68    d2hParms.dstPtr = make_cudaPitchedPtr ((void *) h_hist.get (), ↩
          sizeof (int) * bins, bins, 1);
69    d2hParms.dstPos = make_cudaPos (0, 0, 0);
70    d2hParms.extent = make_cudaExtent (sizeof (int) * bins, 1, 1);
71    d2hParms.kind = cudaMemcpyDeviceToHost;
72
73    cudaGraphAddMemcpyNode (&d2h, gr, NULL, 0, &d2hParms);
74    //------------------------------
75    // Dependencies
76    cudaGraphNode_t from[] = { h2d, dset, kern };
77    cudaGraphNode_t to[]   = { kern, kern, d2h };
78
79    cudaGraphAddDependencies (gr, from, to, 3);
80
81    //**********************************************************
82    // Instantiation phase
83    cudaGraphNode_t errorNode;
84    cudaGraphExec_t instance;
85    const int LOGSIZE = 100;
86    char log[LOGSIZE];
87    cudaGraphInstantiate (&instance, gr, &errorNode, log, LOGSIZE);
88
89    //**********************************************************
90    // Execution phase
91    cudaGraphLaunch (instance, str);
92
93    cudaStreamSynchronize (str);
94    . . .
```

The above code is lengthy but rather straightforward. The three phases of creation (lines 12–79), instantiation (lines 83–87), and execution (line 91) are clearly distinguishable, as well as the setup work for each of the four nodes required. A few points are worth further elaboration:

- If the kernel is expecting pointers to device memory, the kernelParams field of the cudaKernelNodeParams structure should contain pointers to those pointers, and not their values, hence the code of line 19.
- As we are using the *Ptr fields to specify the source and destination of the memory transfers, the *Array fields of the cudaMemcpy3DParms instances must be set to NULL (lines 35, 38, 64, and 67).
- The graph dependencies established using the code of lines 76–79 connect one element of the from array with the corresponding element of the to array, e.g., to[2] depends on from[2], etc. There is no limit on the number of times a node will appear in these arrays, as long as there is no cycle formed.
- The execution of the graph is asynchronous, like most GPU-submitted work. To check for the termination of the graph, synchronization with the corresponding stream is required (line 93).

Notably, this version of the code is slightly slower than the implementation in Listing 6.26, due to the extra work required to set up and validate the graph. As mentioned earlier, graph implementations make sense for repetitive workloads, where the same sequence of actions needs to be executed over and over.

6.8.2 Creating a graph by capturing a stream

The previous graph creation approach is the most flexible one but it is also the most elaborate and error-prone, requiring substantial programmer effort. An easier way is to "record" work submission to one or more streams and generate a graph from the recording. This is how stream capture works.

In order to capture a stream submission, one has to put the stream into capture mode with:

```
cudaError_t cudaStreamBeginCapture(
    cudaStream_t stream,          // Stream to capture (IN)
    cudaStreamCaptureMode mode);  // Capture mode (IN)
```

The capture mode controls what kind of calls are allowed to be made during a capture session. The default option, which is cudaStreamCaptureModeGlobal, prohibits the capture of events (i.e., API calls) that could be potentially unsafe. An example of such a call is cudaMalloc, which is not enqueued in a stream. So it would be a logical mistake to expect that this event would be captured and become part of the graph.

The stream capture ends when the cudaStreamEndCapture call is made. Up to that moment, all submitted requests to that stream are just recorded but not executed.

```
cudaError_t cudaStreamEndCapture(
    cudaStream_t stream,    // Stream that is being captured (IN)
    cudaGraph_t *pGraph);   // Pointer to graph object to receive the
                            // captured graph (IN/OUT)
```

Stream capture works on all but the default (NULL) stream. Once the graph is captured, the instantiation and execution phases are identical to the one detailed in the previous section.

Admittedly, creating the graph explicitly is the best way to expose all the potential concurrency. Capturing a stream does not offer this flexibility. To counter this deficiency, capturing is allowed to cover multiple streams. Also, in order to be able to establish interstream dependencies, it is allowed to make a stream wait for an event in another stream with the function:

```
cudaError_t cudaStreamWaitEvent(
    cudaStream_t stream,    // Stream to wait for an event (IN)
    cudaEvent_t event,      // Event to wait for (IN)
    unsigned int flags);    // Operation parameters (should be zero) (↵
        IN)
```

Obviously, the event has to be triggered in another stream for this to work.

The stream capture has to be initiated on one stream (called the *origin stream*). Creating/recording an event on a stream that is being captured creates a *captured event*. Another (non-captured) stream which is made to wait for a captured event is also placed in capture mode, and the operations submitted to it become part of the captured graph.

The origin stream is the one that should trigger the initiation of all computations and the one that should finish last, i.e., wait for all other streams to finish.

As an example, consider the graph in Fig. 6.22(a). Ideally we would like to run the six kernels in two different streams.

Operations placed in a stream execute in their placement order. So there is no need to make C explicitly wait for A if they are placed in the same stream. However, for C to wait for B, if B is placed in another stream, an event has to be generated/recorded after B finishes execution and this event has to be anticipated before C can commence. For this orchestration to materialize, four events are used:

- `startEvent`: Recorded in the origin stream and waited-for in the second stream, placing the latter in capture mode as well. The event is also used to initialize the execution of the second stream operations.
- `finishEvent`: Recorded in the second stream and waited-for in the origin stream, effectively signaling the end of the graph execution.
- `eventC2D`: Recorded in the origin stream and waited-for in the second stream, triggering the execution of the D kernel.
- `eventB2C`: Recorded in the second stream and waited-for in the origin stream, triggering the execution of the C kernel.

The code implementing the graph capture is shown below:

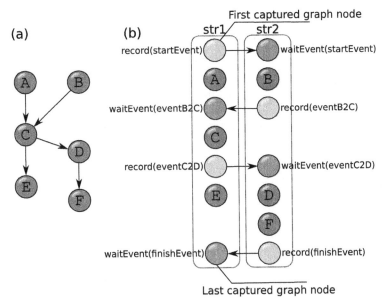

FIGURE 6.22

(a) Example graph with six kernels and their dependencies. (b) Execution of the graph in two streams str1 and str2, with event recording and event waiting nodes enforcing the dependencies. str1 is the origin stream. Symbols refer to the Listing 6.31 code.

Listing 6.31: CUDA stream capture code for the graph in Fig. 6.22.

```
1   // File : graphCaptureExample.cu
2   . . .
3   __global__ void A() { // Just for demo purposes
4     printf ("A\n");
5   }
6   . . .
7   int main ()
8   {
9     cudaStream_t str1, str2, execStream;
10
11    cudaStreamCreate(&str1);
12    cudaStreamCreate(&str2);
13    cudaStreamCreate(&execStream);
14    cudaGraph_t gr;
15    cudaEvent_t eventB2C, eventC2D, startEvent, finishEvent;
16    cudaEventCreate(&eventB2C);
17    cudaEventCreate(&eventC2D);
18    cudaEventCreate(&startEvent);
19    cudaEventCreate(&finishEvent);
20
21    // origin stream
22    cudaStreamBeginCapture(str1, cudaStreamCaptureModeGlobal);
```

```
23   cudaEventRecord(startEvent, str1);
24   A<<<1,1,0,str1>>>();
25   cudaStreamWaitEvent(str1, eventB2C,0);
26   C<<<1,1,0,str1>>>();
27   cudaEventRecord(eventC2D, str1);
28   E<<<1,1,0,str1>>>();
29
30   // second captured stream
31   cudaStreamWaitEvent(str2, startEvent,0);
32   B<<<1,1,0,str2>>>();
33   cudaEventRecord(eventB2C, str2);
34   cudaStreamWaitEvent(str2, eventC2D,0);
35   D<<<1,1,0,str2>>>();
36   F<<<1,1,0,str2>>>();
37   cudaEventRecord(finishEvent, str2);
38
39   cudaStreamWaitEvent(str1, finishEvent,0);
40   cudaStreamEndCapture(str1, &gr);
41
42   // *******************************************************
43   // Instantiation phase
44   cudaGraphExec_t instance;
45   cudaGraphInstantiate (&instance, gr, NULL, NULL, 0);
46
47   // *******************************************************
48   // Execution phase
49   cudaGraphLaunch (instance, execStream);
50   cudaStreamSynchronize(execStream);
51   . . .
```

The key points of the above code are:

- Line 22 puts the `str1` stream in capture mode, making it the origin stream. The second stream (str2) enters capture mode when it is made to wait for the `startEvent` event (line 31).
- The capture ends on line 40, with the creation of the CUDA graph.
- The last captured operation is the wait for the `finishEvent` (line 39), which effectively becomes the last node in the graph. This event is generated upon the termination of the operations in the second stream (line 37).
- The graph instantiation and execution phases are identical to the ones discussed in the previous section. The only difference is on line 45, where no diagnostic information is collected (no log buffer or node address is provided).

6.9 Warp functions

Warp functions (also known as warp intrinsics or warp primitives) are functions that allow the threads of a warp to communicate/exchange data and perform simple calcu-

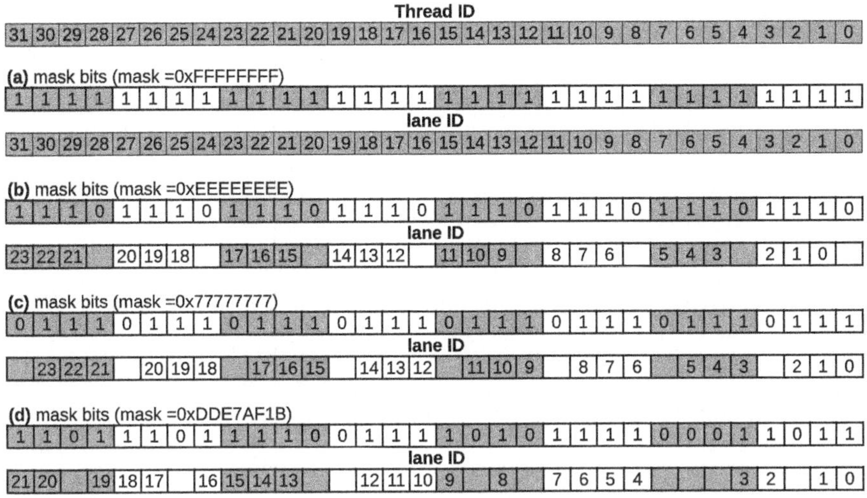

FIGURE 6.23

Examples of masks and corresponding lane IDs. The threads with no lane ID do not participate in a warp primitive.

lations without the use of shared memory, only through registers. This feature makes warp functions a very effective tool in the optimization process of a kernel.

In the context of the warp primitives, the threads that comprise a warp are called *lanes*. Each lane has a unique ID in the range [0, 31]. Most of the warp primitives receive a so-called *mask* parameter, which identifies which of the lanes will participate in the corresponding operation by assigning a bit to each of the lanes. So, if we would like to have all the lanes participating, the value of the mask should be 0xFFFFFFFF or $2^{32} - 1$.

The influence of the mask on the lane IDs is explained with the examples in Fig. 6.23.

Warp functions are categorized as:

- vote functions to collectively query all lanes,
- shuffle functions for data exchange,
- match function for broadcasting and comparing a value across all selected lanes, and
- matrix functions that use the tensor cores introduced in Volta/Fermi to accelerate matrix operations.

As an example, let us consider the odd-counting kernel of Listing 6.16, which performs a manual reduction of the results, shown for clarity below:

Listing 6.32: A kernel for counting odd numbers, repeated from Listing 6.15.

```
// File : odd_maxActive.cu
__global__ void countOdds (int *d, int N, int *odds)
```

```
{
  extern __shared__ int count[];

  int myID = blockIdx.x * blockDim.x + threadIdx.x;
  int localID = threadIdx.x;
  count[localID] = 0;
  if (myID < N)
    count[localID] = (d[myID] % 2);
  __syncthreads ();

  // reduction phase: sum up the block
  int step = 1;
  int otherIdx = localID | step;
  while ((otherIdx < blockDim.x) && ((localID & step) == 0) )
    {
      count[localID] += count[otherIdx];
      step <<= 1;
      otherIdx = localID | step;
      __syncthreads ();
    }

  // add to global counter
  if (localID == 0)
    atomicAdd (odds, count[0]);
}
```

The reduction phase can be accomplished by utilizing the "shuffle down"
__shfl_down_sync function to perform the reduction in two phases: one for collecting the result within a warp and two for accumulating the partial warp results:

Listing 6.33: A kernel for counting odd numbers using warp primitives.

```
1  // File : odd_warpPrim.cu
2  __global__ void countOdds (int *d, int N, int *odds)
3  {
4    extern __shared__ int count[];
5
6    int myID = blockIdx.x * blockDim.x + threadIdx.x;
7    int totalThr = blockDim.x * gridDim.x;
8    int localID = threadIdx.x;
9    count[localID] = 0;
10   for(int i=myID; i < N; i+= totalThr)
11     count[localID] += (d[i] % 2);
12   __syncthreads ();
13
14   // reduction phase 1: sum up the warp results
15   unsigned mask = 0xffffffff;
16   int val = count[localID];
17   for(int offset=16;offset >0;offset/=2)
18     {
19       val += __shfl_down_sync(mask, val, offset);
20     }
21   if(localID % 32 ==0) // lane 0 in all warps
```

```
22      count[localID]=val;
23
24      __syncthreads ();
25
26      // reduction phase 2: sum up the warp leaders results
27      int step = 32;
28      int otherIdx = localID | step;
29      while ((otherIdx < blockDim.x) && ((localID & step) == 0) )
30        {
31          count[localID] += count[otherIdx];
32          step <<= 1;
33          otherIdx = localID | step;
34          __syncthreads ();
35        }
36
37      // add to global counter
38      if (localID == 0)
39        atomicAdd (odds, count[0]);
40 }
```

During the first phase (lines 15–22), all the threads in a warp (mask is set to 0xFFFFFFFF on line 15) perform a pairwise exchange and accumulation at distance offset (line 19). Once the loop of lines 17–20 is complete, the warp-local result is "property" of the lane with ID 0, which it then saves to shared memory (lines 21–22).

During the second phase, the partial results stored in locations 0, 32, 64, etc., are reduced to the single block-local result, starting with results that are 32 places apart (line 27). It is feasible to merge the two reduction phases into one, by repeating shuffling down operations on the partial results. This is left as an exercise to the reader.

To illustrate further how the "shuffle down" primitive works, Fig. 6.24 shows the execution of the first phase loop for two different initial states of the count array. The signature of the __shfl_down_sync function is:

```
// Returns the value of "var" held by another lane, identified by ↩
     adding the "delta" to the lane ID of the caller
T __shfl_down_sync(
    unsigned mask,           // "mask" for participating threads (IN)
    T var,                   // Value contributed by each lane (IN)
    unsigned int delta,      // Distance from "source" lane (IN)
    int width = warpSize)    // If width is less than warpSize, warp is
                             // split into sections, with each section
                             // having lane IDs starting from 0 (IN)
```

It should be noted that for lanes where the source is outside the width boundaries (i.e., $laneID + delta \geq width$), the shuffle operation returns the value of the same lane. This is clearly shown in Fig. 6.24 to lead to "garbage" accumulating in the higher lanes of the warp, despite the example in Fig. 6.24(a) wrongly hinting to all the lanes

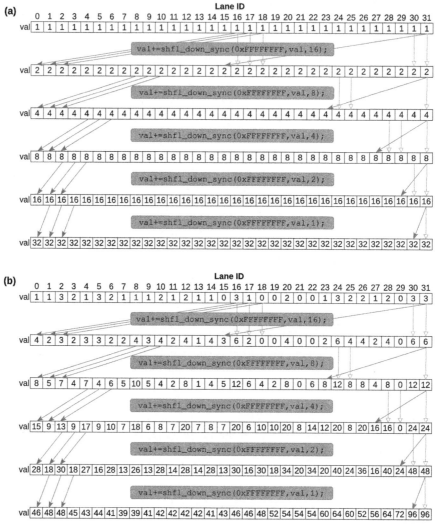

FIGURE 6.24

Tracing the first reduction phase loop of Listing 6.33 and the operation of
`__shfl_down_sync`, for (a) the case where all the initial values are 1 and (b) the case where
46 total odd numbers are in the input data. Hollow arrows indicate lanes that do not have a
source lane to get data from.

getting the same data. This is also the reason why on line 21 we isolate lane 0 as the
one having the desired result.

Shuffling can be also performed in the "up" direction, with `__shfl_up_sync`, and
one can also pick a single lane to be the source of the data with `__shfl_sync`:

```
// Returns the value of "var" held by the source lane. Source lane ←
    ID is calculated as (srcLane % width) in case srcLane is outside←
    the valid range [0,width-1]
T __shfl_sync(
    unsigned mask,        // "mask" for participating threads (IN)
    T var,                // Value contributed by each lane (IN)
    int srcLane,          // Lane to broadcast "var" (IN)
    int width = warpSize) // If width is less than warpSize, warp
                          // is split into sections,
                          // with each section having lane IDs
                          // starting from 0 (IN)
```

Shuffling up would allow the coding of scan/prefix-sum operations if it wasn't for the issue of no-source lanes that leads to data corruption in our shuffle down example (an example of prefix-sum is shown in Fig. 7.10).

An easy fix would be a kernel logic similar to the following:

Listing 6.34: A kernel for calculating a summation scan, using warp primitives.

```
41  // File : warpScan.cu
42  __global__ void scan (int *d, int N, int *res)
43  {
44     extern __shared__ int shm[];
45     __shared__ int *toadd;          // what to add to each warp partial ←
            results
46     toadd = shm + blockDim.x;       // find beginning of toadd array
47
48     int myID = threadIdx.x;
49     int warpID = myID / 32;
50     if (myID % 32 == 0)
51        toadd[warpID] = 0;
52
53     shm[myID] = 0;
54     if (myID < N)
55        shm[myID] = d[myID];
56     __syncthreads ();
57
58     //─────────────────────────────────────────
59     // Scan phase 1: partial warp results
60     unsigned mask = 0xffffffff;
61     int val = shm[myID];
62     for (int offset = 1; offset < 32; offset *= 2)
63        {
64           int tmp = __shfl_up_sync (mask, val, offset);
65           if (myID % 32 - offset >= 0) // source exists?
66              val += tmp;
67        }
68     shm[myID] = val;
69     __syncthreads ();
70
71     //─────────────────────────────────────────
```

```
72    // Scan phase 2: get lane 0 in each warp to find what to add to ↩
             each warp partial results
73    if (myID % 32 == 0)
74      {
75        for (int i = myID + 32; i < blockDim.x; i += 32)
76          atomicAdd (toadd + (i / 32), shm[myID + 31]);    // multiple ↩
               warps may be running
77      }
78    __syncthreads ();
79
80    //————————————————————————————————————————————
81    // Scan phase 3: complete calculation
82    if (warpID > 0)
83      shm[myID] += toadd[warpID];
84
85    // Store in global memory
86    if (myID < N)
87      res[myID] = shm[myID];
88  }
89  . . .
90  scan <<< gridSize, blockSize, (blockSize + (blockSize/32+1)) * ↩
           sizeof (int) >>> (da, N, dres);
91  . . .
```

The scan is performed in three phases:

(1) Intrawarp calculation, where the partial results limited to 32 successive elements are calculated.

(2) The partial results have to be offset by what is coming before them, i.e., the partial sums stored in the elements before lane 0 in each warp. These partial sums are accumulated under the control of lane 0 of the warp that produced them on lines 73–77. As we do not control when or how many warps will run concurrently, the atomic addition of line 76 is mandatory to avoid a data race. The produced offsets are stored in the toadd array, which has as many elements as the number of warps in the block (see execution configuration on line 90).

(3) Finally, the offsets are added to all the results except the ones produced by warp 0 (lines 82 and 83).

The key to making the shuffling up work as intended is the conditional update of a lane's data based on the existence of a source lane (line 65). The only problem with the above kernel is that it works only for a single block, so our input data is limited to 1024 elements (the maximum block size). Fortunately, the size does not have to be a multiple of the warp size, or a power of 2, or any other number. To go beyond one block without having to use multiple kernels, we need interblock coordination, which is examined in Section 6.10.2.

Please note that the following alternative for lines 62–67 is wrong, on account of warp primitives being collective operations. Unless all lanes identified in the mask call them, they block:

```
. . .
  for (int offset = 1; offset < 32; offset *= 2)
    {
      if (myID % 32 − offset >= 0)
        val += __shfl_up_sync (mask, val, offset);
    }
. . .
```

Other notable members of the warp primitives family include:

```
// Returns a non−zero value if all the lanes have a non−zero
// predicate
int __all_sync (
    unsigned mask,  // Mask identifying the participating lanes (IN)
    int predicate); // Value to compare   (IN)
//──────────────────────────────────────────────
// Returns a mask with all the lanes that have "predicate" evaluate
// to non−zero
unsigned int __ballot_sync (
    unsigned mask,  // Mask identifying the participating lanes (IN)
    int predicate); // Value to check if it is zero or not  (IN)
//──────────────────────────────────────────────
// Returns a mask with all the lanes that have a value matching the
// calling lane's provided value. This is available to CC 7.x
// devices and above
unsigned int __match_any_sync (
    unsigned mask,  // Mask identifying the participating lanes (IN)
    T value);       // Value to match with other lanes  (IN)
//──────────────────────────────────────────────
// Returns a mask coresponding to the lanes executing the function
unsigned int __activemask ();
```

The last one listed can help us determine the threads that are executing a branch of a decision-making structure. The following example is yet another way to count odd numbers, with a kernel that has one thread assigned per data element:

Listing 6.35: A alternative kernel for counting odd numbers using warp primitives.

```
92  // File : odd_warpFunc2.cu
93  __global__ void countOdds (int *d, int N, int *odds)
94  {
95    extern __shared__ int count[];
96
97    int myID = blockIdx.x * blockDim.x + threadIdx.x;
98    int localID = threadIdx.x;
99    int warpID = localID / 32;
100   count[localID] = 0;
101   __syncthreads ();
102
103   // Phase 1: warp calculation
104   if (myID < N)
105     {
```

```
106          if (d[myID] % 2)
107            {
108              unsigned mask = __activemask ();
109              int tmp = __popc (mask); // count the bits
110              int lsb = __ffs (mask);  // find the first lane to be in ↵
                    this code block
111              if (localID % 32 == lsb - 1)
112                count[warpID] = tmp;
113            }
114          }
115      __syncthreads ();
116
117      // Phase 2: partial results consolidation
118      if(warpID==0)
119      {
120          unsigned mask = 0xffffffff;
121          int val = count[localID];
122          for (int offset = 16; offset > 0; offset /= 2)
123              val += __shfl_down_sync (mask, val, offset);
124
125          if (localID == 0)    // lane 0 in all warps
126              atomicAdd (odds, val);
127      }
128  }
```

The key points of the above kernel are:

- The threads that are assigned odd numbers diverge into the body of the if statement on line 106. The active lanes in that block are discovered on line 108 and counted on line 109 using the __popc primitive. __popc counts the set bits in its argument.[21]
- The partial result is stored in the count array at a location indexed by the warp ID (line 112). The lane responsible for this action is selected by getting the first active lane on line 110. The __ffs primitive returns the position of the first non-zero bit in an integer, with positions starting from 1 (hence the subtraction of 1 on line 111).
- Once the first phase is complete, there are ≤ 32 partial results stored in the beginning of the count shared-memory array. This implies that only one warp needs to perform the second consolidation phase.

Lines 104–115 can be replaced with the following to the same effect:

```
. . .
int predicate=0;
if (myID < N)
    predicate = d[myID] % 2;
```

---

[21] The __popc and __ffs functions used in Listing 6.35 are documented in the "CUDA Math API" document.

```
unsigned mask = 0xffffffff;
unsigned active = __ballot_sync(mask, predicate);
int tmp = __popc (active);
int lsb = __ffs (mask);
if (localID % 32 == lsb - 1)
    count[warpID] = tmp;
__syncthreads ();
. . .
```

6.10 **Cooperative groups**

Cooperative groups is an extension to CUDA initially introduced in v9.0, that allows the user to selectively group threads at all possible levels of granularity, starting from the warp all the way up to *multiple devices*! This is an extremely powerful extension to CUDA, given that up to the introduction of this technology, the only coordination possible was between the threads of a single block.

Cooperative groups provide for this purpose the following facilities:

- A set of data types for representing groups of threads and associated operations for inspecting and managing them (e.g., getting the rank of a thread within a group or splitting a group into more groups).
- Collective functions that operate on the members of a group, such as barriers, shuffle operations and vote operations. The availability of these depends on the granularity of the group. For example, only a barrier operation is available at all levels.

The CUDA 11 SDK documentation identifies two types of groups: **implicit**, which are created by default when a kernel is launched, and **explicit**, which are created by programmer action during kernel execution. In the following sections we follow a different classification, based on the scope of the group actions.

Apart from the unique capabilities that cooperative groups add to the CUDA toolkit, they also promote a shift in CUDA development, as the objects used to represent the groups of threads can be passed as parameters to other device functions. This means that we can elegantly control thread workflow by organizing them in groups instead of checking their placement in the block/grid via the intrinsic variables such as threadIdx and blockIdx.

6.10.1 **Intrablock cooperative groups**

Intrablock cooperative groups are an evolution of the warp functions described in Section 6.9, in that they allow similar functionality to be implemented but with less programmer effort.

In order to create an intrablock cooperative group of threads, one has to start by including the following lines in the source program:

```
#include <cooperative_groups.h>

using namespace cooperative_groups;
```

The hierarchy of classes that are used to manage groups of threads has the class `thread_group` at its base. The `thread_group` class defines the following methods, which are inherited by all the subclasses:

```
// Returns the size of the group
unsigned int size();
//
// Returns an intragroup ID for the calling thread, in the range [0,
    size()-1]
unsigned int thread_rank();
//
// Barrier function
void sync();
```

An intrablock group that is comprised of all the threads in a block can be easily constructed by calling:

```
thread_block b = this_thread_block();
```

If one then calls:

```
b.sync();
```

it would be equivalent to `__syncthreads();`
And if one calls:

```
int myLocalID = b.thread_rank();
```

it would be equivalent to calculating a scalar intrablock identifier for the thread, instead of handling the components of `threadIdx`.

The `thread_block` class adds a few more methods to what is inherited from `thread_group`:

```
// Returns the position of the block in the grid. Equivalent to
    blockIdx
static dim3 group_index();

//
// Returns the position of the thread in the block. Equivalent to
    threadIdx
static dim3 thread_index();

//
// Returns the size of the block. Equivalent to blockDim
static dim3 group_dim();
```

Obviously using a group that contains all the threads in a block does not offer anything new. But once we have a group, it can then be partitioned in subgroups, or, in the jargon of the cooperative groups library, **tiles**, using the following function template:

```
// Returns a tile of threads, the size of parameter tileSize
template <unsigned int tileSize, typename ParentT>
    thread_block_tile<tileSize> tiled_partition(const ParentT& g);
```

The partitioning can be done in tiles with a size which is a power of 2, and up to 32 threads. The threads of the original/parent group are split into tiles according to the outcome of the $\lfloor \frac{g.thread\_rank()}{tileSize} \rfloor$ expression to form a total of $\lceil \frac{g.size()}{tileSize} \rceil$ tiles. Each thread acquires a new rank within the tile it is assigned to, given by `g.thread_rank() % tileSize`.

Working with tiles can be simplified with a number of methods that allow the programmer to retrieve information about the total number of tiles and the position of a tile within a group of tiles:

```
// thread_block_tile<> methods:

// Returns the number of tiles created by the tiled_partition call
unsigned long long meta_group_size() const;

//------------------------------------------------------------
// Returns the position of a tile within a group produced by ↩
    partitioning
unsigned long long meta_group_rank() const;
```

A call to `tiled_partition` is a collective operation, so it will block until all the threads in the parent group make it. The `thread_block_tile<>` instances offer methods similar to warp primitives such as:

```
// List of methods provided by the thread_block_tile class template.
// T can be any primitive 32- or 64-bit data type
// The match_* methods require compute capability 7.x and above

//------------------------------------------------------------
// Returns the var from the thread with rank src_rank
T shfl(T var, unsigned int src_rank)

//------------------------------------------------------------
// Returns var from the thread ranked +delta
T shfl_down(T var, int delta)

//------------------------------------------------------------
// Returns var from the thread ranked -delta
T shfl_up(T var, int delta)

//------------------------------------------------------------
// Returns var from the thread ranked (thread_rank() ^ mask)
T shfl_xor(T var, int mask)

//------------------------------------------------------------
```

```
// Returns a non-zero value if any of the threads in the tile ↩
    provide a non-zero predicate
int any(int predicate)

//─────────────────────────────────────────────
// Returns a non-zero value if all the threads in the tile provide a↩
    non-zero predicate
int all(int predicate)

//─────────────────────────────────────────────
// Returns an integer whose Nth bit is set if the Nth thread in the ↩
    tile provides a non-zero predicate
unsigned int ballot(int predicate)

//─────────────────────────────────────────────
// Returns a mask identifying the set of threads that have the same
//   val. If no other thread has a matching val, only the
//   thread_rank()-th bit will be set
unsigned int match_any(T val)

//─────────────────────────────────────────────
// Returns (1<<size() -1) (a mask with all bits set), if all the
//   threads provide the same val pred is set to true if this
//   condition holds
unsigned int match_all(T val, int &pred)
```

These are identical in functionality to their warp *_sync counterparts. In fact they do use the warp primitives internally. The only differences are that (a) the mask is implicit (the tile itself) and (b) they are adjusted for the – possibly – smaller size of the group of threads. For example, while __ballot_sync returns a 32-bit unsigned integer which has the ith bit set to one if the ith lane provides a non-zero predicate, the ballot() method returns the same type of data, but the ith bit is set to one if the ith *ranked* thread provides a non-zero predicate.

For example, the following kernel code:

```
thread_block b = this_thread_block();
thread_block_tile<4> t = tiled_partition< 4 >( b );
int res = t.match_any(t.thread_rank() %2);
printf("ID %i TileID %i   Result: %i\n", myID, t.thread_rank(), res);
```

compiled with:

```
$ nvcc —arch=compute_70 example.cu
```

would produce

```
ID 0 TileID 0   Result: 5       <= Matching with thread 2
ID 1 TileID 1   Result: 10
ID 2 TileID 2   Result: 5       <= Matching with thread 0
ID 3 TileID 3   Result: 10
ID 4 TileID 0   Result: 5
ID 5 TileID 1   Result: 10
```

```
. . .
```

The final and most powerful way available for managing threads is the `coalesced_group`, which can be constructed with the following statement:

```
coalesced_group cg = coalesced_threads();
```

It consists of all the *threads in a warp* that execute the particular path containing the constructor call. By utilizing a `coalesced_group` we can break the limitation of power-of-two size that the `thread_block_tile` class imposes, while having all the methods listed above at our disposal.

Group partitioning

CUDA 11 introduced two more ways for partitioning a group into more `coalesced_group` objects based on a predicate value. That value can be an integer or a Boolean, leading accordingly to an arbitrary number of groups or a division into two groups.

The corresponding **labeled_partition** and **binary_partition** functions operate on `coalesced_group` or `thread_block_tile` instances to generate the new `coalesced_group` the calling thread belongs to. For example:

```
#include <cooperative_groups/details/partitioning.h>
using namespace cooperative_groups;
. . .

__global__ void foo()
{
  coalesced_group blk = coalesced_threads(); // all threads ↵
      in warp
  int myID = (int) blk.thread_rank();
  bool isOdd= myID % 2;

  coalesced_group part = binary_partition(blk, isOdd);
  . . .
}
```

This functionality requires a minimum of compute capability 7.0 and NVidia states that it is subject to future change.

The cooperative groups and their supported methods are a nice addition to the warp primitives, but they still require additional program logic to help consolidate the results across tiles/groups.

As an example application, let us consider the problem of filtering a dataset, i.e., produce a new dataset where all the input elements not satisfying a predicate function are removed. This is not a trivial problem if the output needs to be compacted, i.e., not have any empty slots where the deleted elements used to be.

To keep things simple, but still get something that could be the foundation of a more complex problem solution, the following program filters out the even numbers from the input array:

Listing 6.36: A cooperative groups-based filtering program for removing the even numbers from an array.

```
1   // File : odd_CGfilter.cu
2   #include <cooperative_groups.h>
3   using namespace cooperative_groups;
4   . . .
5   __global__ void countOdds (int *d, int N, int *oddBlockCount)
6   {
7     __shared__ int count;
8
9     int myID = blockIdx.x * blockDim.x + threadIdx.x;
10    int localID = threadIdx.x;
11    bool isOdd=false;
12    if(localID==0)
13      count=0;
14    __syncthreads ();
15
16    if (myID < N)
17      isOdd = d[myID] % 2;
18
19    if(isOdd)
20     {
21       coalesced_group active = coalesced_threads();
22       if(active.thread_rank()==0)
23         atomicAdd (&count, active.size());
24     }
25
26    __syncthreads ();
27
28    if (localID == 0)
29      oddBlockCount[blockIdx.x] = count;
30  }
31
32  //——————————————————————————————
33  __global__ void moveOdds (int *src, int N, int *dest, int *↵
         oddBlockCount)
34  {
35    int myID = blockIdx.x * blockDim.x + threadIdx.x;
36    bool isOdd=false;
37    if (myID < N)
38      isOdd = src[myID] % 2;
39
40    if(isOdd)
41     {
42       coalesced_group active = coalesced_threads();
43       int offset;
44       if(active.thread_rank() == 0)
45         offset = atomicAdd(oddBlockCount + blockIdx.x, active.size())↵
             ;
46       offset = active.shfl(offset,0);
47       dest[offset + active.thread_rank() ] = src[myID];
48     }
```

```
49    }
50
51    //————————————————————————————————
52    int main (int argc, char **argv)
53    {
54      int N = atoi (argv[1]);
55
56      unique_ptr<int[]> h_a; // host (h*) and
57      unique_ptr<int[]> h_odd;
58      unique_ptr<int[]> h_blockCounts;
59      int *d_a;                   // device (d*) pointers
60      int *d_odd;
61      int *d_blockCounts;
62
63      h_a = make_unique<int[]>(N);
64      . . .
65      cudaMalloc ((void **) &d_a, sizeof (int) * N);
66      cudaMemcpy (d_a, h_a.get(), sizeof (int) * N, ↩
            cudaMemcpyHostToDevice);
67
68      // calculate the execution configuration
69      int blockSize, gridSize;
70      cudaOccupancyMaxPotentialBlockSize (&gridSize, &blockSize, (void ↩
            *) countOdds, sizeof(int), N);
71      gridSize = ceil (1.0 * N / blockSize);
72
73      // allocate as many counters as blocks
74      h_blockCounts = make_unique<int[]>(gridSize);
75      cudaMalloc ((void **) &d_blockCounts, sizeof (int) * gridSize);
76
77      // first count what each block is supposed to handle
78      countOdds <<< gridSize, blockSize >>> (d_a, N, d_blockCounts);
79
80      cudaMemcpy (h_blockCounts.get(), d_blockCounts, sizeof (int)*↩
            gridSize, cudaMemcpyDeviceToHost);
81
82      // exclusive scan or prescan calculation
83      int toAdd=0;
84      for(int i=0;i<gridSize;i++)
85      {
86         int tmp = h_blockCounts[i];
87         h_blockCounts[i] = toAdd;
88         toAdd += tmp;
89      }
90
91      // offsets for each block copied back to the device
92      cudaMemcpy (d_blockCounts, h_blockCounts.get(), sizeof (int)*↩
            gridSize, cudaMemcpyHostToDevice);
93
94      // allocate memory for the result-holding array
95      h_odd = make_unique<int[]>(toAdd);
96      cudaMalloc ((void **) &d_odd, sizeof (int) * toAdd);
```

```
97
98    moveOdds <<< gridSize, blockSize>>> (d_a, N, d_odd, d_blockCounts)↵
      ;
99
100   cudaMemcpy (h_odd.get(), d_odd, sizeof (int)*toAdd, ↵
      cudaMemcpyDeviceToHost);
101   . . .
```

Listing 6.36 is structured around two kernels that need to be called in succession. This is mandated by the need to compute the destination offsets where the data will be moved, which is a computation that involves the whole input dataset and the grid that processes it. Without the ability to perform a grid-wide synchronization, we are forced to break the whole process into two kernels.

The input data are assigned on a one-to-one basis to kernel threads. The key points of Listing 6.36 are:

- The countOdds kernel is responsible for calculating the number of odd numbers found in each block. To this end, a cooperative group is created for each warp that consists of the threads that discover odd numbers. The size of the group is atomically added to a shared memory counter (defined on line 7 and initialized on lines 12–13). When all the threads in the block are done (line 26), the value of the counter is stored in the element of the oddBlockCounts array that corresponds to the block index (line 29).
- The d_blockCounts array, which will hold the counts found in the countOdds kernel, needs to have as many elements as the size of the grid. For this reason it is allocated (line 75) only after the execution configuration is found (line 71).
- Once the countOdds kernel completes execution, the block counts can be used in an exclusive prefix-sum summation operation (i.e., a scan where an element is not added to the previous elements sum) in order to calculate the block offsets. This can be done on the GPU (that would require a third kernel invocation) or the CPU, which is the design alternative implemented above. The block counts are moved to the host (line 80), the exclusive prefix-sum calculated on lines 83–89, and the results moved back to the device (line 92) prior to calling the second kernel.
- The moveOdds kernel completes the operation by moving the filtered data to a new destination array. The destination array is allocated to the exact size needed after the prefix-sum calculation is complete (line 96). The moveOdds kernel again diverges threads that are assigned odd numbers to the if block starting at line 42 to form a coalesced_group. The leader of the coalesced_group, i.e., the thread ranked 0, atomically adds the size of the group to the offset assigned to the block and retrieves the previous value (line 45), which is effectively the group-specific offset. This offset is propagated to the other group of threads with the shuffle operation of line 46, before each thread moves its assigned data to the destination array (line 47). Each thread is using its rank to advance beyond the group-specific offset in the destination array.

There are two major issues with the program of Listing 6.36. First, two kernels need to be involved, interleaved with device-to-host and host-to-device memory copies, which do not include the input and output copies. This is far from following the kernel fusion guideline. Second, the data can be reordered during the copy to the destination array, as the order of warp executions is unspecified. This is something that might not be acceptable in a different application scenario.

In Section 6.10.2 we show how both of these issues can be addressed.

6.10.1.1 Coalesced group reduction

CUDA 11 has introduced a long-awaited feature in the coalesced groups functionality: the ability to perform reduction at the `thread_block_tile` and `coalesced_group` level.

This is still some way off having reduction at the block or grid level, but it is a welcome addition to the CUDA toolkit. In Section 6.10.3 we show how this limitation can be overcome.

Reduction is performed via the `reduce` function template:

```
template <typename ArgType, typename OperType, typename GroupType>
auto reduce(
        const GroupType& group, // Group that participates in the
                                //    reduction (IN)
        ArgType&& val,          // Value to be reduced. Has to be (IN)
        OperType&& op)          // Operator to apply (IN)
        -> decltype(op(val,val));
```

On compute capability 8.0 devices this is a hardware-accelerated operation for 32-bit scalars.

Reduction is available only if the type of the operand is trivially copyable (i.e., `is_trivially_copyable<ArgType>::value` should be true) and its size is up to 32 bytes.

The available built-in *function objects* that can be used for the reduction are `plus()`, `less()`, `greater()`, `bit_and()`, `bit_xor()`, and `bit_or()`, with self-explanatory semantics. As these are function templates, when `reduce` is called, an object has to be constructed with explicit reference to `ArgType`.

For example, if we were summing up doubles, we should have:

```
double localSum;
. . .
res = reduce( group, localSum, plus<double >() );   // anonymous plus<↵
    double> object created
```

We can also supply our own function object to `reduce`. All that is needed is a `struct` with a binary `operator()` defined. For example:

Listing 6.37: A simple custom reduction function object.

```
template <typename T>
struct customReduction
{
    __device__ __host__
    T operator()(T a, T b)
```

```
  {
    . . .
  };
};

//-------------------------------------------
__global__ void foo (. . .)
{
  res = reduce (tile, localRes, customReduction< int >());
  . . .
```

Non-template function objects can be used as well.

A simple example of the `reduce` function template is given in Listing 6.38 in the following section.

6.10.1.2 Asynchronous memory copy to shared memory

Proper use of shared memory is one of the most critical factors in getting the most performance out of a GPU. A typical scenario (full discussion in Section 6.7.3) is to have a block's threads initialize a section of shared memory and synchronize before it is put to use.

CUDA 11 offers the capability to perform the transfer from global to shared memory *asynchronously*, using the **memcpy_async** function templates. The transfer is truly asynchronous on compute capability 8.0 devices (special hardware support is required) and on the condition that the source and destination addresses have 4-, 8-, or 16-byte alignment. When we use the regular global to shared memory copy pattern discussed in Section 6.7.3, e.g.:

```
__global__ void foo(int *data, ...)
{
  __shared__ int buff[M];

  for(int i=0 ; i < M ; i += blockDim.x)
     buff[i] = data[i];
     . . .
}
```

then the transfer takes place over several steps: the data first move to the L2 cache, then the L1 cache, and then to an SM register, before reaching shared memory (see Fig. 6.25(a)).

In compute capability 8.0 where **memcpy_async** is hardware-accelerated, the copy happens in fewer steps, as it is possible to complete the move without going through SM registers [32] (see Fig. 6.25(b)).

The `memcpy_async` function templates mimic the operation of the C standard library `memcpy` function[22]:

---

[22] ◈ **Pitfall**: The `memcpy` function expects the copy size in bytes. However, the `memcpy_async`, being templates, expect counts in number of elements. A failure to comply can lead to abruptly terminated kernels.

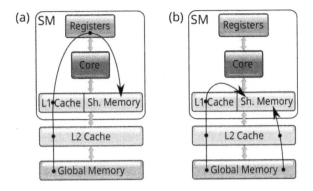

FIGURE 6.25

(a) Regular move of global data to shared memory. (b) Asynchronous memory copy using `memcpy_async`. In case (b) there are two possible movement paths, both skipping SM registers.

```
// Returns the size of the transferred block in number of elements
template <class GroupType, class ElemType>
size_t memcpy_async(
      GroupType &group,        // Reference to thread group (IN)
      ElemType *dst,           // Shared memory address (IN)
      size_t dstCount,         // Size of dst buffer in elements (IN)
      const ElemType *src,     // Global memory address (IN)
      size_t srcCount);        // Size of src buffer in elements (IN)
```

The size of the data block transferred is the minimum of `dstCount` and `srcCount`.

Once a `memcpy_async` has been initiated by the member threads of a block (it is a collective operation), threads can perform other actions until it is time to use the shared memory. The completion of the operation can be checked with the **wait** function:

```
template <class GroupType>
void wait(
      GroupType & group);    // Reference to thread group (IN)
```

The `wait` function will block until all pending transfers have been completed.

A scenario that would really put this feature to use would be to operate on different parts of the global memory data in a stream-like fashion, where an asynchronous transfer would overlap with the processing of the data from the previous transfer. The limited size of the shared memory makes this "multi-installment" technique the only viable approach to caching global data in shared memory (unless a small volume of data is involved).

In order to facilitate this scenario, we need to utilize the alternative forms of the `memcpy_async` and `wait` function templates, so that individual transfers can be identified and waited upon:

```
template <class GroupType, class ElemType>
size_t memcpy_async(
     GroupType &group,        // Reference to thread group (IN)
     ElemType *dst,           // Shared memory address (IN)
     size_t dstCount,         // Size of dst buffer in bytes (IN)
     const ElemType *src,     // Global memory address (IN)
     size_t srcCount          // Size of src buffer in bytes (IN)
     nvcuda::experimental::pipeline & pipe); // Object to associate
                              // transfer with (IN)
//————————————————————————————————
template <class GroupType>
void wait(
     GroupType & group,       // Reference to thread group (IN)
     nvcuda::experimental::pipeline & pipe, // Object associated
                              // with transfer (IN)
     size_t stage);           // Distance between last initiated
                              // transfer and the transfer on which
                              // to wait for. Setting this to 1
                              // means the immediate previous one (IN)
```

The `nvcuda::experimental::pipeline` object that is required as a parameter in these variants is used for queueing the transfers to be performed. A group may initiate multiple such transfers, each targeting a different section of shared memory.

The following code shows how we can overlap processing and data transfers of the input data. The calculation performed is mundane (counting the odd numbers) but it is just right for showing the relevant techniques:

Listing 6.38: A cooperative groups-based kernel that uses asynchronous memory copy from global to share memory to overlap computation and data transfer.

```
1  // File : CGasync.cu
2  #include <cooperative_groups.h>
3  #include <cooperative_groups/memcpy_async.h>
4  #include <cooperative_groups/reduce.h>
5  #include <cuda_pipeline.h>
6
7  using namespace cooperative_groups;
8  using namespace nvcuda::experimental;
9
10 const int BLKSIZE = 256;
11
12 //————————————————————————————————
13 __global__ void countOdds (int *src, int N, int *odd)
14 {
15   pipeline p;
16   __shared__ int cache[2][BLKSIZE];
17   int tranferred[2];
18   int whichBank = 0;
19   int oddCount = 0;
20
21   thread_block blk = this_thread_block ();
```

```
22    grid_group grd = this_grid ();
23
24    int myID = grd.thread_rank ();
25    int localID = blk.thread_rank ();
26    int totalThr = grd.size ();
27    int localIdx = blockIdx.x * blockDim.x; // starting point for data↩
          copy
28
29    // initiate the first transfer
30    tranferred[whichBank] = memcpy_async (blk, &(cache[whichBank][0]),↩
          BLKSIZE, src + localIdx, N - localIdx, p);
31    p.commit ();  // start the operation
32    localIdx += totalThr;
33    whichBank ^= 1;
34    while (localIdx < N)
35      {
36        // initiate the next transfer
37        tranferred[whichBank] = memcpy_async (blk, &(cache[whichBank↩
              ][0]), BLKSIZE, src + localIdx, N - localIdx, p);
38        p.commit ();  // start the operation
39        localIdx += totalThr;
40        whichBank ^= 1;
41
42        // wait on the previous transfer to end
43        wait (blk, p, 1);
44
45        if (localID < tranferred[whichBank]) // check if there are ↩
              actual data to process
46          oddCount += (cache[whichBank][localID] % 2);
47      }
48
49    // process the last batch of data
50    whichBank ^= 1;
51    wait (blk, p, 1);
52    if (localID < tranferred[whichBank])
53      oddCount += (cache[whichBank][localID] % 2);
54
55    // reduction on a per-warp basis (tile is 32 threads)
56    thread_block_tile < 32 > tile = tiled_partition < 32 > (blk);
57    oddCount = reduce (tile, oddCount, cooperative_groups::plus < int ↩
          >());
58
59    // first thread in the tile group adds to global counter
60    if (tile.thread_rank () == 0)
61      atomicAdd (odd, oddCount);
62  }
63  . . .
```

Lines 2–5 contain all the include directives required to access the desired functionality (and the reduce function template). All the included functions belong to the cooperative_groups namespace, apart from the pipeline object, which is part of nvcuda::experimental.

To achieve the computation/data transfer overlap, we create two sets of every object/data required. Each set consists of a shared memory buffer (cache defined on line 16) and an integer holding the number of elements to be transferred (transferred defined on line 17). Each set is selected by the whichBank integer defined on line 18. Once we initiate a transfer to the cache[whichBank] array, we can switch to the other set and process the corresponding data once they are available. Just one pipeline object (p defined on line 15) is required. The commit operation performed on lines 31 and 38 submits all async-copy operations as a batch. In our case there is just one pending.

Other key points of the Listing 6.38 code are:

- After the initial transfer is initiated (lines 30–31), a while loop is used to initiate the next transfer (lines 37–38) and then wait for the completion of the previous transfer (line 43). Once this barrier is reached, the fetched data can be processed (lines 45–46).
- Each block of threads "walks over" the input data by transferring a block and advancing the next position from which it will transfer (localIdx) by the number of total threads (lines 32 and 39).
- The last data to be transferred are processed on lines 52–53.
- The size of the buffers is set to BLKSIZE, which is also the execution configuration block size. This is not a requirement in general, so the buffer size is application-specific or constrained by the size of available shared memory.
- As the global data are not required to be a multiple of BLKSIZE, it is essential to check that each thread has actual data to process (checks on lines 45 and 52).
- The cooperative_groups namespace qualification for the plus<>() function template on line 57 is required because of a naming clash with standard C++ library code.
- Each thread collects its own result for the data it processes in variable oddCount (line 19).
- The reduction operation at line 57 is tile-based, so we get a result for each warp of threads, as the tile size is set to 32 (line 56). The "leader" of each tile (thread ranked 0) is responsible for adding the local warp result to the global counter (lines 60–61).

The reduction at the final stage of the kernel can be further improved to avoid doing multiple atomic additions to global memory. This is left as an exercise.

6.10.2 Interblock cooperative groups

The intrablock cooperative groups are a welcome addition to the warp primitives that improve the readability and performance of CUDA kernels. The interblock cooperatives groups though add a totally different – and very welcome – addition to CUDA programming: grid-level and cross-device-level synchronization. This capability is available to compute capability 6.0 devices and above. Cross-device synchronization is not covered here, but it shares many similarities to grid synchronization.

In order to be able to synchronize threads across the grid, all that is needed are two statements:

```
grid_group g = this_grid();
g.sync();
```

However, there is a trade-off: the angular brackets kernel launch has to be replaced by a call to this function:

```
cudaLaunchCooperativeKernel(
    const T *func,           // Kernel to call (IN)
    dim3 gridDim,            // Execution configuration param. (IN)
    dim3 blockDim,
    void **args,             // Pointer to array of pointers to
                             // kernel parameters (IN)
    size_t sharedMem = 0,    // Dynamically allocated shared memory
                             // in bytes (IN)
    cudaStream_t stream = 0  // Stream for submission (IN)
);
```

Launches are still asynchronous. The parameter requiring more explanation is the `args` one. In fact it is identical in semantics to the `kernelParams` field of the `cudaKernelNodeParams` structure explained in Section 6.8.1. So, `args` is a pointer to an array of pointers, each pointing to a parameter required for the launch of the `func` kernel. The type and size of the data that are pointed at are inferred from `func`'s signature.

There are two additional requirements: (a) the source code must be compiled with relocatable device code enabled, i.e., using the `-rdc=true` switch, and (b) care should be taken in picking the grid size, as the use of grid synchronization puts a restriction on the maximum number of blocks that can be launched. For the grid to synchronize, all the blocks should be able to execute (more precisely, to be resident) at the same time, which means we can have between one block per SM and the maximum resident blocks allowed by the compute capability of the target device, subject to shared memory and register availability.

Equipped with the `grid_group` class, we can solve the filtering problem of the previous section with just one kernel:

Listing 6.39: A kernel that uses grid synchronization for removing the even numbers from an array.

```
1  // File : odd_CGfilter2.cu
2  #include <cooperative_groups.h>
3  using namespace cooperative_groups;
4  . . .
5
6  __global__ void filterOdds (int *src, int *dest, int N, int *←
       oddWarpCount)
7  {
8    int myID = blockIdx.x * blockDim.x + threadIdx.x;
9    int warpID = myID / 32;          // global warp index
```

```
10    int totalWarps = blockDim.x * gridDim.x / 32;
11    int *toAddToBlock = oddWarpCount + totalWarps;
12    bool isOdd = false;
13
14    // init block offsets
15    if (myID < gridDim.x)
16      toAddToBlock[myID] = 0;
17
18    //----------------------------------------------
19    // Step 1: find the number of odds assigned to each warp
20    if (myID < N)
21      isOdd = src[myID] % 2;          // false for thread beyond N-1
22
23    if (isOdd)
24      {
25        coalesced_group active = coalesced_threads ();
26        if (active.thread_rank () == 0)
27          oddWarpCount[warpID] = active.size ();
28      }
29
30    grid_group g = this_grid ();
31    g.sync ();
32
33    //----------------------------------------------
34    // Step 2: calculate the prefix-sum of the counts
35    if (myID < totalWarps)
36      {
37        int val = oddWarpCount[myID];
38        coalesced_group cg = coalesced_threads ();
39
40        for (int offset = 1; offset < 32; offset *= 2)
41          {
42            int tmp = cg.shfl_up (val, offset);
43            if (cg.thread_rank () >= offset)          // source exists?
44              val += tmp;
45          }
46        oddWarpCount[myID] = val;
47      }
48    g.sync ();
49
50    //----------------------------------------------
51    // Step 3: Find by how much to offset each block
52    if (myID < gridDim.x)
53      {
54        int toAdd = oddWarpCount[myID * 32 + 31];
55        for (int i = myID + 1; i < gridDim.x; i++)
56          atomicAdd (toAddToBlock + i, toAdd);   // multiple warps ↩
                  may be running
57      }
58    g.sync ();
59
60    // Adjust the warp offsets accordingly
```

```
61    if (myID < totalWarps)
62      oddWarpCount[myID] += toAddToBlock[myID / 32];
63
64    g.sync ();
65
66    //---------------------------------------------------
67    // Step 4: move data
68    if (isOdd)
69      {
70        coalesced_group active = coalesced_threads ();
71        int offset;
72        if (warpID == 0)
73          offset = active.thread_rank ();
74        else
75          offset = oddWarpCount[warpID - 1] + active.thread_rank ();
76        dest[offset] = src[myID];
77      }
78  }
```

The filterOdds kernel processes one data item per thread, in 1024-thread blocks. It operates in four phases/steps which are separated by grid synchronization statements (lines 31, 48, and 64), ensuring that different blocks execute and produce results in a coordinated fashion:

Step 1: Coalesced threads are grouped together and the size of the group is effectively the number of odd numbers discovered by the corresponding warp. This warp-specific count is stored in the oddWarpCount array, indexed by the corresponding warp index (warpID, found on line 9).

Step 2: A prefix-sum calculation for every 32 warps (i.e., the warps of a block) produces an offset relative to the beginning of the block for each warp for the placement of its assigned odd numbers. The last of the counts computed is essentially the number of odds found by that block (used on line 54).

Step 3: Each block needs the offset in the destination array space, where it can move its data. There is a separate counter per block, assigned in array toAddtoBlock, and a prefix-sum of the block counts is performed. Once these block-specific offsets are calculated (line 58), the warp offsets are adjusted on line 62. The first element of the toAddtoBlock array is the ((blockDim.x * gridDim.x)/32)-th element of oddWarpCount (line 11).

toAddtoBlock is allocated as part of the oddWarpCount array by the host (see line 107 in Listing 6.40), to avoid having to do extra allocations/deallocations and requiring an extra kernel parameter.

Step 4: Finally the move of the selected data can be performed. Each member of the coalesced group uses its group rank to calculate the proper position in the destination array.

The main function that calls the filterOdds kernel is shown below:

Listing 6.40: The main function for calling the kernel of Listing 6.39.

```
79  // File : odd_CGfilter2.cu
80  int main (int argc, char **argv)
81  {
82    unique_ptr < int[] > h_a;        // host (h*) and
83    unique_ptr < int[] > h_odd;
84    int *d_a;                        // device (d*) pointers
85    int *d_odd;
86    int *d_blockCounts;
87
88    h_a = make_unique < int[] > (N);
89    cudaMalloc ((void **) &d_a, sizeof (int) * N);
90
91    numberGen (N, MAXVALUE, h_a.get ());
92
93    cudaMemcpy (d_a, h_a.get (), sizeof (int) * N, ←
            cudaMemcpyHostToDevice);
94
95    int blockSize = 1024, gridSize;
96    cudaDeviceProp pr;
97    cudaGetDeviceProperties (&pr, 0);        // replace 0 with ←
            appropriate ID in case of a multi-GPU system
98    int SM = pr.multiProcessorCount;
99    int numBlocksPerSm;
100   cudaOccupancyMaxActiveBlocksPerMultiprocessor (&numBlocksPerSm, ←
            filterOdds, blockSize, 0);
101
102   gridSize = ceil (1.0 * N / blockSize);
103   assert(gridSize <= SM * numBlocksPerSm); // make sure we can ←
            launch
104
105   int warpPerBlock = blockSize / 32;
106   // allocate as many counters as warps and blocks
107   cudaMalloc ((void **) &d_blockCounts, sizeof (int) * gridSize * (←
            warpPerBlock + 1)); // one for each warp, plus one for every ←
            block
108   h_odd = make_unique < int[] > (N);
109   cudaMalloc ((void **) &d_odd, sizeof (int) * N);
110
111   void *args[] = { &d_a, &d_odd, &N, &d_blockCounts };
112   cudaLaunchCooperativeKernel ((void *) filterOdds, gridSize, ←
            blockSize, args, 0);        // Instead of  filterOdds <<< ←
            gridSize, blockSize >>> (d_a, N, d_odd, d_blockCounts);
113
114   int toGet; // how many odds to retrieve from the device
115   cudaMemcpy (&toGet, d_blockCounts + gridSize * warpPerBlock - 1, ←
            sizeof (int), cudaMemcpyDeviceToHost);
116
117   cudaMemcpy (h_odd.get (), d_odd, toGet * sizeof (int), ←
            cudaMemcpyDeviceToHost);
118   . . .
```

The `main` function shown above is unremarkable with the exception of one major item: the calculation of the execution configuration. The statement on line 100 establishes how many blocks are allowed to be launched per SM. While `filterOdds` uses no shared memory and only 40 registers (as reported by `nvcc`), line 100 returns a value of one (1) when the program executes on a Turing device (an RTX 2060 Super in particular). This significantly limits the size of the dataset that can be fed to the kernel. For example, on the test device used which comes with 34 SMs, a maximum of $34 \cdot 1024 = 34,816$ integers can be filtered. This is unfortunately a trade-off for grid synchronization. The kernels in Listing 6.36 have no such problem size/grid size restriction.

Line 103 is there to protect against an attempt to launch a bigger grid, which if allowed would result in a program that produces the wrong or no output.

As a last clarification point, line 115 retrieves the total amount of odds found, which is stored by step 3 of the `filterOdds` kernel in the last element of the `toAddtoBlock` array (line 56). As mentioned previously, `toAddtoBlock` is an alias for the last elements of the `d_blockCounts` array. This allows us to minimize the total communicated data during the last device-to-host transfer (line 117).

6.10.3 Grid-level reduction

The `reduce` function template is only available as a `thread_block_tile` or a `coalesced_group` collective, which limits the results to a maximum of `warpSize=32` threads. Getting reduction to work at the block or grid level requires that the tile/group-level results are consolidated with subsequent rounds of reduction.

The following code implements a grid-level reduction over four steps. The process is graphically presented in Fig. 6.26:

Listing 6.41: A block- and grid-level reduction based on the `reduce` collective. Addition is assumed to be the reduction operation.

```
1   // File : CGreduce_grid.cu
2   . . .
3   //-----------------------------------------------
4   __global__ void countOdds (int *src, int N, int *odd, int *perBlock)
5   {
6     int oddCount = 0;
7     __shared__ int cache[32];        // maximum possible warps
8
9     thread_block blk = this_thread_block ();
10    grid_group grd = this_grid ();
11
12    int myID = grd.thread_rank ();
13    int localID = blk.thread_rank ();
14    int totalThr = grd.size ();
15
16    // calculate local result
17    for (int i = myID; i < N; i += totalThr)
18      oddCount += (src[i] % 2);
```

```
19
20      //—————————
21      // Step 1: reduction on a per—warp basis (tile is 32 threads)
22      thread_block_tile < 32 > tile = tiled_partition < 32 > (blk);
23      oddCount = reduce (tile, oddCount, cooperative_groups::plus < int ↩
            >());
24
25      // store the tile results in shared memory
26      if (tile.thread_rank () == 0)
27          cache[tile.meta_group_rank ()] = oddCount;
28      blk.sync ();
29
30      //—————————
31      // Step 2: reduce the block results into one. First warp in block ↩
            employed for this
32      if (tile.meta_group_rank () == 0 && localID < (blk.size () + ↩
            warpSize — 1) / warpSize)
33      {
34          coalesced_group activeWarps = coalesced_threads ();
35          oddCount = cache[localID];
36          oddCount = reduce (activeWarps, oddCount, cooperative_groups::↩
                plus < int >());
37
38          // store block result in global memory
39          if (activeWarps.thread_rank () == 0)
40              perBlock[blk.group_index ().x] = oddCount;
41      }
42      grd.sync ();
43
44      //—————————
45      // Step 3: reduce grid results using the first block in the grid
46      if (blk.group_index ().x == 0)
47      {
48          oddCount = 0;
49          for (int i = localID; i < grd.group_dim ().x; i += blk.size ()↩
                )
50              oddCount += perBlock[i];
51          oddCount = reduce (tile, oddCount, cooperative_groups::plus < ↩
                int >());
52          blk.sync ();
53
54          // save warp results to shared memory
55          if (tile.thread_rank () == 0)
56              cache[tile.meta_group_rank ()] = oddCount;
57          blk.sync ();
58
59          //—————————
60          // Step 4: first warp in block produces the final result
61          if (tile.meta_group_rank () == 0 && localID < (blk.size () + ↩
                warpSize — 1) / warpSize)
62          {
63              coalesced_group activeWarps = coalesced_threads ();
```

```
64          oddCount = cache[localID];
65          oddCount = reduce (activeWarps, oddCount, ↩
                cooperative_groups::plus < int >());
66          *odd = oddCount;
67      }
68    }
69 }
70
71 //────────────────────────────────────
72 int main (int argc, char **argv)
73 {
74   int N = atoi (argv[1]);          // size of array to process
75
76   unique_ptr < int[] > h_a;        // host (h*) and
77   int *d_a;                        // device (d*) pointers
78   int h_odd;
79   int *d_odd;
80   int *d_perBlock;
81
82   // allocate and initialize host data
83   h_a = make_unique < int[] > (N);
84   . . .
85   CUDA_CHECK_RETURN (cudaMalloc ((void **) &d_a, sizeof (int) * N));
86   CUDA_CHECK_RETURN (cudaMemcpy (d_a, h_a.get (), sizeof (int) * N, ↩
        cudaMemcpyHostToDevice));
87
88   int blockSize = BLKSIZE, gridSize;
89   . . .
90   CUDA_CHECK_RETURN (cudaMalloc ((void **) &d_odd, sizeof (int)));
91   CUDA_CHECK_RETURN (cudaMemset (d_odd, 0, sizeof (int)));
92   CUDA_CHECK_RETURN (cudaMalloc ((void **) &d_perBlock, sizeof (int)↩
        * gridSize));
93
94   void *args[] = { &d_a, &N, &d_odd, &d_perBlock };
95   cudaLaunchCooperativeKernel ((void *) countOdds, gridSize, ↩
        blockSize, args, 0);
96
97   CUDA_CHECK_RETURN (cudaMemcpy (&h_odd, d_odd, sizeof (int), ↩
        cudaMemcpyDeviceToHost));
98   . . .
```

The kernel in Listing 6.41 works in four steps. The last two are mirroring the first two. In detail:

Step 1: The thread-local results are accumulated by splitting the block into tiles of 32 threads each (line 22) and calling the reduce collective function. The block is represented by the blk variable (defined on line 9). The partial results are stored in the cache shared-memory array defined on line 7 by the "leader," i.e., the thread ranked 0, of each tile (lines 27–28). As the maximum block size is 1024 threads, there can be no more than 32 32-thread tiles, hence the hardcoded size of the cache array.

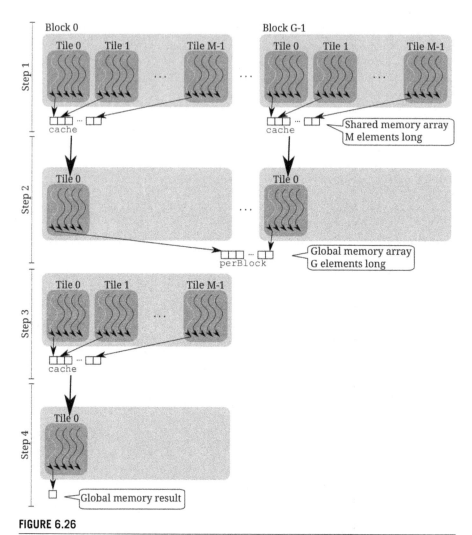

FIGURE 6.26

Grid-level reduction using cooperative groups. The names shown reflect the code in Listing 6.41. In step 1 the thread-local results are reduced using tiles and saved in shared memory. In the second step, a block-wide reduction is performed by the first tile in each block and the result is saved to global memory. During step 3 the first block in the grid reads the partial results stored in global memory and produces tile-partial results. The final fourth step uses the first tile of the first block to reduce the final result.

Step 2: The first tile of each block reads the `cache` array and reduces the result into an element of the shared-memory `perBlock` array, positioned at the index of the `blk` group (line 40). The complex condition of line 32 ensures that (a) only the first tile in each block executes the `if` body and (b) data exist for reduction. The second requirement is why a `coalesced_group` is defined (line 34) and used in the reduction instead of the regular tile created previously.

Step 3: The first block reads in the `perBlock` data and produces tile-wide results (lines 49–51). Tile-wide reduction results are produced on line 51 and saved by the tile leaders in the `cache` array.

Step 4: Similarly to step 3 being a mirror of step 1, this step is a mirror of step 2. The first tile in the first block reads the `cache` array data and reduces the final grid-wide result. Again the second part of the if condition on line 61 exists to ensure that threads read and process actual data. Using the `tile` group on line 65 instead of the `activeWarps` coalesced group would be justified only if the block had 1024 threads.

Between the different steps block (lines 28, 52, and 57) and grid synchronizations (line 42) ensure that operations are completed in the proper order before the next ones can begin.

The shared-memory array that holds the intermediate block results after step 2 has to be explicitly allocated by the host (line 92) and passed as a kernel parameter (line 94).

As grid synchronization is utilized, the kernel launch has to be performed with the `cudaLaunchCooperativeKernel` function on line 95.

The execution configuration calculations are not shown in Listing 6.41. What is imperative though is that the grid size has to be calculated/set so that *all blocks can be resident at the same time*. Otherwise, there cannot be a grid-level barrier and the kernel will fail to complete its execution.

6.11 Dynamic parallelism

Dynamic parallelism is a mechanism that was introduced with compute capability 3.5 devices, and it enables the launch of kernels from the device. This means that the divide-and-conquer decomposition pattern discussed in Section 2.3.2 can be conveniently implemented in CUDA with minimum effort. A kernel can use the same syntax that the host is using, i.e., the triple angular brackets $<<<>>>$, to asynchronously launch other kernels.

A grid that is launched by a CUDA thread is considered a *child grid*. The grid of the launcher is called the *parent grid*. Child grids execute asynchronously, as if they were launched by the host. However, typical nesting rules apply, i.e., a parent grid is not considered finished (even if its threads have exited the kernel) until all the child grids launched by its threads are also finished.

Device-launched kernels can be only monitored from threads belonging to the same block as the launcher thread. It is this particular block that is not considered finished until the child grids are complete. Even if a `cudaDeviceSynchronize` call is not explicitly used, synchronization is automatically invoked at the end of the parent block. Calling the cudaDeviceSynchronize function from a thread causes the thread to block until all the previous child grids submitted *by the same block* are complete.

Streams and events can be used to synchronize and control dependencies between different launches via a subset of the API that is available for the host (e.g., event timing is not supported). However, the launches cannot target another GPU device in a multi-GPU system. This is still host-only territory.

As far as memory management is concerned, a child grid launch can be passed references to global data, but not to shared memory, since shared memory is private to a specific SM. The same applies to local memory, as it is private to a thread.

As an example of dynamic parallelism, Listing 6.42 holds a CUDA implementation of the quicksort algorithm.

Listing 6.42: A CUDA implementation of quicksort that utilizes dynamic parallelism.

```
1  // File : quicksort_dynamic.cu
2  . . .
3  const int MAXRECURSIONDEPTH=16;
4
5  // *************************************************
6  void numberGen (int N, int max, int *store)
7  {
8    int i;
9    srand (time (0));
10   for (i = 0; i < N; i++)
11     store[i] = rand () % max;
12 }
13
14 // *************************************************
15 __device__ void swap (int *data, int x, int y)
16 {
17   int temp = data[x];
18   data[x] = data[y];
19   data[y] = temp;
20 }
21
22 // *************************************************
23 __device__ int partition (int *data, int N)
24 {
25   int i = 0, j = N;
26   int pivot = data[0];
27
28   do
29     {
30       do
31         {
32           i++;
33         }
34       while (pivot > data[i] && i < N);
35
36       do
37         {
```

```
38           j--;
39         }
40       while (pivot < data[j] && j > 0);
41       swap (data, i, j);
42     }
43   while (i < j);
44   // undo last swap
45   swap (data, i, j);
46
47   // fix the pivot element position
48   swap (data, 0, j);
49   return j;
50 }
51
52 // ************************************************
53 __device__ void insertionSort (int *data, int N)
54 {
55   int loc=1;
56   while(loc < N)
57   {
58     int temp = data[loc];
59     int i=loc-1;
60     while(i>=0 && data[i] > temp)
61     {
62       data[i+1]=data[i];
63       i--;
64     }
65     data[i+1] = temp;
66     loc++;
67   }
68 }
69
70 // ************************************************
71 __global__ void QSort (int *data, int N, int depth)
72 {
73   if(depth == MAXRECURSIONDEPTH)
74   {
75     insertionSort(data, N);
76     return ;
77   }
78
79   if (N <= 1)
80     return ;
81
82   // break the data into a left and right part
83   int pivotPos = partition (data, N);
84
85   cudaStream_t s0, s1;
86   // sort the left part if it exists
87   if (pivotPos > 0)
88     {
89       cudaStreamCreateWithFlags (&s0, cudaStreamNonBlocking);
```

```
90          QSort <<< 1, 1, 0, s0 >>> (data, pivotPos, depth+1);
91          cudaStreamDestroy (s0);
92        }
93
94      // sort the right part if it exists
95      if (pivotPos < N - 1)
96        {
97          cudaStreamCreateWithFlags (&s1, cudaStreamNonBlocking);
98          QSort <<< 1, 1, 0, s1 >>> (&(data[pivotPos + 1]), N - pivotPos↩
                - 1, depth+1);
99          cudaStreamDestroy (s1);
100       }
101   }
102
103   //─────────────────────────────────────────────────────────────
104   int main (int argc, char *argv[])
105   {
106     if (argc == 1)
107       {
108         fprintf (stderr, "%s N\n", argv[0]);
109         exit (0);
110       }
111     int N = atoi (argv[1]);
112     int *data;
113     cudaMallocManaged ((void **) &data, N * sizeof (int));
114
115     numberGen (N, 1000, data);
116
117     QSort <<< 1, 1 >>> (data, N, 0);
118
119     cudaDeviceSynchronize ();
120
121     // clean up allocated memory
122     cudaFree (data);
123     return 0;
124   }
```

The majority of the code in Listing 6.42 is a straightforward implementation of the well-known sequential quicksort and insertion sort algorithms. For this reason we will not comment on the inner workings of the partition and insertionSort functions. The key points are as follows:

- The main function reads from the standard input the size N of the data array of integers to be sorted. It proceeds to allocate a block of unified memory for this task (line 113) and initialize the data to random values (line 115).
- The host launches the QSort kernel with a grid of one block, with the block made up of one thread. The concurrency is the outcome of asynchronously launching two more such grids on lines 90 and 98, after the data are partitioned using the partition __device__ function. The partition function (lines 23–50) returns the location in the sorted array of the element used to split the data in two (the

pivot element), allowing QSort to decide whether the parts hold any data or not (condition checks on lines 87 and 95).

- The child grids are launched using two separate streams. Launching them into the default stream would force their sequential execution.
- The cudaStreamDestroy calls of lines 91 and 99 are non-blocking. The associated streams will be destroyed once the work items deposited in them are complete. Still, the parent grid cannot terminate before the child grids are complete.
- The recursion is limited by monitoring the depth of the child grids generated (line 73). The depth parameter is incremented whenever a child grid is launched. If it matches the threshold specified by the MAXRECURSIONDEPTH constant, we switch to the insertion sort algorithm (lines 53–68).

It should be noted that Listing 6.42 is just a demonstration of dynamic parallelism in action, and it is not meant to serve as a fast sorting implementation. After all, the design of quicksort is inherently unsuitable for GPU execution. Even if we were not launching one-block grids of one thread, the unavoidable thread divergence would hinder any performance gains.

As a last note, in order to compile the program of Listing 6.42, the following command is required, as the code must be relocatable:

```
$ nvcc quicksort_dynamic.cu —rdc=true —o quicksort_dynamic
```

6.12 Debugging CUDA programs

CUDA applications can be debugged using:

- The Eclipse integrated debugger for GUI-based operation under Linux. Under Windows, Visual Studio provides similar capabilities.
- CUDA-GDB (cuda-gdb) is a command-line debugger based on GNU's debugger (gdb) and it is available for the Linux platform. Putting aside the awkward interface, CUDA-GDB offers all the conveniences of a modern debugger, such as single-step execution, breakpoints in kernel code, inspection of individual threads, etc. Additionally, because it shares the same commands with the GNU debugger, it can be used in tandem with front-ends such as DDD, eliminating the need for someone to memorize its commands. For example, the following instructs DDD to use cuda-gdb for a debugging session:

```
$ ddd —debugger cuda—gdb myCudaProgram
```

Actually, in Linux Eclipse is just a front-end for CUDA-GDB.

Originally, debugging CUDA programs suffered from a major drawback that stems from the peculiarity of using a display device for computations: two GPUs were required, one for running the application under development and one for regular display. The former GPU may be hosted in the same machine or a remote one.

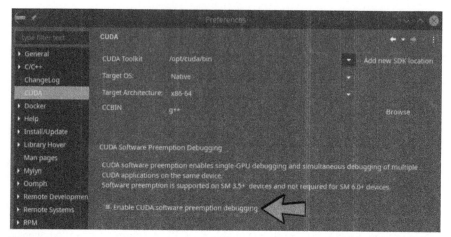

FIGURE 6.27

Partial view of the CUDA plugin options in the Eclipse Preferences dialog.

Most users would find themselves in the second scenario, i.e., using a remote machine (e.g., a shared server) for debugging purposes.

Currently this limitation has been removed for devices of compute capability 3.5 and above by allowing the debugger to release the GPU for display purposes when a breakpoint in kernel code is reached. This functionality had to be explicitly enabled by one of the following command shell actions in CUDA 10:

```
$ set cuda software_preemption on
# OR
$ export CUDA_DEBUGGER_SOFTWARE_PREEMPTION=1
```

Starting with CUDA 11, this is an option that should be enabled within the Eclipse IDE as shown in Fig. 6.27 for devices below compute capability 6.0.

In this section we will explore how Nsight Eclipse Plugins Edition can be used for remote debugging, following one of the most probable scenarios that one can encounter in HPC or cluster environments.

A remote debugging session can be initiated by selecting to use the remote NVidia CUDA GDB as shown in Fig. 6.28.

The next dialog, which is shown in Fig. 6.29, controls how the remote system will get the application. Unless a common filesystem, e.g., an NFS volume, is used, this has to be done by uploading the compiled binary. If the remote system is used for the very first time, pressing "Manage" allows the user to specify the connection details.

The connection details, including the DNS name or IP address of the remote machine, the connection protocol and port, the user credentials, and the paths of the needed executables (cuda-gdbserver) and libraries, can be supplied with the sequence of dialogs shown in Fig. 6.30.

Typically, the defaults on the dialogs should serve well the majority of the users.

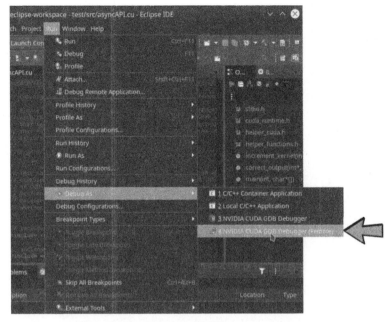

FIGURE 6.28

Starting a remote debugging session in Nsight Eclipse Plugins Edition.

CAUTION: It is a good idea to use the same CUDA SDK in both the local and remote hosts in order to avoid errors caused by missing or different version libraries.

6.13 Profiling CUDA programs

Profiling is an integral part of parallel program development, more so in the case of CUDA programs where the idiosyncrasies of the underlying hardware deviate from what programmers think to be typical behavior. In the case of a sequential program, profiling can help us pinpoint the parts of the program that contribute the most to the execution time. In the case of a GPU program, profiling can help us understand what are the factors limiting/preventing the GPU from achieving its peak performance.

NVidia provides profiling functionality via the following tools:

- `nvprof` is a command-line-based utility for profiling CUDA programs. A number of switches enable control over the profiling process (e.g., what kind of metrics to collect). It is the tool of choice for profiling remote systems.
- NVidia Visual Profiler (`nvvp`) is a GUI-based tool for visualizing the execution timeline of a CUDA program. `nvvp` can provide a plethora of analyses, guiding the development of a CUDA program. `nvvp` can also be used for the visualization of data collected from `nvprof`. The Visual Profiler can be used as a stand-alone tool

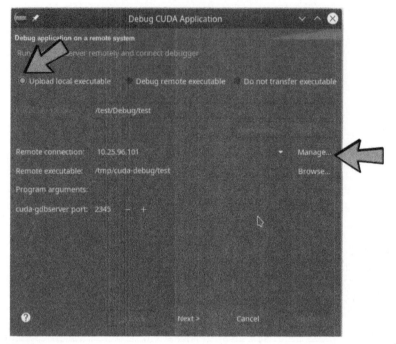

FIGURE 6.29

Dialog for selecting how the application will reach the remote system (typically by uploading). By pressing "Manage" a user can specify the remote system connection parameters.

or embedded within Nsight Eclipse Plugins Edition. It can be used from within the IDE by invoking "Run → Profile As → NVidia Visual Profiler" (this option is available in the C/C++ view of Eclipse).

- Nsight Compute is a kernel profiler suitable for devices of compute capability 7.5 and above. It comes in both GUI (`nv-nsight-cu`) and CLI (`nv-nsight-cu-cli`) flavors. Nsight Compute does not support tracing, which means that it can provide execution metrics (such as occupancy) but no timing information.
- Nsight Systems is a tool capable of profiling the whole system performance, including both CPU and GPU code. It also comes as a GUI or CLI command and it comes bundled with the CUDA SDK. In contrast to Nsight Compute, this is a tool that can produce tracing output.

Nsight Compute and Nsight Systems are the latest generation of profiling tools from NVidia. In terms of their functionality, they share similarities with the Scalasca and Tau tools, respectively (see Section 5.21). Scalasca and Tau can also be used for GPU profiling. On the other hand, NVidia Visual Profiler and `nvprof` are officially deprecated and they will not support new features added to future GPU architectures.

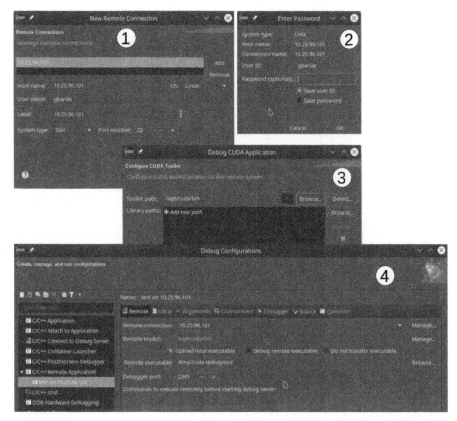

FIGURE 6.30

Nsight Eclipse Plugins Edition dialogs for supplying remote system (1) connection information, (2) user credentials, and (3) location of the CUDA debugger and other libraries that might be required by the application to be debugged. In (3) the "Detect" button can be used to validate the user choices. (4) "Debug Configurations" dialog for editing previously set up configurations.

The starting point in profiling a program is to decide which are the parts to be examined. Profiling is a process that is characterized by:

1. The potential generation of huge amounts of – visual – data that increase monotonically as a function of the execution time. Extracting useful information from long runs can be very challenging. It is a better idea to focus on specific parts of the program.
2. The profiler can influence the execution of the program by altering the timing of operations and the amount of I/O generated.
3. The profiler's results can be influenced by irregular operations timing. Because the profiler may need to run the program several times in order to collect reliable

statistics, it is desirable, especially in the case of multi-threaded host programs that use different contexts/streams, to have a single CPU thread generate all the GPU operations in the same sequence every time.

The above problems can be minimized or eliminated by performing focused instead of whole-program profiling. In **focused profiling** only parts of the program which are executed between calls to the `cudaProfilerStart()` and `cudaProfiler-Stop()` functions will be profiled, i.e., profiling is controlled programmatically from within the profiled program. The skeleton of a focused profiled program would be similar to:

```
#include <cuda_profiler_api.h>  /* necessary include file */
. . .
cudaProfilerStart();

// calls to CPU and GPU routines

cudaProfilerStop();
. . .
```

The Visual Profiler when run as a stand-alone program can also perform **guided analysis**, i.e., it can run an analysis phase where a set of problem areas are identified in the program, and solutions are proposed. An example of the results of the guided analysis is shown in Fig. 6.31. A detailed example of how a profiler can be used to guide our design decisions is provided in Section 6.15.

This facility is not available for compute capability 7.5 and above devices, as it has been delegated to Nsight Compute. Nsight Compute can be executed in a variety of configurations, including in the form of a client-server setup, where the CLI profiles an application under the control of the GUI interface for interactive profiling sessions. Upon launching `nv-nsight-cu`, a user can use the "Quick Launch" shortcut to specify the profiler execution settings (see Fig. 6.32).

Upon running the profiler, the results are stored in an `.nsight-cuprof-report` file that can be opened separately by the GUI front-end. The profiler can also be executed by copying-and-pasting the "Command Line" textbox contents (see Fig. 6.32②) in a console window, which allows for more flexibility, e.g., running the profiler remotely or using special permissions (superuser).

Nsight Systems mirrors the design philosophy of Nsight Compute, providing a CLI utility (`nsys`) and a GUI front-end (`nsight-sys`), but at the moment of this writing the GUI component is a bit spartan. Fortunately, one can use `nsys` to do the profiling and `nsight-sys` for inspecting the outcome.

In order to use focused profiling with `nsys`, the "`-c cudaProfilerApi`" switch needs to be employed. For example:

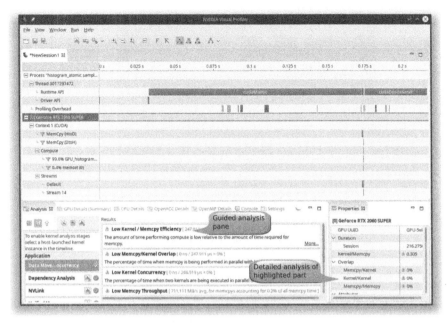

FIGURE 6.31

A sample screenshot of NVidia's Visual Profiler in action.

```
$ nsys profile —c cudaProfilerApi —o log ./fooProg sample.pgm
# Or for full program profiling
$ nsys profile —o log ./fooProg sample.pgm
```

The outcome is a log.qdrep file that can be inspected as shown in Fig. 6.33. The benefit of using the GUI front-end is that it can automatically run the application multiple times and collect statistics.

6.14 CUDA and MPI

A GPU can be a formidable tool for speeding up a computation. So, it is only natural to expect that we could do more and we could go further by employing multiple GPUs. NVidia's NVLink and NVSwitch technologies allow up to 16 GPUs to be interlinked in a fully connected topology. CUDA allows the transfer of data directly between the memories of NVLink-connected GPUs (see Section 6.7.4.2 on unified memory) and cooperative groups allow kernel launches across multiple devices.

If, on the other hand, someone desires to use the GPUs in a multi-GPU system individually, the cudaSetDevice() function can be used to specify the target device:

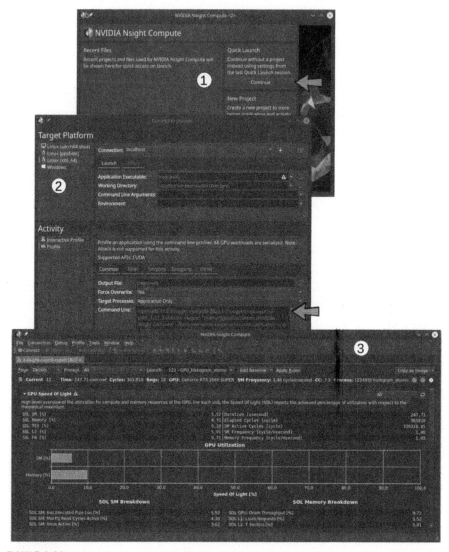

FIGURE 6.32

Nsight Compute screenshots: ① Initial dialog. Selecting "Quick Launch" allows the user to enter the application-to-be-profiled information in ②. The "Command Line" textbox in ② contains the command that will be executed upon pressing "Launch." ③ Profiling results and analysis.

```
cudaError_t cudaSetDevice (int device);  // device is a number ↩
    between 0 and the number_of_GPUs - 1
```

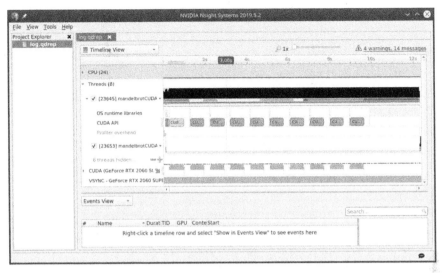

FIGURE 6.33

A sample screenshot of Nsight Systems, inspecting the output of a profile session.

In most scenarios a 16-GPU beast will probably be enough to satisfy the most demanding applications. However, such a machine requires a substantial investment. Most institutions rely on intranets of GPU-equipped machines or cloud-provisioned GPU clusters.

Mastering the power of these systems requires the use of MPI (see Chapter 5) for communication purposes. MPI is designed to essentially transfer data between host buffers, making the transfer of data residing in GPU memory space a problem. There are two possible solutions, based on whether MPI is CUDA-aware or not:

(i) **MPI is not CUDA-aware**: Data are explicitly transferred from the device to the host before making the desired MPI call. On the receiving side these actions have to be repeated in reverse.

(ii) **MPI is CUDA-aware**: MPI can access device buffers directly, hence pointers to device memory can be used in MPI calls. An example of a CUDA-aware MPI implementation is OpenMPI.

To illustrate the differences between the two approaches, Listing 6.43 shows a modified version of a ping-pong program that is typically used to gauge the communication characteristics in MPI installations.

Listing 6.43: A variation of an MPI ping-pong program, where the source and destination buffers are in GPU memory, without MPI being aware of this.

```
// File : ping_pong.cu
. . .
  char *d_data;    // allocate host and device memory
```

```
4    unique_ptr<char[]> h_data;
5    cudaMalloc ((void **) &d_data, MAX_MESG);
6    h_data = make_unique<char[]>(MAX_MESG);
7
8    if (rank == 0)
9      {
10       for (int mesg_size = 0; mesg_size <= MAX_MESG; mesg_size += ↩
             1000)
11         {
12           start_time = MPI_Wtime ();
13           for (int i = 0; i < REP; i++)
14             {
15               // get data from device
16               cudaMemcpy (h_data.get (), d_data, mesg_size, ↩
                   cudaMemcpyDeviceToHost);
17               // send it to other host
18               MPI_Send (h_data.get (), mesg_size, MPI_CHAR, 1, tag, ↩
                   MPI_COMM_WORLD);
19               // wait to collect response
20               MPI_Recv (h_data.get (), MAX_MESG, MPI_CHAR, 1, ↩
                   MPI_ANY_TAG, MPI_COMM_WORLD, &status);
21               // forward data to device
22               cudaMemcpy (d_data, h_data.get (), mesg_size, ↩
                   cudaMemcpyHostToDevice);
23             }
24
25           end_time = MPI_Wtime ();
26           printf ("%i %lf\n", mesg_size, (end_time − start_time) / 2↩
             / REP);
27         }
28
29       tag = END_TAG;
30       MPI_Send (h_data.get (), 0, MPI_CHAR, 1, tag, MPI_COMM_WORLD);
31     }
32   else
33     {
34       while (1)
35         {
36           // get message
37           MPI_Recv (h_data.get (), MAX_MESG, MPI_CHAR, 0, MPI_ANY_TAG↩
             , MPI_COMM_WORLD, &status);
38           // filter−out end tag
39           if (status.MPI_TAG == END_TAG)
40             break;
41
42           // get size of message and sent it to the device
43           MPI_Get_count (&status, MPI_CHAR, &mesg_size);
44           cudaMemcpy (d_data, h_data.get (), mesg_size, ↩
                   cudaMemcpyHostToDevice);
45
46           // get response from the device
```

```
47        cudaMemcpy (h_data.get(), d_data, mesg_size, ←
              cudaMemcpyDeviceToHost);
48        // and send it back
49        MPI_Send (h_data.get(), mesg_size, MPI_CHAR, 0, tag, ←
              MPI_COMM_WORLD);
50      }
51    }
52 . . .
```

The above program can be compiled with a single command using the nvcc compiler driver, just by including the MPI dynamic library (-lmpi) and specifying the location of the corresponding include files (e.g., -I/usr/include/mpi):

```
$ nvcc ping_pong.cu -lmpi -I/usr/include/mpi -o ping_pong
```

The explicit movement between host and device buffers is clear on lines 16, 22, 44, and 47. The program does not do anything particularly useful, as it is only meant to report the time it takes for the exchange to take place.

The second solution entails the use of 64-bit operating systems for the host and the use of 64-bit compilation mode for the device (affecting memory pointers), so that UVA can be enabled. UVA uses 64-bit addressing (actually 49 bits are used on AMD64 architectures) to unify the address space of the host along with the address spaces of any CUDA devices in the system. The value of a memory pointer can then be used to deduce exactly where the corresponding data reside (host or device and on which device). A CUDA-aware MPI implementation can then proceed to perform the transfer from the device to an MPI buffer, saving at least one memory copy on the sending and one memory copy on the receiving side.

The ping-pong implementation for a CUDA-aware MPI is shown in Listing 6.44 (it can be compiled via an identical nvcc command-line as the program of Listing 6.43).

Listing 6.44: A variation of an MPI ping pong program for device data, where MPI is CUDA-aware and UVA is enabled.

```
53 // File : ping_pong_CUDAaware.cu
54  . . .
55    char *d_data;
56    cudaMalloc ((void **) &d_data, MAX_MESG);
57
58    if (rank == 0)
59      {
60        for (int mesg_size = 0; mesg_size <= MAX_MESG; mesg_size += ←
              1000)
61        {
62          start_time = MPI_Wtime ();
63          for (int i = 0; i < REP; i++)
64            {
65              // send data to other host
66              MPI_Send (d_data, mesg_size, MPI_CHAR, 1, tag, ←
                  MPI_COMM_WORLD);
```

```
67                    // wait to collect response
68                    MPI_Recv (d_data, MAX_MESG, MPI_CHAR, 1, MPI_ANY_TAG, ↩
                         MPI_COMM_WORLD, &status);
69                  }
70
71            end_time = MPI_Wtime ();
72            printf ("%i %lf\n", mesg_size, (end_time - start_time) / 2↩
                 / REP);
73          }
74
75        tag = END_TAG;
76        MPI_Send (d_data, 0, MPI_CHAR, 1, tag, MPI_COMM_WORLD);
77      }
78   else
79      {
80        while (1)
81          {
82            // get message
83            MPI_Recv (d_data, MAX_MESG, MPI_CHAR, 0, MPI_ANY_TAG, ↩
                 MPI_COMM_WORLD, &status);
84            // filter-out end tag
85            if (status.MPI_TAG == END_TAG)
86              break;
87
88            // get size of message and sent it to the device
89            MPI_Get_count (&status, MPI_CHAR, &mesg_size);
90
91            // send response back
92            MPI_Send (d_data, mesg_size, MPI_CHAR, 0, tag, ↩
                 MPI_COMM_WORLD);
93          }
94      }
95   . . .
```

Obviously, the second one is the method of choice, given the benefits of having a simpler program logic and streamlining any required memory copies. The striking difference between Listing 6.44 and 6.43 is the absence of a host buffer and the passing of device pointers directly to MPI_Send and MPI_Recv functions (lines 66, 68, 83, and 92).

The details of how a CUDA-aware MPI implementation will behave upon request to operate on a device buffer depend to a large degree on the compute capability of the device. Since 2010, NVidia has introduced a set of technologies, collectively referred to as **GPUDirect**, that provide the following:

- **Faster communication with network and storage devices**: By using pinned memory, the CUDA driver and third-party device drivers can share a buffer, eliminating the need to make an extra copy of the data.

- **Peer-to-peer**[23] **transfers between GPUs** on the same PCIe bus, without going through the host's memory.
- **Peer-to-peer memory access**: A GPU can access the memory of another GPU, using NUMA-style access. The difference between this and the previous item is the volume of data involved: the previous item involves a `cudaMemcpy()` call in order to transfer a memory region instead of a single item.
- **Remote DMA (RDMA)**: A GPU buffer can be copied directly over a network to a remote GPU.

Just to clarify the difference between UVA and GPUDirect, UVA enables the simplification of the source code by allowing the value of a pointer to designate the memory space where the data reside. Library functions, both CUDA and third-party, can use this information to stage the appropriate memory copy operations in the background. GPUDirect on the other hand is a technology completely transparent to the application programmer (but not to the device driver or library developer) that enables fast access or communication of device data without the need for intermediate holding buffers.

The traffic generated by a plain-vanilla MPI implementation for a single send–receive pair of commands involving device buffers is illustrated and contrasted with the one generated by a CUDA-aware, RDMA-assisted MPI implementation in Fig. 6.34. Data to be transferred via DMA by a controller other than the CPU (e.g., PCIe south bridge, Ethernet controller, Infiniband, etc.) need to reside on non-swappable (i.e., pinned) memory. This results in the operation shown in Fig. 6.34(a) needing no less than six (!) memory copies before the data reach their destination. In Fig. 6.34(b) RDMA bypasses all this overhead by allowing direct access to the source and destination buffers.

Even if one uses a CUDA-**un**aware MPI implementation, if the host memory is pinned, we can get away with only two memory copies as shown in Fig. 6.34(c), despite having to explicitly call `cudaMemcpy()`.

6.15 Case studies

In this section we explore the potential of CUDA with a number of easy to understand applications. The goal is to show how we can use CUDA to accelerate our computations while at the same time exercise the tools that are provided with the CUDA SDK.

In the following sections we revert to the primitive but convenient CUDA error checking that a preprocessor macro can provide, as identified in Section 6.6. This is currently the safest bet for catching early errors occurring on the GPU. Although we purposefully omitted error checking before, this was done for the sake of clarity and is obviously not recommended.

---

[23] "Peer" in this context refers to another GPU hosted on the same machine. No networking is involved.

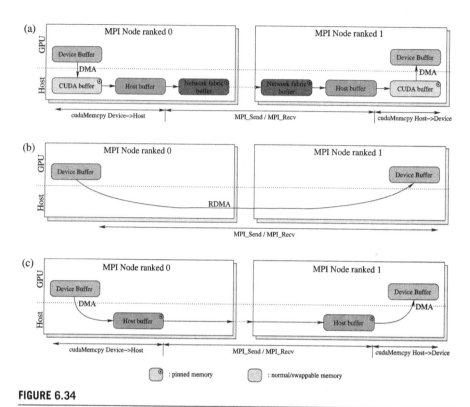

FIGURE 6.34

Traffic generated for device-to-device communication by (a) a plain-vanilla MPI implementation, (b) a CUDA-aware MPI implementation using the GPUDirect RDMA mechanism, and (c) an MPI implementation taking advantage of pinned host memory. The network fabric buffer is a buffer used by a networking controller such as, e.g., Ethernet or Infiniband.

6.15.1 Fractal set calculation

In this section we present the design of a Mandelbrot fractal set generator. The particular application has been discussed extensively in this book (see Sections 3.12 and 5.25.1) so we will proceed directly with just a brief explanation.

The Mandelbrot set is a set of points $c = x + i \cdot y$ on the complex plane that produce a bounded sequence of numbers $z_0, z_1, z_2, \dots$ when the recursive formula $z_{n+1} = z_n^2 + c$ with $z_0 = c$ is applied, i.e., $|z_n| = \sqrt{x_n^2 + y_n^2} < \infty \ \forall n$. In order to produce a graphical depiction of the Mandelbrot set, we must apply the recursive formula on each point of the complex plane that corresponds to an image pixel, until z_{n+1} diverges ($|z_n| > 2$) or n exceeds a preset threshold.

We explore and evaluate three possible design approaches that can be considered an evolution sequence:

1. Using one CUDA thread per pixel, with normal host and device memory allocations.
2. Using one CUDA thread per pixel, with pitched device memory allocation and pinned host memory.
3. Using one CUDA thread per block of pixels, with pitched device memory allocation and pinned host memory.

6.15.1.1 Version #1: One thread per pixel

The application of the recursive formula suggests an uneven computational cost for each point in the set, but an easy migration to a CUDA solution would be to just spawn a thread per point/pixel. This approach is shown in Listing 6.45.

Listing 6.45: A CUDA thread-per-pixel solution for the calculation of the Mandelbrot set.

```
1  // File : mandelCUDA_v1/kernel.cu
2  #include <QImage>
3  #include <QRgb>
4  . . .
5  static const int MAXITER = 1024;
6
7  //**************************************************************
8  // Checks to see how many iterations takes for (cx, cy) to diverge
9  __device__ int diverge (double cx, double cy)
10 {
11    int iter = 0;
12    double vx = cx, vy = cy, tx, ty;
13    while (iter < MAXITER && (vx * vx + vy * vy) < 4)
14      {
15        tx = vx * vx - vy * vy + cx;
16        ty = 2 * vx * vy + cy;
17        vx = tx;
18        vy = ty;
19        iter++;
20      }
21    return iter;
22 }
23
24 //**************************************************************
25 // Each CUDA thread calculates the result for one point. The pitch ↩
       parameter is identical to resX in this solution
26 __global__ void mandelKernel (unsigned char *d_res, double upperX, ↩
       double upperY, double stepX, double stepY, int resX, int resY, ↩
       int pitch)
27 {
28    int myX, myY;
29    myX = blockIdx.x * blockDim.x + threadIdx.x;  // get the thread's ↩
          grid coordinates
30    myY = blockIdx.y * blockDim.y + threadIdx.y;
31    if (myX >= resX || myY >= resY)
32      return;
```

```
33
34    double tempx, tempy;
35    tempx = upperX + myX * stepX;    // translate the thread's ID into ↩
          a point in the complex plane
36    tempy = upperY - myY * stepY;
37    int color = diverge (tempx, tempy);
38    d_res[myY * pitch + myX] = color % 256;
39  }
40
41  //***********************************************************
42  // Host front-end function that allocates the memory and launches ↩
        the GPU kernel
43  double hostFE (double upperX, double upperY, double lowerX, double ↩
        lowerY, QImage * img, int resX, int resY)
44  {
45    int blocksX, blocksY;
46    blocksX = (int) ceil (resX / 16);
47    blocksY = (int) ceil (resY / 16);
48    dim3 block (16, 16);
49    dim3 grid (blocksX, blocksY);
50    int pitch;
51
52    unique_ptr<unsigned char[]> h_res;
53    unsigned char *d_res;
54
55    pitch = resX;
56    auto t1 = high_resolution_clock::now();
57
58    CUDA_CHECK_RETURN (cudaMalloc ((void **) &d_res, resX * resY));
59    h_res = make_unique<unsigned char []>(resY * pitch);
60
61    double stepX = (lowerX - upperX) / resX;
62    double stepY = (upperY - lowerY) / resY;
63
64    // launch GPU kernel
65    mandelKernel <<< grid, block >>> (d_res, upperX, upperY, stepX, ↩
        stepY, resX, resY, pitch);
66
67    // get the results
68    CUDA_CHECK_RETURN (cudaMemcpy (h_res.get(), d_res, resY * pitch, ↩
        cudaMemcpyDeviceToHost));
69    auto t2 = high_resolution_clock::now();
70    auto dur = t2-t1;
71
72    //copy results into QImage object
73    for (int j = 0; j < resY; j++)
74      for (int i = 0; i < resX; i++)
75        {
76          int color = h_res[j * pitch + i];
77          img->setPixel (i, j, qRgb (256 - color, 256 - color, 256 - ↩
              color));
78        }
```

```
79
80    // clean up allocated memory
81    CUDA_CHECK_RETURN (cudaFree (d_res));
82    return duration_cast<milliseconds>(dur).count();
83  }
```

The code of Listing 6.45 consists of three functions:

- The hostFE() function (starting at line 43) is called by the host's main() function to run the GPU code. It is responsible for allocating memory, spawning the CUDA threads, setting up the requested image (lines 73–78), and clearing up memory. The execution configuration uses an ad hoc arrangement of 16×16-thread blocks, making up a 2D grid. The grid dimensions are calculated based on the image resolution (lines 46 and 47). hostFE() returns the time it takes for the GPU operations to take place, excluding freeing up memory.
- The diverge() function (line 9) is identical to the one used in the examples of Chapters 3 and 5. It is just "decorated" by the __device__ qualifier, which means it is only callable from device code.
- The mandelKernel() function (line 26) first locates the position of a thread in the overall grid, before mapping this position to the complex plane (lines 35 and 36) and calling diverge(). The number of iterations required before a point diverges (or MAXITER if it does not) is stored in a global array (line 38). As these data are accessed only once, no provision for involving the shared memory is made. The mandelKernel() function signature is consistent across all three implementations.

Listing 6.46 shows a variation of the hostFE() function, using unified memory.

Listing 6.46: A unified memory variation of the code in Listing 6.45.

```
84    // File : mandelCUDA_v1_unified/kernel.cu
85    . . .
86    double hostFE (double upperX, double upperY, double lowerX, double ←
          lowerY, QImage * img, int resX, int resY)
87    {
88      int blocksX, blocksY;
89      blocksX = (int) ceil (resX / 16);
90      blocksY = (int) ceil (resY / 16);
91      dim3 block (16, 16);
92      dim3 grid (blocksX, blocksY);
93      int pitch;
94
95      // single pointer to results array
96      unsigned char *res;
97
98      pitch = resX;
99      auto t1 = high_resolution_clock::now();
100     CUDA_CHECK_RETURN (cudaMallocManaged ((void **) &res, resX * resY)←
          );
101
102     double stepX = (lowerX - upperX) / resX;
```

```
103    double stepY = (upperY − lowerY) / resY;
104
105    // launch GPU kernel
106    mandelKernel <<< grid, block >>> (res, upperX, upperY, stepX, ←
           stepY, resX, resY, pitch);
107
108    // wait for GPU to finish
109    CUDA_CHECK_RETURN (cudaDeviceSynchronize ());
110    auto t2 = high_resolution_clock::now();
111    auto dur = t2−t1;
112
113    //copy results into QImage object from host−side managed memory
114    for (int j = 0; j < resY; j++)
115      for (int i = 0; i < resX; i++)
116        {
117           int color = res[j * pitch + i];
118           img−>setPixel (i, j, qRgb (256 − color, 256 − color, 256 − ←
               color));
119        }
120
121    // clean up allocated memory
122    CUDA_CHECK_RETURN (cudaFree (res));
123    return duration_cast<milliseconds>(dur).count();
124  }
```

As can be seen on line 100, only a single memory allocation is made and there is no memory copy operation required prior to launching the kernel on line 106.

6.15.1.2 Version #2: Pinned host and pitched device memory

There are two issues that can be improved in Listing 6.45 as per the techniques listed in Section 6.7: (a) we can use pinned host memory to improve the communication time over the PCIe interface between the host and the device and (b) we can use pitched memory allocation on the device, so that each image row occupies a multiple of 32 bytes of memory, allowing coalescing of memory accesses when line 38 in function mandelKernel() is executed. The latter change will impact performance only if the width of our image resX is not a multiple of 32.

These changes require only a small modification of the hostFE() function, as shown in Listing 6.47. The only lines that are different from Listing 6.45 are 18, 20, and 42, as a pitch variable was already used in Listing 6.45, but it was set to resX.

Listing 6.47: A CUDA thread-per-pixel solution for the calculation of the Mandelbrot set using pinned host memory and pitched device memory allocation. Only the differences from Listing 6.45 are shown.

```
1    // File : mandelCUDA_v2/kernel.cu
2    . . .
3    //==============================================================
4    // Host front−end function that allocates the memory and launches ←
          the GPU kernel
5    void hostFE (double upperX, double upperY, double lowerX, double ←
          lowerY, QImage * img, int resX, int resY)
```

```
6   {
7     int blocksX, blocksY;
8     blocksX = (int) ceil (resX / 16.0);
9     blocksY = (int) ceil (resY / 16.0);
10    dim3 block (16, 16);
11    dim3 grid (blocksX, blocksY);
12    int pitch;
13
14    unsigned char *h_res;
15    unsigned char *d_res;
16    auto t1 = high_resolution_clock::now();
17    // make sure each row of the 2D array d_res, occupies a multiple ←
          of 32 bytes
18    CUDA_CHECK_RETURN (cudaMallocPitch ((void **) &d_res, (size_t *) &←
          pitch, resX, resY));
19    // allocate pinned host memory
20    CUDA_CHECK_RETURN (cudaHostAlloc (&h_res, resY * pitch, ←
          cudaHostAllocMapped));
21
22    double stepX = (lowerX — upperX) / resX;
23    double stepY = (upperY — lowerY) / resY;
24
25    // launch GPU kernel
26    mandelKernel <<< grid, block >>> (d_res, upperX, upperY, stepX, ←
          stepY, resX, resY, pitch);
27
28    // get the results
29    CUDA_CHECK_RETURN (cudaMemcpy (h_res, d_res, resY * pitch, ←
          cudaMemcpyDeviceToHost));
30    auto t2 = high_resolution_clock::now();
31    auto dur = t2—t1;
32
33    //copy results into QImage object
34    for (int j = 0; j < resY; j++)
35      for (int i = 0; i < resX; i++)
36        {
37          int color = h_res[j * pitch + i];
38          img->setPixel (i, j, qRgb (256 — color, 256 — color, 256 — ←
              color));
39        }
40
41    // clean up allocated memory
42    CUDA_CHECK_RETURN (cudaFreeHost (h_res));
43    CUDA_CHECK_RETURN (cudaFree (d_res));
44    return duration_cast<milliseconds>(dur).count();
45  }
```

6.15.1.3 Version #3: Multiple pixels per thread

The use of one thread per pixel seems like an overkill if one considers that a modest 1024×768 image results in 768k threads, or $4 \times 768 = 3072$ blocks given the grid and block arrangement used (16×16 image blocks require 256-thread blocks). These figures do not exceed the specifications of GPU capabilities, but they have a side effect: so many blocks cannot be resident on the device (e.g., for compute capability 7.5 devices the maximum number of resident blocks is 16 per SM), so the CUDA runtime has to distribute them as the SMs complete previously assigned blocks. This is a fact that we will consider again when we evaluate the performance of the three designs.

In order to process a block of points[24] a nested for-loop is set up inside `mandelKernel()` as seen in Listing 6.48 (lines 15–28). The (`myX`, `myY`) pair which constitutes the ID of a thread is mapped to the upper left corner of the block to be processed. The size of the block is fixed, determined by the `THR_BLK_X` and `THR_BLK_X` constants defined on lines 3 and 4.

The only other modification that is required is the grid configuration calculations that take place in `hostFE()` on lines 36 and 37. Besides those two lines, `hostFE()` is identical to the function in Listing 6.47.

Listing 6.48: A CUDA thread-per-block of pixels solution for the calculation of the Mandelbrot set. Only the differences from Listing 6.45 are shown.

```
1   // File : mandelCUDA_v3/kernel.cu
2   . . .
3   static const int THR_BLK_X = 4; // pixels per thread, x-axis
4   static const int THR_BLK_Y = 4; // pixels per thread, y-axis
5   static const int BLOCK_SIDE = 16;  // size of 2D block of threads
6   . . .
7   //==================================================================
8   __global__ void mandelKernel (unsigned char *d_res, double upperX, ←
        double upperY, double stepX, double stepY, int resX, int resY, ←
        int pitch)
9   {
10    int myX, myY;
11    myX = (blockIdx.x * blockDim.x + threadIdx.x) * THR_BLK_X;
12    myY = (blockIdx.y * blockDim.y + threadIdx.y) * THR_BLK_Y;
13
14    int i, j;
15    for (i = myX; i < THR_BLK_X + myX; i++)
16      for (j = myY; j < THR_BLK_Y + myY; j++)
17        {
18          // check for "outside" pixels
19          if (i >= resX || j >= resY)
20            continue;
21
22          double tempx, tempy;
23          tempx = upperX + i * stepX;
24          tempy = upperY - j * stepY;
25
```

---

[24] This effectively corresponds to a 2D partitioning of the workload. A 1D partitioning is also possible, whereas a thread processes a vertical or horizontal line of points.

```
26        int color = diverge (tempx, tempy);
27        d_res[j * pitch + i] = color % 256;
28      }
29 }
30
31 // ===============================================================
32 // Host front-end function that allocates the memory and launches ↩
       the GPU kernel
33 double hostFE (double upperX, double upperY, double lowerX, double ↩
       lowerY, QImage * img, int resX, int resY)
34 {
35   int blocksX, blocksY;
36   blocksX = (int) ceil (resX * 1.0 / (BLOCK_SIDE * THR_BLK_X));
37   blocksY = (int) ceil (resY * 1.0 / (BLOCK_SIDE * THR_BLK_Y));
38   dim3 block (BLOCK_SIDE, BLOCK_SIDE);
39   dim3 grid (blocksX, blocksY);
40
41   int pitch;
42
43   unsigned char *h_res;
44   unsigned char *d_res;
45   auto t1 = high_resolution_clock::now();
46   CUDA_CHECK_RETURN (cudaMallocPitch ((void **) &d_res, (size_t *) &↩
           pitch, resX, resY));
47   CUDA_CHECK_RETURN (cudaHostAlloc (&h_res, resY * pitch, ↩
           cudaHostAllocMapped));
48
49   double stepX = (lowerX - upperX) / resX;
50   double stepY = (upperY - lowerY) / resY;
51
52   // launch GPU kernel
53   mandelKernel <<< grid, block >>> (d_res, upperX, upperY, stepX, ↩
           stepY, resX, resY, pitch);
54
55   // get the results
56   CUDA_CHECK_RETURN (cudaMemcpy (h_res, d_res, resY * pitch, ↩
           cudaMemcpyDeviceToHost));
57   auto t2 = high_resolution_clock::now();
58   auto dur = t2-t1;
59
60   //copy results into QImage object
61   for (int j = 0; j < resY; j++)
62     for (int i = 0; i < resX; i++)
63       {
64         int color = h_res[j * pitch + i];
65         img->setPixel (i, j, qRgb (256 - color, 256 - color, 256 - ↩
               color));
66       }
67
68   // clean up allocated memory
69   CUDA_CHECK_RETURN (cudaFreeHost (h_res));
70   CUDA_CHECK_RETURN (cudaFree (d_res));
```

```
71    return duration_cast<milliseconds>(dur).count();
72  }
```

6.15.1.4 Performance comparison

A convenient way to evaluate the performance of a CUDA program is to use the Nsight Systems profiler. As can be observed in Fig. 6.33, the profiler times all CUDA calls and reports detailed information about the performance of a kernel and the utilization of the GPU. Fig. 6.33 actually shows the timing of an execution of our third solution, running the image generation 10 times. There is just one problem: GPU operations are dominated by the transfer of the image data from the device to the host, which does not allow for concrete conclusions to be reached about which version is performing best and under which conditions.

The only way around this problem is to benchmark each program under a variety of inputs and configurations. Admittedly, the evaluation performed here is not as thorough as it should be for a production situation, but it does depict the correct strategy to deal with this problem.

The main() function shown in Listing 6.49 is common for all the versions shown above, as it is only responsible for I/O operations and calling the front-end function hostFE() in kernel.cu. The Qt library is used for image I/O (lines 28 and 40). The details of how this can be accomplished in terms of properly compiling and linking the code are given in Section E.3.

Listing 6.49: The main() function of the CUDA programs for the calculation of the Mandelbrot set.

```cpp
1  // File : mandelCUDA_v[123]/main.cpp
2  #include <QImage>
3  #include <QRgb>
4  #include <QTime>
5  . . .
6  int main (int argc, char *argv[])
7  {
8    double upperCornerX, upperCornerY;
9    double lowerCornerX, lowerCornerY;
10
11   upperCornerX = atof (argv[1]);
12   upperCornerY = atof (argv[2]);
13   lowerCornerX = atof (argv[3]);
14   lowerCornerY = atof (argv[4]);
15
16   // support for timing the operation
17   int iterations = 1;
18   if (argc > 5)
19     iterations = atoi(argv[5]);
20
21   int imgX = 3840, imgY = 2160;
22   if (argc > 7)
23   {
```

```
24      imgX = atoi(argv[6]);
25      imgY = atoi(argv[7]);
26    }
27
28    QImage *img = new QImage (imgX, imgY, QImage::Format_RGB32);
29
30    QTime t;
31    t.start();
32
33    int i = iterations;
34    double gpuOpsTime=0;
35    while (i--)
36      gpuOpsTime += hostFE (upperCornerX, upperCornerY, lowerCornerX, ↩
              lowerCornerY, img, imgX, imgY);
37
38    cout << "Time (ms) per iteration: " << t.elapsed()*1.0/iterations ↩
            << " " << " GPU only: " << gpuOpsTime / iterations << endl;
39
40    img->save ("mandel.png", "PNG", 0);
41    return 0;
42  }
```

The program is called by supplying the upper-left and lower-right corner coordinates of the complex plane to be investigated as command-line parameters. for example:

```
$ ./mandelCUDA -.75 0.131 -.74 0.121
```

In order to support accurate evaluation of the three solutions, the call to hostFE() on line 29 is inside a while-loop that can be optionally run more than one time (if there is a fifth argument in the command-line, as per the condition on line 18) and report the average execution time by line 38. This feature was not utilized in our tests, as it leads to lower reported times, because the CUDA runtime is initialized only once.

Two more optional parameters can be used to specify the desired image resolution, which defaults to 4K.

The following settings were used for testing:

- Block size was fixed to 256 threads.
- Three different image resolutions were tested: HD, 4K, and 8K.
- Two regions of the plane were calculated:
  - One covering the whole Mandelbrot set, between corners $(-1.5, 1.25)$ and $(1, -1.25)$, identified as "Low detail."
  - One covering a small portion of the set, between corners $(-.75, 0.131)$ and $(-.74, 0.121)$, identified as "High detail." The first takes less time to calculate but features very diverse computing requirements per point/pixel, while the second takes more computational time but the differences in the number of iterations between points are less extreme.

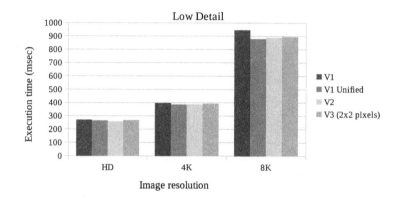

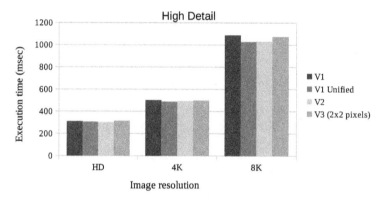

FIGURE 6.35

Average GPU execution duration for different CUDA implementations of the Mandelbrot set calculation on an RTX 2060 Super GPU.

- A total of 100 runs were performed for each test.
- For the third version we used a configuration assigning a 2×2 block of points per thread.

The results are shown in Fig. 6.35.

Unsurprisingly, the first CUDA version is the one performing worse than every other across all test settings. Version 3 is the second worst, a fact which is easy to explain: assigning multiple points per thread has the undesirable effect of increasing the circumstances where warp threads diverge in their execution, leading to under-utilization of the SMs.

The best versions are V1 with unified memory and V2. The former is marginally better in higher resolutions, while the latter is ahead again by a narrow margin in HD. The reason comes down to the relative cost of the operations that the GPU is required to carry out. As can be seen in Fig. 6.36, version 3 utilizes the CUDA cores better by producing a slightly smaller kernel execution time. However, this is not

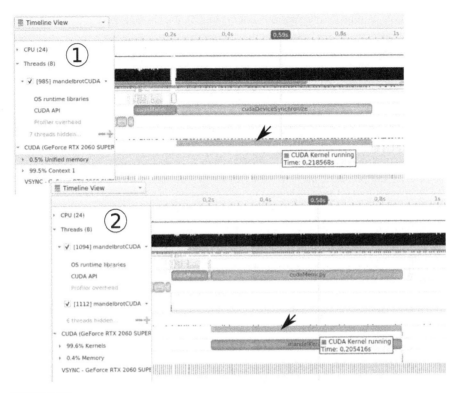

FIGURE 6.36

Nsight Systems screenshots for ① version 1 with unified memory of the Mandelbrot set calculator and ② version 3. Arrows point to the kernel executions.

enough to grant superiority to version 3. The different costs of the memory allocation and management calls (possibly affected by driver optimizations) are the ones that dictate the outcome.

The results demonstrate just how challenging CUDA program optimization can be: something that works for one situation does not work for another. This extends also to different devices, as new architectures can require a shift in the optimization approach. Proper testing of design alternatives is the recommended strategy.

6.15.2 Block cipher encryption

In this section we explore the use of CUDA and MPI for the encryption of large volumes of data on a cluster of GPU nodes, using the Advanced Encryption Standard (AES) algorithm.

AES was established in 2000 by the U.S. National Institute of Standards and Technology (NIST) as the successor to the Data Encryption Standard (DES) for the encryption of digital information. Encryption is the process of encoding data in a way that prevents unauthorized users from accessing the data. Encryption algorithms are also known as *ciphers*. The original data are called *plaintext* and the encrypted output of a cipher is called *ciphertext*. Data can be restored to their original form by the reverse process, which is known as decryption.

Encryption and decryption typically need one or more keys, e.g., a pass phrase or a number, that are used in the transformation from plaintext to ciphertext and back. AES is a symmetric-key cipher, i.e., it uses the same key for both processes. The key should be obviously kept secret as it enables the decryption to take place.

AES (also known as the Rijndael cipher) is a block cipher, i.e., it operates on blocks of the plaintext that are 16 bytes long. The data to be encrypted have to be broken up into 16-byte-long pieces, before having AES operate independently on each piece. The key is a number that can be 128, 192, or 256 bits long. Each 16-byte block is treated as if arranged in a 4 × 4 matrix, and it is subjected to multiple rounds of repetitive manipulations. The number of rounds depends on the length of the encryption key, i.e., we have 10 rounds for a 128-bit key, 12 rounds for a 192-bit key, and 14 rounds for a 256-bit key. The 16-byte block is called the *state* of the cipher.

Each AES encryption round is a sequence of the following operations:

- **KeyExpansion**: The encryption key is expanded, i.e., a bigger key is created, so that individual, disjoint parts of it can be used in the subsequent rounds.
- First round applied to the state of the algorithm:
  - **AddRoundKey**: Each byte of the state is combined with a part of the expanded key using bitwise XOR.
- Second to next-to-last rounds:
  - **SubBytes**: A lookup table is used to replace each byte of the state with another value.
  - **ShiftRows**: Each row of the state is shifted a number of steps based on its location.
  - **MixColumns**: A linear transformation step that operates on the state's columns.
  - **AddRoundKey**: Same as above.
- Final round (missing a MixColumns step):
  - **SubBytes**
  - **ShiftRows**
  - **AddRoundKey**

Fig. 6.37 displays how the four operations that constitute AES operate on the state. AES is covered thoroughly in a large number of online and printed documentation (Wikipedia's article at http://en.wikipedia.org/wiki/Advanced_Encryption_Standard is quite informative). In this section we only focus on the aspects which are relevant to the GPU deployment of the algorithm.

The AES operations can be sped up considerably by using lookup tables to perform them. The following are snippets of the AES reference implementation

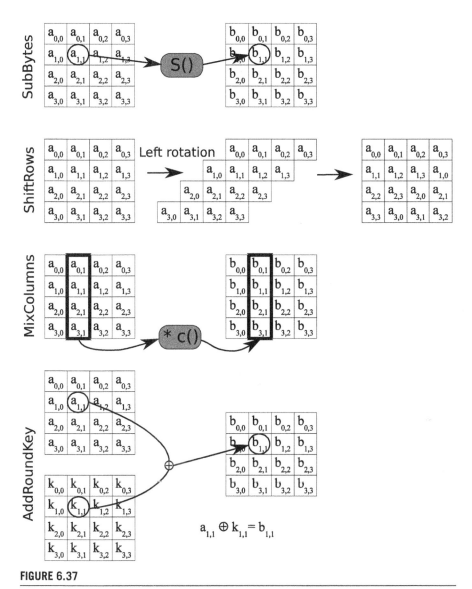

FIGURE 6.37

A demonstration of how the four elementary operations of AES modify the state of the algorithm. S() is a substitution function, while c() is a polynomial that is multiplied by each column of the state to produce a new column.

(https://embeddedsw.net/zip/Rijndael_Original.zip, last accessed in December 2021) that show how this is accomplished in C code. The KeyExpansion phase is implemented by the function:

```
int rijndaelSetupEncrypt(
        unsigned long *rk,          // expanded key (OUT)
        const unsigned char *key,   // original encryption key (IN)
        int keybits);               // size of original key (IN)
```

that is called once, before the encryption phase. The rounds of AddRoundKey, Syb-Bytes, ShiftRows, etc., for each group of 16 bytes are performed by the function:

```
void rijndaelEncrypt(
        const unsigned long *rk,      // pointer to the expanded key (IN↩
        )
        int nrounds,                  // number of rounds to perform (IN↩
        )
        const unsigned char plaintext[16], // original "state"    (IN↩
        )
        unsigned char ciphertext[16]); // final "state" storage (OUT↩
        )
```

A short sample of the AES reference implementation is shown below:

Listing 6.50: A sample of the AES reference implementation.

```
1  // File : AES_MPI/Rijndael_Original/rijndael.c
2  typedef unsigned long u32;
3  typedef unsigned char u8;
4
5  static const u32 Te0[256] =
6  {
7    0xc66363a5U, 0xf87c7c84U, 0xee777799U, 0xf67b7b8dU, . . .};
8
9  static const u32 Te1[256] =
10 {
11   0xa5c66363U, 0x84f87c7cU, 0x99ee7777U, 0x8df67b7bU, . . .};
12
13 static const u32 Te2[256] =
14 {
15   0x63a5c663U, 0x7c84f87cU, 0x7799ee77U, 0x7b8df67bU, . . .};
16
17 static const u32 Te3[256] =
18 {
19   0x6363a5c6U, 0x7c7c84f8U, 0x777799eeU, 0x7b7b8df6U, . . .};
20
21 static const u32 Te4[256] =
22 {
23   0x63636363U, 0x7c7c7c7cU, 0x77777777U, 0x7b7b7b7bU, . . .};
24
25 . . .
26
27 #define GETU32(plaintext) (((u32)(plaintext)[0] << 24) ^ \
28                   ((u32)(plaintext)[1] << 16) ^ \
29                   ((u32)(plaintext)[2] <<  8) ^ \
30                   ((u32)(plaintext)[3]))
```

```
31
32  #define PUTU32(ciphertext, st) { (ciphertext)[0] = (u8)((st) >> 24);←
        \
33                      (ciphertext)[1] = (u8)((st) >> 16); \
34                      (ciphertext)[2] = (u8)((st) >>  8); \
35                      (ciphertext)[3] = (u8)(st); }
36  . . .
37  void rijndaelEncrypt(const u32 *rk, int nrounds, const u8 plaintext←
        [16], u8 ciphertext[16])
38  {
39    u32 s0, s1, s2, s3, t0, t1, t2, t3;
40    . . .
41    /*
42     * map byte array block to cipher state
43     * and add initial round key:
44     */
45    s0 = GETU32(plaintext     ) ^ rk[0];
46    s1 = GETU32(plaintext +  4) ^ rk[1];
47    s2 = GETU32(plaintext +  8) ^ rk[2];
48    s3 = GETU32(plaintext + 12) ^ rk[3];
49
50  #ifdef FULL_UNROLL
51    /* round 1: */
52    t0 = Te0[s0 >> 24] ^ Te1[(s1 >> 16) & 0xff] ^ Te2[(s2 >>  8) & 0←
        xff] ^ Te3[s3 & 0xff] ^ rk[ 4];
53    t1 = Te0[s1 >> 24] ^ Te1[(s2 >> 16) & 0xff] ^ Te2[(s3 >>  8) & 0←
        xff] ^ Te3[s0 & 0xff] ^ rk[ 5];
54    t2 = Te0[s2 >> 24] ^ Te1[(s3 >> 16) & 0xff] ^ Te2[(s0 >>  8) & 0←
        xff] ^ Te3[s1 & 0xff] ^ rk[ 6];
55    t3 = Te0[s3 >> 24] ^ Te1[(s0 >> 16) & 0xff] ^ Te2[(s1 >>  8) & 0←
        xff] ^ Te3[s2 & 0xff] ^ rk[ 7];
56    /* round 2: */
57    s0 = Te0[t0 >> 24] ^ Te1[(t1 >> 16) & 0xff] ^ Te2[(t2 >>  8) & 0←
        xff] ^ Te3[t3 & 0xff] ^ rk[ 8];
58    s1 = Te0[t1 >> 24] ^ Te1[(t2 >> 16) & 0xff] ^ Te2[(t3 >>  8) & 0←
        xff] ^ Te3[t0 & 0xff] ^ rk[ 9];
59    s2 = Te0[t2 >> 24] ^ Te1[(t3 >> 16) & 0xff] ^ Te2[(t0 >>  8) & 0←
        xff] ^ Te3[t1 & 0xff] ^ rk[10];
60    s3 = Te0[t3 >> 24] ^ Te1[(t0 >> 16) & 0xff] ^ Te2[(t1 >>  8) & 0←
        xff] ^ Te3[t2 & 0xff] ^ rk[11];
61    /* round 3: */
62    t0 = Te0[s0 >> 24] ^ Te1[(s1 >> 16) & 0xff] ^ Te2[(s2 >>  8) & 0←
        xff] ^ Te3[s3 & 0xff] ^ rk[12];
63    t1 = Te0[s1 >> 24] ^ Te1[(s2 >> 16) & 0xff] ^ Te2[(s3 >>  8) & 0←
        xff] ^ Te3[s0 & 0xff] ^ rk[13];
64    t2 = Te0[s2 >> 24] ^ Te1[(s3 >> 16) & 0xff] ^ Te2[(s0 >>  8) & 0←
        xff] ^ Te3[s1 & 0xff] ^ rk[14];
65    t3 = Te0[s3 >> 24] ^ Te1[(s0 >> 16) & 0xff] ^ Te2[(s1 >>  8) & 0←
        xff] ^ Te3[s2 & 0xff] ^ rk[15];
66    /* round 4: */
67    . . .
68    s0 =
```

```
69        (Te4[(t0 >> 24)       ] & 0xff000000) ^
70        (Te4[(t1 >> 16) & 0xff] & 0x00ff0000) ^
71        (Te4[(t2 >>  8) & 0xff] & 0x0000ff00) ^
72        (Te4[(t3     ) & 0xff] & 0x000000ff) ^
73        rk[0];
74     PUTU32(ciphertext     , s0);
75     s1 =
76        (Te4[(t1 >> 24)       ] & 0xff000000) ^
77        (Te4[(t2 >> 16) & 0xff] & 0x00ff0000) ^
78        (Te4[(t3 >>  8) & 0xff] & 0x0000ff00) ^
79        (Te4[(t0     ) & 0xff] & 0x000000ff) ^
80        rk[1];
81     PUTU32(ciphertext +  4, s1);
82     . . .
83  }
```

The above snippet exposes the key features of the reference implementation code that we can use to create an efficient CUDA derivative:

- The state of the algorithm (the 16 bytes) is read in four variables s0, s1, s2, and s3 (lines 45–48). The state is updated by exchanging these values between the s? and t? variables, as shown on lines 52–65.
- The four operations that constitute each round of AES are performed via five lookup tables Te0[] to Te4[], each made up of 256 32-bit unsigned integers (lines 5–23). The decoding process employs five tables (not shown above) also of the same size as the ones used in encoding.
- The GETU32 and PUTU32 macros ensure that the data are treated as if they were processed in a big-endian architecture.

The sample encrypt.c file from the AES reference implementation reveals the sequence that should be followed for the encryption of a set of data (see Listing 6.51).

Listing 6.51: Part of a main() function that highlights the sequence of calls required for encrypting a set of data, using the AES reference implementation.

```
84  // File : AES_MPI/Rijndael_Original/encrypt.c
85  . . .
86  int main(int argc, char **argv)
87  {
88     unsigned long rk[RKLENGTH(KEYBITS)];    // expanded key
89     unsigned char key[KEYLENGTH(KEYBITS)]; // encryption key
90     int i;
91     int nrounds;
92     . . .
93     nrounds = rijndaelSetupEncrypt(rk, key, 256);  // key expansion
94     while (!feof(stdin)) // while there are more input data
95     {
96        // read a 16-byte block
97        unsigned char plaintext[16];
98        unsigned char ciphertext[16];
99        int j;
```

```
100   for (j = 0; j < sizeof(plaintext); j++)
101   {
102     int c = getchar();
103     if (c == EOF)
104       break;
105     plaintext[j] = c;
106   }
107   if (j == 0)
108     break;
109   for (; j < sizeof(plaintext); j++)  // replace any missing data ↩
          with spaces
110     plaintext[j] = ' ';
111
112   rijndaelEncrypt(rk, nrounds, plaintext, ciphertext); // encrypt ↩
          plaintext block
113
114   if (fwrite(ciphertext, sizeof(ciphertext), 1, output) != 1)
115   {
116     fclose(output);
117     fputs("File write error", stderr);
118     return 1;
119   }
120   }
121   fclose(output);
122 }
```

In the following paragraphs we describe three AES implementations: two stand-alone and one cluster-based. The compilation of the sources can be done via the provided makefile in the AES_MPI directory. The details of how the makefile is put together can be found in Appendix E.3. Also, a short description of the files used in the following sections and the dependencies between them are shown in Fig. 6.38.

6.15.2.1 *Version #1: The case of a stand alone GPU machine*

Our ultimate goal is the development of a solution capable of utilizing a cluster of GPUs for AES encryption. This can be a tall order however, as the detection of bugs can become a daunting task. For this reason, we set as our first stepping stone the development of a stand-alone GPU solution. A working CUDA program subsequently allows us to narrow down any required debugging efforts on the MPI-side only.

The characteristics identified in the previous section allow us to develop a CUDA solution that minimizes access to global memory for the input and output data and maximizes the memory subsystem throughput by using cached constant memory and registers.

The primary components of the kernel solution, as shown in Listing 6.52, are:

- Constant memory is utilized for holding the tables that are used for speeding up the encoding and decoding processes. The total constant memory requirements sum up to a little over 10 KiB if one factors in the ten 1-KiB tables and the memory where the expanded encryption/decryption key is stored (array defined

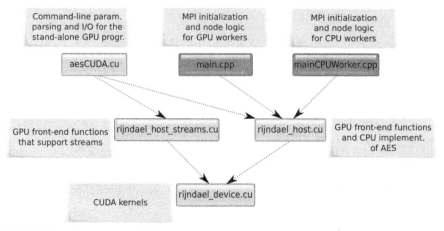

FIGURE 6.38

Dependencies between the files that make up the AES implementations described in Section 6.15.2. A different subset of these files is used to generate each of the presented programs.

on line 20). However, during encryption only half of this is necessary, making the 8 KiB constant memory cache more than sufficient.

- The automatic variables used in `rijndaelGPUEncrypt()` need only a small number of registers per thread. The `nvcc` compiler driver automatically places the `s?` and `t?` variables on registers, as the output in Fig. 6.39 reveals.
- The signature of the `rijndaelGPUEncrypt()` kernel is substantially different from the one used by the `rijndaelEncrypt()` reference function, although they both operate on a single 16-byte block. The reasons are:
  - In order to avoid the overhead of allocating a separate memory region for the output data, the input data are just overwritten upon the completion of the encryption/decryption.
  - The type of the input array is changed from `unsigned char` to `unsigned int` in order to reduce the global memory access overhead by performing one 32-bit instead of four 8-bit accesses. Especially for the latter part, the `GETU32` and `PUTU32` macros are replaced by the `RESHUFFLE` macro (defined on line 22), which is functionally identical but operates on a 32-bit integer variable instead of a four-element array of characters.
  - The expanded or rounds key is stored in constant memory so it can be reused through a series of kernel invocations. The `d_rk` array defined on line 20 is used to hold the rounds key. This array should be initialized by the host prior to calling the encryption/decryption kernels.
  - Finally, as the kernel is executed by a bunch of threads operating collectively on multiple 16-byte blocks, the size of the input array in bytes is also supplied in the form of the `N` parameter (line 28).

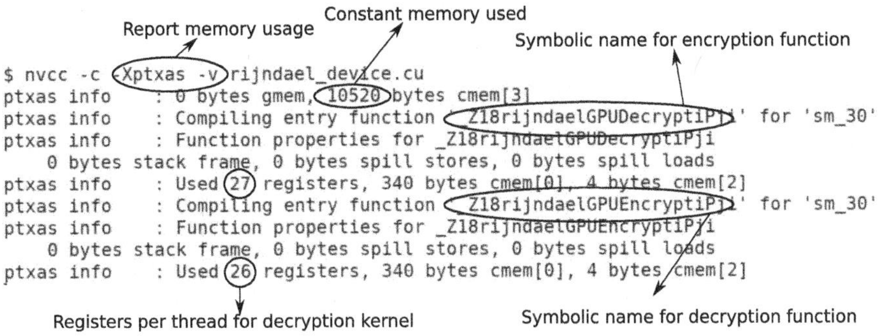

FIGURE 6.39

Compiler report for the device memory allocation related to the AES encryption and decryption kernel functions.

- The only major addition to the `rijndaelGPUEncrypt()` kernel compared to the original `rijndaelEncrypt()` function is the code calculating the location of the data that a thread should operate upon on lines 34–39. The thread ID calculation assumes a configuration of a 1D grid of 1D blocks. Once the grid-wide thread ID is established on line 34, a simple multiplication by 4 (the number of 32-bit integers per block) produces the `data` array offset to be used for input/output.

Listing 6.52: Major parts of the AES encryption CUDA implementation. Only the changes affecting the reference implementation code are shown. Also, the parts related to decryption are omitted for brevity.

```
1   // File : AES_MPI/rijndael_device.cu
2   . . .
3   __constant__ u32 Te0[256] = {
4     0xc66363a6U, 0xf87c7c84U, 0xee777799U, 0xf67b7b8dU, . . .};
5
6   __constant__ u32 Te1[256] = {
7     0xa5c66363U, 0x84f87c7cU, 0x99ee7777U, 0x8df67b7bU, . . .};
8
9   __constant__ u32 Te2[256] = {
10    0x63a5c663U, 0x7c84f87cU, 0x7799ee77U, 0x7b8df67bU, . . .};
11
12  __constant__ u32 Te3[256] = {
13    0x6363a5c6U, 0x7c7c84f8U, 0x777799eeU, 0x7b7b8df6U, . . .};
14
15  __constant__ u32 Te4[256] = {
16    0x63636363U, 0x7c7c7c7cU, 0x77777777U, 0x7b7b7b7bU, . . .};
17
18  . . .
19
20  __constant__ u32 d_rk[RKLENGTH (256)];  // allocate the maximum ↩
        possible needed space for the expanded key
21
```

```
22  #define RESHUFFLE(i) (((i & 0xFF) << 24) | \
23                        ((i & 0xFF00) << 8) | \
24                        ((i & 0xFF0000) >> 8) | \
25                        ((i & 0xFF000000) >> 24 ))
26
27  //=====================================================================
28  __global__ void rijndaelGPUEncrypt (int nrounds, u32 * data, int N)
29  {
30    u32 s0, s1, s2, s3, t0, t1, t2, t3;
31    const u32 *rk = d_rk;          // to avoid changing d_rk in the ↩
          code
32    u32 aux;
33
34    int myID = blockIdx.x * blockDim.x + threadIdx.x;
35    // check if there is a block to process
36    if (myID >= (N >> 4))
37      return;
38
39    int myDataIdx = myID << 2;    // *4 to offset 16 bytes
40
41  #ifndef FULL_UNROLL
42    int r;
43  #endif /* ?FULL_UNROLL */
44    /*
45     * map byte array block to cipher state
46     * and add initial round key:
47     */
48    aux = data[myDataIdx];   s0 = RESHUFFLE(aux) ^ rk[0];
49    aux = data[myDataIdx+1]; s1 = RESHUFFLE(aux) ^ rk[1];
50    aux = data[myDataIdx+2]; s2 = RESHUFFLE(aux) ^ rk[2];
51    aux = data[myDataIdx+3]; s3 = RESHUFFLE(aux) ^ rk[3];
52
53  #ifdef FULL_UNROLL
54    /* round 1: */
55    t0 = Te0[s0 >> 24] ^ Te1[(s1 >> 16) & 0xff] ^ Te2[(s2 >> 8) & 0xff↩
         ] ^ Te3[s3 & 0xff] ^ rk[4];
56    t1 = Te0[s1 >> 24] ^ Te1[(s2 >> 16) & 0xff] ^ Te2[(s3 >> 8) & 0xff↩
         ] ^ Te3[s0 & 0xff] ^ rk[5];
57    t2 = Te0[s2 >> 24] ^ Te1[(s3 >> 16) & 0xff] ^ Te2[(s0 >> 8) & 0xff↩
         ] ^ Te3[s1 & 0xff] ^ rk[6];
58    t3 = Te0[s3 >> 24] ^ Te1[(s0 >> 16) & 0xff] ^ Te2[(s1 >> 8) & 0xff↩
         ] ^ Te3[s2 & 0xff] ^ rk[7];
59    /* round 2: */
60    . . .
61    s0 = (Te4[(t0 >> 24)] & 0xff000000) ^ (Te4[(t1 >> 16) & 0xff] & 0↩
         x00ff0000) ^ (Te4[(t2 >> 8) & 0xff] & 0x0000ff00) ^ (Te4[(t3) ↩
         & 0xff] & 0x000000ff) ^ rk[0];
62    data[myDataIdx] = RESHUFFLE(s0);
63
64    s1 = (Te4[(t1 >> 24)] & 0xff000000) ^ (Te4[(t2 >> 16) & 0xff] & 0↩
         x00ff0000) ^ (Te4[(t3 >> 8) & 0xff] & 0x0000ff00) ^ (Te4[(t0) ↩
         & 0xff] & 0x000000ff) ^ rk[1];
```

```
65    data[myDataIdx + 1] = RESHUFFLE(s1);
66
67    s2 = (Te4[(t2 >> 24)] & 0xff000000) ^ (Te4[(t3 >> 16) & 0xff] & 0↩
          x00ff0000) ^ (Te4[(t0 >> 8) & 0xff] & 0x0000ff00) ^ (Te4[(t1) ↩
          & 0xff] & 0x000000ff) ^ rk[2];
68    data[myDataIdx + 2] = RESHUFFLE(s2);
69
70    s3 = (Te4[(t3 >> 24)] & 0xff000000) ^ (Te4[(t0 >> 16) & 0xff] & 0↩
          x00ff0000) ^ (Te4[(t1 >> 8) & 0xff] & 0x0000ff00) ^ (Te4[(t2) ↩
          & 0xff] & 0x000000ff) ^ rk[3];
71    data[myDataIdx + 3] = RESHUFFLE(s3);
72    }
```

The key expansion is a procedure that needs to be done only once for the encryption/decryption, regardless of the number of 16-byte groups that need to be processed. For this reason, the key is expanded by the host and stored in constant memory for all subsequent kernel launches. The main() function as shown in Listing 6.53 computes the expanded key, calculates the size of the input data (lines 111–113), reads the input data in a single call (line 117), calls a host function that serves as a front-end for the kernel invocations (line 121), and saves the ciphertext data (line 126) after releasing any memory reserved on the device (line 123).

Reading the whole file in one go is a controversial step; the operating system can do this faster than in multiple steps, but on the other hand we cannot overlap host I/O with GPU computation, making the overall program duration potentially longer. At the end, this was chosen so a proper evaluation of the different design approaches could be conducted on the basis of how much time was spent on the actual computation, without contamination from the I/O overhead.

Listing 6.53: The main() function used in the CUDA implementation of the AES encryption.

```
73    // File : AES_MPI/aesCUDA.cu
74    . . .
75
76    static const int keybits = 256;
77
78    //==========================================================================
79    int main (int argc, char *argv[])
80    {
81      int lSize = 0;
82      FILE *f, *f2;
83      unsigned char *iobuf;
84
85      if (argc < 4)
86        {
87          fprintf (stderr, "Usage : %s inputfile outputfile ↩
                threadsPerBlock\n", argv[0]);
88          exit (1);
89        }
90
```

```
91   // encryption key
92   unsigned char key[32] = { 1, 2, 3, 4, 5, 6, 7, 8, 9, 10, 11, 12, ↵
         13, 14, 15, 16, 17, 18, 19, 20, 21, 22, 23, 24, 25, 26, 27, ↵
         28, 29, 30, 31, 32 };
93   u32 rk[RKLENGTH (keybits)];
94   // expanded key preparation
95   int nrounds = rijndaelSetupEncrypt (rk, key, keybits);
96
97   if ((f = fopen (argv[1], "r")) == NULL)
98     {
99       fprintf (stderr, "Can't open %s\n", argv[1]);
100      exit (EXIT_FAILURE);
101    }
102
103  if ((f2 = fopen (argv[2], "w")) == NULL)
104    {
105      fprintf (stderr, "Can't open %s\n", argv[2]);
106      exit (EXIT_FAILURE);
107    }
108
109  int thrPerBlock = atoi (argv[3]);
110
111  fseek (f, 0, SEEK_END); // calculate size of required buffer
112  lSize = ftell (f);
113  rewind (f);
114
115  iobuf = new unsigned char[lSize];
116  assert (iobuf != 0);
117  fread (iobuf, 1, lSize, f);
118  fclose (f);
119
120  // encrypt an lSize-long block located at iobuf
121  rijndaelEncryptFE (rk, keybits, iobuf, iobuf, lSize, thrPerBlock);
122
123  rijndaelShutdown ();   // release device memory
124
125  // save ciphertext
126  fwrite(iobuf, 1, lSize, f2);
127  fclose(f2);
128
129  delete[]iobuf;   // release host memory
130  return 0;
131 }
```

The `rijndaelEncryptFE()` front-end function as shown in Listing 6.54 is responsible for:

- Allocating device memory: the allocation is done when the function is called for the first time (lines 163 and 164). The amount of device memory allocated is fixed, determined by the `DEVICEMEMSIZE` constant.
- Copying the rounds key to constant memory (line 168).

- Copying data to global memory (line 179) and back (line 189): the input data are split into DEVICEMEMSIZE-sized subblocks and transferred to the device.
- Calculating the grid configuration (line 182) based on the specified threads-per-block value and the number of data blocks to be encrypted (line 175). There is one kernel thread assigned to each data block, hence the expression for finding the size of the grid on line 182.

Listing 6.54: Host code for launching the AES encryption kernel. The nearly identical decryption-related parts are not shown.

```
132  // File : AES_MPI/rijndael_host.cu
133  . . .
134  // Host-side copies of the arrays used in key expansion.
135  // Identifiers are the same as in the AES_MPI/rijndael_device.cu ↩
         file, but there is no naming conflict as the arrays are declared↩
         as static
136  static const u32 Te4[256] =
137  {
138    0x63636363U, 0x7c7c7c7cU, 0x77777777U, 0x7b7b7b7bU, . . .};
139
140  static const u32 Td0[256] =
141  {
142    0x51f4a750U, 0x7e416553U, 0x1a17a4c3U, 0x3a275e96U, . . .};
143
144  . . .
145  //================================================================
146  // Expands the encryption key and returns the number of rounds for ↩
         the given key size
147  int rijndaelSetupEncrypt(u32 *rk, const u8 *key, int keybits)
148  {
149    // This function in not shown here as it is identical to the one ↩
         provided by the reference implementation
150    . . .
151  }
152  //================================================================
153
154  const int DEVICEMEMSIZE=(1<<24); // 16 MiB
155  u32 *d_buffer=NULL;
156  extern __constant__ u32 d_rk[RKLENGTH(256)]; // externally defined ↩
         symbol, allocated in device constant memory
157  //================================================================
158  // Host FE function responsible for calling the device
159  // Setups the grid of blocks and calls the kernel
160  // N is the size of the plaintext in bytes and it should be a ↩
         multiple of 16
161  void rijndaelEncryptFE(const u32 *rk, int keybits, unsigned char *↩
         plaintext, unsigned char *ciphertext, int N, int thrPerBlock↩
         =256)
162  {
163      if(d_buffer == NULL)
```

```
164         CUDA_CHECK_RETURN(cudaMalloc((void **)&d_buffer, ←
               DEVICEMEMSIZE));
165
166     int nrounds = NROUNDS(keybits);
167
168     CUDA_CHECK_RETURN(cudaMemcpyToSymbol (d_rk[0], (void *)rk, ←
               RKLENGTH(keybits)*sizeof(u32)));
169
170     // data to be encrypted are broken up into DEVICEMEMSIZE chunks ←
               and sent to the device
171     int dataPos;
172     for(dataPos=0; dataPos<N; dataPos += DEVICEMEMSIZE)
173     {
174         int toSend = (N − dataPos < DEVICEMEMSIZE) ? N−dataPos : ←
               DEVICEMEMSIZE;   // how much data to send to the device
175         int numDataBlocks = (int)ceil(toSend /16.0);
176         toSend = numDataBlocks * 16;
177
178         // copy data to device
179         CUDA_CHECK_RETURN(cudaMemcpy(d_buffer, plaintext + dataPos, ←
               toSend, cudaMemcpyHostToDevice));
180
181         // grid calculation
182         int grid = ceil(numDataBlocks *1.0/ thrPerBlock);
183
184         rijndaelGPUEncrypt<<< grid, thrPerBlock >>>(nrounds, ←
               d_buffer, toSend);
185
186         // wait for encyption to complete
187         CUDA_CHECK_RETURN(cudaDeviceSynchronize());
188         // retrieve encypted data
189         CUDA_CHECK_RETURN(cudaMemcpy(ciphertext + dataPos, d_buffer,←
               toSend, cudaMemcpyDeviceToHost));
190     }
191 }
192
193 //===============================================================
194 // Called to clean up memory allocation on the device
195 void rijndaelShutdown()
196 {
197     if(d_buffer != NULL)
198         CUDA_CHECK_RETURN(cudaFree((void *)d_buffer));
199     d_buffer = NULL;
200     CUDA_CHECK_RETURN (cudaDeviceReset ());
201 }
```

The `rijndaelShutdown()` function releases the device memory, so it should be called after the encryption/decryption completes.

The program receives as command-line parameters the filenames of the input and output data, as well as the number of threads per block to be used in the kernel execution configuration. For example:

```
$ ./aesCUDA in.data out.data 256
```

This allows us to easily experiment with alternative configurations, without the need to recompile the code.

6.15.2.2 Version #2: Overlapping GPU communication and computation

The application at hand is one requiring the transfer of massive amounts of data across the PCIe bus. A design strategy that can effectively "hide" the communication overhead is the use of streams (see Section 6.7.5), at least as long as the target device supports concurrent kernel and memory copy executions.

The introduction of streams into the CUDA code presented in the previous section requires only small modifications to the host front-end functions `rijndaelEncryptFE()` and `rijndaelDecryptFE()`, as well as the `main` function. The `rijndaelShutdown()` is also affected but it is only of minor concern as it merely cleans up the allocated memory and destroys the stream objects.

The modification to the main function has to do with the allocation of pinned memory; otherwise we cannot achieve kernel execution and data transfer concurrency. This means that lines 115 and 129 in Listing 6.53 have to be replaced by:

Listing 6.55: Main function modifications for allocating pinned memory.

```
1   // File : AES_MPI/aesCUDA.cu
2   . . .
3      cudaMallocHost(&iobuf, lSize);
4   . . .
5    cudaFreeHost(iobuf);
6   . . .
```

The remaining modifications that need to be carried out are shown below:

Listing 6.56: Host code for launching the AES encryption kernel using streams. Only the changes from Listing 6.54 are shown. The function names remain the same, allowing the compilation of the new program without mandating any modifications to the other source code files in the project.

```
1   // File : AES_MPI/rijndael_host_streams.cu
2   . . .
3   static u32 *d_buffer[2] = { 0 }; // two buffers, one for each stream
4   static cudaStream_t str[2];
5
6   //==========================================================
7   void rijndaelEncryptFE (const u32 * rk, int keybits, unsigned char *↵
          plaintext, unsigned char *ciphertext, int N, int thrPerBlock = ↵
          256)
8   {
9     if (d_buffer[0] == NULL)
10      {
11        CUDA_CHECK_RETURN (cudaMalloc ((void **) &d_buffer[0]), ↵
              DEVICEMEMSIZE));
```

```
12        CUDA_CHECK_RETURN (cudaMalloc ((void **) &(d_buffer[1]), ↵
              DEVICEMEMSIZE));
13        CUDA_CHECK_RETURN (cudaStreamCreate (&(str[0])));
14        CUDA_CHECK_RETURN (cudaStreamCreate (&(str[1])));
15     }
16
17   int nrounds = NROUNDS (keybits);
18
19   CUDA_CHECK_RETURN (cudaMemcpyToSymbol (d_rk[0], (void *) rk, ↵
         RKLENGTH (keybits) * sizeof (u32)));
20
21   // data to be encrypted are broken up into DEVICEMEMSIZE chunks ↵
         and sent to the device
22   int dataPos;
23   int whichStream = 0;
24   for (dataPos = 0; dataPos < N; dataPos += DEVICEMEMSIZE)
25     {
26        int toSend = (N - dataPos < DEVICEMEMSIZE) ? N - dataPos : ↵
              DEVICEMEMSIZE; // how much data to send to the device
27        int numDataBlocks = (int) ceil (toSend / 16.0);
28        toSend = numDataBlocks * 16;
29
30        // copy data to device
31        CUDA_CHECK_RETURN (cudaMemcpyAsync (d_buffer[whichStream], ↵
              plaintext + dataPos, toSend, cudaMemcpyHostToDevice, str[↵
              whichStream]));
32
33        // grid calculation
34        int grid = ceil (numDataBlocks * 1.0 / thrPerBlock);
35
36        rijndaelGPUEncrypt <<< grid, thrPerBlock, 0, str[whichStream] ↵
              >>> (nrounds, d_buffer[whichStream], toSend);
37
38        // retrieve encpted data
39        CUDA_CHECK_RETURN (cudaMemcpyAsync (ciphertext + dataPos, ↵
              d_buffer[whichStream], toSend, cudaMemcpyDeviceToHost, str↵
              [whichStream]));
40        whichStream = !whichStream;
41     }
42   // wait for encption to complete
43   CUDA_CHECK_RETURN (cudaStreamSynchronize (str[0]));
44   CUDA_CHECK_RETURN (cudaStreamSynchronize (str[1]));
45 }
46
47 //==============================================================
48 // Called to clean up memory allocation on the device
49 void rijndaelShutdown ()
50 {
51   if (d_buffer[0] != NULL)
52     {
53        CUDA_CHECK_RETURN (cudaFree ((void *) d_buffer[0]));
54        CUDA_CHECK_RETURN (cudaFree ((void *) d_buffer[1]));
```

```
55        CUDA_CHECK_RETURN (cudaStreamDestroy (str[0]));
56        CUDA_CHECK_RETURN (cudaStreamDestroy (str[1]));
57      }
58    d_buffer[0] = NULL;
59    CUDA_CHECK_RETURN (cudaDeviceReset ());
60  }
```

The differences can be boiled down to the allocation of two separate device buffers and the construction of two streams that are fed alternating pieces of the input data. The whichStream variable is used to change the target stream in every iteration of the for-loop of lines 24–41. In order to utilize the two stream objects that are created on lines 13 and 14, the cudaMemcpy() calls are replaced with cudaMemcpyAsync() calls and the kernel invocation of line 36 carries a fourth parameter that references the target stream. The synchronization is performed only once for each stream, past the end of the for-loop on lines 43 and 44.

6.15.2.3 Version #3: Using a cluster of GPU machines

Having a working CUDA program from the previous sections simplifies the task of moving to a cluster solution tremendously. The design of the cluster implementation in this section follows the master–worker paradigm: extending the data breakup practiced in both rijndaelEncryptFE() functions above, a master process breaks up the input data in fixed-sized chunks and distributes them on a first-come, first-served basis to the worker nodes. The workers return the ciphertext before getting one more piece of the plaintext, etc., until all the data are encrypted.

This technique provides an easy path to load balancing; however, internode communication can no longer overlap with computation. Nevertheless, we proceed with this approach, more as a teaching aid for the techniques involved, and less as a performance improvement. This approach is convenient but it has been shown to be inferior to more elaborate partitioning attempts [14]. This issue is addressed in more detail in Chapter 11.

The only change that needs to be carried out in the code of the previous section lies in the main() function, so that communication between nodes can be orchestrated. The new main function is shown in Listing 6.57.

The protocol used for the communication between the master and worker nodes is shown in the form of a UML sequence diagram in Fig. 6.40. The protocol involves the exchange of three types of messages, as identified by their tag[25]:

- TAG_DATA: The message carries data to be processed (coming from the master) or data that have been processed already (coming from a worker). A TAG_DATA message is always preceded by one of the other types of messages.

---

[25] A protocol can be established that uses only two types of messages for the exchange. The key is making the messages that carry the data offset redundant. This would also reduce the overall message count by a factor of 2. This can be accomplished by having the master process maintain a record of what piece of the data has been assigned to each worker. This modification is left as an exercise.

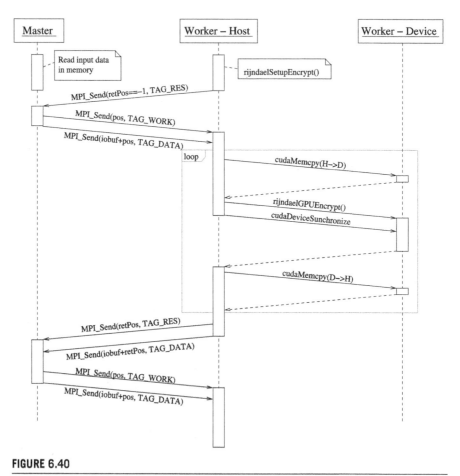

FIGURE 6.40

UML sequence diagram of the master–worker exchanges in the MPI-based AES implementation of Listing 6.57.

- TAG_RES: A "result" message sent by a worker that acts as a prolog to a TAG_DATA message. This message carries the offset in the output data array, where the processed data are to be deposited.
- TAG_WORK: A "work item" message that is sent by the master to a worker. This message carries the offset/position in the input array of the data to be processed that are subsequently sent in a TAG_DATA message.

The conversation between the master and a worker is triggered by the latter. A worker announces its availability by sending a TAG_RES message with a negative data offset (line 104). The master will then respond by sending a block of input data to the worker (lines 69 and 70). When the worker receives a work item, it calls the rijndaelEncryptFE() function (line 111) after determining the exact size of the data to be processed (line 110). This function in turn sets up and carries through a sequence of kernel invocations in order to encrypt all the input data. Once `rijndae-lEncryptFE()` returns, the worker sends a `TAG_RES` followed by a `TAG_DATA` message (lines 112 and 113) and awaits its next assignment (line 116).

Once all the data have been assigned by the master (end of while-loop of lines 60–73), the master sends a `TAG_WORK` message to each worker with a negative data offset (lines 77–86), as soon as they report back with the results of their last assignment (lines 80–82). The negative data offset acts as a flag to the end of the computation (line 106).

Listing 6.57: Main function for handling the interaction between nodes in an MPI cluster implementation of the AES encryption/decryption. Time measurement-related code is omitted for brevity.

```cpp
// File : AES_MPI/main.cpp
. . .
#define TAG_RES   0
#define TAG_WORK  1
#define TAG_DATA  2

static const int keybits = 256;

//========================================================================
int main (int argc, char *argv[])
{
  int rank;
  unsigned char *iobuf;

  int lSize = 0;
  FILE *f;

  int comm_size = 0;
  MPI_Status status;
  MPI_Init (&argc, &argv);
  MPI_Comm_rank (MPI_COMM_WORLD, &rank);
  MPI_Comm_size (MPI_COMM_WORLD, &comm_size);
  MPI_Request req;
  MPI_Status stat;

  if (argc < 5)
    {
      if (rank == 0)
        fprintf (stderr, "Usage : %s inputfile outputfile ↩
            workItemSize threadsPerBlock\n", argv[0]);

      exit (1);
    }

  //encryption key
  unsigned char key[32] = { 1, 2, 3, 4, 5, 6, 7, 8, 9, 10, 11, 12, ↩
      13, 14, 15, 16, 17, 18, 19, 20, 21, 22, 23, 24, 25, 26, 27, ↩
      28, 29, 30, 31, 32 };
```

```
36    u32 rk[RKLENGTH (keybits)];
37    rijndaelSetupEncrypt (rk, key, keybits);
38
39    if (rank == 0)
40      {
41        if ((f = fopen (argv[1], "r")) == NULL)
42          {
43            fprintf (stderr, "Can't open %s\n", argv[1]);
44            exit (EXIT_FAILURE);
45          }
46
47        int workItemSize = atoi (argv[3]);
48
49        fseek (f, 0, SEEK_END);
50        lSize = ftell (f);
51        rewind (f);
52
53        iobuf = new unsigned char[lSize];
54        assert (iobuf != NULL);
55        fread (iobuf, 1, lSize, f);
56        fclose (f);
57
58        // master main loop
59        int pos = 0;
60        while (pos < lSize)
61          {
62            int retPos;
63            MPI_Recv (&retPos, 1, MPI_INT, MPI_ANY_SOURCE, TAG_RES, ↩
                  MPI_COMM_WORLD, &stat);
64            if (retPos >= 0)          // if not the first dummy worker ↩
                  call
65              MPI_Recv (iobuf + retPos, workItemSize, ↩
                    MPI_UNSIGNED_CHAR, stat.MPI_SOURCE, TAG_DATA, ↩
                    MPI_COMM_WORLD, &stat);
66
67            // assign next work item
68            int actualSize = (workItemSize < lSize − pos) ? ↩
                  workItemSize : (lSize − pos);
69            MPI_Send (&pos, 1, MPI_INT, stat.MPI_SOURCE, TAG_WORK, ↩
                  MPI_COMM_WORLD);
70            MPI_Send (iobuf + pos, actualSize, MPI_UNSIGNED_CHAR, stat↩
                  .MPI_SOURCE, TAG_DATA, MPI_COMM_WORLD);
71
72            pos += actualSize;
73          }
74
75        // wait for last results
76        pos = −1;
77        for (int i = 1; i < comm_size; i++)
78          {
79            int retPos;
```

```
80          MPI_Recv (&retPos, 1, MPI_INT, MPI_ANY_SOURCE, TAG_RES, ←
                MPI_COMM_WORLD, &stat);
81          if (retPos >= 0)          // if not the first dummy worker ←
                call
82            MPI_Recv (iobuf + retPos, workItemSize, ←
                  MPI_UNSIGNED_CHAR, stat.MPI_SOURCE, TAG_DATA, ←
                  MPI_COMM_WORLD, &stat);
83
84          // indicate end of operations
85          MPI_Send (&pos, 1, MPI_INT, stat.MPI_SOURCE, TAG_WORK, ←
                MPI_COMM_WORLD);
86        }
87
88      FILE *fout;
89      if ((fout = fopen (argv[2], "w")) == NULL)
90        {
91          fprintf (stderr, "Can't open %s\n", argv[2]);
92          exit (EXIT_FAILURE);
93        }
94      fwrite(iobuf, 1, lSize, fout);
95      fclose (fout);
96    }
97  else                              // GPU worker
98    {
99      int workItemSize = atoi (argv[3]);
100     int thrPerBlock = atoi (argv[4]);
101     int pos = -1;
102     iobuf = new unsigned char[workItemSize];
103
104     MPI_Send (&pos, 1, MPI_INT, 0, TAG_RES, MPI_COMM_WORLD);
105     MPI_Recv (&pos, 1, MPI_INT, 0, TAG_WORK, MPI_COMM_WORLD, &stat←
              );
106     while (pos >= 0)
107       {
108         MPI_Recv (iobuf, workItemSize, MPI_UNSIGNED_CHAR, 0, ←
                TAG_DATA, MPI_COMM_WORLD, &stat);
109         int actualSize;
110         MPI_Get_count(&stat, MPI_UNSIGNED_CHAR, &actualSize);
111         rijndaelEncryptFE (rk, keybits, iobuf, iobuf, actualSize, ←
                thrPerBlock);
112         MPI_Send (&pos, 1, MPI_INT, 0, TAG_RES, MPI_COMM_WORLD);
113         MPI_Send (iobuf, actualSize, MPI_UNSIGNED_CHAR, 0, ←
                TAG_DATA, MPI_COMM_WORLD);
114
115         // get next work item start
116         MPI_Recv (&pos, 1, MPI_INT, 0, TAG_WORK, MPI_COMM_WORLD, &←
                stat);
117       }
118     rijndaelShutdown();
119   }
120
121   MPI_Finalize ();
```

```
122
123    delete [] iobuf;
124    return 0;
125  }
```

The program receives as command-line parameters the filenames of the input and output data, the work item size, i.e., the size of the parts communicated to the workers, and the number of threads per block to be used in the kernel execution configuration. An example run with three GPU worker nodes would be:

```
$ mpirun —np 4 ./aesMPI in.data out.data 1000000 256
```

Again, the goal is to easily experiment with alternative configurations, without the need to recompile the code.

In order to accommodate both GPU and CPU worker nodes, without complicated initialization procedures and extensive code modifications, we resorted to creating a version of the program in Listing 6.57 for CPU worker nodes only and using an MPMD launch configuration. The only modification that needs to be carried out is in the else-block of lines 97–119. The resulting code is shown in Listing 6.58, constructed so that it utilizes the AES reference implementation function rijndaelEncrypt(), which has been renamed for clarity to rijndaelCPUEncrypt():

Listing 6.58: Part of the main() function that is targeting AES encryption on CPU worker nodes. The remaining code is identical to the one shown in Listing 6.57.

```
126  // File : AES_MPI/mainCPUWorker.cpp
127  . . .
128    else                        // CPU worker
129    {
130        int workItemSize = atoi (argv[3]);
131        int thrPerBlock = atoi (argv[4]);
132        int pos = -1;
133        workItemSize = (workItemSize / 16 + 1) * 16;    // making ↩
                sure enough space for zero—padding is available
134
135        iobuf = new unsigned char[workItemSize];
136        int nrounds = NROUNDS (keybits);
137
138        // report for duty!
139        MPI_Send (&pos, 1, MPI_INT, 0, TAG_RES, MPI_COMM_WORLD);
140        // get 1st assigned block location
141        MPI_Recv (&pos, 1, MPI_INT, 0, TAG_WORK, MPI_COMM_WORLD, &stat↩
                );
142        while (pos >= 0)
143          {
144            MPI_Recv (iobuf, workItemSize, MPI_UNSIGNED_CHAR, 0, ↩
                   TAG_DATA, MPI_COMM_WORLD, &stat);
145            int actualSize;
146            MPI_Get_count (&stat, MPI_UNSIGNED_CHAR, &actualSize);
147
```

```
148     // Padding is added at the end of the array, to produce an↩
            integer
149     // number of 16-byte blocks
150     int paddedSize = ceil (actualSize / 16.0) * 16;
151     for (int k = actualSize; k < paddedSize; k++)
152       iobuf[k] = ' ';
153
154     // Assigned data block is processed in 16-byte blocks at a↩
            time
155     int dataPos;
156     for (dataPos = 0; dataPos < actualSize; dataPos += 16)
157       {
158         // encrypt 16-byte block
159         rijndaelCPUEncrypt (rk, nrounds, iobuf + dataPos, ↩
              iobuf + dataPos);
160       }
161
162     // Return results, and their location in the overall ↩
            ciphertext
163     MPI_Send (&pos, 1, MPI_INT, 0, TAG_RES, MPI_COMM_WORLD);
164     MPI_Send (iobuf, actualSize, MPI_UNSIGNED_CHAR, 0, ↩
            TAG_DATA, MPI_COMM_WORLD);
165
166     // get next work item start
167     MPI_Recv (&pos, 1, MPI_INT, 0, TAG_WORK, MPI_COMM_WORLD, &↩
            stat);
168     }
169   }
170
171   MPI_Finalize ();
172
173   delete [] iobuf;
174   return 0;
175 }
```

In summary, the files used in our three AES encryption implementations and their dependencies are shown in Fig. 6.38.

As stated above, Listings 6.57 and 6.58 are used to generate two executables, one targeting GPU workers and one targeting CPU workers, respectively. These are jointly used in order to be able to support the deployment of the program over a network of mixed capability nodes. Fig. 6.41 shows an example of a mixed machines cluster that we will use to illustrate how an MPMD program deployment can be performed. An application file (appfile) detailing the destination of each executable and the number of processes spawned in each machine is all that is needed, as shown below:

Listing 6.59: Appfile for spawning 13 MPI processes, i.e., 1 master, 2 GPU workers, and 10 CPU workers, on the two desktops of the intranet in Fig. 6.41.

```
-host achilleas -np 2 aesMPI in512.dat ciphertext.dat 16777216 512
-oversubscribe -host achilleas -np 3 aesMPICPUWorker in512.dat ↩
    ciphertext.dat 16777216 512
```

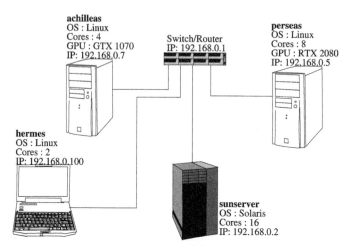

FIGURE 6.41

Intranet example used for explaining the MPMD deployment of an MPI program that utilizes GPU-equipped, multicore nodes.

```
-host perseas -np 1 aesMPI in512.dat ciphertext.dat 16777216 512
-oversubscribe -host perseas -np 7 aesMPICPUWorker in512.dat ↩
    ciphertext.dat 16777216 512
```

The "-oversubscribe" switch prevents the MPI runtime from complaining about trying to use an already occupied node. The above lines need to be stored in an application file (e.g., "encryptionMPMD.conf") and used in the following fashion[26]:

```
$ mpirun -app encryptionMPMD.conf
```

MPI numbers the spawned processes in the order they are listed in the appfile. So, the appfile in Listing 6.59 produces the processes shown in Table 6.9. The quad-core achilleas machine is scheduled to run five MPI processes, as the master process is mostly idle in terms of CPU time, dedicated to exchanging messages with the workers.

6.15.2.4 Performance comparison

Compared to the previous case study, AES encryption has the additional characteristic of putting a big emphasis on I/O. In this section we explore not only the issue of GPU code optimization, but also the issue of overall efficiency, especially in comparison with a CPU implementation. In order to produce a quantitative answer to this question, the code presented in the previous sections is structured so that file I/O is

---

[26] MPI requires that the node from which the launch is done is included in the execution. If the user is using hermes for launching the program, the above appfile will fail. A remote launch is possible via an ssh session running on achilleas.

Table 6.9 MPI processes generated in response to the appfile of Listing 6.59.

Appfile line	MPI processes generated
`-host achilleas -np 2 aesMPI ...`	0 : master 1 : GPU worker
`-host achilleas -np 3 aesMPICPUWorker ...`	2-4 : CPU workers
`-host perseas -np 1 aesMPI ...`	5 : GPU worker
`-host perseas -np 7 aesMPICPUWorker ...`	6-11 : CPU workers

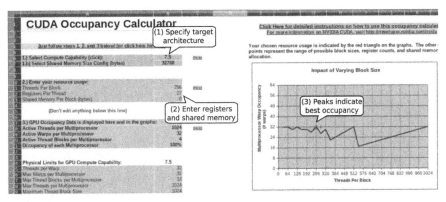

FIGURE 6.42

Occupancy calculation for the `rijndaelGPUEncrypt()` kernel.

completely decoupled from the encryption process. The same approach is used in order to measure the CPU execution time.

The test platform used was an AMD Ryzen 3900X processor, with 32 GiB of DDR4 RAM and an RTX 2060 Super GPU card with 8 GiB of DDR6 RAM. A PCIe 3.0 interface provided the interconnect between the GPU and its host. As shown in Fig. 6.39, the `rijndaelGPUEncrypt()` and `rijndaelGPUDecrypt()` kernels use 27 and 26 registers, respectively. The CUDA occupancy calculator for a compute capability 7.5 device reveals the optimum settings for the number of threads per block (see Fig. 6.42) as being 64, 128, 256, 512, or 1024, so our tests covered all these alternatives.

The size of the data blocks that are processed per grid was set to 1 MiB, 16 MiB, or 32 MiB, in order to support streaming. Two files of randomly generated data were used for timing the execution, one 128 MiB and one 512 MiB. These were produced by utilizing the `dd` command and the `/dev/urandom` Linux device:

```
$ dd if=/dev/urandom of=in128.dat bs=1M count=128
```

The correctness of the GPU code was tested by decrypting the data and checking them against the original input.

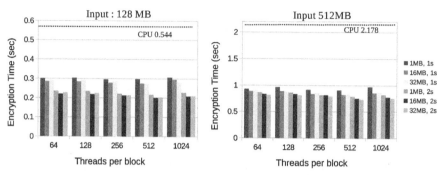

FIGURE 6.43

Average AES encryption times on a Ryzen 3900X and an RTX 2060 Super. Bars are colored according to the data block size per grid (1 MiB, 16 MiB, or 32MiB) and the number of streams used (1 or 2).

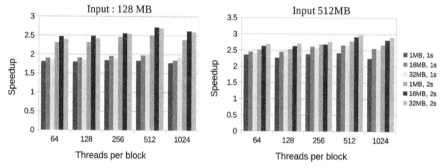

FIGURE 6.44

Speedup of the AES GPU-based encryption compared to the CPU-based one.

The average encryption-only execution times (averaged over 100 runs) are shown in Fig. 6.43. The software setup included GCC 7.4, CUDA 10.2, and OpenMPI 4.0.2. Optimization was turned on using the "-O2" switch.

As the times are difficult to quantify in relative terms, Fig. 6.44 shows the corresponding speedup achieved.

The results suggest that the best configuration consists of processing the data in batches of 16 MiB or 32 MB, based on the size of the input, and by grids of 512-thread blocks. Additionally, Figs. 6.43 and 6.44 reveal a noticeable boost in performance by the use of the dual streams. The relative reduction in execution time compared with the single-stream case ranges between 6.5% and nearly 30%.

Fig. 6.45 reveals why this gain is possible and why it is not bigger. One may be tempted to think that two streams could reduce the time in half, but this would be a naive misconception.

While the roughly 2.5× speedup offered by the CUDA solution is not negligible, one could argue that we were using only one of the available CPU cores. A multi-

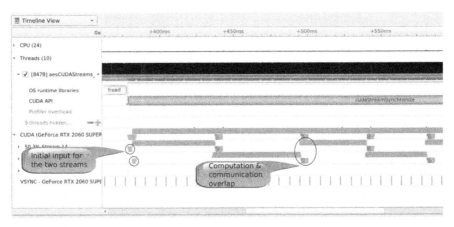

FIGURE 6.45

A screenshot of Nsight Systems displaying the data captured during a profiling session of the AES encryption using two streams. A small overlap between kernel executions is also visible. As the SMs finish the blocks from one stream, they can begin executing the blocks from the other.

threaded version of the CPU version would most certainly be faster than the GPU one, without even considering using the AES-NI instruction set. The AES-NI set provides hardware support for the AES standard, speeding up the encryption/decryption process as much as sixfold [29].

However, the proper point of view is that a GPU is just another computational resource at our disposal, one that should be used in tandem and not in isolation with whatever is available in a system. In that respect, the MPI version of the AES encoder that tries to integrate all available computational resources is a step in the right direction.

The performance potential of the cluster solution was tested on the same single-machine environment used for generating the results of the GPU-only solutions (the explanation for not testing on an actual cluster is given shortly). The outcome averaged over 100 runs is shown in Fig. 6.46. As can be observed, performance is only marginally better than that of the stand-alone GPU solution, and this is only feasible if the size of the work item is relatively small to the size of the overall load to allow load balancing to take place.

A seemingly odd observation in Fig. 6.46 is that the MPI implementation is inferior to the stand-alone GPU one when identical hardware resources are involved, i.e., when only one GPU worker is used. The reason for this behavior comes down to the way MPI programs are made up: as message exchanging processes. In the MPI implementation the host–device–host overhead is augmented with the master–worker exchange costs, bogging down the execution.

Only when multiple CPU workers are involved and the grain of the work item is fine enough to allow them to get an appropriate slice of the workload does the MPI solution start to offer a small advantage. Clearly, the increased communication over-

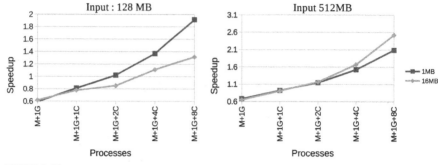

FIGURE 6.46

Speedup offered by the AES MPI implementation compared to the stand-alone GPU implementation when the input data are distributed as 1 MiB and 16 MiB work items. The x-axis labels indicate the composition of the processes taking part in the computation, namely "M" for master, "G" for GPU worker, and "C" for CPU worker.

head, even for processes sharing memory (!), evaporates any potential performance gains from adding more computational resources. This is the reason why in the absence of a very fast communication medium such as Infiniband, we chose not to test over a cluster.

Exercises

1. An array of type float elements is to be processed in a one-element-per-thread fashion by a GPU. Suggest an execution configuration for the following scenarios:
   a. The array is 1D and of size N. The target GPU has 8 SMs, each with 16 SPs.
   b. The array is 2D and of size $N \times N$. The target GPU has 5 SMs, each with 48 SPs.

   For each of the above scenarios, calculate what is the minimum size that N should satisfy to make the GPU computation a desirable alternative to CPU computation.

2. A reduction is an operation frequently encountered in a many algorithms: summing up the elements of an array, finding the minimum, maximum, etc. One possible solution to a CUDA kernel that calculates the sum of an array would be:

```
__global__ void sum(float *in, float *out)
{
    __shared__ float localStore[];  // to speed up data access

    int globalID = threadIdx.x + blockIdx.x * blockDim.x;
    int localID = threadIdx.x;
```

```
localStore[localID] = in[globalID];    // copy to shared ↩
    memory
for(int i=1; i< blockDim.x ; i*=2)
  {
    if(localID % (2*i) == 0)
      localStore[localID] += localStore[localID + i];
    __syncthreads ();
  }
if(localID == 0)
  out[blockIdx.x] = localStore[0];
}
```

The above needs to be called multiple times, each time reducing the size of the data by the number of threads in a block. Data at each kernel launch should be multiples of the block size.

Analyze the above code in relation to the following criteria and how they reflect on the execution speed: thread divergence, memory coalescing, and use of SPs within a warp. Suggest modifications that would improve the performance.

3. The reduction operation discussed in the previous exercise is a special case of the "scan" or prefix-sum operation that can be applied to the elements of a vector or list. In general, the operator applied can be any of summation, minimum, maximum, etc. Implement a CUDA kernel capable of performing a prefix-sum operation. The "Prefix-Sums and Their Applications" paper by Guy Blelloch, available at http://www.cs.cmu.edu/~guyb/papers/Ble93.pdf, is a wonderful resource for learning more on the topic.

4. Create CUDA implementations of the `gsl_stats_mean()` and `gsl_stats_variance()` functions offered by the GNU Scientific Library that produce the mean and variance statistics of an array of type `double` data. Their signatures are:

```
double gsl_stats_mean (const double DATA[], // Pointer to input ↩
    data
                       size_t STRIDE,        // Step used to read ↩
                         the input. Normally this should be ↩
                         set to 1.
                       size_t N);            // Size of DATA ↩
                         array
double gsl_stats_variance (const double DATA[], // Same as above ↩

                           size_t STRIDE,
                           size_t N);
```

Assuming that the `STRIDE` is 1, create a memory access pattern that utilizes coalescing. Suggest ways to deal with the problem if the `STRIDE` is not 1.

5. Design and implement a CUDA program for calculating the histogram of a 24-bit color image. In this case, three separate histograms will be produced, one for each color component of the image.

6. Create a variation of the program in Listing 6.28 to discover and plot the memory copy speed for host-to-device and device-to-host operations and for all the available types of host memory allocations: pageable, pinned, and mapped. In order to test the last type of allocation, you will have to call a kernel that will try to access the memory, triggering the transfer. Compare your results with the ones returned by the $CUDA/samples/1_Utilities/bandwidthTest sample program.

7. The Mandelbrot set calculators of Section 6.15.1 are limited to a maximum of 1024 iterations per pixel. However, the beauty of the Mandelbrot set is revealed for thousands or millions of iterations. Modify one or more of the solutions of Section 6.15.1 so that up to $2^{16} - 1$ iterations can be performed for each pixel. Profile your program and analyze its performance. What is the grid/block arrangement that yields the best performance?

8. Examine the following modifications for improving the stand-alone CUDA AES implementations of Section 6.15.2:

    a. *Move the tables from constant to shared memory*: The constant memory cache is faster than global memory, but it is still slower than shared memory. Will the speed improvement offset the need to copy the tables to constant memory for every block of threads?

    b. *Process multiple 16-byte blocks per thread*: Turning rijndaelGPUEncrypt() into a __device__ function and introducing another __global__ function as a front-end to it, to be called by rijndaelEncryptFE(), should require the smallest possible effort.

    Modify the source code of the Version #2 program in order to introduce your chosen changes and measure the performance improvement obtained. Which change offers the biggest – if any – performance improvement?

9. The MPI cluster AES implementations of Section 6.15.2 do not provide overlapping of communication and computation. This issue could be addressed if a new "work item" was downloaded by the worker nodes while the GPU was processing an already downloaded part. Modify the MPI solution to provide this functionality. Do you expect any problems with the load balancing of the modified solution?

10. Modify the MPI cluster AES implementations of Section 6.15.2 so that only two types of messages are needed for data exchange, instead of the current three. How can this be combined with the modification of the previous exercise?

11. The whole point of the multicore "adventure" is to accelerate our programs. This should be our sole focus, beyond any mis- or preconceptions. The evaluation of the different AES parallel implementations conducted in Section 6.15.2.4 considered only the encryption process, disregarding any I/O costs incurred. Perform your own experiment where the overall execution time is considered and not just the encryption time. Make sure that the file cache provided by the operating system is not utilized by:

- either calling the following from the command-line (root permissions are required):

```
$ sync ; echo 3 > /proc/sys/vm/drop_caches
```

- or calling the `posix_fadvice()` function from within your program, prior to any I/O:

```
#include <unistd.h>
#include <fcntl.h>
int main(int argc, char *argv[]) {
  int fd;
  fd = open(argv[1], O_RDONLY); // Open the file holding the ↩
    input data
  fdatasync(fd);
  posix_fadvise(fd, 0,0,POSIX_FADV_DONTNEED); // clear cache
  close(fd);
  . . .
}
```

Analyze your findings.

12. Modify the program shown in Listing 6.33 so that the reduction phases are shortened to one using the shuffling down operation multiple times.

13. Listing 6.39 presents a kernel that uses grid synchronization for filtering an array of numbers. The problem is that we can only launch one block per SM, and given that each thread processes one data element, this limits the maximum problem size we can handle. Write a modified version of the kernel in Listing 6.39 that processes multiple elements per thread. Are there any shortcomings that you will have to deal with?

GPU and accelerator programming: OpenCL

7

In this chapter you will:

- Learn how to write an OpenCL program that can target a wide variety of accelerators including GPUs and FPGAs.

- Understand how memory is organized in the OpenCL standard and how each level of the memory hierarchy can be utilized.

- Learn how computations are mapped to work items in OpenCL using ranges and work groups.

- Learn how to use queues and events to maximize the utilization of an accelerator and satisfy dependencies in computational tasks.

- Combine OpenCL and C++11 threads to perform hybrid computations, maximizing the utilization of a platform.

- Learn how OpenCL can be used to seamlessly assign work to both host and device.

7.1 The OpenCL architecture

The **Open C**omputing **L**anguage (OpenCL) is an open, royalty-free standard for programming almost every computing device available today (with the possible exception of quantum computers). OpenCL can be used to program CPUs, GPUs, Field Programmable Gate Arrays (FPGAs), and Digital Signal Processors (DSPs), taking advantage of the unique characteristics that each computing platform can offer.

OpenCL 1.0 was originally developed and released by Apple in 2009 as part of their MacOS system. Apple submitted the initial OpenCL specification proposal to the Khronos Group[1] in 2008. The Khronos Group in collaboration with AMD, IBM, Qualcomm, Intel, and NVidia published the OpenCL 1.0 specification in 2009.

While the original specification was based on the C99 language standard, since version 2.0 the standard is based on C++11, allowing the use of classes, templates, and other features one can expect from a modern OO language, as well as the atomics operators introduced in the C++11 standard. The latest version, version 3.0, which was released in September 2020, allows the use of C++17 features for kernel (i.e., a program running on an OpenCL device) development.

---

[1] The Khronos Group is a nonprofit technology consortium (http://www.khronos.org).

Multicore and GPU Programming. https://doi.org/10.1016/B978-0-12-814120-5.00016-0

The major change in OpenCL 3.0 versus previous versions is the adoption of a flexible architecture, where all functionality beyond OpenCL 1.2 is split into optional features whose availability can be queried by the 3.0 API. This allows OpenCL vendors to pick and choose which features to support, while also allowing for future extensions to be incrementally introduced into the standard.

At the moment of this writing (January 2021), there are no OpenCL 3.0 implementations available. For this reason, in this chapter we follow the OpenCL 2.x standard, which means that the provided source code examples might not compile using an OpenCL 1.x software platform.

Contrary to NVidia's CUDA platform, which can only run on their own devices, OpenCL is an open standard that can run on any accelerator architecture and multi-core CPUs, as long as the manufacturer provides an OpenCL "driver." The *Installable Client Driver* (ICD), in OpenCL terminology, is responsible for on-line compilation and execution of OpenCL programs on the corresponding device.

From the three mainstream hardware vendors, we have the following OpenCL implementations:

- AMD: provides OpenCL 2.0-compatible drivers for their FirePro and Radeon lines of GPUs, as well as their APUs (available at https://support.amd.com/en-us/download/, last accessed December 2021), but not their CPUs.
- Intel: provides ICDs for their multicore CPUs (earliest supported architecture is their fifth-generation Core one) and integrated HD Graphics GPUs. Intel also provides an SDK that includes an offline compiler, a debugger, and other tools (available at https://software.intel.com/en-us/articles/opencl-drivers, last accessed December 2021). Intel ICDs support OpenCL 1.2, 2.0, and 2.1.
- NVidia: since CUDA v.9, OpenCL support has migrated from the CUDA SDK to the display drivers. Unfortunately, at the moment of this writing support is provided for OpenCL 1.2 only.

In order to cater for such a wide gamut of target devices, OpenCL is defined as a set of four models that describe different aspects of the system operation:

- The Platform Model: describes the composition of a system at the hardware level.
- The Execution Model: describes how OpenCL programs are launched and executed.
- The Programming Model: describes how an OpenCL program is mapped to hardware resources.
- The Memory Model: describes how memory is managed and data are transferred between memory spaces.

Fig. 7.1 shows how these models relate to the overall system operation, as it pertains to a typical host machine equipped with an OpenCL device/accelerator with a separate memory, along with the sections covering them in detail. As we cover each one in succession, we will delve deeper step-by-step into OpenCL development. We use the C bindings for this purpose. The OpenCL standard also provides C++ bind-

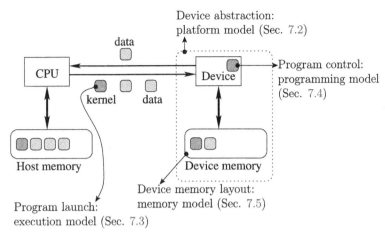

FIGURE 7.1

Overview of the OpenCL models and how they relate to the operation of a heterogeneous system consisting of a CPU and an OpenCL device/accelerator with discrete memory.

ings, which do offer significant benefits by making the source shorter and easier to comprehend. However, these are too extensive to cover in this chapter.

The examples in this chapter have been tested with two compiler suites, Intel's 19.1 (which is available for free for education purposes) and GNU's 9.3, and the NVidia ICD.

7.2 The platform model

OpenCL assumes that the target execution platform is made of a **host** (typically a CPU) and a number of attached/hosted **devices** (typically one or more accelerators). Each device is composed of a number of **compute units** (CUs), which are in turn made of a number of **processing elements** (PEs). One can think of CUs as vector processors, or the equivalent of CUDA streaming multiprocessors (SMs), and of PEs as the equivalent of CUDA streaming processors (SPs).

Fig. 7.2 illustrates this high-level system view. Each of the devices can execute a different OpenCL program, under the control of the host. Each CU can execute a different OpenCL program, but all PEs in a CU must execute the same program. The PEs of a CU are not required to execute the same sequence of instructions (this is a source of inefficiency as will be discussed later), which is identified as a **diverged** control flow.

The problem with the OpenCL heterogeneous platform architecture is that each device may demand its own binary executable code. Such a binary can be generated:

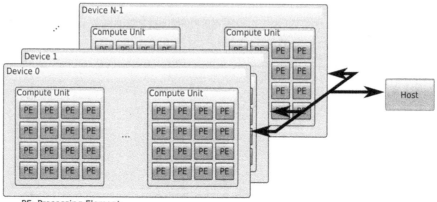

PE: Processing Element

FIGURE 7.2

An illustration of the OpenCL platform model.

- On-line: the OpenCL C/C++ code is compiled during program execution, by supplying the source code to the device's compiler. The compilation overhead is an unwanted burden, but it means that OpenCL programs can run on any device without prior (re)compilation, as long as an online compiler is provided.
- Off-line: the OpenCL code is compiled prior to execution and can be made available to the device immediately. The device code can be statically linked with the host executable code in a single file.

An OpenCL program can be also compiled into an intermediate form of an assembly-like language called the **S**tandard **P**ortable **I**ntermediate **R**epresentation (SPIR), which is similar to CUDA's PTX. The current version, published in 2015, is SPIR-V. SPIR requires an online compiler, but it has a reduced compilation overhead as it is much closer to the hardware than C/C++. This means that certain optimizations can take place beforehand, i.e., during the translation to SPIR-V.

OpenCL provides an API for querying the available devices in a system. The code shown in Listing 7.1 illustrates two of these functions, namely `clGetPlatformIDs` and `clGetDeviceIDs`.

Listing 7.1: Discovering the OpenCL devices.

```
1  // File : deviceList.cpp
2  #include <stdio.h>
3  #ifdef __APPLE__
4  #include <OpenCL/cl.h>
5  #else
6  #include <CL/cl.h>
7  #endif
8
9  using namespace std;
10
```

```
11   const int MAXNUMDEV=10;
12   int main()
13   {
14       cl_int errNum;
15       cl_uint numPlatforms;
16       cl_platform_id firstPlatformId;
17       cl_device_id devID[MAXNUMDEV];
18       cl_uint numDev;
19
20       // Get a reference to an object representing a platform
21       errNum = clGetPlatformIDs(1, &firstPlatformId, &numPlatforms);
22       if (errNum != CL_SUCCESS || numPlatforms <= 0)
23       {
24           cerr << "Failed to find any OpenCL platforms." << endl;
25           return 1;
26       }
27
28       // Get the device IDs matching the CL_DEVICE_TYPE parameter, up ←
             to the MAXNUMDEV limit
29       errNum = clGetDeviceIDs( firstPlatformId,CL_DEVICE_TYPE_ALL, ←
             MAXNUMDEV, devID, &numDev);
30       if (errNum != CL_SUCCESS || numDev <= 0)
31       {
32           cerr << "Failed to find any OpenCL devices." << endl;
33           return 2;
34       }
35
36       char devName[100];
37       size_t nameLen;
38       for(int i=0;i<numDev;i++)
39       {
40         errNum = clGetDeviceInfo(devID[i], CL_DEVICE_NAME, 100, (void←
               *)devName, &nameLen);
41         if(errNum == CL_SUCCESS)
42             cout << "Device " << i << " is " << devName << endl;
43       }
44       return 0;
45   }
```

The code in Listing 7.1 can be compiled with the following command line:

```
$ g++ deviceList.cpp -lOpenCL -o deviceList
$ ./deviceList
Device 0 is pthread-AMD Ryzen 9 3900X 12-Core Processor
```

which indicates that OpenCL does not mandate any special support from the host compiler, as it is just like any other third-party library. As can be seen above, the program lists the OpenCL-capable devices. For the above command to work, make sure that the OpenCL include directory and library path are included in the environment variables.

Table 7.1 OpenCL primitive data types. Two's complement representation is used for the signed types.

Data type	Bits	Description
cl_char	8	Signed 8-bit integer
cl_uchar	8	Unsigned 8-bit integer
cl_short	16	Signed 16-bit integer
cl_ushort	16	Unsigned 16-bit integer
cl_int	32	Signed 4-byte integer
cl_uint	32	Unsigned 4-byte integer
cl_long	64	Signed 8-byte integer
cl_ulong	64	Unsigned 8-byte integer
cl_half	16	Half-precision floating point number
cl_float	32	Single-precision floating point number
cl_double	64	Double-precision floating point number

The source code in Listing 7.1 provides an opportunity to highlight some common traits in OpenCL code:

- Lines 3–7 show that all functions are defined in the cl.h header file. The #ifdef preprocessor control structure serves to differentiate the include path based on whether the host is an Apple OS or not. If one wishes to use the OpenCL C++ bindings, then the CL/cl.hpp file should be included instead. Also, if OpenCL 2.x is required, the appropriate include file is CL/cl2.hpp.
- The definitions on lines 14–18 show that to ensure cross-platform data compatibility, OpenCL introduces a number of data types, including primitives ones (like cl_uint). A list of the most common ones is shown in Table 7.1.
- Most OpenCL functions return an error code that serves to check error conditions. As long as the returned integer is 0 (CL_SUCCESS), the function executed without error.

In terms of functionality, all the interesting parts happen at lines 21, 29, and 40: clGetPlatformIDs has the following signature:

```
// Returns OpenCL platform IDs in the second parameter
cl_int clGetPlatformIDs(cl_uint capacity, // Size of IDs array (IN)
            cl_platform_id * IDs,   // Array where platform
                                    // IDs will be deposited
                                    // (IN/OUT)
        cl_uint * numPlatforms );// Actual IDs deposited
                                    // in the 'IDs' array
                                    // (IN/OUT)
```

clGetDeviceIDs has the following signature:

```
// Returns the OpenCL devices of the supplied platform ID
cl_int clGetDeviceIDs(cl_platform_id pID, // Platform ID (IN)
            cl_device_type type,      // Type of devices
```

```
                                               // desired. E.g.,
                                               // CL_DEVICE_TYPE_GPU (IN)
              cl_uint capacity,                // 'devIDs' array size(IN)
              cl_device_id *devIDs,            // Placeholder for device
                                               // IDs (IN/OUT)
              cl_uint *numDev);                // Number of device IDs
                                               // actually placed in
                                               // 'devIDs' (IN/OUT)
```

On lines 38–43 we iterate over the retrieved device IDs and extract and print out their name via the `clGetDeviceInfo` call:

```
// Returns a user-specified property of the supplied device ID
cl_int clGetDeviceInfo(cl_device_id  ID,  // Device ID (IN)
               cl_device_info spec,         // Constant identifying the
                                            // desired property to
                                            // retrieve, e.g.,
                                            // CL_DEVICE_VENDOR (IN)
               size_t s,                    // Size in bytes of the
                                            // 'buffer' array (IN)
               void * buffer,               // Address of repository to
                                            // hold the property value
                                            // (IN/OUT)
               size_t *stored);             // Actual bytes used from
                                            // the buffer array(IN/OUT)
```

The `size_t` type maps to a 64-bit unsigned integer if the device supports 64-bit addresses or to a 32-bit one otherwise.

In Listing 7.1 we only get a single platform. If one wants to get all the available platforms, calling the `clGetPlatformIDs` function with the second parameter set to NULL returns in `numPlatforms` the number of available platforms. Thus, getting references to all the platforms requires this sequence:

```
cl_int errNum;
cl_uint numPlatforms;
cl_platform_id *platformIds;

errNum = clGetPlatformIDs(1, NULL, &numPlatforms);
// allocate sufficient space
platformIds = malloc( sizeof(cl_platform_id) * numPlatforms );

// in second call the third parameter can be NULL
errNum = clGetPlatformIDs(numPlatforms, platformIds, NULL);
```

In the following sections we will report on the most commonly used OpenCL functions. The definitive reference material is provided by the Khronos Group at https://www.khronos.org/files/opencl30-reference-guide.pdf (last accessed in December 2021).

7.3 The execution model

OpenCL programs are typically broken down into two components:

- A host program that is controlling execution of the device code and providing I/O facilities.
- One or more device programs that are called **kernels**.

When a kernel is launched by the host, it executes on a device in the form of **work items** (equivalent to CUDA threads). Each work item executes on a PE, and there can be multiple work items mapped to a PE, executing one at a time. Work items are grouped into **work groups** (equivalent to CUDA blocks) and each work group is mapped to a CU.

The launch of a kernel is performed via a **command-queue** and it can be asynchronous, i.e., the host can continue working without having to wait for the completion of a kernel's execution. OpenCL provides functions for checking the state of a kernel's execution. Blocking commands are also possible.

Since OpenCL 2.0, a kernel can place requests in command-queues, enabling a device to request kernel executions from other devices. The kernel that makes the request is called the **parent kernel** and the enqueued kernels are called **child kernels**. This is similar to dynamic parallelism in CUDA, but it is much more powerful, because the child kernel can execute on a completely different device. The execution of a parent kernel does not complete before its child kernels complete as well.

Each enqueued OpenCL command goes in sequence through the following states:

1. Queued: Command is placed on a host-side queue.
2. Submitted: Command has moved to the device.
3. Ready: Command is ready to execute. Commands may have dependencies/precedence, so this state indicates that all conditions for execution are met.
4. Running: One or more work groups associated with the command are running on the device.
5. Ended: All work groups have finished execution.
6. Complete: The command and all its child commands have finished execution.

The states and the transitions between them are also shown in Fig. 7.3.

In the presence of prerequisites, an OpenCL command-queue does not necessarily behave as a FIFO structure, allowing commands to execute *out-of-order*, i.e., out of the order they were enqueued. This allows OpenCL to maximize the utilization of a device.

OpenCL devices do not necessarily run full-fledged operating systems. Some may even restrict the kernels that can run to a number of vendor-predefined ones. In order for the OpenCL runtime to keep track of all the resources utilized (host or device side), it uses a **context**, i.e., a special object for managing all the related resources. Examples of such resources include command-queues, memory regions, kernel objects, and others.

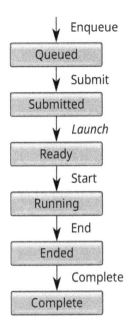

FIGURE 7.3

The states and transitions that a kernel goes through in the OpenCL execution model. All the transitions can be profiled, as explained in Section 7.9, except the "Launch" one.

As expected, after one gets the available devices as described in the previous section, a context should be created. The OpenCL function used for this purpose is shown below:

```
// Creates and returns an OpenCL context object
cl_context clCreateContext (
    const cl_context_properties *prop,   // Null-terminated array of
                                         // desired property names
                                         // and their values(IN)

    cl_uint num_devices,                 // Number of devices (IN)
    const cl_device_id *devices,         // Array of device IDs that
                                         // will be associated with
                                         // the context (IN)

    void (CL_CALLBACK*pfn_notify)        // Pointer to call-back
        (const char *errinfo,            // function, to be called
        const void *private_info,        // upon the detection of an
        size_t cb,                       // error during the creation
        void *user_data),                // of the context. Can be
                                         // set to NULL (IN)

    void *user_data,                     // Data to be passed to the
                                         // call-back function. Can
                                         // be set to NULL.(IN)

    cl_int *errcode);                    // Placeholder for error
```

```
                                                        // code (IN/OUT)
```

The essential property that needs to be specified with the creation of a context is the platform ID, as shown below:

```
1  cl_int errNum;
2  cl_platform_id firstPlatformId;
3  cl_device_id devID[MAXNUMDEV];
4  cl_uint numDev;
5
6  // Getting platform and device IDs
7  . . .
8
9  cl_context_properties prop[] = {
10         CL_CONTEXT_PLATFORM,
11         (cl_context_properties)firstPlatformID,
12         0                                    // termination
13 };
14
15 cl_context cont = clCreateContext (prop,
16                                    numDev,
17                                    devID,
18                                    NULL,    // no call—back function
19                                    NULL,    // no data for callback
20                                    &errNum);
21 if (errNum != CL_SUCCESS)
22 {
23   cerr << "Failed to create a context." << endl;
24   return 3;
25 }
```

In a similar fashion to a new/delete sequence, the termination of an OpenCL program requires the release of the associated context with a call to the clReleaseContext function:

```
// Releases the resources of a context
cl_int clReleaseContext (cl_context context);
```

Once the context is established, a command-queue can be created for entering device commands. Functionally a command-queue is equivalent to a CUDA stream. The following function is used for the creation:

```
// Creates and returns an OpenCL command—queue for the specified ↩
     device
cl_command_queue
   clCreateCommandQueueWithProperties (
         cl_context context,     // Context for created queue (IN)
         cl_device_id device,    // Device to be targeted by
                                 // queue (IN)
         const cl_command_queue_properties *prop, // Null—termina—
                                 // ted array of desired proper—
                                 // ties and their values (IN)
         cl_int *errcode);       // Returned error code (IN/OUT)
```

The properties that can be specified for the creation of a command-queue are just listed in the prop array as symbolic constants followed by the corresponding values. The two properties that can be specified are CL_QUEUE_SIZE, which is the size of the queue in bytes, and CL_QUEUE_PROPERTIES, which is a bitfield of flags enabling specific functionalities, like profiling and out-of-order execution. Properties can be set to NULL, in which case device-specific default values are used. For example:

```
cl_command_queue q;
cl_queue_properties qprop[]={
    CL_QUEUE_PROPERTIES,
    CL_QUEUE_OUT_OF_ORDER_EXEC_MODE_ENABLE,
    0};

q = clCreateCommandQueueWithProperties(
        cont,     // context
        devID[0], // and device ID are required
        qprop,    // this can be NULL if defaults are OK
        &errNum);
if (errNum != CL_SUCCESS)
{
    cerr << "Failed to create a command queue" << endl;
    return 4;
}
```

The CL_QUEUE_OUT_OF_ORDER_EXEC_MODE_ENABLE option allows the queue to reorder the enqueued actions for maximum device utilization. In that case though, the programmer must ensure that action dependencies are satisfied by describing said dependencies in the form of events (see Section 7.9 for more). Leaving the qprop parameter NULL defaults the queue operation to a FIFO mode.

Fig. 7.4 summarizes the relationship of all the entities discussed so far: platforms, contexts, queues, etc. A system may sport multiple platforms, each providing a collection of devices. A host can create multiple contexts, where each context is used to manage the resources associated with a subset of a single platform's devices. Work can be assigned to a device via a command queue. A device can be fed by multiple queues, allowing different parts of the device's hardware to be utilized, e.g., executing a kernel while transferring data. Queues can also be configured to serve work in an out-of-order fashion. Multiple contexts related to a specific platform can also exist, although this is not recommended for a single application. We could have multiple contexts when different applications access the same platform.

7.4 The programming model

Once a command-queue has been set up, kernel execution can be requested and performed on an OpenCL device. A kernel is defined as a normal C function, with the added decoration of the __kernel/kernel keyword. A kernel function cannot return

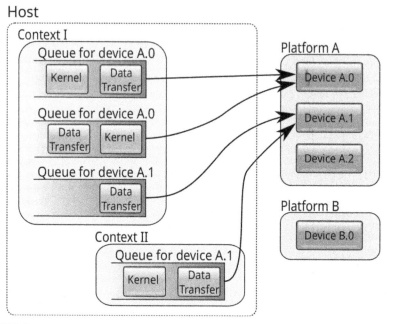

FIGURE 7.4

OpenCL platforms, devices, contexts, queues, and their association. The shown context relates to platform A only. Platform B would need a separate context.

anything directly to the host which invoked it, so it must be declared as returning `void`.

Kernels are typically compiled on-line i.e., after the host program begins execution. For this reason, they have to be declared as strings. As such they can either be statically defined character arrays, or they can reside in separate text files that are loaded prior to their compilation.

Once a kernel function is compiled, the device executable is generated, which in OpenCL jargon is called the **program object** (represented by the `cl_program` data type). The program object, combined with the associated arguments, forms a **kernel object** that can be placed in the appropriate command-queue.

The compilation of the OpenCL source code is a two-step process:

1. Create a program object using the kernel source(s). Multiple kernel sources in separate strings can be provided:

```
// Creates a program object and returns an index/reference to it
cl_program clCreateProgramWithSource(
     cl_context context,    // Valid context   (IN)
     cl_uint count,         // Number of supplied strings in
                            // following argument (IN)
     const char **strings   // Points to array of source code
```

```
                                      // strings. It is a pointer to an
                                      // array of pointers (IN)
        const size_t *lengths,//  Pointer to array of program string
                                      // lengths. Can be NULL if the
                                      // strings are NULL-terminated  (IN)
        cl_int *errcode_ret);  // Place holder for error code
                                      // (IN/OUT)
```

2. Compile the program for one or more target OpenCL devices using:

```
// Compiles (and links) the provided sources for the target
// devices. Returns error code or CL_SUCCESS
cl_int clBuildProgram(
        cl_program program,    // Program object reference (IN)
        cl_uint num_devices,   // Number of targeted devices (IN)
        const cl_device_id *devlist, // Pointer to array of device
                                      // IDs (IN)
        const char *options,   // String of build options for OpenCL
                                      // compiler (IN)
        void (CL_CALLBACK *pfn_notify) // Pointer to call-back
              (cl_program program,     // function to be called
               void *user_data),       // when compilation is
                                        // complete. Can be NULL(IN)
        void *user_data);      // Data to be passed to call-back
                                      // function. Can be NULL (IN)
```

The `options` parameter can be used to control the compiler flags. For example, enabling OpenCL 2.0-specific features requires the option `"-cl-std=CL2.0"`.

A program may contain multiple kernel functions, which mandates the use of a separate object for identifying the function that will actually execute on a device. OpenCL uses a `cl_kernel` structure for this purpose. A kernel object can be created using:

```
// Creates and returns a kernel object from a compiled program.
cl_kernel clCreateKernel(
        cl_program program,          // Reference to compiled program (IN)
        const char *kernel_name,  // String identifying the kernel
                                      // function (IN)
        cl_int *errcode_ret);      // Placeholder for error code
                                      // (IN/OUT)
```

Multiple instances of a kernel can execute at the same time, each on a separate PE, as a work item. Each work item can be identified by two identifiers: a global one that is unique and a local one that differentiates work items within the same work group. These identifiers are 3D vectors, but not all dimensions need to be utilized. This depends on the launch configuration of a kernel.

Upon enqueueing a kernel object in a command-queue, the programmer must specify the 1D, 2D, or 3D index space over which work items will be generated. In OpenCL terms, this index space is called an **N-dimensional range** or **NDRange**, with N being 1, 2, or 3. An NDRange is also used to specify a work group size, which in turn is used to partition the work items into work groups.

The index space is specified as an array of type `size_t` data, with one, two, or three elements, each holding the number of work items in the corresponding dimension. The *dimensions* of the work groups can be equal to or less than the dimensions of the global index space. This does not apply to the *arrays* used to specify the index space and the work group size: these have to be of the same size.[2] Some examples are shown in Fig. 7.5.

Only the work items that map to valid vertices of the index space are generated, which means that contrary to CUDA, work groups need not be uniform in size. The work groups that are at the boundaries of the index space can have fewer work items, depending on whether the dimensions of the work group do or do not evenly divide the corresponding dimensions of the index space.[3]

Another peculiarity of OpenCL relative to CUDA is that the `NDRange` values do not need to start from 0. Each dimension can start from its own specific offset. An array equal in size to the array describing the index space can be used to specify the "global offsets" for each dimension. If this is omitted, the offsets default to zero.

The launch of a kernel is performed by enqueueing it in a device's queue via the function:

```
cl_int clEnqueueNDRangeKernel (
        cl_command_queue queue,         // Queue for placement (IN)
        cl_kernel kernel,               // Kernel to execute (IN)
        cl_uint workDim,                // Size of the following three
                                        // arrays(IN)
        const size_t *globalOffset,     // Points to a 1D array for
                                        // global offsets, i.e.,
                                        // starting values for NDRange
                                        // IDs. Offsets default to zeros
                                        // if this is NULL.(IN)
        const size_t *globalSize,       // Vector for global work item
                                        // size (IN)
        const size_t *localSize,        // Vector for work group size(IN)
        cl_uint numEventsInWaitList,    // Size of following vector (IN)
        const cl_event *eventWaitLst,   // Vector of event objects that
                                        // need to be "triggered" before
                                        // the kernel can execute, i.e.,
                                        // a list of prerequisites. It
                                        // can be NULL (IN)
        cl_event *event);               // Address of event object that
                                        // will be initialized so that it
                                        // could be used to query the
```

---

[2] ◈ **Pitfall**: CUDA programmers are accustomed to having different dimensions for the grid and the block in an execution configuration, as these are distinct entities. This is not allowed in OpenCL, where a work group is a "slice" of the index space and it must have the same declared dimensions, even if some of them are unused by setting them equal to 1.

[3] This is an OpenCL 2.0 feature. In OpenCL 1.x work groups are identical in size.

(a)

NDRange   Work group

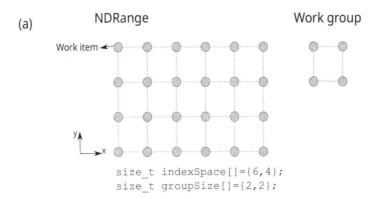

```
size_t indexSpace[]={6,4};
size_t groupSize[]={2,2};
```

(b)

NDRange   Work group

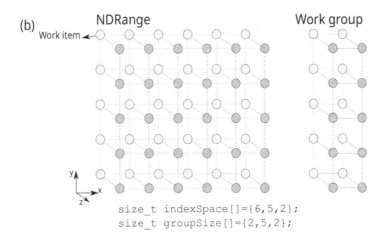

```
size_t indexSpace[]={6,5,2};
size_t groupSize[]={2,5,2};
```

(c)

NDRange   Work group

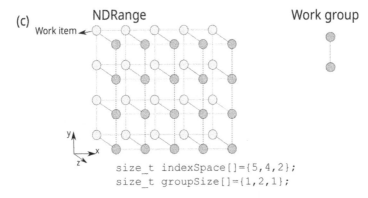

```
size_t indexSpace[]={5,4,2};
size_t groupSize[]={1,2,1};
```

FIGURE 7.5

Three examples of NDRange and the corresponding work group size definitions. In case (a) we have the 24 work items grouped into six groups, while in case (b) we have a total of three work groups. In (c) we have a 3D index space split into 20 2D work groups.

```
                                        // execution status of the
                                        // kernel. (IN/OUT)
```

The clEnqueueNDRangeKernel call is asynchronous, i.e., it returns right after enqueueing the kernel, and does not wait for the device to complete execution. The issue of passing parameters to a kernel is discussed in Section 7.5, in conjunction with how memory is managed by OpenCL.

The last argument of the function provides a way to check when the kernel is complete by using an **event**. An event is a special OpenCL object that encapsulates the state of a command. It can be used to query information about a command or to force the host or another command to wait until an operation is complete. A more detailed discussion on events is presented in Section 7.9.

A number of built-in functions are available for querying the work item identifiers as well as other index space- and work group-related information. Their availability depends on the supported OpenCL specification. The ones introduced in OpenCL 2.0 are separated in the list below. The *global IDs* position a work item in the complete index space, while the *local IDs* position a work item within a work group:

```
uint get_work_dim();                      // Returns the number of
                                          // dimensions in use
size_t get_global_size(uint dim);         // Returns the number of global
                                          // work-items in the given
                                          // dimension
size_t get_global_id(uint dim);           // Returns the global work item
                                          // position in the given
                                          // dimension
size_t get_local_size(uint dim);          // Returns the size of work group
                                          // in the given dimension, if
                                          // work-group size is uniform
size_t get_local_id(uint dim);            // Returns the local work item ID
                                          // in the given dimension
size_t get_num_groups(uint dim);          // Returns the number of work
                                          // groups in the given dimension
size_t get_group_id(uint dim);            // Returns the work group ID in
                                          // the given dimension
size_t get_global_offset(uint dim);       // Returns the global offset for
                                          // the specified dimension
//------------------------------------------------
// Introduced in OpenCL 2.0

size_t get_global_linear_id();            // Returns the work item's global
                                          // ID, mapped to 1D
size_t get_local_linear_id();             // Returns the work item's local
                                          // ID, mapped to 1D
size_t get_enqueued_local_size(uint dim); // Returns the number
                                          // of local work items, even if
                                          // work group size is non-uniform
```

Fig. 7.6 shows an example of what some of the above functions would return when invoked by a work item, given an index range and global offsets.

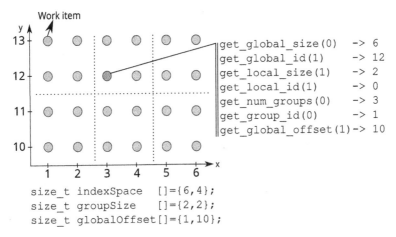

FIGURE 7.6

An example of what the highlighted work item would receive upon using the query functions shown about its position in a 2D index space. The index space, work group size, and global offset settings are also shown.

The information provided by the above functions allows the programmer to control the logic of the kernel functions with minimum effort. There is some redundancy in these functions as a number of them can be computed from others. For example, calculating the global linear ID of a work item can be done with the following code snippet:

```
size_t globaLinearlID = 0;
uint numDim = get_work_dim();
while(numDim >=0)
{
  numDim--;
  globaLinearlID *= get_global_size(numDim);
  globaLinearlID += get_global_id(numDim) - get_global_offset(numDim↩
      );
}
```

The while loop above ensures that we get a proper calculation regardless of the dimensions of the NDRange. The global linear ID is equivalent to retrieving the offset of an element in an array defined as (assuming a 3D index space):

```
T workItems[ get_global_size(2) ] [ get_global_size(1) ] [ ↩
    get_global_size(0) ];
```

The "Hello World" program in Listing 7.2 is a good starting point for illustrating the so far discussed topics, before we move into the specifics of OpenCL memory management.

Listing 7.2: A "Hello World" program in OpenCL.

```
1   // File : hello.cpp
2   . . .
3   string kernSource = "                    \
4   kernel void hello ()     \
5   {                                   \
6      int ID = get_global_id(0);  \
7      int grID = get_group_id(0);   \
8      printf(\"Work item %i from group %i says hello !\\n\", ID, grID);\
9   }";
10
11  //=============================================
12  void cleanUp (cl_context c, cl_command_queue q, cl_program p, ↩
        cl_kernel k)
13  {
14     if (k != 0)
15        clReleaseKernel (k);
16
17     if (p != 0)
18        clReleaseProgram (p);
19
20     if (q != 0)
21        clReleaseCommandQueue (q);
22
23     if (c != 0)
24        clReleaseContext (c);
25  }
26  //=============================================
27  int main ()
28  {
29     cl_int errNum;
30     cl_uint numPlatforms;
31     cl_platform_id firstPlatformId;
32     cl_device_id devID[MAXNUMDEV];
33     cl_uint numDev;
34     cl_context cont = 0;            // initialize to 0 for cleanup check
35     cl_command_queue q = 0;
36     cl_program pr = 0;
37     cl_kernel kernel = 0;
38
39     // Get platform and device IDs
40     . . .
41
42     cl_context_properties prop[] = {
43        CL_CONTEXT_PLATFORM,
44        (cl_context_properties) firstPlatformId,
45        0                           // termination
46     };
47
48     cont = clCreateContext (prop, numDev, devID, NULL,    // no ↩
           callback
49                            NULL, // no data for callback
```

```
50                          &errNum);
51   if (errNum != CL_SUCCESS)
52     {
53       cerr << "Failed to create a context." << endl;
54       cleanUp (cont, q, pr, kernel);
55       return 1;
56     }
57
58   q = clCreateCommandQueueWithProperties (cont, devID[0], NULL, &←
         errNum);
59   if (errNum != CL_SUCCESS)
60     {
61       cerr << "Failed to create a command queue" << endl;
62       cleanUp (cont, q, pr, kernel);
63       return 1;
64     }
65
66   const char *src = kernSource.c_str ();
67   size_t len = kernSource.size ();
68   pr = clCreateProgramWithSource (cont, 1, (const char **) (&src), &←
         len, &errNum);
69   if (errNum != CL_SUCCESS)
70     {
71       cerr << "Failed to create program." << endl;
72       cleanUp (cont, q, pr, kernel);
73       return 1;
74     }
75
76   errNum = clBuildProgram (pr, 1, devID, NULL, NULL, NULL);
77   if (errNum != CL_SUCCESS)
78     {
79       cerr << "Failed to build program" << endl;
80       cleanUp (cont, q, pr, kernel);
81       return 1;
82     }
83
84   kernel = clCreateKernel (pr, "hello", &errNum);
85   if (errNum != CL_SUCCESS || kernel == NULL)
86     {
87       cerr << "Failed to create kernel" << endl;
88       cleanUp (cont, q, pr, kernel);
89       return 1;
90     }
91
92   // work item index space and group size setup
93   size_t idxSpace[] = { 12 };
94   size_t localWorkSize[] = { 3 };
95
96   cl_event completeEv;
97   errNum = clEnqueueNDRangeKernel (q, kernel, 1, NULL, idxSpace, ←
         localWorkSize, 0, NULL, &completeEv);
98
```

```
 99     // wait for enqueued command to finish
100     clWaitForEvents (1, &completeEv);
101
102     cleanUp (cont, q, pr, kernel);
103     return 0;
104   }
```

The key features of Listing 7.2 are:

- The device code is defined as a static global string variable on lines 3–9. This is an impractical approach for anything but very small kernels. As will be shown later, it is standard practice to store OpenCL programs in separate files and load them in strings during program execution. A separate file also allows compilation checks to be performed prior to building and running the whole program.
- The cleanup function, defined on lines 12–25, is called upon the detection of an error (e.g., condition on lines 51–56) or at the end of execution in order to release all the resources allocated by the program. Resource release is a critical component of OpenCL programs, as devices typically lack full-blown operating systems that can reclaim resources. Releasing resources in a planned fashion avoids having to reboot a system to reclaim its full use.
- The OpenCL source code is used to create a program object on line 68, and the source is compiled on line 76.
- A kernel object that identifies the kernel to run on the device is created on line 85. The name of the kernel function is clearly seen as the second parameter of the clCreateKernel call.
- The kernel launch parameters are set up and the kernel enqueued on lines 93–97.
- Finally we wait for the kernel to finish execution by waiting for the one event that is triggered upon its completion on line 100. Normally this is not required as the execution of a kernel is typically followed by a blocking device-to-host memory transfer. In that case, when control is returned to the main program the device queue is empty.

There is however a caveat in the "build on-line" approach employed by OpenCL: if a compilation error happens, how can it be reported and fixed?

OpenCL provides the clGetProgramBuildInfo function, which can be used to get the build error description:

```
cl_int clGetProgramBuildInfo(
        cl_program program,           // Program object reference (IN)
        cl_device_id device,          // Device ID (IN)
        cl_program_build_info param, // Symbolic name of desired
                                      // parameter to retrieve (IN)
        size_t param_value_size,      // Size of buffer "param_value"(IN)
                                      // This is ignored if set to 0.
        void* param_value,            // Address of buffer to hold the
                                      // returned value (IN/OUT)
                                      // Ignored if set to NULL.
        size_t* param_value_size);    // Address of integer to hold the
```

```
                              // actual size of "param" (IN/OUT)
                              // Ignored if set to NULL.
```

The parameter name required for getting the compilation log is `CL_PROGRAM_BUILD_LOG`. The size of the error description string is unknown, so there are two alternatives: (a) allocate a buffer big enough for any error or (b) run a sequence of two calls, one for getting the error string size and one for getting the actual string. The latter approach is shown below:

```
size_t logSize;
// Retrieve message size in "logSize"
clGetProgramBuildInfo(program, deviceID, CL_PROGRAM_BUILD_LOG, 0, ↩
    NULL, &logSize);

// Allocate the necessary buffer space
char *logMsg = (char *)malloc(logSize);

// Retrieve the actual error message
clGetProgramBuildInfo(program, deviceID, CL_PROGRAM_BUILD_LOG, ↩
    logSize, logMsg, NULL);
printf("Error : %s\n", logMsg);
```

In Section 7.4.1 we show how this aspect of the development process can be simplified.

7.4.1 Summarizing the structure of an OpenCL program

At this point we can summarize the skeleton of an OpenCL program sans the error checking logic, as illustrated in Listing 7.3.

Listing 7.3: An OpenCL C skeleton program.

```
1  // File : skeleton.cpp
2  ...
3  #include <CL/cl.h>
4
5  string kernSource = ""; // static OpenCL source, or it can be read ↩
       from a file
6
7  //================================================
8  void cleanUp (cl_context c, cl_command_queue q, cl_program p, ↩
       cl_kernel k)
9  {
10    if (k != 0) clReleaseKernel (k);
11
12    if (p != 0) clReleaseProgram (p);
13
14    if (q != 0) clReleaseCommandQueue (q);
15
16    if (c != 0) clReleaseContext (c);
17
18    // add other device resources that need to be released
```

```
19  }
20  //=============================================
21  int main ()
22  {
23    cl_int errNum;
24    cl_uint numPlatforms;
25    cl_platform_id firstPlatformId;
26    cl_device_id devID[MAXNUMDEV];
27    cl_uint numDev;
28    cl_context cont = 0;              // initialize for cleanup check
29    cl_command_queue q = 0;
30    cl_program pr = 0;
31    cl_kernel kernel = 0;
32
33    // Get a reference to an object representing a platform
34    errNum = clGetPlatformIDs (1, &firstPlatformId, &numPlatforms);
35
36    // Get the device IDs matching the CL_DEVICE_TYPE parameter, up to ↵
          the MAXNUMDEV limit
37    errNum = clGetDeviceIDs (firstPlatformId, CL_DEVICE_TYPE_ALL, ↵
          MAXNUMDEV, devID, &numDev);
38
39    cl_context_properties prop[] = {
40      CL_CONTEXT_PLATFORM,
41      (cl_context_properties) firstPlatformId,
42      0                              // termination
43    };
44
45    // create a context for the devices detected
46    cont = clCreateContext (prop, numDev, devID, NULL, NULL, &errNum);
47
48    // create a command queue
49    q = clCreateCommandQueueWithProperties (cont, devID[0], NULL, &↵
          errNum);
50
51    // create a program object with supplied OpenCL source
52    const char *src = kernSource.c_str ();
53    size_t len = kernSource.size ();
54    pr = clCreateProgramWithSource (cont, 1, (const char **) (&src), &↵
          len, &errNum);
55
56    // compile the program
57    errNum = clBuildProgram (pr, 1, devID, NULL, NULL, NULL);
58
59    // create a kernel object
60    kernel = clCreateKernel (pr, "hello", &errNum);
61
62    // allocate memory on the target device and copy data from the  ↵
          host to it
63
64    // specify the parameters that will be used for the kernel ↵
          execution
```

```
65
66    // set up the work item index space and group size
67    size_t idxSpace[] = { N };
68    size_t localWorkSize[] = { K };
69
70    // enqueue kernel execution request
71    errNum = clEnqueueNDRangeKernel (q, kernel, 1, NULL, idxSpace, ↵
          localWorkSize, 0, NULL, &completeEv);
72
73    // collect the results by copying them from the device to the host↵
          memory
74
75    // release resources
76    cleanUp (cont, q, pr, kernel);
77    return 0;
78  }
```

It must be stressed that after each and every OpenCL call, the returned error code should be checked to allow for early detection of any anomalies. Adding these checks in the above code would result in an even bigger footprint for essentially setup code that does not relate to useful work, distracting the programmer from the more critical parts of the program.

In order to reduce the effort required to write an OpenCL program and also reduce the cognitive effort for readers to work out the examples in the rest of the chapter, we introduce a number of helper functions. The aim is to compress as much as possible the code required for error checking, device setup, and program compilation. The signatures of these functions are shown below, while the full implementation and commentary is given in Appendix F.

Listing 7.4: Helper function signatures for OpenCL program coding. The full implementation is in the `cl_utility.h` file.

```
// Reads device code from a file and returns a pointer to the buffer
// holding it
char * readCLFromFile(
        const char* file);   // File name holding the device source
                             // code (IN)
/*─────────────────────────────────*/
// Returns false if status is CL_SUCCESS
bool isError(
        cl_int status,       // Status returned by an OpenCL
                             // function (IN)
        const char *msg);    // Message to be printed if status is
                             // not CL_SUCCESS (IN)
/*─────────────────────────────────*/
// If status is not CL_SUCCESS, it prints the message, calls the
// clean up function, and exits the program
void handleError(
        cl_int status,       // Status returned by an OpenCL
                             // function (IN)
        const char *msg,     // Message to be printed if status is
```

```
                                   // not CL_SUCCESS (IN)
                 void (*cleanup)());// Pointer to clean up function
/*————————————————————————*/
// Retrieves the compilation errors
char *getCompilationError (
             cl_program & pr,      // Reference to program object that
                                   // failed to compile (IN)
             cl_device_id & id)    // Target device ID (IN)
/*————————————————————————*/
void setupDevice(
             cl_context &cont,     // Reference to context to be
                                   // created (IN/OUT)
             cl_command_queue &q,  // Reference for queue to be created
                                   // (IN/OUT)
             cl_queue_properties *qprop, // Array to queue properties
                                   // (IN/OUT)
             cl_device_id &id);    // Reference to device to be
                                   // utilized. Defaults to the first
                                   // one listed by the ↩
                                       clGetPlatformIDs
                                   // call (IN/OUT)
/*————————————————————————*/
// Returns true if program was compiled successfully
bool setupProgramAndKernel(
         cl_device_id &id,  // Reference to the device to be
                            // targeted (IN)
         cl_context cont,   // Reference to the context to be
                            // utilized (IN)
         const char *programFile, // Pointer to file name holding the
                            // source code (IN)
         cl_program &pr,    // Reference to program object to be
                            // created (IN/OUT)
         const char *kernelName, // Pointer to string identifying the
                            // kernel function (IN)
         cl_kernel &kernel);//Reference to kernel object to be
                            // created (IN/OUT)
```

The only thing that is not addressed by this collection of functions is the cleanup at the end of the execution, as this is a program-specific sequence that is primarily concerned with memory management and resource release.

Equipped with the above list, we can rewrite Listing 7.3 in the following form:

Listing 7.5: An OpenCL C skeleton program using the `cl_utility.h` functions.

```
1  // File : skeleton2.cpp
2  ...
3  #include "cl_utility.h"
4  ...
5  //================================================
6  int main ()
7  {
8    cl_int errNum;
9    cl_context cont = 0;              // initialize for cleanup check
```

```
10    cl_command_queue q = 0;
11    cl_program pr = 0;
12    cl_kernel kernel = 0;
13    cl_device_id devID;
14
15    // retrieve platform and device information. Create content and ↵
          queue
16    setupDevice(cont, q, NULL, devID);
17
18    // read program source, build it and create kernel object for ↵
          identified function
19    if(!setupProgramAndKernel(devID, cont, "deviceSource.cl", pr, "↵
          kernelName", kernel))
20    {
21        if(pr!=0)
22            printf("Error: %s\n", getCompilationError(pr, devID));
23        cleanUp (cont, q, pr, kernel);
24        return 1;
25    }
26
27    // allocate memory on the target device and copy data from the ↵
          host to it
28
29    // specify the parameters that will be used for the kernel ↵
          execution
30
31    // set up the work item index space and group size
32    size_t idxSpace[] = { N };
33    size_t localWorkSize[] = { K };
34
35    // enqueue kernel execution request
36    errNum = clEnqueueNDRangeKernel (q, kernel, 1, NULL, idxSpace, ↵
          localWorkSize, 0, NULL, &completeEv);
37
38    // collect the results by copying them from the device to the host↵
          memory
39
40    // release resources
41    cleanUp (cont, q, pr, kernel);
42    return 0;
43 }
```

The above is arguably significantly easier to navigate and comprehend.

7.5 **The memory model**

OpenCL's memory model is an abstraction of all the possible ways memory can be organized on a device. It closely reflects current GPU memory hierarchies, but it is generic enough to allow individual OpenCL platforms to select how to map model entities to actual hardware components.

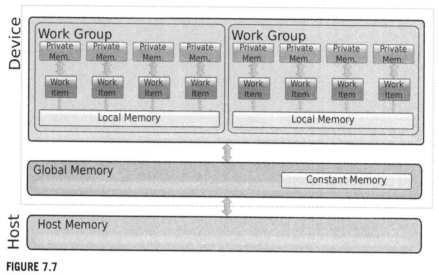

FIGURE 7.7

OpenCL memory regions.

Device memory is divided into the following **memory regions**:

- **Global memory**: memory which is accessible from all work items. It is typically used for holding input data to kernels and output data from the kernel execution. It is the only device memory that can be accessed by the host using appropriate OpenCL calls.
- **Constant memory**: a part of global memory (hence universal access by all work items) that is meant to be read-only. For example, it can be used to hold tables of immutable values. The benefit of distinguishing constant memory as a separate entity from the global memory is that devices may have special support (e.g., dedicated caches) for this type of data. NVidia GPUs do have such dedicated caches.
- **Local memory**: memory which is local to a work group. Local memory is used to share data by the work items of a group, and as such it would be mapped to on-chip memory, making a low-latency, high-bandwidth option. On an NVidia GPU this would be equivalent to SM shared memory, as work groups map to SMs.
- **Private memory**: memory that is exclusive to a work item. It is used to hold the automatic variables of a kernel and it is typically implemented by registers.

Fig. 7.7 summarizes the available memory regions and their relationships with work groups and work items.

Getting a data item to reside at a particular region can have a substantial impact on performance, as each region can have wildly different speed and latency characteristics. Comparing Fig. 7.7 to Fig. 6.9, which shows typical performance figures for NVidia GPU memory regions, reveals, apart from a striking (and obviously expected)

Table 7.2 OpenCL memory regions access and lifetime.

Region	Host access	Kernel access	Definition	Lifetime
Global memory	R/W	R/W	`global` or `__global`	Program
Constant memory	R/W	R	`constant` or `__constant`	Program
Local memory	-	R/W	`local` or `__local`	Work group execution
Private memory	-	R/W exclusive to work item	Local variables and non-pointer kernel arguments	Work item execution

similarity, this part of the program design (i.e., data placement) to be of critical importance.

The placement and scope of device data can be controlled by using appropriate keywords or by how data are defined within a kernel. A summary of the memory regions characteristics is presented in Table 7.2.

OpenCL manages device data in the form of three types of objects, which can reside in global or constant memory:

- **Buffers**: a buffer is the equivalent of a 1D array in C.
- **Images**: designated for storing image data. The exact storage arrangement depends on the device specifics. Image objects are supposed to provide accelerated access to image data by utilizing the specialized hardware provided by a device.
- **Pipes**: placeholders for arbitrary data chunks called **packets**. Pipes behave as FIFO queues and they are designed for supporting producer–consumer software designs.

The memory region qualifiers listed in Table 7.2 are used in combination to the aforementioned objects to control device memory data placement. In the following section we discuss the setup and management of buffer objects. Images and pipes are discussed in Sections 7.5.3 and 7.5.4, respectively.

7.5.1 Buffer objects

OpenCL devices can have distinct memory spaces from the CPUs that host them. In order for input data to become available to them and for computation results to be collected by the host, data need to be transferred between the host and the device.

Transfers can be implicit or explicit. Transfers do not take place if a device shares the host's RAM, as for example is the case for integrated GPUs. However, for the sake of consistency, data movements need to be programmed in a program's logic regardless. The OpenCL runtime can take care of the specifics of the data movements, while the programmer needs to address their timing by sequencing them properly in regard to kernel executions.

Creating a buffer can be done with the following function:

```
cl_mem clCreateBuffer (
      cl_context context,// Context associated with memory obj.(IN)
      cl_mem_flags flags,// Flags used for the type of
                         // allocation(IN)
      size_t size,       // Size of required memory in bytes (IN)
      void *hostPtr,     // Pointer to host memory to be copied
                         // over to the device for initialization.
                         // Its size has to be at least equal to
                         // 'size' if it is utilized. Could be set
                         // to NULL. (IN)
      cl_int *errcode);  // Address for storing the returned error
                         // code (IN/OUT)
```

If the host pointer is not NULL, the device's data can be initialized by an implicit transfer following the allocation of the proper memory space. The `flags` argument is a bitfield that controls the type of allocation to be performed. Several types can be bitwise-ORed together to the desired effect. Some of the symbolic constants that can be used for this argument are:

- `CL_MEM_READ_WRITE`: Kernel will be allowed to read and write to the allocated memory (default).
- `CL_MEM_READ_ONLY`: Kernel will be allowed read-only access. `CL_MEM_WRITE_ONLY` is also available.
- `CL_MEM_HOST_WRITE_ONLY`: Host will be only allowed to write to the device memory, using appropriate OpenCL calls. The alternative is `CL_MEM_HOST_READ_ONLY`.
- `CL_MEM_HOST_NO_ACCESS`: Host will have no access to the allocated memory.
- `CL_MEM_USE_HOST_PTR`: When `hostPtr` is not NULL, the contents of the host memory will be used to initialize the device memory. A copy is conditional based on the system capabilities (see shared virtual memory in Section 7.6).
- `CL_MEM_COPY_HOST_PTR`: When `hostPtr` is not NULL, memory will be allocated in order to hold a copy of the contents of the host memory.

As an example, if we had a 1D array of `float` data that we wanted to process on a device, given the following definitions:

```
float h_data[N]; // data residing in host memory

cl_mem d_data;   // reference to an OpenCL buffer
```

transferring the data to the device memory so that they can become available to a kernel is as simple as:

```
size_t dataSize = N*sizeof(float);   // size of memory to be ↩
    allocated in bytes

// allocation and initialization
d_data = clCreateBuffer (context, CL_MEM_READ_WRITE | ↩
    CL_MEM_USE_HOST_PTR, dataSize, h_data, &errNum);
```

As a matter of convention, and for avoiding errors and keeping programs easily readable, we will be using the `h_` prefix for data residing on the host and the `d_` prefix for data residing on a device.

It should be emphasized that the allocation plus initialization combination works only if the `CL_MEM_USE_HOST_PTR` flag is specified. The alternative is to perform the data transfer past the device memory allocation:

```
size_t dataSize = N*sizeof(float);

// allocation
d_data = clCreateBuffer (context, CL_MEM_READ_WRITE, dataSize, NULL,↩
    &errNum);

// data transfer enqueued
errNum = clEnqueueWriteBuffer(queue, d_data, CL_TRUE, 0, dataSize, ↩
    h_data, 0, NULL, NULL);
```

The `clEnqueueWriteBuffer` function has the following signature:

```
// Returns an error code for the status of the operation
cl_int clEnqueueWriteBuffer(
    cl_command_queue queue, // Queue associated with operation (IN)
    cl_mem buffer,          // Reference to device memory (IN)
    cl_bool blockingWrite,  // Either CL_TRUE or CL_FALSE. If set
                            // to CL_TRUE the fuction will return
                            // when the operation is complete (IN)
    size_t offset,          // Starting position in buffer, to
                            // write to (IN)
    size_t size,            // Number of bytes to transfer (IN)
    const void *ptr,        // Host location to copy from (IN)
    cl_uint numEvents,      // Number of events in the following
                            // array (IN)
    const cl_event *evList, // Pointer to array of events that
                            // need to be complete before the
                            // operation can start (IN)
    cl_event *event);       // Pointer to event object that can be
                            // used to query the status of the
                            // transfer. Can be set to NULL. (IN)
```

The opposite data movement, i.e., from the device to the host, can be accomplished with the `clEnqueueReadBuffer` function which has an identical signature to `clEnqueueWriteBuffer`.

A buffer can be initialized from the host without an explicit memory transfer, by calling the `clEnqueueFillBuffer` function:

```
// Returns an error code for the status of the operation
cl_int clEnqueueFillBuffer(
    cl_command_queue queue, // Queue associated with operation (IN)
    cl_mem buffer,          // Reference to device memory (IN)
    const void *pattern,    // Sequence that will be used to fill
                            // up the buffer (IN)
    size_t patt_size,       // Size of the pattern in bytes (IN)
```

```
size_t offset,          // Start of buffer location that will
                        // be filled. Must be a multiple of
                        // 'patt_size' (IN)
size_t size,            // Buffer bytes that will be filled.
                        // Must be a 'patt_size' multiple (IN)
cl_uint numEvents,      // Number of events in 'evList'
                        // array (IN)
const cl_event *evList, // Pointer to array of events that
                        // need to be complete before the
                        // operation can start (IN)
cl_event *event);       // Pointer to event object that can be
                        // used to query the status of the
                        // transfer. Can be set to NULL. (IN)
```

This is significantly faster than performing a memory copy, and it comes handy when we just need to initialize the allocated buffer to some predetermined state.

As an example, if we wish to initialize a buffer to zeros before the invocation of a kernel, we can do:

```
cl_mem d_data = 0;
d_data = clCreateBuffer (cont, CL_MEM_READ_WRITE, N*sizeof (float), ↵
    NULL, &errNum);
float pattern = 0;
clEnqueueFillBuffer (q, d_data, (void *)&pattern, sizeof(float), 0, ↵
    N*sizeof(float), 0, NULL, NULL);
```

A peculiarity of how OpenCL launches programs on a device is the argument passing procedure. Assuming we have a kernel defined as:

```
kernel void deviceDoSmt(int N, global float *in, global float *out);
```

then each of the parameters must be individually specified before the kernel can be invoked, using the clSetKernelArg function:

```
// Returns an error code for the status of the operation
cl_int clSetKernelArg(
    cl_kernel kernel,       // Reference to kernel object (IN)
    cl_uint argIndex,       // Position of the argument in the
                            // kernel's signature (numbering
                            // starts from 0) (IN)
    size_t argSize,         // Number of bytes used to represent
                            // value (IN)
    const void *argValue);  // Pointer to argument value (IN)
```

If the argument to be passed is a memory object (e.g., a buffer), then argValue should point to the corresponding OpenCL object (e.g., cl_mem) and the argSize should be set to the number of bytes used for the particular type (e.g., sizeof(cl_mem)). The kernel signature should contain a pointer with a global or constant specifier, as these are the only regions that the host can access.

For our above example kernel, the resulting code would be similar to:

```
int numData;
cl_mem d_in;
cl_mem d_out;

errNum = clSetKernelArg(kernel, 0, sizeof(int), &numData);
errNum = clSetKernelArg(kernel, 1, sizeof(cl_mem), &d_in);
errNum = clSetKernelArg(kernel, 2, sizeof(cl_mem), &d_out);
```

An easy example of how the above can be utilized is shown in Listings 7.6 and 7.7 in the form of a vector addition program.

The device part of the code can be supplied as a separate file:

Listing 7.6: OpenCL vector addition kernel.

```
1  // File : vectorAdd.cl
2  kernel void vecAdd(global int *a, global int *b, global int *c)
3  {
4      size_t ID = get_global_id(0);
5      if(ID < get_global_size(0))
6          c[ID] = a[ID] + b[ID];
7  }
```

The kernel is designed for executing one work item per result vector element. The work items are arranged on a 1D range that matches the size of the input vectors. Line 5 ensures that the work item has a valid assignment by comparing the global ID with the size of the vectors/index range. This is a mandatory check in case the vector size is not evenly divided by the work group size.

The host part of the program is shown in Listing 7.7, and it is rather short with the assistance of the functions supplied in cl_utility.h. The first part of the listing is occupied with the cleanUp function, which is responsible for releasing any of the acquired resources. The clRelease* functions are conditionally executed depending on the stage at which cleanUp is called, e.g., at the end of execution or because of a critical error during setup. The conditional logic is supported by the initialization performed on lines 43–47.

Listing 7.7: OpenCL vector addition host code.

```
8   // File : vectorAdd.cpp
9   . . .
10  #include "cl_utility.h"
11
12  const int VECSIZE = 100;
13  const size_t DATASIZE = VECSIZE*sizeof(int);
14
15  //================================================
16  void cleanUp (cl_context c, cl_command_queue q, cl_program p, ↩
17          cl_kernel k, cl_mem d_A, cl_mem d_B, cl_mem d_C)
18  {
19      if(d_A != 0)
        clReleaseMemObject(d_A);
```

```
20
21    if(d_B != 0)
22      clReleaseMemObject(d_B);
23
24    if(d_C != 0)
25      clReleaseMemObject(d_C);
26
27    if (k != 0)
28      clReleaseKernel (k);
29
30    if (p != 0)
31      clReleaseProgram (p);
32
33    if (q != 0)
34      clReleaseCommandQueue (q);
35
36    if (c != 0)
37      clReleaseContext (c);
38 }
39 //================================================
40 int main ()
41 {
42    cl_int errNum;
43    cl_context cont = 0;              // initialize for cleanup check
44    cl_command_queue q = 0;
45    cl_program pr = 0;
46    cl_kernel kernel = 0;
47    cl_mem d_A=0, d_B=0, d_C=0;
48    cl_device_id devID;
49
50    int *h_A, *h_B, *h_C;
51    h_A = new int[VECSIZE];
52    h_B = new int[VECSIZE];
53    h_C = new int[VECSIZE];
54
55    assert(h_A != NULL && h_B != NULL && h_C != NULL);
56    for(int i=0;i<VECSIZE; i++)
57      h_A[i] = h_B[i] = i;
58
59    setupDevice(cont, q, NULL, devID);
60
61    // create device memory objects
62    d_A = clCreateBuffer (cont, CL_MEM_READ_ONLY | CL_MEM_USE_HOST_PTR ↩
         , DATASIZE, h_A, &errNum);
63    d_B = clCreateBuffer (cont, CL_MEM_READ_ONLY | CL_MEM_USE_HOST_PTR ↩
         , DATASIZE, h_B, &errNum);
64    d_C = clCreateBuffer (cont, CL_MEM_WRITE_ONLY, DATASIZE, NULL, &↩
         errNum);
65
66    // read program source and build it
67    if(!setupProgramAndKernel(devID, cont, "vectorAdd.cl", pr, "vecAdd↩
         ", kernel))
```

```
68  {
69      cleanUp (cont, q, pr, kernel, d_A, d_B, d_C);
70      return 1;
71  }
72
73  // set up kernel parameters
74  errNum = clSetKernelArg(kernel, 0, sizeof(cl_mem), &d_A);
75  errNum |= clSetKernelArg(kernel, 1, sizeof(cl_mem), &d_B);
76  errNum |= clSetKernelArg(kernel, 2, sizeof(cl_mem), &d_C);
77  if (isError(errNum, "Failed to set kernel parameters"))
78      {
79      cleanUp (cont, q, pr, kernel, d_A, d_B, d_C);
80      return 1;
81      }
82
83  // work item index space and group size setup
84  size_t idxSpace[] = { VECSIZE };
85  size_t localWorkSize[] = { 64 };
86
87  errNum = clEnqueueNDRangeKernel (q, kernel, 1, NULL, idxSpace, ↵
          localWorkSize, 0, NULL, NULL);
88
89  errNum = clEnqueueReadBuffer(q, d_C, CL_TRUE, 0, DATASIZE, h_C, 0,↵
          NULL, NULL);
90
91  if(!isError(errNum, "Failed to get result vector"))
92  {
93      for(int i=0;i<VECSIZE;i++)
94          cout << h_C[i] << " " ;
95      cout << endl;
96  }
97  cleanUp (cont, q, pr, kernel, d_A, d_B, d_C);
98
99  delete [] h_A;
100 delete [] h_B;
101 delete [] h_C;
102
103 return 0;
104 }
```

Following the allocation and initialization of the host memory vectors on lines 50–57 (and the setup of a target device on line 59), we allocate and at the same time initialize their corresponding device counterparts on lines 62–64.

Once the kernel object is available past lines 67–71, we can set up the kernel arguments (lines 74–76). Since CL_SUCCESS is a symbolic name for 0, we can perform a bitwise OR of the codes returned by the clSetKernelArg calls and check them collectively at line 77.

The 1D index range and group size are set on lines 84 and 85, respectively, before the kernel execution is enqueued on line 87. The resulting vector can be retrieved by enqueueing a device-to-host reading action on line 89. As the call is blocking one (check third parameter), by line 91 we are certain that the queue is empty and barring an error, the results can be reported.

A device buffer can be "mapped" to host memory, i.e., become visible to the host, by using the `clEnqueueMapBuffer` function:

```
// Returns a host memory pointer, through which the device memory ←
    object is accessible
void* clEnqueueMapBuffer(
    cl_command_queue queue,   // Queue associated with operation (IN)
    cl_mem buffer,            // Reference to device memory obj. (IN)
    cl_bool blocking,         // Either CL_TRUE or CL_FALSE. If set
                              // to CL_TRUE the function will return
                              // when the operation is complete (IN)
    cl_map_flags flags,       // Bitfield for how the mapping will be
                              // done (IN)
    size_t offset,            // Starting position in buffer, to map
                              // from (IN)
    size_t size,              // Number of bytes to map (IN)
    cl_uint numEvents,        // Number of events in the 'evList'
                              // array (IN)
    const cl_event *evList,   // Pointer to array of events that need
                              // to be complete before the operation
                              // can start (IN)
    cl_event *event,          // Pointer to the event object that can
                              // be used to query the status of the
                              // map. Can be set to NULL. (IN)
    cl_int* errcode);         // Placeholder for error code (IN/OUT)
```

The mapping may or may not entail the actual copy of the data, based on the architecture of the memory subsystem. For example, APUs with their integrated GPU have a common CPU-GPU address space. As a result, using `clEnqueueMapBuffer` can be faster than using `clEnqueueReadBuffer` to get access to the results of a kernel computation.

The mapping, based on the setting of the `flags` parameter, can be one of:

- `CL_MAP_READ`: The mapped region will be read by the host.
- `CL_MAP_WRITE`: The mapped region will be modified by the host.
- `CL_MAP_WRITE_INVALIDATE_REGION`: The mapped region will be modified by the host and the device memory contents are to be discarded. This setting is incompatible with the two previous ones. The reason this is different from a simple `CL_MAP_WRITE` is that the original buffer contents do not need to be retrieved.

A mapped memory region can be released back to the device by the `clEnqueue-UnmapMemObject` function:

```
// Unmaps a buffer object from the host's memory space
// Returns an error code or CL_SUCCESS
cl_int clEnqueueUnmapMemObject(
    cl_command_queue queue,   // Queue associated with operation (IN)
    cl_mem memobj,            // Reference to device memory obj. (IN)
    void* mapped_ptr,         // Host pointer returned by
```

```
                                  // clEnqueueMapBuffer (IN)
     cl_uint numEvents,           // Number of events in the 'evList'
                                  // array (IN)
     const cl_event *evList,      // Pointer to array of events that need
                                  // to be complete before the operation
                                  // can start (IN)
     cl_event *event);            // Pointer to the event object that can
                                  // be used to query the status of the
                                  // unmap. Can be set to NULL. (IN)
```

A typical sequence involves pairing clEnqueueMapBuffer with clEnqueueUnmap-
MemObject. Fig. 7.8 shows a possible allocation and initialization sequence for a
device memory object using mapping. The actual operations taking place are system-
specific.

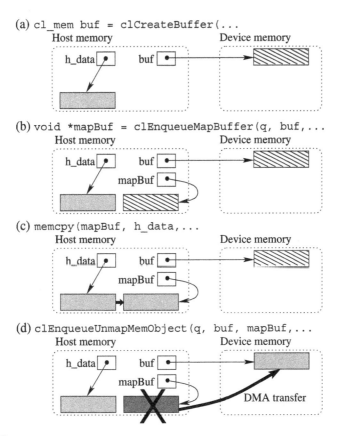

FIGURE 7.8

Mapping a buffer object in the case of a discrete memory device. (a) Creation of an
uninitialized device buffer. (b) Mapping device memory to host memory. (c) Initializing
mapped buffer. (d) Update of device buffer and release of mapped region.

7.5.2 Local memory

Local memory is a fast addressable memory that can be shared between the work items of a work group. It is equivalent to CUDA's shared memory, but because OpenCL targets a much wider gamut of accelerators, it is a feature that is conditionally available. Also the size of the local memory is device-specific. One can get the size of the available local memory by utilizing the clGetDeviceInfo function. For example:

```
cl_ulong size;
clGetDeviceInfo(deviceID, CL_DEVICE_LOCAL_MEM_SIZE, sizeof(cl_ulong)↩
    , &size, 0);
```

Nevertheless, it is a feature that can speed up access to frequently used data and intrawork group communications significantly.

Local memory can be statically or dynamically allocated. *Static allocation* requires the declaration (but not initialization) of kernel-scoped automatic variables, qualified with the __local/local reserved name. The initialization of local memory variables has to be done explicitly by the work items. For example:

```
const int N=...;
kernel void foo(...)
{
  local int counters[N];
  for(int i=get_local_id(0); i<N; i+= get_local_size(0))
    counters[i] = 0;
  work_group_barrier(CLK_LOCAL_MEM_FENCE);
  . . .
```

The barrier call that follows the for loop ensures that initialization is complete in all work items before execution can continue beyond that point. More details on the work_group_barrier function are covered in Section 7.7.

Dynamic allocation requires the use of a kernel pointer parameter, again qualified using __local/local:

```
kernel void foo(local int *c, int N...)
{
  . . .
```

Initialization is pretty much identical with the static allocation case. The only difference is that we have to pass the size of the array as a parameter, or the kernel must be able to determine that from other parameters.

The size of the allocated local memory has to be specified by the host, by setting the size of the corresponding kernel parameter:

```
csSetKernelArg(kernel, 0, N*sizeof(int), NULL);
csSetKernelArg(kernel, 1, sizeof(int), &N);
```

Note that the argument value parameter (the fourth one) in the first of the above calls is set to NULL, as is mandated for local memory objects.

An example on the use of local memory is provided in Section 7.5.4.

7.5.3 **Image objects**

OpenCL provides special facilities for working with images, simplifying pixel subsampling and image boundary access. OpenCL images are opaque objects in the sense that one can access the data only via the built-in functions. The upside to this encapsulation is that OpenCL can utilize the hardware facilities provided by devices to speed up access to image data.

Since version 2.0, OpenCL supports 1D, 2D, and 3D "images," which are represented by the following symbolic constants:

* CL_MEM_OBJECT_IMAGE1D: one-dimensional data,
* CL_MEM_OBJECT_IMAGE1D_ARRAY: a linear sequence of 1D "images,"
* CL_MEM_OBJECT_IMAGE1D_BUFFER: one-dimensional data, but without the capability of using a sampler,
* CL_MEM_OBJECT_IMAGE2D: data stored as a linear sequence of adjacent scan lines,
* CL_MEM_OBJECT_IMAGE2D_ARRAY: a sequence of 2D images,
* CL_MEM_OBJECT_IMAGE3D: a sequence of 2D images.

In order to allocate and possibly initialize an image object, the following function can be utilized:

```
// Returns a reference to a memory object containing an image
cl_mem clCreateImage(
        cl_context context,   // Reference to a valid context (IN)
        cl_mem_flags flags,   // Bitfield specifying the access mode
                              // (read/write) (IN)
        const cl_image_format *image_format, // Pointer to a
                              // structure describing the image format
                              // (see below) (IN)
        const cl_image_desc *image_desc, // Pointer to structure
                              // describing the image dimensions (IN)
        void *host_ptr,       // Pointer to host data that can be used
                              // to initialize the image (IN)
        cl_int *errcode_ret); // Address for the returned error code
                              // (IN/OUT)
```

In terms of representation, an image object is still referenced by a cl_mem instance on the *host side*.

The first two parameters are identical to the ones used in clCreateBuffer.

The data provided by the host for the initialization of the image object should be a linear sequence of scan lines in the case of a 2D image and a linear sequence of 2D images in the case of a 2D array or 3D image types.

How each pixel of a scan line is structured depends on the cl_image_format parameter, which is a structure defined as having two fields:

```
typedef struct cl_image_format {
    cl_channel_order image_channel_order;     // Specifies which color
                                              // components are avail-
                                              // able for each pixel
    cl_channel_type image_channel_data_type;// Specifies the size of
```

```
                                                   // each color channel
} cl_image_format;
```

Symbolic constants that could be used for the channel order include CL_RGB, CL_RGBA, CL_ARGB, CL_LUMINANCE – for grayscale images – and others (cl_channel_order is actually an enumerated type). The first example mentioned describes pixels made up of three channels. CL_RGBA and CL_ARGB convey the presence of four color components (three plus alpha). Table 7.3 lists a sample of these constants and what they convey about the pixel formats.

The channel data type is also an enumerated type that specifies the resolution or possible range of values for each of the channels. Samples of the possible values that can be used for this field are listed in Table 7.4. The CL_UNORM_SHORT_555 type is one of several alternatives that exhibit composite pixel representations, where each channel occupies a set of bits (5 in this case) in an unsigned 16- or 32-bit integer.

The final component making up the description of an image is the cl_image_desc structure, which establishes the dimensions and memory allocated per scan line

Table 7.3 A sample of image channel order symbolic constants. A value of 0 or 1 means that the corresponding component is not present and it is assumed to be 0 or 1, respectively. A value of 1 for the alpha channel corresponds to 100% opacity. In CL_LUMINANCE the luminance value is replicated in the red, green, and blue components.

Symbolic name	Format (R,G,B,A)
CL_R	(X,0,0,1)
CL_A	(0,0,0,X)
CL_LUMINANCE	(X,X,X,1)
CL_RG	(X,Y,0,1)
CL_RGBA	(X,Y,Z,W)

Table 7.4 A sample of image channel types.

Symbolic name	Description
CL_SNORM_INT8	Normalized signed 8-bit integer
CL_UNORM_INT8	Normalized unsigned 8-bit integer
CL_UNORM_SHORT_555	Normalized x-5-5-5 4-channel xRGB
CL_SIGNED_INT8	Signed 8-bit integer
CL_SIGNED_INT16	Signed 16-bit integer
CL_UNSIGNED_INT8	Unsigned 8-bit integer
CL_UNSIGNED_INT16	Unsigned 16-bit integer
CL_UNSIGNED_INT32	Unsigned 32-bit integer
CL_HALF_FLOAT	16-bit float
CL_FLOAT	Single-precision float

and/or image in the case of a 2D array or 3D image. The field names make them pretty much self-explanatory:

```
struct cl_image_desc {
    cl_mem_object_type image_type,// 1D, 2D etc.
    size_t image_width;           // Width in pixels
    size_t image_height;          // Height in pixels
    size_t image_depth;           // Depth in pixels. Only used for
                                  // 3D images
    size_t image_array_size;      // Number of images in an image
                                  // array.
                                  // Used only for 1D or 2D array
                                  // types
    size_t image_row_pitch;       // Size of a scan line in bytes
                                  // Must be 0 is host_ptr is not
                                  // NULL. If it is 0, it is calcu-
                                  // lated as
                                  // image_width * sizeof(pixel)
    size_t image_slice_pitch;     // Size of an image in bytes.
                                  // Applies only to 1D, 2D arrays
                                  // or 3D
                                  // If set to 0, it is calculated as
                                  // image_row_pitch * image_height
    cl_uint num_mip_levels;       // Should be set to 0
    cl_uint num_samples;          // Should be set to 0
    cl_mem mem_object;            // Either NULL or a reference to
                                  // a valid buffer or image object
                                  // Allows the creation of multiple
                                  // image objects that share the
                                  // same data
};
```

Getting images in and out of a device requires data transfer similar to the setup used for buffer objects. For example, copying an image object to device memory is the purpose of function:

```
// Transfers image data from the host to a device image object
// Returns an error code or CL_SUCCESS
cl_int clEnqueueWriteImage (
        cl_command_queue queue,  // Queue associated with operation (IN)
        cl_mem image,            // Reference to device memory obj. (IN)
        cl_bool blocking_write,  // Either CL_TRUE or CL_FALSE. If set
                                 // to CL_TRUE the fuction will return
                                 // when the operation is complete (IN)
        const size_t *origin,    // Points to an array of three offsets
                                 // (x,y,z) that define the starting
                                 // position of the copy. If y and/or z
                                 // are not needed because of the image
                                 // type, they should be set to 0 (IN).
        const size_t *region,    // Points to a three-element array,
                                 // that define the width, height and
                                 // depth of the data to copy. If height
                                 // and/or depth are not needed because
```

```
                              // of the image type, they should be
                              // set to 1 (IN).
    size_t row_pitch,         // Length of each row in bytes. Can be
                              // set to 0, which results in its
                              // calculation (IN).
    size_t slice_pitch,       // Size in bytes of 2D slice in a 3D
                              // image, or 2D image array. Can be
                              // set to 0 for auto calc. (IN).
    const void * ptr,         // Host address to copy from (IN).
    cl_uint num_events,       // Number of events in following array
                              // (IN)
    const cl_event *evlist,   // Pointer to array of events that
                              // need to be complete before the
                              // operation can start (IN)
    cl_event *event);         // Pointer to event object that can be
                              // used to query the status of the
                              // transfer. Can be set to NULL. (IN)
```

On the *device side*, an image object is represented by one of `image1d_t`, `image2d_t`, or `image3d_t`, depending on the type of image used.

Transferring an image from a device to the host requires the use of the `clEnqueueReadImage` function, which has an identical signature with `clEnqueueWriteImage`. Of course in the case of `clEnqueueReadImage` image is the source and `ptr` is the destination.

Finally, once an image is moved to a device, accessing the individual pixels requires the use of a *sampler object*. A sampler is responsible for handling access beyond the boundaries, fractional or normalized pixel coordinates (i.e., in the range [0, 1]), as well as performing interpolation when required. A sampler can be created with:

```
// Returns a sampler object created to specifications
cl_sampler clCreateSamplerWithProperties (
    cl_context context,             // Context to associate with
                                    // object (IN)
    const cl_sampler_properties *prop,// Null-terminated array of
                                    // desired properties and
                                    // their values (IN)
    cl_int *errcode_ret);           // If not NULL, will be used
                                    // as a placeholder for the
                                    // error code if any (IN/OUT)
```

The properties list is something we have seen before, e.g., in the creation of a context and a command queue. It is an array containing symbolic names of properties, followed by their assigned value. In the case of a sampler, the available properties are shown in Table 7.5.

A sampler can be also created as a constant in the kernel source, outside the actual kernels, so we do not have to pass it as a kernel parameter with all the additional statement overhead. For example:

Table 7.5 Properties for the creation of a sampler object.

Symbolic name	Alternative values
CL_SAMPLER_NORMALIZED_COORDS	CL_TRUE (default)
	CL_FALSE
CL_SAMPLER_ADDRESSING_MODE	CL_ADDRESS_MIRRORED_REPEAT
	CL_ADDRESS_REPEAT
	CL_ADDRESS_CLAMP_TO_EDGE
	CL_ADDRESS_CLAMP (default)
	CL_ADDRESS_NONE
CL_SAMPLER_FILTER_MODE	CL_FILTER_NEAREST (default)
	CL_FILTER_LINEAR

```
const sampler_t s = CLK_NORMALIZED_COORDS_FALSE | ↵
    CLK_ADDRESS_CLAMP_TO_EDGE | CLK_FILTER_LINEAR;
```

Please note the different symbolic constants that have to be used in this case.

OpenCL provides a collection of `read_image*` and `write_image*` functions for handling *device-side* image I/O. The former require the use of a sampler, while the latter work only with integer pixel coordinates.

For example, the following function returns an array of four signed 32-bit integers corresponding to the four color/channel components of a pixel:

```
int4 read_imagei(
    read_only image2d_t image, // Image object reference (IN)
    sampler_t sampler,         // Sampler reference (IN)
    int2 coord);               // Pixel coordinates (x,y) (IN)
```

The `int4` type corresponds to a four-element array of integers, `int2` to a two-element array, etc.

The `coord` parameter has to be a type matching the kind of image read or written. So for 1D images it should be a scalar (`int` or `float`), for 2D images it has to be an `int2` or `float2`, and for 3D images it has to be an `int4` or `float4`, with the last element of the vector ignored.

The `int4`, `float2`, etc., data types can be used inside kernel code. In the host code the equivalent OpenCL-supplied types are `cl_int4`, `cl_float2`, etc., as defined in the `cl_platform.h` header file. The OpenCL-defined vector data types can be any of `cl_char<n>`, `cl_short<n>`, `cl_int<n>`, `cl_long<n>`, `cl_float<n>`, and `cl_double<n>` (as well as the unsigned variants of the integer types), where n can be 2, 3, 4, 8, or 16.

The individual components of a vector type can be accessed by treating them as fields in a structure. The field names can be `.xyzw` (for up to four components), `.rgba` (for up to four components in OpenCL 3.0), or `.s[x]`, with x being an integer from 0 up to n-1. For example:

```
// in device code:
float2 coord;
coord.s[0]=1;
coord.s[1]=1;
float2 coord2 = {0.1, 0.2};

// in host code:
cl_int4 color;
color.r = 255;
color.g = 0;
color.b = 0;
```

The following function returns four float numbers in the range [0, 1] for images created with a channel type of CL_UNORM_INT8 or CL_UNORM_INT16. If the channel type is signed (i.e., CL_SNORM_INT8 or CL_SNORM_INT16) the color components are in the range [−1, 1].

```
float4 read_imagef(
    read_only image3d_t image, // Image object of type 3D (IN)
    sampler_t sampler,         // Sampler reference (IN)
    float4 coord);             // Array of pixel coordinates (x,y,z).
                               // The fourth coordinate is ignored
                               // (IN)
```

A kernel that is trying to read pixels from an image object to which it is passed a reference should have the image declared as read_only/__read_only. Mirroring this, an image object that is used for output duties should be declared in the kernel parameter list as write_only/__write_only. These conventions are mandatory as they generate compilation errors if they are not satisfied.

Since OpenCL 2.0, a read_write /__read_write qualifier is available, which means that an image can be processed in place, without the need to allocate a duplicate-sized memory object.

In order to set the pixel value in a 2D image, one can use:

```
// Suitable for images with normalized signed or unsigned pixel
// values, like, e.g., CL_SNORM_INT8. Floating point colors in
// the range [0,1] or [-1,1] will be converted accordingly
void write_imagef(
    write_only image2d_t image, // Image object of type 3D (IN)
    int2 coord,                 // Pixel coordinates (x,y) (IN)
                                // x must be in the range
                                // [0, width -1]. y must be in
                                // the range [0, height -1]
    float4 color)               // Color components (IN)
//-------------------------------------------------
// Suitable for images with unnormalized signed pixel values
// like, e.g., CL_SIGNED_INT8
void write_imagei(
    write_only image2d_t image,
    int2 coord,
```

```
     int4 color)                    // <== Signed color components
//————————————————————————————————————————————————————
// Suitable for images with unnormalized unsigned pixel values
// such as CL_UNSIGNED_INT8
void write_imageui (
     write_only image2d_t image,
     int2 coord,
     uint4 color)                   // <== Unsigned color components
```

It should be clear that the suffix in the `write_image*` function name specifies what kind of color values are expected and that all coordinates must be integer values within the image boundaries.

The list of `read_image*` and `write_image*` functions is quite long and they have preconditions based on the type of image they operate on and the type of pixel values supplied (floating point or integer). Mentioning all the variations is beyond the scope of this book. The interested reader should look up the OpenCL API reference.

In order to put all the above to use, we will examine the application of image convolution, which we first explored in terms of design in Section 2.2. Image convolution is considered to be a low-level image processing operation that manipulates the input image pixels by "multiplying" each pixel and its immediate neighborhood with a fixed-size, square matrix called a kernel (nothing to do with an OpenCL kernel). Based on the selection of kernel cell values, a wide variety of filtering operations can be performed, including blurring, edge detection, sharpening, etc.

If we feed the input and output image objects to an OpenCL kernel, alongside the convolution filter/kernel values, we can have the following implementation:

Listing 7.8: OpenCL kernel for image convolution. Each work item corresponds to one input image pixel.

```
1   // File : imageConv.cl
2   kernel void imageConv (
3            read_only image2d_t in,   // Input imae object
4            int w,                     // Input width in pixels
5            int h,                     // Input height in pixels
6            constant float *filter,    // Conv. kernel cell values
7            int fdim,                  // Conv. matrix side
8            write_only image2d_t out,  // Output image object
9            sampler_t s)               // Sampler for retrieving the ↩
                  input pixels
10  {
11     int xID = get_global_id (0);
12     int yID = get_global_id (1);
13     // check if work item is corresponding to an actual pixel
14     if (xID < w && yID < h)
15        {
16           int filtCenter = fdim / 2;
17           int filtIdx = 0;
18           float newPixel = 0;
19           int2 coord = { xID, yID };
20           for (int yOff = -filtCenter; yOff <= filtCenter; yOff++)
```

```
21      {
22          coord.y = yID + yOff;
23          coord.x = xID — filtCenter;
24          for (int xOff = —filtCenter; xOff <= filtCenter; xOff++)
25          {
26              int4 oldP = (int4) read_imagei (in, s, coord);
27              newPixel += oldP.x * filter[filtIdx];
28              filtIdx++;          // works only if the inner loop is ↩
                    for x—axis iteration
29              coord.x++;
30          }
31      }
32
33      coord.x = xID;
34      coord.y = yID;
35      int4 newP = { (int) newPixel, 0, 0, 0 };
36      write_imagei (out, coord, newP);
37  }
38  }
```

The `coord` structure is used above to access pixels in the input and output images. Each work item is dedicated to one image pixel, whose coordinates are identified by lines 11 and 12. The two nested *for* loops starting at line 20 iterate over the pixels centered around (`xID`, `yID`), multiplying each pixel with the corresponding filter weight and accumulating the results (line 27).

Line 26 retrieves four color components (individually accessed as mandated by the `read_image*` functions), although our image is using only the R channel (see `oldP.x` on line 27). Similarly, the final new pixel color is saved on line 36, again using four color components, of which just the x field is set.

A noteworthy feature of the `imageConv` kernel is that the `filter` parameter is declared as `constant`, which allows OpenCL to utilize constant specific caches if available on the target device.

A simple blurring operation can be performed by using this 3×3 kernel:

$$K = \frac{1}{16} \cdot \begin{vmatrix} 1 & 2 & 1 \\ 2 & 4 & 2 \\ 1 & 2 & 1 \end{vmatrix}. \tag{7.1}$$

Such a matrix is defined on lines 80–83 of the following host code that "drives" the OpenCL kernel:

Listing 7.9: Host code for invoking the kernel of Listing 7.8.

```
39  // File : image_conv.cpp
40  #include "cl_utility.h"
41  #include <CL/cl2.hpp>
42  #include "common/pgm.cpp"
43  . . .
44
45  static cl_context cont = 0;          // initialize for cleanup check
```

```
46   static cl_command_queue q = 0;
47   static cl_program pr = 0;
48   static cl_kernel kernel = 0;
49   static cl_mem d_inImg = 0, d_outImg = 0, d_filter = 0;
50
51   //================================================
52   void cleanUp()
53   {
54     if (d_inImg != 0)
55       clReleaseMemObject (d_inImg);
56     . . .
57   }
58
59   //================================================
60   int main (int argc, char **argv)
61   {
62     cl_int errNum;
63     cl_device_id devID;
64     cl_event filtTrans, imgTrans, kernComplete;
65
66     setupDevice (cont, q, NULL, devID);
67
68     //------------------------------------------------
69     // read program source and build it
70     if (!setupProgramAndKernel (devID, cont, "imageConv.cl", pr, "↩
           imageConv", kernel))
71       {
72         cleanUp();
73         return 1;
74       }
75
76     //------------------------------------------------
77     // host-side memory allocation & I/O
78     PGMImage inImg (argv[1]);
79
80     float filter[] = { 1.0 / 16, 2.0 / 16, 1.0 / 16,
81       2.0 / 16, 4.0 / 16, 2.0 / 16,
82       1.0 / 16, 2.0 / 16, 1.0 / 16
83     };
84     int filterSize = 3;
85
86     //------------------------------------------------
87     // allocate memory on the target device and copy data from the ↩
           host to it
88
89     // image specification
90     cl_image_desc imgDescr;
91     imgDescr.image_type = CL_MEM_OBJECT_IMAGE2D;
92     imgDescr.image_width = inImg.x_dim;
93     imgDescr.image_height = inImg.y_dim;
94     imgDescr.image_row_pitch = 0;
95     imgDescr.num_mip_levels = 0;
```

```
96     imgDescr.num_samples = 0;
97     imgDescr.mem_object = NULL;
98
99     cl_image_format imgFmr;
100    imgFmr.image_channel_order = CL_R;
101    imgFmr.image_channel_data_type = CL_UNSIGNED_INT8;
102
103    // Input image
104    d_inImg = clCreateImage (cont, CL_MEM_READ_ONLY | ↩
           CL_MEM_COPY_HOST_PTR, &imgFmr, &imgDescr, inImg.pixels, &↩
           errNum);
105    if (isError (errNum, "Failed to create device input image"))
106      {
107        cleanUp();
108        return 1;
109      }
110
111    // Output image
112    d_outImg = clCreateImage (cont, CL_MEM_WRITE_ONLY, &imgFmr, &↩
           imgDescr, NULL, &errNum);
113    if (isError (errNum, "Failed to create device output image"))
114      {
115        cleanUp();
116        return 1;
117      }
118
119    // Device filter
120    d_filter = clCreateBuffer (cont, CL_MEM_READ_ONLY | ↩
           CL_MEM_COPY_HOST_PTR, 9 * sizeof (float), &(filter[0]), &↩
           errNum);
121    if (isError (errNum, "Failed to create device filter buffer"))
122      {
123        cleanUp();
124        return 1;
125      }
126
127    // Image sampler
128    cl_sampler_properties prop[] = { CL_SAMPLER_NORMALIZED_COORDS, ↩
           CL_FALSE, 0 };
129    cl_sampler sampler = clCreateSamplerWithProperties (cont, prop, &↩
           errNum);
130    if (isError (errNum, "Failed to create sampler"))
131      {
132        cleanUp();
133        return 1;
134      }
135
136    //--------------------------------------------------
137    // specify the parameters that will be used for the kernel ↩
           execution
138    // set up the work item index space and group size
```

```
139    size_t idxSpace[] = { (size_t) inImg.x_dim, (size_t) inImg.y_dim ←
           };
140    size_t localWorkSize[] = { 16, 16 };
141
142    // enqueue kernel execution request
143    errNum = clSetKernelArg (kernel, 0, sizeof (cl_mem), (void *) &←
           d_inImg);
144    errNum |= clSetKernelArg (kernel, 1, sizeof (int), (void *) &(←
           inImg.x_dim));
145    errNum |= clSetKernelArg (kernel, 2, sizeof (int), (void *) &(←
           inImg.y_dim));
146    errNum |= clSetKernelArg (kernel, 3, sizeof (cl_mem), (void *) &←
           d_filter);
147    errNum |= clSetKernelArg (kernel, 4, sizeof (int), (void *) &←
           filterSize);
148    errNum |= clSetKernelArg (kernel, 5, sizeof (cl_mem), (void *) &←
           d_outImg);
149    errNum |= clSetKernelArg (kernel, 6, sizeof (cl_sampler), (void *)←
            &sampler);
150    if (isError (errNum, "Failed to set kernel parameters"))
151      {
152        cleanUp();
153        return 1;
154      }
155
156    errNum = clEnqueueNDRangeKernel (q, kernel, 2, NULL, idxSpace, ←
           localWorkSize, 0, NULL, &kernComplete);
157    if (isError (errNum, "Failed to launch kernel"))
158      {
159        cleanUp();
160        return 1;
161      }
162
163    //----------------------------------------------------------------
164    // collect the results by copying them from the device to the host←
           memory
165    size_t origin[] = { 0, 0, 0 },
166    size_t region[] = { (size_t) inImg.x_dim, (size_t) inImg.y_dim, 1 ←
           };
167    cl_event waitList[] = { kernComplete };
168    clEnqueueReadImage (q, d_outImg, CL_TRUE, origin, region, 0, 0, ←
           inImg.pixels, 1, waitList, NULL);
169
170    inImg.write (argv[2]);
171
172    // release resources
173    cleanUp();
174
175    return 0;
176  }
```

A critical part of the above listing is the error handling logic, which is essentially repeated after each and every OpenCL function call the host makes, in order to detect errors as soon as they occur. The same pattern is repeated on lines 105–109, lines 113–117, etc., which is basically a check for the returned error code. If the error code fails to match CL_SUCCESS, the supplied message is printed, followed by the release of all the device resources allocated (by calling the cleanUp function) and the termination of the program.

In order to simplify the cleanUp function and the code needed to call it, all device resources are declared as static global variables (lines 45–49). Being static means that they do not pollute the namespace of other modules, staying only visible to the code of the same file.

The core logic of Listing 7.9 consists of the following steps:

(1) The OpenCL context and queue are initialized on line 66. The program and kernel objects are set up on line 70. The setupDevice and setupProgramAndKernel helper functions are documented in Appendix F.

(2) The input PGM-formatted image is read on line 78.

(3) The image object specifications, e.g., dimensions, channel order, resolution, etc., are set on lines 90–101 prior to creating the actual image objects. Extra caution is required so that the values specified match the input image residing in host memory.

(4) The memory objects required on the device, namely the input and output images, and the convolution kernel data are allocated on lines 90–125. By setting the flags of the clCreateImage call on line 104 to include the CL_MEM_COPY_HOST_PTR option, we can allocate and copy the image data to the device in one step. This eliminates the need for a separate clEnqueueWriteImage call.

(5) The sampler that is used to read the input image pixels is initialized on lines 128–134. Only the properties that deviate from the default settings need to be specified (line 128).

(6) The index space and work group sizes are set on lines 139 and 140. Then the kernel parameters are set prior to enqueueing the kernel invocation on line 156.

(7) As the kernel is asynchronously executed, we wait for the event of its completion (kernComplete), prior to transferring the output image from the device to the host (line 168). Waiting for the event is actually redundant, because the setupDevice call on line 66 creates a command queue that executes submitted requests in order (the default setting).

Image objects can also be mapped to host memory with the clEnqueueMapImage function. The unmapping is done with the clEnqueueUnmapMemObject function mentioned in the previous section.

7.5.4 **Pipe objects**

Pipe memory objects were added to the OpenCL 2.0 standard, designed to facilitate the implementation of the producer–consumer pattern. A pipe is essentially a FIFO queue holding user-defined items called *packets*. A packet can be any primitive data type, any type provided by OpenCL (e.g., int4), or any user-defined type.

Pipes are meant to be used as a communication medium between kernels running concurrently, and as such they reside by default in global memory. The host can create a pipe by calling:

```
cl_mem clCreatePipe(
    cl_context context,    // Valid context associated with pipe (IN)
    cl_mem_flags flags,    // Flags used for the pipe creation (IN)
    cl_uint packet_size,   // Size in bytes of pipe packet (IN)
    cl_uint max_packets,   // Maximum number of resident packets (IN)
    const cl_pipe_properties *prop,// Must be NULL in OpenCL 2.2(IN)
    cl_int *errcode_ret)   // Placeholder for returned error code
                           // (IN/OUT)
```

The flags parameter is a bitfield where the following bits can be set: CL_MEM_READ_WRITE and CL_MEM_HOST_NO_ACCESS. If flags is set to 0, it defaults to CL_MEM_READ_WRITE | CL_MEM_HOST_NO_ACCESS.

As a cl_mem type is used for referencing pipe objects, their release is similarly accomplished to buffers and images, via a call to clReleaseMemObject.

Once the host creates a pipe, it can be passed to a kernel as a pipe-type parameter. Each kernel can have either read or write access to a pipe, by qualifying the corresponding parameter as __read_only/read_only or __write_only/write_only. The read_write qualifier, which is allowed for image objects, is prohibited in this context. This does not prevent a kernel from having read access to one pipe and write access to another one.

The final component in the declaration of a pipe parameter is the type of the packet. For example:

```
void fooMonteCarlo( read_only pipe int2 coordPipe,
                    write_only pipe bool inCircle)
{...
```

Pipes, as images, are opaque objects. The only way their contents can be accessed is via the OpenCL-provided functions:

```
// Reads a packet of type "gentype" from "p". Returns 0 on success,
// or a negative number on failure (e.g., the pipe is empty)
int read_pipe(
    read_only pipe gentype p, // Pipe to read from (IN)
    gentype *ptr);            // Address for placing the dequeued
                              // packet (IN/OUT)
//--------------------------------------------------
// Enqueues a packet of type "gentype" to "p". Returns 0 on success,
// or a negative number on failure (e.g., the pipe is full)
int write_pipe(
```

```
    write_only pipe gentype p,   // Pipe to write to (IN)
    const gentype *ptr);         // Address of packet to enqueue (IN)
```

A work item can ensure that the pipe has enough packets to read or enough space to write by reserving space ahead of time. The reservation is performed via the functions:

```
// Reserves packets for reading. Returns reservation identifier
reserve_id_t reserve_read_pipe(
    read_only pipegentype p,    // Pipe to read from (IN)
    uint num_packets);          // Packets that are reserved for
                                // reading (IN)
//------------------------------------------------
// Reserves packet space for writing. Returns reservation identifier
reserve_id_t reserve_write_pipe(
    write_only pipe gentype p,  // Pipe to write to (IN)
    uint num_packets);          // Reserved packet space (IN)
```

The above functions return a reservation identifier that can be used to read/write from/to the reserved packets. Once the reservation is done, the reserved packets/space can be consumed by using these modified versions of the read_pipe and write_pipe functions:

```
// Reads one of the "num_packets" reserved packets, as identified by
// "index". Returns 0 on success.
int read_pipe(
    read_only pipe gentype p,   // Pipe to read from (IN)
    reserve_id_t reserve_id,    // Reservation ID (IN)
    uint index,                 // Number of reserved packet to read
                                // (IN). It should be in the range
                                // [0,num_packets)
    gentype *ptr);              // Address for storing read packet
                                // (IN/OUT)
//------------------------------------------------
// Enqueues a packet of type "gentype" to "p" at reserved position
// "index". Returns 0 on success.
int write_pipe(
    write_only pipe gentype p,  // Pipe to write to (IN)
    reserve_id_t reserve_id,    // Reservation ID (IN)
    uint index,                 // Number of reserved packet space
                                // to use (IN). It should be in the
                                // range [0,num_packets)
    const gentype *ptr);        // Address of packet to enqueue (IN)
```

Finally, the reservation should be canceled when the corresponding reads/ writes are complete (so that the corresponding pipe space can be reused) by calling:

```
void commit_read_pipe(
    read_only pipe gentype p,   // Pipe that was read from (IN)
    reserve_id_t reserve_id);   // Reservation ID (IN)
//------------------------------------------------
void commit_write_pipe(
```

```
       write_only pipe gentype p,  // Pipe that was written to (IN)
       reserve_id_t reserve_id);  // Reservation ID (IN)
```

A simple example that illustrates the pipe operation principles is the following application for calculating the mode of a set of integers. In terms of design, this is obviously not the best or most efficient way to perform this statistical calculation.

In order to find the mode of a set, we can accumulate the occurrences of all the individual numbers and then proceed to find the most frequent one. These two kernels perform this computation in two stages: one for accumulating the occurrences over subsets of the input set (freqCount) and one for consolidating the partial results and reducing the mode (modeFind):

Listing 7.10: Kernels for finding the mode of a set of integer. The kernels communicate using a pipe.

```
1  // File : pipe_mode.cl
2  kernel void freqCount (global int *data, int N, write_only pipe int2↩
        countsPipe, int st, int end, local int *counts)
3  {
4    int ID = get_global_id (0);
5    int totalWorkItems = get_global_size (0);
6    int localID = get_local_id (0);
7    int groupSize = get_local_size (0);
8
9    // initialize local counts
10   int totalCounts = end − st + 1;
11   for (int i = localID; i < totalCounts; i += groupSize)
12     counts[i] = 0;
13   work_group_barrier (CLK_LOCAL_MEM_FENCE);
14
15   for (int i = ID; i < N; i += totalWorkItems)
16     {
17       int v = data[i] − st;
18       atom_add (counts + v, 1);
19     }
20
21   // wait for all counts to be done
22   work_group_barrier (CLK_LOCAL_MEM_FENCE);
23
24   for (int i = localID; i < totalCounts; i += groupSize)
25     {
26       if (counts[i] > 0)  // only non−zero counts are placed in the ↩
            pipe
27         {
28           int2 pair = { i, counts[i] };
29           write_pipe (countsPipe, &pair);
30         }
31     }
32  }
33
34  // ================================================================
35  // Assumes a 256−work item group
```

```
36   kernel void modeFind (read_only pipe int2 countsPipe, global int *↩
        res, int N, int st, int end, local int *counts)
37   {
38     int localID = get_local_id (0);
39     int groupSize = get_local_size (0);    // this should be 256
40     local int bestIdx[256];
41     local int bestCount[256];
42     local int total;
43     if (localID == 0)
44       total = 0;
45
46     // initialize local counts
47     int totalCounts = end - st + 1;
48     for (int i = localID; i < totalCounts; i += groupSize)
49       counts[i] = 0;
50
51     work_group_barrier (CLK_LOCAL_MEM_FENCE);
52
53     // start collecting partial results from the pipe
54     int2 pipeItem;
55     while (total != N)
56       {
57         int res = read_pipe (countsPipe, &pipeItem);
58         if (res == 0)
59           {
60             atomic_add (counts + pipeItem.x, pipeItem.y);
61             atomic_add (&total, pipeItem.y);
62           }
63       }
64
65     // find the mode
66     if (localID < totalCounts)
67       {
68         bestIdx[localID] = localID;
69         bestCount[localID] = counts[localID];
70       }
71     else
72       {
73         bestIdx[localID] = 0;
74         bestCount[localID] = 0;
75       }
76
77     work_group_barrier (CLK_LOCAL_MEM_FENCE);
78
79     // find local maximum from counts
80     for (int i = localID + groupSize; i < totalCounts; i += groupSize)
81       if (bestCount[localID] < counts[i])
82         {
83           bestIdx[localID] = i;
84           bestCount[localID] = counts[i];
85         }
86
```

```
87      work_group_barrier (CLK_LOCAL_MEM_FENCE);
88
89      // reduce mode
90      int step = 1;
91      bool cont = true;
92      while (step < groupSize)
93        {
94          int otherID = localID | step;
95          if (localID & step != 0)
96            cont = false;
97          if (cont && otherID < groupSize)
98            {
99              if (bestCount[localID] < bestCount[otherID])
100               {
101                 bestIdx[localID] = bestIdx[otherID];
102                 bestCount[localID] = bestCount[otherID];
103               }
104            }
105          step *= 2;
106
107          work_group_barrier (CLK_LOCAL_MEM_FENCE);
108        }
109
110     if (localID == 0)
111       {
112         res[0] = bestIdx[0] + st;
113         res[1] = bestCount[0];
114       }
115   }
```

The fine points of the above kernels are:

- The counts of the numbers are maintained as an array dynamically allocated in local memory. Both kernels use such an array, so their first lines are devoted to initializing the corresponding local memory (lines 10–13 and 47–51). The freqCount kernel uses the counts array for holding the partial frequencies of the data items examined by the for loop on lines 15–19. Each work group has its own counts array, but because each array is shared between the work items, a data race is possible. This is the reason line 18 uses an atomic increment to the concerned counts element (see more on OpenCL atomics in Section 7.7).
- The size of the local memory array (totalCounts, lines 10 and 47) depends on the range of the numbers in the data array. This is why the range [st, end] endpoints are passed as parameters to both kernels.
- Once the input data are examined by all work items in a group (line 22), the for loop of lines 24–30 enqueues in the countsPipe the counts that were not found to be zero. The counts of number no are enqueued as the pair of (no-st, counts[no-st]), in the form of an int2 vector.
- The modeFind kernel is supposed to run as a single work group made up of 256 work items. It is responsible for consolidating the counts placed in the pipe and reducing the mode.

- `modeFind` reads from the pipe on lines 54–63, each time having a successful read (check on line 58) followed by an atomic update of the local `counts` elements (line 60).
- A critical aspect of `modeFind`'s operation is to determine when it is time to stop reading from the pipe. This is done by keeping a count of all the items accounted for in the `total` local memory variable. Once `total` reaches the input size N the pipe is empty.
- Lines 65–108 implement a reduction algorithm, where each work item selects the best candidate between the one it holds and the one held by another work item with a local ID at a `step` distance from its local ID (calculation of `otherID` at line 94). The `step` distance is incremented exponentially at the end of each step, until it covers the work group. The algorithm is covered in detail in Section 5.11.3. Lines 65–85 constitute the initialization of the best candidate for each work item, before the reduction takes place in the while loop starting at line 92. It should be stressed that all the work items execute all the while loop iterations, even if they are not part of the reduction process (lines 95–96 determine when a work item is "retired"). Otherwise the collective barrier of line 107 would block.

An illustration of the inner workings of Listing 7.10 is shown in Fig. 7.9.

A critical observation about OpenCL pipes is that the read and write operations (even the reserved ones) are not blocking. So if a work item is trying to read from a pipe that is empty, it will not block until a packet becomes available.

In order for the pipe to be functional in our example, we must ensure two things:

(1) The kernel that deposits packets in the pipe should have enough space to do so, even if the "consumer" kernel is not running, which would reduce the pipe's memory requirements. So the pipe should be sufficiently big to fit all that could be produced from the "producer" work items.

(2) The kernel that removes packets from the pipe should know when to stop doing so, either by checking some universal condition, or knowing a priori the number of packets present or expected. The code in Listing 7.10 uses the former approach. An alternative would be to have `freqCount` deposit all the counts in the pipe, even the zero ones, which means that the exact number of packets would be known ahead of time to `modeFind`.

The first condition is satisfied by lines 178–180 below, where during the construction of the pipe the maximum possible number of packets is chosen for the size:

Listing 7.11: Host driver program for the kernels in Listing 7.10.

```
116  // File : pipe_mode.cpp
117  #include "cl_utility.h"
118  #include <CL/cl2.hpp>
119
120  static cl_context cont = 0;       // initialize for cleanup check
121  static cl_command_queue q = 0;
122  static cl_program pr = 0;
123  static cl_kernel countKernel = 0, reduceKernel;
```

```
124  static cl_mem d_mode = 0, d_countsPipe = 0, d_data = 0;
125
126  //================================================
127  void cleanUp ()
128  {
129  . . .
130  }
131
132  //================================================
133  int main (int argc, char **argv)
134  {
135    cl_int errNum;
136    cl_device_id devID;
137
138    if (argc < 4)
139      {
140        printf ("%s #num_data lowerValue higherValue\n", argv[0]);
141        return 0;
142      }
143    int N = atoi (argv[1]);
144    int st = atoi (argv[2]);
145    int end = atoi (argv[3]);
146
147    // context and queue setup
148    setupDevice (cont, q, NULL, devID);
149
150    //------------------------------------------------
151    // read program source and build it
152    if (!setupProgramAndKernel (devID, cont, "pipe_mode.cl", pr, "↵
         freqCount", countKernel))
153      {
154        if (pr != 0)
155          printf ("Error: %s\n", getCompilationError (pr, devID));
156        cleanUp ();
157        return 1;
158      }
159
160    // second kernel build from the same source
161    reduceKernel = clCreateKernel (pr, "modeFind", &errNum);
162    if (isError (errNum, "Failed to create reduce kernel."))
163      {
164        cleanUp ();
165        return 1;
166      }
167
168    //------------------------------------------------
169    // host-side memory allocation & I/O
170    int *h_data = new int[N];
171    srand (clock ());
172    for (int i = 0; i < N; i++)
173      h_data[i] = st + rand () % (end - st + 1);
174
```

```
175    //------------------------------------------------
176    // allocate memory on the target device and copy data from the  ↵
           host to it
177    int totalWorkItems = (N / 10 + 1);
178    int numWorkGroups = (totalWorkItems+255)/256;
179    int pipeSize = numWorkGroups * (end - st + 1);
180    d_countsPipe = clCreatePipe (cont, 0, 2 * sizeof (int), pipeSize, ↵
           NULL, &errNum);
181    if (isError (errNum, "Failed to create pipe"))
182      {
183        cleanUp ();
184        return 1;
185      }
186
187    // Device input data
188    d_data = clCreateBuffer (cont, CL_MEM_READ_ONLY | ↵
           CL_MEM_USE_HOST_PTR, N * sizeof (int), h_data, &errNum);
189    if (isError (errNum, "Failed to create device input data buffer"))
190      {
191        cleanUp ();
192        return 1;
193      }
194
195    // Device mode result
196    d_mode = clCreateBuffer (cont, CL_MEM_READ_WRITE, 2 * sizeof (int)↵
           , NULL, &errNum);
197    if (isError (errNum, "Failed to create device mode storage"))
198      {
199        cleanUp ();
200        return 1;
201      }
202
203    //------------------------------------------------
204    // specify the parameters that will be used for the kernel ↵
           execution
205    // set up the work item index space and group size
206    size_t idxSpace_k1[] = { totalWorkItems };
207    size_t localWorkSize_k1[] = { 256 };
208
209    size_t idxSpace_k2[] = { 256 };
210    size_t localWorkSize_k2[] = { 256 };
211
212    // enqueue kernel execution request
213    errNum = clSetKernelArg (countKernel, 0, sizeof (cl_mem), (void *)↵
           &d_data);
214    errNum |= clSetKernelArg (countKernel, 1, sizeof (int), (void *) &↵
           N);
215    errNum |= clSetKernelArg (countKernel, 2, sizeof (cl_mem), (void ↵
           *) &(d_countsPipe));
216    errNum |= clSetKernelArg (countKernel, 3, sizeof (int), (void *) &↵
           st);
```

```
217    errNum |= clSetKernelArg (countKernel, 4, sizeof (int), (void *) &↵
           end);
218    errNum |= clSetKernelArg (countKernel, 5, 256 * sizeof (int), NULL↵
           );
219    if (isError (errNum, "Failed to set kernel parameters for ↵
           freqCount"))
220    {
221        cleanUp ();
222        return 1;
223    }
224
225    errNum = clSetKernelArg (reduceKernel, 0, sizeof (cl_mem), (void ↵
           *) &d_countsPipe);
226    errNum |= clSetKernelArg (reduceKernel, 1, sizeof (cl_mem), (void ↵
           *) &d_mode);
227    errNum |= clSetKernelArg (reduceKernel, 2, sizeof (int), (void *) ↵
           &N);
228    errNum |= clSetKernelArg (reduceKernel, 3, sizeof (int), (void *) ↵
           &st);
229    errNum |= clSetKernelArg (reduceKernel, 4, sizeof (int), (void *) ↵
           &end);
230    errNum |= clSetKernelArg (reduceKernel, 5, 256 * sizeof (int), ↵
           NULL);
231    if (isError (errNum, "Failed to set kernel parameters for modeFind↵
           "))
232    {
233        cleanUp ();
234        return 1;
235    }
236
237    errNum = clEnqueueNDRangeKernel (q, countKernel, 1, NULL, ↵
           idxSpace_k1, localWorkSize_k1, 0, NULL, NULL);
238    if (isError (errNum, "Failed to launch freqCount"))
239    {
240        cleanUp ();
241        return 1;
242    }
243
244    errNum = clEnqueueNDRangeKernel (q, reduceKernel, 1, NULL, ↵
           idxSpace_k2, localWorkSize_k2, 0, NULL, NULL);
245    if (isError (errNum, "Failed to launch modeFind"))
246    {
247        cleanUp ();
248        return 1;
249    }
250
251    //───────────────────────────────────────────────
252    // collect the results by copying them from the device to the host↵
           memory
253    int h_res[2];
254    errNum = clEnqueueReadBuffer (q, d_mode, CL_TRUE, 0, 2 * sizeof (↵
           int), h_res, 0, NULL, NULL);
```

```
255    if (isError (errNum, "Failed to get the results"))
256      {
257        cleanUp ();
258        return 1;
259      }
260
261    printf ("Mode %i with %i occur.\n", h_res[0], h_res[1]);
262    // release resources
263    cleanUp ();
264    delete[]h_data;
265    return 0;
266  }
```

The device setup and error checking/cleanup procedures in the above listing follow the design approach established in Section 7.4.1 and practiced in the previous examples of this chapter.

The host allocates three device memory objects, a buffer for the input data (d_data, line 188), a buffer for the mode item and its frequency (d_mode, line 196), and a pipe of int2 packets (countsPipe, line 180).

The host assigns roughly 10 input numbers per work item on line 177 and uses a 1D index space for kernel freqCount. Both kernels also have 256-size work groups. The only difference is that modeFind is assigned only one work group (line 209). Both kernels are placed in the same device queue (lines 237 and 244), which means that they will run in sequence. Different queues can also be employed, as well as queues of different devices, e.g., run freqCount on a GPU and modeFind on a CPU. The context however has to be the same, as the pipe, in line with all memory objects, is associated with a specific context.

The memory transfer of line 254 completes the result collection by the host. Please note that the d_mode buffer object, which is of type int2, can be retrieved by using a two-element int array (line 253) or a cl_int2 variable.

7.6 Shared virtual memory

Shared virtual memory (SVM) is an addition to the standard as OpenCL 2.0 enables the unification of the virtual memory spaces of host and device. As such, a pointer to memory would be valid if it were used by either of them. The consequences of SVM are quite dramatic: not only host-to-device and vice versa transfers become irrelevant, but also complex pointer-based structures such as linked lists are readily available system-wide, including the host and any devices. Of course, one of the preconditions for SVM to work is that the host and the device(s) have the same endianness, i.e., data types are laid out in the same way in memory.

This is the ideal scenario, but it requires support both at the hardware and system software level. For this reason OpenCL provides three different levels of SVM support:

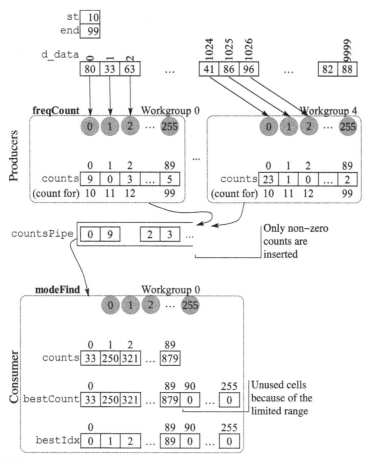

FIGURE 7.9

An example of how 10,000 integers in the range [10, 99] are processed by the kernels of Listing 7.10. A total of five work groups of 256 work items each (see line 178 in Listing 7.11 to know why) are generated to run the freqCount kernel. A single work group is assigned to run the modeFind kernel. Because the range of numbers is less than the size of this work group, parts of the bestCount and bestIdx arrays are not utilized.

- *Coarse grain sharing*: Memory is shared at the level of a buffer. Shared memory has to be allocated using the clSVMAlloc function and freed using clSVMFree:

```
// Allocates a shared virtual memory space as per the "size"
// parameter. Returns a pointer or NULL if the allocation fails.
void* clSVMAlloc(
    cl_context context,       // Valid context to associate
                              // allocated memory with (IN)
    cl_svm_mem_flags flags,   // Allocation flags (IN)
    size_t size,              // Size of block in bytes (IN))
```

```
        cl_uint alignment);     // Allocation alignment in bytes. If
                                // set to 0 it will default to the
                                // size of the largest build-in
                                // OpenCL type (IN)
//--------------------------------------------
// Releases a SVM memory block
void clSVMFree(
        cl_context context,     // Valid context (IN)
        void* svm_pointer);     // Pointer to allocated memory (IN)
```

The flags parameter can be one of CL_MEM_READ_ONLY, CL_MEM_WRITE_ONLY, or CL_MEM_READ_WRITE, which are the same symbolic constants examined in Section 7.5.1.

A pointer acquired using clSVMAlloc can be sent as a parameter to a kernel. A different function has to be used for this purpose:

```
// Sets the "arg_index" kernel parameter to the provided pointer.
// Returns an error code or CL_SUCCESS
cl_int clSetKernelArgSVMPointer(
        cl_kernel kernel,       // Kernel reference (IN)
        cl_uint arg_index,      // Parameter position (IN)
        const void* ptr);       // SVM pointer (IN)
```

Host and device will have a consistent view of the shared memory at synchronization points.[4]

The synchronization points that cause the updates to be visible in the case of coarse-grained SVM are the mapping and unmapping of memory and kernel start and completion events. Mapping SVM memory is accomplished via the clEnqueueSVMMap and clEnqueueSVMUnmap functions, which are similar to their buffer object counterparts, covered in Section 7.5.1.

As an example of the above functions, consider the following kernel:

Listing 7.12: Host driver program for the kernels in Listing 7.10.

```
1  // File : svm_coarse.cl
2  kernel void initKernel (global int *data, int N)
3  {
4    int ID = get_global_id (0);
5    if(ID<N) data[ID] = ID;
6  }
```

If it is invoked by the host program in Listing 7.13, it will initialize the data array to a sequence of integers starting from 0, without any explicit memory transfer taking place:

---

[4] A **synchronization point** is a command that forces the host or device to wait for some action to complete. Such commands could be the work_group_barrier function in a kernel or a clEnqueue* function executed by the host that has a list of events that have to be triggered before it can start.

Listing 7.13: Host driver program for the kernels in Listing 7.10.

```
7    // File : svm_coarse.cpp
8    . . .
9    int main (int argc, char **argv)
10   {
11     int N = atoi (argv[1]); // size of array determined by CLI ↩
           parameter
12     . . .
13     // Allocate SVM array
14     int *data = (int *)clSVMAlloc(cont, CL_MEM_READ_WRITE, N*sizeof↩
           (int),0);
15     if (data == NULL)
16       {
17         cleanUp ();
18         return 1;
19       }
20
21     //——————————————————————————————
22     // specify the parameters that will be used for the kernel ↩
           execution
23     size_t idxSpace[] = { N };
24     size_t localWorkSize[] = { 256 };
25
26     // enqueue kernel execution request
27     errNum = clSetKernelArgSVMPointer(kern, 0, data);
28     errNum |= clSetKernelArg (kern, 1, sizeof (int), (void *) &N);
29     . . .
30     errNum = clEnqueueNDRangeKernel (q, kern, 1, NULL, idxSpace, ↩
           localWorkSize, 0, NULL, &kernComplete);
31     . . .
32     cl_event evlist[]={ kernComplete };
33     errNum = clWaitForEvents(1, evlist);
34
35     for( int i=0;i<N;i++)
36         printf("%i ",data[i]); // sequence will be printed
37     printf("\n");
38
39     // release resources
40     clSVMFree(cont, data);
41     . . .
```

The synchronization point that makes the device modifications visible to the host is line 33, where we wait for the completion of the kernel execution. Past this line, the new contents of the data array will be visible to the host.

- *Fine-grained sharing at the buffer level*: The difference between this and the previous support level is that updates become visible at any synchronization point (not just when a kernel starts and when it finishes), without the need for a map/unmap sequence. The buffer has to be allocated by clSVMAlloc still.

Additionally, if the optional atomic operations are supported (see Section 7.7), using them results in a consistent view of the SVM buffer across host/device, without other barriers or synchronization points.

- *Fine-grained sharing at the system level*: This is the support level that enables memory allocated with `malloc` or `new` to be visible to devices without any explicit or implicit action. Memory consistency, as is the case for most contemporary multicore CPU architectures, is only guaranteed if the – optional – atomics are used. Otherwise, data races and race conditions are still possible. In other words, it is like providing the device with equal footing access to main memory as any CPU core.

An OpenCL 2.x-compliant library implementation has to provide support for the coarse-grained SVM. The other two types are optional. A user can query the supported SVM level by calling the `clGetDeviceInfo` function with a specification parameter of `CL_DEVICE_SVM_CAPABILITIES`. The returned value will be a bitfield set to one of the following: `CL_DEVICE_SVM_COARSE_GRAIN_BUFFER`, `CL_DEVICE_SVM_FINE_GRAIN_BUFFER`, or `CL_DEVICE_SVM_FINE_GRAIN_SYSTEM`. Additionally, if the `CL_DEVICE_SVM_ATOMICS` bit is set, the optional atomic operations are supported.

Another example of SVM is provided in Section 7.8.

7.7 Atomics and synchronization

Work items running on separate processing elements are no different in terms of data access to threads running on regular CPU cores: they can produce data races and race conditions if they operate in an uncoordinated fashion. Since OpenCL 2.0 the standard provides barriers and atomics operations to deal with these issues. These atomics are largely based on their C11 counterparts.

A barrier is a mechanism operating within a work group, and it is a collective operation in the sense that all work items *must* reach the barrier statement. This means that special care needs to be given to barrier placement. Placing one inside a conditional block (e.g., an `if`/`else` statement or a `while` loop) will lead to a deadlock if some work items do not enter the block.

Barriers are implemented in OpenCL with these functions:

```
// Work—group barrier function
void work_group_barrier(
    cl_mem_fence_flags flags);
//
// Work—group barrier function, with memory scope specification
void work_group_barrier(
    cl_mem_fence_flags flags,
    memory_scope scope);
```

The `flags` parameter in the above functions specifies the address space affected by the barrier. The possible options correspond to which memory updates become visible to the work group. These are:

- `CLK_LOCAL_MEM_FENCE`: All local memory updates become visible to the work group.
- `CLK_GLOBAL_MEM_FENCE`: All global memory updates become visible to the work group.
- `CLK_IMAGE_MEM_FENCE`: All image object updates become visible to the work group.

For example, having a local memory array initialized prior to using it requires a code snippet similar to:

```
local int counters[N];
for(int i=get_local_id(0); i<N; i+= get_local_size(0))
    counters[i]=0;
work_group_barrier(CLK_LOCAL_MEM_FENCE);
```

The fourth line ensures that the initialization has been performed and the changes are observable by all the work items in the group.

The `scope` parameter in the second barrier function specifies whether the changes will become available or not beyond a single work group. The `memory_scope` is an enumerated type and the symbolic constants available as options for the `scope` parameter are:

- `memory_scope_work_group`: Updates become available to the work group. This is equivalent to just using the first barrier function.
- `memory_scope_device`: Updates become visible to all work groups running on the same device.
- `memory_scope_all_svm_devices`: Updates become visible to all the devices that have SVM capability. This implies that the corresponding devices are all managed as part of the same context. Otherwise this has no meaning.

It should be clarified that the last two options do not mean that a barrier needs to be executed across all work groups or across all devices. Also, updates to local memory do not concern any work items other than the ones belonging to the same work group. As such, the last two options cannot be paired with a `CLK_LOCAL_MEM_FENCE` flag.

Barriers are in general costly operations that compromise performance potential. An alternative for keeping a consistent view of the data is to use atomic operations. Since OpenCL 2.0 we have a set of atomic data types as shown in Table 7.6 that are based on the C11 standard.

The 64-bit atomic data types have to be explicitly enabled (*if supported* by the target device) by including the following lines in the device source code:

```
#pragma OPENCL EXTENSION cl_khr_int64_base_atomics : enable
#pragma OPENCL EXTENSION cl_khr_int64_extended_atomics : enable
```

All atomic data types have the same memory representation and footprint as their non-atomic counterparts. For this reason, if we would like to have the host allocate and pass to a kernel an atomic variable, we can perform the allocation (and subsequent memory transfers) as if it was just a regular variable.

Table 7.6 OpenCL 2.0 (and above) atomic data types. Support for 64-bit types is conditional, based on the availability of 64-bit device support. The `atomic_flag` is a Boolean data type.

Type	OpenCL support
atomic_int	Yes
atomic_uint	Yes
atomic_flag	Yes
atomic_float	Yes
atomic_long	Provisional
atomic_ulong	Provisional
atomic_double	Provisional
atomic_size_t	Provisional
atomic_intptr_t	Provisional
atomic_uintptr_t	Provisional
atomic_ptrdiff_t	Provisional

An atomic variable can be initialized in three ways, two by the device and one by the host:

(1) Using the `ATOMIC_VAR_INIT` preprocessor macro. For example:

```
atomic_int counter = ATOMIC_VAR_INIT(0);
kernel void foo(...)
{
  local atomic_int local_cnt;
  if(get_local_id(0)==0)
    local_cnt = ATOMIC_VAR_INIT(0);
  ...
```

(2) Using the `atomic_init` function. The function name is misleading, as this is not really an atomic operation. The function is overloaded to cover all the atomic types, and its signature is:

```
// Initializes an atomic variable of type A to a compatible
// value of type C
void atomic_init(
        volatile A *var, // Address of atomic variable (IN)
        C value);        // Value for initialization (IN)
```

For example:

```
kernel void foo(...)
{
  local atomic_int local_cnt;
  if(get_local_id(0)==0)
    atomic_init(&local_cnt, 0);
  ...
```

A barrier might be required afterwards in this case to ensure that initialization is complete before any work item attempts to access the atomic variable.

(3) Using the `clEnqueueFillBuffer` function (see Section 7.5.1) after allocation and before invoking the kernel that will use the atomic variable.

Basic access to an atomic variable is provided by a set of overloaded functions, which mirror the methods of the atomic classes reported in Chapter 3. Please note that in the following signatures A refers to an atomic type and C to a compatible non-atomic type:

```
// Stores val in *var
void atomic_store(
      volatile A *var,
      C val);
//----------------------------------------
// Returns the current value of *var
C atomic_load(
      volatile A *var);
//----------------------------------------
// Returns the current value of *var and replaces it with val
C atomic_exchange(
      volatile A *var,
      C val);
//----------------------------------------
// Compares the value of *var and if it matches *expectedV, it
// replaces it with val. Returns true if the match is successful.
// In the case of failure, it returns false and stores the value
// found in *var in *expectedV
bool atomic_compare_exchange_strong(
      volatile A *var,
      C *expectedV,
      C val;
//----------------------------------------
// Performs the same operation as atomic compare_exchange_strong,
// but it may fail spuriously, i.e., it may return false even if
// *var==*expectedV.
bool atomic_compare_exchange_weak(
      volatile A *var,
      C *expectedV,
      C val;
```

The weak variant of the compare and exchange function can offer performance benefits and/or it may suit architectures that use load-link and store-conditional (LL/SC)-based implementations. For a complete discussion on the benefits and drawbacks of the strong and weak variants, please see Section 3.8.

OpenCL also offers a set of fetch-and-modify functions as listed below:

Listing 7.14: Signature of fetch-and-modify OpenCL atomic functions. The "X" can be any of `add`, `sub`, `or`, `xor`, `and`, `min`, and `max`. The Boolean operators are bitwise.

```
// Stores the result of applying binary operation X on *var and val
// in *var. Returns the value of *var before the operation
C atomic_fetch_X(
    volatile A *var,
    C val);
```

The `atomic_fetch_X` functions apply only to integer atomic types, e.g., `atomic_int`, `atomic_long`, `atomic_intptr`, etc. In order to provide similar functionality to non-integer types, the compare-and-exchange functions have to be utilized.

For example, in order to perform atomic addition to an `atomic_float` we can employ the following pattern:

```
void atomic_float_addition(volatile atomic_float *ptr, float a)
{
    float oldv=atomic_load(ptr); // get the old value
    float newv=oldv+a;           // calculate the updated one
    while(!atomic_compare_exchange_strong(ptr, &oldv, newv))
        newv=oldv+a;             // in case of failure, oldv
                                 // holds the "unexpected"
                                 // value of *ptr
}
```

which should be familiar from the lock-free structures material in Section 4.3.

All the aforementioned atomic functions, bar `atomic_init`, come in variants that specify the memory order, e.g., `fetch_and_add_explicit`, `atomic_compare_exchange_strong_explicit`, etc. These functions receive an extra parameter of type `memory_order` that specifies how the atomic operations will be arranged by the OpenCL compiler relative to the non-atomic surrounding operations.

Memory ordering is a topic that is examined also for C++11 in Section 3.8.1, so the discussion here serves only for describing the OpenCL specifics. OpenCL provides the following memory orderings:

- `memory_order_relaxed`: There are no synchronization or ordering constraints imposed on other work items' reads or writes.
- `memory_order_acquire`: Used in a load operation to make sure that all writes to the concerned atomic variable are visible in the current work item.
- `memory_order_release`: Used in a store operation to ensure that the changes applied become visible in other work items that acquire/read the same atomic variable.
- `memory_order_acq_rel`: Used in a read–modify–write operation (e.g., `compare_exchange_*`), where both an acquire operation is performed for the read part and a release operation is performed for the write part.
- `memory_order_seq_cst`: Short for "sequentially consistent," i.e., a load operation performs an acquire and a write operation performs a release. This is the most strict ordering, and it is the default one in order to ensure program correctness.

Compared with the corresponding C++11 list, the above list is missing the `memory_order_consume` option, which is not supported.

Although it is not mandatory or necessary, `memory_order_release` and `memory_order_acquire` are typically used in pairs. Once a work item executes a `memory_order_release` on an atomic variable X, all changes become visible to any work item that subsequently executes an operation with a `memory_order_acquire` on X.

The default `memory_order_seq_cst` ordering is the safest to use for development. The other options can be tested for maximizing performance, once program correctness has been established.

Synchronization can be also performed on a work item basis, instead of a work group basis. OpenCL provides the following fence operation:

```
// Imposes a consistent view of memory for a work item, as specified
// by the parameters
void atomic_work_item_fence(
    cl_mem_fence_flags flags, // Bitfield or ORed specifiers, such as
                              // CLK_GLOBAL_MEM_FENCE (IN)
    memory_order order,       // Memory order, e.g.,
                              // memory_order_acquire (IN)
    memory_scope scope);      // Memory scope, e.g.,
                              // memory_scope_device (IN)
```

A typical use of the `atomic_work_item_fence` function is for synchronizing image writes with reads (suitable only for image objects declared as `read_write`). The OpenCL standard specifies that the results of a write to an image object without a sampler are not guaranteed to be viewed even by the work item that initiated it. In that case, the following statement is required prior to any read operations:

```
atomic_work_item_fence( CLK_IMAGE_MEM_FENCE,  memory_order_acquire, ↩
    memory_scope_device );
```

7.8 Work group functions

Work group functions are collective functions that allow the easy and efficient implementation by a work group of a number of essential primitives, such as voting, broadcasting, reduction, and scanning.

Work group functions in OpenCL are similar to the cooperative groups functions in CUDA. The difference is that while CUDA cooperative groups can operate on a subset of a block of threads, work group functions are collective operations that must involve all the work items in a group. OpenCL 2.0 also defines a set of optional subgroup functions, such as `sub_group_all()`. However, the creation of the subgroups themselves is not part of the standard, and it is left up to the individual vendors for implementation.

The functions provided by OpenCL are shown below, where T represents one of the types: `half`, `int`, `uint`, `long`, `ulong`, `float` or `double`, and OP can be one of `add`, `min`, or `max`:

```
// Returns a non-zero value if the "predicate" evaluates to an
// non-zero value in all the work items
int work_group_all(
    int predicate);
//----------------------------------------------
// Returns a non-zero value if the "predicate" evaluates to an
// non-zero value in at least one work item
int work_group_any(
    int predicate);
//----------------------------------------------
// Broadcasts the value "a" at the work item identified by the
// local_id parameter, to all the work items. Three different
// versions cover the cases of 1D, 2D and 3D index ranges.
T work_group_broadcast(
    T a,
    size_t local_id);
T work_group_broadcast(
    T a,
    size_t local_id_x,
    size_t local_id_y);
T work_group_broadcast(
    T a,
    size_t local_id_x,
    size_t local_id_y,
    size_t local_id_z);
//----------------------------------------------
// Returns the result of performing reduction using the OP operator,
// on all the values x provided by the work items
T work_group_reduce_OP(
    T x);
//----------------------------------------------
// Performs an exclusive scan on the provided x values, using the
// OP operator. Each work item receives a different result
T work_group_scan_exclusive_OP(
    T x);
//----------------------------------------------
// Performs an inclusive scan on the provided x values, using the
// OP operator. Each work item receives a different result
T work_group_scan_inclusive_OP(
    T x);
```

As an example application of the above, we will examine the problem of filtering a dataset, i.e., producing a subset of the input data, where all the elements not satisfying a predicate function are removed. This is the same problem examined in Section 6.10.1, so the interested reader can compare the OpenCL versus the CUDA solution, although the CUDA version does not utilize unified memory.

This is not a trivial problem for an accelerator to solve, especially if the output needs to be compacted, i.e., produce a new array without the eliminated elements, while keeping them in their original relative order. The reason is that the copy of the condition-satisfying elements to the new set *in parallel* requires a prefix-sum calculation for finding the appropriate offsets.

The following two kernel functions implement these steps:

Listing 7.15: Two kernels that utilize work group functions for calculating the number of odd numbers assigned to a work group (countOdds) and for moving the odd numbers to a new array (moveOdds).

```
1   // File : filter_reduction.cl
2   inline bool predicate(int i)
3   {
4       return i % 2;
5   }
6
7   //----------------------------------------
8   kernel void countOdds(global int *data, int N, global int *↩
          groupCount)
9   {
10      int ID = get_global_id (0);
11      int haveOdd = predicate(data[ID]); // no check for ID vs N, ↩
             implies OpenCL 2.0
12
13      int totalForThisGroup = work_group_reduce_add(haveOdd);
14      if(get_local_id(0)==0)
15          groupCount[get_group_id(0)+1] = totalForThisGroup;
16  }
17
18  //----------------------------------------
19  kernel void moveOdds(global int *src, int N, global int *dest, ↩
          global int *groupOffsets)
20  {
21      int ID = get_global_id (0);
22      int haveOdd = predicate(src[ID]);
23      int localOffset = work_group_scan_exclusive_add(haveOdd);
24
25      if(haveOdd)
26          dest[ localOffset + groupOffsets[get_group_id(0)] ] = src[ID];
27  }
```

The filtering is based on the outcome of the predicate function (line 2), so modifying it would allow an easy adaptation of the code for other applications.

The two kernels are designed on the basis of one data element per work item. In the countOdds kernel, each work item examines its assigned array element (line 11), and the total count for the work group is determined on line 13 by calling work_group_reduce_add. A representative of the group (the one with local ID 0) proceeds to store this at an appropriate location (indexed by the group ID) in the supplied groupCounts array (line 15).

The moveOdds kernel receives the source and destination array pointers alongside the work group-specific offsets where the filtered data will be deposited. The offsets are calculated based on the groupCounts array results by having the host perform an exclusive prefix-sum (see lines 99–101 in Listing 7.16).

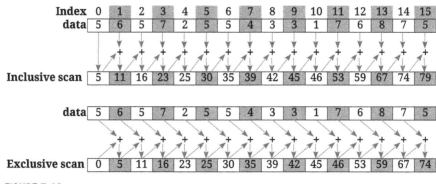

FIGURE 7.10

An example of the inclusive and exclusive scan calculations. As can be observed, the latter is a shifted-by-1 version of the former.

By making the group offsets available, each work item has to only calculate its group-relative offset by using the `work_group_scan_exclusive_add` function on line 23. An example of an exclusive scan operation is shown in Fig. 7.10.

These two kernels are invoked by the following host program:

Listing 7.16: Host program for filtering the odd numbers from an input array. The error handling code is omitted for brevity.

```
28  // File : filter_reduction.cpp
29  . . .
30  static cl_context cont = 0;        // initialize for cleanup check
31  static cl_command_queue q = 0;
32  static cl_program pr = 0;
33  static cl_kernel kern1=0;
34  static cl_kernel kern2=0;
35  static int *data=0;
36  static int *filteredData=0;
37  static int *groupCounts=0;
38  . . .
39  //=================================================
40  int main (int argc, char **argv)
41  {
42    cl_int errNum;
43    cl_device_id devID;
44    cl_event countKernComplete, moveKernComplete;
45
46    if (argc < 2)
47      {
48        printf ("%s #num_data\n", argv[0]);
49        return 0;
50      }
51    int N = atoi (argv[1]);
52
53    // context and queue setup
```

```
54    setupDevice (cont, q, NULL, devID);
55
56    //---------------------------------------------------
57    // read program source and build it
58    if (!setupProgramAndKernel (devID, cont, "filter_reduction.cl", pr↩
          , "countOdds", kern1))
59      {
60        if (pr != 0)
61          printf ("Error: %s\n", getCompilationError (pr, devID));
62        cleanUp ();
63        return 1;
64      }
65
66    // second kernel build from the same source
67    kern2 = clCreateKernel (pr, "moveOdds", &errNum);
68
69    //---------------------------------------------------
70    // SVM memory allocation
71    int *data = (int *) clSVMAlloc (cont, CL_MEM_READ_WRITE, N * ↩
          sizeof (int), 0);
72    for (int i = 0; i < N; i++)
73      data[i] = i;
74
75    int *filteredData = (int *) clSVMAlloc (cont, CL_MEM_READ_WRITE, N↩
          * sizeof (int), 0);
76
77    int numWorkGroups = (N + 255) / 256;
78    int *groupCounts = (int *) clSVMAlloc (cont, CL_MEM_READ_WRITE, (↩
          numWorkGroups + 1) * sizeof (int), 0);
79
80    //---------------------------------------------------
81    // specify the parameters that will be used for the kernel ↩
          execution
82    // set up the work item index space and group size
83    size_t idxSpace[] = { N };
84    size_t localWorkSize[] = { 256 };
85
86    // enqueue kernel execution request
87    errNum = clSetKernelArgSVMPointer (kern1, 0, data);
88    errNum |= clSetKernelArg (kern1, 1, sizeof (int), (void *) &N);
89    errNum |= clSetKernelArgSVMPointer (kern1, 2, groupCounts);
90
91    errNum = clEnqueueNDRangeKernel (q, kern1, 1, NULL, idxSpace, ↩
          localWorkSize, 0, NULL, &countKernComplete);
92
93    //---------------------------------------------------
94    // wait for the kernel to finish
95    cl_event evlist[] = { countKernComplete };
96    errNum = clWaitForEvents (1, evlist);
97
98    //---------------------------------------------------
99    // calculate the prefix-sum for the group offsets
```

```
100    groupCounts[0] = 0;
101    for (int i = 0; i < numWorkGroups; i++)
102      groupCounts[i + 1] += groupCounts[i];
103
104    //------------------------------------------------------------
105    // set parameters and call the second kernel
106    errNum = clSetKernelArgSVMPointer (kern2, 0, data);
107    errNum |= clSetKernelArg (kern2, 1, sizeof (int), (void *) &N);
108    errNum |= clSetKernelArgSVMPointer (kern2, 2, filteredData);
109    errNum |= clSetKernelArgSVMPointer (kern2, 3, groupCounts);
110
111    errNum = clEnqueueNDRangeKernel (q, kern2, 1, NULL, idxSpace, ↵
           localWorkSize, 0, NULL, &moveKernComplete);
112
113    //------------------------------------------------------------
114    // wait for the kernel to finish
115    cl_event evlist2[] = { moveKernComplete };
116    errNum = clWaitForEvents (1, evlist2);
117    . . .
```

The host program reads from the command-line the size of the array to be processed (line 51). In the spirit of keeping things simple and most importantly tractable, the input data array is initialized to a sequence of numbers (lines 72–73), making the check of the program output a trivial matter (it should be $1, 3, 5, ...$).

The host allocates three arrays on SVM (lines 71, 75, and 78), in order to hold the input data, the filtered output, and the per-group counts that will be utilized for offset calculations. The filtered data array can also be allocated once the total number of odds is known (after the group counts are accumulated by the loop of lines 100–102), if trimming the array sizes down is a priority.

The SVM allocation means that no explicit data movement needs to take place. Instead, the host only has to wait for the called kernels to finish to ensure that memory is consistent across both host and device. The two synchronization points are lines 96 and 116, where we wait for the kernel termination events.

As we are assigning one work item per input array element, we can calculate the total number of work groups as the group size is fixed to 256 (line 77). The expression on line 77 is just the ceiling calculation $\lceil \frac{N}{256} \rceil$, without the use of floating point arithmetic.

The host participates in the computation on lines 100–102, calculating the group offsets based on the outcome of the first kernel execution. The breakup of the overall operation into two kernels is certainly inefficient, but it is dictated by the absence of intergroup synchronization mechanisms: the offsets can only be calculated if all the group counts are known, and there is no way of knowing when they are, other than the end of the first kernel's execution. If we relax the keeping-the-relative-order requirement for the filtered data, then the whole operation can be done with one kernel, without the interim contribution of the host. This is left as an exercise.

7.9 **Events and profiling OpenCL programs**

In this section we explore the profiling capabilities afforded by the OpenCL library. Profiling OpenCL applications is relatively simple given that both the TAU and Scalasca profiling toolkits (see Section 5.21) support OpenCL. However, utilizing the OpenCL API allows relatively simple and inexpensive profiling that can go hand-in-hand with on-line algorithm optimization, e.g., optimizing kernel parameters during runtime based on the performance measured during previous executions.

In the previous sections we have already used events to properly enforce dependencies between device-enqueued commands. Events can also carry timing information if the device queue is created with the flag that enables profiling support, i.e.:

```
cl_queue_properties qprop[]={
    CL_QUEUE_PROPERTIES, CL_QUEUE_PROFILING_ENABLE,
    0};
q = clCreateCommandQueueWithProperties(...
```

The timing information associated with an event object can be queried with the `clGetEventProfilingInfo` function:

```
// Retrieves the time instance a particular occurrence associated
// with the supplied event object took place.
// Returns CL_SUCCESS upon successful execution.
cl_int clGetEventProfilingInfo(
    cl_event event,               // Target event (IN)
    cl_profiling_info param_name,// Symbolic name for desired time
                                  // info (IN)
    size_t param_value_size,      // Memory block size for
                                  // param_value (IN)
    void* param_value,            // Placeholder for requested value
                                  // (IN/OUT)
    size_t* param_actual_size);   // Actual memory used in
                                  // param_value (IN/OUT)
                                  // Ignored if set to NULL
```

All the possible parameter names return a 64-bit unsigned long value (`cl_ulong`) that corresponds to the device's time counter in nanoseconds. The available parameter names are listed in chronological order; the corresponding times are recorded below:

- `CL_PROFILING_COMMAND_QUEUED`: time when the command was enqueued.
- `CL_PROFILING_COMMAND_SUBMIT`: time when the command was submitted to the device.
- `CL_PROFILING_COMMAND_START`: execution start time.
- `CL_PROFILING_COMMAND_END`: execution end time.
- `CL_PROFILING_COMMAND_COMPLETE`: execution end time, which includes the completion of any spawned child commands.

The following example calculates the execution time of a kernel using this facility:

Listing 7.17: Calculating the duration of a kernel's execution phases using an event object.

```
// File : vectorAdd_profile.cpp
. . .
  // enable queue profiling
  cl_queue_properties qprop[] = {
    CL_QUEUE_PROPERTIES, CL_QUEUE_PROFILING_ENABLE,
    0
  };
  setupDevice(cont, q, qprop, devID);
. . .
  cl_event kernExec;
  clEnqueueNDRangeKernel (q, kernel, 1, NULL, idxSpace, ←
      localWorkSize, 0, NULL, &kernExec);

  // ensure that the kernel is finished
  clEnqueueReadBuffer(q, d_C, CL_TRUE, 0, DATASIZE, h_C, 0, NULL, ←
      NULL);

  cl_ulong enqTime, submitTime, startTime, endTime;
  clGetEventProfilingInfo(kernExec, CL_PROFILING_COMMAND_QUEUED, ←
      sizeof(cl_ulong), &enqTime, NULL);
  clGetEventProfilingInfo(kernExec, CL_PROFILING_COMMAND_SUBMIT, ←
      sizeof(cl_ulong), &submitTime, NULL);
  clGetEventProfilingInfo(kernExec, CL_PROFILING_COMMAND_START, ←
      sizeof(cl_ulong), &startTime, NULL);
  clGetEventProfilingInfo(kernExec, CL_PROFILING_COMMAND_END, sizeof←
      (cl_ulong), &endTime, NULL);
  cout << "Queueing time (ns) " << submitTime − enqTime << endl;
  cout << "Submit time (ns) "<< startTime − submitTime << endl;
  cout << "Execution time (ns) "<< endTime − startTime << endl;
. . .
```

The differences reported on lines 21–23 are in nanosecond units. This does not mean that the timer resolution is 1 ns though. The actual timer resolution can be retrieved using the clGetDeviceInfo function with the CL_DEVICE_PROFILING_TIMER_RESO-LUTION parameter name, as shown below:

```
// File : vectorAdd_profile.cpp
. . .
  size_t timerResol;
  clGetDeviceInfo (devID, CL_DEVICE_PROFILING_TIMER_RESOLUTION, ←
      sizeof(size_t), &timerResol, NULL);
  cout << "Timer resolution (ns) " << timerResol << endl;
. . .
```

7.10 **OpenCL and other parallel software platforms**

OpenCL device code is packaged as separate files that are compiled during runtime. This arrangement means that OpenCL can live alongside any of the other parallel software platforms examined in this book.

Additionally, all OpenCL calls are thread-safe, which means that they can be called by multiple host threads without any ill effect. The only exception to this rule are OpenCL calls that modify the state of a kernel object, such as clSetKernelArg and clSetKernelArgSVMPointer. However, this is an issue only if, e.g., clSetKernelArg is called on the same cl_kernel object.

Thus, if one would like to develop a multi-threaded host application that uses OpenCL to execute compute-intensive parts of the application on one or more devices, the only precaution required if *the same kernel function* is to be called by multiple host threads is to either (a) protect the argument setting and launch of a kernel by a mutex or (b) have each host thread create its very own kernel object from the same source code. The second option does not require recompilation as the clCloneKernel function can be utilized to generate a copy:

```
// Returns a shallow copy of the provided kernel. Only the data
// internal to the kernel object are copied. Available in OpenCL
// 2.1 and above.
cl_kernel clCloneKernel (
     cl_kernel source_kernel , // Original kernel object (IN)
     cl_int* errcode_ret);     // Placeholder for returned error code
                               // (IN/OUT)
```

An example of the first design approach is shown below:

Listing 7.18: Using the same kernel object from multiple host threads.

```
1   // File : host_threads_v1.cpp
2   . . .
3   #include <thread>
4   #include <mutex>
5   #include <memory>
6   . . .
7   static cl_kernel kern=0;
8   static mutex l;
9   . . .
10  // ==============================================
11  void hostThr(int ID)
12  {
13    int errNum;
14    cl_event kernComplete;
15    //----------------------------------------------
16    // specify the parameters that will be used for the kernel
17    // execution and set up the work item index space and group size
18    size_t idxSpace[] = { 16 };
19    size_t localWorkSize[] = { 16 };
20
21    l.lock();
```

```
22    // enqueue kernel execution request
23    errNum = clSetKernelArg (kern, 0, sizeof (int), (void *) &ID);
24    if (isError (errNum, "Failed to set kernel parameters"))
25      {
26        l.unlock();
27        return ;
28      }
29
30    errNum = clEnqueueNDRangeKernel (q, kern, 1, NULL, idxSpace, ←
          localWorkSize, 0, NULL, &kernComplete);
31    if (isError (errNum, "Failed to launch kernel"))
32      {
33        l.unlock();
34        return ;
35      }
36    l.unlock();
37
38    //------------------------------------------------
39    // wait for the kernel to finish
40    cl_event evlist[]={kernComplete};
41    clWaitForEvents(1, evlist);
42  }
43
44  //================================================
45  int main (int argc, char **argv)
46  {
47    . . .
48    // Set up context and queue for device,
49    // read OpenCL program source and build it
50    . . .
51    // create host threads
52    unique_ptr<thread> thr[N];
53    for(int i=0;i<N;i++)
54      thr[i] = make_unique<thread>(hostThr, i);
55
56    // wait for host threads to finish
57    for(int i=0;i<N;i++)
58      thr[i]->join();
59    . . .
60  }
```

The threads which are created on lines 52–54 use the global cl_kernel object (defined on line 7) to enqueue kernel execution requests (line 30). The kernel parameter setup (line 23) and the enqueueing of the kernel are in a critical section protected by a mutex (defined on line 8). Waiting for the kernel to complete execution is done outside the critical section, which ends at line 36.

The second option is illustrated in the following code, which requires OpenCL 2.1 to run:

Listing 7.19: Using copies of the same kernel object from multiple host threads (requires OpenCL 2.1 and above).

```cpp
61  // File : host_threads_v2.cpp
62  . . .
63  void hostThr (int ID, cl_kernel * kern)
64  {
65    int errNum;
66    cl_event kernComplete;
67    //----------------------------------------------
68    // specify the parameters that will be used for the kernel
69    // execution and set up the work item index space and group size
70    size_t idxSpace[] = { 16 };
71    size_t localWorkSize[] = { 16 };
72
73    // enqueue kernel execution request
74    errNum = clSetKernelArg (*kern, 0, sizeof (int), (void *) &ID);
75    if (isError (errNum, "Failed to set kernel parameters"))
76        return;
77
78    errNum = clEnqueueNDRangeKernel (q, *kern, 1, NULL, idxSpace, ↩
            localWorkSize, 0, NULL, &kernComplete);
79    if (isError (errNum, "Failed to launch kernel"))
80        return;
81
82    //----------------------------------------------
83    // wait for the kernel to finish
84    cl_event evlist[] = { kernComplete };
85    clWaitForEvents (1, evlist);
86  }
87
88  //=============================================
89  int main (int argc, char **argv)
90  {
91    . . .
92    // Set up context and queue for device,
93    // read OpenCL program source and build it
94    . . .
95
96    // create host threads
97    unique_ptr < thread > thr[N];
98    cl_kernel kernCopies[N];
99    for (int i = 0; i < N; i++)
100     {
101       kernCopies[i] = clCloneKernel (kern, &errNum); // copy kernel ↩
              object
102       if (isError (errNum, "Failed to copy kernel"))
103         {
104           cleanUp ();
105           return 1;
106         }
107 
```

```
108        thr[i] = make_unique < thread > (hostThr, i, &(kernCopies[i]))←
                ;
109        }
110
111     // wait for host threads to finish
112     for (int i = 0; i < N; i++)
113        thr[i]->join ();
114     . . .
115  }
```

The change in Listing 7.19 is that a copy of the initial `cl_kernel` object is obtained on line 101 for each of the host threads to execute and passed by reference to the thread constructor (line 108). The result is that no critical section is required for launching effectively the same kernel.

MPI also does not need any special treatment, as OpenCL looks like an ordinary library to the compiler. So the following line should suffice for compiling an MPI-OpenCL combination:

```
$ mpic++ myprog.cpp -lOpenCL -o myprog
```

A Multiple-Program, Multiple-Data (MPMD) design is not necessary even if the machines participating in the computation are equipped with different accelerators, as long as the appropriate *dynamic* OpenCL library is available for them to load at runtime.

7.11 Case study: Mandelbrot set

The generation of the Mandelbrot set is an embarrassingly parallel workload that also produces eye candy. For this reason, it is utilized in multiple case studies in this book. The particular application is discussed extensively in Sections 3.12 and 5.25.1, so we will proceed directly with just a brief explanation.

The Mandelbrot set is made up of the points $c = x + i \cdot y$ on the complex plane that produce a bounded sequence of numbers $z_0, z_1, z_2, \ldots$ when the recursive formula $z_{n+1} = z_n^2 + c$ with $z_0 = c$ is applied, i.e., $|z_n| = \sqrt{x_n^2 + y_n^2} < \infty \; \forall n$. In order to produce a graphical depiction of the Mandelbrot set, we must apply the recursive formula on each point of the complex plane that corresponds to an image pixel, until z_{n+1} diverges ($|z_n| > 2$) or n exceeds a preset threshold.

We explore and evaluate two possible design approaches:

1. Using just OpenCL to do the calculation.
2. Combining OpenCL and C++11 to enable the combined use of the device and the host.

7.11.1 **Calculating the Mandelbrot set using OpenCL**

A high-resolution Mandelbrot set image can consist of millions of pixels, each corresponding to an application of the $z_{n+1} = z_n^2 + c$ recursive formula. As the number of iterations required to achieve divergence is unknown, we experiment in this section with varying workload assignment per work item.

The OpenCL source code is a derivation of the code in Listing 3.42:

Listing 7.20: OpenCL device code for the calculation of the Mandelbrot set.

```
 1  // File : mandelOpenCL/kernel.cl
 2  #include "const.h"
 3
 4  // ***********************************************************
 5  int diverge (double cx, double cy)
 6  {
 7    int iter = 0;
 8    double vx = cx, vy = cy, tx, ty;
 9    while (iter < MAXITER && (vx * vx + vy * vy) < 4)
10      {
11         tx = vx * vx - vy * vy + cx;
12         ty = 2 * vx * vy + cy;
13         vx = tx;
14         vy = ty;
15         iter++;
16      }
17    return iter;
18  }
19
20  // ***********************************************************
21  kernel void mandelKernel (global unsigned char *d_res, double upperX ↵
      , double upperY, double stepX, double stepY, int resX, int resY)
22  {
23    int myX = get_global_id (0);
24    int myY = get_global_id (1);
25    int advX = get_global_size(0);
26    int advY = get_global_size(1);
27
28    int i, j;
29    for (i = myX; i < resX; i+= advX)
30      for (j = myY; j < resY; j+= advY)
31        {
32           double tempx, tempy;
33           tempx = upperX + i * stepX;
34           tempy = upperY - j * stepY;
35
36           int color = diverge (tempx, tempy);
37           d_res[j * resX + i] = color % 256;
38        }
39  }
```

The const.h header file included on line 2 contains a set of essential constants which are shared by the host and device code, such as the number of maximum iterations MAXITER.

Of the two functions defined in Listing 7.20, only mandelKernel is decorated with the kernel keyword, as the diverge function is never called from the host.

Each work item iterates over the whole target image (of resolution resX × resY), with the two nested for loops of lines 29 and 30. The number of pixels that will be processed is determined by the size of the 2D index space used for launching the kernel. The dimensions of the index space are retrieved on lines 25 and 26, and they are utilized as increment parameters in the for loops, effectively providing a staggered traversal of the image by each work item. For example, if the index space dimensions match the image resolution, only one pixel will be processed by each work item, the one corresponding to its 2D global identifier.

The execution of the kernel is managed by the following program, which reveals how one can go about adjusting the host code based on the capabilities of the target device. The capability in question is the support for SVM. SVM can have an impact on performance, while at the same time simplifying the host proceedings.

Listing 7.21: Host code for the calculation of the Mandelbrot set.

```
40  // File : mandelOpenCL/main.cpp
41  . . .
42  #include <QImage>
43  #include <QRgb>
44  #include "../cl_utility.h"
45  #include "const.h"
46
47  static cl_context cont = 0;      // initialize for cleanup check
48  static cl_command_queue q = 0;
49  static cl_program pr = 0;
50  static cl_kernel kern = 0;
51  static bool OCL2support = true;
52  static unsigned char *data = 0;  // image data
53  static cl_mem d_data = 0;        // image data if OpenCL 2.0 is not ←
        supported
54
55  // ************************************************************
56  void cleanUp ()
57  {
58      . . .
59      if (cont != 0)
60         {
61           if (OCL2support)
62             clSVMFree (cont, data);
63           else
64             clReleaseMemObject (d_data);
65           clReleaseContext (cont);
66         }
67  }
68
```

```
69   // ****************************************************************
70   // Host front—end function that allocates the memory and launches ↩
          the GPU kernel
71   double hostFE (double upperX, double upperY, double lowerX, double ↩
          lowerY, QImage * img, int resX, int resY)
72   {
73     auto t1 = high_resolution_clock::now ();
74
75     cl_int errNum;
76     cl_device_id devID;
77     cl_event kernComplete;
78
79     // context and queue setup
80     setupDevice (cont, q, NULL, devID);
81
82     //————————————————————————————————
83     // read program source and build it
84     if (!setupProgramAndKernel (devID, cont, "kernel.cl", pr, "↩
          mandelKernel", kern))
85       {
86         if (pr != 0)
87           printf ("Error: %s\n", getCompilationError (pr, devID));
88         cleanUp ();
89         return 1;
90       }
91
92     // check if SVM is supported
93     char attr[20];
94     size_t attrLen;
95     clGetDeviceInfo (devID, CL_DEVICE_VERSION, 20, (void *) attr, &↩
          attrLen);
96     if (attr[7] == '1')              // Character at position 7 is the ↩
          OpenCL major version
97       OCL2support = false;
98
99     if (OCL2support)
100      data = (unsigned char *) clSVMAlloc (cont, CL_MEM_READ_WRITE, ↩
             resX * resY * sizeof (unsigned char), 0);
101    else
102      {
103        d_data = clCreateBuffer (cont, CL_MEM_READ_WRITE, resX * resY ↩
               * sizeof (unsigned char), NULL, &errNum);
104        data = new unsigned char[resX * resY];
105      }
106
107    double stepX = (lowerX — upperX) / resX;
108    double stepY = (upperY — lowerY) / resY;
109
110    if (OCL2support)
111      errNum = clSetKernelArgSVMPointer (kern, 0, data);
112    else
```

```
113    errNum = clSetKernelArg (kern, 0, sizeof (cl_mem), (void *) &↵
           d_data);

114
115    errNum |= clSetKernelArg (kern, 1, sizeof (double), (void *) &↵
           upperX);
116    errNum |= clSetKernelArg (kern, 2, sizeof (double), (void *) &↵
           upperY);
117    errNum |= clSetKernelArg (kern, 3, sizeof (double), (void *) &↵
           stepX);
118    errNum |= clSetKernelArg (kern, 4, sizeof (double), (void *) &↵
           stepY);
119    errNum |= clSetKernelArg (kern, 5, sizeof (int), (void *) &resX);
120    errNum |= clSetKernelArg (kern, 6, sizeof (int), (void *) &resY);
121    if (isError (errNum, "Failed to set kernel parameters"))
122      {
123        cleanUp ();
124        return 1;
125      }

126
127    int threadX, threadY;
128    threadX = (int) ceil (resX * 1.0 / THR_BLK_X);
129    threadY = (int) ceil (resY * 1.0 / THR_BLK_Y);
130    threadX = ((threadX + BLOCK_SIDE - 1) / BLOCK_SIDE) * BLOCK_SIDE; ↵
           // make sure that a work item divides the idxSpace evenly
131    threadY = ((threadY + BLOCK_SIDE - 1) / BLOCK_SIDE) * BLOCK_SIDE;

132
133    size_t idxSpace[] = { threadX, threadY };
134    size_t localWorkSize[] = { BLOCK_SIDE, BLOCK_SIDE };

135
136    // launch GPU kernel
137    errNum = clEnqueueNDRangeKernel (q, kern, 2, NULL, idxSpace, ↵
           localWorkSize, 0, NULL, &kernComplete);
138    if (isError (errNum, "Failed to launch kernel"))
139      {
140        cleanUp ();
141        return 1;
142      }

143
144    if (!OCL2support)
145      errNum = clEnqueueReadBuffer (q, d_data, CL_TRUE, 0, resX * resY↵
           * sizeof (unsigned char), data, 0, NULL, NULL);
146    else
147      {
148        //--------------------------------------------------
149        // wait for the kernel to finish
150        cl_event evlist[] = { kernComplete };
151        errNum = clWaitForEvents (1, evlist);
152        if (isError (errNum, "Failed to wait for event"))
153          {
154            cleanUp ();
155            return 1;
156          }
```

```
157        }
158
159      //copy results into QImage object
160      for (int j = 0; j < resY; j++)
161        for (int i = 0; i < resX; i++)
162          {
163              int color = data[j * resX + i];
164              img->setPixel (i, j, qRgb (256 - color, 256 - color, 256 - ↩
                      color));
165          }
166
167      // clean up allocated memory
168      cleanUp ();
169      auto t2 = high_resolution_clock::now ();
170      auto dur = t2 - t1;
171      return duration_cast < milliseconds > (dur).count ();
172    }
173
174    // ************************************************************
175    int main (int argc, char *argv[])
176    {
177      double upperCornerX, upperCornerY;
178      double lowerCornerX, lowerCornerY;
179
180      upperCornerX = atof (argv[1]);
181      upperCornerY = atof (argv[2]);
182      lowerCornerX = atof (argv[3]);
183      lowerCornerY = atof (argv[4]);
184
185      int imgX = 3840, imgY = 2160;
186      if (argc > 6)
187        {
188            imgX = atoi (argv[5]);
189            imgY = atoi (argv[6]);
190        }
191
192      QImage *img = new QImage (imgX, imgY, QImage::Format_RGB32);
193      double gpuOpsTime = hostFE (upperCornerX, upperCornerY, ↩
                  lowerCornerX, lowerCornerY, img, imgX, imgY);
194      img->save ("mandel.png", "PNG", 0);
195    . . .
```

The `main` function of the program is reserved for I/O duties, i.e., reading the CLI parameters and saving the computed image (line 194). The CLI parameters consist of the top-left and bottom-right corner coordinates in the complex plane, which delimit the part of the set to be computed. Optionally, the image resolution can also be specified (defaulting otherwise to 4K). The `QImage` object used for handling the image data is defined on line 192 and passed by reference to the front-end function responsible for managing the device.

The `hostFE` function starts by setting up the device (line 80) and compiling the kernel (line 84), before detecting the device's capabilities (lines 93–97). Calling the clGetDeviceInfo function with a CL_DEVICE_VERSION parameter returns a string describing the OpenCL version supported by the device. The eighth character in that string is the major version number. Hence, the if statement on line 96 determines if SVM is supported or not. The outcome is saved in the OCL2support global variable declared on line 51, as it is required by various parts of the program, including the cleanUp function (see line 61).

If a device is known for supporting OpenCL 2.0 (otherwise CL_DEVICE_SVM_CA-PABILITIES is not available), one can query the SVM capabilities by using a different call, similar to the one shown below:

```
cl_device_svm_capabilities svm;  // bitfield for supported ↩
    functionality
clGetDeviceInfo (devID, CL_DEVICE_SVM_CAPABILITIES, sizeof(svm), (↩
    void *) &svm, NULL);
SVMsupport = (svm | CL_DEVICE_SVM_FINE_GRAIN_SYSTEM );  // checking ↩
    for required flag
```

Based on the OCL2support flag, either shared or host plus device memory blocks are allocated (lines 99–105) for holding the computed divergence data.

The 2D index space is computed on lines 127–133, based on the size of the block of pixels assigned to each work item and the image dimensions. The per-work-item block is constant, set to THR_BLK_X by THR_BLK_Y. The index space is forcibly made into a multiple of the block size on lines 130 and 131. The alternative (i.e., not being a multiple) is only supported by OpenCL 2.0. The work group is fixed at $16 \times 16 = 256$ work items, which is a modest choice.

After launching (or rather requesting the launch of) the kernel on line 137, OCL2support is checked to decide whether detecting the end of the kernel's execution will require waiting for the associated event (cl_event object kernComplete on lines 147–157) or it will be implied by the blocking device-to-host data transfer of line 145.

The hostFE function completes after color-coding the results in the QImage object (lines 159–165). It returns the total execution time of the activities involving the device, including setup, compilation, and image postprocessing.

Listing 7.21 employs the Qt library for performing image I/O. Combining the Qt and OpenCL libraries is a matter of a simple one-line addition to the .pro project file, as shown below:

```
# File : mandelOpenCL/oclAndQt.pro
LIBS+= —lOpenCL —lpthread
. . .
```

The OpenCL version has been tested for blocks of 1×1, 2×2, and 4×4 pixels per work item, with the 2×2 version yielding a very minor performance advantage,

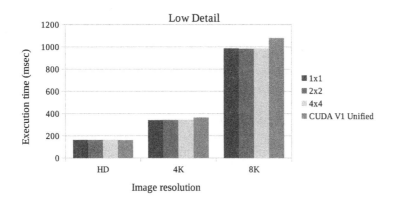

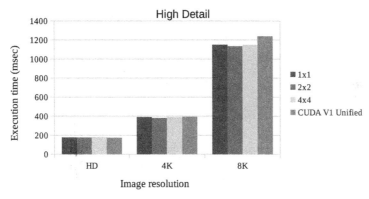

FIGURE 7.11

Average GPU execution time on an RTX 2060 Super GPU, for different pixel block size assignment per work item, for the Mandelbrot set calculation. The results for the CUDA V1 unified memory version of Section 6.15.1.1 are shown for comparison.

as shown in Fig. 7.11. Since this particular application is also used as a demonstration tool in Chapter 6, we use the same experimental setup as detailed in Section 6.15.1.4 to be able to compare the relative performance of OpenCL versus the best version of CUDA (the "V1 unified" as presented in Section 6.15.1.1).

The CUDA variant outperforms OpenCL on the same hardware for the HD resolution by a very narrow margin, but the ranking is reversed for higher resolutions. Given that the program logic and load distribution per CUDA thread and OpenCL work item are nearly identical, this discrepancy could be possibly attributed to differences in library optimizations concerning data transfers. The software platform used included GCC 9.3 (with identical optimization settings, i.e., -02), CUDA 11.2, and the 450.102 NVidia Linux driver. The CUDA times shown here include the data copy to the `QImage` object, as this is part of the OpenCL timings as well.

7.11.2 Hybrid calculation of the Mandelbrot set using OpenCL and C++11

In an effort to show how OpenCL can be integrated with C++11 host threads and the benefits that can be harvested, in this section we present a variation of the previous program, where the load is dynamically shared between the host and the device.

The effective partitioning of the target image between the host and the device can be an intricate problem on its own. For this reason we adopt a dynamic load balancing approach akin to the producers–consumers pattern employed in Section 3.12, splitting the image in blocks that are assigned on a first-come, first-served order to the computing threads. One of the host threads is dedicated to the management of the device.

However, because the load that should be assigned to the device has to be of different granularity (i.e., bigger) than the load assigned to the host threads, the size of the block is determined on the spot, based on the type of thread requesting it. So, instead of a buffer holding block specifications that are placed there from a producer thread a priori, we have a monitor class that is publishing an API for getting a "slice" of the target image according to the type of thread making the request.

The partitioning can be performed using geometric decomposition (see Section 2.3.3) in one or two dimensions. 1D groups of columns or rows offer the least complicated approach. In this section we break up the target image in sets of rows of varying height.

The LoadMonitor class responsible for this action is shown below:

Listing 7.22: Host code for the combined calculation of the Mandelbrot set by host and device: the load partitioning class.

```
1   // File : mandelOpenCL_hybrid_Cpp11/main.cpp
2   . . .
3   #include <atomic>
4
5   atomic<int> cpuBlocks(0); // for counting what is assigned to CPU/↩
        GPU
6   int gpuBlocks=0;
7   // ************************************************************
8   struct BlockDescr
9   {
10    double upperX, upperY, stepX, stepY;
11    int width, height;
12    int startCol=0;
13    int startRow=0;
14  };
15  // ************************************************************
16  const int DEVICEALLOC = 64;
17  const int CPUALLOC = 16;
18
19  class LoadMonitor
20  {
21  private:
22    mutex l;
```

```
23      int width, height;
24      double upperX, upperY;//, lowerX, lowerY;
25      int currentCol = 0;
26      int currentRow = 0;
27      double xStep, yStep;
28   public:
29      LoadMonitor (double uX, double uY, double lX, double lY, int w, ←
            int h):upperX (uX), upperY (uY), width (w), height (h)
30      {
31        xStep = (lX - upperX) / width;
32        yStep = (upperY - lY) / height;
33      }
34      bool getNextBlock (BlockDescr & d, bool isDevice = false);
35   };
36   //—————————————————————————
37   // returns true if the d structure is populated. False if work is ←
        done
38   bool LoadMonitor::getNextBlock (BlockDescr & d, bool isDevice)
39   {
40      lock_guard < mutex > lg (l);
41
42      if (currentRow == height)
43        return false;
44
45      // row-wise partitioning
46      d.upperY = upperY - yStep * currentRow;
47      d.upperX = upperX ;
48      d.stepX = xStep;
49      d.stepY = yStep;
50      d.width = width;
51      d.startRow = currentRow;
52      if (isDevice)
53        {
54          if (height - currentRow < DEVICEALLOC)
55            return false;
56          currentRow += DEVICEALLOC;
57          d.height = DEVICEALLOC;
58        }
59      else
60        {
61          int toAlloc = (height - currentRow >= CPUALLOC) ? CPUALLOC : ←
              height - currentRow;
62
63          currentRow+=toAlloc;
64          d.height = toAlloc;
65        }
66
67      return true;
68   }
69   . . .
```

Each thread calls the getNextBlock method (definition starts at line 38) of a shared LoadMonitor instance, which is initialized with the image dimensions and the opposing corners' (upper-left and lower-right) coordinates in the complex plane (constructor on lines 29–33).

The code is instrumented so that the load collectively assigned to the CPU cores or the GPU can be reported at the end. The counter variables defined on lines 5 and 6 are used towards this goal. Finding how the load shifts to the CPU or the GPU based on the load characteristics, i.e., which device will dominate in load consumption, is left as an exercise.

The type of device (CPU or GPU) controlled by the calling thread is passed as a parameter to the getNextBlock method, allowing the monitor to assign DEVICEALLOC rows at a time to the GPU or CPUALLOC (or less if not enough remain, as per line 61) rows at a time to a CPU thread. The monitor fills in an instance of the BlockDescr structure (defined on lines 8–14) as supplied by the calling thread to indicate the part of the target image assigned.

The values of the DEVICEALLOC and CPUALLOC symbolic constants are just educated guesses.

Finally, getNextBlock returns false if all the image parts have been assigned, prompting the termination of the calling thread.

The remaining modifications over the OpenCL program in Listing 7.21 are shown below:

Listing 7.23: Host code for the combined calculation of the Mandelbrot set by host and device: the C++ threads and the OpenCL front-end.

```
70  // File : mandelOpenCL_hybrid_Cpp11/main.cpp
71  . . .
72  //****************************************************************
73  int diverge(double cx, double cy) {
74  . . .
75  }
76  //----------------------------------------------------------------
77  void hostThread (shared_ptr < QImage > img, shared_ptr < LoadMonitor↩
        > mon)
78  {
79    BlockDescr work;
80    while (mon->getNextBlock (work))
81      {
82      cpuBlocks.fetch_add(1);
83      for (int i = 0; i < work.width; i++)
84          for (int j = 0; j < work.height; j++) {
85              double tempx, tempy;
86              tempx = work.upperX + i * work.stepX;
87              tempy = work.upperY - j * work.stepY;
88              int color = diverge(tempx, tempy);
89              img->setPixel(work.startCol + i, work.startRow + j, qRgb↩
                  (256 - color, 256 - color, 256 - color));
90          }
91      }
```

```
 92    }
 93
 94    // *********************************************************
 95    // OpenCL related parts
 96
 97    // *********************************************************
 98    // Host front-end function that allocates the memory and launches ←
          the GPU kernel
 99    void hostFE (shared_ptr < QImage > img, shared_ptr < LoadMonitor > ←
          mon)
100    {
101      BlockDescr work;
102      cl_int errNum;
103      cl_device_id devID;
104      cl_event kernComplete;
105
106      // context and queue setup
107      setupDevice (cont, q, NULL, devID, CL_DEVICE_TYPE_GPU);
108
109      //--------------------------------------------------
110      // read program source and build it
111      if (!setupProgramAndKernel (devID, cont, "kernel.cl", pr, "←
          mandelKernel", kern))
112        {
113          if (pr != 0)
114            printf ("Error: %s\n", getCompilationError (pr, devID));
115          cleanUp ();
116          return;
117        }
118
119      // check if SVM is supported
120      char attr[20];
121      size_t attrLen;
122      clGetDeviceInfo (devID, CL_DEVICE_VERSION, 20, (void *) attr, &←
          attrLen);
123      if (attr[7] == '1')                     // Character at position 7 is the ←
          OpenCL major version
124        OCL2support = false;
125
126      int threadX, threadY;
127
128      //--------------------------------------------------
129      // main thread loop
130      while (mon->getNextBlock (work, true))
131        {
132          gpuBlocks++;
133          // memory allocation and some initializations done only during←
              the first iteration
134          if (data == 0)
135            {
136              if (OCL2support)
```

```
137          data = (unsigned char *) clSVMAlloc (cont, ↵
                 CL_MEM_READ_WRITE, work.width * work.height * sizeof↵
                 (unsigned char), 0);
138        else
139          {
140            d_data = clCreateBuffer (cont, CL_MEM_READ_WRITE, work↵
                 .width * work.height * sizeof (unsigned char), ↵
                 NULL, &errNum);
141            data = new unsigned char[work.width * work.height];
142          }
143        threadX = (int) ceil (work.width * 1.0 / THR_BLK_X);
144        threadY = (int) ceil (work.height * 1.0 / THR_BLK_Y);
145        threadX = ((threadX + BLOCK_SIDE - 1) / BLOCK_SIDE) * ↵
                 BLOCK_SIDE;        // make sure that a work item divides ↵
                 the idxSpace evenly
146        threadY = ((threadY + BLOCK_SIDE - 1) / BLOCK_SIDE) * ↵
                 BLOCK_SIDE;
147      }
148
149    if (OCL2support)
150      errNum = clSetKernelArgSVMPointer (kern, 0, data);
151    else
152      errNum = clSetKernelArg (kern, 0, sizeof (cl_mem), (void *) ↵
             &d_data);
153
154    errNum |= clSetKernelArg (kern, 1, sizeof (double), (void *) &↵
           work.upperX);
155    errNum |= clSetKernelArg (kern, 2, sizeof (double), (void *) &↵
           work.upperY);
156    errNum |= clSetKernelArg (kern, 3, sizeof (double), (void *) &↵
           work.stepX);
157    errNum |= clSetKernelArg (kern, 4, sizeof (double), (void *) &↵
           work.stepY);
158    errNum |= clSetKernelArg (kern, 5, sizeof (int), (void *) &↵
           work.width);
159    errNum |= clSetKernelArg (kern, 6, sizeof (int), (void *) &↵
           work.height);
160    if (isError (errNum, "Failed to set kernel parameters"))
161      {
162        cleanUp ();
163        return ;
164      }
165
166    size_t idxSpace[] = { threadX, threadY };
167    size_t localWorkSize[] = { BLOCK_SIDE, BLOCK_SIDE };
168
169    // launch GPU kernel
170    errNum = clEnqueueNDRangeKernel (q, kern, 2, NULL, idxSpace, ↵
           localWorkSize, 0, NULL, &kernComplete);
171    if (isError (errNum, "Failed to launch kernel"))
172      {
173        cleanUp ();
```

```
174              return;
175            }
176
177        if (!OCL2support)
178          errNum = clEnqueueReadBuffer (q, d_data, CL_TRUE, 0, work.↵
                  width * work.height * sizeof (unsigned char), data, 0, ↵
                  NULL, NULL);
179        else
180          {
181            //─────────────────────────────────
182            // wait for the kernel to finish
183            cl_event evlist[] = { kernComplete };
184            errNum = clWaitForEvents (1, evlist);
185            if (isError (errNum, "Failed to wait for event"))
186              {
187                cleanUp ();
188                return ;
189              }
190          }
191
192        //─────────────────────────────────
193        //copy results into QImage object
194        for (int j = 0; j < work.height; j++)
195          for (int i = 0; i < work.width; i++)
196            {
197              int color = data[j * work.width + i];
198              img->setPixel (work.startCol + i, work.startRow + j, ↵
                    qRgb (256 - color, 256 - color, 256 - color));
199            }
200      }
201    // clean up allocated memory
202    cleanUp ();
203 }
204
205 // ************************************************************
206 int main (int argc, char *argv[])
207 {
208   double upperCornerX, upperCornerY;
209   double lowerCornerX, lowerCornerY;
210
211   upperCornerX = atof (argv[1]);
212   upperCornerY = atof (argv[2]);
213   lowerCornerX = atof (argv[3]);
214   lowerCornerY = atof (argv[4]);
215
216   int imgX = 3840, imgY = 2160;
217   if (argc > 6)
218     {
219       imgX = atoi (argv[5]);
220       imgY = atoi (argv[6]);
221     }
222
```

```
223    shared_ptr < QImage > img = make_shared < QImage > (imgX, imgY, ↩
           QImage::Format_RGB32);
224    shared_ptr < LoadMonitor > mon = make_shared < LoadMonitor > (↩
           upperCornerX, upperCornerY, lowerCornerX, lowerCornerY, imgX, ↩
           imgY);
225
226    // create and start the host threads
227    int numHostThr = thread::hardware_concurrency () - 1; // One will ↩
           be used to control the device
228    unique_ptr < thread > hostThr[numHostThr];
229    for (int i = 0; i < numHostThr; i++)
230      hostThr[i] = make_unique < thread > (hostThread, img, mon);
231
232    hostFE (img, mon);                    // use the master thread to control ↩
           the device
233
234    // wait for remaining threads to finish
235    for (int i = 0; i < numHostThr; i++)
236      hostThr[i]->join ();
237
238    img->save ("mandel.png", "PNG", 0);
239    . . .
```

The main function (starting at line 206) begins by creating the two objects shared by all the threads, i.e., the QImage instance for managing the image data (line 223) and the LoadMonitor instance for partitioning the load (line 224). A number of threads equal to the number of logical cores minus the one handling the device/GPU (line 227) is created and initialized by the loop of lines 229–230.

The CPU threads execute the hostThread function (lines 77–92). The latter uses a while loop to call the monitor's getNextBlock method and processes its assigned set of rows with the nested loops of lines 83–90.

The main thread is used to manage the device by calling the host front-end hostFE function on line 232. The hostFE function (lines 99–203) goes through the same steps as the hostFE function of Listing 7.21, with the exception that operations are split into two groups: a group for device setup and code compilation (lines 107–124) and another group inside the "monitor-polling" while loop of lines 130–200 that sets up the kernel parameters, invokes the kernel, and collects the results.

7.11.3 Hybrid calculation of the Mandelbrot set using OpenCL on both host and device

A feature that sets OpenCL apart from CUDA is that OpenCL can also be used to target CPUs. The only thing that is required is a driver, as explained in Section 7.1.

Equipped with a CPU driver, we can have the functional equivalent of the previous program, by *explicitly* defining only two threads: one for handling the OpenCL device deployment and one for handling the OpenCL CPU execution. The Intel OpenCL driver can be used for that purpose (available at https://software.intel.com/content/www/us/en/develop/articles/opencl-drivers.html, last accessed December 2021).

The code in the following listing does exactly this, by encapsulating all the OpenCL-related variables and code inside the HostFE class which starts at line 22. The goal is to be able to instantiate two objects from this class: one for the CPU (line 76) and one for the GPU (line 78). Line 76 creates the first unnamed object that is responsible for instantiating an OpenCL CPU device (CL_DEVICE_TYPE_CPU) and passes it to a thread. The main thread handles the GPU device instantiation by calling the operator() method of the second object on line 79.

The BlockDescr structure is identical to the one reported in Listing 7.22. The only difference for the LoadMonitor class is that there is no distinction between device and host anymore when getNextBlock is called, as the load to be given to the CPU concerns all the cores and not a single one.

Listing 7.24: Host code for the combined calculation of the Mandelbrot set using hybrid execution.

```
1   // File : mandelOpenCL_hybrid/main.cpp
2   . . .
3   bool LoadMonitor::getNextBlock (BlockDescr & d)
4   {
5     lock_guard < mutex > lg (l);
6
7     if (currentCol == width)
8       return false;
9
10    d.upperY = upperY;
11    d.upperX = upperX + xStep * currentCol;
12    d.stepX = xStep;
13    d.stepY = yStep;
14    d.height = height;
15    d.startCol = currentCol;
16    int toAlloc = (width - currentCol >= DEVICEALLOC) ? DEVICEALLOC : ←
          width - currentCol;
17    currentCol+=toAlloc;
18    d.width = toAlloc;
19    return true;
20  }
21  // ************************************************************
22  class HostFE
23  {
24  private:
25    cl_context cont = 0;        // initialize for cleanup check
26    cl_command_queue q = 0;
27    cl_program pr = 0;
28    cl_kernel kern = 0;
29    bool OCL2support = true;
30    unsigned char *data = 0;   // image data
31    cl_mem d_data = 0;         // image data if OpenCL 2.0 is not ←
          supported
32    shared_ptr < QImage > img;
33    shared_ptr < LoadMonitor > mon;
34    cl_device_type t;
```

```
35
36   public:
37     int colsProcessed=0;
38     HostFE(shared_ptr < QImage > img, shared_ptr < LoadMonitor > mon, ↵
           cl_device_type t)
39     {
40         this ->img=img;
41         this ->mon=mon;
42         this ->t=t;
43     }
44     void operator()();
45     void cleanUp();
46   };
47
48   //─────────────────────────────────────────────
49   void HostFE::cleanUp ()
50   {
51     . . .
52   }
53
54   // *************************************************************
55   // Host front-end function that allocates the memory and launches ↵
          the GPU kernel
56   void HostFE::operator()()
57   {
58     BlockDescr work;
59     cl_int errNum;
60     cl_device_id devID;
61     cl_event kernComplete;
62
63     // context and queue setup
64     setupDevice (cont, q, NULL, devID, t);
65     . . .
66   }
67
68   // *************************************************************
69   int main (int argc, char *argv[])
70   {
71     . . .
72     shared_ptr < QImage > img = make_shared < QImage > (imgX, imgY, ↵
           QImage::Format_RGB32);
73     shared_ptr < LoadMonitor > mon = make_shared < LoadMonitor > (↵
           upperCornerX, upperCornerY, lowerCornerX, lowerCornerY, imgX, ↵
           imgY);
74
75     // create a thread for handling the host as an OpenCL device
76     thread hostThr(std::move(HostFE(img, mon, CL_DEVICE_TYPE_CPU)));
77
78     HostFE gpu(img, mon, CL_DEVICE_TYPE_GPU);
79     gpu(); // use the master thread to control the GPU device
80
81     // wait for CPU handling thread to finish
```

```
82    hostThr.join ();
83    img->save ("mandel.png", "PNG", 0);
84    . . .
```

The `hostFE` function of Listing 7.23 is now the `operator()` method of the `HostFE` class. This is the reason why the rest of the code is not shown. The only difference concerns the device to be targeted for setup on line 64. The device is determined upon construction of a `HostFE` instance as seen on lines 76 and 78. The `cleanUp` method starting at line 49 is also a verbatim copy of the corresponding function shown previously.

Listing 7.24 clearly shows that hybrid computation can be easily supported with very little extra effort beyond the construction of the OpenCL code. The benefits of hybrid computation are of course application-specific.

7.11.4 Performance comparison

The Mandelbrot set is only used as motivational eye candy in this book, but having all the different implementations discussed above gives us the ability to perform some limited form of performance comparison between the software platforms covered so far.

The results presented here should by no means be used as a definitive guide for choosing one platform or design technique over another. Optimization was never a priority in any of the above implementations. And the mix of double-precision arithmetic with large data volume transfers is never a good one for discrete GPUs.

Fig. 7.12 shows the average execution time over 100 runs, using the same software and hardware setup as in Section 7.11.1. The combined use of the CPU and the GPU produces a welcome performance boost. However, the OpenCL-for-all version shows a number of "anomalies": the execution for HD resolution takes longer than in the plain OpenCL case, and the execution in 8k is way faster than the OpenCL plus C++11 version!

The first irregularity can be attributed to the cost of initializing the OpenCL runtimes and compiling the kernels. In the OpenCL plus C++11 version, the same cost prevents the GPU from processing any significant part of the load. In fact, the computation takes place almost exclusively on the CPU in HD resolution. In the 8k scenario, it is probably the highly optimized Intel OpenCL library that helps boost performance beyond what the "plain-vanilla" C++11 threads can accomplish by taking advantage of vector instruction sets such as AVX2.

Exercises

1. Write a device query program that will report all the OpenCL devices present in your computer, along with the version of OpenCL they support, the number of compute units, the size of the global memory, and the size of the local memory available in each one.

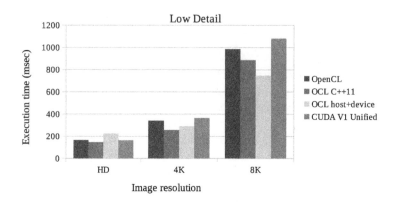

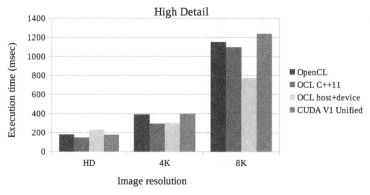

FIGURE 7.12

Average execution time on a machine equipped with a Ryzen 3900x CPU and an RTX 2060 Super GPU, using different software platforms for calculating the Mandelbrot set.

2. Implement the trapezoid rule integration technique in OpenMP for an arbitrary function $f()$. As explained in Section 3.7.2.2, the definite integral between $[a, b]$ of $f()$ can be approximated by the formula

$$h\left(\frac{f(a) + f(b)}{2} + \sum_{i=1}^{n-1} f(x_i)\right),$$

where n is the number of divisions and $h = \frac{b-a}{n}$. Explore the following possibilities. (a) Have the device calculate the target function's $f(x_i)$ values and the host accumulate the sum. (b) Have the device perform all the calculations, including the *reduction* of the final result. For the latter approach employ work group functions.

3. Use the solution of the previous exercise to calculate π. It is known that $\pi = 4\int_0^1 \frac{1}{x^2+1}dx$. Test your program with single and double floating point precision arithmetic. How does this change influence the accuracy and performance?

4. Write an OpenCL program to calculate the outer product of two vectors. If we have two vectors $U = (u_1, u_2, \ldots, u_n)$ and $V = (v_1, v_2, \ldots, v_m)$, their outer product is a matrix nxm:

$$U \otimes V = \begin{bmatrix} u_1v_1 & u_1v_2 & \ldots & u_1v_m \\ u_2v_1 & u_2v_2 & \ldots & u_2v_m \\ \vdots & \vdots & \ddots & \vdots \\ u_nv_1 & u_1v_2 & \ldots & u_nv_m \end{bmatrix}. \tag{7.2}$$

Make your program accept as command-line parameters the n and m sizes, so that you can experiment with different workloads.

5. Write an OpenCL program to calculate the inner product of two vectors. If we have two vectors $U = (u_1, u_2, \ldots, u_n)$ and $V = (v_1, v_2, \ldots, v_n)$, their inner or dot product is a scalar defined as the sum $U \cdot V = \sum_{i=1}^{n} u_i \cdot v_i$. Experiment with two kernels: one that assigns one work item per product $u_i \cdot v_i$ and one that assigns multiple products per work item. Which of the two kernels performs best?

Also try running your program with different work group sizes, e.g., 32, 64, 128, 256, 512. How is the execution time affected?

6. Write an OpenCL program for calculating the histogram of a grayscale image. Use an OpenCL image object to represent the input data. Use one work item per pixel.

7. Modify the program of the previous exercise so that you process multiple pixels per work item.

8. Modify the histogram calculation of the previous exercise so that your kernel uses local memory to speed up the process. How does your new version compare with the previous one in terms of execution time?

9. Create OpenCL implementations of the gsl_stats_mean() and gsl_stats_vari-ance() functions offered by the GNU Scientific Library that produce the mean and variance statistics of a supplied array. To avoid issues with 64-bit extension support, you can settle for the following signatures:

```
float gsl_stats_mean (const float DATA[], // Pointer to input ↩
      data
                      size_t STRIDE,     // Step used to read ↩
                          the input. Normally this should be set↩
                          to 1.
                      size_t N);         // Size of DATA array
float gsl_stats_variance (const float DATA[], // Same as above.
                      size_t STRIDE,
                      size_t N);
```

10. In the filtering example of Section 7.8, two kernels are employed in order to get the filtered data in order in the output array. Solve the problem using one kernel by relaxing the keeping-the-order constraint.

11. Conduct an experiment to find out how changing the image resolution and/or the values of the symbolic constants DEVICEALLOC and CPUALLOC influences the distribution of the load in the hybrid Mandelbrot set calculation program of Section 7.11.2.

12. The hybrid Mandelbrot calculator of Section 7.11.3 partitions the target image row-wise. Modify the code so that the partitioning is done column-wise. As there are more columns than rows in an image, do you think this will allow for better load balancing and faster execution?

Higher-level parallel programming

Shared-memory programming: OpenMP

8

In this chapter you will:

- Learn how to use OpenMP compiler directives to introduce concurrency in a sequential program.

- Learn the most important OpenMP #pragma directives and associated clauses for controlling the concurrent constructs generated by the compiler.

- Understand which loops can be parallelized with OpenMP directives.

- Address the dependency issues that OpenMP-generated threads face using synchronization constructs.

- Learn how to use OpenMP to create function-parallel programs.

- Learn how to write thread-safe functions.

- Understand the issue of cache false-sharing and learn how to eliminate it.

- Learn how to use OpenMP to offload work to GPUs and/or take advantage of SIMD CPU extensions.

8.1 Introduction

Parallel program development is a tedious endeavor, even when it targets shared-memory machines. It requires careful planning and it is full of caveats. The use of patterns as the ones covered in Chapter 3 (e.g., producers–consumers) can help to a certain degree, but it is still an exercise outside the comfort zone of most programmers, who are usually accustomed to sequential programs only.

There is also the issue of the extensive library of existing sequential programs that drive the world's economic, industrial, and scientific institutions. How can this software take advantage of multicore hardware, without the need to rewrite it completely? A rewrite would face several hurdles, both cost- and correctness-wise. A parallel version of a sequential program must not only run faster, but also produce identical results as its sequential counterpart.

OpenMP is the answer to this problem: a technology capable of allowing the *incremental* conversion of sequential programs to parallel ones. OpenMP's support for C/C++ and Fortran is also evidence to its target audience. OpenMP stands for Open

Multi-Processing and it is an industry standard controlled by the OpenMP Architecture Review Board (ARB), which is a nonprofit corporation. The latest version of the OpenMP standard[1] is currently 5.2, published in November 2021. In the latest iterations of the standard, new directives have been introduced to allow OpenMP to take advantage of all the hardware features offered by a platform, including SIMD execution on CPUs and offloading work to co-processors such as GPUs.

As far as GNU C++ compiler support is concerned, given that this is the development platform used by our examples, as of GCC 6.1 there is full support for the OpenMP 4.5 specification, whereas OpenMP 5.0 has been partially supported since GCC 9.1. GPU offloading support is a bit sketchy, given that CUDA started to provide support for GCC 9.x only in CUDA 11.

In OpenMP, the compiler is responsible for handling all the "ugly" implementation details associated with spawning, initiating, and terminating threads. The trade-off – typical of similar approaches – is that programmer control is sacrificed for convenience. The OpenMP Application Program Interface (API) consists of compiler directives, library routines, and environment variables. OpenMP uses what it calls **work-sharing constructs** to direct the compiler to start threads and have them perform a specific task. The work-sharing constructs range from automated loop parallelization to explicit task description.

In an OpenMP program the execution profile follows the Globally Sequential Locally Parallel structure (see Section 2.4). In effect, we have a sequential program that – ideally – has its most time-consuming parts parallelized by the compiler, with the elementary assistance of the programmer. Obviously, this is not the most flexible model for introducing concurrency, but it works well with existing sequential programs and it is also faster to produce results in terms of development cost.

8.2 Your first OpenMP program

As mentioned in the introduction, OpenMP relies on the compiler to generate threads. Nowadays, most C/C++ compilers offer OpenMP support, often with the specification of an appropriate switch.

The instructions to the compiler come in the form of `#pragma` preprocessor directives. Pragma directives allow a programmer to access compiler-specific preprocessor extensions. For example, a common use of pragmas is in the management of include files. The following pragma directive:

```
#pragma once
```

will prevent the compiler from including the same file more than once. It is equivalent to having "include guards" in each file, as in:

```
#ifndef __FILE_H_
#define __FILE_H_

. . . // code

#endif
```

The following program illustrates some of the essential components that make up an OpenMP program, namely:

- The inclusion of the header file that declares the OpenMP library functions (line 4).
- A #pragma omp directive (line 12). The #pragma omp parallel line launches multiple threads, each executing the *block of statements* that follows. Pragma directives typically have a number of optional clauses that modify their behavior. Clauses can be comma- or white space-separated. In our example, the num_threads clause modifies the number of threads that will be spawned.
- OpenMP library function calls to inspect or modify the state of the OpenMP runtime. The omp_get_thread_num() function on line 13 returns the ID of the thread executing that statement. This can be used to diversify the action of each thread, in a similar fashion like the one examined in Chapter 3.

The parallel directive is called in OpenMP jargon a **single program, multiple data** (SPMD) directive, as we have the same program code run by multiple threads, each applying its logic on a separate dataset.

Listing 8.1: "Hello World" in OpenMP.

```
1   // File : hello.cpp
2   #include <iostream>
3   #include <stdlib.h>
4   #include <omp.h>
5
6   using namespace std;
7
8   int main (int argc, char **argv)
9   {
10      int numThr = atoi (argv[1]);
11
12   #pragma omp parallel num_threads(numThr)
13      cout << "Hello from thread " << omp_get_thread_num () << endl;
14
15      return 0;
16   }
```

The compilation of this sample program can be done with GNU C++:

```
$ g++ hello.cpp -fopenmp -o hello
```

with -fopenmp being the switch that activates the OpenMP extensions. If you are using a different compiler, you should check the corresponding documentation for the appropriate switch (e.g., the Intel Compiler requires an -openmp switch). The output of a run is similar to:

```
$ ./hello 4
Hello from thread Hello from thread Hello from thread 12

0
Hello from thread 3
```

with the output out-of-order and mangled, as there is no control on when each thread executes and there is no coordination for access to the console. As the "Hello from thread" string is output at a different instance than the value returned from the omp_get_thread_num() call, they can become separated. The only thing common between the output of multiple runs would be that there always are as many lines as the number of threads.

But how exactly does the program in Listing 8.1 execute? OpenMP programs have a Globally Sequential Locally Parallel structure (see Section 2.4), which means there is a main sequential flow of control that forks to multiple threads. These threads subsequently join back to the main thread, and this process can be repeated. This is also known as fork-join parallelism. The operating system, upon launching the hello program, starts a **master thread** that will – based on the pragma directives – spawn more threads to execute in parallel parts of the program. These parallel parts are called **parallel regions** and these threads are called **child threads**. Collectively, the master and child threads constitute a **team of threads**. When the flow of execution transitions from a parallel region back to a sequential part of the program, the master thread waits for all the child threads to terminate, in what is effectively an implicit **barrier**. Fig. 8.1 visualizes this process in the form of a UML sequence diagram.

OpenMP makes a distinction between regions and constructs. A region is the *dynamic* sequence of statements produced during the execution of an OpenMP construct. A construct is the combination of an OpenMP pragma directive and the structured block of statements that follows it. Hence, a construct may be part of multiple regions based on the program flow.

During the execution of a region, a thread has access to a set of variables that are either shared with other threads or private/exclusive to that thread. All these variables are collectively called a **data environment** in OpenMP jargon. Data environments exist for any computing device present in a heterogeneous platform (e.g., one with accelerators), including the host. Also the main program thread that executes outside any OpenMP construct has its own data environment.

Parallel constructs can be nested, i.e., we can have nested parallel pragmas, in which case a child thread can spawn more threads. This would result in a tree hierarchy of threads, with the master thread at the root of the tree. OpenMP uses tree terminology to describe the relationships between the threads, such as parent, child, ancestor, or descendant.

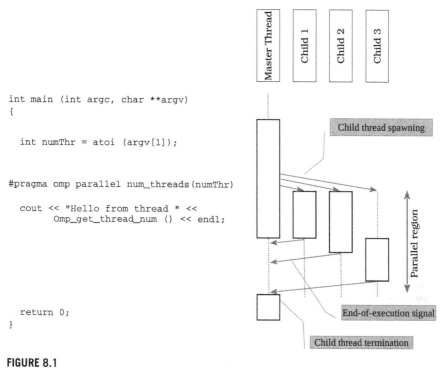

```
int main (int argc, char **argv)
{

  int numThr = atoi (argv[1]);


#pragma omp parallel num_threads(numThr)

  cout << "Hello from thread " <<
       Omp_get_thread_num () << endl;




  return 0;
}
```

FIGURE 8.1

UML sequence diagram of a possible execution of our "Hello World" program with four threads.

OpenMP will by default use as big a team of threads as the number of available cores in the system. The size of the team can be controlled:

- **Universally**, i.e., for all OpenMP programs, via the OMP_NUM_THREADS environment variable:

```
$ echo ${OMP_NUM_THREADS}  # to query the value
$ export OMP_NUM_THREADS=4 # to set it in BASH
```

- At the **program level**: via the omp_set_num_threads function:

```
void omp_set_num_threads(int n); // size of the team of threads (↩
    IN)
```

The omp_get_num_threads call returns the active threads in a parallel region. If it is called in a sequential part it returns 1.

- At the **pragma level**: via the num_threads clause, as seen in Listing 8.1, line 12.

The lower an item is in the above list, i.e., the more specific it is, the higher precedence it has.

All the above actions for controlling the size of the team of threads are ultimately modifying an internal control variable (ICV) of the OpenMP runtime. In fact, OpenMP comes with a large collection of ICVs that control the various aspects of converting the pragma directives into executable code. For example, the size of the team of threads can be dynamically adjusted by OpenMP during execution. A related Boolean ICV exists for enabling or disabling this feature, and this ICV can be modified by calling the `omp_set_dynamic` function, with a parameter that evaluates to true/false.

Parallel regions are allowed to be nested, e.g., have one parallel region inside another or inside a function called by a parallel region. The question is what happens then with regard to threads? Do we have the generation of a new team of threads to handle the new parallel region? The answer is that it actually depends on a related ICV, which can be controlled/queried with the following functions:

```
// Sets the maximum number of active nested parallel regions
void omp_set_max_active_levels( int n );
//------------------------------------------------
// Gets the maximum number of active nested parallel regions
int omp_get_max_active_levels( );
```

If a parallel region exceeds the maximum nested level, no new threads are generated and the nested parallel region is executed by a single thread. The effect of `omp_set_max_active_levels` is actually implementation-specific: if the supplied parameter exceeds the OpenMP's implementation limit, then it is ignored. For example, the program in Listing 8.2 will produce the following output on a Ryzen 9 3900x CPU with 24 hardware threads:

```
$ g++ −fopenmp nested.cpp −o nested    # Compilation with GCC
$ ./nested 2
Parallel at lvl 0 with thread team of 24
Parallel at lvl 1 with thread team of 1
Parallel at lvl 2 with thread team of 1
$ icc −fopenmp nested.cpp −o nested    # Compilation with Intel ↩
    compiler in GCC compatibility mode
$ ./nested 2
Parallel at lvl 0 with thread team of 24
Parallel at lvl 1 with thread team of 24
Parallel at lvl 2 with thread team of 1
```

Listing 8.2: A program for testing the number of threads generated in nested parallel regions.

```
17  // File : nested.cpp
18  #include <omp.h>
19  . . .
20  void testPar (int curLvl, int maxLvl)
21  {
22    if (curLvl == maxLvl)
23      return;
```

```
24        else
25          {
26   #pragma omp parallel
27          {
28   #pragma omp single
29            {
30                cout << "Parallel at lvl " << curLvl << " with thread team←
                      of " << omp_get_num_threads () << endl;
31                testPar (curLvl + 1, maxLvl);
32            }
33          }
34        }
35   }
36
37   int main (int argc, char **argv)
38   {
39     int nestedLvl = atoi (argv[1]);     // read the parameter to use in ←
             omp_set_max_active_levels from CLI
40     omp_set_max_active_levels (nestedLvl);
41     testPar (0, nestedLvl + 1);          // recursive execution for a ←
             nestedLvl+1 depth
42     return 0;
43   }
```

The `single` pragma directive on line 28 above makes the associated block execute by one thread only. This is covered in more detail in Section 8.6.

Compilers that do not support particular pragmas ignore the corresponding statements. This means that it is possible for an OpenMP program to be compiled by a non-supporting compiler, albeit without concurrency support. So, it is critical that one does not forget the compiler switches that activate OpenMP! The program in Listing 8.1 would fail to compile in that case, because the code in the `omp.h` header file does not allow the declaration of the OpenMP library functions if OpenMP is not enabled, causing in turn a compilation error (an undefined reference to "omp_get_thread_num").

8.3 Variable scope

When a parallel region is executing, each of the threads in the team execute a copy of the designated block of statements. The question is: what kind of access do threads have to the variables declared outside the block? How about the variables that are declared inside the block? Are these variables shared or not? And if they are shared, how can we coordinate access to them so that there is no race condition?

Outside the parallel regions, normal scope rules apply. OpenMP specifies the following types of variables:

• **Shared**: All variables declared outside a parallel region are by default shared.

- **Private**: All variables declared inside a parallel region are allocated in the runtime stack of each thread. So we have as many copies of these variables as the size of the thread team. Private variables are destroyed upon termination of a parallel region.
- **Reduction**: A special type of shared variable that is actually a private one! The contradiction is not real: a reduction variable gets individual copies for each thread running the corresponding parallel region. Upon termination of the parallel region, an operation is applied to the individual copies (e.g., summation) to produce the value that will be stored in the shared variable.

The default scope of variables can be modified by clauses in the pragma lines.

An example will help us illustrate the purpose of the above list. We start from a sequential program that calculates the definite integral of a given function:

Listing 8.3: Sequential program for calculating the integral of a function.

```cpp
1   // File : integration_seq.cpp
2   . . .
3   //-----------------------------------------------
4   double testf (double x)
5   {
6     return x * x + 2 * sin (x);
7   }
8
9   //-----------------------------------------------
10  double integrate (double st, double en, int div, double (*f) (double ↩
        ))
11  {
12    double localRes = 0;
13    double step = (en - st) / div;
14    double x;
15    x = st;
16    localRes = f (st) + f (en);
17    localRes /= 2;
18    for (int i = 1; i < div; i++)
19      {
20        x += step;
21        localRes += f (x);
22      }
23    localRes *= step;
24
25    return localRes;
26  }
27
28  //-----------------------------------------------
29  int main (int argc, char *argv[])
30  {
31    if (argc == 1)
32      {
33        cerr << "Usage " << argv[0] << " start end divisions\n";
34        exit (1);
```

```
35      }
36      double start, end;
37      int divisions;
38      start = atof (argv[1]);
39      end = atof (argv[2]);
40      divisions = atoi (argv[3]);
41
42      double finalRes = integrate (start, end, divisions, testf);
43
44      cout << finalRes << endl;
45      return 0;
46  }
```

There is nothing special to mention about Listing 8.3, other than that it is a straight-forward implementation of the trapezoid rule. A few simple optimizations in the loop of lines 18–22 avoid repeated calculations (see Section 3.7.2.2 for more information on the trapezoid rule). The program reads three command-line parameters, two for the endpoints of the integration interval and one for the number of subdivisions to use in the calculation.

Any function can be used for testing. The one shown in Listing 8.3 has a known solution, $\int (x^2 + 2 \cdot \sin(x)) \, dx = \frac{1}{3}(x^3 - 6 \cdot \cos(x))$, which makes the verification of the computed results easier.

In the following section we examine three possible OpenMP derivatives of this program, progressing towards a version that better captures the ethos of OpenMP.

8.3.1 OpenMP integration V.0: manual partitioning

Partitioning the work done by the `integrate()` function in Listing 8.3, line 10, could be done by calling the function multiple times from different threads, but with different parameters. Effectively it is like breaking up the integration interval in as many pieces as the number of threads N, as seen in Fig. 8.2. We can use the thread ID returned from the `omp_get_thread_num()` library function to derive distinct parameters for each thread $i \in [0, N-1]$, using the formulas

$$local\,Start = start + ID \cdot local\,Div \cdot step \qquad (8.1)$$

and

$$local\,End = local\,Start + local\,Div \cdot step, \qquad (8.2)$$

where $local\,Div$ is the number of divisions assigned to each thread: $local\,Div = \frac{divisions}{N}$.

The resulting program is shown in Listing 8.4, with modifications pertaining only to the invocation of the `integrate()` function, which is now located inside a parallel region.

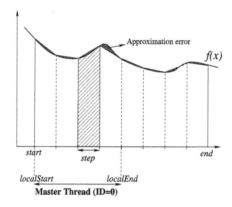

FIGURE 8.2

An illustration of how the trapezoid rule can be applied in parallel, by evenly breaking up the integration interval [*start*, *end*], among the team of threads (made up of two threads in our figure). The red (dark gray in print version) area represents the approximation error.

Listing 8.4: OpenMP-based program for calculating the integral of a function. This version suffers from a race condition. Only the changes from Listing 8.3 are shown.

```cpp
// File : integration_omp_V0.cpp
. . .
//————————————————————————————————————
int main (int argc, char *argv[])
{
  if (argc == 1)
    {
      cerr << "Usage " << argv[0] << " start end divisions\n";
      exit (1);
    }
  double start, end;
  int divisions;
  start = atof (argv[1]);
  end = atof (argv[2]);
  divisions = atoi (argv[3]);

  // get the number of threads for next parallel region
  int N = omp_get_max_threads ();
  divisions = (divisions / N) * N;    // make sure divisions is a ↵
      multiple of N
  double step = (end − start) / divisions;

  double finalRes = 0;
#pragma omp parallel
  {
     int localDiv = divisions / N;
     int ID = omp_get_thread_num ();
     double localStart = start + ID * localDiv * step;
     double localEnd = localStart + localDiv * step;
```

```
29        finalRes += integrate (localStart, localEnd, localDiv, testf);
30    }
31
32    cout << finalRes << endl;
33
34    return 0;
35 }
```

The block between lines 24 and 30 is executed by multiple threads, all having (by default) shared access to the variables declared outside: `start`, `end`, `step`, `finalRes`, etc. Each thread retrieves its own ID (the master thread's ID is always 0) on line 26 and proceeds to calculate the limits of its own part of the integration interval (lines 27 and 28).

The number of threads that will be used in a parallel region, in the absence of a modifier (e.g., a `num_threads` clause), can be queried with the `omp_get_max_threads()` function, as seen on line 18. The reasoning behind lines 18 and 19 is that `divisions` must be a multiple of the number of threads. Otherwise the `step` variable will not match the `localDiv` subdivisions used by each thread to cover its part of the integration interval.

All the variables declared inside the parallel block are private, and they cease to exist once the parallel region terminates. For this reason, we need one or more shared scope variables so that the calculated partial integrals from line 29 can be saved and made available beyond the block. For this purpose, we are using the `finalRes` variable, but there is a catch: there is no coordination between the threads. The resulting race condition makes our first attempt a failure! But there is an easy fix, as shown in the next section.

8.3.2 OpenMP integration V.1: manual partitioning without a race condition

The race condition of Listing 8.4 can be fixed if each thread could store the results it calculates at a separate repository: the `partial` shared array defined on line 24 of Listing 8.5 holds as many elements as the size of the thread team. Line 31 uses a thread's ID to store its partial result to its "own" array element. Once the parallel block terminates, we only need to *reduce* the partial results to the final one, via the loop of lines 35–37.

Listing 8.5: OpenMP-based program for calculating the integral of a function, with a shared array holding per-thread partial results. Changes relative to Listing 8.3 are limited to the `main` function of the program.

```
1 // File : integration_omp_V1.cpp
2 . . .
3 //─────────────────────────────
4 int main (int argc, char *argv[])
5 {
6
7    if (argc == 1)
```

```
8     {
9         cerr << "Usage " << argv[0] << " start end divisions\n";
10        exit (1);
11    }
12    double start, end;
13    int divisions;
14    start = atof (argv[1]);
15    end = atof (argv[2]);
16    divisions = atoi (argv[3]);
17
18    // get the number of threads for next parallel region
19    int N = omp_get_max_threads ();
20    divisions = (divisions / N) * N;      // make sure divisions is a ↩
          multiple of N
21    double step = (end − start) / divisions;
22
23    // allocate memory for the partial results
24    unique_ptr< double[] > partial = make_unique< double[] >(N);
25 #pragma omp parallel
26    {
27        int localDiv = divisions / N;
28        int ID = omp_get_thread_num ();
29        double localStart = start + ID * localDiv * step;
30        double localEnd = localStart + localDiv * step;
31        partial[ID] = integrate (localStart, localEnd, localDiv, testf);
32    }
33
34    // reduction step
35    double finalRes = partial[0];
36    for (int i = 1; i < N; i++)
37        finalRes += partial[i];
38
39    cout << finalRes << endl;
40
41    return 0;
42 }
```

Listing 8.5 is a working program, but it does not really feel like this is the "easy way" to transform a sequential program into a multi-threaded one, as it required extensive changes to the original source code. Fortunately, OpenMP provides an easier way, as shown next.

8.3.3 OpenMP integration V.2: implicit partitioning with locking

Listing 8.5 constitutes a design approach that is familiar territory to programmers exposed to the traditional "manual" way of managing threads. But it is totally over-the-top for OpenMP! As the bulk of the work is typically done in loops, OpenMP provides a "parallel for" construct for breaking up the iterations of a `for` loop and assigning them to different threads. There are a number of conditions on the form of the loop, but we leave this discussion for a later section.

The `parallel for` construct can only be applied on a `for` loop (including nested `for` loops) and not a block of statements like the `omp parallel` pragma. By heading the `for` loop of line 14 in Listing 8.6, with a `parallel for` pragma, OpenMP launches multiple threads that execute the loop's iterations in some system-specific fashion (more details are given in Section 8.4.3).

The accumulation of the results (something that was problematic in the previous versions of the program) is accomplished via a shared local variable, `localRes`. This avoids the necessity of having to keep a separate partial sum for each thread, but we need to make any changes to the `localRes` variable atomic (otherwise we end up with a race condition like in Listing 8.4). A `critical` pragma is employed for this purpose, as shown on line 18 of Listing 8.6.

Listing 8.6: OpenMP-based program for calculating the integral of a function using a critical section. Only changes relative to Listing 8.3 are shown. The `main` function remains unchanged.

```
1   // File : integration_omp_V2.cpp
2   . . .
3   //----------------------------------------
4   double integrate (double st, double en, int div, double (*f) (double↩
        ))
5   {
6      double localRes = 0;
7      double step = (en - st) / div;
8      double x;
9      x = st;
10     localRes = f (st) + f (en);
11     localRes /= 2;
12
13  #pragma omp parallel for private(x)
14     for (int i = 1; i < div; i++)
15        {
16           x = st + i * step;
17           double temp = f (x);
18  #pragma omp critical
19           localRes += temp;
20        }
21
22     localRes *= step;
23
24     return localRes;
25  }
26  . . .
```

The `critical` construct restricts execution of the associated block to a single thread at a time.

The "private" clause in the `parallel for` construct of line 13 modifies the scope of variable "x." Note that "x" needs to be private as each thread must use it to obtain the value of the function to be integrated at a different location. In fact, it could also be declared inside the `for` loop with less drama.

There is also a more subtle change from Listing 8.3, involving the calculation of "x." The original statement shown below:

```
x += step;
```

is completely inappropriate, as it requires a shared variable and a sequential execution of the loop: there are **loop-carried dependencies**. If child thread 1 was assigned the iterations from, e.g., 100 to 200, during its first execution of the loop's body, it would not be able to get the proper value for "x," nor for any subsequent iterations. The form used on line 16 eliminates any such dependencies, as the value of "x" depends only on the loop variable and not the execution sequence. The role of dependencies in for loop parallelism is examined in more detail in Section 8.4.1.

8.3.4 OpenMP integration V.3: implicit partitioning with reduction

We can still improve on the version of the previous section: if each thread could calculate its own partial sum that we accumulate at the end of the loop, there would not be any reason to use the performance-sapping critical section. A reduction clause can help us achieve this, as shown in Listing 8.7.

Listing 8.7: OpenMP-based program for calculating the integral of a function using a *reduction variable*. Only changes relative to Listing 8.3 are shown. The main function remains unchanged.

```
1   // File : integration_omp_V3.cpp
2   . . .
3   //————————————————————————————————
4   double integrate (double st, double en, int div, double (*f) (double↩
        ))
5   {
6     double localRes = 0;
7     double step = (en − st) / div;
8     double x;
9     x = st;
10    localRes = f (st) + f (en);
11    localRes /= 2;
12
13  #pragma omp parallel for private(x) reduction(+: localRes)
14    for (int i = 1; i < div; i++)
15      {
16        x = st + i * step;
17        localRes += f (x);
18      }
19
20    localRes *= step;
21
22    return localRes;
23  }
24  . . .
```

Table 8.1 List of the available operators for the `reduction` clause, along with the initial value of the reduction variable's private copies [3]. Since OpenMP 5.2 the minus ("-") operator is deprecated.

Operator	Private copy initial value
+, −, |, ||, ^	0
*, &&	1
&	`0xFFFF...FFF`, i.e., all bits set to 1
max	Smallest possible number that can be represented by the type of the reduction variable
min	Largest possible number that can be represented by the type of the reduction variable

Note that `localRes` is defined outside the parallel region so it would be normally shared. However, by introducing the `reduction` clause on line 13, each thread creates a local copy of `localRes`, which is initialized to zero (the initial value depends on the reduction operation). Each thread accumulates its partial result in its local `localRes` copy. Upon termination of the parallel region, the operation specified in the reduction clause (addition in our example) is repeatedly applied to produce the final result, which is subsequently stored in the shared `localRes`.

The syntax of the `reduction` clause is:

```
reduction( reduction_identifier : variable_list)
```

where `variable_list` is a comma-separated list of variable identifiers and `reduction_identifier` is one of the following binary arithmetic and Boolean operators: +, *, −, &, &&, |, ||, ^, max, and min. The specified operator is applied between the private copies of the threads and the shared variable declared outside the parallel block, until a single value is obtained. The initial value of the private copies depends on the chosen operator, as shown in Table 8.1.

As an example of a different reduction operator, the following parallel for loop can be used to determine the maximum of an array of elements in parallel:

Listing 8.8: Calculating the maximum of an array in parallel via reduction.

```
  int maxElem = data[0];
#pragma omp parallel for reduction(max : maxElem)
  for (int i = 1; i < sizeof (data) / sizeof (int); i++)
    if (maxElem < data[i])
      maxElem = data[i];

  cout << "Maximum is : " << maxElem << endl;
```

The reduction operation is a really significant asset in a parallel program designer's toolbox. The mechanisms through which it can be implemented in parallel, plus more elaborate uses of it, are examined in Sections 5.11.3 and 10.4.3.

8.3.5 Final words on variable scope

Variable scope rules for parallel regions are rather simple. The problem is that race conditions can arise without careful consideration from the programmer. Read-only variables pose no threat, but variables that need to be modified must do so in an orderly fashion. OpenMP does not warn of such potential problems, so it is prudent to act proactively. What this translates to is that we should explicitly declare the desired type of access to all shared variables (i.e., variables declared outside the parallel block) inside a parallel construct.

The `default(none)` clause causes OpenMP to ignore all symbols declared outside of a parallel construct that are missing explicit access declarations. Using this clause in the code of Listing 8.7 would mandate the following additional changes[2]:

```
#pragma omp parallel for default(none) \
            shared(step, div, st, f) \
            private(x)    \
            reduction(+: localRes)
  for (int i = 1; i < div; i++)
    {
      x = st + i * step;
      localRes += f (x);
    }
```

The following list summarizes the OpenMP clauses (a.k.a. **data-sharing** clauses) that modify the scope of a variable, or variables, as they can take as parameter a comma-delimited list of identifiers. These are common (with a few exceptions) to most OpenMP parallel constructs:

- **shared**: The default behavior for variables declared outside of a parallel block. It needs to be used only if `default(none)` is also specified.
- **reduction**: A reduction operation is performed between the private copies and the "outside" object. The final value is stored in the "outside" object.
- **private**: Creates a separate copy of a variable for each thread in the team. Private variables are not initialized, so one should not expect to get the value of the variable declared outside the parallel construct.
- **firstprivate**: Behaves the same way as the `private` clause, but the private variable copies are initialized to the value of the "outside" object.
- **lastprivate**: Behaves the same way as the `private` clause, but the thread finishing the last iteration of the sequential block (for the final value of the loop control variable that produces an iteration) copies the value of its object to the "outside" object.
- **threadprivate**: Creates thread-specific, *persistent* storage (i.e., for the duration of the program) for *global* data. In contrast, a `private` clause only creates parallel-block storage that is automatic, i.e., data are destroyed upon block termination.

---

[2] Pragmas, like all other preprocessor directives, are supposed to occupy a single line only. Long lines, like the one used in this example, can be split in several lines by "escaping" the change of line with a \.

The threadprivate clause is used outside a parallel construct, typically immediately after the declaration of the corresponding variables.

A private clause only masks/hides global data, while a threadprivate clause creates a private-per-thread copy for each thread in a team.

- **linear**: Used in loop directives to indicate that the listed variables have a linear relationship with the loop control variable. In terms of semantics, it is very similar to the private clause.

  Its syntax is: linear(list_variables : step) with the optional step defaulting to one if omitted. The linear clause has a peculiar behavior based on the type of directive it is attached to. A number of examples are shown in Sections 8.4.1.1 and 8.8, but it should be noted that this clause has been deprecated since OpenMP 5.2.

OpenMP also offers a couple of clauses for **data copying** between threads:

- **copyin**: Used in conjunction with the threadprivate clause to initialize the thread private copies of a team of threads, from the master thread's variables.
- **copyprivate**: Used to broadcast the value of a private variable of a task (see Section 8.5 for what a task stands for) to the copies of other tasks that belong to the same parallel region. This clause is typically attached to a single construct, and the copy is performed at the end of the single's structured block and before the parallel region is complete.

The difference between copyin and copyprivate is that the former is used to make the copy at the very beginning of a construct, while the latter can make the copy at any point of a parallel region's execution.

For example, the following function could be executed by the master thread to read from the user and initialize the other threads' copies of x and y, after they begin execution:

```
float x, y;
#pragma omp threadprivate(x, y)

void init() {
#pragma omp single copyprivate(x,y)
  {
    scanf("%f %f", &x, &y);
  }
}
```

Examples for the clauses we have not covered so far are reserved for subsequent sections.

8.4 Loop-level parallelism

In the examples of the previous section, we sampled the parallel for construct to derive a multi-threaded version of a sequential program with a handful of changes.

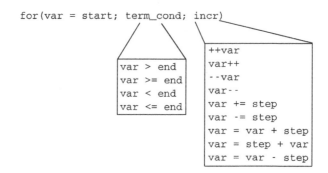

FIGURE 8.3

Canonical loop form. Expressions/variables `start`, `end`, and `step` must be loop-invariant and of compatible type to `var`.

But can we use the same approach on any `for` loop? The answer is, unfortunately, no. The `for` loop has to satisfy certain conditions, which in OpenMP jargon are called the **canonical form**.

These are the restrictions of the canonical form:

- The loop control variable has to be an integer type (signed or unsigned), a pointer type (e.g., base address of an array), or a random access iterator (for C++). The loop control variable is made `private` by default, even if it is declared outside the loop.
- The loop control variable must not be modified in the body of the loop.
- The limit against which the loop control variable is compared against to determine the truth of the termination condition must be loop-invariant, i.e., they cannot change during the loop's execution. The following loop, which eliminates the even numbers from a `data` array of size `M`, violates both this and the previous rule:

```
for (int i = 0; i < M; i++)
   {
   if(data[i] % 2 == 0)
      {
         data[i] = data[M−1]; // copy over
         M−−; // limit modified
         i−−; // loop control var change
      }
   }
```

- The increment/decrement step of the loop control variable must be loop-invariant.
- The logical and arithmetic operators allowed in the `for` statement are limited to the ones shown in Fig. 8.3.
- No program logic that transfers control outside the loop body is allowed. This includes `break`, `goto`, and `throw` statements. One can use `goto` and `throw` only if the destination address and the exception handling, respectively, take place within the loop body.

- The program is allowed to terminate from within the loop body via an `exit` call.

The last two requirements are common to all blocks handled by OpenMP constructs. The transition to the code outside a parallel region can only take place after all the team threads are synchronized. This extends to code entry (which is more or less obvious for loops), i.e., you cannot jump inside a parallel block. OpenMP calls these blocks **structured**. A structured block has a single point of entry and a single point of exit.

The purpose of the canonical form is to ensure that the number of iterations can be computed a priori, i.e., before the loop executes. This way, OpenMP can distribute the iterations to the team of threads and produce a result consistent with the corresponding sequential `for` loop.

As a final word, the `parallel for` directive is actually a shortcut for the following *nested* directives:

```
#pragma omp parallel
#pragma omp for
for (...
```

The significance of the above is not in having a separate `for` directive, but in being able to place in the block managed by the `parallel` directive, all sorts of work-sharing constructs, as in:

```
#pragma omp parallel
{
#pragma omp for
    for (. . .
#pragma omp sections
. . .
}
```

We will discuss more about this possibility later in the chapter.

8.4.1 Data dependencies

A loop being in canonical form is the first step in making it available for parallelization. The next step is making sure that the loop body permits "out-of-order" execution of the iterations. The loop-carried dependency we treated in Listing 8.6 is just a hint to the bigger problem.

Let us assume that we have a loop body with two statements S1 and S2 that operate on a common memory location:

```
for(i =...
{
  S1 : operate on a memory location x
  ...
  S2 : operate on a memory location x
}
```

The kind of operations performed, e.g., read or write, determines the kind of dependency formed between the two statements. When such dependencies are limited within the execution of the same iteration, there are no problems in the parallel execution of the loop by a `parallel for` directive.[3]

The four kinds of dependencies are [21]:

- **Flow dependence**: when S1 writes x and S2 reads x (read after write [RAW]), denoted by $S1 \, \delta^f \, S2$. The name stems from the notion that the value produced by S1 is transmitted/flows to S2. For example:

```
x = 10;          // S1
y = 2 * x + 5;  // S2
```

- **Anti-dependence**: when S1 reads x and S2 writes x (write after read [WAR]), denoted by $S1 \, \delta^\alpha \, S2$. This is the antithesis of the flow dependence. For example:

```
y = x + 3;      // S1
x ++ ;          // S2
```

- **Output dependence**: when S1 writes x and S2 writes x (write after write [WAW]), denoted by $S1 \, \delta^o \, S2$. For example:

```
x = 10;          // S1
x = x + c ;     // S2
```

- **Input dependence**: when S1 reads x and S2 reads x (read after read [RAR]), denoted by $S1 \, \delta^i \, S2$. For example:

```
y = x + c;       // S1
z = 2 * x + 1;  // S2
```

This is not considered a real dependence, so it is not examined further below.

These dependencies are transformed into **loop-carried dependencies** if S1 and S2 depend explicitly (using an expression of the loop control variable i) or implicitly (via an iteration sequence or a condition on i) on different values of the loop control variable. For example, S1 could write a location during iteration i that is read by S2 during iteration j.[4] It should be noted that in loop-carried dependencies, the relationship between S1 and S2 is characterized based on their sequential *execution* order and not only on their sequence in the code. This is a critical point when arrays are involved.

---

[3] Dependencies in general cause problems for vectorizing compilers, i.e., compilers that attempt to concurrently execute the dependent statements within an iteration. However, this is a topic for a compiler book [8].

[4] In principle, we could have nested loops, in which case i and j are vectors representing the values of the control variables going from the outer to the inner loop. In this section we keep things simple by working mostly with single-level loops.

Each dependency type requires a different elimination approach, so it is essential that we recognize its type. In the following sections we provide examples of how we treat each dependence type. However, in the case of flow dependencies, a successful elimination is far from guaranteed. Often, an algorithmic change is necessary to ensure that parallel execution is possible.

When a dependency cannot be eliminated, our only course of action is to try to rewrite the code so that at least some part of the code can be parallelized, while at the same time *honoring* the dependencies that exist. Dependence violation is not an option, as it leads to an incorrect program [8].

8.4.1.1 Flow dependencies

Flow dependencies are the most difficult to remove if at all possible. In this section we progress from simple to more challenging cases of flow dependencies.

Case 1: **Reduction and induction variables**

The following code is a snippet from an integration program, similar to the example we used in Section 8.3:

Listing 8.9: Sequential loop with flow dependencies.

```
double v = start;
double sum=0;
for(int i = 0; i < N; i++)
{
    sum = sum + f(v);    // S1
    v = v + step;        // S2
}
```

We have three flow dependencies:

- $S1 \, \delta^f \, S1$: is caused by a **reduction variable**, sum. The value of sum is read in each iteration, and it is updated with the use of the same operator and an iteration-specific value. As the initial value is produced from the previous iteration, we have a read after a write, which is the definition of the flow dependence.
- $S2 \, \delta^f \, S2$: is caused by an **induction variable**, v. An induction variable is a variable whose value is an affine function of the loop control variable, e.g.,

```
var = a * i + b;
```

  where a and b are loop-invariant expressions. In our example, we have b = start and a = step.
- $S2 \, \delta^f \, S1$: this is also caused by the v induction variable.

A reduction variable-caused dependence is easily treated by use of the reduction clause, which does not actually break the dependence, but it localizes it to each thread.

An induction variable-caused dependence on the other hand can be completely removed if we use the affine formula to update the value of the variable in a loop-independent way.

The resulting code is shown below:

Listing 8.10: OpenMP version of Listing 8.9, with loop-carried flow dependencies treated.

```
double v = start; // now irrelevant. v can be an automatic ↵
    variable declared inside the loop
double sum=0;

#pragma omp parallel for reduction(+ : sum) private(v) shared(↵
    step)
for(int i = 0; i < N; i++)
{
    v = i * step + start;
    sum = sum + f(v);
}
```

A second option for handling induction variables is to utilize the **linear** clause.[5] The linear clause receives as a parameter a list of variables that are going to be treated as firstprivate, and their values for each iteration will be calculated by adding to their initial value outside the loop the position of the iteration in the iteration space. As an optional parameter, the step by which the variable will be incremented can be supplied. The default step is one. The linear clause is restricted to integers or pointer-type variables.

Using the linear clause, we can convert the loop in the following code:

```
int i = 0, j = 1;
float x[N];

for (int k = 0; k < N; k++)
{
    x[k] = i + j * j;
    i++;
    j += 2;
}
```

To this OpenMP variation, as both i and j are induction variables:

```
#pragma omp parallel for linear(i) linear(j:2)
    for (int k = 0; k < N; k++)
    x[k] = i + j * j;
```

Please note that we cannot combine the two linear clauses into a single linear(i, j:2) clause, because although it is legal, it would cause both variables to be incremented by a step of 2.

---

[5] OpenMP 5.2 deprecated the linear clause, so this is bound to be unavailable in future OpenMP implementations.

Case 2: **Loop skewing**

Another technique for removing loop-carried flow dependencies is **loop skewing**, i.e., rearrangement of the loop body's statements. In the following example, we have $S2\ \delta^f\ S1$, as the values of the x array produced during iteration i are consumed during iteration $i + 1$:

Listing 8.11: Sequential program with a flow dependence.

```
for(int i = 1; i < N; i++)
{
    y[ i ] = f( x[ i-1 ] );   // S1
    x[ i ] = x[ i ] + c[ i ];  // S2
}
```

By taking the calculation of a single y element outside of the loop, we can eliminate the obstacle to parallelizing the loop. The modification aims at having the statement that consumes the x[i] value to be executed at the same iteration that computes x[i]:

Listing 8.12: OpenMP version of Listing 8.11 that removes the loop-carried flow dependence via loop skewing.

```
y[ 1 ] = f( x[ 0 ] );
for(int i = 1; i < N - 1; i++)
{
    x[ i ] = x[ i ] + c[ i ];
    y[ i + 1 ] = f( x[ i ] );
}
x[ N - 1 ] = x[ N - 1 ] + c[ N - 1 ];
```

Although the dependence still exists, it is no longer loop-carried.

Case 3: **Partial parallelization**

There may be cases where dependencies cannot be removed. In Listing 8.13 we have two flow dependencies in the body of two nested `for` loops.

Listing 8.13: Sequential code with two flow dependencies in the body of a nested loop.

```
for (int i = 1; i < N; i++)
  for (int j = 1; j < M; j++)
    data[i][j] = data[i - 1][j] + data[i - 1][j - 1];
```

To better appreciate the nature of these dependencies and how they could be dealt with, we can draw the iteration space dependency graph (ISDG). This graph has nodes that represent iterations and edges that represent data flow. The source of an edge is the iteration that produces a value/changes a location in memory, and the sink of the edge is the iteration where this value is utilized. The ISDG of Listing 8.13 is shown in Fig. 8.4. It can be observed that there are no edges between the nodes of the same row. This means that the j loop can be parallelized, in contrast to the i loop, which cannot. For a given value of i, we can execute the iterations of the j loop in parallel as shown in Listing 8.14.

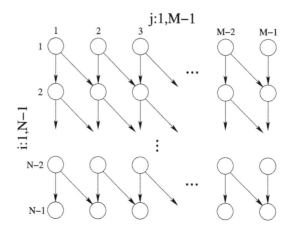

FIGURE 8.4

Iteration space dependency graph for Listing 8.13.

Listing 8.14: Partial OpenMP parallelization of Listing 8.13, affecting only the inner loop.

```
for (int i = 1; i < N; i++)
#pragma omp parallel for
   for (int j = 1; j < M; j++)
      data[i][j] = data[i - 1][j] + data[i - 1][j - 1];
```

Case 4: **Refactoring**

In the following example, we have two nested for loops with three flow dependencies, all involving S1:

Listing 8.15: Sequential code with multiple flow dependencies in the body of a nested loop.

```
// File : nested_flowDep.cpp
. . .
  int N = atoi(argv[1]), M = atoi(argv[2]);
  double **data = new double *[N];
  for (int i = 0; i < M; i++)
    data[i] = new double[M];

  // init data array with sample values
  . . .
  // compute
  for (int i = 1; i < N; i++)
    for (int j = 1; j < M; j++)
      data[i][j] = data[i - 1][j] + data[i][j - 1] + data[i - ↵
         1][j - 1];   // S1
```

The ISDG of Listing 8.15 is shown in Fig. 8.5.

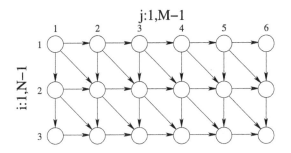

FIGURE 8.5

Iteration space dependency graph for Listing 8.15, for N=4 and M=7.

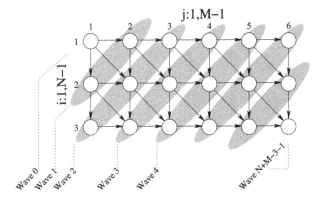

FIGURE 8.6

The iteration space dependency graph of Fig. 8.5, with highlighted groups of iterations that can be executed concurrently. The groups have to be executed in sequence.

At first glance, it does not seem possible that we could ever run the iterations of these nested loops concurrently. But close examination of the graph reveals that there are groups of iterations that are independent of each other, and they could execute in parallel without violating the dependencies of the graph. These groups, highlighted in Fig. 8.6, can be executed in a "wave-like" fashion. The waves have to be executed in sequence, but the iterations of each group/wave can be executed in parallel.

The resulting code is shown below. As can be observed, only the inner loop can be parallelized to ensure correct execution:

Listing 8.16: Parallelized version of Listing 8.15, with groups of iterations executed in parallel.

```
// File : nested_flowDepFixed.cpp
. . .
  int smallDim;
  int largeDim;
```

```
5    if (N > M)
6      {
7         smallDim = M;
8         largeDim = N;
9      }
10   else
11     {
12        smallDim = N;
13        largeDim = M;
14     }
15
16     // compute
17     for (int diag = 1; diag <= N + M - 3; diag++)
18       {
19          int diagLength = diag;
20          if (diag + 1 >= smallDim)
21            diagLength = smallDim - 1;
22          if (diag + 1 >= largeDim)
23            diagLength = (smallDim - 1) - (diag - largeDim) - 1;
24
25   #pragma omp parallel for default(none) shared(data, diag, ↵
        diagLength, N, M)
26          for (int k = 0; k < diagLength; k++)
27            {
28               int i = diag - k;
29               int j = k + 1;
30               if (diag > N - 1)
31                 {
32                    i = N - 1 - k;
33                    j = diag - (N - 1) + k + 1;
34                 }
35               data[i][j] = data[i - 1][j] + data[i][j - 1] + data[i↵
                    - 1][j - 1];
36            }
37       }
```

The important points of the above code are:

- The execution in waves requires a change of loop variables from the original i and j. The new loop control variables represent the wave index (diag in the for statement of line 17) and the member of the wave/group, scanning from bottom left to top right, respectively (k in the for statement of line 26).
- There are exactly $N + M - 3$ waves, but the exact size of each one has to be calculated based on the number of rows (N) and columns (M) of our data table. The size is calculated on lines 19–23 by comparing the wave index with the smaller and bigger of the two dimensions N and M.
- The parallel loop of lines 25–36 transforms the two new loop control variables to the original i and j indices so that the statement of line 35 can be executed.

Case 5: **Fissioning**

The last technique we could employ, before a full-blown change of the underlying algorithm, is **fissioning**, i.e., splitting the loop body into two loops, a parallelizable one and a sequential one. The latter is obviously the holding place of the computations whose dependencies force a sequential computation. An example that requires this treatment is shown in Listing 8.17.

Listing 8.17: Sequential code with a flow dependence that requires fissioning.

```
s = b[ 0 ];
for (int i = 1; i < N; i++)
{
    a[ i ] = a [ i ] + a[ i − 1 ];   // S1
    s = s + b[ i ];
}
```

S1 introduces a loop-carried flow dependence that can be partially treated by splitting the loop in two, as shown in Listing 8.18:

Listing 8.18: Split up version of Listing 8.17 that can be partially parallelized.

```
// sequential part
for (int i = 1; i < N; i++)
    a[ i ] = a [ i ] + a[ i − 1 ];

// parallel part
s = b[ 0 ];
#pragma omp parallel for reduction(+ : s)
for (int i = 1; i < N; i++)
    s = s + b[ i ];
```

Actually, in the above code the first loop constitutes a **prefix-sum** or **scan** calculation that can also be parallelized, but not using just an OpenMP `parallel for` directive! A reduction is a special case of a prefix-sum operation. More details are covered in Section 10.4.4.

Case 6: **Algorithm change**

It is an oddity that a simple example that is usually reserved as an introduction to recursion can also serve as an example of a code that cannot be parallelized. The following code, which computes all the Fibonacci terms up to N, contains two loop-carried flow dependencies:

```
for(int i = 2; i < N; i++)
{
  F[i] = F[i−1] + F[i−2];
}
```

We could rewrite the code as:

```
for(int i = 2 ; i < N; i++)
{
    int x =  F[i−2]; // S1
```

```
    int y =  F[i-1]; // S2
    F[i] =  x + y;   // S3
}
```

$F[i-2]$ is read during iteration i, but it was computed during iteration $i - 2$, which constitutes a flow dependence. Hence we have $S1 \ \delta^f \ S3$ and $S2 \ \delta^f \ S3$. Dependencies in this code cannot be eliminated without modifying the algorithm that computes the terms: instead of using the recursive definition, we could use a closed-form solution based on Binet's formula:

$$F_n = \frac{\varphi^n - (1 - \varphi)^n}{\sqrt{5}}, \tag{8.3}$$

where $\varphi = \frac{1+\sqrt{5}}{2} \approx 1.161803$ is the golden ratio. This allows parallel computation of all terms, without requiring a sequence to be followed.

8.4.1.2 Anti-dependencies

The following sample code contains a loop-carried anti-dependence:

```
for(int i = 0; i < N-1; i++)
{
    a[ i ] = a[ i + 1 ] + c;
}
```

We can rewrite it as:

```
for(int i = 0; i < N-1; i++)
{
    x = a[ i + 1 ];   // S1
    a[ i ] = x + c;   // S2
}
```

The location read by S1 is written to by S2 in the next iteration, thus $S1 \ \delta^\alpha \ S2$.

Anti-dependencies can be eliminated by providing a copy of the data that need to be read prior to their modification. The outcome for our example is as follows, with the a2 array serving as the repository for the "saved" values of the original:

```
for(int i = 0; i < N-1; i++)
{
    a2[ i ] = a[ i + 1 ];
}

#pragma omp parallel for
for(int i = 0; i < N-1; i++)
{
    a[ i ] = a2[ i ] + c;
}
```

The separate loop that copies the data has no loop-carried dependencies, as the a array is not modified during its execution.

This technique of course entails an additional time and space overhead that needs to be evaluated carefully. The objective is to gauge whether the overhead is justified/offset by the speedup offered by the parallel execution.

8.4.1.3 Output dependencies

The following code contains a loop-carried output dependence caused by writing to variable d ($S2 \; \delta^o \; S2$):

```
for(int i = 0; i < N; i++)
{
    y[i] = a * x[i] + c;  // S1
    d = fabs( y[i] );     // S2
}
```

There is also a flow dependence ($S1 \; \delta^f \; S2$), but it is not loop-carried.

Output dependencies can be resolved easily even if the value that is modified is required after the termination of the parallel for block, by making it lastprivate:

```
#pragma omp parallel for shared( a, c ) lastprivate( d )
for(int i = 0; i < N; i++)
{
    y[i] = a * x[i] + c;
    d = fabs( y[i] );
}
```

The lastprivate clause will make the thread executing the last – in sequential order – iteration, to store its private value of d into the location of the external-to-block d.

Listing 8.8 also shows how the output dependence of the following sequential program, which calculates the maximum of an array of values, can be removed by using a reduction variable:

```
int maxElem = data[0];
for (int i = 1; i < sizeof (data) / sizeof (int); i++)
  if (maxElem < data[i])
    maxElem = data[i];

cout << "Maximum is : " << maxElem << endl;
```

8.4.2 Nested loops

As of OpenMP 3.0, perfectly nested loops (i.e., with no statement between the successive for) can be parallelized in unison. OpenMP can "collapse" multiple nested loops into a single one and then proceed to partition this derivative loop between the team of threads. The following matrix multiplication sample has two perfectly nested loops:

```
  double A[K][L];
  double B[L][M];
  double C[K][M];
. . .
#pragma omp parallel for collapse(2)
  for (int i = 0; i < K; i++)
    for (int j = 0; j < M; j++)
      {
        C[i][j] = 0;
        for (int k = 0; k < L; k++)
          C[i][j] += A[i][k] * B[k][j];
      }
```

where the `collapse` clause instructs OpenMP how many of the nested loops should be converted into a single one.

The question is, why should we want to do the collapse in the first place? Multiple reasons can justify such an action:

- The outer loop has too few iterations to balance the workload properly. Imagine that in our matrix multiplication code, we had $K = 5$, $L = 1000$, and $M = 3000$. Parallelizing the outer loop only would translate to having just five work items to give to our threads. How could we evenly distribute these to the eight threads that are the typical team size for quad-core hyperthreaded CPUs? The 15,000 work items that would be produced by the collapse are a different story though.
- It is possible that the execution cost of each loop iteration is different. Collapsed loops are easier to balance in that regard, especially with the clauses that we examine in the next section.

8.4.3 Scheduling

OpenMP can use a variety of ways to assign iterations to a team of threads in a parallel loop, the motivation being that an ad hoc, even split can yield poor performance if the execution cost of each iteration is not more or less the same.

In this section we explain how the available partitioning and scheduling schemes work. To assist in this effort, we will assume that the team is made up of p threads and that the total number of iterations, collapsed or otherwise, to be assigned is N. All schemes can have a parameter called `chunk_size` that determines how the partitioning is done:

- `static`: In this scheme, the loop is broken into groups of `chunk_size` iterations. If `chunk_size` is unspecified, it defaults to $\lceil \frac{N}{p} \rceil$, with the last group possibly being a bit smaller if N is not a multiple of p. The groups are assigned to the threads in a round-robin fashion, in the order of the thread number.
- `dynamic`: This scheme mimics the operation of a dynamic load balancer, where groups of size `chunk_size` are assigned to the threads on a first-come, first-served basis. A thread executes a group, then requests another, etc. If `chunk_size` is unspecified, it defaults to 1.

- guided: The dynamic scheme offers flexibility, but the coordination overhead associated with requesting a new group can deteriorate performance. The guided scheme tries to offset this overhead by using variable-sized groups that shrink over time to allow for load balancing. The group size given out at each new request is equal to the number of *unassigned* iterations divided by p. The chunk_size specifies a lower bound for the size of a group (the very last being an exception obviously). If chunk_size is unspecified, it defaults to 1. The group sizes can be determined by the formula

$$groupSize = min(remainingIter, max(chunk\_size, \lceil \frac{remainingIter}{p} \rceil)).$$

Fig. 8.7 shows how these schemes work for a few example cases. The dynamic and guided schemes cannot be traced exactly, as the group assignment is taking place during runtime. The group sizes in the guided scheme are of particular interest, as they shrink exponentially until the chunk_size limit is reached. The gradually smaller groups serve to fill in gaps in thread utilization.

Upon specifying the scheduling scheme to OpenMP, a programmer has the additional option of setting it to auto, in which case the compiler and/or the OpenMP runtime decide on the best partitioning scheme from the above list.

The programmer can specify the desired scheduling using any of the following methods, going from the most generic to the most specific, the latter always having precedence over the former:

- The OMP_SCHEDULE environment variable. This should be set to a string adhering to the form: static | dynamic | guided | auto [, chunk_size]. Such a setting potentially affects the execution of all OpenMP programs. For example:

```
export OMP_SCHEDULE="static ,1"    # in BASH
export OMP_SCHEDULE="guided"       # in BASH
setenv OMP_SCHEDULE "dynamic,5"    # in TCSH/CSH
```

- The omp_set_schedule function. The syntax is:

```
void omp_set_schedule(omp_sched_t kind, // Scheduling scheme (IN)
                      int chunk_size);  // (IN)
```

The omp_sched_t is just an enumerated type, and the available symbolic constants for the first parameter are: omp_sched_static, omp_sched_dynamic, omp_sched_guided, and omp_sched_auto. For example:

```
omp_set_schedule(omp_sched_guided, 10);
#pragma omp parallel for
for (...
```

In the absence of a schedule clause, this function sets the scheduling for all parallel loops that follow in a program.

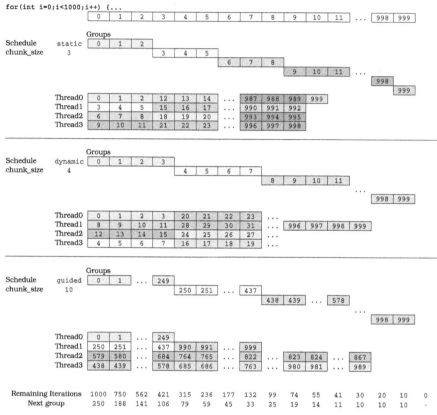

FIGURE 8.7

Examples of resulting iteration partitioning and assignment based on the scheduling scheme for a 1000-iteration `for` loop. We end up with 334 groups for `static`, 250 groups for `dynamic`, and 15 groups for `guided` scheduling, for the given `chunk_size` parameters. Only for the `static` scheme we have a priori knowledge of the iteration group assignment to threads.

• The `schedule` clause. This `parallel for`-exclusive clause accepts parameters in the form: `schedule(static | dynamic | guided | auto | runtime [, chunk_size ])`. The `runtime` option delegates the scheduling decision for the execution of the program, where a previous setting (e.g., via `OMP_SCHEDULE`) can be inspected for suggestions. This is exclusive to the `schedule` clause only. For example:

```
#pragma omp parallel for schedule( dynamic )
for (...
```

A number of optional modifiers exist for the `schedule` clause parameters. One of them is examined in Section 8.8.

How can we use these options in a parallel loop? Which is the best schedule option? As long as the iterations do not differ substantially and *unpredictably* in execution cost, the `static` scheme is a safe option. For example, in the following code, the cost increases linearly as i increases:

```
#pragma omp parallel for schedule( static , 1 )
for(int i = 1; i <= N; i++)
{
    long sum = 0;
    for(int j = 1; j <= i; j++)
        sum += j;
}
```

but a cyclic distribution of iterations, as dictated by the `chunk_size = 1` option, would assign to each thread more or less the same workload.[6] If, on the other hand, there is no way to predict the cost of each iteration, the `dynamic` or the `guided` option would be more suitable. The `guided` option is preferable if the resulting number of groups is very high for the selected `chunk_size` or the per-iteration cost gradually increases as the loop progresses. For a `guided` schedule this means that the first – and largest – group is not overly costly in execution time, so that it causes an imbalance in thread workload.

Finally, if in doubt, a set of simple tests can reveal the ideal strategy. All one has to do is set:

```
#pragma omp parallel for schedule( runtime )
for(. . .
```

and time multiple executions of the program, each with a different `OMP_SCHEDULE` setting. A recompilation would not be required. The following BASH script could automate the whole process:

```
#!/bin/bash
# File : schedule_script.sh

for scheme in static dynamic guided
do
    for chunk in 1 2 4 8 16 32
        do
            export OMP_SCHEDULE="${scheme},${chunk}"
            echo $OMP_SCHEDULE '/usr/bin/time -o tmp.log -p $1 >/dev/↩
                null ; head -n 1 tmp.log | gawk '{print $2}' ' >> $2
        done
done
```

---

[6] If N is evenly divided by the number of threads p, then the master thread would perform $\frac{N}{p} + N\frac{(\frac{N}{p}-1)}{2}$ additions, and the $(p-1)$-th child thread would perform $N + N\frac{(\frac{N}{p}-1)}{2}$ additions. Thus the maximum imbalance would be $N - \frac{N}{p}$ additions. So this clearly depends on the values of N and p.

The script uses the `time` command to measure the overall execution time of the target program. Subsequently, the `head` and `gawk` filters extract the measurement in seconds from the output of the `time` command.

All that is required is that the user passes the name of the executable and the name of the file for storing the results as parameters to the script, as in:

```
$ ./schedule_script.sh ./myProg timingResults.csv
```

Each scheduling option can be tested multiple times if required by nesting a third loop in the script for this purpose.

8.5 Task parallelism

The `parallel for` directive can assist in the parallelization of a data parallel program, i.e., a program where concurrency is derived from processing disjoint subsets of data in parallel. Any data dependencies can spoil this recipe, and that is why we addressed this issue exclusively in Section 8.4.1. On the other hand, we have instances of programs where multiple actions can potentially take place at the same time, not necessarily involving a particular dataset. We call these programs function- or task-parallel (see Section 2.3.1).

OpenMP can support this functionality via the `parallel` directive, but dedicated directives also exist to avoid having to introduce control logic similar to the following:

```
#pragma omp parallel
switch( omp_get_thread_num() )
{
    case 0:
    ...
}
```

into a program.

There is nothing particularly wrong about the above logic. It is perfectly legal and we have already employed something similar in our first two versions of the integration program in Section 8.3. The additional feature that the dedicated "tasking" work-sharing constructs offer, apart from a cleaner code structure, is that they decouple the task description from the task execution. OpenMP may execute the different tasks at different points in time, based on the availability of cores and their execution cost.

8.5.1 The `sections` directive

The `sections` directive is a means for specifying to OpenMP a list of code blocks that are to be executed in parallel. The `sections` directive (as the `for` one) can appear as an element of a parallel region or in combination with a `parallel` pragma as a shortcut:

```
#pragma omp parallel
{
   ...
#pragma omp sections
   ...
}

// OR

#pragma omp parallel sections
{
   ...
}
```

The individual blocks that make up a `sections` directive are defined by embedding one or more `section` directives:

```
#pragma omp parallel sections
{
#pragma omp section
   {
      // concurrent block 0
   }
   ...
#pragma omp section
   {
      // concurrent block M-1
   }
}
```

The `sections` directive can have the same optional clauses as the `parallel` directive, e.g., `shared`, `private`, `num_threads`, etc. The included `section` directives cannot have any clauses, so any required clause additions should be done at the `sections` level.

When OpenMP processes a `sections` directive, it starts a number of threads that execute the section blocks concurrently. The assignment of sections to threads is implementation-specific. There is no restriction between the team size and the number of sections. If the team is bigger than the number of sections, some threads will remain idle, whereas if the number of sections exceeds the size of the team, there will be an OpenMP implementation-specific[7] mapping of sections to threads. There is an implicit barrier at the end of a `sections` block, which means that the statements following it will execute only when all individual `section` blocks are complete.

In the following section we solve the producers–consumers problem, as an application of the `sections` directive.

---

[7] This means that the standard does not specify or enforce a specific behavior in that regard.

8.5.1.1 Producers–consumers in OpenMP

The problem setting is thoroughly established in Section 3.7.1, where we also summarize the semaphore-based solution guidelines (see Table 3.2). OpenMP provides its own implementations of a binary semaphore in the form of the `omp_lock_t` and `omp_nest_lock_t` data types. The two types of locks provided are simple and nestable. The latter is the same as a recursive lock, i.e., a lock that can be locked multiple times by the same thread (for more details see Section 3.6).

A lock can be in three states: uninitialized, locked, and unlocked. OpenMP includes functions for initializing, setting (locking), unsetting (unlocking), testing, and destroying locks[8]:

```
// Initializes an instance of the omp_lock_t structure. It should be
// called prior to any operations with a lock.
void omp_init_lock(omp_lock_t *lock);

// Destroys a lock. Cleanup call at the end of a lock's use.
void omp_destroy_lock(omp_lock_t *lock);

// Acquires a lock. This is a blocking call.
void omp_set_lock(omp_lock_t *lock);

// Releases a lock. This is a non-blocking call.
void omp_unset_lock(omp_lock_t *lock);

// Acquires the lock and returns true if the lock is unlocked.
// Otherwise, false is returned. This is a non-blocking call.
int omp_test_lock(omp_lock_t *lock);
```

However, the omission of a general/counting semaphore implementation is a weak point of the standard. Fortunately, we can utilize the semaphore class that is discussed in Section 3.9.3.

An alternative is to combine OpenMP with the Qt library. This combination would allow us to use the former for thread management, while taking advantage of the rich library of classes provided by the latter. The only requirement is the inclusion of the `-fopenmp` flag in the compiler switches as specified in the Qt's project file. The following example, with the addition of the `QMAKE_CXXFLAGS` and `QMAKE_LFLAGS` lines, accomplishes just that:

```
SOURCES += prodCons.cpp
TARGET = prodCons
CONFIG += qt
QMAKE_CXXFLAGS += -fopenmp
QMAKE_LFLAGS += -fopenmp
```

The following code presents a single-producer, multiple-consumers-based program for integrating a function. As discussed in Section 3.7.1, a semaphore-based

---

[8] There is a matching set of functions for nestable locks.

solution requires two counting semaphores for safely counting space and available items in the shared buffer, and one binary semaphore for coordinating consumer access to the "output" index (variable out):

Listing 8.19: Multi-threaded integration of a function using the sections directive. The producer thread uses "messages" to terminate the consumer threads. Each of the "parties" (producer or consumer) to the program has its own dedicated section.

```cpp
// File : prod_cons/prodCons.cpp
. . .
#include <omp.h>
#include <mutex>
#include "semaphore.h"

using namespace std;

const int BUFFSIZE = 10;
const double LOWERLIMIT = 0;
const double UPPERLIMIT = 10;

const int NUMCONSUMERS = 2;
//------------------------------------------------
struct Slice
{
  double start;
  double end;
  int divisions;
};
//------------------------------------------------
double func (double x)
{
  return fabs (sin (x));
}

//------------------------------------------------
void integrCalc (shared_ptr < vector < Slice > >buffer, semaphore & ↩
    buffSlots, semaphore & avail, mutex & l, int &out, mutex & ↩
    resLock, double &res)
{
  while (1)
    {
      avail.acquire ();          // wait for an available item
      l.lock ();
      // take the item out
      double st = buffer->at (out).start;
      double en = buffer->at (out).end;
      double div = buffer->at (out).divisions;
      out = (out + 1) % BUFFSIZE;       // update the out index
      l.unlock ();

      buffSlots.release ();      // signal for a new empty slot

      if (div == 0)
```

```
44              break;                   // exit
45
46          //calculate area
47          double localRes = 0;
48          double step = (en - st) / div;
49          double x;
50          x = st;
51          localRes = func (st) + func (en);
52          localRes /= 2;
53          for (int i = 1; i < div; i++)
54             {
55                x += step;
56                localRes += func (x);
57             }
58          localRes *= step;
59
60          // add it to result
61          resLock.lock ();
62          res += localRes;
63          resLock.unlock ();
64       }
65  }
66
67  //────────────────────────────────────────────────────
68  int main (int argc, char **argv)
69  {
70    if (argc == 1)
71       {
72          cerr << "Usage " << argv[0] << " #jobs\n";
73          exit (1);
74       }
75    int J = atoi (argv[1]);
76    shared_ptr < vector < Slice > >buffer = make_shared < vector < ↵
        Slice >> (BUFFSIZE);
77    int in = 0, out = 0;
78    semaphore avail, buffSlots (BUFFSIZE);
79    mutex l, integLock;
80    double integral = 0;
81  #pragma omp parallel sections default(none) \
82                      shared(buffer, in, out,\
83                      avail, buffSlots, l, \
84                      integLock, integral, J)
85     {
86  // producer part
87  #pragma omp section
88       {
89          // producer thread, responsible for handing out 'jobs'
90          double divLen = (UPPERLIMIT - LOWERLIMIT) / J;
91          double st, end = LOWERLIMIT;
92          for (int i = 0; i < J; i++)
93             {
94                st = end;
```

```
95          end += divLen;
96          if (i == J - 1)
97            end = UPPERLIMIT;
98
99          buffSlots.acquire ();
100         buffer->at (in).start = st;
101         buffer->at (in).end = end;
102         buffer->at (in).divisions = 1000;
103         in = (in + 1) % BUFFSIZE;
104         avail.release ();
105       }
106
107     // put termination sentinels in buffer
108     for (int i = 0; i < NUMCONSUMERS; i++)
109       {
110         buffSlots.acquire ();
111         buffer->at (in).divisions = 0;
112         in = (in + 1) % BUFFSIZE;
113         avail.release ();
114       }
115     }
116
117 // 1st consumer part
118 #pragma omp section
119     {
120       integrCalc (buffer, buffSlots, avail, 1, out, integLock, ↩
                integral);
121     }
122
123
124 // 2nd consumer part
125 #pragma omp section
126     {
127       integrCalc (buffer, buffSlots, avail, 1, out, integLock, ↩
                integral);
128     }
129   }
130
131   cout << "Result is : " << integral << endl;
132
133   return 0;
134 }
```

The above program follows the same guidelines for load assignment/balancing and termination as Listing 3.15, allowing direct comparison between the C++ and OpenMP solutions. The key points of the above program are:

- The parallel region is enclosed in the block between lines 85 and 129, headed by the sections directive. The items to be shared between the producer and consumer threads are explicitly listed in the shared clause of line 82. This would include even std:cout, if it were to be used.

- As in Listing 3.15, we have a producer thread that generates a sequence of Slice structure instances, each representing a part of the integration range. These are deposited in a shared buffer. The producer thread runs the block between lines 87 and 115. The producer thread also flags the end of the computation to the consumer threads, by enqueueing Slice instances with the number of divisions set to 0.
- In the C++ program of Listing 3.15, the main thread also serves as a producer. In the above program, the OpenMP runtime selects the team thread that will execute the producer section.
- The consumer threads have to be explicitly listed as separate section-headed blocks. As such, we do not have the flexibility of dynamically specifying the number of consumer threads, as we did in the C++ version.
- To shorten the consumer section parts, the consumer code is delegated to the integrCalc() function of lines 28–65. All the data items that need to be shared between the threads (e.g., semaphores, indices, the data buffer, etc.) are passed by reference to the function.
- The code in function integrCalc() is an almost verbatim copy of the consumer thread code of Listing 3.15. The consumer threads keep retrieving Slice instances from the shared buffer, calculating the corresponding area (lines 47–58) and accumulating the results in a shared variable that is accessed inside a critical section (lines 61–63). The function terminates upon retrieving a Slice structure with the number of divisions set to zero (lines 43–44).
- The critical section of lines 61–63 could also be established with a critical directive as:

```
#pragma omp critical
        res += localRes;
```

- The shared buffer is allocated as a shared_ptr to a vector of Slice instances (line 76). The vector size is fixed upon construction to BUFFSIZE elements.

The need to have multiple section blocks, even if the desired threads are supposed to execute the same code, is a shortcoming of the sections work-sharing construct. A solution to this problem exists, and it is described in the next section.

8.5.2 The task directive

The task directive was originally introduced as part of the OpenMP 3.0 standard. OpenMP has been always working internally with "tasks," the name referring to entities consisting of:

- Code: a block of statements designated to be executed concurrently.
- Data: a set of variables/data owned by the task (e.g., local variables).
- Thread reference: references the thread (if any) executing the task.

OpenMP performs two activities related to tasks:

- **Packaging**: creating a structure to describe a task entity.
- **Execution**: assigning a task to a thread.

The `task` directive allows the decoupling of these two activities, which means that *tasks can be dynamically created and queued for later execution*. This not only solves the problem of creating a variable number of concurrent blocks, as expressed in the previous section; it also opens up a rich set of additional possibilities.

The syntax of the `task` directive is:

```
#pragma omp task [clause*]
{
   // Block of code to be assigned to a thread
}
```

where the clauses (apart from the scope clauses listed in Section 8.3) of the optional list are examined later in this section.

As an example, we examine the problem of traversing a linked list of data and applying an operation on each item. An array could be easily handled by a `parallel for` construct, but a linked list demands a sequential traversal. What the `task` construct allows us to do is to conform to a sequential traversal, while spinning off tasks to handle the concurrent processing of the discovered items:

Listing 8.20: Multi-threaded processing of a linked list's elements using the `task` directive.

```
1   // File : linked_list.cpp
2   . . .
3   // template structure for a list's node
4   template <class T>
5   struct Node
6   {
7     T info;
8     shared_ptr<Node<T>> next;
9   };
10
11  //-----------------------------------------
12  // Appends a value at the end of a list pointed by the head *h
13  template <class T>
14  void append (int v, shared_ptr<Node<T>> &h)
15  {
16    shared_ptr<Node<T>> tmp = make_shared<Node<T>> ();
17    tmp->info = v;
18    tmp->next = nullptr;
19
20    shared_ptr<Node<T>> aux = h;
21    if (aux->next == nullptr)              // first node in list
22      h->next = tmp;
23    else
24      {
25        while (aux->next != nullptr)
26          aux = aux->next;
```

```
27          aux->next = tmp;
28        }
29 }
30
31 //————————————————————————
32 // function stub for processing a node's data
33 template <class T>
34 void process (shared_ptr<Node<T>> p)
35 {
36 #pragma omp critical
37   cout << p->info << " by thread " << omp_get_thread_num () << endl;
38 }
39
40 //————————————————————————
41 int main (int argc, char *argv[])
42 {
43   // build a sample list
44   shared_ptr<Node<int>> head = make_shared<Node<int>>();
45   head->next=nullptr;
46   append (1, head);
47   append (2, head);
48   append (3, head);
49   append (4, head);
50   append (5, head);
51
52 #pragma omp parallel
53   {
54 #pragma omp single
55     {
56         shared_ptr<Node<int>> tmp = head->next;
57         while (tmp != nullptr)
58           {
59 #pragma omp task
60           process (tmp);
61           tmp = tmp->next;
62         }
63     }
64   }
65 . . .
```

The `head` shared pointer defined on line 44 points to a sentinel node. So the first list node is actually pointed by `head->next`.

A `task` directive should normally reside inside a `parallel` directive. Otherwise, the generated task is undeferred, i.e., it is executed sequentially by the master thread. This is the justification for nesting the `task` directive inside a `parallel` construct on the above listing.

A new `pragma` is used on line 54: the `single` directive. The `single` directive is typically used in combination with a `parallel` directive to limit a block of code to single-threaded execution. So while the outer `parallel` directive of line 52 sets up the multi-threaded execution of the whole block, the `single` directive forces a sequential traversal of the linked list with the `while` loop of lines 57–62.

The traversal is done in sequence, but the processing of the data items is performed in parallel via the `task` directive of line 59. We cannot be certain about when or by which thread the actual processing of a node will take place. But we do know that when the parallel region finishes, all the generated tasks will have completed as well, due to the implicit barrier at the end of the parallel block.

There is however an issue that we bypassed: how many tasks are we allowed to generate? If the linked list had one million elements, would it make sense to generate one million tasks in one go? Does OpenMP have the appropriate structures for accommodating such a scenario? Would it even be sensible to have something like this, even if it was possible?

OpenMP addresses this issue two ways. Firstly, the OpenMP runtime may suspend the generating task and execute one or more of the generated tasks, if the task "pool" grows too big. Secondly, the programmer may direct OpenMP to suspend the current task and execute the generated task. A number of clauses that can accompany the `task` directive can control this behavior.

The clauses that affect the scheduling of tasks are:

- `if(scalar-expression)`: If the expression evaluates to 0, the generated task becomes **undeferred**, i.e., the current task is suspended, until the generated task completes execution. The generated task may be executed by a different thread. An undeferred task that is executed *immediately* by the thread that generated it is called an **included task**.
- `final(scalar-expression)`: When the expression evaluates to true, the task and all its child tasks (i.e., other tasks that can be generated by its execution) become *final* and *included*. This means that a task and all its descendants will be executed by a single thread.
- `untied`: A task is by default tied to a thread: if it gets suspended, it will wait for the particular thread to run it again, even if there are other idle threads. This, in principle, creates better CPU cache utilization. If the `untied` clause is given, a task may resume execution on any free thread.
- `mergeable`. A **merged task** is a task that shares the data environment of the task that generated it. If the `mergeable` clause is present and an undeferred task is generated (via an `if` or `final` clause), then OpenMP may generate a merged task.

All types of undeferred tasks can suppress run-away programs from generating an extraordinary number of *pending* tasks. The following listing calculates a term of the Fibonacci sequence using the recursive definition. To spice things up, each recursive call constitutes a task:

Listing 8.21: OpenMP-based calculation of the Nth term of the Fibonacci sequence using a `task` work-sharing construct.

```
// File : fibo.cpp
. . .
int fib (int i)
{
  int t1, t2;
```

```
6      if (i == 0 || i == 1)
7        return 1;
8      else
9        {
10   #pragma omp task shared(t1) if(i>25) mergeable
11         t1 = fib (i − 1);
12   #pragma omp task shared(t2) if(i>25) mergeable
13         t2 = fib (i − 2);
14   #pragma omp taskwait
15         return t1 + t2;
16       }
17   }
18
19   //——————————————————————————————
20   int main (int argc, char *argv[])
21   {
22     // build a sample list
23     int N = atoi (argv[1]);
24
25   #pragma omp parallel
26       {
27   #pragma omp single
28         {
29           cout << fib (N) << endl;
30         }
31       }
32
33     return 0;
34   }
```

As in our linked list example, the main function sets up a parallel region with the pragma of line 25 and has a single thread (with the `single` directive of line 27) call the recursive function and print out the result. The `fib` function generates two new tasks for calculating the two previous terms, `t1` and `t2`, with the `task` constructs of lines 10 and 12. Summing up these two terms on line 15 requires that the corresponding tasks are complete. There is an implicit barrier at the end of the parallel region, but this is obviously not sufficient. The `taskwait` directive of line 14 is a barrier for the child tasks of the current task, so it just ensures that `t1` and `t2` have been computed, regardless of what is taking place in other tasks.

The `if` clauses of lines 10 and 12 produce undeferred tasks if the `i` parameter goes below 26, which limits the size of the task pool (the 25 threshold is arbitrary, just for our tests). The `mergeable` clause potentially reduces the memory management overhead, associated with the child tasks, as it permits them to use the data environment of the current task.

An extra optimization to Listing 8.21 would be the elimination of line 12 (the pragma, not the block it controls). As the thread generating the child tasks will become idle until the barrier of line 14 is reached, it makes sense to just let it compute the second term `t2`.

Of course, the optimality of this program is not in question: it is desperately inefficient! If we did eliminate the pragma of line 12, we would have for the calculation of the Nth Fibonacci term the generation of $t(N)$ child tasks, with

$$t(N) = 1 + t(N - 1) + t(N - 2), \tag{8.4}$$

where $t(0) = 0$ and $t(1) = 0$. The 1 term is contributed by the task directive of line 10, and $t(N - 1)$ and $t(N - 2)$ by the recursion.

This recurrence relation produces the sequence $0, 0, 1, 2, 4, 7, 12, \ldots$, which is just the Fibonacci sequence, with terms reduced by 1:

$$t(N) = F(N) - 1. \tag{8.5}$$

As an illustration of how significant the `if` clause can be in our extreme example, calculating $F(40)$ can take less than 1 sec with the `if(i>25)` and `mergeable` clauses and around 108 sec without them,[9] the result of having to schedule a total of 165,580,140 child tasks!

This extreme example serves just one purpose: to raise awareness that dynamic generation of tasks does not come free. It is justified as long as we can create enough tasks to keep the cores of the execution platform busy.

Finally, we can control the priority of the generated tasks by using the `priority` clause. The `priority` clause receives an integer value that signifies the relative priority of the task: the higher this value, the higher the priority. As an example, if we would like to generate a set of tasks with reverse priorities, e.g., the last one generated gets the highest priority, we can have:

```
#pragma omp parallel
#pragma omp single
  {
    for (int i = 0; i < N; ++i)
      {
#pragma omp task priority(i)
        do_work(i);
      }
  }
```

The priority has to be a non-negative number between 0 and the value returned by the `omp_get_max_task_priority()` function.

8.5.3 Task dependencies

Naturally, the `task` construct is the primary tool for modeling function-parallel programs in OpenMP. Such programs, though, typically have dependencies between the

---

[9] As tested on an i7-4700HQ, 2.40 GHz CPU, with the GNU C++ 4.9.1 compiler and the `-O2` compiler switch.

different tasks/functions that can be expressed in the form of a dependency graph. Such dependencies, which essentially translate into an execution precedence, can be enforced through the use of binary semaphores.

Alternatively, since OpenMP 4.0, the standard supports the capability to declare and enforce such dependencies with the depend clause. Dependencies can only be established between sibling tasks, i.e., tasks generated by the same parent task. The syntax of the depend clause is:

```
#pragma omp task [ depend( dependence-type : list ) ]
{
    ...
}
```

where the list contains one or more variable identifiers and/or array sections. The list should contain data items that are either input to the task, or the result of the task computation. The dependence-type describes the nature of these data items, by being one of[10]:

- **in**: The task is dependent on all *previously generated sibling* tasks that reference at least one of the list items in an out or inout dependency type.
- **out, inout**: The task is dependent on all *previously generated sibling* tasks that reference at least one of the list items in an in, out, or inout dependency type.
- **mutexinoutset**: Behaves in the same way as inout, but if two (or more) sibling tasks share the same variable with this dependence type, then they cannot be scheduled to run at the same time (they are mutually exclusive).

The following example shows the use of a loop to generate multiple tasks, with T2 and T3 dependent on T1:

Listing 8.22: An example of establishing dependent tasks using the depend clause. This program requires a compiler implementing OpenMP 4.0 to compile successfully.

```
1  // File : depend_test.cpp
2  ...
3  #pragma omp parallel
4  #pragma omp single
5  {
6      for (int i = 0; i < 3; ++i)
7      {
8  #pragma omp task shared(x) depend(out: x)
9          // T1
10         printf ("T1 %i\n", i);
11 #pragma omp task shared(x) depend(in: x)
12         // T2
13         printf ("T2 %i\n", i);
14 #pragma omp task shared(x) depend(in: x)
```

---

[10] A fifth dependence type exists in the form of depobj (dependency object), but it is not covered in this book.

```
15        // T3
16        printf ("T3 %i\n", i);
17      }
18    }
19  . . .
```

It is worthwhile to note that the variable x used in the depend clauses does not appear in the tasks' blocks, as it is not mandatory to do so. The for loop is executed by a single thread, and while the order of T2 and T3 may be switched (T3 may output before T2), T1 has to be complete before any of them can begin execution. Additionally, there is an interiteration dependence between T1 and T2 and T3: T1 during the second iteration cannot begin before the T2 and T3 tasks generated during the first iteration finish. The same is true for the third iteration as T1 then has to wait for the T2 and T3 that were generated during the second iteration. A sample output of this program is shown below. The clustering of the tasks generated during an iteration verifies our discussion:

```
$ ./depend_test
T1 0
T3 0
T2 0
T1 1
T2 1
T3 1
T1 2
T3 2
T2 2
```

Using dummy variables in the depend clauses serves the purpose of establishing dependencies well, but it might be undesirable from the source maintenance point of view: declaring the variables that are actually shared/communicated between the tasks makes the source code more readable.

We can go as far as listing arrays or array sections in depend clauses. An array section is a subset of an array starting at an arbitrary non-negative offset (more details in Section 8.9.2). OpenMP also offers the capability of using iterators (these are different to C++ STL iterators) as a convenient way to select multiple items from a set/container to base dependencies on. The syntax of the depend clause when accounting for iterators is:

```
depend([iterator-modifier,] dependence-type : identifer-list)
```

The syntax of the iterator-modifier is:

```
iterator(iterator-specifier+)
```

where "+" indicates one or more iterator specifiers. An iterator-specifier is defined as:

```
[iterator-type] identifier = range-specification
```

where the iterator-type is a type name (such as int or float) and range-specification is in the form begin:end[:step]. The identifier supplied will take the values begin, begin+step, etc., all the way up to but excluding end. Note that step can have a negative value, in which case the values decrease from the first one and keep going as long as they are *bigger* than the end.

The following example shows how all these different ways can be used to establish dependencies between sibling tasks:

Listing 8.23: An example of establishing dependencies using array ranges and iterator modifiers.

```cpp
// File : depend_test2.cpp
. . .
const int N = 10;

//------------------------------------------------
void initElem (int *p, int val)
{
  *p = val;
}

//------------------------------------------------
void printAll (int *v, int n)
{
  for (int i = 0; i < n; ++i)
    printf ("%d ", v[i]);
  printf ("\n");
}

//------------------------------------------------
int main ()
{
  int v[N];

//------------------------
// Version 1
#pragma omp parallel
#pragma omp single
  {
    int i;

    for (i = 0; i < N; ++i)
#pragma omp task depend(out: v[i])
      initElem (&v[i], i);
#pragma omp task depend(in: v[0:N])
    printAll (v, N);
  }

//------------------------
// Version 2
#pragma omp parallel
#pragma omp single
```

```
42      {
43        int i;
44
45        for (i = 0; i < N; ++i)
46   #pragma omp task depend(out: v[i])
47          initElem (&v[i], i);
48   #pragma omp task depend(iterator(it = 0:N), in: v[it])
49        printAll (v, N);
50      }
51
52   //————————
53   // Version 3
54   int fooVar;
55   #pragma omp parallel
56   #pragma omp single
57      {
58        int i;
59
60        for (i = 0; i < N; ++i)
61          {
62   #pragma omp task depend(out: fooVar)
63            {
64              if (i == 5)
65                sleep (1);
66              initElem (&v[i], i);
67            }
68          }
69   #pragma omp task depend(in: fooVar)
70        printAll (v, N);
71      }
72   . . .
```

The above program performs the same operations in three different ways. Each version operates on an array of integers by creating one task per element for initialization (for loops on lines 31–33, 45–47, and 60–67). These tasks call the initElem function for this purpose. An extra task is created that depends on these, for printing out the values in the array by calling the printAll function (defined on line 12). Version 1 (starting at line 26) is using an array section (line 34) to establish the dependencies. Version 2 (starting at line 40) is using an iterator-modifier called *it* (see line 48) to make the printing task wait on all the "initializer" tasks.

The third version is using a dummy variable fooVar for the same purpose. To verify that the printing task is not just waiting on a single of the "initializers" before printing, a sleep(1) statement is added to the sixth initializer. Sure enough, the printing task in the third version delays its execution until the sixth initializer is also complete.

8.5.4 The taskloop **directive**

The taskloop is an alternative to the parallel for directive, where a for loop is partitioned amongst tasks instead of a team of threads. This can be a desirable outcome if the execution cost of the loop body varies significantly (so it is a load balancing attempt) or the generated tasks are supposed to coordinate with other tasks which have been generated outside the particular loop (see also how to do reduction over multiple tasks in Section 8.5.5).

The for loop that can be decorated with a taskloop directive has to be in a canonical form, so in terms of conditions the same apply as in the case of the parallel for (see the rules in Section 8.4). Of course, this extends to any loop-carried dependencies, i.e., they need to be fixed before attempting to parallelize the loop.

For taskloop there is no schedule clause that can be used to control the partitioning of the loop. The only available option for this purpose is the grainsize clause, which accepts as a parameter an integer GS which acts as a "hint" to the number of loop iterations that will be assigned per task. The actual loop iterations per task range between GS and $2 \cdot GS - 1$ inclusive.

For example, the following code would generate tasks with between four and seven iterations per task:

```
#pragma omp parallel
{
#pragma omp single
#pragma omp taskloop grainsize(4)
   for(int i = 0; i < N; i++)
       printf("Thread ID #%i : %i\n", omp_get_thread_num(), i);
}
```

All tasks get the same number of iterations, except the last one, which gets whatever remains. The single directive above is essential for getting the loop executed only once. Otherwise, all the threads in the team would generate tasks from the taskloop directive.

The number of tasks can be controlled with the num_tasks clause. The actual number of tasks generated is the minimum of the num_tasks clause parameter and the number of loop iterations (cannot have a task with no iterations assigned). If neither grainsize nor num_tasks are provided, the number of tasks generated is implementation-specific.

Most of the other clauses, especially the ones controlling variable scope, like, e.g., reduction, shared, private, etc., are still available. Also, the generation of tasks can be conditional based on the outcome of an if or a final clause, and the generated tasks can be untied and/or mergeable. The semantics of these clauses are shared with the task directive.

8.5.5 The taskgroup **directive and task-level reduction**

The taskwait directive examined previously sets up a barrier that "collects" all the immediate children of a task. It would be beneficial if we could establish and synchronize groups of tasks that are generated inside a parallel region, without the must-be-siblings restriction. This is the objective of the taskgroup directive, which allows us to synchronize all the tasks generated within its boundaries, regardless if

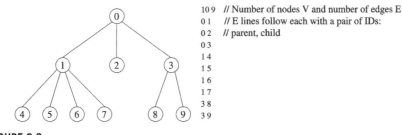

FIGURE 8.8

An example of a 4-ary tree and a possible simple text representation of it.

they are children or descendants of the thread executing the structured block of the taskgroup directive.

The end of a taskgroup directive carries an implicit barrier for all the tasks that were generated in one or the other way inside the associated parallel region.

The taskgroup directive extends the idea of the reduction clause that we have seen in the parallel for and taskloop, with the pair of task_reduction and in_reduction clauses:

- task_reduction(reduction_identifier: list_of_variables): can be used with a taskgroup directive to declare that the tasks participating in the group operate on the listed variables. After the task group terminates, the listed variables will contain the value of the reduction operation.
- in_reduction(reduction_identifier: list_of_variables): can be used with a taskloop or task directives to declare that the corresponding tasks participate in the reduction of the listed variables. The tasks having an in_reduction clause must belong to a taskgroup with a task_reduction clause.

As an example that will showcase all the above material, let us consider the traversal of a k-ary tree. A k-ary tree is a tree that has nodes equipped with a maximum of k children. A binary tree is a special case of a k-ary one for k−2. An example of a 4-ary tree is shown in Fig. 8.8.

A node of a k-ary tree can be represented by the following structure:

Listing 8.24: A structure template for a k-ary tree node.

```
// File : k-ary.cpp
template < typename T > struct Node
{
  T data;
  int parent;
  vector < int >children;
};
```

The structure contains a field for the data associated with the node, along with a "pointer" to the parent node and a vector of "pointers" to its child nodes. As an array is used to hold the tree nodes (see line 25 in Listing 8.25), the "pointers" are actually the indices of the corresponding Node structure instances.

A k-ary tree can be built on top of this Node structure as shown below:

Listing 8.25: A class template for a k-ary tree.

```cpp
 8  //  File  :  k—ary.cpp
 9  static  int  __count;
10
11  //====================================
12  //  Node  0  is  supposed  to  be  the  root
13  template  <  typename  T  >  class  KTree
14  {
15  public:
16    KTree  (int  n);
17    void  setData  (int  i,  T  d);
18    void  addEdge  (int  a,  int  b);
19    void  preOrder  ();
20    int  filterCount  (bool  pred  (T));
21  private:
22    int  N;
23    void  preOrder_aux  (int);
24    void  filterCount_aux  (int,  bool  pred  (T));
25    unique_ptr  <  Node  <  T  >[]  >  nodes;
26  };
27
28  //----------------------------------------
29  template  <  typename  T  >  KTree  <  T  >::KTree  (int  n)
30  {
31    nodes  =  make_unique  <  Node  <  T  >[]  >  (n);
32    nodes[0].parent  =  -1;
33    N  =  n;
34  }
35
36  //----------------------------------------
37  template  <  typename  T  >  void  KTree  <  T  >::setData  (int  i,  T  d)
38  {
39    nodes[i].data  =  d;
40  }
41
42  //----------------------------------------
43  template  <  typename  T  >  void  KTree  <  T  >::addEdge  (int  a,  int  b)
44  {
45    nodes[a].children.push_back  (b);
46    nodes[b].parent  =  a;
47  }
48
49  //----------------------------------------
50  template  <  typename  T  >  void  KTree  <  T  >::preOrder  ()
51  {
52  #pragma  omp  parallel
53    {
54  #pragma  omp  single
```

```
55   #pragma omp taskgroup
56       preOrder_aux (0);
57     }
58   }
59
60   //————————————————————————————
61   template < typename T > void KTree < T >::preOrder_aux (int n)
62   {
63     cout << nodes[n].data << endl;
64   #pragma omp taskloop grainsize(1)
65     for (int i = 0; i < nodes[n].children.size (); i++)
66       preOrder_aux (nodes[n].children[i]);
67   }
68
69   //————————————————————————————
70   template < typename T > int KTree < T >::filterCount (bool pred (T))
71   {
72     __count = 0;
73
74   #pragma omp parallel
75     {
76   #pragma omp single
77       {
78   #pragma omp taskgroup task_reduction(+:__count)
79         filterCount_aux (0, pred);
80       }
81     }
82     return __count;
83   }
84
85   //————————————————————————————
86   template < typename T > void KTree < T >::filterCount_aux (int n, ↩
            bool pred (T))
87   {
88     __count += pred (nodes[n].data);
89
90   #pragma omp taskloop grainsize(1) in_reduction(+:__count)
91     for (int i = 0; i < nodes[n].children.size (); i++)
92       filterCount_aux (nodes[n].children[i], pred);
93   }
94
95   //========================================
96   // Expecting the first line to contain the number of nodes and the ↩
            number of edges E
97   // E lines follow, each having the ID of the parent and the ID of ↩
            the child. IDs start from 0
98   unique_ptr < KTree < int >>readTree (const char *fname)
99   {
100    ifstream fin (fname);
101    int N, E, a, b;
102    fin >> N >> E;
```

```
103    unique_ptr < KTree < int >>tree = make_unique < KTree < int > >(N)↩
       ;
104    for (int i = 0; i < N; i++)
105      tree->setData (i, i);
106    while (E--)
107      {
108        fin >> a >> b;
109        tree->addEdge (a, b);
110      }
111    fin.close ();
112    return move (tree);
113  }
114
115  //========================================
116  bool pred (int n)
117  {
118    return n % 2 == 0;
119  }
120
121  //========================================
122  int main (int argc, char **argv)
123  {
124    unique_ptr < KTree < int >>tree = readTree (argv[1]);
125    tree->preOrder ();
126
127    cout << "Count " << tree->filterCount (pred) << endl;
128    . . .
```

The KTree class template is based on a fixed-size array of Node structures (defined on line 25) that is allocated during the construction of the tree (line 31), hence the need for a parameter in the constructor of line 29 that specifies the number of nodes in the tree. A dynamically grown tree could also be accommodated with some extra effort (e.g., by using a vector of Node instances), but notably we could do so without having to modify the logic of the preOrder method which is supposed to print the tree contents in a preorder fashion. The use of a smart pointer for the nodes field simplifies memory management.

The first node in the nodes array serves as the root of the tree. The addEdge and setData methods serve the purpose of building the tree by establishing the connections between the nodes and populating the nodes with their associated information, respectively.[11] The readTree function starting at line 98 serves the purpose of reading a k-tree from a file and returning a unique pointer to a KTree instance back to the caller. An example of the simple file format expected is shown in Fig. 8.8. For the purposes of our example, we just populate the Node instances with their position in the nodes array (lines 104–105).

The preorder traversal is accomplished across two methods:

---

[11] A KTree instance can be traversed in parallel but it is not designed to be *manipulated* in parallel. Relevant techniques are covered in Chapter 4.

1. The `preOrder` which is defined at line 50 and acts as a front-end. It is used to set up a parallel region (line 52) and create a `taskgroup` for the tasks that will process the tree nodes (line 55). The `single` directive at line 54 is essential, as otherwise all the threads in the team would be executing line 56.

2. The `preOrder_aux` is serving as the back-end method, printing out the data of the parent node (line 63) before using a `taskloop` directive to iterate over the child nodes. All the tasks generated by the directive of line 64 belong to the `taskgroup` initiated on line 55.

A filtering operation where we count the nodes that satisfy a predicate function can be implemented in a similar fashion as observed in the `filterCount` and `filterCount_aux` methods (lines 70–93). `filterCount` and `filterCount_aux` expect a pointer to a predicate function as a parameter. In Listing 8.25 we are just checking if the number stored in a `Node`'s `data` field is an even number (see function `pred` on line 116).

The major addition relative to the preorder methods is the use of the `task_reduction` and `in_reduction` clauses on lines 78 and 90, respectively, that identify that the addition operator will be used to reduce the private per-task copies of the `__count` variable.[12] The `task_reduction` clause is reserved for the `taskgroup` directive and the `in_reduction` clause for the individual tasks generated within the group.

The `grainsize(1)` clause on lines 64 and 90 forces the use of one task per node. This could get wildly off-hand for large trees. A possible solution would be to utilize the depth of the traversal as a deciding factor in the creation of new tasks.

If we assume that we have P CPU cores and the tree is perfect, i.e., all internal nodes have k child nodes, then as the traversal reaches depth d, the number of tasks generated would be equal to

$$0 + k + k^2 + k^3 + \cdots + k^d = (k^d + \cdots + k + k^0) - 1 = \frac{k^{d+1} - 1}{k - 1} - 1. \quad (8.6)$$

The first term on the left expression is zero, as there is no new task generated for the root node.

If we would like to have a maximum of $2 \cdot P$ tasks generated, then the following should hold true:

$$\frac{k^{d+1} - 1}{k - 1} - 1 \leq 2 \cdot P \Rightarrow$$

$$k^{d+1} \leq (2 \cdot P + 1) \cdot (k - 1) + 1 \Rightarrow$$

$$d \leq \frac{log((2 \cdot P + 1) \cdot (k - 1) + 1)}{log(k)} - 1. \quad (8.7)$$

---

[12] ◈ **Pitfall**: The use of a global variable for `__count` may seem odd when a class private data member could be used instead. Unfortunately, during testing for this book and up to the GCC 10.1 compiler, a reduction clause in a task directive *inside a method template* caused an internal compiler error.

The required changes to the class template are minimal, as seen below:

Listing 8.26: Essential modifications to Listing 8.25, so that there is an upper limit on the generated tasks during a tree traversal.

```
129   // File : k-ary2.cpp
130   template < typename T > class KTree
131   {
132    private:
133     int k=0; // for k-ary tree
134     int maxDepth;
135      . . .
136   };
137
138   //—————————————————————————
139   template < typename T > void KTree < T >::addEdge (int a, int b)
140   {
141     nodes[a].children.push_back (b);
142     nodes[b].parent = a;
143     if(k < nodes[a].children.size()) k = nodes[a].children.size(); // ↵
            get the tree degree when building it
144   }
145
146   //—————————————————————————
147   template < typename T > void KTree < T >::preOrder ()
148   {
149     int P = omp_get_num_procs();
150     maxDepth = log( (2*P +1) * (k -1) + 1)/log( k )  -1;
151
152   #pragma omp parallel
153     {
154   #pragma omp single
155   #pragma omp taskgroup
156       preOrder_aux (0, 0);
157     }
158   }
159
160   //—————————————————————————
161   template < typename T > void KTree < T >::preOrder_aux (int n, int ↵
           depth)
162   {
163     cout << nodes[n].data << endl;
164   #pragma omp taskloop grainsize(1) if(depth <= maxDepth)
165     for (int i = 0; i < nodes[n].children.size (); i++)
166       preOrder_aux (nodes[n].children[i], depth+1);
167   }
```

The major changes boil down to line 143, which is used to get the degree of the tree during the construction phase, lines 149–150, which compute the depth threshold of Eq. (8.7), and line 164, which incorporates an if clause in the taskloop directive. The same technique could be used for the filtering operation.

8.6 **Synchronization constructs**

Shared-memory, parallel program correctness hinges on the ability to perform changes to shared data items in a coordinated fashion. OpenMP provides a number of synchronization directives that serve two purposes: mutual exclusion and event synchronization.

Many of the directives presented in this section have been used and explained previously. This section serves to consolidate and complete the relevant discussion in one place.

The mutual exclusion directives ensure that certain blocks of code will be executed as critical sections. This category of directives includes:

- `critical`: Allows only one thread at a time, to enter the structured block that follows. The syntax involves an optional identifier:

```
#pragma omp critical [ ( identifier ) ]
{
    // structured block
}
```

The identifier allows the establishment of *named critical sections*. The identifier serves to group critical sections together: using the same identifier in different `critical` directives means that there can be only one thread at any time, executing any of the corresponding blocks. All critical directives without an identifier are assumed to have the same name. We can think of grouped `critical` constructs as using the same mutex.

Obviously, explicitly naming the `critical` constructs can provide better performance, as it allows threads executing disjoint critical sections to do so concurrently.

- `atomic`: This is a lightweight version of the `critical` construct that uses platform-specific atomic machine instructions (like the Intel x86 CMPXCHG Compare and Exchange) to accelerate the execution of single-statement critical sections. Given that the statement should correlate closely with an atomic CPU instruction, the operations that can be "decorated" by an `atomic` directive are very limited.[13] These are:

```
x++;
x--;
++x;
--x;
x binop= expr;
x = x binop expr;
x = expr binop x;
```

---

[13] The `atomic` directive has a number of optional clauses that extend the types of statements that it can pair with. The OpenMP specification contains more details [3].

where x has to be a variable of scalar type, `binop` can be one of

```
+, *, -, /, &, ^, |, << , or >>
```

and `expr` is a scalar expression.

Caution should be taken in the calculation of the `expr` above. In the following example:

```
#pragma omp atomic
   x += y++;
```

while the update to the x variable is atomic, the update to the y variable is not, and thus it could be the possible cause of a race condition. In that case a `critical` directive should be used instead.

- `master`: Forces only the master thread in a parallel region to execute a block of code. The `master` directive has no associated clauses and no implied barrier on entry to or exit from the corresponding block. This means that when a thread other than the master reaches this construct, it just skips over it.

The `master` directive can be reserved for I/O operations, like, e.g., updating the program status on the console, as the example shown below:

```
int examined = 0;
int prevReported = 0;
#pragma omp for shared( examined, prevReported )
  for( int i = 0 ; i < N ; i++ )
    {
        // some processing

        // update the counter
#pragma omp atomic
        examined++;

        // use the master to output an update every 1000 newly ↵
            finished iterations
#pragma omp master
        {
            int temp = examined;
            if( temp - prevReported >= 1000)
                {
                    prevReported = temp;
                    printf("Examined %.2lf%%\n", temp * 1.0 / N );
                }
        }
    }
```

- `single`: Forces the execution of a block by one thread only. It is similar to the master directive, but for the implicit barrier at the end of the `single` block, which means that the two constructs are not interchangeable in general. The barrier can be eliminated by adding the `nowait` clause to the `single` directive.

We have seen multiple examples of the `single` directive in the previous sections, so we are repeating our discussion here for completeness. The `single` directive is typically paired with a `parallel` construct to limit the execution of certain parts of the code to one thread only. Notably, this problem does not exist with the `sections` or `task` constructs, as each thread is assigned specific work in these cases.

In the following example, the processing of some arbitrary data can start only after they are read from a file. The `single` directive assigns this task to one of the team threads:

Listing 8.27: An example of using the `single` directive to perform I/O prior to the processing of some data.

```
double data[ N ];
#pragma omp parallel shared( data, N )
{

#pragma omp single
  {
    // read data from a file
  }

#pragma omp for
  for(int i = 0; i < N; i++)
    {
        // process the data
    }
}
```

Could we possibly do the same with a `master` directive? The answer is given below, in the discussion of the `barrier` directive.

The second category of synchronization directives deals with events, including coordination, data consistency, and operation ordering:

- `barrier`: Explicit barrier directive that ensures threads begin/continue work after some point in time where certain conditions are met. All threads in a team must reach the `barrier` directive before execution can continue beyond that point. The `barrier` directive has no associated block. It is just placed inside an OpenMP work-sharing construct.

The code in Listing 8.27 could be modified to use the `master` directive if an explicit barrier forced all team threads to wait until the data have been read:

```
double data[ N ];
#pragma omp parallel shared( data, N )
{

#pragma omp master
  {
    // read data from a file
  }

#pragma omp barrier
```

```
#pragma omp for
  for(int i = 0; i < N; i++)
    {
        // process the data
    }
}
```

- taskwait: This is the barrier equivalent for tasks generated from a particular parent task. While the barrier directive applies to a team of *threads*, the taskwait directive applies to a group of *tasks*.

  Listing 8.28 shows how we can utilize taskwait for the postorder traversal of a binary tree. In a postorder traversal, a node is processed only after all its children have been processed.

Listing 8.28: A postorder traversal of a binary tree.

```cpp
1   // File : tree_postOrder.cpp
2   . . .
3   // template structure for a tree node
4   template < class T > struct Node
5   {
6     T info;
7     Node *left, *right;
8
9       Node (int i, Node < T > *l, Node < T > *r) :
10                     info (i), left (l), right (r) { }
11  };
12
13  //————————————————————————————
14  // function stub for processing a node's data
15  template < class T > void process (T item)
16  {
17  #pragma omp critical
18    cout << "Processing " << item << " by thread " << ↵
            omp_get_thread_num () << endl;
19  }
20
21  //————————————————————————————
22  template < class T > void postOrder (Node < T > *n)
23  {
24    if (n == NULL)
25      return ;
26
27  #pragma omp task
28    postOrder (n->left);
29  #pragma omp task
30    postOrder (n->right);
31  #pragma omp taskwait
32
33    process (n->info);
34  }
35
```

```
36   //-------------------------------------------------
37   int main (int argc, char *argv[])
38   {
39       // build a sample tree
40       Node < int >*head =
41       . . .
42
43   #pragma omp parallel
44       {
45   #pragma omp single
46           {
47               postOrder (head);
48           }
49       }
50
51       return 0;
52   }
```

The `parallel` pragma of line 43 sets up the multi-threaded execution of the structured block that follows. Although the `single` directive limits to one the calls to the `postOrder()` function, this in turn creates two new tasks to handle the two children of a node (via the `task` directives on lines 27 and 29). The recursive nature of the `postOrder()` function means that we eventually get one task for every node in the tree. As discussed earlier, we can limit the "explosion" of task creation by using the `if` or `final` clauses in the `task` directives, but this is not the essence of our example.

In order to force a postorder traversal, the tasks associated with the children of a node must be complete prior to processing the node itself via the call of line 33. The `taskwait` directive of line 31 ensures just that, by blocking the execution of the current task running the `postOrder()` function, until all the child tasks it spawned are complete.

• `ordered`: Is used inside a `parallel for` region to enforce the sequential execution of the structured block it heads. So while the iterations of a `for` loop may be partitioned according to the `schedule` clause and assigned to different threads to execute out-of-order, the `ordered` block has to execute as if it was done sequentially. The consequence is that if two threads are assigned successive groups of loop iterations, the second thread will have to block at the entry of its ordered block, until the first thread completes its own ordered block(s).

Any type of schedule can be used in a `parallel for` that contains an `ordered` directive. The only restriction is that the `parallel for` must have an `ordered` clause specified. However, if the `ordered` block is executed in every iteration, a `static` or `dynamic` schedule with a chunk size of 1 should maximize the concurrency potential. On the other hand, a `guided` schedule will result in a mostly sequential execution.

It should be noted that the `ordered` directive does not have to be *lexically* included in a `parallel for`. It can just as well be in a function that is called by the loop. The `ordered` clause should still be included in the `for` pragma. A `for` directive with an ordered clause suffers no consequence, if it does not encounter an ordered block during the execution of its body.

In the following example, we use the ordered directive to ensure that the program's output matches the one produced by the corresponding sequential program:

```
double data[ N ];
#pragma omp parallel shared( data, N )
{

#pragma omp for ordered schedule( static, 1 )
  for(int i = 0; i < N; i++)
    {
        // process the data

        // print the results in order
#pragma omp ordered
        cout << data[i];
    }
}
```

- flush: Is used to make a thread's view of *shared data*[14] *consistent* with main memory. This is an odd statement that requires clarification. Shared data are stored in main memory locations, which are supposed to be accessible by all threads. One would expect that reading or writing to these variables involves data transfer from or modification of the corresponding memory locations. Alas, CPU caches and/or compiler optimizations cause deviations from these expectations: shared data may be held in disjoint, CPU-specific cache memories, or even CPU registers for faster access.

So, when a shared variable is modified, this modification may not propagate to the appropriate main memory location immediately. A thread running on another core may get "stale" data if it tries to access this variable before the other CPU's cache and the main memory become consistent again.

The flush directive is like a *memory fence*: all memory operations, initiated before the flush, must complete before the flush can complete, i.e., the modifications have to propagate from the cache/registers to main memory. All operations that follow the flush directive cannot commence before the flush is complete.

The flush is a stand-alone directive that affects only the thread that executes it. It is only accompanied with an optional list of variables that will be restored to a consistent state:

```
#pragma omp flush [ ( list_of_variables ) ]
```

---

[14] It actually involves all thread-visible data, but it is only the shared ones that are of any consequence. It makes absolutely no difference to a thread what is the state of automatic, private, or threadprivate variables of other threads: it cannot "see" them. That is why we limit our discussion to shared variables.

If the list is missing, *all* thread-visible data return to a consistent state. Both the modified and the unchanged data by a thread are affected: the modified have to be stored to the main memory *before* the flush can complete, and the unchanged have to be read again from the main memory (refreshed) *after* the flush is complete.

An implicit flush operation takes place when one of the following occurs:

- a barrier directive,
- upon entry to and exit from parallel, critical, and ordered regions,
- upon exit from a work-sharing region, unless a nowait clause is specified,
- upon entry to and exit from an atomic operation,
- during any OpenMP lock operation that causes the lock to be set or unset (e.g., omp_set_lock, omp_test_lock, etc.),
- immediately before and immediately after every task scheduling point.

The extent of the above list means that under normal circumstances, an explicit flush directive is not necessary. The flush directive is a low-level synchronization directive as it affects one thread only. This is both an asset, as it can be used to optimize coordination between subsets of threads, and a drawback, as it demands careful design in order to avoid logical programming errors.

In Listing 8.29, we use the flush directive to send a signal between two threads.

Listing 8.29: Using the flush directive to propagate a signal in the form of a shared Boolean between two threads.

```
1  // File : flush_test.cpp
2  . . .
3    bool flag = false;
4  #pragma omp parallel sections default( none ) shared( flag, cout ←
       )
5    {
6
7  #pragma omp section
8      {
9        // wait for signal
10       while (flag == false)
11       {
12  #pragma omp flush ( flag )
13       }
14       // do something
15       cout << "First section\n";
16     }
17
18  #pragma omp section
19      {
20        // do something first
21        cout << "Second section\n";
22        sleep (1);
23        // signal other section
24        flag = true;
25
26  #pragma omp flush ( flag )
```

```
27
28          }
29      }
```

The first `flush` directive on line 12 ensures that an updated value for `flag` is fetched every time from the main memory. The second directive on line 26 makes the main memory consistent with the updated state of the `flag` Boolean.

Would this not work without the `flush` directives? This is a question that cannot be answered outside the context of a particular execution platform. We have to know how the target platform treats cache updates. The `flush` directive allows us to keep memory consistent in a cross-platform way without considering the restrictions of the underlying machine.

8.7 Cancellation constructs

A cancellation construct allows the termination of the innermost region that encloses it. It is a convenient way for controlling the flow of parallel execution when conditions dictate it, but OpenMP restrictions prohibit typical C++ flow control. For example, `parallel for` mandates the use of canonical form loops, i.e., a single point of entry and a single point of exit. There is no way to leave a `parallel for` loop before completing all the iterations, unless we could somehow make all the team threads aware of the termination and make them coordinate accordingly.

Cancellation is implemented with the use of two directives:

1. **cancel**: used to establish/declare to the OpenMP runtime that a parallel region should be canceled.
2. **cancellation point**: allows the executing thread to check if cancellation has been activated.

The use of the **cancellation point** directive is not mandatory. Cancellation can be also detected by a thread when a barrier (explicit or implicit) is encountered. When a thread detects a cancellation event, it transfers execution to the end of the canceled region. When all the team threads reach this implicit barrier, either by discovering the cancellation or by completing their assigned load, normal execution can resume.

The syntax of the two directives involves the naming of the enclosing construct affected:

```
#pragma omp cancel affected_construct [ if ( [ cancel: ] ↩
    logical_expr   ) ]
//─────────────────────────────
#pragma omp cancellation point affected_construct
```

where `affected_construct` can be one of `parallel`, `for`, `sections`, or `taskgroup`.

The following example shows how these constructs work with a `parallel for`:

Listing 8.30: An example of using cancellation constructs to stop a `parallel for` loop.

```
1  bool found=false;
2  #pragma omp parallel firstprivate( found )
3    {
4  #pragma omp for
5      for (int i = 0; i < N; i++)
6        {
7          found = doSmt( i );  // return true if something is ↩
                  accomplished
8
9  #pragma omp cancel for if(found)
10
11 #pragma omp cancellation point for
12      }
13    }
```

Line 9 initiates the cancellation procedure when a thread gets a true value returned by the line 7 call. Other threads can detect the cancellation via line 11.

It should be noted that the cancellation constructs' availability is implementation-specific. They are enabled if the `cancel-var` ICV is set to `true`. One can call the `omp_get_cancellation` function to inspect the value of `cancel-var` (at the moment of this writing the GNU compiler implementation returns `false`). Currently the standard does not have a provision for manipulating this ICV.

8.8 SIMD extensions

In the latest incarnations of the OpenMP standard, there has been a push to take better advantage of the hardware features that have been introduced over the years, including architectural CPU changes (e.g., augmented instruction sets) and coprocessors such as GPUs.

One of the significant changes in the CPU domain was the introduction of extended single instruction, multiple data (SIMD) capabilities, such as the Advanced Vector Extensions (AVX) instruction sets in the x86-64 world or the 128-bit vector instructions in ARM. The AVX-512 implementation in the Intel Phi CPU is capable of processing a 512-bit wide vector of data. So for example, we could process 16 type-`float` data in parallel! Mainstream x86-64 CPUs sport the AVX-256 instructions which could process half of these data in a SIMD fashion, which can still provide a significant performance boost. However, taking advantage of these capabilities requires special compiler optimizations and/or programmer intervention (e.g., by employing special libraries).

OpenMP exposes these capabilities through the `simd` directive, which comes in three flavors:

- **simd** loop directive: This is used to convert a canonical-form loop into a sequence of SIMD instructions.

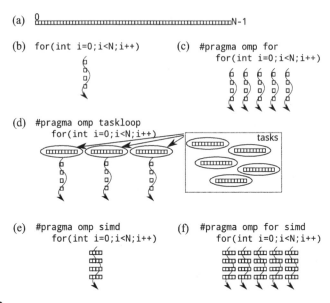

FIGURE 8.9

Five possible ways for processing the array of N elements shown in (a). In (b) a sequential loop processes one element per iteration. In (c) we use a `parallel for` directive to have multiple threads process one element for each of their iterations. In (d) a `taskloop` splits the array into tasks and then assigns the tasks to threads. In (e) we use a `simd` directive to have one thread process multiple elements per iteration as a SIMD vector. (f) effectively combines (c) and (e) with a `for simd` directive to have multiple threads process multiple elements for each of their iterations.

- **for simd** loop directive: This is used to parallelize a loop, where each thread is also employing SIMD instructions for executing its share of the iterations in batches. The loop must be – as always – in a canonical form.
- **declare simd** directive: This is used to declare that a function can be "inlined" and multiple calls to it with different parameters can be executed in a SIMD fashion.

Multiple nested loops can be combined into one by using a `collapse` clause, and results can be combined using a `reduction` clause, in the same fashion as with the `parallel for` construct.

Along with the `simd` directive, OpenMP supports four different ways of parallel execution for loops (plus one for devices that will be examined in Section 8.9). Fig. 8.9 shows how these alternatives translate into different workload partitionings and different execution patterns.

Getting `simd` to work properly might require a bit more work though than just inserting the directive. For example, the execution pattern should translate to processing successive elements in an array (so that they can be treated as a vector). Or the elements to be processed should follow a regular spatial pattern, so that they can be grouped in vectors.

In order to assist the compiler in completing the transformation of a loop into a sequence of SIMD instructions, OpenMP provides the following clauses:

- **simdlen(positive_integer**): Specifies the *preferred* number of iterations to be executed in SIMD fashion. The actual number that OpenMP will use depends on both the hardware platform and the loop to be transformed.
- **safelen(positive_integer**): Specifies the maximum number of successive iterations that can be grouped "safely" together for SIMD execution.

Also the aforementioned declare simd directive can be used to decorate functions that can be "inserted" into a SIMD loop. What this means is that a special version of the function is created that can process multiple arguments (as if called multiple times) from a single invocation in a SIMD loop.

In the following listing, which performs the "sum of *a* times *x* plus *y*" operation on two vectors, i.e., $a \cdot \vec{x} + \vec{y}$ (a.k.a. saxpy), the implementation function is declared to be SIMD-friendly by the directive on line 2. The uniform clause is used to specify that the "a" parameter will be the same for all calls to the saxpy function.

Listing 8.31: Performing the saxpy operation on two vectors using SIMD instructions.

```
1   // File : vectorAdd_simd.cpp
2   #pragma omp declare simd uniform(a)
3   float saxpy (float a, float x, float y)
4   {
5      return a * x + y;
6   }
7
8   int main (int argc, char **argv)
9   {
10     int N = atoi (argv[1]);
11     int useSIMD = atoi (argv[2]);
12
13     unique_ptr < float[] > x = make_unique < float[] > (N);
14     unique_ptr < float[] > y = make_unique < float[] > (N);
15     unique_ptr < float[] > z = make_unique < float[] > (N);
16   #pragma omp parallel for simd if(useSIMD>0)
17     for (int i = 0; i < N; i++)
18        x[i] = y[i] = i;
19
20     float a = 1.0;
21   #pragma omp parallel for simd if(useSIMD>0)
22     for (int i = 0; i < N; i++)
23        z[i] = saxpy (a, x[i], y[i]);
24   . . .
```

The above program reads the size of the vectors from the command-line, plus a flag indicating whether the SIMD extensions should be activated or not (line 11). This parameter is fed to the if clauses of lines 16 and 21 to control whether the SIMD transformations will take place or not.

A programmer can use two additional clauses to assist the work of the compiler:

- **inbranch**: Declares that the function will always be called from within a conditional statement in the body of a SIMD loop. This is obviously a setback.
- **notinbranch**: Declares that the function will never be called from within a conditional statement.

Data memory alignment can be also significant depending on the underlying hardware architecture and the instructions that are used. For example, as stated in Section 14.9 of Intel's software development manual for x86_64 [6], some SIMD instructions have explicit memory alignment requirements (either at 16- or 32-byte boundaries), while others have no such restriction.

Data alignment can be specified when data are declared by using the `alignas` specifier. Also we can declare to OpenMP the data alignment to assist the compiler, by using `simd`'s `aligned` clause. The syntax is:

```
aligned ( list_of_variables [ : alignment ] )
```

where `alignment` is in bytes. If `alignment` is missing, it is assumed to be equal to an implementation-specific default for the SIMD instructions used. For example:

```
alignas(16) float data[N];
#pragma omp parallel for simd aligned( data : alignof(data) )
  for (. . .
```

The C++ `alignof` operator returns the memory alignment of its argument.

When `for simd` is used, it is a good strategy to partition the loop between the threads in multiples of the SIMD vector length. This way we can use the SIMD instructions for processing the entirety of a thread's assigned load. Otherwise, parts that do not fill up a vector or are misaligned are processed as scalars. The partitioning can be done via the schedule clause:

```
const int SIMD_VEC_LEN=64;
#pragma omp parallel for simd schedule(static : SIMD_VEC_LEN)
  for (. . .
```

An alternative is to use the `simd` modifier in the `schedule` clause as shown below:

```
#pragma omp parallel for simd schedule(simd : dynamic)
  for (. . .
```

In that case, all the chunks except possibly the first (due to misalignment) and the last (because the total number of iterations may not be a multiple of the SIMD vector size) have their chunk size fixed to $\lceil \frac{chunk\_size}{simd\_width} \rceil \cdot simd\_width$, where $chunk\_size$ is the chunk size specified by the programmer (or the default if the parameter is omitted) and $simd\_width$ is an implementation-specific constant. The target of this modification is to make sure that the `chunk_size` is a multiple of `simd_width`.

It should be stressed that the `linear` clause behaves differently for the `simd` directive than it does for the work-sharing `for` directive. In the case of the `simd` variants (including the `for simd`), the variables listed in the `linear` clause do not get implicitly modified based on the supplied (or implied) step. This is contrary to how it works for the `for` directive, as we saw in Section 8.4.1.1.

For example, the following code:

```
// File : linear_clause2.cpp
int i=1, j=1;
#pragma omp simd linear(i) linear(j:2)
for (int k = 0; k < 4; k++)
    printf("SIMD %i %i %i\n", k, i, j);

printf("POST LOOP %i %i\n", i, j);

#pragma omp parallel for linear(i) linear(j:2)
for (int k = 0; k < 4; k++)
    printf("FOR %i %i %i\n", k, i, j);

printf("POST LOOP %i %i\n", i, j);
```

produces this output:

```
SIMD 0 1 1
SIMD 1 1 1
SIMD 2 1 1
SIMD 3 1 1
POST LOOP 1 1
FOR 1 2 3
FOR 0 1 1
FOR 3 4 7
FOR 2 3 5
POST LOOP 4 7
```

Noteworthy observations are that the `simd` loop output is in order, while the `parallel for` loop is not. Also, the `i` and `j` variables are modified during the second loop and they keep the value of the last iteration after the loop exits.

If we would like the `simd` loop to exhibit the same exact behavior, then we should have:

```
#pragma omp for simd linear(i) linear(j:2)
for (int k = 0; k < 4; k++)
{
    printf("SIMD %i %i %i\n", k, i, j);
    i++;
    j+=2;
}
i --; // adjuct values after the loop
j -= 2;
```

8.9 Offloading to devices

Since the 4.0 incarnation of the standard, OpenMP supports the migration of workload (so-called offloading) to accelerators such as GPUs or many-core computing devices (such as Intel's Phi).

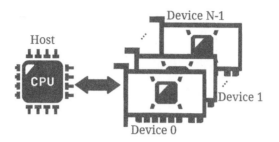

FIGURE 8.10

OpenMP system model for accelerator support.

OpenMP models a heterogeneous platform as consisting of a host (the CPU with one or more cores) and one or more devices (e.g., GPUs), called *targets*, as shown in Fig. 8.10.

A structured block can be offloaded to any of the attached devices, by selecting the "target" of the offloading action. The devices can be queried and selected with the following functions:

```
// Returns the number of available devices
int omp_get_num_devices();

// Returns the number that corresponds to the default device
int omp_get_default_device();

// Sets the default device to be the one identified by "dev_num"
void omp_set_default_device(int dev_num);

// Returns the device number the executing thread is running on
int omp_get_device_num();

// Returns a number identifying the host "device"
int omp_get_initial_device();
```

In addition, OpenMP supports a `device` clause for selecting the target device in the directives that are covered in subsequent paragraphs.

Alternatively, one can define the `OMP_DEFAULT_DEVICE` environment variable for setting which device to be selected by default. For example:

```
$ export OMP_DEFAULT_DEVICE=0  # Works in BASH
```

Each computing device in the heterogeneous platform is associated with a *data environment* that holds the variables residing in its memory space. A variable may exist in multiple data environments, and keeping the copies consistent and up-to-date is one of OpenMP's mandates. The data environments may be distinct (as is the case for discrete GPUs), they may share physical memory (as is the case of APUs), or they may have some automated sharing mechanism like unified memory (available in OpenMP 5.0).

The directives that OpenMP incorporates for device operations support fall into two categories: work-sharing constructs and data managements constructs, as explained in the following sections.

8.9.1 **Device work-sharing directives**

The new set of directives are used in tandem with the ones covered so far in this chapter. The first one is the `target` directive:

```
#pragma omp target
    structured_block
```

which migrates the structured block that follows and the *data required to run it* to a device. A new task is created for running the associated structured block by a single thread.

By default, the scalar data and pointers referenced in the structured block are treated as `firstprivate` (see Section 8.3.5), and the arrays are copied *to* the device before the start of the execution and *from* the device after the execution is complete. In the next section we examine how this behavior can be modified/fine-tuned.

Obviously a single thread executing the structured block would translate to a slowdown and not a speedup! A single thread cannot take advantage of the multiple streaming multiprocessors (SMs) in a CUDA device or the multiple compute units (CUs) in an OpenCL one. The solution is the introduction of another directive:

```
#pragma omp teams
    structured_block
```

The `teams` directive creates a `league`/collection of `teams`/groups of threads. One thread from each team is initially assigned to run the associated structured block. The `teams` is equivalent to the `parallel` directive in the sense that all the initial threads execute the same block.

Each team of threads corresponds to a CUDA block or an OpenCL work group. So the league of teams corresponds to a CUDA grid or an OpenCL index space. All the threads that are initiated by `teams` and its nested directives are called the **contention group**. The official OpenMP definition for the term is "an initial thread and all its descendants."

The size of the league and the size of the individual teams can be controlled with appropriate clauses:

- `num_teams ( [lower-bound:] upper-bound)`: If the optional `lower-bound` is missing, a fixed number of teams are created, equal to the `upper-bound`. Otherwise, the actual number of teams is implementation-specific and within the supplied boundary.
- `thread_limit ( integer-expression )`: Upper limit for the total number of threads for all the teams (not each team individually).

In general, explicit management of the `num_teams` and `thread_limit` clauses creates code that is not platform-agnostic and that will have a hard time delivering decent results on every deployment platform. For this reason, and unless algorithm design concerns impose otherwise, it is advisable to let the OpenMP runtime figure out the best number of teams and their threads.

A thread can recover the number of the team it belongs to by using the `omp_get_team_num()` function. Following OpenMP conventions, the `omp_get_num_teams()` – if called within a `teams` construct – returns the number of teams created.

There are still two major hurdles to overcome in order to fully utilize a GPU: (a) have each team of threads process a different part of the workload and (b) have all the threads in a team (and not just the initial one) participate in the computation.

The first problem can be overcome by using the `omp_get_team_num()` and `omp_get_thread_num()` functions to identify the location of a thread in the contention group and diverge execution accordingly. The `omp_get_thread_num()` function returns the ID of the thread within a team, i.e., something similar to the `get_local_id()` function in OpenCL and the `threadIdx` intrinsic variable in CUDA.

A better solution is using the `distribute` directive, which must be nested inside a `teams` directive and must be immediately followed by a `for` loop. Any code that is between the `teams` and `distribute` directives will be executed by all the initial team threads. Consider the following code snippet:

Listing 8.32: Device matrix multiplication code that utilizes the `target`, `teams`, and `distribute` directives.

```cpp
// File : teamsEx.cpp
int a[N][N], b[N][N], c[N][N];

#pragma omp target
#pragma omp teams
  {
#pragma omp distribute
   for(int i=0;i<N;i++)
#pragma omp parallel for
     for(int j=0;j<N;j++)
       for(int k=0;k<N;k++)
         c[i][j]+= a[i][k]*b[k][j];
  }
```

The result of each of the directives is shown in Fig. 8.11.

Lines 4–9 in Listing 8.32 can be also combined into one directive:

```cpp
#pragma omp target teams distribute parallel for collapse(2)
  for(int i=0;i<N;i++)
    for(int j=0;j<N;j++)
      for(int k=0;k<N;k++)
        c[i][j]+= a[i][k]*b[k][j];
```

As has been extensively discussed in Chapters 6 and 7, GPUs come into their own only if the workload is sufficiently large to justify the deployment overhead. A structured block can be conditionally offloaded to a GPU by using the `if` clause:

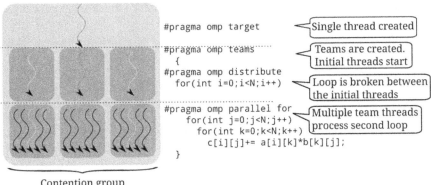

FIGURE 8.11

Generation of threads by the matrix multiplication code in Listing 8.32.

```
#pragma omp target if( boolean-expr )
    structured_block
```

The `target` directive can be also combined with a `depend` clause (see Section 8.5.2) so that it can synchronize with other tasks and a `nowait` clause that creates a new host task to launch the device code asynchronously. An alternative to using the `nowait` clause is to explicitly create a `task` "wrap" around the `target` construct.

The program in Listing 8.32 can be compiled with the following commands, using either the GNU or the CLang C++ compilers:

```
$ g++ -fopenmp -foffload=nvptx-none -fno-stack-protector -foffload=-↵
    lm teamsEx.cpp -o teamsEx
# OR
$ clang++-9 -fopenmp -fopenmp-targets=nvptx64 teamsEx.cpp -o teamsEx
```

The notable additions to the GNU compiler switches are `-foffload=nvptx-none`, which specifies the offload target device (in our case NVidia PTX), and `-fno-stack-protector`, which treats a possible compilation error encountered during the invocation of the cross-compiler (the compiler targeting the device). If your compiler does not have this issue, it can be safely omitted.

By changing the value fed to the `-foffload` switch, we can target AMD GPUs (with "hsa") or Intel's Phi coprocessors (with "x86_64-intelmicemul-linux-gnu").

On the side of the CLang compiler, the produced executable will default to the GPU architecture specified during the compilation of the CLang tools. One can override this default by adding an explicit switch such as "`-Xopenmp-target -march=sm_70`" (see the meaning of the sm_* symbolic names in Section 6.4).

The extra offload switch for the GNU compiler (i.e., "`-foffload=-lm`"), although not required for the particular example, ensures that any math functions that are supposed to run on the device are properly linked and called by the device code.

Of course this raises the question whether user-defined functions require any special treatment to be made available to the device. The short answer is that they do: they must be declared as being part of the code to be offloaded to the device, by placing them inside this pair of directives:

```
#pragma omp declare target
  variable declarations and function definitions
#pragma omp end declare target
```

The same directives can be used to flag variables (or copies of them) as residing in the device memory space. For example:

```
#pragma omp declare target
double testf (double x)
{
  return x * x + 2 * sin (x);
}
double sum=0;
#pragma omp end declare target
```

By default, the function `testf` and the global variable `sum` shown above will be made available to both the host and the device.

The placement of variables and the generation of function code can be fine-tuned with the optional `device_type` clause, which accepts three possible values:

- `any`: The default option, making the enclosed items available to both host and device.
- `host`: Makes the enclosed items available only on the host.
- `nohost`: Availability is limited only to the device.

Both the `teams` and `target` directives can be decorated with a `reduction` clause. However, at the moment of this writing, careful considerations need to be made based on the OpenMP implementation utilized. In general, reductions crossing the boundaries of teams may produce wrong results. A safe way to always yield a correct interteam reduction is to perform individual intrateam reductions and then consolidate the results at a subsequent step.

Considering the integration application that we used in Section 8.3, moving the trapezoid computations to a GPU requires the following directive sequence:

Listing 8.33: OpenMP device-based code for calculating the integral of a function using a team-wise reduction operation. Only changes relative to Listing 8.3 are shown.

```
1  // File : integration_omp_V5.cpp
2  . . .
3  const int numTeams = 100;
4  //————————————————————————————
5  double integrate (double st, double en, int div)
6  {
7    double localRes = 0;
8    double step = (en - st) / div;
```

```
9     unique_ptr < double [] > TR = make_unique < double [] > (numTeams);
10    double *teamResults = TR.get ();
11  #pragma omp target data map(tofrom: teamResults[0:numTeams])
12  #pragma omp target teams num_teams(numTeams)
13    {
14      int teamID = omp_get_team_num ();
15  #pragma omp distribute parallel for reduction(+:teamResults[teamID])
16      for (int i = 1; i < div; i++)
17        {
18          double x = st + i * step;
19          teamResults[teamID] += testf (x);
20        }
21    }
22    // consolidate partial results
23    for (int i = 0; i < numTeams; i++)
24      localRes += teamResults[i];
25
26    localRes += (testf (st) + testf (en)) / 2;
27    localRes *= step;
28    return localRes;
29  }
30
31  . . .
```

The key points of the above program are:

- The intrateam reduction results are saved in an array created before entering the target section, using a smart pointer on line 9. The `make_unique` function template initializes all the array elements to zero.
- The `TR` array is moved to the device before the computation and retrieved after the device computation is complete with the "`target data`" directive on line 11. This directive is explained in the next section.
- To signal to OpenMP that `TR` points to an array, it is cast to a regular pointer on line 10.
- The initial thread of each team identifies the team it belongs to on line 14. Subsequently all threads in that team reduce the results of the for loop execution in the `teamResults[teamID]` element, as instructed by the `reduction` clause of line 15.
- The number of teams is explicitly controlled by the `num_teams` clause on line 12. One could settle for the number of teams created by default by the OpenMP runtime; however, it must be ensured that enough space is allocated in the `TR` array.
- The intrateam results are accumulated by the host at lines 23–24.
- One minor difference with Listing 8.3 that is not easily distinguished above is that the function to be integrated is hardcoded on line 19 instead of passed as a parameter. Otherwise a runtime error is produced as the host does not have a reference to the device-side `testf` function.

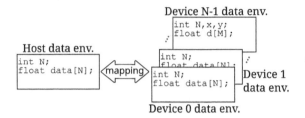

FIGURE 8.12

OpenMP data environments for device offloading. Each data environment can hold copies of the host variables or data exclusively available to the associated device. Mapping works in a bi-directional way.

8.9.2 Device memory management directives

The major obstacle in discrete memory GPU/accelerator use has always been the transfer of data from/to the host machine. Actually, it has been demonstrated in the literature [14,61] that the problem is severe enough to form a kind of "barrier": if the computation-to-communication ratio is not sufficiently high to overcome the data transfer latency, using a GPU is counterproductive.

As a result, the timely transfer (or persistence) of data to/from an accelerator is a critical software design component. In OpenMP a number of directives and clauses can be used to fine-tune data transfer and/or persistence, deviating from the default behavior of moving everything on the device before the computation and collecting everything back to the host after the device computation.

For each device present in a system, OpenMP manages a data environment which consists of all the variables used by the regions executing on the corresponding device, as shown in Fig. 8.12. *Synchronizing* the different copies is the purpose of the mapping directives and clauses used.

The `target data` directive can be used to establish a data environment by surrounding any other `target` constructs. For example:

```
#pragma omp target data
{
// first target construct
#pragma omp target teams
. . .

// no host sync here

// second target construct
#pragma omp target teams
. . .
}
```

The two `teams` constructs shown above share the same data environment, eliminating the need for synchronization with the host between them.

The `target data` directive is typically accompanied by one or more `map` clauses that state how and when the data synchronization will occur between the host and the device data environments. In the following vector addition example, the variables that are not placed in a `map` clause (namely `N`) are treated as `firstprivate`, while the arrays `a` and `b` are transferred to the device (but not back to the host). On the other hand, the `c` array is only transferred to the host from the device after the parallel region is complete.

Listing 8.34: OpenMP device-based vector addition with explicit data mapping.

```
1  // File : vectorAdd.cpp
2  int a[N], b[N], c[N];
3  . . .
4  #pragma target data map(to:a,b) map(from:c)
5  #pragma omp target teams distribute parallel for
6     for(int i=0;i<N;i++)
7        c[i] = a[i]+b[i];
8  . . .
```

The two directives can also be combined into one:

```
#pragma omp target teams distribute parallel for map(to:a,b) map(↩
    from:c)
. . .
```

The `map` clause has the following syntax:

```
map( [ [map-type-modifier[, map-type-modifier [, ...]]] map-type : ]↩
    list)
```

The optional `map-type-modifier` can be one of `always`, `close`, `mapper( mapper_identifier )`, `present`, or `iterator`. The full details of these are covered in the OpenMP reference documentation. The most commonly one used is `always`, which instructs the compiler to always perform the initialization of the device-side variables (if `to` or `tofrom` map types are used) from the host or the other way around (if `from` or `tofrom` map types are used), regardless of the state of the device-side variables (e.g., even if the variables have been allocated prior to that directive).

The optional `map-type` can be one of:

- `to`: The device-side variable is initialized from the host-side one. This is the default map type for scalar data.
- `from`: The device-side variable value is copied to the host-side one.
- `tofrom`: A combination of `to` and `from`. This is the default map type for arrays.
- `alloc`: Allocates (but does not initialize) data on the device.
- `release`: Decrements the reference count of a variable.
- `delete`: Sets the reference count of a variable to zero and deletes the device data.

The reference count mentioned above is associated with the host variables. Every time a host variable is mapped to a device, a reference counter is incremented upon entry to a `target` region and decremented upon exit. When the count gets to zero, the device-side copy is deleted.

The reference count has no relevance for global/static data, as in that case it is equivalent to being infinite.

In the example of Listing 8.34, when the program counter reaches line 8 and the parallel region is complete, the reference counts for the a, b, and c arrays are decremented to zero, and their device-memory copies are deleted.

This may be an undesirable behavior if we would like to reuse the results of the computation. So it would be beneficial if device-side allocations and deallocation could be manually controlled.

This is the goal of the `target enter data` and `target exit data` pair of directives. These are supposed to surround any `target` constructs, offering allocation and deallocation control, respectively. It should be noted that these do not behave as curly brackets do for a block of code: they do not need to be paired and we can have multiple instances of each, based on what needs to be placed in or taken out from the device's data environment.

Finally, a third directive called `target update` can be used inside a `target data` or a `target enter data` and `target exit data` pair construct to synchronize host-side data from device-side ones at user-selected points of execution. It is accompanied by `to` and/or `from` clauses that control the flow of the update.

As an example, the following code builds upon Listing 8.34 to implement the $\vec{a} \cdot \left(\vec{a} + \vec{b}\right)$ vector operation:

Listing 8.35: A multiple-stage device calculation involving vectors.

```
// File : vectorAdd2.cpp
int a[N], b[N], c[N], d[1];
d[0] = 0;
. . .
#pragma target enter data map(to:a,b,d) map(alloc:c)

#pragma omp target teams distribute parallel for
  for (int i = 0; i < N; i++)
    c[i] = a[i] + b[i];

#pragma omp target update from(c)

#pragma omp target exit data map(delete:b)

#pragma omp target teams
  {
#pragma omp distribute parallel for reduction(+:d[0])
    for (int i = 0; i < N; i++)
      d[0] += a[i] * c[i];
  }

#pragma target exit data map(from:d) map(release:a,c)
. . .
```

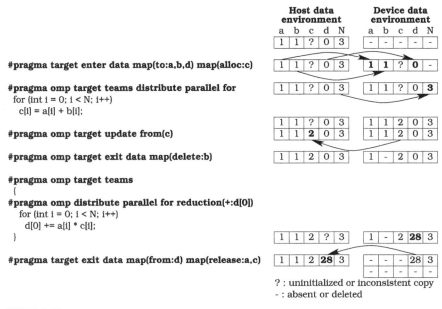

#pragma target enter data map(to:a,b,d) map(alloc:c)

#pragma omp target teams distribute parallel for
  for (int i = 0; i < N; i++)
    c[i] = a[i] + b[i];

#pragma omp target update from(c)

#pragma omp target exit data map(delete:b)

#pragma omp target teams
  {
#pragma omp distribute parallel for reduction(+:d[0])
  for (int i = 0; i < N; i++)
    d[0] += a[i] * c[i];
  }

#pragma target exit data map(from:d) map(release:a,c)

? : uninitialized or inconsistent copy
- : absent or deleted

FIGURE 8.13

A step-by-step trace of Listing 8.35 and how OpenMP directives affect the data environments when processing two vectors $\vec{a} = \vec{b} = \{1, 2, 3\}$. Only the first elements of the vectors are shown.

A notable thing about the above code is that the scalar result of the computation is defined as an array of one element (d on line 2). This allows the retrieval of the result by the host at line 22 using the `target exit data` directive.[15]

On line 5 the `target enter data` directive allocates the a, b, c, and d arrays on the device and copies over the contents of the a, b, and d host values. The value of N is copied over when the teams directive is executed starting at line 7.

Line 11 copies the updated values of c back to the host, before b is deallocated from the device by line 13.

The final result in d[0] is retrieved by line 22, which also decrements the reference counts for a and c. If these counts reach 0, the device data are deleted.

Fig. 8.13 shows the effect of all these pragmas on the host and device data environments during the processing of a set of small vectors.

The map types listed above cannot be used freely with any `target data` directive. Table 8.2 summarizes the legitimate pairings.

---

[15] This should sound familiar with anyone having CUDA experience, as getting results from a CUDA kernel requires that a pointer to a GPU memory location known by both the device and the host is used. Scalars are one-way parameters, i.e., they can be sent from the host to the device but not the other way around.

Table 8.2 `target*` directives and the map types allowed in their `map` clauses.

Map type	`target`	`target data`	`target enter data`	`target exit data`
to	X	X	X	
from	X	X		X
tofrom	X	X		
alloc	X	X	X	
release				X
delete				X

The list in the `map` clause can include arrays and structure fields. If a variable is a structure, then it is treated as if all its members are parts of the list. However, this may not suffice, as illustrated with the example below:

```
struct Measure
{
  int N;
  float *data;
};

Measure inData, outData;

#pragma omp target data map(to:inData) map(to:outData)
#pragma omp target teams distribute parallel for
    for (int i = 0; i < inData.N; i++)
       outData.data[i]= inData.data[i]*2;
. . .
```

The `for` loop above can cause an illegal device memory access error when executed.[16] The problem is that the size of the data accessed through a pointer (`inData.data` and `outData.data` above) is not part of the variable definition, and it may be even unknown until runtime. Hence it is essential that we somehow declare the size of the array to be mapped: this is where **array sections** come into play.

An array section is a subset of an array starting at an arbitrary non-negative offset that may even involve non-contiguous elements. Array sections go beyond the mere handling of pointer-accessed data to allow the transfer to the device (and back) of any part of an array during the mapping process. The `map` clause can accept as parameters the name of an array along with the starting index/offset, the length of the section to be mapped, and the stride, using the following syntax alternatives:

```
array[ start_offset : length : stride] or
array[ start_offset : length : ] or
array[ start_offset : length ] or
```

---

[16] The error may be avoided if unified memory is used, as explained later.

```
array[ start_offset : : stride] or
array[ start_offset : : ] or
array[ start_offset : ] or
array[ : length : stride] or
array[ : length : ] or
array[ : length ] or
array[ : : stride]
array[ : : ]
array[ : ]
```

The above can be extended to multi-dimensional arrays, with the offset, length, and stride specified for each dimension.

In the alternatives where `start_offset` and/or `stride` are missing, they are assumed to be equal to zero and one, respectively. If the `length` is omitted, it defaults to the expression $\lceil \frac{length - start\_offset}{stride} \rceil$.

For example, the clause

```
int data[N];
#pragma omp . .  . map( data[ : N/2 : 2] )
```

would map half of the elements of array `data` to the device, namely `data[0]`, `data[2]`, `data[4]`, etc. At the moment of this writing the GNU compiler does not yet support the `stride` component of the syntax, which is an OpenMP 5.0 added feature.

It should be stressed that *using array sections does not change the way an array is accessed on the device in regard to the offset and limits used.* The statements and expressions should remain valid if the `pragmas` were removed and the code were to run sequentially on the host, as per OpenMP's design philosophy.

This characteristic hides the fact that OpenMP can fine-tune the device memory allocation based on the mapping specification, negating the need to have matching size – to the host – arrays on the device. This can be critical for devices which are typically memory-constrained, especially when compared to the host.

The vector addition example of Listing 8.34 is extended below to show how array sections can be used to control device memory occupancy:

Listing 8.36: Piece-wise device vector addition employing array sections.

```
 1  // File : vectorAdd3.cpp
 2  . . .
 3  const int N=100;
 4  const int chunk=10;
 5  . . .
 6  for(int off=0; off<N; off+=chunk)
 7  #pragma omp target teams distribute parallel for map(to:a[off:chunk↩
       ],b[off:chunk]) map(from:c[off:chunk])
 8    for(int i=0;i<chunk;i++)
 9       c[off+i] = a[off+i]+b[off+i];
10  . . .
```

The outer loop in the above code controls the offset for the array sections to be mapped to the device by the directive of line 7. The arrays allocated on the device are just `chunk` elements long, despite reaching index `N-1` in the statement of line 9.

Finally, we could get "lazy" (or smart) by relying on unified memory mechanism provisions. By incorporating the following directive:

```
#pragma omp requires unified_shared_memory
```

we are forcing the compiler to use *managed memory* (see what this is in Section 6.7.4.2), making all transfers implicit and on a need-to-do basis. The only drawback is that we relinquish some of the fine control that explicit mapping provides over memory transfers that could give room for better performance.

The `requires` directive has to appear at the file scope before any `target` directives, and in all the compilation units of a project. All variables regardless of scope become part of one unified virtual memory space and thus even global/static variables can be accessed in `target` constructs without having to use `declare target` directives.

8.9.3 CUDA interoperability

Using device-specific development platforms like CUDA can avail a large collection of accelerated library functions to the programmer, like, e.g., CUBLAS, nvGRAPH, CUFFT, etc. Being able to switch between CUDA and OpenMP would allow one to leverage both the convenience of the OpenMP directives and the performance of the CUDA library functions.

This is an easy problem to solve if we use the `requires unified_shared_memory` directive as mentioned in the previous section. Here we will explore the alternative of manually handling CUDA- and OpenMP-allocated data.

Doing so requires the use of two clauses:

* `is_device_ptr( list_of_pointers )`: This can be used as part of the `target` directive to establish access to CUDA-allocated data to OpenMP. For example:

Listing 8.37: Using OpenMP to add two vectors on a device that are managed by explicit CUDA calls.

```
1   // File : vectorAdd_cuda.cu
2   . . .
3     unique_ptr<float[]> ha, hb, hc;
4     float *da, *db, *dc;      // host (h*) and device (d*) pointers
5
6     // host memory allocation
7     ha = make_unique<float[]>(N);
8     hb = make_unique<float[]>(N);
9     hc = make_unique<float[]>(N);
10
11    // device memory allocation
12    cudaMalloc ((void **) &da, sizeof (float) * N);
13    cudaMalloc ((void **) &db, sizeof (float) * N);
```

```
14    cudaMalloc ((void **) &dc, sizeof (float) * N);
15    . . .
16    // data transfer, host -> device
17    cudaMemcpy (da, ha.get(), sizeof (float) * N, ↩
         cudaMemcpyHostToDevice);
18    cudaMemcpy (db, hb.get(), sizeof (float) * N, ↩
         cudaMemcpyHostToDevice);
19
20  #pragma omp target is_device_ptr(da,db,dc)
21  #pragma omp teams distribute parallel for
22    for (int i = 0; i < N; i++)
23      dc[i] = da[i] + db[i];
24
25    // data transfer, device -> host
26    cudaMemcpy (hc.get(), dc, sizeof (float) * N, ↩
         cudaMemcpyDeviceToHost);
27    . . .
```

Obviously the use of this clause eliminates the need for the corresponding mapping clauses, as the data transfers have to be explicit.

- use_device_ptr(list_of_pointers): This can be used as part of the target data directive to establish access to OpenMP-managed device data from CUDA functions. For example:

Listing 8.38: Using OpenMP to manage two device vectors that are added using a CUBLAS saxpy function.

```
28  // File : vectorAdd_cuda2.cu
29    . . .
30    unique_ptr<float[]> ha, hb, hc;
31    float *pa, *pb, *pc;       // host (h*) and device (d*) pointers
32    int i;
33
34    // host memory allocation
35    ha = make_unique<float[]>(N);
36    hb = make_unique<float[]>(N);
37    hc = make_unique<float[]>(N);
38
39    pa = ha.get();
40    pb = hb.get();
41    pc = hc.get();
42    . . .
43  cublasHandle_t handle;
44  cublasCreate (&handle);
45  float alpha=1;
46  #pragma omp target data map(tofrom:pa[0:N]) map(tofrom:pb[0:N])
47  #pragma omp target data use_device_ptr(pa, pb)
48    cublasSaxpy(handle, N, &alpha, pa,1, pb,1);
49    . . .
```

In both of the above cases, the source code will have to be compiled with the nvcc compiler front-end.

8.10 The `loop` **construct**

OpenMP 5.0 introduced the `loop` construct as a way to automate and *unify* the concurrent execution of loop iterations using different mechanisms and targeting both CPUs and GPUs.

The `loop` directive can be used on a canonical-form loop the same way a `for` does:

```
#pragma omp parallel
#pragma omp loop
for (...
```

Also multiple nested loops can be combined into one logical index space using the optional `collapse` clause.

The `loop` construct allows for more aggressive compiler optimizations as it carries extra restrictions compared to the `for` construct. In particular, there can be no OpenMP directives or calls to the OpenMP runtime inside the loop body or in any of the functions called by it. The only exceptions are the `loop`, `parallel`, `simd`, and combined constructs for which the first construct is a `parallel` construct.

The `loop` construct introduces the `bind` clause that can be used to *suggest* how the loop will be executed. The available options for the `bind` clause are:

- **parallel**: The loop will be executed on the CPU.
- **teams**: If the innermost region enclosing the construct is a `teams` region, then the loop will be executed on the device.
- **thread**: Binding is not defined. It is up to the compiler.

If the `bind` clause is missing, the compiler will use the type of the closest enclosing region to determine the binding.

For example:

Listing 8.39: Vector addition on the CPU and GPU using the loop construct.

```
1   // File : vectorAdd4.cu
2   . . .
3   // CPU execution
4   #pragma omp parallel
5   #pragma omp loop
6     for(int i=0;i<N;i++)
7       c[i] = a[i]+b[i];
8
9   // GPU execution
10  #pragma omp target teams
11  #pragma omp distribute
12  #pragma omp loop
13    for(int i=0;i<N;i++)
14      c[i] = a[i]+b[i];
15  . . .
```

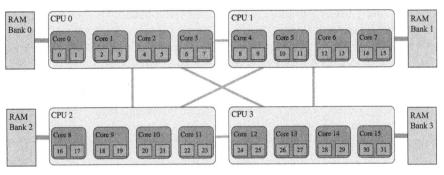

FIGURE 8.14

An example of a NUMA platform consisting of four sockets equipped with quad-core CPUs. Each core supports two hardware threads.

The compilation command has to be differentiated based on the target platform. So, if a teams region is enclosing the loop construct, we should have compiler switches matching device offloading.

8.11 Thread affinity

In OpenMP jargon a **place** is an unordered set of processors on a device. It is the equivalent of a multicore CPU residing in a socket. OpenMP maintains a list of places that can be used to host its threads. Thread affinity refers to the association/binding of a thread with a place or even a specific CPU core. Maintaining a fixed thread affinity translates to better utilization of CPU caches, as even if a thread times out and it surrenders the CPU, it is likely that the cache will preserve some of the contents relevant to this thread when it is scheduled again.

Thread affinity is a big concern for NUMA platforms, i.e., machines equipped with multiple CPUs having non-uniform cost access to memory. These are mostly encountered in HPC installations, where dual- or quad-socket machines are the norm. Even if a thread is not allowed to change its affinity during execution, the initial placement of a thread can have great impact on its performance.

There are two counterarguments to consider. On the one hand, placing threads in different places makes synchronization and data access slow. But the counterargument is that different placement maximizes both the amount of cache available to the application and the aggregate memory bandwidth.

OpenMP allows the programmer to control *where* the threads will be placed and *how* they will be placed. Remember that places are sets of processors.

The allowed places are controlled via the **OMP_PLACES** environment variable. As of OpenMP 5.1, this can be set to one of the following (we are using the platform of Fig. 8.14 as a basis for our examples):

- An explicit list of permitted cores or hardware threads. The list can be in the form of ranges {*start* : *length*[: *stride*]} or in the form of enumerated sets. If the *stride* is missing, it is assumed to be 1. The numbers correspond to the smallest unit of execution exposed by the execution environment, which is typically a hardware thread.

  A collection of sets can also be specified by using the format {*start* : *length*[: *stride*]} : *repeat* : *stride2*, where the first set is repeated *repeat* times (including the first one), each time advancing the numbers by *stride2*. For example:

```
$ export OMP_PLACES="{0},{1},{2},  . . . "          # Having each ↩
    hardware thread as a separate place
$ export OMP_PLACES="{0,1},{2,3},{4,5},  . . . "    # Having each ↩
    core as a separate place
$ export OMP_PLACES="{0:2}:16:2"                    # same as the ↩
    previous example
$ export OMP_PLACES="{0:8:1},{8:8:1},{16:8:1},{24:8:1}"  # each ↩
    socket is a place.
$ export OMP_PLACES="{0:8}:4:8"                     # same ↩
    as the previous line
```

  The last example is equivalent to the fourth one, with the supplied set serving as a template to be repeated four times, with a stride of 8.

- An abstract name from the following list:

  - **threads**: Each place corresponds to a single hardware thread. For the platform in Fig. 8.14 this setting would mean we have 32 places: {0}, {1}, {2}, ...

  - **cores**: Each place corresponds to a single core, possibly supporting multiple hardware threads. For our example we would have 16 places: {0, 1}, {2, 3}, {4, 5}, ...

  - **sockets**: Each place corresponds to a CPU socket. This would translate to four places for our example: {0, 1, . . . , 7}, {8, 9, . . . , 15}, ...

  - **ll_caches**: Each place corresponds to the set of cores that share the last level of CPU caches (e.g., L3). If the last level cache is shared by all the cores in a socket, we will get the same places as in the previous setting. In the case of an AMD Epyc Rome processor, which has the L3 cache shared between four cores, we would be getting two places for each octa-core Core Complex Die (CCD) [42].

  - **numa_domains**: A place is made up of all the cores that share their closest system memory. This memory has to be at the same distance from them. Some platforms permit different NUMA configurations. For example, AMD's Epyc Rome CPU, with its eight memory channels and multiple CCDs, can be configured in four different ways, from treating the whole CPU as a single NUMA domain to breaking it into two NUMA domains per CCD [42].

The *how* of the placement can be controlled in a number of ways:

- Using the **proc_bind** clause with a `parallel` directive. There are three different settings/policies that can be used:

- **master**: All threads in the team are assigned to the same place as the master thread. If fast access to some locally defined data is paramount, this could be the best option.
- **close**: The team threads are placed "close" to the master thread. If T is the number of threads and P the number of places numbered p_0, p_1, etc., there are two cases:
  - $T \leq P$: The threads are distributed in a round-robin fashion amongst the available places, starting with the master thread at p_i, then the thread with the next smallest thread number at p_{i+1}, and so on. Placement wraps around when we reach p_{P-1}.
  - $T > P$: The threads are broken into groups so that each group has threads with consecutive IDs. The group sizes are implementation-specific and non-uniform, but they satisfy the condition $\lfloor \frac{T}{P} \rfloor \leq group\_size \leq \lceil \frac{T}{P} \rceil$. The groups are then assigned to places, starting with the master's group at p_i, then the next group at p_{i+1}, etc.
- **spread**: The team threads are supposed to spread as far as possible from each other. Again based on whether we have more threads or more places the placement goes as follows:
  - $T \leq P$: The parent thread's original places are grouped into T groups, with each group having either $\lfloor \frac{P}{T} \rfloor$ or $\lceil \frac{P}{T} \rceil$ places. Effectively we have a new set of places. Then each thread is assigned to one of these new places, in a round-robin fashion, starting with the master thread, followed by the thread with the next smallest thread number, and so on. The placement is done to the first place in each of the new sets.
  - $T > P$: The threads are placed in the same fashion as if close was chosen.
- Using the **OMP_PROC_BIND** environment variable. In addition to the three previous settings, we can have a value of **false** (no affinity enforced) and a value of **true** (implementation-specific setting used).

Table 8.3 shows several examples of how the master, close, and spread policies affect thread binding when we have four places.

One can easily experiment and observe thread placement by manipulating the OMP_PLACES and OMP_PROC_BIND environment variables and running the program below without having to modify the code or recompile:

Listing 8.40: A simple program for experimenting with thread affinity settings.

```cpp
// File : places.cpp
. . .
int nPlaces = omp_get_num_places ();
cout << "Places : " << nPlaces << endl;
for (int i = 0; i < nPlaces; i++)
   {
      int numProcs = omp_get_place_num_procs (i);
      cout << "\tPlace " << i << " with " << numProcs << endl;
      int IDs[numProcs];
      omp_get_place_proc_ids (i, IDs);
```

```
11        for (int j = 0; j < numProcs; j++)
12            cout << "\t\tCPU with ID : " << IDs[j] << endl;
13        }
14
15    #pragma omp parallel for
16        for (int l = 0; l < omp_get_num_threads (); l++)
17            printf ("Thread %i at place %i\n", omp_get_thread_num (), ↩
                omp_get_place_num ());
18    . . .
```

The part between lines 3 and 13 is responsible for printing out the available places (retrieved by the omp_get_num_places call on line 3) and the IDs of the hardware threads or cores (let us call them processors) that belong to each place. The number of processors for each place is found on line 7 by calling omp_get_place_num_procs, which is then used to set up an array of integers big enough to fit the processor IDs. The array is populated by the omp_get_place_proc_ids call on line 10.

The second part of Listing 8.40 runs a parallel for loop, where each thread prints out the place it is assigned to by calling omp_get_place_num.

As a final note, a thread's affinity can be printed out by calling the omp_display_affinity() function. The output is sent to the standard error stream:

```
#pragma omp parallel
    {
        . . .
        omp_display_affinity (NULL);
        . . .
    }
```

Table 8.3 Placement of threads based on the existence of four places (p_0 to p_3), for different numbers of threads and initial placements of the master thread (MT).

Policy	MT	Threads	Place			
			p_0	p_1	p_2	p_3
master	p_0	4	0,1,2,3			
	p_1	4		0,1,2,3		
	p_2	6			0,1,2,3,4,5	
close	p_0	4	0	1	2	3
	p_1	4	3	0	1	2
	p_0	8	0,1	2,3	4,5	6,7
	p_2	2			0	1
spread	p_0	4	0	1	2	3
	p_1	8	6,7	0,1	2,3	4,5
	p_0	12	0,1,2,3	4,5,6,7	8,9,10,11	12,13,14,15
	p_0	2	0		1	
	p_2	2	1		0	

8.12 **Correctness and optimization issues**

The issues addressed in this section are not unique to OpenMP. In fact, they are generic concerns for all shared-memory parallel programs. They are especially relevant to OpenMP because in OpenMP the development process frequently starts from a sequential program, and not from a design specifically targeting parallel execution. These issues are thread safety and false-sharing.

8.12.1 **Thread safety**

A function or method (or even a block of code in general) is called **thread-safe** if it can be executed concurrently by several threads without any problems.

Thread-safe functions are also – mistakenly – called reentrant, although these are two different qualities. A **reentrant** function can be interrupted while being executed, and then safely called again (reentered) before the previous call or calls are complete. Reentrancy is a concept usually associated with operating system code (like interrupt handlers), and it does not deal with concurrency. A function can be thread-safe, reentrant, both, or neither of the two.

Although being reentrant does not make a function thread-safe, a reentrant function does a good job of isolating its inner workings from the outside world. This is a desirable feature for multi-threaded programs. Usually, making a function reentrant is a step towards making it thread-safe also.

Reentrant functions are all about being available to multiple threads. Thread-safe functions are all about safe access to shared data.

An analogy that allows us to capture the essence of these two properties is the baking recipe one: imagine that a function is a cake recipe, and several chefs are using it (our threads). A reentrant function would allow the chefs to go about their business as long as they use their own materials and cooking utensils (input data). A chef may interrupt his/her preparation and come back to it at a later time without any issue. On the other hand, a thread-safe recipe would allow the chefs to work concurrently, while sharing the oven or other resources (shared data). If a chef can lock the common oven and leave, thread safety is preserved, but the recipe is not reentrant. Unless the chef using the oven returns, the other chefs cannot bake a cake.

The conditions that need to be met by a **reentrant** function are [5]:

- In relation to their **input**: All data required by the function should be provided by the caller. If a program calls a function multiple times, with the same arguments, it is the responsibility of the caller to ensure that the calls are properly done. For example, the `qsort_r` C-library function is a reentrant implementation of the quicksort algorithm that allows additional information to be passed in the form of a pointer to the comparison function, without having to use global data. If two threads call this function with the same input array, the results cannot be predicted:

```
// File : reentrant_test.cpp
// Comparison function for int. The extra argument is unused
int comp(const void *x, const void *y, void *extra)
{
  int a = *(int *)x;
  int b = *(int *)y;
  return a-b;
}
. . .

 int *data = new int[N];

 // populate the array

#pragma omp parallel num_threads(2)
  {
    qsort_r(data, N, sizeof(int), comp, NULL);
  }

// data may not be sorted!
. . .
```

- In relation to **access to data**:
  - The function should not use `static` or global data, i.e., data that are persistent between calls. Global data may be accessed (e.g., hardware status registers), but they should not be modified unless atomic operations are used.
  - In the case of an object method, either the method is an accessor method (does not change the state of the object, also known as a "getter"), or it is a mutator (or "setter") method, in which case the object should be modified inside a critical section.
- In relation to their **output**: The function does not return pointers to static data. If an array needs to be returned, it can be either dynamically allocated or provided by the caller.
- In relation to **other functions**: The function does not call any non-reentrant functions.
- The function does not modify its code, unless private copies of the code are used in each invocation.

The requirement for making a function `thread-safe` is rather simple: provide *linearizable* access (see Section 3.5) to shared data. Whenever a function modifies a shared resource (e.g., a file pointer, a global object, etc.), changes need to be performed in a way that would be consistent with a sequential program. This can be accomplished by using a critical section. Critical sections can be built via an OpenMP lock, a `critical` construct, condition variables, etc.

The `qsort_r` function is just one of many reentrant alternatives to standard C-library functions designed for sequential execution. A programmer should be aware of the availability of these functions and switch the program code to using them instead. Front-end functions with locks can be used in the case where reentrant variants are not available and/or thread safety is required, although this could come at a significant performance penalty.

For example, Listing 8.41 using the non-reentrant strtok[17] parsing function achieves thread safety by blocking access to strtok while it is being used, effectively making the program sequential.

Listing 8.41: A multi-threaded program that uses tasks to parse two strings concurrently. A lock makes sure that only one of the two threads gets to use the strtok function each time.

```
1   // File : thrsafe_strtok.cpp
2   . . .
3   omp_lock_t l;
4   //─────────────────────────────────────
5   void threadSafeParse (char *s, const char *delim)
6   {
7     omp_set_lock (&l);  // acquire the lock
8     char *tok;
9     tok = strtok (s, delim);
10    while (tok)
11      {
12        printf ("Thread %i : %s\n", omp_get_thread_num (), tok);
13        tok = strtok (NULL, delim);
14      }
15
16    omp_unset_lock (&l); // release the lock
17  }
18
19  //─────────────────────────────────────
20  int main (int argc, char *argv[])
21  {
22    if (argc != 4)
23      {
24        fprintf (stderr, "Usage: %s string1 string2 delim\n", argv[0])↩
          ;
25        exit (EXIT_FAILURE);
26      }
27    char *str1 = argv[1], *str2 = argv[2], *delim = argv[3];
28
29  #pragma omp parallel
30    {
31  #pragma omp single
32      {
33  // one task per input string
34  #pragma omp task
35        threadSafeParse (str1, delim);
36
37  #pragma omp task
38        threadSafeParse (str2, delim);
```

---

[17] strtok is not reentrant as it stores a reference to the string being tokenized between successive calls.

```
39        }
40      }
41
42      exit (EXIT_SUCCESS);
43  }
```

Our example is a bit mundane, as we do have a reentrant variant in the form of the strtok_r function. But we will stick with it, in order to answer an interesting question: do we *need* locks to have a thread-safe function?

If you have gone through Chapter 4, you probably know the answer: no, but it is certainly more convenient if we do use locks.

A reentrant string tokenizer function, similar to the strtok_r one, can be constructed as shown below:

Listing 8.42: A reentrant string tokenizer function (strtokV2) and a function strParse that uses it to parse strings.

```
44  // File : thrsafe_strtokV2.cpp
45  . . .
46  char *strtokV2 (char *s, const char *delim, char **aux)
47  {
48    int idx1 = 0, idx2 = -1;
49    char needle[2] = { 0 };
50    char *token = NULL;
51    int i;
52    char *temp = s;
53    if (s == NULL)
54      temp = *aux;
55
56    // iterate over all characters of the input string
57    for (i = 0; temp[i]; i++)
58      {
59        needle[0] = temp[i];
60        // check if a character matches a delimiter
61        if (strstr (delim, needle) != NULL)          // strstr is ↩
            reentrant
62          {
63            idx1 = idx2 + 1;          // get the index boundaries of the ↩
                token
64            idx2 = i;
65            if (idx1 != idx2)        // is it a token or a delimiter ↩
                following another?
66              {
67                temp[i] = 0;
68                *aux = temp + i + 1;
69                token = temp + idx1;
70                break;
71              }
72          }
73      }
74
75    // repeat checks for the token preceding the end of the string
```

```
76     if (!token)
77       {
78         idx1 = idx2 + 1;
79         idx2 = i;
80         if (idx1 != idx2)
81           {
82             *aux = temp + i;
83             token = temp + idx1;
84           }
85       }
86
87     return token;
88   }
89
90   //------------------------------------------------
91   void strParse (char *s, const char *delim)
92   {
93     char *state;
94     char *tok;
95
96     tok = strtokV2 (s, delim, &state);
97     while (tok)
98       {
99         printf ("Thread %i : %s\n", omp_get_thread_num (), tok);
100        tok = strtokV2 (NULL, delim, &state);
101      }
102  }
```

The above `strtokV2` function is a straightforward replacement for `strtok` or `strtok_r`. The code in the `strParse` function (lines 91–102) is identical to a sequential counterpart using the C-library's `strtok_r` function.

`strtokV2`'s exclusive reliance on automatic and caller-provided variables means that it is reentrant. Its operation can be distilled to the following points:

- The `s` (or `*aux` if `s` is `NULL`) pointer is used to initialize a temporary pointer (`temp`) and iterate over the characters of the input until a zero value is encountered (for loop of line 57)
- The `strstr` reentrant function is used to check if the examined character (`temp[i]`) matches any of the specified in the set of delimiters (line 61). The `idx1` and `idx2` indices point to the beginning and end of a detected token. Obviously, if they coincide, we have an empty string that is bypassed (check of line 65).
- If we have a non-zero length token, we mark its end by inserting the end-of-string at the position of the delimiter (line 67) and return the beginning of the search string for the next call to the caller (line 68). The function ends by returning the address of the token.
- Lines 78–84 share much of the logic of lines 63–71, in treating the case of the very last token in the input string.

However, it is *not* thread-safe! If two threads try calling `strtokV2` using the same strings as parameters, the results will be unpredictable. If we were trying to parse the same string by multiple threads, we could be striving for one of two outcomes: (a) all the threads get the same tokens or (b) each token is produced one time only, as threads "walk over" the string. Neither of these two outcomes is feasible with the reentrant strtokV2.

Getting a thread-safe *and* reentrant variation to strtok is challenging, as an array of characters was never designed with concurrency in mind. The following function strikes a compromise in order to offer these features, by changing the function behavior (pre- and postconditions): the first call to the function needs to have the third argument set to NULL (instead of being ignored) and all subsequent calls for the remaining tokens need to provide the address of the original string (instead of NULL). The reason for this is to allow the function to maintain a list of strings currently processed by threads. The same string is not allowed to be processed concurrently by two or more threads. When the last token is extracted from a string, the address of the original string is removed from the list, permitting its future reuse.

Listing 8.43: A reentrant and thread-safe string tokenizer function (strtokV3). Only the changes over Listing 8.42 are shown.

```
103  // File : thrsafe_strtokV3.cpp
104  . . .
105  #include <set>
106  #include <mutex>
107
108  char *strtokV3 (char *s, const char *delim, char **aux)
109  {
110    static set < char *>inProc;
111    static mutex l;
112
113    // add s to the set of strings being processed or return NULL on ↵
           failure
114    unique_lock < mutex > ul (l);
115    if (*aux == NULL && inProc.insert (s).second == false)
116      return NULL;
117    ul.unlock ();
118
119    int idx1 = 0, idx2 = -1;
120    char needle[2] = { 0 };
121    char *token = NULL;
122    int i;
123    char *temp = s;
124    if (*aux != NULL)
125      {
126        temp = *aux;
127        s[0] = 0;
128      }
129
130    // iterate over all characters of the input string
131    for (i = 0; temp[i]; i++)
132      {
133        . . .
134      }
```

```
135
136     // repeat checks for the token preceding the end of the string
137     if (!token)
138       {
139       . . .
140       }
141
142     // remove s from inProc if done
143     ul.lock ();
144     if (token == NULL)
145       inProc.erase (s);
146
147     return token;
148   }
149
150   //————————————————————————————————————————
151   void threadSafeParse (char *s, const char *delim)
152   {
153     char *state = NULL;
154     char *tok;
155
156     tok = strtokV3 (s, delim, &state);
157     while (tok)
158       {
159         printf ("Thread %i : %s\n", omp_get_thread_num (), tok);
160         usleep (1);
161         tok = strtokV3 (s, delim, &state);
162       }
163   }
```

The ellipses at lines 133 and 139 indicate that the same code as on lines 59–72 and 78–84 of Listing 8.42, respectively, is used. The threadSafeParse function follows the guidelines outlined above.

The core changes in function strtokV3 are the entry (lines 114–117) and exit blocks (lines 143–145). The static set of pointers inProc defined at line 110 serves to maintain a record of the strings which are undergoing processing. Upon entry to the function, the mutex l is used to establish a critical section, where we attempt to insert the pointer to the original string *s to the set, on the condition that the third parameter *aux is NULL. *aux being NULL is an indication of the very first call to the function by a thread for the particular s. If the insertion fails, which means another thread is processing this exact string, we exit the function and no token is returned. The lock is released by line 117, permitting the use of the function by multiple threads, even if a thread is interrupted.

In the exit block, we erase s from the inProc set if there has been no token detected. This is again done inside a critical section that terminates with the return from the function.

Still, strtokV3 is not foolproof. If a thread calls the function with a pointer from within a string, e.g., s+1, the entry check will fail to detect the data sharing. Further changes to the function signature and logic would be required to cover this case as well.

8.12.2 False-sharing

Cache memory speeds up access to main memory contents by holding copies of the most frequently used data. Cache memory takes advantage of both *temporal* and *spatial* locality in data access patterns: a data item that has been referenced in the past is likely to be referenced again in the near future, along with other items in neighboring locations.

Cache memory tries to exploit spatial redundancy by fetching data from main memory in fixed-sized blocks called cache lines. The size of the cache line is architecture-specific, but a commonly used value is 64 bytes. Caches hold data aligned at addresses which are integer multiples of the cache line size.

To explain what kind of problem the presence of the extra data in a cache line creates, we will use an example of a dual core system running the following parallel for loop, for calculating the values of a double array:

```
double x[N];
#pragma omp parallel for schedule(static, 1)
  for( int i = 0; i < N; i++ )
    x[ i ] = someFunc( x [ i ] );
```

Given the schedule clause, the L1 caches of the two cores[18] might at some point in time be in the state shown in Fig. 8.15. As the cache can contain data from every available memory location, a cache line consists of the actual data, their address (so the CPU knows where they came from), and a state.

The state is used to implement a **coherency protocol**, i.e., a mechanism that allows data stored in multiple disjoint caches to be kept in a consistent state [48]. For example, if core 0 changes the value of x[10], core 1 should be able to read the updated value and not keep using an outdated one.

A simple state model is MESI, an acronym standing for the four possible cache line states covered by the model: **m**odified, **e**xclusive, **s**hared, and **i**nvalid. An excellent source of information for MESI is the online article by Paul E. McKenney [48]. This is the meaning of these states:

- **Modified**: The CPU has recently changed part of the cache line, and the cache line holds the only up-to-date value of the corresponding item. No other CPU can hold copies of these data, so the CPU can be considered the owner of the data. The pending changes are supposed to be written back to the main memory according to the rules of the CPU architecture.

---

[18] Complexity and efficiency reasons dictate the use of separate L1 caches in multicore CPUs. Most CPUs employ multiple cache hierarchies but for our purposes we can limit our discussion to the L1 cache only.

Main Memory   0x8000 0x8008 0x8010 0x8018 0x8020 0x8028

x| | | | | | | ...

Core 0 Cache

State	Address				Data				
	...								
S	0x8000	**x[0]**	x[1]	**x[2]**	x[3]	**x[4]**	x[5]	**x[6]**	x[7]
	...								

Core 1 Cache

State	Address				Data				
	...								
S	0x8000	x[0]	**x[1]**	x[2]	**x[3]**	x[4]	**x[5]**	x[6]	**x[7]**
	...								

FIGURE 8.15

A possible L1 cache state for two cores processing alternating array elements of type int. We assume that the cache line size is 64 bytes. The elements accessed by each core are highlighted. The state of the cache lines is "shared."

- **Exclusive**: This is similar to the modified state, in that the CPU is considered the owner of the data. No change has been applied though. The main memory and the cache hold identical values.
- **Shared**: At least one more cache holds a copy of the data. Changes to the data can only be performed after coordination with the other CPUs holding copies.
- **Invalid**: This represents an empty cache line. It can be used to hold new data from the main memory.

What is of interest to us is what happens when a *shared* cache line is modified by one of the CPUs using it. The CPU applying the change sends "invalidate" messages to the CPUs that have copies of the cache line and awaits "acknowledge" responses from them, before changing the state from *shared* to *modified*. The CPUs that receive an "invalidate" message clear the corresponding cache line by changing its state to "invalid" and send back an "acknowledge" message. This means that if they wish to access the data that got cleared, they have to either fetch it from the "owning" cache, or *read it again from memory*.

Now that we have covered the basic mechanisms of cache management, let us return to our example: what happens to the state of Fig. 8.15 if core 0 modifies the value of x[0]? Although core 1 does not actually access this item, it shares the cache line that holds it. The resulting "invalidate" message will cause core 1 to dump the cache line and reread from the main memory the items it needs, at a substantial time overhead. This is exactly the definition of **false-sharing**, i.e., sharing cache lines without actually sharing data.

The resulting performance degradation can be very significant [55]. There are three ways for eliminating false-sharing:

- *Pad the data* with extra bytes, so that distinct elements map to distinct cache lines. This is a viable option for data structures where the extra padding will not cause an extreme memory space overhead. For an array and scheduling arrangement like the one in our example, this would cause a sevenfold increase in the memory footprint of array x, which by itself would defeat the benefits of cache memory, if not starve the application of memory. The padding in our example would have to take the form of:

```
double x[N][8];
#pragma omp parallel for schedule(static, 1)
  for( int i = 0; i < N; i++ )
    x[ i ][ 0 ] = someFunc( x [ i ][ 0 ] );
```

so that each array row would occupy a complete cache line.
- Change the *mapping of data* to threads/cores. This is a far simpler and more economical proposition:

```
double x[N];
#pragma omp parallel for schedule(static, 8)
  for( int i = 0; i < N; i++ )
    x[ i ] = someFunc( x [ i ] );
```

- Reduce the sharing by *using private/local variables*. In our example, we can intermediately store a bunch of the results locally, before sending them back to the main memory.[19]

```
// assuming that N is a multiple of 8
double x[N];
#pragma omp parallel for schedule(static, 1)
  for( int i = 0; i < N; i += 8 )
  {
     double temp[ 8 ];
     for(int j = 0; j < 8; j++)
        temp[ j ] = someFunc( x [ i + j] );
     memcpy( x + i, temp, 8 * sizeof( double ));
  }
```

This can be combined with a partial loop unrolling:

```
// assuming that N is a multiple of 8
double x[N];
#pragma omp parallel for schedule(static, 1)
  for( int i = 0; i < N; i += 8 )
  {
```

---

[19] The example is not very good because it is equivalent to a change in the data mapping. For a better example continue reading!

```
    double temp[ 8 ];
    temp[ 0 ] = someFunc( x [ i ] );
    temp[ 1 ] = someFunc( x [ i + 1 ] );
    temp[ 2 ] = someFunc( x [ i + 2 ] );
    temp[ 3 ] = someFunc( x [ i + 3 ] );
    temp[ 4 ] = someFunc( x [ i + 4 ] );
    temp[ 5 ] = someFunc( x [ i + 5 ] );
    temp[ 6 ] = someFunc( x [ i + 6 ] );
    temp[ 7 ] = someFunc( x [ i + 7 ] );
    memcpy( x + i, temp, 8 * sizeof( double ));
}
```

In order to test the severity of the problem false-sharing constitutes and also apply the three elimination techniques shown above, we study the problem of matrix multiplication. Listing 8.44 shows an initial solution that follows the discussion of Section 8.4.2, where it is explained that collapsing the two outer loops is a good choice for load balancing.

Listing 8.44: A simple OpenMP adaptation of a matrix multiplication function. Matrix A is assumed to be $N \times K$ and matrix B is assumed to be $K \times M$ in size.

```
void mmult (double *A, double *B, double *C, int N, int K, int M)
{
#pragma omp parallel for collapse(2) schedule(static, 1)
  for (int i = 0; i < N; i++)
    for (int j = 0; j < M; j++)
      {
        int idx = i * M + j;
        C[idx] = 0;
        for (int l = 0; l < K; l++)
          C[idx] += A[i * K + l] * B[l * M + j];
      }
}
```

But this is clearly not the end of the story, since false-sharing affects the updates to the product matrix C.

Padding the matrix so that there is only one element of C per cache line results in the following code (assuming that the cache line is 64 bytes long):

Listing 8.45: OpenMP matrix multiplication, with padding of the result matrix C, so that each cache line can hold only a single element of C.

```
//------------------------------------------------------------
void mmult (double *A, double *B, double *C, int N, int K, int M)
{
#pragma omp parallel for collapse(2) schedule(static, 1)
  for (int i = 0; i < N; i++)
    for (int j = 0; j < M; j++)
      {
        int idx = (i * M + j) * 8; // using 1 element from each ↩
            group of 8
```

```
        C[idx] = 0;
        for (int l = 0; l < K; l++)
          C[idx] += A[i * K + l] * B[l * M + j];
      }
}
//—————————————————————————————————————————————————————
int main (int argc, char *argv[])
{
    . . .
  double *A = new double[N * K];
  double *B = new double[K * M];
  double *C = new double[N * M * 8]; // 8x the original space
    . . .
```

Changing the data mapping can be accomplished by modifying the `schedule` clause, as shown in Listing 8.46.

Listing 8.46: OpenMP matrix multiplication, with a schedule having a chunk size of 8, so that each cache line holding C elements is exclusive to a core. This is a modification of the data elements mapping to threads/cores.

```
void mmult (double *A, double *B, double *C, int N, int K, int M)
{
#pragma omp parallel for collapse(2) schedule(static, 8)
  for (int i = 0; i < N; i++)
    for (int j = 0; j < M; j++)
      {
        int idx = i * M + j;
        C[idx] = 0;
        for (int l = 0; l < K; l++)
          C[idx] += A[i * K + l] * B[l * M + j];
      }
}
```

Finally, a temporary, automatic variable can be used for accumulating the result in the inner loop, leaving only a single reference to each element of the resulting matrix, as shown in Listing 8.47.[20]

Listing 8.47: OpenMP matrix multiplication, with a temporary variable for the element of C being calculated, that eliminates false-sharing.

```
void mmult (double *A, double *B, double *C, int N, int K, int M)
{
#pragma omp parallel for collapse(2)
  for (int i = 0; i < N; i++)
    for (int j = 0; j < M; j++)
      {
        double temp = 0;
```

---

[20] To be exact, Listing 8.47 combines both a temporary variable and a mapping modification, because OpenMP defaults to a chunk size of $\lceil \frac{N\,M}{p} \rceil$ for p threads.

```
        for (int l = 0; l < K; l++)
          temp += A[i * K + l] * B[l * M + j];
        C[i * M + j] = temp;
    }
}
```

The measured speedup, averaged over 10 runs, is reported in Fig. 8.16. The test platform was a Ryzen 9 3900X, 12-core CPU, with each core supporing two hardware threads (so OpenMP used 24 threads by default). All programs were compiled with the GNU C++ 9.3 compiler and the -O3 compiler switch.

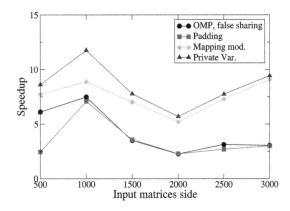

FIGURE 8.16

Matrix multiplication average speedup versus different sides of the square input matrices. Tested programs include the false-sharing OpenMP program and the three variants that eliminate cache false-sharing. Mean values were obtained by running each test 10 times.

The results shown in Fig. 8.16 are astonishing. The plain-vanilla OpenMP version of Listing 8.44 offers a modest speedup over the sequential version that is however a far cry from the true potential of the machine, despite working on a problem that is essentially embarrassingly parallel. The padding approach, being worse than the plain OpenMP version, fails miserably, as it reduces the effectiveness of the cache by filling it up with useless data. Both the mapping alteration and the use of a private variable fare much better than the other two methods. The use of private variables proves to be the best option.

The difference between the "mapping change" and "use of private variables" methods can be explained by how they utilize the cache: the former keeps updating C[idx] in the inner loop, which means that writes have to propagate to the main memory, at a significant overhead. The former uses an automatic variable, which the compiler can place in a register, without needing to send writes to the main memory, but at the end of the inner loop.

8.13 A case study: sorting in OpenMP

Searching and sorting are quintessential operations in algorithm design. In this section we explore how mergesort, a well-known sorting algorithm, can be amended for multi-threaded execution by the OpenMP runtime. Mergesort, in its bottom-up form, is explored in great detail in Section 9.4.5. In the following subsections we will also examine the case of the top-down mergesort, as OpenMP provides the mechanisms that allow both formulations of the algorithm to be parallelized. These also provide a good opportunity for applying the work-sharing constructs listed in this chapter.

8.13.1 Bottom-up mergesort in OpenMP

Fig. 9.1 illustrates how the bottom-up, non-recursive version of mergesort can sort N data items by merging disjoint neighboring blocks in $\Theta(\lceil lg(N) \rceil)$ phases. We can summarize the overall operation as a merging of ever increasing neighboring array parts, starting from a size of 1 (i.e., individual array items) and doubling in size after each phase.

Algorithm 8.1 shows a more concise description of the bottom-up mergesort in pseudocode. In order to keep things short, we assume that N is a power of 2, so that every array part has another part which it can merge with. Obviously a special case needs to be treated inside the loop of lines 3–5 to allow the use of arbitrary N. The $stIdx$ and $nextIdx$ indices point to the start of the array parts that need to be

---

Algorithm 8.1 Bottom-up mergesort: sorting N data items, where N is a power of 2.

1:   $grpSize \leftarrow 1$
2: **while** $grpSize < N$ **do**
3:     **for** $stIdx \leftarrow 0$ to $N - 1$ step $2 \cdot grpSize$ **do**
4:       $nextIdx \leftarrow stIdx + grpSize$
5:       Merge array parts of size $grpSize$, starting at indices $stIdx$ and $nextIdx$
6:     $grpSize \leftarrow grpSize \cdot 2$

---

merged. The actual sorting takes place during the merging operation of line 5, where the resulting conglomeration of items forms an ascending (or descending based on the comparison operator used) sequence.

A sequential implementation of the bottom-up mergesort with the addition of the special case code for arbitrary N and a further optimization concerning the moving of data between the data array and the temporary storage is shown in Listing 8.48.

Listing 8.48: A sequential implementation of the bottom-up mergesort algorithm.

```
template < class T > void mergeList (T * src1, T * src2, int len1, ↩
    int len2, T * dest)
{
  int idx1 = 0, idx2 = 0;
  int loc = 0;                    // starting point in dest array
  while (idx1 < len1 && idx2 < len2)
```

```
6           {
7             if (src1[idx1] <= src2[idx2])
8               {
9                 dest[loc] = src1[idx1];
10                idx1++;
11              }
12            else
13              {
14                dest[loc] = src2[idx2];
15                idx2++;
16              }
17            loc++;
18          }
19
20     // copy the rest
21     for (int i = idx1; i < len1; i++)
22       dest[loc++] = src1[i];
23
24     for (int i = idx2; i < len2; i++)
25       dest[loc++] = src2[i];
26 }
27
28 //─────────────────────────────────────────────────────────
29 template < class T > void mergesort (T * data, int N)
30 {
31   // allocate temporary array
32   unique_ptr<T[]> temp = make_unique<T[]>(N);
33   // pointers to easily switch between the two arrays
34   T *repo1, *repo2, *aux;
35
36   repo1 = data;
37   repo2 = temp.get();
38
39   // loop for group size growing exponentially from 1 element
40   for (int grpSize = 1; grpSize < N; grpSize <<= 1)
41     {
42       for (int stIdx = 0; stIdx < N; stIdx += 2 * grpSize)
43         {
44           int nextIdx = stIdx + grpSize;
45           int secondGrpSize = min (max (0, N - nextIdx), grpSize);
46
47           // check to see if there are enough data for a second ↵
                  group to merge with
48           if (secondGrpSize == 0)
49             {
50               // if there is no second part, just copy the first ↵
                    part to repo2 for use in the next iteration
51               for (int i = 0; i < N - stIdx; i++)
52                 repo2[stIdx + i] = repo1[stIdx + i];
53             }
54           else
55             {
```

```
56              mergeList (repo1 + stIdx, repo1 + nextIdx, grpSize, ↩
                    secondGrpSize, repo2 + stIdx);
57          }
58        }
59
60      // switch pointers
61      aux = repo1;
62      repo1 = repo2;
63      repo2 = aux;
64    }
65
66    // move data back to the original array
67    if (repo1 != data)
68      memcpy (data, temp.get(), sizeof (T) * N);
69 }
```

The key points of the above implementation are:

- The `mergeList()` template function of lines 1–26 is a typical implementation of an array merging operation. It receives the addresses of two array segments (`src1` and `src2`) and their lengths (`len1` and `len2`) and deposits the sorted result in the destination array (`dest`). The loop of lines 5–18 compares the smaller elements of the two segments, before moving the smaller of the two to the destination array. This process continues until either of the two parts is exhausted.

  The two `for` loops that follow just copy whatever elements remain in one of the two subarrays to `dest`. What is different in our implementation from what is discussed in most algorithm books is that the data are not moved back to the source array. The motivation is the minimization of the data movement overhead. The `mergesort()` template function anticipates this "bouncing" of data between repositories and adjusts accordingly.

- The `mergesort()` template function contains two nested for loops: the outer one controls the array segment sizes that get merged and the inner one iterates over the starting index of the first array part to be merged. The starting index of the second part (`nextIdx`) is just `grpSize` distance from the first one.

- The `mergesort()` template function maintains two pointers, `repo1` and `repo2`, that reference the holding place of the input data and the temporary storage used during the merging operation, respectively. These pointers get switched at the end of each merging phase (lines 61–63).

- The only major problem caused by N not being a power of 2 is that there can be array parts with no counterpart to merge with. In order to maintain the data in either of the two repositories as a whole, these "partnerless" parts are just copied to the temporary storage pointed to by `repo2` (lines 51–52).

  A minor issue is also that the very last part to be merged in every phase might not be of `grpSize` length. The adjustment of the second group size takes place on line 45.

- If at the end of the sorting procedure the data reside at the temporary storage, they are copied back to the original array (lines 67 and 68).

Our sequential implementation seems ripe for parallelization, with a `parallel for` construct, given the two nested loops in the `mergesort()` template function. However, only the inner loop can be parallelized in this fashion, as there is a loop-carried flow dependency affecting the outer loop: the array referenced by `repo2` is written during iteration `grpSize`, before being used as an input in iteration `grpSize*2`. As we cannot eliminate this RAW dependency, we have to settle for the inner loop.

Amazingly, the only thing we need to do to turn Listing 8.48 into a multi-threaded implementation is to insert a pragma line between lines 41 and 42, as in:

Listing 8.49: The OpenMP-based multi-threaded version of Listing 8.48 requires only a single additional line.

```
70  // File : mergesort_omp_bottomup.cpp
71  . . .
72    for (int grpSize = 1; grpSize < N; grpSize <<= 1)
73      {
74  #pragma omp parallel for
75        for (int stIdx = 0; stIdx < N; stIdx += 2 * grpSize)
76          {
77  . . .
```

For clarity, we omit in this `pragma` line the recommended `default(none)` and `shared(...)` clauses.

In Section 8.13.3 we compare the performance of our OpenMP-based implementation against the Qt-based one that is described in Section 9.4.5.

8.13.2 Top-down mergesort in OpenMP

Arguably, the most studied version of mergesort is the recursive, top-down one. It does have a number of features in its favor, such as a shorter and easier to describe structure and no need for treatment of special N cases. While relying on the same merging process as the bottom-up algorithm, it partitions the input in a different way. The bottom-up mergesort merges subarrays in a carefully orchestrated manner, so that the subarrays are already sorted when the merging commences. On the other hand, the top-down variant calls itself in order to sort the two halves of the input array, before the merging can be done.

A sequential implementation is shown in Listing 8.50.

Listing 8.50: A sequential implementation of the top-down mergesort algorithm.

```
1  template < class T > void mergeList (T * src1, T * src2, int len1, ↩
       int len2, T * dest)
2  {
3    int idx1 = 0, idx2 = 0;
4    int loc = 0;                      // starting point in dest array
5    while (idx1 < len1 && idx2 < len2)
6      {
7        if (src1[idx1] <= src2[idx2])
```

```
8          {
9              dest[loc] = src1[idx1];
10             idx1++;
11         }
12       else
13         {
14             dest[loc] = src2[idx2];
15             idx2++;
16         }
17       loc++;
18     }
19
20   // copy the rest
21   for (int i = idx1; i < len1; i++)
22     dest[loc++] = src1[i];
23
24   for (int i = idx2; i < len2; i++)
25     dest[loc++] = src2[i];
26
27   memcpy(src1, dest, sizeof(T)*(len1+len2));
28 }
29
30 //---------------------------------------------------------------
31 // sort data array of N elements, using the temp array as temporary ↩
       storage
32 template < class T > void mergesortRec (T * data, T * temp, int N)
33 {
34   // base case
35   if(N < 2)
36     return;
37   else
38   {
39     int middle = N/2;
40     mergesortRec(data, temp, middle);
41     mergesortRec(data+middle, temp+middle, N - middle);
42     mergeList(data, data+middle, middle, N-middle, temp);
43   }
44 }
45 //---------------------------------------------------------------
46 template < class T > void mergesort (T * data, int N)
47 {
48   // allocate temporary array
49   T *temp = new T[N];
50   int middle = N/2;
51
52   mergesortRec(data, temp, middle);
53   mergesortRec(data+middle, temp+middle, N - middle);
54   mergeList(data, data+middle, middle, N-middle, temp);
55
56   delete []temp;
57 }
```

The only difference between the `mergeList()` template function of Listing 8.48 and the one shown above is the inclusion of line 27, which ensures that the input data always stay in their original array. The `mergesort()` front-end function allocates the temporary memory needed for the merging operation and calls the recursive `mergesortRec()` function to sort the two halves of the input before subsequently merging them on line 54.

The recursive function checks for the base cases of no data or one data item only (line 35) so that the recursion can be terminated, before following the same routine as `mergesort()`, i.e., calling itself to sort the two halves of the input before subsequently merging them on line 42.

As the calls to `mergesortRec()` on lines 40, 41, 52, and 53 deal with disjoints parts of the input array, we can use `sections` or `task` directives to allow them to execute concurrently. The only restriction is that the `mergeList()` calls on lines 42 and 54 can only be issued after the preceding sorting operations are complete.

The required modifications, albeit way more extensive than in the bottom-up algorithm, are still straightforward, as shown in Listing 8.51.

Listing 8.51: OpenMP, multi-threaded implementation of the top-down mergesort algorithm.

```
1   // File : mergesort_omp_topdown.cpp
2   . . .
3   template < class T > void mergesortRec (T * data, T * temp, int N)
4   {
5     if (N < 2)
6       return;
7     else
8       {
9         int middle = N / 2;
10  #pragma omp task if(N>10000) mergeable
11        {
12          mergesortRec (data, temp, middle);
13        }
14  #pragma omp task if(N>10000) mergeable
15        {
16          mergesortRec (data + middle, temp + middle, N - middle);
17        }
18
19  #pragma omp taskwait
20
21        mergeList (data, data + middle, middle, N - middle, temp);
22      }
23  }
24
25  //------------------------------------------------------------
26  template < class T > void mergesort (T * data, int N)
27  {
28    // allocate temporary array
29    T *temp = new T[N];
30
```

```
31  #pragma omp parallel
32    {
33
34  #pragma omp single
35      {
36        int middle = N / 2;
37  #pragma omp task
38        {
39          mergesortRec (data, temp, middle);
40        }
41  #pragma omp task
42        {
43          mergesortRec (data + middle, temp + middle, N - middle);
44        }
45
46  #pragma omp taskwait
47
48        mergeList (data, data + middle, middle, N - middle, temp);
49      }
50    }
51
52    delete [] temp;
53  }
```

The `parallel` directive on line 31 of the front-end function sets up the parallel execution of the algorithm. The `task` directives on lines 10, 14, 37, and 41 enable the concurrent sorting of disjoint parts of the array. The `taskwait` directives on lines 19 and 46 guarantee that the parts to be merged have been sorted already.

If left unchecked, lines 10 and 14 would produce a task for every item in the input array! The `if` clauses limit the generation of new tasks to inputs that exceed 10,000 items. The threshold of 10,000 is chosen arbitrarily, and this is a weak point of this implementation.

Could it be possible that we always roughly get an a priori specified number of tasks, regardless of the size of the input?

Let us assume that we target an implementation that will generate a maximum of T tasks. The tasks that are generated by the implementation in Listing 8.51 form a binary tree as the one shown in Fig. 8.17.

One could propose the following formulation in order to limit the number of tasks:

```
. . .
// A global numTasks counter is used to enumerate the number of
// tasks generated and limit the generation of new ones
#pragma omp task if(numTasks < maxTasks) mergeable
    {
#pragma omp atomic
        numTasks++;

        mergesortRec (data, temp, middle);
    }
```

. . .

However, this is a bad idea, as the task tree is not necessarily generated in a breadth-first manner. This way, we could end up with tasks that are very big or very small, and just plain inappropriate for properly load balancing the computation.

A better approach would be to have a variable-size threshold, associated with the overall array size.

If N is a power of 2, then the binary tree of tasks is perfect, and the total number of tasks for a tree of height h is $2^{h+1} - 1$. If h is the maximum height that the tree can grow to before we exceed our maximum number of tasks T, then we have

$$2^{h+1} - 1 \leq T < 2^{h+2} - 1 \tag{8.8}$$

and we can express h as a function of T:

$$2^{h+1} - 1 \leq T \Rightarrow h \leq lg(T + 1) - 1. \tag{8.9}$$

As h has to be an integer, its maximum value has to be

$$h = \lfloor lg(T + 1) \rfloor - 1. \tag{8.10}$$

The smallest size of a subarray to be sorted in such a tree is

$$\frac{N}{2^h} = \frac{N}{2^{\lfloor lg(T+1) \rfloor - 1}} \approx \frac{2 \cdot N}{T + 1}. \tag{8.11}$$

Eq. (8.11) requires no complex computations and can be used conveniently to limit the generation of tasks in our implementation, as shown in Listing 8.52.

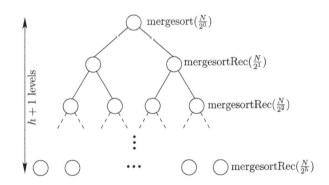

FIGURE 8.17

A binary tree of tasks is formed during the execution of the top-down mergesort function in Listing 8.51. The tree nodes are decorated by the name of the function executed by the corresponding task and the size of the array part to be sorted (assuming N is a power of 2). In this figure we assume that the generation of new tasks stops when the size of the array parts to be sorted falls below $\frac{N}{2^h}$.

Listing 8.52: Modifications to the OpenMP, multi-threaded implementation of the top-down mergesort algorithm in order to limit the number of generated tasks in an input size-agnostic manner.

```cpp
1   // File : mergesort_omp_topdown_v2.cpp
2   . . .
3   const int maxTasks=4096;
4   int _thresh_; // used for the if clauses
5   . . .
6   //──────────────────────────────────────────────────
7   // sort data array of N elements, using the aux array as temporary ↵
          storage
8   template < class T > void mergesortRec (T * data, T * temp, int N)
9   {
10    if (N < 2)
11      return;
12    else
13      {
14        int middle = N / 2;
15  #pragma omp task if(N > _thresh_ ) mergeable
16        {
17          mergesortRec (data, temp, middle);
18        }
19  #pragma omp task if(N > _thresh_ ) mergeable
20        {
21          mergesortRec (data + middle, temp + middle, N - middle);
22        }
23
24  #pragma omp taskwait
25
26        mergeList (data, data + middle, middle, N - middle, temp);
27      }
28  }
29
30  //──────────────────────────────────────────────────
31  template < class T > void mergesort (T * data, int N)
32  {
33    // allocate temporary array
34    T *temp = new T[N];
35    _thresh_ = 2.0 * N / (maxTasks + 1);
36
37  #pragma omp parallel
38    {
39  . . .
```

The only changes required in this updated version of Listing 8.51 are the calculation of the size threshold once in the front-end function (line 35) and the expression of the if clauses on lines 15 and 19. A further improvement to the generation of tasks is left as an exercise (see Exercise 13).

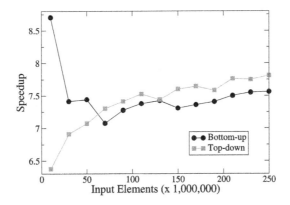

FIGURE 8.18

Average speedup of the bottom-up and top-down parallel mergesort implementations for different input sizes. Mean values were obtained by running each test 30 times.

8.13.3 Performance comparison

The bottom-up, non-recursive sequential version of mergesort is considered more efficient than the corresponding top-down one. But is this performance benefit carried over to the OpenMP implementations?

For this battery of tests we used an AMD Ryzen 9 3900X 12-core CPU, with two hardware threads per core. Our platform run 64-bit Kubuntu Linux 20.04, and all programs were compiled by GCC 9.3 with the `-O2` switch. The sequential sorting times were obtained by using C's `qsort` standard library function. The measured speedup curves are shown in Fig. 8.18.

The results are surprising, as the top-down implementation has a clear margin over the bottom-up one when the input exceeds a threshold, despite being penalized by recursion and the explicit generation and management of tasks. This is even more surprising given that in the previous edition of this book, where a different CPU was used as a testbed, the results were exactly the opposite, with the bottom-up mergesort being superior in all the tests! The cache hierarchy employed by the Ryzen 9 CPU is probably the reason for this behavior.

8.14 A case study: brute-force encryption cracking, combining MPI and OpenMP

This section is a continuation of the DES cracking example in Section 5.24, where we presented performance measurements on a single multicore machine. MPI is perfectly capable of utilizing the computational resources of such platforms, but to purists it may seem inappropriate. The reason is that MPI spawns processes, an action that is orders of magnitude slower than spawning threads. So, in principle, the following deployment scenario promises the best resource utilization: first start a single process for each *physical* node in the system and then spawn as many threads as necessary to fully exploit the multiple cores in that system.

In that setting, we can have MPI implement the first phase and OpenMP take care of the second one. OpenMP is poised as a very good choice in that regard, especially given that the development effort associated with OpenMP parallel constructs is minimal. However, when combined with MPI this advantage is lost. OpenMP requires an additional effort over the already substantial one necessary for dividing the workload amongst distributed memory nodes. One would have to develop the MPI program first and then insert the OpenMP pragmas that would automatically generate threads.

In general, a "hybrid" computation that combines MPI and OpenMP can be accomplished in a variety of ways. We can classify them according to how MPI communications are conducted as [51]:

- **Master-only**: Only one MPI process per machine is launched. The communications are performed only by the master thread, either inside a master construct or outside a parallel region. This design approach can hinder the utilization of cores, as while MPI is being *called*, there can be only one application thread active.
- **Overlapping communication/computation**: Multiple OpenMP threads may make MPI calls. MPI must be specifically compiled to handle this functionality (see also Section 5.19). It is also possible that we can have multiple MPI processes per machine, each using its own team of threads [23].

The naming of the second design approach is a bit misleading though, as making an MPI call and returning from it is not the same as starting and completing the actual communication. MPI provides immediate and locally blocking calls that carry out the communication in the background. So, there can be an overlap between the computation and the communication, even if a "master-only" design is employed.

In the following code, we convert the program of Listing 5.37 into an MPI–OpenMP hybrid using the "master-only" design. The changes are limited to the loop that processes the part of the key search space assigned to a node:

Listing 8.53: OpenMP-based variation of the static, key search space partitioning solution for DES cracking of Listing 5.37. Changes are limited to the main() function.

```
1   // File : decrypt2_omp.cpp
2   #include <omp.h>
3   ...
4   const int BLOCK = 1000000;
5   //————————————————————————————————————
6   int main (int argc, char **argv)
7   {
8       int N, id;
9       long upper = (1L << 56);
10      long found = -1;
11      MPI_Status st;
12      MPI_Request req;
13      int flag = 0;
14      int ciphLen = strlen ((char *) cipher);
```

```
15
16     MPI_Init (&argc, &argv);
17     double start = MPI_Wtime ();
18     MPI_Comm_rank (MPI_COMM_WORLD, &id);
19     MPI_Comm_size (MPI_COMM_WORLD, &N);
20     MPI_Irecv ((void *) &found, 1, MPI_LONG, MPI_ANY_SOURCE, ↵
           MPI_ANY_TAG, MPI_COMM_WORLD, &req);
21     int iterCount = 0;
22
23     long idx = 0;
24     while (idx < upper && found < 0)
25       {
26   #pragma omp parallel for default(none) shared(cipher, ciphLen, found ↵
       , idx, id, N)
27       for (long i = idx + id; i < idx + N * BLOCK; i += N)
28         {
29           if (tryKey (i, (char *) cipher, ciphLen))
30             {
31   #pragma omp critical
32               found = i;
33             }
34         }
35
36       // communicate termination signal
37       if (found >= 0)
38         {
39           for (int node = 0; node < N; node++)
40             MPI_Send ((void *) &found, 1, MPI_LONG, node, 0, ↵
                 MPI_COMM_WORLD);
41         }
42
43       idx += N * BLOCK;
44     }
45
46   // print out the result from node 0
47   if (id == 0)
48     {
49       MPI_Wait (&req, &st);       // in case process 0 finishes before↵
             the key is found
50       decrypt (found, (char *) cipher, ciphLen);
51       printf ("%i nodes in %lf sec : %li %s\n", N, MPI_Wtime () - ↵
             start, found, cipher);
52     }
53   MPI_Finalize ();
54 }
```

There is a key difference between Listing 8.53 and 5.37, in that there is a split of the
for loop in Listing 5.37 into a pair of nested loops (lines 24 and 27) in the above
code. The reason for the split is the need to be able to detect the discovery of the
secret key by another node (an early termination condition).

A `parallel for` loop must have a single point of entry and a single point of exit, which means that it is not possible to break out of the loop when the `found` variable is set using a conditional statement. Additionally, we cannot add the check of the `found` variable in the `for` termination condition, as, e.g.:

```
#pragma omp parallel for default(none) shared(cipher, ciphLen, . . .
    for (long i = idx + id; i < idx + N*BLOCK && found < 0; i += N↩
        )
```

as this violates the canonical form dictated by OpenMP (see Section 8.4).

As it is impossible to cater for the detection of the key discovery in a `parallel for` loop, we are forced to break the loop into smaller fragments. Between the multi-threaded execution of these smaller loops, we can check the `found` flag (line 24) and/or propagate the discovery to other nodes using `MPI_Send` (lines 37–41). The granularity of the split is controlled by the `BLOCK` constant of line 4.

This program can be compiled and run (on a single node in our example) by the following lines:

```
$ mpic++ -fopenmp decrypt2_omp.cpp -o decrypt2_omp
$ mpirun -np 1 ./decrypt2_omp
```

Enabling OpenMP support is just a matter of including the `-fopenmp` switch for the GNU C/C++ compiler, as `mpicc/mpic++` are just compiler front-ends. In comparison, utilizing all the capability of a 12-core CPU, with 24 threads, using just MPI, would require the command:

```
$ mpirun -np 24 ./decrypt2
```

The selection of the `BLOCK` parameter is critical and should not be glossed over, as it influences how frequently we check the termination condition (`BLOCK` should be made smaller for this) and how often we launch a team of threads to run the inner loop (`BLOCK` should be made bigger for this). For example, a setting of `BLOCK=1000` results in an execution time of ~ 9.8 sec on a Ryzen 9 3900x, 12-core CPU, while a setting of `BLOCK=1000000` results in an execution time of ~ 8.9 sec.

It is therefore obvious that the need to start–stop the OpenMP threads in order to check the termination condition acts against the efficiency of the program. Through experimentation we settled for `BLOCK=`10^6, but we still could not beat the runtime of the plain-vanilla MPI program over the same platform. Averaged over 10 runs, we were able to achieve 8.92 ± 0.05 sec for the MPI-OpenMP combination and 7.94 ± 0.07 sec for the MPI version. The larger standard deviation of the MPI program is probably due to the inconsistent startup times of the MPI processes.

We could solve the problem stemming from the split for loop by using `task` constructs instead of a `parallel for`. It is however highly unlikely that any significant performance gains over the plain-vanilla MPI could be materialized. What is certain though is that the complexity of the code will increase.

As closing remarks, we can summarize the benefits and drawbacks of combining OpenMP and MPI as follows:

✓ It lowers the memory footprint, as OpenMP threads reuse the code and the global data of a single process.

✓ It simplifies program deployment as we do not need to know the number of cores in each machine. All we need is the machine's IP or DNS name.

✓ There is no need for intranode communications. OpenMP code can use shared variables.

✓ Intranode load balancing is easy to achieve, by using a "dynamic" or "guided" setting for the `schedule` clause of `parallel for` constructs.

- OpenMP threads do not have distinct ranks/IDs within an MPI communicator. As such, it is cumbersome to establish communication between specific threads running on different physical machines.[21]

- Performance gains are dubious (more on this below). We can expect startup costs to improve, but computationally–heavy applications do not really suffer from startup times.

- Development effort is increased.

In terms of performance benefits, this is an issue that is application- and machine architecture-dependent. There have been many studies on the subject of MPI–OpenMP hybrid software, and the results are generally mixed. For example, in [23], the authors report that pure MPI is superior for small numbers of nodes, while the MPI–OpenMP combination delivers better performance for larger collections of machines.

Exercises

1. Modify the program in Listing 8.1 so that `printf` is used instead of `cout`. Do you see any difference in the output compared to the one reported in Section 8.2? Can you explain it?

2. In the matrix multiplication example of Section 8.4.2 we could get three perfectly nested loops if we initialize the C matrix outside:

```
double A[K][L];
double B[L][M];
double C[K][M];

. . .
#pragma omp parallel for collapse(3)
  for (int i = 0; i < K; i++)
    for (int j = 0; j < M; j++)
      for (int k = 0; k < L; k++)
        C[i][j] += A[i][k] * B[k][j];
```

---

[21] It is cumbersome but not impossible, as message tags can be used to filter messages sent between nodes.

Is the above code correct? If not, what kind of modification is required for fixing it?

3. Draw the iteration space dependency graph for the following program:

```
for (int i = 1; i < K-1; i++)
    for (int j = 0; j < M; j++)
        a[i][j] = a[i-1][j] + a[i+1][j];
```

What kind of dependencies exist? How can you eliminate them?

4. Create a C++ program for visualizing the thread iteration assignment performed by a `parallel for` directive for different `schedule` schemes. Your program should have a per-thread vector that accumulates the loop control variable values assigned to each thread. Use this program and appropriate `schedule` settings to experiment with multiple schemes without recompiling your program. This is a sample of the output you should be able to get for a loop of 100 iterations:

```
$ export OMP_SCHEDULE="static ,5"
$ ./solution
Thread 0: 0 1 2 3 4 40 41 42 43 44 80 81 82 83 84
Thread 1: 5 6 7 8 9 45 46 47 48 49 85 86 87 88 89
Thread 2: 10 11 12 13 14 50 51 52 53 54 90 91 92 93 94
Thread 3: 15 16 17 18 19 55 56 57 58 59 95 96 97 98 99
Thread 4: 20 21 22 23 24 60 61 62 63 64
Thread 5: 25 26 27 28 29 65 66 67 68 69
Thread 6: 30 31 32 33 34 70 71 72 73 74
Thread 7: 35 36 37 38 39 75 76 77 78 79
```

5. In Listing 8.20 we examined the issue of processing a linked list concurrently. Is there a way to improve this program for a doubly linked list? Write the corresponding program.

6. Write a program for traversing and processing the elements of a binary tree in parallel using a preorder, in-order, or postorder traversal. Use the `task` construct to that effect.

7. Modify the program of the previous exercise so that *undeferred tasks* are generated after the traversal has moved beyond the fifth level of the tree (assume that the root sits at level 0).

8. Modify the Fibonacci sequence-calculating program of Listing 8.21 so that it counts the number of child tasks generated.

9. Use the `task` directive to create a solution to the single-producer, multiple-consumers problem with a variable number of consumers, as specified in the command-line.

10. Use the `task` directive and its `depend` clause to model the dependency graph of Fig. 8.19. You can use stub functions to represent each of the tasks in the figure.

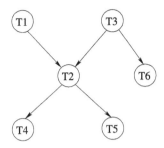

FIGURE 8.19

A dependency graph consisting of six tasks.

11. Finding the odd integers in an array can be accomplished by the following OpenMP code:

```
int data[N];
int oddCount=0;
#pragma omp parallel for
  for (int i = 0; i < N; i++)
       if( data[i] % 2 )
#pragma omp atomic
            oddCount ++;
```

Modify the above code so that there is no need for a `critical` or `atomic` directive by introducing a counter array with one element per thread. Compare the performance of your version with and without cache false-sharing. If we were to use a reduction variable, what false-sharing elimination technique does this correspond to?

12. Quicksort rightfully holds the place of the top performer amongst generic sorting algorithms. Its design can be considered a reflection of mergesort, although both algorithms employ a divide-and-conquer design. Write a sequential implementation of quicksort and proceed to parallelize it using OpenMP constructs. Measure the speedup that can be achieved and compare it to the performance that can be obtained from the bottom-up mergesort of Section 8.13.1.

13. The number of tasks in the top-down mergesort implementation of Listing 8.52 can be further reduced if only one new task is generated for one-half of the data, with the parent task taking up the sorting of the other half, as in the following listing:

```
template < class T > void mergesortRec (T * data, T * temp, int ↩
    N)
{
  if (N < 2)
    return;
  else
    {
      int middle = N / 2;
```

```
#pragma omp task if(N > _thresh_ ) mergeable
    {
        mergesortRec (data, temp, middle);
    }

    mergesortRec (data + middle, temp + middle, N — middle);

#pragma omp taskwait

        mergeList (data, data + middle, middle, N — middle, temp);
    }
}
```

In that case, what should be the size threshold _thresh_ used in the if clause?

14. The following function is supposed to return a pseudorandom number between 0 and 100:

```
unsigned int customRand ()
{
    static unsigned int seed = clock ();
    seed = (seed * 7) % 101;
    return seed;
}
```

- Can it be safely used by multiple threads?
- Can you turn it into a reentrant one? How about a thread-safe one?

15. Is it possible to take out the distribute directive from the code in Listing 8.32 as shown below?

```
#pragma omp target teams
#pragma omp parallel for collapse(2)
    for(int i=0;i<N;i++)
        for(int j=0;j<N;j++)
            for(int k=0;k<N;k++)
                c[i][j]+= a[i][k]*b[k][j];
```

What would be the outcome of this change?

16. Assuming we have a dual-socket platform with 32 cores per CPU, each supporting two hardware threads, write the appropriate environment variable so that the following places are defined:

- **(a)** Each socket is a place.
- **(b)** Each set of four cores constitutes a place.
- **(c)** Each set of 16 hardware threads is a place.

17. The AMD Epyc 7742 CPU comes with 64 cores, each supporting two hardware threads. The cores are organized in the form of CCD chiplets, each hosting eight cores and their dedicated 32 MiB L3 cache. The L3 cache is split between two core complexes (CCXs). Explain what will happen for each of the following settings in terms of thread placement:

(a) OMP_PLACES="ll_caches", OMP_PROC_BIND="close", for 64 threads and the master thread at p_0,

(b) OMP_PLACES="{0:4}:16:4", OMP_PROC_BIND="master", for 256 threads and the master thread at p_1,

(c) OMP_PLACES="{0:8}:8:8", OMP_PROC_BIND="spread", for 16 threads and the master thread at p_2,

(d) OMP_PLACES="{0:8}:8:8", OMP_PROC_BIND="spread", for 256 threads and the master thread at p_3,

(e) OMP_PLACES="cores", OMP_PROC_BIND="spread", for 64 threads and the master thread at p_4,

(f) OMP_PLACES="cores", OMP_PROC_BIND="spread", for 16 threads and the master thread at p_5.

High-level multi-threaded programming with the Qt library

9

In this chapter you will:

- Learn about the high-level thread management facilities provided by Qt.
- Use Qt's built-in thread pool to reduce the overhead of thread construction.
- Utilize the power of multicore CPUs with map, reduce, and filter semantics.
- Explore a number of test cases on the deployment and use of the QtConcurrent facilities.

9.1 Introduction

The Qt library[1] is a cross-platform dual-license library that offers support for UI development, DB connectivity, networking, XML processing, and other things besides providing a very simple-to-use set of classes for managing threads. Qt is made available both as an open source library and as a commercial product for the developers that require closed source development. Currently Qt runs on top of Windows, MacOS X, Linux, and a small collection of embedded operating systems, offering a remarkable flexibility in program deployment.

Although the C++ standard has finally incorporated thread support since the C++11 iteration, Qt offers both a more complete implementation and an easier-to-master philosophy about threading. An added bonus is that Qt's approach to threads is very close to the one used by Java, with the only major differences stemming from how these two languages handle data allocation. For example, creating a thread requires instances of a class derived from the QThread or QRunnable classes. This object-oriented approach allows for a more gentle learning curve.

Qt offers implementations of semaphores (QMutex and QSemaphore), condition variables (QWaitCondition), and all the other bells and whistles that one can expect from a full-fledged concurrency support library. In this chapter we are concerned with the higher-level functionality offered by Qt, in the form of the QThreadPool class and the QtConcurrent module. Similar features have been added to C++17 STL recently. However, because Qt relies on inheritance rather than templates, one tends

---

[1] http://www.qt.io.

Multicore and GPU Programming. https://doi.org/10.1016/B978-0-12-814120-5.00019-6

803

to get less scary error messages, making it a more approachable toolkit. In terms of performance, STL algorithms generally have an edge, as for example, Qt performs reduction sequentially. Of course this all comes down to the design employed as Qt facilities can still produce excellent performance, as attested by the case studies that follow.

In this chapter we do not explicitly address Qt's interoperability with other software platforms. However, this is not an issue, as Qt can be combined with all the tools covered in this book, including C++11 threads, OpenMP, MPI, CUDA, and OpenCL, just by appropriately constructing a `qmake` project file or a `Makefile`. Many of the case studies covered in the previous chapters already employ Qt, although not for its concurrency support.

9.2 Implicit thread creation

It is occasionally the case that a side task needs to be executed without the formality of creating a thread object, starting it, and then waiting for it to finish. Qt supports this scenario with a set of functions in the `QtConcurrent` namespace. The syntax is as follows:

```
#include <QtConcurrent>

extern void foo();
...
QtConcurrent::run(foo);
```

When the static `QtConcurrent::run` function is called, a separate thread is used to run the supplied function. This may look similar to the `async` call in C++11, but there is a major difference: the thread is taken from a pool of Qt-managed threads that are preallocated in order to eliminate the OS overhead associated with starting a thread during program execution. The `QThreadPool` class is responsible for this task.

There are three issues with the use of `QtConcurrent::run`:

- *How to pass parameters*: Since there is no object that can be initialized before the thread is called, the technique used to pass parameters is to list them as parameters to the `QtConcurrent::run` method after the reference to the function. These are copied and passed in turn to the function when the thread runs. This also prevents the function from modifying the original parameters, unless they are passed by reference.
- *How to detect when the thread is done*: The `QtConcurrent::run` function returns a reference to a `QFuture` object that can be used to check the status of the execution and even block until the thread is done. So both polling and blocking checks can be conducted. Some of the most useful methods supported by `QFuture` are:
    - `isStarted()`: returns true if the thread has started execution. The execution may be delayed if there is no available thread in `QThreadPool`.

- isRunning(): returns true if the thread is currently running.
- isFinished(): returns true if the thread has competed execution of the provided function.
- *How to collect the result of the function*: QFuture is a class template that allows also the retrieval of the function return value. The example that follows illustrates how.

Let us consider an MD5-hash calculating program that is supposed to print out the 16-byte checksum for every file specified as a parameter. The twist in Listing 9.1 is that each MD5 calculation is run concurrently:

Listing 9.1: A program that calculates the MD5 hash for each of the files passed as parameters to it, by invoking a Qt-managed thread for handling each file.

```
1   // File : md5Ex/md5Ex.cpp
2   . . .
3   #include "md5.h"
4   #include <QtConcurrentRun>
5   #include <QFuture>
6   . . .
7   int main (int argc, char *argv[])
8   {
9     int N = argc - 1;
10    QFuture < string > f[N];
11    char *buffers[N];
12
13    // scan all the filenames supplied
14    for (int i = 0; i < N; i++)
15      {
16        buffers[i] = 0;
17        FILE *fin;
18        fin = fopen (argv[i + 1], "r");
19        if (fin != 0)        // if the file exists
20          {
21            fseek (fin, 0, SEEK_END);
22            int fileSize = ftell (fin);   // find out the size
23            fseek (fin, 0, SEEK_SET);
24
25            buffers[i] = new char[fileSize + 1];  // allocate enough ↩
                  memory
26            fread (buffers[i], fileSize, 1, fin); // read all of it in↩
                  memory
27            buffers[i][fileSize + 1] = 0;          // terminate by 0 as↩
                  md5() expects a string
28            fclose (fin);
29            string s (buffers[i]);
30            f[i] = QtConcurrent::run (md5, move(s));    // calculate ↩
                  the MD5 hash in another thread
31          }
32      }
33
34    for (int i = 0; i < N; i++)
```

```
35      if (buffers[i] != 0)           // if file existed
36      {
37          f[i].waitForFinished ();  // wait for the calculation to ↩
                complete
38          cout << argv[i + 1] << " : " << f[i].result () << endl;
39          delete [] buffers[i];      // cleanup the buffer
40      }
41    return 0;
42  }
```

The key points of the above program are:

- The md5 function used at line 30 is supplied by a publicly available MD5 source code library based on the reference C implementation. The full code is provided in the book's supplementary material.
- The number of file names supplied at the command-line N is retrieved at line 9. This is subsequently used to allocate an array of QFuture<string> objects (line 10) for accessing the results of each individual thread run.
- Each file is loaded into memory before being processed. The buffer array of pointers (declared at line 11) reference the individual blocks used.
- The size of each file (determined on lines 21–23) is used to allocate space for its contents (line 25) and read it in one go (line 26). Each block is zero-terminated (line 27). It should be noted that the program does not produce correct output for binary files because the md5 function is coded to work on data of type string.
- Line 30 serves to request the execution of the md5 function by a separate thread. The exact time that this will happen is unknown, depending on the availability of free threads.
- The main thread uses the loop of lines 34–40 to wait for each run to complete (line 37), print out the 16-character-long string retrieved from the QFuture object (line 38), and release the memory held by the file contents.

Depending on the version of Qt used, lines similar to the following may need to be added to the .pro file, for a program using QtConcurrent facilities to compile successfully:

```
INCLUDEPATH += /usr/include/x86_64-linux-gnu/qt5/QtConcurrent
LIBS += -lQt5Concurrent
```

It all depends on the directory structure employed by the operating system, and this can change from one release to the next. Using a Qt-aware IDE such as QtCreator can alleviate the hassle associated with properly setting up the project file.

9.3 Qt's pool of threads

As mentioned in the previous section, Qt maintains a pool of threads that are ready to go, without the need for the OS to allocate and initialize a new thread entity. While the overhead of thread creation compared to forking a new process is orders of magnitude smaller, it can still be significant, especially if threads need to be dynamically spawned at runtime. A classic example is that of a **concurrent** web or database server, which listens to incoming requests and dedicates a thread to servicing each one. Instead of creating a new thread for every request, the thread could be reused, taken from a repository of idle threads. This repository is exactly the kind of functionality the QThreadPool class provides, and the one we hand-crafted in Section 3.12.

The QThreadPool class and QtConcurrent namespace functions provide the means for an efficient and easy transition to multi-threaded applications, especially when the threads do not have to share common resources. The only problem is that the functions which are designated to be run by separate threads will only run if there is a free thread available.

As an example to how these can be utilized, the following program is a rewrite of the producers–consumers code of Listing 3.13:

Listing 9.2: Generic solution to the n-producer and m-consumer problem, with a fixed number of iterations, using the QThreadPool class and QtConcurrent::run function. Only the differences from Listing 3.13 are shown.

```
1   // File : qtconcurProdCons.cpp
2   . . .
3       if(N + M > QThreadPool::globalInstance() -> maxThreadCount())
4           QThreadPool::globalInstance() -> setMaxThreadCount (N+M);
5
6       QFuture<void> prodF[N];
7       QFuture<void> consF[M];
8       shared_ptr<Producer<int>> p[N];
9       shared_ptr<Consumer<int>> c[M];
10
11      for (int i = 0; i < N; i++) {
12          p[i] = make_shared<Producer<int>>(i);
13          prodF[i] = QtConcurrent::run(*p[i], &Producer<int>::↵
                operator());
14      }
15      for (int i = 0; i < M; i++) {
16          c[i] = make_shared<Consumer<int>>(i);
17          consF[i] = QtConcurrent::run(*c[i], &Consumer<int>::↵
                operator());
18      }
19
20      for (int i = 0; i < N; i++)
21          prodF[i].waitForFinished();
22
23      for (int i = 0; i < M; i++)
24          consF[i].waitForFinished();
25  . . .
```

As can be easily deduced from the length of the above listing, only minimal changes are required in order to introduce the new functionality. As can be seen on lines 13 and 17, the `QtConcurrent::run` function can also work on an object's method if an object reference is provided first, followed by the address of the method to call. Because threads are unnamed, the main thread has to use the `QFuture` objects returned by `QtConcurrent::run` to wait for them to complete (lines 21 and 24).

A final clarification about the syntax on lines 13 and 17 is that the address-of (&) operator is required because non-static methods cannot be referenced otherwise in the absence of a class instance.

Lines 3–4 ensure that all the requested threads will start running, even if this number is suboptimal according to Qt's criteria. The ideal number of threads is estimated and made available by the `QThread::idealThreadCount()` method, and this is the default setting for the active number of threads. By getting a reference to the intrinsic `QThreadPool` instance, via the `QThreadPool::globalInstance()` static method, the available number of threads can be modified (line 4).

9.4 Higher-level constructs – multi-threaded programming without threads!

Qt goes beyond the elementary provisions of the `QThread`, `QMutex`, and associated classes by providing support for automatic thread creation, job distribution, and result collection. The `QThreadPool` class and `QtConcurrent` functions provide the underpinning for creating multi-threaded programs without ever subclassing the `QThread` class or explicitly managing the execution and termination of threads. Furthermore, a program that uses `QtConcurrent`'s high-level functionality will automatically adjust to the available cores in the execution platform, without any programmer consideration.

The provisions of the **QtConcurrent** namespace functions address embarrassingly parallel problems, i.e., problems that require computations on data items that have no interdependencies. Surprisingly, there are many problems that satisfy this requirement. Qt provides two versions for each of the functions described below: a *blocking/synchronous* and a *non-blocking/asynchronous* variant. The non-blocking version allows the calling thread to continue execution until it needs to check for the termination of the assigned tasks. In that case, a `QFuture` instance is returned and used to handle the check and subsequent result collection.

Table 9.1 lists the available functions. Because the functions discussed in this section are overloaded, their signatures are not reported in this book for brevity. The reader should consult the Qt documentation utility, i.e., `assistant`, for complete and up-to-date (e.g., upgrades) information.

9.4.1 Concurrent map

The `QtConcurrent::map` function applies a supplied function to all the members of a sequence (e.g., vector, list) in parallel. The following example is illustrative:

Table 9.1 A list of the functions provided by the `QtConcurrent` namespace. T represents the type of element that the map/filter/reduce functions apply to.

Function	Result	Modifies original data	Header
blockingFilter	void	✓	QtConcurrentFilter
blockingFiltered	QList<T>		QtConcurrentFilter
blockingFilteredReduced	T		QtConcurrentFilter
blockingMap	void	✓	QtConcurrentMap
blockingMapped	QList<T>		QtConcurrentMap
blockingMappedReduced	T		QtConcurrentMap
filter	QFuture<void>	✓	QtConcurrentFilter
filtered	QFuture<T>		QtConcurrentFilter
filteredReduced	QFuture<T>		QtConcurrentFilter
map	QFuture<void>	✓	QtConcurrentMap
mapped	QFuture<T>		QtConcurrentMap
mappedReduced	QFuture<T>		QtConcurrentMap

Listing 9.3: An example of applying `QtConcurrent::map()` for calculating the value of a function y over all the points x in an array.

```
// File : concurrentmap/map.cpp
#include <QtConcurrentMap>
#include <QFuture>
. . .
const double a = 2.0;
const double b = -1.0;
void func(double &x)
{
    x = a*x + b;
}
//------
int main(int argc, char *argv[])
{
    int N = atoi(argv[1]);
    vector<double> data;
    // populate the input data
    . . .
    QFuture<void> res = QtConcurrent::map(data.begin(),
                                          data.end(),
                                          func);

    res.waitForFinished();
    . . .
```

The `QtConcurrent::map` function operates in-place, i.e., the calculated values are stored in the input container, overwriting the corresponding input data. This has two consequences: (i) the signature of the function to be applied should be:

```
void mapFuncName(T &);
```

where T is the input datatype, i.e., the input should be passed by reference, and (ii) a QFuture<void> reference is returned as on line 18, as no results can be retrieved explicitly. The QFuture<void> reference can be used to check the termination of the "mapping" (as on line 22) or to cancel or pause the task (with methods cancel() and pause(), respectively).

QtConcurrent can work with both STL containers like vector<> and Qt containers like QVector<> and QList<>. Performance is better though if a container that provides random-access iterators is used, like the ones listed above. QtConcurrent can operate on a range of input (as, e.g., specified by the begin() and end() iterators on lines 18 and 19) or a whole container.

If the input data are to be preserved, the QtConcurrent::mapped() function can be used instead as shown below, creating a new container with the results:

Listing 9.4: An example of QtConcurrent::mapped() application. Only the differences with Listing 9.3 are shown.

```
1   // File : concurrentmapped/mapped.cpp
2   . . .
3   double func(const double x)
4   {
5       return a*x + b;
6   }
7   //——————————————————————————————————
8   int main(int argc, char *argv[])
9   {
10      int N = atoi(argv[1]);
11      vector<double> data;
12      // populate the input data
13      for(int i=0;i<N;i++)
14          data.push_back(i);
15
16      QFuture<double> res = QtConcurrent::mapped(data,
17                                                 func);
18
19      res.waitForFinished();
20      QList<double> y = res.results();
21      cout << "Calculated " << y.size() << " results\n";
22      cout << "Results:\n";
23      for(QFuture<double>::const_iterator iter = res.begin(); iter != ↵
            res.end() ; iter++)
24          cout << *iter << endl;
25   . . .
```

The differences from QtConcurrent::map() are limited to the mapping function signature and the treatment of the QFuture<> object returned. The signature has to be:

Listing 9.5: Signature of the mapping function used by `QtConcurrent::mapped()` and `QtConcurrent::blockingMapped()`.

```
T mappedFuncName(const T );
// or
T mappedFuncName(const T &);
```

The results can be retrieved in the form of a `QList<>` collection as done on line 20 from the `QFuture<>` object. Alternatively, the `QFuture<>` object can be queried (e.g., with methods `resultAt()`, `resultCount()`) or traversed with the use of iterators, as shown on lines 23–24.

The blocking variants `QtConcurrent::blockingMap()` and `QtConcurrent::block-ingMapped()` do not return a `QFuture<>` object reference. Instead, one gets nothing/void for the former and a `QList<T>` for the latter function, where `T` is the input datatype. For example, the code of Listing 9.4 modified to work with the blocking function would be:

```
 1   . . .
 2       QList<double> data;
 3       // populate the input data
 4       for(int i=0;i<N;i++)
 5           data.append(i);
 6
 7       QList<double> res = QtConcurrent::blockingMapped(data,
 8                                                        func);
 9
10       cout << "Calculated " << res.size() << " results\n";
11       cout << "Results:\n";
12       for(int i=0;i<res.size(); i++)
13           cout << res.at(i) << endl;
14   . . .
```

9.4.2 Map-reduce

Qt provides a convenient implementation of the map-reduce pattern presented in Section 2.4.4. Reiterating the discussion of that section, map-reduce is a pattern made up of two stages: a mapping stage that applies a function to/transforms the supplied input data and a reduction stage that performs a summary-type operation on the "transformed" data.

Qt's implementation in the form of the `QtConcurrent::mappedReduced()` and `QtConcurrent::blockingMappedReduced()` functions requires two functions to be passed as input, one for performing the mapping and one for performing the reduction. Following the same naming convention as in the previous section, the "mapped" function name prefix implies that a new container is created to hold the results of the mapping procedure.

The signature for the mapping function is the same as the one shown in Listing 9.5. The reduction function should have the following signature, i.e., accepting two parameters and using the first one to return the result of the reduction:

Listing 9.6: Signature of the reduction function used by `QtConcurrent::mappedReduced()` and `QtConcurrent::blockingMappedReduced()`.

```
void reductionFuncName(T & , const T&);
```

As an example, let us consider the problem of finding the variance of a random variable x, using a sample x_i for $i = 0, \ldots, N - 1$, as given by the formula

$$\sigma^2 = \overline{(x - \mu)^2} = \overline{x^2} - \mu^2 = \frac{\sum_{i=0}^{N-1} x_i^2}{N} - \mu^2, \tag{9.1}$$

where $\mu = \overline{x}$.

The following code uses map-reduce to calculate the $\overline{x^2}$ term:

Listing 9.7: A map-reduce Qt implementation of the variance calculation for a set of samples.

```cpp
1  // File : variance.cpp
2  #include <QtConcurrentMap>
3  #include <QList>
4  . . .
5  //*******************************************
6  long powX2 (const long &x)
7  {
8    return x * x;
9  }
10
11 //*******************************************
12 void sumFunc (long &x, const long &y)
13 {
14   x += y;
15 }
16
17 //*******************************************
18 int main (int argc, char *argv[])
19 {
20   // initialize the random-number generator seed
21   srand (time (0));
22
23   // get how big the sample will be
24   int N = atoi (argv[1]);
25
26   // and populate a QList<> with the data
27   QList < long >data;
28   for (int i = 0; i < N; i++)
29     data.append ((rand () % 2000000) - 1000000);
30
31   // calculate the average
32   long sum = 0;
33   for (int i = 0; i < N; i++)
34     sum += data[i];
35   double mean = sum * 1.0 / N;
```

```
36
37   // map-reduce to find the sum of x_i^2
38   long res = QtConcurrent::blockingMappedReduced (data, powX2, ↩
         sumFunc);
39
40   // calculate variance, not forgetting to multiple res by 1.0 to ↩
         avoid truncation when dividing by N
41   double var = res * 1.0 / N - mean * mean;
42   cout << "Average: " << mean << " Variance " << var << endl;
43
44   return 0;
45 }
```

Line 38 is used to compute the term $\sum_{i=0}^{N-1} x_i^2$ by mapping the data collection to data * data via function powX2() (lines 6–9) and summing up the results with the reduction sumFunc() (lines 12–15).

There is just one shortcoming to Qt's implementation: reduction is performed sequentially, as only one reduction operation is allowed to be carried out at any point in time. This is mandated by thread safety considerations, as the reduction function is called in a mutual exclusion fashion. As a result, if the reduction stage constitutes a substantial part of the overall execution time, one should aim at a separate implementation. A user-supplied reduction implementation can still use QThread-Pool::start() to carry out the reduction in parallel. Such an example is provided in Section 9.4.5.

9.4.3 Concurrent filter

Along the lines of the "mapping" functionality, Qt also offers filtering capabilities, i.e., concurrently selecting a subset of items from a collection. The selection/rejection is based on the result of applying a predicate function on each item. Four function variants are provided, following the conventions observed in the previous sections:

- QtConcurrent::filter: Modifies the original collection. Returns a QFuture<void> reference for checking completion of operation.
- QtConcurrent::filtered: Generates a new sequence with the filtered items. Returns a QFuture<T> reference for checking completion of operation and for retrieving the results.

The above are augmented with their blocking variants QtConcurrent::blockingFilter and QtConcurrent::blockingFiltered. The signature of the predicate function required by all the filtering functions is:

Listing 9.8: Signature of the predicate function used by QtConcurrent::filter() and its variants. T is the type of items being filtered.

```
bool filterPredFuncName(const T&);
```

As an example, let us consider the problem of eliminating the outliers from a sample of data. Several methods exist for establishing the criteria on which such a decision can be made, although it is a process that remains controversial. In the code that follows, we just filter out all data that lie outside a supplied range of values [*lower*, *upper*]:

Listing 9.9: An example of how `QtConcurrent`'s filtering capabilities can be used to remove samples that lie outside a given range.

```
1   // File : outliers.cpp
2   #include <QtConcurrentFilter>
3   #include <QList>
4   #include <functional>
5   ...
6   bool filterFunc (const int &x, const int &lower, const int &upper)
7   {
8     if(x>upper)
9       return false;
10    if(x<lower)
11      return false;
12    return true;
13  }
14
15  // ********************************************
16  int main (int argc, char *argv[])
17  {
18    srand (time (0));
19    int N = atoi (argv[1]);
20    int l = atoi (argv[2]);
21    int u = atoi (argv[3]);
22    QList < int >data;
23    for (int i = 0; i < N; i++)
24      data.append ((rand () % 2000000) - 1000000);
25
26    QList<int> out = QtConcurrent::blockingFiltered (data, bind(↩
          filterFunc, placeholders::_1, l, u));
27
28    cout << "Filtered array is " << out.size() << " long\n";
29  ...
```

The predicate function on lines 6–13 requires three parameters, which is in disagreement with the signature of Listing 9.8. One solution would be to replace the second and third parameters with global variables, but this is a bad design choice. Instead, we use the `std::bind()` function to generate a function that meets the requirements of `QtConcurrent::blockingFiltered`, by binding the second and third arguments to the values passed as command-line parameters. The `bind(filterFunc, placeholders::_1, l, u)` call on line 26 generates a unary function that is equivalent to calling `filterFunc(*, l, u)`. The `placeholders::_1` acts as a placeholder, replaced by an actual parameter upon a call to the generated function.

9.4.4 **Filter-reduce**

Similarly to the map-reduce functionality, QtConcurrent offers a pair of filter-reduce methods that first filter elements in a collection before reducing them to a single result.

Qt's implementation in the form of the QtConcurrent::filteredReduced() and QtConcurrent::blockingFilteredReduced() functions requires two functions to be passed as input, one for performing the filtering and one for performing the reduction. The "filtered" function name prefix implies that a new container is created to hold the subset of items generated.

The required signature for the filtering function is the same as the one shown in Listing 9.8, while the reduction step requires a function with the signature shown in Listing 9.6.

The example we examine here is from the realm of statistics: observatories around the world have been trying to discover and track near-earth objects (NEOs), like asteroids and comets, in an attempt to predict and possibly avert a catastrophic collision with Earth. If a collection of such objects were available, one could answer the question of what is the average mass of the ones having a radius above 10 meters with the following code:

Listing 9.10: An example of how Qt's filter-reduce can be applied on a collection of data.

```cpp
// File : NEO.cpp
#include <QtConcurrentFilter>
...
struct NEO
{
    double radius;
    double mass;
    int groupNum;
    ...
};
//----------------------------------------
bool filtFunc(const NEO &x)
{
    return  x.radius >= 10;
}
//----------------------------------------
void reduFunc(NEO &x, const NEO &y)
{
    x.mass += y.mass;
    x.groupNum += y.groupNum;
}
//----------------------------------------
int main (int argc, char *argv[])
{
    QVector<NEO> data;
    ...
    NEO average = QtConcurrent::blockingFilteredReduced(data, filtFunc
        , reduFunc);
```

```
28    cout << "Average " << average.mass / average.groupNum << endl;
29    ...
```

The application filter function `filtFunc()` guides `QtConcurrent::blockingFilteredReduced()` into the creation of a container with the NEO instances that satisfy the condition of line 14. Subsequently, the `reduFunc()` function accumulates the mass of the two NEO instances passed to it and stores it in the first one. The `groupNum` field maintains the number of objects reduced (line 20). The accumulated values are returned as an NEO instance and copied to the `average` structure on line 27.

As mentioned in Section 9.4.2, Qt's reduction implementation suffers from being performed in a sequential manner. The programmer can control the order in which the individual operations are performed, but performance-wise this is clearly a problematic approach. In the following sections, we show how one can work around this problem via two cases studies.

9.4.5 A case study: multi-threaded sorting

Searching and sorting are the most commonly used components for algorithm design. In this section we explore how concurrency can significantly speed up data sorting by using the high-level constructs of the `QtConcurrent` namespace.

Mergesort is an algorithm that can be easily extended to support concurrency, given that the algorithm examines disjoint parts of the input at different stages of its execution. Fig. 9.1 illustrates how the bottom-up, non-recursive version of mergesort processes N data items by merging disjoint neighboring blocks in $\Theta(\lceil lg(N) \rceil)$ phases.

Each of the merging operations during a phase of mergesort is independent of the others, making them candidates for concurrent execution. However, using a thread to only merge two items, as done during the first phase, would produce an extraor-

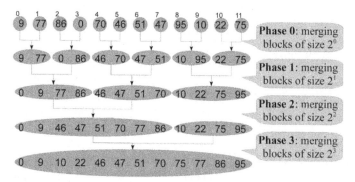

FIGURE 9.1

An illustration of how mergesort operates in a bottom-up fashion, merging ever increasing adjacent blocks of data. Each new phase doubles the size of the blocks merged relative to the previous one.

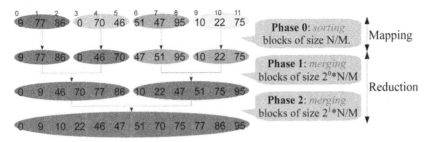

FIGURE 9.2

An example of how mergesort can be run in parallel, with an initial phase where *M* disjoint blocks are sorting individually, followed by merging phases with exponentially increasing sizes. Colors in each phase indicate the maximum number of threads that can be utilized.

dinary amount of housekeeping overhead. An easy adaptation that would eliminate this problem would be to start using threads for merging once the size of the blocks exceeds a certain threshold. An equivalent approach that would allow us to escape the obligation to come up with such a threshold would be to break the input into a predetermined number of blocks and merge these concurrently, after they are individually sorted.

Conceptually, *parallel mergesort can be implemented as a map-reduce operation*: mapping would sort each block individually, and reduction would merge the blocks in a pairwise fashion, until the whole input is sorted.

Fig. 9.2 shows the concept, which can be described by the following algorithm:

Algorithm 9.1 Parallel mergesort: sorting *N* data items by *M* threads.

1: Break the input into *M* blocks of size $\frac{N}{M}$.
2: Sort each of the *M* blocks by a separate thread, using any sequential sorting algorithm.
3: $blockSize \leftarrow \frac{N}{M}$
4: **while** $blockSize < N$ **do**
5:    Use multiple threads to merge adjacent blocks of size $blockSize$
6:    $blockSize \leftarrow blockSize \cdot 2$

Ideally, *M* should be twice the number of available cores in the execution platform, so that maximum CPU utilization can be achieved during the first merging phase, where $\frac{M}{2}$ merge operations occur. It should be noted that there is no design characteristic that would prevent any number of blocks from being used.

The implementation of the parallel mergesort is given below, broken up in separate listings to allow for easier exploration of the code. The main component of the shown solution is the ArrayRange class template that allows the description, sorting, and merging of data blocks (lines 9–121). Each instance of this class carries the starting and ending index of the block it represents (line 14), plus a pointer to the array containing the data (store, line 12) to be sorted. As the merging operation requires the transfer of the data to a temporary array, each `ArrayRange` also has a pointer to such a repository (`temp`, line 13).

In an attempt to minimize the copy operations mandated by merging, the `ArrayRange<>::merge()` method (lines 62–107) does not copy the sorted data from `*temp` back to the `*store` array. Instead, a switch of the pointers is performed (method `ArrayRange<>::switchPointers()` called at line 106, defined at lines 44–50), so that `this->store` always points to the array that contains the valid data of the block with indices [`this->start`, `this->end`).

The only side effect of this optimization strategy is that we may reach a point where blocks residing in different arrays need to be merged (check of line 65). In that case, the smaller of the blocks is moved prior to the merging operation (lines 68–74) by utilizing the `ArrayRange<>::switchStore()` method.

When the merging is complete, the first of the two `ArrayRange` objects passed as parameters assumes responsibility of the merged data (lines 102 and 103). In every other way, the merging operation in `ArrayRange<>::merge()` is a textbook implementation.

Listing 9.11: A parallel mergesort implementation based on the functionalities offered by `QThreadPool` and `QtConcurrent`: block management code.

```cpp
 1  // File : concurrent_mergesort.cpp
 2  . . .
 3  #include <QRunnable>
 4  #include <QThreadPool>
 5  #include <QtConcurrentMap>
 6  #include <QVector>
 7
 8  //****************************************************
 9  template < class T > class ArrayRange
10  {
11  private:
12    T * store;        // where data reside
13    T *temp;          // where they can be shifted for sorting
14    int start, end;   // 'end' points 1 spot further than the last item.
15  public:
16    ArrayRange (T * x, T * y, int s, int e);
17    static void merge (ArrayRange * x, ArrayRange * y);
18    static void sort (ArrayRange * x);
19    int size ();
20    T *getStore ()
21    {
22      return store;
23    }
24    void switchStore ();
25    void switchPointers ();
26  };
27
28  //------------------------------------------------
29  template < class T > int ArrayRange < T >::size ()
30  {
```

```
31       return end - start;
32     }
33
34     //--------------------------------------------------
35     template < class T > void ArrayRange < T >::switchStore ()
36     {
37       for (int i = start; i < end; i++)
38         temp[i] = store[i];
39       switchPointers ();
40     }
41
42     //--------------------------------------------------
43     // Only swaps the pointers
44     template < class T > void ArrayRange < T >::switchPointers ()
45     {
46       T *aux;
47       aux = temp;
48       temp = store;
49       store = aux;
50     }
51
52     //--------------------------------------------------
53     template < class T > ArrayRange < T >::ArrayRange (T * x, T * y, int↩
           s, int e)
54     {
55       store = x;
56       temp = y;
57       start = s;
58       end = e;
59     }
60
61     //--------------------------------------------------
62     template < class T > void ArrayRange < T >::merge (ArrayRange * x, ↩
           ArrayRange * y)
63     {
64       // check if a copy is needed for input data to be in the same ↩
             array
65       if (x->store != y->store)
66         {
67           // determine which is smaller
68           int xlen = x->end - x->start;
69           int ylen = y->end - y->start;
70
71           if (xlen > ylen)
72             y->switchStore ();
73           else
74             x->switchStore ();
75         }
76
77       // now perform merge-list
78       int idx1 = x->start, idx2 = y->start;
79       int loc = min (idx1, idx2);      // starting point in temp array
```

```
80      while (idx1 != x->end && idx2 != y->end)
81        {
82          if (x->store[idx1] <= y->store[idx2])
83            {
84              x->temp[loc] = x->store[idx1];
85              idx1++;
86            }
87          else
88            {
89              x->temp[loc] = x->store[idx2];   // same as y->store[idx2]
90              idx2++;
91            }
92          loc++;
93        }
94
95      // copy the rest
96      for (int i = idx1; i < x->end; i++)
97        x->temp[loc++] = x->store[i];
98
99      for (int i = idx2; i < y->end; i++)
100       x->temp[loc++] = x->store[i];
101
102     x->start = min (x->start, y->start);
103     x->end = max (x->end, y->end);
104
105     // the sorted "stuff" are in temp now, so swap store and temp
106     x->switchPointers ();
107   }
108
109   //----------------------------------------------------
110   int comp (const void *a, const void *b)
111   {
112     int x = *((int *) a);
113     int y = *((int *) b);
114     return x - y;
115   }
116
117   //----------------------------------------------------
118   template < class T > void ArrayRange < T >::sort (ArrayRange * x)
119   {
120     qsort (x->store + x->start, x->end - x->start, sizeof (int), comp)↵
              ;
121   }
```

The stand-alone sorting of a block is supported by the `ArrayRange<>::sort()` method, which in turn calls the `qsort()` C standard library function (line 120). Thus, in the event that someone would like to adapt the code for sorting items of a different datatype T, the only changes/additions that would be required are:

- A function similar to `comp()` (lines 110–115), capable of comparing instances of T.

- Type *T* should support `operator<=()` so that a comparison during merging (line 82) is possible.

`QtConcurrent::mappedReduced()` is poised to be the vehicle of choice for "glue-ing" together our map-reduce formulation of parallel mergesort. Alas, the reduction phase in `QtConcurrent::mappedReduced()` is done sequentially, which would translate to a big performance hit. Instead, our implementation separates the two stages, using the `QThreadPool::start()` method to direct the reduction/merging stages through its $\lceil lg(M) \rceil$ phases.

Listing 9.12: A parallel mergesort implementation: data block "mapping" and "reduction."

```
122  template < class T >
123  void concurrentMergesort (T * data, int N, int numBlocks = -1)
124  {
125    if (numBlocks < 0)
126      numBlocks = 2 * sysconf (_SC_NPROCESSORS_ONLN);
127
128    T *temp = new T[N];
129
130    // 1st step: block setup
131    QVector < ArrayRange < T > *>b;
132    int pos = 0;
133    int len = ceil (N * 1.0 / numBlocks);
134    for (int i = 0; i < numBlocks - 1; i++)
135      {
136        b.append (new ArrayRange < T > (data, temp, pos, pos + len));
137        pos += len;
138      }
139    // setup last block
140    b.append (new ArrayRange < T > (data, temp, pos, N));
141
142    // 2nd step: sort the individual blocks concurrently
143    QtConcurrent::blockingMap (b, ArrayRange < T >::sort);
144
145    //3rd step: "mergelisting" the pieces
146    // merging is done in lg(numBlocks) phases in a bottom-up fashion
147    for (int blockDistance = 1; blockDistance < numBlocks; ↵
         blockDistance *= 2)
148      {
149        for (int startBlock = 0; startBlock < numBlocks - ↵
             blockDistance; startBlock += 2 * blockDistance)
150          {
151            QThreadPool::globalInstance ()->start (new MergeTask < T >↵
                 (b[startBlock], b[startBlock + blockDistance]));
152          }
153        // barrier
154        QThreadPool::globalInstance ()->waitForDone ();
155      }
156
157    // b[0]->store points to the sorted data
```

```
158     if (b[0]->getStore () != data)          // need to copy data from ↩
           temp -> data array
159       b[0]->switchStore ();
160     delete [] temp;
161   }
162
163   //————————————————————————————————————————————————————————————
164   void numberGen (int N, int max, int *store)
165   {
166     int i;
167     srand (time (0));
168     for (i = 0; i < N; i++)
169       store[i] = rand () % max;
170   }
171
172   //————————————————————————————————————————————————————————————
173   int main (int argc, char *argv[])
174   {
175     if (argc < 3)
176       {
177         cout << "Use : " << argv[0] << " numData numBlocks\n";
178         exit (1);
179       }
180
181     int N = atoi (argv[1]);
182     int *data = new int[N];
183     numberGen (N, MAXVALUE, data);
184
185     QTime t;
186     t.start ();
187     concurrentMergesort (data, N, numBlocks);
188     // print-out sorting time in msec
189     cout << t.elapsed () << endl;
190   ...
```

The key points of the `concurrentMergesort()` function (lines 123–161) are:

- The temporary array needed by the merge operations – equal in size to the input array – is allocated at the beginning (line 128).
- Pointers to the input data and the temporary arrays are passed as parameters to the constructor of the `ArrayRange` class, along with the part of these arrays that each `ArrayRange` is responsible for, as delimited by the range [*start*, *end*). So, while each `ArrayRange` manages its own disjoint part of the data, these collectively reside in the same two arrays (`data` or `temp`). This approach eliminates the need for any additional, costly memory management operations that would degrade performance.
- An instance of type `QVector < ArrayRange < T > *>` is used to collectively manage the block representations. The required `ArrayRange` objects are generated with the loop of lines 134–138. The last `ArrayRange` in the sequence is created

separately (line 140) to incorporate the last block in its entirety, without requiring special logic to handle the case where N is not evenly divided by M.

- The "mapping" phase is accomplished on line 143. The $\lceil lg(M) \rceil$ phases of the reduction are controlled by the loop of lines 147–155. Each i reduction phase, for $i = 1, \ldots, \lceil lg(M) \rceil$, initiates $min(1, \lfloor \frac{M}{2^i} \rfloor)$ merging jobs in the form of instances of the MergeTask<> class template (explained below). These are submitted as requests for multi-threaded execution on line 151. The parent thread is blocked until each merging phase is complete (line 154).

Fig. 9.3 traces the execution of the concurrentMergesort() function through the data structures it sets up and maintains.

The final component of our implementation is the MergeTask<> class template shown in Listing 9.13. Its instances act as stubs for the execution of the ArrayRange<T>::merge() method (line 205). This class is so simple that one could wonder why the ArrayRange class is not derived from QRunnable to reduce the length of the code.

Actually, its existence is mandated by the fact that QThreadPool deletes the QRunnable objects passed to the start() method upon execution completion. This would make the reuse of ArrayRange objects impossible if they were used instead of a MergeTask<> instance.

Listing 9.13: A parallel mergesort implementation: task management code.

```
191  template < class T > class MergeTask:public QRunnable
192  {
193  private:
194    ArrayRange < T > *part1;
195    ArrayRange < T > *part2;
196
197  public:
198  MergeTask (ArrayRange < T > *p1, ArrayRange < T > *p2):part1 (p1), ↩
          part2 (p2)   {}
199    void run ();
200  };
201
202  //—————————————————————————————
203  template < class T > void MergeTask < T >::run ()
204  {
205    ArrayRange < T >::merge (part1, part2);
206  }
```

The performance of our implementation in terms of speedup and efficiency is shown in Fig. 9.4. The execution platform used to generate these graphs was an AMD Ryzen 3900x 12-core/24-thread CPU. The baseline, sequential times were calculated by using only one block for the initial data partitioning, resulting in the use of quicksort only.

As can be clearly observed in Fig. 9.4, the speedup reaches a plateau in excess of $12 \times$ at 64 blocks for the larger input size. This is a good result given the characteristics of the CPU and the fact that this is a memory-intensive test.

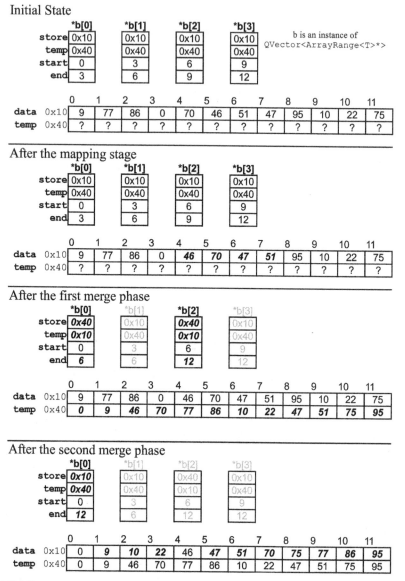

FIGURE 9.3

An example of how the ArrayRange instances generated by the concurrentMergesort() function of Listing 9.12 are initialized to manage the different data blocks and how they evolve over the function's execution. It is assumed that the data array starts at address 0x10 and the temp array at address 0x40. The changes that occur in memory between successive phases are in bold italics font, while the ArrayRange instances that become irrelevant for subsequent steps are grayed out.

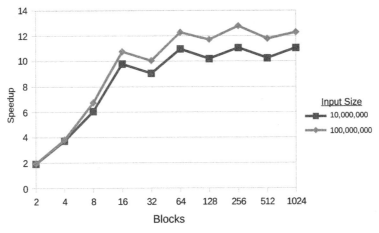

FIGURE 9.4

Speedup of the multi-threaded mergesort of Listing 9.11 over quicksort. Data consisted of type `int` arrays, sized at 10^7 and 10^8 elements. Displayed data points were averaged over 10 runs.

An important observation is that our parallel mergesort does not differ in the total number of comparisons performed from a plain-vanilla mergesort. The first phase where quicksort is used requires $M \frac{N}{M} lg(\frac{N}{M}) = N lg(\frac{N}{M})$ comparisons, while the reduction phase requires $\sum_{i=1}^{lg(M)} \frac{2^i N}{M} \frac{M}{2^i} = N lg(M)$ comparisons in the worst case. The two combined account for a total of $N lg(\frac{N}{M}) + N lg(M) = N lg(N)$ comparisons. This means that the performance gain observed is the result of the parallel execution and does not stem from a fundamental change in the algorithmic approach. Naturally, linear-complexity sorting algorithms like bucket sort could form the basis for extracting much better performance if they are properly formulated for parallel execution.

Comparing the map-reduce Qt implementation with the OpenMP-based merge-sort implementation of Section 8.13 reveals that the extra effort involved in the development of the Qt version paid off. For the map-reduce version we used $M = 256$ blocks based on the previous tests. The measured speedup curves are shown in Fig. 9.5. The performance difference is attributed to the fact that the map-reduce algorithm is a "hybrid" one with quicksort providing a better utilization of the 32 MiB of L3 cache per CCX of the 3900X CPU, for the first phase of the algorithm.

9.4.6 A case study: multi-threaded image matching

The problem of finding among a set of images a subset that best matches a target image is a typically computationally expensive problem that would benefit from parallel execution. In this section, it serves to exemplify the expressive power of the map/reduce/filter formulation.

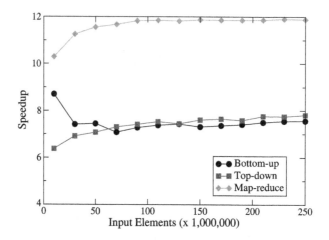

FIGURE 9.5

Comparison of the average speedup of the map-reduce mergesort versus the two OpenMP variants presented in Section 8.13. Mean values were obtained by running each test 30 times.

Whether a match between two images is positive or not depends on the operator used to compare them. A large collection of such operators has been proposed in the literature, such as the absolute and squared differences, the correlation coefficient, the mutual information, and others [12,50]. In this section we will just use the mutual information of two images I and J, which is defined as

$$MI(I, J) = \sum_{\forall x} \sum_{\forall y} p_{xy} log_2 \left(\frac{p_{xy}}{p_x p_y} \right), \tag{9.2}$$

where x represents a gray level in I and y a gray level in J; p_x is the probability of having a pixel in I with a gray level of x (similarly for p_y for J); p_{xy} is the joint probability defined by $p_{xy} = \frac{n_{xy}}{n}$, where n is the total number of pixels in I, J, and $n_x y$ is the number of pixels that have a gray level of x in I and y in J.

Selecting a single image would require a straightforward application of the filter-reduce pattern. In this section we solve a more generic problem that involves the selection of the best candidate images. The selection process could be materialized in a variety of ways: it could be based on meeting certain criteria, e.g., having $MI(I, J)$ exceed an a priori specified threshold, or on sorting the images according to their performance and picking a fixed number of them. In this section, we will use the latter approach.

The solution shown in Listing 9.14 is built around an Image class that provides functionality for reading PGM formatted images and for calculating the probabilities required for finding the mutual information:

Listing 9.14: Mutual information-based image matching implementation that uses `QtConcurrent` namespace functions.

```cpp
// File : image_matching/main.cpp
...
#include <boost/bind.hpp>
#include <QtConcurrentMap>
#include <QThreadStorage>
#include <QVector>

using namespace std;

#define MAXLEVELS 2048
// ****************************************************************
class Image
{
private:
  int width;
  int height;
  int levels;
  unsigned int *pixel;
  double *p;  // probabilities
  double MI;  // mutual information with a target image
  char filename[20];

  // joint probs. This is a per-thread value
  static QThreadStorage < double *>jointProb;
  void calcJointProb (Image * x);

public:
  Image (char *);
  ~Image ();
  static double mutualInformation (Image *, Image *);
  static void calcProb (Image *);
  double getMI () {return MI;}
  char *getFilename () {return filename;}
};

QThreadStorage < double *>Image::jointProb;
//-------------------------------------------------------------
// Used to compare and sort images in descending order of
// the mutual information calculated
bool comp (Image * x, Image * y)
{
  return x->getMI () > y->getMI ();
}

//-------------------------------------------------------------
// Assumes that the file does not contain any comment lines
// starting with #. Allocates the memory for the pixel values
// and the value probabilities
Image::Image (char *fname)
{
```

```
51     FILE *fin;
52     strncpy (filename, fname, 20);
53     filename[19] = 0;
54     fin = fopen (fname, "rb");
55     fscanf (fin, "%*s%i%i%i", &(width), &(height), &(levels));
56
57     pixel = new unsigned int[width * height];
58     // first set all values to 0. This is needed as in 2 of the 3
59     // cases only a part of each pixel value is read from the file
60     memset ((void *) pixel, 0, width * height * sizeof (unsigned int))↩
          ;
61     if (levels < 256)  // each pixel is 1 byte
62       for (int i = 0; i < width * height; i++)
63         fread ((void *) &(pixel[i]), sizeof (unsigned char), 1, fin);
64     else if (levels < 65536) // each pixel is 2 bytes
65       for (int i = 0; i < width * height; i++)
66         fread ((void *) &(pixel[i]), sizeof (unsigned short), 1, fin);
67     else // each pixel is 4 bytes
68       fread (pixel, sizeof (unsigned int), width * height, fin);
69
70     levels++;
71     fclose (fin);
72     p = new double[levels];
73   }
74
75   //----------------------------------------------------------------
76   // Releases memory
77   Image::~Image ()
78   {
79     if (pixel != NULL)
80       {
81         delete [] pixel;
82         delete [] p;
83         pixel = NULL;
84         p = NULL;
85       }
86   }
87
88   //----------------------------------------------------------------
89   void Image::calcProb (Image * x)
90   {
91     int numPixels = x->width * x->height;
92
93     // first set all values to 0
94     memset ((void *) x->p, 0, x->levels * sizeof (double));
95     for (int i = 0; i < numPixels; i++)
96       x->p[x->pixel[i]]++;
97
98     for (int i = 0; i < x->levels; i++)
99       x->p[i] /= numPixels;
100  }
101
```

```cpp
102   //-----------------------------------------------------------
103   // Precondition: images must have the same spatial resolution and ↩
          number of grayscale levels
104   void Image::calcJointProb (Image * x)
105   {
106     double *pij;
107     if (jointProb.hasLocalData ())  // joint probabilities storage ↩
            exist, retrieve its location
108       {
109         pij = jointProb.localData ();
110       }
111     else                            // otherwise allocate it and store ↩
            its address
112       {
113         pij = new double[MAXLEVELS * MAXLEVELS];
114         jointProb.setLocalData (pij);
115       }
116
117     int numPixels = width * height;
118
119     // first set all values to 0
120     memset ((void *) pij, 0, x->levels * x->levels * sizeof (double));
121     for (int i = 0; i < numPixels; i++)
122       pij[pixel[i] * x->levels + x->pixel[i]]++;
123
124     for (int i = 0; i < x->levels * x->levels; i++)
125       pij[i] /= numPixels;
126   }
127
128   //-----------------------------------------------------------
129   // The probabilities must be calculated beforehand
130   double Image::mutualInformation (Image * x, Image * y)
131   {
132     x->calcJointProb (y);
133     double *pij = jointProb.localData (); // the array has been ↩
            created already by the previous statement
134     double mutual = 0;
135     for (int i = 0; i < x->levels; i++)
136       for (int j = 0; j < y->levels; j++)
137         {
138           int idx = i * y->levels + j;
139           if (x->p[i] != 0 && y->p[j] != 0 && pij[idx] != 0)
140             mutual += pij[idx] * log (pij[idx] / (x->p[i] * y->p[j]));
141         }
142     x->MI = mutual / log (2);
143     return x->MI;
144   }
145
146   // ***********************************************************
147   int main (int argc, char *argv[])
148   {
149     int numImages = atoi (argv[1]);
```

```
150    QTime t;
151    t.start ();
152
153    // read the target and all other images
154    Image target ("images/main.pgm");        // target image
155    QVector < Image * >pool;
156    for (int picNum = 0; picNum < numImages; picNum++)
157      {
158        char buff[100];
159        sprintf (buff, "images/(%i).pgm", picNum);
160        pool.append (new Image (buff));
161      }
162    int iodone = t.elapsed ();
163
164    // pixel value probabilities calculation
165    Image::calcProb (&target);
166
167    QtConcurrent::blockingMap (pool, Image::calcProb);
168
169    // mutual information (MI) calculation
170    QtConcurrent::blockingMap (pool, bind (Image::mutualInformation, ↩
           placeholders::_1, &target));
171
172    // sorting of the images according to MI findings
173    qSort (pool.begin (), pool.end (), comp);
174    printf ("%i %i\n", iodone, t.elapsed () - iodone);
175
176    return 0;
177  }
```

The program in Listing 9.14 can be executed by supplying the number of images to compare the target image with:

```
$ ./imageMatch 100
```

The images are stored in PGM format in the `image_matching/images` directory. The same directory holds the target image in a file named `main.pgm`. All the images have been resized to the same spatial (1024×768 pixels) and color resolutions (256 shades of gray).

The key points of the code in Listing 9.14 are:

- The program has been designed so that small modifications would permit the execution in sequence of multiple match operations for different target images, instead of the "one-shot" operation used here. As such, the pixel value probabilities for each image are stored within each `Image` instance.
- The calculation of the joint probabilities p_{xy} for a pair of images I and J requires a matrix with $Levels_I$, $Levels_J$ elements, where $Levels_I$ and $Levels_J$ are the maximum grayscale pixel values of I and J, respectively. This is a matrix that can be reused for every image pair requested, making it a candidate for becoming a

static data member of the `Image` class. However, as multiple threads need to use this storage, a single copy is out of the question.

A separate instance of this matrix is required for each thread using it. The solution to this problem is to use a `QThreadStorage<double *>` reference as part of the `Image` class. The class template `QThreadStorage<>` will store a separate instance of its data[2] for every thread accessing it. The three essential methods of the `QThreadStorage<>` class are:

```
bool hasLocalData ();    // returns true if a data item has been
                         // stored on behalf of the current thread
T localData ();          // retrieves the data item corresponding
                         // to the currently running thread
void setLocalData (T);   // associates a data item with the
                         // currently running thread
```

The pointer to the joint probability matrix is managed on lines 107–115. If the current thread has executed the `Image::calcJointProb()` function before, the pointer is retrieved (line 109). Otherwise, the necessary memory is allocated and its address stored in the `jointProb` variable (lines 113 and 114).

- The `QtConcurrent::blockingMap()` function is used twice, on lines 167 and 170, in order to calculate the pixel probabilities for each individual image and subsequently their mutual information with the target image. The only particular thing about line 170 is that the `bind()` function (see also Section 9.4.3) is utilized to allow a binary function (`Image::mutualInformation()`) to be used in the place of a unary one, as dictated by `QtConcurrent::blockingMap()`.

The performance of the multi-threaded solution, as far as the mutual information computation is concerned, is shown in Fig. 9.6. The execution platform was an AMD Ryzen 3900x, 12-core/24-thread CPU. Speedup increases as more images are used, reaching the modest figure of 22.7 for 256 images, despite the penalty of the sequential execution of lines 165 and 173.

The biggest issue is that the mutual information calculation is dwarfed by the I/O and memory allocation costs of lines 154–161. The overall execution speedup reaches about 1.77 for 256 images, i.e., only roughly 44% reduction over the sequential time is witnessed. However, looking at the bigger picture, this is something that could be expected given the simple nature of the chosen matching operator. In practice, I/O is only a fraction of the overall execution time as more computationally expensive algorithms – and typically multiple ones – are employed.

Finally, it is worth clarifying why the `Image::mutualInformation` and `Image::calcProb` methods are declared as static: normal methods would require the use of a wrapper object for the application of the mapping process on lines 167 and 170. An example of how this could be achieved for the `calcProb()` invocation of line 167 is shown below:

---

[2] **CAUTION**: A `QThreadStorage<>` instance takes ownership of the data held within, and it will delete them upon termination of the threads that use them.

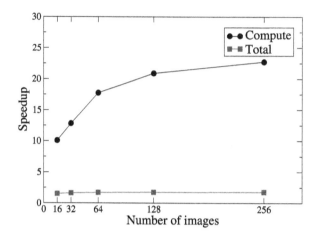

FIGURE 9.6

Speedup achieved by the multi-threaded image matching program of Listing 9.14 for the mutual information computation. Displayed data points were averaged over 100 runs. Overall execution and compute-only speedup are shown.

Listing 9.15: An example of how a non-static method can be used with the QtConcurrent namespace functions. Only the differences to Listing 9.14 are shown.

```
1   // File : image_matching/main_wrapper.cpp
2   ...
3   class Image
4   {
5     ...
6   public:
7     void calcProb();
8     ...
9   };
10  ...
11  // ***************************************************************
12  struct Wrapper
13  {
14    void operator()(Image *x)
15    {
16        x->calcProb();
17    }
18  };
19
20  // ***************************************************************
21  int main (int argc, char *argv[])
22  {
23    ...
24    // pixel value probabilities calculation
25    target.calcProb ();
26
27    Wrapper w;
```

```
28    QtConcurrent::blockingMap (pool, w);
29    ...
```

As can be observed, one just needs to create an instance of a *"wrapper"* class or structure that overloads the parentheses operator (lines 16–19) and pass it as a parameter to the QtConcurrent function being used (line 28). The wrapper's operator() method should have a parameter of type T, where T is the type of the items held in the container used in the mapping/reduction/filtering operation. The same trick could be also used in place of the bind function in case a method with a different signature than the one mandated needs to be used.

Exercises

1. Use the QtConcurrent functionality to implement a prime number checker. Compare it in terms of speed, efficiency, and programming effort to your QThread-based attempt of the previous exercise.

2. Create a big array of randomly generated 2D coordinates (x, y). Each of the coordinates should be a number in the range $[-1000, 1000]$. Use appropriate QtConcurrent functions to find the points that are in a ring of distances between 100 and 200 from the point of origin. Compare the performance of your solution against a sequential implementation.

3. Use the QtConcurrent functionality to implement a parallel bucket sort. Does the number of buckets play a significant role in your implementation's performance?

4. Create a program that utilizes the QtConcurrent functionality to calculate the definite integral of a function within a user-supplied range.

The Thrust template library

10

In this chapter you will:

- Learn how to accelerate the development and ease the maintenance of GPU/multicore programs by using the Thrust library.
- Learn the data types used in Thrust and how to employ them to represent your problem data.
- Learn the algorithms implemented in Thrust and how to use them as building blocks in your own programs.
- Use Thrust with CUDA kernels to simplify CUDA development.

10.1 Introduction

Thrust is a C++ template library, both implementing and facilitating the implementation of parallel algorithms. Thrust's syntax resembles the Standard Template Library (STL), making it easy for seasoned C++ programmers to transition to parallel programming without going through the process of mastering complex tools like CUDA. This chapter assumes that the reader possesses at least some basic knowledge of the STL class templates.

Originally, Thrust was introduced as a CUDA front-end, a library to simplify GPU programming. However, since version 1.6 Thrust includes support for CUDA, OpenMP, Intel Thread Building Blocks (TBB), and standard C++ as "device back-ends." This means that a simple switch (programmatic or compiler command-line) can make the same Thrust-based source code run using any of the listed back-ends, utilizing NVidia GPUs or multicore CPUs in the process. So, although we will be frequently referring to Thrust in the context of GPUs and CUDA, it is without question that Thrust can be used for harnessing the power of multicore CPUs as well.

Thrust provides the means for a developer to describe the computations that need to take place at a very high level, in the form of operations to be applied to a data collection. Thrust takes care of the "ugly" details of partitioning the data, deploying them, spawning the processes/kernels that perform the computation, and collecting the results. Thrust will try to do all these tasks in a near-optimal manner but it can be easily deduced given the complexity of these tasks that it trades off performance for ease-of-use. For example, when using the CUDA back-end, Thrust will try to maximize occupancy, although it has been reported many times in the literature that higher occupancy can lead to lower performance [60]. The exact extent of the trade-

Multicore and GPU Programming. https://doi.org/10.1016/B978-0-12-814120-5.00020-2

off depends on the application being developed. Thankfully, Thrust maintains full interoperability with the back-ends it employs, allowing the programmer to shift between Thrust and CUDA, Thrust and OpenMP, etc., at will. It is even possible to switch between back-ends within the same program. Also, since Thrust 1.8, there is full interoperability between CUDA and Thrust, i.e., Thrust algorithms can be called from inside CUDA kernels. Also, Thrust algorithms can be instructed to launch any kernels they require during execution at specific CUDA streams.

This flexibility elevates Thrust to one of the prime tools for parallel development. Especially the efficient implementations of sorting and reduce operations, among other things, are godsent for CUDA developers. A possible development plan could involve:

1. Using Thrust to quickly prototype an application, regardless of the computing capabilities of the development platform.
2. Profiling the application and identifying the "hotspots" that dominate the execution time.
3. Refining the code that runs inefficiently by using CUDA or other techniques that allow platform awareness to translate to more efficient execution (e.g., explicit use of shared memory, etc.).

The use of templates by Thrust means that (a) the provided algorithms are generic, applicable to any user-defined data type, and (b) there is no need for a binary component that must be installed for the library to function. One can just include the Thrust files in a project and point the compiler to the appropriate include directories to start using Thrust.

Thrust is an open source software (OSS) project released under the Apache License v2.0. Although it is not affiliated with NVidia, its popularity has literally "thrusted" it into NVidia's toolkit. Programmers who download the latest CUDA SDK also get a version – probably not the most recent – of the Thrust library. Anyone interested to have the latest and greatest release can download and install Thrust separately from https://github.com/thrust/thrust. At the time of this writing, CUDA SDK 11.5.1 incorporates the 1.13.1 version of Thrust.

Thrust, being an OSS endeavor, suffers from lack of proper documentation. Fortunately, a large collection of samples is maintained at https://github.com/thrust/thrust/tree/main/examples. Additionally, Thrust's header files typically contain in the form of comments a healthy set of samples that can be used as starting points for someone to get to grips with the Thrust class templates.

10.2 First steps in Thrust

A simple program in Thrust which just allows you to check the version available at your disposal is the following:

```
1   // File : hello.cu
2   #include <iostream>
3   #include <thrust/version.h>
4
5   using namespace std;
6
7   int main()
8   {
9     cout << "Hello World from Thrust v " << THRUST_MAJOR_VERSION << "." ↩
          " << THRUST_MINOR_VERSION << endl;
10    return 0;
11  }
```

The program compiles and runs with the commands:

```
$ nvcc hello.cu -o hello
$ ./hello
```

The program displays the major and minor version numbers of the Thrust library that is accessible by default with the CUDA SDK.[1]

The next example performs something at least remotely useful by computing the average of an array of integers:

Listing 10.1: A Thrust program that calculates the average of an array of random integers. The array size is passed as a command-line parameter.

```
1    // File : sum.cu
2    #include <stdlib.h>
3    #include <time.h>
4    #include <iostream>
5    #include <thrust/device_vector.h>
6    #include <thrust/host_vector.h>
7    #include <thrust/reduce.h>
8
9    using namespace std;
10
11   int main (int argc, char **argv)
12   {
13     srand (time (NULL));
14     int N = atoi (argv[1]);
15     thrust::host_vector < int >h_d (N);
16     for (int i = 0; i < N; i++)
17       h_d[i] = rand () % 10000;   // limit the range to [0, 9999]
18
19     thrust::device_vector < int >d_d (N);
```

---

[1] You can access a more recent or different version of Thrust by either pointing the nvcc compiler driver to the appropriate directory, e.g. (assuming that Thrust is installed in your home directory):

```
$ nvcc hello.cu -o hello -I ~/thrust
```

or by replacing the contents of the SDK's include/thrust directory with the desired library.

```
20    d_d = h_d;    // host -> device transfer
21
22    cout << "Average computed on CPU :" << thrust::reduce (h_d.begin ↩
         (), h_d.end ()) * 1.0 / N << endl;
23
24    cout << "Average computed on GPU :" << thrust::reduce (d_d.begin ↩
         (), d_d.end ()) * 1.0 / N << endl;
25
26    return 0;
27  }
```

Listing 10.1 reveals many of the strengths and idiosyncrasies of working with Thrust. Lines 5–7 show that one has to individually include all the header files corresponding to the functionality required.

All the classes and functions that make up Thrust belong to the `thrust` namespace. As a matter of caution, one should avoid introducing a "`using namespace thrust`" statement in a program to prevent conflicts with STL, since many of the classes and functions provided by Thrust have matching names to their STL counterparts.

Data in Thrust are stored in two types of vectors, which are functionally equivalent to the STL `vector` class template:

- `host_vector<>`: for data residing in host memory and
- `device_vector<>`: for data residing in device memory.

The novelty about using these vector types is that data transfer from the host to the device, or vice versa, is implemented by overloading the assignment operator, as shown on line 20.

Thrust functions operate on vector ranges which are defined by using iterators, following the STL's legacy. Thrust functions, such as the reduction used on lines 22 and 24, automatically call the appropriate code (host or device) based on the type of vector/iterator passed to them. Additionally, the decision on which code to use is made at compile time, avoiding any execution overheads. This is known as **static dispatching**. The only restriction is that when multiple iterators are used (as in multiple vectors), they should all reside in the same memory space (all in host or all in device). Otherwise the compiler will produce an error message. This obviously excludes the functions that copy data between the memory spaces.

Another example that showcases the extremely expressive power of Thrust is shown in Listing 10.2.

Listing 10.2: A Thrust program that calculates the point in a range that produces the smallest value of a function. The range limits and the number of samples taken within the range are passed as command-line parameters.

```
1   // File : min.cu
2   #include <iostream>
3   #include <thrust/device_vector.h>
4   #include <thrust/sequence.h>
```

```
5    #include <thrust/extrema.h>
6
7    #include <stdlib.h>
8    #include <time.h>
9
10   using namespace std;
11   // ****************************************************
12   struct functor
13   {
14     __host__ __device__
15     float operator()(const float &x) const{
16       return x*x;    // just a simple example function
17     }
18   };
19   // ****************************************************
20   int main(int argc, char **argv)
21   {
22     float st, end;
23     st = atof(argv[1]);
24     end = atof(argv[2]);
25     int dataPoints = atoi(argv[3]);
26     float step= (end-st)/dataPoints;
27
28     thrust::device_vector<float> d_x(dataPoints);
29     thrust::device_vector<float> d_y(dataPoints);
30     thrust::sequence(d_x.begin(), d_x.end(), st, step);  // fill up ↩
          array with sequence
31
32     functor f;
33     thrust::transform(d_x.begin(), d_x.end(), d_y.begin(), f);  // ↩
          calculate function for all values in d_x
34
35     int idx= thrust::min_element(d_y.begin(), d_y.end()) - d_y.begin↩
          ();
36     cout << "Function minimum over ["<< st <<"," << end << "] occurs ↩
          at " << d_x[idx] << endl;
37
38     return 0;
39   }
```

A key component of Listing 10.2 is the use of a **functor**. A functor or "**function object**" is the C++ equivalent of a C function pointer. The added benefit that a functor offers over a simple function pointer is that it can have a state, i.e., it can be initialized to perform in a customized fashion that is independent of the parameters on which it operates. Because a functor is just a normal C++ object, it can carry an assortment of data members that allow this customization.

In simple terms, a functor is just an *instance of a class or structure* that overloads the "()" operator. Such a structure is provided on lines 12–18 of Listing 10.2. Because the operator() method should be callable from both device and host code (based on the type of iterator provided to Thrust functions), it has to be decorated by both __host__ and __device__ specifiers. In our example the function computed is $y = x^2$, but we could have used any unary function in Listing 10.2.

The thrust::sequence function on line 30 initializes a device vector (d_x) to the values st, $st + step$, $st + 2 \cdot step$, etc. The resulting vector is then "transformed" on line 33 by applying the f functor (defined on line 32) on all the vector elements (range d_x.begin() to d_x.end()-1 inclusive) and storing the results in the d_y device vector. The thrust::transform function (called an algorithm in Thrust jargon) supports either unary or binary functors only.

It should be noted that the preparation of the input array d_x is not done by the host, but by the device. In fact, the only data exchange between the host and the device takes place on lines 35 and 36. On line 35 an iterator to the minimum element of device vector d_y is found by the call to function thrust::min_element. By subtracting the beginning of d_y, the offset to the d_x value that produced the minimum is found and output by direct access to the corresponding device vector element (line 36).

Thrust provides direct access to device data, but this is a capability that should be used sparingly, since it always results in a call to cudaMemcpy().

10.3 Working with Thrust datatypes

The Thrust vector classes provide the same functionality as the STL vector class template. This means that one can use the [] operator for accessing individual vector elements:

```
int N=100;
thrust::device_vector<int> d_x(N); // allocate a 100-element vector ←
    on the device
d_x[0] = 1;
d_x[1] = 2;
```

Vectors can be resized:

```
d_x.resize(1000);
```

Vectors can queried:

```
cout << "New device vector size : " << d_x.size() << endl;
```

Vectors can be copied in a variety of ways:

```
#include <thrust/copy.h>
. . .
thrust::host_vector<float> h_x(N);
thrust::copy(d_x.begin()+10, d_x.begin()+20, h_x.begin()); // copies ←
    10 elements to the beginning of h_x, starting from the 11th ←
    element of d_x. If N<10, only the first N of the 10 elements are ←
    copied to h_x.
```

```
thrust::host_vector<float> h_y(N);
h_y = d_x;   // h_y will be resized to match the size of d_x
```

Vectors can be inserted in other vectors (the difference with `thrust::copy` is that the target vector can get "enlarged"):

```
thrust::host_vector < int >h_data (10, 0);          // all set to 0
thrust::host_vector < int >h_add (10);

h_data.insert (h_data.begin (), h_add.begin (), h_add.end ()); // ←
    h_data is now 20 elements long
```

Vectors can have part of their content eliminated:

```
// erase all elements from the 13th till the end
h_data.erase(h_data.begin()+12, h_data.end());
```

And they can be initialized by the `thrust::sequence` and `thrust::fill` functions:

```
#include <thrust/fill.h>
#include <thrust/sequence.h>
. . .
thrust::fill(d_x.begin(), d_x.begin()+10, 100);   // fills the first ←
    10 elements of d_x with 100. d_x[10] is excluded.

thrust::sequence(d_x.begin()+10, d_x.begin()+20); // fills the next ←
    10 elements of d_x with the sequence 0, 1, 2, ... d_x[20] is ←
    excluded.

thrust::sequence(d_x.begin(), d_x.end(), 100, 10);// fills the ←
    vector with the sequence 100, 110, 120, ...
```

Thrust provides full interoperability with CUDA, which means that device data can be allocated, manipulated, and passed to kernels/Thrust functions seamlessly. This way, a programmer can always use the best tool for the job at hand.

The only modifications required stem from the need to use an "augmented" data representation in Thrust: a "raw" pointer to an array just does not suffice for Thrust, because it prohibits static dispatching. Data must be encapsulated in a vector class template or referenced by a special type of pointer such as the `thrust::device_ptr` class template. This unavoidably sets the stage for explicit type casting.

In order to use memory allocated by `cudaMalloc` in Thrust, the corresponding pointer must be "wrapped" using the procedure exemplified by Listing 10.3.

Listing 10.3: Casting a raw pointer to a `thrust::device_ptr` datatype so that memory allocated by `cudaMalloc` can be used in Thrust algorithms.

```
1  // File : datatype.cu
2  #include <thrust/device_ptr.h>
3  #include <thrust/reduce.h>
4  #include <thrust/functional.h>
```

```
5    ...
6    int *d_data;
7    int *h_data;
8
9    h_data = new int[N];
10   cudaMalloc(&d_data, N*sizeof(int));
11   ... // populate h_data
12
13   cudaMemcpy(d_data, h_data, sizeof(int)*N, cudaMemcpyHostToDevice);
14
15   thrust::device_ptr<int> thr_d (d_data);
16
17   int sum = thrust::reduce(thr_d, thr_d + N, 0, thrust::plus<int>())↩
     ;
18
19   thrust::device_vector<int> d_vec(thr_d, thr_d + N);
20
21   int sum2 = thrust::reduce(d_vec.begin(), d_vec.end());
22
23   cout << "Sum is " << sum2 << endl;
24   ...
```

The `thrust::device_ptr<int>` type variable defined on line 15 behaves as an iterator as can be seen on line 17. If one prefers to use the Thrust vector types, a conversion is also possible with the constructor called on line 19.

Moving in the opposite direction, i.e., using Thrust to allocate memory and subsequently passing it to a CUDA kernel, can be accomplished by the `thrust::raw_pointer_cast`, as shown in Listing 10.4.

Listing 10.4: Example showing how data allocated by Thrust can be passed to a CUDA kernel.

```
1    ...
2    using namespace std;
3
4    const int BLOCKSIZE = 256;
5    // ************************************************
6    __global__ void foo(int *data, int N)
7    {
8        int gID = blockDim.x * blockIdx.x + threadIdx.x;
9        if(gID < N)
10           data[gID] *= 2;
11   }
12   // ************************************************
13   int main (int argc, char **argv)
14   {
15       int N = atoi (argv[1]);
16
17       //------------------------------------------------
18       // way #1
19       thrust::host_vector<int> h_vec(N);
20       thrust::device_vector<int> d_vec(N);
```

```
21
22   for (int i = 0; i < N; i++)
23     h_vec[i] = rand () % 10000;
24
25   for(int i=0;i<min(10, N);i++)
26     cout << h_vec[i] << " ";
27   cout << endl;
28
29   d_vec = h_vec;
30
31   thrust::device_ptr<int> d_ptr = d_vec.data();
32
33   int *d_data = thrust::raw_pointer_cast(d_ptr);
34
35   dim3 block(BLOCKSIZE);
36   dim3 grid( (N + BLOCKSIZE −1)/BLOCKSIZE ); // equivalent to ceil↩
           (1.0*N/BLOCKSIZE)
37
38   foo<<<grid, block>>>(d_data, N);
39
40   h_vec = d_vec;
41
42   for(int i=0;i<min(10, N);i++)
43     cout << h_vec[i] << " ";
44   cout << endl;
45
46   //—————————————————————————————————————
47   // way #2
48   thrust::device_ptr<int> d_ptr2 = thrust::device_malloc<int>(N);
49   thrust::copy( h_vec.begin(), h_vec.end(), d_ptr2);
50
51 // Allowed but very inefficient
52 //   for (int i = 0; i < N; i++)
53 //       d_ptr2[i] = rand () % 10000;
54
55   int *d_data2 = thrust::raw_pointer_cast(d_ptr2);
56
57   foo<<<grid, block>>>(d_data2, N);
58
59   thrust::copy( d_ptr2, d_ptr2 + N, h_vec.begin());
60   thrust::device_free(d_ptr2);
61   ...
```

In the first part of Listing 10.4 (lines 19–44), memory is allocated and communicated via thrust vectors. Line 31 extracts a pointer to the data of the device vector used and wraps it inside a device_ptr<int> class instance. This can be subsequently cast to a raw pointer on line 33.

In the second part of Listing 10.4 (lines 48–60), memory is allocated with the Thrust equivalent of the malloc() function, thrust::device_malloc<>(), which in turn necessitates the explicit deallocation with the thrust::device_free() function (line 60). Data can still be transferred between Thrust vectors and the allocated memory blocks via the `thrust::copy` algorithm (lines 49 and 59).

10.4 Thrust algorithms

Thrust provides efficient implementations for a number of important algorithms that can be used as building blocks to problem solutions. These include sorting, scanning, subset selection, and reduction implementations. Not only does Thrust boost programmer productivity and program readability and maintenance, but it can also boost performance as it can adjust the execution configuration to the available GPU capabilities and resources.

These algorithms fall into five categories:

- transformations,
- sorting & searching,
- reductions,
- scans/prefix-sums, and
- data management/manipulation.

Some of the above have been already introduced in the previous sections, in an informal manner. In the sections that follow we will examine each category of algorithms and provide a number of examples on their use.

10.4.1 Transformations

Transformations operate on an input sequence by applying a supplied operation on each element. Contrary to a reduction, the produced output is equal in size – in terms of granularity – with the input. The following is a list of Thrust transformations that we got a glimpse of in the previous introductory examples:

- `thrust::fill`: Fills the elements of a vector with a specific value.
- `thrust::copy`: Copies a subvector to another location (actually a data management algorithm, see Section 10.4.5).
- `thrust::sequence`: Initializes the elements of a vector to a sequence specified by an initial value and an optional step.
- `thrust::transform`: Generic form of transformation. Applies a user- or Thrust-supplied operation on every element of a vector.
- `thrust::for_each`: An alternative, simplified form of `thrust::transform`. Applies a unary functor on every element of a single vector, as delimited by the supplied iterators. It is similar to STL's `for_each` algorithm.

As shown in Listing 10.2, `thrust::transform` requires the use of a named (i.e., accessible through a variable) or unnamed functor that will be used to process the elements of one or more vectors. As an example, let us consider the calculation of the "saxpy" operation (short for A*X plus Y), which is a basic linear algebra vector operation:

$$\vec{z} = a \cdot \vec{x} + \vec{y}.$$

An implementation of the double-precision saxpy (DAXPY) vector operation is shown in Listing 10.5.

Listing 10.5: Using `thrust::transform` to perform the DAXPY vector operation.

```
1   // File : daxpy.cu
2   #include <iostream>
3   #include <thrust/host_vector.h>
4   #include <thrust/device_vector.h>
5   #include <thrust/transform.h>
6   #include <thrust/sequence.h>
7   #include <thrust/fill.h>
8
9   using namespace std;
10  // *********************************************************
11  // Helper function template
12  template < typename t >
13  void print (char c, thrust::host_vector < t > &v)
14  {
15    cout << "Version " << c << " : ";
16    thrust::copy (v.begin (), v.end (),
17                  ostream_iterator < t > (cout, ", "));
18    cout << endl;
19  }
20  // *********************************************************
21  struct saxpy
22  {
23    double a;
24    saxpy ():a (1.0)  {};
25    saxpy (double i):a (i)  {};
26
27    __host__ __device__
28    double operator () (double &x, double &y)  {
29      return a * x + y;
30    }
31  };
32  // *********************************************************
33  int main ()
34  {
35    thrust::device_vector < double >d_x (100);
36    thrust::device_vector < double >d_y (100);
37    thrust::device_vector < double >d_res (100);
38    thrust::sequence (d_x.begin (), d_x.end (), 0.0, .1);
39    thrust::fill (d_y.begin (), d_y.end (), 0.5);
40
41    saxpy funct;
42    funct.a = 1.2;
43
44    thrust::transform (d_x.begin (), d_x.end (),
```

```
45                        d_y.begin (),
46                        d_res.begin (),
47                        funct);
48   // Alternative call using an unnamed functor
49   // thrust::transform(d_x.begin(), d_x.end(), d_y.begin(), d_res. ↵
        begin(), saxpy(1.2));
50
51     thrust::host_vector < double >h_res (d_res);
52     print < double >('A', h_res);
53
54     return 0;
55   }
```

The helper function template of lines 12–19 copies the host_vector of type t elements to the standard output stream using the ",_" string as a separator. Line 16 is a convenient alternative to an explicit for loop.

Listing 10.5 shows the use of both a named and an unnamed functor, the latter as part of the commented-out line 49. The unfamiliar notation used (saxpy(1.2)) returns a reference (i.e., a constant pointer) to an instance of class saxpy allocated as a temporary object,[2] in contrast to the more identifiable "new saxpy(1.2)" that would return a pointer to an object allocated in the heap.

The thrust::transform algorithm can operate on one or two vectors, storing the result in a third one. As the second vector and the one that will hold the result must be at least equal in size to the first one, one can omit the iterators pointing to their end. Appropriate overloaded function templates support this functionality, as one can observe by inspecting the contents of the thrust/transform.h header file:

```
template <typename InputIterator,
         typename OutputIterator,
         typename UnaryFunction>
OutputIterator transform(InputIterator first, InputIterator last,
                         OutputIterator result,
                         UnaryFunction op);


template <typename InputIterator1,
         typename InputIterator2,
         typename OutputIterator,
         typename BinaryFunction>
OutputIterator transform(InputIterator1 first1, InputIterator1 last1,
                         InputIterator2 first2,
                         OutputIterator result,
                         BinaryFunction op);
```

A work-around for supporting functors with a longer argument list is possible through the zip_iterator (see Section 10.5).

---

[2] Temporary entities get out-of-scope, i.e., they get destroyed, when the expression that uses them completes execution.

The `operator()` method of line 28 has to be decorated with both __host__ and __device__ directives, so that the CUDA compiler driver can generate code that can be applied to elements of both `host_vector` and `device_vector` containers.

Thrust provides a number of built-in functors that are available in the `thrust/functional.h` header file. These include the following that correspond to basic arithmetic operators:

- `thrust::plus`,
- `thrust::minus`,
- `thrust::negate`,
- `thrust::modulus`,
- `thrust::divides`,
- `thrust::multiplies`.

These are defined as structures, as shown for `thrust::plus` below, with the `operator()` method being the only required component:

```
template <typename T>
struct plus
{
  typedef T first_argument_type;
  typedef T second_argument_type;
  typedef T result_type;
  __host__ __device__  T operator()(const T &lhs, const T &rhs) ↩
      const
    {
      return lhs + rhs;
    }
};
```

The DAXPY example of Listing 10.5 can also be performed with the built-in functors, as shown in Listing 10.6.

Listing 10.6: Using `thrust::transform` and the built-in functors to perform the DAXPY vector operation. Only the changes relative to Listing 10.5 are shown.

```
1  // File : daxpy_builtin.cpp
2  ...
3  #include <thrust/functional.h>
4  ...
5  int main ()
6  {
7    ...
8    thrust::fill (d_y.begin (), d_y.end (), 0.5);
9
10   thrust::transform (d_x.begin (), d_x.end (),
11                      thrust::constant_iterator<double >(1.2),
12                      d_res.begin (), thrust::multiplies<double >());
13   thrust::transform (d_res.begin (), d_res.end (),
14                      d_y.begin(), d_res.begin (),
15                      thrust::plus<double >());
```

```
16
17    thrust::host_vector < double >h_res (d_res);
18    ...
```

Line 11 in Listing 10.6 introduces the `thrust::constant_iterator` class template. Instances of `thrust::constant_iterator` can be used in Thrust algorithms in the place of vector iterators when a constant value needs to be used. The only drawback of Listing 10.6 is that it requires the GPU to perform three read and two write operations to/from global memory for each element of the result vector. In contrast, the solution of Listing 10.5 needs two read operations and one write operation per result element.

Line 13 in Listing 10.6 reveals that it is possible to store the output of a transformation back into the input vector container. In a situation where *in-place* storage of the transformation results is desirable, the `thrust::for_each` algorithm can also be used, as shown in Listing 10.7.

Listing 10.7: A variation of Listing 10.5 that employs `thrust::for_each`.

```
1    // File : daxpy_foreach.cpp
2    #include <thrust/for_each.h>
3    ...
4    // unary functor supported only
5    struct atx
6    {
7      double a;
8      atx ():a (1.0)  {};
9      atx (double i):a (i)  {};
10
11     __host__ __device__
12       void operator () (double &x)  {
13       x *= a;
14     }
15   };
16
17   // ***************************************************************
18   int main ()
19   {
20   ...
21     atx funct;
22     funct.a = 1.2;
23
24     thrust::for_each (d_x.begin (), d_x.end (), funct);
25     thrust::transform(d_x.begin(), d_x.end(),
26                       d_y.begin(), d_res.begin(),
27                       thrust::plus<double >());
28
29     thrust::host_vector < double >h_res (d_res);
30   ...
```

The major difference of the `thrust::for_each` algorithm with the `thrust::transform` is that only unary functors that get called by reference, can be utilized. If the `operator()` function returns anything, it is ignored by `thrust::for_each`.

10.4.2 **Sorting & searching**

Thrust provides efficient GPU implementations of searching and sorting operations in the form of the following algorithms:

- `thrust::sort`
- `thrust::stable_sort`: Guarantees that two equal items will not change relative positioning in the sorted sequence.
- `thrust::sort_by_key`: Sorts two sequences in tandem, one serving as the "values" and one as the "keys."
- `thrust::stable_sort_by_key`: Same as the previous one, but using a stable sort.
- `thrust::is_sorted_until`: Returns an iterator to the first position in the input vector that is out-of-order. If the vector is sorted, the iterator points past the end of the vector.
- `thrust::lower_bound`: Searches an ordered sequence to find the first position where if an item were inserted, it would not violate the ordering of the sequence.
- `thrust::upper_bound`: Searches an ordered sequence to find the last position where if an item were inserted, it would not violate the ordering of the sequence.
- `thrust::binary_search`: Returns true or false based on whether an item can be found in an ordered sequence.
- `thrust::equal_range`: Is a combination of `thrust::lower_bound` and `thrust::upper_bound`, in that it returns a pair of iterators delimiting a range of elements matching a supplied one.

Thrust contains GPU implementations of mergesort and radix sort. The choice of algorithm depends on the type of input data and whether stability is required or not. The library decides at compile time whether to use radix sort (for primitive data types, e.g., `int`, `char`, `float`, etc.) or mergesort (for composite data types or stability).

The searching algorithms have both scalar and vector implementations, in the sense that multiple items can be searched for in an input sequence. A demonstration of these algorithms is given in the form of Listing 10.8.

Listing 10.8: Sample code illustrating how the searching and sorting capabilities of Thrust can be invoked.

```
1   // File : sort_example.cu
2   ...
3   #include <thrust/binary_search.h>
4   #include <thrust/sort.h>
5
6   using namespace std;
7
8   // ****************************************************************
9   template < typename T> void print (char *s, thrust::host_vector < T ↩
        > &v)
10  {
11    cout << s ;
12    thrust::copy (v.begin (), v.end (), ostream_iterator < T > (cout, ↩
        " "));
```

```
13    cout << endl;
14  }
15
16  // *********************************************************
17
18  int main ()
19  {
20    int salary[] = { 1000, 2000, 1001, 2000, 3000, 5000 };
21    int numItems = sizeof (salary) / sizeof (int);
22    thrust::host_vector < int >h_salary (salary, salary + numItems);
23    int SSN[] = { 212, 122, 34, 456, 890, 102 };
24    thrust::host_vector < int >h_SSN (SSN, SSN + numItems);
25
26    thrust::device_vector < int >d_salary (h_salary);
27    thrust::device_vector < int >d_SSN (h_SSN);
28
29    //------------------------------------------------
30    // Example — thrust::sort_by_key
31    thrust::sort_by_key (d_salary.begin (), d_salary.end (), d_SSN.↩
          begin ());
32    h_salary = d_salary;
33    h_SSN = d_SSN;
34    print("Keys : ", h_salary);
35    print("Values : ", h_SSN);
36    // Output is:
37    // Keys : 1000 1001 2000 2000 3000 5000
38    // Values : 212 34 122 456 890 102
39
40    //------------------------------------------------
41    // Example — thrust::is_sorted
42    cout << thrust::is_sorted (h_salary.begin (), h_salary.end ()) << ↩
          endl;
43    // Output is:
44    // 1
45
46    //------------------------------------------------
47    // Searching on the device : SCALAR VERSIONS
48    thrust::device_vector < int >::iterator i = thrust::lower_bound (↩
          d_salary.begin (), d_salary.end (), 1500);
49    cout << "Found at index " << i - d_salary.begin () << " Value " <<↩
          *i << endl;
50    // Output is:
51    // Found at index 2 Value 2000
52
53    i = thrust::upper_bound (d_salary.begin (), d_salary.end (), 2500)↩
          ;
54    cout << "Found at index " << i - d_salary.begin () << " Value " <<↩
          *i << endl;
55    // Output is:
56    // Found at index 4 Value 3000
57
```

```
58   thrust::pair < thrust::device_vector < int >::iterator, thrust::↵
         device_vector < int >::iterator > p;
59   p = thrust::equal_range (d_salary.begin (), d_salary.end (), 2000)↵
         ;
60   cout << "Range equal to item is between indices " << p.first − ↵
         d_salary.begin () << " " << p.second − d_salary.begin () <<↵
         endl;
61   //Output is:
62   // Range equal to item is between indices 2 4
63
64   p = thrust::equal_range (d_salary.begin (), d_salary.end (), 2222)↵
         ;
65   cout << "Range equal to item is between indices " << p.first − ↵
         d_salary.begin () << " " << p.second − d_salary.begin () <<↵
         endl;
66   //Output is:
67   // Range equal to item is between indices 4 4
68
69   cout << thrust::binary_search (d_salary.begin (), d_salary.end (),↵
         1500) << endl;
70   //Output is:
71   // 0
72
73   //—————————————————————
74   // Searching on the host
75   thrust::host_vector < int >::iterator j = thrust::lower_bound (↵
         h_salary.begin (), h_salary.end (), 2000);
76   cout << j − h_salary.begin () << " " << *j << endl;
77   //Output is:
78   // 2 2000
79
80   //—————————————————————
81   // Searching on the device : VECTOR VERSIONS
82   thrust::device_vector<int> itemsToLook(10);
83   thrust::sequence(itemsToLook.begin(), itemsToLook.end(), 0, 500);
84   thrust::device_vector<int> results;
85   thrust::host_vector<int> h_r;
86   results.resize(itemsToLook.size());
87   h_r = itemsToLook;
88   print("Searching for : ", h_r);
89   //Output is:
90   // Searching for : 0 500 1000 1500 2000 2500 3000 3500 4000 4500
91
92   thrust::lower_bound (d_salary.begin (), d_salary.end (), ↵
         itemsToLook.begin(), itemsToLook.end(), results.begin());
93   h_r = results;
94   print("Lower bounds : ", h_r);
95   //Output is:
96   // Lower bounds : 0 0 0 2 2 4 4 5 5 5
97
98   thrust::upper_bound (d_salary.begin (), d_salary.end (), ↵
         itemsToLook.begin(), itemsToLook.end(), results.begin());
```

```
99    h_r = results;
100   print("Upper bounds : ", h_r);
101   // Output is:
102   // Upper bounds : 0 0 1 2 4 4 5 5 5 5
103
104   thrust::binary_search (d_salary.begin (), d_salary.end (), ↵
          itemsToLook.begin(), itemsToLook.end(), results.begin());
105   h_r = results;
106   print("Binary search results : ", h_r);
107   // Output is:
108   // Binary search results : 0 0 1 0 1 0 1 0 0 00
109
110   return 0;
111 }
```

The above code is more or less self-explanatory. There are just two fine details one has to observe. Firstly, the result of searching through a vector is expressed in the form of an iterator, as seen on lines 48, 53, and 75. Secondly, `thrust::equal_range` returns an instance of the `thrust::pair` class template. The two individual items that make up the pair can be accessed via the `first` and `second` data members (see lines 60 and 65).

A more meaningful example that uses the sorting and searching capabilities of Thrust to calculate the histogram of an input sequence is given below. Considering that CUDA requires jumping through a number of hoops to achieve good performance in the calculation of a histogram (see Section 6.6.2), the following program is a much sorter and easier-to-maintain implementation. However, it is suboptimal, as the CUDA version does not have to sort as a preprocessing step.

Listing 10.9: Histogram calculation using `thrust::sort` and `thrust::upper_bound`.

```
1   // File : histogram.cu
2   ...
3   #include <thrust/transform.h>
4   #include <thrust/sort.h>
5   #include <thrust/binary_search.h>
6   #include <thrust/iterator/counting_iterator.h>
7   ...
8   template < typename T > void print (char *s, thrust::host_vector < T↵
        > &v )
9   {
10    cout << s << ":";
11    thrust::copy (v.begin (), v.end (), ostream_iterator < T > (cout, ↵
        " "));
12    cout << endl;
13  }
14
15  // ************************************************************
16  template < typename T > void histogram (thrust::device_vector < T > ↵
        &data, thrust::device_vector < int >&hist )
17  {
18    // start by sorting the data
```

```
19      thrust::sort (data.begin (), data.end ());
20
21      // the data range is now known, allowing the proper sizing of the ↩
            histogram vector
22      T min = data[0];
23      T max = data[data.size () - 1];
24      T range = max - min + 1;
25      hist.resize (range);
26
27      thrust::device_vector < int >aux;
28      aux.push_back (0);
29      aux.resize (hist.size () + 1);
30
31      // a counting_iterator is used to generate all the numbers in the ↩
            range [min, max]
32      thrust::counting_iterator < int >search (min);
33
34      // the vector version of upper_bound calculates for each item in ↩
            the range, the index of the smallest item bigger than it
35      thrust::upper_bound (data.begin (), data.end (), search, search + ↩
            range, aux.begin () + 1);
36
37      // a simple subtraction produces the size of each group of ↩
            identical items, i.e., the histogram
38      thrust::transform (aux.begin () + 1, aux.end (), aux.begin (), ↩
            hist.begin (), thrust::minus < T > ());
39  }
40
41  // ***********************************************************
42  int main (int argc, char **argv)
43  {
44      int N = atoi (argv[1]);
45      thrust::host_vector < int >h_x (N);1
46      thrust::host_vector < int >h_hist;
47      thrust::device_vector < int >d_x;
48      thrust::device_vector < int >d_hist;
49
50      srand (time (0));
51      for (int i = 0; i < N; i++)
52          h_x[i] = rand () % 20;
53
54      d_x = h_x;
55
56      histogram (d_x, d_hist);
57      h_hist = d_hist;
58      print ("Hist ", h_hist);
59
60      return 0;
61  }
```

The inner workings of the histogram() function of Listing 10.9 are traced via a numerical example in Fig. 10.1. Once identical values are clustered following the

Input		Value
data		0 7 5 3 3 7 7 0 2 8 6 8 5
hist		\<empty vector\>

Statement	Output	Value
`thrust::sort (data.begin (), data.end ());`	data	0 0 2 3 3 5 5 6 7 7 7 8 8
`T min = data[0];`	min	0
`T max = data[data.size () - 1];`	max	8
`T range = max - min + 1;`	range	9
`hist.resize (range);`	hist	0 0 0 0 0 0 0 0 0
`thrust::device_vector < int >aux;`	aux	\<empty vector\>
`aux.push_back (0);`	aux	0
`aux.resize (hist.size () + 1);`	aux	0 0 0 0 0 0 0 0 0 0
`thrust::counting_iterator < int >search (min);`	search	0 1 2 ... (not an actual vector)
`thrust::upper_bound (data.begin (), data.e...`	aux	0 2 2 3 5 5 7 8 11 13
`thrust::transform (aux.begin () + 1, aux.e...`	hist	2 0 1 2 0 2 1 3 2

FIGURE 10.1

An example illustrating how the `histogram()` function of Listing 10.9 calculates the histogram of integer data.

sorting of line 19, the `thrust::upper_bound` algorithm essentially produces for every possible value in the input data range (generated by the `counting_iterator` of line 32) the array index that follows the group of items matching that value. Another interpretation of the line 35 results is that they represent the prefix-sum of the histogram array. As such, the transformation of line 38 uses subtraction of neighboring values to yield the histogram array.

10.4.3 Reductions

A reduction algorithm extracts a single value from an input sequence by applying a binary operation. A summation is a simple example of a reduction and it can be performed with the generic `thrust::reduce` algorithm:

```
#include <thrust/reduce.h>
...
  thrust::device_vector<double> d_x;
  ...
  double total = thrust::reduce(d_x.begin(), d_x.end(), 0.0L, thrust↩
      ::plus<double>());
  double total = thrust::reduce(d_x.begin(), d_x.end(), 0.0L);
  double total = thrust::reduce(d_x.begin(), d_x.end());
...
```

All three of the above statements are equivalent as the initial reduction result value (the third parameter) and the reduction functor (the fourth parameter) default to zero and `thrust::plus<>()`, respectively.

Thrust provides a large collection of additional reduction algorithms as shown in the following list:

- `thrust::min_element`: Returns the smallest from a sequence.
- `thrust::max_element`: Returns the largest from a sequence.
- `thrust::is_sorted`: Returns true if the sequence is sorted.
- `thrust::inner_product`: Calculates the inner product of two vectors. In its generic form, this algorithm can be supplied custom "multiplication" (transformation) and custom "addition" (reduction) functors.
- `thrust::count`: Counts the elements matching a given value.
- `thrust::count_if`: Returns the count of elements that satisfy a predicate functor, i.e., a functor with an `operator()` member function that returns a Boolean.
- `thrust::reduce_by_key`: Performs a reduction operation on (key, value) pairs. For each group of consecutive pairs with identical keys, the reduction is done on the corresponding values.

Kernel fusion, i.e., the replacement of multiple, successive kernel invocations by a single one (see Section 6.7.5), is a device optimization technique that aims to eliminate redundant data transfers over the PCIe bus. Kernel fusion is relevant to Thrust also, and in that spirit Thrust designers have provided a fusion of transformation and reduction operations in the form of the `thrust::transform_reduce` and `thrust::inner_product` algorithms. Their difference is that the former applies to a single vector, while the latter applies to two.

The `thrust::inner_product` and `thrust::reduce_by_key` algorithms can be used to calculate the sparse histogram of an array of values, i.e., a histogram where the counts of only encountered values are calculated. The process involves the sorting of the input array so that groups of identical values are formed. Subsequently, groups of identical values are reduced to produce partial sums (the histogram counts) as shown in Listing 10.10.

Listing 10.10: Sparse histogram calculation using `thrust::reduce_by_key` and `thrust::inner_product`. Code shared with Listing 10.9 is not shown.

```
// File : histogram_sparse.cu
...
#include <thrust/reduce.h>
#include <thrust/inner_product.h>
#include <thrust/iterator/constant_iterator.h>
...
template < typename T >
void histogram_sparse (thrust::device_vector < T > &data,
                       thrust::device_vector < T > &value,
                       thrust::device_vector < int >&count)
{
   thrust::sort (data.begin (), data.end ());

   // calculate how many different values exist in the vector
   // by comparing successive values in the sorted data.
   // For every different pair of keys (i.e., a change from one set ↩
       to
   // the next set of keys) a value of 1 is produced and summed up
```

```
18   int numBins = thrust::inner_product (data.begin (), data.end () - ↵
         1,
19                                            data.begin () + 1,
20                                            0,
21                                            thrust::plus < int >(),
22                                            thrust::not_equal_to < T > ()↵
                                                 );
23
24     // output vectors are resized to fit the results
25     value.resize (numBins);
26     count.resize (numBins);
27
28     // the groups of identical keys, get their values (1) summed up
29     // producing as a result a count
30     thrust::reduce_by_key (data.begin (), data.end (),
31                            thrust::constant_iterator < int >(1),
32                            value.begin (),
33                            count.begin ());
34   }
35
36   // ***********************************************************
37   int main (int argc, char **argv)
38   {
39     int N = atoi (argv[1]);
40     thrust::host_vector < int >h_x (N);
41     thrust::host_vector < int >h_value;
42     thrust::host_vector < int >h_count;
43     thrust::device_vector < int >d_x;
44     thrust::device_vector < int >d_value;
45     thrust::device_vector < int >d_count;
46
47     srand (time (0));
48     for (int i = 0; i < N; i++)
49       h_x[i] = rand () % 10000;
50
51     d_x = h_x;
52
53     histogram_sparse (d_x, d_value, d_count);
54     h_value = d_value;
55     h_count = d_count;
56     print ("Values ", h_value);
57     print ("Counts ", h_count);
58
59     return 0;
60   }
```

The key points of the `histogram_sparse()` function are:

1. The number of "bins," i.e., distinct values which are encountered in the input data, needs to be determined in order to resize the output vectors. This is the task accomplished by lines 18–22, where successive data items are compared (the transformation step of `thrust::inner_product`, via functor `thrust::not_equal_to`)

	Input	Value
	data	0 7 5 3 3 7 7 0 2 8 6 8 5
	value	<empty vector>
	count	<empty vector>

Statement	Output	Value
thrust::sort (data.begin (), data.end ());	data	0 0 2 3 3 5 5 6 7 7 7 8 8
int numBins = thrust::inner_product (d...	numBins	7
value.resize (numBins);	value	0 0 0 0 0 0 0
count.resize (numBins);	count	0 0 0 0 0 0 0
thrust::reduce_by_key (data.begin (), d...	value	0 2 3 5 6 7 8
	count	2 1 2 2 1 3 2

FIGURE 10.2

An example illustrating how the histogram_sparse() function of Listing 10.10 calculates the histogram of integer data.

against each other. Unequal pairs contribute +1 to the overall sum produced by the reduction step, afforded by functor thrust::plus. Parameter 0 of line 20 is just the initial value for the reduction.

2. Once the number of bins is found, the sorted input data – treated as keys – are paired with a "value" vector implicitly generated by the anonymous thrust::constant_iterator of line 31. The thrust::constant_iterator sets all the values to 1. The thrust::reduce_by_key algorithm thus counts the cardinality of each group of "keys," effectively producing the desired histogram.

This process is illustrated via a numerical example in Fig. 10.2.

In terms of outright performance, Listing 10.10 is expected to perform more slowly than the corresponding CUDA solution, which does not have to sort the values first. However, it clearly illustrates the conceptual shift required for efficient use of Thrust to solve problems: one has to think in terms of vector/array manipulations.

10.4.4 Scans/prefix-sums

Reduction operations are a special form of prefix-sums, also known as scans. Despite the "sum" part of the name, prefix-sums can be defined for arbitrary operators. The formal definition of a prefix-sum operation calls for the application of a *binary associative* operator $\oplus$ (i.e., one that satisfies $(a \oplus b) \oplus c = a \oplus (b \oplus c)$) on an ordered set of n elements $[a_0, a_1, \ldots, a_{n-1}]$ so that the following set is produced: $[a_0, (a_0 \oplus a_1), \ldots, (a_0 \oplus a_1 \oplus \cdots \oplus a_{n-1})]$.

The output of a scan operation is a vector, in contrast to a reduction operation, where only a single element of that vector is of interest and thus computed.

Scans are a building block of many parallel algorithms. Some of the applications include:

- radix sort,
- polynomial evaluation,
- recurrence evaluation.

Thrust provides a small collection of algorithms for computing prefix-sums. These include:

- `thrust::inclusive_scan`: The result associated with an input element, includes the contribution of that element. The default binary operation is summation.
- `thrust::exclusive_scan`: The result associated with an input element, excludes the contribution of that element. So the output sequence is $[I, a_0, (a_0 \oplus a_1), \ldots, (a_0 \oplus a_1 \oplus \cdots \oplus a_{n-2})]$, where I is the identity value for $\oplus$ (e.g., 0 for summation).
- `thrust::transform_inclusive_scan`: An inclusive scan following the application of a unary functor on the input vector.
- `thrust::transform_exclusive_scan`: A transform followed by an exclusive scan.

The following short program illustrates the results produced by these algorithms:

```
// File : scan_example.cu
...
#include <thrust/scan.h>
...
// ***********************************************************

int main ()
{
  int data[] = { 10, 1, 34, 7, 8, 10, 17 };
  int numItems = sizeof(data)/sizeof(int);
  thrust::host_vector < int >h_data (data, data + numItems);
  thrust::host_vector < int >h_r;

  thrust::device_vector < int >d_data(h_data);
  thrust::device_vector < int >d_r(numItems);

  thrust::inclusive_scan(d_data.begin (), d_data.end (), d_r.begin()←
    );
  h_r = d_r;
  print("Inclusive scan : ", h_r);
  // Output is:
  // Inclusive scan : 10 11 45 52 60 70 87

  thrust::exclusive_scan(d_data.begin (), d_data.end (), d_r.begin()←
    );
  h_r = d_r;
  print("Exclusive scan : ", h_r);
  // Output is:
  // Exclusive scan : 0 10 11 45 52 60 70

  thrust::inclusive_scan(d_data.begin (), d_data.end (), d_r.begin()←
    , thrust::multiplies<int >());
  h_r = d_r;
  print("Inclusive scan product : ", h_r);
  // Output is:
```

```
// Inclusive scan product : 10 10 340 2380 19040 190400 3236800

return 0;
}
```

A more meaningful example of the scan algorithm comes in the form of solving the DNA sequence alignment problem, as described in Section 10.8.2.

10.4.5 Data management and reordering

Thrust provides ways to manipulate the elements of a vector by allowing selective copying, replacement, removal, or partitioning. The supplied algorithms are:

- `thrust::copy`: Copies one vector to another.
- `thrust::remove`: Removes all elements that match a supplied value.
- `thrust::replace`: Replaces all elements that match a supplied value with a new value.
- `thrust::remove_copy`: Removal takes place during copying to another vector.
- `thrust::replace_copy`: Replacement takes place during copying to another vector.
- `thrust::unique`: From each group of identical, consecutive elements, all but the first one are removed.
- `thrust::unique_copy`: During copying to another vector, only the first element of each group of identical consecutive elements is copied.
- `thrust::unique_by_key`: Applies the same operation as `thrust::unique`, but for two vectors, one serving as the keys and one as the values. The keys vector is the one where groups are identified.
- `thrust::unique_by_key_copy`: Identical to the previous one with the exception that the data are copied to two other vectors.
- `thrust::partition`: Reorders the elements of a sequence according to the value of a predicate functor. All the elements for which `true` is returned are placed before the ones for which `false` is returned. The relative order is not preserved among the elements of each group. This is equivalent to the partition function used by quicksort.
- `thrust::partition_copy`: The same as the previous one, but the reordered sequence is stored in another vector.

The above are augmented by versions that perform the filtering action (replacement, removal, etc.) not if a specific value is matched, but if a predicate functor returns true. These include the algorithms `thrust::copy_if`, `thrust::remove_if`, `thrust::replace_if`, `thrust::replace_copy_if`, `thrust::remove_if`, and `thrust::remove_copy_if`.

The algorithms that modify the length of the vector or produce as output a new vector with different size return an iterator that points to the end of the new vector. Any data beyond that point should be ignored.

The following sample program shows how the above algorithms work, as well as the difference between the two groups of algorithms:

```
1    // File : data_manage_example.cu
2    ...
3    #include <thrust/copy.h>
4    #include <thrust/replace.h>
5    #include <thrust/remove.h>
6    #include <thrust/unique.h>
7    #include <thrust/partition.h>
8    ...
9
10   struct evenFunct
11   {
12     __host__ __device__
13     bool operator()(int i)  {
14       return i%2==0;     }
15   };
16   // ************************************************************
17   struct pivotFunct
18   {
19     int pivot;
20     pivotFunct(int p) : pivot(p){}
21
22     __host__ __device__
23     bool operator()(int i)    {
24       return i<pivot;    }
25   };
26   // ************************************************************
27   int main ()
28   {
29     int aux[] = { 5, 1, 3, 3, 2, 4, 2, 7, 6, 7 };
30     char aux2[] = { 'A', 'B', 'C', 'D', 'E', 'F', 'G', 'H', 'I', 'J'};
31     int numItems = sizeof(aux)/sizeof(int);
32     thrust::host_vector < int >h_keys (aux, aux + numItems);
33     thrust::host_vector < char >h_values(aux2, aux2 + numItems);
34
35     thrust::host_vector<int> dest_keys(numItems);
36     thrust::host_vector<char> dest_values(numItems);
37
38     thrust::host_vector<int >::iterator newEnd = thrust::copy_if(h_keys↩
           .begin(), h_keys.end(), dest_keys.begin(), evenFunct());
39     dest_keys.resize( newEnd — dest_keys.begin());
40     print("copy_if : ", dest_keys);
41     // Output is:
42     // copy_if : 2 4 2 6
43
44     dest_keys.resize(numItems);
45     newEnd = thrust::remove_copy(h_keys.begin(), h_keys.end(), ↩
           dest_keys.begin(), 3);
46     dest_keys.resize( newEnd — dest_keys.begin());
47     print("remove_copy : ", dest_keys);
48     // Output is:
```

```
49    // remove_copy : 5 1 2 4 2 7 6 7
50
51    dest_keys.resize(numItems);
52    newEnd = thrust::unique_copy(h_keys.begin(), h_keys.end(), ←
          dest_keys.begin());
53    dest_keys.resize( newEnd − dest_keys.begin());
54    print("unique_copy : ", dest_keys);
55    // Output is:
56    // unique_copy : 5 1 3 2 4 2 7 6 7
57
58    thrust::pair<thrust::host_vector<int>::iterator,
59                thrust::host_vector<char>::iterator> endsPair =
60                thrust::unique_by_key_copy(h_keys.begin(), h_keys.end←
                    (), h_values.begin(), dest_keys.begin(), ←
                    dest_values.begin());
61    dest_keys.resize(endsPair.first − dest_keys.begin());
62    dest_values.resize(endsPair.second − dest_values.begin());
63    print("unique_by_key_copy (keys)   : ", dest_keys);
64    print("unique_by_key_copy (values): ", dest_values);
65    // Output is:
66    // unique_by_key_copy (keys)   : 5 1 3 2 4 2 7 6 7
67    // unique_by_key_copy (values): A B C E F G H I J
68
69    thrust::sort_by_key(h_keys.begin(), h_keys.end(), h_values.begin()←
          );
70    endsPair = thrust::unique_by_key_copy(h_keys.begin(), h_keys.end()←
          , h_values.begin(), dest_keys.begin(), dest_values.begin());
71    dest_keys.resize(endsPair.first − dest_keys.begin());
72    dest_values.resize(endsPair.second − dest_values.begin());
73    print("unique_by_key_copy (keys)   : ", dest_keys);
74    print("unique_by_key_copy (values): ", dest_values);
75    // Output is:
76    // unique_by_key_copy (keys)   : 1 2 3 4 5 6 7
77    // unique_by_key_copy (values): B E C F A I H
78
79    thrust::sort(h_keys.begin(), h_keys.end());
80    dest_keys.resize(numItems);
81    newEnd = thrust::unique_copy(h_keys.begin(), h_keys.end(), ←
          dest_keys.begin());
82    dest_keys.resize( newEnd − dest_keys.begin());
83    print("unique_copy for sorted : ", dest_keys);
84    // Output is:
85    // unique_copy for sorted : 1 2 3 4 5 6 7
86
87    thrust::replace_if(h_keys.begin(), h_keys.end(), evenFunct(), 0);
88    print("replace_if : ", h_keys);
89    // Output is:
90    // replace_if : 1 0 0 3 3 0 5 0 7 7
91
92    thrust::partition(h_keys.begin(), h_keys.end(), pivotFunct( h_keys←
          [0] ));
93    print("partition : ", h_keys);
```

```
94    // Output is:
95    // partition : 0 0 0 0 1 3 3 5 7 7
96
97    return 0;
98  }
```

There are several key points related to the steps shown above:

- When the output of an algorithm is destined for another container/vector, that vector should be large enough to accommodate the data, i.e., it must be properly sized a priori (see lines 35, 36, 44, and 51).
- To avoid problems, the iterator returned by the size-modifying algorithms, like, e.g., thrust::remove, should be used to resize the affected vectors (see lines 39, 46, 53, 61, 62, and 82).
- The inner workings of the thrust::unique_by_key_copy algorithm are revealed by comparing the outputs of lines 66–67 and 76–77. The only difference between the two comes from sorting the two input vectors at line 69, prior to the second copy operation. It is clear that the "uniqueness" test involves only successive input elements, hence producing a truly unique-by-key copy demands a sorting preprocessing step.
- The thrust::*_by_key* family of algorithms that modify the size of their input vectors return a pair of iterators in the form of a thrust::pair<> instance (see lines 58 and 70).

10.5 Fancy iterators

The term "fancy" is used in Thrust to characterize special-purpose iterators that are used either to generate data without having to occupy memory or to combine vectors in an effort to adhere to the Structure of Arrays design principle discussed in Section 6.7.4. We have already seen the thrust::constant_iterator in action in Listing 10.6 and the thrust::counting_iterator in Listing 10.9.

The list of fancy iterators includes:

- thrust::constant_iterator: Returns the same constant value.
- thrust::counting_iterator: Returns a sequence of increasing values. The user can specify the starting value, but the increment step is fixed to 1.
- thrust::transform_iterator: Returns a sequence produced by applying a transformation to the elements of another vector/fancy iterator. It provides a convenient way to combine multiple transformations in one statement, serving the principle of **kernel fusion**.
- thrust::permutation_iterator: Returns a subset of a sequence with its elements retrieved at a user-specified/arbitrary order. It uses two vectors: one serves as a data source and the other as an index map/data selector. The index map vector allows us to use a subset of a data vector as input to an algorithm, while at the same time controlling the order in which the data will be used.

- `thrust::zip_iterator`: Allows the combination of two or more data sequences into a sequence of tuples. In doing so, it allows one to emulate an Array of Structures while storing the data in a Structure of Arrays manner. It also enables having functors with arbitrary parameter lists, since the majority of the algorithms allow only unary or binary functors.

Most of the above iterators have been used in examples in the previous sections. We will proceed to explore the use of the `thrust::zip_iterator` to solve the following problem: given a set of point in 3D space, find the one which is most distant from the origin, i.e., from point $(0, 0, 0)$.

The first issue that needs to be addressed is that of data representation. Having a structure and a functor such as:

```
struct Point3D {
  float x, y, z;
};

struct distanceSqrFunct {
  __host__ __device__
  float operator()(Point3D &p) {
    return p.x*p.x + p.y*p.y + p.z*p.z;
  }
};
```

may be convenient but this solution suffers from two major drawbacks. Firstly, it is counter-efficient for device execution (see memory coalescing in Section 6.7.4). Secondly, using a `thrust::transform_reduce` algorithm on an array of such points would produce the maximum distance, but not the coordinates or index of the corresponding point.

On the other hand, using three different arrays to represent the problem data raises the obstacle that only unary and binary functors are supported by Thrust algorithms. That is until the `thrust::zip_iterator` steps into the picture. Before we delve into the solution of this example, let us see how the zip iterator can be used. Zip iterators are created with the assistance of the `thrust::make_zip_iterator()` function, which in turn requires the use of the `thrust::make_tuple()` function to "glue" together individual arrays into a logical tuple. For example:

```
typedef thrust::device_vector<int >::iterator DVIint;  // typedef can
                                           // shorten the necessary code
typedef thrust::device_vector<float >::iterator DVIfloat;

// tuple instances with 3 elements each
thrust::tuple < DVIint, DVIint, DVIfloat> aTuple, anotherTuple;

// given the above declarations, in the statement below, x and y
// must be device vectors of type int and alpha must be a device
// vector of type float
aTuple = thrust::make_tuple (x.begin(), y.begin(), alpha.begin());
```

```
anotherTuple =thrust::make_tuple (x.begin()+10,
                                   y.begin()+10,
                                   alpha.begin()+10);
```

To access individual elements of a tuple in a functor, the following syntax is required:

```
template < typename Tuple >
__host__ __device__
float operator() (Tuple t)
  {
    int x = thrust::get < 0 > (t);   // get the first component
    int y = thrust::get < 1 > (t);   // get the second comp.
    float alpha = thrust::get < 2 > (t);   // etc.
    return alpha * x + y ;
  }
```

Given a starting tuple, a zip iterator can be used to synchronously and incrementally access the elements of the individual arrays:

```
typedef thrust::tuple < DVIint, DVIint, DVIfloat> tupleDef;
thrust::zip_iterator< tupleDef > ziter;
ziter = thrust::make_zip_iterator(aTuple);

// output the x component of the first tuple
cout << thrust::get < 0 > (ziter[0]) << endl;

// output the y component of the sixth tuple
cout << thrust::get < 1 > (ziter[5]) << endl;
```

Having covered the basic syntax of the Thrust tuple class and the zip iterator, we can proceed to solve the posed problem, as shown in Listing 10.11.

Listing 10.11: Using the `thrust::zip_iterator` to find the coordinates of a point in 3D space that is the most distant from the origin.

```
1  // File : max3d.cu
2  ...
3  #include <thrust/iterator/zip_iterator.h>
4  #include <thrust/iterator/counting_iterator.h>
5  #include <thrust/transform.h>
6  #include <thrust/reduce.h>
7  #include <thrust/random.h>
8  #include <thrust/tuple.h>
9  #include <math.h>
10
11 using namespace std;
12
13 // Calculate the square of the distance
14 struct distSqrFunct
15 {
16   template < typename Tuple >
17   __host__ __device__
18   float operator() (Tuple t)
```

```
19      {
20        int x = thrust::get < 0 > (t);
21        int y = thrust::get < 1 > (t);
22        int z = thrust::get < 2 > (t);
23        return x * x + y * y + z * z;
24      }
25    };
26
27    // **************************************************
28    struct maxFunct
29    {
30      thrust::device_ptr < int >dis;
31        maxFunct (thrust::device_ptr < int >d):dis (d)   {}
32
33      __host__ __device__
34      int operator() (int idx1, int idx2)
35      {
36        if (dis[idx1] > dis[idx2])
37          return idx1;
38        return idx2;
39      }
40    };
41
42    // ***************************************************
43    int main (int argc, char **argv)
44    {
45      // initialize the RNG
46      thrust::default_random_engine rng (time(0));
47      thrust::uniform_int_distribution<int> uniDistr(-10000,10000);
48
49      int N = atoi (argv[1]);
50
51      // generate the data on the host and move them to the device
52      thrust::device_vector < int >x (N);
53      thrust::device_vector < int >y (N);
54      thrust::device_vector < int >z (N);
55      thrust::device_vector < int >dis (N);
56      thrust::host_vector<int> aux(N);
57      for (int i = 0; i < x.size (); i++) aux[i] = uniDistr(rng);
58      x = aux;
59      for (int i = 0; i < x.size (); i++) aux[i] = uniDistr(rng);
60      y = aux;
61      for (int i = 0; i < x.size (); i++) aux[i] = uniDistr(rng);
62      z = aux;
63
64      // "zip" together the 3 arrays into one
65      // typedefs make the code easier to read
66      typedef thrust::device_vector < int >::iterator DVIint;
67      typedef thrust::tuple < DVIint, DVIint, DVIint > tTuple;
68      tTuple a = thrust::make_tuple (x.begin (), y.begin (), z.begin ())↩
                 ;
69      tTuple b = thrust::make_tuple (x.end (), y.end (), z.end ());
```

```
70
71    // calculate the distance for each point
72    thrust::transform (thrust::make_zip_iterator (a),
73                        thrust::make_zip_iterator (b),
74                        dis.begin (),
75                        distSqrFunct ());
76
77    // initialize the functor that will find the maximum distance, so ↩
          that it has access to the distance data
78    maxFunct f (dis.data());
79
80    // reduce the index of the most distant point
81    int furthest = thrust::reduce (thrust::counting_iterator < int ↩
          >(0),
82                                    thrust::counting_iterator < int >(N),
83                                    0,
84                                    f);
85
86    float maxDist = dis[furthest]; // get max distance^2 from the ↩
          device memory
87    cout << "The most distant point is the " << furthest << "-th one, ↩
          with a distance of " << sqrt(maxDist) << endl;
88
89    return 0;
90  }
```

Aside from the part of the program concerned with data generation (lines 57–62) that utilizes the Thrust random number generation (RNG) capabilities (for more details on this topic see Section 10.8.1), the rest of the program involves two steps: the transformation to compute the distances for all the points (lines 72–75) and the reduction to find the one furthest from the origin (lines 81–84).

The details of the solution of Listing 10.11 are:

- In order to allow for device memory coalescing, the coordinates of the data points are held in separate arrays (defined on lines 52–54). The number of points is controlled by command-line input (line 49).
- The data are randomly generated on the host (lines 57, 59, and 61) and then transferred as a single step to the device (lines 58, 60, and 62), thus avoiding extraordinary PCIe traffic. To clarify this point, it is possible that the data were generated as follows:

```
for (int i = 0; i < x.size (); i++) {
    x[i] = uniDistr(rng);
    y[i] = uniDistr(rng);
    z[i] = uniDistr(rng);
}
```

But this would result in a separate PCIe transfer (`cudaMemcpy` operation) for each array element!

- The square of the distance of each point[3] is calculated by the distSqrFunct functor of lines 14–25. The zip iterators created on lines 72 and 73 based on the tuples representing the collective beginning and the collective end of the arrays (lines 68 and 69) permit Thrust to process each point with a unary functor.
- The reduction process involves a bit of a hack, given that the desired output is an index, but the data on which the reduction must be performed are the distances. The solution is to provide the functor access to the distances by passing to its constructor a pointer to the device memory holding them (line 78). Once the memory location of the distances is known, the pair of indices that are passed to the functor during the reduction can be used to fetch and compare the corresponding distances (line 36).

It should be stressed that passing a *reference* to the actual device_vector object as in:

```
struct maxFunct
{
   thrust::device_vector < int > *dis;
     maxFunct (thrust::device_vector< int > *d) : dis(d)  {}

   __host__ __device__
   int operator() (int idx1, int idx2)
   {
     if ((*dis)[idx1] > (*dis)[idx2])
        return idx1;
     return idx2;
   }
};

...
   maxFunct f (&dis);
...
```

is both a logical and a syntax error and it will result in an admittedly cryptic and far from user-friendly long list of compilation error messages. The essence is that while the dis.data() call returns a device memory pointer as the one required to perform the reduction, the dis device_vector *object itself is an entity living in host memory*.

- The reduction requires a list of the point indices. Instead of having an extra vector occupying memory and taking up time to allocate and populate, it suffices to have a pair of thrust::counting_iterators denoting the first (line 81) and beyond-last (line 82) indices to use. The zero index (line 83) serves as our initial reduction value.

---

[3] The calculation of the square root has no significance in finding the greatest distance, thus it constitutes a runtime cost that can be avoided.

- Finally, the greatest distance, as represented by dis[furthest], cannot be output to the console directly. Instead a memory copy from the device to the host must be initiated (line 86) before this action can take place.

10.6 Switching device back-ends

Thrust was originally designed to be a CUDA front-end, i.e., the ultimate compilation of the provided algorithms was relegated to a CUDA compiler driver back-end. However, since Thrust version 1.7, we are allowed to use other back-ends for compilation.

These so-called **device back-ends** are:

- CUDA compiler driver (default),
- OpenMP compiler,
- Intel Thread Building Blocks (TBB) templates,
- standard C++ compiler.

The choice of device back-end is controlled by the THRUST_DEVICE_SYSTEM symbolic name.[4] For example, if one was to compile the histogram program of Section 10.4.2 with the standard C++ compiler, the following line would be required:

```
nvcc histogram.cu —DTHRUST_DEVICE_SYSTEM=THRUST_DEVICE_SYSTEM_CPP —o↩
    histogram_stdc
```

Under certain conditions, it is also possible to switch device back-ends programmatically during runtime, by changing the execution policy. This is discussed in the next section.

The use of the alternative device back-ends may require additional compiler switches, such as library/include file locations, extra libraries to link against, or other compiler directives (these are compiler- and system environment-dependent). Table 10.1 lists the value required for THRUST_DEVICE_SYSTEM and any additional compiler switches for each of the available back-ends. Also, it is advisable to always install the latest Thrust version from the github repository to ensure that the latest bug fixes and features are available.

So, compiling the histogram program for execution using OpenMP or TBB, we would need the commands:

```
#OpenMP
nvcc histogram.cu —DTHRUST_DEVICE_SYSTEM=THRUST_DEVICE_SYSTEM_OMP —↩
    Xcompiler —fopenmp —lgomp —o histogram_omp

#TBB
nvcc histogram.cu —DTHRUST_DEVICE_SYSTEM=THRUST_DEVICE_SYSTEM_TBB —↩
    ltbb —o histogram_tbb
```

---

[4] Older Thrust versions use the THRUST_DEVICE_BACKEND name.

Table 10.1 Thrust device back-ends and their associated compiler switches. GCC is assumed to be the compiler used by `nvcc`.

Device back-end	`THRUST_DEVICE_SYSTEM` **value**	Other compiler switches
CUDA	`THRUST_DEVICE_SYSTEM_CUDA`	N/A
OpenMP	`THRUST_DEVICE_SYSTEM_OMP`	`-Xcompiler -fopenmp -lgomp`
TBB	`THRUST_DEVICE_SYSTEM_TBB`	`-ltbb`
C++	`THRUST_DEVICE_SYSTEM_CPP`	N/A

The difference in performance is immediately apparent between the different back-ends. For instance, calculating the histogram of 10^8 values on a system equipped with an AMD Ryzen R9 3900X processor and a GTX 2060 Super GPU card produced the following execution times[5] with the GCC 7.5 compiler optimizations set to "-O3," and the CUDA 10.2 SDK:

```
$ time ./histogram_cuda 100000000
Hist: 5000401 4998014 4998156 5001767 4999178 5000646 5004777 ↩
    5000649 5003735 4998608 5000312 4995903 4997914 4995985 4998512 ↩
    5003050 5000494 5001308 5000523 5000068

real    0m0,970s
user    0m0,638s
sys     0m0,289s
$ time ./histogram_omp 100000000
Hist: 4998990 5002218 4998932 5003450 5001763 5004416 4999207 ↩
    4996477 5004299 4998787 5000989 4999075 4997855 4998525 4999643 ↩
    4999431 4997868 4999067 4998010 5000998

real    0m1,379s
user    0m3,993s
sys     0m1,408s
$ time ./histogram_stdc 100000000
Hist: 4997651 5000146 4999079 5004062 4999694 4996387 4998252 ↩
    4996115 5001821 4999503 5000113 5003083 4999648 5000785 5003284 ↩
    5000553 5000514 5003098 5000413 4995799

real    0m2,222s
user    0m1,973s
sys     0m0,248s
```

The above times are not indicative of how well a particular back-end will perform under any and all circumstances (especially given the very small execution time that would exaggerate any difference in back-end initialization time). Compiler choice (e.g., `gcc` versus `icc`) and program design can have a big influence on the outcome. For example, if the test was performed for 10^7 values, the CUDA version would be the slowest.

---

[5] Sample outputs are different because each run uses randomly generated data.

10.7 Thrust execution policies and asynchronous execution

By default all Thrust algorithm invocations are synchronous, i.e., the calls return only when their action is complete. Asynchronous execution can be beneficial to performance, so in this section we examine how it can be set up.

One easy way, given that CUDA kernel calls are asynchronous, is to encapsulate the Thrust call inside a kernel, as starting with Thrust 1.8, it is possible to invoke Thrust from device code. This approach is shown below in a variant of Listing 10.2 for finding the minimum of a function.

Listing 10.12: Using a kernel as a front-end to run Thrust asynchronously.

```
1  // File : min_async.cu
2  . . .
3  struct functor
4  {
5    __host__ __device__
6    float operator () (const float &x) const
7    {
8      return x * x;
9    }
10 };
11
12 // ******************************************************
13 template < typename Iterator, typename Functor, typename ResultPtr >
14 _global__ void frontEnd (Iterator xs, Iterator ys, int N, Functor f, ↩
       ResultPtr idx)
15 {
16   thrust::transform (thrust::cuda::par, xs, xs + N, ys, f);
17
18   *idx = thrust::min_element (thrust::cuda::par, ys, ys + N) - ys;
19 }
20
21 // ******************************************************
22 int main (int argc, char **argv)
23 {
24   float st, end;
25   st = atof (argv[1]);
26   end = atof (argv[2]);
27   int dataPoints = atoi (argv[3]);
28   float step = (end - st) / dataPoints;
29
30   thrust::device_vector < float >d_x (dataPoints);
31   thrust::device_vector < float >d_y (dataPoints);
32   thrust::sequence (d_x.begin (), d_x.end (), st, step);
33
34   // first way
35   thrust::device_vector < int >d_res (1);
36   frontEnd <<< 1, 1 >>> (d_x.begin (), d_y.begin (), dataPoints, ↩
       functor (), d_res.data ());
37   cudaDeviceSynchronize ();
```

```
38    cout << "Function minimum over [" << st << "," << end << "] occurs↩
          at " << d_x[d_res.data ()[0]] << endl;
39    . . .
```

Once the data have been allocated and initialized (lines 30–32), we can launch a single CUDA thread (line 36) that will in turn call Thrust (lines 16–18). The tricky parts in this approach are (a) to get all the parameters properly passed to the kernel and (b) to collect the result. The first problem can be simplified by making the kernel function a template, as seen on line 13, which makes the compiler deduce all the appropriate types with minimum programmer effort.

The second problem can be solved by allocating explicit device storage for holding the result, in our case a vector of size 1 (line 35).

A novel – and mandatory in this case – component of the Thrust calls on lines 16 and 18 is the *execution policy*. The execution policy is an optional parameter of many (but currently not all) Thrust algorithms that instructs the library on how and where the computations will be performed. Possible execution policies include:

- `thrust::host`: Computation will be done on the host.
- `thrust::cpp::par`: Computation will be done in parallel, using C++ threads.
- `thrust::omp::par`: Computation will be done in parallel, using OpenMP.
- `thrust::tbb::par`: Computation will be done in parallel, using TBB.
- `thrust::cuda::par`: Computation will be done using multiple CUDA threads.
- `thrust::cuda::par.on(stream)`: The same as the previous one, but all kernels launched will be queued in the specified stream.

Device code invoking Thrust can also use these policies:

- `thrust::seq`: Computation will be done by a single CUDA thread.
- `thrust::cuda::par`: Computation will be done using multiple CUDA threads.
- `thrust::device`: Computation will be done on the device. But it may not involve multiple threads unless dynamic parallelism is available.

Of course, using these execution policies might mandate the use of additional compiler switches to enable the corresponding back-ends, as shown in the previous section.

An alternative and arguably easier way to achieve asynchronous execution is to spawn a host thread to handle the Thrust calls. The full details on C++11 asynchronous threads are covered in Section 3.11.

Listing 10.13: Using an asynchronous host thread for running Thrust.

```
40    // File : min_async.cu
41    . . .
42    #include <future>
43    . . .
44    using namespace std;
45
46    // ***************************************************
47    int main (int argc, char **argv)
```

```
48   {
49     . . .
50     // second way
51     future < long >res = std::async (std::launch::async,[&](){
52               functor f;
53               thrust::transform (d_x.begin (), d_x.end (), d_y.↩
                  begin (), f);
54               return thrust::min_element (d_y.begin (), d_y.end ()↩
                  ) - d_y.begin ();}
55     );
56     int idx = res.get ();
57     cout << "Function minimum over [" << st << "," << end << "] occurs↩
              at " << d_x[idx] << endl;
58     . . .
```

The lambda expression of lines 51–55 covers exactly the actions we need from Thrust. The result can be retrieved by waiting on the `future` object returned by `std::async` (line 56).

10.8 Case studies

10.8.1 Monte Carlo integration

Monte Carlo integration is an approximation technique for calculating definite integrals. It is typically used for higher-dimensional integrals where an analytical solution is impossible.

If we pick N random points x_i with $i \in [0, N - 1]$, uniformly distributed in an n-dimensional space $V \in \Re^n$, then the integral of a function f over V can be approximated by

$$I = \int_V f dx = V\bar{f} \pm V\sqrt{\frac{\overline{f^2} - \bar{f}^2}{N - 1}}, \qquad (10.1)$$

where the overline represents arithmetic mean over the N points, i.e., $\bar{f} = \frac{1}{N} \times \sum_{i=0}^{N-1} f(x_i)$, and the $\pm$ part of the equation represents an error estimate based on the unbiased standard deviation of f.

The error decreases at a rate of $\frac{1}{N}$, which means that the larger the set of points is, the better the accuracy of the result.

If the volume V cannot be calculated, then one can select a space W such that $V \subseteq W$ and proceed to sample W. Then

$$I = \int_V f dx = W\bar{g}, \qquad (10.2)$$

where the function g is defined as

$$g(x) = \begin{cases} f(x), & \text{if } x \in V, \\ 0, & \text{if } x \notin V. \end{cases} \tag{10.3}$$

As an example, let us apply a Monte Carlo approach to the calculation of π. Approximating π can be accomplished by finding the integral

$$I = \int_0^1 \sqrt{1 - x^2} dx. \tag{10.4}$$

The function in this case is the equation of the unit circle ($x^2 + y^2 = 1$), so the integral should be equal to a quarter of the unit circle's area: $\frac{\pi}{4}$.

The pseudocode for a program calculating π in this fashion, given the number of sample points N,[6] is shown in Listing 10.14.

Listing 10.14: Pseudocode of a Monte Carlo-based calculation of π.

```
int inside=0;
for(int i=0;i<N;i++)   {
   double x, y, distance;
   x = rand();     // generate an x and y coordinates in the
   y = rand();     // [0,1]x[0,1] part of the plane
   distance = x*x + y*y;
   if( distance <= 1 )  inside++; // check if it is inside the ←
      circle
   }
double PI = 4.0 * inside / N;
```

A critical component of Monte Carlo methods is the RNG. Most computational methods rely on pseudorandom number generators (PRNGs), i.e., algorithms that produce seemingly random sequences based on an initial "seed" value. The sequence is deterministic, however, as the same seed will always produce the same sequence.

Thrust provides a number of PRNG engines that are used as the back-end to other algorithms that adapt the generated numbers to a specific range or distribution (e.g., uniform, normal, etc.). For example, the default PRNG engine can be used to generate custom distribution numbers as follows:

```
thrust::default_random_engine rng(seed);   // provide seed in case ←
   results need to be reproducible

// generates floating point numbers using a uniform distribution in ←
   the [a,b] interval
thrust::uniform_real_distribution<double> uniDistr(a,b);
double aNum = uniDistr(rng);
```

---

[6] A nice GIF animation that shows the influence of N on the calculation accuracy can be found at http://en.wikipedia.org/wiki/File:Pi_30K.gif.

```
// generates integer numbers using a uniform distribution in the [a,↩
    b] interval
thrust::uniform_int_distribution<long> uniDistrInt(a,b);
long anotherNum = uniDistrInt(rng);

// generates floating point numbers using a normal distribution with↩
    mean a and standard deviation b
thrust::random::normal_distribution<float> normalDistr(a, b);
float thirdNum = normalDistr(rng);
```

The approach used by Thrust is nearly identical to the standard C++11 setup. In fact many of the thrust- and std-namespace engine and distribution class names are identical. The benefit of using the Thrust classes is that they are made available in all the back-ends.

In order to speed up the calculation of the integral, the RNG process should run in parallel as well. To avoid having identical sequences that could taint the results, each point should be generated by an RNG initialized with a different seed. However, this cannot still guarantee that the same subset of an RNG's sequence will not be used.

A better alternative would be to partition a sequence among the threads invoked by Thrust, effectively eliminating the possibility of pseudorandom number reuse. This is a possibility afforded by the discard method of the PRNG provided by Thrust, which allows one to skip over a set of numbers in the sequence, as shown in the implementation of Listing 10.15 (line 27).

Listing 10.15: Thrust implementation of the Monte Carlo π calculation.

```
1   \\ File : pi.cu
2   #include <thrust/device_vector.h>
3   #include <thrust/host_vector.h>
4   #include <thrust/transform_reduce.h>
5   #include <thrust/random.h>
6   #include <thrust/functional.h>
7
8   #include <iostream>
9   #include <iomanip>
10
11  using namespace std;
12
13  //*************************************************************
14  struct MonteCarloPi
15  {
16    int seed;
17    int pointsPerThread;
18
19    MonteCarloPi(int s, int p) : seed(s), pointsPerThread(p){}
20
21    __host__ __device__
22    long operator()(int segment)
23    {
```

```
24     double x, y, distance;
25     long inside=0;
26     thrust::default_random_engine rng(seed);
27     rng.discard(segment * 2 * pointsPerThread);  // skip the parts ←
          of the sequence that belongs to previous threads
28
29     thrust::uniform_real_distribution<double> uniDistr(0,1);
30
31     for(int i=0;i<pointsPerThread;i++)
32     {
33         x = uniDistr(rng);    // generate (x,y) coordinates in the
34         y = uniDistr(rng);    // [0,1]x[0,1] part of the plane
35         distance = x*x + y*y;
36         inside += ( distance <= 1 ); // optimized check
37     }
38     return inside;
39   }
40 };
41
42 // **********************************************************
43 int main (int argc, char **argv)
44 {
45   int N = atoi (argv[1]); // total points to examine
46   int M = atoi (argv[2]); // points per thread
47
48   N = (N+M-1)/M * M; // make sure N is a multiple of M
49
50   long total = thrust::transform_reduce(
51                     thrust::counting_iterator<int>(0),
52                     thrust::counting_iterator<int>(N/M),
53                     MonteCarloPi(0, M),  // transformation functor
54                     0,                    // reduction initial value
55                     thrust::plus<int>());// reduction functor
56   cout << setprecision(15);
57   cout << 1.0L * total / N * 4.0L << endl;
58   return 0;
59 }
```

As indicated by Eq. (10.1), the more random points are used in the calculation, the more accurate are the results produced by Monte Carlo methods. While CUDA allows for millions of threads to be generated, it is also true that increasing the arithmetic density of our kernels (the functors in Thrust) improves the execution efficiency. There is no obstacle against using each functor invocation for calculating the contribution of multiple points in our integral. Hence, the unary functor on lines 31–37 generates and checks a number of pointsPerThread points.

The total number of points N and the M (or pointsPerThread) parameters are controlled by user input (lines 45 and 46). The thrust::counting_iterator parameters of lines 51–52 generate $[0, \ldots, N/M)$ transformation functor invocations, each with its own unique segment number, referring to a distinct part of the PRNG sequence. Once the transformation is complete, a simple summation produces the total number out of the N points examined that fell within the unit circle.

Having both N and M available as inputs enables us to finely control the execution configuration that will be used. This is essential for successfully using a CPU device back-end, which is not as efficient as a GPU in the generation and management of thousands of threads.

10.8.2 DNA sequence alignment

DNA is composed of a sequence of organic molecules called nucleotides, represented by the letters G, A, T, and C, from the initials of their names. Thus a DNA sequence can be effectively represented as a string of these four letters. In bioinformatics, comparing two (or more) DNA sequences allows one to identify regions of similarity between them, which could indicate ancestral relationships, mutations, functional similarities, etc. The comparison is performed by attempting an optimal alignment, i.e., a relative placement between the two sequences, that maximizes the pairs of nucleotides that match. The alignment can involve the introduction of gaps in the sequences, as DNA sequencing technologies are known to produce such inconsistencies (gaps) in their output.

Many possible alignments are typically possible. In order to compute the best one, we have to come up with an objective function, i.e., a way to measure the quality of the resulting match. The Smith–Waterman algorithm[7] can be used to find the best alignment by applying the following conventions: a weight/score is assigned to each of the formed pairs of nucleotides: $+w$ if they are identical, $-y$ if there is a mismatch or a gap. The score of a particular alignment is the sum of the individual scores.

Assuming that we have two sequences, S and T, of length N and M, respectively, then we can calculate the best score H that can be achieved for two prefices/substrings $S[1, ..., i]$ and $T[1, ..., j]$, with $i \in [1, N]$ and $j \in [1, M]$ as follows:

$$H(j,i) = max \begin{cases} H(j-1,i) - y, & \text{if we insert a gap in } S \\ H(j-1,i-1) + w, & \text{if } S[i] = T[j] \\ H(j,i-1) - y, & \text{if we insert a gap in } T \end{cases}. \quad (10.5)$$

When we are not using any letters from one of the two sequences to calculate H, the score is set to zero:

$$H(j,0) = H(0,i) = 0 \text{ for } \forall i, j. \quad (10.6)$$

The recursive computation described by Eq. (10.5) can be efficiently performed by using dynamic programming. We just have to allocate an $(M+1) \times (N+1)$ matrix

---

[7] See http://en.wikipedia.org/wiki/Smith-Waterman_algorithm, last accessed December 2021.

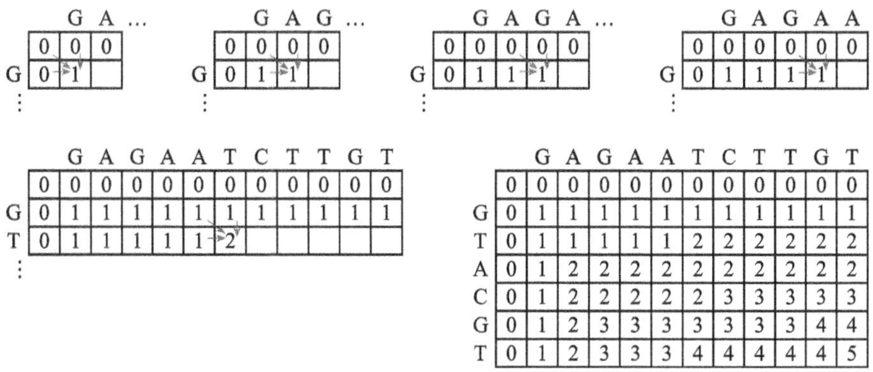

FIGURE 10.3

An example illustrating how the best alignment score of DNA sequences "GAGAATCTTGTA" and "GTACGT" can be calculated in a row-by-row fashion, starting from the top left corner, with $w = 1$ and $y = 0$. The arrows show the dependencies between matrix cells, as mandated by Eq. (10.5).

H and initialize its first row and column to zero (corresponding to the base cases of Eq. (10.6)). Then, the computation can be done row-by-row or column-by-column, so that the previous values required at every step have been calculated. The best score will be deposited at the $H[M][N]$ location. An illustration of the calculation is shown in Fig. 10.3.

The example in Fig. 10.3 seems to indicate that the calculation has to be performed sequentially. However, as the max operator used in Eq. (10.5) is associative and commutative, we can perform the calculation of each row j in two parallelizable steps:

1. Use a transformation algorithm to calculate temporary values for the current row using the previous row according to:

$$H_{temp}(j, i) = max \begin{Bmatrix} H(j-1, i) - y \\ H(j-1, i-1) + w & \text{if } S[i] = T[j] \end{Bmatrix}. \quad (10.7)$$

2. Use a scan algorithm to calculate the final values according to

$$H(j, i) = max \begin{Bmatrix} H_{temp}(j, i) \\ H_{temp}(j, i-1) - y \end{Bmatrix}. \quad (10.8)$$

An example of the successful application of this idea is shown in Fig. 10.4, where the calculation of a row of the H matrix used in Fig. 10.3 is performed.

The row-by-row (or column-by-column) calculation means that if we are only interested in the best score, we need to allocate only two rows (columns). This is the approach followed in Listing 10.16, where it is also assumed that $w = 1$ and $y = 0$, i.e., no penalty is accumulated for inserting gaps.

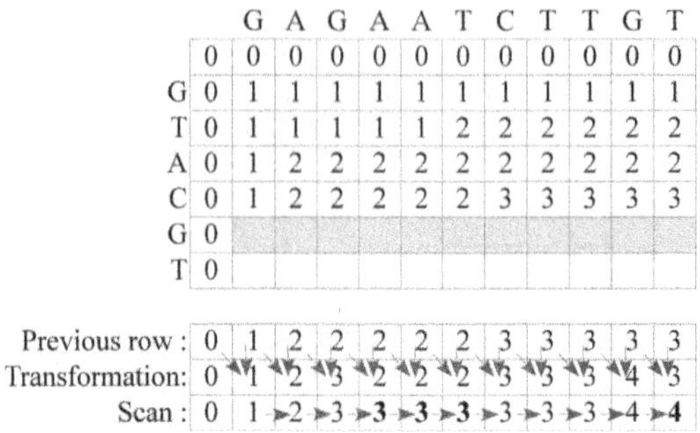

	G	A	G	A	A	T	C	T	T	G	T
	0	0	0	0	0	0	0	0	0	0	0
G 0	1	1	1	1	1	1	1	1	1	1	1
T 0	1	1	1	1	1	2	2	2	2	2	2
A 0	1	2	2	2	2	2	2	2	2	2	2
C 0	1	2	2	2	2	2	3	3	3	3	3
G 0											
T 0											

Previous row : 0 1 2 2 2 2 2 3 3 3 3 3
Transformation: 0 1 2 3 2 2 2 3 3 3 4 3
Scan : 0 1 2 3 3 3 3 3 3 3 4 4

FIGURE 10.4

The calculation of the shaded, fifth row of the H matrix used in Fig. 10.3 with a two-step process, involving a transformation and a scan. The arrows show the data dependencies and the bold text highlights the cells affected by the second step.

Listing 10.16: Thrust implementation of the Smith–Waterman DNA sequence alignment algorithm.

```
1   \\ File : dna.cu
2   ...
3   #include <thrust/transform.h>
4   #include <thrust/scan.h>
5   #include <thrust/fill.h>
6   #include <thrust/iterator/counting_iterator.h>
7   #include <thrust/functional.h>
8
9   using namespace std;
10
11  struct Phase1_funct
12  {
13    thrust::device_ptr < char >S;
14    char T; // T single character used here
15    thrust::device_ptr < int >prev;
16
17    Phase1_funct (thrust::device_ptr < char >s, char t, thrust::↵
          device_ptr < int >p):S (s), T (t), prev (p) {}
18
19    // just finds the maximum that can be obtained from
20    // the two cells from the previous iteration
21    __host__ __device__ int operator () (int j) const
22    {
23      int max = prev[j];
24
25      int tmp = prev[j - 1];
26
27      if (S[j - 1] == T)
28        tmp++;
29      if (max < tmp)
30        max = tmp;
```

```
31
32          return max;
33     }
34    };
35    // *************************************************************
36
37    int main ()
38    {
39      char *S = "GAATTCAGTTA";        // sample data
40      char *T = "GGATCGA";
41      int N = strlen (S);
42      int M = strlen (T);
43
44      // allocate and initialize the equivalent of 2 N+1-length vectors
45      // [0] is used to hold at the end of each iteration, the last
46      // computed row of the matrix
47      thrust::device_vector < int >H[2];
48      H[0].resize (N + 1);
49      H[1].resize (N + 1);
50      thrust::fill (H[0].begin (), H[0].end (), 0);
51
52      // transfer the big DNA strand to the device
53      thrust::device_vector < char >d_S (N);
54      thrust::copy (S, S + N, d_S.begin ());
55
56      thrust::counting_iterator < int >c0 (1);
57      thrust::counting_iterator < int >c1 (N + 1);
58
59      // calculate the rows, one-by-one
60      for (int j = 0; j < M; j++)
61        {
62          char oneOfT = T[j];
63          // first phase using the previous row in the matrix
64          thrust::transform (c0, c1, H[1].begin () + 1, Phase1_funct (←
65              d_S.data (), oneOfT, H[0].data ()));
66
66          // second phase using the current row in the matrix
67          thrust::inclusive_scan (H[1].begin () + 1, H[1].end (), H[0].←
                begin () + 1, thrust::maximum < int >());
68        }
69
70      cout << "Best matching score is " << H[0][N] << endl;
71      return 0;
72    }
```

The program above uses three device vectors to facilitate the calculation of the optimum score: two vectors representing successive *H* matrix rows and one for holding one of the DNA sequences (d_S). The H[0] vector is used to hold the outcome of the last calculation (or the very first row used, initialized to zero on line 50), while the H[1] vector is used to hold the intermediate result of the transformation step on line 64.

The Thrust implementation of Eq. (10.8) hinges on having the functor employed for the task (defined on lines 11–34) satisfy the following conditions:

- The functor that produces each element of the H[1] vector must be aware of the element's position i in the vector/matrix row, in order to be able to locate the two corresponding elements in the previous vector H[0][i] and H[0][i-1].
- The functor should also be aware of the DNA sequence "labeling" the columns of the matrix and the element of the second DNA sequence that "labels" the row (see the illustration in Fig. 10.4).

All the necessary data, including the previous vector H[0], are passed to the constructor of the functor (line 64). The position information is passed by applying the transformation on an integer sequence representing the range of indices $[0, N]$. The range limits are represented by the two counting_iterator objects c0 and c1 defined on lines 56 and 57.

Finally, the second step of the calculation as expressed by Eq. (10.8) is performed by the inclusive_scan algorithm on line 67. Using the H[1] vector as input and the H[0] vector as output allows us to perform the calculation row-by-row while minimizing the device memory requirements.

However, if the actual optimum alignment is required, the whole of matrix H must be kept in memory. The optimum alignment – or at least one of them as multiple ones are typically possible – can be calculated by tracing back the steps taken whenever Eq. (10.5) was applied, starting from the $H[M][N]$ element of the matrix, all the way to the top row or left column. Fig. 10.5 shows how the optimum alignment can be extracted for the example of Fig. 10.3.

In this section we do not address the issue of getting the alignment. However, Listing 10.17 shows how the whole matrix can be obtained by *fusing* the two phases of row calculation via the thrust::transform_inclusive_scan algorithm (see lines 63–66 below):

Listing 10.17: Thrust implementation of the Smith–Waterman DNA sequence alignment algorithm, which employs kernel fusion in the form of a combined transform-and-scan algorithm.

```
1   \\ File : dna_fusion.cu
2   ...
3   #include <thrust/transform_scan.h>
4   #include <thrust/sequence.h>
5   #include <thrust/fill.h>
6   #include <thrust/iterator/counting_iterator.h>
7   #include <thrust/functional.h>
8
9   using namespace std;
10
11  // ****************************************************************
12  template < typename D >
13  struct Pass1_funct
14  {
```

```
15    thrust::device_ptr < char >S;
16    char T;                        // T single character used here
17    thrust::device_ptr< D >prev;
18
19      Pass1_funct (thrust::device_ptr < char >s, char t, thrust::↩
            device_ptr < D >p):S (s), T (t), prev (p) {}
20
21    // just finds the maximum that can be obtained from
22    // the two cells from the previous iteration
23    __host__ __device__ D operator () (const D & j) const
24    {
25      D max = prev[j];
26      // optimized check that avoids path divergence
27      D tmp = prev[j - 1] + (S[j - 1] == T);
28
29      if (max < tmp)  max = tmp;
30
31      return max;
32    }
33  };
34  // *********************************************************
35
36  int main ()
37  {
38    char *S = "GAATTCAGTTA"; // sample data
39    char *T = "GGATCGA";
40    int N = strlen (S);
41    int M = strlen (T);
42
43    // allocate and initialize the equivalent of a (M+1)x(N+1) matrix
44    thrust::device_vector < int >H[M + 1];
45    thrust::device_vector < int >aux;
46    for (int i = 0; i < M + 1; i++)
47      H[i].resize (N + 1);
48
49    thrust::fill (H[0].begin (), H[0].end (), 0);
50    for (int j = 1; j < M + 1; j++)
51      H[j][0] = 0;
52
53    // transfer to the device the big DNA strand
54    thrust::device_vector < char >d_S (N);
55    thrust::copy (S, S + N, d_S.begin ());
56
57    thrust::counting_iterator < int >c (1);
58
59    // fill-in the DP table, row-by-row
60    for (int j = 1; j < M + 1; j++)
61      {
62        char oneOfT = T[j - 1];
63        thrust::transform_inclusive_scan (c, c + N,
64                                          H[j].begin () + 1,
```

```
65                                          Pass1_funct <int >(d_S.data()↩
                                              , oneOfT, H[j − 1].data↩
                                              ()),
66                                          thrust::maximum < int >());
67        }
68
69        cout << "Best matching score is " << H[M][N] << endl;
70        return 0;
71    }
```

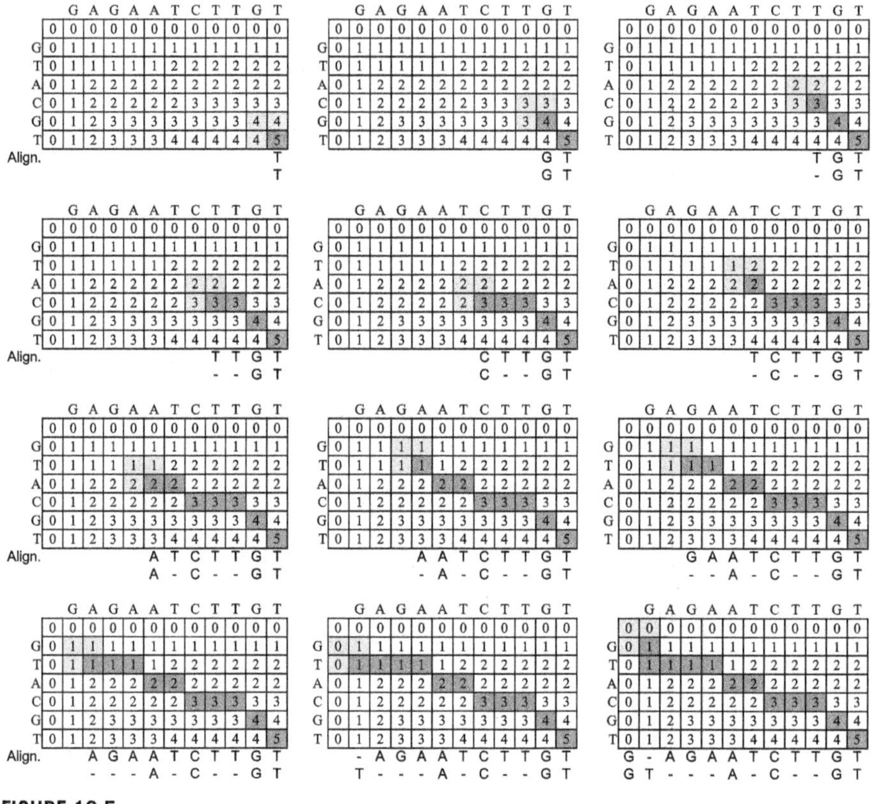

FIGURE 10.5

Calculation of the optimal alignment for the two DNA sequences used in the example shown in Fig. 10.3. The calculation is based on the blue-shaded (dark gray in print version) cells, progressing from the top-left to the bottom-right matrix. Below each matrix, the alignment, as calculated up to that point, is shown.

While following the same guidelines for the construction of the unary functor performing the transformation step (structure Pass1_funct, defined on lines 12–33), as set out in the above paragraphs, the major difference of Listing 10.17 lies in the use of a template syntax for Pass1_funct. This is mandated by the Thrust library for employing the thrust::transform_inclusive_scan algorithm, although the same was not a requirement for using the `Pass1_funct` functor of Listing 10.16 with `thrust::transform`. Missing this detail would result in a large collection of unintelligible compilation error messages.

Another minor change relates to the logic of the unary functor's `operator()` method: by turning the block of lines 25–28 in Listing 10.16 into the statement of line 27 in Listing 10.17, we can avoid path divergence, which is a performance-sapping problem for GPU execution (see Section 6.7.2).

Exercises

1. Develop a Thrust program for calculating the inner product of two vectors by using the `thrust::transform` algorithm and an appropriate functor.
2. Calculate the inner product of two vectors by using the `thrust::inner_product` algorithm. Compare the performance of this version with the performance of a CUDA-based solution.
3. Use Thrust algorithms to find the absolute maximum of an array of values.
4. Write a Thrust program for calculating the sum of two matrices.
5. Write a Thrust program for calculating the definite integral of a function $f(x)$ over a range $[a, b]$ using the trapezoidal rule. Consider a solution that avoids the need to create a vector for all the x-values for which a trapezoid is calculated. The details of the trapezoidal rule can be found in Section 3.7.2.
6. Use Thrust to calculate the mean and variance of a dataset X of cardinality N. For convenience, the corresponding formulas are

$$E[X] = \frac{\sum_{i=0}^{N-1} x_i}{N},$$
(10.9)

$$\sigma^2 = E[X^2] - (E[X])^2.$$
(10.10)

7. Measure the performance of the `thrust::sort` algorithm in Thrust by sorting varying volumes of data. Compare the achieved times with the STL version running on the host. For this purpose create a big array (make sure it is not too big to fit in the GPU's memory) and populate it with random data.
8. Measure the performance hit that an Array of Structures design approach will have in device-based sorting by trying to sort a big vector (e.g., 10^6 elements) of randomly generated instances of the following structure:

```
struct TestStr {
    int key;
    float value;

    __host__ __device__
    bool operator <(const TestStr &o) const
    {
        return this->key < o.key;
```

```
    }
};
```

To measure the performance deterioration, you will have to implement and time a Structure of Arrays alternative.

9. Create a Thrust program for computing the Mandelbrot set. Section 3.12 (starting from page 161) covers the mathematical details of how the set is calculated.

10. A problem related to the furthest-distance point solved in Section 10.5 is the problem of finding the pair of points which are the furthest apart from each other. Create a brute-force solution to this problem, i.e., by examining all pairs of points, using Thrust. Consider the case where the number of points is too big to allow storage of all the calculated distances. You should avoid duplicate calculations since the distance from point A to B is the same as the distance from B to A.

11. The all-pairs shortest paths graph problem can be solved by the dynamic programming algorithm by Floyd and Warshall. Assuming that the graph is described by a $V \times V$ adjacency matrix, where V is the number of vertices, then the pseudocode of the algorithm below shows how the solution can be obtained in V steps. In each kth step, we update the distance matrix by involving the kth vertex as a possible intermediate:

```
// initialization phase
Allocate a VxV distance matrix, and set all elements to infinity
for each vertex v
    distance[v][v] <- 0
for each edge (u,v)
    distance[u][v] <- adj(u,v)   // the weight of the edge (u,v)

// computation phase
for k from 1 to V    // for each k intermediate vertex
    for i from 1 to V  // reconsider each pair of vertices
        for j from 1 to V
            if distance[i][j] > distance[i][k] + distance[k][j]
                distance[i][j] <- distance[i][k] + distance[k][j]
            end if
return distance
```

Create a Thrust program that could perform the V individual stages of the algorithm in parallel, i.e., parallelize the two inner loops of the algorithm.

Advanced topics

Load balancing

11

In this chapter you will:

- Learn how to use static and/or dynamic load balancing for improving the execution time of parallel/multicore programs.
- Understand the trade-off between extra coordination cost and reduced execution time that different load balancing techniques offer.
- Apply divisible load theory techniques to optimally partition the workload to the nodes of a parallel/multicore platform.
- Learn how load balancing can be used to split up workload between heterogeneous computing nodes.

11.1 Introduction

The idea behind load balancing is to shift workload to computational resources that are underutilized, with the ultimate goal of reducing the overall execution time. A lot of research has been devoted to the topic and this trend continues with grid computing and distributed computation. In the realm of multicore computing, though, the notion of load balancing may seem alien. A typical multicore system consists of identical cores that communicate using a shared memory space. The same holds true for GPUs as well. So an even partitioning of the load amongst available cores should suffice to produce a minimum execution time.

However, this argument is easily countered by the fact that we can have a collection of work items, each with different or unknown computation requirements. In that case an even/equal partitioning would be unfeasible. And to top this, a typical multicore system can employ heterogeneous cores, as shown in Fig. 11.1, even without going outside the boundaries of a single system.

If a distributed memory system is employed as an execution platform, communication overheads can become a serious performance concern. In all, properly partitioning the work load is paramount to maximizing performance. Towards this goal, one has to take into consideration as many of the platform (e.g., computational speed) and problem characteristics (e.g., cost of data transmission) as possible. In the following section we will examine both dynamic and static approaches to load balancing. While our coverage is not complete, it is wide enough to allow the reader to make informed decisions about the best design approach for a given problem.

Multicore and GPU Programming. https://doi.org/10.1016/B978-0-12-814120-5.00022-6

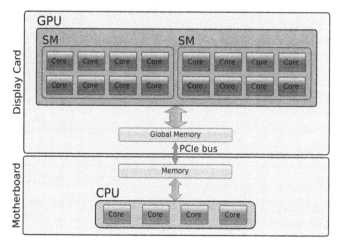

FIGURE 11.1

An example of a single-system heterogeneous computing platform.

Dynamic load balancing refers to a large collection of algorithms that perform or modify load assignments on-line, i.e., during the execution of a program.

Static load balancing, on the other hand, refers to algorithms that assign workload off-line, i.e., either before the beginning or at the very start of the execution.

Dynamic load balancing is characterized by the ability to adapt to changes to the execution platform (e.g., nodes going off-line, communication links becoming congested, etc.) but at the expense of additional coordination overhead. Static load balancing can provide a near-optimal solution to the load partitioning problem, the trade-offs being the inability to adjust to runtime changes and the need to establish intimate knowledge about the performance characteristics of the individual components making up the execution platform.

An example of dynamic load balancing has been presented previously in the master–worker MPI-based implementation of Section 5.25. In this chapter we present a comprehensive view of load balancing, including recent advances in the area of static load balancing.

A particular contribution of this chapter is that CPU-GPU hybrid execution is explicitly tackled.

11.2 Dynamic load balancing: the Linda legacy

Linda is a coordination language that was originally introduced in the mid-1980s [7] as an alternative to message-passing and/or shared-memory operations, which are the primary tools for synchronizing shared-nothing and shared-memory systems, respectively.

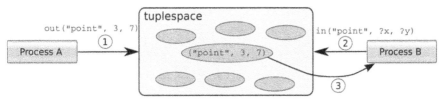

FIGURE 11.2

An example of an interaction of two processes via out (step 1) and in (step 2) tuplespace operations. The "?" prefix represents wildcard components that will be bound once a matching tuple is found (step 3).

Linda creators boast that the language offers orthogonality to computation, completely decoupling the computational nodes in both the spatial and temporal domains. This means that one can have distributed nodes running programs written in different languages and on top of diverse platforms that can coordinate asynchronously. This is accomplished via the use of an entity called **tuplespace**. A tuplespace is a repository of a collection of ordered sequences of data objects called **tuples**. As long as the tuplespace remains operational, nodes can come and go from the computation, thus providing a degree of fault tolerance and adaptability.[1] Linda's tuplespace supports the following basic operations that can be invoked by any process participating in the computation:

- in: Gets/extracts a tuple from tuplespace.
- rd: Reads a tuple but without removing it.
- out: Writes a tuple into tuplespace.
- eval: Creates a new process to evaluate a tuple. The result of the computation is written into tuplespace.

The in operation specifies the tuple to be retrieved using a form of associative memory, whereas some of the fields in the tuple are specified and others are left as wildcards. This form of tuple is called an **antituple** or template. An illustration of the interaction of two processes via a tuplespace is shown in Fig. 11.2. Upon the successful execution of the in operation in Fig. 11.2, variables x and y are set to 3 and 7, respectively. If multiple tuples match the antituple, a randomly chosen one can be returned.

Over the years, more operations have been added to various Linda implementations to enable faster tuplespace manipulation (like, e.g., extracting the "smallest" from a collection of tuples) or non-blocking variants of rd (rdp) and in (inp). Additionally, the tuplespace has been implemented as a single repository or as a distributed one, in order to facilitate better scaling [62].

---

[1] The tuplespace itself is a liability both in terms of fault tolerance and scalability. However, the idea of a distributed tuplespace has been explored in the literature.

In the context of multicore programming, Linda might seem as an overkill given that shared memory allows for substantially faster operations. However, when one considers scaling beyond the boundaries of a single system, Linda can be a viable alternative for coordination and implicit load balancing. Linda does not impose any restrictions on how the tuples are exchanged between the nodes of the system. In fact, MPI can be used quite effectively to that effect!

11.3 Static load balancing: the divisible load theory approach

Dynamic load balancing works reasonably well and it can be (given the right circumstances) the only possible way to accelerate a program using heterogeneous computational resources. There is just one chink in its armor: it requires extensive communication. Communication is a performance drain that needs to be avoided as much as possible.

This performance drain can be minimized if we know a priori, i.e., before the execution or at least before the distribution of the workload, what each of our nodes needs to do. This is the definition of static load balancing. Of course, short of having an oracle, obtaining this knowledge is not a trivial proposition.

Perfect load partitioning can be elusive, but we can still approximate it by a systematic study of the problem at hand.

Divisible load theory[2] (DLT) is a systematic approach to model and solve partitioning and operation sequencing problems for parallel computation and/or data distribution problems in general. Using DLT to load balance a parallel computation hinges on the following conditions:

- The computational load (typically associated with the input data) can be arbitrarily divided and assigned to the nodes of the parallel platform.
- There are no interdependencies between the disjoint parts assigned to the computational nodes.

The above conditions may seem severe, but they are actually honored to a large extent by a big collection of problems that include, among others, low-level image processing [17,58], query processing [17], linear algebra operations (e.g., matrix–vector multiplication) [15,27], DNA sequencing, distributed video-on-demand [18,56], image registration [12], and video transcoding [13,44]. Also, when the first condition is not met, we can still use DLT to derive an approximate solution that can be subsequently adapted to the peculiarities of the problem [16].

The application of DLT typically involves the following steps:

---

[2] Literature also refers to this methodology as divisible load scheduling (DLS), or divisible load analysis (DLA).

- **Modeling costs**: Creating mathematical cost models for each component of a parallel program's execution, including both communication[3] and computation phases.
- **Communication configuration**: Specifying how the load/data reach the compute nodes and whether communication and computation can overlap. This is obviously meaningful in the context of distributed-memory programming. Oddly, this also applies for execution on heterogeneous platforms that combine CPU and GPU resources, since the device's memory is disjoint from the host's memory.
- **Analysis**: Combining the models and the communication setup to predict how the computation load should be partitioned and distributed in order to minimize the overall execution time.

It all comes down to determining the $part_i$ percentages of the computational load that will be assigned to each of the $i \in [0, N - 1]$ nodes of a parallel platform. The parts should be disjoint and sum up to 100%, i.e.,

$$\sum_{i=0}^{N-1} part_i = 1. \tag{11.1}$$

Eq. (11.1) is known as the **normalization equation**.

When communications are involved, it is quite usual that (a) the load/input data are distributed and (b) the output are collected by a central/master node. If the distribution of the load is done in sequence, i.e., each part is communicated sequentially one after the other, then we also have to determine the *optimum distribution/collection sequence* in terms of the overall execution time. This communication configuration is also known as single-port (**1-port**), versus the alternative where all parts are communicated concurrently (**N-port**), in which case the order is irrelevant.

11.3.1 Modeling costs

The problem at hand is how to model the time spent on the individual parts/phases of a parallel program as a function of the problem size. This is similar to how the time and space complexities of algorithms are derived, with one paramount difference: the outcome serves to predict the actual execution time and not for counting the times a basic operation is performed.

The cost models should be preferably linear or affine (i.e., linear with an additional constant overhead). The authors in [19] have shown that divisible loads cannot benefit from parallel execution unless the cost is linearly or close-to-linearly dependent on the size of the data. The reason is that there is a very significant cost left over for the "merging" of the partial results produced by the parallel execution. For

---

[3] Communication cost can be ignored for shared-memory machines. However, shared-memory platforms typically involve homogeneous/identical computing nodes, a scenario which makes static load balancing a piece of cake: just break up the load into equal pieces.

example, if for M inputs we have to perform M^2 operations to calculate the result, splitting the input into N equal pieces and processing them in parallel would result in performing a total of $N\left(\frac{M}{N}\right)^2 = \frac{M^2}{N}$ operations. The resulting deficit of $M^2(1 - \frac{1}{N})$ operations has to be carried out sequentially, which for a large N translates to effectively doing everything sequentially. Of course, this simplistic argument extends to pretty much any workload that is to be executed in parallel.

The counter-argument is that we could devise a data partitioning and distribution method that allows each node to perform $\frac{M^2}{N}$ operations, which means that each node may be receiving more than $\frac{M}{N}$ items. In fact, there have been several publications that show that it is possible to apply DLT for non-linear cost models [35], or even for costs which are approximated by arbitrary continuous functions [36]. The only real shortcoming for non-linear cost models is that they result in complex equations that cannot yield closed-form solutions. Instead, approximations [54] or other heuristic techniques [36] can be employed for solving them.

Amazingly, there have been cases where both non-linear computation loads and closed-form solutions can coexist [15,22], which shows that DLT can be more versatile than originally imagined.

Before we can show an example of how such models are derived, we need to clarify how the volume/size of a computation can be quantified. In the vast majority of cases, this size is intimately connected to the size of the input data. This is not entirely unambiguous though: do we measure the size in number of data items or in bytes? This is not a trivial question: a data representation change, e.g., from `int` to `long`, will double the size in bytes even if the number of items is unchanged.

The answer to this dilemma is simple: because we need to use *compatible* cost models for both the communication and the computation phases and because communication cost is typically expressed as a function of data volume, e.g., bytes, we will also express the computational cost as a function of data volume.

As an example, let us consider the problem of sharpening an image by performing convolution with a *kernel* (a term used to refer to an odd-sized, square, constant matrix). An illustration of the process is shown in Fig. 11.3. Image convolution is discussed in detail in Section 2.2.

The convolution process takes place in the image's luminance plane in order to avoid unwanted chromatic alternations by the sharpen filter. The process is summarized in Listing 11.1.

Listing 11.1: Sequential code for applying a sharpen convolution kernel to an image of resolution $X \times Y$.

```
1   // File : sharpen_sequential/sharper.cpp
2   ...
3      // arrays holding the color components
4      R = new int[X * Y];
5      G = new int[X * Y];
6      B = new int[X * Y];
7      L = new float[X * Y];
8      a = new float[X * Y];
```

```
9    b = new float[X * Y];
10   ...
11   // main body : RGB --> LAB conversion
12   for (j = 0; j < Y; j++)
13     for (i = 0; i < X; i++)
14       {
15         loc = j * X + i;
16         RGB2LAB (R[loc], G[loc], B[loc], L[loc], a[loc], b[loc]);
17       }
18
19   // convolution
20   for (j = 0; j < Y; j++)
21     for (i = 0; i < X; i++)
22       {
23         double temp;
24         temp = 5.0 * pixel_L (i, j);
25         temp -= (pixel_L (i - 1, j) + pixel_L (i + 1, j) + pixel_L (←
             i, j - 1) + pixel_L (i, j + 1));
26
27         loc = j * X + i;
28         new_L[loc] = round (temp);
29         if (new_L[loc] <= 0)  new_L[loc] = 0;
30       }
31
32
33   // LAB --> RGB inverse color conversion
34   for (j = 0; j < Y; j++)
35     for (i = 0; i < X; i++)
36       {
37         loc = j * X + i;
38         LAB2RGB (new_L[loc], a[loc], b[loc], R[loc], G[loc], B[loc])←
             ;
39
40             // Fix conversion under-/overflow which is
41             // just a shortcut replacing proper normalization.
42             // "max_value" represents the maximum value of a
43             // color component
44         if (R[loc] < 0)
45           R[loc] = 0;
46         else if (R[loc] > max_value)
47           R[loc] = max_value;
48         if (G[loc] < 0)
49           G[loc] = 0;
50         else if (G[loc] > max_value)
51           G[loc] = max_value;
52         if (B[loc] < 0)
53           B[loc] = 0;
54         else if (B[loc] > max_value)
55           B[loc] = max_value;
56       }
57   ...
```

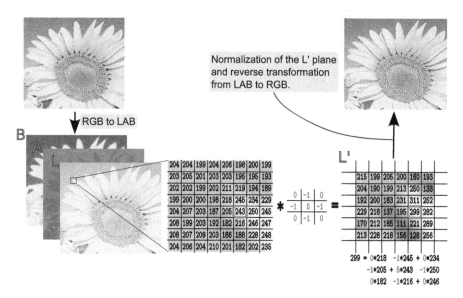

FIGURE 11.3

An illustration of the application of a 3 × 3 convolution kernel for sharpening an image. The calculation for one of the pixels of the "sharpened" luminance plane is shown in detail. A normalization of the new L' plane is required, as the convolution can result in luminance values that are outside the nominal range $[0, 2^n - 1]$, where n are the bits per color component.

The time complexity of the code fragment in Listing 11.1 is clearly a linear function of the number of pixels involved, i.e., $\in \Theta(X \cdot Y)$. A simple timing test also exposes this relationship: measuring the execution time of the above program for different-size (pixel-wise) input images produces the scatter plot of Fig. 11.4.

Fig. 11.4 leaves little doubt on the linear relationship between pixel count and execution time. If we were to express the relationship between execution time and picture size in terms of bytes (i.e., how many bytes it takes to represent the input image), then we could modify the regression equation of Fig. 11.4 as follows:

$$t_{comp} = \frac{1.98 \cdot 10^{-07} \, sec/pixel}{3 \, B/pixel} \cdot L + 0.00028 \, sec \approx 6.6 \cdot 10^{-08} \, sec/B \cdot L, \quad (11.2)$$

where $L = 3X \cdot Y$ is the size of the input, with each pixel being represented by 3 bytes, one per color component.

We should expect to get this linear behavior (bar any discrepancies caused by CPU caches) for *sequential* execution on any contemporary CPU, although the slope of the line would be different based on how fast the CPU is. In general we should expect to get

$$t_{comp} = p \cdot L, \quad (11.3)$$

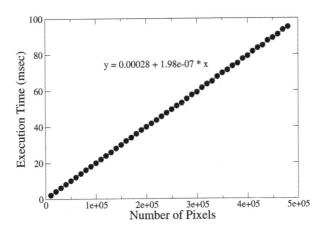

FIGURE 11.4

Execution time of the sharpen convolution in Listing 11.1 on an AMD Ryzen 3900X CPU, versus the input image size. Times are averaged over 100 runs. The regression line coefficients are also shown.

Table 11.1 Symbol table. Examples of typical units are shown.

Symbol	Description	Unit
a	Constant ≥ 1 used in the data distribution cost model. It is greater than 1 when used to account for the extra data that need to be communicated to a node in order to eliminate data interdependencies	N/A
b	The constant overhead associated with load distribution	$Byte$
b_i	A node-specific constant overhead associated with load distribution	$Byte$
c	Constant ≥ 1 used in the result collection cost model that is analogous to a	N/A
d	The constant overhead associated with result collection	$Byte$
e_i	A load-independent computational overhead at node P_i	$Byte$
L	The load that has to be processed/volume of input data	$Byte$
l	Inversely proportional to the speed of the communication links in a homogeneous network	sec/B
l_i	Inversely proportional to the speed of the link connecting P_i and its load-originating node	sec/B
p	Inversely proportional to the processing speed of a processor in a homogeneous platform	sec/B
p_i	Inversely proportional to the speed of P_i	sec/B
$part_i$	Part of the load L assigned to P_i, hence $0 \leq part_i \leq 1$; P_i's total load assignment is $part_i L + e_i$	N/A

where p is a node-specific constant that could be regarded as being inversely proportional to the speed of a node. Table 11.1 summarizes the symbols used in this chapter and their semantics.

Thus, if we were to assign $0 \leq part_i \leq 1$ of an image to a node P_i, we would expect the computation to last for

$$t_{comp}^{(i)} = p_i \cdot part_i \cdot L. \qquad (11.4)$$

One could argue that the model of Eq. (11.4) is lacking: what about the cost of allocating all those big arrays that hold the color components? We can augment our model to accommodate any residual costs e_i, which are *independent of the input*:

$$t_{comp}^{(i)} = p_i(part_i \cdot L + e_i). \qquad (11.5)$$

The overhead e_i is assumed to be node-specific for extra flexibility.

Sending $part_i \cdot L$ volume of data to a remote node and then collecting the outcome of the computation could entail some significant communication cost. Communication cost is generally not application-specific in the sense that what matters is the communicated volume and not the semantics of what is communicated. Thus, a communication cost model needs to be derived only once for a particular installation, as long as the hardware and software communication stack (including any OS and user-space libraries) remain unchanged.

Communication cost can be measured with the assistance of a "ping-pong" program that measures the time elapsed between sending a message, having it bounce at its destination, and receiving it back at its origin. By varying the message size, one can estimate the transmission rate l^4 as the regression line intercept[5]:

$$t_{comm} = l \cdot V, \qquad (11.6)$$

where V is the volume of data communicated.

Eq. (11.6) requires a number of refinements before it is suitable for describing the communication costs in our example. Firstly, it falls short of describing the distribution cost. As shown in Fig. 11.5, because the calculation of each new luminance value of a pixel requires four more surrounding pixels, processing $part_i L$ input requires the presence in node P_i of extra data. Depending on the application, these extra data could be a percent $a - 1$ of the actual data to be processed, or a fixed overhead. In the first case we only need to multiply $part_i L$ by a to find the distribution com-

---

[4] l is actually the inverse of the communication speed as it is expressed in time/volume units, e.g., sec/Byte.

[5] The exact shape of the curve one gets from such an experiment depends heavily on the MPI implementation, the hardware testbed, and the range of message sizes tested. For example, in the measurements reported in [51], bandwidth rose and fell with increasing message sizes. Amazingly, Rabenseifner et al. report cases where internode communications beat intrasocket ones! Fortunately, for an application where the message sizes are not too diverse, we can get a piece-wise linear curve, making the use of a constant l a good approximation.

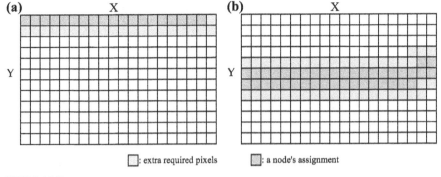

(a) X

Y

(b) X

Y

□: extra required pixels   ▨: a node's assignment

FIGURE 11.5

Two examples of pixel regions that could be assigned to a remote node for processing. Case (a) involves a boundary row of pixels while (b) shows a more generic case. The highlighted regions surrounding the assigned pixels are also required for a convolution with a 3 × 3 kernel.

munication demands: $t_{comm} = l \cdot a \cdot part_i L$. In the latter case, we could incorporate the extra cost into an additional constant b: $t_{comm} = l(part_i L + b)$.

Our image sharpening example does not seem to fit either of the two cases, as the extra data are neither constant (in Fig. 11.5(a) only an extra row is required, while in Fig. 11.5(b) two are needed instead) nor proportional to the $part_i L$.

A simple solution can be given to this problem if we assume that all the nodes will require two extra rows of pixels, thus having $b = 2 \cdot 3 \cdot X$ (each row has X pixels, each with three color components). We can also be more specific if we assume that $b_0 = b_{N-1} = 3 \cdot X$ and $b_j = 2 \cdot 3 \cdot X$ for $\forall j \neq 0, N-1$, if P_0 gets the top and P_{N-1} the bottom rows.

The alternative (i.e., using a) is also possible if we expect to get more or less equal, row-wise partitioning of the data among our N compute nodes. Then, each would process approximately $\frac{Y}{N}$ rows while requiring two extra rows of pixels. Based on this assumption we could have $a = 1 + \frac{2}{\frac{Y}{N}} = 1 + \frac{2N}{Y}$. In the next section we will be using b to refine our communication cost model for the image sharpening example.

In general, we will employ the following data distribution cost model[6]:

$$t_{distr}^{(i)} = l_i(a \cdot part_i \cdot L + b),\tag{11.7}$$

where l_i is the inverse of the communication speed of the link connecting the master node and node P_i.

---

[6] An alternative formulation would be $t_{distr} = l \cdot a \cdot part_i \cdot L + b$, where b is expressed in time units instead of data volume units. However, these are not two different models, but rather variations of the same one. The added benefit of Eq. (11.7) is that it is more convenient for the analysis step shown in Section 11.3.3.

The same treatment should be extended to the data collection cost, although the constants need not be the same:

$$t_{coll}^{(i)} = l_i(c \cdot part_i \cdot L + d). \tag{11.8}$$

The above example serves to show both the kind of cost models we can use in DLT analysis[7] and the process through which they can be derived, i.e., benchmarking. Eqs. (11.5), (11.7), and (11.8) constitute generic costs models that can be customized to reflect specific scenarios. In the following section we show how these models can provide us with both optimization guidelines and an extraordinary insight into the performance behavior of parallel platforms, as they can yield closed-form solutions to the partitioning and distribution problems.

An alternative to establishing the cost models off-line (before parallel execution) is to derive them during runtime. For example, it is possible that the execution cost varies wildly based on the quality of the input data and not just their volume (e.g., video transcoding cost may depend on the genre of the input movie, e.g., adventure, animation, romance, etc., and not just on the resolution and frame rate [13]). Such a scenario would make predetermined model parameters inaccurate, and these would in turn compromise the efficiency of the partitioning.

Runtime model calculation could involve the separation of the execution into two phases (three or more phases may be used to hide the delay between measuring the initial performance and calculating the model parameters and resulting partitioning by the master): an initial benchmarking phase that serves to calculate the cost models and a second processing phase where the remaining workload is partitioned appropriately [13,36].

11.3.2 Communication configuration

Eqs. (11.5), (11.7), and (11.8) constitute generic enough models to capture the computation and communication cost of many applications. Before we can use them to solve the partitioning problem, we must determine the communication setup of the application. We have to answer three questions:

1. How many compute nodes can receive load and return results simultaneously? Possible answers are one (*1-port*) or all (*N-port*). Using a single-port configuration is not really a hardware limitation, but rather a software design feature. Contemporary networking hardware and software stacks allow the buffering and sending of messages to multiple destinations concurrently. However, if this is done via time division multiplexing, communication costs become larger as the capacity of the communication medium has to be shared. In general, an evaluation of possible design approaches should be carried out.

---

[7] Quadratic and other generally non-linear models can be also employed [15,22,35]. The trade-off is a harder-to-perform analysis.

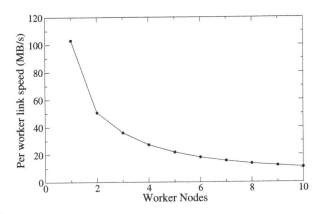

FIGURE 11.6

Average communication speed per node for an N-port setup, for an intranet of PC workstations connected over 1 Gbps Ethernet.

Fig. 11.6 shows the test results of measuring communication speed on an intranet of Linux-running machines connected with 1 Gbps Ethernet. The measurements were conducted over 100 runs with a message size of 10^7 bytes sent via `MPI_Isend` calls. A modified "ping-pong" program was used to measure the times.

2. Is it possible to start the computation prior to the completion of the transfer of the load assigned to a node? If the answer is negative we have *block-type* tasks; if it is positive we have *stream-type* tasks. The decision between the two options depends on the software architecture and the nature of the input data. Stream-type computation is generally more complex to set up and run correctly, as one has to ensure that the part(s) of the input data required for processing are available at the proper time.

3. In how many phases is the distribution and/or collection taking place? In the simplest of cases we have only one phase, but we can also employ multiple ones, especially when block-type computations are involved, in order to minimize the time before the computations can commence. The former case is called *single-installment*, while the latter is called *multiple-installment* distribution. Multiple-installment distribution can be considered a form of "streaming," as it allows the computation to start before all the assigned data become available at a node. Installments may be fixed to an a priori specified size (e.g., the data are split into k equal pieces [49]), or they could be determined based on the optimization of an objective function [12].

Multiple-installment strategies are also referred to in the literature as "multi-round" strategies. In [64] the authors show that the multiple-installment problem is in its general form NP-hard (via reduction from 2-partition). Fortunately, problem-specific conditions (e.g., when no result collection is required) or model simplifications (e.g., assuming homogeneous communication links) allow us to solve this

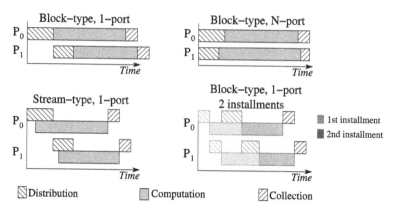

FIGURE 11.7

Gantt charts of four samples from the plethora of possible communication configurations. The graphs are not supposed to be comparable as far as their duration is concerned. Also the optimality of the sequences is not considered here.

problem, either in closed form or using some other exact (e.g., linear programming) or approximation technique.

Fig. 11.7 shows contrasting examples of a subset of the possible arrangements. The one to be selected for the final analysis step depends on the software architecture and the application at hand. For example, stream-type tasks could be used for our image sharpening example: assuming a row-wise distribution of an image, the arrival of three rows is sufficient for the start of the computation if a 3×3 kernel is used. The problem is writing a program that can figure out when rows become "locally" available, i.e., ready for processing.

We might be tempted to conclude that there are only eight[8] possible configurations that need to be examined. However, when multiple installments are used, the number of installments becomes a factor.[9] And the questions do not stop there: Are all the installments identical? Does the first installment need to carry additional data or not? Is the collection also performed in multiple installments? Are all nodes available from the beginning of the execution, or might they become available some time later? Is the master node participating in the processing of the load? If it does, does it have a co-processor that handles all the communications (i.e., equipped with a communication front-end) while it is processing, or does it have to wait until all data are sent out to the workers before it can process its share of the load?

These questions clearly illustrate that there are many possibilities, well beyond the product of the three binary alternatives listed above. A clear understanding of

---

[8] Each of the three questions posed earlier has two possible answers, for a total of 2^3 combinations.
[9] Another dilemma pops up: How many installments are optimal?

the parallel platform and the desired software design is critical for setting the proper specification in this step.

11.3.3 **Analysis**

Performing analysis using equations (11.5), (11.7), and (11.8) can be a challenge. These equations cannot produce closed-form solutions for all the possible communication configurations in their generic form; they need to be simplified.

The procedure used for the analysis is more or less the same regardless of the communication configuration:

1. Establish a relation between $part_i$s and $part_0$.
2. Use the normalization equation (11.1) to derive a closed-form solution for $part_0$.
3. Use the solution to $part_0$ to calculate the other $part_i$s and the overall execution time.[10]

In this section we analyze two cases:

- *N-port, block-type, single installment*: This is a commonly used communication configuration. It is precisely the setup used by a master node that makes MPI_Isend() calls to distribute the input data to the workers of a distributed-memory parallel machine.
- *1-port, block-type, single installment*: We derive the solution for the kernel convolution (e.g., image sharpening) example used in this section. For single-port setups, the optimum sequence also has to be established. This is a more intricate procedure, for which our simple example is well suited to show how it can be performed.

In both cases we assume that the parallel platform is made up of a master and multiple worker nodes arranged in a single-level tree with the master at the root, as shown in Fig. 11.8. We also assume that the master is participating in the computation and it is equipped with a communication front-end, allowing it to compute while communicating with the workers.

11.3.3.1 N-Port, block-type, single-installment solution

Our goal is to minimize the overall execution time. It is obvious that the only arrangement capable of achieving this is the one shown in Fig. 11.9. It is easy to prove that any other configuration that allows nodes to terminate at different times is liable to further reduction in execution time, by taking load from the nodes that finish last and assigning it to the nodes that finish first. So the only optimum configuration is the one where all nodes finish at the same time.

---

[10] **Insight**: the normalization equation and the relationships that connect $part_i$s with $part_0$ or other $part_j$s form a sparse system of N linear equations. This sequence of steps uses the peculiarities of our settings to avoid a typical linear-algebra solution to the system (e.g., using Gauss–Jordan elimination), while also providing the formulas that allow further study of the parallel platform.

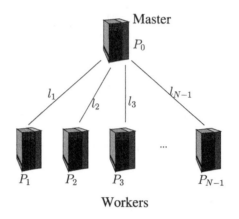

FIGURE 11.8

The target platform for our DLT analysis is composed of N nodes, arranged in a single level tree. P_0 is assumed to serve as the master.

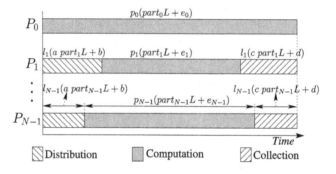

FIGURE 11.9

Optimum configuration for the case of N-port communications and block-type computation.

Forcing the collective duration of all the operations at nodes P_i and P_j for $i, j \in [0, N-1]$ to be equal produces the following:

$$t_{distr}^{(i)} + t_{comp}^{(i)} + t_{coll}^{(i)} = t_{distr}^{(j)} + t_{comp}^{(j)} + t_{coll}^{(j)} = t_{comp}^{(0)} \Rightarrow$$
$$l_i(a\ part_i L + b) + p_i(part_i L + e_i) + l_i(c\ part_i L + d) =$$
$$l_j(a\ part_j L + b) + p_j(part_j L + e_j) + l_j(c\ part_j L + d) =$$
$$p_0(part_0 L + e_0), \quad (11.9)$$

which can be rewritten as

$$part_i L(l_i(a+c) + p_i) + l_i(b+d) + p_i e_i = p_0(part_0 L + e_0) \Rightarrow$$

$$part_i = part_0 \frac{p_0}{l_i(a+c) + p_i} + \frac{p_0 e_0 - p_i e_i - l_i(b+d)}{L(l_i(a+c) + p_i)}. \quad (11.10)$$

By replacing the $part_j$ components of the normalization equation with Eq. (11.10), we get

$$\sum_{j=0}^{N-1} part_j = 1 \Rightarrow$$

$$part_0 \left(1 + \sum_{j=1}^{N-1} \frac{p_0}{l_j(a+c) + p_j}\right) + \sum_{j=1}^{N-1} \frac{p_0 e_0 - p_j e_j - l_j(b+d)}{L(l_j(a+c) + p_j)} = 1 \Rightarrow$$

$$part_0 = \frac{1 + L^{-1} \sum_{j=1}^{N-1} \frac{p_j e_j - p_0 e_0 + l_j(b+d)}{l_j(a+c) + p_j}}{p_0 \sum_{j=0}^{N-1} \left(l_j(a+c) + p_j\right)^{-1}}, \quad (11.11)$$

where in the denominator, 1 is absorbed in the summation with the assumption that $l_0 = 0$ (obviously there is no communication cost from P_0 to P_0).

Eqs. (11.11) and (11.10) allow the calculation of the optimum partitioning and the overall execution duration in linear time $\Theta(N)$. We can also consider that the whole system is behaving as a single equivalent node with characteristics $p_{equiv} = p_0 \, part_0$ and $e_{equiv} = \frac{e_0}{part_0}$.

Both equations allow the production of negative results for $part_i$s. Such an outcome would signify that the corresponding nodes are too slow to be assigned any load. The problem could also lie with slow communication links. This brings up another facet of the load balancing problem that we did not mention before: *finding the optimum set of nodes* on which to run the program. The beauty of Eqs. (11.11) and (11.10) is that they are cheap enough to evaluate multiple times; as many times as would be required by a heuristic or even an exhaustive/brute-force algorithm (for small N) in order to determine this set. We leave the design of such algorithms as an exercise.

If the master node were to not participate in the processing of the workload (i.e., $part_0 = 0$), then we would have for $\forall i \neq j$ and $i, j \neq 0$

$$t_{total} = l_i(a \, part_i L + b) + p_i(part_i L + e_i) + l_i(c \, part_i L + d) =$$
$$l_j(a \, part_j L + b) + p_j(part_j L + e_j) + l_j(c \, part_j L + d) \Rightarrow$$
$$part_i = part_j \frac{l_j(a+c) + p_j}{l_i(a+c) + p_i} + \frac{p_j e_j - p_i e_i + (l_j - l_i)(b+d)}{L(l_i(a+c) + p_i)}, \quad (11.12)$$

which produces for $part_1$ via the normalization equation

$$\sum_{j=0}^{N-1} part_j = 1 \Rightarrow$$

$$part_1 = \frac{1 + L^{-1} \sum_{j=2}^{N-1} \frac{p_j e_j - p_1 e_1 + (l_j - l_1)(b+d)}{l_j(a+c) + p_j}}{(l_1(a+c) + p_1) \sum_{j=1}^{N-1} \left(l_j(a+c) + p_j \right)^{-1}}. \quad (11.13)$$

11.3.3.2 One-port, block-type, single-installment solution

The generic cost models of Eqs. (11.5), (11.7), and (11.8) can be adapted for our kernel convolution example by setting $a = 1$, $c = 1$, $d = 0$, and $e_i = 0$[11] as per the discussion in Section 11.3.1. If we also assume homogeneous communication links $l_i \equiv l$, our models are simplified to

$$t_{comp}^{(i)} = p_i \cdot part_i \cdot L, \quad (11.14)$$

$$t_{distr}^{(i)} = l \cdot (part_i \cdot L + b_i), \quad (11.15)$$

$$t_{coll}^{(i)} = l \cdot part_i \cdot L. \quad (11.16)$$

There is a small change in Eq. (11.15) relevant to Eq. (11.7), in that a node-specific b_i constant is used. In normal circumstances making the cost models more complex than necessary would be ill-advised, since doing so can make our work much more challenging. The reason for this change will become apparent later.

The issue with 1-port communications is that the optimum distribution and collection sequences have to be established. For a platform with N workers, the possible configurations are $(N!)^2$, as each of the distribution and collection sequences can be done in $N!$ different ways!

We consider the problem in its simplest possible form, when only two nodes are involved. In the following discussion, and until explicitly mentioned otherwise, we purposefully ignore the contribution of the master node, as it does not participate in the distribution/collection sequence.

For two workers there are only four possible configurations, as shown in Fig. 11.10. This is a much easier-to-tackle setting that a generic N-node platform, and it can provide us with useful insights about the optimum sequence.

The overall duration of each configuration can be found by calculating $part_1$ from the system of equations produced by combining the normalization Eq. (11.1) and one of:

$$p_1 \, part_1 L = l(part_2 L + b_2) + p_2 \, part_2 L + l \, part_2 L \quad \text{for conf. #1}, \quad (11.17)$$

---

[11] Despite the extra memory allocation overhead, we can assume that the allocation takes place during the initialization of our program, prior to the distribution of the input data. Hence, our computational cost adheres to the model we derived from test data in Eq. (11.2).

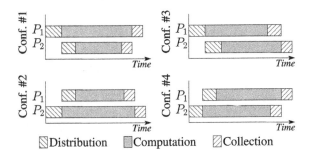

FIGURE 11.10

The four possible distribution/collection sequences for the case of two nodes sharing a load L.

$$p_2 \, part_2 L = l(part_1 L + b_1) + p_1 \, part_1 L + l \, part_1 L \quad \text{for conf. \#2,} \quad (11.18)$$

$$p_1 \, part_1 L + l \, part_1 L = l(part_2 L + b_2) + p_2 \, part_2 L \quad \text{for conf. \#3,} \quad (11.19)$$

$$p_2 \, part_2 L + l \, part_2 L = l(part_1 L + b_1) + p_1 \, part_1 L \quad \text{for conf. \#4.} \quad (11.20)$$

The above equations can be derived directly from the Gantt charts in Fig. 11.10. The same applies for the calculation of the overall execution times (the actual solutions are not shown due to their length):

$$t_{\#1} = l(part_1 L + b_1) + p_1 \, part_1 L + l \, part_1 L, \quad (11.21)$$

$$t_{\#2} = l((1 - part_1)L + b_2) + p_2 \, (1 - part_1)L + l(1 - part_1)L, \quad (11.22)$$

$$t_{\#3} = l(part_1 L + b_1) + p_1 \, part_1 L + l \, L, \quad (11.23)$$

$$t_{\#4} = l((1 - part_1)L + b_2) + p_2(1 - part_1)L + l \, L. \quad (11.24)$$

Calculating the differences in overall execution times yields[12]

$$t_{\#3} - t_{\#1} = -\frac{l^2 \, (L + b_2)}{p_1 + p_2 + 2 \, l} < 0, \quad (11.25)$$

$$t_{\#4} - t_{\#2} = -\frac{l^2 \, (L + b_1)}{p_1 + p_2 + 2 \, l} < 0, \quad (11.26)$$

[12] A computer algebra system such as Maxima (http://maxima.sourceforge.net) can produce the desired results quickly and error-free.

$$t_{\#3} - t_{\#4} = -\frac{l \; (b_2 p_2 - b_1 p_1 + b_2 \, l - b_1 \, l)}{p_1 + p_2 + 2 \, l}. \tag{11.27}$$

The sign of the first two differences is clearly negative, which means that the optimum configuration can be either #3 or #4. If the two nodes are sorted in ascending order of their $b_i (p_i + l)$ property, then Eq. (11.27) becomes negative, and configuration #3 is the optimum one. For two identical b_i constants, we only need to sort the nodes in descending order of their computing power as expressed by p_is.

One could speculate at this point that the same should be true for an arbitrary number of nodes. We will proceed to prove that this is true, in a proper mathematical fashion. The impatient reader may choose to skip the lemmas and theorem that follow and see the net outcome on page 910, in the form of Eq. (11.39).

We can summarize our findings so far with the following lemma.

Lemma 11.3.1. *Given two nodes P_1 and P_2 that are to perform kernel convolution, the minimum execution time is achieved using a configuration where the nodes receive their input and send back the results in ascending order of their $b_i (p_i + l)$ property.*

Proof. The proof is given in the form of Eqs. (11.25), (11.26), and (11.27) shown above. $\qquad\square$

For the discussion that follows we will assume that $b_2(p_2 + l) \geq b_1(p_1 + l)$, making configuration #3 the optimum one.

The overall execution time for configuration #3 can be found to be

$$t_{\#3} = \frac{p_1 p_2 L + 2 \, l \; p_2 L + 2 \, l \; p_1 L + 3 \, l^2 L + b_1 p_2 l + l \, b_2 p_1 + l \, b_1 p_1 + b_2 l^2 + 2 \, b_1 l^2}{p_1 + p_2 + 2 \, l}, \tag{11.28}$$

which can be rewritten in the following form:

$$t_{\#3} = l(L + b_1 + b_2) + \frac{p_1 \; p_2 \; L - l^2 \; L - b_2 \, l \; p_2 - b_2 \, l^2}{(p_1 + p_2 + 2 \, l) \; L} L + l \, L. \tag{11.29}$$

Eq. (11.29) expresses the total time as the time it would take a node **equivalent** (a.k.a. aggregate) to the two original ones to process the input at the same time, while incurring the exact same communication overhead:

$$t_{distr}^{(equiv)} = l(L + b_1 + b_2), \tag{11.30}$$

$$t_{coll}^{(equiv)} = l \, L, \tag{11.31}$$

$$t_{comp}^{(equiv)} = L \frac{p_1 p_2 L - l^2 L - l \, b_2 p_2 - b_2 l^2}{(p_1 + p_2 + 2 \, l) \, L}. \tag{11.32}$$

We could describe the equivalent node as having $p_{equiv} = \frac{p_1 p_2 L - l^2 L - l\, b_2 p_2 - b_2 l^2}{(p_1 + p_2 + 2\,l)L}$ and $b_{equiv} = b_1 + b_2$ (this is where the switch from b to b_i in Eq. (11.15) comes in handy).

The equivalent node also has the following property:

$$b_2(p_2 + l) - b_{equiv}(p_{equiv} + l) =$$
$$\frac{(p_2 + l)\,(L(b_2(p_2 + l) - b_1(p_1 + l)) + b_2 l(b_1 + b_2))}{(p_1 + p_2 + 2\,l)\,L} > 0. \quad (11.33)$$

The outcome of Eq. (11.33) is positive as by definition we have $b_2(p_2 + l) \geq b_1(p_1 + l)$.

We have just added one more component in our mathematical arsenal that will assist us in proving how to optimize N nodes.

Lemma 11.3.2. *Given two nodes P_1 and P_2, assumed without loss of generality to have $b_1(p_1 + l) \leq b_2(p_2 + l)$, that are to perform kernel convolution on L data in an optimum configuration, they collectively behave as an equivalent node P_{equiv} that incurs the same communication costs and sports properties $p_{equiv} = \frac{p_1 p_2 L - l^2 L - l\, b_2 p_2 - b_2 l^2}{(p_1 + p_2 + 2\,l)L}$ and $b_{equiv} = b_1 + b_2$, such that $b_{equiv}(p_{equiv} + l) \leq b_2(p_2 + l)$.*

Proof. The proof is given in the form of Eqs. (11.29) and (11.33) shown above. □

The process of replacing a pair of nodes with an equivalent one can be applied iteratively when an arbitrary number of nodes exist. We can assume without loss of generality that after sorting the nodes in ascending order of their $b_i(p_i + l)$ property, we get the sequence P_1, P_2, P_3, etc. (after all, it is just a labeling issue). Then, we can replace the pair of P_1, P_2 with their equivalent $P_{equiv}^{(1,2)}$, then the pair of $P_{equiv}^{(1,2)}$, P_3 with their equivalent $P_{equiv}^{(1,2,3)}$, and so on. Configuration #3 will remain the optimum in every case as the new equivalent nodes preserve the sorting order according to Lemma 11.3.2.

This constitutes the basis of our proof for the optimum sequence theorem.

Theorem 11.3.3. *Given a single-level tree of N worker nodes and a load L that is big enough to guarantee the usage of all the nodes (more on this later), the optimum sequence for load distribution and result collection in 1-port, block-type computation of kernel convolution is produced by sorting the nodes in non-decreasing order of the quantity $b_i(p_i + l)$.*

Proof. We will prove this theorem by induction. We have already proven the theorem for $N = 2$ via Lemma 11.3.1. We will assume that it is true for k nodes and show that it holds for $k + 1$. We can assume without loss of generality that after sorting the k nodes in ascending order of their $b_i(p_i + l)$ property, we get the sequence $P_1, P_2, ..., P_k$. The first k nodes can be replaced by their equivalent P_{equiv}, for which we have two possibilities: (a) $b_{equiv}(p_{equiv} + l) < b_{k+1}(p_{k+1} + l)$ or (b) $b_{equiv}(p_{equiv} + l) \geq b_{k+1}(p_{k+1} + l)$.

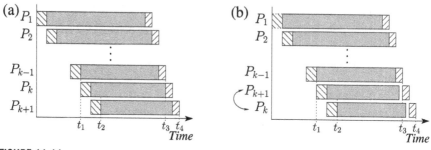

FIGURE 11.11

Switching the order of nodes P_k and P_{k+1} in the distribution and collection sequences reduces their computation time, while keeping their communication time unchanged, if $b_k(p_k + l) > b_{k+1}(p_{k+1} + l)$.

In case (a), configuration #3 is optimum for the pair of P_{equiv}, P_{k+1} and we have either $b_k(p_k + l) \leq b_{k+1}(p_{k+1} + l)$, which satisfies the theorem, or $b_k(p_k + l) > b_{k+1}(p_{k+1} + l)$. If the latter is true we can switch the order of P_k and P_{k+1} in the distribution and collection sequence and reduce the overall execution time of the part of the load that is assigned to them. As depicted in Fig. 11.11, rearranging the P_k and P_{k+1} nodes (going from the state shown in Fig. 11.11(a) to the state in Fig. 11.11(b)), communication times are unchanged ($t_2 - t_1$ for distribution and $t_4 - t_3$ for collection), but changing the configuration of the pair from – what is effectively – #4 to #3 reduces the pair's computation time. This means that an overall redistribution of the load is possible that will reduce the overall execution time.

This can continue until we find a node P_X that satisfies $b_X(p_X + l) \leq b_{k+1}(p_{k+1} + l)$ or P_{k+1} becomes the first node in the sequence, which proves the theorem.

In case (b), configuration #4 is optimum and thus P_{k+1} should precede P_{equiv} in the sequence. If $b_{k+1}(p_{k+1} + l) \leq b_1(p_1 + l)$, the theorem is satisfied. Otherwise, we can follow the same process as before but in reverse, e.g., swapping P_{k+1} and P_1 if $b_1(p_1 + l) > b_{k+1}(p_{k+1} + l)$, etc. The swapping of nodes in the sequence can only stop when the order speculated by the theorem holds, which completes the proof. $\quad\square$

Theorem 11.3.3 allows us to derive a solution beyond the two-node case. For every pair of successive nodes P_i and P_{i+1} in the distribution/collection sequence, the following should hold:

$$t_{comp}^{(i)} + t_{coll}^{(i)} = t_{distr}^{(i+1)} + t_{comp}^{(i+1)} \Rightarrow$$

$$p_i \, part_i L + l \, part_i L = l(part_{i+1}L + b_{i+1}) + p_{i+1} \, part_{i+1} L \Rightarrow$$

$$part_{i+1} = part_i \frac{p_i + l}{p_{i+1} + l} - \frac{lb_{i+1}}{L(p_{i+1} + l)}. \quad (11.34)$$

Now that we have figured out the optimum sequence of the workers, we can also consider the role of the master node. If P_0 is participating in the computation, then

Eq. (11.34) holds for $i \in [1, N - 2]$ and we also have the following relation between P_0 and P_1:

$$t_{comp}^{(0)} = t_{distr}^{(1)} + t_{comp}^{(1)} + \sum_{j=1}^{N-1} t_{coll}^{(j)} \Rightarrow$$

$$p_0 \, part_0 L = l(part_1 L + b_1) + p_1 \, part_1 L + l \, L(1 - part_0) \Rightarrow$$

$$part_0 L(p_0 + l) = part_1 L(p_1 + l) + l(b_1 + L) \Rightarrow$$

$$part_1 = part_0 \frac{p_0 + l}{p_1 + l} - \frac{lb_1}{L(p_1 + l)} - \frac{l}{p_1 + l}. \quad (11.35)$$

Eq. (11.35) allows us to express the other $part_i$s as a function of $part_0$:

$$part_2 = part_1 \frac{p_1 + l}{p_2 + l} - \frac{lb_2}{L(p_2 + l)} =$$

$$\left(part_0 \frac{p_0 + l}{p_1 + l} - \frac{l(b_1 + L)}{L(p_1 + l)} \right) \frac{p_1 + l}{p_2 + l} - \frac{lb_2}{L(p_2 + l)} =$$

$$part_0 \frac{p_0 + l}{p_2 + l} - \frac{lb_1}{L(p_2 + l)} - \frac{lb_2}{L(p_2 + l)} - \frac{l}{p_2 + l}, \quad (11.36)$$

$$part_3 = part_2 \frac{p_2 + l}{p_3 + l} - \frac{lb_3}{L(p_3 + l)} =$$

$$\left(part_0 \frac{p_0 + l}{p_2 + l} - \frac{l(b_1 + L)}{L(p_2 + l)} - \frac{lb_2}{L(p_2 + l)} \right) \frac{p_2 + l}{p_3 + l} - \frac{lb_3}{L(p_3 + l)} =$$

$$part_0 \frac{p_0 + l}{p_3 + l} - \frac{l(b_1 + L)}{L(p_3 + l)} - \frac{lb_2}{L(p_3 + l)} - \frac{lb_3}{L(p_3 + l)} =$$

$$part_0 \frac{p_0 + l}{p_3 + l} - \frac{lb_1}{L(p_3 + l)} - \frac{lb_2}{L(p_3 + l)} - \frac{lb_3}{L(p_3 + l)} - \frac{l}{(p_3 + l)} =$$

$$part_0 \frac{p_0 + l}{p_3 + l} - \frac{l}{L(p_3 + l)} \sum_{j=1}^{3} b_j - \frac{l}{p_3 + l}, \quad (11.37)$$

or in general

$$part_k = part_0 \frac{p_0 + l}{p_k + l} - \frac{l}{L(p_k + l)} \sum_{j=1}^{k} b_j - \frac{l}{p_k + l}. \quad (11.38)$$

The normalization equation can then provide us with the answer for $part_0$:

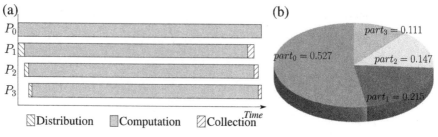

FIGURE 11.12

(a) Gantt chart for a four-node heterogeneous platform example that performs kernel image convolution as predicted by DLT-based analysis. (b) Pie chart of the percentages $part_i$.

$$\sum_{k=0}^{N-1} part_k = 1 \Rightarrow$$

$$part_0 \sum_{k=0}^{N-1} \frac{p_0 + l}{p_k + l} - \sum_{k=1}^{N-1} \left(\frac{l}{L(p_k + l)} \sum_{j=1}^{k} b_j \right) - \sum_{k=1}^{N-1} \frac{l}{p_k + l} = 1 \Rightarrow$$

$$part_0 = \frac{1 + \sum_{k=1}^{N-1} \left(\frac{l}{L(p_k+l)} \sum_{j=1}^{k} b_j \right) + \sum_{k=1}^{N-1} \frac{l}{p_k+l}}{(p_0 + l) \sum_{k=0}^{N-1} (p_k + l)^{-1}}. \quad (11.39)$$

Eq. (11.39) allows the calculation of $part_0$ and the overall execution time (equal to $p_0 part_0 L$) in linear time complexity $\Theta(N)$.

As an example of the application of our analysis, we consider an instance of the kernel convolution problem with the following characteristics:

- A parallel platform made up of four nodes, with $p_0 = 6.6 \cdot 10^{-8}$, $p_1 = 2 \cdot (6.6 \cdot 10^{-8})$, $p_2 = 3 \cdot (6.6 \cdot 10^{-8})$, and $p_3 = 4 \cdot (6.6 \cdot 10^{-8})$, all in sec/B. P_0 is considered the master node holding the input data. The parameters are derived from the result reported in Eq. (11.2), in order to represent a heterogeneous machine.
- An input image of UHD resolution, i.e., 3840 × 2160 pixels, with 24-bit color accuracy. This translates to $L = 3840 * 2160 * 3 \; B = 23.73$ MiB.
- A network with 102.98 MiB/sec speed, or $l = 9.26 \cdot 10^{-9}$ sec/B.
- The cost model is completed with $b_1 = b_2 = 2 \cdot 3 \cdot 3840 \; B$ and $b_3 = 3 \cdot 3840 \; B$, given the length of the image row.

Fig. 11.12 illustrates the results produced by Eqs. (11.39) and (11.38). It is obvious that in real life these results can only be expected in the most ideal of situations. The side effects of additional workloads, network activity, CPU cache utilization, and other factors will invariably cause deviations from this ideal scenario.

This weakness does not diminish the usefulness of DLT as a modeling and load balancing tool. The beauty of these equations is that they can be quickly evaluated to either guide partitioning decisions or even allow performance estimation at an abstract level.

11.3.4 Summary – short literature review

The three-stage process outlined above can provide elegant closed-form solutions that can guide the design of both parallel software and hardware. It is not uncommon in DLT literature to encounter optimal arrangement theorems where the authors derive the optimal hardware configuration in regard to the examined application or setting [54,57]. These typically come in the form of how to pair communication and computation resources.

However, this three-stage process is not rigid. It is possible that the outcome of the modeling and communication configuration phases does not allow the derivation of analytical solutions. In such cases, researchers have resorted to linear programming [12,28], genetic algorithms [11], or other heuristics [37] in order to get the desired partitioning and operations schedules.

Fig. 11.13 puts into perspective samples of DLT domain publications, relative to the design choices outlined above.

Recent research efforts have focused, apart from the ever growing set of applications targeted, on the following key areas:

(a) Non-linear cost functions: A number of applications, including classical problems such as, e.g., matrix multiplication or sorting, do not conform to a linear or an affine cost model. Expanding the DLT framework to cover these cases can significantly enhance the impact of the methodology.

(b) Multiple load-originating nodes: A typical characteristic in networking, but also in parallel file systems, is that data may reside in disjoint nodes. Taking into account this platform characteristic changes significantly how load distribution should be conducted, which is a very significant performance parameter.

(c) Processing of multiple loads: Computation clouds and high-performance computing facilities employ job queues in order to perform long-term scheduling. Processing multiple loads is a different problem than processing a single one, needing to take into consideration, among other things, resource consumption and node release times, i.e., when machines become free to process something new.

Beaumont et al. have shown in [19] that non-linear cost functions present a problem for parallel execution, especially in the context of a map-reduce pattern. The reduction phase, which is typically less amenable to parallelization than mapping, can negate any gains that the parallel execution of the mapping phase may yield. Beaumont et al. show that problems can be overcome by replicating data, e.g., sending "augmented" datasets to the compute nodes. This effectively shifts the burden from computation to communication.

One of the first breakthroughs came from Hung and Robertazzi [35], who were able to use quadratic and power-of-x computational cost models for multi- and single-

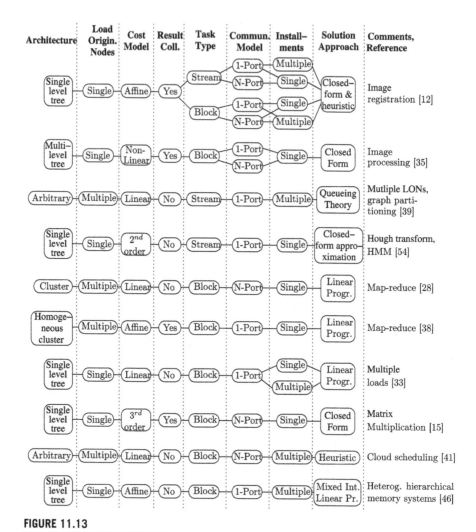

FIGURE 11.13

Samples of DLT bibliography, in reference to key problem modeling factors.

level trees, respectively. Suresh et al. [54] were able to prove "optimal sequencing"[13] and "optimal arrangement"[14] theorems for partitioning a second-order cost workload on a single-level tree. Suresh et al. used a 1-port configuration and stream-type tasks to derive closed-form approximations under certain problem assumptions. Also in

---

[13] "Sequencing" translates to the order in which nodes receive load.
[14] "Arrangement" translates to how nodes and communication links should pair with each other, as in during hardware setup.

[15] third-order cost workload, namely matrix multiplication, was solved in a closed form for a single-level tree of heterogeneous machines, including accelerators.

Ilic and Sousa propose in [36] a two-phase scheduling algorithm consisting of an initial benchmarking phase called "initialization phase," which serves to calculate the cost models, and a second processing phase, called the "iterative phase." During the initialization phase the load is equally partitioned among the available machines. Upon termination, the measured execution times are used to establish cost models that are applied and refined during subsequent executions (iterative phase). A major novelty of their work is the use of continuous generic cost functions that combine both communication and computation costs.

In [39] the authors study two scheduling strategies that partition the graph representing the network joining sources (a.k.a. load-originating nodes [LONs]) and sinks (workers) into disjoint subgraphs. A limitation of the proposed strategies is that each of the sources carries a separate, disjoint queue of individual loads. This hinders their application in the case of parallel file systems or in cases where the sources share a load. The same limitation applies to the work presented in [59], where the authors suggest three resource-aware scheduling schemes that implicitly use multiple installments to process the loads present at the sources under deadline considerations. The size of the installments is dictated by the buffer space available in the workers at any given time.

Multiple LONs have been also examined in the context of map-reduce computations. Gu et al. [28] use linear programming to calculate how the input data resident at multiple LONs should be partitioned among "mapper" nodes (i.e., nodes that perform the mapping phase). Berlinska and Drozdowski [38] use a homogeneous computation with varying communication costs model to propose two heuristic methods for the load partitioning in a map-reduce context, but without using multiple LONs. The timing constraints produced, involving both the mapping and reduction phases, are solved with a linear programming solver.

The processing of multiple loads that are enqueued at a single LON is the subject of the work by Hu and Veeravalli in [33]. Hu and Veeravalli propose static and dynamic scheduling strategies that differ in how the release of a node from a previous assignment is detected. In the static strategy, the release times are assumed to be known a priori, while in the dynamic strategy the workers signal the LON upon finishing their work. The dynamic strategy resorts to multiple installments to be able to incorporate newly released nodes into the working set for a job.

Hu and Veeravalli have also worked on the joined scheduling of divisible and indivisible (i.e., sequential) loads on clusters [34] by proposing a heuristic algorithm called hybrid load scheduling (HMS). HMS tries to fill in the "gaps" (i.e., time periods of idleness) left over from the computation of the indivisible tasks that are scheduled first, with divisible loads. A similar "greedy" approach to scheduling multiple loads on a multi-cloud system is proposed in [41], where the finish times of nodes are used to derive a multi-installment/multi-phase partitioning heuristic.

Finally, DLT has also been used to optimize the time and energy consumption in the processing of a load by a heterogeneous system organized as a single level tree.

Piece-wise linear approximations of the "in RAM" and "out of core" costs for each node are combined with a mixed-integer linear programming approach to produce a multi-installment delivery schedule in [46].

11.4 DLTLib: a library for partitioning workloads

A large number of application scenarios have been studied over the years under the prism of DLT. In the previous sections we explored two relatively straightforward cases that illustrate the analysis approach and challenges involved. In this section we present a software library that can assist in the application of the work that has been done over the years, without the need for a programmer to implement the "scary" looking equations.

Our DLTlib library incorporates only a subset of the published results, but because it is released under the GNU GPL V3 Open Source Software License, it can serve as a starting point for anyone willing to experiment and/or augment it.

DLTlib operations depend on two classes/structures: `Node`, which represents a computing node and contains as data members all the node-specific information needed, and class `Network`, which is supposed to be a container of `Node` instances. The `Network` class provides all the methods that calculate the partitioning of a load based on the problem circumstances. Node instances are connected with a parent–child relationship to form a multi-level tree, although most of the supplied methods can operate on single-level trees only.

Appendix G contains detailed information about the functionality provided by DLTlib. In this section we describe the basic steps needed for incorporating it in a project, which include the following:

1. Declare an instance of the `Network` class.
2. Add to the `Network` instance all the compute nodes that make up the parallel machine. These nodes are assumed to be organized in a tree. The first node to be inserted should be the root of the tree. The insertion requires the specification of the node-specific attributes, i.e., p_i, l_i, and e_i.
3. Call a `Network` method to solve the partitioning problem. Any application-specific parameters (e.g., L, a, b, etc.) are passed at this point to the library.
4. Iterate over the `Network`'s collection of `Node` structures to query about their assigned part.

As an example we will use the problem of image registration, i.e., finding among a pool of images the one that best suits a target image (this is a common problem in medical informatics). This is an application that can be parallelized by following the map-reduce pattern (see Section 2.4.4), where the "mapping" step involves the calculation of comparison metrics between the target and each pool image, while the reduction step involves the selection of the best image. We will ignore the reduction step in our partitioning as it is typically substantially smaller in cost than the mapping step.

We will assume that the problem attributes are:

- A pool of 1000 images, each 1 MiB bytes in size. A target image of the same size.
- Three CPU nodes, each node capable of comparing two images in $p_{cpu} = 0.01$ sec/image. One of them serves as the host.
- A GPU capable of comparing two images in $p_{gpu} = 0.005$ sec/image.
- All nodes are connected with a network capable of 100 MiB/sec transfer rates, or $l = 0.01$ sec/image.[15]

Listing 11.2 implements the sequence of steps shown above:

Listing 11.2: A demonstration of `DLTlib` in action.

```
1   // File : DLTlib/DLTdemo.cpp
2   ...
3   //———————————————————————————————————
4   // DLTlib specific definitions that need to be used by the library.
5   // Control of the seed allows manipulation of the output of any
6   // pseudorandom generated structures in case repetitive tests
7   // are needed.
8   long global_random_seed;
9
10  #include "dltlib.cpp"
11  //———————————————————————————————————
12
13  int main ()
14  {
15    double p_cpu = 0.01;
16    double p_gpu = 0.005;
17    double l = 0.01;
18    long int L = 1000;
19    int M = 2;                // number of installments
20
21    // STEP 1
22    Network platform;         // object representing parallel platform
23
24    // STEP 2
25    // insert one-by-one the nodes that make up the machine
26    // LON stands for load-originating node. It can be considered to
27    // be equivalent to the file server as it does not compute
28    platform.InsertNode ((char *) "LON", p_cpu, 0, (char *) NULL, 1, ←
          true);
29    platform.InsertNode ((char *) "GPU", p_gpu, 0, (char *) "LON", 1, ←
          true);
30    platform.InsertNode ((char *) "CPU0", p_cpu, 0, (char *) "LON", 1, ←
          true);
31    platform.InsertNode ((char *) "CPU1", p_cpu, 0, (char *) "LON", 1, ←
          true);
```

---

[15] The units used here are different than the ones used in earlier examples. However, they are still "time/-data volume" units. As long as they are consistent across all the constants employed, no problem exists.

```
32   platform.InsertNode ((char *) "CPU2", p_cpu, 0, (char *) "LON", 1, ↩
         true);
33
34   // STEP 3
35   // Solve the partitioning problem for 1-port, block-type
36   // computation and M installments
37   double execTime = platform.SolveImageQuery_NInst (L, 1, 0, M);
38
39   // print out the results, if the solution is valid
40   if (platform.valid == 1)
41     {
42       cout << "Predicted execution time: " << execTime << endl;
43
44       // STEP 4
45       // Compute nodes are stored in a public linked list that
46       // allows rearrangement to the order of distribution and
47       // collection
48       cout << "Solution in terms of load percent:\n";
49       Node *h = platform.head;
50       while (h != NULL)
51         {
52           // For a single installment case, the following statement ↩
                  should be used instead
53           //cout << h->name << " " << h->part << endl;
54
55           cout << h->name;
56           for (int i = 0; i < M; i++)
57             cout << "\t" << h->mi_part[i]; // array mi_part holds ↩
                      the parts for each installment
58           cout << endl;
59           h = h->next_n;
60         }
61
62       cout << "Solution in terms of images:\n";
63       h = platform.head;
64       while (h != NULL)
65         {
66           cout << h->name;
67           for (int i = 0; i < M; i++)
68             cout << "\t" << h->mi_part[i] * L;
69           cout << endl;
70           h = h->next_n;
71         }
72     }
73   else
74     cout << "Solution could not be found\n";
75   return 0;
76 }
```

DLTlib depends on the GNU Linear Programming Toolkit for compilation. Hence it needs access to the corresponding header file (glpk.h) and shared library (libglpk.so). The following command line would suffice for compiling and linking our sample program:

```
$ g++ DLTdemo.cpp —1stdc++ —1glpk —o DLTdemo
```

The output generated is shown in Listing 11.3.

Listing 11.3: Output of the program in Listing 11.2.

```
$ ./DLTdemo
Predicted execution time: 10.1106
Solution in terms of load percent:
LON      0         0
GPU      0.635698           0
CPU0     0.172554           0.028259
CPU1     0.0928417          0.0141295
CPU2     0.0494532          0.00706475
Solution in terms of images:
LON      0         0
GPU      635.698 0
CPU0     172.554 28.259
CPU1     92.8417 14.1295
CPU2     49.4532 7.06475
```

As a final word, DLTlib has evolved over a span of many years. It has been used as a research tool and a validation platform by the author. Although much effort has been devoted to making it bug-free, we cannot provide guarantees for its correctness or appropriateness for any software project. We hope that its release under the GNU GPL V3 software license will spur its growth with the assistance of the community.

11.5 Case studies

11.5.1 Hybrid computation of a Mandelbrot set "movie": a case study in dynamic load balancing

In this section we show how dynamic load balancing can be used to speed up the calculation of the Mandelbrot set in the context of heterogeneous or hybrid computational resources (combining GPU and CPU computation). The details of the Mandelbrot set are covered in Section 3.12. As large portions of the code used in this project have appeared before (see Chapters 3 and 6), in the paragraphs that follow we mainly focus on the problem of how the computation can be efficiently partitioned in order to achieve the minimum possible execution time. Non-essential information, such as how the pixels are pseudocolored, etc., is not covered to avoid bloating this section.

In contrast to the case studies of previous chapters that employed the particular fractal, in this one we consider the problem of generating an animation, i.e.,

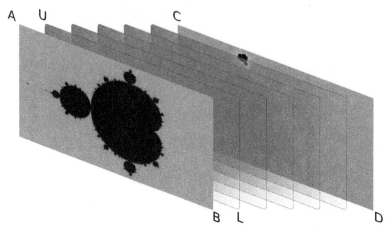

FIGURE 11.14

The corners of the starting and ending frames A, B, C, and D, are used to interpolate the corner coordinates U and L of each intermediate frame.

a sequence of images, of the Mandelbrot fractal, as we pan and zoom between two regions of the complex plane, as shown in Fig. 11.14.

Given the opposing corner coordinates of the first (A, B) and last (C, D) images in the sequence, the corner coordinates of the intermediate frames are linearly interpolated. So for the jth frame in an N-frame sequence, with $j \in [0, N - 1]$, the upper and lower corner points are calculated as

$$U(j) = A + j \cdot \frac{C - A}{N - 1}, \tag{11.40}$$

$$L(j) = B + j \cdot \frac{D - B}{N - 1}. \tag{11.41}$$

The same methodology is applied for figuring out the maximum number of iterations to be performed.[16]

The calculation still relies on the direct application of the recurrence formula of Eq. (3.2) for every pixel of the target image(s).

Bringing out the detail of the fractal requires the increase of the maximum number of iterations, way beyond the 1024 limit employed in Section 6.15.1. This however introduces a new problem for GPU deployment: high variability in the number of iterations needed for convergence in neighboring pixels leads to CUDA thread di-

---

[16] In the actual implementation in Listing 11.4, a slightly bigger denominator is used (i.e., N) to avoid round-off errors that can prohibit the rendering of the last image in the sequence by making corners U and L cross.

vergence (i.e., some threads finish earlier than others), effectively diminishing the utilization of the GPU's SMs.

To address this deficiency, we evaluate how appropriate a region is for GPU processing by calculating the number of iterations needed to process its four corners. If their variation (as measured by the difference between the maximum and minimum number of iterations) is too big, the region is broken into four equal pieces that are in turn examined individually. A region is considered suitable for GPU processing if the following criterion is satisfied:

$$maxIter - minIter < diffThres \cdot maxIter, \tag{11.42}$$

where $maxIter = max_{\forall i}(cornerIter[i])$ and $minIter_{\forall i} = min(cornerIter[i])$ for $i \in [0, 3]$ and $diffThres < 1$ is an ad hoc specified fixed threshold.

This subdivision process is repeated until the condition (11.42) is met or until a region's pixel count falls below a fixed threshold $pixelSizeThresh$. Through experimentation, we found that $diffThres = 0.5$ and $pixelSizeThresh = 32,768$ are reasonably good choices, at least for the test platform and setup reported here.

In the listings that follow, each frame/image to be calculated is represented by an instance of the MandelFrame class shown in Listing 11.4.

Listing 11.4: Class used to represent an image.

```
1   // File : mandelbrot_hybrid / mandelframe .h
2   ...
3   class MandelFrame
4   {
5   public:
6       int MAXITER;
7       double upperX, upperY;          // complex plane corners
8       double lowerX, lowerY;
9       double stepX, stepY;
10      int pixelsX, pixelsY;           // image resolution
11      QImage *img;                    // object holding pixel values
12      char fname[MAXFNAME+1];         // filename used for storage
13      std::atomic_int remainingRegions; // atomic counter for regions
14                                      // left to be computed
15      MandelFrame(double, double, double, double, int, int, char*, int ↩
            );
16      void regionSplit();
17      void regionComplete();
18  };
```

Each of the subregions that make up a frame is represented by an instance of the MandelRegion class, as shown in Listing 11.5.

Listing 11.5: Class used to represent a part of an image.

```
19  // File : mandelbrot_hybrid / mandelregion .h
20  ...
21  class MandelRegion
```

```
22  {
23  private :
24    int diverge (double cx, double cy); // calculates the number
25                                          // of iterations for a pixel
26    double upperX, upperY;  // complex plane coordinates of region
27    double lowerX, lowerY;
28    int imageX, imageY;     // location in target image
29    int pixelsX, pixelsY;   // and pixel dimensions
30    int cornersIter[4];     // iterations for the four corners
31    shared_ptr<MandelFrame> ownerFrame;
32    static QRgb *colormap;  // used for pseudocoloring the pixels
33    static double diffThresh;  // thresholds that trigger calculation
34    static int pixelSizeThresh;
35
36  public :
37      MandelRegion (double, double, double, double, int, int, int, int ↩
             , shared_ptr<MandelFrame>);
38    void compute (bool onGPU);       // calculates a region's pixels
39    void examine (WorkQueue &, bool onGPU); // evaluates the suitabi-
40                                           // lity of a region for
41                                           // computing on a GPU
42    bool operator< (const MandelRegion & a);
43    static void initColorMapAndThrer (int, double, int);
44  };
```

Each MandelFrame is originally made up of just one MandelRegion that is inserted in an instance of the WorkQueue class, which is shown in Listing 11.6.

Listing 11.6: Thread-safe FIFO queue class for managing regions to be computed.

```
45  // File : mandelbrot_hybrid/workqueue.h
46  ...
47  class WorkQueue
48  {
49  private :
50    mutex l; // lock ensuring thread safety
51    deque<unique_ptr<MandelRegion> > queue;//container
52
53  public :
54    void append(unique_ptr<MandelRegion>);
55    unique_ptr<MandelRegion> extract();
56    int size();
57  };
```

Each worker thread (executing a functor/instance of the CalcThr class) extracts a MandelRegion object from the work queue and proceeds to either process it or subdivide it and place the pieces back in the queue. Once all the pieces of a frame have been calculated, the frame is saved to the filesystem in the form of a PNG image.

The main part of the program is shown in Listing 11.7.

Listing 11.7: Main part of the hybrid Mandelbrot animation calculation program.

```cpp
58   // File : mandelbrot_hybrid/main.cpp
59   ...
60   // ********************************************************
61   class CalcThr
62   {
63   private:
64     WorkQueue * que;
65     bool isGPU;
66
67   public:
68     CalcThr (WorkQueue * q, bool gpu):que (q), isGPU (gpu)
69     {
70     }
71     void operator()();
72   };
73
74   void CalcThr::operator()()
75   {
76     unique_ptr<MandelRegion> t;
77     while ((t = que->extract ()) != nullptr)
78         t->examine (*que, isGPU);
79   }
80
81   // ********************************************************
82   // Expects an input file with the following data:
83   //   numframes resolutionX resolutionY imageFilePrefix.
84   //   upperX upperY lowerX lowerY maxIterations  ; for first frame
85   //   upperX upperY lowerX lowerY maxIterations  ; for last frame
86   //
87   // Command-line param.:  spec_file numThr GPUenable diffT pixelT
88   //          spec_file : file holding the parameters mentioned above
89   //          numThr : number of threads (optional, defaults to the
90   //                   number of cores)
91   //          GPUenable : 0/1, 1(default) enables the GPU code (opt.)
92   //          diffT pixelT : optional thresholds for frame
93   //                   partitioning heuristics
94   int main (int argc, char *argv[])
95   {
96     int numframes, resolutionX, resolutionY;
97     char imageFilePrefix[MAXFNAME - 8];
98     double upperCornerX[2], upperCornerY[2], lowerCornerX[2], ↩
           lowerCornerY[2];
99     int maxIterations[2];
100    double diffT = 0.5;
101    int pixT = 32768;
102
103    if (argc < 2)
104      {
105        cerr << "Usage : " << argv[0] << "spec_file numThr GPUenable [↩
               diffT pixelT ]\n";
106        exit (1);
```

```
107        }
108
109     int numThreads = sysconf (_SC_NPROCESSORS_ONLN);
110     if (argc > 2)
111       numThreads = atoi (argv[2]);
112
113     bool enableGPU = true;
114     if (argc > 3)
115       enableGPU = (bool) atoi (argv[3]);
116
117     if (argc > 4)
118       diffT = atof (argv[4]);
119
120     if (argc > 5)
121       pixT = atoi (argv[5]);
122
123     ifstream fin (argv[1]);
124     fin >> numframes >> resolutionX >> resolutionY;
125     fin >> imageFilePrefix;
126     fin >> upperCornerX[0] >> upperCornerY[0] >> lowerCornerX[0] >> ↵
            lowerCornerY[0] >> maxIterations[0];
127     fin >> upperCornerX[1] >> upperCornerY[1] >> lowerCornerX[1] >> ↵
            lowerCornerY[1] >> maxIterations[1];
128     fin.close ();
129
130     // generate the pseudocolor map to be used for all frames
131     int MAXMAXITER = max (maxIterations[0], maxIterations[1]);
132     MandelRegion::initColorMapAndThrer (MAXMAXITER, diffT, pixT);
133
134     WorkQueue workQ;
135
136     // generate the needed frame objects and the corresponding regions
137     unique_ptr< shared_ptr<MandelFrame>[] > fr = make_unique< ↵
            shared_ptr<MandelFrame>[] >(numframes);
138     double uX = upperCornerX[0], uY = upperCornerY[0];
139     double lX = lowerCornerX[0], lY = lowerCornerY[0];
140     int iter = maxIterations[0];
141     double sx1, sx2, sy1, sy2;
142     int iterInc;
143
144     // steps sx1 and sx2 are a little bit smaller to avoid round-off
145     // errors causing the last image to not render
146     sx1 = (upperCornerX[1] - upperCornerX[0]) / numframes;
147     sx2 = (lowerCornerX[1] - lowerCornerX[0]) / numframes;
148     sy1 = (upperCornerY[1] - upperCornerY[0]) / numframes;
149     sy2 = (lowerCornerY[1] - lowerCornerY[0]) / numframes;
150     iterInc = (maxIterations[1] - maxIterations[0]) * 1.0 / numframes;
151     char fname[MAXFNAME];
152     for (int i = 0; i < numframes; i++)
153       {
154         sprintf (fname, "%s%04i.png", imageFilePrefix, i);
```

```
155    fr[i] = make_shared<MandelFrame>(uX, uY, lX, lY, resolutionX, ↩
             resolutionY, fname, iter);
156    workQ.append (make_unique<MandelRegion>(uX, uY, lX, lY, 0, 0, ↩
             resolutionX, resolutionY, fr[i]));
157    uX += sx1;
158    uY += sy1;
159    lX += sx2;
160    lY += sy2;
161    iter += iterInc;
162  }
163
164  // generate the threads that will process the workload
165  unique_ptr< thread > thr[numThreads];
166  for (int i = 1; i < numThreads; i++)
167    thr[i] = make_unique< thread > ( move(CalcThr (&workQ, false) ↩
             ));
168
169  // use the main thread to run one of the workers
170  if (enableGPU)
171  {
172    CUDAmemSetup (resolutionX, resolutionY);
173    CalcThr(&workQ, true)();
174    CUDAmemCleanup ();
175  }
176  else
177    CalcThr(&workQ, false)();
178
179  for (int i = 1; i < numThreads; i++)
180    thr[i]->join ();
181
182  return 0;
183 }
```

The main program reads the input parameters from the command-line and the associated file (lines 103–128), generates the MandelFrame instances that correspond to the frames that need to be calculated (lines 137–162), and spawns the worker threads that will process the workload (lines 165–167).

Once the setup is complete, the master thread proceeds to serve as a worker (there is no reason why it should be idle for the duration of the computation) by creating and calling an instance of a CalcThr functor (lines 170–177). If GPU computation is enabled, the master thread allocates the device memory required (line 172) prior to calling the functor.

Each thread, as mentioned previously, extracts a MandelRegion object from the work queue (line 77) and assesses what should be done next by calling the MandelRegion::examine() method, shown on lines 232–297 of Listing 11.8. The size and statements' length of this method might look intimidating, but the actual logic is very simple: lines 237–260 calculate (if not previously done during the evaluation of the "parent" region) the number of iterations required for the four corners of the region to diverge (or not) and evaluate the condition described by Eq. (11.42) on line 263.

If the condition is satisfied, the pixels of the regions are calculated by calling the MandelRegion::compute() method. Otherwise, the region is split into four equally sized subregions (lines 269–296) which are appended into the work queue. The information for the four corners of the parent region is preserved in the new MandelRegion instances via lines 282, 285, 288, and 291.

The MandelRegion::compute() method (lines 186–228) performs the calculation on either the GPU (lines 194–212) or the CPU (lines 214–227), according to a thread-supplied parameter (onGPU).

Listing 11.8: The core part of the MandelRegion class, which is responsible for carrying out the computations.

```
184   // File : mandelbrot_hybrid/mandelregion.cpp
185   ...
186   void MandelRegion::compute (bool onGPU)
187   {
188     double stepX = ownerFrame->stepX;
189     double stepY = ownerFrame->stepY;
190     QImage *img = ownerFrame->img;
191     int MAXGRAY = ownerFrame->MAXITER;
192
193     if (onGPU)
194       {
195         unsigned int *h_res;
196         int pitch;
197
198         hostFE (upperX, upperY, lowerX, lowerY, pixelsX, pixelsY, &↵
                   h_res, &pitch, MAXGRAY);
199         pitch /= sizeof (int);
200
201         //copy results into QImage object
202         for (int i = 0; i < pixelsX; i++)
203           for (int j = 0; j < pixelsY; j++)
204             {
205               int color = h_res[j * pitch + i];
206               if (color == MAXGRAY)
207                 img->setPixel (imageX + i, imageY + j, qRgb (0, 0, 0))↵
                     ;
208               else
209                 img->setPixel (imageX + i, imageY + j, colormap[color↵
                     ]);
210             }
211
212       }
213     else                            // CPU execution
214       {
215         for (int i = 0; i < pixelsX; i++)
216           for (int j = 0; j < pixelsY; j++)
217             {
218               double tempx, tempy;
219               tempx = upperX + i * stepX;
220               tempy = upperY - j * stepY;
```

```
221            int color = diverge (tempx, tempy);
222            if (color == MAXGRAY)
223              img->setPixel (imageX + i, imageY + j, qRgb (0, 0, 0))↩
                 ;
224            else
225              img->setPixel (imageX + i, imageY + j, colormap[color↩
                 ]);
226          }
227      }
228 }
229
230 //————————————————————————————————————————————————
231 // if the region is small enough, process it, or split it in 4 ↩
       regions
232 void MandelRegion::examine (WorkQueue & q, bool onGPU = false)
233 {
234    int minIter = INT_MAX, maxIter = 0;
235
236    // evaluate the corners first
237    for (int i = 0; i < 4; i++)
238      {
239        if (cornersIter[i] == UNKNOWN)
240          {
241            switch (i)
242              {
243              case (UPPER_RIGHT):
244                cornersIter[i] = diverge (lowerX, upperY);
245                break;
246              case (UPPER_LEFT):
247                cornersIter[i] = diverge (upperX, upperY);
248                break;
249              case (LOWER_RIGHT):
250                cornersIter[i] = diverge (lowerX, lowerY);
251                break;
252              default:                 // LOWER_LEFT
253                cornersIter[i] = diverge (upperX, lowerY);
254              }
255          }
256        if (minIter > cornersIter[i])
257          minIter = cornersIter[i];
258        else if (maxIter < cornersIter[i])
259          maxIter = cornersIter[i];
260      }
261
262    // either compute the pixels or break the region in 4 pieces
263    if (maxIter − minIter < diffThresh * maxIter || pixelsX * pixelsY ↩
         < pixelSizeThresh)
264      {
265        compute (onGPU);
266        ownerFrame->regionComplete ();
267      }
268    else
```

```
269       {
270           double midDiagX1, midDiagY1;        // data for determining the ↵
                   new subregions
271           double midDiagX2, midDiagY2;
272           int subimageX, subimageY;
273           subimageX = pixelsX / 2;  // concern the upper left quad.
274           subimageY = pixelsY / 2;
275           midDiagX1 = upperX + (subimageX - 1) * ownerFrame->stepX;
276           midDiagY1 = upperY - (subimageY - 1) * ownerFrame->stepY;
277           midDiagX2 = midDiagX1 + ownerFrame->stepX;
278           midDiagY2 = midDiagY1 - ownerFrame->stepY;
279
280           unique_ptr<unique_ptr<MandelRegion>[]> sub = make_unique<↵
                   unique_ptr<MandelRegion>[]>(4);
281           sub[UPPER_LEFT] = make_unique<MandelRegion> (upperX, upperY, ↵
                   midDiagX1, midDiagY1, imageX, imageY, subimageX, subimageY ↵
                   , ownerFrame);
282           sub[UPPER_LEFT]->cornersIter[UPPER_LEFT] = cornersIter[↵
                   UPPER_LEFT];
283
284           sub[UPPER_RIGHT] = make_unique<MandelRegion> (midDiagX2, ↵
                   upperY, lowerX, midDiagY1, imageX + subimageX, imageY, ↵
                   pixelsX - subimageX, subimageY, ownerFrame);
285           sub[UPPER_RIGHT]->cornersIter[UPPER_RIGHT] = cornersIter[↵
                   UPPER_RIGHT];
286
287           sub[LOWER_LEFT] = make_unique<MandelRegion>(upperX, midDiagY2,↵
                   midDiagX1, lowerY, imageX, imageY + subimageY, subimageX,↵
                   pixelsY - subimageY, ownerFrame);
288           sub[LOWER_LEFT]->cornersIter[LOWER_LEFT] = cornersIter[↵
                   LOWER_LEFT];
289
290           sub[LOWER_RIGHT] = make_unique<MandelRegion> (midDiagX2, ↵
                   midDiagY2, lowerX, lowerY, imageX + subimageX, imageY + ↵
                   subimageY, pixelsX - subimageX, pixelsY - subimageY, ↵
                   ownerFrame);
291           sub[LOWER_RIGHT]->cornersIter[LOWER_RIGHT] = cornersIter[↵
                   LOWER_RIGHT];
292
293           for (int i = 0; i < 4; i++)
294               q.append (move(sub[i]));
295           ownerFrame->regionSplit ();
296       }
297   }
298   ...
```

The CPU code is a straightforward nested loop, iterating over all the possible pixels of a region in sequence. The GPU code, administered by the hostFE() function shown in Listing 11.9, is nearly identical to the code shown in Listing 6.45.

The single most significant difference between the two programs is in **device memory management**: whereas in Listing 6.45, a single allocation and deallocation are required for the one-time kernel launch, in this section, multiple kernel invocations have to be carried out. Multiple allocations/deallocations would severely penalize performance in this case. For this reason, the maximum amount of global device memory that could be ever needed is allocated a priori (function CUDAmem-Setup(), lines 349–354). Based on the width (resX) of the region to be processed by hostFE(), the memory pitch (ptc) is calculated on-the-fly (lines 366–368) in order to keep memory accesses coalesced.

Listing 11.9: Kernel and front-end functions used for carrying out the GPU computations.

```
299  // File : mandelbrot_hybrid/kernel.cu
300  ...
301  static const int BLOCK_SIDE = 16;         // size of 2D block of ←
          threads
302
303  // *********************************************************
304  __device__ int diverge (double cx, double cy, int MAXITER)
305  {
306    int iter = 0;
307    double vx = cx, vy = cy, tx, ty;
308    while (iter < MAXITER && (vx * vx + vy * vy) < 4)
309      {
310        tx = vx * vx — vy * vy + cx;
311        ty = 2 * vx * vy + cy;
312        vx = tx;
313        vy = ty;
314        iter++;
315      }
316    return iter;
317  }
318
319  // *********************************************************
320  __global__ void mandelKernel (unsigned *d_res, double upperX, double←
          upperY, double stepX, double stepY, int resX, int resY, int ←
          pitch, int MAXITER)
321  {
322    int myX, myY;
323    myX = blockIdx.x * blockDim.x + threadIdx.x;
324    myY = blockIdx.y * blockDim.y + threadIdx.y;
325    if (myX >= resX || myY >= resY)
326      return;
327
328    double tempx, tempy;
329    tempx = upperX + myX * stepX;
330    tempy = upperY — myY * stepY;
331    int color = diverge (tempx, tempy, MAXITER);
332    d_res[myY * pitch/sizeof(int) + myX] = color;
333  }
334
335  // *********************************************************
336  int maxResX = 0;
337  int maxResY = 0;
```

```
338  int pitch = 0;
339  unsigned int *h_res;
340  unsigned int *d_res;
341  // ************************************************************
342  extern "C" void CUDAmemCleanup ()
343  {
344    CUDA_CHECK_RETURN (cudaFreeHost (h_res));
345    CUDA_CHECK_RETURN (cudaFree (d_res));
346  }
347
348  // ************************************************************
349  extern "C" unsigned int *CUDAmemSetup (int maxResX, int maxResY)
350  {
351    CUDA_CHECK_RETURN (cudaMallocPitch ((void **) &d_res, (size_t *) &↩
            pitch, maxResX * sizeof (unsigned), maxResY));
352    CUDA_CHECK_RETURN (cudaHostAlloc (&h_res, maxResY * pitch, ↩
            cudaHostAllocMapped));
353    return h_res;
354  }
355
356  // ************************************************************
357  // Host front-end function that allocates the memory and launches ↩
         the GPU kernel
358  extern "C" void hostFE (double upperX, double upperY, double lowerX,↩
            double lowerY, int resX, int resY, unsigned int **pixels, int *↩
            currpitch, int MAXITER)
359  {
360    int blocksX, blocksY;
361    blocksX = (int) ceil (resX * 1.0/ BLOCK_SIDE);
362    blocksY = (int) ceil (resY * 1.0/ BLOCK_SIDE);
363    dim3 block (BLOCK_SIDE, BLOCK_SIDE);
364    dim3 grid (blocksX, blocksY);
365
366    int ptc = 32;
367    while (ptc < resX * sizeof (unsigned))
368      ptc += 32;
369
370    double stepX = (lowerX - upperX) / resX;
371    double stepY = (upperY - lowerY) / resY;
372
373    // launch GPU kernel
374    mandelKernel <<< grid, block >>> (d_res, upperX, upperY, stepX, ↩
            stepY, resX, resY, ptc, MAXITER);
375
376    // get the results
377    CUDA_CHECK_RETURN (cudaMemcpy (h_res, d_res, resY * ptc, ↩
            cudaMemcpyDeviceToHost));
378    *pixels = h_res;
379    *currpitch = ptc;
380  }
```

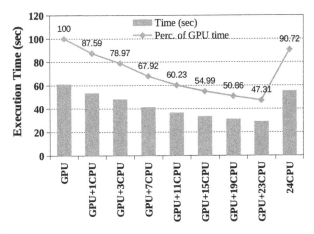

FIGURE 11.15

Average execution time (bars) for the calculation of a 100-frame full-HD resolution sequence, for a variety of thread configurations. The line and number labels represent the time as a percentage of the execution time achieved by the GPU alone.

Our program was tested on a Linux platform, equipped with an AMD Ryzen 3900X 12-core, 24-thread CPU and an RTX 2060 Super GPU card. Fig. 11.15 illustrates the average timing results over 10 runs for the generation of 100 frames at HD resolution (1920×1080). The starting frame was set to a maximum iteration limit of 100, and the ending frame was set to a maximum iteration limit of 10,000.

Fig. 11.15 clearly illustrates that the utilized CPU and GPU are roughly on par for the problem at hand. So it comes to no surprise that combining both of them cuts in half the execution time that either of them can achieve.

In conclusion, the above configuration for the hybrid computation of the Mandelbrot set is one of many possible designs. For example, the task queue/tuple space can be active and not passive, i.e., it could detect/pick the tasks appropriate for a type of machine and "push" them along, in contrast to the "pull" setup described above. Although our design is not a tuplespace approach, it does illustrate the potential of this paradigm and it can hopefully spark ideas about improved hybrid/heterogeneous computation designs.

Additionally, several improvements could be incorporated into this initial approach. For example, preallocation and explicit memory management of the `MandelRegion` objects would eliminate much of the host-memory allocation overhead. However, this and other potential improvements just go beyond the scope of the application at hand, which was meant as a concept illustration tool.

11.5.2 Distributed block cipher encryption: a case study in static load balancing

The problem of encrypting large volumes of data on a cluster of GPU nodes using the AES algorithm has been explored in Section 6.15.2. In that case study, a dynamic load balancing approach that involved a handshake between the master and worker nodes was utilized, but with only mediocre results. In this section we will extend this work by balancing the load statically. The analysis is generic enough to apply to any block cipher and not just AES.

In Section 5.24 we examined the problem of statically partitioning a 2^{56}-sized key space in a quest to decrypt a DES-encrypted ciphertext. The DES brute-force cracking case study featured a partitioning scheme that assigned equal parts of the key space to every compute node, regardless of their relative power. This is an obvious shortcoming that can compromise performance.

Here we will tackle the balancing problem by using divisible load analysis. The first step, as mentioned in Section 11.3, is to establish the cost model parameters that relate input size and execution time. This comes down to encrypting plain-texts of varying sizes and determining the corresponding execution time. The results, which averaged over 100 runs, are shown in Fig. 11.16. The execution platform, both hardware- and software-wise, is identical to the one used in Section 6.15.2. For this reason we used 512 threads per CUDA block, as this has been shown to be the best choice (see Fig. 6.44).

It is clear that a linear or affine model is not a good fit to the entirety of either the CPU or the GPU curves. What is intriguing is that the GPU is way slower than the CPU for small to medium-size messages, compromised by the need to transfer the data over the PCIe bus. It is not until inputs start exceeding the 100 MiB mark that the GPU starts to offer a tangible advantage.

The curves can be considered piecewise linear, as for the range of [64 kiB, 256 MiB] for the CPU and [16, 256] MiB for the GPU, a line is a reasonable approximation, with

$$t_{CPU} = 3.975 \cdot 10^{-9} \frac{sec}{Byte} L + 8.788 \cdot 10^{-5} \text{ sec} \qquad (11.43)$$

and

$$t_{GPU} = 9.133 \cdot 10^{-10} \frac{sec}{Byte} L + 0.25 \text{ sec}, \qquad (11.44)$$

where L is the plaintext size.

These ranges are suitable for our analysis, as we will be breaking up the input in larger chunks than the ones used in Section 6.15.2. Furthermore these affine equations match the computation model of Eq. (11.5), i.e., $t_{comp} = p_i(part_i L + e_i)$ if we use

$$p_{CPU} = 3.975 \cdot 10^{-9} \frac{sec}{B} \text{ and } e_{CPU} = \frac{8.788 \cdot 10^{-5} s}{3.975 \cdot 10^{-9} s/B} = 22107 B, \qquad (11.45)$$

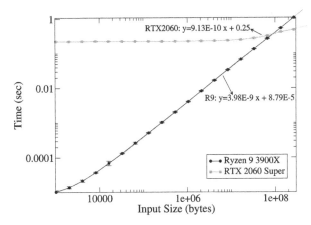

FIGURE 11.16

Log-log graph of the average execution time on a single CPU core and a GPU versus the plaintext size. Message sizes range from 2^{10} to 2^{28} bytes in exponential steps. Error bars correspond to the standard deviation for the associated set of experiments.

$$p_{GPU} = 9.133 \cdot 10^{-10} \frac{s}{B} \quad \text{and} \quad e_{GPU} = \frac{0.25 \, s}{9.133 \cdot 10^{-10} \, s/B} = 273919467 \, B.$$
(11.46)

A similar procedure (via a ping-pong program, see Exercise 4 in Chapter 5) can produce the communication model parameters. For two MPI processes running on the same Ryzen 9 3900X host, we get a least squares line: $y = 9.899 \cdot 10^{-11} \cdot x - 5.071 \cdot 10^{-6}$. This linear equation translates to the following communication parameters: $l = 9.899 \cdot 10^{-11} \, s/B$ and $b = d = -51231 \, B$. The negative intercept is a result of the regression approximation, because the CPU cache hierarchy results in a piece-wise linear communication cost (longer messages get slower communication speeds).

If 1-port, single-installment distribution and block-type computation were chosen (e.g., by using MPI_Ssend calls for distributing the workload) and as b and d are small enough to be ignored, the problem setting would fit the "image processing" class of problems that have known DLT solutions, as identified in Section G.1.3. In that case, we could use the methods described in Appendix G as part of the DLTlib to calculate the partitioning.

In this section we follow an alternative route by using parallel I/O operations for all workers, making the communication configuration an N-port, single-installment, block-type computation one. The program in the case study of Section 6.15.2 reads the whole input file in the local memory of the master node before distributing the pieces to the workers in a first-come, first-served basis. In this section we calculate the single-piece-per-worker part of the input using DLT analysis and communicate to the workers only the start index and length of their assignment, i.e., only a description of which part of the input they are supposed to process. Each worker then proceeds to perform I/O in parallel. The cost of communicating the assignment descriptions is

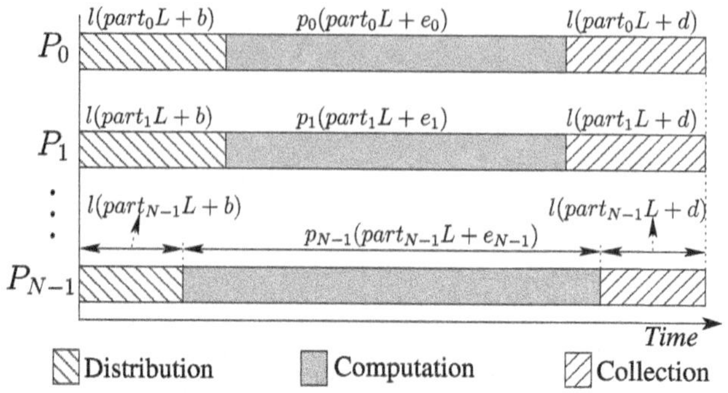

FIGURE 11.17

An illustration of the optimum N-port, single-installment, block-type computation, configuration for block-cipher encryption.

insignificant relevant to the massive I/O costs incurred, and for this reason it can be safely ignored.

As the I/O for both the distribution and collection phases is done in parallel, we can apply the analysis of Section 11.3.3.1 and Eqs. (11.12) and (11.13). The reasoning is that the bulk of the communications concerns I/O operations done in parallel, and thus, the sequence of events matches the one shown in Fig. 11.17. Adapting Eqs. (11.12) and (11.13) to our particular problem means setting the parameters as follows: $a = 1$, $c = 1$, $l_i = l$. Also given that there is no master node as far as the I/O is concerned, so that node 0 in our setting is the equivalent of worker 1 in Eqs. (11.12) and (11.13), we can simplify them to

$$(11.12) \Rightarrow part_i = part_0 \frac{2 \cdot l + p_0}{2 \cdot l + p_i} + \frac{p_0 e_0 - p_i e_i}{L(2 \cdot l + p_i)} \tag{11.47}$$

and

$$(11.13) \Rightarrow part_0 = \frac{1 + \sum_{j=1}^{N-1} \frac{p_j e_j - p_0 e_0}{L(2 \cdot l + p_j)}}{(2 \cdot l + p_0) \sum_{j=0}^{N-1} \left(2 \cdot l + p_j\right)^{-1}}. \tag{11.48}$$

It should be noted that l, as measured by the ping-pong process *on the same host*, corresponds essentially to a memory-to-memory copy. This is sufficient for our testing/benchmarking purposes, as the operating system disk cache typically ends up holding the entire input file. As a result, repeated tests with the same input only read from the main memory without needing to access a secondary memory device. Special management of the disk cache (e.g., clearing it prior to every single test) should be conducted if the "communication" parameters are supposed to reflect real-life scenarios.

The implementation of Eqs. (11.47) and (11.48) is given in Listing 11.10.

Listing 11.10: Code implementing the DLT partitioning Eqs. (11.47) and (11.48).

```cpp
// File : AES_MPI_nodatacopy/partition.cpp
...
// ********************************************************************
// Returns the predicted execution time
// and the calculated parts in array part[]
double nPortPartition(double *p, double *e, long L, double l, double ↩
    b, double d, double *part, int N)
{
  // temporary arrays for speeding up the calculation
  double lacp[N];
  double sumTerms[N];

  lacp[0]=1.0/p[0];
  for(int i=1;i<N;i++)
    lacp[i] = 1.0/(l*2+p[i]);

  // sumTerms[0] is not utilized
  for(int i=1;i<N;i++)
    sumTerms[i] = (p[0]*e[0] - p[i]*e[i]-l*(b+d)) * lacp[i] / L;

  // calculate the nominator and denominator for finding part_0
  double nomin=1, denom=0;
  for(int i=1;i<N;i++)
  {
    nomin -= sumTerms[i];
    denom += lacp[i];
  }
  denom*=p[0];
  denom++;

  part[0] = nomin/denom;

  // calculate the other parts now
  for(int i=1;i<N;i++)
    part[i] = part[0] * p[0]*lacp[i] + sumTerms[i];

  // sanity check - always a good idea!
  double sum=0;
  for(int i=0;i<N;i++)
    sum += part[i];
  assert(fabs(sum -1)<0.001);

  // return the exec. time
  return l*(2*part[0] + b+d) + p[0]*(part[0]*L+e[0]);
}
// ********************************************************************
// returns the assigned load in array assign[], that are multiples ↩
    of quantum (assuming L is also a multiple of quantum)
void quantize(double *part, long L, int quantum, int N, long *assign↩
    )
{
```

```
49    int totAssigned=0;
50    for(int i=1;i<N;i++)
51    {
52      // truncate the parts assigned to all workers but node 0
53      assign[i] = ((long)floor(part[i]*L/quantum))*quantum;
54      totAssigned += assign[i];   //accummulate
55    }
56    // node 0 gets everything else
57    assign[0] = L - totAssigned;
58  }
```

The function `nPortPartition()` is called by node 0 (it would be superficial to call it the master node), followed by a call to function `quantize()` so that the parts to be assigned are integer multiples of the load "quantum," which in our case is a 16-byte-long block (AES processes data in 16-byte blocks).

Before the optimum partitioning can be calculated, node 0 collects from every other node their respective p and e parameters. In our code, these parameters are hardcoded in the source code targeting the different types of nodes: There are two dedicated source code files, for GPU and CPU nodes, respectively. Of course, there are many alternatives to having fixed, a priori determined computing parameters:

- p and e can be derived on-line by, e.g., having each node calculate them based on the outcome of processing a small part of the data.
- Interpolation or extrapolation could be used to estimate p and e based on the parameters of a prototypical node. For example, if $p_{10\ SM} = 1$ for a GPU having 10 SMs, another GPU of the same architecture (e.g., Turing) and clock frequency, with 20 SMs, could be estimated as having $p_{20\ SM} = 0.5$ (i.e., twice as fast).
- A database could be used to hold the past performance of each node and use these figures to estimate p and e.

The `quantize()` function on lines 47–58 truncates the load assigned to all worker nodes indexed between 1 and $N - 1$, leaving the rest of the load to be assigned to node 0, assuming that node 0 is a GPU. This is not the optimum procedure for this task. More elaborate algorithms are described in [16] and implemented in DLTlib.

A large portion of the source code is shared with the project of Section 6.15.2. The only difference, apart from the addition of the partitioning functions described above, is the `main` function structure as shown in Listing 11.11.

Listing 11.11: Main module holding the logic to be executed by GPU nodes.

```
59  // File : AES_MPI_nodatacopy/main.cpp
60  // Assumes that the encryption will take place on GPU nodes
61  ...
62  #include "rijndael.h"
63  #include "partition.cpp"
64
65  using namespace std;
66
67  #define TAG_MODEL 0
```

```
68   #define TAG_WORK 1
69
70   const double modelParams[]={9.1330538834295E-10, 273919466.799488}; ↩
          // p_i and e_i
71   const double l= 9.8993099309931E-11;// speed for a single transfer
72   const double b= -51230.9967752103;
73   const double d= -51230.9967752103;
74
75   static const int keybits = 256;
76
77   //*******************************************************************
78   int main (int argc, char *argv[])
79   {
80     int rank;
81     unsigned char *iobuf;
82
83     int lSize = 0;
84     FILE *f;
85
86     int comm_size = 0;
87     MPI_Status status;
88     MPI_Init (&argc, &argv);
89     MPI_Comm_rank (MPI_COMM_WORLD, &rank);
90     MPI_Comm_size (MPI_COMM_WORLD, &comm_size);
91     MPI_Request req;
92     MPI_Status stat;
93
94     if (argc < 4)
95       {
96         if (rank == 0)
97           fprintf (stderr, "Usage : %s inputfile outputfile ↩
                   threadsPerBlock\n", argv[0]);
98
99         exit (1);
100       }
101
102     //encryption key
103     unsigned char key[32] = { 1, 2, 3, 4, 5, 6, 7, 8, 9, 10, 11, 12, ↩
            13, 14, 15, 16, 17, 18, 19, 20, 21, 22, 23, 24, 25, 26, 27, ↩
            28, 29, 30, 31, 32 };
104     u32 rk[RKLENGTH (keybits)];
105     rijndaelSetupEncrypt (rk, key, keybits);
106
107     // node 0 is reserved for the GPU
108     if (rank == 0)
109       {
110         if ((f = fopen (argv[1], "r")) == NULL)
111           {
112             fprintf (stderr, "Can't open %s\n", argv[1]);
113             exit (EXIT_FAILURE);
114           }
115
```

```
116        fseek (f, 0, SEEK_END);
117        lSize = ftell (f);
118        rewind (f);
119
120        // allocate the arrays needed for calculating the partitioning
121        double *p=new double[comm_size];
122        double *e=new double[comm_size];
123        double *part=new double[comm_size];
124        long *assignment = new long[comm_size];
125        long *offset = new long[comm_size];
126        long *indLenPairs = new long[comm_size*2];
127        MPI_Request *rq = new  MPI_Request[comm_size];
128
129        // get the characteristics of each node
130        p[0] = modelParams[0];
131        e[0] = modelParams[1];
132        double temp[2];
133        for(int i=1;i<comm_size;i++)
134        {
135            MPI_Recv (temp, 2, MPI_DOUBLE, MPI_ANY_SOURCE, TAG_MODEL, ←
                    MPI_COMM_WORLD, &stat);
136            int idx = stat.MPI_SOURCE;
137            p[idx] = temp[0];
138            e[idx] = temp[1];
139        }
140        // calculate the assignment. Communication speed is divided ←
                between the N-1 workers
141        double predTime = nPortPartition(p, e, lSize, l*(comm_size-1),←
                b, d, part, comm_size);
142
143        quantize(part, lSize, 16, comm_size, assignment);
144
145        // calculate the start_offset, length of the assignment parts
146        long pos = 0;
147        for(int i=0;i<comm_size;i++)
148        {
149            indLenPairs[2*i] = pos;
150            indLenPairs[2*i+1] = assignment[i];
151            pos +=assignment[i];
152        }
153
154        // communicate the assigned plaintext start_off, length pairs
155        for(int i=1;i<comm_size;i++)
156            MPI_Isend (indLenPairs +2*i, 2, MPI_LONG, i, TAG_WORK, ←
                    MPI_COMM_WORLD, &req);
157
158        iobuf = new unsigned char[assignment[0]];
159        assert (iobuf != NULL);
160        fread (iobuf, 1, assignment[0], f);
161        fclose (f);
162
163        // process part0 of the input on the GPU
```

```
164        int thrPerBlock = atoi (argv[3]);
165        rijndaelEncryptFE (rk, keybits, iobuf, iobuf, assignment[0], ←
              thrPerBlock);
166
167        rijndaelShutdown ();
168
169        FILE *fout;
170        if ((fout = fopen (argv[2], "w")) == NULL)
171          {
172             fprintf (stderr, "Can't open %s\n", argv[2]);
173             exit (EXIT_FAILURE);
174          }
175        fwrite(iobuf, 1, assignment[0], fout);
176        fclose (fout);
177
178        MPI_Barrier(MPI_COMM_WORLD);
179
180        delete[] p;
181        delete[] e;
182        delete[] part;
183        delete[] assignment;
184        delete[] offset;
185        delete[] rq;
186        delete[] indLenPairs;
187      }
188    else                            // GPU worker
189      {
190        long indLenPairs[2];
191
192        // send model parameters
193        MPI_Send ((void*)modelParams, 2, MPI_DOUBLE, 0, TAG_MODEL, ←
              MPI_COMM_WORLD);
194
195        // get size of assignment and allocate appropriate buffer
196        MPI_Recv (indLenPairs, 2, MPI_LONG, 0, TAG_WORK, ←
              MPI_COMM_WORLD, &stat);
197
198        long jobSize = indLenPairs[1];
199        iobuf = new unsigned char[jobSize];
200        FILE *f;
201        if ((f = fopen (argv[1], "r")) == NULL)
202          {
203             fprintf (stderr, "Can't open %s\n", argv[1]);
204             exit (EXIT_FAILURE);
205          }
206        fseek(f,indLenPairs[0], SEEK_SET);
207        fread(iobuf, 1, indLenPairs[1], f);
208        fclose (f);
209
210        int thrPerBlock = atoi (argv[3]);
211
```

```
212         rijndaelEncryptFE (rk, keybits, iobuf, iobuf, jobSize, ↵
                thrPerBlock);
213         rijndaelShutdown();
214
215         FILE *fout;
216         if ((fout = fopen (argv[2], "w")) == NULL)
217           {
218             fprintf (stderr, "Can't open %s\n", argv[2]);
219             exit (EXIT_FAILURE);
220           }
221         fseek(f,indLenPairs[0], SEEK_SET);
222         fwrite(iobuf, 1, jobSize, fout);
223         fclose (fout);
224
225         MPI_Barrier(MPI_COMM_WORLD);
226       }
227  ...
```

We have already outlined the steps involved in the execution of this program. The following list contains the main points of Listing 11.11 in more detail:

- Node 0 is using the loop of lines 133–139 to collect the p and e parameters of all nodes and populate the p[] and e[] arrays defined on lines 121 and 122.
- The p and e parameters of each node are held in the modelParams array defined on line 70. The array is convenient for allowing easy communication of said parameters on lines 193 (sender) and 135 (receiver).
- Node 0 calculates the parts that should be assigned to each node (lines 141–143) and then converts these figures to (start-index, length) integer pairs that identify which part of the input data each node will process (lines 146–152).
- The (start-index, length) pairs are stored in the same array (indLenPairs) in consecutive positions (lines 149 and 150) for easy communication to the worker nodes (lines 155 and 156).
- The communication of the (start-index, length) pairs could also be done by an MPI_Scatter call. The MPI_Isend call on line 156 allows node 0 to proceed to the actual input processing sooner.
- The input processing takes place on the GPU via a call to the front-end function rijndaelEncryptFE().
- Once a node has the details of its assignment (past line 196 for nodes other than 0), it allocates the necessary memory (lines 158 and 199) and reads the input data (lines 160 and 207).
- The input data buffer is also used to hold the ciphertext result, which is stored in the proper location of the output file (line 175 for node 0 and lines 221 and 222 for all the others).

A file similar to the one shown in Listing 11.11 targeting CPU execution is also supplied in the project directory (AES_MPI_nodatacopy/mainCPUWorker.cpp). Its only differences are the values of the p and e constants as defined on line 70 and the use of a plain for loop to go over the assigned part of the input in 16-byte blocks.

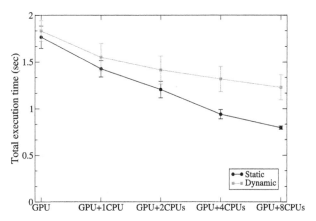

FIGURE 11.18

Average total execution times and corresponding standard deviation for dynamic and static load balancing, for encrypting 512 MiB of data.

The actual code, part of which is shown in Listing 11.11, contains statements for measuring the execution time. These lines are not shown for brevity.

The program can be executed by utilizing an application file, so that the GPU can be reserved by a single process, avoiding unnecessary resource contentions. For example, if we were to run four processes on a host, one utilizing the GPU, we should create an application file similar to:

```
# GPU node 0
—oversubscribe —host 127.0.0.1 —np 1 aesMPI in512 cipher 512

# 3 more CPU nodes
—oversubscribe —host 127.0.0.1 —np 3 aesMPICPUWorker in512 cipher ↩
    512
```

The expected command-line parameters are the input filename, the output filename, and the number of threads per block, the latter being essential for the GPU node only.

The execution can then be performed by calling:

```
$ mpirun ——app applFile
```

Fig. 11.18 compares the averaged-over-100-runs performance results of the parallel I/O design, with DLT-based partitioning outlined in this section, against the dynamic load balancing design of Section 6.15.2, running on the same hardware, i.e., an AMD Ryzen 9 3900X CPU and an RTX 2060 Super GPU. The times reported are the total execution times, including I/O, and not just the encoding times.

The results displayed in Fig. 11.18 clearly show the performance deterioration caused by the master–worker negotiating process that dynamic load balancing commands. The negative effect of this load-handling process becomes more prominent the more nodes are involved, as evident by the widening gap between static and dynamic designs. The latter also shows a higher variability in the execution times, which is not ideal.

Another factor contributing to the performance discrepancy is the parallel I/O that the static partitioning enables, allowing nodes to start and keep processing their assigned loads much faster.

Ideally, a software engineer should evaluate the circumstances of the execution platform, e.g., machine load and resource availability (like memory) variations in a multi-user environment, network traffic, etc., and the application requirements, in order to establish the best strategy for minimizing the execution time.

Exercises

1. Design a brute-force/exhaustive algorithm for determining the optimum subset of N nodes/processors in the case of static load balancing. What is the complexity of your algorithm?

2. Design a greedy algorithm for determining the optimum subset of N nodes/processors in the case of static load balancing. Will you always get the same solution as the one provided by an exhaustive algorithm?

3. The closed-form solutions in Section 11.3.3.1 for the N-port communication setup are based on the assumption that the master participates in the processing of the load. Derive the equations that would govern the solution if the master abstained from this task, facilitating only I/O functionality instead.

4. Write a program that calculates $part_0$ from Eqs. (11.11) and (11.39) in a linear number of steps.

5. Solve the example at the end of Section 11.3.3.2 by reversing the computing power of the nodes: $p_0 = 4 \cdot 6.6 \cdot 10^{-8}$, $p_1 = 3 \cdot (6.6 \cdot 10^{-8})$, $p_2 = 2 \cdot (6.6 \cdot 10^{-8})$, and $p_3 = (6.6 \cdot 10^{-8})$.

6. An alternative to having the master node distribute the load is to have all the nodes access a network filesystem and retrieve the data from there. What kind of communication configuration would correspond to such an arrangement? Calculate the partitioning that would be produced in this case, for the same problem setting as the previous question.

7. The partitioning performed using DLT in the kernel convolution example returns the percentage of the input bytes that should be assigned to each node. How can we convert this number to pixels? One may argue that we should instead use image rows. How can we convert the result of our analysis to rows?

8. Use the `tiobench` utility available at http://sourceforge.net/projects/tiobench/ to measure the performance you can get by concurrent access to a network filesystem (e.g., an NFS volume). Calculate the collective throughput of the server versus the number of threads used.

9. One way that can be used to improve the distribution cost of input data is to compress them. What kind of compression algorithms could be used in this case? How could we adapt the cost models to reflect this change?

10. Use the DLTlib library to calculate the optimum partitioning for a "query processing" application, where the communication cost is independent of the workload, consisting of a query during distribution and the result during the collection. You can assume that $b = d = 1$, the workload consists of $L = 10^6$ items, and the parallel platform is made of 10 compute nodes connected in a single-level tree, with $p_i = (i + 1) \cdot 0.01$ sec/item $\forall i \in [0, 9]$ and $l = 0.001$ sec/item. What would happen if the communication was 10 times slower?

11. Derive the equivalent of Eqs. (11.47) and (11.48) for arbitrary a and c, and implement them as part of a partitioning function.

12. The DLT examples presented in Sections 11.3.3.1 and 11.3.3.2 do not address an aspect of the problem which is significant: what is the optimum subset of nodes to use to process a load? Implement the heuristic algorithm you came up with in Exercise 2 to derive such a set.

Hint: nodes that should not be part of this set get a negative load assignment $part_i$.

Creating Qt programs

A.1 Using an IDE

Using an Integrated Development Environment is the best choice for beginning to explore Qt's functionality. Qt can be easily integrated with Eclipse or Microsoft's Visual Studio. One can also use the Qt Creator IDE supplied by The Qt Company, which is a lightweight alternative to the aforementioned IDEs. The IDEs take care of the library dependencies and include directory locations, which are needed for compiling a Qt program.

For experimenting with Qt threads, only a console application project needs to be created as shown in Fig. A.1.

A.2 The qmake utility

The qmake utility (supplied as part of the Qt tool chain) solves the problem of tracking dependencies across different platforms. A short project description (in the form of a text file with a .pro extension) is all that is needed. As an example, let us assume that a project consists of the following files:

```
main.cpp
client.cpp
calc.h
```

Then, the .pro file (e.g., myapp.pro) has to contain the following self-explanatory directives:

```
CONFIG += qt
HEADERS += calc.h
SOURCES += main.cpp
SOURCES += client.cpp
TARGET = myapp
```

Running the qmake command:

```
$ qmake myapp.pro
```

will produce the Makefile necessary for compiling the source files and linking them with the required libraries (Qt). Running the qmake utility is necessary only when the set of files making up the project is modified (added to or removed from). Once qmake

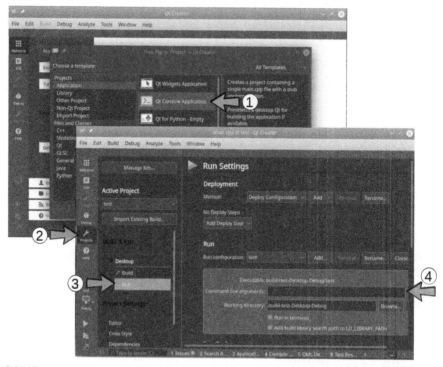

FIGURE A.1

After ① creating a "Qt Console Application," one can control the CLI parameters by ② selecting "Projects," ③ selecting the "Run" options, and ④ entering the required parameters.

is run, every subsequent compilation of the project requires only an execution of the make utility.

Running MPI programs: preparatory and configuration steps

B

B.1 Preparatory steps

The problem with having a network of workstations (NoW) as a parallel platform is that each of the workstations must provide a mechanism for remotely starting a process. The usual way of doing this is either through Remote Shell (RSH) or through Secure Shell (SSH). The former is obsolete as it is highly insecure (passwords are communicated in plaintext form).

SSH would normally require an interactive login process to take place on each of the workstations in order for an MPI program to execute! This lengthy and tedious procedure can be avoided by having an authentication agent perform the login transaction on our behalf. The following steps achieve this goal:

1. Create an authentication key, i.e., a number that will uniquely identify your user account:

```
$ ssh-keygen -t dsa
```

You will be prompted for a pass phrase that controls access to your keys. This does not have to be the same as your user account password. The ssh-keygen command generates two files holding a public and a secret key, respectively (the ~ sign represents your home directory):

```
~/.ssh/id_dsa
~/.ssh/id_dsa.pub
```

2. Copy the public key ~/.ssh/id_dsa.pub file:

```
$ cp ~/.ssh/id_dsa.pub ~/.ssh/authorized_keys2
```

3. Make sure that the copied file has the correct permissions:

```
$ chmod go-rwx ~/.ssh/authorized_keys2
```

4. Steps 1–3 have to be done only once (unless you forget the pass phrase!). Before each MPI session, you need to start the agent program:

```
$ ssh-agent bash
```

or

```
$ ssh—agent $SHELL
```

5. Handing over the keys to the agent is done via the command:

```
$ ssh—add
```

Now, you are – almost – ready to run your first parallel program. Using an NoW as a parallel platform entails one more step outlined in the next section.

B.2 Computing nodes discovery for MPI program deployment

Deploying an MPI program over an NoW requires a list of the corresponding IP addresses or DNS names. For the lucky few that have access to dedicated clusters or supercomputing facilities, the problem of node availability is largely solved and governed by the policies of their institution. However, when a generic intranet with dynamic IP machines is utilized, the list of machines might have to be compiled again every time, prior to the launch of a program. This section describes the steps that can be used for the generation of this list.

B.2.1 Host discovery with the nmap utility

The **Network Map**per (nmap) program is a security scanner developed to discover hosts and the services they support on a computer network. It has been primarily used for vulnerability detection, and as such it has been used by both system administrators (for securing systems) and hackers alike (for breaking in). For this reason, the use of nmap over an intranet may be monitored and/or controlled. It is a good idea to discuss your planned fair use of nmap with your site sysadmin before attempting the commands/scripts that are described below.

For the problem at hand, nmap will be used to detect the hosts available in a user-supplied range of IPs and enumerate the open ports on these machines. The latter is needed for safe identification of the machines that run sshd, as the OS detection supported by nmap is not always accurate. Additionally, for security reasons many operating systems spoof their replies to the calls used by nmap to deduce their identities.

If we assume that the machines that will be used to run our MPI program lie in the IP ranges of 10.25.32.* and 10.25.34.*, then the following sequence will produce a list of machines that are candidates for deployment:

```
$ nmap —oG hosts 10.25.32.* 10.25.34.*
$ grep ssh hosts | gawk —F " " '{print $2}' > hostsWithSSH
```

The "-oG" switch of the first line is used to save the output of nmap to a file ("hosts" is specified) in a text format that can be filtered with the grep utility. The next command line does just that, i.e., filter the output for lines containing `ssh`. These are in turn passed to the `gawk` utility for extracting their second column which contains the IP of the corresponding host.

The hosts can be subsequently verified, i.e., checking that the user credentials are appropriate for logging on, via the following line, which attempts to run an `echo` command in each of them:

```
$ for f in `cat hostsWithSSH`; do ssh $f echo $f; done
```

The above line should be attempted only after the SSH agent has started, as shown in Section B.1.

B.2.2 Automatic generation of a hostfile

An MPI hostfile can potentially hold the number of processes each of the hosts can support. An obvious reason for doing this is to maximize the hosts' utilization, as the number of cores can be incorporated into MPI's deployment process.

The following script combines the steps explained in the previous section and the information available in the /proc pseudofilesystem of Linux to automatically generate an appropriate hostfile:

```
 1  #!/bin/bash
 2  # File : hostBuild.sh
 3
 4  uname=`whoami`
 5  tmpFile=/tmp/hosts_${uname}
 6  tmpFile2=/tmp/hosts2_${uname}
 7
 8  # Discover all the hosts matching the supplied IP pattern(s)
 9  nmap -oG ${tmpFile} $* >/dev/null
10
11  # Get the IP of the localhost. It has to participate in the launch
12  ifconfig | head -n 2 | tail -n 1 | gawk -F "addr:" '{print $2}' | ←
         gawk '{print $1}' > ${tmpFile2}
13
14  # Filter out the hosts not supporting SSH
15  grep ssh ${tmpFile} | gawk -F " " '{print $2}' >> ${tmpFile2}
16
17  # Remove -if it exists- a duplicate entry for localhost
18  uniq ${tmpFile2} ${tmpFile}
19
20  # Get the cores for each host in the temporary file
21  for h in `cat ${tmpFile}`
22  do
23      res=`ssh -o ConnectTimeout=5 -o BatchMode=yes -o ←
             StrictHostKeyChecking=no $h cat /proc/cpuinfo 2>/dev/null |←
             grep processor | wc | gawk '{print $1}'`
24
25      # Output the IP only if there is a valid response from the ←
             previous command
```

```
26        if [ "${res:-0}" -ne 0 ]
27            then
28            echo "$h slots= ${res}"
29        fi
30    done
31    rm ${tmpFile} ${tmpFile2}
```

The lines that constitute something new in the above script are the following:

- Line 12: Inserts the IP of the host running the script to the hostfile.
- Line 18: Uses the uniq utility to remove any duplicate entries from the hostfile. This involves only the localhost.
- Lines 21–30: The loop iterates over all entries in the temporary hostfile and outputs the ones that respond to the command issued via ssh on line 23. Hosts which do not respond are ignored.
- Line 23: Runs the ssh command non-interactively (-o BatchMode=yes), with a maximum waiting period of 5 seconds (-o ConnectTimeout=5) and without performing strict key checking (-o StrictHostKeyChecking=no). Each host is required to run the "cat /proc/cpuinfo | grep processor | wc | gawk '{print $1}'" pipeline, which if successful returns the number of cores as recognized by the OS. There is no distinction between cores based on their support for hardware threads.

The script can simply be used in the fashion shown in the following example, i.e., by providing a space-separated list of IP patterns and redirecting the output to a file:

```
$ bash hostBuild.sh 10.25.32.* 10.25.34.*  > myHosts
```

For the script to execute properly, the ssh agent must be started before, as explained in Section B.1.

Time measurement

C.1 Introduction

High-resolution time measurement is a critical capability for calculating performance and keeping track of events in your system. This can serve both profiling and debugging purposes. After all, the bottom-line is how much time one can gain by introducing threads, GPU computation, and the like in an application.

Time measurement can be identified as absolute or relative. The concept of absolute or universal time is dated back to Isaac Newton, and many will argue that in the post-general relativity era there is no such thing as absolute time! In our context, absolute time has no place either, as we are concerned with time spans.

A common pattern that is used in all the sections that follow is that of subtracting time stamps. The time functions that are provided by the various libraries typically measure time from a fixed point in time, e.g., the beginning of program execution, the bootup time of the system, or the distance to a fixed point in time (usually 00:00 Jan 1, 1970).

It should be noted that *system clocks can be modified by time adjustments performed by the operating system*. Many systems run daemons that periodically synchronize the system time with Internet time servers via the NTP protocol. Real-time clock adjustments are typically done once on a daily basis, but they can produce wild time differences, e.g., measured durations can be very big, or even negative! In such an event, the results should be discarded as bogus and the experiment repeated.

C.2 POSIX high-resolution timing

Portable Operating System Interface for UniX (POSIX) is an IEEE standard that defines a set of APIs. POSIX was designed to provide cross-platform compatibility at the source-code level. Program written to use POSIX functions can be recompiled and executed in any system offering POSIX compatibility.

POSIX defines a set of function for high-resolution timing:

```
int clock_getres(clockid_t clk_id, struct timespec *res);  // ↩
    returns the clock resolution of the specified clock

int clock_gettime(clockid_t clk_id, struct timespec *tp);  // return↩
    the time according to the specified clock
```

The functions are defined in the header file time.h, and the -lrt switch has to be used during the linking process of a program.

Both functions return 0 for success and −1 for failure, and they operate on a pair of parameters of type:

- clockid_t: an integer identifying the clock to be queried. A number of clocks can be supported, either system-wide or process-specific, or even thread-specific. The most important ones, represented by symbolic constants, are:
  - CLOCK_REALTIME : system-wide real-time clock.
  - CLOCK_MONOTONIC : represents time since an unspecified starting point.
  - CLOCK_PROCESS_CPUTIME_ID : process-specific timer.
- struct timespec: contains two integer fields representing seconds and nanoseconds, respectively:

```
struct timespec {
    time_t    tv_sec;        /* seconds */
    long      tv_nsec;       /* nanoseconds */
};
```

Given an instance of ts of struct timespec, the time is ts.tv_sec + ts.tv_nsec/1000000000.0.

Equipped with the above functions, we can write a set of functions for conveniently measuring the time from a specified moment in the execution of a program. The time can be expressed in nanoseconds as an integer or in seconds as a floating point quantity, as shown in Listing C.1.

Listing C.1: An example of how the POSIX high-resolution timing functions can be utilized to measure execution times. The hrclock_sec (hrclock_nsec) function returns the time since the time0_sec (time0_nsec) variable was initialized in seconds (nanoseconds).

```
1   // File : clock_example.cpp
2   . . .
3   #include <time.h>
4
5   long time0_nsec = 0;
6
7   double time0_sec = 0;
8
9   //************************************************
10  double hrclock_sec ()
11  {
12      timespec ts;
13      clock_gettime (CLOCK_REALTIME , &ts);
14      double aux = ts.tv_sec + ts.tv_nsec / 1000000000.0;
15      return aux − time0_sec;
16  }
17
18  //************************************************
```

```
19
20   long hrclock_nsec ()
21   {
22     timespec ts;
23     clock_gettime (CLOCK_REALTIME, &ts);
24     long aux = ts.tv_sec * 1000000000 + ts.tv_nsec;
25     return aux - time0_nsec;
26   }
27
28   // *************************************************
29
30   int main ()
31   {
32     time0_nsec = hrclock_nsec ();
33
34     time0_sec = hrclock_sec ();
35     sleep (1);
36     cout << hrclock_nsec () << endl;
37     cout << hrclock_sec () << endl;
38     return 0;
39   };
```

C.3 Timing in C++11

C++ has been evolving in leaps and bounds during the last decade, with the introduction of new language features and standard library functionalities. C++20 introduced yet more features in the form of extensions to the chrono library, which are mainly focused on calendar and time-zone functionalities. In this section we discuss the chrono library that became part of the C++11 standard.

The <chrono> header file provides a high_resolution_clock class that we can use for timing purposes by calling its now() static method. The latter returns an std::chrono::time_point instance, which represents the current value of the clock.

The difference between two time_point objects is a duration object that can be converted to different time units by utilizing the duration_cast template function:

```
#include <chrono>

using namespace std::chrono;
. . .
auto t1 = high_resolution_clock::now();
// do something
auto t2 = high_resolution_clock::now();
auto dur = t2-t1;

cout << duration_cast<milliseconds>(dur).count() << endl;
```

The duration class overloads all the basic arithmetic and relational operators, allowing for easy manipulation of time spans. The milliseconds symbolic constant in the above statement is part of the set provided by the chrono library for controlling the casting outcome. The set includes:

- `std::chrono::nanoseconds`
- `std::chrono::microseconds`
- `std::chrono::milliseconds`
- `std::chrono::seconds`
- `std::chrono::minutes`
- `std::chrono::hours`

The `count()` method returns the duration in the specified time units.

C.4 Timing in Qt

Qt provides a convenient class for timing events: `QTime`. The most useful methods supported are:

```
void QTime::start();    // Set the time in the QTime object to the ←
    current time.
int QTime::elapsed ();  // Returns the number of milliseconds passed ←
    since the previous call to start() of restart().
int QTime::restart ();  // Set the time in the QTime object to the ←
    current time, and returns the elapsed time in milliseconds since ←
    the previous call to start() of restart().
```

Using QTime for timing purposes is straightforward as the following example shows:

```
...
QTime t;
t.start();

do_something();

printf("Time elapsed %i (ms)\n", t.elapsed());
```

C.5 Timing in OpenMP

OpenMP provides a timing function in the form of

```
double omp_get_wtime( void );
```

that returns the time elapsed from "some time in the past."

The resolution of the timer used is reported by:

```
double omp_get_wtick( void );
```

The duration of a portion of a program can be estimated by subtracting two readings of the `omp_get_wtime()` function, as in the example shown below:

```
double timeStart, timeEnd;
timeStart = omp_get_wtime();
. . . . // do something
timeEnd = omp_get_wtime();
cout << "Total time spent : " << timeEnd - timeStart << endl;
```

C.6 Timing in MPI

In terms of timing, MPI provides two functions: `MPI_Wtime` (wall time) and `MPI_Wticks`. The first reads the system clock, while the second returns the clock's resolution in seconds per tick. Their syntax is the following:

```
double MPI_Wtime( void );
double MPI_Wtick( void );
```

`MPI_Wtime` returns the time since an unspecified time in the past. Therefore, a single returned value has no meaning, but by subtracting two readings of the function, we can measure a time span.

```
double timeStart, timeEnd;
timeStart = MPI_Wtime();
. . . . // do something
timeEnd = MPI_Wtime();
cout << "Total time spent : " << timeEnd - timeStart << endl;
```

C.7 Timing in CUDA

Timing in CUDA is inherently tied to the use of events and streams, as explained in Section 6.7.5.1. CUDA kernel launches are asynchronous, i.e., the host returns immediately without waiting for the GPU to complete its assignment. The host can measure the timing of events on the GPU by inserting `cudaEvent_t` objects in streams.

An example of how events can be used to instrument a CUDA program is provided in Listing C.2.

Listing C.2: An example of how a CUDA program can be instrumented with the use of events.

```
1   . . .
2   cudaStream_t str;
3   cudaEvent_t startT, endT;
4   float duration;
5
```

```
6    // initialize two events
7    cudaEventCreate (&startT);
8    cudaEventCreate (&endT);
9
10   // enclose kernel launch between startT and endT events
11   cudaEventRecord (startT, str);
12   doSmt <<< grid, block, 0, str >>>(...);   // launch request has to be ←
         placed in a stream
13   cudaEventRecord (endT, str);
14
15   // wait for endT event to take place
16   cudaEventSynchronize (endT);
17
18   // calculate elapsed time
19   cudaEventElapsedTime (&duration, startT, endT);
20   printf("Kernel executed for %f\n", duration);
21
22   // clean-up allocated objects and reset device
23   cudaStreamDestroy (str);
24   cudaEventDestroy (startT);
25   cudaEventDestroy (endT);
26   cudaDeviceReset ();
27   . . .
```

It should be noted that cudaEventRecord() on lines 11 and 13 (and subsequently the kernel launch of line 12) can be performed without an explicit stream parameter str. In that case, the cudaEventSynchronize() call of line 16 will return when all the preceding operations in the CUDA context have been completed. These may include operations created by different host threads.

Boost.MPI

D.1 Mapping from MPI C to Boost.MPI

Table D.1 lists the most commonly used MPI functions and constants and their respective Boost.MPI counterparts. Only a subset of MPI functions are available through the Boost.MPI classes, but a program is allowed to have a mix of Boost.MPI methods and MPI C calls.

Table D.1 MPI functions and constants and their Boost.MPI counterparts.

MPI	Boost.MPI
Various functions	
MPI_Abort	environment::abort
MPI_Comm_size	communicator::size
MPI_Comm_rank	communicator::rank
MPI_Finalize	called by environment destructor
MPI_Init	called by environment constructor
Point-to-point communications	
MPI_Bsend	N/A
MPI_Buffer_attach	N/A
MPI_Buffer_detach	N/A
MPI_Get_count	status::count
MPI_Ibsend	N/A
MPI_Iprobe	communicator::iprobe
MPI_Irsend	N/A
MPI_Isend	communicator::isend
MPI_Issend	N/A
MPI_Irecv	communicator::irecv
MPI_Probe	communicator::probe
MPI_Recv	communicator::recv
MPI_Rsend	N/A
MPI_Send	communicator::send
MPI_Ssend	N/A
MPI_Test	request::test

continued on next page

Table D.1 (*continued*)

MPI	Boost.MPI
MPI_Testall	test_all
MPI_Testany	test_any
MPI_Wait	request::wait
MPI_Waitall	wait_all
MPI_Waitany	wait_any
Constants	
MPI_ANY_SOURCE	any_source
MPI_ANY_TAG	any_tag
Collective communications	
MPI_Allgather	all_gather
MPI_Allgatherv	all_gatherv
MPI_Allreduce	all_reduce
MPI_Alltoall	all_to_all
MPI_Alltoallv	N/A
MPI_Barrier	communicator::barrier
MPI_Bcast	broadcast
MPI_Gather	gather
MPI_Gatherv	gatherv
MPI_Reduce	reduce
MPI_Scan	scan
MPI_Scatter	scatter
MPI_Scatterv	scatterv

Setting up CUDA

E.1 Installation

CUDA SDK installation is typically a trouble-free experience. NVidia has shifted in recent SDK releases to a single-archive approach: you just have to download a single file from https://developer.nvidia.com/cuda-downloads and either run it if you select the executable one or feed it to your system software administration tool in the case of Linux. The single archive contains the NVidia tool chain in addition to reference documentation (manual pages), sample programs, and an updated display driver.

NVidia's site is the ultimate source of information for proper installation steps. In this section we just highlight some of the pitfalls that can plague someone making their first steps in the CUDA world:

- Always install the NVidia display driver that accompanies the CUDA release you select to install or a newer one. Failure to do so may cause your CUDA programs or even the samples that come with the toolkit to fail to run, even if they manage to compile without a problem. Having said that, recent SDKs do allow the use of older drivers and NVidia publishes the minimum driver specification required.
- In multi-user systems like Linux, a CUDA sample programs installation on a system-wide location (e.g., /opt or /usr) will create problems for users that try to compile or modify these programs, due to permission limitations. In that case, one has to copy the entire samples directory to their home directory to perform any of these actions.

E.2 Issues with GCC

The NVidia CUDA Compiler driver (nvcc) has been known to have incompatibility problems with newer GCC versions. The remedy for a properly working tool chain is to install an older GCC version. In the case of the Ubuntu Linux distribution, the following commands will accomplish just that. For the particular example GCC version 7 is used, but the ultimate choice depends on the CUDA SDK installed and the particular Linux distribution:

```
$ sudo apt—get install gcc—7 g++—7
$ sudo update—alternatives ——install /usr/bin/gcc gcc /usr/bin/gcc—7↩
    50
$ sudo update—alternatives ——config gcc
```

The response to the last command is the following prompt that allows the switch to the alternate C compiler:

```
There are 2 choices for the alternative gcc (providing /usr/bin/gcc)↩


    Selection    Path              Priority   Status
  * 0            /usr/bin/gcc—9    50         auto mode
    1            /usr/bin/gcc—7    50         manual mode
    2            /usr/bin/gcc—9    50         manual mode

Press enter to keep the current choice[*], or type selection number:
```

The same sequence should be repeated separately for the C++ compiler:

```
$ sudo update—alternatives ——install /usr/bin/g++ g++ /usr/bin/g++—7↩
    50
$ sudo update—alternatives ——config g++
```

As mentioned above, this is a CUDA SDK version-specific issue, so your mileage may vary. For example, CUDA 11.5 is able to work properly with GCC 11, compiling successfully all NVidia-supplied CUDA sample projects.

E.3 Combining CUDA with third-party libraries

NVidia offers Nsight Eclipse Plugins (NEP) as the primary IDE for CUDA development, on all supported platforms. However, it does not accommodate easy integration of other tools like, e.g., Qt's toolchain into a project. While the sequence of commands is straightforward, making NEP or Qt's qmake generate this sequence is a challenge. For this reason we present a makefile that can perform this task while at the same time being easy to modify and adapt.

The key points are:

- Have all .cu files *compiled* separately by nvcc. The compilation has to generate relocatable device code (-device-c). This is a requirement for projects made up of several CUDA files.
- Have all the .c/.cpp files that do not contain device code *compiled* separately by gcc/g++.
- Have all the object files .o, *linked* by nvcc. The linking has to generate relocatable device code (-rdc=true).

During compilation all the necessary include file directories should be supplied. Similarly, during the linking process all the library directories and dynamic/static libraries needed must be specified.

We will use the fractal generation test case of Section 6.15.1 as an example. That particular project is made up of the following files:

- `kernel.cu`: Contains device code for calculating the Mandelbrot fractal set. It also contains a host front-end function for launching the kernel, copying the results from the device to the host and using them to color the pixels of a `QImage` object. Hence it needs to include Qt header files.
- `kernel.h`: Header file containing the declaration of the host function that launches the GPU kernel. Needed by `main.cpp`.
- `main.cpp`: Program entry point, responsible for parsing user input, calling the host front-end function in `kernel.cu`, and saving the output with the assistance of Qt.

Given the above, the following makefile can be used to compile and link the project:

```
NVCC = nvcc
CC = g++

CUDA_COMPILE_FLAGS = --device-c -arch=compute_75 -code=sm_75
CUDA_LINK_FLAGS =  -rdc=true -arch=compute_75 -code=sm_75

QT_COMPILE_FLAGS = -I/usr/include/qt5/QtCore  -I/usr/include/qt5/↵
    QtGui -I/usr/include/qt5
QT_LINK_FLAGS = -L/usr/lib/x86_64-linux-gnu -lQtGui -lQtCore -↵
    lpthread

mandelbrotCUDA : main.o kernel.o
        ${NVCC} ${CUDA_LINK_FLAGS} ${QT_LINK_FLAGS} $^ -o $@

main.o : main.cpp kernel.h
        ${CC} ${QT_COMPILE_FLAGS} -c main.cpp

kernel.o : kernel.cu kernel.h
        ${NVCC} ${CUDA_COMPILE_FLAGS} ${QT_COMPILE_FLAGS} -c kernel.↵
            cu

clean:
        rm *.o
```

In the above, the automatic variable `$@` represents the target, i.e., `mandelbrotCUDA`, for that particular rule, and `$^` represents all the dependencies listed.

A similar procedure can be applied for integrating MPI and CUDA, or any other possible combination of tools. As an example, let us consider the makefile used in the MPI-CUDA implementation of the AES block cipher described in Section 6.15.2. This makefile describes the creation of three targets, two stand-alone GPU implementations `aesCUDA` and `aesCUDAStreams`, and the MPI-enhanced version `aesMPI`:

```
NVCC = nvcc
CC = g++
CUDA_LINK_FLAGS = -rdc=true -arch=compute_75 -code=sm_75
CUDA_COMPILE_FLAGS = --device-c -arch=compute_75 -code=sm_75
CC_COMPILE_FLAGS = -O3 -I/usr/include/openmpi
CC_LINK_FLAGS = -lm -lstdc++ -lmpi -L/usr/lib -lpthread -lmpi_cxx


all : aesMPI aesCUDA aesCUDAStreams

aesMPI : main.o rijndael_host.o rijndael_device.o
        ${NVCC} ${CUDA_LINK_FLAGS} ${CC_LINK_FLAGS} $^ -o $@

main.o : main.cpp rijndael.h
        ${CC} ${CC_COMPILE_FLAGS} -c main.cpp

rijndael_host.o : rijndael_host.cu rijndael.h rijndael_device.h
        ${NVCC} ${CUDA_COMPILE_FLAGS} ${CC_COMPILE_FLAGS} -c ↩
            rijndael_host.cu

rijndael_device.o : rijndael_device.cu rijndael.h rijndael_device.h
        ${NVCC} ${CUDA_COMPILE_FLAGS} ${CC_COMPILE_FLAGS} -c ↩
            rijndael_device.cu

aesCUDA : aesCUDA.o rijndael_host.o rijndael_device.o
        ${NVCC} ${CUDA_LINK_FLAGS} ${CC_LINK_FLAGS} $^ -o $@

aesCUDA.o : aesCUDA.cu rijndael.h
        ${NVCC} ${CUDA_COMPILE_FLAGS} ${CC_COMPILE_FLAGS} -c aesCUDA↩
            .cu

aesCUDAStreams : aesCUDA.o rijndael_host_streams.o rijndael_device.o
        ${NVCC} ${CUDA_LINK_FLAGS} ${CC_LINK_FLAGS} $^ -o $@

rijndael_host_streams.o : rijndael_host_streams.cu rijndael.h ↩
    rijndael_device.h
        ${NVCC} ${CUDA_COMPILE_FLAGS} ${CC_COMPILE_FLAGS} -c ↩
            rijndael_host_streams.cu

clean:
        rm *.o
```

An issue that can be encountered is that the third-party libraries to be linked with your project require the generation of "position-independent code." This can be accomplished by the use of the -fPIC or -fPIE compiler flags. These flags cannot be passed directly to nvcc, but they have to "pass through" to the GCC compiler. The appropriate nvcc flag to achieve this is -Xcompiler '-fPIC'.

OpenCL helper functions

OpenCL uses a long procedure for setting up the interaction between host and device. This sequence of elementary steps that has to be repeated for every OpenCL program is a burden on the programmer. In this section we describe in detail a number of simple functions that are designed to reduce the programmer effort. All the functions are provided as part of the cl_utility.h file.

F.1 **Function** readCLFromFile

OpenCL device code is typically compiled on-line. While having the device code as a static string presents no problems, keeping it in a separate file allows the use of the sophisticated programming editors we have all become accustomed to for writing this code. The readCLFromFile function shown below reads the device code from a file and returns it as a C string to the caller for subsequent compilation.

Listing F.1: OpenCL helper function readCLFromFile.

```
1   // Reads device code from a file and returns a pointer to the buffer↩
        holding it
2   char * readCLFromFile(
3           const char* file)  // File name holding the device source ↩
                code (IN)
4   {
5       FILE *f=fopen(file,"rt");
6       if(f==NULL)
7       {
8           printf("Failed to open file %s for reading\n", file);
9           return NULL;
10      }
11
12      fseek(f, 0, SEEK_END);
13      long fsize = ftell(f);
14      fseek(f, 0, SEEK_SET);
15
16      char *buffer = (char*)malloc(sizeof(char)*(fsize+1));
17      if(buffer==NULL)
18      {
19          printf("Failed to allocate memory for reading file %s\n", file↩
                );
```

```
20        return NULL;
21    }
22
23    fread(buffer, fsize, 1, f);
24    buffer[fsize]=0;
25
26    fclose(f);
27    return buffer;
28 }
```

The function works by retrieving the size of the file (line 12) and allocating a buffer capable of holding the entire file contents and the terminating null value (line 16). The file is read in one go at line 23. The buffer which is dynamically allocated should be released by the caller.

F.2 **Function** isError

An OpenCL function returns the outcome of the requested action either as the result of the function or by storing it at a supplied cl_int address location. This outcome needs to be checked immediately for easy and early error detection. The detection of an error also typically entails the output of a message, although an immediate termination is up to the host program logic. The isError function is supposed to print the supplied message if the status argument does not match CL_SUCCESS. The returned Boolean also indicates whether an error was detected.

In terms of functionality it is very simple, but it can reduce the effort involved in error checking and reporting following every single OpenCL function invocation.

Listing F.2: OpenCL helper function isError.

```
1  // Returns false if status is CL_SUCCESS
2  bool isError(
3              cl_int status,   // Status returned by an OpenCL
4                               // function (IN)
5              const char *msg)// Message to be printed if status is
6                               // not CL_SUCCESS (IN)
7  {
8      if(status == CL_SUCCESS)
9          return false;
10     else
11     {
12         printf("%s\n",msg);
13         return true;
14     }
15 }
```

F.3 **Function** getCompilationError

This is a function that returns the address of a string containing the compilation error of the OpenCL code that was used in the generation of the program "pr." If no error happens, the string will be empty.

Listing F.3: OpenCL helper function getCompilationError.

```
char *getCompilationError (cl_program & pr, // Reference to program
                                             // object that failed
                                             // to compile (IN)
                           cl_device_id &id)// Target device ID (IN)
{
  size_t logSize;
  // Retrieve message size in "logSize"
  clGetProgramBuildInfo (pr, id, CL_PROGRAM_BUILD_LOG, 0, NULL, &↵
      logSize);
  // Allocate the necessary buffer space
  char *logMsg = (char *) malloc (logSize);
  // Retrieve the actual error message
  clGetProgramBuildInfo (pr, id, CL_PROGRAM_BUILD_LOG, logSize, ↵
      logMsg, NULL);
  return logMsg;
}
```

F.4 **Function** handleError

This is a function that extends the isError functionality to include program cleanup and termination. A pointer to a function that returns nothing and accepts no parameters must be provided.

Listing F.4: OpenCL helper function handleError.

```
// Calls the cleanup function if status is not CL_SUCCESS,
// after printing message
void handleError(
          cl_int status,     // Status returned by an OpenCL
                             // function  (IN)
          const char *msg,   // Message to be printed if status
                             // is not CL_SUCCESS (IN)
          void (*cleanup)())// Pointer to cleanup function
{
    if(status != CL_SUCCESS)
    {
        printf("%s\n",msg);
        (*cleanup)();
        exit(1);
    }
}
```

F.5 **Function** setupDevice

Preparing an OpenCL device for executing a kernel involves the identification of the OpenCL-supporting platform that contains the device, the identification of the device, the creation of a context for handling the associated resource management, and the creation of a command-queue.

The setupDevice function shown below performs these steps (as explained in Section 7.3), defaulting to the first available platform (line 20) and the first available device (line 25). Upon success, the selected device ID, the context, and the command-queue are returned to the caller.

Listing F.5: OpenCL helper function setupDevice.

```
1   void setupDevice(
2                   cl_context &cont,     // Reference to context to be
3                                         // created (IN/OUT)
4                   cl_command_queue &q, // Reference for queue to be
5                                         // created (IN/OUT)
6                   cl_queue_properties *qprop, // Array to queue
7                                         // properties (IN/OUT)
8                   cl_device_id &id)     // Reference to device to be
9                                         // utilized. Defaults to the
10                                        // first one listed by
11                                        // clGetPlatformIDs (IN/OUT)
12  {
13    cl_uint numPlatforms;
14    cl_platform_id firstPlatformId;
15    cl_device_id devID[MAXNUMDEV];
16    cl_uint numDev;
17    cl_int errNum;
18
19    // Get a reference to an object representing a platform
20    errNum = clGetPlatformIDs (1, &firstPlatformId, &numPlatforms);
21    if (isError(errNum,"Failed to find any OpenCL platforms.") || ↩
          numPlatforms <= 0)
22      exit(1);
23
24    // Get the device IDs matching the CL_DEVICE_TYPE parameter, up to ↩
          the MAXNUMDEV limit
25    errNum = clGetDeviceIDs (firstPlatformId, CL_DEVICE_TYPE_ALL, ↩
          MAXNUMDEV, devID, &numDev);
26    if (isError(errNum, "Failed to find any OpenCL devices.") || ↩
          numDev <= 0)
27      exit(2);
28
29    char devName[100];
30    size_t nameLen;
31    for (int i = 0; i < numDev; i++)
32      {
33        errNum = clGetDeviceInfo (devID[i], CL_DEVICE_NAME, 100, (void↩
              *) devName, &nameLen);
34        if (errNum == CL_SUCCESS)
```

```
35        printf("Device %i is %s\n",i,  devName);
36      }
37
38   cl_context_properties prop[] = {
39     CL_CONTEXT_PLATFORM,
40     (cl_context_properties) firstPlatformId,
41     0                          // termination
42   };
43
44   cont = clCreateContext (prop, numDev, devID,
45                           NULL,   // no callback function
46                           NULL,   // no data for callback
47                           &errNum);
48   if (isError(errNum, "Failed to create a context. "))
49     {
50         exit(3);
51     }
52
53   q = clCreateCommandQueueWithProperties (cont, devID[0], qprop, &↩
          errNum);
54
55   if (isError(errNum, "Failed to create a command queue"))
56     {
57         clReleaseContext (cont);
58         exit(4);
59     }
60
61   // return chosen device ID
62   id = devID[0];
63 }
```

F.6 **Function** setupProgramAndKernel

This function serves the runtime compilation of an OpenCL program, supplied in a file named by the programFile argument. A program object serves to encapsulate the details (line 19). The compilation of the program (line 24) targeting the device identified by the id parameter is not the end of the story, as a program can contain multiple kernel functions. Selecting the desired one (identified by the kernelName string) and packaging it as a cl_kernel object on line 28 is the final step.

It is noteworthy to mention the inclusion of line 23, so that OpenCL2.0-specific features, such as pipes, can be compiled properly.

This function is appropriate for simple device programs that have just a single kernel function.

Listing F.6: OpenCL helper function setupProgramAndKernel.

```
1  // Returns true if program was compiled successfully
2  bool setupProgramAndKernel(
```

```
3          cl_device_id &id,          // Reference to device to be
4                                     // targeted (IN)
5          cl_context cont,           // Reference to context to be
6                                     // utilized (IN)
7        const char *programFile,     // Pointer to file name
8                                     // holding the source code (IN)
9          cl_program &pr,            // Reference to program object
10                                    // to be created (IN/OUT)
11       const char *kernelName,      // Pointer to string identifying
12                                    // the kernel function (IN)
13         cl_kernel &kernel)         // Reference to kernel object to
14                                    // be created (IN/OUT)
15  {
16      cl_int errNum;
17      char *source = readCLFromFile(programFile);
18
19      pr = clCreateProgramWithSource (cont, 1, (const char**)&source, ↵
            NULL, &errNum);
20      if(isError(errNum, "Failed to create program."))
21          return false;
22
23      char options[]="-cl-std=CL2.0";
24      errNum = clBuildProgram (pr, 1, &id, options, NULL, NULL);
25      if(isError(errNum, "Failed to build program."))
26          return false;
27
28      kernel = clCreateKernel (pr, kernelName, &errNum);
29      if (isError(errNum, "Failed to create kernel."))
30          return false;
31
32      return true;
33  }
```

DLTlib

G.1 DLTlib functions

The library does break good software engineering practices by making a number of data members public. The reason for this violation is just convenience, given the use of the library as a research tool primarily.

The mathematical underpinnings of the library have been published in [17] and [12]. These publications contain a far more extended analysis than the one allowed by a reference appendix.

The library provides methods for solving the partitioning and optimum node subset problems for three categories of problems:

- **Query processing**: Class of problems where the communication cost does not depend on the workload. Conceptually, it is similar to running a query on the records of a database. The overall execution time depends on the size of the tables, but the communication involves only a query statement and a result set.
- **Image processing**: Class of problems where the communication is linearly dependent on the size of the workload. Low-level image filtering is a characteristic example.
- **Image registration** (a.k.a. image query): A mix of the previous two cases where the distribution cost depends on the workload but the collection cost does not. Distribution cost entails the communication of the images against which a comparison is made, while the collection cost only accounts for the indices (and possibly comparison metrics) of the best matches.

The library is built around two classes: Node and Network. Tables G.1 and G.2 list the most significant data components of Node and Network, respectively. The notations used in these tables refer to the cost models of Section 11.3.1, i.e., Eqs. (11.5), (11.7), and (11.8), that we also list below for convenience:

$$t_{comp}^{(i)} = p_i(part_i \cdot L + e_i),$$

$$t_{distr}^{(i)} = l_i(a \cdot part_i \cdot L + b),$$

$$t_{coll}^{(i)} = l_i(c \cdot part_i \cdot L + d).$$

Table G.1 Short reference of structure `Node`. Fields are listed in alphabetical order.

Field	Type	Description
child	Node *[]	Array of pointers to children nodes.
collection_order	int	Used in the 1-port image query to encode the suggested collection order.
degree	int	The number of children of this `Node`.
e0	double	The constant part of the computation.
L	double	The load assigned to *tree* rooted at this node.
Lint	long	The "quantized" load assigned to this node (not to subtree).
l2par	double	Link to parent, i.e., l_i.
mi_part	double[]	Array of parts, one for each installment.
name	char[]	Identifier used for this node.
next_n	Node *	Pointer to the next `Node` structure in a linked list.
parent	Node *	Pointer to the parent `Node`.
part	double	The part of the computation assigned to a `Node`, in the case of one installment only.
power	double	Corresponds to p_i.
through	char	A value of 1 indicates that the `Node` is not participating in the computation (e.g., too slow), instead sending all of its received load to its children.

Table G.2 Short reference of data members of class `Network`.

Field	Type	Description
head	Node *	Points to the first in a linked list of `Node` instances. Can be used to traverse the list and examine a solution.
valid	char	Set to 1 by the methods, to indicate if a solution to a partitioning problem is feasible and correct. It should be checked immediately after a partitioning is attempted.
clipping	char	Set by `Quantify` method to 1, if the set of current nodes has redundant items, i.e., a subset should be used.

In the following subsections we summarize the most important methods offered by the `Network` class, categorized by the target partitioning problem they address.

G.1.1 Class `Network`: **generic methods**

```
// Removes Nodes with no assigned load from a Network
void ClipIdleNodes();

// Generates a random tree according to the given parameters
void GenerateRandomTree(
            bool ImageOrQuery,  // 0: query, 1: image proc.
            int N,              // number of nodes
            float min_p,        // minimum p_i
```

```
                    float max_p,         // maximum p_i
                    float min_l,         // minimum l_i
                    float max_l,         // maximum l_i
                    float min_e,         // minimum e_i
                    float max_e,         // maximum e_i
                    bool fultree=false,  // If true, the internal nodes
                                         // will be filled up with
                                         // children up to the maximum
                                         // degree specified by the
                                         // MAX_NODE_DEGREE constant
                    bool all_fe=false);  // All nodes have a communi-
                                         // cation front-end?

// Inserts a Node in a Network and returns a reference to it
Node* InsertNode(char *c,               // Name of node
                 double speed,          // p_i
                 double e,              // e_i
                 char *parent,          // Name of parent
                 double link2parent,    // l_i
                 bool fe = false,       // Comm. front-end equipped?
                 bool thru = false);    // Is it a "conductor" node?
                                        // I.e., does it participate in
                                        // the computation?

// Overloaded version of the previous method. A reference to the
    parent Node is passed instead of its name
Node* InsertNode(char *c,
                 double speed,
                 double e,
                 Node *parent,
                 double link2parent,
                 bool fe = false,
                 bool thru = false);

// Prints to standard output a description of the Node objects
    managed by a Network
void PrintNet(void);

// Prints the assigned parts to a Network's nodes
void PrintSolution(bool quantized = 0); // If set to true, the Lint
    field is used

// Rounds the assigned loads, to integer quantities. It returns the
    estimated execution time
double Quantify( bool ImageOrQuery, // 0: query, 1: image processing
                 double ab,          // contains the 'a' parameter
                                     // for image, or 'b' otherwise
                 double cd);         // contains the 'c' parameter
                                     // for image, or 'd' otherwise
```

```
// Generates a random tree by reusing the existing nodes of a ←
     Network. Parameters are identical to the GenerateRandomTree ←
     method
void ReUseRandomTree(
                    bool ImageOrQuery,
                    float min_p,
                    float max_p,
                    float min_l,
                    float max_l,
                    float min_e,
                    float max_e,
                    bool full_tree = false,
                    bool all_fe = false);
```

G.1.2 **Class** Network: **query processing**

The term "query processing" refers to a scenario where the communication costs are independent from the workload that is to be partitioned. In other words, we have $a = c = 0$ in Eqs. (11.7) and (11.8). The following methods assume the use of 1-port communications and a single-installment load distribution, but they can solve the problem for arbitrary trees of Node instances.

```
// Uses a greedy algorithm to find the best subset from the ←
     available nodes, that can process a workload. The algorithm adds←
     nodes one-by-one, as long as the execution time decreases.
void GreedyQuery(Network &s, // Reference to the best performing
                              // subset of nodes (OUT)
                long L,       // Workload
                double b,     // Comm. model parameters
                double d);    //

// Similar to GreedyQuery, with the exception that the algorithm ←
     starts from the complete machine and attempts to remove leaf ←
     nodes one-by-one, as long as the execution time decreases.
void GreedyQueryRev(
                Network &s, // Reference to the best performing
                            // subset of nodes (OUT)
                long L,       // Workload
                double b,     // Comm. model parameters
                double d);    //

// Implements an exhaustive algorithm for finding the optimum node ←
     subset. It can be very time-consuming
void OptimumQuery(
                Network &s, // Reference to the optimum performing
                            // subset of nodes (OUT)
                long L,       // Workload
                double b,     // Comm. model parameters
                double d);    //
```

```
// Determines the execution time for a load that has been ←
    partitioned already , not necessarily using DLT
double SimulateQuery(
                double b,        // Comm. model parameters
                double d,        //
                bool output = 1);  // By default results are also
                                   // dumped to standard output


// Applies the DLT formulas for calculating the optimum assignement ←
    to a given set of nodes. Calculated parts are stored in the "←
    part" field of each Node structure
void SolveQuery( long L,          // Workload
                double b,        // Comm. model parameters
                double d,        //
                bool plain = 0);  // Should be set to 0 or omitted


// Similar to the GreedyQuery method , but specifically addressing ←
    homogeneous parallel platforms , p_i=p, l_i=l
void UniformQueryGreedy(
                Network &s, // Reference to the best performing
                            // subset of nodes (OUT)
                long L,      // Workload
                double b,    // Comm. model parameters
                double d);   //
```

G.1.3 **Class** Network: **image processing**

The term "image processing" refers to a scenario where the communication costs are linearly dependent on the workload that is to be partitioned. In other words, we have $b = d = 0$ in Eqs. (11.7) and (11.8). Additionally, it is assumed that the communication media are uniform, i.e., $l_i \equiv l$, at least as far as the children of each individual node are concerned.

The following methods assume the use of 1-port communications and a single installment load distribution, but they can solve the problem for arbitrary trees of Node instances.

```
// Uses a greedy algorithm to find the best subset from the ←
    available nodes , that can process a workload. The algorithm adds←
    nodes one—by—one , as long as the execution time decreases .
void GreedyImage(Network &s,  // Reference to the best performing
                              // subset of nodes (OUT)
                long L,      // Workload
                double a,    // Comm. model parameters
                double c);


// Uses a greedy algorithm to find the best subset from the ←
    available nodes , that can process a workload. The algorithm ←
    starts from the complete machine and attempts to remove leaf ←
    nodes one—by—one , as long as the execution time decreases .
void GreedyImageRev(
```

```
                Network &s,   // Reference to the best performing
                              // subset of nodes (OUT)
                long L,       // Workload
                double a,     // Comm. model parameters
                double c);

// Implements an exhaustive algorithm for finding the optimum node ↩
//    subset. It can be very time-consuming
void OptimumImage(
                Network &s,   // Reference to the optimum performing
                              // subset of nodes (OUT)
                long L,       // Workload
                double a,     // Comm. model parameters
                double c);

// Determines the execution time for a load that has been ↩
//    partitioned already, not necessarily using DLT
double SimulateImage(
                double a,             // Comm. model parameters
                double c,             //
                bool output = 1);     // By default results are also
                                      // dumped to standard output

// Applies the DLT formulas for calculating the optimum assignement ↩
//    to a given set of nodes. Calculated parts are stored in the "↩
//    part" field of each Node structure
void SolveImage( long L,           // Workload
                double a,          // Comm. model parameters
                double c,          //
                bool plain = 0);// Should be set to 0 or omitted


void UniformQueryGreedy(
                Network &s,   // Reference to the best performing
                              // subset of nodes (OUT)
                long L,       // Workload
                double b,     // Comm. model parameters
                double d);    //

// Similar to the GreedyImage method, but specifically addressing ↩
//    homogeneous parallel platforms, p_i=p, l_i=1
void UniformImageGreedy(
                Network &s,   // Reference to the best performing
                              // subset of nodes (OUT)
                long L,       // Workload
                double a,     // Comm. model parameters
                double c);    //
```

G.1.4 **Class** Network**: image registration**

In this case, which is also known as image query, the distribution cost depends on the workload, but the collection cost does not. The following methods cover almost all possible communication setups, but they can solve the problem for single-level node trees only. By default, all methods assume single-installment distribution, using 1-port communications and block-type computation. The naming convention used for methods covering other scenarios is to add one or more of the following extensions:

- NInst: using $M \geq 2$ installments,
- NPort: N-port communication,
- ST: stream-type computation.

A major difference of the following methods compared to the ones listed in Sections G.1.2 and G.1.3 is that they can cater for multiple executions, where the workload is distributed during the first execution, and possibly rebalanced during subsequent ones. The key idea is that each time a new image is to be compared against a pool of images, the latter do not have to be communicated again to the compute nodes. The term used here is "embedding," i.e., making the previously used images a part of the local/resident workload. The resident load is represented by the e_i parameter of the Node objects (field e0).

```
// Makes workload L, part of the resident load
void ImageQueryEmbed(long L);

// Makes workload L that was distributed over M installments, part ←
    of the resident load
void ImageQueryEmbed_Ninst(
                long L,   // Workload
                int M);   // Number of installments


// Estimates and returns the execution time, for arbitrarily ←
    partitioned loads
double SimulateImageQuery_Nport(
                long L,                     // Workload
                long b,                     // Comm. model parameters
                double d,                   //
                bool isstream = false);     // Set to true for
                                            // stream-type computation

// Estimates and returns the execution time, for arbitrarily ←
    partitioned loads
double SimulateImageQuery_ST(
                long L,   // Workload
                long b,   // Comm. model parameters
                double d);//

// Estimates and returns the execution time, for arbitrarily ←
    partitioned loads
double SimulateImageQuery(
```

```
                long L,       // Workload
                long b,       // Comm. model parameters
                double d);  //

// Solves the partitioning problem, for multiple installments and N←
    port. Returns the execution time.
double SolveImageQuery_NInst_NPort(
                long L,       // Workload
                long b,       // Comm. model parameters
                double d, //
                int M);     // Number of installments

// Solves the partitioning problem for multiple installments ←
    optimally, and returns the execution time. Distribution and ←
    collection sequences are found via exhaustive search. L and b ←
    parameters may be modified in the case of stream−type ←
    computation for proper timing. Works for single installment as ←
    well.
double SolveImageQuery_NInst_Optimum(
                long &L,                    // Workload (IN/OUT)
                long &b,                    // Comm. model parameters
                                            // (IN/OUT)
                double d,                   //
                int M,                      // Number of installments
                bool blocktype = true,  // Selects between
                                            // block and stream type
                double *worstp = NULL);// Execution time of worst
                                            // possible sequences. Just
                                            // for comparison (OUT)

// Solves the partitioning problem for multiple installments and ←
    returns the execution time. Distribution and collection ←
    sequences are heuristically found. L and b parameters may be ←
    modified for timing purposes, if the nodes hold no resident load←

double SolveImageQuery_NInst_ST(
                long &L,  // Workload (IN/OUT)
                long &b,  // Comm. model parameters (IN/OUT)
                double d, //
                int M);   // Number of installments

// Solves the partitioning problem for multiple installments and ←
    returns the execution time. Distribution and collection ←
    sequences are heuristically found.
double SolveImageQuery_NInst(
                long L,   // Workload
                long b,   // Comm. model parameters
                double d, //
                int M);   // Number of installments

// Solves the partitioning problem for a single installment, stream−←
    type computation, and returns the execution time.
```

```
double SolveImageQuery_NPort_ST(
                long &L,     // Workload(IN/OUT)
                long b,      // Comm. model parameters
                double d);   //

// Solves the partitioning problem for a single installment, N-port ↩
    communications, and returns the execution time. L is passed by ↩
    reference to allow resident load rebalancing
double SolveImageQuery_NPort(
                long &L,     // Workload(IN/OUT)
                long b,      // Comm. model parameters
                double d);   //

// Solves the partitioning problem for a single installment, 1-port ↩
    communications, and returns the execution time. L is passed by ↩
    reference to allow resident load rebalancing
double SolveImageQuery(
                long &L,                    // Workload (IN/OUT)
                long b,                     // Comm. model parameters
                double d,                   //
                bool blocktype = true,      // Selects block- (default)
                                            // or stream-type computation
                bool firstcall = false,     // Set to true to indicate
                                            // the first image query run
                bool equalLoad = true);     // If true, causes the load
                                            // to be equally partitioned.
                                            // This is reserved for runs
                                            // following the first one.

// Simplified version of method SolveImageQuery, for homogeneous ↩
    platforms
double SolveImageQueryHomogeneous(
                long &L,                    // Workload (IN/OUT)
                long b,                     // Comm. model parameters
                double d,                   //
                bool firstcall);            // If true, causes the load to be
                                            // equally partitioned. This is
                                            // reserved for runs following the
                                            // first one.
```

G.2 DLTlib files

Table G.3 contains a list of the files that make up the library. These can reside either within the directory of the project that uses them or at a system-wide centralized location (e.g., /usr/include and /usr/lib) for all users to access.

Table G.3 A list of the files that make up the DLTlib library.

File	Description
dltlib.cpp	Contains the source code of all the required methods. This is the only file that needs to be included if the library is compiled as part of another source code file.
dltlib.h	Only file that needs to be included if dltlib.cpp is compiled separately.
node_que.cpp	Contains a Queue class definition which is used for Node management.
random.c	Contains a number of pseudorandom number generation functions. The file is included directly in dltlib.cpp
random.h	Header file for random.c. This file needs to be included only if a program needs to use the supplied functions directly.

Glossary

activation frame A memory block reserved in the runtime stack that serves for storing function parameters and the return address upon calling a function.

activation record See activation frame.

communicator A group of processes in MPI. Processes inside a communicator are sequentially indexed starting from 0. The default communicator that incorporates all processes is `MPI_COMM_WORLD`.

functor A C++ function object, i.e., an instance of a class that overloads `operator()`, the "function call" operator.

ICD Installable client driver.

ICV Internal control variable: an internal variable of the OpenMP runtime that controls how it operates.

iteration space dependency graph A graph used to visualize the iterations performed by a loop or a set of nested loops and the data dependencies between them. The nodes in this graph represent iterations and the edges represent flow of data.

JIT Just-in-time compilation: a compilation technique that translates the source or intermediate code right before it is executed on the target platform. Originally popularized by Java.

kernel fusion The action of combining two or more CUDA kernels into one, so that memory access and transfer overheads are eliminated.

managed memory Term used to describe two memory regions, one on the CPU/host and one on the GPU/device, that are maintained so they stay coherent (i.e., holding the same data) by the device driver.

Message-Passing Interface A standard specification for a library aimed at writing portable programs for distributed memory platforms.

MPI See Message-Passing Interface.

MPMD See multiple program, multiple data.

multiple program, multiple data A software construction parading for distributed-memory machines, where each node runs a different program while also operating on different data.

NoW Network of Workstations, a term loosely used to describe an intranet of computers running parallel software.

occupancy The ratio of resident warps in a GPU, over the maximum possible resident warps.

RAII Resource Acquisition Is Initialization: a programming technique that binds the life cycle of a resource that needs to be acquired before its use (e.g., a chunk of memory) to the lifetime of an object. Object construction and destruction are implicitly managing the allocation and deallocation of the corresponding resource, avoiding memory leaks in the process.

SIMD See single instruction, multiple data.

SIMT See single instruction, multiple threads.

single instruction, multiple data One of the categories of Flynn's computer taxonomy, where multiple processing elements operate on multiple data, following the same instruction sequence.

single instruction, multiple threads NVidia's GPU execution model, where multiple threads operating on different data are executing synchronously the same instruction sequence.

single program, multiple data A software construction paradigm for distributed-memory machines, where the same program runs on all the nodes, but it operates on different data.

SM See streaming multiprocessor.

SP See streaming processor.

SPMD See single program, multiple data.

streaming multiprocessor A group of CUDA cores that execute under the control of a single control unit, i.e., all running the same instruction at any time instance.

streaming processor Also referred to as CUDA core.

warp A set of CUDA threads that run on an SM as a unit, i.e., executing synchronously the same instruction.

Bibliography

[1] BeeGFS Parallel Cluster File System, https://www.beegfs.io/content/. (Accessed September 2020).

[2] Lustre Parallel File System, https://lustre.org/. (Accessed September 2020).

[3] OpenMP Application Programming Interface, Version 5.2, https://www.openmp.org/wp-content/uploads/OpenMP-API-Specification-5-2.pdf. (Accessed December 2021).

[4] Parallel Virtual File System V2, https://web.archive.org/web/20160701052501/http://www.pvfs.org/. (Accessed September 2020).

[5] Writing reentrant and threadsafe code, IBM Knowledge Center, https://www.ibm.com/support/knowledgecenter/ssw_aix_71/generalprogramming/writing_reentrant_thread_safe_code.html. (Accessed September 2020).

[6] Intel 64 and IA-32 Architectures Software Developer's Manual, Vol. 1: Basic Architecture, http://www.intel.com/content/dam/www/public/us/en/documents/manuals/64-ia-32-architectures-software-developer-vol-1-manual.pdf, September 2016. (Accessed September 2020).

[7] Sudhir Ahuja, Nicholas Carriero, David Gelernter, Linda and friends, IEEE Computer 19 (8) (August 1986) 26–34.

[8] Randy Allen, Ken Kennedy, Optimizing Compilers for Modern Architectures: A Dependence-based Approach, 1st edition, Morgan Kaufmann, ISBN 978-1558602861, 2001.

[9] D.H. Ballard, Generalizing the Hough transform to detect arbitrary shapes, Pattern Recognition 13 (2) (1981) 111–122.

[10] Savina Bansal, Padam Kumar, Kuldip Singh, An improved duplication strategy for scheduling precedence constrained graphs in multiprocessor systems, IEEE Transactions on Parallel and Distributed Systems 14 (6) (June 2003) 533–544.

[11] G.D. Barlas, Khaled El-Fakih, A GA-based movie-on-demand platform using multiple distributed servers, Multimedia Tools and Applications 40 (3) (December 2008) 361–383.

[12] Gerassimos Barlas, An analytical approach to optimizing parallel image registration/retrieval, IEEE Transactions on Parallel and Distributed Systems 21 (8) (August 2010) 1074–1088.

[13] Gerassimos Barlas, Cluster-based optimized parallel video transcoding, Parallel Computing 38 (4–5) (April-May 2012) 226–244.

[14] Gerassimos Barlas, Ahmed Hassan, Yasser Al Jundi, An analytical approach to the design of parallel block cipher encryption/decryption: a CPU/GPU case study, in: Proc. of PDP 2011, Ayia Napa, Cyprus, Febr. 9–11, 2011, pp. 247–251.

[15] Gerassimos Barlas, Lamees El Hiny, Closed-form solutions for dense matrix-matrix multiplication on heterogeneous platforms using divisible load analysis, in: PDP, Cambridge, UK, March 21–23, 2018, pp. 376–384.

[16] Gerassimos Barlas, Bharadwaj Veeravalli, Quantized load distribution for tree and bus connected processors, Parallel Computing 30 (7) (July 2004) 841–865.

[17] Gerassimos D. Barlas, Collection-aware optimum sequencing of operations and closed-form solutions for the distribution of a divisible load on arbitrary processor trees, IEEE Transactions on Parallel and Distributed Systems 9 (5) (May 1998) 429–441.

[18] Gerassimos D. Barlas, Bharadwaj Veeravalli, Optimized distributed delivery of continuous-media documents over unreliable communication links, IEEE Transactions on Parallel and Distributed Systems 16 (10) (October 2005).

[19] Olivier Beaumont, Hubert Larcheveque, Loris Marchal, Non linear divisible loads: there is no free lunch, in: 2013 IEEE 27th International Symposium on Parallel & Distributed Processing, 2013, pp. 863–873.

[20] Guy E. Blelloch, Prefix sums and their applications, Technical Report CMU-CS-90-190, Carnegie Mellon University, 1990.

[21] Rohit Chandra, Leo Dagum, David Kohr, Dror Maydan, Jeff McDonald, Ramesh Menon, Parallel Programming in OpenMP, Morgan Kaufmann, ISBN 1-55860-671-8, 2001.

[22] C. Chen, C. Chu, Divisible nonlinear load distribution on heterogeneous single-level trees, IEEE Transactions on Aerospace and Electronic Systems 54 (4) (2018) 1664–1678.

[23] Martin J. Chorley, David W. Walker, Performance analysis of a hybrid MPI/OpenMP application on multi-core clusters, Journal of Computational Science 1 (3) (2010) 168–174.

[24] Shane Cook, CUDA Programming: A Developer's Guide to Parallel Computing with GPUs, 1st edition, Morgan Kaufmann, ISBN 978-0124159334, 2012.

[25] Luke Durant, Olivier Giroux, Mark Harris, Nick Stam, Inside Volta: The World's Most Advanced Data Center GPU, NVidia Developer Blog, https://developer.nvidia.com/blog/inside-volta/, May 2017. (Accessed September 2020).

[26] Ian Foster, Designing and Building Parallel Programs: Concepts and Tools for Parallel Software Engineering, Addison-Wesley, ISBN 978-0201575941, 1995. Available at http://www.mcs.anl.gov/dbpp/. (Accessed September 2020).

[27] D. Ghose, H.J. Kim, Load partitioning and trade-off study for large matrix-vector computations in multicast bus networks with communication delays, Journal of Parallel and Distributed Computing 55 (1) (1998) 32–59.

[28] Tao Gu, Qun Liao, Yulu Yang, Tao Li, Scheduling divisible loads from multiple input sources in MapReduce, in: IEEE 16th International Conference on Computational Science and Engineering, 2013, pp. 1263–1270.

[29] Tom's Hardware Guide, AES-NI Performance Analyzed, Limited To 32nm Core i5 CPUs, http://www.tomshardware.com/reviews/clarkdale-aes-ni-encryption,2538-5.html, February 2010. (Accessed September 2020).

[30] Maurice Herlihy, Nir Shavit, The Art of Multiprocessor Programming, Morgan Kaufmann, ISBN 978-0123973375, 2012.

[31] W.D. Hillis, G.L. Steele Jr., Data parallel algorithms, Communications of the ACM 29 (1986) 1170–1183.

[32] Markus Hrywniak, CUDA 11 and A100 - What's new?, https://www.fz-juelich.de/SharedDocs/Downloads/IAS/JSC/EN/slides/msa-seminar/2020-06-23-a100-hrywniak.pdf?__blob=publicationFile, June 2020. (Accessed December 2021).

[33] Menglan Hu, Bharadwaj Veeravalli, Requirement-aware strategies with arbitrary processor release times for scheduling multiple divisible loads, IEEE Transactions on Parallel and Distributed Systems 22 (10) (October 2011) 1697–1704.

[34] Menglan Hu, Bharadwaj Veeravalli, Scheduling hybrid divisible and indivisible loads on clusters, in: 17th IEEE International Conference on Networks (ICON), December 2011, pp. 141–146.

[35] Jui Tsun Hung, Thomas G. Robertazzi, Scheduling nonlinear computational loads, IEEE Transactions on Aerospace and Electronic Systems 44 (3) (July 2008) 1169–1182.

[36] Aleksandar Ilic, Leonel Sousa, On realistic divisible load scheduling in highly heterogeneous distributed systems, in: 20th Euromicro International Conference on Parallel, Distributed and Network-based Processing, 2012, pp. 426–433.

[37] J. Berlinska, M. Drozdowski, Heuristics for multi-round divisible loads scheduling with limited memory, Parallel Computing 36 (4) (2010) 199–211.

[38] J. Berlinska, M. Drozdowski, Scheduling divisible MapReduce computations, Journal of Parallel and Distributed Computing 71 (3) (March 2011) 450–459.

[39] Jingxi Jia, Bharadwaj Veeravalli, Jon Weissman, Scheduling multi-source divisible loads on arbitrary networks, IEEE Transactions on Parallel and Distributed Systems 21 (4) (April 2010) 521–531.

[40] Zhe Jia, Marco Maggioni, Jeffrey Smith, Daniele Paolo Scarpazza, Dissecting the NVidia Turing T4 GPU via Microbenchmarking, Technical report, Citadel, March 2019, https://arxiv.org/pdf/1903.07486.pdf. (Accessed September 2020).

[41] Seungmin Kang, Bharadwaj Veeravalli, Khin Mi Mi Aung, Dynamic scheduling strategy with efficient node availability prediction for handling divisible loads in multi-cloud systems, Journal of Parallel and Distributed Computing 113 (2018) 1–16.

[42] Anre Kashyap, High Performance Computing: Tuning Guide for AMD EPYC 7002 Series Processor, Technical report 56827, AMD, January 2020, http://developer.amd.com/wp-content/resources/56827-1-0.pdf. (Accessed September 2020).

[43] Ronny Krashinsky, Olivier Giroux, Stephen Jones, Nick Stam, Sridhar Ramaswamy, NVIDIA Ampere Architecture In-Depth, NVidia Developer Blog, https://developer.nvidia.com/blog/nvidia-ampere-architecture-in-depth/, May 2020. (Accessed September 2020).

[44] Li Ping, Bharadwaj Veeravalli, Ashraf A. Kassim, Design and implementation of parallel video encoding strategies using divisible load analysis, IEEE Transactions on Circuits and Systems for Video Technology 15 (9) (September 2005) 1098–1112.

[45] Fujitsu Limited, FUJITSU Supercomputer PRIMEHPC FX1000, An HPC System Opening Up an AI and Exascale Era, https://www.fujitsu.com/downloads/SUPER/primehpc-fx1000-hard-en.pdf. (Accessed September 2020).

[46] Jędrzej Marszałkowski, Maciej Drozdowski, Gaurav Singh, Time–energy trade-offs in processing divisible loads on heterogeneous hierarchical memory systems, Journal of Parallel and Distributed Computing 144 (2020) 206–219.

[47] Timothy G. Mattson, Beverly A. Sanders, Berna Massingill, Patterns for Parallel Programming, Addison-Wesley, ISBN 0-321-22811-1, 2005.

[48] Paul E. McKenney, Memory Barriers: a Hardware View for Software Hackers, http://www.rdrop.com/users/paulmck/scalability/paper/whymb.2009.04.05a.pdf, April 2009. (Accessed September 2020).

[49] M. Drozdowski, M. Lawenda, Multi-installment divisible load processing in heterogeneous distributed systems, Concurrency and Computation: Practice and Experience 19 (17) (December 2007) 2237–2253.

[50] J. Montagnat, H. Duque, J.M. Pierson, V. Breton, L. Brunie, I.E. Magnin, Medical image content-based queries using the grid, in: Proc. of HealthGrid 03, 2003.

[51] Rolf Rabenseifner, Georg Hager, Gabriele Jost, Hybrid MPI/OpenMP parallel programming on clusters of multi-core SMP nodes, in: 17th Euromicro Int. Conf. on Parallel, Distributed and Network-based Processing, February 2009, pp. 427–436.

[52] Toshiyuki Shimizu, Post-K Supercomputer Development, https://www.fujitsu.com/global/Images/post-k-supercomputer-development.pdf. (Accessed September 2020).

[53] John SingLee, Nee Helgeson, Introduction Guide to the IBM Elastic Storage System, IBM Redbooks, 2020, http://www.redbooks.ibm.com/redpapers/pdfs/redp5253.pdf. (Accessed September 2020).

[54] S. Suresh, Cui Run, Hyoung Joong Kim, Thomas G. Robertazzi, Young-Il Kim, Scheduling second-order computational load in master-slave paradigm, IEEE Transactions on Aerospace and Electronic Systems 48 (1) (January 2012) 780–793.

[55] Herb Sutter, Eliminate False Sharing, https://www.drdobbs.com/parallel/eliminate-false-sharing/217500206, May 2009. (Accessed September 2020).

[56] Bharadwaj Veeravalli, Gerassimos Barlas, Distributed Multimedia Retrieval Strategies for Large Scale Networked Systems, Springer, ISBN 0-387-28873-2, 2006.

[57] Bharadwaj Veeravalli, D. Ghose, V. Mani, T.G. Robertazzi, Scheduling Divisible Loads in Parallel and Distributed Systems, IEEE Computer Society Press, Los Alamitos, California, 1996.

[58] Bharadwaj Veeravalli, Li Xiaolin, Ko Chi Chung, Efficient partitioning and scheduling of computer vision and image processing data on bus networks using divisible load analysis, Image and Vision Computing 18 (11) (1999) 919–938.

[59] Sivakumar Viswanathan, Bharadwaj Veeravalli, Thomas G. Robertazzi, Resource-aware distributed scheduling strategies for large-scale computational cluster/grid systems, IEEE Transactions on Parallel and Distributed Systems 18 (10) (October 2007) 1450–1461.

[60] Vasily Volkov, Better Performance at Lower Occupancy, https://www.nvidia.com/content/GTC-2010/pdfs/2238_GTC2010.pdf, September 2010. (Accessed September 2020).

[61] Vasily Volkov, Understanding Latency Hiding on GPUs, PhD thesis, EECS Department, University of California, Berkeley, Aug. 2016, http://www.eecs.berkeley.edu/Pubs/TechRpts/2016/EECS-2016-143.html. (Accessed September 2020).

[62] George Wells, Coordination languages: back to the future with Linda, in: Proc. of WCAT'05, 2005, pp. 87–98.

[63] Anthony Williams, C++ Concurrency in Action, Practical Multithreading, 1st edition, Manning, ISBN 9781933988771, 2012.

[64] Yang Yang, Henri Casanova, Maciej Drozdowski, Marcin Lawenda, Arnaud Legrand, On the Complexity of Multi-Round Divisible Load Scheduling, Technical Report 6096, INRIA, January 2007.

[65] Jerry Zhao, Jelena Pjesivac-Grbovic, MapReduce: The programming model and practice, Tutorial, http://static.googleusercontent.com/media/research.google.com/en//archive/papers/mapreduce-sigmetrics09-tutorial.pdf, 2009. (Accessed September 2020).

Index